Jeannette M. Wing   Jim Woodcock
Jim Davies (Eds.)

FM'99 – Formal Methods

World Congress on Formal Methods
in the Development of Computing Systems
Toulouse, France, September 20-24, 1999
Proceedings, Volume I

Springer

Series Editors

Gerhard Goos, Karlsruhe University, Germany
Juris Hartmanis, Cornell University, NY, USA
Jan van Leeuwen, Utrecht University, The Netherlands

Volume Editors

Jeannette M. Wing
Carnegie Mellon University, Computer Science Department
5000 Forbes Avenue, Pittsburgh, PA 15213, USA
E-mail: wing@cs.cmu.edu

Jim Woodcock
Jim Davies
Oxford University Computing Laboratory
Software Engineering Programme
Wolfson Building, Parks Road, Oxford OX1 3QD, UK
E-mail: {jim.woodcock, jim.davies}@ comlab.ox.ac.uk

Cataloging-in-Publication data applied for

Die Deutsche Bibliothek - CIP-Einheitsaufnahme

Formal methods : proceedings / FM '99, World Congress on Formal Methods in the
Development of Computing Systems, Toulouse, France, September 20 - 24, 1999 /
Jeannette M. Wing ... (ed.). - Berlin ; Heidelberg ; New York ; Barcelona ;
Hong Kong ; London ; Milan ; Paris ; Singapore ; Tokyo : Springer

Vol. 1. - (1999)
 (Lecture notes in computer science ; Vol. 1708)
 ISBN 3-540-66587-0

CR Subject Classification (1998): F.3, D.2, F.4.1, D.3, D.1, C.2, C.3, I.2.3, B,
J.2

ISSN 0302-9743
ISBN 3-540-66587-0 Springer-Verlag Berlin Heidelberg New York

© Springer-Verlag Berlin Heidelberg 1999
Printed in Germany

Typesetting: Camera-ready by author
SPIN: 10704999   06/3142 – 5 4 3 2 1 0   Printed on acid-free paper

Preface

Formal methods are coming of age. Mathematical techniques and tools are now regarded as an important part of the development process in a wide range of industrial and governmental organisations. A transfer of technology into the mainstream of systems development is slowly, but surely, taking place.

FM'99, the First World Congress on Formal Methods in the Development of Computing Systems, is a result, and a measure, of this new-found maturity. It brings an impressive array of industrial and applications-oriented papers that show how formal methods have been used to tackle real problems.

These proceedings are a record of the technical symposium of *FM'99*: alongside the papers describing applications of formal methods, you will find technical reports, papers, and abstracts detailing new advances in formal techniques, from mathematical foundations to practical tools.

The World Congress is the successor to the four Formal Methods Europe Symposia, which in turn succeeded the four VDM Europe Symposia. This succession reflects an increasing openness within the international community of researchers and practitioners: papers were submitted covering a wide variety of formal methods and application areas.

The programme committee reflects the Congress's international nature, with a membership of 84 leading researchers from 38 different countries. The committee was divided into 19 tracks, each with its own chair to oversee the reviewing process. Our collective task was a difficult one: there were 259 high-quality submissions from 35 different countries.

Each paper was reviewed within a track, the track chairs resolved conflicts between reviewers, and the recommendations of each track chair were considered by the executive programme committee. This resulted in 92 papers being accepted, along with 15 abstracts describing work in progress and industrial applications.

We thank all those members of the programme and organising committees for their hard work, carried out under necessarily short deadlines. Thanks are due also to our able administrators, Maureen York and Anna Curtis; they did an excellent job and they deserve our gratitude for their contribution.

Finally, thanks to all those who submitted papers and attended the Congress: it is your hard work that has made it such a timely and important event.

July 1999

Jeannette Wing
Jim Woodcock
Jim Davies

Technical Tracks

The tracks that structure the technical symposium may be divided into three groups. First, there are application areas:

- Avionics
- Co-design
- Open information systems

- Safety
- Security
- Telecommunications

Second, there are processes and techniques:

- Composition and synthesis
- Integration
- Model checking
- Software architecture

- Object orientation
- Program verification
- Refinement
- Testing

Finally, there are groups of users and researchers:

- European Association for Theoretical Computer Science
- Foundations of System Specification
- Formal Description of Programming Concepts
- Abstract State Machines

- European Theory and Practice of Software
- Algebraic Methods in Software Technology
- OBJ / CafeOBJ / Maude
- The B method

Our five distinguished invited speakers are Tony Hoare of the University of Oxford, Cliff Jones of the University of Manchester, Amir Pnueli of the Weizmann Institute, Joseph Sifakis of Verimag, John Rushby of SRI International, and Michael Jackson, independent consultant.

Symposium Committee

Keijiro Araki, Japan
Egidio Astesiano, Italy
Albert Benveniste, France
Didier Bert, France
Dines Bjørner, Denmark
Robin Bloomfield, UK
Dominique Bolignano, France
Egon Börger, Italy
Jonathan Bowen, UK
Wilfried Brauer, Germany
Ed Brinksma, NL
Manfred Broy, Germany
Andrew Butterfield, Ireland
Jacques Cazin, France
Edmund Clarke, USA
Dan Craigen, Canada
Jorge Cuéllar, Germany
Aristides Dasso, Argentina
Jim Davies, UK
Tim Denvir, UK
Jin Song Dong, Singapore
Steve Dunne, UK
Hartmut Ehrig, Germany
John Fitzgerald, UK
Laure Pauline Fotso, Cameroon
Birgitte Fröhlich, Austria
Kokichi Futatsugi, Japan
David Garlan, USA
Marie-Claude Gaudel, France
Chris George, Macau
David Gries, USA
Henri Habrias, France
Armando Haeberer, Brazil
Nicolas Halbwachs, France
Kirsten Mark Hansen, Denmark
Anne Haxthausen, Denmark
Ian Hayes, Australia
Rick Hehner, Canada
Valérie Issarny, France
Rene Jacquart, France
Randolph Johnson, USA
Bengt Jonsson, Sweden
Leonid Kalinichenko, Russia
Kanchana Kanchanasut, Thailand

Kyo Chul Kang, Korea
Marite Kirikova, Latvia
Derrick Kourie, South Africa
Souleymane Koussoube, Burkina Faso
Reino Kurki-Suonio, Finland
Axel van Lamsweerde, Belgium
Jean-Claude Laprie, France
Peter Gorm Larsen, Denmark
Shaoying Liu, Japan
Peter Lucas, Austria
Micheal Mac an Airchinnigh, Ireland
Tom Maibaum, UK
Zohar Manna, USA
Lynn Marshall, Canada
Kees Middelburg, NL
Markus Montigel, Austria
Peter Mosses, Denmark
Friederike Nickl, Germany
Nikolai Nikitchenko, Ukraine
Roger Noussi, Gabon
Ernst-Rüdiger Olderog, Germany
José Nuno Oliveira, Portugal
Fernando Orejas, Spain
Paritosh Pandya, India
Jan Peleska, Germany
Frantisek Plásil, Czech Republic
Igor Prívara, Slovakia
Hans Rischel, Denmark
Ken Robinson, Australia
Teodor Rus, USA
Augusto Sampaio, Brazil
Georgy Satchock, Belarus
Kaisa Sere, Finland
Natarajan Shankar, USA
Joseph Sifakis, France
Doug Smith, USA
Radu Soricut, Rumania
Andrzej Tarlecki, Poland
T.H. Tse, Hong Kong
Bogdan Warinski, Rumania
Jeannette Wing, USA
Jim Woodcock, UK
Pamela Zave, USA
Zhou Chaochen, Macau

Congress General Chair
  Dines Bjørner

Programme Committee Co-chairs
  Jeannette Wing and Jim Woodcock

Organisation Committee Chair
  Rene Jacquart

Local Organisation and Publicity
  Jacques Cazin

Congress Public Relations Officer
  Jonathan Bowen

Congress Sponsors

AMAST	France Telecom
Aérospatiale Airbus	IFIP
Alcatel Space	INRIA
CCIT	IPSJ
CEPIS	IRIT
CNES	JSSST
CNRS	LAAS
Cap Gemini	Mairie de Toulouse
Carnegie-Mellon University	Matra Marconi Space
Conseil Regional Midi-Pyrenees	ONERA
DGA	Technical University of Delft
EATCS	Technical University of Denmark
ESA	Technical University of Graz
ETAPS	Translimina
European Union	University of Oxford
FACS	University of Reading
FME	

Table of Contents

Model Checking

The B Method

Composition and Synthesis

Telecommunications

Table of Contents, Volume II

Refinement

Safety

Works-in-Progress

Industrial Experience

Theories of Programming: Top-Down and Bottom-Up and Meeting in the Middle

Oxford University Computing Laboratory
Wolfson Building, Parks Road, Oxford, OX1 3QD
`tony.hoare@comlab.ox.ac.uk`

1 Introduction

The goal of scientific research is to develop an understanding of the complexity of the world which surrounds us. There is certainly enough complexity out there to justify a wide range of specialist branches of science; and within each branch to require a wide range of investigatory styles and techniques.

For example, among the specialists in Physics, cosmologists start their speculations in the vast distances of intergalactic space, and encompass the vast time-scales of the evolution of the stars. They work methodically downward in scale, until they find an explanation of phenomena that can be observed more or less directly by the naked eye.

At the other end of the scale, particle physicists start with the primitive components of the material world, currently postulated to be quarks and gluons. They then work methodically upward in scale, to study the composition of baryons, hadrons, and leptons, clarifying the laws which govern their assembly into atoms and molecules. Eventually, they can explain the properties of materials that we touch and smell and taste in the world of every day.

In spite of the difference in scale of their starting points, and in the direction and style of their investigations, there is increasing excitement about the convergence and overlap of theories developed by cosmologists and by particle physicists. The point at which they converge is the most significant event in the whole history of the universe, the big bang with which it all started.

The same dichotomy between top-down and bottom-up styles of investigation may be found among mathematicians. For example, category theorists start at the top with a study of the most general kind of mathematical structure, as exemplified by the category of sets. They then work downward to define and classify the canonical properties that distinguish more particular example structures from each other.

Logicians on the other hand start from the bottom. They search for a minimal set of primitive concepts and notations to serve as a foundation for all of mathematics, and a minimal collection of atomic steps to define the concept of a valid proof. They then work methodically upward, to define the more familiar concepts of mathematics in terms of the primitives, and to justify the larger proof steps which mathematicians need for efficient prosecution of their work.

J. Wing, J. Woodcock, J. Davies (Eds.): FM'99, Vol. I, LNCS 1708, pp. 1–27, 1999.
© Springer-Verlag Berlin Heidelberg 1999

Fortunately in this case too, the top-down and the bottom-up styles of investigation both seek a common explanation of the internal structure of mathematics and clarification of the relationship between its many branches. Their ultimate goal is to extend the unreasonable power of mathematical calculation and make it more accessible to the experimental scientist and to the practicing engineer.

Computer science, like other branches of science, has as its goal the understanding of highly complex phenomena, the behaviour of computers and the software that controls them. Simple algorithms, like Euclid's method of finding the greatest common divisor, are already complex enough; a challenge on a larger scale is to understand the potential behaviour of the million-fold inter-linked operating systems of the world-wide computing network.

As in physics or in mathematics, the investigation of such a system may proceed in a choice of directions, from the top-down or from the bottom-up. In the following exposition, this dichotomy will be starkly exaggerated. In any particular scientific investigation, or on any particular engineering project, there will be a rapid alternation or mixture of the two approaches, often starting in the middle and working outward. A recommendation to this effect is made in the conclusion of the paper.

An investigation from the top-down starts with an attempt to understand the system as a whole. Since software is a man-made artifact, it is always relevant to ask first what is its purpose? Why was it built? Who is it for? What are the requirements of its users, and how are they served?

The next step is to identify the major components of the system, and ask how they are put together? How do they interact with each other? What are the protocols and conventions governing their collaboration? How are the conventions enforced, and how does their observance ensure successful achievement of the goals of the system as a whole?

A top-down theory of programming therefore starts by modelling external aspects of the behaviour of a system, such as might be observed by its user. A meaningful name is given to each observation or measurement, so that the intended behaviour of the system can be described briefly and clearly, perhaps in a user manual for a product, or perhaps even in a specification agreed with the user prior to implementation.

The set of observations is extended to include concepts needed to describe the internal interfaces between components of the system. The goal of the theory is to predict the behaviour of a complex assembly by a calculation based only on descriptions of the behaviour of its major components. The collection of formulae used for these calculations effectively constitutes a denotational semantics for the languages in which a system is specified, designed, and eventually implemented.

The programming language used for ultimate implementation is defined by simply selecting an implementable subset of the mathematically defined notations for describing program behaviour. The correctness of a program simply means that all possible observations of its behaviour under execution are included in the range defined by its specification.

The development of the theory starts from the denotational definitions and continues by formalisation and proof of theorems that express the properties of all programs written in the language. The goal is to assemble a collection of mathematical laws (usually equations and inequations) that will be useful in the top-down design of programs from their specifications, and ensure that the resulting code is correct by construction.

Investigation of a complex system from the bottom-up starts with an attempt to discover a minimum collection of primitive components from which it has been made, or in principle could have been. These are assembled into larger components by primitive combinators, selected again from a minimal set. The notations chosen to denote these primitives and combinators constitute the syntax of a simple programming language.

Since programs are intended for execution by a machine, their operational meaning is defined by enumerating the kinds of primitive step that will be taken by the machine in executing any program that is presented to it. The theory may be further developed by investigation of properties of programs that are preserved by all the possible execution steps; they are necessarily preserved throughout execution of any program.

The resulting classification of programs is presented as a set of axioms that can be used in proofs that a program enjoys the relevant property. The properties are often decidable, and the axioms can be used as a type system for the programming language, with conformity checkable by its compiler.

In favourable cases, the type system allows unique or canonical types to be inferred from an untyped program. Such inference can help in the understanding of legacy code, possibly written without any comprehensible documentation describing its structure or purpose (or worse, the original documentation often has not been kept up to date with the later changes made to the code).

The benefits of a top-down presentation of a theory are entirely complementary to those of a bottom-up presentation. The former is directly applicable to discussion and reasoning about the design of a program before it has been written, and the latter to the testing, debugging, and modification of code that has already been written. In both cases, successful application of the theory takes advantage of a collection of theorems proved for this purpose. The most useful theorems are those which take the form of algebraic laws.

The advantages of both approaches can be confidently combined, if the overlap of laws provided by both of them is sufficiently broad. The laws are a specification of the common interface where the two approaches meet in the middle. I suggest that such a convergence of laws developed by complementary approaches and applied to the same programming language should be a rigorous scientific criterion of the maturity of a theory and of a language, when deciding whether it is ready for practical implementation and widespread use.

2 Top-Down

A top-down presentation of a theory of programming starts with an account of a conceptual framework appropriate for the description of the behaviour of a running program as it may be observed by its users. For each kind of observation, an identifier is chosen serve as a variable whose exact value will be determined on each particular run of the program.

Variables whose values are measured as a result of experiment are very familiar in all branches of natural science; for example in mechanics, x is often declared to denote the displacement of a particular object from the origin along a particular axis, and $\bullet\ x$ denotes the rate of change of x. We will find that such analogies with the normal practice of scientists and engineers provide illumination and encouragement at the start as well as later in the development of theories of programming.

There are two special times at which observation of an experiment or the run of a program are especially interesting, at the very beginning and at the very end. That is why the specification language VDM introduces special superscript arrow notations: $\overleftarrow{x}$ to denote the initial value of the global program variable x, and $\overrightarrow{x}$ to denote its final value on successful termination of the program. (The Z notation uses x and x' for these purposes).

Fragments of program in different contexts will update different sets of global variables. The set of typed variables relevant to a particular program fragment is known as its *alphabet*. In the conventional sequential programming paradigm, the beginning and the end of the run of a program are the only times when it is necessary or desirable to consider the values of the global variables accessed and updated by it. We certainly want to ignore the millions of possible intermediate values calculated during its execution, and it is a goal of the theory to validate this simplification.

A full understanding of a description of program behaviour requires prior specification of its alphabet, and agreement on the way in which the value of each variable in it can be determined by experiment. To interpret the meaning of a program without knowing its alphabet is as impossible as the interpretation of a message in information theory without knowing the range of message values that might have been sent instead.

Not all the relevant parameters of program behaviour have to be directly observable from outside the computer; some may be observable only indirectly, by their effect on other programs. Actually, even the values of the program variables inside the computer are inaccessible to a user; they can be controlled or observed only with the aid of an input-output package, which is written in the same language as the program under analysis. The indirect observations are needed to make successful predictions about the behaviour of larger programs, based on knowledge of the behaviour of their components parts.

Successful termination is one of the most important properties of a program to predict, so we need a special variable (called $\overrightarrow{ok}$) which is true just if and when termination occurs. The corresponding initial variable $\overleftarrow{ok}$ indicates that the program has started. Of course a false value of $\overrightarrow{ok}$ will never be conclusively observed; but that doesn't matter, because the intention of the theorist and the programmer alike is to ensure it that $\overleftrightarrow{ok}$ is necessarily true, and to prove it. Such a proof would be vacuous if the possibility of its falsity were not modelled in the theory.

In general, for serious proof of total correctness of programs, it is essential to model realistically all the ways in which a program can go wrong, even if not directly observable. In fact, the progress of science is marked by acceptance of such unobservable abstractions as force and mass and friction as though they were directly measurable quantities. As Einstein pointed out, it is the theory itself which determines what is observable.

In the interactive programming paradigm, the most important observable component of program behaviour is an interaction between the system and its environment. Each kind of interaction has a distinct name. For example, in the process algebra CCS [6] the event name *coin* may stand for the insertion of a pound coin in the slot of a vending machine, and the event name *choc* may stand for the selection and extraction of a chocolate bar by the user.

The CSP [7] variant of process algebra allows the user to record a *trace* of the sequence in which such events have occurred while the machine is running; so $\langle coin, choc, coin \rangle$ is a value of *trace* observed in the middle of the second transaction of the machine; the empty trace $\langle \rangle$ is the value when the machine is first delivered.

We also model the possibility of deadlock (hang-up) by recording the set of events currently offered by the machine's environment, but which it refuses to accept. For example, initially the machine refuses $\{choc\}$ because it has not been paid (or perhaps because it has run out of chocolates). A deadlocked machine is one that refuses all the events offered by its environment.

Practical programming of useful systems will involve a combination of interactive and imperative programming features; and the relevant alphabet must include both internal variable names and external event names. The special variable $\overrightarrow{ok}$ should be reinterpreted as successful stabilisation, or avoidance of livelock (divergence). A new special variable $\overrightarrow{wait}$ is needed to distinguish those stable states in which the program is waiting for an interaction with its environment from those in which it has successfully terminated.

An important achievement in the theory of programming has been to formalise separate models for sequential and for interactive programs, and then to combine them with only a minimum of extra complexity.

A top-down theory of programming is highly conducive to a top-down methodology for program design and development. The identifiers chosen to denote the relevant observations of the ultimate program are first used to describe the intended and permitted behaviour of a program, long before the detailed programming begins. For example, a program can be specified not to decrease the value of x by the statement

$$\overleftarrow{x} \leq \overrightarrow{x}$$

A precondition for termination of a program can be written as the antecedent of a conditional

$$(\overleftarrow{x} < 27 \wedge \overleftarrow{ok}) \Rightarrow \overrightarrow{ok}$$

The owner of a vending machine may specify that the number of *choc* events in the *trace* must never exceed the number of *coin* events. And the customer certainly requires that when the balance of coins over chocs is positive, extraction of a chocolate will not be refused.

Explicit mention of refusals is a precise way of specifying responsiveness or liveness of a process, without appeal to the concept of fairness. But there is nothing wrong with fairness: it can be treated simply by allowing traces to be infinite. A fair trace is then one that contains an infinite number of occurrences of some relevant kind of event.

It is not an objective of a programming theory to place finitary or other restrictions on the language in which specifications are written. Indeed, our goal is to place whole power of mathematics at the disposal of the engineer and scientist, who should exercise it fully in the interests of utmost clarity of specification, and utmost reliability in reasoning about correctness. We will therefore allow arbitrary mathematical statements as predicates: as in the mu-calculus, we will even allow the definition of weakest fixed points of monotonic predicate transformers.

In an observational semantics of a programming language, the meaning of an actual computer program is defined simply and directly as a mathematical predicate that is true just for all those observations that could be made of any execution of the program in any environment of use.

For example, let x, y, and z be the entire alphabet of global variables of a simple program. The assignment statement $x := x + 1$ has its meaning completely described by a predicate stating that when it is started, the value of x is incremented, and that termination occurs provided the value of x is not too large. The values of all the other global program variables remain unchanged

$$\overleftarrow{x} < max \wedge \overleftarrow{ok} \quad \Rightarrow \quad \overrightarrow{ok} \wedge \overrightarrow{x} = \overleftarrow{x} + 1 \wedge \overrightarrow{y} = \overleftarrow{y} \wedge \overrightarrow{z} = \overleftarrow{z}$$

Similarly, the behaviour of the deadlock process in a process algebra can be described purely in terms of its trace behaviour—it never engages in any event, and so the trace remains forever empty

$$trace = \langle \rangle$$

(Here and in future, we will simplify our treatment of processes by ignoring issues of divergence).

This kind of definition of programming concepts enables us to regard both specifications and programs as predicates placing constraints on the range of values for the same alphabet of observational variables; the specification restricts the range of observations to those that are permitted; and the program defines exhaustively the full range of observations to which it could potentially give rise.

As a result, we have the simplest possible explanation of the important concept of program correctness. A program P meets a specification S just if the predicate describing P logically implies the predicate describing S. Since we can identify programs and specifications with their corresponding predicates, correctness is nothing but the familiar logical implication

$$P \Rightarrow S$$

For example, the specification of non-decreasing x is met by a program that increments x, as may be checked by a proof of the implication

$$\overleftarrow{ok} \wedge \overleftarrow{x} < max \wedge x := x + 1 \quad \Rightarrow \quad \overleftarrow{x} \leq \overrightarrow{x} \wedge \overrightarrow{ok}$$

This simple notion of correctness is obviously correct, and is completely general to all top-down theories of programming. Furthermore it validates in complete generality all the normal practices of software engineering methodology.

For example, stepwise design develops a program in two (or more) steps. On a particular step, the engineer produces a design D which describes the properties of the eventual program P in somewhat greater detail than the specification S, but leaving further details of the eventual program to be decided in later steps.

The general design method is defined and justified by the familiar *cut rule* of logic, expressing the mathematical property of transitivity of logical implication

$$\frac{D \Rightarrow S \quad P \Rightarrow D}{P \Rightarrow S}$$

In words this rule may be read: if the design is correct relative to the specification, and if the program meets its design requirement, then the program also meets its original specification.

The most useful method of constructing the specification of a large system is as the conjunction of its many requirements. Programs and designs can also be combined by conjunction, provided that they have completely disjoint alphabets. In that case, the conjunction can generally be implemented by parallel execution of its operands.

Such a parallel implementation is also possible when programs share parts of their alphabet, provided that these include observations of all the ways in which the programs can interact with each other during their execution. In these cases, the stepwise approach to implementation can be greatly strengthened if each step is accompanied by a decomposition of the design D into separately implementable parts D_1 and D_2.

The correctness of the decomposition can be checked before implementation starts by proof of the implication

$$D_1 \wedge D_2 \Rightarrow D$$

Further implementation of the designs D_1 and D_2 can be progressed independently and even simultaneously to deliver components P_1 and P_2. When the components are put together they certainly will meet the requirements of the original design D.

The proof principle that justifies the method of design by parts is just the expression of the monotonicity of conjunction with respect to implication

$$\frac{P_1 \Rightarrow D_1 \quad P_2 \Rightarrow D_2}{P_1 \wedge P_2 \;\Rightarrow\; D_1 \wedge D_2}$$

An even more powerful principle is that which justifies the reuse of a previously written library component, which has been fully described by the specification L. We want to implement a program P which uses L to help achieve a specification S. What is the most general description of a design for P that will achieve this goal in the easiest way? The answer is just $S \vee \overline{L}$, as described by the proof rule

$$\frac{P \;\Rightarrow\; S \vee \overline{L}}{P \wedge L \;\Rightarrow\; S}$$

The Boolean term $S \vee \overline{L}$ is often written as an implication (e.g., $L \supset S$); indeed, the above law, together with the inference in the opposite direction, is used in intuitionistic logic to define implication as an approximate inverse (Galois connection) of conjunction. An implication is always a predicate, but since it is antimonotonic in its first argument, it will rarely be a program.

The identification of programs with more abstract descriptions of their behaviour offers a very simple and general explanation of a number of important programming concepts. For example, a non-deterministic program can be constructed from two more deterministic programs P and Q by simply stating that you do not care which one of them is selected for execution on each occasion. The strongest assertion you can make about any resulting observation is that it must have arisen either from P or from Q.

So the concept of non-determinism is simply and completely captured by the disjunction $P \vee Q$, describing the set union of their observations. And the proof rule for correctness is just the familiar rule for disjunction, defining it as the least upper bound of the implication ordering

$$\frac{P_1 \Rightarrow D \quad P_2 \Rightarrow D}{P_1 \vee P_2 \;\Rightarrow\; D}$$

In words, if you want a non-deterministic program to be correct, you have to prove correctness of both alternatives. This extra labour permits the most general (demonic) interpretation of non-determinism, offering the greatest opportunities for subsequent development and optimisation.

Existential quantification in the predicate calculus provides a means of concealing the value of a variable, simultaneously removing the variable itself from the alphabet of the predicate. In programming theory, quantification allows new variables local to a particular fragment of program to be introduced and then eliminated.

In a process algebra, local declaration of event names ensures that the internal interactions between components of an assembly are concealed, as it were in a black box, before delivery to a customer. Observations of such interactions are denoted by some free variable, say x occurring in the formula P_x ; on each execution of P_x this variable must have some value, but we do not know or care what it is. The value and even the existence of the variable can be concealed by using it as the dummy variable of the quantification $(\exists\, x.P_x)$.

An important example of concealment is that which occurs when a program component P is sequentially composed with the component Q, with the effect that Q does not start until P has successfully terminated. The assembly (denoted $P;\ Q$) has the same initial observations as P, and the same final observations as Q. Furthermore, we know that the initial values of the variables of Q are the same as the final values of the variables of P.

But in normal sequential programs we definitely do not want to observe these intermediate values on each occasion that execution of the program passes a semicolon. Concealment by existential quantification makes the definition of sequential composition the same as that of composition in the relational calculus

$$(P;\ Q)\ =_{df}\ \exists x.P(\overleftarrow{x},x) \wedge Q(x,\overrightarrow{x})$$

Here we have written x and its superscripted variants to stand for the whole list of global variables in the alphabet of P and Q. In a procedural programming language sequential composition is the commonest method of assembling small components. The definition given above shows that the properties of the assembly can be calculated from a knowledge of its components, just as they can for conjunction.

Surprisingly, sequential composition is like conjunction also in admitting an approximate inverse, —a generalisation of Dijkstra's weakest precondition [3]. $L \setminus S$ is defined as the weakest specification [4] of a program P such that $P;\ L$ is guaranteed to meet specification S. There is also a postspecification, similarly defined. Such inverses can be invaluable in calculating the properties of a design, even though they are not available in the eventual target programming language.

In the explanation of stepwise composition of designs, we used conjunction to represent assembly of components. Conjunction of program components is not an operator that is generally available in a programming language. The reason is that it is too easy to conjoin inconsistent component descriptions, to produce a description that is logically impossible to implement, for example,

$$(x := x + 1) \wedge (x := x + 2), \qquad \text{which equals } \textbf{false}$$

So a practical programming language must concentrate on operators like sequential composition, which are carefully defined by conjunction and concealment to ensure implementability. Negation must also be avoided, because it turns **true**, which is implementable, to **false**, which is not.

That is why prespecifications, which are antimonotonic in their first argument, cannot be allowed in a programming language. But there is a compensation. Any operator defined without direct or indirect appeal to negation will be monotonic, and the programmer can use for the newly defined operator the same rules for stepwise decomposition that we have described for conjunction. The whole process of software engineering may be described as the stepwise replacement of logical and mathematical operators used in specifications and designs by the implementable operators of an actual programming language.

Ideally, each step should be small and its correctness should be obvious. But in many interesting and important cases, the structure of the implementation has to differ radically from the usual conjunctive structure of the specification, and the validity of the step must be checked by a more substantial proof. You do not expect to build an engine that is fast, eco-friendly, and cheap from three simpler components, each of which enjoy only one of these properties. A mismatch with implementation structure can throw into question the value of prior specification. But it should not; indeed, the value of specification to the user is greatest just when it is fundamentally and structurally simpler than its delivered implementation.

The simplest implementable operator to define is the conditional, in which the choice between components P and Q depends on the truth or falsity of a boolean expression b, which is evaluated in the initial state. So b can be interpreted as a predicate $\overleftarrow{b}$, in which all variables are replaced by their initial values.

$$\textbf{if } b \textbf{ then } P \textbf{ else } Q =_{df} \overleftarrow{b} \wedge P \vee \neg \overleftarrow{b} \wedge Q$$

All the mathematical properties of the conditional follow directly from this definition by purely propositional reasoning.

The most important feature of a programming language is that which permits the same portion of program to be executed repeatedly as many times as desired; and the most general way of specifying repetition is by recursion.

Let X be the name of a parameterless procedure, and let $F(X)$ be the body of the procedure, written in the given programming language, and containing recursive calls on X itself. Since F is monotonic in the inclusion ordering of the sets of observations desribed by predicates, and since these sets can be regarded as a complete lattice, we can use Tarski's fixed point theorem to define the meaning of each call of X as the weakest possible solution of the implication $X \Rightarrow F(X)$.

This definition applies also to recursively defined specifications. Incidentally, if F is expressed wholly in programming notations, it will be a continuous function, and an equivalent definition can be given as the intersection of a descending chain of iterates of F applied to **true**.

A non-terminating recursion can all too easily be specified as a procedure whose body consists of nothing but a recursive call upon itself. Our choice of the weakest fixed point says that such a program has the meaning **true**, a predicate satisfied by all observations whatsoever. The programmer's error has been punished in the most fitting way: no matter what the specification was (unless it was also trivally **true**), it will be impossible to prove that the product is correct.

This interpretation of divergence does not place any obligation on an implementor of the programming language actually to exhibit the full range of allowable observations. On the contrary, the implementor may assume that the programmer never intended the divergence, and on this assumption may validly perform many useful optimisations on the program before executing it.

$$P \vee Q = Q \vee P$$
$$P \vee (Q \vee R) = (P \vee Q) \vee R$$
$$P \vee \mathbf{false} = P$$
$$P \vee \mathbf{true} = \mathbf{true}$$
$$P \wedge (Q \vee R) = (P \wedge Q) \vee (P \wedge R)$$
$$P;\ (Q \vee R) = (P;\ Q) \vee (P;\ R)$$
$$(Q \vee R);\ P = (Q;\ P) \vee (R;\ P)$$

Table 1. Basic algebra of non-determinism

As a result of such optimisations, the program may even terminate, for example,

while $x \leq 0$ **do** $x := x - 1$; $x := abs(x)$

can be optimised to nothing, because the optimiser assumes that the intention of the while loop was to terminate, which only happens when x starts positive. The anomalous terminating behaviour of the optimised program for negative x is allowed by the semantics, and is entirely attributed to the fault of the programmer. Our theory of programming, whose objective is to avoid non-termination, can afford to treat all instances of non-termination as equally bad; and the whole theory can often be simplified just by regarding them as equal.

After definition of the relevant programming concepts, the next stage in the top-down exploration of the theory of programming is the formalisation and proof of the mathematical properties of programs. The simplest proprieties are those that can be expressed as algebraic laws, either equations or inequations; they are often pleasingly similar to algebraic properties proved of the familiar operators of the arithmetic of numbers, which are taught at school.

For example, it is well known that disjunction—used to define non-determinism in programming—is like multiplication: it is associative and commutative, with **false** serving as its unit and **true** as its zero. Furthermore, conjunction distributes through disjunction, and so do most simple programming combinators, including sequential composition: see Table 1. Laws are the basis for algebraic reasoning and calculation, in which professional engineers often develop considerable skill.

The same principles of programming language definition apply to process algebras, which have the observational variable *trace* in their alphabet. One of the risks of interactive programming is deadlock; and the worst deadlock is the process that never engages in any recordable action, no matter what events the environment may offer to engage in at the same time. As a result, its trace is always empty

$$\mathbf{0} =_{df} trace = \langle \rangle$$

This definition is equally applicable to the process *STOP* in CSP.

A fundamental operation of a process algebra is external choice $P + Q$, which allows the environment to choose between its operands by appropriate selection of the first event to occur. It has an astonishingly simple definition

$$P + Q \ =_{df}\ (P \wedge Q \wedge \mathbf{0}) \vee (\overline{\mathbf{0}} \wedge (P \vee Q))$$

While the trace is empty, an event can be refused by $P + Q$ just if it can be refused by both of them. When the trace is non-empty, the subsequent behaviour is determined by either P or Q, whichever is consistent with the first event in the trace. If both are, the result is non-deterministic.

As in the case of the conditional, the algebraic properties of this simple definition can be simply verified by truth tables. External choice is commutative, idempotent and associative, with unit $\mathbf{0}$; and it is mutually distributive with non-deterministic union. The corresponding operator $\square$ in CSP has the same properties, but its definition has been made a little more complicated, to take account of the risk of divergence of one of its two operands. The top-down approach to both theories helps to elucidate exactly how two very similar theories may in some ways be subtly different.

The aim of the top-down method of system development is to deliver programs that are correct. Assurance of correctness is obtained not just by testing or debugging the code, but by the quality of the reasoning that has gone into its construction. This top-down philosophy of correctness by construction is based on the premise that every specification and every design and every program can be interpreted as a description of some subset of a mathematically defined space of observations. But the converse is certainly not true. Not every subset of the observation space is expressible as a program. For example, the empty predicate **false** represents a specification that no physical object could ever implement: if it did, the object described would be irretrievably unobservable.

The question therefore arises, what are the additional characteristics of those subsets of observations that are in fact definable in the restricted notations of a particular programming language? The answer would help us to distinguish the feasible specifications that can be implemented by program from the infeasible ones that cannot.

The distinguishing characteristics of implementable specifications have been called *healthiness conditions* [Dijkstra]. They act like conservation laws or symmetry principles in physics, which enable the scientist quickly to dismiss impossible experiments and implausible theories; and similarly they can protect the engineer from many a wild-goose chase. As in the natural sciences, healthiness conditions can be justified by appeal to the real-world meaning of the variables in the alphabet. Analysis of termination gives a good example.

A characteristic feature of a program in any programming language is that if its first part fails to terminate, any fragment of program which is written to be executed afterwards will never be started, and the whole program will also fail to terminate. In our top-down theory, the non-terminating program is represented by the predicate **true**; so the relevant healthiness condition can be neatly expressed as an algebraic law, stating that **true** is a left zero for sequential composition

> **true**; P = **true**,   for all programs P

This law is certainly not true for all *predicates* P; for example, when P is false, we have

> **true**; **false** = **false**

This just means that the healthiness condition is succeeding in its primary purpose of showing that unimplementable predicates like **false** can never be expressed as a program.

The majority of simple algebraic laws that are applicable to programs can be proved once-for-all as mathematical theorems about sets of observations; and they can be applied equally to designs and even to specifications. But healthiness conditions, as we have seen, are just not true for arbitrary sets: they cannot be proved and they must not be applied to specifications. Their scope is mainly confined to reasoning about programs, including program transformation and optimisation. It is therefore an obligation on a programming theorist to prove that each healthiness condition holds at least for all programs expressible in the restricted notations of the programming language, and perhaps to certain design notations as well.

The method of proof is essentially inductive on the syntax of the language. All the primitive components of a program must be proved to satisfy the healthiness condition; furthermore, all the operators of the language (including recursion) must be proved to preserve the health of their operands. Here is a proof that union and sequential composition preserve the healthiness condition that they respect non-termination: for union,

> **true**; $(P \lor Q)$
> = (**true**; P) $\lor$ (**true**; Q)
>> relational composition distributes through disjunction
> = **true** $\lor$ **true**   by induction hypothesis, P and Q are healthy
> = **true** $\lor$ is idempotent

and for sequential composition,

> **true**; $(P;\ Q)$
> = (**true**; P); Q composition is associative
> = **true**; Q by inductive hypothesis, P is healthy
> = **true**   by inductive hypothesis, Q is healthy

Algebraic laws are so useful in reasoning about programs, and in transforming them for purposes of optimisation, that we want to have as many laws as possible, provided of course that they are valid.

How can we know that a list of proven laws is complete in some appropriate sense? One possible sense of completeness is given by a normal form theorem, which shows that every program in the language can be reduced (or rather expanded) to a normal form (not necessarily expressible in the programming language).

A normal form should be designed so that the identity of meaning of non-identical normal forms is quite easy to decide, for example, merely by rearranging their sub-terms. Furthermore, if two normal forms are unequal, it should always be possible to find an observation described by one of them but not the other.

Unfortunately, there may be *no* finite set of algebraic laws that exactly characterises all true facts about the programming language. For example, even the simple relational calculus has no complete finite axiomatisation. One interpretation of the Church-Turing hypothesis states that no top-down analysis can ever exactly characterise those sets of observations that are computable by programs from those that are not. It is only by modelling computation steps of some kind of machine that we can distinguish the computable from the incomputable.

Specifications are inherently incomputable. It is their negations that are recursively enumerable: and they need to be, because we want to be able to prove by counterexample that a program is *not* correct. If your chief worry is accidental description of something that is incomputable or even contradictory, top-down theory development does not immediately address this concern. Complete protection can be obtained only by starting again from the bottom and working upward.

3   Bottom-Up

A bottom-up presentation of a theory of programming starts with a definition of the notations and syntactic structure of a particular programming language. Ideally, this should be rather a small language, with a minimum provision of primitive features; the hope is that these will be sufficiently expressive to define the additional features of more complex languages.

As an example language, we choose a subset of the pi-calculus at about the level of CCS. Figure 1 expresses its syntax in the traditional Backus-Naur form, and Figure 2 gives an informal specification of the meaning.

The traditional first example of a process expressed in a new process algebra is the simple vending machine *VM*: see Figure 3. It serves an indefinite series of customers by alternately accepting a *coin* and emitting a chocolate. The expected behaviour of a single customer engaging in a single transaction is

$$cust \ =_{df} \ \overline{coin}.choc.\mathbf{0}$$

The behaviour of the whole population of customers is modelled by the unbounded set !*cust*. This population can insert an indefinite number of coins; and at any time a lesser number of chocolates can be extracted.

But we plan to install a simple *VM* that can serve only one customer at a time. To implement this sequentialisation, we need an internal control signal nx, by which the machine signals to itself its own readiness for the next customer; a complete definition of the vending machine is given in Figure 3.

$$\langle event \rangle ::= \langle identifier \rangle \mid \overline{\langle identifier \rangle}$$

$$\langle process \rangle ::= \mathbf{0} \mid \langle event \rangle.\langle process \rangle$$
$$\mid \ (\langle process \rangle \mid \langle process \rangle) \mid !\langle process \rangle$$
$$\mid \ (\mathbf{new}\langle identifier \rangle) \ \langle process \rangle$$

Fig. 1. Syntax

- $\mathbf{0}$ is the deadlock process: it does nothing.
- $coin.P$ is a process that first accepts a $coin$ and then behaves like P.
- $\overline{nx}.\mathbf{0}$ first emits a control signal nx and then stops.
- $nx.Q$ first accepts a control signal nx and then behaves as Q.
- $P \mid Q$ executes P and Q in parallel. Signals emitted by one may be accepted by the other.
- $!P$ denotes parallel execution of an unbounded number of copies of P: $P \mid P \mid P \mid \ldots$
- $(\mathbf{new}\ e)\ P$ declares that e is a local event used only for interactions within its scope P.

Fig. 2. Explanation

$$one =_{df} nx.coin.\overline{choc}.\overline{nx}.\mathbf{0}$$
$$many =_{df} (!one) \mid (\overline{nx}.\mathbf{0})$$
$$VM =_{df} (\mathbf{new}\ nx)\ many$$

Fig. 3. Vending machine

The operational semantics of the programming language is presented as a collection of formulae, describing all the permitted steps that can be taken in the execution of a complete program. Each kind of step is described by a transition rule written in the form $P \to Q$, where P gives a pattern to be matched against the current state of the program, and Q describes how the program is changed after the step. For example, the rule

$$(e.P) \mid (\overline{e}.Q) \to (P \mid Q)$$

describes an execution step in which one process accepts a signal on e which is sent by the other. Emission and acceptance of the signal are synchronised, and their simultaneous occurrence is concealed; the subsequent behaviour is defined as parallel execution of the rest of the two processes involved.

The reduction shown above can be applied directly to a complete program consisting of a pair of adjacent processes written in the order shown and separated by the parallel operator $|$. But we also want to apply the reduction to processes written in the opposite order, to processes which are embedded in a larger network, and to pairs that are not even written adjacently in that network.

Such reductions can be described by a larger collection of formulae: e.g.,

$$(\overline{e}.Q) \mid (e.P) \rightarrow Q \mid P$$
$$((\overline{e}.Q) \mid (e.P)) \mid R \rightarrow (Q \mid P) \mid R$$
$$(e.Q \mid R) \mid (\overline{e}.P) \rightarrow (Q \mid R) \mid P$$

But even this is only a small subset of the number of transition rules that would be needed to achieve communication in all circumstances. A much easier way to deal with all cases is to just postulate that $|$ is a commutative operator, that it is associative, and that it has unit $\mathbf{0}$.

$$P \mid \mathbf{0} = P$$
$$P \mid Q = Q \mid P$$
$$P \mid (Q \mid R) = P \mid (Q \mid R)$$

(These equations are more usually written with equivalence ($\equiv$) in place of equality, which is reserved for syntactic identity of two texts. They are called structural *congruences*, because they justify substitution in the same way as equality.)

These are called *structural* laws in a process calculus. They represent the *mobility* of process, because the implementation may use the equations for substitution in either direction, and so move a process around until it reaches a neighbour capable of an interaction with it. In a bottom-up presentation, these laws are just postulated as axioms that define a particular calculus; they can be used in the proof of other theorems, but they themselves are not susceptible of proof, because there is no semantic basis from which such a proof could be constructed.

The laws governing reduction apply only to complete programs; and they need to be extended to allow reduction steps to take place locally within a larger context. For example a local reduction can occur anywhere within a larger parallel network, as stated by the rule

if $P \rightarrow P'$ then $(P \mid Q) \rightarrow (P' \mid Q)$

A similar law applies to hiding.

if $P \rightarrow P'$ then $(\mathbf{new}\ e)P \rightarrow (\mathbf{new}\ e)P'$

But there is no similar rule for $e.P$. A reduction of P is not permitted until after e has happened. It is only this omission of a rule that permits terminating programs to be distinguished from non-termination.

One of the main objectives of a theory of programming is to model the behaviour of computing systems that exist in the world today. The world-wide network of interconnected computers is obviously the largest and most important such system.

Any of the connected computers can emit a communication into the network at any time. There is reasonable assurance that the message will be delivered at some later time at some destination that is willing to accept it (if any). But the exact order of delivery does not necessarily reflect the order of sending: messages in the net can overtake each other.

This aspect of reality is very simply encoded in the calculus by adding a single new reduction step. This just detaches a message from its sender, and allows the message to proceed independently in its own timescale through the network to its destination.

$$\overline{e}.P \to (\overline{e}.0) \mid P$$

This means that the sender P is not delayed if the receiver is unready at the time of sending. The subsequent actions of the sender proceed in parallel with the journey undertaken by its message.

A calculus with such a reduction rule is called *asynchronous*, and output prefixing is usually omitted from its syntax. That is why the algebraic laws for an asynchronous calculus are different from those of a synchronous one.

Structural laws are also used in addition to reductions to formalise the intended meaning of the constructions of the language. For example, the repetition operator $(!P)$ denotes an unbounded set of parallel instances of the same process P. The addition of a new instance of P therefore makes no difference, as stated in the unfolding law

$$!P = P \mid (!P)$$

This law can be applied any number of times

$$P \mid (!P) = P \mid P \mid (!P) = \ldots$$

If each application allows a reduction, we can generate an infinite reduction sequence leading to potential non-termination. Consider for example the process P that reduces in one step to the empty process

$$P =_{df} (e.0 \mid \overline{e}.0) \to 0 \mid 0 = 0$$

This can be put into a repetition

$$!P = (e.0 \mid \overline{e}.0) \mid !P \to 0 \mid !P = !P$$

It follows that $!P$ can be subjected to an infinite series of reductions, without ever engaging in a useful interaction with its environment. This is just what is known as divergence or livelock, and it is clearly and obviously definable on the basis of an operational semantics. A top-down presentation cannot give such an obviously appropriate *definition* of non-termination, and has to postulate that the artificial variable $\overset{\rightharpoonup}{ok}$ is mysteriously allowed to take the value **false** whenever there is a risk of divergence.

Another useful definition in operational semantics is that of a labelled transition, in which the transition relation $\rightarrow$ is labelled by a trace of interactions with the environment that can occur during the evolution of the process.

$$P \overset{\langle\rangle}{\longrightarrow} Q =_{df} P \overset{*}{\rightarrow} Q$$

$$P \overset{(e)^\frown s}{\longrightarrow} Q =_{df} \exists P'.P \overset{*}{\rightarrow} e.P' \wedge P' \overset{s}{\rightarrow} Q$$

where $\overset{*}{\rightarrow}$ is the reflexive transitive closure of $\rightarrow$.

Now we can trace the evolution of our vending machine, using a few structural laws which seem reasonable

$$
\begin{aligned}
&many\\
&= \quad \overline{nx}.\mathbf{0} \mid \,!one &\\
&= \quad \overline{nx}.\mathbf{0} \mid (nx.coin.\overline{choc}.\overline{nx}.\mathbf{0}) \mid \,!one &\text{expanding }!\\
&\rightarrow \quad \mathbf{0} \mid (coin.\overline{choc}.\overline{nx}.\mathbf{0}) \mid \,!one &\text{reduction}\\
&= \quad coin.\overline{choc}.\overline{nx}.\mathbf{0} \mid \,!one &\mathbf{0}\text{ is unit of }!\\
&\rightarrow \quad coin.(\overline{choc}.\overline{nx}.\mathbf{0} \mid \,!one) &\text{reduction}\\
&\overset{coin}{\rightarrow} \quad \overline{choc}.\overline{nx}.\mathbf{0} \mid \,!one &\text{def } \overset{coin}{\rightarrow}\\
&\overset{choc}{\rightarrow} \quad \overline{nx}.\mathbf{0} \mid \,!one &\text{similarly}
\end{aligned}
$$

$$\therefore \quad many \overset{\langle coin, \overline{choc}\rangle}{\longrightarrow} many \qquad\qquad \text{local reduction}$$

$$\therefore \quad VM = ((\mathbf{new}\ nx)\ many \overset{\langle coin,\overline{choc}\rangle}{\longrightarrow} VM)$$

This mathematical derivation is a close simulation of the execution of the program. But does it prove that the program is correct? And what does correctness mean for a programming language that has been defined only in terms of its internal execution rather than what can be observed from outside?

The usual answer to the more general question is that a program is adequately specified in the programming language itself by displaying the equations that it should satisfy. For example, perhaps what we really want to prove about the vending machine is

$$VM = coin.\overline{choc}.VM$$

(In a more abstract language like CCS or CSP, such an equation would be permitted as a recursive definition of VM).

In constructing the proof of such equations, free use may be made of all the structural laws of the calculus. But in general the structural laws are deliberately restricted to transformations on the static shape of a formula, and they do not give enough information about equality of dynamically evolving behaviour. Such reasoning would require a set of laws much larger than those postulated by the calculus. What laws should they be? And how are they justified?

The solution to this problem is of startling originality. The user of the calculus is allowed to extend its set of laws by any new equations that may be desired, provided that this does not lead to a contradiction. A contradiction is defined as the proof of an equation between processes that obviously ought to be different, like a divergent process and a non-divergent one. For example, an equation $P = Q$ leads to contradiction if you can find some program $C[P]$ containing P which does not diverge, but when P is replaced by Q, $C[Q]$ actually can diverge.

Finer discriminations may be imposed by defining a function $obs(P)$, which maps a program P to some simple set of observations that may be made of it. For example, $obs(P)$ might map P onto the set of environments in which it might deadlock. In each case, one might observe the set of events offered by the environment but refused by the process. Then a contradiction is defined as a law that equates two programs with different observable refusal sets. An equation established in this way is called a *contextual equivalence*.

Proving that a proposed law $P = Q$ leads to contradiction is quite a challenge, because the context $C[]$ that reveals it may be very large. But proving that something is *not* a contradiction can be even harder, because it involves consideration of the infinite set of all possible contexts that can be written around P and Q; such a universal hypothesis requires an inductive case analysis over all the combinators of the calculus. Sometimes, only a reduced set of contexts is sufficient; this fact is established by proof of a *context lemma*.

As a result of their syntactic orientation, proofs by induction tend to be specific to a particular calculus, and care is needed in extending their results to calculi with a slightly different syntax, different reductions, or different structural laws. For this reason, each new variation of a familiar calculus is usually presented from scratch.

Heavy reliance on induction certainly provides a strong motive for keeping down the number of notations in the original syntax to an inescapable core of primitives, even if this makes the language less expressive or efficient in practical use. The pursuit of minimality tends to favour the design of a language at a relatively low level of abstraction. The power of such a language matches that of machine code, which offers enormous power, including the opportunity for each instruction to interfere with the effect of any other.

In the presence of multi-threading or non-determinacy, understanding of the behaviour of an arbitrary program becomes rapidly impossible. And there are few general theorems applicable to arbitrary programs that can aid the understanding, or permit optimising transformations that preserve behavioural equivalence. The solution to this problem is to confine attention to programs that follow defined protocols and restrictive conventions to limit their mutual interaction.

The meaning of conformity with the convention is defined by means of a *type system*, which is also usually presented in a bottom-up fashion. The syntax gives a notation for expressing all the types that will be needed. Then a collection of axioms and proof rules provide a means of deducing which parts of each program can be judged to belong to a particular type. In a higher level programming language the programmer may be required or allowed to provide adequate type information for variables and parameters; but most of the labour of type checking or even type inference can be delegated to a compiler.

The consistency of the typing system is established by showing that pairs of programs equated by the structural laws have the same type, and that each reduction step in execution preserves the proper typing of its operand. This is called a *subject reduction* theorem. Subsequent development of the theory can then be confined to properly typed programs.

A type system based on an operational model may be designed to supply information that is highly relevant to program optimisation. For example, it can detect dead code that will never be executed, and code that will be executed at most once. Other type systems can guarantee absence of certain kinds of programming error such as deadlock. If it is known that no type can be deduced for such an erroneous program, then type consistency ensures that the error can never occur a run time.

Because type systems enforce disciplined interaction, well-typed programs often obey additional laws, useful both for comprehension and for optimisation. Type systems thereby raise the level of abstraction of an operationally defined programming language; their role in the bottom-up development of a theory is complementary to that of healthiness conditions, which in a top-down development bring abstract denotational specifications closer to implementable reality.

Operational presentations of semantics are particularly appropriate for analysis of security aspects of communication in an open distributed network, where co-operation between a known group of agents is subject at any time to accidental or deliberate interference by an outsider. The main role of the language is to define and limit the capabilities of the outsider.

For example, the localisation operator (**new** e) enables an agent in the system to invent an arbitrary secret code or a *nonce*, and the structural laws of the language are designed to ensure that it remains secret except to those who have received it in an explicit communication. It is then the responsibility of an implementation of the language to enforce this level of secrecy by choice of an appropriate cryptographic method. Furthermore, if the proof of security of a protocol depends on observance of type constraints, it is essential at run time to check the types of any code written by an outsider before executing it in a sensitive environment.

The purpose of a secure protocol can often be described most clearly by an equation $P = Q$, where P describes the situation before some desired interaction takes place, and Q describes the desired result afterwards. For example, we might use the equation

$$(e.P \mid \overline{e}.Q) = P \mid Q$$

to describe the intended effect of transmission of a signal e from Q to P. But this is not a valid equation in the calculus, because it is not secure against interference by an outsider R, which can intercept and divert the signal, as permitted by the reduction

$$e.P \mid \overline{e}.Q \mid e.R \;\rightarrow\; e.P \mid Q \mid R$$

This reduction will be inhibited if the name e is kept secret from the outside, so it is valid to equate

$$(\textbf{new } e)\,(e.P \mid \overline{e}.Q) \;=\; (\textbf{new } e)\,(P \mid Q)$$

Since it is assumed that the outsider is limited to the capabilities of the programming language, an arbitrary attack can be modelled by a context $C[]$ placed around both sides of the equation. A standard proof of contextual equivalence would be sufficient to show that there is no such context. That is exactly what is needed to show that no outsider can detect or affect the desired outcome described by the equation.

As in this example, the required protection is often achieved with the aid of the **new** operator, which prevents an outsider from detecting or communicating a signal with the new name. It is much more difficult to design a top-down theory for application to problems of security, privacy and authentication. A top-down theory has to start with a decision of exactly what an intruder could observe of another agent in the system, and what attacks are possible upon it. But this understanding is exactly what the security analysis seeks to develop; it cannot be postulated in advance.

A great deal of research effort has been expended on designing proof techniques that are simpler to apply and more efficient to mechanise than proof by non-contradiction. Many of these methods use a variation of the technique of bisimulation [6]. A bisimulation is a postulated equivalence between programs that is respected by the individual steps of the operational semantics of the language, i.e., if two programs belong to the same equivalence class before the step, they belong to the same equivalence class afterwards.

For particular calculi and for particular kinds of bisimulation, theorists have proved that the postulation of the bisimulation as an equality will not lead to a contradiction. Then that kind of bisimulation may safely be used to prove equality of arbitrary programs in the language. For a well-explored calculus, there may be a whole range of bisimulations of varying strength, some suitable for mechanisation, and some suitable for quick disproof. They are all approximations to the truly intended notion of equality, which is defined by the more elusive concept of contextual equivalence.

As described above, much of the effort in a bottom-up theory goes into the determination of when two programs are equal. This is absolutely no problem in a top-down theory, where normal mathematical equality of sets of observations is used throughout. Conversely, much of the effort of a top-down theory goes into determination of which subsets of observations correspond to implementations. This is absolutely no problem in a bottom-up theory, where programs are always by definition computable. In each case the theorist approaches the target by a series of approximations. In the happy circumstance that they are working on the same language and the same theory, top-down and bottom-up will eventually meet in the middle.

4   Meeting in the Middle

A brief summary of the merits and deficiencies of top-down and bottom-up presentations show that they are entirely complementary.

- A top-down presentation of a theory of programming gives excellent support for top-down development of programs, with justifiable confidence that they are correct by construction.

  By starting with observable system properties and behaviour, it permits and encourages the advance specification of a system yet to be implemented, and the careful design of the interfaces between its major components. It provides concepts, notations and theorems that can be used throughout the design and implementation of software systems of any size and complexity.

  On the other hand, an abstract denotational semantics gives no help at all in the debugging of incorrect programs. It is therefore useless in the analysis of legacy systems, many of which have been written and frequently changed without regard to general design principles, clarity of structure, or correctness of code.

- A bottom-up presentation of a theory of programming gives excellent support for reasoning about the execution of programs that have already been written.

  By starting with a definition of the individual steps of execution, it models directly the run-time efficiency of programs. Execution traces provide the primary diagnostic information on debugging runs of incorrect programs.

  On the other hand, an operational semantics gives no help at all in relating a program to its intended purpose. It is therefore useless in reasoning about programs before they have been written in the notations of a particular programming language.

If programming theory is ever to make its full contribution to the practice of programming, we must offer all the benefits of both styles, and none of the deficiencies. Neither approach could be recommended by itself. It is clearly foolish to provide a conceptual framework for program design if there is no way of executing the resulting program step by step on a computer. It would be equally unsatisfactory to present an operationally defined theory if there is no way of describing what a program is intended to do.

In the natural sciences, it is a necessary condition of acceptability of a theory that it should agree with experiment. Experiments are equally important in validation of theories of programming. They test the efficiency with which a new programming concept can be implemented and the convenience with which it can be used. An experiment which requires the design, implementation and use of a completely new programming language is prohibitively time-consuming.

For rapid scientific progress, it is preferable just to add a single new feature to an existing programming language, its compiler and its run time system. The first trial applications may be conducted by a group of experimental programmers, who have accepted the risk that the new feature may soon be changed or withdrawn. Even such a limited experiment is expensive; and worse, it is difficult to interpret the results, because of uncontrollable factors such as the skill and the experience of the people involved.

That is why it is advisable to restrict experimentation to test only theories that have shown the highest initial promise. The promise of a theory is not judged by its popularity or by its novelty or by its profitability in competition with rival theories. Quite the reverse: it is by its coherence and close agreement with other theories that a new theory can be most strongly recommended for test. Such agreement is much more impressive if the theories are presented in radically differing styles.

From the practical point of view, it is the stylistic differences that ensure complementarity of the benefits to the user of the programming language. And the results of the experiment are much more convincing if the implementors and trial users are completely independent of the original theorists, as they usually are in more mature branches of Science.

The unification of theories is not a goal that is easy to achieve, and it often requires a succession of adjustments to the details of the theories, and in the way they are tested. The development of an abstract denotational model to match a given operational semantics is known as the problem of full abstraction. It took many years to discover fully abstract models for PCF, a simple typed functional programming language that was presented by an operational semantics.

A recent model [1, 5] represents a type of a programming language by the rules of a two-person game, and a function by a strategy for playing the game. A large and complex collection of healthiness conditions is imposed on the games and strategies to ensure that every strategy that satisfies them can be denoted by a program expressed in the syntax of PCF.

It is generally considered sufficient to prove this just for finite games, which correspond to programs that do not use recursion or any other form of unbounded iteration. That is the best that can be done, because it is impossible within an abstract model to formulate healthiness conditions that will select exactly those sets of observations that are implementable as iterative programs.

In the practical development and analysis of programs, it is quite uncommon to make a direct appeal to the definition of the programming language, whether denotational or operational. Much more useful are theorems that have been based on those definitions; many of these take the form of algebraic laws, either proven from definitions or postulated as healthiness conditions. The importance of laws is recognised both by top-downers and by bottom-uppers, who measure progress in their chosen direction by accumulation of larger collections of useful laws.

When both theories have been adequately developed, I suggest that an appropriate measure of successful meeting in the middle is provided by the overlap of the two collections of laws. Adjustments can (and should) then be made to the details of both theories, until the overlap is sufficiently broad to meet all the needs of practice. If the practitioner uses just the appropriate laws in the appropriate circumstances, the merits of both approaches can be safely combined.

In a perfect meeting, the laws derived from the top-down and from the bottom-up would be exactly the same. In fact, this is not necessary. All that is needed is that the operationally defined axioms and laws should be a subset of those provable from the denotational definitions. Then all the remaining laws proveable from the denotations will be contextual equivalences. The existence of the denotational model guarantees their consistency, even without the need for an exhaustive inductive argument on contexts.

Identity of differently derived theories is not the only goal; and when applying the same derivational techniques to different programming paradigms, differences in the algebraic laws are to be expected and even welcomed. It turns out that a great many algebraic laws are common to nearly all paradigms, but it is the laws that they do not share that are even more interesting. The fundamental property that distinguishes two paradigms is often very neatly expressed by an algebraic law, free of all the clutter of detail involved in a formal definition, and unaltered when the detail changes.

For example, functional programming languages are classified as lazy or non-lazy. In a non-lazy language, each function evaluates its arguments first, so if an argument aborts, so does the function call. As a consequence, functional composition (denoted by semicolon) has abortion as its left zero:

true; $P = $ **true**

However, a lazy functional language does not satisfy this law. It allows a constant function K to deliver its answer without even looking at its argument:

true; $K = K$

However, a lazy language still satisfies a right zero law:

P; **true** = **true**

So does a non-lazy language, unless it allows an argument E to raise an exception or jump. In this case the aborting function does not get the chance to start, so E; **true** $= E$.

Discussion of such laws is highly relevant to the selection and design of a programming language, as well as its implementation and optimisation. Future texts on comparative programming languages will surely exploit the power of algebra to explain the fundamental principles of the subject.

Fascination with the elegance and expressive power of laws was what inspired the development of abstract algebra as a branch of modern mathematics. Since the earliest days, mathematics has been primarily concerned with the concept of number. Its progress has been marked by the discovery of new and surprising varieties. Starting with positive integers, even the discovery of zero was a major advance. Then come negative numbers, fractions, reals, and complex numbers.

In modern times, study of the foundations of mathematics has given a denotational semantics to each of these different kinds of number. Natural numbers are defined as sets, integers and fractions as pairs, and reals as sequences. Correspondingly different definitions are given for the arithmetic operations that are performed on the different kinds of number.

In each case, algebraic laws are proved on the basis of the definitions. In spite of the fact that the definitions are so different, most of the laws turn out to be the same. It is the sharing of laws that justifies the use of the same arithmetic operator to denote operations with such radically different definitions. The laws have then inspired the development of other interesting mathematical structures, like quaternions and matrices, for which algebraically similar operations can be defined. Algebra, among all branches of mathematics, is the one that takes reusability as its primary goal.

Computing Science makes progress by discovery of new patterns and paradigms of programming. These are embodied in new programming languages, and subjected to the test of trial implementation and use. The procedural paradigm was among the earliest, and still has the widest application. Now there is also a declarative paradigm, which already splits into two major branches, the logical paradigm which permits backtracking, and the functional paradigm that does not. The functional paradigm splits into lazy and non-lazy varieties.

The advent of multiprocessors and networking has introduced a new paradigm of distributed computing, with even more variations. Some of them are based on sharing of global random access memory, and others on explicit communication. Communications may be ordered or unordered; they may be global or directed along channels; and they may be synchronised or buffered.

In addition to notations traditionally recognised in the community as programming languages, we should consider the languages used for database queries, spreadsheets, menu generators, and other complex interfaces that are coming into wide-spread use. A significant challenge for programming theory is to bring some order into this growing range of tools, and develop an understanding to assist in the selection of an appropriate tool for each purpose, and for using them in combination when necessary.

For purposes of classification, comparison, and combination, both denotational and operational semantics have far too much detail to convey the desired understanding and illumination. It is only the algebra that captures the essence of the concepts at an appropriately high level of abstraction. It is perhaps for the same reason that algebraic laws are also the most useful in practice for engineering calculation.

The primary role of algebraic laws is recognised in the most abstract of branches of algebra, namely category theory. Categories provide an excellent source of elegant laws for programming. Its objects nicely represent the types of a programming language, and its basic operation of composition of arrows is a model for the combination of actions evoked by parts of a program.

Additional important operators and their types are specified entirely by the algebraic laws that they satisfy. The specification of an operator is often accompanied by a proof that there is only one operator that satisfies it – at least up to isomorphism. This gives assurance that the stated laws are complete: no more are needed, because all other categorial properties of the operator can be proved from them. Finally, a wide range of differing categories can be explored and classified simply by listing the operators which they make available and the laws which they satisfy.

These considerations suggest a third approach to the development of programming theory, one that starts with a collection of algebraic laws as a definitive presentation of the semantics of a programming language [2]. The theory then develops by working outwards in all directions. Working upwards explores the range of denotational models for languages which satisfy the laws. Working downwards explores the range of correct implementations for these languages. And working sideways explores the range of similar theories and languages that might have been chosen instead.

The work of the theorist is not complete until the consequences of theory have been fully developed in all relevant directions. Such an ambitious programme can be achieved only by collaboration and accumulation of results by members of different research traditions, each of whom shares an appreciation of the complementary contributions made by all the others.

5   Acknowledgements

The views put forward in this paper evolved during a long collaboration with He Jifeng on research into unifying theories of programming. They contribute towards goals pursued by the partners in the EC Basic Research Project CONCUR; and they have been subjected to test in the EC Basic Research Project PROCOS. They are more fully expounded in [4], which contains a list of 188 further references. Significant contributors to this work at Oxford include Carroll Morgan, Jeff Sanders, Oege de Moor, Mike Spivey, Jeff Sanders, Annabelle McIver, Guy McCusker, and Luke Ong.

Other crucial clarifications and insights were obtained during a sabbatical visit to Cambridge in conversations with Robin Milner, Andy Pitts, Martin Hyland, Philippa Gardner, Peter Sewell, Jamey Leifer, and many others. I am also grateful to Microsoft Research Limited for supporting my visit to Cambridge, and to researchers at Microsoft who have devoted their time to my further education, including Luca Cardelli, Andy Gordon, Cedric Fournet, Nick Benton and Simon Peyton-Jones.

The organisers of POPL 1999 in San Antonio invited me to present my thoughts there, and the participants gave useful encouragement and feedback. Krzysztof Apt and John Reynolds have suggested many improvements that have been made since an earlier draft of the paper, and more that could have been.

References

[1] S. Abramsky, R. Jagadeesan and P. Malacaria. *Full abstraction for PCF*. To appear in *Information and Computation*.

[2] J. C. M. Baeten and W. P. Weijland. *Process Algebra*. CUP 1990, ISBN 0521 400430.

[3] E. W. Dijkstra. *A Discipline of Programming*. Prentice Hall 1976, ISBN 013 215871X.

[4] C. A. R. Hoare and He Jifeng. *Unifying Theories of Programming*. Prentice Hall 1998, ISBN 0-13-458761-8.

[5] J. M. E. Hyland and C. H. L. Ong. *On Full Abstraction for PCF: I, II and III*. To appear in *Informatics and Computation*.

[6] R. Milner *Communication and Concurrency*. Prentice Hall 1989, ISBN 013 1150073.

[7] A. W. Roscoe. *Theory and Practice of Concurrency*. Prentice Hall 1998, ISBN 013 6744095.

Scientific Decisions which Characterize VDM

Cliff B. Jones

Department of Computer Science
Manchester University
M13 9PL, UK
cliffjones@acm.org

Dedicated to the memory of Heinz-Peter Chladek

Abstract. The formal description and development method known as
VDM has been used extensively, its specification language is now an ISO
standard, and it has influenced other specification languages. The origins
of VDM are normally placed in language description or semantics but it
is probably best known in the wider arena of formal methods for (general)
program specification and design. This paper sets out a personal view
of some of the key technical decisions which characterize the Vienna
Development Method.

VDM is generally believed to stand for *Vienna Development Method*. The
programming language description aspects of VDM were forged in the heat of a
compiler development project in the IBM Laboratory in Vienna between 1973
and 1976; the technical decisions which characterize this work are outlined in
Section 2. VDM is also a general formal method in that it can be applied to programs or systems other than compilers; scientific decisions relating to this more
general area are discussed in Section 3. Preceding these substantive sections, the
scene is set in Section 1. Some conclusions are offered in Section 4.

1   Background

It must be a relatively small proportion of scientific developments whose progress
is defined by large discontinuities. In my opinion, progress in research on 'formal
methods' has built steadily since the 1960s and the identification of new ideas
has nearly always benefited from earlier work and has rarely forced a complete
revolution in thinking. It is therefore worth reviewing the background pre-VDM.[1]

During the 1960s, there was a growing awareness that programming languages were complex enough that their semantics needed to be described formally. This proved to be a less straightforward task than had been devising BNF
to fix the context-free syntax of programming languages. A seminal conference
was organised by Heinz Zemanek in Baden-bei-Wien in September 1964 (the

---

[1] The papers identified here as important not only represent a personal choice but
their selection hass also been influenced by accessibility.

J. Wing, J. Woodcock, J. Davies (Eds.): FM'99, Vol. I, LNCS 1708, pp. 28–47, 1999.

proceedings [73] contain transcripts of some interesting discussions). One of the clearest semantic approaches proposed was to write a function which, for a given program and starting state, computes the corresponding final state[2] (see for example [61][3]). Of course, this is what an *interpreter* does. An *abstract interpreter* was made (shorter and) more perspicuous by defining an abstract form of both the program and the state. Devising an abstract syntax for a language basically required choosing an abstraction of parse trees (but even here there are some detailed issues on which further comments are made in Section 2.1). Defining states abstractly involved finding convenient mathematical abstractions such as using a set of things in preference to a list if the semantics did not depend on the order.[4]

In the 1960s, IBM was developing (see [77, Part XII]) a new programming language which became known as 'PL/I'. In conjunction with members of the UK Hursley laboratory, the IBM Vienna Laboratory set out to provide a complete formal specification of the semantics of PL/I. This was a heroic effort resulting in many hundreds of pages of formulae (and special software for printing them). They called the work 'Uniform Language Description III' but JAN Lee coined the term *Vienna Definition Language* and it is 'VDL' rather than 'ULD-III' which stuck. The most readable description of this work is [57].

Technically, the definition of PL/I was an abstract interpreter whose intent was similar to [62].[5] But the 'richness' of the PL/I language posed enormous challenges to the ingenuity of the definers. For example, PL/I programs could change their locus of execution both by goto statements and by an exception mechanism. Furthermore, in the original version of the language, a 'tasking' concept permitted parallel execution of portions of program which shared a common state. The basic abstract interpreter idea was extended and these concepts were modelled by keeping a whole control tree in the 'state'. The idea worked in that the abstract interpreter could arrive at any of the intended final states but –as we shall see below– it made it difficult to reason about the definition.

There was in fact another impediment to reasoning about the VDL abstract interpreters. The concept of passing parameters by reference had been modelled by the (now universal) wheeze of splitting a mapping from names (program identifiers) to values into an *environment* which maps names to locations and a *store* which maps locations to values. *Locations* were an abstract surrogate for the

---

[2] In its most obvious form, this was clearly limited to deterministic programs.

[3] Note use of the word 'description' rather than 'specification' in McCarthy's title; Mosses has also made the point that whether or not something is a specification is a question for standards organisations; in nearly all cases, formalists are producing descriptions.

[4] This might sound trivial but, when the ECMA/ANSI committee used a method which revolved around an abstract machine, they eschewed the use of difficult abstractions like sets; the consequence was that if a state component was a list, the implementors had to search the entire definition to ascertain if any essential use was made of the order before they could decide on the design of their run-time state.

[5] The Vienna group always insisted on also remembering the stimulus from that wonderful gentleman C C Elgot.

machine addresses which an implementation might use. So far, so good. Unfortunately it was found necessary to retain the whole stack of active environments in the state.

Although the VDL definitions were operational in the sense that they computed a (set of) final outcome(s) for a given pair of program and initial state, they were certainly not *Structured Operational Semantic* descriptions. This negative statement goes beyond the contrast with the neat inference rule style of [70]; it is more aimed at the way in which complex machinery had crept into the state.

It must however be remembered that we are talking about the mid-60s, that PL/I was by far the most complex language about at that time, that other languages which had had their semantics formalised were trivial by comparison, and –most tellingly of all– this was the first real formal description of a concurrent language. It must also be said that the process of writing the descriptions did something to clean up the language.[6]

It is also interesting to note that the basic abstract machine idea was embroidered with axiomatic extensions. For example, PL/I left a compiler freedom as to how compound variables such as structures were mapped onto store. The Vienna group used an implicit or axiomatic characterization of their storage model to capture this. The initial work was done in the mid-60s but is most easily read about in [10] which tackles a more general storage model.

Personally, I came into this story in 1968 when I persuaded IBM to send me on assignment to Vienna. I'd been working on testing techniques for the first PL/I product and had become convinced that *post-facto* testing of such complex software was never going to yield a reliable product and I wanted to see how formal descriptions could be used in a reasoned design process.

Vienna changed my life in many ways and I owe a huge debt of gratitude to the wonderful group that I joined in 1968. Peter Lucas was already working on compiler correctness proofs and his 'twin machine' idea [56] –applied to a non-trivial proof of the equivalence of ways of referring to variables– was a great starting point. We went on to give correctness proofs of standard compiler algorithms [29, 53]; to detect bugs in IBM products [28, 31]; and to devise new implementations based on the models of languages and target machines (e.g. [32]).[7] Another important contribution by Lucas from this phase was his insistence that we try to separate *language concepts*.

In spite of the successes, we were paying a high price for the excessive machinery in the VDL-style of definition. One of the most troublesome lemmas in [53] stated that the interpretation of a single statement from the source language left the environment component of the state unchanged. The proof was non-trivial

---

[6] One amusing example is the reluctant acceptance of what the Hursley implementors referred to as 'Bekič recursion' for proper static scoping rules.

[7] It is unfortunate that much of the material was published only in IBM reports. The most accessible contemporary source was [53]: a testing collaboration which surprisingly led to friendship rather than (my) murder. That paper also contains further references.

because the statement could be a block or a procedure call either of which did in fact install new environments; one had to show that they were popped properly.

So by the end of my first sojourn in Vienna, we had a clear notion of what was making it difficult to use operational definitions as a basis for compiler design. I had also proposed an exit idea which was to be the seed from which the exit combinator of VDM was to grow (here again, the early documentation was only in a report [30]). Essentially, the idea –in VDL terms– was to obviate the need for the entire program being in the state by having a way of testing for abnormal return and taking appropriate action. The state of the abstract interpreter was smaller but, more importantly, what could *not* happen during interpretation was clearer.

Another interesting example of saying more by saying less came from proofs about abstract objects. Although this was to have more impact on the non-language research, the first application related to compiling algorithms. Lucas's 'twin machine' [56] approach tackled the job of proving the equivalence of two algorithms which employed different data structures. His approach was to define a new abstract interpreter which 'twinned' the data structures and prove that a predicate (which we came later to call a *datatype invariant*) remained true. Having shown that a certain relationship was preserved between the two data structures, one could then prove by induction over the computation that two functions always gave the same result. The final step was to 'erase' the unwanted components. I realised that –at least in this example– one of the data structures was more abstract than the other and that it could be recovered from the more detailed one. The proof in [38] called the function m (I did not use the term *homomorphism*) but the approach is similar to that in [65, 36].

There were also other seeds waiting to bear fruit. The Baden conference had been the genesis of IFIP's Working Group 2.2 and there had been an exciting meeting in Vienna in April 1969.[8] Following on from that meeting, Dana Scott came back to the Vienna Lab. for a stimulating visit in August 1969. We had actually invited him to help us make sense of Floyd's [22] (about which I still had questions after visiting CMU with Ted Codd as my IBM minder!). In fact, Scott gave us a first glimpse of the then new *Denotational Semantics* ideas in [18]. Hans Bekič went to work with Peter Landin at QMC from November 1968– November 1969. Landin's role in the development of denotational semantics is often under-estimated but anyone who has read [54, 55] will have no doubt as to his seminal contributions.[9]

When I returned to IBM Hursley in late 1970, it was to manage my own 'Ad Tech' group which meant that I could send others crazy with my ideas.

---

[8] Among other things, this was one of Tony Hoare's first attempts to describe an *axiomatic method*. Even I must have said something about post-conditions because I remember Belnap joking one lunch time that I should just pay at the beginning if I was only interested in the post-condition.

[9] There was a fascinating workshop at Essex University in July 1971; John Laski was the organiser and most of the key members of the Vienna group came over; Landin was a key discussant.

In the following three years, we initiated much of what was to comprise the non-language parts of VDM.

The first thing I wanted to do was to test out a 'small state' approach to semantics. In particular, because of the difficulties with [53], I wanted to show that while the state was an argument and result of most semantic functions, the environment only need to be an argument since it could not be modified. Furthermore, the exit idea gave us a way of defining what it meant to execute a goto without the heavy mechanism used in VDL. After some intense efforts to convince my new colleagues, we set about employing these ideas on Algol 60 and wrote [3]. I like to call this a *functional semantics* but it is actually close in spirit to Plotkin's *Structured Operational Semantics* [70] without the clear advantage of his rule notation. Furthermore, we had ducked the problem of concurrency. This work was to come to fruition in VDM.

Let us turn now to the efforts on developing 'ordinary' (non-compiler) programs. We needed for other reasons a table-driven parser and my colleagues had produced and debugged a nice implementation of Earley's recogniser which they challenged me to prove correct. I tried and failed! I was mirroring Tony Hoare's experience in his proof of FIND [35] in that the step from specification to design was too big to bridge in one stage; we both needed marry the advantages of formalism with a stepwise design approach. I finally constructed my own reasoned development of Earley's recogniser in 1971 and it was published externally as [39]. Data refinement was crucial to this formal development. Interestingly, this paper did not employ the homomorphic mapping of both later and earlier VDM work but used a careful analysis of the properties required of abstract datatypes and a subsequent check that these properties were preserved in the representations. Having developed my program (which my colleagues insisted on being the first to test) a comparison with their code uncovered bugs in the latter.

VDM's separation of pre-conditions from post-conditions as well as the use of post-conditions of two states date from [40]. In fact, the struggle with avoiding angelic composition is graphically clear in [40, Section 3.5].

So, by the time the 'VDM group' formed in 1973[10] there was a lot from which to work.

2   Denotational Semantics

I vividly remember the call from Peter Lucas in late 1972 asking me if I'd like to come back to Vienna and try out formal methods on a full blown PL/I compiler for a completely new machine architecture. I said 'yes' with an alacrity which ignored the fact that my son Peter was due to arrive in the world. We also plotted who else we could get and agreed that I should call Dines Bjorner[11] who

---

[10] Most of the Vienna group were diverted onto looking for hidden parallelism in FORTRAN programs whilst I was enjoying myself in the UK.

[11] Dines and I can still never agree where we first met!

proved equally reluctant to join the team. I moved to Vienna in March 1973 on a 'permanent' transfer.

Even before the group fully assembled, we exchanged style proposals and there was a rapid and almost unanimous vote to write a formal semantics for (ECMA/ANSI) PL/I in the denotational style, a naive assumption that the IBM machine architecture would be more stable than the output from the standards committee, and an equally optimistic assumption that the formal definition of the machine architecture promised from Poughkeepsie would be adequate for our object-time design.

The remainder of this section discusses some of the technically interesting decisions which were made in the two years or so in which we were trying to design a compiler, refine our methods, and correct some of the wilder peculiarities of the object machine architecture.

2.1 Superficial Points

The PL/I definition [8] is an interesting document: the base definition (Part I) is a fraction of the size of the VDL definition[12] and is matched by a Part II which contains a commentary of about the same size. Anyone wishing to see the style, might find it easier to tackle the ALGOL 60 description in [33] or that for Pascal in [4].

The obvious comparison is with the 'Oxford style' of writing denotational descriptions (see [67, 64, 75, 23]. One immediate –but superficial– difference is the use in the Vienna descriptions of longer names for functions and their parameters. I believe this comes from tackling larger specificands and reflects a tendency which is familiar to all who have written large pieces of software.

The Vienna group experimented with different document structures for presenting descriptions: [8] starts with the whole (abstract) syntax, followed by the so-called context conditions, then the state or auxiliary objects and finally all of the semantic functions. In [33], we tried to group the material (syntax, context conditions, semantic functions) by language construct. Similarly, [8] separated all of the commentary into a separate volume whereas Bjorner and his colleagues pioneered a style of numbering lines of formulae and keying comments to those line numbers after each substantial chunk of formalism (see for example their landmark description of Ada [14]).

Even with the abstract syntax, Vienna managed to depart from orthodoxy. As mentioned above, an abstract syntax defines a set of trees which contain the essential information in a program with none of the syntactic clues which make it possible for a parser to get at the information. This leaves the issue of how one distinguishes sub-trees with similar content. The 'standard' approach is to put the load on a disjoint union operator as in

$$Stmt = Assign + Goto + Call + \ldots$$

---

[12] The ECMA/ANSI decision to drop PL/I's tasking was a relief and clearly helps the comparison.

We chose to use a simple set union and have a form of definition which forced a constructor:

$$Stmt = Assign \cup Goto \cup Call \cup \dots$$

$$\begin{aligned} Assign \; :: \quad & lhs \; : \; Var \\ & rhs \; : \; Expr \end{aligned}$$

Such 'composite object' definitions give rise to a convenient set of constructor and selector functions:

$$mk\text{-}Assign\colon Var \times Expr \to Assign$$
$$s\text{-}lhs\colon Assign \to Var$$
$$s\text{-}rhs\colon Assign \to Expr$$

which can be used in defining, *unter anderen*, semantic functions by cases as in:

$$M[\![mk\text{-}assign(l, r)]\!] = \dots$$
$$M[\![mk\text{-}Goto(id)]\!] = \dots$$

The Vienna style owes much to McCarthy's ideas on abstract syntax: in [61] he gave an axiomatic characterization of constructors and selectors.

Another minor observation relates to what we originally called *context conditions*. While the sort of syntax described above succeeds in abstracting from the trivia of concrete syntax, it is still *context free*: just as in Floyd's [21], there is no way –for example– of requiring that declarations and use of variables match. There is, however, a significant advantage in defining that subset of *Program* which the meaning function is expected to map to a denotation: the semantics is not clouded with the definition of context dependencies.[13] In the definitions written in Vienna and shortly thereafter, it was normal to define the context conditions as a recursive function over (a static environment and) the syntax tree:

$$is\text{-}wf[\![mk\text{-}Assign(l, r)]\!]\rho = \dots$$

An issue which was by no means minor or superficial was concurrency but I do not intend to go into it in this paper. As explained, the languages we described turned out to be sequential. Hans Bekič did propose a concurrent combinator but a full discussion of his work would require a comparison of the posthumous collection of his writings [7] with ideas like Plotkin's *Power Domains* [69] and that is well beyond the intended scope of this review.

2.2   Use of Combinators

Why is denotational semantics viewed as purer than operational semantics? Why is it better to define:

$$M\colon Program \to (\Sigma \to \Sigma)$$

---

[13] The terms *static semantics* and *dynamic semantics* have been used for what is here referred to as 'context conditions' and 'semantics'.

than

$$I: Program \times \Sigma \to \Sigma$$

I suppose that the respectable answer uses the argument of *full abstraction*; my view is less absolute! Recall that we were writing a language description as the basis for a compiler design. We certainly did not want to have mechanisms in the definition (state) which would not be present in our implementation: we hoped that the abstractions in the definition would have one or more representations in our object-time store but that the implementation would never conflate two abstract states. It was actually unlikely that having the state-to-state function as the denotation for a sequence of statements would simplify the problem of justifying any cross-statement optimizations.[14] What was crucial was the adoption of a 'small state' semantics (in contrast to VDL's 'grand state'): we needed a minimum of information in the state objects which were in the range of the (functional) denotations. With

$$Env = Id \to Loc$$

$$\Sigma = Loc \to Val$$

It seems to me, that there is an *essential* distinction between

$$M: Program \to (Env \to (\Sigma \to \Sigma))$$

and

$$I: Program \times State \to State$$

$$State = Env \times \Sigma$$

because one needs to be able to see immediately that environment-like information could not be changed by executing statements. Furthermore, we certainly had to eschew any tricks like putting the program text in Σ.

One could in fact ask whether we needed a denotational definition at all. I believe that the answer was 'yes, to keep us honest' rather than the importance of having fully abstract procedure denotations. Had Plotkin's nice SOS notation in [70] been known to us (rather than the heavier notation in [3]), I think we would have tried it although there would have still been a need for more notational invention to prevent the reduction rules becoming obscured by the need to have several auxiliary parameters for a PL/I description.

Well, that's probably enough heresy for now.

Less controversially, we chose to use combinators to represent the compositions of denotations. Thus with

$$M: Stmt \to Env \to (\Sigma \to \Sigma)$$

$$M[\![s1; s2]\!]\rho = m[\![s2]\!]\rho^\circ M[\![s1]\!]\rho$$

---

[14] Optimizations are an interesting issue in formal design of compilers – see [45].

was written as:

$$M[\![s1; s2]\!]\rho = M[\![s1]\!]\rho; m[\![s2]\!]\rho$$

Where the second semicolon was defined (for the moment) in the obvious way. We pushed the combinator idea further and half a dozen such combinators are carefully defined in [12]. I have no doubt that they made our definitions easier to grasp.

2.3 The exit Idea

The largest single distinction between the Oxford and Vienna styles came about with the description of statements which caused exceptional changes to the flow of control. For ease, we'll focus here on goto statements but modelling PL/I's exception mechanism (On statements etc.) presented the same challenge. This problem had been seen in the early in the work on 'mathematical semantics' and the idea of *continuations* was invented more-or-less independently by Mazurkiewicz71 [60], Lockwood Morris [66][15] and Chris Wadsworth [76][16].

Basically, by defining

$$Cont = \Sigma \rightarrow \Sigma$$

the semantics of statements could be defined

$$M_c\colon Statement \rightarrow Env \rightarrow (Cont \rightarrow Cont)$$

with the trick that

$$M_c[\![s_1; s_2]\!]\rho\theta = M_c[\![s_1]\!]\rho(M_c[\![s_2]\!]\rho\theta)$$

$$M_c[\![mk\text{-}Goto(id)]\!]\rho\theta = \rho(id)$$

We were aware of continuations in 1973 (probably via Bekič but I had attended some Oxford lectures by Christopher Strachey during my 1970–72 stay in Hursley and Lockwood Morris had also spent some time with me in Hursley). But I pushed hard to use a development of the exit idea from my first stay in Vienna. I remember some tough debates and I doubt that we would have used exits if the evidence of [3] had not been available: fortunately it was clear that exits could handle abnormal termination. Again to oversimplify somewhat, the idea was to use

$$M\colon Statement \rightarrow (\Sigma \rightarrow \Sigma \times Abn)$$

and then test where appropriate for a non-nil abnormal return value (*nil* marked normal return, non-nil values gave some indication of what was to be done next).

---

[15] Morris' title plays on Landin's [55].

[16] Peter Lucas has recently informed me that he first heard about continuations from van Wijngaarden.

The notation that I had used in Hursley was ugly because it made every test explicit but the combinator idea came to our rescue and gave a surprising bonus. We defined a combinator which performed exactly the right combination of the denotations of $s1$ and $s2$ to get the denotation of $s1; s2$ where either might have terminated abnormally.

What was this combinator? We redefined the (semantic) semicolon operator

$$f; g = (\lambda(\sigma, a) \cdot \textbf{if } a = \textbf{ nil then } g(\sigma) \textbf{ else } (\sigma, a))^\circ f$$

This is more than a symbol saving exercise. Prompted by Lucas' insistence to think about language concepts, we had all recognised that it was unreasonable to have to completely redefine a language when new concepts were added: for example, why did the semantics of expressions and assignment statements have to be defined differently depending whether the language had goto statements or not? The redefinition of the combinator seemed a more apposite way to reflect the distinction.[17]

The difference between continuations and exits excited considerable debate. No one who was at the delightful Winter School organised by Bjørner at Lyngby in 1979 (see [11] for proceedings), will forget Joe Stoy's *Deus es machina* drawing which expressed his distaste at the alleged operational exit; even in the paper in the proceedings, Joe catches his writing 'taking on a doctrinal flavour'. I could never understand this argument. I can see clearly that continuations are powerful; they can model co-routines which exits can't. But power is not necessarily a virtue: putting the whole program text in the VDL states was powerful in some sense. The limitation of exits appeared to me to be an advantage: where the weaker idea was adequate, employing it might say more.

Of course, there was a legitimate mathematical question about the relationship of these two approaches. In general, they could not be equivalent but definitions of what were intended to be the same language using the two styles ought correspond in some way. I took on the challenge of proving that *exit* and *continuation* definitions of a representative language correspond in [43] and [13, Chapter 5]. As one might guess from the multiple attempts, the proof was not simple and the process of teasing it into manageable steps is enlightening. For example, it is easily overlooked that one consequence of a continuation style definition is the need to put things in the environment which are not required for exit-style definitions.

2.4   Use in Proofs

As has been made clear, the Vienna work was not just an experiment in definition style; nor was the definition of a large language an end in itself: our goal was to use the PL/I definition [8] as a basis for the design of a compiler. While it lasted, the project was successful. We wrote the definition of the source language; we

---

[17] Peter Mosses has commented verbally that our approach influenced his early thinking on what was to become *Action Semantics* [68].

also wrote definitions of the key parts of the novel object machine architecture; a formal mapping from our object-time state back to the state of the PL/I description was not only written but uncovered errors in our design; we used a similar *retrieve function* to record the relationship between the concrete and abstract syntaxes (thus creating a specification of the front end).

Unfortunately, in February 1975, IBM decided to cancel the machine architecture and our project no longer had a target machine. I'll make some comments about the diaspora which followed below but before it occurred, the essential ideas were written up in [9, 41]. These documents certainly suffer from the confusion surrounding the redirection of the Vienna Laboratory but they did serve as some sort of contemporary record. Fortunately, those who moved on spent time producing more polished examples of the key ideas which originated in those three exciting years.

2.5   Use and Dissemination of VDM for Languages

The main books on the denotational semantics work from Vienna were [12, 13].

Dines Bjørner moved back to (what he just about remembered was) his home country of Denmark. His team at the university and later the colleagues he advised at the Danish Datamatik Center pushed the ideas on language work forward. A major achievement was the creation of the first European Ada complier to receive official validation; the definition was first published as [14].[18]

3   Specification and Formal Development of Programs

Although compilers play a critical role in the creation of software, they comprise a small percentage of the total population of programs. A development method which addressed only language description and processors would not receive wide circulation. Concepts like data abstraction and justified development steps permeate all applications of VDM but there are many technical commitments specific to the design of programs outside the compiler arena which deserve comment. This section discusses some of the decisions which relate to the specification and justified development of such software. Judging –for example– by the number of books which have been published, this aspect of VDM is now considerably more widely known than its specific application to formal semantics descriptions.

One pervasive idea is *compositional development*. This is not as easy to define as one might think at first sight. Assume that a (specified) component C is to be created and that its designer decides that a series of sub-components, say sc_i are needed. The essence of a compositional method is that the specifications of the sc_i should say all that it is necessary to insulate the development of the sc_i from the design of C. This means that the designer of C can verify its design without

---

[18] Subsequent research together with Egidio Astesiano's team led to SMoLCS. Comments on the RAISE work are given in Section 4 as are references to their work on database descriptions.

knowing the implementations of the sc_i and that the developers of the sc_i should not have their work rejected on any grounds other than those recorded in their specifications. In clear contrast is a development method which requires some extra proof obligation to be discharged once the development of all of the sc_i are available. There are however ways of meeting the above formal requirement without meeting its spirit. These issues become more delicate with concurrency so we'll leave them for now.

3.1   Why Models?

A computer system contains a model of something in the physical world.[19] For example, a database application might record information about students and courses or a process control system might maintain information about the required and expected values of measurement devices. Such a system provides a number of functions or operations which can be accessed via some interface. Such operations might change the state of the model inside the computer or simply access some (derived) values from that model. To describe or specify such a system is to pin down precisely the observable effects of these operations. There are two ways of tackling this. Operations can either be described solely in terms of each other by relating their input and output values or the operations can be described individually with respect to (an abstraction of) a state. Let's agree to use the terms *property-oriented* and *model-oriented* descriptions respectively for these two approaches.

The property-oriented approach has the potential advantage that a system might be described solely in terms of its visible behaviour. The archetypical example of a successful property-oriented specification is a *stack*: one can say that the last value pushed is what is returned by a pop and that pop/push pair leave the stack unchanged. Although not widely circulated, the first example of such a specification that I saw was from Lucas and Walk in their 'Documentation of Programming Ideas' which was presented to patent experts in 1969: they specified a stack in exactly this way[20]. The more influential references on this approach were by Guttag, Horning and Zilles around 1975 and this led to more than a decade of intense research on Algebraic specification methods (an up-to-date overview of this work with many references can be found in [5]).

The potential advantage of property-oriented descriptions is, however, sometimes unrealisable. There are formal difficulties like coping with non-deterministic and partial operations. It can also be shown that there are systems for which no finite set of axioms (without hidden functions) can capture their behaviour.

But it was pragmatic arguments which led VDM to adopt the model-oriented approach to the description of data types and systems. With an awareness of the advantages of implicit storage models (cf. Section 1) and of the basic idea

---

[19] For the purposes of the current discussion, we can ignore the extent to which the computer system becomes a significant part of the real world system which –we are here arguing– is abstracted by the computer model.

[20] This was published a couple of years later as [58].

My insistence on using post-conditions which were predicates of two states (initial and final) made it impossible to achieve this brevity. Furthermore, the rules in [46] were unnecessarily heavy.[24] It took the intervention of Peter Aczel [2] to show that rules could be formulated for the relational case that were almost as brief as in Hoare's system

$$\boxed{\textit{While-A}} \quad \frac{\{P \wedge b\}\, S\, \{P \wedge R\}}{\{P\}\ \textbf{while}\ b\ \textbf{do}\ S\ \textbf{end}\ \{R^r \wedge \neg b\}}\ R\ \text{twf}$$

These rules actually have an advantage in that the well-foundedness of R automatically ensures termination. (In some ways this is a neat generalisation of the 'variant function' of weakest pre-condition systems.)

Soundness proofs of the rules used in [48] and subsequently are given –in terms of relations– in [49].

3.4   Data Reification

Since the main points of the story of the data reification work are related in [50], this section can be brief. The transition from Lucas' 'twin machine' approach to the retrieve function idea is first recorded in Vienna in 1970; after the diversion of the more axiomatic approach used in the proof of Earley's recogniser, the idea of a 'retrieve function' (a homomorphism from the representation to the abstraction) became a key part of VDM's notion of *data reification*. Coupled with this was the important concept of *adequacy*.

The VDM books were I believe the first to give due importance to this aspect of program design. The idea of engineering handbooks for software was again the motivation behind the proposal to build up *theories* of data types [44].

3.5   LPF

Here again, much has been written about the work on logics which handle partial functions (or undefined terms). Although this is now a distinctive part of VDM, the reader is referred to [6, 15, 52] for further discussion of the *Logic of Partial Functions* (LPF).

3.6   Concurrency

A review paper is planned of the concurrency work in the near future. Suffice it here to say that the original rely/guarantee idea of [47] was progressed significantly in [74, 16, 17] and that subsequent work on the difficult issue of achieving compositionality in the presence of interference has gone in the direction of concurrent object-based languages [51, 37].

---

[24] Although they did permit discussion of some interesting distinctions between 'up' and 'down' loops.

4   Conclusions

After what the trade press called the 1975 'St Valentine's day massacre', many of those who had been involved in the PL/I compiler project in IBM Vienna –and thus the real solidifying of VDM– dispersed. At one point, the acronym 'VDM' was claimed to have stood for 'Vienna, Denmark and Manchester'; at another 'Very Diverse Methods'; my preference was for 'Vorsprung durch Mathematik'. The real origin of the name owes more to Dines's cocktails than anything else (or was that only the even worse 'Meta-IV'?). There was some concern that 'VDM' was too close to 'VDL' and this did indeed confuse the unwary.

Be that as it may, at least the description part of VDM has made it to an ISO standard and this is one reason for now looking back on the venture.

I confess, that I personally preferred to see the whole exercise as more like the foundation of a 'school' than a single specific notation which was to be carved on tablets of stone. I had some doubts about the motives of some of the early standardisation effort and only got fully involved when I saw that (a) it was going ahead anyway and (b) some rather odd decisions were being made. The development of LPF is one example of something that was by no means fixed early in VDM's history; concurrency is an issue which still requires more work.

One pleasing outcome of the the work has been its influence on other specification notations. It is worth mentioning at least VVSL [63], Irish VDM [59] Larch [26], RAISE [24, 25] and B [1]. The significant omission from this list is –of course– Z [72]. Jean-Raymond Abrial and I arrived at Oxford's 'Programming Research Group' at almost the same time in 1979. We worked well together in a mixture of notations and I can't help suspecting that VDM and Z could have become closer had Jean-Raymond have retained control of Z. Some evidence for this suspicion is that his Abstract Machine Notation in B [1] does fit more closely with aspects of VDM than Z.

It is fair to address the question of what –with the benefit of hindsight– one would have wished had been done differently.

I should have liked to have seen less emphasis on notation and more on concepts (for example, [27] discusses some of the more arbitrary divergences between Z and VDM). The RAISE effort was probably mistimed in the sense that cleaning up VDM first might have had the twin benefit of giving RAISE a better starting point and postponing the start on the concurrency aspects of RAISE (which must rate as its most difficult to use).

In spite of a number of efforts, projects to provide tool support have never been easy to justify.

Perhaps what remains –and might be seen as significant in years to come– is that there are many useful descriptions (and some specifications) around. Not all of these descriptions are public and I applaud Brian Monahan's recent proposal to encourage a 'open source' approach to descriptions of widely used systems. In my own teaching, I moved to trying to communicate the idea of *abstract modelling* as a way of understanding computer systems.

Above all –for me at least– it was a great way to work on some real problems and with some wonderful colleagues. It is to all of them that I dedicate this paper.

Acknowledgements

This paper was drafted whilst I was still at Harlequin: I am grateful for the time made available for the work.

Peter Lucas was kind enough to comment on a draft of this paper for which I am very thankful.

References

[1] J.-R. Abrial. *The B-Book: Assigning programs to meanings.* Cambridge University Press, 1996.

[2] P. Aczel. A note on program verification. manuscript, January 1982.

[3] C. D. Allen, D. N. Chapman, and C. B. Jones. A formal definition of ALGOL 60. Technical Report 12.105, IBM Laboratory Hursley, August 1972.

[4] D. Andrews and W. Henhapl. Pascal. In *[13]*, pages 175–252. 1982.

[5] E. Astesiano, H.-J. Kreowski, and B. Krieg-Brueckner, editors. *Algebraic Foundations of System Specification.* Springer Verrlag, 1999.

[6] H. Barringer, J.H. Cheng, and C. B. Jones. A logic covering undefinedness in program proofs. *Acta Informatica*, 21:251–269, 1984.

[7] H. Bekič. *Programming Languages and Their Definition: Selected Papers of H. Bekič*, volume 177 of *Lecture Notes in Computer Science*. Springer-Verlag, 1984.

[8] H. Bekič, D. Bjørner, W. Henhapl, C. B. Jones, and P. Lucas. A formal definition of a PL/I subset. Technical Report 25.139, IBM Laboratory Vienna, December 1974.

[9] H. Bekič, H. Izbicki, C. B. Jones, and F. Weissenböck. Some experiments with using a formal language definition in compiler development. Technical Report LN 25.3.107, IBM Laboratory, Vienna, December 1975.

[10] H. Bekič and K. Walk. Formalization of storage properties. In *[20]*, pages 28–61. 1971.

[11] D. Bjørner, editor. *Abstract Software Specifications: 1979 Copenhagen Winter School Proceedings*, volume 86 of *Lecture Notes in Computer Science*. Springer-Verlag, Berlin, 1980.

[12] D. Bjørner and C. B. Jones, editors. *The Vienna Development Method: The Meta-Language*, volume 61 of *Lecture Notes in Computer Science*. Springer-Verlag, 1978.

[13] D. Bjørner and C. B. Jones. *Formal Specification and Software Development.* Prentice Hall International, 1982.

[14] D. Bjørner and O. N. Oest, editors. *Towards a Formal Description of Ada*, volume 98 of *Lecture Notes in Computer Science*. Springer-Verlag, Berlin, 1980.

[15] J. H. Cheng and C. B. Jones. On the usability of logics which handle partial functions. In C. Morgan and J. C. P. Woodcock, editors, *3rd Refinement Workshop*, pages 51–69. Springer-Verlag, 1991.

[16] Pierre Collette. *Design of Compositional Proof Systems Based on Assumption-Commitment Specifications – Application to UNITY.* PhD thesis, Louvain-la-Neuve, June 1994.

[17] Pierre Collette and Cliff B. Jones. Enhancing the tractability of rely/guarantee specifications in the development of interfering operations. Technical Report UMCS-95-10-3, Manchester University, 1995.

[18] J. W. de Bakker and D. Scott. A theory of programs. Manuscript notes for IBM Seminar, Vienna, August 1969.

[19] E. W. Dijkstra. *A Discipline of Programming*. Prentice-Hall, 1976.

[20] E. Engeler. *Symposium on Semantics of Algorithmic Languages*. Number 188 in Lecture Notes in Mathematics. Springer-Verlag, 1971.

[21] R. W. Floyd. On the nonexistence of a phrase structure grammar for ALGOL 60. *Communications of the ACM*, 5:483–484, 1962.

[22] R. W. Floyd. Assigning meanings to programs. In *Proc. Symp. in Applied Mathematics, Vol.19: Mathematical Aspects of Computer Science*, pages 19–32. American Mathematical Society, 1967.

[23] M.J.C. Gordon. *The Denotational Description of Programming Languages*. Springer-Verlag, 1979.

[24] The RAISE Language Group. *The RAISE Specification Language*. BCS Practitioner Series. Prentice Hall, 1992. ISBN 0-13-752833-7.

[25] The RAISE Method Group. *The RAISE Development Method*. BCS Practitioner Series. Prentice Hall, 1995. ISBN 0-13-752700-4.

[26] John V. Guttag and James J. Horning. *Larch: Languages and Tools for Formal Specification*. Texts and Monographs in Computer Science. Springer-Verlag, 1993. ISBN 0-387-94006-5/ISBN 3-540-94006-5.

[27] I. J. Hayes, C. B. Jones, and J. E. Nicholls. Understanding the differences between VDM and Z. *ACM Software Engineering News*, 19(3):75–81, July 1994.

[28] W. Henhapl. A proof of correctness for the reference mechanism to automatic variables in the F-compiler. Technical Report LN 25.3.048, IBM Laboratory Vienna, Austria, November 1968.

[29] W. Henhapl and C. B. Jones. The block concept and some possible implementations, with proofs of equivalence. Technical Report 25.104, IBM Laboratory Vienna, April 1970.

[30] W. Henhapl and C. B. Jones. On the interpretation of GOTO statements in the ULD. Technical Report LN 25.3.065, IBM Laboratory, Vienna, March 1970.

[31] W. Henhapl and C. B. Jones. Some observations on the implementation of reference mechanisms for automatic variables. Technical Report LR 25.3.070, IBM Laboratory, Vienna, May 1970.

[32] W. Henhapl and C. B. Jones. A run-time mechanism for referencing variables. *Information Processing Letters*, 1(1):14–16, 1971.

[33] W. Henhapl and C. B. Jones. A formal definition of ALGOL 60 as described in the 1975 modified report. In *[12]*, pages 305–336. 1978.

[34] C. A. R. Hoare. An axiomatic basis for computer programming. *Communications of the ACM*, 12(10):576–580, 583, October 1969.

[35] C. A. R. Hoare. Proof of a program: FIND. *Communications of the ACM*, 14:39–45, January 1971.

[36] C. A. R. Hoare. Proof of correctness of data representations. *Acta Informatica*, 1:271–281, 1972.

[37] Steve J. Hodges and Cliff B. Jones. Non-interference properties of a concurrent object-based language: Proofs based on an operational semantics. In Burkhard Freitag, Cliff B. Jones, Christian Lengauer, and Hans-Jörg Schek, editors, *Oject Orientation with Parallelism and Persistence*, pages 1–22. Kluwer Academic Publishers, 1996.

[38] C. B. Jones. A technique for showing that two functions preserve a relation between their domains. Technical Report LR 25.3.067, IBM Laboratory, Vienna, April 1970.

[39] C. B. Jones. Formal development of correct algorithms: an example based on Earley's recogniser. In *SIGPLAN Notices, Volume 7 Number 1*, pages 150–169. ACM, January 1972.

[40] C. B. Jones. Formal development of programs. Technical Report 12.117, IBM Laboratory Hursley, June 1973.

[41] C. B. Jones. Formal definition in compiler development. Technical Report 25.145, IBM Laboratory Vienna, February 1976.

[42] C. B. Jones. Implementation bias in constructive specification of abstract objects. typescript, September 1977.

[43] C. B. Jones. Denotational semantics of goto: An exit formulation and its relation to continuations. In *[12]*, pages 278–304. 1978.

[44] C. B. Jones. Constructing a theory of a data structure as an aid to program development. *Acta Informatica*, 11:119–137, 1979.

[45] C. B. Jones. The Vienna Development Method: Examples of compiler development. In M. Amirchahy and D. Neel, editors, *Le Point sur la Compilation*, pages 89–114. IRIA-SEFI, 1979.

[46] C. B. Jones. *Software Development: A Rigorous Approach*. Prentice Hall International, 1980. ISBN 0-13-821884-6.

[47] C. B. Jones. *Development Methods for Computer Programs including a Notion of Interference*. PhD thesis, Oxford University, June 1981. Printed as: Programming Research Group, Technical Monograph 25.

[48] C. B. Jones. *Systematic Software Development Using VDM*. Prentice Hall International, 1986.

[49] C. B. Jones. Program specification and verification in VDM. In M. Broy, editor, *Logic of Programming and Calculi of Discrete Design*, volume 36 of *NATO ASI Series F: Computer and Systems Sciences*, pages 149–184. Springer-Verlag, 1987.

[50] C. B. Jones. Data reification. In J. A. McDermid, editor, *The Theory and Practice of Refinement*, pages 79–89. Butterworths, 1989.

[51] C. B. Jones. Process algebra arguments about an object-based design notation. In A. W. Roscoe, editor, *A Classical Mind*, chapter 14, pages 231–246. Prentice-Hall, 1994.

[52] C. B. Jones. TANSTAAFL with partial functions. In William Farmer, Manfred Kerber, and Michael Kohlhase, editors, *Proceedings of the Workshop on the Mechanization Of Partial Functions*, pages 53–64, 1996.

[53] C. B. Jones and P. Lucas. Proving correctness of implementation techniques. In *[20]*, pages 178–211. 1971.

[54] P. J. Landin. A correspondence between ALGOL-60 and Church's lambda-notation. Parts I and II. *Communications of the ACM*, 8:89–101, 158–165, 1965.

[55] P. J. Landin. The next 700 programming languages. *Communications of the ACM*, 9:157–166, 1966.

[56] P. Lucas. Two constructive realizations of the block concept and their equivalence. Technical Report TR 25.085, IBM Laboratory Vienna, June 1968.

[57] P. Lucas and K. Walk. *On The Formal Description of PL/I*, volume 6 of *Annual Review in Automatic Programming Part 3*. Pergamon Press, 1969.

[58] Peter Lucas. On the semantics of programming languages and software devices. In Randall Rustin, editor, *Formal Semantics of Programming Languages*, pages 41–57, Englewood Cliffs, NewJersey, 1972. Prentice Hall. Proceedings of the Courant Computer Science Symposium 2.

[59] M. Mac an Airchinnigh. Tutorial Lecture Notes on the Irish School of the VDM. In *[71]*, pages 141–237, 1991.

[60] A. W. Mazurkiewicz. Proving algorithms by tail functions. *Information and Control*, 18(3):220–226, April 1971.

[61] J. McCarthy. A formal description of a subset of ALGOL. In *[73]*, pages 1–12, 1966.

[62] J. McCarthy. A basis for a mathematical theory for computation. In P. Braffort and D. Hirschberg, editors, *Computer Programming and Formal Systems*, pages 33–70. North-Holland Publishing Company, 1967.

[63] Cornelius A. Middelburg. *Logic and Specification: Extending VDM-SL for advanced formal specification.* Chapman and Hall, 1993.

[64] R. Milne and C. Strachey. *A Theory of Programming Language Semantics.* Chapman and Hall, 1976.

[65] R. Milner. An algebraic definition of simulation between programs. Technical Report CS-205, Computer Science Dept, Stanford University, February 1971.

[66] F. L. Morris. The next 700 formal language descriptions. Manuscipt, 1970.

[67] P. D. Mosses. The mathematical semantics of Algol 60. Technical Monograph PRG-12, Oxford University Computing Laboratory, Programming Research Group, January 1974.

[68] Peter D. Mosses. *Action Semantics.* Number 26 in Cambridge Tracts in Theoretical Computer Science. Cambridge University Press, 1992.

[69] G. D. Plotkin. A powerdomain construction. *SIAM J. Comput.*, 5(3), 1976.

[70] G. D. Plotkin. A structural approach to operational semantics. Technical report, Aarhus University, 1981.

[71] S. Prehn and W. J. Toetenel, editors. *VDM'91 – Formal Software Development Methods. Proceedings of the 4th International Symposium of VDM Europe, Noordwijkerhout, The Netherlands, October 1991, Vol.2: Tutorials*, volume 552 of *Lecture Notes in Computer Science.* Springer-Verlag, 1991.

[72] J.M. Spivey. *The Z Notation: A Reference Manual.* Prentice Hall International, second edition, 1992.

[73] T. B. Steel. *Formal Language Description Languages for Computer Programming.* North-Holland, 1966.

[74] K. Stølen. *Development of Parallel Programs on Shared Data-Structures.* PhD thesis, Manchester University, 1990. available as UMCS-91-1-1.

[75] J.E. Stoy. *Denotational Semantics: The Scott-Strachey Approach to Programming Language Theory.* MIT Press, 1977.

[76] C. Strachey and C. P. Wadsworth. Continuations – a mathematical semantics for handling jumps. Monograph PRG-11, Oxford University Computing Laboratory, Programming Research Group, January 1974.

[77] R. L. Wexelblat. *History of Programming Languages.* Academic Press, 1981.

Mechanized Formal Methods: Where Next?*

John Rushby

Computer Science Laboratory
SRI International
333 Ravenswood Avenue
Menlo Park, CA 94025, USA
rushby@csl.sri.com

1 Where Are We Now?

An author who elects to use the phrase "Where Next?" in a title clearly has predictive or prescriptive intent. In my case it is the latter: I cannot say how formal methods will develop in the next few years, still less whether or how they will be adopted in practice, but I do have views on how they *should* develop and what ought to encourage their adoption in practice, and this World Congress seems an excellent opportunity to impose these views on the public.

To offer a prescription for the future requires the presumption to assess the present and my bias here is indicated in the first part of my title: "mechanized formal methods." While mathematically-based methods can provide several benefits and have elucidated the basic concepts of our field—what it means for a design to be correct with respect to a specification, or for one design to refine another, or for a proof to establish one or another of these relationships—the value, to my mind, of specifically *formal* methods is that they allow some properties of a software or hardware system to be deduced from its design or specification by a process of *mechanized logical calculation*, in much the same way that mechanized numerical calculation is used to predict the properties of traditional engineering artifacts such as bridges and turbine blades. I find engineering calculations a more illuminating analogy for the role of formal methods in computer science than formalized mathematics or logic as practiced by mathematicians and logicians. In particular, the engineering perspective highlights the necessity of efficient, automated, calculation: the stresses in a bridge are calculated by computer, not by pencil and paper, and the calculations are used during design exploration, not just for verification.

So, I consider the most useful technical developments in formal methods to have been those that provide efficient mechanized calculation in logical domains: static analysis, model checking, decision procedures, and so on. And I consider the most useful formal methodologies to be those that help cast analysis of significant properties of a design (or of certain types of design) into forms that allow effective use of these mechanized logical calculations: abstract interpretation,

* Based on research supported by DARPA through USAF Rome Laboratory Contract F30602-96-C-0204, and by the National Science Foundation contract CCR-9509931.

J. Wing, J. Woodcock, J. Davies (Eds.): FM'99, Vol. I, LNCS 1708, pp. 48–51, 1999.

extended static checking, well-formedness checks for tabular specifications, and a host of domain-specific methods for pipelines and other hardware structures, for railroad switching, for translation validation, and for protocols and certain other classes of concurrent systems.[1]

These tools and methods have demonstrated a certain effectiveness, and have been voluntarily adopted by industry to a modest degree (most notably for hardware and communications protocols).

2   Where Should We Go Next?

My prescription for further development of mechanized formal methods is a continuation of the successful trends identified above. I break it into several related headings.

2.1   Mechanize Everything

Some current formal methods, for example those that use model checkers or SAT solvers, are described as "automatic," meaning that they perform their logical calculations without needing interactive guidance (unlike, for example, a tactic-based theorem prover). However, this is a very narrow interpretation of automation, since considerable human guidance and ingenuity is generally required to transform the original problem to a form where the final "push button" automation can be applied. The transformation often requires: translating the description of the problem from a programming or design notation such as C, Java, Verilog, or UML into the input format of the tool concerned; extracting the part of the overall description that is relevant to the problem or property concerned; and reducing the extracted description to a form (e.g., finite-state) consistent with the capabilities of the tool concerned.

Much current research aims to mechanize the manual steps in this process. For example, methods based on backward slicing can yield just the part of a large system specification that is relevant to a given property, and combinations of abstract interpretation and partial evaluation can create a conservative finite-state (or other special-form) approximation from a given program or specification. Techniques employing decision procedures can calculate more precise property-preserving abstractions. These methods work better if provided with invariants of the program or specification concerned; such invariants can be calculated by static analysis or by reachability analysis (a capability of most symbolic model checkers) applied to another abstraction (the reachable states characterize the strongest invariant of that abstraction; their concretization is an invariant—and plausibly a strong one—of the original). This last suggests iterated application of these techniques (one abstraction is used to calculate an invariant that helps calculate another abstraction, and so on), which in turn suggests a blackboard

---

[1] I omit references due to lack of space; they are provided in a version available at http://www.csl.sri.com/~rushby/fm99.html.

architecture in which a common intermediate representation is used to accumulate useful properties and abstractions of a design in a form that many different tools can both use and contribute to. A common intermediate representation also provides a way to support many source notations without inordinate cost.

The first of my prescriptions is to continue and extend this line of development so that the human verification engineer will direct and select a sequence of mechanized calculations, rather than manually create input for a single tool. A radical element of this proposal is that it shifts the focus of formal analysis from verification (or refutation) to the calculation of *properties* that can assist further analyses: for example, a static analyzer will be used to calculate (rather than verify) the range of values that a variable can assume, and a model checker will be used to calculate an invariant rather than verify a property.

2.2   Mechanize More Powerfully

Traditional techniques for mechanized formal methods were based on interactive theorem proving. As the role of automated deduction in this activity came to be recognized as more closely resembling calculation in engineering than proof in mathematics, so more powerful automation such as decision procedures came to be accepted. But the overall pattern of activity was (and is) still that of an interactively-guided proof, where the main activity is one of generating and reducing subgoals to the point where they can be discharged by decision procedures or other automation. In contrast, techniques that combine automated abstraction, invariant generation, and model checking in the manner outlined above, even though they may be undertaken in the context provided by a theorem prover, have a rather different character: the steps are bigger, and fewer, and are aimed at quickly reducing the problem to a single decidable subgoal. The effectiveness of this approach depends on having techniques for "reduction" (e.g., abstraction and invariant generation) and a decidable class of formulas (e.g., μ-calculus formulas over finite transition systems) that are well-suited to the class of problems at hand.

Different classes of problems need different underlying capabilities in order to use this "big step" approach. For example, translation validation and certain kinds of pipeline correctness arguments need massively efficient decision procedures for the combination of propositional calculus with equality over uninterpreted function symbols (whereas a traditional theorem prover will generally provide a less efficient decision procedure for a richer combination of theories).

The second of my prescriptions is to develop and exploit new and highly efficient decision procedures or other algorithmic techniques for pragmatically useful combinations of theories. These need to be tens of thousands of times faster, and to scale better, than the techniques employed in current verification systems: the efficiency is to be gained by more precise targeting of the theories to be decided, thereby allowing better data structures and better algorithms. As suitable theories are identified and a customer base develops, an industry may emerge to supply the necessary components, much as BDD packages and SAT solvers are becoming commodities today.

2.3   Make Mechanized Formal Analysis Ubiquitous

Tools with the capabilities described in the last two sections can serve wider purposes than classical verification or refutation. For example, they can be used to support testing: either by generating test cases (e.g., using counterexamples generated by a model checker for the negation of the property of interest), pruning test cases (e.g., do not use tests that are provably satisfied by a conservative approximation of the design), or by serving as a test oracle. Another example is static analysis, where decision procedures can be used to increase the strength of typechecking, or to improve the precision of slicing. And another example is use of these techniques to examine security properties of mobile code (e.g., "proof carrying code").

Thus, my third prescription is to use mechanized logical calculation in all aspects of software and hardware development: I suspect that almost every tool used in development could be improved if it made some use of mechanized formal analysis. We should aim to make our techniques ubiquitous throughout software and hardware engineering; this particularly means that we should attempt to serve all stages of the development lifecycle—from requirements analysis through maintenance—and all classes of products (not just those deemed "critical").

2.4   Adapt to Engineering Practice

Successful transition from research to practice is unpredictable, and especially so where methodology, rather than technology, is concerned. While it is possible that formally-based methods will become widespread (and the possibility will surely be greater if they are supported by tools that offer compelling advantages over those of other methods), a more plausible scenario uses tools made possible by mechanized formal analysis to *add value* to existing (or modestly enhanced) practices: this may mean finding more bugs, or higher-value bugs, more quickly than otherwise, increasing the quality of test-cases, or verifying the satisfaction of certain properties. These accomplishments are rather far from the proofs of correctness that were among the original goals of formal methods, and from the view that programming and hardware design should become mathematical activities, but they are consistent with the way mathematics and calculation are used in other engineering disciplines.

I suggest we envisage and work towards a scenario where designers (or specialist verification or test engineers) equipped with an eclectic knowledge of formal methods and familiarity with several tools will turn to these methods and tools, much as they currently turn to traditional tools such as test coverage analyzers, when the need or opportunity arises. Only by adapting to existing "design flows" and by coexisting with traditional tools and methods will our methods have a chance to be assimilated into the normal state of practice. By developing the more powerful, flexible, and integrated mechanization suggested earlier, I believe that formal methods of analysis could increase their value added and reduce the cost incurred so significantly that they would then have a chance to become a dominant part of that normal practice.

Integration, the Price of Success
Extended Abstract

J. Sifakis

Verimag, Centre Equation, 2 rue Vignate, Gières, France

Formal methods and their acceptance

It is generally recognized that formal techniques have a limited impact on current industrial practice. Several reasons often had been advocated to explain this fact: youth of the discipline, intrinsic limitations due to complexity and undecidability, lack of trained practitioners and engineers. All these are factors limiting the application of formal techniques. However, a reason that is less frequently suggested is the relevance of our contribution to current industrial practice. Clearly, Informatics is a scientific discipline with its own evolution laws and proper objectives. However, as an experimental discipline it should find inspiration and validation in applications whose development is also driven by external needs, technologic, economic and ultimately social. The recognition and the success of our discipline is intimately related to the capability to address problems raised by the fast evolving practice.

Many theoretical results, concepts and methods have been integrated in current engineering practice so perfectly that their use is completely transparent: automata and formal languages theory in compiler technology, or more recently, circuit verification by model-checking. On the other hand, it is clear that most of the existing theoretical results will not find a direct application in the foreseeable future while at the same time software and systems engineering techniques develop on a more empirical and technology driven basis. It is remarkable that pessimistic predictions about limitations of the current industrial practice to produce reliable software and systems, have been falsified. In fact, the rapid increase of complexity and the introduction of new technologies arising from the integration of reactive systems satisfying hard real-time requirements, did not result in significant changes of the current practice.

These facts should make us question the direction of our work, in particular, its role and the relevance of its contribution to Informatics. Without abandoning promising theoretical research directions, it is important that a stronger connection with practice is sought for two reasons: to defend Informatics as a basic emerging experimental discipline and more importantly, to validate results, methods and ideas by confrontation with practice.

Research on formal methods has essentially been motivated by the study of formal languages and their semantics including languages for the description of systems (executable languages) and of their properties (usually logical languages). In this context, two important and related classes of methods have been extensively studied. Synthesis methods which allow the computation of

J. Wing, J. Woodcock, J. Davies (Eds.): FM'99, Vol. I, LNCS 1708, pp. 52-55, 1999.

a system satisfying a given property and verification methods which allow the satisfaction of a property by a system to be checked. The effective use of formal techniques by software and system developers requires their integration in existing support environments. There are two major impediments to such an integration. One is the distance between formal languages and languages used by practitioners in different application areas. The other is non scalability of existing formal methods.

Connection with practically used languages

Industrial practice is based on the use of sets of languages covering the development cycle from requirements, to specification, programming and integration. A remarkable fact about the evolution of languages over the last twenty years, is the common use of a few implementation languages and the emergence of executable description and development languages specific to application areas. For each of them, complex technologies with commercially available support tools have been developed. For HW design, there exist CAD tools dedicated to languages such as Verilog and VHDL. For real-time systems, two different technologies emerged, one based on ADA and multi-tasking and one based on synchronous programming. For telecommunications protocols, a complex technology for specification and testing is being developed around standards such as SDL (executable specifications) MSC (service specifications) TTCN (test case description format) defined by ITU. Finally, for distributed systems standards such as CORBA, IDL and UML are promoted due to the concerted action of leading software companies and organizations. Clearly, most of the mentioned formalisms and languages are not impeccable and sometimes do not satisfy elementary rigorousness and optimality requirements. However, their impurity very often hides interesting problems that are crucial for modeling complex systems. The study of executable languages for systems design and modeling as well as their combination in methodologies is becoming the most important research direction in Formal Methods. We identify below some interesting problems:

- Combination in co-design methodologies of hardware description languages with system description languages, such as SDL.
- For real-time systems engineering, the combination of the synchronous approach with asynchronous multi-tasking approaches requires a deep understanding of the underlying models. In the same area, we need methods for combining description of real-time controllers with models of their asynchronous timed environment involving continuous state variables.
- For distributed systems, we need languages with dynamically changing structure, process creation and mobility. Another important problem is the introduction of a "reasonable" notion of time in specification languages such as SDL or UML. Finally, the definition of languages for general distributed systems raises a multitude of questions about optimal combination of different approaches and description styles as illustrated by the definition of UML.

Scalable (partial) methods

Most of the synthesis and verification methods are not tractable for real systems and non trivial properties. Even though in some applications such as circuits or simple real-time controllers, current model checking technology may suffice, in other applications involving complex data and asynchrony available tools are severely limited. Furthermore, it is anticipated that the complexity of systems will increase rapidly while methods are subject to intrinsic complexity or undecidability limitations.

Research on synthesis and verification techniques focused so far on general methods for powerful languages of properties. Prototype tools have been often developed with a concern for generality which is valid in research terms, but is incompatible with efficiency. To get synthesis and verification techniques accepted, another approach would be to develop methods that allow current industrial practice to be improved by respecting tractability criteria. This practically means restriction to very simple classes of properties such as reachability and invariance and preference to partial methods that can be combined smoothly with other more empirical techniques. We identify below some interesting work directions:

- Combination of model-checking and of static analysis techniques with debugging and simulation techniques to validate complex systems. Discovering design errors by model-checking for safety properties does not require an exhaustive exploration of the state space. The use of on-the-fly techniques as well as approximate symbolic analysis techniques such as convergence acceleration and abstraction can drastically help validating complex systems provided they are integrated in support environments.
- Improving testing technology, especially functional testing. Testing is the validation technique used to check experimentally, by application of test cases, that the behavior of a system agrees with some reference property. Testing is a work intensive activity and in many application areas test cases are written by experts from requirements expressed as "test purposes". Test case generation for a given test purpose and a given system to be tested, can be formulated as a synthesis problem. However, for test purposes expressing simple reachability properties efficient automatic test case generation techniques have been developed and are now available in commercial tools. These techniques share a common technology with model-checking and can be drastically improved by symbolic analysis.
- Use of synthesis techniques in design methodologies. Standard engineering practice consists in decomposing the system to be designed into a set of cooperating components. A key problem is the coordination of the components in order to ensure that the global behavior satisfies given properties. In some application areas synthesis techniques can be used to solve the coordination problem by computing a controller that adequately restricts the behavior of the components. We believe that such a combination of synthesis

and design methodologies is particularly interesting for scheduling real-time applications or in general to design hard real-time systems.

Discussion

The effective integration of formal techniques in design methodologies and support environments is a significant criterion of success. For more than three decades formal methods have been developed rather as an alternative to some industrial practice which it was envisaged would disappear. Instead of the expected revolution, we observe a slow integration of those results that improve incrementally a well-established practice. This process is determined by needs and rules that lie mostly outside our area of action. It favors the integration of formal techniques which are the most ripe for transfer: tool supported techniques based on executable languages.

It is necessary that we participate in this process by focusing on new challenging work directions. This implies a deeper understanding of current practice, methodologies and technological results that are at the basis of software and systems engineering. This requires in some cases, critical mass and organization of the effort on a different basis. Our success and credibility depend on our capability to take up the integration challenge.

The Role of Formalism in Method

Michael Jackson

101 Hamilton Terrace, London NW8 9QY, England
AT&T Research, 180 Park Avenue, Florham Park NJ 07932, USA
jacksonma@acm.org | mj@doc.ic.ac.uk

Wider use of formal methods in the development of computing systems promises better quality in general, and in particular safer and more reliable systems. But we must recognise that formalisation and formal reasoning are not goals in themselves: they are partial means to our goals.

Any useful computing system interacts with the world outside the computer. In problems of a mathematical nature, such as problems in graph theory or cryptography, interaction with the world is a negligible part of the problem: the gravamen lies in the manipulation of the formal mathematical abstractions. But in many problems the balance is different: the quality of the solution must be judged by its effects in the physical world of people, chemical plants, lifts, libraries, telephone networks, aeroplanes—or wherever the problem is located. Unlike the abstract world of mathematics, these real-world domains are not formal; it is not always obvious how—or even whether—formal methods can and should be applied to them.

One possible response is to exclude such domains from the scope of development method. Let the domain experts determine what is required in the domain, what domain properties can be exploited, and what computer behaviour at the interface with the world will satisfy the requirements. We, as software developers, will start from a specification of that computer behaviour, carefully avoiding the messy and irritating informality of the world outside the computer.

But this response is ineffective for two related reasons. First, a specification strictly confined to the computer behaviour at the interface is unintelligible. Such a specification of software to control a lift would be expressed purely in terms of values of shared registers and signals on lines connecting the computer to the electro-mechanical equipment of the lift. No-one could understand such a specification. Second, the domain experts, unaided, are scarcely ever able to produce such a specification to the required degree of formality and precision. As software developers we are compelled to involve ourselves in their work.

We therefore cannot escape a major share of responsibility for determining and bounding the problem that the system is to solve in the world. Inevitably we are led into classifying and structuring real-world problems, and into formalising real-world domains and reasoning about them within the large structures appropriate to the class of problem in hand. We must understand and practise effective techniques of formalising informal domains, and recognise the approximate nature of the resulting formalisations and the limitations of formal reasoning based upon them. And in dealing with the world outside the computer, we must accept that formalisation and formal methods can show the presence of errors, but never their absence.

J. Wing, J. Woodcock, J. Davies (Eds.): FM'99, Vol. I, LNCS 1708, pp. 56–56, 1999.
© Springer-Verlag Berlin Heidelberg 1999

Formal Design for Automatic Coding and Testing: The ESSI/SPACES Project

Eric Conquet[1] , Jean-Luc Marty[2]

Matra Marconi Space, Data Processing and On-Board SW Division,
31 Avenue des Cosmonautes, 31402 Toulouse Cedex 4 - France.
[1]Tel : +33 5 62 19 51 36
eric.conquet@tls.mms.fr
[2]Tel : +33 5 62 19 91 82
jean-luc.marty@tls.mms.fr

Abstract. Embedded software in the space domain must satisfy a set of strong constraints related to behaviour and performance, to fulfil user requirements. Moreover, due to the cost reduction trend in the domain and to the global necessity of increasing the quality of complex software systems, early design validation has become a real challenge for software designers. Currently used methods such as HOOD lacks support for behaviour description. Moreover, design validation is not feasible with such methods and first validation has to be made when the coding phase has sufficiently advanced. This occurs too late in the development phase especially when coding is essentially manual. This calls for the adoption of new development strategies based on formal description of the behaviour, on the use of simulation techniques to check the proposed design solution and on automatic code and tests generation techniques to increase productivity.
Following a preliminary successful experience in the context of an ESTEC R&D study called DDV(Dms Design Validation) [1] , the SDL and MSC languages and the ObjectGeode tool have been successfully applied on real projects. To complete those first applications of the technique, a PIE project (Process Improvement Experiment) in the ESSI program [2] has been proposed and accepted by the European Community. That project, called SPACES [3], aims at measuring improvement of development processes through the use of automatic coding and testing from a SDL model. This paper tells the complete story of SDL in our on-board division and focuses on the SPACES project and its current achieved results.

1 Introduction

For many years, development of software in different domains of industry has mainly focused on the choice and best use of programming languages. Then, to face with the increasing size and complexity of software systems, specification and design methods and tools have emerged. Their first purpose was to propose a common formalism, different from the programming language, to support the design process and ease the communication within the design team and with the customer. They helped very

J. Wing, J. Woodcock, J. Davies (Eds.): FM'99, Vol. I, LNCS 1708, pp. 57-75, 1999.
© Springer-Verlag Berlin Heidelberg 1999

much especially on large projects with different contractors where a precise description of SW interfaces and SW role is mandatory.

Although having been very helpful to support the design process, those methods have suffered from one major limitation : they were limited to the static description of the SW. Even if different methods promoted the extensive use of informal language to support the behaviour description, they were limited by the ambiguousness and lack of precision of such languages.

Then come the time of formal languages with their cortege of attractive concepts, hopes of powerful verification means and easiness of use. Needless to say that not every formal language fully meets those requirements. Especially when comes the time of industrial use which makes the availability of a powerful, robust and complete tool a must have if a real use on a project is foreseen.

Executable specifications and designs through the use of formal methods is very helpful during SW development since it eases early validations through simulations and automatic coding.

This paper tells the story of the successful use of SDL in the On-Board SW division of MMS through the very first experiments to the SPACES project, an ESSI PIE (Process Improvement Experiment) which is currently on-going and already gave interesting results.

- Section 1 describes the SDL language, how it has been selected for use on our projects, and its application on the VTC/SW project,
- Section 2 describes the current results obtained on different projects where SDL has been used,
- Section 3 presents the SPACES project, its objectives and development plan,
- Section 4 presents the results obtained so far in SPACES and what is expected from the next project phases,
- And finally, section 5 presents the expected impact of SPACES on our SW development processes.

2   SDL AND MSC at MMS: The Story Began with the VTC Experiment

2.1 Description of the SDL and MSC Languages and the ObjectGeode Product

SDL stands for Specification and Design Language. It originates from an IUT standard which evolves every four years. The 1992 release [4], which is now supported by the currently available tools, introduced the Object Oriented concepts into the language. Originally, the language has been defined to cover the specific needs of the telecommunication domain related to the specification and description of protocols [5] [6].

The SDL language is made of three different views :

• A hierarchical view where a root block constitutes the top of the hierarchy and includes other blocks. Terminal blocks are called processes since they contain the automaton which describes the behaviour.

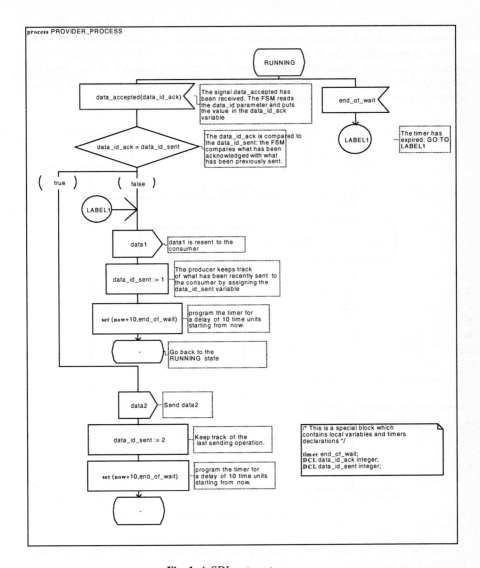

Fig. 1. A SDL automaton.

- A communication view where, for each level of the block hierarchy, a set of channels are defined connecting the blocks of the current level. Those channels carry signals which are used by the processes to communicate.
- An automaton view, where the behaviour of each process can be described. The automaton is made of transitions which can be fired when a specified signal has been received by the process. The figure 1 shows an example of such an automaton in SDL. It is sufficiently commented and should not require any additional explanation.

The MSC formalism is complementary to the SDL one. MSC stands for Message Sequence Charts and is used to describe the sequences of exchange between SDL entities. A set of MSC sheets can be combined with specific operators to define more complex scenario. Those operators express alternative, parallelism or sequence between MSC sheets. The figure 2 shows a simple example of such an MSC which describes a small sequence of interaction between two SDL blocks.

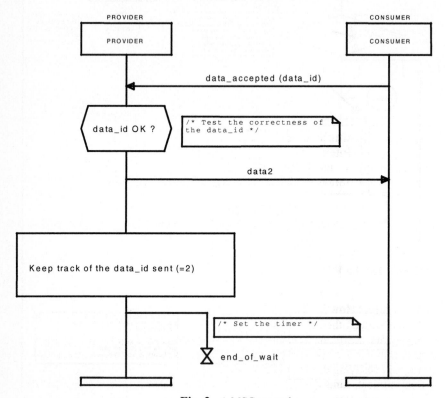

Fig. 2. A MSC example.

The ObjectGeode tool [7] is one of the tools which support the SDL/MSC formalism. It includes :
- A SDL graphical editor to build SDL models,
- A MSC graphical editor supporting the combination operators to build large scenarios,
- A SDL simulator which can use a set of MSCs as observers to verify the behaviour of the SDL model,
- An exhaustive simulator to verify model properties with a full analysis of model states,
- A document generator which supports different formats,
- A code generator which produces C code from the SDL model.

The figure 3 shows the different modules of the ObjectGeode tool.

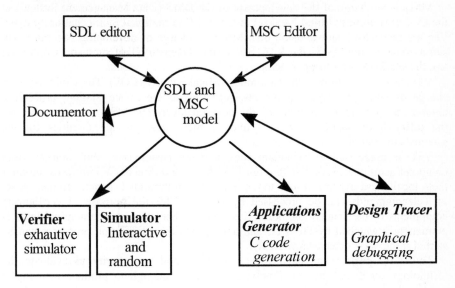

Fig. 3. Architecture of the ObjectGeode tool.

2.2 Selected for the VTC/SW Project

The DDV Project How SDL/ObjectGeode Has Been

MMS has studied the interest of modelling languages and simulations techniques for many years. Different techniques have been evaluated and applied on many projects mainly for performance evaluation of computer systems but more recently for analysing and verifying the behaviour of critical systems.

A R&D project, funded by ESA (European Space Agency), has been particularly fruitful in the selection process of a modelling environment which can be used on a real project for the purpose of modelling, documenting, verifying and sub-contracting a SW specification and design. This project called DDV (DMS Design Validation) [8] began in 1995 and analysed a large set of modelling formalisms with the purpose of selecting the most appropriate one for modelling and verifying a DMS architecture in the specification and design phase. The selection phase, led with a strong support of the VERIMAG laboratory in Grenoble, France, concluded on the appropriateness of the SDL formalism and on the maturity of the commercial tools.

The formalism has been applied during the specification phase where we modelled the architecture of an avionics system. Both the hardware architecture and the DMS layer were modelled and a set of properties were verified with the exhaustive simulator of ObjectGeode. Then, the specification model has been delivered to the designer team (Dornier Satelliten System Gmbh) who refined the model and verified the same properties. The global conclusions of the study were very positive and convinced MMS to apply the formalism on a real project.

The VTC/SW of the COF/DMS Was a Good Candidate

MMS is in charge of the development of the DMS (Data Management System) of the COF (Columbus Orbital Facility) in the ISS (International Space Station) project. The On-board Software division of MMS is in charge of developing two main SW sub-systems in the DMS: the VTC SW (Vital Telemetry/Telecommand Controller) and the MSW (Master Support SW).

VTC is a corner stone of the Columbus Orbital Facility (COF). The vital layer is in charge of managing vital equipments, reporting to the Space Station, processing commands, starting and monitoring the nominal layer. The MSW is responsible for the different on-board experiences and as such must provide facilities for the scientists to operate these experiences.

VTC is made of two redundant computers in master/slave configuration. Both computer acquire sensors data through 1553 buses and direct HW interfaces, monitor them locally and transmit results to the space station through Telemetry frames. A set of Telecommands can be processed by the VTC for the purpose of configuring equipments or the acquisition/monitoring process. The status of the nominal layer is permanently watched by the VTC and appropriate reconfiguration processes can be started if the VTC detects an anomaly.

The VTC project has been for us a very good opportunity to evaluate the technology on a real project. Firstly, it was large enough to produce meaningful results which could be used to convince other teams of the interest of the technology. Secondly, it is a critical part of the DMS in charge of controlling the vital layer of the COF. As such, it has been classified by ESA as a category B SW. This indicates that the SW contains a set of mechanisms on which the safety of the COF relies. Consequently, there is the opportunity to analyse and validate the behaviour of some critical mechanisms in the SW, which is just why formal languages have been defined. Thirdly, the Columbus standards, taking into account the critical dimension of the SW, proposed to complement the HOOD methodology with a formalism addressing the objectives of behaviour modelling and verification. The selected formalism was Petri Nets for which a coupled use with HOOD was described. Having no experience with Petri, and considering that the commercial tools when they existed were not mature enough, MMS proposed to DASA (the COF project manager) to replace Petri with SDL supported by the ObjectGeode tool. That proposal has been accepted after some needed clarifications from MMS. And, last but not least, the project team was really motivated by the experience which reveals a real mind openness to new technologies in our division.

This has been the first stone of the first industrial use of SDL at MMS and this is the story that we are going to tell in the rest of the paper.

2.3 Use of SDL on the VTC Project

First Step : Which Modelling Strategy to Apply ?

Although a standard existed preliminary to the decision to use SDL, it was appropriate to Petri Nets and proposed only a limited use of the modelling technique. We have considered that our knowledge and experience with SDL could be a good basis for a larger experimentation of the technology.

The selection of a modelling language and tool is just the first step in the elaboration of a methodology which can guarantee satisfying results. Formalisms such as SDL and MSC, and the facilities provided by the ObjectGeode tool, can be applied on different types of projects, with different goals, to provide different kinds of results.

A very light use of those technologies may be sufficient for either small projects or projects for which a full use of a modelling and simulation technology would be oversized with respect to the real needs. For such projects, formalisms such as SDL and MSC can be used only for documentation purposes by focusing on the visual and legible aspects of their graphical representations.

Another possible use is to combine the visual dimension of the formalism with the power of interactive simulation in order to run different scenarios and to produce traces under the form of MSCs. This strategy is interesting when the global behaviour of a system must be understood and analysed to demonstrate that the proposed architecture fulfils the user requirements.

A more formal approach consists in using the formalism, and the tool features, to prove that a given set of properties is fulfilled by the model. Exhaustive simulation is the ideal candidate for such purpose but although being very performing it has several limitations and cannot be considered as a push-button verification strategy. First of all, due to the nature of the technology itself (exhaustive simulation means a complete exploration of all the system states), the size of the model must be reasonable, which generally means small. Secondly, before verifying properties, they have to be written by using either the same formalism as the one used for modelling, or another one more dedicated to the task. There is a true properties modelling activity which requires the same level of attention as the system modelling.

In the case of VTC, we've decided to adopt the second modelling strategy described above : a complete modelling of the SW architecture and a set of verifications by using interactive and random simulation.

SDL and MSC with HOOD in the VTC/SW Project

One major characteristic of the SDL experience in VTC is that the HOOD methodology has been kept as the main design method. This introduced some constraints on the use of SDL but gave us interesting results on the comparison between the two methods.

The experiment [9] took place during the Architectural Design phase of the project where the whole software architecture is designed. The experience consisted in four majors phases as depicted in figure 4:

- A complete modelling of the SW functions with MSC diagrams,
- A complete modelling of the SW architecture with SDL,
- A simulation of the system functions and analysis of the SW behaviour with the ObjectGeode simulator,
- A generation of the complete MSC traces produced by the simulator after execution of the system functions. Those traces should be used to ease the elaboration of the integration test plan.

In the first phase of the experiment, each function of the system, the cyclic activities and the asynchronous operations (TC processing), have been described with the MSC formalism. Due to the complexity of the behaviour, and to the size of interactions sequences between the different SW entities, the scenarios have been broken down into small MSC leaves which have been organised into larger scenarios with the combination operators. The elaboration of MSCs has been performed at each successive level of the HOOD architectural design, to provide a full traceability between the system functions and the use of HOOD operations visible at each level.

In the second phase, the complete architectural design of VTC/SW has been modelled.

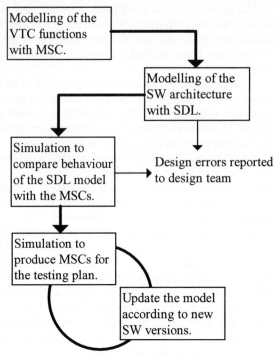

Fig. 4. The SDL experiment on VTC.

Although only the dynamic behaviour of the application was concerned by the modelling, it could have been sufficient to restrict the model to only terminal and active objects. We have considered that the model should also be a complete representation of the HOOD design with a more precise and complete description of the behaviour. For those reasons, the SDL model is structured just like the HOOD design, it contains only the active objects and limits the level of details to those absolutely needed for modelling behaviour. For example, details of data structures have not been represented when they were not essential to fulfil the modelling/simulation objectives.

In the third phase, having a detailed model in SDL and a description of the functions to be performed by the system, in MSC, we were ready to start a simulation campaign for demonstrating the correct behaviour of the proposed design. The MSCs which have been initially written for documentation purposes have been lightly rewritten to satisfy the constraints imposed by the simulator. The model has been compiled with each interesting MSC and the simulator used for verifying that the behaviour described in the MSC was exhibited by the model. If not, a detailed scenario was automatically generated which gave the complete sequence of interactions leading to a discrepancy between the actual behaviour and the expected one. Such a process perfectly worked even with very complex MSCs made of different sequences combined with operators. Such a capability of the ObjectGeode tool considerably reduced the time spent in the verification phase.

Those three above steps already formed the basis of a very positive experience. And, in fact, that experience should have stop here. But, without anticipating on the conclusions, we can say that the experience has gone further than initially scheduled mainly because of the positive results it gave and the increased interest of the project team in the technology. The last step consisted in the generation of the MSC traces for each function performed by the VTC/SW and modelled in SDL. One major interest of such traces is that they give, in a very simple and easy-to-read form, a complete description of the interactions between SW entities (Objects or tasks) which occur when a given function is executed. Those traces are very helpful for documentation purpose, especially when new designers join the team or during the maintenance phase. Moreover, they can also be used for elaborating the test plan for the integration phase since they contain all the requested details.

3   The VTC/SW Successful Experiment Convinced New Project

3.1 Major Conclusions of the VTC/SW Experiment

A Positive Experiment
If the challenge is to use the smallest number of words as possible for summarising the conclusions after the experiment, we would say « it is a very positive experience ». To say more, we can list here above the major conclusions :

- SDL and MSC are visual and formal languages which make them rather easy to read and non ambiguous.
- SDL and MSC are not very complex to use. They can be easily manipulated by any SW designers. This is a major advantage compared to other formal languages.
- SDL and MSC significantly improved the communication within the design team, especially when new members joined the group. This is specially due to the great legibility of the formalisms. The use, by the designers, of the SDL model to write the ADA pseudo code is a good demonstration of the real legibility of the formalism.
- The SDL modelling activity provided interesting feedback to the designers and helped in identifying incompleteness and inconsistencies in the HOOD design. This shows that elaborating an executable model with a formal language forces the designer to enter a higher level of detail and helps him to trap design errors earlier.
- The MSC descriptions of VTC functions has been found very clear and precise and the SDL model has greatly emphasised the description of the tasks, especially from the behavioural point of view.
- The level of confidence on the quality of the SW design has been increased according to all project members. This is due to both the results of the analysis phase with SDL, where inconsistencies have been found, and to the verification phase where all the nominal behaviours, as described with MSC diagrams, have been checked with the simulator.
- The final customers (ESA and DASA) have very much appreciated the content of the Architectural Design Document, which contained the SDL model. It

allowed them to more deeply understand the architecture of the VTC/SW, especially from the behavioural point of view.

- The SDL model, initially elaborated for the Architectural Design Phase, has been continuously maintained since its very first version and is now completely in phase with the current release of the SW. This is a direct consequence of the positive conclusions above described and it is a decision of the project manager to ease the integration testing phase with the help of MSC diagrams generated by simulation.

Some Limitations Found

Although having been very positive, the VTC/SW experiment raised some limitations in the domain covered by the tool or some difficulties in the introduction of the technology in our processes.

- The SDL/MSC formalisms are much appropriate for modelling the SW behaviour, but when performance or Real Time behaviour of the target must be analysed, some limitations appear. The formalisms, and the supporting tool, are not appropriate for such tasks, even if it is always possible to model HW resources or operating system but at the price of a substantial model modification. This has been a major limitation during the experiment since performance of the SW was also a major concern. Consequently, there is here a place for SW gateways between SDL tools and true performance evaluation tools such as OPNET.
- The major problem of any modelling activity is the selection of the right modelling level. Obviously, not all the system features can be modelled, and the model must be adapted to the real needs. This point has to be discussed before the modelling activity starts.
- Our experiment has taken the HOOD design as the main driver of the modelling activity, and most of the HOOD model has been translated into SDL. The mapping has been quite easy to establish due to the closeness of concepts from the two methods. As a result, there are many redundancies between the SDL model and the HOOD design. This will lead us to deeply investigate the problem of using SDL from the methodological point to view, and to study how a smooth transition from HOOD to SDL for example can be put into practice.

3.2 Applications of SDL/MSC after the Successful VTC Experiment

Considering the very positive results we obtained on the VTC/SW project, we have decided to enter a new phase in the integration of the SDL technology in our SW development process. It has been concretised by different types of actions : application of SDL to existing projects, deeper analysis of new features of the ObjectGeode tool and a more general evaluation of the potential impact of the technology on our processes.

New Applications of SDL

After the VTC experiment, which is still running to maintain the model up to date, a new project has been selected to use the SDL and MSC formalisms. It is the SPOT5/HELIOS2 Central Flight Software which was also designed in HOOD. But the application to this project has been very different from the first experiment on VTC/SW. As most of the code was reused from the SPOT4/HELIOS1 version, it has been considered as not mandatory to build a SDL model of the SW but to focus more on MSC for improving the description of the dynamic behaviour of the SW. For that reason, only some parts of the SW has been selected, generally those for which the dynamic behaviour was complex to describe. The results on that project have also been very positive, for the project team as well as from the customer point of view. This project confirms that those modelling technologies can be easily adapted to the project needs.

Following that successful experiences, another projects decided to use the SDL/MSC languages for different purposes.

- On ARIANE V project, we decided to use SDL and MSC to monitor and master the re-design of the IMU (Inertial Measurement Unit) SW of the launcher. The specification and design activities are performed outside MMS by Sextant Avionique. We expect from the use of SDL to better understand the proposed design and to improve our role of SW architect. This is an on-going project and the first conclusions already showed that some inconsistencies in the informal specification can be found by modelling it with SDL.

- On the MSW (another part of the COF Data Management System) we have used MSCs to describe tests sequences to be executed during integration phase. MSCs are easy to build and to understand, and ease the understanding of the SW dynamic, especially for some complex behaviours.

- We are also trying to convince the project to use simulation to verify the design and code generation to generate a prototype of the application able to run on VXWORKS targets.

Entering SPACES

Those on-going use of the SDL/MSC formalisms and ObjectGeode tool are concrete applications of our development processes which recommend those languages to support, when needed, the SW development phases. The SDL/MSC and ObjectGeode features whose interest has been demonstrated are recommended for use on real projects. As process improvement is a continuous activity, always aiming at defining better processes, there is clearly a need to investigate unexplored features of a given technology.

In the ObjectGeode tool there are at least two features which seems interesting: the code generator and the capacity of producing test sequences. The past and current applications on real projects did not use all of the ObjectGeode features, either because they were not really needed, or our experience with them was not sufficient to start a real use on a project. To complete our knowledge of the real tool capabilities, we sent a proposal to the European Commission in the framework of the ESSI program (European System and Software Initiative). That proposal, called SPACES (Software Production using Automatic Code Generation for Embedded Systems) has been selected for funding by the commission and started in November 98.

4   The SPACES Project

SPACES is a PIE project according to the ESSI program. A PIE (Process Improvement Experiment) "provides the opportunity for an organisation to demonstrate the benefits of process improvement, through a controlled, limited experiment. The PIE is undertaken in conjunction with a real software project (the baseline project) which forms part of the normal business of the organisation" according to the ESSI web site [2]

"A PIE allows an organisation to try out new procedures, new technologies and organisational changes before taking the decision as to whether or not they should be replicated throughout the software developing unit" [2].

According to that definition, a PIE project must:
1.   Define process Improvement Objectives from business and technical point of views,
2.   Select a set of limited changes whose impact have to be evaluated with respect to the selected objectives,
3.   Choose a baseline project on which the experiment will be performed. A PIE is not a complementary funding source for the baseline project but a mean for evaluating the interest of a new development strategy which is applied on a real project.

4.1 The SPACES Objectives and Development Plan

One of the major objective of the SPACES project is to demonstrate if code and test generation techniques can significantly increase our productivity and reduce the time to market of our space systems. This objective is mainly business oriented since the introduction of a new technology in a development process has an interest for an industrial company if it can significantly improve its capacity to develop its core business and its market share. In the SPACES project, we targeted a reduction of almost 30% of the SW development effort by using automatic code and test generation techniques. Moreover, by using those techniques, we expect a significant increase of the confidence level that we and our customer have in our systems.

Naturally, this business objective is directly related to technical ones. Proving that those techniques can increase the productivity of our teams implies to demonstrate that they are really applicable in our projects. The main question from the technical point of view is the following: are we able to produce real code for on-board applications with real-time constraints?

Four Phases in SPACES

According to those objectives, the SPACES project is made of four major phases:
- Apply code generator to the VTC model and analyse the qualities of the generated code. This requires the addition of design details in the model, specially at data and algorithmic levels which are very simplified in the model. The quality of the generated code is evaluated from the quality standards point of view and also with respect to performance. The time to produce the final code is also measured and compared with the figures from the baseline project.

- Optimise the generated code. The first versions of the generated code will probably not match the quality standards we expect for embedded SW. As direct modifications of the generated code must be avoided, there are two different kinds of solutions. The first one consists in defining modelling rules at SDL level which forbid the use of some SDL statements whose translation into code is not optimal. The second one consists in modifying the code generator itself by providing new translation rules for some SDL statements. Technically speaking, the second solution is totally feasible thanks to a real openness of the ObjectGeode code generator. But it must be performed carefully since the new code generator can violate SDL semantic.

- Produce automatically tests sequences and generate the testing monitors. Testing is generally a painful task. First, the tests sequences must be defined from the testing objectives. Then, they must be executed on the target and their results analysed. This process is generally manual and consumes time and money. Our purpose in SPACES is to demonstrate that appropriate test sequences can be automatically generated from a model. Given a test objective, the ObjectGeode simulator is used to produce the test sequences which match the test objective. Those sequences are described as MSC diagrams to document the testing activity. And they are also used to produce the testing monitors which will capture data from the running code and verify if the test passed.

- Perform cross-testing on the final target. Our main goal in this task is to compare the coverage level of automatic and manual tests sequences. The manual code will be tested with the automatic tests sequences, and the automatic code will be tested with both manual and automatic tests sequences. By comparing the number of errors found in each case, we will have an idea of the respective quality of the tests sequences and the codes. By crossing those figures with the time spent on setting up each testing strategy, we can estimate the gain in terms of productivity to reach a given quality level.

5   SPACES: Already Positive Results and Other Expected

5.1 First Results from SPACES Now Available on Earth

At the present time, the SPACES project has almost reached the end its first phase and some results already exist.

From Model to Code in an Incremental Way

- The list of discrepancies between the model and the existing ADA code has been produced. For each of those discrepancies, a solution has been defined to update the model.

- An incremental approach has been set up to evaluate the code generation technique. Three versions of generated code have been defined as shown on Figure 5: V0 which is the initial version of the model, V1 which integrates some facilities for entering TCs and which also produces TM flows in the correct format, and finally V2 which will improve the TC interface by including decoding mechanisms which take a CCSDS message on input.

Successful Code Generation on Various Platforms

- The version V0 has been generated and executed on UNIX platform. No problem have been found during this first trial. Thanks to the structure of the code generator, generating code from a SDL model on any of the supported platform is really a push-button activity. The behaviour of the generated code is identical to the model1 and this can be checked either manually through traces produced by the code, or more easily with MSC and SDL model animations generated at run time and processed by the Design Tracer tool.

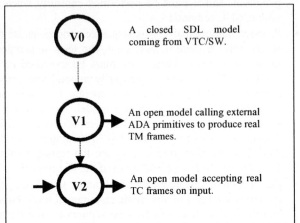

- To demonstrate the capability of the code generation, we have also try to generate and execute the code on another platform. The

Fig. 5. The different produced versions of the generated code.

test has been performed on Windows NT platforms, and once again, a simple push-button action has been sufficient to produce the code which exhibited the same behaviour as on Unix.

- The V0 version has also been ported to a true real-time target: a Force Computer board with the VXWORKS operating system. Porting has not been very difficult since the code generator is already customised for that environment. The generated code run perfectly the first time it was loaded on the target. Moreover, thanks to a complete integration between ObjectGeode and the Tornado development environment, debugging at SDL level is possible and really operational. Debugging trace at code level are used to locate SDL statements in the model, and breakpoints can be put directly in the SDL model through SDL editor.

Subsequent Versions to Be Closer to Real Targets

- The production of the V1 version required use of external ADA code which implement primitives used to build telemetry packets from internal data. That code is produced automatically by the Production Program which takes on input information coming from the system data base and generate the primitives.

---

[1] There are some differences due to some SDL concepts which are nice from the theory point of view but not realistic. This concern especially the way time is managed in SDL.

Modelling this mechanism with SDL is not very appropriate, so we decide to couple the C code generated by ObjectGeode with the ADA code generated by the Production Program.

- For what concerns the V2 version, it has been completely developed and successfully tested on Unix platforms. That version introduces an interesting feature by directly processing real TC messages (CCSDS frames) instead of abstract representations through SDL signals. It means that the produced code can be easily integrated with real hardware and specially with bus controllers from which it can get the CCSDS frames.
- Our experience also showed that integrating external code at simulation level was almost as easy than with generated code. This is an interesting result since it will allow our development teams to perform early design generation by introducing in an incremental way external code.

Success in Code Generation Impacts the Reuse Policy

- For now we can consider that code production through automatic generators has really been demonstrated at least for prototypes. For what concerns the possible use for embedded applications, a deeper analysis on the quality, conformity to the standards, performance, and size of the generated code has to be performed. Some preliminary analysis showed that with easy to use optimisation techniques, code size can be dramatically decreased (30% gained by a very simple optimisation rule: precise for each SDL process that only one instance is authorised at execution time).
- For what concerns the productivity issues, it is clear that the code generation task, with or without integration of external code, is not time consuming. One day at most has been necessary to get a code whose behaviour has been checked with respect to the original model. Moreover, changing the target platform, or even the system architecture, by introducing multiple processors, is not really a major problem, since the code generator already addresses those issues.
- The code generator integrated in ObjectGeode only produces C code when ADA is preferred and imposed for embedded systems. Our analysis show that the target language has least importance when code generation is automatic. In classical development strategies, the assembly code is merely analysed or modified (unless performance optimisation are needed or when parts of code are directly written in that language). Constraints which exist at ADA level, and which are verified by the compiler, can be put at SDL level instead.
- From the reuse point of view, we think that a combined use of SDL modelling and automatic code generation techniques can improve a lot the reuse process. If reuse is limited to piece of codes, it cannot be optimal since code is generally very much related to a given target. If reuse takes place at design level, complete parts of SDL model can be reused and combined to produce new models which can be verified through simulation and used to produce new implementations for other targets or even different architectures.

5.2 SPACES: Second Stage Ready for Ignition

Ready for Testing

The second stages of the SPACES project is now ready for ignition and will start as soon as the first stage is completely finished. First results obtained during first stage operational phase are very promising for the project's future and at the time this paper will be presented, we can expect many positive conclusions.

The second stage will address two important issues:

• Automatic generation of tests sequences by model analysis.
• Automatic generation of tests procedures to monitor the target code.

SPACES aims at reducing the duration of the testing phase and improving its efficiency. There are three major problems during testing: find the most accurate tests sequences, write the test procedures and apply them to the real code. Testing is critical but generally painful and it is certainly the place where productivity can be most easily increased.

Verification and Validation Testing

As an exhaustive test of the code is generally not feasible, appropriate tests sequences have to be selected trying to find all potential or real bugs. There are two kinds of tests (not to be mixed with testing levels: unit and integration): verification and validation. Verification testing aims at proving that the SW design does not introduce improper behaviours leading to code crash, validation testing aims at proving the SW fulfils its specification.

We think that the use of a formal model, and SDL is a formal language, can help in elaborating those tests sequences. For what concern verification testing, the knowledge of the model architecture and of the code structure, should be sufficient to produce tests sequences by techniques of model analysis. The purpose of those tests sequences is to test most of the possible behaviours of the code as identified through the model. Validation testing requires the knowledge of the tests objectives and of the model and generated code structure. Tests objectives cannot be automatically derived at validation level, and it is not desirable for them to be derived since tests would be defined by the same tool which produce the code. Those objectives must be given by the testing team and derived from the SW specification. Use of MSC, SDL, logical assertions or GOAL[2] models are possible means for defining such objectives and the list is certainly not exhaustive. By using those high level objectives and mastering SDL model and generated code, tests sequences matching the objectives can be derived.

Another painful activity in testing is writing tests sequences which have to be executed on the target. Use of a dedicated testing language or a classical programming one does not significantly change the nature of problem. Our solution consists in starting from tests sequences, written in MSC for example and produced either manually or automatically, generate the testing code and execute it automatically either on the target or on a testing platform which monitors the target. The activity of producing appropriate test code is then significantly reduced and testing can be almost made automatically.

---

[2] GOAL is a language used in the ObjectGeode tool to define model observers.

The SPACES project is an experiment of those techniques and has to prove their interest and efficiency on real projects. For testing issues we have to demonstrate that the solutions described above can be put into practice at a reasonable cost and can save time and money with keeping the same quality level or reaching a higher level. Especially, we would like to demonstrate that tests sequences generated from the model, either at verification or validation phase, are at least as efficient than the manually produced one to capture bugs. To verify that we will apply the automatic tests sequences both on manual and on automatic code.

6   What Do Exist after SPACES ? A New Development Process

The SPACES project has already produced some interesting results by demonstrating that executable code can be easily generated from a SDL model. A more detailed analysis has to be performed to confirm use of code generation techniques for embedded Software. But the main challenge of SPACES is not technical but organisational. Proving that a method, a technique or a tool is really powerful is one thing, but making it efficient on real projects is really a matter of organisation. The focus must be put on software development processes: how must they evolve to integrate a new technology? This is specially hard for code generation technique since it is not a simple box replacing manual coding. Introduction of such techniques requires important modifications of the whole process, especially during the design phase where more time shall be spent on software modelling.

For what concerns the specification and design phases, SDL has shown that it can be used for modelling a complete SW design, verifiable by simulation and usable for producing code able to run on a final target. But SDL has also some limitations, especially when data and algorithms have to be defined. The ObjectGeode method guidelines proposes an integration with OMT/UML class diagrams to address that issue.

The SPACES experience raised the problem of the evolution from HOOD to new design methodologies such as UML which is now arriving with a lot of promises. Due to the very recent release of a stable version of the UML notation [10], there is no available tool fully supporting it. But there are a lot of plans to provide new generation of tools which will implement several views of the notation, and some of them will be more dedicated to real-time systems [11]. VERILOG has such plans to provide a UML tool using the SDL and MSC notation to describe the behaviour.

It is clear that a full use of SDL to support the design phase will completely change the look of that phase. More time will be spent in it to validate the design and to produce executable prototypes on development or targets platforms. The development will be more incremental but at each design step, the implementation can be quickly verified.

During testing phase, we really think productivity can be increased with the same quality level. Automatic production of tests suites directly from the model, and automatic execution on the target will significantly reduced time wasted in painful task, giving more time to execute more tests.

7   Conclusion

People sometimes think that modelling tools require few efforts and produce a lot of interesting results that no human can produce. If the tool does not satisfy those requirements, it is not a good tool and investment will not be profitable. Those miracle tools do not exist and ObjectGeode is not an exception. But with the appropriate level of project and people investment, those tools can help a lot in the documentation of the project, in the communication within the team and with the customer, and are very helpful for early validation of a SW architecture.

The SPACES project shows that, not only formal methods such as SDL are powerful enough to almost completely support the SW design phase, but also that with proper use of powerful tools such as ObjectGeode, code can be produced and easily ported on various platforms. Moreover, even if the project did not prove yet that generated code is ready for direct integration in embedded systems, it has proven that working prototypes integrating external code can be automatically produced. If SPACES also proves that the testing phase can be improved, we will consider that ESSI experiment as fully successful. If the results are not fully satisfactory, the experiment will help us in defining rules for successfully applying the technology, taking its limit into account.

We are now convinced that such techniques, and their integration in the UML world, constitute the basis of new SW design processes. They will surely increase the productivity of the designers and significantly improve the confidence level that system providers and customers can reasonably put into the delivered products. We have now to be prepared to improve our development processes to be more cost effective and more competitive and those modelling techniques are one of the key of our success.

8   References

1. E. Conquet, Ph Humbert, V. Debus, J. Sifakis - Data Management System Design Validation - Final report - 09/96 - ESA contract N° 9558/91/NL/JG, WO N°20.

2. European System and Software Initiative -web site: www.cordis.lu/esprit/src/stessi.htm.

3. Matra Marconi Space - SPACES, Software Production through Automatic Coding for Embedded Systems. Project Programme V2.1 – 08/98.

4. ITU-T, Recommendation Z.100, Specification and Description language (SDL), COM X-R 17-E, Geneva, March 1992.

5. Systems Engineering Using SDL-92 , A. Olsen, O. Færgemand, B. Møller-Pedersen, R. Reed and J. R. W. Smith. North-Holland 1994, ISBN 0 444 898727.

6. SDL - formal object-oriented language for communicating systems, J. Ellsberger, D. Hogrefe and A. Sarma. Prentice Hall 1997, ISBN0-13-621384-7.

7. VERILOG, ObjectGeode method guidelines, version 1.0 – VERILOG - 1996.

8. S. Ayache, E. Conquet, Ph. Humbert – Specification and early validation of autonomous spacecraft fault tolerance using SDL – DASIA 96 – Roma, May 1996

9. E. Conquet, G. Touet - « Modélisation et validation d'un logiciel critique en phase de conception, une expérience d'utilisation de LDS/ObjectGeode » - EC/NT/LB/97.092 - 01/98.

10. UML Notation Guide version 1.1, Rational Corp, et.al., OMG, Sept. 1997

11. Doing Hard Time, Bruce Powel Douglass, Addison Wesley, 1998, ISBN 0-201-49837-5

A Business Process Design Language

Henk Eertink, Wil Janssen, Paul Oude Luttighuis,
Wouter Teeuw, Chris Vissers

Telematics Institute, P.O. Box 589, 7500 AN Enschede, The Netherlands
{eertink,janssen,luttighu,teeuw,vissers}@telin.nl

Abstract. Business process modelling and analysis puts specific requirements on models used and the language for expressing those models. The models should be easily understandable and analysable. In this paper we study the requirements for such a language and introduce a language that satisfies those requirements to a large extent. It was developed in the Testbed project, which aims at developing a systematic approach to business process change.

The language, called AMBER, has a graphical representation, and allows to model processes, data, and the organisation and people involved in a uniform and integrated way. On the basis of a formal foundation of the language, different analyses and tool support are available. We illustrate our approach with a realistic example.

1 Introduction

Organisations are complex artefacts. They involve different customer groups, business units, people, resources and systems. They stretch over numerous different processes that interact in a seemingly chaotic way. When trying to change business processes within organisations one is confronted with that complexity. In order to cope with that complexity and improve the grip on changing business processes, a systematic and controlled approach is needed.

The Testbed project develops a systematic approach to handle change of business processes, particularly aimed at processes in the financial service sector (Franken, Janssen, 1998). A main objective is to give *insight* into the structure of business processes and the relations between them. This insight can be obtained by making *business process models* that clearly and precisely represent the *essence* of the business organisation. These models should encompass different levels of organisational detail, thus allowing to find bottlenecks and to assess the consequences of proposed changes for the customers and the organisation itself; see also Jacobson et al. (1995) and Ould (1995). Formal methods allow for detailed analysis of models and tool support in this process.

J. Wing, J. Woodcock, J. Davies (Eds.): FM'99, Vol. I, LNCS 1708, pp. 76–95, 1999.

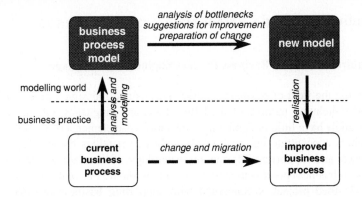

Figure 1. A model-based approach to business process change

As shown in Figure 1, business processes models can be used for analysis and manipulation of business processes without having to actually build these processes first. This model-based approach allows to identify the effects of changes before implementing them. The models constitute an important means for the preparation and actual implementation of organisation and IT change.

In order for such models to be of real help, they have to combine different, competing requirements. On the one hand, they have to be easily accessible and highly understandable to serve as a means of communication between people involved. The primary users of the models are business analysts. They are not especially trained in modelling or formal languages. Moreover, they have to discuss the results with management and people in the shop floor. Thus, the representation should be a *graphical* one: textual representations are not acceptable for the intended users. Moreover, the language should be based on concepts that are relevant to the domain of discourse. It should have a clear *architectural* meaning for business modelling (Vissers, 1994).

On the other hand, the models should be analysable using computer tools and serve as a starting point for (information) systems design. This implies that the models should have a rigorously defined meaning and syntax. Mathematical rigour and communicability are qualities that are not often found in close companionship.

In this paper we introduce a language designed for business process engineering, called AMBER (*Architectural Modelling Box for Enterprise Redesign*). We show the ingredients of the language and how it fulfils the larger part of the requirements needed for business process modelling and analysis. The emphasis in this paper is on the language, and not on the tools and the methodology that support it.

This paper is structured as follows. In section 2 we define requirements for a business process modelling language. Thereafter we mention a number of current approaches and match them to these requirements. Section 3 then gives an overview of AMBER and the means of specialising the language for specific purposes. Section 4 illustrates the approach using a larger example. We end with a summary of our findings and an overview of the current state and plans for (tool) support.

2   Requirements and Current State

2.1   Requirements for a Business Process Engineering Language

When entering the field of business process analysis and redesign, one is confronted with an overwhelming number of modelling tools and languages. Often, these languages and tools have little in common. Some emphasise elements of workflow in the models, others concentrate on quantitative analysis, yet others try to integrate business processes and supporting information technology. If there are so many different viewpoints on business process modelling, then how should one make a choice?

As the Testbed project is concerned with supporting business process analysts throughout a BPR project, we have judged modelling languages and BPR tools for their suitability in different stages. From this perspective an evaluation framework was developed (Janssen et al., 1997). It has four dimensions of evaluation criteria (see Figure 2).

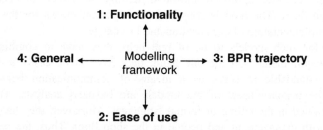

Figure 2. The dimensions of the evaluation framework

The most prominent dimension for modelling languages is *functionality*. It covers:
- *Expressiveness*: we want to express activities and their relations, repetition, and co-operation;
- *Structuring*: the language must support abstraction levels and decomposition;
- *Analysis*: formal semantics are required, extensibility with respect to required analysis parameters;
- *Relevance*: all concepts should be relevant to the domain being modelled.

A second dimension is *ease of use*. This dimension is partly conflicting with the previous one: high functionality often leads to difficulties in using the language due to the number and complexity of the language concepts. As we are aiming at business analysts or business consultants to build and use models, the language should be highly intuitive and communicable.

The third dimension is the *BPR-trajectory*. Modelling business processes is only a small part of BPR. In a BPR-trajectory different steps are distinguished, from developing a corporate strategy to the introduction and implementation of new, redesigned processes. Whether or not languages and tools are helpful in different steps in the BPR trajectory is vital for their applicability. This dimension is often overlooked when evaluating tools and languages. This includes modelling for *design, redesign and migration*: language support for component-based design, sharing model parts, sequences (trajectory) of models.

The last dimension considers *general properties* of (especially) tools supporting the language, e.g. cost, user support and market acceptance. In general, tool support is a prerequisite for broad acceptance. Though processes can be visualised using drawing tools such as ABC Flowcharter, more extensive support is needed to tackle complexity and ensure maintainability.

2.2   Current Approaches to Business Process Modelling

The problem of understanding complex system behaviour and the challenge of developing easy-to-use models are apparent in the field of business processes. Until recently, many organisations used only spreadsheet models to forecast the implications of change. Nowadays, more sophisticated modelling and analysis techniques —often based on simulation or workflow techniques— are used in predicting the effects of change.

A simulation model represents a (discrete event) system, setting (input) parameters and observing output parameters and the way they behave in time. For this purpose, many tools have been built, for example based on simulation languages like Simula '67 (Dahl et al., 1970) or SIMAN (Pegden et al., 1995). Arena (Systems Modelling Corporation) and SimProcess (CACI Products Company) are examples of such tools. The resulting simulation models are often used for problem solving in organisations (Dur, 1992).

For some purposes, simulation is less suited, because it is too time-consuming or does not deliver the level of completeness required. In such cases, analytical techniques for quantitative analysis (Lazowska et al., 1984) can be used. Especially for computer systems performance modelling such techniques are well suited.

Workflow approaches (Lawrence, 1997) tend to use activity models like Petri-nets or role activity diagrams or non-standard modelling techniques to define the business processes and their relations. Workflow is often used to automate or streamline business processes.

When considering people and their positions in an organisation, it is not sufficient to focus only on the procedural aspects of process definition. Aspects of responsibility and accountability must also be taken into account. The theoretical framework of Flores and Winograd (1986), commonly referred to as *speech-act theory*, provides concepts for modelling these issues (Scherr, 1993). Examples of methods and tools built on this theory are ActionWorkflow (Medina-Mora et al., 1992), DEMO (Rijst, Dietz, 1994), and SAMPO (Auramaki et al., 1988).

The Unified Modelling Language UML (Rational, 1997) provides a set of concepts and language elements for different aspects: use-case diagrams show the actors, class and object diagrams define objects and their behaviour, state or scenario diagrams show life-cycles and scenarios, etc. Although the approach was originally developed for software process design, the application of object-oriented design principles as provided by UML for the (re)design of business processes is extensively described by Jacobson (Jacobson et al, 1995).

A limited number of more systematic approaches to *business process design* are found in the literature. One of the most extensive ones is STRIM (Systematic Technique for Role and Interaction Modelling) (Ould, 1995). This method uses Role Activity Diagrams (RADs) to graphically model processes. The method comprises a global approach to model a process, and more detailed guidelines for specific situations. It defines process patterns (a kind of templates) for frequently occurring process types. The Architecture of Integrated Information Systems approach, supported by the tool Aris, can be regarded as a systematic approach (Scheer, 1998) as well. Aris allows for different visualisations of processes for different purposes. Moreover, it provides a powerful repository that can serve a kind of collective organisational memory. The conceptual basis of the approach has certain similarities to the language we use in Testbed. Due to lack of formal foundation, however, analysis is limited. Simulation is possible, but other types of analysis are missing.

If we place the above approaches along the dimension of the evaluation framework, we can see that all of them provide ingredients applicable to business process modelling and analysis. They provide expressiveness (simulation languages, Petrinets), analysability (simulation, analytical techniques), insight (STRIM, speech-act theory), relative ease of use (workflow modelling tools). However, none of them combine those aspects in a uniform way. Moreover, the fact that business process change involves a series of models (plateaux, migration stages) is missing from almost all approaches mentioned (Janssen et al., 1997).

We may conclude that the existing modelling languages each emphasise some elements, but do not provide an overall solution for business process engineering. This is partially caused by the fact that most of these methods originate from information system development. In the next section we define AMBER and illustrate how this language aims at fulfilling the requirements stated, in a unified, graphical yet formally defined language.

3   AMBER Explained

Business modelling languages may be deployed for many different purposes. Not only do they supply a sound foundation for communicating and discussing business process designs, they may be used as well for e.g.

- *analysis* of business processes, that is, assessment of qualities and properties of business process designs, either in quantitative or qualitative terms;
- *model checking*, that is, providing answers to functional queries posed on business models, e.g. "Will every customer request result in an answer?";
- *export to implementation platforms*, such as workflow management and enterprise resource planning systems;
- *job design*, that is, designing detailed job specifications and generating job instructions; and

- *domain-specific modelling*, that is, incorporating concepts specifically for a certain application domain, such as a business sector.

Every specific purpose of a business modelling language brings about its own specific demands on the language. Yet, it should be possible to use the language for only a limited purpose, without being burdened with the peculiarities of other purposes. Therefore, AMBER was designed to have a lean core language, containing the basic concepts underlying any of the purposes served. On top, it can be tailored for specific purposes by means of a specialisation mechanism called 'profiles'. The top of the pie holds the modelling and analysis extensions, the bottom contains the extensions that can be used to map models to real-world implementations. This design makes AMBER flexible, extendible, and comprehensible (Figure 3).

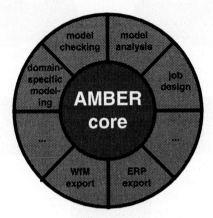

Figure 3. AMBER's pie-wise design

3.1   The Core Language

The core of the business modelling language contains concepts that enable basic reasoning about business processes. AMBER recognises three aspect domains:

- the *actor* domain, which allows for describing the organisations, departments, systems, and people carrying out business processes;
- the *behaviour* domain, which allows for describing what happens in a business process;
- the *item* domain, which allows for describing the items handled in business processes.

The Actor Domain

The basic concept in the actor domain is the *actor*. It designates a resource (used for) carrying out a business process. Actors are structured: they may contain other actors. Also, they are related. Therefore, actors are equipped with *interaction points*, indicating physical or logical locations at which the actor may interact with its environment. They are the hooks where interaction-point relations couple actors. Interaction points may be involved in multiple relations. Also, an interaction-point relation may involve more than two interaction points.

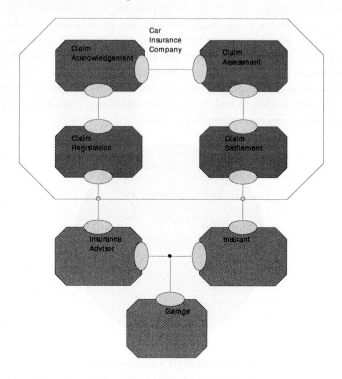

Figure 4. A typical actor model

Figure 4 depicts a typical actor model, showing the parties involved in car insurance claims. It includes a triple interaction-point relation, between the insurant, his garage, and his insurance adviser. It also shows the internal structure of the car insurance company, that is, the four departments involved in processing the claim. The legend of this domain is given in Figure 5. Note that colours have no formal meaning in these models.

Actions, Relations, and Behaviour Structuring

The basic concept in the behaviour domain is *action*. It models a unit of activity in business processes. Actions carry two essential attributes: the actors involved in the action and the result in terms of their outputs.

An action can only happen when its *enabling condition* is satisfied. These conditions are formulated in terms of other actions having occurred yet, or not. The most simple is the enabling relation. When put between actions *a* and *b*, it models the fact that *b* cannot happen but after *a* has finished. Its mirror image is the disabling relation, modelling that *b* cannot happen any more, once *a* has occurred.

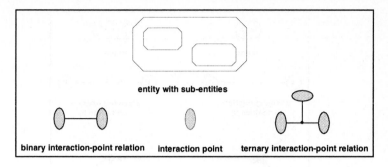

entity with sub-entities

binary interaction-point relation   **interaction point**   **ternary interaction-point relation**

Figure 5. Ingredients of the actor domain

Causality relations can be composed using Boolean-like operators. Also, they can be supplied with additional *constraints*, which further restrict the relation with conditions on attribute values of preceding actions.

A special kind of action, used in many business process models, is a *trigger*. Triggers are like actions, accept that they have no causality condition, that is, they are immediately enabled.

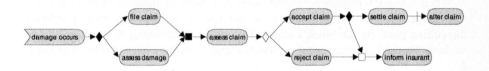

Figure 6. A typical unstructured behaviour model

Figure 6 depicts a typical behaviour model, containing a sequence of actions, related by enabling conditions. The occurrence of damage triggers both the filing of a claim as well as the assessment of the damage. Only when both have been carried out, the claim is assessed and then either accepted or rejected. In any case, the insurant is informed about the outcome. Only in case of acceptance, the claim is settled. After settlement, the claim cannot be changed. We did not model what happens when claims are altered. The legend is shown in Figure 7.

Extensive modelling of all relevant actions in a business process, and their enabling conditions, will result in huge and cluttered models for any serious business process. Therefore, structuring concepts are included in AMBER to tackle the complexity of behaviour models.

Behaviour can be grouped in *blocks*. Like actors, blocks can be nested. There are basically two points at which some behaviour can be separated from its environment. One is *between* actions, the other is *inside* actions.

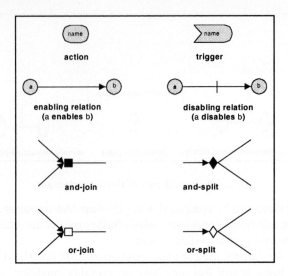

Figure 7. Actions and enabling conditions

When a block separates behaviour between actions, a causality relation is cut. A so-called entry or exit, depending on the direction of the causality relation, indicates the cutting point (at the block's edge). This type of structuring is typically, but not exclusively, used for structuring in phases. Figure 8 shows a phased version of Figure 6.

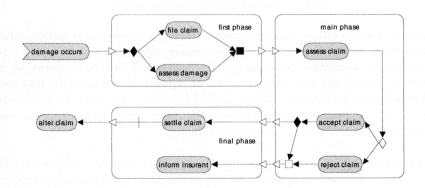

Figure 8. A phased behaviour model

When a block separates behaviour inside actions, the action is divided in a number of *interactions*. Interactions are related like interaction points in the actor domain. An interaction can only happen simultaneously with all of its related interactions, which must therefore all be enabled. This type of structuring is typically used for modelling interaction between model elements. Figure 9 shows a version of Figure 6, in which this type of structuring is used.

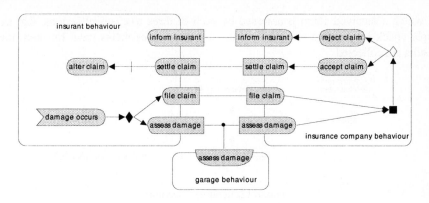

Figure 9. Interacting blocks

Although separately introduced here, phased and interaction-based structured may be arbitrarily mixed.

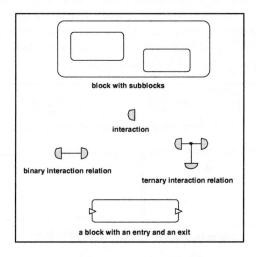

Figure 10. Behaviour structuring

Next to structuring, another way to tackle complexity in business models is to allow similar elements to be described at once, as a group, instead of having to copy each of them out individually. AMBER offers two facilities for this: replication and iteration.

Figure 11. A replicated action

Replication can be used for actors, actions, interactions, and blocks, and indicates that a number of replicas exist next to each other. Figure 11 shows a typical example, in which a received claim is assessed by each of three assessment actions, e.g. as a triple check for high-value claims. When all three assessments have finished, their results are collected.

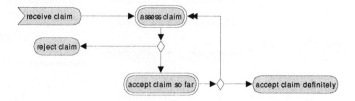

Figure 12. Iterative behaviour

Iteration is used for modelling repeated behaviour, that is, the repeated occurrence of similar behaviour over time. Figure 12 shows an example. Here, different assessment actions are carried out subsequently, for instance for checking different aspects of the claim in different turns. Every assessment may result in (definite) rejection of the claim, or in partial acceptance. When all aspects have been assessed, partial accep-tance may result in definite acceptance. Notice that all actions involved in the loop carry double edges and a double-headed arrow separates different loop traversals. The legend of replication and iteration is shown in Figure 13.

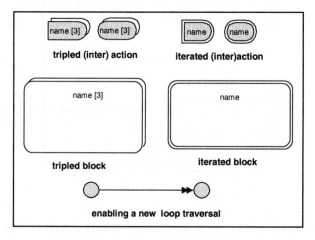

Figure 13. Replication and iteration

The Item Domain
The item domain enables to model the items on which the behaviour is performed. In the actor and behaviour models, items can be included and coupled to the various elements of these models. In the actor domain, items are coupled to interaction point relations, indicating that at the interaction point relation involved, the indicated item is used. Figure 14 shows a straightforward example.

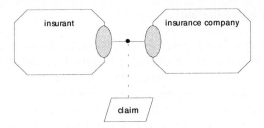

Figure 14. An item coupled to an interaction point relation

Coupling items to elements of behaviour models is different in two ways. First, the items are coupled to actions and interactions, instead of to interaction relations. This is because interaction point relations are symmetric (that is, the interaction points involved cannot have different roles), whereas interaction relations are not: each interaction involved may have its own distinctive contribution to the relation.

Second, item coupling in behaviour models distinguishes between five modes: create, read, change, read/change, and delete. This mode indicates what type of action is performed on the item involved. Figure 15 shows an example in which these respective modes occur, from left to right.

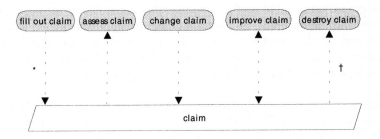

Figure 15. An item, coupled to actions in five ways

Notice that the example includes one single item, coupled to different actions. This way of representing an item in an actor or behaviour model is called an *item bar* and is very much like in IBM's LOVEM (Helton et al., 1995). It is possible to use a different item bar for each coupling and let each of them refer to the same item.

Currently, AMBER does not include an item modelling language. Hence, so far items are not structured, nor related. At the moment, the inclusion of such a language is matter of investigation. A subset of UML will be used, extended with the link to process models.

3.2   Profiles for Specialisation[1]

The concept of 'profile' is introduced in AMBER to allow for more tailored definitions of concepts, even by end-users. This tailoring is useful for a variety of reasons:

- Export mechanisms. For instance, when a model is being translated into a model for a workflow engine, additional parameters should be given for actions, like the executable that should be started for an end-user.
- Specific analysis tools. For quantitative analysis, for instance, aspects like average waiting time, or costs per activity or per resource are necessary. It is only useful to specify these attributes if the analysis is used. When modelling for a workflow engine, cost-aspects are rarely necessary and therefore do not need to be part of the model.
- Context-specific information. Some companies may have a need to specify company-specific information (like additional information for organisational units). Such information is only useful for models that are relevant in that company, and should therefore be visible only in these models.

The profile concept allows us to realise the structure visualised in Figure 3, where the AMBER core is re-used for various analyses and/or export mechanisms. Typically, for each of these pie charts one or more profiles are defined that contain the additional attribute definitions necessary to perform the analysis techniques or generate specific export formats. The profile concept makes it possible to use the same basic model for different purposes, by associating the necessary information with modelling concepts. Models need not contain all information, but only that information required for the analyses or exports desired. The Testbed methodology helps the business engineer in determining his or her information and analysis needs.

A profile is defined in a profile definition language containing type-definition constructs (for re-usable types) and supports sub-classing of profile definitions.

```
type Money     = alias real;
type TimeCat = enum {hour,  day,  week,  month,
year};
type Rate = struct {
        Money            amount;
        TimeCat          period;
};

Profile Costs {
  assignable to Actor;
  Money        fixed = 0.0;
  Rate variable ={amount:100.0,  period:hour};
};
```

The example above shows that there are a number of means to define types (aliasing of built-in types, definitions via structures, unions, enumerations, and collections). The syntax resembles that of the C-programming language. We also support

---

[1] patent pending

a notion of single inheritance in the profile definitions. For instance, to declare a cost-profile that by default has a fixed rate and an empty variable rate you would define:

```
Profile FixedCosts isA Costs {
    Money        fixed = 25.0;
    Rate variable;
};
```

3.3   Formalisation for Analysis

One of the requirements for our language is *analysability*. The AMBER language combines organisational, behavioural, and data elements. For all these elements analysis should be possible, preferably in combination. Formal methods provide analysability. The current state of affairs, however, is that there in no sound mathematical model available in the literature that combines those different elements and still allows for tool supported analysis.

We therefore have taken a different approach. Instead of thriving for a single, unified semantic foundation, different non-conflicting semantic models are used for different aspects. Thus it becomes possible to develop means of analysis that function for realistic business cases. One loses, however, the possibility to analyse relations between aspects that are in different semantic domains.

Many structural analyses are not really based on the underlying semantics, but on the formal syntax. Such analyses, called *views*, allow to highlight specific structural aspects of models, such as "what activities can precede this action?", or show the relationship between different modelling domain ("show what actors perform the activities", or a dataflow view of behaviour). These views make extensive use of information in profiles associated with objects in the model.

An operational semantics has been defined to analyse certain behavioural properties. It defines the meaning of processes in terms of state automata (Janssen et al., 1998). It allows for both an interleaving interpretation as well as a multistep interpretation. The operational semantics forms the basis of the stepwise simulation in the tool. Functional analysis using model checking is derived from the same semantics. We have defined a translation from the finite-state fragment of AMBER to the input language of the model checker Spin, called Promela (Holzman, 1997). This allows for a full state space verification of temporal properties of AMBER models (Janssen et al., 1998). To define verification properties for functional analysis a pattern-based interface is defined, allowing to check for sequences of activities, necessary precedence or consequence, and combinations of occurrences. (Janssen et al., 1999). These patterns are then translated to linear-time temporal logic and thereafter transformed to Spin queries (never claims).

For quantitative properties such an operational semantics is of no use. Instead, we use analytical techniques for performance analysis, based on queuing theory, graph models and hybrid models (Jonkers et al., 1998). Analysis of completion times, critical paths, resource utilisation, and cost analysis are currently available.

As our data language is not fully developed as yet, no particular means of analysis, other than structural analysis, are provided for items.

Finally, the tool allows to transform models to emphasise properties of the model. A powerful concept is that of *process lanes*. A business process model can be automatically structured with respect to any attribute. For example, a process can be structured into a single block (sub-process) for every actor involved, showing the change in responsibility in a process. Alternatively, the process could be structured with respect to the business function associated with an activity, or whether the activity belongs to the primary or secondary part of the process.

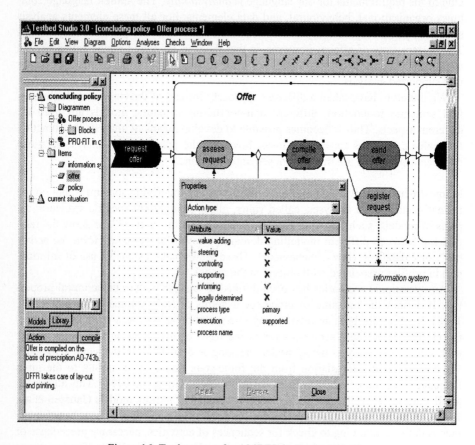

Figure 16. Tool support for AMBER in Testbed Studio

3.4   Tool Support

The language is supported by an integrated set of tool components, together referred to as *Testbed Studio*.

Testbed Studio has the following functionality:
- easy editing of models;
- quantitative analysis of models using various analysis methods;
- functional analysis of models using model checking;
- report generation;
- different views on models;
- step-by-step animation of models;
- management of trajectories of models (refinement of models, versioning);
- component libraries, to allow for re-use of business models.

Testbed Studio runs in the Windows environment. An example screen is shown in Figure 16.

4   AMBER Illustrated

During the past three years, AMBER has been applied in over 30 pilot studies within the Testbed project. These pilots have actually been the steering wheel of the project. Initially, the pilots have been used to study the essential concepts of business process and formulate requirements on languages, methods and tools that should support the business consultants. Later on, the pilots were used for validating results. Only by doing real-life projects and solving real business problems one can optimise its languages, methods, and tools. Gradually, the cases became more complex, evolving from modelling to analysis to redesign and implementation studies. Sample projects concern decreasing the completion time of a insurance process with 30%, modelling and analysing a business function architecture, analysis of the relationship between a pension process and the organisations in its context it depends upon and so on/

In this section we present an imaginary redesign case concerning a car insurance company. It is a realistic case because it is a generalisation of real-life cases. In the following, we restrict ourselves to only one aspect of the overall Testbed approach for business process analysis and redesign: the use of modelling. The overall approach is discussed in Franken and Janssen (1998).

4.1   Modelling for Analysis

Consider RR, a company selling property insurance for cars. Recently, insurance sales have been decreasing. Only 25% of the quotation requests result in an insurance policy. The norm is 40%, however. Testbed and AMBER are used to find the bottlenecks, suggest improvements, and analyse the impact of changes. From RR management we find out that the service level provided is the most important success factor of RR. Costs are in second place. A constraint is that the division of RR in departments should not be changed. Finally, we get the suggestion that state-of-the-art technology should be used. We first model the actors involved (Figure 17).

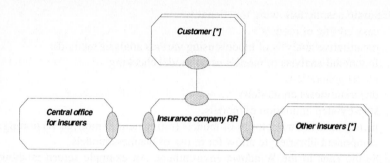

Figure 17. Actors involved in Claim Handling process

Next, we determine the service provided by RR and elaborate the internal processes (Figure 18)

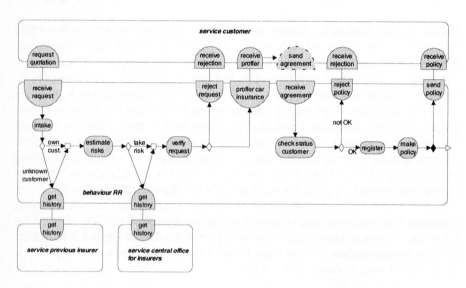

Figure 18. The Claim Handling process

The above behaviour is a *logical* model because it abstracts from physical implementation features. It just shows the request for quotation process. The exit shows the
process continues (with the payment collection, which we omitted in the figure).

Using a number of iterations, the model may be extended and improved. For example, the department 'Sales', 'Policy Management' and 'Finance' may be distinguished and the behaviour may be structured correspondingly. The duration of actions may be specified, and probabilities may be added to each or-split. The resulting
model is a *physical* model, showing the current implementation of activities. This
model, with the *profile* for execution times filled out, can be used as input for analysis
tools showing the critical path or response times.

4.2   Model-Based Analysis

The physical models are not shown, but in Figure 19 some results are presented to give an impression of Testbed analyses. The left plot shows the response time from 'request quotation' until either 'receive rejection' or 'receive proffer'. The average response time is 12.7 days, with 50% and 90% percent of the request handled in 13 respectively 18 days.

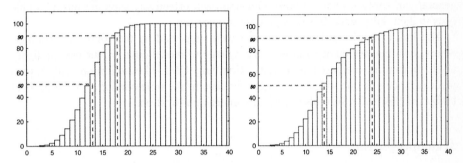

Figure 19. Completions times of Claim Handling proces

The right plot shows the response time from 'request quotation' till either 'receive rejection' or 'receive policy' or 'receive proffer' (in case of no customer response). The average response time is 15.3 days, with 50% and 90% percent of the request handled in 14 respectively 24 days.

These results were analytically obtained using completion time analysis in Testbed Studio. It does not require extensive simulation.

Modelling and analysis reveal the following facts:
- *Customer satisfaction* — Response to quotation request takes 12.7 days. After customer agreement, policy may be rejected.
- *The number of customer interactions* — Customer interacts with all three departments. Customer may be contacted twice before receiving quotation (not shown in the model above).
- *Performance indicators* — 25% of request results in policy. Overall response time is 15.3 days.
- *The logical flow of processes* — All customers are treated equally.

These facts are a starting point for the development of improved processes on the basis of the models of the current situation. The models of the improved situation can then be compared to the original situation, to assess the impact on people, throughput, cost, completion times and so on.

5   Conclusions and Future Work

In this paper a language was presented, suited to model, analyse, and redesign business processes. Using different semantic models for the language, and embedding the language in a methodology for business process redesign supported by tools, has lead to a powerful integrated approach. The approach has proven itself in numerous cases and shows that people that are not aware of intricacies of applying formal methods in general can apply formal methods. Our approach effectively supports business analysts in their daily work: business process engineering.

The link to implementation is not yet well supported by the approach. Amongst others, this requires incorporation of a language to model data. In our user audience UML is gaining increased popularity. Combing UML-like definition with formal process models is one of the challenges we face in the time coming. On the basis of UML, the link to CASE tools is currently under investigation.

Acknowledgement

We would like to thank the anonymous referees for detailed suggestions and Henry Franken for general comments on the paper.

This paper results from the Testbed project, a 120 man-year research initiative that focuses on a virtual test environment for business processes. The Testbed consortium consists of ABP, the Dutch Tax Department, ING Group, IBM and the Telematica Instituut (The Netherlands) and co-operates with several Dutch universities and research institutes. The project is financially supported by the Dutch Ministry of Economic Affairs. We appreciate to acknowledge all Testbed contributors.

References

Auramaki, E., E. Lehtinen, and K. Lyytinen, A speech-act-based office modelling approach, *ACM Transactions on Office Information Systems*, Vol. 6), No. 2, April 1988, 126-152.

Browne, J., P. Bradley, S. Jackson, and H. Jagdev, Business process re-engineering (BPR) - A Study of the software tools currently available. *Computers in Industry*, 25 (1995), p. 309-330.

Dahl, O.-J., B. Myrhrhaug, and K. Nygaard. *SIMULA 67 Common Base Language*. Norwegian Computing Centre, Oslo, 1970, Publication N. S-22.

Dur, R.C.J., *Business reengineering in information intensive organisations*. Ph.D. Thesis, Delft University of Technology, 1992.

Franken, H.M., and W. Janssen, Get a grip on changing business processes, *Knowledge & Process Management* (Wiley), Winter 1998.

Hansen, G. A., Tools for business process reengineering. *IEEE Software*, September 1994, p. 131-133.

Helton, A., E. Zulaybar, and P. Soper. *Business Process Engineering and Beyond*. IBM Redbook. Publication No. SG24-2590-00, 1995.

Holzman, G.J., The model checker SPIN, *IEEE Transactions on Software Engineering*, Vol. 23, No. 5, May 1997, 279-295.

Jacobson, I., M. Ericsson, and A. Jacobson, *The Object Advantage - Business Process Reengineering with Object Technology*, ACM Books, 1995.

Janssen, W., H. Jonkers, and J.P.C. Verhoosel, What makes business processes special? An evaluation framework for modelling languages and tools in Business Process Redesign. In Siau, Wand and Parsons (eds.), *Proceedings 2nd CAiSE/IFIP 8.1 international workshop on evaluation of modelling methods in systems analysis and design*, Barcelona, June 1997. (Available as http://www.telin.nl/publicaties/1997/caise97_final.doc)

Janssen, W., R. Mateescu, S. Mauw, and J. Springintveld, Verifying Business Processes using Spin. In G. Holzman, E. Najm, and A. Serhrouchni (eds.), Proceedings 4th International SPIN Workshop. Report ENST 98 S 002, pp. 21-36. Ecole Nationale Superieure des Telecommunications, Paris, France. November, 1998.

Janssen, W., R. Mateescu, S. Mauw, P. Fennema, and P. van der Stappen, Model checking for managers. In Proceedings 6th International SPIN Workshop on Practical Aspects of Model Checking. Toulouse, France. September 1999.

Jonkers, H., W. Janssen, A. Verschut, and E. Wierstra, A unified framework for design and performance analysis of distributed systems. Paper released to *IPDS'98, IEEE International Performance and Dependability Symposium*, Durham, NC, USA, 7-9 September 1998.

Lawrence, P. (Ed.), *Workflow Handbook*, John Wiley & Sons Ltd, Chichester, UK, 1997.

Lazowska, E.D., J. Zahorjan, G. Graham, and K. Sevcik, *Quantitative System Performance: Computer System Analysis Using Queueing Network Models*. Prentice-Hall, 1984.

Medina-Mora, R., T. Winograd, R. Flores, and F. Flores, The action workflow approach to workflow management technology. In *Proceedings of CSCW '92*, November 1992, pp. 281-288.

Ould, M.A., *Business Processes: Modelling and analysis for re-engineering and improvement*, John Wiley & Sons, Chichester, England, 1995.

Pegden, C.D., R.R. Shannon, and R.P. Sadowski, *Introduction to Simulation Using SIMAN*. Second ed. McGraw-Hill, 1995.

Quartel, D.A.C., L. Ferreira Pires, M.J. van Sinderen, H.M. Franken, and C.A. Vissers, On the role of basic design concepts in behaviour structuring, *Computer Networks and ISDN Systems* 29:4, March 1997, pp. 413-436.

Rational Software Corporation, *Unified Modeling Language, Version 1.0*, 1997 [Unpublished report]. http://www.rational.com/ot/uml/1.0/index.html.

Rijst, N.B.J. van der, and J.L.G. Dietz, Expressing production control principles in the DEMO communication model. In: A. Verbraeck, H.G. Sol and P.W.G. Bots (Eds.), *Proceedings of the Fourth International Working Conference on Dynamic Modelling of Information Systems*, Delft University Press, Delft, The Netherlands, 1994, pp 171-186.

Scheer, A.-W., *ARIS – Business Process Frameworks*. Springer-Verlag, 1998.

Scherr, A.L., A new approach to business processes, *IBM Systems Journal*, Vol. 32, No. 1, 1993, pp. 80-98.

Vissers, C.A., Report on the architectural semantics workshop. In: J. de Meer, B. Mahr and S.Storp (eds.), Proceeding of International Conference on Open Distributed Processing, IFIP, pp. 367-386. North-Holland, 1994.

Winograd, T., and F. Flores, *Understanding computers and cognition: A new foundation for design*, Ablex, Norwood, NJ, 1986.

Refinement of Pipe-and-Filter Architectures

Jan Philipps and Bernhard Rumpe

Institut für Informatik,
Technische Universität München,
D-80290 München,
www4.in.tum.de/∼{philipps,rumpe}

Abstract. Software and hardware architectures are prone to modifications. We demonstrate how a mathematically founded powerful refinement calculus for a class of architectures, namely pipe and filter architectures, can be used to modify a system in a provably correct way. The calculus consists of basic rules to add and to remove filters (components) and pipes (channels) to a system. A networking example demonstrates some of the features of our calculus.

The calculus is simple, flexible and compositional. Thus it allows us to build more complex and specific rules that e.g. embed models of existing architectures or define design patterns as transformation rules.

1 Introduction

Only in recent years, fueled through the survey [10] and greatly enhanced by [16], notations to define software architectures have been developed (see [12] for an overview). One specific kind of architecture description style — the pipe and filter approach —, is especially useful for asynchronously communicating, distributed processes.

The architecture of a software or hardware system influences its efficiency, its adaptability, and the reusability of software components. Especially the adaptation to new requirements causes frequent changes in the architecture while the system is developed, or when it is later extended. However, the definition of architecture is still rather informal in the software engineering community, and the question of how to properly modify an architecture has not been adequately addressed so far.

In this paper, we examine how pipe and filter achitectures can be modified, so that the new system is a provably correct refinement of the original system. Filters are units of concurrency and computation, connected only through pipes to asynchronously send and receive messages along them. This model corresponds to data flow networks and we therefore will interchangeably use the words "component" and "filter" as well as "channel" and "pipe". In fact, we prefer the term component over filter throughout this paper, as it fits better to the hierarchic nature and the explicitly defined interfaces of these units. Also the the term channel is preferred over pipe. Our work is based on a precise mathematical model [4, 5, 6] for data flow networks. An earlier version of this calculus [14] is improved and its powerful features demonstrated in a networking

J. Wing, J. Woodcock, J. Davies (Eds.): FM'99, Vol. I, LNCS 1708, pp. 96–115, 1999.
© Springer-Verlag Berlin Heidelberg 1999

example, where a previously given architecture is optimized. Our model gives a compositional semantics to data flow networks (pipe and filter architectures with feedback), and hence components can be composed to build hierarchical models of a system. Thus, our semantic model does not only contain pipe and filters but also asynchronous communication processes and event based systems, all three listed as different architectural styles in [16].

The semantic model is simple, yet powerful: when specifying a component behavior, certain aspects can be left open. We refer to this style as *underspecification*. The reduction of this underspecification immediately gives a refinement relation for blackbox behaviors of components.

In addition to blackbox or *behavioral* refinement, two other classes of refinement relations are established today, namely *structural refinement* (glassbox refinement) and *signature refinement*. While blackbox refinement only relates blackbox behaviors of not further detailed components, structural refinement allows us to refine a blackbox behavior by a subsystem architecture. Signature refinement deals with the manipulation of the system or component interfaces. As shown in [2], both structural and signature refinement can be reduced to behavioral refinement. In Section 2 we will see that behavioral refinement is a simple subset relation.

Neither of these three refinement classes, however, allows architectural refinement in the sense that two glassbox architectures are related. In [14], we introduced a concept for glassbox refinement; again, it can be defined in terms of behavioral refinement. For the practical application of architectural refinement, we defined a rule system to incrementally change an architecture, e.g. by adding new components or channels.

In this paper, we demonstrate in detail how the rule system can be applied to a concrete example. It is structured as follows. In Sections 2 and 3 we present the mathematical foundations and define the concepts of component and system. In Section 4 we summarize the rules introduced in [14]. Section 5 describes the refinement of a simple data acquisition system. Section 6 concludes.

2   Semantic Model

In this section we introduce the basic mathematical concepts for the description of systems. We concentrate on interactive systems that communicate asynchronously through channels. A component is modeled as a relation over input and output communication histories that obeys certain causality constraints. We assume that there is a given set of channel identifiers, $\mathbb{C}$, and a given set of messages, M.

Streams. We use *streams* to describe communication histories on channels. A stream over the set M is a finite or infinite sequence of elements from M. By M^* we denote the finite sequences over the set M. The set M^* includes the empty sequence that we write as $\langle \rangle$. The set of infinite sequences over M is denoted by M^∞.

Communication histories are represented by *timed streams*: $M^\aleph =_{def} (M^*)^\infty$ The intuition is that the time axis is divided into an infinite stream of time intervals, where in each interval a finite number of messages may be transmitted. In Fig. 1, a prefix of such a stream is visualized. It is based on the messages $\{a, b, c\}$ which occur several times during the first six units of time.

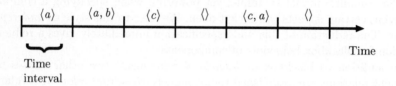

Fig. 1. Prefix of a communication history

These intervals can be considered to be of a fixed duration, such as months or days for reports in business information systems, or milliseconds in more technical applications. Their duration need not be fixed, however: the intervals could also span the time between certain events that are of interest to the system, such as the pressing of a button. In each interval, the order of the messages is fixed, but the exact arrival time of a message is unknown.

For $i \in \mathbb{N}$ and $x \in M^\aleph$ we denote by $x{\downarrow}i$ the sequence of the first i sequences in the stream x. When writing specifications, we sometimes abstract from the interval boundaries, and regard a stream as the finite or infinite sequence of messages that results from the concatenation of all the intervals. We then use the syntax $a \, \& \, r$ to split a stream into its first element a, and the remaining sequence r.

A *named stream tuple* is a function $\mathbb{C} \to M^\aleph$ that assigns histories to channel names. For $C \subseteq \mathbb{C}$ we write $\vec{C}$ for the set of named stream tuples with domain C. For $x \in \vec{C}$ and $C' \subseteq C$, the named stream tuple $x \mid_{C'} \in \vec{C'}$ denotes the restriction of x to the channels in C':

$$\forall \, c \in C' : x \mid_{C'} (c) = x(c)$$

We extend operators like $\downarrow$ and $\mid$ in the usual pointwise style to stream tuples and sets over stream tuples.

Behaviors. We model the interface behavior of a component with the set of input channels $I \subseteq \mathbb{C}$ and the set of output channels $O \subseteq \mathbb{C}$ by a function

$$\beta : \vec{I} \to \mathbb{P}(\vec{O})$$

Intuitively, β maps the incoming input on I to the set of possible outputs on O, and thus describes the visible behavior of a component with input channels I and output channels O. Equivalently, β can be seen as a relation over the named stream tuples in $\vec{I}$ and the named stream tuples in $\vec{O}$. β is called a *behavior.* Since for every input history multiple output histories can be allowed by a behavior, it is possible to model nondeterminism, or equivalently, to regard relations with multiple outputs for one input as underspecified.

A function $f \in \overrightarrow{I} \to \overrightarrow{O}$ can be seen as a special case of a deterministic relation. We say the f is *time guarded*, iff for all input histories x and y, and for all $i \in \mathbb{N}$

$$x{\downarrow}i = y{\downarrow}i \Rightarrow (f\ x){\downarrow}(i+1) = (f\ y){\downarrow}(i+1)$$

A time guarded function f is called a *strategy* for a behavior β if for all x we have $f(x) \in \beta(x)$. If β has at least one strategy, we say that β is *realizable*.

Time guardedness reflects the notion of time and causality. The output at a certain time interval may only depend on the input received so far, and not on future input.

Interface adaption. Given a behavior $\beta : \overrightarrow{I} \to \mathbb{P}(\overrightarrow{O})$, we can define a behavior with a different interface by extending the set of input channels, and restricting the set of output channels. If $I \subseteq I'$ and $O' \subseteq O$, then $\beta' = \beta{\uparrow}_{O'}^{I'}$ is again a behavior with $\beta'(i) = (\beta(i\ |_I))\ |_{O'}$.

This corresponds to the change of the component interface by adding input channels that are ignored by the component, and by removing output channels that are ignored by the environment.

Composition. Behaviors can be composed by a variety of operators. Sequential and parallel composition, as well as a feedback construction is introduced in [11]. For our work, we use a generalized operator $\otimes$ that composes a finite set of behaviors

$$B = \{\beta_1 : \overrightarrow{I_1} \to \mathbb{P}(\overrightarrow{O_1}), \ldots, \beta_n : \overrightarrow{I_n} \to \mathbb{P}(\overrightarrow{O_n})\}$$

in parallel with implicit feedback. We define

$$O = \cup_{1 \le k \le n} O_k$$
$$I = (\cup_{1 \le k \le n} I_k) \setminus O$$

where O is the union of all component outputs, and I is the set of those inputs, that are not connected to any of the components' outputs. Then the relation $\otimes B \in \overrightarrow{I} \to \mathbb{P}(\overrightarrow{O})$ is characterized by:

$$o \in (\otimes B)(i) \Leftrightarrow$$
$$\exists l \in \overrightarrow{(I \cup O)}:$$
$$l\ |_O = o \wedge l\ |_I = i \wedge$$
$$\forall k \in \{1, \ldots n\}: \ l\ |_{O_k} \in \beta_k(l\ |_{I_k})$$

If all behaviors in B are realizable, then so is $\otimes B$. The proof follows [11]; it relies on the time guardedness of strategy functions. It is easy to express parallel and sequential composition of behaviors with the $\otimes$ operator.

Refinement. Intuitively, a behavior describes the externally observable relation between the input and the output that the clients of a component may rely on. Refining a behavior in a modular way means that the client's demands are still met, when the component behavior is specialized. Formally, the refinement relation in our framework is defined as follows. Given two behaviors $\beta_1, \beta_2 \in \vec{I} \to \mathbb{P}(\vec{O})$ we say that β_1 is refined by β_2, iff

$$\forall i \in \vec{I} : \beta_2(i) \subseteq \beta_1(i)$$

Refinement means in our context that each possible channel history of the new component is also a possible channel history of the original component.

3   Components and Systems

In this section, we define an abstract notion of system architecture. Basically, a system consists of a set of *components* and their *connections*. We first define components, and then introduce the architectural or glassbox view, and the blackbox view of a system.

Components. A *component* is a tuple $c = (n, I, O, \beta)$, where n is the name of the component, $I \subseteq \mathbb{C}$ is the set of input channels, and $O \subseteq \mathbb{C}$ the set of output channels. Moreover, $\beta : \vec{I} \to \mathbb{P}(\vec{O})$ is a behavior. The operators name.c, in.c, out.c and behav.c yield n, I, O and β, respectively. The name n is introduced mainly as a convenience for the system designer. The channel identifiers in.c and out.c define the interface of the component. This interface can be visualized as shown in Fig. 2.

Architectural view of a system. In the architectural view, a system comprises a finite set of components. A connection between components is established by using the same channel name.

A system is thus a tuple $S = (I, O, C)$, where $I \subseteq \mathbb{C}$ is the input interface, and $O \subseteq \mathbb{C}$ is the output interface of the system. C is a finite set of components. Like single components, a system can be visualized, describing the structure of the connections between its components, as given in Fig. 3.

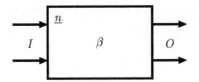

Fig. 2. Component diagram for (n, I, O, β)

We want to be able to decompose systems hierarchically. In fact, as we will see, a system can be regarded as an ordinary component. Therefore systems need

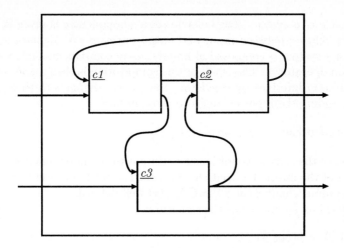

Fig. 3. System structure diagram

not be closed, and we introduce the interface channels I and O to distinguish external from internal channels. We define the operators in.S, out.S, arch.S to return I, O and C, respectively. In addition, we write:

$$\text{in.}C =_{def} \cup_{c \in C}(\text{in.}c)$$
$$\text{out.}C =_{def} \cup_{c \in C}(\text{out.}c)$$

for the union of the input or output interfaces, respectively, of the components of S.

The following consistency conditions ensure a meaningful architectural view of a system S. For all components $c_1, c_2 \in$ arch.S with $c_1 \neq c_2$, we require the following properties:

1. Different components have different names: name.$c_1 \neq$ name.c_2
2. Each channel is controlled by only one component: out.$c_1 \cap$ out.$c_2 = \emptyset$
3. Input channels of the system interface are controlled by the environment, not by a component: in.$S \cap$ out.$C = \emptyset$
4. Each input channel of a component is controlled by either a component or by the environment: in.$C \subseteq$ out.$C \cup$ in.S
5. Each channel of the output interface is controlled by a component: out.$S \subseteq$ out.C.

Note that we allow that input channels are in more than one interface: a channel can have multiple readers, even broadcasting is possible. Not every channel of the system input interface has to be connected to a component, since condition 4 only requires the subset relation instead of equality. We allow a component to read and write on the same channel if desired; as a consequence of conditions (3) and (5), however, input and output of a composed system are disjoint.

Blackbox view of a system. The behavior of a component c is given in terms of its relation behav.c between input and output streams. We define the *blackbox behavior* of a system S composed of finitely many components arch.S using the composition operator $\otimes$. The result of this composition is then made compatible with the system interface by restricting the output channels to those in out.S, and by extending the input channels to those in in.S:

$$[\![S]\!] = (\otimes\{\ \text{behav}.c\ \mid\ c \in \text{arch}.S\ \})\!\uparrow^{\text{in}.S}_{\text{out}.S}$$

Because of the context conditions for systems the composition is well-defined. The hiding of the internal output channels out.$C \setminus$ out.S and the extension with the unused input channels in.$S \setminus$ in.C is also well-defined.

The blackbox behavior has the signature:

$$[\![S]\!] : \overrightarrow{\text{in}.S} \to \mathbb{P}(\overrightarrow{\text{out}.S})$$

Thus, the blackbox behavior can now be used as a component description itself. Introducing a fresh name n, we define the component c_S as:

$$c_S = (n, \text{in}.S, \text{out}.S, [\![S]\!])$$

In this way, a hierarchy of architectural views can be defined and iteratively refined and detailed. Later on we need a more detailed definition of this semantics. By expanding the definitions of the $\otimes$ and $\updownarrow$ operators, we obtain the following equivalent characterisation of $[\![(I, O, C)]\!]$:

$$o \in [\![(I, O, C)]\!](i) \Leftrightarrow$$
$$\exists\, l \in \overrightarrow{(I \cup \text{out}.C)} :$$
$$l\,|_O = o \wedge l\,|_I = i \wedge$$
$$\forall\, c \in C : l\,|_{\text{out}.c} \in (\text{behav}.c)(l\,|_{\text{in}.c})$$

This expanded characterisation says, that o is an output of the system for input i (line 1), iff there is a mapping l of all channels to streams (line 2), such that l coincides with the given input i and output o on the system interface channels (line 3) and feeding the proper submapping of l into a component results also in a submapping of l.

4   Refinement of Architectures

When a system architecture is refined, it must not break the interaction with its environment. The observable behavior of a refined system architecture must be a refinement of the behavior of the original system architecture. In this paper, we leave the interface of the system architecture unchanged. Interface refinements that affect the signature of a system S are described in [2] for blackbox behaviors; they can be adapted to our architectural framework. We also ignore aspects of realizability. The techniques used to prove that a component specification is realizable are orthogonal to the rules presented here, and will not be considered in this paper. We therefore define the refinement relation on system architectures as a behavioral refinement on the given interface:

$$S \leadsto S' \Leftrightarrow_{def} \forall i \in \overrightarrow{\text{in.}S} : [\![S']\!](i) \subseteq [\![S]\!](i)$$

As explained above, we tacitly assume that $\text{in.}S = \text{in.}S'$ and $\text{out.}S = \text{out.}S'$. Stepwise refinement is possible, since the refinement relation is transitive:

$$S \leadsto S' \wedge S' \leadsto S'' \Rightarrow S \leadsto S''$$

In [14], we defined and justified a set of constructive refinement rules that allows refinements of system architectures. The rules allow us to add and remove components, to add and remove channels, to refine the behavior of components, and to refine single components to subsystems and vice versa. In the sequel, we summarize these rules; in Section 5 we apply them to a simple example. Each rule refines a system architecture $S = (I, O, C)$ into another system architecture $S' = (I, O, C')$. We use the syntax

$$S \text{ WITH } C := C'$$

to denote the architecture (I, O, C'). In addition, we write

$$S \text{ WITH } c := c'$$

to denote the architecture $(I, O, (C \setminus \{c\}) \cup \{c'\})$. To create a component with the same name and interface as $c = (n, I, O, \beta)$, but with a different behavior β', we use the syntax

$$c \text{ WITH behav.} c := \beta'$$

to denote the component (n, I, O, β'). Similarly, we can change the name or interface of a component. The refinement rules are presented in the syntax

$$\frac{(Premises)}{(Refinement)}$$

where the premises are conditions to be fulfilled for the refinement relation to hold.

Behavioral refinement. Systems can be refined by refining the behavior of their components. Let $c \in C$ be a component. If we refine the behavior of c to β, we get a refinement of the externally visible, global system behavior:

$$\frac{c \in C \quad \forall i \in \overrightarrow{\text{in.}c} : \beta(i) \subseteq \text{behav.}c(i)}{S \leadsto S \text{ WITH behav.}c := \beta}$$

In some cases, to prove the behavioral refinement of c some assumptions on the contents of c's input channels are necessary. Then this simple rule cannot be used.

To overcome this problem, we introduce the notion of behavioral refinement in the context of an *invariant*. An invariant is a predicate Ψ over the possible message flows within an architecture $S = (I, O, C)$:

$$\Psi : \overrightarrow{(I \cup \text{out.}C)} \to \mathbb{B}$$

An invariant is valid within an architecture, if it holds for all named stream tuples l defining the system's streams. This can be formally expressed similar to the expanded definition of the system semantics $[\![S]\!]$ presented in Section 3:

$$\forall l \in \overrightarrow{(I \cup \text{out.}C)} :$$
$$(\forall c \in C : l \mid_{\text{out.}c} \in (\text{behav.}c)(l \mid_{\text{in.}c})) \Rightarrow \Psi(l)$$

Note that invariants are not allowed to restrict the possible inputs on channels from I, but only characterize the internal message flow.

Let us now assume that we want to replace the behavior of component c by a new behavior β. The latter is a refinement of behav.c under the invariant Ψ, when:

$$\forall l \in \overrightarrow{(I \cup \text{out.}C)} :$$
$$\Psi(l) \Rightarrow \beta(l \mid_{\text{in.}c}) \subseteq (\text{behav.}c)(l \mid_{\text{in.}c})$$

Thus, the complete refinement rule is as follows. The two premises express that Ψ is a valid invariant, and that β refines behav.c under this invariant.

$$
\begin{array}{|l}
\forall l \in \overrightarrow{(I \cup \text{out.}C)} : \\
\quad (\forall c \in C : l \mid_{\text{out.}c} \in (\text{behav.}c)(l \mid_{\text{in.}c})) \Rightarrow \Psi(l) \\
\forall l \in \overrightarrow{(I \cup \text{out.}C)} : \\
\quad \Psi(l) \Rightarrow \beta(l \mid_{\text{in.}c}) \subseteq (\text{behav.}c)(l \mid_{\text{in.}c}) \\
\hline
S \rightsquigarrow S \ \text{WITH behav.}c := \beta
\end{array}
$$

This rule is the only one that requires global properties of a system as a premise. The other rules only deal locally with one affected component. However, since Ψ is used only for a single application of this rule, it is often sufficient to prove its invariance with respect to a relevant subset of all the system components.

Behavioral refinement of a component usually leads to true behavioral refinement of the system architecture. This is in general not the case for the following architectural refinements, which leave the global system behavior unchanged.

Adding and removing output channels. If a channel is neither connected to a system component, nor part of the system interface, it may be added as a new output channel to a component $c \in \text{arch.}S$:

$$p \in \mathbb{C} \setminus (I \cup \mathsf{out}.C)$$
$$\beta \in \overrightarrow{\mathsf{in}.c} \to \mathbb{P}(\overrightarrow{\mathsf{out}.c \cup \{p\}})$$
$$\forall\, i, o: \ o \in \beta(i) \Leftrightarrow o \mid_{\mathsf{out}.c} \in \mathsf{behav}.c(i)$$

$S \rightsquigarrow S$ WITH
$$\mathsf{out}.c := \mathsf{out}.c \cup \{p\}$$
$$\mathsf{behav}.c := \beta$$

The new behavior β does not restrict the possible output on channel p. Hence, the introduction of new output channels increases the nondeterminism of the component. It does not, however, affect the behavior of the composed system, since p is neither part of the system interface nor connected to any other component. The contents of the new channel can be restricted with the behavioral refinement rule.

Similarly, an output channel $p \in \mathsf{out}.c$ can be removed from the component c, provided that it is not used elsewhere in the system architecture:

$$p \notin O \cup \mathsf{in}.C$$
$$\beta = \mathsf{behav}.c\!\uparrow^{\mathsf{in}.c}_{\mathsf{out}.c \setminus \{p\}}$$

$S \rightsquigarrow S$ WITH
$$\mathsf{out}.c := \mathsf{out}.c \setminus \{p\}$$
$$\mathsf{behav}.c := \beta$$

The new behavior β is the restriction of the component behavior $\mathsf{behav}.c$ to the remaining channels.

Adding and removing output channels are complementary transformations. Consequently, both rules are behavior preserving. This is not surprising, since the channel in question so far is not used by any other component.

Adding and removing input channels. An input channel $p \in \mathbb{C}$ may be added to a component $c \in C$, if it is already connected to the output of some other component or to the input from the environment:

$$p \in I \cup \mathsf{out}.C$$
$$\beta = \mathsf{behav}.c\!\uparrow^{\mathsf{in}.c \cup \{p\}}_{\mathsf{out}.c}$$

$S \rightsquigarrow S$ WITH
$$\mathsf{in}.c := \mathsf{in}.c \cup \{p\}$$
$$\mathsf{behav}.c := \beta$$

The behavior β now receives input from the new input channel p, but is still independent of the data in p.

If the behavior of a component c does not depend on the input from a channel p, the channel may be removed:

$$\forall i, i' \in \overrightarrow{\mathsf{in}.c} : \ i \mid_{\mathsf{in}.c \backslash \{p\}} = i' \mid_{\mathsf{in}.c \backslash \{p\}}$$
$$\Rightarrow \mathsf{behav}.c(i) = \mathsf{behav}.c(i')$$
$$\forall i \in \overrightarrow{\mathsf{in}.c} : \ \beta(i \mid_{\mathsf{in}.c \backslash \{p\}}) = \mathsf{behav}.c(i)$$

$S \rightsquigarrow S$ WITH
$$\mathsf{in}.c := \mathsf{in}.c \backslash \{p\}$$
$$\mathsf{behav}.c := \beta$$

Because the component does not depend on the input from p (first premise), there is a behavior β satisfying the second premise. The rule for removing input channels might seem useless — why should a component have an input it does not rely on? However, note that it is possible to first add new input channels that provide basically the same information as an existing channel, then to change the component's behavior so that it relies on the new channels instead. Finally, the old channel can safely be reduced. As with output channels, adding and removing input channels are complementary transformations and thus behavior preserving. This is because the input channels do not influence the component's behavior, and therefore the global system behavior is unchanged, too.

Adding and removing components. A component can be added without changing the global system behavior if we ensure that it is not connected to the other components, or to the system environment. Later, we may successively add input or output channels, and refine the new component's behavior with the previously given rules.

$$\forall c \in C : \ \mathsf{name}.c \neq n$$
$$S \rightsquigarrow S \text{ WITH } C := C \cup \{(n, \varnothing, \varnothing, \alpha)\}$$

The premise simply ensures that the name n is fresh; the new behavior α is somewhat subtle: it is the unique behavior of a component with no input and no output channels: $\{()\} = \alpha(())$. Similarly, components may be removed if they have no output ports that might influence the functionality of the system.

$$\mathsf{out}.c = \varnothing$$
$$S \rightsquigarrow S \text{ WITH } C := C \backslash \{c\}$$

Note that the addition of a component without input and output channels necessarily does not affect the system behavior. The trivial behavior of this component can made less deterministic by adding channels and more deterministic by refining its behavior.

Expanding and Folding. As we have seen, components can be defined with the blackbox view of system architectures. In this way system architectures can be decomposed hierarchically: a single component of a system is replaced by another system. We therefore define a rule for expansion of components. Assume a given system architecture $S = (I_S, O_S, C_S)$ contains a component $c \in C_S$.

This component c is itself described by an architecture $T = (I_T, O_T, C_T)$. The names of the components in T are assumed to be disjoint from those in S; through renaming this can always be ensured. The expansion of T in S takes the components and channels of T and incorporates them within S.

$$c = (n, I_T, O_T, [\![T]\!])$$
$$\mathsf{out}.C_T \cap \mathsf{out}.C_S = \mathsf{out}.c$$
$$\mathsf{out}.C_T \cap I_S = \varnothing$$

$$S \leadsto S \text{ WITH } C_S := C_S \setminus \{c\} \cup C_T$$

The first premise means that the architecture T describes the component c. The other two premises require that the internal channels of T, which are given by $\mathsf{out}.C_T \setminus O_T$, are not used in S. In general, this can be accomplished through a renaming rule, which it would be straightforward to define.

The complementary operation to the expansion of a component is the folding of a subarchitecture $T = (I_T, O_T, C_T)$ of a given system $S = (I, O, C)$. This rule is equipped with several context conditions that are mainly concerned with the identification of a correct subarchitecture to be folded.

T is a subarchitecture of S, if

- the components C_T are a subset of the components C of S;
- the inputs I_T of T contain at least the channels that are needed, but not provided by components of T: $\mathsf{in}.C_T \setminus \mathsf{out}.C_T \subseteq I_T$;
- the inputs I_T may contain more input channels, but only those who are provided from outside: $I_T \subseteq I \cup \mathsf{out}.C$, $I_T \cap \mathsf{out}.C_T = \varnothing$;
- similarly, the outputs O_T are a subset of the component outputs $\mathsf{out}.C_T$: $O_T \subseteq \mathsf{out}.C_T$;
- the outputs O_T include at least those outputs from $\mathsf{out}.C_T$ that are needed by a component outside of T: $\mathsf{out}.C_T \cap \mathsf{in}.(C \setminus C_T) \subseteq O_T$;
- and the outputs O_T include those outputs from $\mathsf{out}.C_T$ that are part of the interface of S: $\mathsf{out}.C_T \cap O \subseteq O_T$.

The folding rule is then defined as follows, containing a compact description of the above stated requirements for I_T and O_T:

$$C_T \subseteq C$$
$$\mathsf{in}.C_T \setminus \mathsf{out}.C_T \subseteq I_T \subseteq (I \cup \mathsf{out}.C) \setminus \mathsf{out}.C_T$$
$$\mathsf{out}.C_T \cap (O \cup \mathsf{in}.(C \setminus C_T)) \subseteq O_T \subseteq \mathsf{out}.C_T$$
$$\forall c \in C \setminus C_T : \ \mathsf{name}.c \neq n$$

$$S \leadsto S \text{ WITH } C := C \setminus C_T \cup \{(n, I_T, O_T, [\![T]\!])\}$$

The first three premises are the conditions mentioned above; the fourth premise requires that the name n of the new component is not used elsewhere in the resulting system. In practice, such a folding is done simply by selecting a subset of the components of S and pushing an appropriate "folding"-button.

Most of the rules presented might seem to be simple. However, as demonstrated in the next section, because of the transitivity of the refinement relation the refinement rules can be composed to complex system modifications. This allows to group rules together to derive complex rules as best-practice rules often used as refinement steps.

5 Refinement Example

In this section, we demonstrate how our refinement rule system can be used in practice. Our example architecture is shown in Fig. 4; it models a small data acquisition system. A similar example was carried out in [17].

This example covers a simple, yet frequent architecture modification, which is problematic for the usual functional decomposition techniques. We apply eight refinement steps in this example. Most of them are very simple; they could be carried out by clicking within an appropriate diagram-based tool. No "proof-support" in the stricter sense is necessary. One rule, however, uses a kind of invariant, that resembles both a provision of the changed component as well as an assumption about a part of the environment. We prove this invariant by hand. In practice, the correctness of the refinement could be done by tool support, or just by reviewing the generated proof conditions.

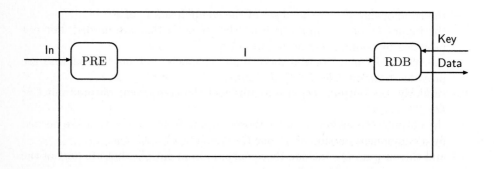

Fig. 4. Database example

The system reads input via an input In; the messages on In consist of pairs of a key and some data to be stored under this key; new data values for the same key overwrite old values. Concurrently, the system answers request for the data of a certain key that is input via channel Key by transmitting the data stored in the database under this key via channel Data. Internally, the system consists of two components: a preprocessor PRE, and a database RDB. The data from the environment first undergoes some transformations in PRE, and is then forwarded via the internal channel I to the remote database.

Let *Key* be the set of possible keys for the database, and *Data* the set of possible data values. Then, *Entry* = *Key* × *Data* is the set of possible entries for the database. The database itself is modeled as a function $M : Key \rightarrow Data$. We write $M(k)$ for the data item stored under key k. If there is not yet a proper item stored under k, then $M(k)$ should return an otherwise unused item $\perp$. By $M[k \mapsto d]$ we denote the updated database M', where $M'(j) = d$ if $j = k$, and $M'(j) = M(j)$ otherwise.

The two components PRE and RDB are specified as state machines (Fig. 5(a), 5(b)). We assume that there is a given function $f : Data \to Data$, that handles the preprocessing for a single datum.

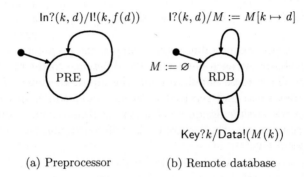

$$\mathsf{In}?(k, d)/\mathsf{I}!(k, f(d)) \qquad \mathsf{I}?(k, d)/M := M[k \mapsto d]$$

$$M := \emptyset$$

PRE   RDB

$$\mathsf{Key}?k/\mathsf{Data}!(M(k))$$

(a) Preprocessor   (b) Remote database

Fig. 5. Component specifications

In order to reduce the transmission time for the entries, we now want to transmit for each entry only the difference of the entry's data with respect to the already stored data for that key; the differences are assumed to be smaller in size than the data itself. Of course, the first entry for each key will need to be transmitted completely.

We are not interested in the algorithmic aspects of the computation of the difference between old data and new data; we just assume that the difference between two data items is itself an element of $Data$, and that there is a function

$$\Delta : Data \times Data \to Data$$

that computes the difference between old and new data. Another function

$$\rho : Data \times Data \to Data$$

reconstructs the new data given old data and the difference. We require that

$$\rho(d_{old}, \Delta(d_{old}, d_{new})) = d_{new} \qquad (\dagger)$$

To simplify our specifications, we also assume that

$$\Delta(\perp, d) = d, \quad \rho(\perp, \delta) = \delta$$

These two functions can be extended to streams, where they take a database M as an additional parameter:

$$\Delta_M^* \left(\langle \rangle \right) = \langle \rangle$$
$$\Delta_M^* \left((k, d) \,\&\, x \right) = (k, \Delta(M(k), d)) \,\&\, \Delta_{M[k \mapsto d]}^* (x)$$

$$\rho_M^* \left(\langle \rangle \right) = \langle \rangle$$
$$\rho_M^* \left((k, \delta) \,\&\, x \right) = (k, \rho(M(k), \delta)) \,\&\, \rho_{M[k \mapsto \rho(M(k), \delta)]}^* (x)$$

Informally, the system modification is simple: the preprocessor is extended with a local database; for each new entry the difference to the old is computed and forwarded. The remote database reads the input, computes the new value out of the stored value and received difference, and stores this new value in its database. One possible design for this modification is to introduce encoding and decoding components, that compute the differences and reconstruct the original data, respectively.

In the sequel, we show how this refinement can be justified with our rule system. The modification consists of eight steps.

Step 1: Adding components. First, we introduce two new components to the system by two applications of the refinement rule. The new components, ENC and DEC, are not connected to any other component in the system.

After this refinement step, the system looks as follows:

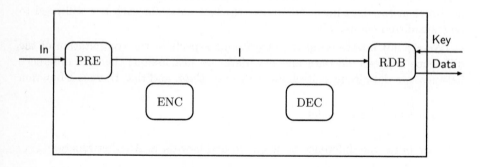

Step 2: Adding output channels. Now we add an output channel D to ENC, and an output channel R to DEC. Since these channels are neither part of the system interface, nor previously connected to any component, the premises of the refinement rule for the addition of channels are satisfied. Note that the contents of the channel are so far completely undefined, and the components ENC and DEC are therefore now nondeterministic. Nevertheless, the behavior of the system itself is unchanged, since the data on the new channels is unused throughout the system.

The following figure depicts the system after this refinement step:

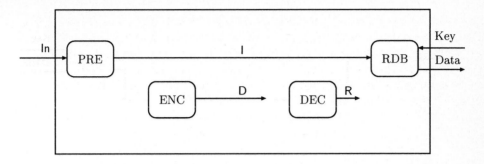

Step 3: Adding input channels. We now connect the channel I to the encoder ENC. The encoder still ignores the additional input, however, and hence the output D of ENC is still arbitrary. Similarly, we connect D to the decoder.

The system now looks like this:

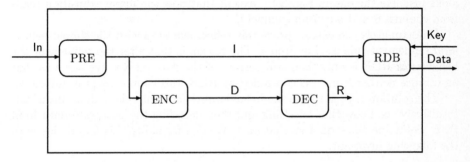

Step 4: Behavioral refinement. Now we constrain the channels D and R to carry the differences of the data on I and the reconstructed data, respectively. This is accomplished by restricting the behavior of ENC and DEC, and we can use the simple behavioral refinement rule for this step.

The encoder component is now specified as follows:

$$(ENC, \{I\}, \{D\}, \beta)$$

where

$$\forall l : l \mid_{\{D\}} \in \beta(l \mid_{\{I\}}) \Leftrightarrow l(D) = \Delta_{\emptyset}^{*}(l(I))$$

Thus, the encoder just applies the difference function Δ^* to its input stream I.

Similarly, we define the behavior of DEC as an application of the restoration function ρ^*. Since until now the behavior of the components was completely unspecified, this refinement is obviously correct.

The structure of the system remains unchanged.

Step 5: Adding an input channel. We now connect the channel R to the remote database. The behavior of RDB still ignores the additional input, however.

This step gives us the following system:

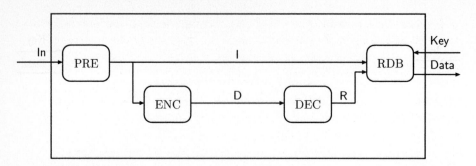

Step 6: Behavioral refinement with invariant. Now we want the remote database to store the data transmitted on R instead of that on I. Conversely, the input via I should be ignored.

The new behavior can again be specified as a state transition diagram; it looks just like the one in Fig. 5(b), except that now the upper transition reads from channel R and not from channel I.

Unfortunately, we cannot prove this refinement step with the simple behavioral refinement rule used in Step 4. The reason is that after the refinement the behavior of RDB is only then still correct, if the data on R is the same as that on I. Since neither R nor I is controlled by RDB, this cannot be proven locally.

The solution here is to use the behavioral refinement rule with an invariant. Intuitively, we know that encoding and then decoding the processed data from PRE yields the same data as that on I. We can formalize this knowledge with the following invariant:

$$\Psi(l) =_{def} l(\mathsf{I}) = \rho_\varnothing^*(\Delta_\varnothing^*(l(\mathsf{I})))$$

To show that Ψ is indeed an invariant we prove the following stronger property, which implies Ψ:

$$\forall\, x, \forall\, M : \rho_M^*(\Delta_M^*(x)) = x$$

The proof is by induction on x:

- If $x = \langle\,\rangle$, we have for all M: $\Delta_M^*(x) = \langle\,\rangle$, and hence $\rho_M^*(\Delta_M^*(\langle\,\rangle)) = \langle\,\rangle$.
- If $x = (k, d)\,\&\,y$, then for an arbitrary M:

$$\rho_M^*(\Delta_M^*((k, d)\,\&\,y)) =$$
$$\rho_M^*((k, \Delta(M(k), d))\,\&\,\Delta_{M[k\mapsto d]}^*\,(y)) =$$
$$(k, \rho(M(k), \Delta(M(k), d)))\,\&$$
$$\rho_{M[k\mapsto\rho(M(k),\Delta(M(k),d))]}^*(\Delta_{M[k\mapsto d]}^*\,(y)) =$$
$$(k, d)\,\&\,\rho_{M[k\mapsto d]}^*(\Delta_{M[k\mapsto d]}^*\,(y)) =$$
$$(k, d)\,\&\,y$$

The first two equalities follow from the definition of Δ^* and ρ^*, respectively; the third equality follows from the property (†) on page 109. The fourth equality uses the induction hypothesis.

It is straightforward to then prove the premises of the behavioral refinement rule with invariant for Ψ. The structure of the system remains unchanged.

Step 7: Removing an input channel. The new behavior of RDB now depends only on the data on R, and not on that in I. (An easy syntactical criterion is that RDB's state machine does not read from R any more.) Thus, we can disconnect I from RDB. The channel I now only feeds the encoder.

The new system looks as follows:

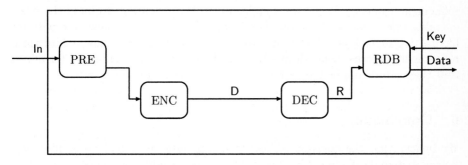

Step 8: Folding subsystems. In the last refinement step, we fold the two components PRE and ENC to a new component PRE′, and DEC together with RDB to a new component RDB′:

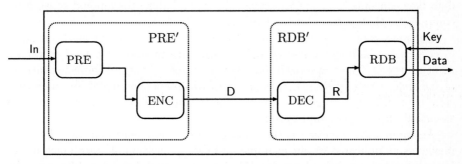

Comments on the transformation. The refinement steps described above are not fully formal; they cannot be, since we did not use a properly formalized description of the component behaviors. Of course, state transition diagrams can be given a mathematical semantics [3], and in [15] a refinement calculus for state transition diagrams is defined. Still, we hope that the example shows that although each individual refinement rule is quite simple, they can be used together for complex system transformations.

In fact, the example can be regarded as the derivation of a more complex refinement pattern: We now know how to transform systems as in our example, provided we have encoding and decoding functions Δ and ρ that enjoy the property (†) on page 109.

As expected, the behavioral rule with invariant is the most complex rule to apply. In general, it is a difficult task for the system designer to find a proper invariant Ψ that is both easy to establish and sufficiently strong to use. The maximal invariant $\Psi(l) = \mathit{True}$ leads to our initially given simple refinement rule without an invariant. The minimal possible Ψ gives an exact description of the internal behavior of a system, but it is often difficult to find and too complex to use.

In practice, the invariant Ψ often only affects a subset of the system channels, and typically forms an abstract environment of the component to modify. In our case, the invariant refers only to components introduced and removed in the refinement sequence. When we combine our rule applications to build the more complex rule mentioned above, we can therefore apply this new rule without having to prove the invariant again. We expect that there are many architectural refinement patterns, where invariants can be shown to hold once and for all, so that they can be applied in case tools without further proof obligations.

6   Conclusion

We believe that the question of how to manipulate and adapt an architecture during system development has not been adequately addressed so far. In particular, a precise calculus, dealing with simple addition and removing of channels and components in a data flow-based architectural style has—to our knowledge—not been considered before. This is somewhat surprising given the long history of data flow concepts in computer science [7, 18] and given the amount of work on components that partly also treat refinement [8, 16, 9, 1].

The most promising attempt at architecture refinement so far has been given in [13], where different software architectures are related by a kind of refinement mapping. Their approach, however, requires a "faithful implementation" of one architecture by the other, which makes the refinement definition somewhat complicated. In our approach, which supports underspecification, refinement is essentially just logical implication.

An interesting direction is the description of component behaviors by state machines as indicated in our example and the application of state machine refinement rules (as defined e.g. in [15]) for component behavior refinement. A concrete description technique for component behavior is essential for the proof of the invariant in the behavior refinement rule. For state machine refinement rules, too, underspecification is essential.

The simplicity and the compositionality of the calculus allow us to build a set of more powerful and more specific rules that describe design patterns as transformations, or embed newly defined data flow structures into a given architecture.

Of course refinement is not limited to pipe and filter architectures as used in this paper, but can be applied to a variety of styles, such as rule-based systems, interpreters, communicating systems or event based systems [16]. Finally, architecture refinement is by no means limited to software systems. A promising application area is hardware design and in particular the codesign of hardware and software components, where frequently a basic design has been changed because of cost or performance issues. Moreover, the simpler description techniques used in hardware design and the finite-state nature of such systems open the door to automatic verification of the refinement rule premises.

Acknowledgement This work originates from the SYSLAB project (supported by the DFG Leibniz program, by Siemens-Nixdorf and by Siemens Corporate Research), from FORSOFT (supported by the Bayerische Forschungsstiftung) and from the Sonderforschungsbereich 342 (supported by the DFG).

References

[1] R. Allen and D. Garlan. Formal connectors. Technical Report CMU-CS-94-115, Carnegie Mellon University, 1994.

[2] M. Broy. Interaction refinement the easy way. In M. Broy, editor, *Program Design Calculi. Springer NATO ASI Series, Series F: Computer and System Sciences, Vol. 118*, 1993.

[3] M. Broy. The specification of system components by state transition diagrams. Technical Report TUM-I9729, Institut für Informatik, TU München, 1997.

[4] M. Broy, F. Dederichs, C. Dendorfer, M. Fuchs, T. F. Gritzner, and R. Weber. The Design of Distributed Systems — An Introduction to FOCUS – revised version –. SFB-Bericht 342/2-2/92 A, TU München, 1993.

[5] M. Broy and K. Stølen. Specification and Refinement of Finite Dataflow Networks — a Relational Approach. In *Proc. FTRTFT'94*, LNCS 863, pages 247–267. Springer-Verlag, Berlin, 1994.

[6] M. Broy and K. Stølen. Focus on System Development. Book manuscript, 1999.

[7] T. DeMarco. *Structured Analysis and System Specification*. Yourdon Press, 1978.

[8] D. D'Souza and A. Wills. *Objects, Components and Frameworks with UML – the Catalysis Approach*. Addison-Wesley, 1998.

[9] D. Garlan. Formal approaches to software architecture. In D.A. Lamb and S. Crocker, editors, *Proceedings of the Workshop on Studies of Software Design*, 1993.

[10] D. Garlan and M. Shaw. *Advances in Software Engineering and Knowledge Engineering*, volume I, chapter An Introduction to Software Architecture. World Scientific Publishing Company, 1993.

[11] R. Grosu and K. Stoelen. A Model for Mobile Point-to-Point Data-flow Networks without Channel Sharing . In Martin Wirsing, editor, *AMAST'96*. LNCS, 1996.

[12] Ch. Hofmann, E. Horn, W. Keller, K. Renzel, and M. Schmidt. The field of software architecture. TUM-I 9641, Technische Universität München, 1996.

[13] M. Moriconi, Xiaolei Qian, and R. Riemenschneider. Correct architecture refinement. *IEEE Transaction on Software Engineering*, 21(4):356–372, April 1995.

[14] J. Philipps and B. Rumpe. Refinement of information flow architectures. In M. Hinchey, editor, *ICFEM'97*. IEEE CS Press, 1997.

[15] B. Rumpe. *Formale Methodik des Entwurfs verteilter objektorientierter Systeme*. PhD thesis, Technische Universität München, 1996.

[16] M. Shaw and D. Garlan. *Software Architecture*. Prentice Hall, 1996.

[17] N. Soundarajam. Interaction refinement in the design of OO systems. In H. Kilov, B. Rumpe, and I. Simmonds, editors, *OOPSLA'97 Workshop on OO Behavioral Semantics*. Technische Universität München, 1997.

[18] E. Yourdon and L.L. Constantine. *Structured Design*. Yourdon Press, 1975.

A Formalization of Software Architecture

John Herbert, Bruno Dutertre, Robert Riemenschneider, and
Victoria Stavridou

Dependable System Architecture Group
System Design Laboratory
SRI International
Menlo Park CA 94025
USA
{herbert, rar, victoria, bruno}@sdl.sri.com
http://www.sdl.sri.com/dsa/

Abstract. Software architecture addresses the high level specification, design and analysis of software systems. Formal models can provide essential underpinning for architectural description languages (ADLs), and formal techniques can play an important role in analysis.

While formal models and formal analysis may always enhance conventional notations and methods, they are of greatest benefit when they employ tractable models and efficient, mechanisable techniques. The novelty in our work has been in the effort to find and mechanise a general semantic framework for software architectures that can provide tractable models and support architectural formal analysis.

The resultant semantic framework is a layered one: the core is a simple model of the elements and topology, which provides the basis for general architectural theorems and proof techniques; the structural core is augmented by semantic layers representing the semantics of relevant properties of the design.

The model has been implemented in the higher-order logic proof tool PVS, and has been used in correctness proofs during a case study of a distributed transaction protocol.

1 Introduction

Software architecture research has resulted in a range of formalisms for modelling architectures including [16, 11, 2, 7, 8, 6]. The formal models of software architecture make possible formal analysis. Formal analysis is especially important for software architectures since operational models, amenable to conventional techniques, may be absent at this abstract level.

Formal verification of real-world designs is difficult. Apart from the use of model-checkers for hardware designs, formal verification is usually a tour de force effort. The success of model-checking relies on problems where the state space can (in effect) be enumerated and exhaustively checked. The abstract levels of design addressed by software architectures require more general proof methods such as induction.

J. Wing, J. Woodcock, J. Davies (Eds.): FM'99, Vol. I, LNCS 1708, pp. 116–133, 1999.
© Springer-Verlag Berlin Heidelberg 1999

For formal analysis of real-world designs to be effective one must have tool support, and the tools must provide efficient proof procedures. The kind of analysis, and consequently tool support, depends on the choice of underlying semantic model. The following describes our exploration of two approaches to the embedding of semantics.

1.1 A Precise Semantic Embedding

SADL (Structural Architectural Description Language) [11] is an example of a current architectural description language (ADL). Like similar ADLs, it has a rich type system and allows one to describe designs at various levels of abstraction. Appendix A presents a high level description in SADL of a software architecture. It describes a set of components and their connections; the configuration is illustrated in figure 2.

Aspects of SADL were inspired by the logic of PVS [12] so it is not surprising that a very precise semantic model can be constructed in PVS. Here is a fragment of the SADL description in Appendix A, followed by a translation into PVS. It illustrates the declaration of types, component types, an instance of a component and a connection.

```
...
tx_commands, tx_responses: TYPE
...
ap:  TYPE <= Function [ap_in1: ar_resources, ap_in2: tx_responses
                          -> ap_out1: ar_requests, ap_out2: tx_commands]
...
the_ap:  ap
...
ar_1: CONNECTION =
         (EXISTS c: Channel<ar_requests>)
           Connects(c, the_ap.ap_out1, the_rms.rm_in1)
...
```

```
...
tx_commands, tx_responses: TYPE
...
ap: TYPE =  Fun[[# ap_in1: ar_resources, ap_in2: tx_responses #],
               [# ap_out1: ar_requests, ap_out2: tx_commands #]]
...
the_ap: VAR  ap
...
ar_1: AXIOM
EXISTS (c: Channel[ar_requests]):
Connects(c, ap_out1(rng(the_ap)), rm_in1(dom(the_rms)))
...
```

There are a number of good points to note about this PVS translation: the syntax closely follows the SADL thus offering the advantage of transparency; the expressiveness of PVS, including the rich type system, matches that of SADL.

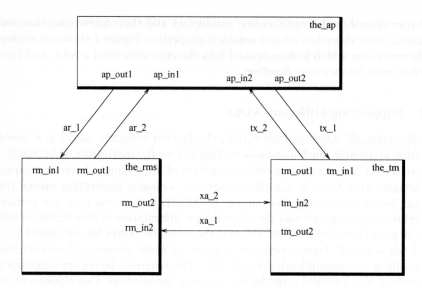

the_ap

ap_out1   ap_in1   ap_in2   ap_out2

ar_1   ar_2   tx_2   tx_1

rm_in1 rm_out1 the_rms   tm_out1 tm_in1 the_tm

rm_out2   xa_2   tm_in2

rm_in2   xa_1   tm_out2

Fig. 2. Software structure: SDTP architecture example

embedding semantics. Formal analysis based on the semantics benefits from the
high degree of automation in PVS.

(The PVS examples use the syntax of the prover: FORALL, EXISTS, IMPLIES, AND
and IFF for the non-ascii $\forall, \exists, \supset, \wedge$ and $\Leftrightarrow$.

a:bool shows type decoration; comp:(INST(comp_ty)) shows type dependency.
bool is the type of booleans in PVS and appears in definitions as the domain
when predicates are defined.

(: :) can denote a list and also a set via the implicit list2set coercion. It is used
here to repesent a set, for example (:output1,output2:).)

2.1 Components

Component families are declared using MK_COMP. This is defined as follows in
PVS:

```
comp_ty: VAR COMP_TY
comp: VAR COMP
inputs: VAR setof[INPUT]
outputs: VAR setof[OUTPUT]
MK_COMP(comp_ty,inputs,outputs): bool =
   FORALL(comp:(INST(comp_ty))):
     (FORALL ip:
       INPUT_OF(comp)(ip) IFF member(ip,inputs)) AND
     (FORALL op:
       OUTPUT_OF(comp)(op) IFF member(op,outputs))
```

`COMP_TY` is a PVS type, an instance of which represents a component type; `COMP` is a PVS type, an instance of which represents an individual component. `INPUT` and `OUTPUT` are PVS types representing inputs and outputs.

For a family of component types `comp_ty` the definition of `MK_COMP` simply states that the only inputs and outputs of any component instance are those given by sets `inputs` and `outputs`.

The interaction points of component types and components are referred to as *inputs* and *outputs*. The fully qualified names for component instances are called *input ports* and *output ports* and are given by expressions such as: `port(the_ap,ap_in1)` and `port(the_ap,ap_out2)`, where `the_ap` is a component instance and `ap_in1` and `ap_out2` are declared as input and output, respectively, of the component type.

Instances of component families are declared using an uninterpreted constant[3] `INST`. Components may also have constraints which can be stated by predicates on the input and outputs. The following example: declares a type `box_ty` to have one input and two outputs; makes an assertion that the values of one output depend on the input values while the values of the other output do not; declares `the_box` to be an instance of `box_ty`.

```
MK_COMP(box_ty,(:input:),(:output1,output2:))
FORALL(box:(INST(box_ty))):
    DependsOn(port(box,output1),port(box,input)) AND
    NOT(DependsOn(port(box,output2),port(box,input)))
INST(box_ty)(the_box)
```

2.2 Connections

A general type of connections, `CONN_TY`, and an uninterpreted constant `CONNECTS`, describing an unconstrained connection between an output port and input port, are declared.

A one-to-one connection is defined by:

```
CONNECTS11(conn,port(c1,output),port(c2,input)) =
(FORALL p1, p2:
 CONNECTS(conn,p1,p2) IFF (p1=port(c1,output)) AND (p2=port(c2,input)))
 AND
(FORALL conn1, p2:
 CONNECTS(conn1,port(c1,output),p2) IFF (conn1=conn)) AND
(FORALL conn1, p1:
 CONNECTS(conn1,p1,port(c2,input)) IFF (conn1=conn))
```

This states that: the only ports connected by `conn` are those given by the arguments; the only connection from the given output port is `conn`; the only connection to the given input port is `conn`.

---

[3] An uninterpreted constant is one with a type signature but without a defining axiom.

References

[1] Hubert Garavel. Open/caesar: An open software architecture for verification, simulation, and testing. In *Proceedings of the First International Conference on Tools and Algorithms for the Construction and Analysis of Systems TACAS'98*, March 1998.

[2] D. Garlan, R. T. Monroe, and D. Wile. Acme: An archiectural description interchange language. In *Proceedings of CASCON '97*, November 1997.

[3] David Garlan, Robert T. Monroe, and David Wile. Acme: An architecture description interchange language. In *Proceedings of CASCON'97*, pages 169–183, Toronto, Ontario, November 1997.

[4] David Garlan and Zhenyu Wang. A case study in software architecture interchange. Submitted for publication to the Workshop on Software and Performance 98, March 1998.

[5] John Herbert. Abstraction for architectural proof. SRI CSL Dependable System Archiecture Group, Working Paper, December 1998.

[6] V. Issarny and C. Bidan. Aster: A framework for sound customization of distributed runtime systems. In *Proceedings of the Sixteenth IEEE International Conference on Distributed Computing Systems*, 1996.

[7] D. C. Luckham, L. M. Augustin, J. J. Kenney, J. Vera, D. Bryan, and W. Mann. Specification and analysis of system architecture using Rapide. *IEEE Transactions on Software Engineering*, 21(4):314–335, April 1995.

[8] J. Magee, S. Eisenbach, and J. Kramer. *Modelling Darwin in the π-Calculus*, volume 938 of *LNCS*. Springer-Verlag, 1995.

[9] Jose Meseguer. Semantic foundations for compositions. DARPA ITO Project Summary, 1998.

[10] M. Moriconi, X. Qian, R. A. Riemenschneider, and L. Gong. Secure software architectures. In *Proceedings of the 1997 IEEE Symposium on Security and Privacy*, pages 84–93, May 1997. Available at http://www.csl.sri.com/sadl/sp97.ps.gz.

[11] M. Moriconi and R. A. Riemenschneider. Introduction to SADL 1.0: A language for specifying software architecture hierarchies. Technical Report SRI-CSL-97-01, Computer Science Laboratory, SRI International, March 1997. Available at http://www.csl.sri.com/sadl/sadl-intro.ps.gz.

[12] S. Owre, J. M. Rushby, and N. Shankar. PVS: A prototype verification system. In Deepak Kapur, editor, *11th International Conference on Automated Deduction (CADE)*, volume 607 of *Lecture Notes in Artificial Intelligence*, pages 748–752, Saratoga, NY, June 1992. Springer-Verlag.

[13] R. A. Riemenschneider. Checking the correctness of architectural transformation steps via proof-carrying architectures. In *Proceedings of SIGSOFT '98*, 1998. Available at http://www.csl.sri.com/sadl/pca.ps.gz.

[14] Jason E. Robbins, Nenad Medvidovic, David F. Redmiles, and David S. Rosenblum. Integrating architecture description languages with a standard design method. Technical Report ICS-TR-97-35, University of California, Irvine, Department of Information and Computer Science, aug 1997.

[15] M. Shaw, R. DeLine, D. V. Klein, T.L. Ross, D. M. Young, and G. Zelesnik. Abstractions for software architecture and tools to support them. *IEEE Transactions on Software Engineering*, 21(4):314–335, April 1995.

[16] Mary Shaw and Paul Clements. A field guide to boxology: Preliminary classification of architectural styles for software systems. In *Proceedings of COMPSAC97*, pages 6–13, August 1997.

[17] X/Open Company, Apex Plaza, Forbury Road, Reading, Berkshire RG1 1AX, U.K. *Distributed Transaction Processing: Reference Model*, November 1993.

Appendix: Abstract Level of SDTP in SADL

```
x_open_abstract_df: ARCHITECTURE [ -> ]
IMPORTING ALL FROM Dataflow_style
BEGIN
  ar_requests: TYPE
  ar_resources: TYPE
  tx_commands, tx_responses: TYPE
  xa_commands, xa_responses: TYPE
COMPONENTS
  ap:  TYPE <= Function [ap_in1: ar_resources, ap_in2: tx_responses
                      -> ap_out1: ar_requests, ap_out2: tx_commands]
  rms: TYPE <= Function [rm_in1: ar_requests, rm_in2: xa_commands
                      -> rm_out1: ar_resources, rm_out2: xa_responses]
  tm:  TYPE <= Function [tm_in1: tx_commands, tm_in2: xa_responses
                      -> tm_out1: tx_responses, tm_out2: xa_commands]
  the_ap:  ap
  the_rms: rms
  the_tm:  tm
CONFIGURATION
  ar_1: CONNECTION =
          (EXISTS c: Channel<ar_requests>)
             Connects(c, the_ap.ap_out1, the_rms.rm_in1)
  ar_2: CONNECTION =
          (EXISTS c: Channel<r_resources>)
             Connects(c, the_rm.rm_out1, the_ap.ap_in1)
  tx_1: CONNECTION =
          (EXISTS c: Channel<tx_commands>)
             Connects(c, the_ap.ap_out2, the_tm.tm_in1)
  tx_2: CONNECTION =
          (EXISTS c: Channel<tx_responses>)
             Connects(c, the_tm.tm_out1, the_ap.ap_in2)
  xa_1: CONNECTION =
          (EXISTS c: Channel<xa_commands>)
             Connects(c, the_tm.tm_out2, the_rms.rm_in2)
  xa_2: CONNECTION =
          (EXISTS c: Channel<xa_responses>)
             Connects(c, the_rms.rm_out2, the_tm.tm_in2)
END x_open_abstract_df
```

The crucial problem in this process is that component refinements should remain composable into a total specification, preserving all (safety and liveness) properties introduced in them. To make the role of interface refinements in this process more concrete, consider the schematic illustration in Fig. 2, where boxes and ellipses stand for variables and actions, respectively, and A is an interface action between the two components. Although assigned to component 1, A may access and modify variables in both components, which means that some cooperation is involved in its execution. In refining component 1 one may wish, for instance, to split A into more elementary interface actions, which then affects also component 2. On the other hand, in refining component 2 one may wish, for instance, to temporarily refuse interaction A, which means disabling of an action that belongs to component 1. Obviously, the composability of such component refinements is not evident.

Component 1   Component 2

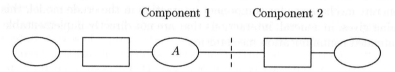

Fig. 2. Illustration of a component interface.

The formal basis for investigating these problems in this paper is Temporal Logic of Actions (TLA) [8]. In their work on TLA, Abadi and Lamport have analyzed the relationship between open and closed systems, and derived composability conditions for component refinements [1]. The problems investigated here are, however, somewhat different. Allowing component refinements to affect also external interface actions in other components makes the problem more general, but is essential for effective interface refinement. On the other hand, to achieve traceability of actions between different levels of abstraction, certain conventions are adopted for the use of TLA. Due to associated restrictions on the fairness properties that are expressible, the problem becomes manageable.

The structure of the rest of the paper is as follows. Section 2 is an introduction to TLA and its use in layered specifications. Composition of layered specifications is defined so that conventional composition of independently specified components can also be understood in terms of it. Component structure is imposed on specifications in Sect. 3. The core of the paper is in Sect. 4, where sufficient conditions are derived for the composability of component refinements, and in Sect. 5, where the approach is applied to interface refinement. The paper ends with some concluding remarks and a brief discussion on related work in Sect. 6.

2 Layered TLA-Based Specifications

The reader is assumed to be familiar with the basic notions and terminology of temporal logic. Some of the special characteristics of TLA [8] are briefly explained in this section, together with conventions that support its use in layered specifications.

2.1   TLA Formulas

TLA is a linear-time logic, where expressions are evaluated for *behaviors*, which are infinite sequences of *states*. *Variables* that are used to model system properties are *state functions*, which have unique values in each state. For a state function or state predicate p, its evaluation in state s will be denoted by $s[\![p]\!]$.

Corresponding to a state change, an ordered pair of states is a *step*, and *actions* are "step predicates" that are evaluated for steps. Variables in the first and the second state of a step are denoted by unprimed and primed variable names, respectively.

For an action A, state predicate *Enabled A* expresses that there exists a possible next state which, together with the given state, gives a step that satisfies A. This predicate is called the enabling condition or *guard* of action A.

A *stuttering* step, where all variables in a given set X retain their values, is denoted by $Stut_X$,

$$Stut_X \ =_{\mathrm{def}} \ \forall x \in X : x' = x,$$

and the stuttering extension of any action A is denoted by $[A]_X$,

$$[A]_X \ =_{\mathrm{def}} \ A \vee Stut_X.$$

In TLA, an action is allowed to appear only in *Enabled* state predicates and in contexts of the form $\Box[A]_X$. Since no "next state" operator is used, this makes the satisfaction of TLA formulas insensitive to stuttering. That is, addition and/or deletion of stuttering steps becomes inessential for behaviors, and logical implication can therefore be taken as the *refinement* relation between TLA specifications.

As usually, "$\Diamond$" will denote the dual of "$\Box$",

$$\Diamond E \ =_{\mathrm{def}} \ \neg\Box\neg E.$$

The dual of $\Box[A]_X$ will be denoted by $\Diamond\langle A\rangle_X$, where

$$\langle A\rangle_X \ =_{\mathrm{def}} \ A \wedge \neg Stut_X.$$

As a derived operator we will use "$\leadsto$" (leads to),

$$E_1 \leadsto E_2 \ =_{\mathrm{def}} \ \Box(E_1 \Rightarrow \Diamond E_2),$$

and shorthand notations will be used for strong and weak *fairness* conditions with respect to actions,

$$\mathrm{SF}_X(A) \ =_{\mathrm{def}} \ \Box\Diamond\langle A\rangle_X \vee \Diamond\Box\neg Enabled\ \langle A\rangle_X,$$
$$\mathrm{WF}_X(A) \ =_{\mathrm{def}} \ \Box\Diamond\langle A\rangle_X \vee \Box\Diamond\neg Enabled\ \langle A\rangle_X.$$

When subscripts X are understood from the context, they will be omitted in the following. Hiding of state variables by quantification will not be discussed in this paper.

2.4   Data Refinement in Superposition

In refinement it is often necessary to replace "abstract" data structures, which are suitable for mathematical manipulation, by "concrete" data structures that are more appropriate for efficient implementation.

Variables for new data representation can be introduced in superposition, but old variables cannot be removed. However, if one proves an invariant

$$\Box(x = f(y))$$

between an old variable x and other variables y, then x no longer needs explicit representation. Therefore, x can then be understood to have become a non-primitive state function, which henceforth provides only an abstract view on the concrete data structures by which it has been replaced.

Similarly, if an action with enabling guard g accesses but does not modify variable x, and invariant

$$\Box(g \Rightarrow x = f(y))$$

can be proved, x can be locally replaced by $f(y)$ in the action, making the action independent of x.

2.5   Composition of Layered Specifications

When two superposition refinements of the same specification (2) are given,

$$T_1 = Q_1 \wedge \Box[\mathcal{B}_1]_{Y_1} \wedge {}^s\mathcal{G}_1 \wedge {}^w\mathcal{G}_1,$$
$$T_2 = Q_2 \wedge \Box[\mathcal{B}_2]_{Y_2} \wedge {}^s\mathcal{G}_2 \wedge {}^w\mathcal{G}_2,$$

it is assumed that the new variables introduced in them are different, $Y_1 \cap Y_2 = X$. Two actions $B_1 \in \mathcal{B}_1$, $B_2 \in \mathcal{B}_2$, are then said to be *compatible*, if they have the same ancestor in $\mathcal{A} \cup \{Stut_X\}$. An action $B_1 \in \mathcal{B}_1$ with ancestor $Stut_X$ is also said to be compatible with $Stut_{Y_2}$, and similarly for $B_2 \in \mathcal{B}_2$ and $Stut_{Y_1}$.

By *composition* $T_1 \oplus T_2$ (see Fig. 4) we then understand the following superposition on both T_1 and T_2, and hence also on S:

$$T_1 \oplus T_2 = (Q_1 \wedge Q_2) \wedge \Box[\mathcal{B}]_{Y_1 \cup Y_2} \wedge {}^s\mathcal{G} \wedge {}^w\mathcal{G}, \tag{4}$$

where

- $\mathcal{B}$ consists of conjoined actions $B_i \wedge B_j$ for all compatible pairs $B_i \in \mathcal{B}_1 \cup \{Stut_{Y_1}\}$, $B_j \in \mathcal{B}_2 \cup \{Stut_{Y_2}\}$,
- ${}^s\mathcal{G}$ consists of those actions in $\mathcal{B}$ for which an ancestor in either $\mathcal{B}_1$ or $\mathcal{B}_2$ belongs to ${}^s\mathcal{G}_1$ or ${}^s\mathcal{G}_2$, respectively, and
- ${}^w\mathcal{G}$ consists of those actions in $\mathcal{B}$ for which an ancestor in either $\mathcal{B}_1$ or $\mathcal{B}_2$ belongs to ${}^w\mathcal{G}_1$ or ${}^w\mathcal{G}_2$, respectively.

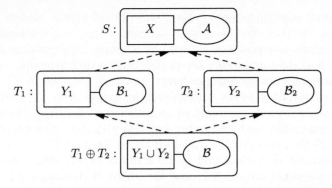

Fig. 4. Illustration of superposition relations in composition.

Obviously, "$\oplus$" is commutative and associative. Notice that it is an operation between layered specifications, not of mere TLA expressions, since the compatibility of actions in T_1 and T_2 depends on their refinement histories.

Under the above assumptions, layered specifications T_1 and T_2 are said to be *composable*, if their composition (4) is an operational expression and a refinement of both T_1 and T_2, i.e., $Q_1 \wedge Q_2$ is satisfiable, and all safety and liveness properties of both T_1 and T_2 hold in (4). In the special case of a dummy S (i.e., $X = \mathcal{A} = \emptyset$), T_1 and T_2 are independent and therefore always composable. The following Lemma is also obvious:

Lemma 1. *If T_1 and T_2 are superposition refinements of S, and no action in S is given explicit refinements in both of them, then T_1 and T_2 are composable.*

From a theoretical viewpoint one would not need to restrict to compatible pairs in the conjoined actions in (4). For a specification process it is desirable, however, that ancestor histories of actions are traceable to all levels of abstraction. For an operational interpretation it is also an advantage that conjoined actions are guaranteed not to have conflicting "assignments" to variables.

2.6   Composition of Independent Specifications

Composition of layered specifications is a generalization of composition in its conventional meaning, since the latter can be understood as the reduced case of composing mutually independent specifications. In this case it is often convenient to use parameterized actions of the form

$$A = \exists x : A(x),$$

where $A(x)$ is a step predicate that depends on parameter x.

In superposition, when $A = \exists x : A(x)$ is an ancestor of a refined action $B = \exists x : B(x)$, direct correspondence will be assumed between their parameters so that $B(x) \Rightarrow A(x)$. Obviously, if the value of x is not uniquely determined by the guard of A, further constraints can be introduced for it in B.

When "open" components are "closed" into closed-system models, parameterized actions provide effective means to describe their communication with their environments. Composition, followed by a simple superposition step, can then describe how the components act as each other's environments.

As an example, consider independently specified components T_1 and T_2, where T_1 gives output x to its environment by action $A = \exists x : A(x)$, and T_2 receives input y from its environment by action $B = \exists y : B(y)$. Since actions A and B are compatible with each other and also with stuttering actions, composition $T_1 \oplus T_2$ then contains the conjoined action $\exists x, y : A(x) \wedge B(y)$ and also (default refinements of) both A and B. By a simple superposition step, where the default refinements are deleted[1] and the guard of the conjoined action is strengthened with $x = y$, all output from T_1 is directed to T_2 as such, and all input to T_2 is taken from T_1.

Obviously, if T_1, for instance, contains a fairness requirement with respect to action A, the above construction need not preserve this liveness property. This would be the case, for instance, if action B in T_2 would not accept all output produced by A in T_1. In the following we will study this problem in a slightly different and more general setting.

3   Components in Closed Systems

Although closed-system specifications can be used in a bottom-up manner as outlined in Sect. 2.6, their main advantages come up when the top-down direction needs to be supported. Proceeding from top down is most natural in the specification of reactive systems; in fact it sounds paradoxical to specify components of a reactive system and their interfaces before specifying what they should do together [7].

In a top-down specification process, a closed-system model is partitioned into components at some stage. In this section we discuss such partitionings and their role in the specification process.

3.1   Partitioning of State

With k components in a closed-system specification, the *global state* consists of the *local states* of these components, $s = (s_1, \ldots, s_k)$. Correspondingly, the set of variables X is partitioned into disjoint subsets

$$X = X_1 \cup \cdots \cup X_k, \quad X_i \cap X_j = \emptyset \text{ for } i \neq j,$$

so that variables in X_i are assigned to the *responsibility* of component i. Each X_i is partitioned further into *shared* and *private* variables, $X_i = X_i^{\mathrm{shd}} \cup X_i^{\mathrm{pvt}}$, so that external accesses (i.e., accesses by actions in other components) are allowed only to shared variables.

---

[1] An action is deleted in superposition by strengthening its guard to be identically false.

A crucial property of superposition is that no new write accesses can be introduced for any old variables, but read accesses can. To model situations where also external read accesses are restricted to those actions that have already been provided for that purpose, *hidden* variables X_i^{hdn} are defined as a subset of X_i^{shd} for which even no new external read accesses are allowed.

In the presence of components, the initial condition P is assumed to be *separable* into conditions on the local states of the components. Denoting the global state by a pair $s = (s_i, t)$, where the first component is the local state of component i, and t denotes the rest of the state, this assumption can be formulated as

$$(s_i, t)[\![P]\!] \wedge (u_i, v)[\![P]\!] \Rightarrow (s_i, v)[\![P]\!]. \tag{5}$$

The initial condition P is then effectively a conjunction of local conditions for the components.

3.2   Partitioning of Actions

The *responsibility* for each action is also assigned to some component, yielding a partitioning

$$\mathcal{A} = \mathcal{A}_1 \cup \cdots \cup \mathcal{A}_k, \quad \mathcal{A}_i \cap \mathcal{A}_j = \emptyset \text{ for } i \neq j.$$

This induces also an associated partitioning of fairness conditions,

$${}^{\mathrm{s}}\mathcal{F} = {}^{\mathrm{s}}\mathcal{F}_1 \cup \cdots \cup {}^{\mathrm{s}}\mathcal{F}_k, \qquad {}^{\mathrm{w}}\mathcal{F} = {}^{\mathrm{w}}\mathcal{F}_1 \cup \cdots \cup {}^{\mathrm{w}}\mathcal{F}_k,$$

so that ${}^{\mathrm{s}}\mathcal{F}_i$ and ${}^{\mathrm{w}}\mathcal{F}_i$ contain only actions in $\mathcal{A}_i$.

In principle, each TLA action involves all variables in X, independently of whether it changes their values or not. In an operational interpretation, however, an action does not need to access all variables in X. A notion of *dependence* on variables is therefore needed in the following.

Intuitively, an action A *write depends* on variable $x \in X$, if it may modify the value of x, and it *read depends* on x, if its guard *Enabled A* or its effect on other variables may depend on the value of x. More precisely, we define these dependencies by occurrences of x' resp. x in the given textual representation (where "stuttering assignments" $x' = x$ are omitted), independently of whether these occurrences are semantically significant or not. Therefore, these dependencies fall outside of TLA, and may in some situations be changed without affecting the TLA meaning of actions.

Actions in $\mathcal{A}_i$ that are allowed to depend on shared variables in other components are called *interface actions* and are denoted by $\mathcal{A}_i^{\mathrm{ifc}}$. Other actions in $\mathcal{A}_i$ are *local* to component i. From the viewpoint of component i, actions in $\mathcal{A}_i^{\mathrm{ifc}}$ are *internal* interface actions in it, while those in $\mathcal{A}_j^{\mathrm{ifc}}$, $i \neq j$, are *external* to it.

3.3   Partitioning of Action Parameters

Parameterized actions are often useful as interface actions. In simple situations a parameter then models an input/output value that is transmitted from one component to others.

In general, parameter values need not be uniquely determined, and they may depend on variables in several components. Instead of input or output, one might then talk about "interput." Obviously, an implementation may then need complex communication, in which the components agree on an appropriate "interput" value. Partitioning into components requires, however, that the *responsibility* for each parameter is assigned to one of the components involved. Intuitively this is the component that makes the final decision on the value.

Analogously to separability of initial conditions, guards of interface actions are assumed to be *separable* with respect to parameters assigned to the responsibility of different components. More precisely, if $\exists x, y : g(x, y)$ is the guard of an interface action, where x denotes parameters that are the responsibility of one component, and y denotes the other parameters, we require

$$g(x, y) \wedge g(u, v) \Rightarrow g(x, v). \tag{6}$$

3.4   Utilizing Components

A refinement of a partitioned specification should normally preserve or refine its component structure. Honoring this structure means that the partitioning of variables and actions into components remains compatible with their old partitionings. Similarly, compatible partitionings are required in composition of partitioned systems, and actions in different components should then be taken as mutually incompatible.

To serve a useful purpose, component structure should not be a mere add-on to a closed-system specification. In particular, partitioning into components should make it possible to work on the components independently in parallel paths of refinement. Because of interactions, component specifications are never, however, completely independent, since they always make some assumptions about their environments. Therefore, when proceeding to lower levels of abstraction, it should be possible to make also these assumptions more concrete.

To decide what the role of components should be in a (closed-system) specification process, we start from their role in implementation:

In implementation, the purpose of components is to provide modularity, where component implementations are composable into an implementation of the total system.

For specification we then adopt the analogous view:

In specification, the purpose of components is to provide modularity, where component refinements are composable into a refined specification of the total system.

Notice that this statement makes no reference to implementations. Therefore, although a specification component may focus on what corresponds to an eventual implementation component, such a correspondence is not necessary.

4   Component Refinements

In this section we discuss component refinements that serve the purpose out-lined above. First we discuss simple component refinements, in which only those actions are refined that are the responsibility of the refined component, and show that these are insufficient for some practical needs. Then we formulate a robustness condition that allows also refinement of external interface actions but still guarantees composability. Throughout the section it will be tacitly assumed that component refinements conform to the given partitioning, and that new variables and actions are introduced only to the component being refined.

4.1   General Assumptions

Given an operational specification S with k components, the idea is to refine the components in S independently, yielding closed-system specifications T^i, $i = 1, \ldots, k$, which are composable into

$$T = T^1 \oplus \cdots \oplus T^k, \tag{7}$$

which then is a refinement of each T^i and hence also of S.[2]

Let P be the initial condition in S, and let Q_i be the strengthened initial condition in T^i. To guarantee separability (5) of the initial condition $Q_1 \wedge \cdots \wedge Q_k$ in T, we require

$$(s_i, t)[\![Q_i]\!] \wedge (u_i, v)[\![P]\!] \Rightarrow (s_i, v)[\![Q_i]\!]. \tag{8}$$

For interface actions we make the simplifying assumption that only one (ex-plicit or implicit) refinement is given in T^i for each of them. (Since fairness requirements are associated with individual actions, this constrains the fairness properties that can be expressed.) No new fairness requirements are allowed for actions in other components, and all new parameters introduced in T^i must be the responsibility of component i. We also assume that only those parameters are constrained in T^i that are the responsibility of component i, and that the separability condition (6) is preserved. Therefore, if $\exists x, y : g(x, y)$ is the guard of a parameterized interface action, where x denotes the parameters that are the responsibility of component i, and $\exists x, y : h_i(x, y)$ is the corresponding refined guard in T^i, we require

$$h_i(x, y) \wedge g(u, v) \Rightarrow h_i(x, v). \tag{9}$$

4.2   Simple Component Refinements

By a *simple component refinement* of component i we understand a refinement that satisfies the above general assumptions and in which only those actions are explicitly refined that are the responsibility of component i. On account of (8) and Lemma 1 such refinements are always composable:

---

[2] Actions introduced as new actions in different T^i are considered mutually incompat-ible in this composition.

Theorem 1. *Simple component refinements are composable.*

Obviously, simple component refinements are sufficient in situations where accesses to external interface variables need not be modified. In addition, they allow restricted interface refinement by additional read dependencies on external interface variables. Still, they are insufficient in many situations that arise in practice.

As an example, consider specification of a data storage with external actions $Put(x)$ and $Get(x)$ for storing and retrieving data values x, respectively. At a high level of abstraction an abstract data structure can be used for data storage, and actions *Put* and *Get* can then be enabled whenever there is room for more data or the storage is nonempty, respectively. At a lower level of abstraction with concrete data structures, the data storage component may, however, sometimes need internal storage reorganization. In a refined specification, the need for such reorganization may therefore enable a new action *Reorg* and disable *Put* and *Get* temporarily, until reorganization by *Reorg* has taken place (see Fig. 5). Therefore, what intuitively is just a refinement of the data storage component would also refine external interface actions to it.

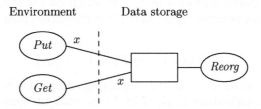

Fig. 5. Need for temporary refusal of external interface actions.

The reason for this phenomenon is that, although each interface action is assigned to some component, its execution requires cooperation from other components involved. When this cooperation is made more explicit at lower levels of abstraction, interface refinement is needed. In this example a simple kind of interface refinement is sufficient: the data storage component should be able to refuse external interface actions, which requires strengthening of their guards. We also notice that without a fairness requirement for *Reorg* such a component refinement would not be composable with environment refinements that add fairness requirements for *Put* and *Get*.

4.3   Robust Component Refinements

For reasons explained above, we allow a component refinement also to refine external interface actions to the component. Additional fairness requirements are not, however, allowed to be introduced for them.

By T_0^i we will denote the reduction of component refinement T^i where fairness assumptions are restricted to concern only local actions in component i. We then have the following Lemma:

Lemma 2. *If a property holds in the reduction T_0^i of some component refinement T^i, it also holds in the composition $T = T^1 \oplus \cdots \oplus T^k$.*

Proof. For safety properties this is obvious. Liveness properties in T_0^i are expressed by fairness requirements for local actions in component i. Since (the ancestors of) these actions cannot be refined in any other component refinement T^j, $j \neq i$, their guards are the same in T and T_0^i. Therefore, the lemma holds also for liveness properties.   □

As a consequence, composition T is a refinement of all T^i iff it satisfies those fairness requirements that each T^i gives for internal interface actions.

Next we formalize the idea that a component refinement can only temporarily refuse an external interface action. Let A be an external interface action to component i in specification S, let g be the guard of A, and let h_i be the guard of its refinement in component refinement T^i. (Possible parameters are existentially quantified within A, g and h_i.) We say that T^i is *insistent* on A, if condition

$$\Box \Diamond g \Rightarrow \Box \Diamond \langle A \rangle \vee \Diamond \Box (g \Rightarrow h_i) \tag{10}$$

holds in T_0^i.

A simpler condition that implies (10) and is often applicable is that h_i can be represented in the form $h_i = g \wedge r_i$ such that conditions

$$g \rightsquigarrow r_i,$$
$$\Box[r_i \Rightarrow r_i' \vee A]$$

hold in T_0^i.

A component refinement T^i is now called *robust* if, in addition to the general assumptions given above, T^i is insistent on all external interface actions. We have:

Theorem 2. *Robust component refinements are composable.*

Proof. It is sufficient to consider fairness properties of interface actions. Let $A = \exists x : A(x)$ be an internal interface action in component i in S, with x denoting its parameters collectively, and let $g = \exists x : g(x)$ and $h_i = \exists x : h_i(x)$ be the guards of A and its refinement in T^i, respectively. For each component j, $j \neq i$, for which A is an external interface action, let $h_j^{\text{ext}} = \exists x : h_j^{\text{ext}}(x)$ be the guard of its refinement in T^j.

The guard of the corresponding conjoined action in composition T is then

$$h = \exists x : (h_i(x) \wedge \bigwedge_j h_j^{\text{ext}}(x)).$$

It is now sufficient to prove that

$$\Box\Diamond h_i \Rightarrow \Box\Diamond\langle A\rangle \vee \Diamond\Box(h_i \Rightarrow h) \tag{11}$$

holds in T, since this would imply that a (weak or strong) fairness property associated with (the refinement of) A in T^i would be satisfied also in T. Since $h_i \Rightarrow g$, insistence condition (10) and Lemma 2 give us a weaker implication

$$\Box\Diamond h_i \Rightarrow \Box\Diamond\langle A\rangle \vee \Diamond\Box(h_i \Rightarrow (\exists x : h_i(x) \wedge \bigwedge_j \exists x : h_j^{\mathrm{ext}}(x))),$$

where the different parameter values for which $h_i(x)$ and $h_j^{\mathrm{ext}}(x)$ are true at the same time may be different. By parameter independence assumptions (6) and (9) there must then, however, exist also common parameter values for them, which leads to (11). $\qquad\Box$

In the example outlined in Sect. 4.2, weak fairness on action *Reorg* is obviously sufficient for making the suggested refinement of the data storage component insistent on external interface actions *Put* and *Get*. Therefore, this refinement is composable with unknown environment refinements.

5   Interface Refinement

When interactions have been defined at a high level of abstraction, they need not be realistic for direct implementation. Therefore, the need may arise to refine "abstract interactions" into more elementary "concrete interactions." In this section we discuss how component refinements can be used for this purpose.

Above it was assumed that component refinements totally conform to the original partitioning of variables and actions into components. In interface refinement this assumption needs to be relaxed. Another interesting point is that, since both internal and external interface actions can be refined in robust component refinements, the interface between two components can often be refined by refining either one of them.

By interface refinement we understand refinements that affect interface actions. The following important varieties of it can be distinguished:

- Representation of interface data can be changed by data refinement.
- External interface actions can be temporarily refused.
- The atomicity of an interaction can be refined by splitting it into more elementary actions. The responsibilities for these may be assigned to the parties involved, and the synchronization of the parties may be loosened.

In this section we will sketch out generic examples to discuss problems associated with atomicity refinement of interactions.

5.1   Changes in Responsibilities

Although each interface action is assigned to the responsibility of a specific component, its implementation requires some cooperation from each of the components involved. In refining an interface action the roles of other components may therefore become explicit in actions that are assigned to their responsibility, and this may also affect the partitioning of variables and actions. Since components have no significance in terms of TLA, composable refinements remain composable independently of such changes.

Obviously, for components to have any significance, arbitrary changes to the partitioning should not be allowed. The principles that we adopt are that a component refinement can reallocate only responsibilities of the refined component to other components, and that all such changes honor the general requirements for partitionings, even when composed with unknown component refinements. For instance, the responsibility for an action in $\mathcal{A}_i$ cannot be moved to another component if it depends on variables in X_i^{pvt}. Similarly, a necessary condition for changing a public variable to become private is that it belongs to X_i^{hdn}.

As an extreme example of changes in responsibilities, consider the following. If it is decided in an environment refinement that a real environment will be replaced by a simulated one, then all variables and actions of the environment part are moved to the system part. Such an environment refinement can then be composed with a system refinement, yielding a refined specification with a simulated environment.

Conversely, we can think of a system refinement that moves all its responsibilities to the external environment. This would reflect the decision that a separate system part will not be used, and everything will be implemented by rules and activities imposed on the environment. This demonstrates that, although an interface refinement can be carried out as a refinement of one component, its feasibility cannot be judged without considering all parties concerned.

5.2   Example: Simplifying an Interface Action

In a high-level specification an external interface action may directly execute some computation that an implementation should assign to local actions. As an example, consider a closed system consisting of an environment component (component 1) and a system component (component 2), where system variable $x \in X_2^{\text{hdn}}$ (initialized as 0) is used to accumulate information given by an environment action $A \in \mathcal{A}_1^{\text{ifc}}$,

$$A(i : \text{integer}) : \textit{true}$$
$$\rightarrow x' = f(i, x),$$

where f denotes some integer-valued function. In the notations, an arrow is used to separate the guard of an action from its "assignments," and "stuttering assignments" are not given explicitly.

The problem with this interface is that all computing, i.e., each evaluation of function f, is done by the environment, which therefore also needs access to the accumulated value x. A robust system refinement can, however, be given, which refines the interface so that variable x is effectively removed, and evaluation of f is moved to take place in a system action (see Fig. 6).

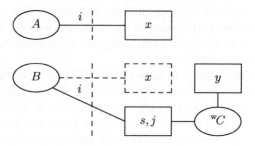

Fig. 6. Example of interface simplification.

As for variables, new system variables $s, j \in X_2^{\text{shd}}$ and $y \in X_2^{\text{pvt}}$ are introduced in this refinement, initialized as *true*, 0 and 0, respectively. Interface action A, which is external to the system component, is refined into B,

$$B(i : \text{integer}) : A(i)$$
$$\wedge\ s = \textit{true}$$
$$\rightarrow j' = i$$
$$\wedge\ s' = \textit{false},$$

and a new local system action ^wC is introduced,

$$^wC : s = \textit{false}$$
$$\rightarrow y' = f(j, y)$$
$$\wedge\ s' = \textit{true}.$$

Prefix ^{w} on ^wC expresses a weak fairness requirement, which ensures that this refinement is, indeed, a robust component refinement of the system part.

Obviously, invariant $\Box(x = (\text{if } s = \textit{true} \text{ then } y \text{ else } f(j, y)))$ now makes x redundant and, since no additional dependencies on x can be introduced in potential environment refinements, x can be removed. Evaluation of function f has then been effectively moved from the environment to the system part, and environment access to x has been removed.

5.3   Example: Refinement of Communication

The normal method to refine the atomicity of an action A is to introduce new actions which together with a refined action B accomplish what was originally done by A alone. Compared to A, the enabling of B is then delayed until the new actions have done all the preparatory work. Here we illustrate how this technique can be used for refining the atomicity of communication between components.

Consider the situation illustrated in the upper part of Fig. 7. There, the environment part gives an integer x to the system part in an atomic action A. For simplicity it is assumed that action A updates no environment variables. Removing this restriction will be discussed below.

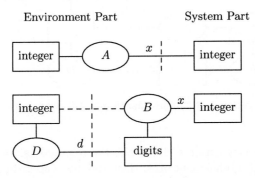

Fig. 7. Example of atomicity refinement.

Assuming that an implementation cannot transmit an entire integer atomically, a refinement is needed where the digits of x are transmitted one by one. This can be expressed as an environment refinement, which can be outlined as follows (see lower part of Fig. 7). The digits d of x are given to the system part by a new environment action D. Once all of them have been transmitted, action B, which is a refinement of A, can reconstruct x from them. By proving the invariant that this integer is indeed x, the dependence of B on environment variables (shown by a dashed line) can be removed, and B can be changed into a local system action.

5.4   Loosening of Component Synchronization

In the previous example it was assumed that action A did not update any environment variables. Otherwise the dependence of B on environment variables could not have been removed. In general, an interface action may update variables in all parties involved, and an implementation may therefore need communication in each direction, and refinement of atomicity then needs loosening of synchronization between the components.

To sketch how this affects the refinement of interface atomicity, consider a situation where an interface action A models two-way communication between two components, updating variables x and y in them (see upper part in Fig. 8).

To get rid of synchronous updating of x and y, one of them (x) has to be transformed into a non-primitive state function. Therefore, let z be a new variable whose value will "almost always" agree with that of x. The functions of action A can then be split into more elementary actions as follows (see lower

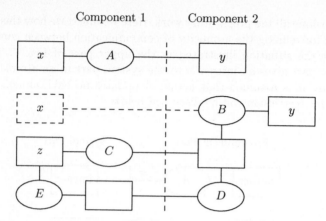

Fig. 8. Loosening of synchronization in two-way communication.

part of Fig. 8): a new action C transmits the required values to component 2, action B, which is a refinement of A, then updates y accordingly and computes the feedback, which is subsequently returned to component 1 by another new action D, and still another new action E finally updates z.

For the correctness of such a refinement it is essential that x has, indeed, become a non-primitive state function that needs no explicit representation, i.e., x is needed in component 1 only when its value is present in z. Another aspect that needs attention is that the enabling of A (and hence also of B) may depend on variables in component 2. Therefore, action C may be executed also in situations where its effects need to be canceled.

6   Concluding Remarks

The idea of layered specifications, as presented in Sect. 2, was developed in connection with the DisCo specification language [4, 5]. Technically, an import clause in DisCo takes the composition of one or more layered specifications as a basis for superposition. Partitioning into components and component refinements, as discussed in this paper, are not supported by the language. The layered structure of DisCo specifications has been utilized in an aspect-oriented manner, where different aspects of the specification are addressed in parallel paths of superposition refinement. Preservation of liveness properties in the composition of the resulting refinements has been treated on a case-by-case basis.

Another approach to TLA-based specifications has been developed in cTLA [3]. Instead of layered specifications, cTLA supports composition of independent specifications (and subsequent superposition) in the manner outlined in Sect. 2.6. Similarly to DisCo, preservation of liveness properties needs to be considered on a case-by-case basis. In the event-based formal framework of LOTOS, where fairness properties are not specified, essentially the same technique is known as the constraint-oriented specification style [2].

Object-oriented concepts have not been used in this paper. In DisCo, state variables are given in terms of classes and objects, actions are parameterized by the objects that can "participate" in them, and inheritance of single-object methods has been generalized into inheritance of capabilities to participate in such multi-object actions [6]. DisCo specifications are therefore patterns of interactive object systems. The results of this paper can be generalized also to this object-oriented situation, where components are collections (or patterns) of objects with associated actions.

Unlike conventional approaches to modularity, layered specifications make it possible to start formal modeling at a high level of abstraction, where component interfaces have not yet been fixed. Components can then be considered as different "aspects," on which the focus is set in parallel refinement paths. In particular, component interfaces can also be refined in this process. Conditions for the composability of such component refinements have been investigated in this paper. The approach seems natural for codesign, for instance, where the joint activities of the components should be specified before deciding on exact partitioning and concrete interfaces [10].

The viewpoint of this paper has been that of a top-down specification process. Therefore, attention has not been paid to techniques for component reuse. Layered specifications make it possible, however, to reuse specifications also at a high level of abstraction, where the operands of composition do not focus on implementation components. Need for reuse at such levels is apparent in design patterns, for instance, to which layered specifications and the object-oriented inheritance mechanism of DisCo have been applied in [11].

References

[1] Abadi, M., Lamport, L.: Conjoining specifications. ACM TOPLAS **17** (May 1995) 507–534

[2] Bolognesi, T., Brinksma, E.: Introduction to the ISO specification language LOTOS. Computer Networks and ISDN Systems **14** (1987) 25–59

[3] Herrmann, P., Krumm, H.: Compositional specification and verification of high-speed transfer protocols. In Protocol Specification, Testing and Verification XIV (Eds. S. T. Vuong and S. T. Chanson), Chapman & Hall 1994, 339–346

[4] Järvinen, H.-M.: The Design of a Specification Language for Reactive Systems. Tampere University of Technology, Publication 95, 1992

[5] Järvinen, H.-M., Kurki-Suonio, R., Sakkinen, M, Systä, K.: Object-oriented specification of reactive systems. Proc. 12th Int. Conf. on Software Eng., IEEE Computer Society 1990, 63–71

[6] Kurki-Suonio, R.: Fundamentals of object-oriented specification and modeling of collective behaviors. In Object-Oriented Behavioral Specifications (Eds. H. Kilov and W. Harvey), Kluwer 1996, 101–120

[7] Kurki-Suonio, R., Mikkonen, T.: Harnessing the power of interaction. In Information Modelling and Knowledge Bases X (Eds. H. Jaakkola, H. Kangassalo and E. Kawaguchi), IOS Press 1999, 1–11

[8] Lamport, L.: The temporal logic of actions. ACM TOPLAS **16** (May 1994) 872–923

[9] Lamport, L.: Composition: a way to make proofs harder. Compaq Systems Research Center, Technical Note 1997-030a, January 1998

[10] Mikkonen, T.: A development cycle for dependable reactive systems. In Proc. IFIP International Workshop on Dependable Computing and its Applications, DCIA98. Available at http://www.cs.wits.ac.za/research/workshop/ifip98.html

[11] Mikkonen, T.: Formalizing design patterns. Proc. 20th Int. Conf. on Software Eng., IEEE Computer Society 1998, 115–124

Semantics of First Order Parametric Specifications

Duško Pavlović

Kestrel Institute, Palo Alto, USA
dusko@@kestrel.edu

Abstract. Parametricity is one of the most effective ways to achieve compositionality and reuse in software development. Parametric specifications have been thoroughly analyzed in the algebraic setting and are by now a standard part of most software development toolkits. However, an effort towards classifying, specifying and refining algorithmic theories, rather than mere datatypes, quickly leads beyond the realm of algebra, and often to full first order theories. We extend the standard semantics of parametric specifications to this more general setting.

The familiar semantic characterization of parametricity in the algebraic case is expressed in terms of the free functor, i.e. using the initial models. In the general case, initial models may not exist, and the free functor is not available. Various syntactic, semantic, and abstract definitions of parametricity have been offered, but their exact relationships are often unclear. Using the methods of categorical model theory, we establish the equivalence of two well known, yet so far unrelated, definitions of parametricity, one syntactic, one semantic. Besides providing support for both underlying views, and a way for aligning the systems based on each of them, the offered general analysis and its formalism open several avenues for future research and applications.

1 Introduction

1.1 Parametric Specifications

The idea of *parametric polymorphism* goes back to Strachey [26] and refers to code reusable over any type that may be passed to it as a parameter. If a type is viewed as a set of logical invariants of the data, this idea naturally extends to the software specifications, as the logical theories capturing requirements and allowing their refinement. The idea of parametric specifications was proposed early on and became a standard part of specification theory (cf. e.g. [8, 12, 13] and the references therein).

A standard nontrivial example of a parametric specification is a presentation of the theory of vector spaces, with the theory of fields as its parameter. The idea is that refining the parameter, in this case the subtheory referring to scalars, yields a consistent refinement of the larger theory, usually called the *body*. Formally, we are given a theory VecSp and a distinguished subtheory Field $\hookrightarrow$ VecSp. The refinement is realized by the pushout in the category of specifications [4, 11].

J. Wing, J. Woodcock, J. Davies (Eds.): FM'99, Vol. I, LNCS 1708, pp. 155–172, 1999.
© Springer-Verlag Berlin Heidelberg 1999

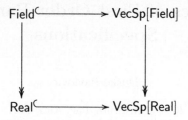

The functoriality of the pushout operation ensures the compositionality of the refinements.

Of course, not every interpretation of one specification in another allows this. For instance, if instead of Field, just the theory of rings is taken as the parameter of VecSp, some consistent refinements of the parameter will induce inconsistencies in the body. Some models of the parameter therefore do not correspond to models of the body.

Some syntactic parametricity conditions, ensuring that consistent refinements of the parameter induce consistent refinements of the body, were proposed early on [9, 14]. However, the analogous semantic characterizations, ensuring that models of the parameter induce models of the body, were given only in terms of free functors, which only exist for (essentially) algebraic specifications, i.e. those stated using just operations and equations (and simple implications between them). In [9], cofree functors were analyzed as well, but for a general first order theory, they may not exist either. E.g., the theories of fields, Hilbert spaces, or linear orders do not have either intial or final models.

Algebraic specifications do suffice for great many practical tasks and offer a fruitful ground for theory [8]. However, when it comes to systems for code synthesis, like SPECWARE™ [28], where it is essential to compositionally refine and implement not only abstract datatypes, but also abstract algorithmic theories, algebraic specifications become increasingly insufficient, and initial and final semantics do not apply.

On one hand, a syntactic form of parametricity for general specifications has been used in practice and in the literature [12, 13]. On the other hand, in [6], a semantical definition of parametricity was proposed, independent of the existence of initial or final models. However, it seems that neither the semantic characterization of the former nor the syntactic characterization of the latter have been worked out. Abstracting away from the concrete meaning of parametricity, some interesting structures have been built, applicable to parametric specifications in general [5, 25], yet no statement tieing together the syntactic and the semantic intuitions seems to have been proved. The purpose of the present paper is to try to bridge this gap, while providing some evidence of the applicability of *categorical model theory* to the study of general software specifications.[1]

---

[1] In contrast, the purported algebraicizing of general specifications in higher order logic by presenting the first order theorems as higher order equations only shifts the problems from the large but familiar area of first order model theory to the scarcely cultivated field of higher order algebra.

1.2   Elements of Categorical Model Theory

The functorial semantics of algebraic theories goes back to the sixties, to Lawvere's thesis [16]. The theory of categorical universal algebra which arose from it is summarized in [22]. An important step beyond algebra is the study of locally presentable categories [10], which come about as the model categories of limit theories, a wider, yet essentially restricted class. The full scope of first order logic was covered by categorical model theory rather slowly, throughout the seventies and eighties, as some parts tend to be technically rather demanding. Good accounts of the more accessible parts are [1, 20, 21].

The main idea of functorial semantics is to

- present logical theories as *classifying* categories with structure, so as to
- obtain their models as structure preserving functors to Set, with homomorphisms between them as natural transformations.

The resulting categories of models will always be *accessible*, i.e. have directed colimits and a suitable generating set. Conversely, every accessible category can be obtained as the category of models of a first order theory, possibly infinitary. Categorical model theory is thus the study of accessible categories and the way they arise from theories. There is a very general Stone-type duality between the first order theories, presented as categories, and the induced categories of models [19], but it is quite involved in thechnical details, and it is not clear whether it can be brought into a practically useful form.

But without going into the formal duality, one can still systematically explore the relationships between the *syntactic* and the *semantic* aspects of theories, by analyzing functors between their categorical presentations. In particular, for any two first order theories $\mathbb{A}$ and $\mathbb{B}$, presented as classifying categories, one can align the properties of the logical interpretations, which can be captured as functors $F : \mathbb{A} \longrightarrow \mathbb{B}$, and the induced forgetful, or "reduct", functors $F^{\#} : \mathsf{Mod}(\mathbb{B}) \longrightarrow \mathsf{Mod}(\mathbb{A})$ between the corresponding categories of models.

This is a typical task for the semantics of software specifications: analyze how a particular class of syntactical manipulations with theories is reflected on their models, and on the computations that may be built on top. We shall show that a syntactic definition of parametric specification, viewed as a property of the interpretation functor $F : \mathbb{A} \longrightarrow \mathbb{B}$, is equivalent to an independent semantic definition, stated in terms of the "reduct" functor $F^{\#} : \mathsf{Mod}(\mathbb{B}) \longrightarrow \mathsf{Mod}(\mathbb{A})$.

1.3   Outline of the Paper

In the next section, we describe the concrete constructions of classifying categories, explain how interpretations are captured as functors between them, and how the idea of parametricity fits into this setting.

In section 3 we list some abstract preliminary results that align the syntactic and semantic properties of functors.

Finally, in section 4, we derive the main result: the equivalence of a syntactic form of parametricity, in the spirit of [12, 13], and a semantic form, as in [6], both adapted only to a common categorical setting.

2   Theories and Models, Categorically

2.1   Classifying Categories

The simplest classifying category is the *Lawvere clone* $\mathbb{C}_T$ of an algebraic theory T, say single sorted. Its objects can be viewed as natural numbers (*viz* the arities), while a morphism from m to n is an n-tuple of the elements of the free algebra in m generators, i.e. a function $n \longrightarrow Tm$, where T denotes the free algebra constructor.[2] A crucial observation from Lawvere's thesis [16] is that $\mathbb{C}_T$ classifies T-algebras, in the sense that they exactly correspond to the product preserving functors $\mathbb{C}_T \longrightarrow$ Set, while the T-homomorphisms correspond to the natural transformations between them. Indeed, since n in $\mathbb{C}_T$ appears as the product of n copies of 1, the product preservation ensures that the functors $\mathbb{C}_T \longrightarrow$ Set trace the operations with the correct arities. The equations of T are then enforced by functoriality. Detailed explanations of the functorial semantics of algebraic theories can be found e.g. in [22].

If models of more general theories are to be captured as functors, some additional preservation properties will be needed, in order to enforce the satisfaction of formulas that are not mere equations, i.e. that express more than just commutativity conditions. There are several well known frameworks for building suitable classifying categories and developing functorial semantics for general first order theories, the most "categorical" being probably sketches [3, 20]. We shall however work in the setting of *coherent categories* [21], closest to the original geometric spirit of categorical logic, because they seem to allow the quickest and perhaps the most intuitive approach to the matters presently of interest.

2.2   Coherent Categories

Let T be a multisorted first order theory with equality. For simplicity, we assume that it is purely relational: operations are captured by their graphs. Moreover, T is assumed to be generated by a set of axioms in *coherent* logic, i.e. using finitary $\wedge$ and $\vee$, including the empty ones, $\top$ and $\bot$, and the quantifier $\exists$. The underlying logic can be classical or intuitionistic. We cannot go into the details here, but reducing finitary first order logic to its coherent fragment is a fairly standard technical device (see [1, 2, 21] and especially the informative introduction of [20]). The extension to infinitary logic is justified by stable and natural categories of models and is routinely handled by extending the classifying constructions. However, some of the proofs presented below essentially depend on the finiteness assumption.

Formally, the theory T can be viewed as a preorder: the underlying set $|T|$ of well-formed formulas is generated by its language, while the entailment preorder $\vdash$ is generated by its axioms. The rough idea is to capture the well-formed formulas of T as the objects of the classifying category $\mathbb{C}_T$, and the theorems of T as the morphisms of $\mathbb{C}_T$.

---

[2] So if T is presented by the monad T, the classifier $\mathbb{C}_T$ is the dual of the induced Kleisli category, restricted to natural numbers.

The passage from the formulas of $\mathcal{T}$ to the objects of $\mathbb{C}_{\mathcal{T}}$ requires an adjustment: the formulas must be viewed modulo variable renaming, i.e. α-conversion $\phi(x) \sim \phi(y)$, where x and y are vectors of variables. Note that this is not a congruence with respect to the logical operations, because e.g. $\phi(x) \wedge \phi(y) \not\sim \phi(x) \wedge \phi(x)$.

The passage from theorems of $\mathcal{T}$ to morphisms of $\mathbb{C}_{\mathcal{T}}$ requires a similar adjustment: modulo the logical equivalence $\varphi \dashv\vdash \psi$, which means that $\varphi \vdash \psi$ and $\psi \vdash \varphi$. The definition is thus

$$|\mathbb{C}_{\mathcal{T}}| = |\mathcal{T}|/\sim$$
$$\mathbb{C}_{\mathcal{T}}\,(\alpha(x), \beta(y)) = \{\vartheta(x,y) \in \mathcal{T} \mid \vartheta(x,y) \vdash \alpha(x) \wedge \beta(y),$$
$$\alpha(x) \vdash \exists y.\ \vartheta(x,y),$$
$$\vartheta(x,y') \wedge \vartheta(x,y'') \vdash y' \equiv y''\}/\dashv\vdash$$

where x and y are disjoint strings of variables, always available by renaming[3], and $\equiv$ is the equality predicate in $\mathcal{T}$. The identities in $\mathbb{C}_{\mathcal{T}}$ are induced by the equality predicates, and the composition of $\vartheta(x,y)$ and $\varrho(y,z)$ is $\exists y.\ \vartheta(x,y) \wedge \varrho(y,z)$.

The logical structure of $\mathcal{T}$ induces the categorical structure of $\mathbb{C}_{\mathcal{T}}$:

- *finite limits* are constructed using conjunction and variable tupling, starting from the true predicates $\top(x)$ over each sort;
- *regular epi-mono factorisations* are constructed using the existential quantifier; and finally
- *joins of the subobjects* correspond to the disjunctions.

These three structural components constitute a coherent category and are preserved by coherent functors. Theories in coherent logic generate coherent classifying categories; conversely, each small coherent category classifies a coherent theory. Coherent functors preserve the truth of the theorems in coherent logic. The reader may wish to work out the details of this correspondence or to consult some of the mentioned references.

A reader familiar with the functorial semantics of algebra has perhaps already noticed that the coherent classifier of an algebraic theory contains the corresponding Lawvere clone as a full subcategory, namely the one spanned by the true formulas $\top(x)$, one for each arity x. Indeed, the coherent classifier of an algebraic theory is the coherent completion of its Lawvere clone. The coherent classifiers have a richer set of objects, in order to impose the preservation of more general axioms; but simpler theories can be captured by smaller classifiers.

2.3   Interpretations and Models

The upshot of coherent classifying categories is thus that the coherent functors, preserving the coherent structure, preserve the coherent logic, and thus enforce the satisfaction of the coherent theorems, represented as the morphisms in coherent categories. A coherent functor $\mathbb{C}_{\mathcal{T}} \longrightarrow \mathbb{C}_{\mathcal{U}}$ can thus be viewed as a sound

---

[3] By the abuse of notation, $\alpha(x)$, $\beta(y)$ and $\vartheta(x,y)$ denote their equivalence classes $[\alpha]$, $[\beta]$ and $[\vartheta]$ modulo $\sim$.

interpretation of the theory $\mathcal{T}$ in the theory $\mathcal{U}$. But since every small coherent category $\mathbb{A}$ can be obtained as the classifier $\mathbb{C}_\mathcal{T}$ of some coherent theory $\mathcal{T}$, every coherent functor $F : \mathbb{A} \longrightarrow \mathbb{B}$ can be understood logically, as such an interpretation.

Although it is not small, Set has all the coherent structure, and the coherent functors $\mathbb{C}_\mathcal{T} \longrightarrow$ Set are exactly the models of $\mathcal{T}$. The natural transformations are the $\mathcal{T}$-homomorphisms, preserving all the definable operations. For every small coherent $\mathbb{A}$, we shall denote by $\mathsf{Mod}(\mathbb{A})$ the category of coherent functors $\mathbb{A} \longrightarrow$ Set. This is the category of models of $\mathbb{A}$. As pointed out before, categories of the form $\mathsf{Mod}(\mathbb{A})$ are accessible, and by allowing infinite disjunctions, one could get (an equivalent version of) every accessible category in this form [1, ch. 5].

On the other hand, by precomposition, every coherent functor $F : \mathbb{A} \longrightarrow \mathbb{B}$ induces a *"reduct"* $F^\# : \mathsf{Mod}(\mathbb{B}) \longrightarrow \mathsf{Mod}(\mathbb{A})$, reinterpreting a model $N : \mathbb{B} \longrightarrow$ Set of $\mathbb{B}$ as a model $NF : \mathbb{A} \longrightarrow$ Set of $\mathbb{A}$. This is the arrow part of the Mod-construction, which yields an indexed category $\mathsf{Mod} : \mathsf{Coh}^{op} \longrightarrow \mathsf{CAT}$, where Coh is the category of small coherent categories and functors, and CAT is the metacategory of categories. Mod thus assigns a semantics to each coherent theory $\mathcal{T}$, classified by a coherent category $\mathbb{C}_\mathcal{T}$; in other words, it maps each theory $\mathcal{T}$ to its category of models, captured as coherent functors $\mathbb{C}_\mathcal{T} \longrightarrow$ Set.

The semantical functor Mod is an instance of a *specification frame* in the sense of Ehrig and Große-Rhode [6]. Specification frames are indexed categories, construed as some abstract model category assignments, like Mod. In these terms, Ehrig and Große-Rhode proposed a semantical definition of parametric specifications, which will be analyzed in the sequel.

2.4   Parametrized Specifications as Functors: Syntactic vs Semantic Definitions

A reader unfamiliar with coherent logic may wish to write down, as a quick exercise, say, the coherent theories of fields and vector spaces and analyze their classifying categories. The classifying category Field is of course a subcategory of the classifying category VecSp. The obvious functor Field $\hookrightarrow$ VecSp is full and faithful. This means that the theory of vector spaces is conservative over the theory of fields: no new theorems about the scalars can be proved using the vectors. Moreover, Field $\hookrightarrow$ VecSp is also a powerful functor: each subobject of an object in the image is also in the image. This means that every predicate about the scalars, expressible in the theory of vector spaces, is already expressible in the theory of fields.

The embedding Field $\hookrightarrow$ VecSp is a typical parametric specification, defined syntactically, as in [12, 13]. Viewed in the setting of classifying categories, a parametric specification is thus a coherent functor $F : \mathbb{A} \longrightarrow \mathbb{B}$, which is full, faithful and powerful.

On the semantic side, as already mentioned, Ehrig and Große-Rhode [6] have proposed an abstract definition of parametricity, applicable to the functor Mod : $\mathsf{Coh}^{op} \longrightarrow \mathsf{CAT}$. Omitting the presentation details, a parametric specification is, according to this definition, an interpretation $F : \mathbb{A} \longrightarrow \mathbb{B}$, such that the induced functor $F^{\#} : \mathsf{Mod}(\mathbb{B}) \longrightarrow \mathsf{Mod}(\mathbb{A})$ is a retraction, i.e. there is a functor $\Phi : \mathsf{Mod}(\mathbb{A}) \longrightarrow \mathsf{Mod}(\mathbb{B})$ with $F^{\#} \circ \Phi \cong \mathsf{Id}$. In words, Φ maps each model M of the parameter $\mathbb{A}$ into a model $N = \Phi M$ of the body $\mathbb{B}$ in such a way that the forgetful functor $F^{\#}$ restores an isomorphic copy[4] of M. Such a functor Φ, which nondestructively expands a model, is said to be *persistent* [8, sec. 10B].

In the present paper, we shall show that the above two definitions are equivalent: a coherent functor $F : \mathbb{A} \longrightarrow \mathbb{B}$ is full, faithful and powerful if and only if $F^{\#} : \mathsf{Mod}(\mathbb{B}) \longrightarrow \mathsf{Mod}(\mathbb{A})$ is a retraction, i.e. has a right inverse.

Completeness View. When an indexed family of sets $\{B_x | x \in A\}$ is represented as a function $f : B \longrightarrow A$, with $B_x = f^{-1}(x)$, an indexed element $b \in \prod_{x \in A} B_x$ becomes a splitting $\phi : A \longrightarrow B$, $f \circ \phi = \mathsf{id}$, with $b_x = \phi(x) \in B_x$.

Similarly, a specification $\mathbb{B}$ parametrized over $\mathbb{A}$ can be thought of as a family of the instances of $\mathbb{B}$ indexed over the instances of $\mathbb{A}$. In particular, the functor $F^{\#} : \mathsf{Mod}(\mathbb{B}) \longrightarrow \mathsf{Mod}(\mathbb{A})$ can be construed as a family of $\mathbb{B}$-models indexed over $\mathbb{A}$-models. A splitting $\Phi : \mathsf{Mod}(\mathbb{A}) \longrightarrow \mathsf{Mod}(\mathbb{B})$, $F^{\#} \circ \Phi \cong \mathsf{Id}$, then becomes an indexed model of $\mathbb{B}$, parametrized over $\mathbb{A}$.

According to this view, a persistent functor is thus an indexed model. The parametricity of theories lifts to the parametricity of their models: the semantical definition of parametric specification, described above, boils down to the requirement that there is a parametric model of the body indexed over the models of the parameter.

The equivalence of the semantic and the syntactic definitions of parametricity, which we are about to establish, thus becomes a soundness-and-completeness theorem, in indexed form.

3   Syntactic vs Semantic Properties of Functors

3.1   Preliminaries

We begin by listing some useful terminology and facts from the general functorial calculus.

Definition 1. *A functor $F : \mathbb{A} \longrightarrow \mathbb{B}$ is said to be*

embedding: *if it is full and faithful;*

subcovering: *if for every object $B \in \mathbb{B}$ there is a finite diagram D in $\mathbb{B}$, such that (1) B is the colimit of D, and (2) for every node D_i of D there is some A_i in $\mathbb{A}$ and a monic $D_i \rightarrowtail F A_i$ in $\mathbb{B}$;*

subobject covering: *if every $B \in \mathbb{B}$ is a subobject of some $F A, A \in \mathbb{A}$ (in other words, if it is subcovering and the diagrams D can be chosen to have one node and no edges);*

---

[4] The original definition actually requires that M is recovered on the nose, i.e. that the strict equality $F^{\#} \circ \Phi = \mathsf{Id}$ holds. But in abstract functorial calculus, this is almost never possible.

powerful: *if all subobjects[5] of FA in $\mathbb{B}$ lie in the image of F. More precisely, for every monic $D \xrightarrow{d} FA$ in $\mathbb{B}$ there is a monic $S \xrightarrow{s} A$ in $\mathbb{A}$ and an isomorphism $i : D \xrightarrow{\sim} FS$ such that $d = Fs \circ i$.*

Lemma 1. *A powerful and subobject covering functor is essentially surjective.*

Lemma 2. $F : \mathbb{A} \longrightarrow \mathbb{B}$ *is faithful if and only if*

$$F(\varphi) \vdash F(\psi) \Longrightarrow \varphi \vdash \psi \tag{1}$$

As the converse of (1) is always true, a faithful coherent functor F always induces an "order isomorphism" on the subobject lattices.

To *prove* lemma 2, use the fact that $\varphi \vdash \psi$ if and only if $\varphi = \varphi \wedge \psi$.

Proposition 1. *A coherent functor must be full as soon as it is both faithful and powerful.*

Proof. Since F is powerful, the graph of any $h : FA \longrightarrow FA'$ must be in the essential image of F: there must be a monic $\kappa \rightarrowtail A \times B$ in $\mathbb{A}$ the F-image of which is isomorphic with the graph $\chi = \langle \mathrm{id}, h \rangle : FA \longrightarrow FA \times FB$. The relation $F\kappa$ thus satisfies;

$$\delta_{FA} \vdash F\kappa \,; F\kappa^{op}$$
$$F\kappa^{op} \,; F\kappa \vdash \delta_{FB}$$

which respectively tell that it is total and single valued. Taking into account that for the identity relation $\delta = \langle \mathrm{id}, \mathrm{id} \rangle$ holds $\delta_{FX} = F\delta_X$, and using (1), we conclude that κ is a total and single valued relation in $\mathbb{A}$. In any regular category, such a relation must be isomorphic to one in the form $\langle \mathrm{id}, k \rangle : A \longrightarrow A \times B$. Since clearly $F\langle \mathrm{id}, k \rangle = \langle \mathrm{id}, h \rangle$, we conclude that $Fk = h$. □

3.2   Basic Results

In the sequel, we assume that $F : \mathbb{A} \longrightarrow \mathbb{B}$ is a coherent functor between coherent categories, and $F^\# : \mathrm{Mod}(\mathbb{B}) \longrightarrow \mathrm{Mod}(\mathbb{A})$ is the functor induced by the precomposition. We use and extend some results from [21]. Note that some of them essentially depend on strong model theoretic assumptions, such as compactness. The proofs are thus largely non-constructive, as they depend on the axiom of choice.

Proposition 2. F *is faithful if and only if* $F^\#$ *is essentially surjective.*

---

[5] Recall that subobjects are *isomorphism classes* of monics.

Proof. By lemma 2, F is faithful if and only if

$$F\varphi \vdash F\psi \Longleftrightarrow \varphi \vdash \psi$$

By the completeness theorem [21, thm. 5.1.7] $F\varphi \vdash F\psi$ holds if and only if

$$\forall N \in \mathsf{Mod}(\mathbb{B}). \ NF\varphi \subseteq NF\psi$$

whereas $\varphi \vdash \psi$ holds if and only if

$$\forall M \in \mathsf{Mod}(\mathbb{A}). \ M\varphi \subseteq M\psi$$

The last two statements are clearly equivalent if $F^{\#}$ is essentially surjective, i.e.

$$\forall M \in \mathsf{Mod}(\mathbb{A}) \exists N \in \mathsf{Mod}(\mathbb{B}). \ M \cong F^{\#}N$$

Conversely, if there is $M \in \mathsf{Mod}(\mathbb{A})$ different from $F^{\#}N$ for all $N \in \mathsf{Mod}(\mathbb{B})$, one can use compactness to construct a formula ψ such that $NF\psi$ is true for all models N of $\mathbb{B}$, whereas $M\psi$ is not. $\qquad\square$

Definition 2. $F^{\#} : \mathsf{Mod}(\mathbb{B}) \longrightarrow \mathsf{Mod}(\mathbb{A})$ *is said to be* subfull *if every $\mathbb{A}$-homomorphism* $h : F^{\#}N' \longrightarrow F^{\#}N''$ *preserves all $\mathbb{B}$-subobjects, i.e. for every monic* $D \overset{d}{\rightarrowtail} FA$ *in $\mathbb{B}$ holds*

$$hA(N'D) \subseteq N''D$$

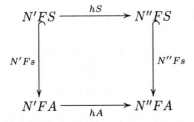

$$\tag{2}$$

Proposition 3. *F is powerful if and only if $F^{\#}$ is subfull.*

Proof. By definition, F is powerful if and only if every $D \overset{d}{\rightarrowtail} FA$ is in the essential image of F, i.e. $d \cong Fs$ for some $S \overset{s}{\rightarrowtail} A$. So (2) must commute because it is isomorphic with the square

$$
\begin{array}{ccc}
N'FS & \overset{hS}{\longrightarrow} & N''FS \\
{\scriptstyle N'Fs}\Big\uparrow & & \Big\uparrow{\scriptstyle N''Fs} \\
N'FA & \underset{hA}{\longrightarrow} & N''FA
\end{array}
$$

which commutes by the naturality of h.

The other way around, the fact that the subfullness of $F^{\#}$, i.e. the commutativity of squares (2) implies that F is powerful is one of the main constituents of the Makkai-Reyes conceptual completeness theorem [21, ch. 7§1]. The proof can be extracted from [21, thms. 7.1.4–4'], and essentially depends on compactness. □

Proposition 4. *F is subcovering if and only if $F^{\#}$ is faithful.*

Proof. Suppose F is subcovering and let $F^{\#}g = F^{\#}h$ for some $\mathbb{B}$-homomorphisms $g, h : N' \longrightarrow N''$. The equation $F^{\#}g = F^{\#}h$ means that $gFA = hFA : N'FA \longrightarrow N''FA$ for all $A \in \mathbb{A}$.

I claim that then $gB = hB : N'B \longrightarrow N''B$ must hold for every $B \in \mathbb{B}$. Since F is subcovering, for each B there is a finite diagram D, with (1) a colimit cocone to B, i.e. a jointly epimorphic family $\{D_i \overset{b_i}{\to} B\}_{i=1}^n$, and (2) the inclusions $\{D_i \overset{d_i}{\rightarrowtail} FA_i\}_{i=1}^n$ for some objects $A_1, \ldots A_n \in \mathbb{A}$. Hence

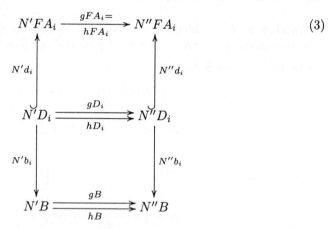

$$(3)$$

Naturality of g and h now yields

$$N''d_i \circ gD_i = gFA_i \circ N'd_i$$
$$= hFA_i \circ N'd_i$$
$$= N''d_i \circ hD_i$$

But since models are left exact, each $N''d_i$ is still a monic, and therefore $gD_i = hD_i$, for all $i = 1, \ldots, n$.

Using naturality again, we get

$$gB \circ N'b_i = N''b_i \circ gD_i$$
$$= N''b_i \circ hD_i$$
$$= hB \circ N'b_i$$

But since models preserve the finite unions of subobjects $\{N'b_i\}_{i=1}^n$ must be jointly monic again, and therefore $gB = h_b$. Thus $g = h$, and $F^{\#}$ is faithful.

For the converse, one assumes that there is $B \in \mathbb{B}$ not subcovered by F, and, using compactness, constructs models N' and N'' and two homomorphisms $g \neq h : N' \longrightarrow N''$ such that $F^{\#}g = F^{\#}h$. The details are in [21, thms. 7.1.6–6']. $\square$

Logical Meaning. Proposition 2 tells that each $\mathbb{A}$-model extends back along $F^{\#}$ to some $\mathbb{B}$-model if and only if $F : \mathbb{A} \longrightarrow \mathbb{B}$ is faithful. However, this does not guarantee that every $\mathbb{A}$-homomorphism between $\mathbb{A}$-models will extend to a $\mathbb{B}$-homomorphism between their extensions. Indeed, according to proposition 3, a necessary condition for this is that $F : \mathbb{A} \longrightarrow \mathbb{B}$ is powerful.

Together, these conditons provide a basis for aligning syntactical and the semantical definitions of parametricity, as described in section 2.4.

4   Characterizing Parametric Specifications

Theorem 1. *For a coherent functor* $F : \mathbb{A} \longrightarrow \mathbb{B}$ *and the induced "reduct"* $F^{\#} : \mathsf{Mod}(\mathbb{B}) \longrightarrow \mathsf{Mod}(\mathbb{A})$, *the following statements are equivalent.*

(a) F *is a powerful embedding.*

(b) $F^{\#}$ *is subfull and essentially surjective.*

(c) $F^{\#}$ *has a right inverse.*

If $\mathsf{Mod}(\mathbb{B})$ *has coproducts, then the above conditions are also equivalent with*

(d) $F^{\#}$ *has a left adjoint right inverse.*

Note that, since $\mathsf{Mod}(\mathbb{B})$ is finitely accessible, it has coproducts if and only if it is locally finitely presentable, i.e. when $\mathbb{B}$ classifies an essentially algebraic theory [1, sec. 3D].

Proof. **(a)**$\Leftrightarrow$**(b)** By proposition 1, it suffices to check that F is faithful and powerful. By proposition 2, F is faithful if and only if $F^{\#}$ is essentially surjective. By proposition 3, F is powerful if and only if $F^{\#}$ is subfull.

To simplify the proof of **(b)**$\Rightarrow$**(c)**, we shall freely use the established equivalence **(a)**$\Leftrightarrow$**(b)**. Given that $F^{\#}$ is essentially surjective and subfull, we thus know that F is full, faithful and powerful. Using all that, we define $\Phi : \mathsf{Mod}(\mathbb{A}) \longrightarrow \mathsf{Mod}(\mathbb{B})$, such that $F^{\#} \circ \Phi \cong \mathrm{Id}$.

Since $F^{\#}$ is essentially surjective, for every M in $\mathsf{Mod}(\mathbb{A})$, there is some L in $\mathsf{Mod}(\mathbb{B})$ such that $M \cong F^{\#}L$. But the homomorphisms to or from M may not extend to every such L, so we cannot simply take $\Phi M = L$.

On the other hand, like any functor, $M : \mathbb{A} \longrightarrow \mathsf{Set}$ has the right Kan extension, a functor $F_{\#}M : \mathbb{B} \longrightarrow \mathsf{Set}$ [18], defined

$$F_{\#}M(B) = \varprojlim M \circ \mathsf{Cod}\,(B/F) \tag{4}$$

where B/F is the comma category, spanned by the arrows in the form $B \xrightarrow{a} FA$ in $\mathbb{B}$. A morphism from $B \xrightarrow{a} FA$ to $B \xrightarrow{c} FC$ is an arrow $g : A \longrightarrow C$ in $\mathbb{A}$ such that $Fg \circ a = c$. The image of $B \in \mathbb{B}$ along $F_{\#}M$ is thus the limit of the diagram $B/F \xrightarrow{\text{Cod}} \mathbb{A} \xrightarrow{M} \text{Set}$.

The construction $F_{\#}$ is functorial and it is not hard to see that $F^{\#} \circ F_{\#} \cong \text{Id}$ holds if and only if F is faithful. So $F_{\#}M$ might be a candidate for $\varPhi M$. But the assumption that $M : \mathbb{A} \longrightarrow \text{Set}$ is coherent does not generally follow for $F_{\#}M : \mathbb{B} \longrightarrow \text{Set}$. The $F_{\#}$-image of an $\mathbb{A}$-model M may not be a $\mathbb{B}$-model, and the functor $F_{\#} : \text{Set}^{\mathbb{A}} \longrightarrow \text{Set}^{\mathbb{B}}$ does not restrict to a functor $\text{Mod}(\mathbb{A}) \longrightarrow \text{Mod}(\mathbb{B})$.

But the desired model $\varPhi M : \mathbb{B} \longrightarrow \text{Set}$ can actually be "interpolated" between the Kan extension $F_{\#}M : \longrightarrow \text{Set}$, and the arbitrary model $L : \mathbb{B} \longrightarrow \text{Set}$ such that $F^{\#}L \cong M$.

First of all, since $F^{\#} \dashv F_{\#}$, every $F^{\#}L \longrightarrow M$ induces $L \longrightarrow F_{\#}M$. Given $L \cong F^{\#}M$, for every $a : B \longrightarrow FA$ in $\mathbb{B}$ there is $La : LB \longrightarrow LFA \cong MA$. Hence a cone $\langle La \rangle_{a \in B/F} : LB \longrightarrow M \circ \text{Cod}(B/F)$. By definition (4), this cone induces a unique arrow $\phi B : LB \longrightarrow F_{\#}M(B)$.

Let the functor $\varPhi M : \mathbb{B} \longrightarrow \text{Set}$ be defined as the monic image of $\phi : L \longrightarrow F_{\#}M$, i.e.

$$\phi B \ : \ LB \longrightarrow\!\!\!\!\!\rightarrow \varPhi M(B) \lhook\joinrel\longrightarrow F_{\#}M(B) \tag{5}$$

This $\varPhi M$ will indeed be a model. Although $F_{\#}M : \mathbb{B} \longrightarrow \text{Set}$ is not a model, when $F : \mathbb{A} \longrightarrow \mathbb{B}$ and $M : \mathbb{A} \longrightarrow \text{Set}$ preserve (finite) limits, then $F_{\#}M : \mathbb{B} \longrightarrow \text{Set}$ weakly preserves them: for every (finite) diagram $\varDelta : I \longrightarrow \mathbb{B}$, the set $F_{\#}M(\varprojlim \varDelta)$ is a weak limit of $F_{\#}M(\varDelta)$ and thus contains $\varprojlim F_{\#}M(\varDelta)$ as a retract.

Together with the coherence of $L : \mathbb{B} \longrightarrow \text{Set}$, this weak preservation property of $F_{\#}M$ suffices for the coherence of $\varPhi M : \mathbb{B} \longrightarrow \text{Set}$. E.g., it preserves the products because the map from $\varPhi M(B) \times \varPhi M(D)$ to $\varPhi M(B \times D)$ on

$$\tag{6}$$

must be both surjective and injective.

The object part of $\varPhi : \text{Mod}(\mathbb{A}) \longrightarrow \text{Mod}(\mathbb{B})$ is thus determined by (5). Notice that $\varPhi$ is not unique, as the definition depends on the choice of L, $F^{\#}L \cong M$.

To define the arrow part of $\varPhi$, take an arbitrary $\mathbb{A}$-homomorphism $h : M' \longrightarrow M''$. It surely induces a natural transformation $F_{\#}h : F_{\#}M' \longrightarrow F_{\#}M''$, and we can find $\mathbb{B}$-models L' and L'' that map by $F^{\#}$ to M' and M'', and determine $\mathbb{B}$-models $\varPhi M'$ and $\varPhi M''$; but $h : M' \longrightarrow M''$ in general does not lift to a homomorphism $L' \longrightarrow L''$. However, $\Phi h : \Phi M' \longrightarrow \Phi M''$ can be derived from $F_\# h : F_\# M' \longrightarrow F_\# M''$ alone.

To simplify notation, write $N' = \Phi M'$ and $N'' = \Phi M''$ and $k = \Phi h$ for the desired homomorphism.

We are given a natural family $hA : M'A \longrightarrow M''A$ and we want to extend it to $kB : N'B \longrightarrow N''B$, so that $kFA = hA$. In other words, we have the subfamily of functions $kFA : N'FA \longrightarrow N''FA$, $A \in \mathbb{A}$, and we need to complete it to a natural family $kB : N'B \longrightarrow N''B$, $B \in \mathbb{B}$.

Consider first, for each $B \in \mathbb{B}$, the set $\mathcal{E}_B$ of regular epimorphisms $e : B \longrightarrow FA_e$ in $\mathbb{B}$. The e-th component of the limit cone $F_\# M(B) \longrightarrow M \circ \mathsf{Cod}(B/F)$ is a function $F_\# M(B) \longrightarrow MA_e$. Hence the map

$$F_\# M(B) \longrightarrow \prod_{e \in \mathcal{E}_B} MA_e \tag{7}$$

Since $F : \mathbb{A} \longrightarrow \mathbb{B}$ is powerful, this map is injective. By postcomposing (5) with it, one gets

$$\langle Le \rangle_{e \in \mathcal{E}_B} \; : \; LB \longrightarrow \Phi M(B) \hookrightarrow \prod_{e \in \mathcal{E}_B} LFA_e \tag{8}$$

because $MA_e = LFA_e$. Of course, since L is coherent, each $Le : LB \longrightarrow LFA_e$ is a surjection. The set $\Phi M(B)$ can thus also be obtained by taking the product of all sets LFA_e, such that there is some regular epi $e : B \longrightarrow FA_e$ in $\mathbb{B}$, and then extracting from this product the image of the tuple formed by all epis $Le : LB \longrightarrow LFA_e$.

The construction of $kB : N'B \longrightarrow N''B$ now proceeds by the following steps:

(i) define a function

$$\kappa B : N'B \longrightarrow \wp(N''B)$$

such that

$$\kappa FA(x) = \{hA(x)\}$$

(ii) show that $\kappa B(x)$ is nonempty for every $x \in N'B$;
(iii) show that $\kappa B(x)$ has at most one element for every $x \in N'B$; writing $kB(x)$ for the only element of $\kappa B(x)$, we get the function $kB : N'B \longrightarrow N''B$;
(iv) prove that the obtained family $kB : N'B \longrightarrow N''B$, $B \in \mathbb{B}$ is natural, i.e. forms $k : N' \longrightarrow N''$.

(i) Using the same set $\mathcal{E}_B$ of regular epis $e : B \longrightarrow FA$ as above, define

$$\kappa^e B(x) = (N''e)^{-1} \circ hA \circ N'e(x)$$
$$\kappa B(x) = \bigcap_{e \in \mathcal{E}_B} \kappa^e B(x)$$

For $B = FA$, $\kappa^{\mathrm{id}} FA(x) = \{hA(x)\}$. Moreover, for every $e \in \mathcal{E}_{FA}$ holds

$$\kappa^{\mathrm{id}} FA(x) \subseteq \kappa^e FA(x) \tag{9}$$

Indeed, since F is full, the naturality of h implies that the square

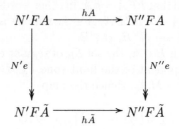

commutes. Hence (9), and thus $\kappa FA(x) = \{hA(x)\}$, as asserted.

(ii) For every $B \in \mathbb{B}$, the set $\mathcal{E}_B$ is nonempty because it surely contains the regular epi part $B \twoheadrightarrow FI \rightarrowtail F1 \cong 1$. $F1$ is terminal because F is coherent; the regular image of $B \longrightarrow F1$ is in the image of F because F is powerful.

Moreover, since N'' is coherent, and $B \longrightarrow FI$ is a cover (regular epi) $N''B \longrightarrow N''FI$ must be a surjection. So if $N''B$ is empty, $N''FI$ must be empty, and hence $N'FI$ must be empty, because there is a function $hI : N'FI \longrightarrow N''FI$. But there is also a function $N'B \longrightarrow N'FI$, and thus $N'B$ must be empty as well, so there is a unique $kB : N'B \longrightarrow N''B$, and we are done.

With no loss of generality, we can thus assume that $N''B$ is nonempty. Since $N''e : N''B \longrightarrow NFA$, $e \in \mathcal{E}_B$, is a surjection, all NFA are nonempty, and *moreover*, every $\kappa^e(x) = (N''e)^{-1} \circ hA \circ N'e(x)$ is nonempty.

Finally, for any $e_0 : B \longrightarrow FA_0$ and $e_1 : B \longrightarrow FA_1$ from $\mathcal{E}_B$ the intersection $\kappa^{e_0} \cap \kappa^{e_1}$ is nonempty as well. Toward a proof, consider the pair $\langle e_0, e_1 \rangle : B \longrightarrow FA_0 \times FA_1 \cong F(A_0 \times A_1)$ in $\mathbb{B}$. Factoring, and using once again the assumption that F is powerful, we get $e_2 : B \twoheadrightarrow FA_2$, with a pair $\langle p_0, p_1 \rangle : A_2 \longrightarrow A_0 \times A_1$ in $\mathbb{A}$ such that $e_i = Fp_i \circ e_2$, $i = 0, 1$. But $N''e_i = N''Fp_i \circ N''e_2$ implies

$$\kappa^{e_2}(x) \subseteq \kappa^{e_0}(x) \cap \kappa^{e_1}(x)$$

for all $x \in N'B$. Since $\kappa^{e_2}(x)$ has been proved nonempty, $\kappa^{e_0}(x) \cap \kappa^{e_1}(x)$ is.

A similar reasoning applies to any finite intersection of κ^es. But for the quotients $e \in \mathcal{E}_B$ in a coherent category $\mathbb{B}$ the compactness applies: if any finite family is consistent, then the whole set together is. Therefore, $\kappa B(x)$ is nonempty.

(iii) So we can surely chose $kB(x) \in \kappa B(x)$. No matter which element we choose, the equation

$$N''e \circ kB = kFA \circ N'e \tag{10}$$

will hold for every $e \in \mathcal{E}_B$, because $kFA = hA$ and the definition of κB implies

$$N''e \circ \kappa B = hA \circ N'e$$

On the other hand, recall that $N''B = \Phi M''B$ was defined so as to make the function $\langle N''e \rangle_{e \in \mathcal{E}_B}$ injective. But this means that the set of equations (10), for all $e \in \mathcal{E}_B$, together determine at most one $kB(x)$, since the functions $N''e$ are jointly injective.

So the family $hA : N'FA \longrightarrow N''FA$, $A \in \mathbb{A}$, extends to a uniquely determined family $kB : N'B \longrightarrow N''B$, $B \in \mathbb{B}$.

(iv) To prove that the family $kB : N'B \longrightarrow N''B$ is natural, take an arbitrary arrow $g : B_0 \longrightarrow B_1$ in $\mathbb{B}$ and an arbitrary $e_1 : B_1 \longrightarrow\!\!\!\rightarrow FA_1$ from $\mathcal{E}_{B_1}$. Let e_0 be the coimage of $e_1 \circ g$

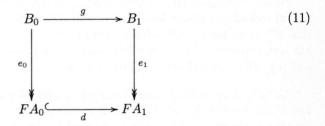

$$(11)$$

The codomain of e_0 is in the image of F because it is powerful.

We want to prove that the upper square in the diagram

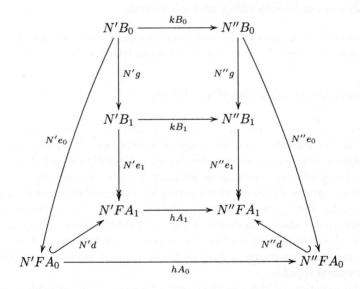

commutes. The lower square and the large outside trapezoid surely commute by the definition of kB. The small trapezoid commutes by the naturality of h, and the two triangles simply as the images of (11). Chasing, one concludes that

$$N''e_1 \circ kB_1 \circ N'g = N''e_1 \circ N''g \circ kB_0$$

But e_1 was taken as an arbitrary element of $\mathcal{E}_{B_1}$, so the last equation holds for all such. Since they are, by the construction of $N'' = \Phi M''$, jointly monic,

$$kB_1 \circ N'g = N''g \circ kB_0$$

follows.

This completes the proof of **(b)**⇒**(c)**. The converse **(c)**⇒**(b)** can be proved by modifying [21, thm. 7.1.4–4']. The argument is lengthy, based on the Los-Tarski theorem, and I do not see a way to improve on it, so the reader may wish to consult the original.

Finally, to connect **(d)** with the other three conditions, note that the assumption of coproducts makes $\mathsf{Mod}(\mathbb{B})$ into a locally finitely presentable category, so that $F^\#$ must have a left adjoint, like in [10, § 5], obtained by restricting the left Kan extension of F. Hence **(d)**⇔**(a)**. But a proof of this was already in [9] and [14], albeit in a slightly different setting.   □

An immediate consequence of theorem 1 and proposition 4 is a precise syntactic characterisation of *definitional extensions*, the interpretations F which induce an equivalence $F^\#$ between the model categories. The class is essentially larger than assumed in any of the implemented versions.

Corollary 1. $F^\# : \mathsf{Mod}(\mathbb{B}) \longrightarrow \mathsf{Mod}(\mathbb{A})$ *is an equivalence if and only if* $F : \mathbb{A} \longrightarrow \mathbb{B}$ *is a powerful embedding, and subcovering.*

A proof of this can also be derived from Makkai-Reyes' *conceptual completeness* theorem [21, thm. 7.1.8], which is the main result of their book.

5   Conclusions and Further Work

The research reported in this paper was originally motivated by the questions arising from the semantics and the usage of SPECWARE™, a tool for the automatic synthesis of software systems, developed at Kestrel Institute. In particular, the original semantics of pspecs as an abstract family of arrows [25] needed to be refined into a precise syntactic characterisation and verified semantically. This task took us far afield, into nontrivial model theory and functorial calculus, and brought about the above theorem relating two extant notions of parametricity. As suggested at the end of section 2.4, it can be viewed as an indexed completeness result. Formalizing this view might lead to various conceptual and meta-theoretical insights.

But the question of the practical repercussions of the presented material, or of their absence, seems even more interesting. The immediate task should probably be to analyze closely related families of coherent functors, capturing the instantiations and the implementations of theories. The practice of parametric specification is based upon them as much as upon the family of pspecs, studied in the present paper. Some important issues of refinement directly require this further analysis.

However, as we are not very far in any of these tasks, the main point of presenting this work currently is not this or that particular result, but showing categorical model theory at work in the software specification framework and suggesting a first step or two toward developing specific tools for analyzing and designing specification frameworks.

If, as is often stated, the increasing complexities and dynamics of evolving software development tasks make semantical analyses increasingly important, even indispensable in critical cases, then mathematical methods of the kind presented here may come to play an increasingly important role, as they may provide enough abstraction to resolve the concrete problems where formal methods are genuinely needed.

Acknowledgement. Most of what I have managed to learn about software is due in one way or another to the Kestrel people; what I have managed not to learn is also due in part to their tolerance. David Espinosa carefully read an earlier version of the paper and suggested many improvements. Theo Dimitrakos has provided very helpful and extensive comments.

References

[1] J. Adámek and J. Rosický, *Locally Presentable and Accessible Categories.* LMS Lect. Note Series 189 (Cambridge Univ. Press 1994)

[2] J. Adámek, P.T. Johnstone, J.A. Makowsky and J. Rosický, Finitary sketches, *J. Symbolic Logic* 62(1997) 699–707

[3] M. Barr and C. Wells, *Category Theory for Computing Science.* (Prentice Hall 1990)

[4] R. Burstall and J. Goguen, The semantics of Clear, a specification languge. In: D. Bjorner, ed., *Proceedings, 1979 Copenhagen Winter School on Abstract Software Specification.* Lecture Notes in Computer Science 86 (Springer 1980)

[5] Th. Dimitrakos, *Formal Support for Specification Design and Implementation.* Thesis (Univ. of London 1998)

[6] H. Ehrig and M. Große-Rhode, Functorial theory of parametrized specifications in generalized specification framework, *Theoret. Comput. Sci.* 135(1994) 221–266

[7] H. Ehrig and H.J. Kreowski, Parameter passing commutes with implementation of parametrized data types. In [23] 197–211

[8] H. Ehrig and B. Mahr, *Fundamentals of Algebraic Specification 2. Module Specifications and Constraints.* EATCS Monographs in Theor. Comp. Sci., vol. 21 (Springer 1990)

[9] H. Ganzinger, Parametric specifications: parameter passing and implementations with respect to observability. *ACM Trans. on Prog. Lang. and Syst.* 5(1983) 318–354

[10] P. Gabriel and F. Ulmer, *Lokal Präsentierbare Kategorien.* Lecture Notes in Mathematics 221 (Springer 1971)

[11] J. Goguen and R.M. Burstall, CAT, a system for the structured elaboration of correct programs from structured specifications. Tech. report CSL-118 (SRI 1980)

[12] J. Goguen, Parametrized programming. *Trans. on Software Engineering* 10-5(1984) 528–543

[13] J. Goguen, Principles of parametrized programming. In: *Software Reusability. Vol I: Concepts and Models.* (Addison-Wesley 1989) 159–225

[14] J. Goguen and J. Meseguer, Universal realization, persistent interconnection and implementation in abstract modules. In [23] 265–281

[15] J. Goguen, J. Meseguer and D. Plaisted, Programming with parametrized abstract objects in OBJ. In: D. Ferrari et al., eds., *Theory and Practice of Software Technology* (North-Holland 1983) 163–193

[16] F.W. Lawvere, *Functorial Semantics of Algebraic Theories.* Thesis (Columbia Univ. 1963)

[17] M. Löwe and U. Wolter, Parametric algebraic specifications with Gentzen formulas — from quasi-freeness to free functor semantics. *Math. Structures Comput. Sci.* 5(1995) 69–111

[18] S. Mac Lane, *Categories for the Working Mathematician.* Graduate Texts in Mathematics 5 (Springer 1971)

[19] M. Makkai, Stone duality for first order logic. *Advances in Math.* 65(1987)

[20] M. Makkai and R. Paré, *Accessible Categories: The Foundations of Categorical Model Theory.* Contemporary Mathematics 104 (AMS 1989)

[21] M. Makkai and G. Reyes, *First Order Categorical Logic.* Lecture Notes in Mathematics 611 (Springer 1977)

[22] E. Manes, *Algebraic Theories.* (Springer 1976)

[23] M. Nielsen and E.M. Schmidt, eds., *Proceedings of Ninth ICALP.* Lecture Notes in Computer Science 140 (Springer 1982)

[24] D. Sanella and M. Wirsing, Implementation of parametrized specifications. In [23] 473–488

[25] Y.V. Srinivas, Refinement of parametrized algebraic specifications. In: R. Bird and L. Meertens, eds., *Algorithmic Languages and Calculi.* (Chapman & Hall 1997) 164–186

[26] C. Strachey, Fundamental concepts in programming languages, *unpublished lecture notes,* 1967

[27] J.W. Thatcher, E.G. Wagner and J.B. Wright, Data type specification: parametrization and the power of specification techniques. *ACM Trans. of Prog. Lang. and Syst.* 4(1982) 711–732 (earlier version: *Proc. of 10th SIGACT Symp. on Theory of Computing* (1978) 119–132)

[28] R. Waldinger, L. Blaine, D. Espinosa, L.-M. Gilham, A. Goldberg, C. Green, R. Jüllig, J. Liu, J. McDonald, D.R. Smith, Y.V. Srinivas, T.C. Wang and S. Westfold, SPECWARE^{TM} *Language Manual* (Kestrel Institute 1998) — available upon request from keep@@kestrel.edu

A Perfecto Verification: Combining Model Checking with Deductive Analysis to Verify Real-Life Software[*]

Yonit Kesten[1], Amit Klein[2], Amir Pnueli[3], and Gil Raanan[2]

[1] Dept. of Communication Systems Engineering, Ben Gurion University, Beer-Sheva, Israel, ykesten@bgumail.bgu.ac.il
[2] Perfecto Technologies Ltd. 103 Medinat Hayehudim St. Herzelia 46733, Israel, (http://www.PerfectoTech.Com), {Amit.Klein|Gil.Raanan}@PerfectoTech.Com
[3] Weizmann Institute of Science

Abstract. The paper presents an approach to the formal verification of a complete software system intended to support the flagship product of Perfecto Technologies which enforces application security over an open communication net.

Based on initial experimentation, it was decided that the verification method will be based on a combination of model-checking using SPIN with deductive verification which handles the more data-intensive elements of the design. The analysis was that only such a combination can cover by formal verification all the important aspects of the complete system.

In order to enable model checking of large portions of the design, we have developed an assume-guarantee approach which supports compositional verification. We describe how this general approach was implemented in the SPIN framework.

Then, we explain the need to split the verification activity into the model-checking part which deals with the control issues such as concurrency or deadlocking and a deductive part which handles the data-intensive elements of the design.

Keyword: models, verification (deductive methods, assume-guarantee, compositional) model checkers (SPIN, PROMELA), concurrent systems, Security, safety properties, Telecommunications, Object Oriented, Network protocols

1 Introduction

The electronic commerce market has a growth potential that may bring it to revolutionize the world economy. The potential is based on the connectivity enabled by the Internet on one hand, and the willingness of customers and clients to do business on the net, on the other hand. The issue of willingness to do business on the Internet is mainly determined by how secure the customers

---

[*] This research was supported in part by the Minerva Center for Verification of Reactive Systems

J. Wing, J. Woodcock, J. Davies (Eds.): FM'99, Vol. I, LNCS 1708, pp. 173–194, 1999.
© Springer-Verlag Berlin Heidelberg 1999

feel when they engage in their business transactions. This is where security (safety, assurance) comes into play, and it can be plainly seen that as the major concerns of the clients are security, privacy and assurance, then addressing these issues in a precise and scientific manner can result in both a robust solution to the technical problems, and a high assurance and confidence level on the side of the clients. In our understanding, formal methods are an enabling technology for security of large scale systems, especially software projects. As a software analysis and improvement tool, formal methods provide the fullest and most complete scientific means for safety and assurance. From the customer point of view, formal verification means high assurance, which is a key feature in the decision to use e-commerce. The paper describes the application of formal methods for the verification of a software product, which delivers e-commerce security for the Internet. The work is an ongoing effort that combines both the company's staff, and academic researchers. Results of the research are used as a feedback into the software development process, as well as improving our understanding of formal verification of a software project.

The rest of the paper is organized as follows. In section 2 we give a short description of both the hardware platform, and the software to be verified.

In section 3 we present the verification framework, discussing our choice of verification tools, system description languages and property specification languages. We discuss problems encountered with these languages in today's existing verification tools, explaining our choice of perform deductive verification manually.

In section 4 we present a compositional model-checking verification of the Top Level Design (TLD) of our system, using the SPIN tool. We present our methodology for using the well known assume-guarantee paradigm, tailored for the specific characteristics of our system and the SPIN tool.

In section 5 we discuss the verification of the detailed design of our system, combining model-checking and deductive proof techniques.

We conclude in section 6 with a summary of the presentation and some advice to developers of tools for deductive verification.

2   Description of Application

The software to be verified is an e-commerce Internet security server ("the product"). The software is usually placed between the e-commerce server (typically a web-server which provides a web-enabled interface to the e-commerce engine - database server, application server, etc.) and the Internet, usually on the seller's premises (see Fig. 1). The Internet connection of the e-commerce server must pass through the security server (the product). Clients of the e-commerce applications access the e-commerce server across the Internet, and through the seller's Internet gateway (routers, firewalls, etc.), and finally through the security server. The product, therefore, completely controls all the e-commerce transactions. Monitoring is performed at the application level, that is, the product "understands" the protocol used for the transactions.

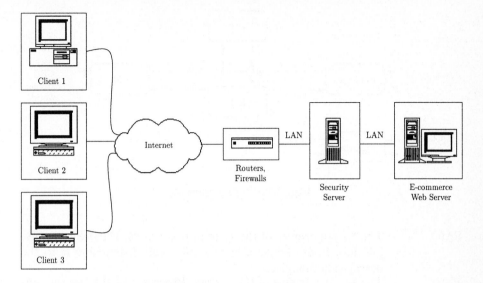

Fig. 1. Product Orientation.

The product consists only of software, running on top of an operating system. The hardware platform may consist of two CPU's, connected through a dedicated bus. A typical configuration would be two PC's connected via an Ethernet cable, but many other configurations are possible.

The product's logical architecture (patent pending) consists of a *Reducer* module and an *Enforcer* module, where the Reducer receives requests from the insecure zone (e.g. Internet) and *reduces* them into a proprietary simple protocol which represents the requests in a plain, unambiguous and robust manner; the Enforcer then *enforces* security rules on this representation and finally synthesizes the requests and transmits them over to the secure zone (the destination Web-Server). Coupling the logical architecture with the suggested physical architecture, such that the Reducer runs on one CPU, and the Enforcer runs on the other, enables the total separation of security functions (carried out by the Enforcer) and non-security functions (carried out by the Reducer), such that the non-security functions cannot compromise the security of the system. Hence, it is required to verify only the Enforcer, relieving us from the need to verify the Reducer.

As presented in Fig. 2, the security functions comprise of the following modules:

CM   — This module interfaces with the physical device driver of the bus which connects the two CPU's. Data to be transmitted to the insecure CPU are handed to the CM (by the RM), and data that arrives from the insecure CPU is handled in the CM, which relays it to the RM.

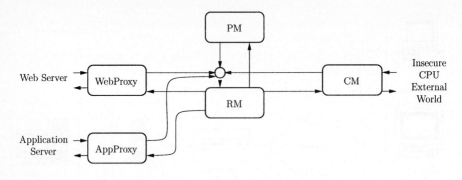

Fig. 2. System structure.

RM   — The "nerve center" of the system. It is a data dispatcher, receiv-
               ing data from various other modules and dispatching it to the
               destination modules.
PM   — The security engine of the system. Processes all the transactions
               to/from the e-commerce server.
WebProxy — This is a proxy module which communicates with the web (e-
               commerce) server. The WebProxy receives data from the RM
               and relays it (typically over TCP/IP) to the web (e-commerce)
               server.
AppProxy — A proxy module which provides a function similar to that of
               WebProxy, for a non web-enabled server.

Incoming data (from the insecure CPU connected to the external, potentially
adversary, world) arrives at the CM, which relays it to the RM, which routes it to
the PM. The PM processes the data, ensures that it is safe, and returns it to the
RM, which moves it to the WebProxy, which delivers it to the final destination,
the e-commerce server. The software is written mostly in C++ (with some GUI
functions in Java), containing tens of thousands lines of code. It is important
to note that not all the code is relevant to the verification effort: there are
some functions, notably the GUI (Graphic User Interface), which have nothing
to do with the (security) properties to be demonstrated, thus are irrelevant to
the whole verification process. These functions are not included in the above
description.

3   The Verification Framework

As claimed in [MP95], a framework for formal verification should consist of the
following components:

- A *computational model*, providing a common semantic base for the system
  and the properties we wish to establish for it.
- A *specification language* in which we can express the properties that need to
  be verified.

- A *system description language* in which we can describe the system whose properties need to be verified.
- A family of *verification techniques* by which such a verification can be successfully carried out. These usually include model checking, methods for deductive verification, and combinations thereof.

For our verification effort, we use the computational model of *fair discrete system* (FDS) ([KP98, KPR98]) which is slightly modified variant of the *fair transition system* (FTS), which is presented in [MP95] and underlies the *stanford temporal verifier* (STeP [BBC+95]).

The main specification language we use is *(linear) temporal logic* (LTL) [MP95]. However, in the context of verification by SPIN, we often express temporal properties by the corresponding automaton. In this paper we report only about the verification of *safety properties*.

For the set of verification techniques, we use model checking by SPIN, and manual deductive verification, using the deductive verification methodology expounded in [MP95] and implemented in STeP. Eventually, we intend to switch to computer-aided deductive verification by the STeP tool.

Currently, we use two system description languages according to the verification technique applied. For model checking with SPIN [Hol91], we use the SPIN system description language PROMELA. For deductive verification, the natural candidate is SPL, the system description language of STeP (and the one recommended in [MP95]).

A major problem we had to solve is how to provide an adequate and faithful representation of the concurrency programmed in our product (which is programmed in C++) within the framework of SPL, where the main difficulty was to represent dynamic creation and annihilation of processes. A solution to this difficulty is presented in the next Subsection.

While working on this representation and perfecting the deductive methods to handle our case studies within STeP, we meanwhile reverted to manual deductive verification, where we use SPL or sometimes even the actual C++ program as the system description language. As soon as we finalize the deductive methods to be used, we intend to incorporate computer-aided deduction, using the STeP tool into our process.

3.1   Dynamic Process Creation within SPL

The SPL modeling language was designed to accommodate *static* concurrency. That is, the number of processes running in parallel must be fixed at compile time, or at most, depend on an input parameter. To accommodate dynamic process creation, we declare in the SPL program an *infinite array* of processes, all of which await activation from a calling customer. A special *allocator* process hands around fresh indices in this array to all requesters. Given a process index, a requester may now communicate with the indexed server process.

To illustrate the application of this representation, consider the C++ program SUM-SQUARES, presented in Fig. 3.

```
class Number
{  // Number object, with the obvious interface
   public:
     Number(int v) // Constructor
     {  num=v; }
     // arithmetic operators, etc.
     int square()
     {  return num*num; }
   private:
     int num;
};
void main()
{  int n,sum=0;
   // Sum the first 10 squares
   for(n=1;n<=10;n++)
   {  Number x(n); //construct a Number object named x, initialized to n
      sum+=x.square(); // call the square member function
   }
}
```

Fig. 3. A C++ program SUM-SQUARES

In Fig. 4, we present the SPL representation of program SUM-SQUARES.

Note that the class *Number* is represented by a parameterized process *Number*[i] and the member functions of this C++ object have been implemented by the (synchronous) channels *cNumber* and *csquare*, which are local to *Number*[i]. While being local, implying that there are individual instances of these channels for each *Number*[i], they are also *public* in the sense that any external agent which knows the process-id i can send and receive messages through them referring to *Number*[i].*cNumber* and *Number*[i].*csquare*. Note that, according to this representation, processes are not really created but exist from the beginning of the run of the program.

In addition, there is an allocation process *allocate* whose role is to keep supplying new process-id's. The act of process creation is thus translated to making a possible client process aware of the name of a new process, by providing the client process with the index of that process. Most server processes keep waiting for some client to invoke their methods and until that happens they take no action.

The C++ invocation Number x(n) by the client (*main*) of the principal method *Number* has been separated into an allocation call providing the server-id which *main* saves in the local variable x, followed by a synchronous output of the value of n to channel *cNumber*[x]. Similarly, the C++ invocation x.square() has been translated to a synchronous input from channel *csquare*[x].

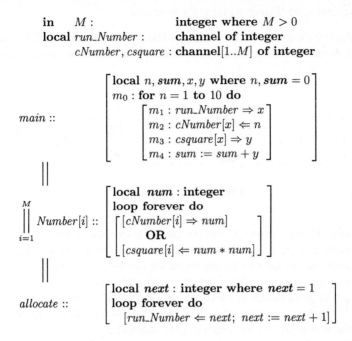

in M :   **integer where** $M > 0$
local run_Number :   **channel of integer**
$\quad cNumber, csquare$: **channel**$[1..M]$ **of integer**

$main$ ::
$$\begin{bmatrix} \textbf{local } n, \textit{\textbf{sum}}, x, y \textbf{ where } n, \textit{\textbf{sum}} = 0 \\ m_0 : \textbf{for } n = 1 \textbf{ to } 10 \textbf{ do} \\ \begin{bmatrix} m_1 : run\_Number \Rightarrow x \\ m_2 : cNumber[x] \Leftarrow n \\ m_3 : csquare[x] \Rightarrow y \\ m_4 : sum := sum + y \end{bmatrix} \end{bmatrix}$$

$\parallel$

$\displaystyle\mathop{\parallel}_{i=1}^{M} Number[i] ::$
$$\begin{bmatrix} \textbf{local } \textit{\textbf{num}} : \textbf{integer} \\ \textbf{loop forever do} \\ \begin{bmatrix} [cNumber[i] \Rightarrow num] \\ \textbf{OR} \\ [csquare[i] \Leftarrow num * num] \end{bmatrix} \end{bmatrix}$$

$\parallel$

$allocate$ ::
$$\begin{bmatrix} \textbf{local } \textit{\textbf{next}} : \textbf{integer where } \textit{\textbf{next}} = 1 \\ \textbf{loop forever do} \\ [run\_Number \Leftarrow next; \ next := next + 1] \end{bmatrix}$$

Fig. 4. The SPL representation of program SUM-SQUARES

4   Model Checking the TLD

Our first formal verification effort concentrated on the verification of the top level design (TLD) of the system. Through this experiment, we hoped to identify a method powerful enough to handle the verification of the complete system. In this experiment, we chose to use the model checker SPIN which was advertised as being specially designed for the verification of software and communication protocols, in particular.

Unfortunately, in spite of the high abstraction we applied in deriving the TLD view of the system, it was still too big to be completely verified in one go. This forced us to revert to compositional model checking based on the assume-guarantee paradigm. This paradigm is very well known and many variants have been developed over the years, e.g., [CM81], [Jon83], [BK85], [Pnu85], [dR85], [Zwi89], [PJ91], [AL93], [Jon94], [KM95], [AL95], [CC95], [CGL96], and [XdRH97]. Yet, for the use of this paradigm in our context we had to develop our own variant (heavily inspired by all this previous work).

In this section, we report about our approach to the verification of the top-level design of our system, using compositional model checking with the SPIN tool.

4.1   Systems and Their Safety Properties

We will illustrate our approach to compositional verification on the simple case
of two processes communicating by synchronous channels, as depicted in Fig. 5.

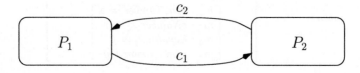

Fig. 5. Two Processes.

We assume that processes in the system are presented as PROMELA programs,
where communication is restricted to synchronous (rendezvous) channels. The
computational model we use for representing the behavior of systems and their
specifications assumes V a finite set of typed *state variables*. In particular, for
each channel c_i with range of messages R_i, the set V includes a corresponding
variable C_i which ranges over $R_i \cup \bot$, where the special value $\bot$ denotes a state
in which there was no communication over channel c_i.

A system *state* is any valuation of the state variables consistent with their
types. For a state s and a state variable $x \in V$, we denote by $s[x]$ the value
assumed by x in state s. A *run* of a system S is a finite non-empty sequence
of states $r : s_0, s_1, \ldots$ such that s_0 satisfies the initial condition, and for every
j, $0 < j < |r|$, the state s_j can be obtained from s_{j-1} by executing one of
the statements in the program for the system S which is enabled on s_{j-1}. In
particular, $C_i = m \neq \bot$ in state s_j iff the statement executed in passing from
s_{j-1} to s_j sent the message m on channel c_i, e.g., by a sender executing $c_i! m$
jointly with a receiver executing $c_i? y$.

For a subset of the state variables $U \subseteq V$ and a state s, we denote by $s\downarrow_U$ the
projection of the state s on the subset U. That is, $s\downarrow_U$ is the U-state obtained by
removing from the state s the valuation of the variables which belong to $V - U$.
In particular, $s\downarrow_{C_i}$ retains only the value assumed by the variable C_i, namely, the
message sent on channel c_i in the step leading to this state (we write $s\downarrow_{C_i}$ as an
abbreviation for $s\downarrow_{\{C_i\}}$). For a run $r : s_0, s_1, \ldots$, we denote by $r\downarrow_U$ the projected
run $s_0\downarrow_U, s_1\downarrow_U, \ldots$. Finally, for a run r and a channel variable C_i, we denote
by $r\Downarrow_{C_i}$ the *compressed projected run* obtained by removing from $r\downarrow_{C_i}$ all the
bottom elements. For a run r, $r\Downarrow_{C_i}$ represents the list of messages emitted on
channel c_i during the run in the order of their emission. In the CSP terminology,
this is called the c_i-restricted trace of r [Hoa84].

In this study, we were mainly interested in the study of *safety properties*
[Lam77]. This is why it is sufficient to consider the semantics of a system as
given by the set of all of its runs, and consider as properties to be verified only
safety properties. The main feature of a safety property φ is that if it is violated
by a run r then it cannot be satisfied by any run extending r. A typical example

is the property specifiable by the formula $\varphi : \Box(x > 0)$ stating that, at all states of all runs, the value of x is always positive. It is obvious that if a run r violates φ then one of the states in r must have a non-positive value of x and, therefore, no extension of r can satisfy the requirement "x is always positive".

We write $r \models \varphi$ to denote that the run r satisfies the property φ, and write $S \models \varphi$ if φ is S-*valid*, i.e., all runs of S satisfy r.

A safety formula φ is said to be a *channel property* of channel c if

C1. $r \models \varphi$ for every r such that $r{\Downarrow}_C$ is the empty sequence. That is, φ holds over all runs which did not send even a single message on channel c.

C2. If r_1 and r_2 are runs such that $r_1{\Downarrow}_C = r_2{\Downarrow}_C$, then $r_1 \models \varphi$ iff $r_2 \models \varphi$. That is, the truth value of φ on a run r is fully determined by $r{\Downarrow}_C$, the sequence of messages transmitted by the run r on channel c.

4.2 A Compositional Proof Rule

Normally, there is no chance of being able to verify, using model checking techniques, any of the properties of the system by submitting the entire system to a model checker such as SPIN. A frequently used approach, to which we refer as the *compositional approach* is to consider modules (processes) of the system separately and verify every property by considering only the processes which are responsible for the variables on which the property depends.

For example, in the system of Fig. 5 we may wish to prove two safety properties: φ_1 and φ_2, where each φ_i depends only on the variables determined by process P_i, for $i = 1, 2$. This suggests that property φ_1 should be model-checked on a model consisting of process P_1 alone. Unfortunately, while the property φ_1 may depend only on variables manipulated by process P_1 the range of behaviors of P_1 when run alone may differ radically from its behaviors when coupled with P_2. In particular, when run in isolation it may produce a behavior which violates the property φ_1, while such a behavior is impossible in the real system due to the interaction with P_2. There is a danger that we may erroneously conclude that property φ_1 is not valid over the system while, in fact, it is valid.

To overcome this difficulty, we never study any of the processes in complete isolation. Instead, we identify channel properties, say I_1 and I_2 which capture the properties of the communication on channels c_1 and c_2 which (for our application) is the only way the two processes can interact with one another.

As a first step in the application of this idea, it is necessary to confirm that the proposed channel properties are indeed valid for all computations of the joint system $P_1 \| P_2$. This can be done using rule COMP presented in Fig. 6.

$$
\begin{array}{ll}
\text{L1.} & P_1 \models (I_2 \rightarrow I_1) \\
\text{L2.} & P_2 \models (I_1 \rightarrow I_2) \\
\hline
& P_1 \| P_2 \models I_1 \wedge I_2
\end{array}
$$

Fig. 6. Rule COMP.

Such a rule is often described as an *assume-guarantee* paradigm. Premise L1 of the rule can be interpreted by saying that, under the *assumption* that the environment maintains the property I_2 on channel c_2, process P_1 *guarantees* to maintain the property I_1 on channel c_1. Premise L2 states the symmetric obligation for process P_2. The rule claims that if these two obligations hold then both I_1 and I_2 will be maintained in all runs of the combined system $P_1 \| P_2$.

This rule is not sound for arbitrary properties I_1 and I_2. In the general case, the most general conclusion that can be inferred from premises L1 and L2 is $(I_1 \rightarrow I_2) \wedge (I_2 \rightarrow I_1)$ which does not necessarily imply $I_1 \wedge I_2$. However, in our case we are guaranteed of the following assumptions:

A1. $s_0[C_1] = s_0[C_2] = \bot$, for every initial state s_0. That is, no message has been transmitted on entering the initial state.

A2. I_1 and I_2 are safety channel properties for channels c_1 and c_2, respectively.

A3. At most one message can be transmitted at any execution step. That is, either $s[C_1] = \bot$ or $s[C_2] = \bot$ for every state s appearing in a run of $P_1 \| P_2$.

As we will now show, these assumptions guarantee that rule COMP is sound.

Claim. Under the assumptions A1–A3, rule COMP is sound.

Proof: Assume, to the contrary, that rule COMP is unsound. Let $r : s_0, s_1, \ldots, s_n$ be one of the shortest counter examples to the rule. That is, r satisfies premises L1 and L2 but does not satisfy the conclusion $I_1 \wedge I_2$.

For $k \leq n$, we denote by $r^{(k)}$ the k-prefix $r^{(k)} : s_0, \ldots, s_k$ of r. Obviously, $n > 0$. This is because, due to assumption A1, $r^{(0)} \Downarrow_{C_1} = r^{(0)} \Downarrow_{C_2}$ is the empty sequence, and by clause C1 of the definition of a channel property, both I_1 and I_2 should hold over $r^{(0)}$.

Since r is one of the shortest counter-examples, we can assume that $r^{(n-1)} \models I_1 \wedge I_2$. By assumption A3, either $s_n[C_1] = \bot$ or $s_n[C_2] = \bot$, and we assume, with no loss of generality, that $s_n[C_2] = \bot$. Consequently, $r^{(n)} \Downarrow_{C_2} = r^{(n-1)} \Downarrow_{C_2}$ and, due to clause C2 of the definition of a channel property and the fact that $r^{(n-1)}$ satisfies I_2, it follows that also $r^{(n)} = r$ satisfies I_2. Applying premise L1 to r, we conclude that I_1 holds over r. Thus, both I_1 and I_2 are satisfied by r, contradicting our hypothesis that r does not satisfy $I_1 \wedge I_2$. $\square$

Once we establish I_1 and I_2 as valid channel properties for the system $P_1 \| P_2$ we can use them for model-checking any local property φ_1 which only refers to the variables manipulated by process P_1. To do so, we model check the validity of the implication $I_2 \rightarrow \varphi_1$ over process P_1. Note that all necessary verification tasks apply model checking to a single process rather than to the complete system. This is the main advantage of the compositional approach.

Obviously, the method described here can be applied to a system consisting of an arbitrary number of processes, as long as every channel connects a unique sender to a unique receiver.

4.3   Implementing the Compositional Verification in SPIN

Since our application involves more than two communicating modules, we decompose the TLD into clusters of processes, each cluster small enough so that it can be locally verified by SPIN. Having defined such a cluster, we identify the incoming and outgoing channels, connecting the cluster to the rest of the design.

In Fig. 7 we present the general setup of a typical cluster.

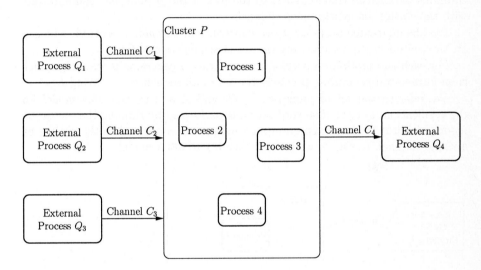

Fig. 7. Decomposition

The general form of the local verification that has to be applied to each of the clusters is

$$P \models (I_1 \wedge I_2 \wedge \ldots \wedge I_n \rightarrow J), \tag{1}$$

where $I_1, \ldots, I_n$ are the *assumptions* for the behavior on the incoming channels, such as $C_1, \ldots, C_3$ in Fig. 7, and J is the property that the cluster *guarantees* on its output channel, such as C_4 in Fig. 7. It is assumed that $I_1, \ldots, I_n, J$ are channel safety properties. The composition rule requires that we associate a unique invariant $I_{i,j}$ with every channel $C_{i,j}$ connecting cluster P_i to cluster P_j. The invariant $I_{i,j}$ will appear as an assumption (one of the I_k's) in the verification task for cluster P_j and as a guarantee (the J) in the verification task for cluster P_i.

Let us consider how to represent the verification task (1) for a representative cluster P to the SPIN tool. Obviously, we can represent the cluster of processes P as a set of concurrent PROMELA processes. The remaining question is how to represent the assumptions $I_1, \ldots, I_n$ and the guarantee J where, up to now, we considered these specifications as temporal formulas.

In theory, SPIN provides a special mechanism for representing non-trivial temporal properties. This is the *never* claim which identifies a single automa-

ton (represented as a PROMELA process) which runs in synchronous parallelism
to the application and monitors its behavior. Unfortunately, this mechanism is
too restricted for us since we need to attach to the cluster a set of automata
corresponding to the assumptions and the guarantee.

Consequently, we decided to construct our own processes which represent automata and monitor for the satisfaction of their corresponding temporal properties. Unlike the single *never* automaton, these automata processes run in asynchronous parallelism (interleaving) to the rest of the system, but communicate
with the cluster via synchronous channels.

For the guarantee property J, we construct an *acceptor process* A, which is
an automaton *accepting* precisely the set of sequences satisfying J.

For each assumption property I_i we construct a *generator process* G_i, which
is an automaton *generating* precisely the set of all sequences satisfying I_i.

We refer to the set of processes P, G_i and A as the PROMELA *model* for
the verification task (1). The verification is performed by running the PROMELA
model within SPIN. Each generator and acceptor is connected to the cluster by
a single channel. In Fig. 8, we present such a PROMELA model.

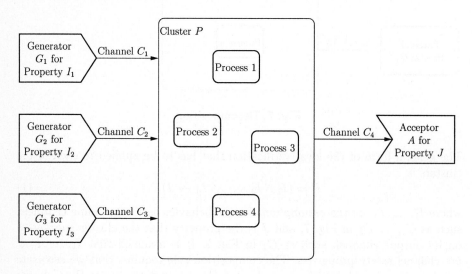

Fig. 8. A PROMELA model for a cluster.

4.4   Construction of Acceptors and Generators

Since each channel $C_{i,j}$ is associated with a single channel safety property $I_{i,j}$,
we have to construct for such a channel first an acceptor $A_{i,j}$ which accepts all
the behaviors satisfying $I_{i,j}$, and then a generator $G_{i,j}$ which generates precisely
the set of all sequences satisfying $I_{i,j}$.

Acceptors: Construction of acceptors is fairly easy. Assume the channel name is "c", and it should comply with a channel safety property J. We assume that we know how to construct for the property J a finite state deterministic automaton over the finite alphabet of c, with a single error state E (where all other states are accepting), which accepts precisely the sequences satisfying J. The translation of this automaton to PROMELA is straightforward. Every non-error node of the automaton is represented by the input statement $c?y$, followed by a case selection statement branching to different locations according to the value of the input y. The error state is represented by the statement assert(0) which aborts the computation, announcing an error.

For the simplest cases, this *explicit state* representation of the automaton for J and its PROMELA translation is adequate. However, in many cases, the alphabet is structured, such as the integers in the range 0..255 and the conditions are often expressed succinctly by predicates over the alphabet, such as $y < 128$. In these cases, the PROMELA acceptor is represented more compactly using auxiliary variables to represent part of the state.

For example, in Fig. 9, we present a PROMELA acceptor that accepts all sequences of permutations of $\{1, 2, 3\}$.

```
active proctype accept_c()
{       byte x,y,z;
        atomic {
        do
        :: c?x -> assert((1<=x) && (x<=3));
           c?y -> assert((1<=y) && (y<=3) && (y!=x));
           c?z -> assert((1<=z) && (z<=3) && (z!=x) && (z!=y));
        od;    }
        unless end_ver;
}
```

Fig. 9. An acceptor for all permutations over $\{1, 2, 3\}$.

Note that this automaton may reject the input at three locations. It rejects after the first input iff this input is not in the range [1..3]. It rejects after the second input iff this input is not in the range [1..3] or it is equal to the first input. Finally, the last input is rejected iff it is not in the range or it equals one of the previous input. Note that the explicit state automaton corresponding to this PROMELA process will have at least 8 states and 21 edges.

Generators   Construction of Generators is less straightforward. An important element in the construction of generators is that we should have a systematic way of translating an acceptor to a generator, automatically if possible. This is important because, as we have already mentioned, for each channel $C_{i,j}$ we need an acceptor $A_{i,j}$ and a generator $G_{i,j}$. The soundness of the composition rule hinges on the assumption that the set of sequences generated by $G_{i,j}$ is equal to the set of sequences accepted by $A_{i,j}$, i.e. that they refer to the same property.

For the case that the acceptor is derived from an explicit-state automaton, the conversion from acceptor to generator is straightforward. Every edge connecting automaton state q_i to $q_j \neq E$ and labeled by the letter A, should be translated to the PROMELA statement $c!A$ connecting the locations corresponding to q_i to q_j. In the case that q_j equals E, the error state, we omit the corresponding output statement. Such a generator will never generate a wrong output.

The situation is more involved in the case the acceptor process uses auxiliary variables, such as the acceptor of Fig. 9. Due to space limitations, we will only present in Fig. 10 the generator obtained by applying our systematic conversion to this acceptor.

```
active proctype generate_c()
{       byte x,y,z;
        atomic {
        do
        :: x = random(1,3); c!x;
           y = random(1,3); end_var = (y==x); c!y;
           z = random(1,3); end_var = ((z==x) || (z==y)); c!z;
        od;     }
        unless end_ver;
}
```

Fig. 10. A generator for all permutations over $\{1, 2, 3\}$.

The way this generator operates is that it first draws a random number in the range 1..3 and outputs it. Next it draws a second random number y in the same range. After drawing it, the generator applies the same test to y relative to x. If y should be rejected, the automaton does not cause an error abortion of the complete system by asserting *false*. Instead, it raises a special boolean flag end_var which causes the complete system to terminate immediately but in a non-error state. Technically, immediate termination is ensured by enclosing all processes in the system by the unless end_var clause which interrupts and terminates all processes as soon as the flag end_var is raised.

4.5   Results of the TLD Verification

The case study described below served to demonstrate the strength of the method together with its limitations. Eventually, it was decided to discontinue the application of this method, although the techniques developed may be of some use in further developments.

The case study included the 5 modules presented in Fig. 2 : WebProxy, PM, CM, RM, and AppProxy, plus an additional trivial module that has been added for technical reasons. The data transmitted over the channels connecting these modules contains 3 or 4 fields (depending on the channel): a "destination" field, a "session" field, and a "data" field, with sometimes a "from" field. In the table below, we summarize for each module the number of incoming and outgoing channels, and the number of overall processes (including acceptors and generators) which were involved in its modular verification:

Module Name	Incoming Channels	Outgoing Channels	Overall Processes
CM	2	2	7
RM	1	4	7
PM	1	1	4
WebProxy	2	2	7
AppProxy	2	2	7

The results from the verification, carried out by SPIN, were all positive. However, the execution (on a Pentium-II/333MHz, 100MHz bus, 512KB L2 cache, 256MB SDRAM, SPIN-3.2.3/Linux-2.0.29, -DSAFETY, -DMA=117 used) took too long (6 hours and 46 minutes for the most complex module - RM). The experiment is considered, therefore, to be unsuccessful in that it appears to reveal a scalability problem inherent to the implementation of the Acceptors/Generators scheme. While we gained a lot of expertise and insight by developing and applying this technique, and managed to verify a certain portion of the TLD, we decided not to use this method for the verification of the detailed design.

5   Detailed Design Verification: Combining Model Checking with Deductive Methods

The results reported in the last section demonstrated that SPIN alone cannot meet the challenge posed by a complex software system. At the beginning we thought that the problem was inherent to an explicit-state model checker such as SPIN, and that switching to a symbolic model checking, such as SMV [BCM+92], may solve the scalability problem. Indeed, we tried SMV on a subset of the case studies and observed a speedup factor of about 1000:1. However we soon realized that no matter how fast they are, no model checking tool is able to handle the complete problem, in particular, it cannot handle data intensive problems.

5.1   Why Combine the Methods?

It appears that the most versatile and powerful method of handling data-intensive problems is by using a deductive method. The main candidate tools for supporting deductive verification are STEP [BBC+95] and PVS [OSR93]. After some preliminary attempts we ran into the problem that none of these tools provided us with a system description language that fits our needs, namely analyzing multi-threaded programs written in C++.

The PVS tool requires translating the program into formulas of high-order logic, and if we wish to perform verification of temporal properties, it is also necessary to include the theory of temporal logic.

At first glance it seems that STeP is more user friendly since it has its own system description language SPL. When we tried to use STeP, it became clear very quickly that, while SPL is quite adequate for dealing with distributed systems, the representation of dynamic object creation, as explained in Section 3, requires a special translation which hinders its application for verifying C++ programs.

Obviously, the problems we complain about are purely technical, and all that is needed to solve them is a translator from C++ to either high-order logic or to SPL. Given enough time, we probably would have constructed such a translator and then continued to use these powerful tools. Being under intense time pressure, our final decision was to use the temporal deductive methodology proposed in [MP95] but conduct the proofs *manually*.

The strategy we have formulated and applied so far consists of a combination of *model checking* with *deductive verification*, where

- *Model checking* is used for handling *control-related* issues of deadlocks, mutual exclusion, and non-interference. It is applied to a simplified model of the system in which almost all data has been abstracted away.
- *Deductive verification* is used for analyzing the data-intensive parts of the system.

Besides separation of concerns, the main interaction between the two methods is that a thorough analysis of non-interference can lead to a significant simplification of the deductive verification task. In particular, when a certain segment in a given object's member function is known to be "isolated" from outside interference, we can verify its data transformations as though it were a sequential program.

5.2 Augmenting Deductive Verification by Model Checking

The chief purpose of employing Model Checking in our scheme is to resolve concurrency issues automatically. The immediate candidates are the following:

- Mutual Exclusiveness (Non-Interference)
- Deadlocks

For the purpose of verifying the security of our system, we are not interested in deadlock freedom properties, since if the system enters a deadlock state, security is not breached (although performance drops to zero). However, in order to verify that while the software is running, it does only what it is supposed to do, we lean heavily on non-interfernce properties. Non-Interference is crucial for the deductive phase: then, it is very helpful to know that some variables can change only by the thread being analyzed (and not by any concurrent thread). To some extent, non-interference can be thought of as "serializing" threads, and making them independent of each other (in limited code segments), with the obvious benefits for the deductive analysis.

The basic temporal formula that represents non-interference is:

$$\Box(at\_\ell_i \wedge at'\_\ell_i \rightarrow x = x') \tag{2}$$

This can be proven using SPIN in the following way: the system to be analyzed is represented as a set of PROMELA processes. Then, for each variable x for which the above formula should hold (at label 1 of process P with process identity i) an analysis is carried out, and each transition that writes on x is marked by a label. The SPIN equivalent of the above formula then takes the following form (for each label a in process Q with process identity j):

```
[](P[i]@l -> !Q[j]@a)
```

This formula can be checked as a **never** claim by SPIN , for each (Q,j,a) tuple. Note that we abstract away all the data manipulations.

The analysis can be extended naturally to cases in which even *access* to a variable should not occur while a certain thread is in a certain state.

Below, we illustrate the use of model-checking for establishing non-interference. The example is a system of threads accessing a shared data object, using locking mechanism to synchronize the access to the object. Threads can read, write or destroy the data object. An object can be read concurrently by several threads. However, when a data object is written or destroyed by one thread, it must not be read by other threads. A "group" is a special object, containing validity information for the data object. Due to implementation restrictions, the data object's validity must be ensured via a lookup in the group object before the data object is accessed. The group object itself is accessible directly, and can be both read and written.

There are K "user" threads in the system, which write the data object, and a "garbage collection" thread, which destroys inaccessible objects. These are, of course, simplified versions (for the sake of the example) of the actual threads, that may read and write nondeterministically to several objects, repeatedly.

Model checking provides the necessary non-interference assurance, stating that the data object cannot be written (or destroyed) while it is read, nor can it be destroyed and written at the same time.

The PROMELA code is as follows:
The "user" threads:

```
active [K] proctype user()
{
        ReadLock(group);
        /* pointer to object */
        if
        :: object_exists ->
           WriteLock(object);
           ReadUnlock(group);
           do
           :: skip -> /* may choose this branch */
```

```
write:              skip; /* perform writing */
                    WriteUnlock(object);
                    /* give up control */
                    /* resume control */
                    WriteLock(object);
                :: skip -> /* may choose this branch */
                    WriteUnlock(object);
                    break;
            od;
        :: else ReadUnlock(group);
        fi;
}
```

The "garbage collection" thread:

```
active proctype remove()
{
        WriteLock(group);
        WriteLock(object);
        object_exists=false;
        WriteUnlock(group);
        WriteUnlock(object);
        /* perform removal */
destroy: skip;
}
```

This code uses the four following macros for semaphore simulations:

```
#define ReadLock(var) atomic {!var.WRITE -> var.READ++ }
#define ReadUnlock(var) {var.READ--}
#define WriteLock(var) atomic {!var.WRITE && !var.READ ->     \
                                    var.WRITE=true}
#define WriteUnlock(var) {var.WRITE=false}
```

Note that the "user" threads release and re-acquire their lock on the object as necessary. This is an optimization applied to the original locking design, wherein the threads held their lock on the object throughout the writing phase. The outcome of this optimization is revealed once SPIN is used to re-assess the safety properties (assume K=2):

```
[] !(user[1]@write && user[2]@write)
[] !(user[1]@write && remove[0]@destroy)
[] !(user[2]@write && remove[0]@destroy)
```

Contrary to the original design, SPIN reports a **never** claim violation for this system. Examining the error trail uncovers the following flaw: the basic assumption of the design is that a "user" thread accesses an object only after checking that its existence bit (in the group object) is up. This no longer holds for the modified system: the `remove` thread may engage in deletion operation (once a "user thread" gives up his lock on the object), with a "user" thread re-acquiring the lock and writing data on the object, a scenario which violates the second or the third LTL formula of the above.

This resulted in a complete redesign of the whole locking scheme.

5.3   Deductive Verification of Data Transformations

Having verified non-interference between threads (equation 2), we can now verify heavy data transformations in single threads, as though they are sequential programs. We give two examples using the deductive verification rules presented in [MP95].

Example 1: Using the WAIT rule to ensure a proper implementation of a procedure. Assume a procedure of the following structure:

$$\begin{bmatrix} E : (entry \quad point) \\ B : \quad \cdots \\ X : \end{bmatrix}$$

We write $\Box((at\_E \wedge precondition) \rightarrow (at\_E \vee at\_B) \; \mathcal{W} \; (at\_X \wedge postcondition))$ to state the fact that once control is in the routine then control remains within the procedure body B until it gets to the exit point X, with the postconditions satisfied, thus guaranteeing the proper $(precondition \rightarrow postcondition)$ action of the procedure.

For instance, this rule can be used to verify a sort algorithm, provided the array it sorts does not change (while program counter is inside the sort code) by other threads. The $precondition$ may be identically T in this case, and the $postcondition$ would require a sorted array which is a permutation of the original array.

Example 2: Using the BACK-TO rule to ensure that if a procedure terminates successfully, then some expected action has been previously executed. Assume a procedure of the following structure:

$$\begin{bmatrix} \cdots \\ \textbf{if } (\cdots) \textbf{ then} \\ \quad \begin{bmatrix} G_1 : \text{an action, in case of } true \\ G_2 : \cdots \\ G_3 : return\_code := GOOD; \\ G_4 : \textbf{go to } X; \end{bmatrix} \\ \textbf{else} \\ \quad \begin{bmatrix} B_1 : \cdots \\ B_2 : return\_code := BAD; \\ B_3 : \textbf{go to } X; \end{bmatrix} \\ X : \end{bmatrix}$$

We write:

$$\Box((at\_X \wedge return\_code = GOOD) \rightarrow ((at\_G_3 \vee at\_G_4) \; \mathcal{B} \; at\_G_2)),$$

Then we write:

$\square$ $(at\_G_2 \qquad\qquad\qquad\qquad \rightarrow \quad postcondition)$
$\square$ $(at\_G_2 \wedge postcondition) \quad \rightarrow \quad (postcondition\ \mathcal{W}\ at\_X \wedge postcondition)$

Combining them into the desired property:

$$\square((at\_X \wedge return\_code = GOOD) \rightarrow postcondition)$$

If *postcondition* involves global (shared) variables, then for the third property to hold, it is necessary to establish that these variables are protected from interference by other threads.

We used the above rules, in the manner described in the examples, to verify non-trivial data transformations, some as complex to analyze as the sort algorithm. The verification relied heavily on the non-interference LTL formulae verified by SPIN . The combination of the two methods resulted in a core module of the product being successfully verified.

6   Conclusions and Further Research

In this paper, we have reported about the experience of Perfecto Technologies in the application of formal verification to their security server software product, and the lessons we learned from this experience.

Starting with model checking by SPIN, we succeeded to verify a certain portion of the TLD of the system. To do so, we have developed a compositional approach, specially geared to verification by SPIN. One of the conclusions we reached was that model checking alone cannot scale up to verify the detailed design, but may suffice for the verification of the top-level design, provided one uses compositionality and abstraction.

For verification of the detailed design, we finally settled on a combination of model checking for the control-intensive part and manual deductive verification for the data-intensive part. The two methods interact by the deductive verification benefiting from proofs of non-interference established by model checking.

The preference for manual verification was forced on us because none of the existing support tools for deductive verification provides a system description language fully adequate for modeling multi-threaded C++ programs. We indicate in Section 3 how such a system description language may be developed with minimal extensions. We call upon developers of tools for deductive verification to pay more attention to providing a convenient interface language if they wish to attract users from the C++ community.

Acknowledgements

The authors would like to thank Eran Reshef (Perfecto Technologies Ltd.) and Eilon Solan (Northwestern University, IL., USA) for their continuous help and advice, and Elad Shahar (The Weizmann Institute of Science) for his help with the SMV system.

References

[AL93]   M. Abadi and L. Lamport. Composing specifications. *ACM Trans. Prog. Lang. Sys.*, 15:73–132, 1993.

[AL95]   M. Abadi and L. Lamport. Conjoining specifications. *ACM Trans. Prog. Lang. Sys.*, 17(3):507–534, 1995.

[BBC$^+$95] N. Bjørner, I.A. Browne, E. Chang, M. Colón, A. Kapur, Z. Manna, H.B. Sipma, and T.E. Uribe. STeP: The Stanford Temporal Prover, User's Manual. Technical Report, Stanford University, 1995.

[BCM$^+$92] J.R. Burch, E.M. Clarke, K.L. McMillan, D.L. Dill, and J. Hwang. Symbolic model checking: 10^{20} states and beyond. *Information and Computation*, 98(2):142–170, 1992.

[BK85]   H. Barringer and R. Kuiper. Hierarchical development of concurrent systems in a temporal logic framework. In *Proc. of Seminar on Concurrency*, LNCS 197, 1985.

[CC95]   P. Collete and A. Cau. Parallel composition of assumption-commitment specifications: A unifying approach for shared variables and distributed message passing concurrency. *Acta Informatica*, 1995.

[CGL96]   E.M. Clarke, O. Grumberg, and D.E. Long. Model checking. In *Model Checking, Abstraction and Composition*, volume 152 of *Nato ASI Series F*, pages 477–498. Springer-Verlag, 1996.

[CM81]   K.M. Chandy and J. Misra. Proofs of networks of processes. *IEEE Trans. Software Engin.*, 7(4):417–426, 1981.

[dR85]   W.-P. de Roever. The quest for compositionality — a survey of assertion-based proof systems for concurrent programs, part i: Concurrency based on shared variables. In *The Role of Abstract Models in Computer Science*, pages 181–206. IFIP, North Holland, 1985.

[Hoa84]   C.A.R. Hoare. *Communicating Sequential Processes*. Prentice-Hall, 1984.

[Hol91]   G.J. Holzmann. *Design and Validation of Computer Protocols*. Prentice Hall, Engelwood Cliffs, NJ, 1991.

[Jon83]   C.B. Jones. Tentative steps towards a development method for interfering programs. *ACM Trans. Prog. Lang. Sys.*, 5(4):596–619, 1983.

[Jon94]   B. Jonsson. Compositional specification and verification of distributed systems. *ACM Trans. Prog. Lang. Sys.*, 16(2):259–303, 1994.

[KM95]   R.P. Kurshan and K.L. McMillan. A structural induction theorem for processes. *Information and Computation*, 117:1–11, 1995.

[KP98]   Y. Kesten and A. Pnueli. Deductive verification of fair discrete systems. Technical report, Weizmann Institute, 1998.

[KPR98]   Y. Kesten, A. Pnueli, and L. Raviv. Algorithmic verification of linear temporal logic specifications. In ICALP'98 pages 1–16.

[Lam77]   L. Lamport. Proving the correctness of multiprocess programs. *IEEE Trans. Software Engin.*, 3:125–143, 1977.

[MP90]   Z. Manna and A. Pnueli. A hierarchy of temporal properties. In *Proc. 9th ACM Symp. Princ. of Dist. Comp.*, pages 377–408, 1990.

[MP95]   Z. Manna and A. Pnueli. *Temporal Verification of Reactive Systems: Safety*. Springer-Verlag, New York, 1995.

[OSR93]   S. Owre, N. Shankar, and J.M. Rushby. User guide for the PVS specification and verification system. SRI International, Menlo Park, CA, 1993.

[PJ91]   P.K. Pandya and M. Joseph. P-A logic – a compositional proof system for distributed programs. *Dist. Comp.*, 5:37–54, 1991.

[Pnu85]   A. Pnueli. In transition from global to modular temporal reasoning about programs. In *Logics and Models of Concurrent Systems*, sub-series F: Computer and System Science, pages 123–144. Springer-Verlag, 1985.

[XdRH97]   Q.W. Xu, W.-P. de Roever, and J.-F. He. The rely-guarantee method for verifying shared variable concurrent programs. *Formal Aspects of Computing*, 9(2):149–174, 1997.

[Zwi89]   J. Zwiers. *Compositionality Concurrency and Partial Correctness*, volume 321 of *Lect. Notes in Comp. Sci.* Springer-Verlag, 1989.

Error Detection with Directed Symbolic Model Checking

Frank Reffel[1] and Stefan Edelkamp[2]

[1] Institut für Logik, Komplexität und Deduktionssysteme, Universität Karlsruhe,
reffel@ira.uka.de
[2] Institut für Informatik, Albert-Ludwigs-Universität Freiburg,
edelkamp@informatik.uni-freiburg.de

Abstract. In practice due to entailed memory limitations the most important problem in model checking is state space explosion. Therefore, to prove the correctness of a given design binary decision diagrams (*BDDs*) are widely used as a concise and symbolic state space representation. Nevertheless, *BDDs* are not able to avoid an exponential blow-up in general. If we restrict ourselves to find an error of a design which violates a safety property, in many cases a complete state space exploration is not necessary and the introduction of a heuristic to guide the search can help to keep both the explored part and the associated *BDD* representation smaller than with the classical approach.

In this paper we will show that this idea can be extended with an automatically generated heuristic and that it is applicable to a large class of designs. Since the proposed algorithm can be expressed in terms of *BDDs* it is even possible to use an existent model checker without any internal changes.

1 Introduction

To formulate the specification properties of a given design many different temporal logics are available, each of them with a different expressive power: (Fair-) CTL [6] is a branching time logic, LTL [18] is a linear time logic and CTL* [13] is a superset containing both of them. CTL* itself is a subset of the μ-calculus [17] which in addition allows to verify bisimulation and other more complex properties.

In practice, however, the characteristics people mainly try to verify are simple safety properties that are expressible in all of the logics mentioned above. They can be checked through a simple calculation of all reachable states. Unfortunately, this computation can become intractable for systems consisting of several asynchronously interacting modules.

Although *BDDs* [5] allow a succinct representation of a system they cannot always avoid an increase in *BDD*-sizes caused by the typical exponential blow-up of states. However, model checking is not only used to show the correctness of a complete system, but also as a very efficient method to find errors during the construction phase in order to avoid cost intensive correction phases later on.

J. Wing, J. Woodcock, J. Davies (Eds.): FM'99, Vol. I, LNCS 1708, pp. 195–211, 1999.
© Springer-Verlag Berlin Heidelberg 1999

In early design phases a system typically contains many errors such that nobody would expect a successful verification. We should try to detect these errors as soon as possible to avoid the calculation of the entire state space. Local model checking methods [14] attempt to exploit only a small part of the state space while global model checking techniques usually calculate all reachable states. Moreover, their fix-point calculation requires a backward traversal and a lot of work is spent in treating unreachable states. Hence, in order just to detect an error local model checking methods [24] can be more efficient. So a suitable application of model checking can replace parts of the classical debugging and testing work because it allows the detection of more errors in less time.

The method proposed in this paper focuses on safety properties. Starting with the set of initial states it performs a forward traversal of the system and exploits only that part of the set of reachable states that is most likely to lead to an error state. This is sufficient to construct a counter example of the violated property helping the designer to understand and fix the failure of the system. To guide the search a heuristic estimates the number of transition steps necessary to reach the error state. If the heuristic fulfills a certain property it guarantees the detection of a minimal counter example.

Our algorithm detects errors in systems unable to be verified by traditional symbolic model checking since the *BDDs* exhaust the available memory resources. Even if we assume pure forward traversal, after several iterations not containing an error state the large amount of states that has to be stored by an unguided search becomes too big; while heuristic search finds the error within an acceptable amount of time without suffering from memory problems.

Since all states have to be visited, our method fails to entirely validate a correct system, but this should be postponed until the end of the construction phase when most of the errors have been removed and the correctness of the system is more probable. The successful verification of large systems can be a very time consuming work which requires elaborated methods and a lot of experience. This results in a manually driven process with a lot of expertise demanding a specialist. We recommend a distinction of a verification to prove the correctness of a system and the use of a model checker as debugging tool, since the ultimate goal is to tediously prove the system only once and not after every detection and correction of an error.

The paper is structured as follows. In Section 2, we introduce some basics about *BDDs*. Section 3 addresses traditional symbolic model checking and Section 4 its proposed enhancement with a heuristic. The automatic inference of the heuristic is the topic of Section 5. Finally, Section 6 presents our results in verifying a buggy design of the tree-arbiter and the DME.

2   *BDD* Basics

Ordered binary decision diagrams (*OBDDs*) introduced by Bryant [5] are a graphical representation for boolean functions. A *BDD* $G(f, \pi)$ with respect to the function f and the variable ordering π is an acyclic graph with one source and two sinks labelled with *true* and *false*. All other (internal) nodes are labelled with a boolean variable x_i of f and have two outgoing edges *left* and *right*. For all edges from an x_i labelled node to an x_j labelled node we have $\pi(i) < \pi(j)$, such that on every path in G the variables are tested in the same order and at most once. Reduced *BDDs* with respect to a fixed variable ordering are a canonical representation for boolean functions. A *BDD* is reduced if isomorphic sub-*BDDs* are merged and nodes whose outgoing edges lead to the same successor are omitted. Reduced *BDDs* are build directly, integrating the reduction rules into the construction algorithm. The variable ordering π can be choosen freely, but it has a great influence on the size of the *BDDs*, e.g. there are functions which have *BDDs* of linear size for a "good" and of exponential size for a "bad" ordering. The determination of an optimal ordering is an NP-hard problem but, for most applications, there exist several heuristics for non-optimal but "good" orderings [2]. Another method to improve the ordering is dynamic variable reordering [23] which is applied during the verification in case the *BDDs* become too large. In the following we will only speak of *BDDs*, however, we always mean reduced ordered *BDDs*.

In model checking *BDDs* help to overcome the memory limitations of explicit state representation methods [19]. They represent both the sets of states and the transition relation. Model checking temporal logic properties can be reduced to the calculation of fix-points. This calculation can be performed efficiently treating lots of states in each iteration step.

An important task is to determine the set of reachable states. Starting with the set of initial states the fix-point iteration corresponds to a breadth-first-search until no more new states are found. This is sufficient to check safety and simple reachability properties. To verify more complicated properties typically a backward state traversal is applied to calculate the necessary fix-points. As a drawback many unreachable states have to be represented because the reachability status of a given state is not known at the beginning of the verification.

3   Model Checking

First we expose the structure of the transition relation and examine the calculations that have to be performed to check safety properties with a classical symbolic model checker. Thereafter, we discuss alternative methods that try to overcome the weaknesses of the breadth-first-search approach.

3.1   Traditional Symbolic Model Checking

In order to apply a model checker we need a description of the system and the safety property to be verified. The μ-calculus is an example of a logic in which both descriptions can be expressed. The two predicates *Start* and *Goal* describe the set of initial states and the set of error states, respectively. In addition a predicate *Trans* is required that evaluates to *true* if and only if there is a transistion between two successive states. For an interleaving model the predicate *Trans* is defined by the following equation:

$$Trans(State\ s, State\ t) = \bigvee_{i=1}^{n} Trans_i(s, t_i) \wedge CoStab_i(s, t).$$

Systems typically consist of several interacting modules. The interaction can be synchronous, asynchronous or interleaving. Here the verification of an interleaving model is described while for the verification of the other two models only small changes in the transition relation have to be made.

The predicate $CoStab_i$ describes that all modules except module i preserve their state and the predicate $Trans_i$ describes the transition relation of the single module i that might depend on the states of up to all other (n) modules but that only changes its own state s_i into t_i. The state of a single module consists of several (m) variables of type: bool, enumerated or integer (with limited values) or a combination of them. They are all translated into boolean variables such that for all modules we end up with an expression of the form:

$$Trans_i(State\ s, ModuleState\ t_i) = \bigwedge_{j=1}^{m} T_{i,j}(s, t_{i,j}),$$

where $t_{i,j}$ describes the state of variable j in module i. The transition $T_{i,j}$ of a single variable $s_{i,j}$ describes the possibility to change its value according to its input variables or to persist in its state. A backward traversal of the system then calculates the following fix-point:

$$\mu\ F_{Goal}(State\ s).Goal(s) \vee (\exists State\ succ.Trans(s, succ) \wedge F_{Goal}(succ)).$$

After determining the set of states satisfying this fix-point we check if it contains the initial state. As said above, the disadvantage of this approach is that many unreachable states have to be stored. The alternative is to start with the set of initial states and to make a forward traversal calculating the transitive closure *Reach* of the transition relation:

$$\mu\ Reach(State\ s).Start(s) \vee (\exists State\ prev.Trans(prev, s) \wedge Reach(prev)).$$

The efficiency can be improved: After each fix-point iteration we check if the set contains an error state in which case the verification can be aborted. Based on an interleaving (asynchronous) combination of modules, however, each order of transitions of the single modules has to be taken into account leading to state space explosion. Therefore, the sole calculation of reachable states might be impossible.

3.2   Other Approaches

An attempt to overcome the disadvantage of the unreachable states to be stored in a backward traversal is *local model checking* [7, 24]. It applies a depth-first search allowing an intelligent choice of the next state to be expanded. It significantly reduces the verification time in case properties are checked that do not necessarily require the traversal of the whole state space. In general, local model checking uses an explicit state representation such that it cannot take profit from the elegant and space efficient representation based on *BDDs*.

An attempt to combine *Partial order reduction* with *BDDs* was made in [1]. Nevertheless, it was not yet as successful as global *BDD*-model checking.

Bounded model checking performs symbolic model checking without *BDDs* using *SAT* decision procedures [4]. The transition relation is unrolled k steps for a bounded k. The bound is increased until an error is found or the bound is large enough to guarantee the correctness of a successful verification. The major disadvantage of bounded model checking is the fact that it is difficult to guarantee a successful verification, since the necessary bound will be rather large and difficult to determine. Therefore, similar to our approach the most important profit of this method is a fast detection of errors.

Validation with guided search [25] is the only other approach known to the authors which tries to profit from a heuristic to improve model checking. The measure is the Hamming distance, i.e. the minimum number of necessary bit-flips to transfer a given bit-vector of a state to an erroneous one. For our purposes this heuristic is too weak. The lower bound presented in Section 5 has a larger range of values leading to a better selection of states to be expanded. Furthermore, the pure effect of the heuristic is not clearly evaluated. The authors compare the number of visited and explored states with a breadth-first-search, but unfortunately the *BDD*-sizes for the state representation, the key performance measure, are not mentioned. It does not become clear which parts of the verification are performed with *BDDs* and which parts are dealt otherwise. The proposed approach is combined with two other methods: *target enlargements* and *tracks*. The former corresponds to a certain kind of bidirectional search, which is not a heuristic but a search strategy close to perimeter search [10] and the latter seems to be highly manually driven and not suitable for automatisation, one of our principal aims. The combination of their methods to find an error leads to good results, but in our opinion, it seems that the heuristic only contributes a small part to this advancement.

In contrast our algorithm entirely utilizes the *BDD* data structure such that the only interesting point are the sizes of the *BDDs* and not the number of states represented by it. In the examples of Section 6 the overall time and memory efficiency of our approach is shown to outperform traditional *BDD* breadth-first-search.

4   Directed Model Checking

In *BDD* based breadth-first-search all states on the search horizon are expanded in one iteration step. In contrast our approach is directed by a heuristic that determines a subset of the states on the horizon to be expanded which most promisingly leads to an error state. Non-symbolic heuristic search strategies are well studied. A* [15] is an advancement of Dijkstra's algorithm [8] for determining the shortest paths between two designated states within a graph.

The additional heuristic search information helps to avoid a blind breadth-first-search traversal but still suffers from the problem that a huge amount of states has to be stored. In this section an algorithm similar to A* is proposed to improve symbolic model checking.

4.1 *BDDA**

Edelkamp and Reffel have shown how *BDDs* help to solve heuristic single-agent search problems intractable for explicit state enumeration based methods [11]. The proposed algorithm *BDDA** was evaluated in the Fifteen-Puzzle and within Sokoban.

The approach exhibits a new trade-off between time and space requirements and tackles the most important problem in heuristic search, the overcoming of space limitations while avoiding a strong penalty in time. The experimental data suggests that *BDDA** challenges both breadth-first-search using *BDDs* and traditional *A**. Sokoban is intractable to be solved with explicit state enumeration techniques (unless very elaborated heuristics, problem graph compressions and pruning strategies are applied) and the Fifteen-Puzzle cannot be solved with traditional symbolic search methods. It is worthwhile to note that especially in the Sokoban domain only very little problem specific knowledge has been incorporated to regain tractability.

The approach was successfully applied in AI-planning [12]. The authors propose a planner that uses *BDDs* to compactly encode sets of propositionally represented states. Using this representation, accurate reachability analysis and backward chaining are apparently be carried out without necessarily encountering exponential representation explosion. The main objectives are the interest in optimal solutions, the generality and the conciseness of the approach. The algorithm is tested against a benchmark of planning problems and lead to substantial improvements to existing solutions. The most difficult problems in the benchmark set were only solvable when additional heuristic information in form of a (fairly easy) lower bound was given.

4.2 Heuristics and *A**

Let $h^*(s)$ be the length of the shortest path from s to a goal state and $h(s)$ its estimate. A heuristic is called *optimistic* if it is always a lower bound for the shortest path, i.e., for all states s we have $h(s) \leq h^*(s)$. It is called *consistent* if we have $h(u) \leq h(v) + 1$, with v being the successor of u on any solution path. Consistent heuristics are optimistic by definition and optimistic heuristics are also called *lower bounds*.

Heuristics correspond to a reweighting of the underlying problem graph. In the uniformly weighted graph we assign the following assignment to the edges $w(u, v) = 1 - h(u) + h(v)$. Fortunately, up to an additional offset the shortest paths values remain the same and no negative weighted loops are introduced.

Consistent heuristics correspond to a positively weighted graph, while optimistic heuristics may lead to negative weighted edges.

In A^* there are three sets. The set *Visited* of states already expanded, the set *Open* containing the states next to be expanded and the states which have not yet been encountered. During the calculation every state always belongs to exactly one of these sets. When a state is expanded it is moved from *Open* to *Visited* and all its successors are moved to *Open* unless they do not already belong to *Visited*. In this case they are inserted back to *Open* only if the current path is shorter than the one found before. This is done until the goal state is encountered or the set *Open* is empty. In the later case there exists no path between an initial state and a goal state. The correctness result of A^* states that given an optimistic estimate the algorithm terminates with the optimal solution length.

4.3   Tailoring $BDDA^*$ for Model Checking

In the *BDD* version of A^* the set *Visited* is omitted. To preserve correctness the successors of the expanded states are always inserted into *Open*. This relates to the expansion of the entire search tree corresponding to the reweighted graph. The closely related explicit state enumeration technique is iterative deepening A^*, IDA^* for short [16]. With an increasing bound on the solution length the search tree is traversed in depth-first manner. Note, IDA^* was the first algorithm that solved the Fifteen Puzzle. The admissibility of BDDA* is inherited by the fact that Korf has shown that given an optimistic heuristic IDA* finds an optimal solution.

For model checking omitting the set *Visited* turns out not to be a good choice in general such that the option to update the set of visited states in each iteration has been reincarnated. In difference to A^*, however, the length of the minimal path to each state is not stored. The closest corresponding single-state space algorithm is IDA^* with transposition tables [22]. Transposition tables store already encountered states to determine that a given state has already been visited. This pruning strategy avoids so-called *duplicates* in the search. However it is necessary to memorize the corresponding path length to guarantee admissibility for optimistic heuristics. Fortunately one can omit this additional information when only consistent heuristics are considered. In this case the resulting cost-function obtained by the sum of path length g and heuristic value h is monotone.

The set *Open* is a priority queue sorted according to the costs of the states. The costs of a state s is the sum of the heuristic and the number of steps necessary to reach s. The priority queue *Open* can be symbolically represented as a *BDD* *Open*(costs, state) in which the variables for the binary representation of the costs have smaller indices than those for the representation of states. In Figure 1 the algorithm is represented in pseudo code. The *BDD* *Open* corresponds to a partitioning of the states according to their costs.

Due to the variable ordering a new *BDD* operation (not included in standard *BDD* libraries) might efficiently combine three steps in the algorithm: the determination of the set of states with minimal costs contained in the queue, its costs f_{min}, and the new queue without these states. The function follows the path from the root node by always choosing the left successor – provided it does not directly lead to *false* – until the first state variable is encountered. This node is the root of *Min*, the persecuted path corresponds to the minimal costs f_{min}. The set *Open* excluding the just expanded states is obtained when *Min* is replaced by *false* probably followed by some necessary applications of the *BDD*-reduction rules.

Note, that the range of the costs has to be chosen adequately to avoid an overflow. To determine the set *Succ* the costs of the new states have to be calculated. As in *Open* only the costs of a state are stored and not the path-length the new costs are the result of the formula $f' - h' + 1 + h$ with f' and h' being the costs and the heuristic value of the predecessor. The value 1 is added for the effected transition and h is the estimate for the new state. Afterwards it remains to update the set *Visited* which is merged with *Min*. Furthermore the new states *Succ* are added to *Open* which should contain no states comprised in *Visited*.

Input *BDD Start* of the initial, *BDD Goal* of the erroneous states, *BDD Trans* representing the transition relation, and *BDD Heuristic* for the estimate of the entire search space.

Output "Error state found!" if the algorithm succeeds in finding the erroneous state, "Complete Exploration!", otherwise.

$Visited$(State s) := *false*
$Open$(Costs f, State s) := $Start$(s) $\wedge$ $Heuristic$(f,s)
while ($\exists$ s_1,f_1. $Open$(f_1,s_1))
    if ($\exists$ s',f'. $Open$(f',s') $\wedge$ $Goal$(s')) **return** "Error state found!"
    Min(f,s) := $Open$(f,s) $\wedge$ f=f_{min}
    $Succ$(f,s) := $\exists$ f',s',h,h'. $Heuristic$(h,s) $\wedge$ $Heuristic$(h',s') $\wedge$
        Min(f',s') $\wedge$ $Trans$(s',s) $\wedge$ f=f'$-$h'$+1+$h
    $Visited$(s) := $Visited$(s) $\vee$ $\exists$ f. Min(f,s)
    $Open$(f,s) := ($Open$(f,s) $\vee$ $Succ$(f,s)) $\wedge$ $\neg$ $Visited$(s)
return "Complete Exploration!"

Fig. 1. Heuristic based algorithm in Model Checking.

5   Inferring the Heuristic

The heuristic estimates the distance (measured in the number of transition steps) from a state to an error state. According to the type of the system such a step can have different meanings. For a synchronous system one step corresponds to one step in each module. In an asynchronous system a subset of all modules can perform a step and finally for an interleaving model exactly one module executes a transition. The challenging question is how to find a lower bound estimate (optimistic heuristic) for typical systems.

First of all, $h \equiv 0$ would be a valid choice, but in this case A^* exactly corresponds to breadth-first-search. Therefore, the values of the heuristic have to be positive to serve as an effective guidance in the search: The more diverse the heuristic values the better the classification of states. In this case we select most promising states for failure detection and distinguish them from the rest. As an effect in each iteration only a few states have to be expanded.

The next intuitive heuristic is the Hamming distance mentioned above. The measure is optimistic if in one transition only one x_i can change. Unfortunately, this is not true in general. The main drawback of this heuristic, however, is that in general the number of variables necessary to define an error state are few in comparison to the number of state variables. Hence, the Hamming distance typically has a small range of values and the number of different partitions of states are too less to significantly reduce the number of states to be expanded.

In the sequel we propose an automatic construction of a heuristic only based on the safety property and the structure of the transition function. We assume that the formula f describing the error states is a boolean formula using $\wedge$ and $\vee$ while negation is only applied directly to variables. In CTL the safety property with respect to the property f is denoted by $AG(\neg f)$.

5.1   Definition

Table 1 describes the transformation of the formula f into a heuristic Heu_f. In the first two cases the sub-formulas f_k must not contain another $\vee$-operator (respectively $\wedge$) at the top level.

$$
Heu_f(s) = \begin{cases}
\min_{k=1,\ldots,n} Heu_{f_k}(s), & \text{if } f = f_1 \vee \cdots \vee f_n \\
\max_{k=1,\ldots,n} Heu_{f_k}(s), & \text{if } f = f_1 \wedge \cdots \wedge f_n \\
Heu_{s_{i,j}}(s), & \text{if } f = s_{i,j} \\
Heu_{\overline{s_{i,j}}}(s), & \text{if } f = \overline{s_{i,j}}
\end{cases}
$$

Table 1. Property-dependent determination of heuristic values.

With this construction the heuristic value depends only on $Heu_{s_{i,j}}(s)$ and $Heu_{\overline{s_{i,j}}}(s)$ which rely on the structure of the transition relation. As explained in Section 3.1 the transition of variable j in module i is described by $T_{i,j}(s, t_{i,j})$. The devices $T_{i,j}$ are typically some standard electronic elements such as the logical operators *or, and, xor*, etc. In a general setting, however, they can be arbitrary formulas.

Table 2 exemplarily depicts the values for the function $Heu_{s_{i,j}}$ for every binary boolean formula. For a general boolean function $s_{i,j} = g : B^n \mapsto B$ with n arguments the sub-function $Heu_{s_{i,j}}(s)$ has the following value:

$$
\min_{x \in B^n | g(x)=1} \{ \max_{i \in \{1..n\}} \{\text{number of transitions necessary until } s_i = x_i\}\}
$$

Lemma 1. $\text{Heu}_{s_{i,j}}(s)$ *is a lower bound for the number of transitions which are necessary to reach a state from s where $s_{i,j} = true$.*

Proof. The property will be shown by induction on the refinement depth:

Refinement depth 0: In this case we have $\text{Heu}_{s_{i,j}} = \text{if }(s_{i,j})\text{ then }0\text{ else }1$.
(The argumentation for negated variables $\overline{s_{i,j}}$ is similar.) If $s_{i,j}$ is *true* no transition step is necessary. Hence, $\text{Heu}_{s_{i,j}}(s) = 0$. In case $s_{i,j}$ is *false* at least one transition step has to be made to change its value. Therefore, $\text{Heu}_{s_{i,j}}(s) = 1$ is a lower bound.

Refinement depth k: We will suppose that for a refinement depth less than k the functions $\text{Heu}_{s_{i,j}}$ fulfill the desired property. After the first application of a rule from Table 2 for the introduced formulae Heu_{x_i} we have a refinement depth of $k - 1$. This implies that it takes at least Heu_{x_i} steps to change the values of the involved variables. It depends on the formula $g(x_1, x_2)$ which changes the value of $s_{i,j}$ that it is necessary for both variables x_1 and x_2 to have a certain value, or that it is sufficient that one of them has a certain value. This determines if the minimum or the maximum of the involved functions Heu_{x_i} is used. In both cases after the variables x_1 and x_2 have been assigned to a value, which allows g to change the value of $s_{i,j}$ from *false* to *true*, at least one additional step is necessary. Therefore, 1 can be added and $\text{Heu}_{s_{i,j}}$ still remains a lower bound.   ∎

Using Lemma 1 it it quite easy to prove that Heu_f according to the construction introduced above is a lower bound estimate.

Theorem 1. *The function Heu_f is optimistic.*

Proof. It remains to show that the rules of Table 1 lead to an optimistic heuristic since the sub-functions $\text{Heu}_{s_{i,j}}$ underestimate the number of transitions necessary to achieve the desired value for $s_{i,j}$. This can be shown easily by induction on the number of applications of the rules of Table 1 so we will only explain the main idea for the proof.

It is based on the fact that for an $\vee$-formula it is sufficient that one of the f_i becomes *true*, so the minimum of the Heu_{f_i} is chosen and for an $\wedge$-formula all f_i have to be fulfilled so the maximum of the Heu_{f_i} can be chosen for the heuristic value.   ∎

Note, that for an asynchronous or a synchronous system in one transition step the values of various variables can change, therefore it is not possible to summarize over the Heu_{f_i} for example in case of an $\wedge$-formula. In contrast, for an interleaving model the sum could be used if the f_i depend on variables in different modules because only one module can change its state in a single transition.

As already indicated to guarantee the computation of the minimal counterexample in the proposed extension to $BDDA^*$ it is not sufficient to use an optimistic heuristic. Fortunately, it is possible to show the consistency of our automatically constructed heuristic:

Theorem 2. *The function* Heu_f *is consistent.*

Proof. We have to show that

$$\forall State\ s, t.\ Trans(s, t) \Rightarrow Heu_f(s) \leq 1 + Heu_f(t).$$

This property follows directly from the fact that for all variables x we have

$$\forall State\ s, t.\ Trans(s, t) \Rightarrow Heu_x(s) \leq 1 + Heu_x(t).$$

We will prove this by induction on the refinement depth similar to Lemma 1. For a refinement depth of 0 there is nothing to prove because $Heu_x(s) \leq 1$. For refinement depth k we will show the property for the operator $\wedge$ (cf. Table 2). In this case $Heu_x(s)$ is defined as $1 + \max\{Heu_{x_1}(s), Heu_{x_2}(s)\}$. For Heu_{x_1} and Heu_{x_2} we have a refinement depth of $k - 1$ so the property holds for these formulas:

$$Heu_x(s) \leq 1 + \max\{1 + Heu_{x_1}(t), 1 + Heu_{x_2}(t)\}$$
$$\leq 1 + (1 + \max\{Heu_{x_1}(t), Heu_{x_2}(t)\})$$
$$\leq 1 + Heu_x(t)$$

The proof for the other operators of Table 2 is analogue expect for the operator $\not\leftrightarrow$. The interesting case is a transition where in state s the variables x_1 and x_2 are assigned to *true* and in state t both variables are assigned to *false*. In this case the structure of the formula changes: For state s we have

$$Heu_x(s) = 1 + \min\{Heu_{\overline{x_1}}(s), Heu_{\overline{x_2}}(s)\}$$

and in state t we establish

$$Heu_x(t) = 1 + \min\{Heu_{x_1}(t), Heu_{x_2}(t)\}.$$

The circumstance that there is a transition from s to t which changes the values of x_1 and x_2 from *true* to *false* implies that $Heu_{\overline{x_1}}(s) = Heu_{\overline{x_2}}(s) = 1$ and $Heu_x(s) = 2$ while for state t we have $Heu_{x_1}(t), Heu_{x_2}(t) \geq 1$. Therefore, the following equation completes the proof:

$$Heu_x(t) = 1 + \min\{Heu_{x_1}(t), Heu_{x_2}(t)\} \geq 1 + \min\{1, 1\} = 2 = Heu(s)$$

∎

Note, that breadth-first-search finds the error state in the minimal number of iterations. In contrast in the heuristic search approach several states remain unexpanded in each iteration such that the number of necessary iteration steps increases. In the worst case we have a quadratic growth in the number of iterations [11]. On the other hand, especially for large systems, a transition step expanding only a small subset of the states is much faster than a transition based on all states. Therefore, this apparent disadvantage even turns out to be very time-efficient surplus as the examples in the next section will show.

6   Experimental Results

In our experiments we used the μ-calculus model checker μcke [3] which accepts the full μ-calculus for its input language [20]. The *while*-loop has to be converted into a least fix-point. As it is not possible to change two sets (*Open, Visited*) in the body of one fix-point the *Visited* set is simulated by one slot in the *BDD* for *Open*. The next problem is that the function for *Open* is not monotone because states are deleted from it after they have been expanded. Monotony is a sufficient criterion to guarantee the existence of fix-points. The function for *Open* is not a syntactic correct μ-calculus formula but as the termination of the algorithm is guaranteed by the monotony of the set *Visited* we can apply the standard algorithm for the calculation of μ-calculus fix-points.

Unfortunately, we cannot take advantage of the special *BDD* operation determining the set of states with minimal costs in this case. These calculations have to be simulated by standard operations leading to some unnecessary overhead that in the visible future has to be avoided in a customized implementation.

For the evaluation of our approach we use the example of the tree-arbiter [9] a mechanism for distributed mutual exclusion: $2n$ user want to use a resource which is available only once and the tree-arbiter manages the requests and acknowledges avoiding a simultaneous access of two different users. The tree-arbiter consists of $2n - 1$ modules of the same structure such that it is very easy to scale the example. Since we focus on error detection we experiment with an earlier incorrect version – also published in [9] – using an interleaving model.

The heuristic was devised according to the description in Section 5 with a refinement-depth of 6. We also experimented with larger depths which implied a reduction neither in time nor in size. Since the algorithm for the automatic construction of the heuristic has not yet been implemented and since the number of different errors increases very fast with the size of the tree-arbiter we searched for the detection of a special error case. Table 4 shows the results in comparison with a classical forward breadth-first-search. To guarantee the fairness of the comparison we terminated the search at the time the error state has first been encountered.

For the tree-arbiter with 15 modules or less the traditional approach is faster and less memory consuming, but for larger systems its time and memory efficiency decreases very fast. On the other hand, the heuristic approach found the error even in large systems, since its memory and time requirements increases slowly. For the tree-arbiter with 23 modules the error could not be found with breadth-first-search and already for the version with 21 modules 9 garbage collections were necessary not to exceed the memory limitations, whereas the first garbage collection with the heuristic method was invoked at a system of 27 modules. For the tree-arbiter with 27 modules we also experimented with the heuristic. When we double its values the heuristic fails to be optimistic, but the error detection becomes available without any garbage collection. Moreover, although more than three times more iterations were necessary only about 8% more time was consumed. This illustrates that there is much room for further research in refinements of the heuristic.

# Mod	#it	BFS max nodes	time	depth	#it	Heuristic max nodes	time
15	30	991374	46s	4	104	10472785	483s
				6	127	5715484	288s
17	42	18937458	3912s	6	157	7954251	476s
19	44	22461024	6047s	6	157	8789341	540s
21	44	26843514	24626s(9)	6	157	9097823	530s
23	>40	-	>17000s	6	157	9548269	516s
25	-	-	-	6	169	21561058	1370s
27	-	-	-	6	169	25165795	1818s(1)
				6(x2)	593	23798202	1970s

Table 4. Results for the tree-arbiter. In parenthesis the number of garbage collections is given.

The second example we used for the evaluation of our approach is the asynchronous DME [9]. Like the tree-arbiter it consists of n identical modules and it is also a mechanism for distributed mutual exclusion. The modules are arranged in a ring structure whereas the modules of the tree-arbiter form a pyramid. In this case we also experimented with the set *Visited* and it turns out that it was more efficient to omit it like proposed in [11]. For this variation only a small change in the calculation of *Open* is necessary. Like in the previous example the results in Table 5 show that the heuristic approach is more memory efficient and less time-consuming. The first experiment in the Table uses the set *Visited* that was omitted in the other experiments. This led to a greater iteration depth because several states are visited more than once. Nevertheless this turned out to be more time and memory efficient. The increase of the refinement-depth to 7 allows to reduce the verification time and no garbage collection remains necessary.

# Mod	#it	BFS max nodes	time	depth	#it	Heuristic max nodes	time
6	23	26843514	5864s(5)	6v	35	29036025	2207s(4)
				6	53	25165795	1009s(1)
				7	53	25159862	813s(0)

Table 5. Results for the asynchronous DME. In parenthesis the number of garbage collections is given.

7   Conclusion and Discussion

We presented how a heuristic can successfully be integrated into symbolic model checking. It is recommended to distinguish between the use of a model checker in order to prove a property and the use as a debugging tool. For debugging exhaustive search of the reachable state space can be avoided and the heuristic can decrease both the number of expanded states and the *BDD*-sizes which allows the treatment of bigger systems. It was shown how a heuristic can be automatically designed for a large class of systems allowing the application of this method also for non-experts.

The experiments demonstrated the effectiveness of the approach and we plan to test the algorithm with more example data and to evaluate further refinements of the heuristic and its construction.

There are lots of choices for an experienced user to modify and improve the estimate or even to use non-optimistic heuristics allowing a better partitioning of the state space. This can be more important than the determination of the minimal counter-example. Pearl [21] discusses limits and possibilities of over-estimations in corresponding explicit search algorithms. One proposed search scheme, called $WIDA^*$, considers costs of the form $f = \alpha g + (1-\alpha)h$. If $\alpha \in [.5, 1]$ the algorithm is admissible. In case $\alpha \in [0, .5)$ the algorithm searches according to overestimations of the heuristic value compared to the path length g. The literature clearly lacks theoretical and practical results for symbolic searches according to non-optimistic heuristics.

Acknowledgments

F. Reffel is supported by DFG within the graduate program on *Controllability of Complex Systems*. S. Edelkamp is associated member in a DFG project entitled *Heuristic Search and Its Application in Protocol Verification*.

We thank the anonymous referees for the interesting comments and suggestions.

References

[1] R. Alur, R. Brayton, T. Henzinger, S. Qaderer, and S. Rajamani. Partial-order reduction in symbolic state space exploration. In *Computer Aided Verification*, volume 1254 of *LNCS*, pages 340–351, 1997.

[2] A. Biere. *Effiziente μ-Kalkül Modellprüfung mit Binären Entscheidungsdiagrammen*. PhD thesis, Fakultät für Informatik, Universität Karlsruhe, 1997.

[3] A. Biere. mucke - efficient μ-calculus model checking. In *Computer Aided Verification*, volume 1254 of *LNCS*, pages 468–471, 1997.

[4] A. Biere, A. Cimatti, E. Clarke, and Y. Zhu. Symbolic model checking without BDDs. In *Tools and Algorithms for the Construction and Analysis of Systems*, 1999. to appear.

[5] R. Bryant. Graph based algorithms for boolean function manipulation. *IEEE Transactions on Computers*, C-35(8):677–691, 1986.

[6] E. Clarke, O. Grumberg, and D. Long. Verification tools for finite-state concurrent systems. In *A Decade of Concurrency*, volume 803 of *LNCS*, pages 124–175. REX School Symposium, Springer, 1993.

[7] R. Cleaveland. Tableau-based model checking in the propositional μ-calculus. *Acta Inf.*, 27:725–747, 1990.

[8] E. W. Dijkstra. A note on two problems in connection with graphs. *Numerical Mathematics*, 1(5):269–271, 1959.

[9] D. L. Dill. *Trace Theory for Automatic Hierarchical Verification of Speed-Independent Circuits*. An ACM Distinguished Dissertation. The MIT Press, 1988.

[10] J. F. Dillenburg and P. C. Nelson. Perimeter search (research note). *Artificial Intelligence*, 65(1):165–178, Jan. 1994.

[11] S. Edelkamp and F. Reffel. OBDDs in heuristic search. In O. Herzog and A. Günter, editors, *Proceedings of the 22nd Annual German Conference on Advances in Artificial Intelligence (KI-98)*, volume 1504 of *LNAI*, pages 81–92. Springer, 1998.

[12] S. Edelkamp and F. Reffel. Deterministic state space planning with BDDs. Technical Report 120, Institut für Informatik, Universität Freiburg, 1999.

[13] E. A. Emerson and J. Srinivasan. Branching time temporal logic. In *REX workshop*, volume 354 of *LNCS*, pages 123–172. Springer-Verlag, 1989.

[14] J. C. Fernandez, L. Mounier, C. Jard, and T. Jéron. On-the-fly verification of finite transition systems. *Formal Methods in System Design*, 1:251–273, 1992.

[15] P. Hart, N. Nilsson, and B. Raphael. A formal basis for the heuristic determination of minimum cost paths. *IEEE Transactions of Systems Science and Cybernetics*, SCC-4(2):100–107, 1968.

[16] R. E. Korf. Depth-first iterative-deepening: An optimal admissible tree search. *Artificial Intelligence*, 27(1):97–109, 1985. reprinted in Chapter 6 of *Expert Systems, A Software Methodology for Modern Applications*, P.G. Raeth (Ed.), IEEE Computer Society Press, Washington D.C., 1990, pp. 380-389.

[17] D. Kozen. Results on the propositional μ-calculus. *Theoretical Computer Science*, 27:333–354, 1983.

[18] O. Lichtenstein and A. Pnueli. Checking that finite state concurrent programs satisfy their linear specification. In *Proceedings of the Twelfth Annual ACM Symposium on Principles of Programming Languages*, pages 97–107, New York, 1985. ACM.

[19] K. McMillan. *Symbolic Model Checking*. Kluwer Academic Press, 1993.

[20] D. Park. Concurrency and automata on infinite sequences. In P. Deussen, editor, *Theoretical Computer Science, 5th GI Conference*, volume 104 of *LNCS*, pages 167–183. Springer, 1981.

[21] J. Pearl. *Heuristics : Intelligent search strategies for computer problem solving*. Addison-Wesley series in Artificial Intelligence. Addison-Wesley, 1984.

[22] A. Reinefeld and T. A. Marsland. Enhanced iterative-deepening search. *IEEE Transactions on Pattern Analysis and Machine Intelligence*, 16(7):701–710, 1994.

[23] R. Rudell. Dynamic variable ordering for ordered binary decision diagrams. In *International Conference on Computer-Aided Design*, pages 139–144. IEEE, 1993.

[24] C. Stirling and D. Walker. Local model checking in the modal μ-claculus. *Theoretical Computer Science*, 89:161–177, 1991.

[25] C. H. Yang and D. Dill. Validation with guided search of the state space. In *35nd Design Automation Conference*, 1998.

Formal Modeling and Analysis of Hybrid Systems: A Case Study in Multi-robot Coordination

R. Alur[1], J. Esposito[2], M. Kim[1], V. Kumar[2], and I. Lee[1]

[1] Department of Computer and Information Science, University of Pennsylvania.
alur,moonjoo,lee@cis.upenn.edu
[2] Department of Mechanical Engineering and Applied Mechanics,
University of Pennsylvania.
jme,kumar@grip.cis.upenn.edu

Abstract. The design of controllers for hybrid systems (i.e. mixed discrete-continuous systems) in a systematic manner remains a challenging task. In this case study, we apply formal modeling to the design of communication and control strategies for a team of autonomous robots to attain specified goals in a coordinated manner. The model of linear hybrid automata is used to describe the high-level design, and the verification software HyTech is used for symbolic analysis of the description. The goal of the project is to understand tradeoffs among various design alternatives by generating constraints among parameters using symbolic analysis. In this paper, we report on difficulties in modeling a team of robots using linear hybrid automata, results of analysis experiments, promise of the approach, and challenges for future research.

1 Introduction

A hybrid system typically consists of a collection of digital programs that interact with each other and with an analog environment. Examples of hybrid systems include manufacturing controllers, automotive and flight controllers, medical equipment, micro-electro-mechanical systems, and robots.

Designing reliable hybrid systems is a challenging task. Control theoretic tools enable the design of continuous controllers in a single mode of operation. While nonlinear switching controllers have been designed for systems with several modes of operation (see [Bra95, Utk77, ZB98]), the techniques are generally only applicable for simple systems with relatively few modes. Nonlinear systems are, in general, solved on a case by case basis. Even when solutions exist, the properties of the design such as stability, convergence and reachability only apply within certain limited operating regimes. Typically the state-space for hybrid systems can be partitioned into many regions so that within each region a different control law with predictable performance can be designed. Variations on this theme can be found in the literature on variable structure systems [Utk77] and on multimodal systems [NBC95]. By selecting the state-space partitions so

J. Wing, J. Woodcock, J. Davies (Eds.): FM'99, Vol. I, LNCS 1708, pp. 212–232, 1999.

that regions of interest overlap and by designing controllers with stable equilibrium points which lie in the overlap, it is possible to control the transition from mode to mode with predictable performance. However, requiring stable equilibria to lie in the given regions is difficult in all but the simplest topological spaces. A game-theoretic approach to designing controllers for hybrid systems with a hierarchical structure is shown to be applicable to automated highway systems [LGS95, TPS97]. However, the the hierarchy is designed manually, and the solution often requires very strict assumptions and constraints.

Inspired by the success of automated formal methods in discovering subtle errors in hardware designs (cf. [CK96]), a current trend is to investigate if these techniques can be generalized to obtain design aids for hybrid systems (the proceedings of the workshops on hybrid systems provide an excellent survey of emerging trends [GNRR93, AKNS95, AHS96, Mal97, HS98]).

The methodology advocated by formal approaches to system design requires construction of a high-level description or a (mathematical) *model* of the system. The model can then be subjected to a variety of mathematical analyses such as simulation, model checking, and performance evaluation. Such modeling and analysis can be performed in early stages of the design, and offers the promise of a more systematic approach and greater automation during the design phase.

The formal analysis of the mixed digital-analog nature of hybrid systems requires a mathematical model that incorporates the discrete behavior of computer programs with the continuous behavior of environment variables such as time, position, and temperature. The model of our choice is the *hybrid automaton*—a finite automaton augmented with a finite number of real-valued variables that change continuously, as specified by differential equations and differential inequalities [ACH+95]. Algorithmic analysis of hybrid systems is a challenging problem since the presence of continuous variables results in an infinite statespace, and even the simplest analysis problems turn out to be undecidable. However, useful analysis can be performed for a class of hybrid systems called *linear hybrid automata*. The analysis procedure involves symbolic fix-point computation over state-sets that are represented by linear constraints over system variables, and can be implemented using routines to manipulate convex polyhedra. The procedure has been implemented in the tool HYTECH [AHH96, HHW97], and has been applied to case studies such as audio-control protocol [HW95] and steam boiler [HW96].

In this paper, we explore the application of formal modeling and analysis to design of multi-robot coordination based upon an experimental testbed of a system of autonomous, mobile robots. We consider a task that involves exploring a room with unknown geometry and with obstacles, and identifying and locating an obstacle. The experimental system and the task is motivated by military applications (scouting, reconnaisance, and surveillance) and the need to minimize human intervention in hazardous environments a wide range of civilian applications including space and nuclear facilities. Typically, the sensory capabilities of each robot yield only imperfect information about the world and in particular, each robot has only estimates about the positions of the obstacles. Our robots are equipped with omnidirectional cameras, and they operate in a two-dimensional world. We make the realistic assumption that the errors in estimates of the position and geometry of a candidate object (target or obstacle) decrease as the robot gets closer to the object. The control of a single robot requires image processing algorithms for interpreting the visual information, computer vision algorithms for building a model of the objects around the robot and for localizing the position of the robot, and planning algorithms for selecting a local direction for steering or for selecting a control law. We can abstract this problem and reduce it to the two subproblems of building estimates of the positions and shapes of objects around the robot and of planning a path around the objects to a target goal. When there are multiple robots that can communicate with one another, they can communicate and share knowledge about the world. For instance, two robots can exchange their individual estimates about a specific obstacle, conclude that the obstacle must lie within the region consistent with both the estimates, and employ this information for better path planning. The challenge, then, is to design communication protocols, in conjunction with control strategies, so that the team of robots achieves its goal in a coordinated and optimal manner. This design problem is not unlike the design problems encountered in a wide range of hybrid systems including intelligent vehicle systems and flight management systems.

Traditionally, verification tools such as KRONOS [DOTY96], UPPAAL [LPY97] and HYTECH have been used to detect logical errors by checking whether a high-level model satisfies a temporal logic requirement. For us, the goal of formal modeling and analysis is to explore and compare various design alternatives. For instance, even for simple communication and control strategies, we need to set various parameters such as the number of robots, the initial positions of the robots, the frequency of communication, the cost of communication (e.g., time required to process messages), and the positions of obstacles and target. Standard simulation, using a tool like MATLAB (see www.mathworks.com), requires fixed setting of all such parameters. In a verification tool such as HYTECH, such parameters can be left unspecified, and the tool performs an *exhaustive symbolic search* for all possible settings of the parameters. The information computed by the tool, then, can be used to understand the various tradeoffs.

After reviewing the basics of formal verification of hybrid automata and the state of the art in design of hybrid controllers in Section 2, we explain the general scenario of experimental testbed of coordinating robots in Section 3. The main effort in this case study concerns modeling the application scenario using linear hybrid automata. The modeling issues are discussed in detail in Section 4. Linear hybrid automata require all expressions to be linear, and all differential constraints to be constant rectangular inclusions. It is worth noting that in previous case studies in formal verification of hybrid systems, the challenge in modeling was approximating complex dynamics by rectangular inclusions. For us, the continuous dynamics is quite simple, but a significant approximation is required to make guard conditions and update rules linear. For instance, we model obstacles and their estimates as rectangles, approximate Euclidean distance by

Manhattan distance, and require the robot to move only along horizontal or vertical directions.

The results of the analysis experiments are reported in Section 5. Since the analysis is computationally expensive, we could successfully analyze only special cases of the scenario. In particular, for two robots and one obstacle, HyTech could synthesize the region of the possible positions of the target for which communication improves the distance traveled. While modest, this experiment does yield information that is computed automatically by a general-purpose tool.

In summary, the paper serves two purposes. First, it shows the promise, and the road-map, for applying tools for formal modeling and analysis to the problem domain of multi-robot coordination. Second, we believe that the outlined scenario will serve as a challenge problem to guide the research in formal verification of hybrid systems.

2   Verification of Hybrid Systems

A hybrid automaton [ACH$^+$95] is a formal model to describe reactive systems with discrete and continuous components. Formally, a hybrid automaton H consists of the following components.

- A finite directed multi-graph (V, E). The vertices are called the *control modes* while the edges are called the *control switches*.
- A finite set of real valued variables X. A *valuation* ν is a function that assigns a real value $\nu(x)$ to each variable $x \in X$. The set of all valuations is denoted Σ_X. A *state* q is a pair (v, ν) consisting of a mode v and a valuation ν. The set of all states is denoted Σ. A *region* is a subset of Σ.
- A function *init*, that assigns to each mode v, a set $init(v) \subseteq \Sigma_X$ of valuations. This describes the initialization of the system: a state (v, ν) is initial if $\nu \in init(v)$. The region containing all initial states is denoted σ^I.
- A function *flow*, that assigns to each mode v, a set $flow(v)$ of C^∞-functions from R^+ to Σ_X. This describes the way variables can evolve in a mode.
- A function *inv*, that assigns to each mode v, a set $inv(v) \subseteq \Sigma_X$ of valuations. The system can stay in mode v only as long as the state is within $inv(v)$, and a switch must be taken before the invariant gets violated.
- A function *jump*, that assigns to each switch e, a set $jump(e) \subseteq \Sigma_X \times \Sigma_X$. This describes the enabling condition for a switch, together with the discrete update of the variables as a result of the switch.
- A function *syn*, that assigns to each switch e, a label $syn(e)$ from a set of labels (names). When different components of a complex system are described individually by hybrid automata, the event-labels on switches of different components are used for synchronization.

The hybrid automaton H starts in an initial state. During its execution, its state can change in one of the two ways. A *discrete* change causes the automaton to change both its control mode and the values of its variables. Otherwise, a *continuous* activity causes only the values of variables to change according to the specified flows while maintaining the invariants. The operational semantics of the hybrid automaton are captured by defining transition relations over the state space Σ. For a switch $e = (v, v')$, we write $(v, \nu) \rightarrow_e (v', \nu')$ if $(\nu, \nu') \in jump(e)$. For a mode v and a time increment $\delta \in R^+$, we write $(v, \nu) \rightarrow_\delta (v, \nu')$ if there exists a function $f \in flow(v)$ such that $f(0) = \nu$, $f(\delta) = \nu'$, and $f(\delta') \in inv(v)$ for all $0 \leq \delta' \leq \delta$. The transition relations $\rightarrow_e$ capture the discrete dynamics, while the transition relations $\rightarrow_\delta$ capture the continuous dynamics.

A key operation on hybrid automata is the *product* operation. For two hybrid automata H_1 and H_2, the product $H_1 \| H_2$ is defined to be another hybrid automaton that describes the behavior of the composite system with two concurrent components. The formal definition of product can be found in [AHH96]. Note that the component automata can have shared variables to communicate, and in addition, can synchronize transitions using common labels on jumps.

Algorithms for symbolic reachability analysis of hybrid automata manipulate regions. Let σ be a region of H. The *successor region of* σ, denoted $post(\sigma)$, contains states q' such that $q \rightarrow_e q'$ for some $q \in \sigma$ and some switch e, or $q \rightarrow_\delta q'$ for some $q \in \sigma$ and some $\delta \in R^+$. A state q is said to be reachable if $q \in post^i(\sigma^I)$ for some natural number i. The set of reachable states of a hybrid automaton H is denoted $reach(H)$.

The central problem in algorithmic formal verification of hybrid systems is to compute the set of reachable states of a given hybrid automaton. The set of all reachable states of a hybrid automaton can be computed by repeatedly applying *post* to the initial region. For a special class of automata, called *linear hybrid automata*, all the regions encountered during the computation can be described by boolean combinations of linear inequalities over automaton variables.

A hybrid automaton $H = (V, E, X, init, flow, jump, syn)$ is called *linear* if

1. For each mode v, the sets $init(v)$ and $inv(v)$ are described by boolean combinations of linear inequalities over the variables X.
2. For each switch e, $jump(e)$ is described by a boolean combination of linear inequalities over the variables $X \cup X'$, where the primed variables X' refer to the values of the variables in X after the switch.
3. For each mode v, allowed flows at a mode v are specified by a conjunction of linear inequalities over the set $\dot{X}$ of dotted variables representing the first derivatives of the corresponding variables in X. That is, a C^∞-function f belongs to $flow(v)$ iff the first derivative $\dot{f}$ of f with respect to time satisfies each linear inequality for all times $\delta \in R^+$.

The above requirements ensure that for each i, the set $post^i(\sigma^I)$ can be described by a boolean combination of linear inequalities [ACH+95]. Furthermore, such sets can be computed effectively. The software HYTECH [AHH96, HHW97] supports model checking of hybrid systems based on the above principles. The implementation is based on routines to manipulate convex polyhedra.

The input of HYTECH consists of two parts: system description section and analysis section. The system description section has a textual representation of linear hybrid automata. The user describes a system as the composition of a collection of components. The analysis section verifies the system against user-defined properties. This section contains definitions of regions, each of which represents a set of states in the system and commands for manipulating these regions. Properties are checked by reachability test of region. For example, to verify a property that a robot never collides with obstacles, we define a region of collision states. Then we show this region is not reachable from the initial region.

The input to HyTech can include *design parameters*—symbolic constants with unknown, but fixed values. Such parameters are treated just like any other system variables. Given a correctness requirement, HyTech uses the symbolic computation to determine necessary and sufficient constraints on the parameters under which violations of the requirement cannot occur. This feature of *parametric analysis* is central to our application as discussed later in Section 4.

3   Multirobot Coordination

3.1   A Typical Scenario

Consider the scenario in which a small team of robots enters a room with obstacles, identifies and locates a target object, and retrieves this object from the room as shown in Figure 1. In the figure, the team consists of five robots, designated as R_1 through R_5. The obstacles are denoted by A through E and the target is denoted by T. In order to keep the problem simple we assume that the geometry is two dimensional. Each robot is equipped with a camera that allows it to identify other robots, obstacles and the target. The sensor has errors in estimating the position of objects (obstacles, targets and other robots) that decrease as the robot approaches the object. Typically, it is necessary for the robot to get within some threshold distance before it can make a positive identification. In addition, each robot has the ability to determine its own position and orientation. This may come from an independent sensor or from the camera and landmarks in the environment. The robots are able to communicate over a wireless local area network. However, because of the bandwidth limitations and the possible clandestine nature of the mission, the communication either may not be possible, or may be limited to sporadic broadcast of a small volume of data. Each robot is controlled independently and is able to move in the room. Although there is no central controller, it is possible to have a situation in which a robot assumes the role of the leader, issues commands to and obtains reports from all other robots in the team, and thus all the decision making is centralized. Finally, the target's shape and size are such that it requires at least two robots to cooperatively transport the object.

As shown in the initial configuration in Figure 1, the team of small robots enters the room. They may or may not have a nominal model of the room. Even if they have a nominal model, there will always be a need to identify and locate features (obstacles, targets and the walls) in the room. The robots disperse to search the room. As they search the room, they identify and locate obstacles. The communication protocol allows the robots to exchange information about

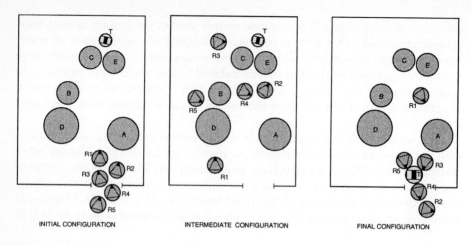

INITIAL CONFIGURATION   INTERMEDIATE CONFIGURATION   FINAL CONFIGURATION

Fig. 1. A robot team searching a room with obstacles, to locate and retrieve a target

their position and orientation, the identity and the position of objects in the room. They may also be able to communicate with each other, and thus, the actions of one can depend on the plans of others.

One of the robots (R_3) eventually locates the target as shown in the intermediate configuration in the figure. When the other robots get this information, they stop searching for the target and organize themselves into a formation. Two or three robots (R_4, R_3, and R_5 in the figure) organize themselves around the target object in order to move the object. The other robot(s) (R_2 in the figure) may lead the robots with the target object and act as scouts as shown in the possible final configuration in the figure. It is quite possible that one or more robots may fail. As shown in the figure, robot R_1, the team leader in the initial configuration, has an actuator failure and is left stranded. However, the team, which now consists of the four remaining robots, successfully completes the mission.

In this scenario, each robot is driven by actuators and sensors that are intrinsically continuous. The dynamics are derived from laws of physics and are represented by continuous mathematics. Therefore the robot behavior is continuous. However, this behavior changes, possibly discontinuously, as new information becomes available or as new events occur. For example, a robot pursuing the identification of an object that is possibly the target object, abandons this course of action when it is told that another robot has identified the target. The exchange of information changes the behavior of the robot. A robot approaching a target changes its control strategy when it makes contact with the target. The event of making contact changes the behavior (dynamics) of the robot.

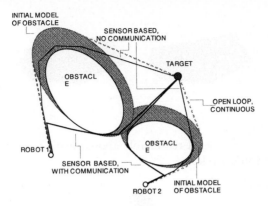

Fig. 2. A simple scenario that illustrates how cooperation between two robots can improve the performance of the team in locating and reaching a target in a partially known environment.

3.2 The Specific Example

In the specific case used in formal modeling, we consider two robots, two static convex obstacles and a goal target position for both robots as shown in Figure 2. The solid lines indicate the actual obstacle location while the dotted lines indicate the initial obstacle model. Note that in the initial model the two obstacles appear to overlap. An open loop control for each robot without any communication or sensing yields the dotted paths labeled "open loop: continuous." Each robot follows a continuous control law. There is only a single control mode. When each robot gets sensory information from its camera and refines its world model, we get discrete changes in the path as shown by the black lines labeled "sensor based: no communication." Now the robot controllers are hybrid controllers. The performance, judged by the length of the path has improved but not significantly. There is still no interaction between the robots. In the third case, the two robots exchange information about their world models at discrete intervals. The corresponding paths followed by the robots are labeled "sensor based: with communication." Because the robots pool their information, the path followed is more efficient — they are able to take advantage of the narrow opening between the two obstacles while avoiding collisions.

3.3 Assumptions

While it is possible to analyze the problems discussed above via simulation, our goal is to pursue symbolic methods and to develop verified control strategies. In order to keep the analysis of the problem simple, we will make a number of simplifying assumptions.

First, we will restrict our attention to mobile robots operating in planar environments. Robots will modeled as points in $\Re^2$. In other words, we ignore

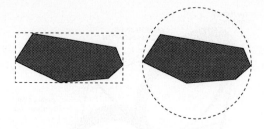

Fig. 3. A rectangle provides a reasonable approximation to most convex polygons, as compared to a circle.

Fig. 4. Non-convex shapes can be well approximated with several overlapping rectangles

the orientation of the robot. We also ignore the nonholonomic constraints that may limit the robots' direction of motion, as in the case of wheeled carts. Further, we will model the dynamics by a set of first order differential equations:

$$\dot{x} = u_1$$
$$\dot{y} = u_2$$

where (x, y) are the coordinates of a robot and (u_1, u_2) are the control inputs, in this case velocities. Note the equations are linear, which would not be the case if the orientation of the robot is included in the description.

Second, we will discretize our model of the robots' environment. We will superimpose a grid on the $x - y$ plane and assume that robots can only move along the grid. Thus, arbitrary point-to-point straight line paths are not possible and must be approximated by "stair case"-like motions consisting of an alternating series of left/right and forward/back steps. Note that successively finer directional discretizations could be made to describe complicated trajectories at the price of computation time.

Another implication of this assumption is that models of obstacles are limited to rectangles or unions of rectangles. As shown in Figures 3 and 4, the use of rectangles to describe objects in the workspace is not necessarily a limitation. Most general polygons can be reasonably approximated by a rectangle. Note that non-convex obstacles can be approximated using multiple overlapping rectangles.

In the grid world, we will use the so-called Manhattan metric or the L_1 norm to measure the distance between two points. The Euclidean metric makes the distance a nonlinear function of the state, but the Manhattan distance is linear. The Manhattan distance, D_M, from Point A to Point B is simply:

$$D_M(\overline{AB}) = \mid X_A - X_B \mid + \mid Y_A - Y_B \mid . \tag{1}$$

Finally, we make some assumptions about the model for sensing and estimation. Each robot is assumed to have some prior *qualitatively* correct knowledge of the workspace (e.g. provided by satellite imagery or a human user). The information is qualitatively correct in that it accurately reflects the number of obstacles in the environment and their general shape; however, their exact position, size or geometry is unknown. In other words, we assume that is possible to parameterize the uncertainties and the unknown information is limited to the value of certain parameters. Further we assume that the robot sensor allows the estimation of these unknown parameters and the estimates improve as the distance between the robot and the obstacle decreases. Such uncertainty models are reasonable approximations of sensor systems where errors are primarily geometric in origin.

For example, in vision applications in a two-dimensional world without occlusions and problems due to segmentation, the accuracy is limited by CCD resolution, especially at long ranges, and the estimates improve as the distance to target decreases. This is also true with sonars. In Figure 5, a mobile robot (black circle) is shown with a sonar array with a rectangular obstacle (shown in gray). Here we have a situation where the robot has reasonably accurate information about some of the obstacle's parameters, while information about the other parameters is subject to a considerable amount of uncertainty. The sonar readings only indicate that there is an object within ensonification cones 2 and 3 at a certain distance, while cones 1 and 4 are empty. The robot's worst case approximation is shown as a dashed rectangle. As the robot approaches the object and the distance between them decreases the uncertainty in the measurement also decreases.

4 Modeling

4.1 Robots

Each robot is described by coordinates (x, y). In our model of the robot and the grid world, the robot only has four distinct modes of travel:

$$
\begin{aligned}
right: &\quad \dot{x} = v_{max}, \quad \dot{y} = 0 \\
left: &\quad \dot{x} = -v_{max}, \dot{y} = 0 \\
forward: &\quad \dot{x} = 0, \qquad \dot{y} = v_{max} \\
back: &\quad \dot{x} = 0, \qquad \dot{y} = -v_{max}
\end{aligned}
\tag{2}
$$

where v_{max} is the robot's maximum speed. Since we are primarily concerned with optimal motions (least time or shortest path), the restriction of the speed to v_{max} does not create any limitations.

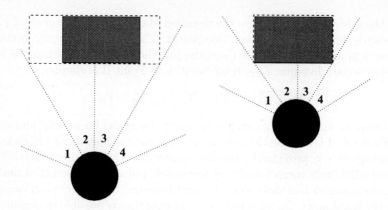

Fig. 5. An overhead view of a mobile robot equipped with sonar arrays detecting a rectangular obstacle. The sonars return the closest distance to an object which lies somewhere within the ensonification cone. At greater distances (left figure) the uncertainty can be rather large since the robot only knows that something lies within cones 2 and 3, while cones 1 and 4 are free. As the robot approaches the obstacle (right) however its estimates get better.

4.2   Obstacles and Workspace

Consider the problem of a team of such mobile robots R_i, for $i = 1,\ldots,N$ navigating an environment toward their respective goal configurations (G_x^i, G_y^i). The environment is populated with multiple polygonal obstacles O_j, for $j = 1,\ldots,M$ which occupy closed sets in $\Re^2$. Note that these obstacles are assumed to be in fixed positions. Therefore, the collision free space through which the robot is permitted to move is:

$$\mathcal{W} = \Re^2 - \cup_j O_j. \tag{3}$$

As discussed in Section 3.3, to ensure linearity and computational feasibility, the obstacles are modeled as rectangles rather than arbitrary polygons. Each rectangle can be completely described using only four parameters. In addition, certain geometric operations that we are concerned with, such as shrinking, growing, and intersection, can be performed on rectangles using strictly linear functions. The importance of these operations will be described later.

4.3   Sensor Model

Let $Y_j^i(t)$ be a closed set in the plane which represents the ith robot's estimate of the jth obstacle at time t. As discussed in Section 3.3, the initial map, $Y_j^i(0)$, and any subsequent estimates, $Y_j^i(t)$, are strictly worst case representations with no stochastic uncertainty. In other words, the uncertainty in a given estimate is bounded in such a way that

$$Y_j^i(t) \supseteq O_j, \forall t \geq 0. \tag{4}$$

Although it is not known *where* O_j lies in $Y_j^i(t)$, it is certain that $O_j \cap (\neg Y_j^i(t)) = \emptyset$. As a consequence of the bounded uncertainty assumption, robots can always determine if a new estimate is better than a previous one by comparing the area of the two, the estimate enclosing the smaller area being superior.

The sensor also has the property that its estimation of the obstacles improves as the distance from the robot to the obstacles decreases. In the limit, as the robot touches the obstacle, $Y_j^i \longrightarrow O_j$.

Allowing all four parameters of the rectangular obstacle to vary proved to be too computationally expensive, so the x coordinates of the right and left sides of the obstacle were taken to be the only information subject to uncertainty. This model was abstracted in HyTech as

$$X_L^O(t) = X_L^A + \underbrace{(X_L^O(0) - X_L^A)\frac{d}{d_0}}_{error}, \forall t \geq 0. \tag{5}$$

$$X_R^O(t) = X_R^A + \underbrace{(X_R^O(0) - X_R^A)\frac{d}{d_0}}_{error}, \forall t \geq 0. \tag{6}$$

here, X_L and X_R denote the X coordinates of the left and right sides of the rectangle, superscripts O and A indicate observed and actual quantities, respectively. The distance at which the measurement is taken is d and d_0 refers to the distance from the robot to the obstacle at time zero.

One limitation of the sensor model is its inability to capture the nonlinearities that appear in real life. However, we argue that the above model captures the essential characteristics of sensor model and higher dimensional linear approximations to sensor models can be used to improve the accuracy. A more serious limitation is due to the use of the Manhattan distance. A sensor reading taken at a point whose true distance to the obstacle is small may be no different from a reading taken further away if the distances are deemed equal in the Manhattan sense. Thus it is possible the robot's estimate will not strictly improve as the robot approaches an obstacle along certain paths.

4.4   Coordination

The robots collectively represent a team and therefore it may be advantageous for them to exchange information periodically. For instance, at discrete time intervals, robot R_i may send its current map of the environment to robot R_k. Robot R_k must then fuse that information with its own representation of the obstacles. Again, as a consequence of the bounded uncertainty assumption this fusion is accomplished by, for all obstacles j,

$$Y_j^k new = Y_j^i \cap Y_j^k. \tag{7}$$

R_k's resulting estimate of obstacle j, $Y_j^k new$, will naturally have an area less than or equal to R_k's previous estimate making it at least as accurate. This new estimate is also guaranteed to completely contain the obstacle. Note that the parameters describing the updated estimates are linear functions of the parameters describing the two old estimates.

4.5   Control Strategy

The term control strategy is used here in reference to a mapping from the currently available information to a collision free kinematic trajectory. The planning algorithm used here is essentially an exact cell decomposition approach. A complete explanation of the algorithm can be found in [Lat91] . For this scenario, the workspace decomposition used is shown in Figure 6.

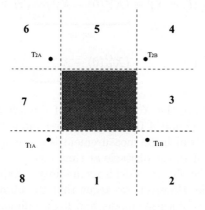

Fig. 6. Illustration of the exact cell decomposition planning method. The dark rectangle represents the obstacle while the numbered regions are free cells in the workspace.

For a point robot navigating amidst rectangular obstacles, only two separate cases need to be considered. First, suppose the robot is currently in cell 1 (the cases for cell 3, 5, or 7 follow by symmetry). When the goal is in any adjacent cell (8, 1, or 2), no special planning is needed since adjacency guarantees that a collision free path exists. If the goal lies in cells 7 or 6 (or 3 or 4), a temporary goal T_{1A} (or T_{1B}) is set. ¿From that point a collision free path to the target exists. However, if the goal resides in region 5 the robot first proceeds to T_{1A} (or T_{1B}), then it sets a new temporary goal T_{2A} (or T_{2B}) based on which intermediate point will result in the shortest overall path. Once it reaches T_{2A} (or T_{2B}), it can proceed to region 5 unobstructed.

The second case occurs when the robot is initially in a corner cell such as 8 (2, 4, or 6). In this case, collision free paths exist when the goal lies in cells 6, 7, 1, or 2. Paths to regions 5 or 3 are determined, similar to the previous case, by setting temporary goals in cells 6 or 2 respectively. The degenerate case occurs when the goal lies in the corner cell opposite to the robot's starting position, cell

4 in this case. Due to the lack of Euclidean metric and the fact that the robot may only move in four directions, the clockwise and anti-clockwise paths around the obstacle will always be of the same Manhattan distance. In this case, the robot chooses the path nondeterministically. This cell decomposition algorithm is *optimal* because it compares various choices of paths based on the length and selects the shortest one. [1]

A complete description of the robot's behavioral algorithm as a finite state machine appears in Figure 7. The behavior can be sketched as follows

```
while (reachedGoal == False) {
    1.   Use sensors to update the map of the world
    2.   Send or Process communication if appropriate
    3.   Plan a path
    4.   Travel for some time period
}
```

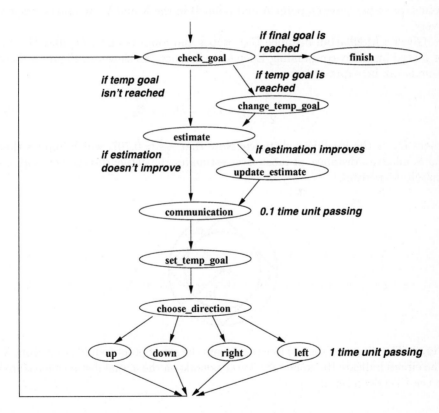

Fig. 7. Representation of the robot's behavioral algorithm as a Finite State Machine.

---

[1] This cell decomposition algorithm is optimal in the Manhattan metric, not in the Euclidean metric.

4.6   Cost Model

As mentioned in the previous section the robots attempt to choose behaviors which minimize some type of cost function. In this model, the cost function indicates sum of the time taken to travel a path and the time taken to communicate.

The shortest path between two points is not unique when using the Manhattan distance even in the absence of obstacles, Due to the fact that sensor and communication information are only updated at discrete intervals and that the robot's speed is constant - it turns out that the robot essentially travels on an equi-spaced grid. In this case, when traveling from grid point (X_A, Y_A) to grid point (X_B, Y_B) there are

$$\frac{(N+M)!}{N! \cdot M!} \tag{8}$$

distinct shortest paths, provided there are no obstacles in the region $[X_A, X_B] \times [Y_A, Y_B]$. Here N and M are positive integers indicating the number of grid points, or steps, between point A and point B in the X and Y directions, respectively.

Given a Manhattan distance D_M, upper and lower bounds, D_u and D_l, can be placed on the corresponding Euclidean distance. As shown in Figure 8 these bounds can be expressed as

$$D_l = \frac{\sqrt{2}}{2} D_M \le D_E \le D_M = D_u \tag{9}$$

where D_E is the Euclidean distance. Note that $\frac{\sqrt{2}}{2} \approx 0.707$, which implies that the Manhattan distance, at most, over estimates the actual distance by approximately 41 percent.

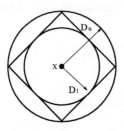

Fig. 8. The diamond shaped line represents the set of points equidistant from X. The circles indicate the upper and lower bounds on the actual distance measured in the Euclidean sense

It is also assumed that communication is a potentially expensive operation, either due to the computational cost of processing the information, bandwidth limitations or for security reasons. To reflect this, a time penalty ρ_{comm} is added to the overall cost function each time a message is sent over the network.

If f is the frequency of communication, the overall performance index J^i which indicates a total time for R^i to reach the goal can be expressed as

$$J^i = \frac{D^i_M}{v_i} + \rho_{comm} \cdot f \cdot \frac{D^i_M}{v_i} \tag{10}$$

where D^i_M is a total distance traveled by R^i in the sense of the Manhattan metric and v_i is the speed of R^i.

5   Results

5.1   Example

Our scenario contains three identical robots (R_1, R_2 and R_3), one fixed obstacle and one fixed goal. R_1 and R_2 collaborate via communication, while R_3 works by itself. The initial positions of R_1 and R_3 are the same. Communication takes a fixed amount of time for each time message exchanged. Thus, unnecessarily frequent communication may increase the time to reach the goal. For verification purposes, the work space was restricted to a bounded rectangle with dimensions of 150 by 160 units. Since optimal motions are of primary concern, all paths can be expected to lie within the bounded region.

Initially R_1 and R_3 are located at (20,0). R_2 is located at (60,10). The target is located at (80,50). The obstacle is located somewhere within the region whose corner-points are (20,20) and (60,40). Let us call the x position of left end of the obstacle x_1, and the x position of right end of the obstacle x_2. Similarly y_1 is the y position of bottom end of the obstacle and y_2 is the y position of top end of the obstacle. R_1 and R_3 estimate x_1 as 10 and x_2 as 120 initially. R_2 estimates x_1 as -30 and x_2 as 70 initially. In other words, R_1 and R_3 estimate the obstacle to be far larger toward right hand side, but R_2 estimates the obstacle far larger toward left hand side. All robots estimate y_1 as 20 and y_2 as 40 initially (i.e., all robots have correct values for y_1 and y_2 as estimates). The direction of movement is determined at the end of each iteration. A robot moves for 1 time unit once direction is determined (see Figure 7). A robot moves 10 units of distance in 1 time unit. R_1 and R_2 communicate every time unit. Communication has a cost of 0.1 time unit.

Initially R_3 sets up a temporary goal as (0,10). It is because the estimated length of left path toward the goal is shorter than the length of right path. It chooses left path for reaching the goal. However, R_1 gets a good estimation of x_2 by communicating with R_2. It sets a temporary goal at (80,10) then chooses a right path. R_3 takes 13 time units to reach the goal (80,50), whereas R_1 takes 12.1 time units including communication overhead; it is verified that collaboration between R_1 and R_2 helps R_1 to reach the goal faster than R_3 in this scenario.

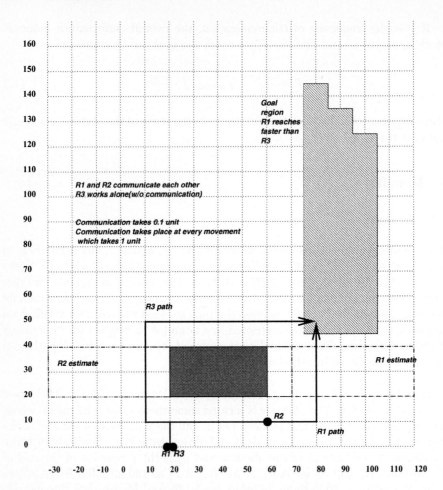

Fig. 9. The scenario of robot modeling

5.2   Parametric Analysis

Setting x and y positions of the goal as parameters, we can compute the geometric region in which R_1 reaches faster than R_3 with the help of communication (see figure 9). With the help of communication, R_1 can choose a shorter path which saves two time units compared to R_3, when the goal lies in the shaded region shown. However, R_1 constantly communicates with R_2 and this communication overhead accumulates so that this overhead cancels out the saving after 20 movements. That is why the region has a stair-like shape.

Also, we can compute the optimal frequency of communication for reaching the goal. Setting the *period* of communication as a parameter, we modified the model so that a robot communicates only every *period* number of iterations. A domain of *period* is finite because period should be less than time for robots to reach the goal. Thus, we can choose the frequency which leads to the minimal total elapsed time.

We get a result that when R_1 and R_2 communicate once in two unit times, R_1 takes 11.5 time units to reach the goal (80,50).

In addition, two safety properties for a robot controller are verified. First, a robot never collides with the obstacle while it navigates to reach any valid goal position. A valid goal position is any position outside of the 5 units extension of the initially estimated obstacle. We added a monitor automaton to the description so that the monitor can check whether a position of a robot is overlapped with the estimate of the obstacle. Second, the verification establishes that a robot *does* reach any valid goal position in the work space

5.3   Limitations of the Analysis

We had to make several simplifications in order to make the analysis tractable. For example, we had to model only one obstacle in the scenario because when we modeled two obstacles, HyTech generated a memory overflow error. Also, only two parameters of the obstacle's geometry were estimated by the sensor in our model due to similar limitations. We could not allow more than three robots in the verification. We limited the range of x between -30 and 120 and the range of y between 0 and 160. Furthermore, we had to divide this region into 21 partitions to make the analysis tractable. The robot model description is around 1700 lines. We verified this description using Sun Enterprise 3000 (4 X 250 Mhz UltraSPARC) with 1GB physical memory. Verifying each region took up to 1.3 GB memory space and one hour[2].

Another limitation is the internal arithmetic overflow error of HyTech when HyTech manipulates a complex region. A region is defined by a set of linear constraints. A linear region becomes more and more complex at each iteration of computation. Although linear constraints in the model description do not look complex, HyTech can eventually generate an overflow error after many iterations. Therefore, we have to be careful to make the linear equations as simple as possible. In modeling a sensor, linear equations can be complex depending on which number we choose for a initial position of robot and obstacle. For example, estimated x position of the obstacle is formulated as

$$x = x_{real} + (x_{init} - x_{real}) \times \frac{|(x_r - x_{real})| + |(y_r - y_{real})|}{d_{init}}$$

where x_r, x_y are position of a robot. Let us see the equation of estimation of x_1 by R_1, where x_1 is a x position of left end of the obstacle. In the scenario $x_{real} = 20, y_{real} = 20, x_{init} = 10, d_{init} = 20$. It generates a simple equation $x = \frac{x_{r1}}{2} + \frac{y_{r1}}{2}$ when the obstacle is at the upper right side of R_1. However, if this equation becomes a little more complex, HyTech generates "Library overflow" error even with enough free memory.

---

[2] We used **top** for checking memory usage.

6 Conclusions

We have reported a case study in applying formal modeling and analysis aimed at exploring alternatives in the design of multi-robot coordination systems. Simultaneous design of control strategies and coordination protocols for interacting dynamical systems is a significant challenge. We believe that tools for high-level design and analysis can greatly aid the design process.

The gist of our approach is to describe the system as interacting hybrid automata, and then employ symbolic analysis to compute the constraints among various parameters for a given objective. Note the generality of this approach compared to prevalent methods in simulation in which either the parameters need to be set to specific values or the computation of the constraints for the specific problem needs to be programmed. Even though we have reported only modest success in the goals of the exercise, we hope that it illustrates the potential of the approach.

It should come as no surprise that significant advances in the formal verification technology are needed for it to be applicable to our problem in its full generality. Two specific obstacles are

Computational requirements. As reported in Section 5, all the parameters had be scaled down to be able to get feedback from HyTech. Improving the efficiency of polyhedra-based analysis remains a significant challenge.

Expressiveness. As described in Section 4, the linearity requirement forces us to do a variety of approximations. While the issue of approximating complex dynamics by rectangular inclusions has received attention in literature, for us, issues such as approximating Euclidean distance by Manhattan distance were particularly unsatisfactory. This problem suggests directions for further research and tool development for more general classes of problems.

We conclude by noting that this is, to our knowledge, the first use of formal methods in the analysis of multirobot coordination and communication. This problem is particularly complicated because of the use of continuous controllers and planners with discrete protocols for communication and for refining world models. Our approach points a way to analyze the role of communication in multirobot coordination, and to establish the dependence of the team performance on the number of team members and on the rate of communication.

Acknowledgements We gratefully acknowledge the support of NSF grant CISE CDS 97-03220-001, NSF CAREER award CCR-9734115, NSF CCR-9619910, ARO DAAG55-98-1-0393, ARO DAAG55-98-1-0466, ONR N00014-97-1-0505 and the DARPA ITO/MARS program. J. Esposito was supported by a Department of Education fellowship.

References

[ACH+95]   R. Alur, C. Courcoubetis, N. Halbwachs, T.A. Henzinger, P. Ho,
            X. Nicollin, A. Olivero, J. Sifakis, and S. Yovine. The algorithmic analysis
            of hybrid systems. *Theoretical Computer Science*, 138:3–34, 1995.

[AHH96]   R. Alur, T.A. Henzinger, and P.-H. Ho. Automatic symbolic verifica-
            tion of embedded systems. *IEEE Transactions on Software Engineering*,
            22(3):181–201, 1996.

[AHS96]   R. Alur, T.A. Henzinger, and E.D. Sontag, editors. *Hybrid Systems III:
            Verification and Control*. LNCS 1066. Springer-Verlag, 1996.

[AKNS95]   P. Antsaklis, W. Kohn, A. Nerode, and S. Sastry, editors. *Hybrid Systems
            II*. LNCS 999. Springer-Verlag, 1995.

[Bra95]   M. S. Branicky. *Studies in Hybrid Systems: Modeling, Analysis, and Con-
            trol*. PhD thesis, Massachusetts Institute of Technology, 1995.

[Bro93]   R. W. Brockett. Hybrid models for motion control systems. In H. L.
            Trentelman and J. C. Willems, editors, *Essays in Control: Perspectives in
            the Theory and its Applications*, pages 29–53. Birkhäuser, 1993.

[CK96]   E.M. Clarke and R.P. Kurshan. Computer-aided verification. *IEEE Spec-
            trum*, 33(6):61–67, 1996.

[DOTY96]   C. Daws, A. Olivero, S. Tripakis, and S. Yovine. The tool KRONOS. In
            Hybrid Systems III: Verification and Control, LNCS 1066, pages 208–219.
            Springer-Verlag, 1996.

[GNRR93]   R. Grossman, A. Nerode, A. Ravn, and H. Rischel, editors. *Hybrid Sys-
            tems*. LNCS 736. Springer-Verlag, 1993.

[HHW97]   T.A. Henzinger, P. Ho, and H. Wong-Toi. HYTECH: a model checker for
            hybrid systems. *Software Tools for Technology Transfer*, 1, 1997.

[HS98]   T. Henzinger and S. Sastry, editors. *Hybrid Systems: Computation and
            Control*. LNCS 1386. Springer-Verlag, 1998.

[HW95]   P.H. Ho and H. Wong-Toi. Automated analysis of an audio control pro-
            tocol. In *Proceedings of the Seventh Conference on Computer-Aided Ver-
            ification*, LNCS 939, pages 381–394. Springer-Verlag, 1995.

[HW96]   T. Henzinger and H. Wong-Toi. Using HYTECH to synthesize control pa-
            rameters for a steam boiler. In *Formal Methods for Industrial Applications:
            Specifying and Programming the Steam Boiler Control*, LNCS 1165, pages
            265–282. Springer-Verlag, 1996.

[Lat91]   J.-C. Latombe. *Robot motion planning*. Kluwer Academic Publishers,
            1991.

[LGS95]   J. Lygeros, D. N. Godbole, and S. Sastry. A game-theoretic approach to
            hybrid system design. In *Hybrid Systems III. Verification and Control*,
            pages 1–12. Springer-Verlag, 1995.

[LPY97]   K. Larsen, P. Pettersson, and W. Yi. UPPAAL in a nutshell. *Springer
            International Journal of Software Tools for Technology Transfer*, 1, 1997.

[Mal97]   O. Maler, editor. *Hybrid and Real-Time Systems*. LNCS 1201. Springer-
            Verlag, 1997.

[NBC95]   K. S. Narendra, J. Balakrishnan, and K. Ciliz. Adaptation and learn-
            ing using multiple models, switching and tuning. *IEEE Control Systems
            Magazine*, pages 37–51, 1995.

[TPS97]   C. Tomlin, G. J. Pappas, and S. Sastry. Conflict resolution for air traffic
            management: A study in multi-agent hybrid systems. *IEEE Transactions
            on Automatic Control*, August 1997. Accepted as a regular paper.

[Utk77]   V. I. Utkin. Variable structure systems with sliding modes. *IEEE Transactions on Automatic Control*, Vol. 22(2):212–222, 1977.

[ZB98]   M. Zefran and J. Burdick. Stabilization of systems with changing dynamics. In *Hybrid Systems*, 1998.

[ZDK96]   M. Zefran, J. Desai, and V. Kumar. Continuous motion plans for robotic systems with changing dynamic behavior. In *2nd Int. Workshop on Algorithmic Foundations of Robotics*, 1996.

On-the-Fly Controller Synthesis
for Discrete and Dense-Time Systems

Stavros Tripakis and Karine Altisen

[1] Verimag, currently at UC Berkeley,
stavros@eecs.berkeley.edu
[2] Verimag,
altisen@imag.fr

Abstract. We present novel techniques for efficient controller synthesis for untimed and timed systems with respect to invariance and reachability properties. In the untimed case, we give algorithms for controller synthesis in the context of finite graphs with *controllable* and *uncontrollable* edges, distinguishing between the actions of the system and its environment, respectively. The algorithms are *on-the-fly*, since they return a controller as soon as one is found, which avoids the generation of the whole state space.

In the timed case, we use the model of *timed automata* extended with controllable and uncontrollable discrete transitions. Our controller-synthesis method here is only half on-the-fly, since it relies on the a-priori generation of a finite model (graph) of the timed automaton, as quotient of the *time-abstracting bisimulation*. The quotient graph is essentially an untimed graph, upon which we can apply the untimed on-the-fly algorithms to compute a timed controller.

Keywords. Controller Synthesis, On-The-Fly Algorithms, Timed Automata, Time-Abstracting Bisimulation.

1 Introduction

An embedded system can be usually considered as a reactive machine that cooperates with an environment to provide a service. The environment generates input events triggering actions that change the state of the machine, which may in turn produce output events that affect the environment. The formal analysis of such systems requires models and techniques that take into account not only the properties of the embedded machine, but also the characteristics of the environment, and in particular, the unpredictable (sometimes even hostile) nature of the latter.

In formal verification (or *model-checking*) there is no distinction between actions of the system and those of the environment. Usually the model of the system is "closed" by descriptions of the environment and the model-checking procedure checks that *all* execution sequences of the closed model satisfy a set of

J. Wing, J. Woodcock, J. Davies (Eds.): FM'99, Vol. I, LNCS 1708, pp. 233–252, 1999.

properties. In such an approach, the description of the system must be complete (often deterministic) at the time of verification, and there is little or no possibility at all of exploiting non-determinism of the system's description to perform "fine-tuning" of the application.

An alternative approach is to start from an "open" model where actions of the system and actions of the environment are distinguished. Such a model can be considered as "incomplete" in the sense that it describes a more liberal behavior and usually the question arises of "closing" the system so that the requirements are met. This is the problem of *controller synthesis* [RW87]. It consists in computing a controller which observes the state/actions of the environment and restricts the choices of the system, ensuring that the given property is satisfied no matter how the environment behaves.

Although more interesting (and more general) than verification, controller synthesis is also a more difficult problem. On the other hand, a number of heuristics which have improved the efficiency of model-checking, such as *on-the-fly* techniques, have not been developed, to our knowledge, in the context of controller synthesis. This is perhaps the reason why the latter has not found so much application in practice as model-checking has.

In this paper we propose on-the-fly methods for controller synthesis for discrete (i.e., finite-state) and dense-time systems, with respect to *invariance* and *reachability* properties. A controller for invariance tries to keep the system inside a set of "safe" states. A controller for reachability tries to lead the system to a set of "target" states.

For the description of discrete systems we use *game graphs* (GG), that is, finite graphs with edges marked as *controllable* or *uncontrollable*, modeling the actions of the system (and possible choices of the controller) and those of the environment, respectively. For game graphs we define the notion of *strategies*, which are sub-graphs representing the choices of the controller for each possible choice of the environment. Controller synthesis consists in computing a strategy with respect to invariance (all nodes are safe) or reachability (all paths lead to the target nodes).

Our method in the untimed case is fully on-the-fly, that is, game graphs can be implicitly represented using a higher-level formalism and generated at the same time as the calculation of the strategy. A strategy is returned as soon as it found, which means that the whole state space does not necessarily have to be generated. The method is based on a forward reachability analysis using a depth-first search and its worst case complexity is $O(n + m)$, where n and m is, respectively, the number of nodes and edges in the graph.

In the timed case, we describe systems using the model of *game timed automata* (GTA) [MPS95], [AMP95], which are simply timed automata (TA) [ACD93], [HNSY94] with discrete transitions marked as controllable or uncontrollable. We define *timed strategies*, a notion similar to the untimed case but adapted to take into account the density of the time domain, as well as the fact that "time can be in favor of both the controller and the environment" [MPS95].

Our controller-synthesis method in the timed case is only half on-the-fly, since it involves two steps: first, we generate a finite-state model of the GTA (a graph); then we apply the on-the-fly untimed synthesis algorithms on this graph. The latter is the *quotient* of the GTA with respect to the *time-abstracting bisimulation* defined in [TY96]. This equivalence abstracts away exact time delays while preserving all properties of interest. We show how the time-abstracting quotient graph of a GTA can be viewed as a game graph so that GTA controller synthesis is reduced to GG controller synthesis.

We illustrate our approach on a toy-example, the Train-Gate-Controller system of [Alu91] (viewed as a GTA). We show how a strategy can be obtained for this system in an on-the-fly manner, that is, without having to explore the whole quotient graph.

Relation to the Literature

Controller synthesis is close to the theory of *games*. In the domain of formal methods, pioneering have been the works of [RW87, PR89], who studied the problem in the untimed case. Algorithms for this theory have been given based on a backward fix-point calculation of a predecessor operator which returns the set of states which can be led to a set of target states independently of uncontrollable actions. *Symbolic* versions of this algorithm (i.e., reasoning in terms of sets of states instead of single states) have been presented in [HW92, Le 93, MPS95, AMP95] and prototype implementations in [WM99]. The fix-point algorithms are not on-the-fly, since the fix-point calculation has to terminate in order for the (maximal) strategy to be computed. Moreover, the method is based on a predecessor operator, therefore, may needlessly consider states which are not reachable. To our knowledge, on-the-fly algorithms for controller synthesis have not been presented before in the literature.

In the timed case, [HW91] use the framework of [RW87] to solve controller synthesis for deterministic TA. [MPS95] present a fix-point controller-synthesis algorithm for general TA and with respect to a large class of properties, including invariance and reachability. The main drawback in the above works is the implementation of the symbolic predecessor operator, which is expensive in the dense-time case (it involves the exponential-cost operation of complementation of polyhedra).

Organization of the Paper

In section 2, we treat the problem in the untimed case. We introduce game graphs and strategies, we define the problem of controller synthesis in terms of a search for strategies and we present the two on-the-fly algorithms for strategies with respect to invariance and reachability. In section 3, we review timed automata and the time-abstracting bisimulation and define the quotient graph with respect to this relation. In section 4, we extended timed automata to game timed automata and define timed strategies and controller synthesis in the timed case. We also show how the on-the-fly algorithms of section 2 can be applied on the quotient graph in order to solve the problem for the timed case. Section 5 presents our conclusions.

2   On-the-Fly Controller Synthesis for Finite Discrete-State Systems

In this section we give an on-the-fly solution to the controller-synthesis problem for the untimed case. We first present our model and its semantics in terms of strategies. Then we give two algorithms for computing on-the-fly strategies with respect to invariance or reachability.

2.1   The Model: Finite Graphs with Controllable/Uncontrollable Edges

We would like to describe finite-state systems which involve an unpredictable (or even hostile) environment. To model such systems we use finite graphs the edges of which are labeled as controllable or uncontrollable, to model the actions of the system and its environment, respectively.

More formally, a *game graph* (GG) is a finite labeled graph $G = (V, v_0, \rightarrow)$, where V is a finite set of nodes, $v_0 \in V$ is the initial node and $\rightarrow \subseteq V \times \{c, u\} \times V$ is a set of edges. For two nodes $v, w \in V$, we write $v \xrightarrow{c} w$ (resp. $v \xrightarrow{u} w$) if $(v, c, w) \in \rightarrow$ (resp. $(v, u, w) \in \rightarrow$). An edge $v \xrightarrow{c} w$ is called *controllable* and w is a controllable *successor* of v. An edge $v \xrightarrow{u} w$ is called *uncontrollable* and w is a uncontrollable successor of v.

We assume that a GG does not contain any nodes without any controllable successor, that is, for each $v \in V$ there exists $w \in V$ such that $v \xrightarrow{c} w$. This is not a restriction to the model since "dummy" self-looping controllable edges can be added to nodes without controllable successors. Notice that this assumption implies that a GG does not contain any *sink* nodes, that is, nodes with no successors.

Example. Figure 1 shows two game graphs. Their nodes are numbered 0 to 3 and 0 to 4, respectively.

Remark 1. The model of game graphs is at least as general as the game-theoretic model where controllable and uncontrollable actions *alternate*, that is, AND-OR graphs: AND nodes correspond to game-graph nodes having only uncontrollable successors (except the self-loop controllable edge) and OR nodes correspond to game-graph nodes having only controllable successors.

Strategies. We are interested in controlling game graphs with respect to two types of properties, namely, *invariance* (where the controller tries to keep the system inside a set of safe states) and *reachability* (where the controller tries to lead the system to a set of target states).

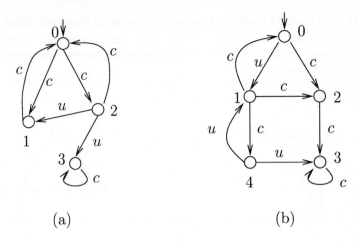

Fig. 1. Two game graphs.

Consider a GG $G = (V, v_0, \rightarrow)$ and a set of nodes $\hat{V} \subseteq V$.

A *strategy of G with respect to invariance of $\hat{V}$* is a graph $G_1 = (V_1, v_0, \rightarrow_1)$ such that:

1. $V_1 \subseteq \hat{V}$ and $\rightarrow_1 \subseteq \rightarrow$.
2. For each node $v \in V_1$, if $v \xrightarrow{u} w$, then $w \in V_1$ and $v \xrightarrow{u}_1 w$.
3. For each node $v \in V_1$, there is an edge $v \xrightarrow{c}_1 w$.

In other words, a strategy with respect to invariance is a subgraph of G restricted to the "safe nodes" $\hat{V}$ (condition 1), and such that for each node, all its uncontrollable successors (condition 2) and at least one of its controllable successors (condition 3) are kept. Condition 1 also ensures that the system remains in the set of safe states. All nodes in V_1 are said to be *winning* with respect to invariance of $\hat{V}$.

A *strategy of G with respect to reachability of $\hat{V}$* is a graph $G_1 = (V_1, v_0, \rightarrow_1)$ such that:

1. $V_1 \subseteq V$ and $\rightarrow_1 \subseteq \rightarrow$.
2. For each node $v \in V_1 \setminus \hat{V}$, if $v \xrightarrow{u} w$, then $w \in V_1$ and $v \xrightarrow{u}_1 w$.
3. For each node $v \in V_1 \setminus \hat{V}$, there is an edge $v \xrightarrow{c}_1 w$.
4. For each node $v \in V_1$, there exists a path $v \xrightarrow{c}_1 v_1 \xrightarrow{c}_1 \cdots \xrightarrow{c}_1 v_n$ such that $v_n \in \hat{V}$.

In other words, a strategy with respect to reachability is a subgraph of G (condition 1) such that each node can reach the "target nodes" $\hat{V}$ by a path of controllable edges (condition 4), and for each non-target node, all its uncontrollable successors (condition 2) and at least one of its controllable successors (condition 3) are kept. Condition 4 ensures that the controller can lead the system to the set of target states. All nodes in V_1 are said to be *winning* with respect to reachability of $\hat{V}$.

Example. Figure 2(a) shows a strategy for the game graph of figure 1(a) with respect to invariance of $\{0, 1, 2\}$. Notice that the controllable edge $0 \xrightarrow{c} 2$ is eliminated, since from node 2 the system can be led to the unwanted node 3 by an uncontrollable edge.

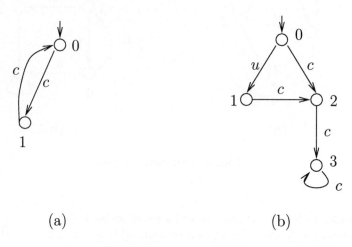

(a)   (b)

Fig. 2. Two strategies.

Figure 2(b) shows a strategy for the game graph of figure 1(b) with respect to reachability of $\{3\}$. The controller, being at node 1, chooses to move to node 2, from where reachability of node 3 is guaranteed.

Controller Synthesis for Game Graphs. Given a GG $G = (V, v_0, \rightarrow)$ and a set of nodes $\hat{V} \subseteq V$, the controller-synthesis problem for G with respect to invariance (resp. reachability) of $\hat{V}$ is to find a strategy (if one exists) with respect to invariance (resp. reachability) of $\hat{V}$.

Remark 2. Notice that the controller-synthesis problems for reachability and invariance are *almost* dual. As we see below the algorithms for the two problems are similar, however, we cannot encode one problem as the negation of the other by simply changing controllable edges to uncontrollable and vice-versa. This is because of the assumption that the environment is "faster" than the controller: in a node where both controllable and uncontrollable actions are possible, our definition of strategy assumes that the environment can force an uncontrollable action before the controller can make a choice.

2.2   The On-the-Fly Algorithms for Invariance and Reachability

Based on the definition of strategies we derive two algorithms, shown in figures 3 and 4, for computing a strategy with respect to invariance and reachability, respectively. The algorithms are on-the-fly in the sense that they return a strategy as soon as one is found. Therefore, the input graph need not be fully generated/explored, which can result in significant savings in performance.

Both algorithms use a depth-first search (DFS) on the input GG. In the figures, the DFS is represented by procedures calling each other in a recursive manner. In practice, a stack is used to eliminate recursion and implement the DFS directly. This stack holds the currently visited path. The set of nodes which are in the stack is denoted *Stack*.

The DFS is adapted to the definition of a strategy, so that whenever a node is explored, all its uncontrollable successors and at least one controllable successor are also explored. Nodes are marked with a *controllability status* during the search. In the algorithm for invariance, a node is initially marked *maybe*, until it is found that it cannot be winning, whereupon its mark is updated to *no*. Dually, in the algorithm for reachability, a node is initially marked *maybe*, until it is found that it is winning, whereupon its mark is updated to *yes*. The sets *Maybe*, *No* and *Yes* are used to store visited nodes and represent their marks.

The algorithms also use a set of edges *Strat* representing the strategy. The set of edges *NegStrat* in the algorithm for invariance represents the "counter-strategy" showing how the environment can lead the system out of the set of safe nodes. This can be used as diagnostics in case a strategy for the controller does not exist. In the case of reachability, such a special structure is not needed, since the explored graph is also the counter-example.

The Algorithm for Invariance. Intuitively, the invariance algorithm works as follows. Procedure Reach explores the graph in depth-first order. For each newly visited node v, the uncontrollable successors of v are explored first. If not all of them are winning then v cannot be winning either, and control moves to procedure UndoMaybe (line 1). Otherwise, its controllable successors are explored by procedure CheckControllable (line 2). If none of them is winning then again v cannot be winning. Procedure UndoMaybe updates a node v which was falsely assumed to be winning, as well as all predecessors of v, since their computed strategies are no longer valid. In particular, all uncontrollable predecessors of v are not winning. Also, if w is a controllable predecessor of v, then a new controllable successor should be found for w (line 10). This is done by procedure CheckControllable, which explores the remaining controllable successors of v.

At the end of the algorithm, and if the answer is not *no*, then the sub-graph represented by the set of edges *Strat* contains the strategy. If the answer is *no*, then *NegStrat* contains a counter-example, that is, a "counter-strategy" showing that the controller has no way to avoid the environment leading the system to a bad state.

The Algorithm for Reachability. The algorithm for reachability works in a dual manner. A difference is that edges which are inserted in *Strat* are no longer removed. A node v is inserted in *Yes* (procedure UndoMaybe) only if all its uncontrollable successors and at least one controllable successor are already in *Yes*. When v is inserted in *Yes*, its predecessors are also updated: if v was

```
FindStrategyForInvariance ((V, v₀, →), V̂) {
  No := Maybe := {} ;
  Strat := NegStrat := {} ;
  Controllable := {v₁ --c--> v₂ | v₁, v₂ ∈ V} ;
  if (Reach(v₀) = no) then return "No strategy exists" ;
  else return "Found strategy Strat" ;

  Reach(v) {
    if (v ∈ No or v ∉ V̂) then return no ;
    if (v ∈ Maybe) then return maybe ;
    Maybe := Maybe ∪ {v} ;    /* new node */
    for each (v --u--> w) do
      if (Reach(w) = no) then
        NegStrat := NegStrat ∪ {v --u--> w} ;
        goto FAIL ;                                          (1)
    end for
    if (CheckControllable(v) ≠ no) then
      Strat := Strat ∪ {v --u--> v' | v' ∈ V} ;            (2)
      return maybe ;
    else NegStrat := NegStrat ∪ {v --c--> w | w ∈ V} ;
  FAIL:
    UndoMaybe(v) ;
    return no ;
  }
  CheckControllable(v) {
    while (∃v --c--> w ∈ Controllable) do                  (3)
      Controllable := Controllable \ {v --c--> w} ;
      if (Reach(w) ≠ no) then                               (4)
        Strat := Strat ∪ {v --c--> w} ;                    (5)
        return maybe ;
    end while
    return no ;                                              (6)
  }
  UndoMaybe(v) {    /* Update from Maybe to No */
    Maybe := Maybe \ {v} ;                                  (7)
    No := No ∪ {v} ;                                        (8)
    while (∃w ∈ Maybe \ Stack . w → v ∈ Strat) do          (9)
      Strat := Strat \ {w → v} ;
      NegStrat := NegStrat ∪ {w → v} ;
      if (w --u--> v) then                                  (10)
        UndoMaybe(w) ;
      elsif (CheckControllable(v) = no) then
        UndoMaybe(w) ;
    end while
  }
}
```

Fig. 3. On-the-fly controller synthesis for invariance.

the single "missing" successor for a node w to be winning (line 6), then procedure UndoMaybe is called recursively for w; otherwise, the remaining unexplored successors of w are explored (line 7). Another difference from the algorithm for invariance is that here the counter-example strategy is not explicitly shown: this is because the explored graph itself is a counter-example.

Example. Consider again the game graphs of figure 1. Suppose that the nodes are numbered in the order they are visited by a DFS (for instance, the edge $0 \xrightarrow{c} 1$ in the graph (a) is visited before the edge $0 \xrightarrow{c} 2$). Then, the on-the-fly algorithms presented above compute the strategies shown in figure 2 without exploring the whole graphs. In particular, the algorithm for invariance only visits nodes 0 and 1 of graph (a) and algorithm for reachability avoids visiting node 4 and the corresponding edges.

A more realistic example demonstrating the on-the-fly aspect of the algorithms is given in sections 3 and 4 where we apply the technique to controller synthesis for timed automata.

Complexity. The worst-case complexity of the algorithms is $O(n + m)$, where n and m are, respectively, the number of nodes and edges in the graph. Let us see why this is so, for the case of invariance. Each node and edge is considered at most twice: one time when they are inserted in *Maybe* or *Strat* and possibly a second time to be removed. This costs $O(n+m)$. In the worst case, when a node is removed by procedure UndoMaybe, all its previously explored predecessors which are not in the stack need to be examined (line 9 of figure 3). This also means that at most m predecessors are going to be considered during the backtracking procedure. In practice, the complexity of the algorithms can be reduced by using clever book-keeping to mark predecessors of a node that are likely to be updated.

3   Timed Automata and Time-Abstracting Bisimulations

In this section we briefly review the model of timed automata and define the time-abstracting bisimulation which reduces the infinite state space of timed automata into a finite graph which preserves most properties of interest. In the next section, we show how this graph can be used for controller synthesis in the timed context.

3.1   Timed Automata

Clocks, Bounds, and Polyhedra. Let R be the set of non-negative reals and $\mathcal{X} = \{x_1, ..., x_n\}$ be a set of variables in R, called *clocks*. An $\mathcal{X}$-*valuation* is a function $\mathbf{v} : \mathcal{X} \mapsto$ R. For some $X \subseteq \mathcal{X}$, $\mathbf{v}[X := 0]$ is the valuation $\mathbf{v}'$, such that $\forall x \in X$. $\mathbf{v}'(x) = 0$ and $\forall x \notin X$. $\mathbf{v}'(x) = \mathbf{v}(x)$. For every $\delta \in$ R, $\mathbf{v} + \delta$ is a valuation such that for all $x \in \mathcal{X}$, $(\mathbf{v} + \delta)(x) = \mathbf{v}(x) + \delta$.

```
FindStrategyForReachability ((V, v₀, →), V̂) {
    Yes := Maybe := {} ;
    Strat := ExploredEdges := {} ;
    if (Reach(v₀) = yes) then return "Found strategy Strat" ;
    else return "No strategy exists" ;

    Reach(v) {
        if (v ∈ Yes or v ∈ V̂) then return yes ;
        if (v ∈ Maybe) then return maybe ;
        Maybe := Maybe ∪ {v} ;    /* new node */
        for each (v →ᵘ w ∉ ExploredEdges) do
            ExploredEdges := ExploredEdges ∪ {v →ᵘ w} ;
            if (Reach(w) ≠ yes) then return maybe ;              (1)
        end for
        if (CheckControllable(v) = yes) then                    (2)
            UndoMaybe(v) ;                                       (3)
            return yes ;
        end if
        return maybe ;
    }

    CheckControllable(v) {
        for each (v →ᶜ w ∉ ExploredEdges) do
            ExploredEdges := ExploredEdges ∪ {v →ᶜ w} ;
            if (Reach(w) = yes) then
                Strat := Strat ∪ {v →ᶜ w} ;                     (4)
                return yes ;
            end if
        end for
        return maybe ;
    }

    UndoMaybe(v) {    /* Update from Maybe to Yes */
        Maybe := Maybe \ {v} ;
        Yes := Yes ∪ {v} ;
        Strat := Strat ∪ {v →ᵘ v' | v' ∈ V} ;                   (5)
        while (∃w ∈ Maybe \ Stack . w → v) do
            if (w →ᶜ v ∧ ∀w →ᵘ v' . v' ∈ Yes) then              (6)
                Strat := Strat ∪ {w →ᶜ v} ;
                UndoMaybe(w) ;
            else                                                (7)
                Maybe := Maybe \ {w} ;
                if (Reach(w) = yes) then UndoMaybe(w) ;
            end if
        end while
    }
}
```

Fig. 4. On-the-fly controller synthesis for reachability.

A *bound* [Dil89] over $\mathcal{X}$ is a constraint of the form $x_i \sim c$ or $x_i - x_j \sim c$, where $1 \le i \ne j \le n$, $\sim \in \{<, \le, \ge, >\}$ and $c \in \mathsf{N} \cup \{\infty\}$. An $\mathcal{X}$-valuation $\mathbf{v}$ satisfies the bound $x_i \sim c$ (resp. $x_i - x_j \sim c$) if $\mathbf{v}(x_i) \sim c$ (resp. $\mathbf{v}(x_i) - \mathbf{v}(x_j) \sim c$).

An $\mathcal{X}$-*polyhedron* ζ is a set of $\mathcal{X}$-valuations satisfying a conjunction of bounds over $\mathcal{X}$. We use the conjunction of bounds to refer to the $\mathcal{X}$-polyhedron itself, for instance, if ζ is the set of valuations satisfying $x \le 5 \wedge x \le y$ then we write $x \le 5 \wedge x \le y$ instead of $\{\mathbf{v} \mid \mathbf{v}(x) \le 5 \wedge \mathbf{v}(x) \le \mathbf{v}(y)\}$. If the bounds of ζ are unsatisfiable, ζ defines the empty valuation set.

Syntax of Timed Automata. A *timed automaton* [ACD93, HNSY94] (TA) is a tuple $A = (\mathcal{X}, Q, q_0, E, I)$, where:

- $\mathcal{X}$ is a finite set of clocks.
- Q is a finite set of *discrete states*.
- q_0 is the initial discrete state.
- E is a finite set of *edges* of the form $e = (q, \zeta, X, q')$, where $q, q' \in Q$ are the *source* and *target* discrete states, ζ is an $\mathcal{X}$-polyhedron, called the *guard* of e, and $X \subseteq \mathcal{X}$ is a set of clocks to be reset.
- I is a function associating at each discrete state $q \in Q$ an $\mathcal{X}$-polyhedron $I(q)$ called the *invariant* of q.

Given an edge $e = (q, \zeta, X, q')$, we write $\mathsf{guard}(e)$ and $\mathsf{reset}(e)$ for ζ and X, respectively. Given a discrete state q, we write $\mathsf{in}(q)$ for the set of edges of the form $(\_, \_, \_, q)$.

Semantics of Timed Automata. A *state* of A is a pair $(q, \mathbf{v})$, where $q \in Q$ is a location, and $\mathbf{v}$ is an $\mathcal{X}$-valuation such that $\mathbf{v} \in I(q)$. $s_0 = (q_0, \mathbf{0})$ is the initial state of A, where $\mathbf{0}$ is the valuation assigning zero to all clocks in $\mathcal{X}$.

The semantics of a TA A are given in terms of the *semantic graph* G_A, which is generally an infinite (non-enumerable) structure, due to the density of the time domain. The nodes of G_A are states of A, the initial node being s_0. G_A has two types of edges: *discrete* edges of the form $(q, \mathbf{v}) \xrightarrow{e} (q', \mathbf{v}')$, where $e \in E, e = (q, \zeta, X, q')$ such that $\mathbf{v} \in \zeta$ and $\mathbf{v}' = \mathbf{v}[X := 0]$; *time* edges of the form $(q, \mathbf{v}) \xrightarrow{\delta} (q, \mathbf{v} + \delta)$, where $\mathbf{v} + \delta \in I(q)$. This graph has by definition the following properties of *time continuity* and *additivity*:

$$s \xrightarrow{\delta} s + \delta \text{ implies } s \xrightarrow{\delta'} s + \delta', \text{ for all } \delta' < \delta \qquad (1)$$

$$s \xrightarrow{\delta} s + \delta \text{ and } s + \delta \xrightarrow{\delta'} s + \delta + \delta' \text{ imply } s \xrightarrow{\delta + \delta'} s + \delta + \delta' \qquad (2)$$

For simplicity, we consider in the sequel only *deadlock-free* TA, that is, where for each state s there exists some $\delta \in \mathsf{R}$ and an edge $e \in E$ such that $s \xrightarrow{\delta} s + \delta \xrightarrow{e} s'$.

Example. Timed automata can be composed in parallel, so that systems with more than one components can be described more easily. We do not define formally the parallel composition here, due to lack of space (see, for instance, [Tri98] for more details). Instead, we present a well-known example of a system composed by three TA (figure 5). The example is about a simple railway-crossing system where a controller commands a gate to lower and raise according to the arrivals and departures of a train. Assuming the usual parallel composition operation with synchronization of edges with same labels, the composite timed automaton modeling the global system is shown in figure 6.

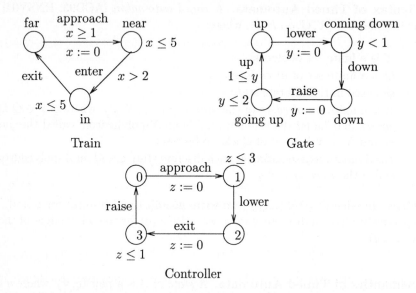

Fig. 5. The Train–Gate–Controller example.

3.2   Time-Abstracting Bisimulation and Quotient Graph

In order to apply algorithmic procedures to timed automata, we need a semantic model which is finite. For this purpose, we define the *time-abstracting bisimulation*, an equivalence which abstracts away from the quantitative aspect of time: we know that *some* time passes, but not how much. Given a TA, the time-abstracting bisimulation induces a finite graph, the *quotient*, which preserves all properties of interest, and can be therefore used for controller synthesis in the timed setting, as we show in the following section.

Time-Abstracting Bisimulation. Consider a TA A with set of edges E. A binary relation $\approx$ on the states of A is a (strong) *time-abstracting bisimulation* (TaB) if for all states $s_1 \approx s_2$, the following conditions hold:

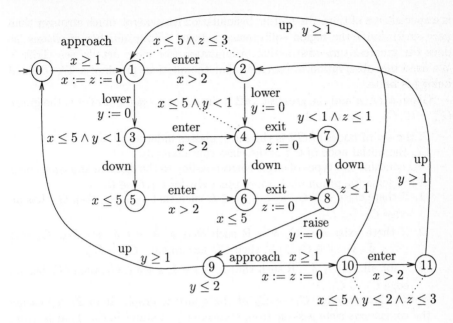

Fig. 6. The composite TA for the Train–Gate–Controller system.

1. if $s_1 \xrightarrow{e_1} s_3$, for some $e_1 \in E$, then there exists $e_2 \in E$ such that $s_2 \xrightarrow{e_2} s_4$ and $s_3 \approx s_4$;

2. if $s_1 \xrightarrow{\delta_1} s_3$ then there exists $\delta_2 \in \mathbb{R}$ such that $s_2 \xrightarrow{\delta_2} s_4$ and $s_3 \approx s_4$;

3. the above conditions also hold if the roles of s_1 and s_2 are reversed.

The definition is illustrated in figure 7 (left). The states s_1 and s_2 are said to be Ta-bisimilar. In general, two TA A_1 and A_2 are said to be Ta-bisimilar if there exists a TaB $\approx$ on the states of A_1 and A_2, such that $s_0^1 \approx s_0^2$, where s_0^i is the initial state of A_i.

Given a set of states $\hat{S}$ of A and a TaB $\approx$ on A, we say that $\approx$ *respects* $\hat{S}$ if for any $s_1 \approx s_2$, $s_1 \in \hat{S}$ iff $s_2 \in \hat{S}$.

Fig. 7. Time-abstracting bisimulations.

Time-Abstracting Quotient Graph. Being an equivalence, a TaB induces a *partition* C of the state space of a TA into *equivalence classes*. We can prove that C has finite cardinality, by showing that the *region equivalence* of [ACD93] is a special case of time-abstracting bisimulation (in general, much stronger than necessary). Since the region equivalence induces a finite number of classes, so does the greatest time-abstracting bisimulation (for more details, see [Tri98]). We need this observation to conclude that the quotient graph of a TA (defined below) is finite.

Given a TA A and the greatest TaB $\approx$ on A, the $\approx$-*quotient* of A is the graph $G_A^{\approx} = (\mathcal{C}, C_0, \rightarrow_{\approx})$, such that:

- $\mathcal{C}$, the set of nodes of $G_A^{\approx}$ is the set of classes induced by $\approx$.
- C_0, the initial node of $G_A^{\approx}$ is the class containing s_0.
- $\rightarrow_{\approx}$ contains two types of edges corresponding to the discrete and time edges of the semantic graph of A. More precisely, for $C_1, C_2 \in \mathcal{C}$,
  1. if there exist $s_1 \in C_1, s_2 \in C_2, e \in E$ such that $s_1 \xrightarrow{e} s_2$, then $G_A^{\approx}$ has an edge $C_1 \xrightarrow{e}_{\approx} C_2$,
  2. if there exist $s \in C_1, \delta \in \mathsf{R}$ such that $s \xrightarrow{\delta} s + \delta$, $s + \delta \in C_2$ and $\forall \delta' < \delta \cdot s + \delta' \in C_1 \cup C_2$, then $G_A^{\approx}$ has an edge $C_1 \xrightarrow{\tau} C_2$.
  3. if for all $s \in C_1, \delta \in \mathsf{R}$ such that $s \xrightarrow{\delta} s + \delta$, $s + \delta \in C_1$, then $G_A^{\approx}$ has an edge $C_1 \xrightarrow{\tau} C_1$.

Notice that an edge $C_1 \xrightarrow{\tau} C_2$ of the quotient graph (item 2) represents the *continuous time passage* from states in C_1 to states in C_2. That is, from each state in C_1 time can pass until the system moves to C_2, without passing from any other class meanwhile. Also, for classes containing all their time successors we add a self-looping τ edge (item 3).

It is worth noting that other definitions of the quotient graph are possible, especially concerning the choices of the set of τ edges (for instance, we could consider taking the transitive closure of the τ-edge relation, which corresponds to the additivity of time successors in the semantic level). Defining the quotient graph as we did above is essential for the correctness of the method to reduce TA controller synthesis to controller synthesis for game graphs, presented in section 4.

A technique to generate the time-abstracting quotient of a TA has been presented in [TY96]. The technique consists in starting from an initial partition of the set of states (possibly respecting a set of initial constraints) and then *refining* the partition until it becomes *stable* with respect to discrete and time edges. The final stable partition induces an equivalence which is a TaB. The technique has been implemented in the module `minim`, part of the real-time verification tool KRONOS [DOTY96, BDM$^+$98].

Example. Applying `minim` to the Train–Gate–Controller system of figure 6, we obtain the quotient graph shown in figure 8 (self-looping τ-edges are not shown, for clarity).

Some of the nodes of the quotient graph are detailed in table 1. Being equivalence classes with an infinite number of states each, the nodes are shown in *symbolic* form $(\mathbf{q}, \zeta)$, where $\mathbf{q}$ is a vector of discrete states (one for each TA) and ζ is a polyhedron representing the set of valuations associated in this discrete state. In other words, $(\mathbf{q}, \zeta)$ represents the set of states $\{(\mathbf{q}, \mathbf{v}) \mid \mathbf{v} \in \zeta\}$.

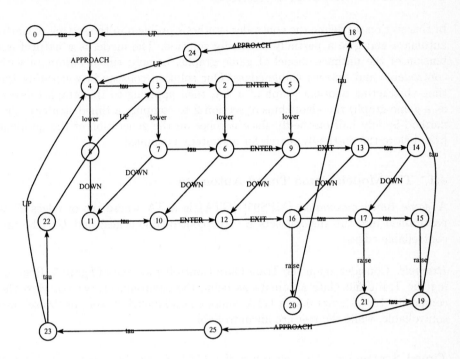

Fig. 8. The time-abstracting quotient graph of the Train–Gate–Controller example.

$$
\begin{array}{ll}
0: (\text{far}, \quad \text{up}, & 0,\, x < 1) \\
1: (\text{far}, \quad \text{up}, & 0,\, x \geq 1) \\
4: (\text{near}, \text{up}, & 1,\, x \leq 1 \wedge z < x + 1) \\
8: (\text{near}, \text{coming down}, & 2,\, y < 1 \wedge x \leq y + 1 \wedge x < z + 2) \\
10: (\text{near}, \text{down}, & 2,\, 2 < x \leq 5) \\
11: (\text{near}, \text{down}, & 2,\, x \leq 2) \\
12: (\text{in}, \quad \text{down}, & 2,\, x \leq 5) \\
16: (\text{far}, \quad \text{down}, & 3,\, x = 0 \wedge z \leq x) \\
18: (\text{far}, \quad \text{going up}, & 0,\, x \geq 1 \wedge 1 \leq y \leq 2) \\
20: (\text{far}, \quad \text{going up}, & 0,\, x < 1 \wedge x = y) \\
24: (\text{near}, \text{going up}, & 1,\, y \leq 2 \wedge x + 1 \leq y \wedge z < x + 1)
\end{array}
$$

Table 1. Some of the nodes of the time-abstracting quotient of figure 8.

4   Timed Controller Synthesis

In this section we define the controller synthesis problem in the setting of timed automata and give a partially on-the-fly solution. The model is a natural extension of the untimed model of game graphs, namely, timed automata with controllable and uncontrollable edges. Our solution consists in generating the time-abstracting quotient graph of a TA, then applying to this graph (viewed as a game graph) the algorithms of section 2 to compute a timed strategy. The method is only half on-the-fly since it relies on the generation of the quotient first, before the on-the-fly search for a strategy is applied.

4.1   The Model: Game Timed Automata

A *game timed automaton* [MPS95] (GTA) is a TA whose set of edges E is partitioned into two disjoint sets E^c (the controllable edges) and E^u (the uncontrollable edges).

Example. Consider again the Train-Gate-Controller system of figure 5. Regarding the Train and Gate automata as being the environment, we can view the composite TA of figure 6 as a GTA where edges labeled "lower" or "raise" are controllable, while the rest are uncontrollable.

Timed Strategies. The semantics of a GTA A are given in terms of *timed strategies*, which are extensions of strategies to account for the density of the time domain. Consider a GTA A, its semantic graph G_A, and a subset of its states $\hat{S}$.

A timed strategy with respect to invariance of $\hat{S}$ is a sub-graph G_1 of G_A, which satisfies the time continuity and additivity conditions 1 and 2, as well as the following conditions:

1. s_0 (the initial state of A) is the initial node of G_1.
2. If s is a node of G_1 and $s \xrightarrow{e_u} s'$ is an edge of G_A, for some $e_u \in E^u$, then $s \xrightarrow{e_u}_1 s'$ is an edge of G_1.
3. If s is a node of G_1 and $s \xrightarrow{\delta} s + \delta$ is an edge of G_A, for some $\delta \in \mathsf{R}$, then:
   - either $s \xrightarrow{\delta}_1 s + \delta$ is an edge of G_1,
   - or there exist $\delta' < \delta$ and $e_c \in E^c$, such that $s \xrightarrow{\delta'}_1 s + \delta'$ and $s + \delta' \xrightarrow{e_c}_1 s''$ are edges of G_1.
4. Every node of G_1 belongs to $\hat{S}$.

(Notice that when we say that $s \to_1 s'$ is a node of G_1, this implies that s' must be an edge of G_1.) Intuitively, condition 2 makes sure that the controller does not "cheat" : if the environment can make a move in the original graph then it can also make this move in the strategy graph. Condition 3 deals with the passage of time : if δ time units can elapse in the original graph then δ time units should be able to elapse in the strategy graph, unless if the controller can make a move earlier, at $\delta' < \delta$. Finally, condition 4 ensures that the system remains in the set of safe states.

A timed strategy with respect to reachability of $\hat{S}$ is a sub-graph G_1 of G_A, which satisfies the time continuity and additivity conditions 1 and 2, as well as the following conditions:

1. s_0 (the initial state of A) is the initial node of G_1.
2. If $s \notin \hat{S}$ is a node of G_1 and $s \xrightarrow{e_u} s'$ is an edge of G_A, for some $e_u \in E^u$, then $s \xrightarrow{e_u}_1 s'$ is an edge of G_1.
3. If $s \notin \hat{S}$ is a node of G_1 and $s \xrightarrow{\delta} s + \delta$ is an edge of G_A, for some $\delta \in R$, then:
   - either $s \xrightarrow{\delta}_1 s + \delta$ is an edge of G_1,
   - or there exist $\delta' < \delta$ and $e_c \in E^c$, such that $s \xrightarrow{\delta'}_1 s + \delta'$ and $s + \delta' \xrightarrow{e_c}_1 s''$ are edges of G_1.
4. For each node s of G_1 there exists a path $s \xrightarrow{\delta_1}_1 \xrightarrow{e_1}_1 s_1 \xrightarrow{\delta_2}_1 \xrightarrow{e_2}_1 \cdots \xrightarrow{\delta_n}_1 \xrightarrow{e_n}_1 s_n$ such that $e_1, ..., e_n \in E^c$ and $s_n \in \hat{S}$.

Conditions 2 and 3 differ from the case of invariance strategies in that for the target states $\hat{S}$ there is no requirement to continue the game. Condition 4 ensures that the controller can lead the system to the set of target states.

Controller Synthesis for Game Timed Automata. Given a GTA A and a set of states $\hat{S}$, the controller-synthesis problem for A with respect to invariance (resp. reachability) to find a timed strategy (if one exists) with respect to invariance (resp. reachability) of $\hat{S}$.

4.2 Reducing Game-Timed-Automata Synthesis to On-the-Fly Game-Graph Synthesis

We are now going to use the on-the-fly algorithms of section 2 to solve the controller-synthesis problem for GTA. Consider a GTA A with set of edges $E = E^c \cup E^u$ and a set $\hat{S}$ of states of A. Let $G_A^{\approx} = (\mathcal{C}, C_0, \to_{\approx})$ be the quotient graph of A with respect to the greatest time-abstracting bisimulation respecting $\hat{S}$.

From $G_{\approx}$ we build the game graph $G = (\mathcal{C}, C_0, \xrightarrow{c} \cup \xrightarrow{u})$, where $\xrightarrow{c}$ and $\xrightarrow{u}$ are constructed as follows:

1. For each edge $C \xrightarrow{e}_{\approx} C'$, for some $e \in E^c$, the edge $C \xrightarrow{c} C'$ is added to G.
2. For each edge $C \xrightarrow{e}_{\approx} C'$, for some $e \in E^u$, the edge $C \xrightarrow{u} C'$ is added to G.
3. For each edge $C \xrightarrow{\tau}_{\approx} C'$, the edge $C \xrightarrow{c} C'$ is added to G.

In other words, discrete transitions do not change controllability status, while time transitions are considered controllable. The intuition behind this choice is the following. Consider a τ-edge $C \xrightarrow{\tau}_{\approx} C'$. There are two possibilities:

- Either C also has a controllable discrete edge $C \xrightarrow{e_c}_\approx C''$, $e_c \in E^c$. Then the controller has a choice, either to let time pass, waiting for the environment to make a move (this comes down to picking $C \xrightarrow{\tau}_\approx C'$ as the controllable edge), or moving to C'' (this comes down to picking $C \xrightarrow{e_c}_\approx C''$). Thus, $C \xrightarrow{\tau}_\approx C'$ can be considered controllable.
- Or C has no controllable discrete edge in the quotient graph. Then the controller has no choice but to wait for the environment to make a move (recall that the TA is assumed deadlock-free). Therefore, also in this case, $C \xrightarrow{\tau}_\approx C'$ can be considered controllable as it is the controller's only choice.

We claim that the above construction is enough to reduce timed controller synthesis to the untimed case. Let $\hat{C} = \{C \mid C \subseteq \hat{S}\}$ (i.e., $\hat{C}$ is the set of all classes whose states satisfy $\hat{S}$).

Proposition 1. *A has a strategy with respect to invariance (resp. reachability) of $\hat{S}$ iff G has a strategy with respect to invariance (resp. reachability) of $\hat{C}$.*

The strategy of G corresponds to a timed strategy of A given in symbolic form. At each symbolic state (class) the controller chooses either to let time pass (τ-edge) or make a move (e-edge). In the latter case, the move can also be delayed (that is, the strategy is not time-deterministic) as long as the system remains in the same symbolic state.

Example. We illustrate the on-the-fly algorithm for invariance on the Train–Gate–Controller example of figure 6. The game graph corresponding to this system is obtained from the quotient graph of figure 8 by simply marking all edges labeled "tau", "lower" or "raise" as controllable and the rest as uncontrollable.

We are interested in computing a controller keeping the system in a set of safe states where whenever the train is in the crossing the gate is down. That is, we want to solve the controller synthesis problem with respect to the above invariance property. The property holds at all nodes of the graph of figure 8 except nodes 5 and 9.

Based on proposition 1, we solve the problem by applying the algorithm of figure 3 on the game graph of figure 8, with set of safe nodes $\hat{V} = \overline{\{5, 9\}}$.

Assuming that in the DFS order (procedure `CheckControllable`) the "tau"-edges are explored last [1], the algorithm yields the strategy shown in figure 9. In node 4, the controller chooses the action "lower" instead of the "tau"-edge and a similar choice is made in node 16. For each node, all its uncontrollable successors are included in the strategy, according to the semantics (for instance, see node 18). It is worth noticing that this strategy corresponds exactly to the part of the graph explored during the DFS, which demonstrates that the algorithm is on-the-fly: no other nodes except those belonging to the computed strategy were needed to be explored, thus no other nodes were visited.

---

[1] This can sometimes be a good heuristic, since it corresponds to exploring first the "as-soon-as-possible" policy: indeed, "tau"-edges correspond to the passage of time (while the controller is waiting).

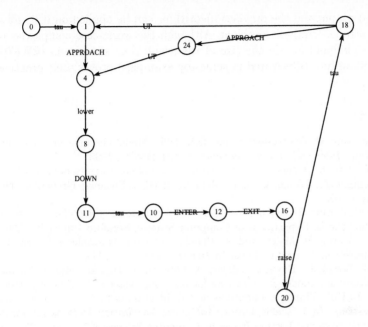

Fig. 9. A strategy for the graph of figure 8.

Examining the symbolic states corresponding to the nodes of the strategy (see table 1) we get some intuition about the timing constraints induced by the controller. For instance, node 4 corresponds to the symbolic state (near, up, 1, $x \leq 1 \wedge z < x + 1$). The discrete part (near, up, 1) corresponds to the Controller having just received the signal "approach" from the Train. The bound $z < x + 1$ means that the Controller waits less than 1 time unit before sending the command "lower" to the gate (whereas in the initial automaton of figure 5, it could wait up to 3 time units).

In a more methodological way, we can use the symbolic representation of the timed strategy in order to *restrict* the input GTA and obtain a *closed* system (but still, possibly non-deterministic) which satisfies the given invariance/reachability property. Restricting the initial GTA means replacing, for each controllable edge $(q, \zeta, X, q') \in E^c$, its guard ζ by $\zeta \cap \zeta'$, where (q, ζ') is the node in the strategy corresponding to the discrete state q. (If there is no winning node corresponding to q, then ζ can be replaced by the empty polyhedron.) The approach is explained in more detail in [Alt98].

5   Conclusions

We have presented on-the-fly techniques for controller synthesis of untimed and timed systems with respect to invariance and reachability. The technique in the untimed case uses DFS-based algorithms which return a strategy as soon as one is computed. In the timed case the technique relies on the generation of the time-abstracting quotient of a timed automaton. The quotient can be viewed as an untimed graph, and the previous algorithms can be applied on it to solve the timed controller-synthesis problem. Although the worst-case complexity of the algorithms is quadratic in the size of the graph (i.e., same as in [RW87]), their on-the-fly nature (illustrated in some toy examples) proves their practical interest.

References

[ACD93]   R. Alur, C. Courcoubetis, and D.L. Dill. Model checking in dense real time. *Information and Computation*, 104(1):2–34, 1993.

[Alt98]   K. Altisen. Génération automatique d'ordonnancements pour systèmes temporisés. Technical report, Mémoire de DEA, Ensimag, Grenoble, 1998. In french.

[Alu91]   Rajeev Alur. *Techniques for Automatic Verification of Real-Time Systems*. PhD thesis, Department of Computer Science, Stanford University, 1991.

[AMP95]   E. Asarin, O. Maler, and A. Pnueli. Symbolic controller synthesis for discrete and timed systems. In *Hybrid Systems II*, 1995.

[BDM+98]   M. Bozga, C. Daws, O. Maler, A. Olivero, S. Tripakis, and S. Yovine. KRONOS: a model-checking tool for real-time systems. In *CAV'98*, 1998.

[Dil89]   D.L. Dill. Timing assumptions and verification of finite-state concurrent systems. In J. Sifakis, editor, *Automatic Verification Methods for Finite State Systems*, Lecture Notes in Computer Science 407, pages 197–212. Springer–Verlag, 1989.

[DOTY96]   C. Daws, A. Olivero, S. Tripakis, and S. Yovine. The tool KRONOS. In *Hybrid Systems III, Verification and Control*, volume 1066 of *LNCS*, pages 208–219. Springer-Verlag, 1996.

[HNSY94]   T.A. Henzinger, X. Nicollin, J. Sifakis, and S. Yovine. Symbolic model checking for real-time systems. *Information and Computation*, 111(2):193–244, 1994.

[HW91]   G. Hoffmann and H. Wong Toi. The input-output control of real-time discrete event systems. In *30th IEEE Conf. on Decision and Control*, 1991.

[HW92]   G. Hoffmann and H. Wong Toi. Symbolic synthesis of supervisory controllers. In *American Control Conference*, 1992.

[Le 93]   M. Le Borgne. *Dynamical Systems over finite fields*. PhD thesis, Université de Rennes, 1993. In French.

[MPS95]   O. Maler, A. Pnueli, and J. Sifakis. On the synthesis of discrete controllers for timed systems. In *STACS '95*, 1995.

[PR89]   A. Pnueli and R. Rosner. On the synthesis of a reactive module. In *ACM Symp. POPL*, 1989.

[RW87]   P. Ramadge and W. Wonham. Supervisory control of a class of discrete event processes. *SIAM J. Control Optim.*, 25(1), January 1987.

[Tri98]   S. Tripakis. *The formal analysis of timed systems in practice*. PhD thesis, Université Joseph Fourrier de Grenoble, 1998.

[TY96]   S. Tripakis and S. Yovine. Analysis of timed systems based on time–abstracting bisimulations. In *Proc. 8th Conference Computer-Aided Verification, CAV'96, Rutgers, NJ*, volume 1102 of *LNCS*, pages 232–243. Springer-Verlag, July 1996.

[WM99]   W. Wonham and C. Meder. The TTCT tool. Personal communication, 1999.

On-the-fly Verification of Linear Temporal Logic

Jean-Michel Couvreur

LaBRI, Université de Bordeaux I, Talence, France
couvreur@labri.u-bordeaux.fr

Abstract. In this paper we present two new practical and pragmatic algorithms for solving the two key on-the-fly model-checking problems for linear temporal logic: on demand construction of an automaton for a temporal logic formula; and on-the-fly checking for whether the automata resulting from the product of the program and the property is empty.

1 Introduction

Automatically checking whether a finite state program satisfies its linear specification is a problem that has gained a lot of attention during the last 15 years. Linear temporal logic is a powerful specification language for expressing safety, liveness, and fairness properties. However, the model-checking problem is known do be PSPACE-complete [18]. In practice, model-checking methods face complexity related limits: the size of the state space program, the size of the underlying automaton that represents the formula, and the size of the product automaton on which model-checking algorithms are applied. Many techniques have been designed to avoid the state explosion problem. By representing programs and automata of formulas using binary decision diagram [1], [3], [4], it is possible to check very large concurrent systems [5]. Another optimizing approach is on-the-fly verification [7], [9], [11], [13], which consists in constructing the program state space, the negation of the property, and the product automaton while checking for the emptiness of the product automaton. An advantage of this approach is that the algorithm can give an answer before the full program state space and the property automaton have been constructed. On-the-fly verification can be combined with methods [10], [14], [17], [22], [23] that avoid the exploration of the complete state space by performing reductions using partial order semantics. Success stories for both methods clearly demonstrate the effectiveness of automatic verification, even for fairly large-scale industrial applications.

In this paper we present new practical and pragmatic algorithms designed for solving the two key on-the-fly model-checking problems for linear temporal logic:

- Constructing on demand an automaton for a temporal logic formula;
- Checking on-the-fly whether the automaton resulting from the product of the program and the property is empty.

Both of these problems have already been solved in an efficient way. The automaton construction algorithm in [9] appears to produce reasonable sized automata

J. Wing, J. Woodcock, J. Davies (Eds.): FM'99, Vol. I, LNCS 1708, pp. 253–271, 1999.

for temporal logic formulas and it operates on-the-fly. Algorithms in [7], [11], [12], [13] check on-the-fly for the emptiness of the product automaton.

Our new automata construction is always better than the one in [9]. It appears to produce smaller automata. From a pragmatic point of view, we build is a variant of Büchi automata, namely transition Büchi automata. As opposed to simple Büchi automata, which have only one set of accepting states [20], transition Büchi automata have multiple sets of accepting transitions. As was proven in [15], ω-automata with accepting conditions on transitions are simpler than ω-automata with accepting conditions on nodes. Automaton construction is very similar than the one proposed in [9]. It is also based on tableau procedures [25], [26]. The key point of our method is the use of symbolic computation, which allows us to simplify expressions in a natural way and then to reduce the number of nodes. Moreover, the implementation can be done efficiently and easily using Binary Decision Diagrams [1], [3], [4].

The new checking algorithm is a simple variation of the Tarjan algorithm. It has the following features:

- The algorithm is designed to run on-the-fly, that is, during the traversal of the product automaton, failure is detected as soon as a failure component is encountered.
- The algorithm works directly on transition Büchi automata with multiple accepting conditions, that is, no expansion of the transition Büchi automaton into a simple Büchi automaton is needed.
- The algorithm can be used for checking temporal properties under fairness assumptions of the form $\bigwedge_i GFp_i$, without needless overhead.

Previously existing algorithms [7], [11], [13] do not have any of the interesting properties mentioned above.

The rest of the paper starts with some preliminaries defining finite state programs, temporal logic, and its interpretations. Section 3 presents transition Büchi automata and the automata construction for a temporal logic formula. Section 4 gives the model-checking algorithm. The paper finishes with some concluding remarks.

2   Preliminaries

Let AP be a set of atomic propositions. We write as 2^{AP} the mapping set $AP \rightarrow \{False, True\}$ and $2^{2^{AP}}$ the mapping set $2^{AP} \rightarrow \{False, True\}$. We may note that 2^{AP} can also be defined just as easily as the set of subsets of AP and $2^{2^{AP}}$ as the set of propositional formulas induced by atomic propositions. Sometimes we will consider an element p of AP as a propositional formula: $\forall y \in 2^{AP} p(y) \equiv (p \in y)$.

A finite state program P consists of the following components:

- S is a finite set of states;
- $\rightarrow \subseteq S \times 2^{AP} \times S$ is a transition relation;
- s_0 is an initial state ($s_0 \in S$).

Intuitively, the set S represents the set of states the system may enter. The relation $\rightarrow$ describes the actions available to states and the state transitions that may result upon execution of the actions. AP is used to associate atomic properties with transition relations. Without loss of generality (as in [16]), one can add loop transition relations, labeled $\{Dead\}$, to every terminal state. In this case every state has some enabled action. A run of P is an infinite sequence of states

$$\rho = s_0 \xrightarrow{x_0} s_1 \xrightarrow{x_1} s_2 \xrightarrow{x_2} \ldots$$

such that for every $j \geq 0 : (s_j, x_j, s_{j+1}) \in \rightarrow$. We call a trace of ρ the infinite word over the alphabet 2^{AP} such that $trace(\rho) = x_0 \cdot x_1 \cdot x_2 \ldots$

We use linear temporal logic (LTL) for our specification language. It defines a logic for the trace set of a program. We will say that program P fulfils a linear temporal property iff every trace of P fulfils f. The formal syntax for LTL is given below.

1. Every atomic proposition $p \in AP$ is a LTL formula.
2. If f and g are LTL formulas, then so are $\neg f$, $f \wedge g$, Xf, fUg.

An interpretation for a LTL formula is an infinite word $\sigma = x_0.x_1.x_2 \ldots$ over the alphabet 2^{AP}. We use the standard notation $\sigma \models f$ to indicate the truth of a LTL formula f for an infinite word σ. We write σ_i, for the suffix of σ starting at x_i. The relation $\models$ is defined inductively as follows:

1. $\sigma \models p$ if $x_0(p)$ for $p \in AP$;
2. $\sigma \models \neg f$ if $\neg(\sigma \models f)$;
3. $\sigma \models f \wedge g$ if $\sigma \models f$ and $\sigma \models g$;
4. $\sigma \models Xf$ if $\sigma_1 \models f$;
5. $\sigma \models fUg$ if $\exists i \geq 0 : \sigma_i \models g \wedge (\forall j < i : \sigma_j \models f)$.

The standard boolean operators, $true$ and $false$ can also be used to construct LTL formulas. We also use the following abbreviations: $F\varphi = trueU\varphi$, $G\varphi = \neg F\neg\varphi$ and $fVg = \neg(\neg fU\neg g)$.

Remark 1. Every LTL formula can be rewritten as an equivalent LTL formula where the $\neg$ unary operator is applied only to atomic propositions. In the following, we will consider only such formulas.

Remark 2. Programs can also be constructed using parameterized transition systems [2]. In such programs, atomic propositions can also be associated with states. This model is useful but does not give any extension when using LTL formulas for the specification language: the atomic propositions of a state can be moved to all its output transitions.

3   A Tableau Construction

Our goal is to build an automaton that generates all infinite words satisfying a given formula f. The automaton we build is a transition Büchi automaton. As opposed to simple Büchi automata that have only one set of accepting states [20], transition Büchi automata have multiple sets of accepting transitions.

Formally a transition Büchi automaton $< Q, Acc, \rightarrow, q_0 >$ has the following components:

- Q is a finite set of states;
- Acc is a finite set of accepting conditions;
- $\rightarrow \subseteq S \times 2^{2^{AP}} \times 2^{Acc} \times S$ is a transition relation;
- q_0 is an initial state ($q_0 \in Q$).

An infinite word $\sigma = x_0.x_1.x_2 \ldots$ over the alphabet 2^{AP} is accepted by a transition Büchi automaton iff there exists an infinite path

$$\rho = q_0 \xrightarrow{(X_0, A_0)} q_1 \xrightarrow{(X_1, A_1)} q_2 \xrightarrow{(X_2, A_2)} \ldots$$

such that $\forall i \geq 0 : ((q_i, X_i, A_i, q_{i+1}) \in \rightarrow) \wedge (\forall a \in Acc, \forall i \geq 0, \exists j \geq i : a \in A_j)$.

The automaton construction is very similar to the one proposed in [9]. It is also based on tableau procedures [25], [26]. The nodes of the graph are labeled by a set of formulas and the transitions are obtained by expanding the temporal operators in order to distinguish what has to be true immediately from what has to be true from the next state on. The fundamental assertions, which are used for this expansion, are:

$$fUg = g + f \cdot X(fUg)$$
$$fVg = f \cdot g + g \cdot X(fVg)$$

where $+$ is the boolean "or" operator and . is the boolean "and" operator.

Our automata construction is based on symbolic computation over a set of boolean variables constructed as follows:

- Every atomic proposition is a boolean variable,
- If f is a LTL formula then r_f is a boolean variable,
- If fUg is a LTL formula then a_{fUg} is a boolean variable.

Intuitively, for an infinite word $\sigma = x_0 \cdot x_1 \cdot x_2 \ldots$ over the alphabet 2^{AP}, r_f corresponds to $f \models \sigma$ and a_{fUg} corresponds to $(\sigma \models fUg) \wedge \neg(\sigma \models g)$. The fundamental identities of Boolean variables r_f and a_{fUg} are:

$$r_{fUg} = r_g + a_{fUg} \cdot r_f \cdot r_{X(fUg)}$$
$$r_{fVg} = r_f \cdot r_g + r_g \cdot r_{X(fVg)}$$
$$r_{f \wedge g} = r_f \cdot r_g$$
$$r_{f \vee g} = r_f + r_g$$
$$r_p = p$$
$$r_{\neg p} = \neg p$$

Using the fundamental identities, and given a LTL formula f, variable r_f can be expressed in an expression which only uses variables of the form p, $\neg p$, a_g and r_{Xg}, where variables p are atomic propositions and g are subformulas of f. Proposition 1 is the application of this property to a set of formulas F.

Proposition 1. *Let F be a set of formulas. $\Delta(F) = \prod_{f \in F} r_f$ can be expanded to the form:*

$$\prod_{f \in F} r_f = \sum_{(X, Nacc, Next) \in L_F} \left(X \cdot \prod_{g \in Nacc} a_g \cdot \prod_{h \in Next} r_{Xh} \right)$$

with

$$L_F \subseteq 2^{2^{AP}} \times \{gUh \in Sub(f)\}$$
$$\times \{\{gUh \in Sub(f)\} \cup \{gVh \in Sub(f)\} \cup \{g \in Sub(f) : Xg \in Sub(f)\}\}.$$

Proof. Obvious.

A transition Büchi automaton that accepts exactly the infinite words satisfying formula f, is obtained by expanding formulas of the form $\prod_g r_g$. The set of accepting condition for the automaton is composed of the subformulas gUh in f. The automata construction starts by each expanding variable r_f. Each implicant of this expansion defines a transition $(f, X, Acc \setminus NAcc, Next)$. We then expand $\prod_{g \in Next} r_g$ to produce new nodes and new transitions in the same manner. Theorem 1 formalizes the resulting automaton.

Theorem 1. *Let f be a LTL formula. Let $Bu(f)$ be the transition Büchi automaton defined by:*

- *$Q = \{F \subseteq \{gUh \in Sub(f)\} \cup \{gVh \in Sub(f)\} \cup \{g \in Sub(f) : Xg \in Sub(f)\} \cup \{f\}\}$;*
- *$Acc = \{gUh \in Sub(f)\}$;*
- *$\rightarrow = \{(F, X, Acc \setminus NAcc, Next) : (X, NAcc, Next) \in L_F\} \cup \{(\emptyset, true, Acc, \emptyset)\}$*
- *$\{f\}$ is an initial state.*

Then $Bu(f)$ accepts exactly the infinite words over the alphabet 2^{AP} that satisfy f.

Proof. ($\Rightarrow$) Let $\sigma = x_0 \cdot x_1 \cdot x_2 \ldots$ be an infinite word accepted by $Bu(f)$. Let us prove that σ satisfies formula f.

By definition, there exists an infinite path in $Bu(f)$

$$\rho = q_0 \xrightarrow{(X_0, A_0)} q_1 \xrightarrow{(X_1, A_1)} q_2 \xrightarrow{(X_2, A_2)} \ldots$$

such that $\forall i \geq 0 : ((q_i, X_i, A_i, q_{i+1}) \in \rightarrow) \wedge (\forall a \in Acc, \forall i \geq 0, \exists j \geq i : a \in A_j)$.

For each transition (q_i, X_i, A_i, q_{i+1}), consider the boolean variables $r[i]_g$ for each LTL formula g, and boolean variable $a[i]_{gUh}$ for each accepting condition gUh.

Let the sets $r[i]_{Xg} = [g \in q_{i+1}]$, $r[i]_p = [p \in x_i]$ for $p \in AP$, $a[i]_{gUh} = [gUh \in A_i]$. Using fundamental identities, we deduce the value of each variable $r[i]_g$ for any LTL formula g. By the construction of $Bu(f)$, $r[i]_g$ is true for any formula in q_i. Indeed, the initial value of the implicant associated with transition was *true*, so $\prod_{g \in q_i} r[i]_g$ must be *true*.

We can establish by induction on the size of the formula that, if $r[i]_g$ is *true*, then the suffix word σ_i satisfies g. This will conclude the first part of the proof.

- If p is an atomic proposition and $r[i]_p$ is true then $p \in x_i$ and then σ_i satisfies p;
- If $r[i]_{g \wedge h}$ is *true* then $r[i]_{g \wedge h} = r[i]_g \cdot r[i]_h = true$ and by induction σ_i satisfies g and h;
- If $r[i]_{g \vee h}$ is *true* then $r[i]_{g \vee h} = r[i]_g + r[i]_h = true$ and by induction σ_i satisfies g or h;
- If $r[i]_{gUh}$ is *true* then $r[i]_{gUh} = r[i]_h + a[i]_{gUh} \cdot r[i]_g \cdot r[i]_{X(gUh)} = true$; if $r[i]_h = true$ then by induction σ_i satisfies h and thus gUh; otherwise $r[i]_{X(gUh)} = true$ and $r[i]_g = true$, by definition $gUh \in q_{i+1}$ and then $r[i+1]_{gUh} = true$ and by induction σ_i satisfies g. In the latter case one can apply the same deduction for $j > i$ until $r[j]_h = true$. This procedure will eventually stop at least when $a[j]_{gUh}$ is false ($gUh \in A_j$).
- If $r[i]_{gVh}$ is *true* then $r[i]_{gVh} = r[i]_g \cdot r[i]_h + r[i]_h \cdot r[i]_{X(gVh)} = true$; if $r[i]_g = r[i]_h = true$ then by induction σ_i satisfies g and h, and thus gVh; otherwise $r[i]_{X(gVh)} = true$ and $r[i]_h = true$, by definition $gVh \in q_{i+1}$ and then $r[i+1]_{gVh} = true$ and by induction σ_i satisfies h. In the latter case one can apply the same deduction for $j > i$ until $r[j]_g = true$. This procedure can stop or proceed infinitely; in both case, we deduce that σ_i satisfies gVh.

($\Leftarrow$) Let $\sigma = x_0 \cdot x_1 \cdot x_2 \ldots$ be an infinite word satisfying formula f. Let us prove that σ is accepted by $Bu(f)$.

One can construct an infinite path in $Bu(f)$

$$\rho = q_0 \xrightarrow{(X_0, A_0)} q_1 \xrightarrow{(X_1, A_1)} q_2 \xrightarrow{(X_2, A_2)} \ldots$$

such that $\forall i \geq 0 : X_i(x_i); \forall g \in q_i, \sigma_i$ satisfies g, and if σ_i satisfies $h \vee \neg(gUh)$ then $gUh \in A_i$.

Each transition (q_i, X_i, A_i, q_{i+1}) corresponds to a *true* implicant in formula $\prod_{g \in q_i} r_g$ when setting variables: $r_{Xg} = [\sigma_{i+1} \models g]$, $r[i]_p = [p \in x_i]$ for $p \in AP$, $a_{gUh} = (\sigma_i \models gUh) \wedge \neg(\sigma_i \models h)$. Any accepting condition gUh appears infinitely often in the path. Otherwise there exists an $i > 0$ and a formula gUh such that $\forall j > i, \sigma_j$ satisfies $\neg h \wedge (gUh)$.

Example 1. Construction of an automaton for formula $f = pU(qUs)$

Let $g = qUs$. We deduce $Acc = \{f, g\}$. The fundamental identities used in the construction are:

$$r_f = r_g + a_f \cdot p \cdot r_{Xf}$$

$$r_g = s + a_g \cdot q \cdot r_{Xg}$$

Firstly, one can expand variable r_f:

$$r_f = r_g + a_f \cdot p \cdot r_{Xf} = s + a_g \cdot q \cdot r_{Xg} + a_f.p.r_{Xf}$$

This expansion produces 3 transitions:

$$(\{f\}, s, \{f, g\}, \emptyset)$$

$$(\{f\}, q, \{f\}, \{g\})$$

$$(\{f\}, p, \{g\}, \{f\})$$

Secondly, one has to produce the successors of states $\{g\}$ and $\emptyset$. The expansion of r_g is immediate: $r_g = s + a_g \cdot q \cdot r_{Xg}$ and produces transitions:

$$(\{g\}, s, \{f, g\}, \emptyset)$$

$$(\{g\}, q, \{f\}, \{g\}).$$

The transition for state $\emptyset$ is always $(\emptyset, true, \{f, g\}, \emptyset)$. Figure 1 gives the resulting automaton.

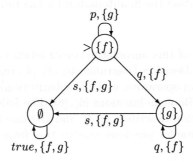

p, {g}

$>(\{f\})$

$q, \{f\}$

$s, \{f, g\}$

$\emptyset$ $s, \{f, g\}$ $\{g\}$

$true, \{f, g\}$ $q, \{f\}$

Fig. 1. A transition Büchi automaton for the formula $pU(qUs)$

Example 2. Construction of an automaton for Formula $f = GXFp$
Let $g = Fp$. We deduce $Acc = \{g\}$.
The fundamental identities used in the construction are:

$$r_f = r_{Xg} \cdot r_{Xf}$$

$$r_g = p + a_g \cdot r_{Xg}$$

First, we expand the variable r_f:

$$r_f = r_{Xg} \cdot r_{Xf}$$

This expansion produces the transition $(\{f, true, \{g\}, \{f, g\}\})$.

emptiness. A classic improvement of this procedure is on-the-fly model checking: construction of nodes for the program automaton and the transition Büchi automaton is be done on demand, while constructing the product automaton and checking its for emptiness. Thus, it is possible to stop the procedure when a violation of the checked property is detected.

To construct all of the successors of node (s, q), one has to build for every transition (s, x, s') of the program, all the transitions (q, X, A, q') of the transition Büchi automaton which match (s, x, s'), i.e $x \in X$. A simple procedure is to build all the successors of q and then select the ones which match. However, this procedure can be improved by just expanding $\Delta(F)(x)$, i.e. $\Delta(F)$ where variables of AP are bounded to Boolean value $[x \in X]$:

$$\prod_{f \in F} r_f = \sum_{(X, Nacc, Next) \in L_F} \left(\prod_{g \in Nacc} a_g \cdot \prod_{h \in Next} r_{Xh} \right)$$

In the underlying transition Büchi automaton this procedure considers that every propositional formula X of each implicant is a mapping x of 2^{AP}. As a proof of the efficiency of this procedure, $Bu(\bigwedge_i GF p_i)$ has a single node and an exponential number of transitions, and only one matching transition for a program transition (s, x, s').

4   Checking Algorithm

To check whether the transition Büchi automaton $P \times Bu(\neg f)$ is nonempty, one has to check whether there exists a failure cycle in $P \times Bu(\neg f)$, that is a cycle that contains at least one transition for each accepting condition and which is reachable from the initial state (s_0, q_0). Note that it is not necessary to consider all possible cycles of $P \times Bu(\neg f)$: it is sufficient to check if $P \times Bu(\neg f)$ contains a failure component, that is a strongly connected component that is reachable from the initial state and which includes at least one transition for each accepting condition.

Searching for maximal strongly connected components can be done with the Tarjan algorithm [19], [21]. This algorithm is based on a depth-first search. It uses two additional variables with each node NFNUMBER and LOWLINK: NFNUMBER gives the order of the first visit of a node and LOWLINK characterizes roots of strongly connected components as nodes with NFNUMBER=LOWLINK. During the depth-first search, values of NFNUMBER and LOWLINK are updated. When a node with NFNUMBER=LOWLINK is reached by backtracking, a strongly connected component is computed and removed from the graph. Any property on a strongly connected component can be checked when it is removed. The main problem of this algorithm is that a strongly connected component is first completely traversed before it is checked. The algorithm cannot detect graph failures in the fly, that is, stop the algorithm when the traversed graph contains a failure cycle.

The new checking algorithm presented in the section is a simple variation of the Tarjan algorithm. The LOWLINK node variables are replaced by a stack of the NFNUMBER values of the roots of strongly connected components of the traversed graph. Each NFNUMBER value of the root stack is associated with the set of accepting conditions of its connected component. During the depth-first search, this stack is updated and then the sets of accepting conditions of strongly connected components of the traversed graph are always known. The algorithm detects graph failures in the fly, and one can stop the computation when the traversed graph contains a failure component.

A description of the new algorithm is given in Figure 3. The data structure we use for representing transition Büchi automata contains sufficient information for the checking algorithm:

- $S0$ is the initial node,
- ACC is the accepting condition set,
- $RELATION \subseteq S \times ACC \times S$ is the transition relation (only accepting conditions are used for the checking algorithm).

The additional data structures of the new algorithm are:

- Num gives the number of nodes of the current graph; it is used to set the order of the first visit of a node,
- $Hash$ is a hash table of pairs $(node, integer)$; it is used to store visiting nodes. The node component is the search key and the integer component gives the node order. When the order $order(v)$ of a node v is null, it means that node v has been already visited and is removed from the graph.
- $Root$ is a stack of pairs $(integer, accepting\ condition\ set)$; it stores the root number of strongly connected components of the current graph and its accepting condition set.
- Arc is a stack of accepting condition sets; it gives the accepting condition set of the arcs which connect strongly connected components of the current graph.

    During the execution of the algorithm, one can consider

- the removed graph: the subgraph containing nodes store in table $Hash$ with order null,
- the current graph: the sub-graph of the traversed graph containing nodes store in table $Hash$ with order non null,
- the search path: the path in the graph induces by the depth-first search.

The new algorithm is designed to preserve the following properties each time a transition is traversed or a new node is visited.

Property 1. The removed graph is a union of nonfailure strongly connected components of the full graph;

Property 2. Stack $Root$ contains only nodes of the search path in the same order;

Moreover the accepting condition set of this component is updated to $\{a\}$. At Line 27, $\{a\} \neq \{a, b\}$ and so no error is reported.

5. The transition $C \to D$ is traversed. D is also a new node and Lines 12-17 are executed.

6. The transition $D \to E$ is traversed. E is also a new node and Lines 12-17 are executed.

7. The transition $E \to D$ is traversed. D is a node with order 4 and then Lines 20-27 are executed. *Root* and *Arc* are popped until the head of *Root* is less than or equal to 4. This operation merges components $\{D\}$ and $\{E\}$ into one strongly connected component.

8. All the successor transitions of Node E have been already traversed. Lines 30-31 check whether Node E is a root of a strongly connected component. This is not the case and the Node E are just backtracked.

9. All the successor transitions of Node D have been already traversed. Lines 30-31 check if Node D is a root of a strongly connected component. It is the case and then Lines 32-36 are executed: this operation removes the strongly connected component $\{D, E\}$ from the current graph. In the calling procedure *Remove* (Lines 39-44), $Hash.testset0(v)$ return *false* if the order of v is 0 (v is already removed) else sets the order of v to 0 and return *true*.

10. The transition $C \to F$ is traversed. F is a new node and Lines 12-17 are executed.

11. The transition $F \to G$ is traversed. G is a new node and Lines 12-17 are executed.

12. The transition $G \to F$ is traversed. F is a node with order 4 and then Lines 20-27 are executed. *Root* and *Arc* are popped until the head of Stack *Root* is less or equal to 4. This operation merges components $\{F\}$ and $\{G\}$ into one strongly connected component $\{F, G\}$. At this point, the accepting condition set is updated to $\{b\}$.

13. The transition $G \to H$ is traversed. H is a new node and Lines 12-17 are executed.

14. The transition $H \to F$ is traversed. F is a node with order 4 and then Lines 20-27 are executed. *Root* and *Arc* are popped until the head of Stack *Root* is less than or equal to 4. This operation merges components $\{F, G\}$ and $\{H\}$ in one strongly connected component $\{F, G, H\}$. The accepting condition set is updated to $\{a, b\}$. At Line 27, an error is reported and the algorithm stops: $\{F, G, H\}$ is a failure connected component.

Theorem 2. *If there exists at least one failure connected component in a transition Büchi automaton, the checking algorithm will report an error. Moreover, the checking algorithm reports an error as soon as the traversed graph contains a failure component.*

Proof. The proof is simple but tedious. One has simply to verify the assertion properties 1-4 set on lines:

- Line 8 : before Procedure *Explore* is called
- Line 9 : before selecting a transition

Table 3. Execution of the checking algorithm

	Node	Transition	Root	Arc	Hash
1	A.1		1.∅	∅	A.1
2	A.1	A→B	1.∅, 2.∅	∅ ∅	A.1, B.2
3	B.2	B→C	1.∅, 2.∅, 3.∅	∅ ∅ a	A.1, B.2, C.3
4	C.3	C→A	1.{a}	∅	A.1, B.2, C.3
5	C.3	C→D	1.{a}, 4. ∅	∅ ∅	A.1, B.2, C.3, D.4
6	D.4	D→E	1.{a}, 4.∅, 5.∅	∅ ∅ ∅	A.1, B.2, C.3, D.4, E.5
7	E.5	E→D	1.{a}, 4.{b}	∅ ∅	A.1, B.2, C.3, D.4, E.5
8	E.5		1.{a}, 4.{b}	∅ ∅	A.1, B.2, C.3, D.4, E.5
9	D.4		1.{a}	∅	A.1, B.2, C.3, D.0, E.0
10	C.3	C→F	1.{a}, 4.∅	∅ {b}	A.1, B.2, C.3, F.4, D.0, E.0
11	F.4	F→G	1.{a}, 4.∅,5.∅	∅ {b} ∅	A.1, B.2, C.3, F.4, G.5, D.0, E.0
12	G.5	G→F	1.{a}, 4.{a}	∅ {b}	A.1, B.2, C.3, F.4, G.5, D.0, E.0
13	G.5	G→H	1.{a}, 4.{a}, 6.∅	∅ {b} ∅	A.1, B.2, C.3, F.4, G.5, H.6, D.0, E.0
14	H.6	H→G	1.{a}, 4.{a,b}	∅ {b}	A.1, B.2, C.3, F.4, G.5, H.6, D.0, E.0

- Line 18 : after visiting of a new node
- Line 27 : after visiting of a current node
- Line 28 : after checking for a failure component
- Line 30 : after visiting all the successor transitions
- Line 37 : after removing a possible non-failure strongly connected component
- Line 38 : at the end of Procedure *Explore*

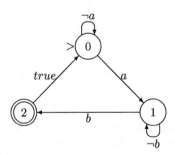

Fig. 5. Counter automaton

The previous algorithms [7], [13], [11] work an on-fly-way only for simple Büchi automata (one accepting condition). They consist of two depth-first searches. In the nicest and lastest version, the magic algorithm [11], each time an accepting state is backtracked by the first search, the second search checks if the accepting state is reachable from itself through a nontrivial path (see [11] for a complete presentation of this algorithm). This algorithm reduces the size of the required memory and is compatible with efficient partial verification techniques such as bit-state hashing techniques [12]. However it needs some adaptation in order to manipulate multiple accepting conditions, which increases the size of the graph (linear time in the number of accepting conditions). Moreover, if a part of the traversed graph contains a failure, this algorithm does not necessary detect it immediately.

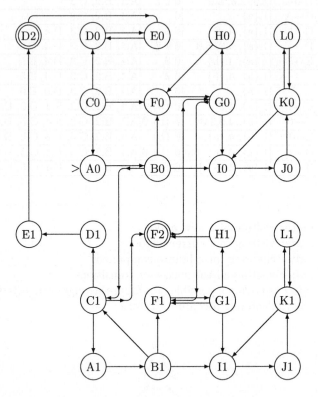

Fig. 6. Expansion of the product transition Büchi automaton

Example To apply the magic algorithm [11] to the transition Büchi automaton presented in Figure 4, one need first to expand it in a simple Büchi automaton (only one accepting condition associated with states, that is, a set of accepting states). This can be done by synchronizing it with the counter automaton (Figure 5). Figure 6 gives the resulted product Büchi automaton.

Table 4 traces the execution of the first depth-first search of the magic algorithm [11]. The second depth-first search starts when F2 is backtracked and detects the failure cycle $F2 \to G0 \to F1 \to G1 \to H1 \to F2$. At Step 13 of the execution of first search, all the transitions of the nontrivial path have been traversed and the magic algorithm does not immediately detect the failure.

Table 4. First depth search of the magic algorithm

	Node	Transition	Hash
1	A0		A0
2	A0	A0→B0	A0,B0
3	B0	B0→C1	A0,B0,C1
4	C1	C1→A1	A0,B0,C1,A1
5	A1	A1→B1	A0,B0,C1,A1,B1
6	B1	B1→C1	A0,B0,C1,A1,B1,C1
7	B1	B1→F1	A0,B0,C1,A1,B1,C1,F1
8	F1	F1→G1	A0,B0,C1,A1,B1,C1,F1,G1
9	G1	G1→F1	A0,B0,C1,A1,B1,C1,F1,G1
10	G1	G1→H1	A0,B0,C1,A1,B1,C1,F1,G1, H1
11	H1	H1→F2	A0,B0,C1,A1,B1,C1,F1,G1, H1,F2
12	F2	F2→G0	A0,B0,C1,A1,B1,C1,F1,G1, H1,F2,G0
13	G0	G0→F1	A0,B0,C1,A1,B1,C1,F1,G1, H1,F2,G0
14	G0	G0→H0	A0,B0,C1,A1,B1,C1,F1,G1, H1,F2,G0,H0
15	H0	H0→F0	A0,B0,C1,A1,B1,C1,F1,G1, H1,F2,G0,H0, F0
16	F0	F0→G0	A0,B0,C1,A1,B1,C1,F1,G1, H1,F2,G0,H0, F0
17	F0		
18	H0		
19	G0	G0→I0	A0,B0,C1,A1,B1,C1,F1,G1, H1,F2,G0,H0, F0,I0
20	I0	I0→J0	A0,B0,C1,A1,B1,C1,F1,G1, H1,F2,G0,H0, F0,I0,J0
21	J0	J0→K0	A0,B0,C1,A1,B1,C1,F1,G1, H1,F2,G0,H0, F0,I0,J0,K0
22	K0	K0→I0	A0,B0,C1,A1,B1,C1,F1,G1, H1,F2,G0,H0, F0,I0,J0,K0
23	K0	K0→L0	A0,B0,C1,A1,B1,C1,F1,G1, H1,F2,G0,H0, F0,I0,J0,K0,L0
24	L0	L0→K0	A0,B0,C1,A1,B1,C1,F1,G1, H1,F2,G0,H0, F0,I0,J0,K0,L0
25	L0		
26	K0		
27	J0		
28	I0		
29	G0		
30	F2		

5 Concluding Remarks

We have presented two new practical and pragmatic algorithms designed for solving the two key on-the-fly model-checking problems for linear temporal logic. The new automata construction has the same nice characteristics than the one in [9]: it is simple, it appears to produce reasonablly-sized automata and it operates on-the-fly. The new construction is always better: in that it produces smaller automata. The key point of our method is the use of symbolic computation. It allows us simplify expressions in a natural way and thus to reduce the number of nodes. A simple and efficient implementation can be done using Binary Decision Diagrams.

The new checking algorithm has the following features:

- The algorithm is designed to run on the fly, i.e., as soon as the traversed product automaton contains a failure component, the failure is detected.
- The algorithm works directly on transition Büchi automata with multiple accepting conditions, i.e, no expansion of the transition Büchi automaton into a simple Büchi automaton is need.
- The algorithm can be used for checking temporal properties under fairness assumptions of the form $\bigwedge_i GFp_i$, without needless overhead: a program running under a fairness assumption introduces accepting conditions (i.e. a program is viewed as a transition Büchi automaton) and the product automaton will still have the same size with new accepting conditions.

Previously existing algorithms [7], [11], [13] do not have any of the interesting properties mentioned above. However the new algorithm is not compatible with efficient partial verification as bit-state hashing technique [12]. For exhaustive verification, the storage of an additional integer with each state is not a problem in practical cases: usually the space to store a program state which is many order of magnitude larger than the space to store an integer. We claim that our algorithm is compatible with partial order methods [10], [17], [22], [23]. It does not need any modification as does the magic algorithm [14]. Moreover, our model-checking algorithm can be adapted in order to solve a classical partial order technique problem: When building a reduced state space, one has to assume some fairness properties in the construction. Informally an action must be executed if it is enabled forever; otherwise safety and liveness properties are not preserved.

References

[1] B. Akers. Binary decision diagrams. *IEEE Transactions on Computers*, 27(6):509–516, 1978.

[2] A. Arnold. *Finite transition systems. Semantics of communicating systems.* Prentice-Hall, 1994.

[3] K. S. Brace, R. L. Rudell, and R. E. Bryant. Efficient Implementation of a BDD Package. In *27th ACM/IEEE Design Automation Conference*, pages 40–45, Orlando, Florida, June 1990. ACM/IEEE, IEEE Computer Society Press.

[4] R. Bryant. Graph based algorithms for boolean function manipulation. *IEEE Transactions on Computers*, 35(8):677–691, 1986.

[5] E. Clarke, O. Grumberg, and D. Long. Verification tools for finite-state concurrent systems. *Lecture Notes in Computer Science*, 803, 1994.

[6] O. Coudert and J. C. Madre. Implicit and incremental computation of primes and essential implicant primes of boolean functions. In *Proceedings of the 29th ACM/IEEE Design Automation Conference*, pages 36–39, 1992.

[7] C. Courcoubetis, M. Y. Vardi, P. Wolper, and M. Yannakakis. Memory efficient algorithms for the verification of temporal properties. *Formal Methods in System Design*, 1:275–288, 1992.

[8] Y. Dutuit and A. Rauzy. Exact and truncated computations of prime implicants of coherent and non-coherent fault trees within aralia. *Reliability Engineering and System Safety*, 58:127–144, 1997.

[9] R. Gerth, D. Peled, M. Y. Vardi, and P. Wolper. Simple on-the-fly automatic verification of linear temporal logic. In *Proc. 15th Work. Protocol Specification, Testing, and Verification*, Warsaw, June 1995. North-Holland.

[10] P. Godefroid. *Partial-Order Methods for the Verification of Concurrent Systems.* Springer, Berlin, 1996.

[11] P. Godefroid and G. J. Holzmann. On the verification of temporal properties. In *Proc. 13th Int. Conf on Protocol Specification, Testing, and Verification, INWG/IFIP*, pages 109–124, Liege, Belgium, May 1993.

[12] G. J. Holzmann. An improved protocol reachability analysis technique. *Software, Practice & Experience*, 18(2):137–161, February 1988.

[13] G. J. Holzmann. *Design and Validation of Computer Protocols.* Prentice-Hall, Englewood Cliffs, New Jersey, 1991.

[14] G. J. Holzmann, D. Peled, and M. Yannakakis. On nested depth first search. In *The Spin Verification System*, pages 23–32. American Mathematical Society, 1996. Proc. of the Second Spin Workshop.

[15] B. Lessaec. *Etude de la reconnaissabilité des langages de mots infinis.* PhD thesis, Université Bordeaux I, 1986.

[16] O. Lichtenstein and A. Pnueli. Checking the finite-state concurrent programs satisfy their linear specifications. In *popl85*, pages 97–107, 1985.

[17] D. Peled. All from one, one from all: on model checking using representatives. In *Proceedings of the 5th International Conference on Computer Aided Verification, Greece*, number 697 in Lecture Notes in Computer Science, pages 409–423, Berlin-Heidelberg-New York, 1993. Springer.

[18] A. P. Sistla and E. M. Clarke. The complexity of propositional linear temporal logic. *Journal of the Association for Computing Machinery*, 32(3):733–749, July 1985.

[19] R. E. Tarjan. Depth-first search and linear algorithms. *SIAM J. Computing*, 1(2):146–160, 1972.

[20] W. Thomas. Automata on infinite objects. In *Handbook of theoretical computer science, Volume B : Formal models and semantics*, pages 165–191. Elsevier Science Publishers, 1990.

[21] J. D. Ullman, A. V. Aho, and J. E. Hopcroft. *The Design and Analysis of Computer Algorithms.* Addison-Wesley, 1974.

[22] A. Valmari. Stubborn sets for reduced state space generation. *Lecture Notes in Computer Science*, 483:491–515, 1990.

[23] A. Valmari. On-the-fly verification with stubborn sets representatives. In *Proceedings of the 5th International Conference on Computer Aided Verification, Greece*, number 697 in Lecture Notes in Computer Science, pages 397–408, Berlin-Heidelberg-New York, 1993. Springer.

[24] M. Y. Vardi and P. Wolper. An automata-theoretic approach to automatic program verification. In *Proceedings of the First Symposium on Logic in Computer Science*, pages 322–331, Cambridge, June 1986.

[25] P. Wolper. Temporal logic can be more expressive. *Information and Control*, 56(1–2):72–99, 1983.

[26] P. Wolper. The tableau method for temporal logic: An overview. *Logique et Analyse*, (110–111):119–136, 1985.

Symbolic Model Checking with Fewer Fixpoint Computations

David Déharbe* and Anamaria Martins Moreira

Universidade Federal do Rio Grande do Norte
Departamento de Informática e Matemática Aplicada
Campus Universitário — Lagoa Nova
59072-970 Natal, RN, Brazil
{david,anamaria}@dimap.ufrn.br
http://www.dimap.ufrn.br/~david,~anamaria

Abstract. Symbolic model checking, *smc*, is a decision procedure that verifies that some finite-state structure is a model for a formula of Computation Tree Logic (CTL). *smc* is based on fixpoint computations. Unfortunately, as the size of a structure grows exponentially with the number of state components, *smc* is not always powerful enough to handle realistic problems.

We first show that a subset of CTL formulas can be checked by testing simple sufficient conditions, that do not require any fixpoint computation. Based on these observations, we identify a second, larger, subset of CTL that can by verified with fewer fixpoint computations than *smc*. We propose a model checking algorithm for CTL that tests the identified sufficient conditions whenever possible and falls back to *smc* otherwise. In the best (resp. worst) case, the complexity of this algorithm is exponentially better (resp. the same) in terms of state components than that of *smc*.

1 Introduction

Model checking is an algorithm for computing the truth of a formula expressed in some logic in a given model. [4] and [15] presented independently a fully automatic model checking algorithm for the branching time temporal logic CTL in finite-state transition systems, linear in the size of the formula and in the size of the model. This algorithm has been used to verify systems of up to several million states and transitions [5], which is enough in practice only for small systems.

A big step forward was made when [14] proposed a new model checking algorithm for CTL, based on fixpoint computations of sets of states. In this algorithm, called symbolic model checking, binary decision diagrams [3] are used to represent both the transitions and the states of the model. Since sets of states are represented in intention by their characteristic functions, the size of the verified

---

* The research presented in this paper has been partially financed by CNPq.

J. Wing, J. Woodcock, J. Davies (Eds.): FM'99, Vol. I, LNCS 1708, pp. 272–288, 1999.
© Springer-Verlag Berlin Heidelberg 1999

model is not bound by the memory of the computer running the verification and it is possible to verify systems that have several orders of magnitude more states.

However, most of the systems designed today are much larger and, in order to achieve verification, symbolic model checking must be combined, often manually, with other techniques, such as abstraction and composition [6]. It is important to note that most of the involved techniques are only good in a heuristic sense: although theoretically their computational complexity is extremely large, practically, on many examples, they prove to be efficient [7, 1]. Successful verification of real-world hardware, software and protocols has been achived with these techniques. However, even with these combinations, the verification of large and complex designs often requires too much resources and is either not possible, due to the complexity of the computations involved in the fixpoint computations, or requires human expertise.

In spite of this handicap, usually known as the "state explosion problem", model checking is probably the most successful trend in formal verification today, particularly in the hardware design community. Given this context, research is being carried out with the goal of potentially increasing the number of systems that can be verified through model checking. We can identify three possible ways to attack this problem: reducing the size of the model (e.g. with abstraction [6], symmetry [8], decomposition [12]), reducing the size of the formulas (with a rewrite system) [9], and developping more efficient verification algorithms where the size of the model and of the formula have a smaller impact on the verification activity [11, 2].

The research presented in this paper belongs to the latter. We propose heuristics for verifying an important class of temporal properties (a subset of CTL), with a smaller number of fixpoint computations than the decision procedures that we are aware of. As the traditional algorithm is basically composed of nested fixpoint computations, the complexity of the verification depends directly on the length of these fixpoint computations. We identify a class of properties that may be checked without any fixpoint computations. However, the presented heuristics do not always provide definite results: for a class of formulas, they may give a false positive or a false negative answer. In those identified cases, traditional verification must be carried out. Fortunately, the computational complexity of the heuristics is significantly smaller than those of the traditional algorithm. Experience shows that the performance of the verification process is significantly better when the heuristics works, and that the time and space penalty is unnoticeable to the user when it does not.

These results constitute a generalization of [10], where a similar approach is applied to the class of invariants[1]. Much in the same way, but for a larger class of properties, we present sufficient conditions for these properties to be true in a given model. We also show how the CTL model checking algorithm is to be modified so that it first checks the validity of these conditions before going on with more complex decision procedures.

---

[1] A property is an invariant of a model if it holds for every reachable state.

Outline: In Sections 2 to 3, we overview the foundations of symbolic model checking: Kripke structures, the class of models considered; and binary decision diagrams, an efficient data structure to represent such structures. We then present in Section 4 syntax and semantics of computation tree logic (CTL) and we define the subsets of CTL which are dealt with by our optimization heuristics. In Section 5, we present the main results of the paper: sufficient conditions for formulas in these subsets to be valid in a given model. We also show, in Section 6, how to incorporate the computation of these sufficient conditions in CTL model checking.

2   Kripke Structures

Let P be a finite set of boolean propositions. A Kripke structure over P is a quadruple $M = (S, T, I, L)$ where:

- S is a finite set of states.
- $T \subseteq S \times S$ is a transition relation, such that $\forall s \in S, \exists s' \in S, (s, s') \in T$.
- $I \subseteq S$ is the set of initial states.
- $L : S \rightarrow 2^P$ is a labeling function. L is injective and associates with each state a set of boolean propositions true in the state.

A path π in the Kripke structure M is an infinite sequence of states $s_1, s_2, \ldots$ such that $\forall i \geq 1, (s_i, s_{i+1}) \in T$. $\pi(i)$ is the ith state of π. The set of states reachable from I, denoted RS, is the set of states s such that there is a path from an initial state to this state:

$$RS = \{s \in S \mid \exists \pi, ((\pi(1) \in I) \land \exists i \geq 1, (\pi(i) = s))\} \qquad (1)$$

A property f is an *invariant* of M, if f is true of each state s of RS.

2.1   Characteristic Functions

Let $M = (S, T, I, L)$ be a Kripke structure over $P = \{v_1, \ldots, v_n\}$. Let $\mathbf{v}$ denote $(v_1, \ldots v_n)$. The characteristic function of a state $s \in S$, denoted $[s]$, is defined as:

$$[s](\mathbf{v}) = \left(\left(\bigwedge_{v_i \in L(s)} v_i \right) \land \left(\bigwedge_{v_i \notin L(s)} \neg v_i \right) \right)$$

The definition of the characteristic function is extended to sets of states with the following definitions:

$$[\{\}](\mathbf{v}) = \mathit{false}$$
$$[\{x\} \cup X](\mathbf{v}) = [x](\mathbf{v}) \lor [X](\mathbf{v})$$

Let $P' = \{v'_1, \ldots v'_n\}$ be a set of fresh boolean propositions. The characteristic function of a transition $t = (s_1, s_2) \in T$, denoted $[t]$, is defined as:

$$[t](\mathbf{v}, \mathbf{v}') = [s_1](\mathbf{v}) \wedge [s_2](\mathbf{v}')$$

This definition can be extended to represent sets of transitions as for sets of states.

To simplify notations, in the rest of the paper we will identify $[X]$ with X.

2.2 State Space Traversal

Let $M = (S, T, I, L)$ be a Kripke structure over P. The image of a set of states $X \subseteq S$ is the set of states that can be reached in one transition from X:

$$\{s \in S \mid \exists s' \in X, (s', s) \in T\}$$

The characteristic function of the image of X, denoted $Forward(X)$, is:

$$Forward(X)(\mathbf{v}') = \exists \mathbf{v}, X(\mathbf{v}) \wedge T(\mathbf{v}, \mathbf{v}')$$

Conversely, the inverse image of a set of states $X \subseteq S$, is the set of states from which X can be reached in one transition:

$$\{s \in S \mid \exists s' \in X, (s, s') \in T\}$$

The characteristic function of the inverse image of a set of states X, denoted $Backward(X)$, is:

$$Backward(X)(\mathbf{v}) = \exists \mathbf{v}', X(\mathbf{v}') \wedge T(\mathbf{v}, \mathbf{v}')$$

3 Binary Decision Diagrams

Binary Decision Diagrams (BDDs for short) form a heuristically efficient data structure to represent formulas of the propositional logic. Let P be a totally ordered finite set of boolean propositions. Let f be a boolean formula over P, $bdd(f)$ is the BDD representing f, and $|bdd(f)|$ is the size if this BDD. [3] showed that BDDs are a canonical representation: two equivalent formulas are represented with the same BDD:

$$f \Leftrightarrow g \text{ iff } bdd(f) = bdd(g)$$

Moreover, most boolean operations can be performed efficiently with BDDs. Let $|b|$ denote the size of BDD b:

- $bdd(\neg f)$ is computed in constant time [2] $O(1)$.
- $bdd(f \vee g)$ is realized in $O(|bdd(f)| \times |bdd(g)|)$.
- $bdd(\exists x, f)$ is performed in $O(|bdd(f)|^2)$.

In this paper, we will use usual boolean operators to denote the corresponding operation on BDDs, e.g. $bdd(f) \vee bdd(g) = bdd(f \vee g)$.

We explain the basic principles of the BDD representation on an example. Fig. 1 presents the binary decision tree for the 2-bit comparison: $x_1 \Leftrightarrow y_1 \wedge x_2 \Leftrightarrow y_2$. The binary tree representation of a formula is exponential in the number of free boolean propositions in the formula.

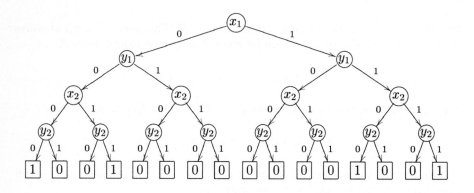

Fig. 1. Binary tree for $x_1 \Leftrightarrow y_1 \wedge x_2 \Leftrightarrow y_2$.

The corresponding BDD is obtained by repeatedly applying the following rules:

- remove duplicate terminal vertices,
- remove duplicate vertices bottom-up,
- remove opposite vertices,
- remove redundant tests.

Fig. 2 presents the BDD of the 2 bit comparator with ordering $x_1 < y_1 < x_2 < y_2$ (dotted edges indicate that the target function shall be negated). For an n-bit comparator, the BDD representation is linear with ordering $x_1 < y_1 < \ldots < x_n < y_n$ and thus is exponentially better than the binary tree representation. However, with ordering $x_1 < \ldots < x_n < y_1 < \ldots < y_n$, the BDD representation is exponential.

---

[2] Actually, negation on BDDs as presented in [3] is a linear operation. However, [13] proposed a slight modification of the data structure that resulted in reducing the negation to a constant operation. Schematically, the modification consists in tagging edges and identifying the representations of f and $\neg f$. Current BDD packages integrate this modification.

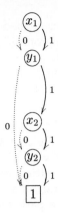

Fig. 2. BDD for $x_1 \Leftrightarrow y_1 \wedge x_2 \Leftrightarrow y_2$.

[3] showed that some functions have an exponential BDD representation for any variable ordering, and that finding the optimum variable ordering is NP-hard. However, in practice, heuristic methods generally achieve a good variable ordering, when such ordering exists.

In a Kripke structure, states, transitions and sets thereof can be characterized with propositional logic formulas. These formulas can be represented and manipulated via their BDD representation.

4   Temporal Logics

We start this section on temporal logics by a quick overview of CTL (Computation Tree Logic), the specification logic associated to symbolic model checking. We then define a hierarchy of proper sub-logics of CTL, named STL (Step Temporal Logic — Section 4.2), NF-CTL (No Fixpoint Temporal Logic — Section 4.3) and FF-CTL (Fewer Fixpoints Temporal Logic — Section 4.4). These logics are such that there is a proper inclusion of the corresponding sets of well-formed formulas.

The results in this paper apply to the verification of both NF-CTL and FF-CTL.

4.1   CTL: Computation Tree Logic

Syntax The set $T_{\mathsf{CTL}}(P)$ of Computation Tree Logic (CTL for short) formulas over a non-empty set of propositions P is the smallest set such that $P \subseteq T_{\mathsf{CTL}}(P)$ and, if f and g are in $T_{\mathsf{CTL}}(P)$, then $\neg f$, $f \wedge g$, $\mathbf{EX}f$, $\mathbf{AX}f$, $\mathbf{EG}f$, $\mathbf{AG}f$, $\mathbf{EF}f$, $\mathbf{AF}f$, $\mathbf{E}[f\mathbf{U}g]$, $\mathbf{A}[f\mathbf{U}g]$, $\mathbf{E}[f\mathbf{R}g]$ and $\mathbf{A}[f\mathbf{R}g]$ are in $T_{\mathsf{CTL}}(P)$.

Each temporal logic operator is composed of:

- a path quantifier: $\mathbf{E}$, for all paths, or $\mathbf{A}$, for some path;
- followed by a state quantifier: $\mathbf{E}$, next state on the path, $\mathbf{U}$, until, $\mathbf{G}$, globally, $\mathbf{F}$, eventually, or $\mathbf{R}$, release.

Semantics The semantics of CTL is defined with respect to a Kripke structure $M = (S, T, I, L)$ over a set of atomic propositions P. If f is in $T_{\mathsf{CTL}}(P)$, $M, s \models f$ means that f holds at state s of M.

Let f and g be in $T_{\mathsf{CTL}}(P)$, then

1. $M, s \models p$ iff $p \in L(s)$.
2. $M, s \models \neg f$ iff $M, s \not\models f$.
3. $M, s \models f \wedge g$ iff $M, s \models f$ and $M, s \models g$.
4. $M, s \models \mathbf{EX} f$ iff there exists a state s' of M such that $(s, s') \in T$ and $s' \models f$. I.e. s has a successor where f is valid.
5. $M, s \models \mathbf{EG} f$ iff there exists a path π of M such that $\pi(1) = s$ and $\forall i \geq 1, M, \pi(i) \models f$. I.e. s is at the start of a path where f holds globally.
6. $M, s \models \mathbf{E}[f \mathbf{U} g]$ iff there exists a path π of M such that $\pi(1) = s$ and and $\exists i \geq 1, M, \pi(i) \models g \wedge \forall j, i > j \geq 1, M, \pi(j) \models f$. I.e. s is at the start of a path where g holds eventually and f holds until g becomes valid.

Other temporal logic operators can be defined in terms of **EX**, **EG** and **E[U]**:

$$\mathbf{AX} f = \neg \mathbf{EX} \neg f$$
$$\mathbf{AG} f = \neg \mathbf{EF} \neg f$$
$$\mathbf{AF} f = \neg \mathbf{EG} \neg f$$
$$\mathbf{EF} f = \mathbf{E}[true \mathbf{U} f],$$
$$\mathbf{A}[f \mathbf{U} g] = \neg \mathbf{E}[\neg g \mathbf{U} \neg f \wedge \neg g] \wedge \neg \mathbf{EG} \neg g$$
$$\mathbf{A}[g \mathbf{R} f] = \neg \mathbf{E}[\neg g \mathbf{U} \neg f]$$
$$\mathbf{E}[g \mathbf{R} f] = \neg \mathbf{A}[\neg g \mathbf{U} \neg f]$$

Two operators are of special interest in the context of this paper:

- $\mathbf{E}[\mathbf{R}]$, where $M, s \models \mathbf{E}[f \mathbf{R} g]$ iff there exists a path π of M such that $\pi(1) = s$ and $\forall i \geq 1, M, \pi(i) \models f$ or $\exists i \geq 1, M, \pi(i) \models g \wedge \forall j, i \geq j \geq 1, M, \pi(j) \models f$. I.e. s is at the start of a path where f holds until g becomes valid (note that f must be valid in s and that g may never turn valid along π):

$$\mathbf{E}[g \mathbf{R} f] = \mathbf{E}[f \mathbf{U}(f \wedge g)] \vee \mathbf{EG} f;$$

- $\mathbf{A}[\mathbf{R}]$, the universal counterpart of $\mathbf{E}[\mathbf{R}]$.

A formula f is valid in structure M if it is valid for all initial states:

$$M \models f \text{ iff } \forall s \in I, M, s \models f.$$

CTL symbolic model checking uses the BDD representations of the characteristic functions of sets of states and transitions. The algorithm is based on the fixpoint characterization of the different temporal operators of CTL, as defined in [4]. For instance,

$$\mathbf{A}[f \mathbf{U} g] = \mathbf{lfp} Z[g \vee (f \wedge \mathbf{AX} Z)]$$

The number of iterations required to reach a fixpoint depends on two factors: the size of the model and the size of the formula.

4.2 STL: Step Temporal Logic

STL is a branching-time temporal logic that does not allow unbounded state quantifiers **G**, **F**, **U** and **R**. Therefore it only contains those formulas that assert exact timing properties, such as "in two steps, necessarily f", which can be written **AXAX**f, or "in two to three steps, necessarily f" (expressed as **AXAX**$(f \vee \textbf{AX} f)$).

Formally, the set $T_{\mathsf{STL}}(P)$ of Step Temporal Logic (STL for short) formulas over a set of propositions P is the smallest set such that $P \subseteq T_{\mathsf{STL}}(P)$ and, if f and g are in $T_{\mathsf{STL}}(P)$, then $\neg f$, $f \wedge g$ and **EX**f are in $T_{\mathsf{STL}}(P)$[3]. Note that $T_{\mathsf{STL}}(P) \subset T_{\mathsf{CTL}}(P)$ and the semantics of STL formulas with respect to a Kripke structure is the same as corresponding CTL formulas.

The symbolic model checking algorithm for CTL also applies to STL. However, none of the STL formulas requires a fixpoint computation. The number of iterations is bounded by the size of the formula (more precisely, it is equal to the number of **EX** operators in the formula), and is independent of the size of the model.

4.3 NF-CTL: No Fixpoint Computation Tree Logic

NF-CTL is a branching time temporal logic whose terms can be model checked without any fixpoint computation. Below, we formally define NF-CTL and discuss its expressive power.

Definition The set $T_{\mathsf{NF\text{-}CTL}}(P)$ of Iterationless Computation Tree Logic (NF-CTL for short) formulas over a set of propositions P is the smallest set such that:

- $T_{\mathsf{STL}}(P) \subseteq T_{\mathsf{NF\text{-}CTL}}(P)$ and,
- if f and g are in $T_{\mathsf{STL}}(P)$, then $\mathbf{E}[g\mathbf{R}f]$, $\mathbf{A}[g\mathbf{R}f]$, $\mathbf{AG}(f \Rightarrow \mathbf{E}[g\mathbf{R}f])$ and $\mathbf{AG}(f \Rightarrow \mathbf{A}[g\mathbf{R}f])$ are in $T_{\mathsf{NF\text{-}CTL}}(P)$.
- if f and g are in $T_{\mathsf{NF\text{-}CTL}}(P)$, then $\neg f$, $f \wedge g$, are in $T_{\mathsf{NF\text{-}CTL}}(P)$.

Note that $T_{\mathsf{NF\text{-}CTL}}(P) \subset T_{\mathsf{CTL}}(P)$ and the semantics of NF-CTL formulas with respect to a Kripke structure is the same as corresponding CTL formulas.

In the following, we call $\mathbf{A}[g\mathbf{R}f]$ and $\mathbf{AG}(f \Rightarrow \mathbf{A}[g\mathbf{R}f])$ *universal NF-CTL* formulas; $\mathbf{E}[g\mathbf{R}f]$ and $\mathbf{AG}(f \Rightarrow \mathbf{E}[g\mathbf{R}f])$, *existential NF-CTL* formulas; and $\neg f$ and $f \wedge g$, *connective NF-CTL* formulas.

Expressive Power Although at first look, NF-CTL seems restricted, important classes of CTL formulas can be expressed in this subset:

- always: $\mathbf{AG}f = \mathbf{A}[\mathit{false}\mathbf{R}f]$;
- almost always: $\mathbf{AG}(f \Rightarrow \mathbf{AG}f) = \mathbf{AG}(f \Rightarrow \mathbf{A}[\mathit{false}\mathbf{R}f])$;

---

[3] Here and in the following definitions of temporal logics, we use the standard equations to relate basic operators **EX**, **EG** and **E**[**U**] with the other operators. The same remark applies to boolean operators.

- release: $\mathbf{A}[g\mathbf{R}f]$;
- handshaking: $\mathbf{AG}(Req \Rightarrow \mathbf{A}[Ack\mathbf{R}Req])$;
- eventually: $\mathbf{AF}f = \neg\mathbf{EG}\neg f = \neg\mathbf{E}[false\mathbf{R}f]$.

4.4   FF-CTL: Fewer Fixpoints Computation Tree Logic

FF-CTL is a branching time temporal logic whose terms can be model checked with fewer fixpoint computations than in McMillan's algorithm. FF-CTL basically consists of CTL formulas where some subterms not embedded in temporal operators, are NF-CTL formulas.

Definition The set $T_{\mathsf{FF\text{-}CTL}}(P)$ of Fewer Fixpoints Computation Tree Logic (FF-CTL for short) formulas over a set of propositions P is the smallest set such that:

- $T_{\mathsf{NF\text{-}CTL}}(P) \subseteq T_{\mathsf{FF\text{-}CTL}}(P)$ and,
- if f and g are in $T_{\mathsf{CTL}}(P)$, then $\mathbf{E}[g\mathbf{R}f]$, $\mathbf{A}[g\mathbf{R}f]$, $\mathbf{AG}(f \Rightarrow \mathbf{E}[g\mathbf{R}f])$ and $\mathbf{AG}(f \Rightarrow \mathbf{A}[g\mathbf{R}f])$ are in $T_{\mathsf{FF\text{-}CTL}}(P)$.
- if f is in $T_{\mathsf{FF\text{-}CTL}}(P)$ and g in $T_{\mathsf{CTL}}(P)$, then $\neg f$, $f \wedge g$, are in $T_{\mathsf{FF\text{-}CTL}}(P)$.

Note that $T_{\mathsf{NF\text{-}CTL}}(P) \subset T_{\mathsf{FF\text{-}CTL}}(P) \subset T_{\mathsf{CTL}}(P)$ and the semantics of FF-CTL formulas for a given Kripke structure is the same as the corresponding CTL formulas.

Expressive Power To evaluate the practical expressive power of FF-CTL, we have made a small statistical study based on a publicly available list of SMV examples [16]. On a total of 107 CTL formulas, 41 (38%) are syntactically NF-CTL formulas, and 49 (46%) are syntactically FF-CTL formulas, even though the $\mathbf{A}[\mathbf{R}]$ and $\mathbf{E}[\mathbf{R}]$ operators are not directly available in SMV specification language.

5   Sufficient Conditions for FF-CTL Formulas

Since FF-CTL is a subset of CTL, standard model checking algorithms for CTL formulas can also be used to check FF-CTL formulas. However, in this section we show heuristics for verifying FF-CTL formulas with fewer fixpoint computations. In the following, for each class of FF-CTL formulas, we present sufficient conditions that guarantee they are valid of a Kripke structure. We then provide proofs for these conditions and, in section 6, show how an alternative model checking algorithm can make use of these results.

5.1   Conditions

Table 1 presents sufficient conditions for universal FF-CTL formulas to be true of a Kripke structure. For instance, if $Forward(f \wedge \neg g) \subseteq f$ holds, then we can conclude that the FF-CTL formula $\mathbf{AG}(f \Rightarrow \mathbf{A}[g\mathbf{R}f])$ is valid. If, additionally,

$I \models f$ holds, then $\mathbf{A}[g\mathbf{R}f]$ is also valid. When $I \not\models f$, then $\mathbf{A}[g\mathbf{R}f]$ does not hold. Otherwise, we cannot conclude.

Standard model checking verification of these formulas requires one (in the case of $\mathbf{A}[g\mathbf{R}f]$) or two (in the case of $\mathbf{AG}(f{\Rightarrow}\mathbf{A}[g\mathbf{R}f])$) additional fixpoint computations than testing the above requirements. Particularly, if both f and g are STL formulas, no fixpoint computation is needed to test the sufficient conditions.

$I \subseteq f$	$Forward(f \wedge \neg g) \subseteq f$	$\mathbf{AG}(f{\Rightarrow}\mathbf{A}[g\mathbf{R}f])$	$\mathbf{A}[g\mathbf{R}f]$
false	false	?	false
false	true	true	false
true	false	?	?
true	true	true	true

Table 1. Sufficient conditions for universal FF-CTL formulas

Table 2 gives sufficient conditions for existential FF-CTL formulas to hold in a Kripke structure. Again, the interesting part of this table lays in the second and fourth lines. If it can be shown that $f \wedge \neg g \subseteq Backward(f)$ is true, we can conclude that the FF-CTL formula $\mathbf{AG}(f{\Rightarrow}\mathbf{E}[g\mathbf{R}f])$ is valid. Furthermore, if we have $I \models f$, then $\mathbf{E}[g\mathbf{R}f]$ is also valid. Again, standard model checking verification of these formulas requires more fixpoint computations than checking the above requirements. As above, if the formula also belongs to NF-CTL, then no fixpoint computation is needed at all.

$I \subseteq f$	$f \wedge \neg g \subseteq Backward(f)$	$\mathbf{AG}(f{\Rightarrow}\mathbf{E}[g\mathbf{R}f])$	$\mathbf{E}[g\mathbf{R}f]$
false	false	?	false
false	true	true	false
true	false	?	?
true	true	true	true

Table 2. Sufficient conditions for existential FF-CTL formulas

5.2 Proofs for Table 1

Proposition 1. Let $M = (S, T, I, L)$ be a Kripke structure. If the image of $f \wedge \neg g$ in M is a subset of f ($Forward(f \wedge \neg g) \subseteq f$), then $M \models \mathbf{AG}(f{\Rightarrow}\mathbf{A}[g\mathbf{R}f])$.

Proof. We prove the contrapositive of this formula, that is:

If a Kripke structure M is such that $M \models \neg\mathbf{AG}(f{\Rightarrow}\mathbf{A}[g\mathbf{R}f])$ then $Forward(f \wedge \neg g) \not\subseteq f$.

First, we rewrite formula $\neg\mathbf{AG}(f\Rightarrow\mathbf{A}[g\mathbf{R}f])$ as follows:

$$
\begin{aligned}
\neg\mathbf{AG}(f\Rightarrow\mathbf{A}[g\mathbf{R}f]) &\equiv \neg\neg\mathbf{EF}(\neg(f\Rightarrow\mathbf{A}[g\mathbf{R}f]))\\
&\equiv \mathbf{EF}(\neg(f\Rightarrow\mathbf{A}[g\mathbf{R}f]))\\
&\equiv \mathbf{EF}(\neg(\neg f\vee\mathbf{A}[g\mathbf{R}f]))\\
&\equiv \mathbf{EF}(f\wedge\neg\mathbf{A}[g\mathbf{R}f]))\\
&\equiv \mathbf{EF}(f\wedge\neg(\neg\mathbf{E}[\neg g\mathbf{U}\neg f]))\\
&\equiv \mathbf{EF}(f\wedge\neg(\neg\mathbf{E}[\neg g\mathbf{U}\neg f]))\\
&\equiv \mathbf{EF}(f\wedge\mathbf{E}[\neg g\mathbf{U}\neg f])
\end{aligned}
$$

The semantics of operator $\mathbf{EF}$ states that if $\mathbf{EF}(f\wedge\mathbf{E}[\neg g\mathbf{U}\neg f])$ holds, then, there is a finite path $\pi_1,\pi_2,\ldots\pi_n, n\geq 1$ of M such that:

$$
\pi_1\in I \text{ and } \pi_n\models f\wedge\mathbf{E}[\neg g\mathbf{U}\neg f].
$$

Therefore,

$$
\pi_n\models f \text{ and } \pi_n\models\mathbf{E}[\neg g\mathbf{U}\neg f].
$$

The semantics of $\mathbf{E}[\mathbf{U}]$ states that if $\mathbf{E}[\neg g\mathbf{U}\neg f]$ holds for π_n, then, there is a finite path $\pi_n,\pi_{n+1},\ldots\pi_m, m\geq n$ of M such that:

$$
\pi_m\models\neg f \text{ and } \forall i, n\leq i< m : \pi_i\models f\wedge\neg g.
$$

Since $\pi_n\models f$, then $\pi_m\neq\pi_n$ and $m>n$. Therefore $\pi_{m-1}\models f\wedge\neg g$ and $\pi_m\models\neg f$. In conclusion, $Forward(f\wedge\neg g)\not\subseteq f$.   □

Proposition 2. *Let* $M=(S,T,I,L)$ *be a Kripke structure. If the image of* $f\wedge\neg g$ *in* M *is a subset of* f *($Forward(f\wedge\neg g)\subseteq f$), and* f *is valid for all initial states ($I\subseteq f$), then* $M\models\mathbf{A}[g\mathbf{R}f]$.

Proof. By hypothesis, in M, $Forward(f\wedge\neg g)\subseteq f$ holds and Proposition 1 applies. Therefore, $M\models\mathbf{AG}(f\Rightarrow\mathbf{A}[g\mathbf{R}f])$, and, by weakening, we can infere that $M\models f\Rightarrow\mathbf{A}[g\mathbf{R}f]$. Since, by hypothesis, $M\models f$, through *modus ponens* we get $M\models\mathbf{A}[g\mathbf{R}f]$.   □

5.3   Proofs for Table 2

Lemma 1. *Let* f *and* g *be two arbitrary CTL formulas. Then,*

$$
\mathbf{A}[f\mathbf{U}g]\equiv\mathbf{A}[(f\wedge\neg g)\mathbf{U}g]
$$

Proof. Using the fixpoint characterization of operator $\mathbf{A}[\mathbf{U}]$, the proof of this lemma is straightforward:

$$
\begin{aligned}
\mathbf{A}[f\mathbf{U}g] &\equiv \mathbf{lfp}K[g\vee(f\wedge\mathbf{AX}K)]\\
&\equiv \mathbf{lfp}K[g\vee(f\wedge\neg g\wedge\mathbf{AX}K)]\\
&\equiv \mathbf{A}[(f\wedge\neg g)\mathbf{U}g]
\end{aligned}
$$

Proposition 3. *Let M be a Kripke structure. If the inverse image of f in M is a subset of $f \wedge \neg g$ ($f \wedge \neg g \subseteq Backward(f)$), then $M \models \mathbf{AG}(f \Rightarrow \mathbf{E}[g\mathbf{R}f])$.*

Proof. Again, we prove the contrapositive of this formula, that is:

If a Kripke structure M is such that $M \models \neg\mathbf{AG}(f \Rightarrow \mathbf{E}[g\mathbf{R}f])$ then

$$f \wedge \neg g \not\subseteq Backward(f).$$

We shall show that whenever $M \models \neg\mathbf{AG}(f \Rightarrow \mathbf{E}[g\mathbf{R}f])$, there exists a state of M where $f \wedge \neg g$ holds and f holds in none of its successors.

First, we rewrite formula $\neg\mathbf{AG}(f \Rightarrow \mathbf{E}[g\mathbf{R}f])$ as follows:

$$\begin{aligned}
\neg\mathbf{AG}(f \Rightarrow \mathbf{E}[g\mathbf{R}f]) &\equiv \mathbf{EF}\neg(f \Rightarrow \mathbf{E}[g\mathbf{R}f]) \\
&\equiv \mathbf{EF}(f \wedge \neg\mathbf{E}[g\mathbf{R}f]) \\
&\equiv \mathbf{EF}(f \wedge \mathbf{A}[\neg g\mathbf{U}\neg f]) \\
&\equiv \mathbf{EF}(f \wedge (\neg f \vee (\neg g \wedge \mathbf{AXA}[\neg g\mathbf{U}\neg f]))) \\
&\equiv \mathbf{EF}(f \wedge \neg g \wedge \mathbf{AXA}[\neg g\mathbf{U}\neg f])
\end{aligned}$$

The semantics of operator $\mathbf{EF}$ states that if $\mathbf{EF}(f \wedge \neg g \wedge \mathbf{AXA}[\neg g\mathbf{U}\neg f])$ holds, then, there is a finite path $\pi_1, \pi_2, \ldots \pi_n, n \geq 1$ of M such that:

$$\pi_1 \in I \text{ and } \pi_n \models f \wedge \neg g \wedge \mathbf{AXA}[\neg g\mathbf{U}\neg f].$$

Therefore, using Lemma 1:

$$\pi_n \models f \wedge \neg g \text{ and } \pi_n \models \mathbf{AXA}[(f \wedge \neg g)\mathbf{U}\neg f].$$

Let $\pi = \pi_n, \pi_{n+1}, \ldots$ be a path starting at state π_n and let $l(\pi) = \min(\{k|\pi_k \models \neg f\})$ be the index of the first state of such path where $\neg f$ holds. Note that, on any path π starting at π_n, the formula $\mathbf{A}[(f \wedge \neg g)\mathbf{U}\neg f]$ is valid in states $\pi_{n+1}, \ldots \pi_{l(\pi)}$.

Let $m = \max(\{l(\pi) \mid \pi = \pi_n, \pi_{n+1}, \ldots\})$. So $m - n$ is the length of the longest path prefix (c.f. fig. 3), starting at π_n, such that $f \wedge \neg g$ holds on every state $\pi_n, \pi_{n+1}, \ldots \pi_{m-1}$. $\neg f$ holds in state π_m.

Note that $\pi_{m-1} \models \mathbf{A}[(f \wedge \neg g)\mathbf{U}\neg f]$ and $\pi_{m-1} \models \neg f$. Therefore:

$$\pi_{m-1} \models \mathbf{AXA}[(f \wedge \neg g)\mathbf{U}\neg f]$$

Let π'_m be an arbitrary successor of π_{m-1}: $\pi'_m \models \mathbf{A}[(f \wedge \neg g)\mathbf{U}\neg f]$.

Suppose $\pi'_m \models f$, and consequently $\pi'_m \models f \wedge \neg g$. Therefore the path prefix $\pi_n\pi_{n+1}\cdots\pi_{m-1}\pi'_m$ starts at state π_n, is of length $1 + m - n$, and $f \wedge \neg g$ holds on every state of the path, which is a contradiction. In conclusion, no successor π'_m of π_{m-1} is such that $\pi'_m \models f$.

Since $\pi_{m-1} \models f \wedge \neg g$, then $f \wedge \neg g \not\subseteq Backward(f)$,

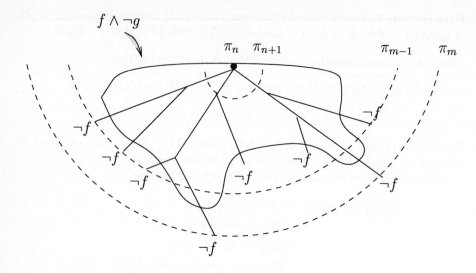

Fig. 3. Paths from π_n where $f \wedge \neg g$ holds

Proposition 4. *Let M be a Kripke structure. If the inverse image of f in M is a subset of $f \wedge \neg g$ ($f \wedge \neg g \subseteq Backward(f)$), and f is valid for all initial states ($I \subseteq f$), then $M \models \mathbf{E}[g\mathbf{R}f]$.*

The argument is similar to proof of Proposition 2:

Proof. By hypothesis, $f \wedge \neg g \subseteq Backward(f)$ holds in M. Therefore, Proposition 3 applies and $M \models \mathbf{AG}(f \Rightarrow \mathbf{E}[g\mathbf{R}f])$. By weakening, we can infere that $M \models f \Rightarrow \mathbf{E}[g\mathbf{R}f]$. Since $M \models f$ (by hypothesis), through *modus ponens* we get $M \models \mathbf{E}[g\mathbf{R}f]$.

6   Algorithms

Figure 4 contains the new CTL symbolic model checking algorithm, named *ModelCheck*. It takes as parameters m, a BDD-based representation of a finite-state transition system, and f, a CTL formula. $m.I$ denotes the characteristic function of the initial states of the system.

ModelCheck uses three subroutines:

- *ModelCheck*FF-CTL is presented in Figure 5 and is further detailed in the following. It basically implements symbolic model checking for FF-CTL, and yields a boolean result.
- *ModelCheck*CTL is McMillan's symbolic model checking algorithm. Given a BDD-based representation of the transition system and a CTL formula, it returns the BDD of the characteristic function of the set of states where the formula is valid.

– *bdd_implies* is a boolean predicate and tests if its first argument implies its second argument (both arguments are BDDs).

Line 3, *ModelCheck* tests if there is a FF-CTL formula f' equivalent to f. If this is the case, then $ModelCheck_{\mathsf{FF\text{-}CTL}}$ is called with f' (line 4), otherwise $ModelCheck_{\mathsf{CTL}}$ is called with f, and the result is checked against the initial states of M (line 6).

```
1 function ModelCheck(m : Model, f : T_CTL) : boolean
2 begin
3     if ∃f' ∈ T_FF-CTL | f' ≡ f then
4         return ModelCheck_FF-CTL(m, f')
5     else
6         return bdd_implies(m.I, ModelCheck_CTL(m, f))
7 end
```

Fig. 4. Algorithm for *ModelCheck*

$ModelCheck_{\mathsf{FF\text{-}CTL}}$, the symbolic model checking algorithm for FF-CTL, is given in Figure 5. Its parameters are m, a BDD-based representation of a finite-state transition system, and f, a FF-CTL formula. f is matched against the different possible patterns of FF-CTL formulas, and action is taken accordingly:

– When f is a negation (lines 6 and 7), the result is the negation of the model checking for the formula argument f_1.
– When f is a conjunction (lines 8 and 9), the result is the conjunction of the model checking for the formula arguments f_1 and f_2.
– When f is a $\mathbf{A}[f_2\mathbf{R}f_1]$ universal FF-CTL formula (lines 10 to 19), we first check that f_1 is valid in the initial states. If not, the formula is already proven false in m, otherwise we go on with the verification by model checking f_2 and testing the corresponding sufficient condition. If this condition is verified, the result is *true*. Otherwise, we cannot conclude, and McMillan's symbolic model checking is invoked on f.
– If on the other hand, f is a $\mathbf{AG}(f_1{\Rightarrow}\mathbf{A}[f_2\mathbf{R}f_1])$ universal FF-CTL formula (lines 20 to 26), both arguments f_1 and f_2 are model checked accordingly and the corresponding sufficient condition is then tested. If verified, the result is *true*. Otherwise, we cannot conclude, and McMillan's symbolic model checking is invoked on f^4.
– The procedure is much the same when f is an existential FF-CTL formula (lines 27 to 43).

---

[4] It is important to note that using a standard *caching* policy, the result of model checking subformulas of f is kept in a table and reused when needed in the verification of f.

```
1  function ModelCheck_FF-CTL(m : Model, f : T_FF-CTL) : boolean
2  var
3      f_1, f_2 : T_CTL
4      F1, F2 : BDD
5  begin
6      if f = ¬f_1 then
7          return ¬ModelCheck(m, f_1)
8      elsif f = f_1 ∧ f_2 then
9          return ModelCheck(m, f_1) ∧ ModelCheck(m, f_2)
10     elsif (f = A[f_2Rf_1]) then      --Table 1, Column 4
11         F_1 ← ModelCheck_CTL(m, f_1)
12         if bdd_implies(m.I, F_1) then
13             F_2 ← ModelCheck_CTL(m, f_2)
14             if bdd_implies(m.I, Forward(m, bdd_and(F_1, bdd_not(F_2))), F_1) then
15                 return true      --Table 1, Column 4, Line 4
16             else
17                 return ModelCheck_CTL(m, f)
18         else
19             return false
20     elsif f = AG(f_1 ⇒ A[f_2Rf_1]) then      --Table 1, Column 3
21         F_1 ← ModelCheck_CTL(m, f_1)
22         F_2 ← ModelCheck_CTL(m, f_2)
23         if bdd_implies(m.I, Forward(m, bdd_and(F_1, bdd_not(F_2))), F_1) then
24             return true      --Table 1, Column 3, Line 4
25         else
26             return ModelCheck_CTL(m, f)
27     elsif (f = E[f_2Rf_1]) then      --Table 2, Column 4
28         F_1 ← ModelCheck_CTL(m, f_1)
29         if bdd_implies(m.I, F_1) then
30             F_2 ← ModelCheck_CTL(m, f_2)
31             if bdd_implies(m.I, bdd_and(F_1, bdd_not(F_2)), Backward(m, F_1)) then
32                 return true      --Table 2, Column 4, Line 4
33             else
34                 return ModelCheck_CTL(m, f)
35         else
36             return false
37     elsif f = AG(f_1 ⇒ E[f_2Rf_1]) then      --Table 2, Column 3
38         F_1 ← ModelCheck_CTL(m, f_1)
39         F_2 ← ModelCheck_CTL(m, f_2)
40         if bdd_implies(m.I, bdd_and(F_1, bdd_not(F_2)), Backward(m, F_1)) then
41             return true      --Table 2, Column 3, Line 4
42         else
43             return ModelCheck_CTL(m, f)
44 end
```

Fig. 5. Algorithm for $ModelCheck_{FF\text{-}CTL}$

6.1   Complexity

To validate our approach, we shall compare the complexity of our algorithm $ModelCheck$ with McMillan's $ModelCheck_{CTL}$.

The best case occurs when f is a FF-CTL formula and the corresponding sufficient conditions hold. In this case, it saves a fixpoint computation of length at most linear in the size of M (i.e. $|S|$, the number of states of M). Since, at each step of the computation, $ModelCheck_{CTL}$ invokes $Backward$ or $Forward$ once, the complexity of $ModelCheck$ is $|S|$ times better ($Forward$ and $Backward$ are equally complex).

The worst case occurs when f is a FF-CTL formula and the corresponding sufficient conditions do not hold. In this case, the additional cost is that of computing of the sufficient conditions, which is that of $Backward$. The resulting complexity of the whole algorithm is still linear in $|S|$. Moreover, it is possible to optimize the algorithm and reuse the backward computation required in testing the sufficient condition, as a first step in the fixpoint computation of $ModelCheck_{CTL}$.

7   Conclusion and Future Work

We have defined NF-CTL, a subset of CTL formulas that can be checked by testing simple sufficient conditions, and do not involve any fixpoint computation, as opposed to previously published symbolic model checking for CTL [14] or subsets thereof [11].

We then identified FF-CTL, a second, larger, subset of CTL that can by verified using fewer fixpoint computations than [14]. Based on these results, we developed a new model checking algorithm for CTL that tests the identified sufficient conditions wherever relevant and uses [14] otherwise. The complexity of the new algorithm with respect to [14] is then discussed.

We have started to implement the proposed model checking algorithm into existing verification tools that use [14]. Preliminary results show that the incurred time penalty is so small that it cannot be quantified (that is, is smaller than the precision of the time measurement of our computing platforms). Also, in the case of invariant formulas (a special case of FF-CTL formulas), we often get positive results when testing sufficient conditions, and therefore are able to save fixpoint computations. We plan to complete this study considering the whole FF-CTL logic. We are also studying a rewrite system for CTL that finds equivalent formulas in FF-CTL wherever possible, and otherwise attempts to find an equivalent CTL formula with fewer temporal operators.

References

[1] R. J. Anderson, P. Beame, S. Burns, W. Chan, F. Modugno, D. Notkin, and R. Reese. Model checking large software specifications. In 4th *Symposium on the Foundations of Software Engineering*, pages 156–166. ACM/SIGSOFT, Oct. 1996.

[2] A. Biere, A. Cimatti, E. Clarke, and Y. Zhu. Symbolic model checking without bdds. In *TACAS'99*, Lecture Notes in Computer Science. Springer Verlag.

[3] R.E. Bryant. Graphbased algorithm for boolean function manipulation. *IEEE Transactions Computers*, C(35):1035–1044, 1986.

[4] E.M. Clarke and E. A. Emerson. Design and synthesis of synchronization skeletons for branching time temporal logic. In *Logics of Programs: Workshop*, volume 131 of Lecture Notes in Computer Science, pages 52–71. Springer Verlag, 1981.

[5] E.M. Clarke, E.A. Emerson, and A.P. Sistla. Automatic verification of finitestate concurrent systems using temporal logic specifications. *ACM Transactions On Programming Languages and Systems*, 8(2):244–263, Apr. 1986.

[6] E.M. Clarke, O. Grumberg, and D.Long. Model checking and abstraction. In *19th Annual ACM Symposium on Principles of Programming Languages*, 1992.

[7] E.M. Clarke, O. Grumberg, H. Hiraishi, S. Jha, D.E. Long, K.L. McMillan, and L.A. Ness. Verification of the futurebus+ cache coherence protocol. In *L. Claesen, editor, 11th International Symposium on Computer Hardware Description Languages: CHDL'93*. NorthHolland, 1993.

[8] E.M. Clarke, T. Filkorn, and S. Jha. Exploiting symmetry in temporal logic model checking.

[9] D. Déharbe. *Vérification Symbolique de Modèle pour la logique CTL: Étude et Application au Langage VHDL*. PhD thesis, Université Joseph Fourier-Grenoble 1, Nov. 1996.

[10] D. Déharbe and A. Martins Moreira. Using induction and BDDs to model check invariants. In Hon F. Li and David K. Probst, editors, *CHARME'97: Correct Hardware Design and Verification Methods*, Montréal, Canada, Oct. 1997. Chapman & Hall.

[11] H. Iwashita, T. Nakata, and F. Hirose. CTL model checking based on forward state traversal. In *ICCAD'96*, page 82, 1996.

[12] Bernhard Josko. MCTL – an extension of CTL for modular verification of concur rent systems. pages 165–187, 1987.

[13] J.C. Madre. *PRIAM Un outil de vérification formelle des circuits intégrés digitaux*. PhD thesis, Ecole nationale supérieure des télécommunications, Paris, France, June 1990. 90 E 007.

[14] K.L. McMillan. *Symbolic Model Checking*. Kluwer Academic Publishers, 1993.

[15] J.P. Queille and J. Sifakis. Specification and verification of concurrent systems in CESAR. In *Procs. 5th international symposium on programming*, volume 137 of Lecture Notes in Computer Science, pages 244–263. Springer Verlag, 1981.

[16] B. Yang. Fmcad'98 benchmark traces.
     http://www.cs.cmu.edu/~bwolen/fmcad98.

Formula Based Abstractions of Transition Systems for Real-Time Model Checking

Roberto Barbuti[1], Nicoletta De Francesco[2], Antonella Santone[2], and Gigliola Vaglini[2]

[1] Dipartimento di Informatica, Università di Pisa, I-56125 Pisa, Italy
barbuti@di.unipi.it
[2] Dipartimento di Ingegneria dell'Informazione, Università di Pisa, I-56126 Pisa, Italy
{nico,santone,gigliola}@iet.unipi.it

Abstract. When verifying concurrent systems described by transition systems, state explosion is one of the most serious problems. If quantitative temporal information (expressed by clock ticks) are considered, state explosion is even more serious. In this paper we present a non-standard (abstract) semantics for the ASTP language able to produce reduced transition systems. The important point is that the abstract semantics produces transition systems equivalent to the standard ones for what concerns the satisfiability of a given set of formulae of a temporal logic with quantitative modal operators. The equivalence of transition systems with respect to formulae is expressed by means of $\langle \rho, n \rangle$-equivalence: two $\langle \rho, n \rangle$-equivalent transition systems give the same truth value to all formulae such that the actions occurring in the modal operators are contained in ρ, and with time constraints whose values are less than or equal to n.

1 Introduction

In this paper we address the problem of verifying systems in which time plays a fundamental role for a correct behaviour. We refer to the *Algebra of Timed Processes* (ATP) [22] as a formalism able both to model time dependent systems and to prove their properties. ATP is an extension of traditional process algebras in order to capture *discrete quantitative timing aspects* with respect to a global clock.

The semantics of such a language is given in terms of labeled transition systems where some transitions are labeled by the special action χ, called *time action*. Such an action represents the progress of time and can be viewed as a clock tick.

One widely used method for verification of properties is *model checking* [8, 7, 18, 23]. Model checking is a technique that proves the correctness of a system specification with respect to a desired behavior by checking whether a structure, representing the specification, satisfies a temporal logic formula describing the expected behavior. Most existing verification techniques, and in particular those

J. Wing, J. Woodcock, J. Davies (Eds.): FM'99, Vol. I, LNCS 1708, pp. 289–306, 1999.

defined for concurrent calculi, like CCS [21], are based on a representation of the system by means of a labeled transition system. In this case, model checking consists in checking whether a labeled transition system is a model for a formula.

When representing systems specifications by transition systems, state explosion is one of the most serious problems: often we have to deal with transition systems with a prohibitive number of states. In such cases model checking is inapplicable. Moreover, when in system specifications quantitative temporal information (expressed by clock ticks) is considered, state explosion is even more serious, the reason for this being that a new state is generated for every clock tick. Fortunately, in several cases, to check the validity of a property, it is not necessary to consider the whole transition system, but only an abstraction of it that maintains the information which "influences" the property. This consideration has been used in the definition of abstraction criteria for reducing transition systems in order to prove properties efficiently. Abstraction criteria of such kind are often based on equivalence relations defined on transition systems: minimizations with respect to different notions of equivalence are in fact used in many existing verification environments (see, for instance, [10, 13, 16]).

In this paper we present a notion of abstraction of transition systems, where the abstraction is driven by the formulae of a quantitative temporal logic. This logic, which we call *qu-mu-calculus*, is similar to the mu-calculus [19] (in particular to a variant of it [4]), in which the modal operators are redefined to include the definition of time constraints. Many logics have been defined to deal with time aspects, see, for example [2, 14]. Although all of them handle quantitative time aspects, they can be used either in conjunction with a dense time domain [1, 3, 20] or with a discrete time domain [15, 14]. A fundamental feature of qu-mu-calculus is that its formulae can be used to drive the abstraction: in particular, given the actions and the time constraints occurring in the modal operators of a formula ϕ of the qu-mu-calculus, we use them in defining an abstract (reduced) transition system on which the truth value of ϕ is equivalent to its value on the standard one.

Equivalence of transition systems with respect to formulae is expressed by means of $\langle \rho, n \rangle$-equivalence: two transition systems are $\langle \rho, n \rangle$-equivalent if and only if they give the same truth value to all formulae such that the actions occurring in the modal operators are contained in ρ, and with time constraints whose values are less than or equal to n. Some interesting properties of such an equivalence are presented.

In the paper we present also a non-standard (abstract) semantics for the ASTP [22] language able to produce abstract transition systems. ASTP is the sequential subset of ATP; actually, this is not a limitation: our abstract semantics is easily applicable to the concurrent operators and its ability in reducing the transition system can be suitably investigated also on the sequential part. Though the paper addresses the problem of defining, for an ASTP program and a formula, ϕ, a reduced transition system preserving ϕ at a very abstract level, such an abstract definition can be usefully exploited as a guide in implementing an algorithm to build the reduced system.

After the preliminaries of Section 2, we introduce our logic in Section 3 and the abstract semantics in Section 4. Section 5 concludes.

2   Preliminaries

2.1   The Algebra of Timed Processes

Let us now quickly recall the main concepts about the Algebra of Timed Processes [22], which is used in the specification of real-time concurrent and distributed systems.

For simplicity, we consider here only the subset of ATP, called ASTP (Algebra of Sequential Timed Processes), not containing parallel operators.

The syntax of *sequential process terms* (*processes* or *terms* for short) is the following:

$$p ::= 0 \mid x \mid \alpha p \mid p \oplus p \mid \lfloor p \rfloor(q)$$

where α ranges over a finite set of *asynchronous actions* $\mathcal{A}^\alpha = \{a, b, ...\}$. We denote by $\mathcal{A}$ the set $\mathcal{A}^\alpha \cup \{\chi\}$, ranged over by $\mu, \nu \ldots$. The action χ (*time action*) is not user-definable and represents the progress of time. x ranges over a set of *constant* names: each constant x is defined by a constant definition $x \overset{def}{=} p$. We denote the set of process terms by $\mathcal{P}$.

The standard *operational semantics* [22] is given by a relation $\longrightarrow \subseteq \mathcal{P} \times \mathcal{A} \times \mathcal{P}$, where $\mathcal{P}$ is the set of all processes: $\longrightarrow$ is the least relation defined by the rules in Figure 1.

Rule **Act** manages the prefixing operator: αp evolves to p by a transition labeled by α. The operator $\oplus$ behaves as a standard nondeterministic choice for processes with asynchronous initial actions (rule **Sum$_1$** and the symmetric one not shown). Moreover, if p and q can perform a χ action reaching respectively p' and q', then $p \oplus q$ can perform a χ action, reaching $p' \oplus q'$ (rule **Sum$_2$**). The process $\lfloor p \rfloor(q)$ can perform the same asynchronous initial actions as p (rule **Delay$_1$**). Moreover $\lfloor p \rfloor(q)$ can perform a χ action, reaching the process q (rule **Delay$_2$**). Finally, rule **Con** says that a constant x behaves as p if $x \overset{def}{=} p$ is its definition. Note that there is no rule for the process 0, which thus cannot perform any move.

A *labeled transition system* (or *transition system* for short) is a quadruple $T = (\mathcal{S}, \mathcal{A}, \longrightarrow_T, p)$, where $\mathcal{S}$ is a set of states, $\mathcal{A}$ is a set of transition labels (actions), $p \in \mathcal{S}$ is the initial state, and $\longrightarrow_T \subseteq \mathcal{S} \times \mathcal{A} \times \mathcal{S}$ is the transition relation. If $(p, \mu, q) \in \longrightarrow_T$, we write $p \overset{\mu}{\longrightarrow}_T q$.

If $\delta \in \mathcal{A}^*$ and $\delta = \mu_1 \ldots \mu_n, n \geq 1$, we write $p \overset{\delta}{\longrightarrow}_T q$ to mean $p \overset{\mu_1}{\longrightarrow}_T \cdots \overset{\mu_n}{\longrightarrow}_T q$. Moreover $p \overset{\lambda}{\longrightarrow}_T p$, where λ is the empty sequence. Given $p \in \mathcal{S}$, with $\mathcal{R}_{\longrightarrow_T}(p) = \{q \mid p \overset{\delta}{\longrightarrow}_T q, \ \delta \in \mathcal{A}^*\}$ we denote the set of the states reachable from p by $\longrightarrow_T$.

$$\mathbf{Act} \quad \frac{}{\alpha p \xrightarrow{\alpha} p}$$

$$\mathbf{Sum_1} \quad \frac{p \xrightarrow{\alpha} p'}{p \oplus q \xrightarrow{\alpha} p'} \qquad\qquad \mathbf{Sum_2} \quad \frac{p \xrightarrow{\chi} p', \; q \xrightarrow{\chi} q'}{p \oplus q \xrightarrow{\chi} p' \oplus q'}$$

$$\mathbf{Delay_1} \quad \frac{p \xrightarrow{\alpha} p'}{\lfloor p \rfloor (q) \xrightarrow{\alpha} p'} \qquad\qquad \mathbf{Delay_2} \quad \frac{}{\lfloor p \rfloor (q) \xrightarrow{\chi} q}$$

$$\mathbf{Con} \quad \frac{p \xrightarrow{\mu} p'}{x \xrightarrow{\mu} p'} \; x \stackrel{def}{=} p$$

Fig. 1. *Standard operational semantics of ASTP*

Given a process p and a set of constant definitions, the *standard transition system* for p is defined as $S(p) = (\mathcal{R}_{\longrightarrow}(p), \mathcal{A}, \longrightarrow, p)$. Note that, with abuse of notation, we use $\longrightarrow$ for denoting both the operational semantics and the transition relation among the states of the transition system.

On ASTP processes equivalence relations can be defined [22], based on the notion of bisimulation between states of the related transition systems.

3 Quantitative Temporal Logic and Abstractions

In order to perform quantitative temporal reasoning, we define a logic, that we call *qu-mu-calculus*, which is an extension of the mu-calculus [19] and in particular of the selective mu-calculus [4]. The syntax is the following, where Z ranges over a set of variables:

$$\phi ::= \mathbf{tt} \mid \mathbf{ff} \mid Z \mid \phi_1 \vee \phi_2 \mid \phi_1 \wedge \phi_2 \mid [\alpha]_{R,<n} \phi \mid [\alpha]_{R,\geq n} \phi \mid \langle \alpha \rangle_{R,<n} \phi \mid$$
$$\langle \alpha \rangle_{R,\geq n} \phi \mid \nu Z.\phi \mid \mu Z.\phi$$

The satisfaction of a formula ϕ by a state p of a transition system, written $p \models \phi$, is defined as follows: any state satisfies $\mathbf{tt}$ and no state satisfies $\mathbf{ff}$; a state satisfies $\phi_1 \vee \phi_2$ ($\phi_1 \wedge \phi_2$) if it satisfies ϕ_1 or (and) ϕ_2.
$[\alpha]_{R,<n} \phi$, $\langle \alpha \rangle_{R,<n} \phi$ and $[\alpha]_{R,\geq n} \phi$, $\langle \alpha \rangle_{R,\geq n} \phi$ are the quantitative modal operators. For each quantitative operator,

- $R \subseteq \mathcal{A}^\alpha$;
- $n \in N$, where N is the set of natural numbers; n is called *time value*. In $\langle \alpha \rangle_{R,<n} \phi$ and $[\alpha]_{R,<n} \phi$ it must be $n > 0$.

The informal meaning of the operators is the following:

$\langle \alpha \rangle_{R,<n} \phi$ is satisfied by a state which can evolve to a state satisfying ϕ by executing α, not preceded by actions in $R \cup \{\alpha\}$, within n time units.

$[\alpha]_{R,<n} \phi$ is satisfied by a state which, for every execution of α occurring within n time units and not preceded by actions in $R \cup \{\alpha\}$, evolves to a state satisfying ϕ.

$\langle \alpha \rangle_{R,\geq n} \phi$ is satisfied by a state which can evolve to a state satisfying ϕ by executing α, not preceded by actions in $R \cup \{\alpha\}$, after at least n time units.

$[\alpha]_{R,\geq n} \phi$ is satisfied by a state which, for every execution of α occurring after at least n time units and not preceded by actions in $R \cup \{\alpha\}$, evolves to a state satisfying ϕ.

As in standard mu-calculus, a fixed point formula has the form $\mu Z.\phi$ ($\nu Z.\phi$) where μZ (νZ) *binds* free occurrences of Z in ϕ. An occurrence of Z is free if it is not within the scope of a binder μZ (νZ). A formula is *closed* if it contains no free variables. $\mu Z.\phi$ is the least fix point of the recursive equation $Z = \phi$, while $\nu Z.\phi$ is the greatest one. We consider only closed formulae.

The precise definition of the satisfaction of a closed formula ϕ by a state p of a transition system T is given in Table 1. It uses the relation $\Longrightarrow_T^{\rho,n}$:

Definition 1 ($\Longrightarrow_T^{\rho,n}$ relation). *Given a transition system $T = (\mathcal{S}, \mathcal{A}, \longrightarrow_T, p)$, a set of actions $\rho \subseteq \mathcal{A}^\alpha$, and $n \in N$, we define the relation $\Longrightarrow_T^{\rho,n} \subseteq \mathcal{S} \times \rho \times \mathcal{S}$ such that, for each $\alpha \in \rho$*

$$p \stackrel{\alpha}{\Longrightarrow}_T^{\rho,n} q = p \stackrel{\delta\alpha}{\longrightarrow}_T q, \text{ with } \delta \in (\mathcal{A} - \rho)^*, |\delta \downarrow_\chi| = n.$$

where $|\delta \downarrow_\chi|$ is the number of χ actions occurring in δ.

By $p \stackrel{\alpha}{\Longrightarrow}_T^{\rho,k} q$ we express the fact that it is possible to pass from p to q by executing a (possibly empty) sequence of actions not belonging to ρ and containing exactly k χ, followed by the action α in ρ.

A transition system T satisfies a formula ϕ iff its initial state satisfies ϕ. An ASTP process p satisfies a formula ϕ iff $S(p)$ satisfies ϕ.

3.1 Formula Driven Equivalence

A formula ϕ of the qu-mu-calculus can be used to define a bisimulation equivalence between transition systems. The bisimulation is defined by considering only the asynchronous actions occurring in the quantitative operators belonging to the formula (denoted by $\mathcal{O}(\phi)$), and the maximum time value of the quantitative operators occurring in the formula (denoted by $\max(\phi)$). Thus all formulae

$$p \not\models \text{ff}$$

$$p \models \text{tt}$$

$$p \models \phi \wedge \psi \qquad \text{iff } p \models \phi \text{ and } p \models \psi$$

$$p \models \phi \vee \psi \qquad \text{iff } p \models \phi \text{ and } p \models \psi$$

$$p \models [\alpha]_{R,<n}\,\phi \text{ iff } \forall p'.\forall k < n.p \overset{\alpha}{\Longrightarrow}_T^{R \cup \{\alpha\},k} p' \text{ implies } p' \models \phi$$

$$p \models \langle \alpha \rangle_{R,<n}\,\phi \text{ iff } \exists p'.\exists k < n.p \overset{\alpha}{\Longrightarrow}_T^{R \cup \{\alpha\},k} p' \text{ and } p' \models \phi$$

$$p \models [\alpha]_{R,\geq n}\,\phi \text{ iff } \forall p'.\forall k \geq n.p \overset{\alpha}{\Longrightarrow}_T^{R \cup \{\alpha\},k} p' \text{ implies } p' \models \phi$$

$$p \models \langle \alpha \rangle_{R,\geq n}\,\phi \text{ iff } \exists p'.\exists k \geq n.p \overset{\alpha}{\Longrightarrow}_T^{R \cup \{\alpha\},k} p' \text{ and } p' \models \phi$$

$$p \models \nu Z.\phi \qquad \text{iff } p \models \nu Z^m.\phi \text{ for all } m$$

$$p \models \mu Z.\phi \qquad \text{iff } p \models \mu Z^m.\phi \text{ for some } m$$

where, for each m, $\nu Z^m.\phi$ and $\mu Z^m.\phi$ are defined as:

$$\nu Z^0.\phi = \text{tt} \qquad\qquad \mu Z^0.\phi = \text{ff}$$
$$\nu Z^{m+1}.\phi = \phi[\nu Z^m.\phi/Z] \qquad \mu Z^{m+1}.\phi = \phi[\mu Z^m.\phi/Z]$$

where the notation $\phi[\psi/Z]$ indicates the substitution of ψ for every free occurrence of the variable Z in ϕ.

Table 1. *Satisfaction of a formula by a state*

with the same set of occurring actions and the same maximum time value define the same bisimulation.

Given a set $\rho \subseteq \mathcal{A}^\alpha$ of actions and a time value n, the $\langle \rho, n \rangle$-bisimulation equivalence relates states p and q if: i) for each path starting from p, containing $k < n$ time actions and no action in ρ and ending with $\alpha \in \rho$, there is a path starting from q, containing exactly k time actions and no action in ρ and ending with $\alpha \in \rho$, such that the reached states are bisimilar, and ii) for each path starting from p, containing $k \geq n$ time actions and no action in ρ and ending with $\alpha \in \rho$, there is a path starting from q, containing $m \geq n$ (possibly $m \neq k$) time actions and no action in ρ and ending with $\alpha \in \rho$, such that the reached states are bisimilar.

Definition 2 ($\langle \rho, n \rangle$-bisimulation, $\langle \rho, n \rangle$-equivalence).
Let $T = (\mathcal{S}_T, \mathcal{A}, \longrightarrow_T, p)$ and $\Sigma = (\mathcal{S}_\Sigma, \mathcal{A}, \longrightarrow_\Sigma, p')$ be transition systems, let $\rho \subseteq \mathcal{A}^\alpha$ and $n \in N$.

 - *A $\langle \rho, n \rangle$-bisimulation, $\mathcal{B}$, is a binary relation on $\mathcal{S}_T \times \mathcal{S}_\Sigma$ such that $r\mathcal{B}q$ implies:*

$i)$ $r \overset{\alpha}{\Rightarrow}{}^{\rho,j}_T r'$, with $j < n$, implies $\exists q'.q \overset{\alpha}{\Rightarrow}{}^{\rho,j}_\Sigma q'$ with $r' \mathcal{B} q'$; and

$ii)$ $q \overset{\alpha}{\Rightarrow}{}^{\rho,j}_\Sigma q'$, with $j < n$, implies $\exists r'.r \overset{\alpha}{\Rightarrow}{}^{\rho,j}_T r'$ with $r' \mathcal{B} q'$; and

$iii)$ $r \overset{\alpha}{\Rightarrow}{}^{\rho,j}_T r'$, with $j \geq n$, implies $\exists i \geq n, \exists q'.q \overset{\alpha}{\Rightarrow}{}^{\rho,i}_\Sigma q'$, with $r' \mathcal{B} q'$; and

$iv)$ $q \overset{\alpha}{\Rightarrow}{}^{\rho,j}_\Sigma q'$, with $j \geq n$, implies $\exists i \geq n, \exists r'.r \overset{\alpha}{\Rightarrow}{}^{\rho,i}_T r'$, with $r' \mathcal{B} q'$.

- T and Σ are $\langle \rho, n \rangle$-equivalent ($T \approx_{\rho,n} \Sigma$) iff there exists a $\langle \rho, n \rangle$-bisimulation $\mathcal{B}$ containing the pair (p, p').

The following proposition holds, relating equivalences with different ρ and n.

Proposition 1. For each $\rho, \rho' \subseteq \mathcal{A}^\alpha$, $n, n' \in N$, if $\rho \subseteq \rho'$ and $n \leq n'$, then $\approx_{\rho',n'} \subseteq \approx_{\rho,n}$.

Proof. See Appendix.

In order to relate $\langle \rho, n \rangle$-equivalence with quantitative temporal properties, we introduce the following definition, concerning equivalences based on sets of formulae.

Definition 3 (logic-based equivalence). Let T and Σ be two transition systems, and Γ be a set of closed formulae:

$$T \equiv_\Gamma \Sigma \text{ iff } \{\phi \in \Gamma : T \models \phi\} = \{\phi \in \Gamma : \Sigma \models \phi\}$$

The following theorem states that $\langle \rho, n \rangle$-equivalent transition systems satisfy the same set of formulae with occurring actions in ρ and maximum time value less than or equal to n.

Theorem 1. Let $T = (\mathcal{S}_T, \mathcal{A}, \longrightarrow_T, p)$ and $\Sigma = (\mathcal{S}_\Sigma, \mathcal{A}, \longrightarrow_\Sigma, q)$ be transition systems and let $\rho \subseteq \mathcal{A}^\alpha$ and $n \in N$.

$$T \approx_{\rho,n} \Sigma \quad \text{implies} \quad T \equiv_{\Phi^{\rho,n}} \Sigma$$

where

$\Phi^{\rho,n} = \{\phi : \phi$ is a closed formula of the qu-mu-calculus such that $\mathcal{O}(\phi) \subseteq \rho$ and $\max(\phi) \leq n\}$.

Proof. See Appendix.

4   Abstract Transition Systems and Abstract Semantics

In order to reduce the number of states of a transition system for model checking, we now define an abstraction of the transition system on which a formula ϕ can be equivalently checked. Given a transition system T, let us denote as *time path* each path $p_1 \xrightarrow{\chi}_T \cdots \xrightarrow{\chi}_T p_n$ such that

- no $p_i, 1 \leq i \leq n$, occurs more than once in the sequence;
- no $p_i, 1 \leq i \leq n$, is able to perform any asynchronous action.

Let T be a transition system and ϕ be a formula with occurring actions ρ and maximum time value n. A $\langle \rho, n \rangle$-abstraction T' of T has the following properties:

- all asynchronous actions labeling the transitions of T' belong to ρ;
- the length of each time path of T' is less than or equal to n;
- $T' \approx_{\rho,n} T$.

Given an ASTP process p and a pair $\langle \rho, n \rangle$, we define an abstract transition system by means of a non-standard semantics which consists of a set of inference rules that skip actions not in ρ and produce time paths not longer than n.

The non standard rules are shown in Figure 2 (the symmetric rules of $\mathbf{Sum}_1$ and $\mathbf{Sum}_2$ are not shown). They use a transition relation $\longrightarrow_{\rho,n}^m$ parameterized by an integer $m \leq n$. The ideas on which the semantics is based are the following:

- the actions in ρ are always performed (rules $\mathbf{Act}_1$, $\mathbf{Delay}_4$ and $\mathbf{Sum}_1$)
- the actions not in ρ are skipped: when an action not in ρ is encountered, a "look-ahead" is performed in order to reach either an action in ρ or a time action (rules $\mathbf{Act}_2$, $\mathbf{Delay}_3$ and $\mathbf{Sum}_2$);
- when a time action is encountered, it is skipped only if the process we reach by this action can perform a sequence of n time units. In order to count the time units we use the superscript of $\longrightarrow_{\rho,n}^m$: the transition $p \xrightarrow{\mu}_{\rho,n}^m q$ occurs when an action belonging to ρ can be executed after m time actions starting from p. In fact, in order to generate the transition $p \xrightarrow{\mu}_{\rho,n}^m q$, we first prove that $q \xrightarrow{\mu}_{\rho,n}^{m-1} q'$ for some q' (rules $\mathbf{Delay}_1$ and $\mathbf{Delay}_2$, $\mathbf{Sum}_3$ and $\mathbf{Sum}_4$). Successive applications of $\mathbf{Delay}_2$ and $\mathbf{Sum}_4$ allow us to skip all time actions in a sequence but the last n ones.

Note that in the premises of rules $\mathbf{Delay}_3$, $\mathbf{Delay}_4$, $\mathbf{Sum}_1$, $\mathbf{Sum}_2$ $\mathbf{Sum}_3$ and $\mathbf{Sum}_4$ the standard operational relation $\longrightarrow$ is used, in order to know the first action of the process and consequently to respect the standard behavior of the operators, which is different depending on whether the first action is a time action or not.

The following proposition characterizes the transitions of the non-standard semantics:

Proposition 2. *Let $\rho \subseteq \mathcal{A}^{\alpha}$ and $n \in N$. For each ASTP process p,*

1. *$p \xrightarrow{\alpha}{}_{\rho,n}^{j} q$ implies $\alpha \in \rho$ and $j = 0$;*

2. *$p \xrightarrow{\chi}{}_{\rho,n}^{m} q$ implies $1 \leq m \leq n$.*

Proof. See Appendix.

The proposition states that there are two kinds of transitions: the first one represents the execution of action $\alpha \in \rho$; the second one represents both the fact that p can perform a χ action and the fact that a path composed by χ actions starts from q, with length $m - 1$, and reaches a state where an action in ρ can be performed. Moreover the rules ensures that m is always less then or equal to n.

The following results hold, relating the standard transition relation with the non-standard one:

Proposition 3. *Let $\rho \subseteq \mathcal{A}^{\alpha}$ and $n \in N$. For each ASTP process p,*

$$p \xRightarrow{\alpha}{}_{S(p)}^{\rho,j} q \quad \textit{iff}$$

1. *$j \leq n$ and $p \xrightarrow{\chi}{}_{\rho,n}^{j} p_1 \xrightarrow{\chi}{}_{\rho,n}^{j-1} p_2 \cdots p_j \xrightarrow{\alpha}{}_{\rho,n}^{0} q$ or;*
2. *$j \geq n$ and $p \xrightarrow{\chi}{}_{\rho,n}^{n} p_1 \xrightarrow{\chi}{}_{\rho,n}^{n-1} p_2 \cdots p_n \xrightarrow{\alpha}{}_{\rho,n}^{0} q$.*

Proof. See Appendix.

Now we formally define the notion of abstract transition system.

Definition 4 (abstract transition system). *For each ASTP process p, given $\rho \subseteq \mathcal{A}^{\alpha}$ and $n \in N$ the abstract transition system for p is defined as*

$$\mathcal{N}_{\rho,n}(p) = (\mathcal{R}_{\to \mathcal{N}_{\rho,n}(p)}(p), \; \rho \cup \{\chi\}, \; \to_{\mathcal{N}_{\rho,n}(p)}, \; p)$$

where $q \xrightarrow{\mu}_{\mathcal{N}_{\rho,n}(p)} q'$ if and only if $\exists j . q \xrightarrow{\mu}{}_{\rho,n}^{j} q'$.

The following theorem holds, stating that the transition system defined by the non-standard semantics is a $\langle \rho, n \rangle$-abstraction of $S(p)$ for each process p.

Theorem 2. *Let $\rho \subseteq \mathcal{A}^{\alpha}$ and $n \in N$. For each ASTP process p,*

1. *the transitions of $\mathcal{N}_{\rho,n}(p)$ are labeled only either by actions in ρ or by χ;*
2. *the length of each time path without repetition in $\mathcal{N}_{\rho,n}(p)$ is less than or equal to n;*
3. *$S(p) \approx_{\rho,n} \mathcal{N}_{\rho,n}(p)$.*

Proof. *See Appendix.*

Note that, if $n = 0$, the abstract transition system $\mathcal{N}_{\rho,0}(p)$ for a process p does not contain transitions labeled by time actions and expresses only the precedence properties between the asynchronous actions in ρ. The following propositions relates $\approx_{\rho,n}$-equivalences with different ρ and n.

Proposition 4. *Let* $\rho, \rho' \subseteq \mathcal{A}^\alpha$, $n \in N$, $n' \in N \cup \{\omega\}$, $\rho \subseteq \rho'$ *and* $n \leq n'$. *For each ASTP process* p,

$$\mathcal{N}_{\rho,n}(p) \approx_{\rho,n} \mathcal{N}_{\rho',n'}(p).$$

Proof. By Proposition 1 and by Theorem 2.3.

$$\textbf{Act}_1 \quad \frac{}{\alpha p \xrightarrow{\alpha}_{\rho,n}^{0} p} \; \alpha \in \rho \qquad\qquad \textbf{Act}_2 \quad \frac{p \xrightarrow{\mu}_{\rho,n}^{m} p'}{\alpha p \xrightarrow{\mu}_{\rho,n}^{m} p'} \; \alpha \notin \rho$$

$$\textbf{Delay}_1 \quad \frac{q \xrightarrow{\mu}_{\rho,n}^{m} q'}{\lfloor p \rfloor (q) \xrightarrow{\chi}_{\rho,n}^{m+1} q} \; m < n \qquad\qquad \textbf{Delay}_2 \quad \frac{q \xrightarrow{\mu}_{\rho,n}^{n} q'}{\lfloor p \rfloor (q) \xrightarrow{\mu}_{\rho,n}^{n} q'}$$

$$\textbf{Delay}_3 \quad \frac{p \xrightarrow{\alpha} p', \; p' \xrightarrow{\mu}_{\rho,n}^{m} p''}{\lfloor p \rfloor (q) \xrightarrow{\mu}_{\rho,n}^{m} p''} \; \alpha \notin \rho \qquad\qquad \textbf{Delay}_4 \quad \frac{p \xrightarrow{\alpha} p'}{\lfloor p \rfloor (q) \xrightarrow{\alpha}_{\rho,n}^{0} p'} \; \alpha \in \rho$$

$$\textbf{Sum}_1 \quad \frac{p \xrightarrow{\alpha} p'}{p \oplus q \xrightarrow{\alpha}_{\rho,n}^{0} p'} \; \alpha \in \rho \qquad\qquad \textbf{Sum}_2 \quad \frac{p \xrightarrow{\alpha} p', \; p' \xrightarrow{\mu}_{\rho,n}^{m} p''}{p \oplus q \xrightarrow{\mu}_{\rho,n}^{m} p''} \; \alpha \notin \rho$$

$$\textbf{Sum}_3 \quad \frac{p \xrightarrow{\chi} p', \; q \xrightarrow{\chi} q', \; p' \oplus q' \xrightarrow{\mu}_{\rho,n}^{m} r}{p \oplus q \xrightarrow{\chi}_{\rho,n}^{m+1} p' \oplus q'} \; m < n \qquad \textbf{Sum}_4 \quad \frac{p \xrightarrow{\chi} p', \; q \xrightarrow{\chi} q', \; p' \oplus q' \xrightarrow{\mu}_{\rho,n}^{n} r}{p \oplus q \xrightarrow{\mu}_{\rho,n}^{n} r}$$

$$\textbf{Con} \quad \frac{p \xrightarrow{\mu}_{\rho,n}^{m} p'}{x \xrightarrow{\mu}_{\rho,n}^{m} p'} \; x \overset{def}{=} p$$

Fig. 2. *Non-standard operational semantics for ASTP*

Example 1. In the following we use $\chi.p$ to denote the term $\lfloor 0 \rfloor (p)$; this process can perform only the action χ and then becomes the process p. Moreover we define $\chi^n.p$ $(n > 1)$ as:

$$\chi^n.p = \lfloor 0 \rfloor (\chi^{n-1}.p)$$
$$\chi^1.p = \chi.p$$

Let us consider a vending machine with a time-dependent behavior. The machine allows a user to obtain different services: a soft drink immediately after the request; a coffee after a delay of a time unit; a cappuccino after a delay of two time units; a cappuccino with chocolate after a delay of three time units. Moreover, it is possible to recollect the inserted coin, if requested within only one time unit. The *ASTP* specification of the machine is:

$V = coin \lfloor recollect \, \overline{money} \, V \rfloor (V_1)$

$V_1 = coffee \, V_2 \oplus cappuccino \, V_3 \oplus choc\_cappuccino \, V_4 \oplus soft\_drink \, V_5$

$V_2 = \chi.(\overline{collect\_coffee} \, V)$

$V_3 = \chi^2.(\overline{collect\_cappuccino} \, V)$

$V_4 = \chi^3.(\overline{collect\_choc\_cappuccino} \, V)$

$V_5 = \overline{collect\_soft\_drink} \, V$

The standard transition for the vending machine contains 14 states and 18 transitions.

Let us suppose that we have to verify the following two formulae:

$\psi_1 = \nu Z.[coin]_{\emptyset, \geq 0} \langle \overline{collect\_soft\_drink} \rangle_{\emptyset, < 2} Z:$

"it alway holds that, after a coin has been inserted, a soft drink can be collected within two time units".

$\psi_2 = [coin]_{\emptyset, \geq 0} [\overline{money}]_{\{coin\}, \geq 1} \mathtt{ff}:$

" it is not possible to recollect the inserted coin after more than one time unit".

The formula ψ_1 can be checked on the abstract transition system $\mathcal{N}_{\rho_1, n_1}(V)$, with $\rho_1 = \mathcal{O}(\psi_1) = \{coin, \overline{collect\_soft\_drink}\}$ and $n_1 = \max(\psi_1) = 2$, which has 8 states and 14 transitions, while ψ_2 can be checked on $\mathcal{N}_{\rho_2, n_2}(V)$, with $\rho_2 = \mathcal{O}(\psi_2) = \{coin, \overline{money}\}$ and $n_2 = \max(\psi_2) = 1$, which has 6 states and 13 transitions.

5   Conclusions

In this paper we have presented an approach to the problem of the reduction of the number of states of a transition system. Many abstraction criteria for system specifications not including time constraints have been defined, see for example [4, 6, 9, 11, 12]. For real-time systems the work [17] define abstractions for transition systems with quantitative labels, but there the abstraction is not driven by the property to be proved.

We have introduced an abstract semantics for ASTP processes in order to formally define the abstract transition system. The abstract semantics can be implemented in order to design a tool for automatically building an abstract transition system. In the implementation, some care must be taken to manage infinite loops which can occur in the look-ahead process.

The reduction performed by the abstract semantics depends on the set ρ of actions and on the bound n. In particular, the reduction can be significant either when the set ρ is a small subset of $\mathcal{A}$ or when the bound n is small with respect

$$r \overset{\delta\alpha}{\underset{T}{\Longrightarrow}}{}^{\rho',j} r', \text{ for some } \delta \in (\rho' - \rho)^*$$

$$\Rightarrow \qquad\qquad\qquad \{ (r,q) \in \mathcal{B} \}$$

$$\exists i \geq n', \exists q'. \ q \overset{\delta\alpha}{\underset{\Sigma}{\Longrightarrow}}{}^{\rho',i} q', \text{ with } (r',q') \in \mathcal{B}$$

$$\Rightarrow \qquad\qquad\qquad \{ \delta \in (\rho' - \rho)^*, \alpha \in \rho \text{ and } n \leq n' \}$$

$$q \overset{\alpha}{\underset{\Sigma}{\Longrightarrow}}{}^{\rho,i} q' \text{ and } i \geq n.$$

iv) The proof of this condition follows by a symmetric argument.

Proof of Theorem 1

Theorem 1. *Let* $T = (\mathcal{S}_T, \mathcal{A}, \longrightarrow_T, p)$ *and* $\Sigma = (\mathcal{S}_\Sigma, \mathcal{A}, \longrightarrow_\Sigma, q)$ *be transition systems and let* $\rho \subseteq \mathcal{A}^\alpha$ *and* $n \in N$.

$$T \approx_{\rho,n} \Sigma \quad implies \quad T \equiv_{\Phi^{\rho,n}} \Sigma$$

where

$\Phi^{\rho,n} = \{\phi : \phi \text{ is a closed formula of the qu-mu-calculus such that } \mathcal{O}(\phi) \subseteq \rho$
    and $\max(\phi) \leq n\}$.

Proof. We prove that, given a state p belonging to T and a state q belonging to Σ

$$p \approx_{\rho,n} q \quad implies \quad p \equiv_{\Phi^{\rho,n}} q$$

By induction on the structure of the formulae without recursion.
Base. tt, ff: straightforward.
Induction step. Let us suppose that the theorem holds for ϕ and ψ, with $\mathcal{O}(\phi) \subseteq \rho$ and $\mathcal{O}(\psi) \subseteq \rho$.

$- \ \phi \vee \psi$. By inductive hypothesis.

$- \ \phi \wedge \psi$. By inductive hypothesis.

$- \ \langle \alpha \rangle_{R,<n} \phi$.

$$p \models \langle \alpha \rangle_{R,<n} \phi$$

$$\Rightarrow \qquad\qquad\qquad \{ \text{ definition of satisfaction } \}$$

for some $k < n, \ p \overset{\alpha}{\underset{T}{\Longrightarrow}}{}^{R\cup\{\alpha\},k} p'$ with $p' \models \phi$

$\Rightarrow$ $\qquad\qquad$ { Definition 1 and $R \cup \{\alpha\} \subseteq \rho$ }

$$p \xrightarrow{\beta_1}^{\rho,k_1}_T p_1 \cdots p_{r-1} \xrightarrow{\beta_r}^{\rho,k_r}_T p_r \xrightarrow{\alpha}^{\rho,k_{r+1}}_T p_{r+1} = p',$$

$r \geq 0,\ \beta_i \in (\rho - (\{\alpha\} \cup R)),\ k_1 + \cdots + k_{r+1} = k$

$\Rightarrow$ $\qquad\qquad$ { definition of $\langle \rho, n \rangle$-equivalence

$\qquad\qquad\qquad\qquad$ and $k_i < n,\ 1 \leq i \leq r+1$ }

$$q \xrightarrow{\beta_1}^{\rho,k_1}_\Sigma q_1 \cdots q_{r-1} \xrightarrow{\beta_r}^{\rho,k_r}_\Sigma q_r \xrightarrow{\alpha}^{\rho,k_{r+1}}_\Sigma q_{r+1}, \text{with } p_i \approx_{\rho,n} q_i,\ 1 \leq i \leq r+1$$

$\Rightarrow$ $\qquad\qquad$ { Definition 1 }

$$q \xrightarrow{\alpha}^{\{\alpha\}\cup R,k}_\Sigma q_{r+1}$$

$\Rightarrow$ $\qquad\qquad$ { inductive hypothesis $(q_{r+1} \models \phi$)

$\qquad\qquad\qquad\qquad$ and definition of satisfaction }

$q \models \langle \alpha \rangle_{R,<n}\ \phi$. The same holds if $q \models \langle \alpha \rangle_{R,<n}\ \phi$.

- $[\alpha]_{R,<n}\ \phi,\ \langle \alpha \rangle_{R,\geq n}\ \phi,\ [\alpha]_{R,\geq n}\ \phi$. Similar to the $\langle \alpha \rangle_{R,<n}\ \phi$ case.

For $\mu Z.\phi$ (resp. $\nu Z.\phi$) formulae the thesis follows since the truth value of such formulae corresponds (the transition systems we deal with are finite and finitely branching [22]) to the $\vee$ (resp. the $\wedge$) of an enumerable set of finite non-recursive formulae.

Proof of Proposition 2

Proposition 2. Let $\rho \subseteq \mathcal{A}^\alpha$ and $n \in N$. For each ASTP process p,

1. $p \xrightarrow{\alpha}^j_{\rho,n} q$ implies $\alpha \in \rho$ and $j = 0$;

2. $p \xrightarrow{\chi}^m_{\rho,n} q$ implies $1 \leq m \leq n$.

Proof. Both points 1 and 2 can be proved by induction on depth of inference. We prove only point 2. Point 1 can be proved in a similar way.

Point 2. We consider in turn each transition rule as the last rule applied in the inference.

αp $\quad$ **Act$_1$**: is not applicable.

$\qquad$ **Act$_2$**: $p \xrightarrow{\chi}^m_{\rho,n} p'$

$\qquad\qquad \Rightarrow$ $\qquad\qquad\qquad$ { inductive hypothesis }

$1 \leq m \leq n.$

$\Rightarrow$ { application of $\mathbf{Act}_2$ }

$\alpha p \xrightarrow{\chi}{}^m_{\rho,n} p'.$

$\lfloor p \rfloor(q)$ $\mathbf{Delay}_1$: $q \xrightarrow{\chi}{}^m_{\rho,n} q'$

$\Rightarrow$ { inductive hypothesis }

$1 \leq m \leq n.$

$\Rightarrow$ { application of $\mathbf{Delay}_1$ $(m < n)$ }

$\lfloor p \rfloor(q) \xrightarrow{\chi}{}^{m+1}_{\rho,n} q$ and $1 \leq m+1 \leq n.$

$\mathbf{Delay}_2$: $q \xrightarrow{\chi}{}^m_{\rho,n} q'$

$\Rightarrow$ { inductive hypothesis }

$1 \leq m \leq n.$

$\Rightarrow$ { application of $\mathbf{Delay}_2$ $(m = n)$ }

$\lfloor p \rfloor(q) \xrightarrow{\chi}{}^m_{\rho,n} q'$

$\mathbf{Delay}_3$: if $p \xrightarrow{\alpha} p'$ and $p' \xrightarrow{\chi}{}^m_{\rho,n} p''$

$\Rightarrow$ { inductive hypothesis }

$1 \leq m \leq n.$

$\Rightarrow$ { application of $\mathbf{Delay}_3$ }

$\lfloor p \rfloor(q) \xrightarrow{\chi}{}^m_{\rho,n} p''.$

$\mathbf{Delay}_4$: is not applicable.

$p \oplus q, x$ Similarly to proofs above.

5.1   Proof of Proposition 3

Proposition 3. Let $\rho \subseteq \mathcal{A}^\alpha$ and $n \in N$. For each ASTP process p,

$p \xRightarrow{\alpha}{}^{\rho,j}_{S(p)} q$ iff

1. $j \leq n$ and $p \xrightarrow{\chi}{}^j_{\rho,n} p_1 \xrightarrow{\chi}{}^{j-1}_{\rho,n} p_2 \cdots p_j \xrightarrow{\alpha}{}^0_{\rho,n} q$ or;

2. $j \geq n$ and $p \xrightarrow{\chi}{}^n_{\rho,n} p_1 \xrightarrow{\chi}{}^{n-1}_{\rho,n} p_2 \cdots p_n \xrightarrow{\alpha}{}^0_{\rho,n} q$.

Proof. *Point 1.* By induction on j.

Base. $j = 0$. $p \xRightarrow{\alpha}{}^{\rho,0}_{S(p)} q$

$\Leftrightarrow$ \hfill { Definition 1 }

$p \xrightarrow{\delta\alpha} q$, $\delta \in (\mathcal{A} - \rho - \{\chi\})^*$

$\Leftrightarrow$ \hfill { definition of the non standard semantics }

$p \xrightarrow{\alpha}{}^0_{\rho,n} q$

Induction step. Let us suppose that the proposition holds for $j < n$.

$p \xRightarrow{\alpha}{}^{\rho,j+1}_{S(p)} q$

$\Leftrightarrow$ \hfill { Definition 1 }

$p \xrightarrow{\delta_1\chi} p' \xRightarrow{\alpha}{}^{\rho,j}_{S(p)} q$, $\delta_1 \in (\mathcal{A} - \rho - \{\chi\})^*$

$\Leftrightarrow$ \hfill { inductive hypothesis }

$p' \xrightarrow{\chi}{}^j_{\rho,n} p_1 \xrightarrow{\chi}{}^{j-1}_{\rho,n} p_2 \cdots p_j \xrightarrow{\alpha}{}^0_{\rho,n} q$

$\Leftrightarrow$ \hfill { definition of non standard semantics }

$p \xrightarrow{\alpha}{}^{j+1}_{\rho,n} p'$.

Point 2. By induction on $j - n$.

Base. $j - n = 0$. The thesis follows by point 1.

Induction step. Let us suppose that the proposition holds for $j - n = k$. Suppose that $j - n = k + 1$.

$p \xRightarrow{\alpha}{}^{\rho,n+k+1}_{S(p)} q$

$\Leftrightarrow$ \hfill { Definition 1 }

$p \xrightarrow{\delta_1\chi} p' \xRightarrow{\alpha}{}^{\rho,n+k}_{S(p)} q$, $\delta_1 \in (\mathcal{A} - \rho - \{\chi\})^*$

$\Leftrightarrow$ \hfill { inductive hypothesis }

$p' \xrightarrow{\chi}{}^n_{\rho,n} p_1 \xrightarrow{\chi}{}^{n-1}_{\rho,n} p_2 \cdots p_n \xrightarrow{\alpha}{}^0_{\rho,n} q$

$\Leftrightarrow$ \hfill { definition of non standard semantics }

$p \xrightarrow{\alpha}{}^n_{\rho,n} p_1$.

Proof Theorem 2

Theorem 2. Let $\rho \subseteq \mathcal{A}^\alpha$ and $n \in N$. For each ASTP process p,

1. the transitions of $\mathcal{N}_{\rho,n}(p)$ are labeled only either by actions in ρ or by χ;
2. the length of each time path without repetition in $\mathcal{N}_{\rho,n}(p)$ is less than or equal to n;
3. $S(p) \approx_{\rho,n} \mathcal{N}_{\rho,n}(p)$.

Proof.

1. By Proposition 2.
2. Since in the relations $\longrightarrow_{\rho,n}^m$, used to define $\mathcal{N}_{\rho,n}(p)$, we have that $m \leq n$.
3. Let $T = S(p)$ and $\Sigma = \mathcal{N}_{\rho,n}(p)$. We show that $\mathcal{B}$ is a $\langle \rho, n \rangle$-bisimulation, where:

$$\mathcal{B} = \{(p,p) \mid p \in T \text{ and } p \in \Sigma\}$$

   i) $p \overset{\alpha}{\Longrightarrow}_T^{\rho,j} p'$, with $j < n$

      $\Rightarrow$ { Proposition 3 }

    $p \overset{\chi}{\longrightarrow}_{\rho,n}^j p_1 \overset{\chi}{\longrightarrow}_{\rho,n}^{j-1} p_2 \cdots p_j \overset{\alpha}{\longrightarrow}_{\rho,n}^0 p'$

      $\Rightarrow$ { Definition 1 }

    $p \overset{\alpha}{\Longrightarrow}_\Sigma^{\rho,j} p'$.

   ii) The proof of this condition follows by a symmetric argument.

   iii) $p \overset{\alpha}{\Longrightarrow}_T^{\rho,j} p'$, with $j \geq n$

      $\Rightarrow$ { Proposition 3 }

    $p \overset{\chi}{\longrightarrow}_{\rho,n}^n p_1 \overset{\chi}{\longrightarrow}_{\rho,n}^{n-1} p_2 \cdots p_n \overset{\alpha}{\longrightarrow}_{\rho,n}^0 p'$

      $\Rightarrow$ { Definition 1 }

    $p \overset{\alpha}{\Longrightarrow}_\Sigma^{\rho,n} p'$.

   iv) The proof of this condition follows by a symmetric argument.

IF: An Intermediate Representation and Validation Environment for Timed Asynchronous Systems

Marius Bozga[1]*, Jean-Claude Fernandez[2], Lucian Ghirvu[1]**, Susanne Graf[1], Jean-Pierre Krimm[1], and Laurent Mounier[1]

[1] VERIMAG Centre Equation, 2 avenue de Vignate, F-38610 Gières
Marius.Bozga@imag.fr
[2] LSR/IMAG, BP 82, F-38402 Saint Martin d'Hères Cedex
Jean-Claude.Fernandez@imag.fr

Abstract. Formal Description Techniques (FDT), such as LOTOS or SDL are at the base of a technology for the specification and the validation of telecommunication systems. Due to the availability of commercial tools, these formalisms are now being widely used in the industrial community. Alternatively, a number of quite efficient verification tools have been developed by the research community. But, most of these tools are based on simple ad hoc formalisms and the gap between them and real FDT restricts their use at industrial scale.

This context motivated the development of an intermediate representation called IF which is presented in the paper. IF has a simple syntactic structure, but allows to express in a convenient way most useful concepts needed for the specification of timed asynchronous systems. The benefits of using IF are multiples. First, it is general enough to handle significant subsets of most FDTs, and in particular a translation from SDL to IF is already implemented. Being built upon a mathematically sound model (extended timed automata) it allows to properly evaluate different semantics for FDTs, in particular with respect to time considerations. Finally, IF can serve as a basis for interconnecting various tools into a unified validation framework. Several levels of IF program representations are already available via well defined APIs and allow to connect tools ranging from static analyzers to model-checkers.

keywords: asynchrony, timed systems, timed automata, model-checking, static analysis

1 Introduction

Formal Description Techniques, such as LOTOS [ISO88] or SDL [IT94] and related formalisms such as MSC and TTCN are at the base of a technology for the specification and the validation of telecommunication systems. Due to the availability

---

* Verimag is Research Laboratory of CNRS, Université Joseph Fourier and Institut National Polytechnique of Grenoble

** Work partially supported by Région Rhône-Alpes, France

J. Wing, J. Woodcock, J. Davies (Eds.): FM'99, Vol. I, LNCS 1708, pp. 307–327, 1999.
© Springer-Verlag Berlin Heidelberg 1999

of commercial tools, mainly for editing, code generation and testing, and the fact that these formalisms are promoted by ITU and other international standardization bodies, these formalisms are now being widely used in the community of telecommunication systems.

There are also increasing needs for description and validation tools covering as many aspects of system development as possible. This is the reason why the commercial editing tools contain also some verification facilities. Unfortunately, these verification facilities are often quite restricted and the tools are "closed" in the sense that there are only limited possibilities to interface them with others. On the other hand, a number of quite efficient verification tools have been developed by the research community, but they are in general based on ad hoc input formalisms and the gap between them and real FDT restricts their use at an industrial scale. Even if these tools are in general less closed than commercial ones, they have rarely well-defined interfaces. For example, a lot of developments were made around the Spin verification tool [Hol91], but they are based on the availability of the source code and not on *a priori* defined interfaces.

A different approach was followed within CADP [FGK+96], a toolbox for the verification of LOTOS specifications. It was conceived right from the beginning as an open platform for interfacing different algorithms and provides several well-defined and documented interfaces (Application Programming Interfaces, API for short). The initial motivation for the work presented here was the fact that SDL becomes a more and more popular formalism in the telecommunication community, and that we wanted to adapt CADP to deal also with SDL specifications. Since the intermediate program level formalisms used within CADP are not appropriate for SDL specifications, we had to investigate alternative representations. For example CADP is based on a synchronous communication model (rendez-vous), whereas SDL communications are fully asynchronous (via queues).

Another motivation concerns time modeling. Finding a "reasonable" notion of time in asynchronous systems is a non trivial question and this is reflected by the variety of the existing proposals for existing FDTs. For instance, the SDL syntax defines a timer concept, but there is no consensus on how time progresses, and different SDL tools have adopted different choices. Similarly, in the original LOTOS definition there is no particular notion of time, whereas different timed extensions are currently being proposed [LL97, Que98]. Choosing an appropriate timed extension for an FDT should take into account not only technical considerations about the semantics of timed systems but also more pragmatic ones related to the appropriateness for use in a system engineering context. We believe that the different ideas about extensions of the language must be validated experimentally before being adopted to avoid phenomena of rejection by the users.

These problems motivated the development of IF, an intermediate representation for timed asynchronous systems. The requirements on such a formalism are the following ones:

- it must be sufficiently expressive to be used as an intermediate representation for the above mentioned specification formalisms, or at least for reasonably large subsets of them.
- it must have a formally defined operational semantics, and be flexible enough to experiment different choices and extensions.
- it must be supported by a set of well defined APIs, at different levels of program representation, allowing to interface existing validation tools and to experiment new ones.

The paper is organized as follows. First, we define the IF formalism, its main concepts and its operational semantics. We also discuss its expressiveness with respect to other models and specification formalisms, in particular regarding the timing aspects. Then, we present a set of tools interconnected within an open validation environment for IF specifications[1]. Finally, we illustrate the use of IF on a small example, a distributed leader election algorithm on which different kinds of validation are performed.

2   Presentation of IF

In the following sections, we give a brief overview of the main features of IF, its operational semantics in terms of labeled transition systems. A more complete description of IF and of its semantics can be found in [BFG+98].

2.1   Syntax

An IF system is a set of processes communicating either asynchronously through a set of *buffers* or synchronously through a set of *gates*. The timed behavior of a system can be controlled through *clocks* (like in timed automata [ACD93, HNSY94]).

IF System Definition: A system is a tuple $Sys = (glob\text{-}def, \text{PROCS}, \text{S})$ where

- $glob\text{-}def = (type\text{-}def, sig\text{-}def, gate\text{-}def, var\text{-}def, buf\text{-}def)$ is a list of global definitions, where *type-def* is a list of type definitions (enumerated types, arrays, records and also abstract data types[1]) *sig-def* defines a list of parameterized *signals* (as in SDL), *gate-def* defines a list of parameterized *gates* (as in LO-TOS), *var-def* is a list of global variables, and finally, *buf-def* is a list of *buffers* through which the processes communicate by asynchronous signal exchange (as in Promela[Hol91] or SDL). Notice that we allow various types of buffers: FIFO queues, stacks or bags, which can chosen to be unbounded or bounded and reliable or lossy.
- PROCS defines a set of processes described in the following paragraph.

---

[1] where we suppose that the user provides also implementations of the introduced functions, otherwise expressions containing them are handled syntactically

- S is a synchronization expression, as in LOTOS or CSP, telling how the processes defined in PROCS synchronize. Such a synchronization expression is given by the following grammar where C is a (possible empty) set of gates:

  S ::= P∈PROCS | S ⟦C⟧ S

  Thus, a system S is either a process P or a parallel composition of two subsystems S_1 and S_2 with rendez-vous synchronization on the set of gates C. In a system of the form S_1 ⟦C⟧ S_2 transitions concerning a gate in C are executed synchronously in the two subsystems whereas all other transitions are interleaved.

IF Process Definition: Processes are defined by a set of local variables, a set of control states and a set of control transitions. A process P∈PROCS is a tuple P= (*var-def*, Q, CTRANS), where:

- *var-def* is a set of local variable definitions including also clocks[2] (as in timed automata)
- Q is a set of **control states** on which the following attributes are defined:
  - *stable*(q) and *init*(q) are boolean attributes, where the attribute *stable* can be used to control the level of atomicity: only stable states are visible on the semantic level.
  - the attributes *save*(q), *discard*(q) are sets of `filters` of the form
    `signal-list in buf if cond`.
    which filter the buffers contents in this state. For example, *discard*(q) is used to eliminate silently unexpected signals: when consuming the next signal in the FIFO queue `buf`, all signals of `signal-list` preceding it are discarded in the same atomic step, if the boolean expression `cond` evaluates to `true`. These primitives are useful in practice and taken from SDL.
- CTRANS is a set of **control transitions**, between control states q,q'∈Q, which may be of the following types:
  - input transitions which are triggered by some signal read from one of the communication buffers (as in SDL) and internal transitions without input:

  $$q \xrightarrow[\text{(urg)}]{g \;\mapsto\; \{\texttt{input ;}\}\; \texttt{body}} q'$$

  - synchronization transitions which are executed simultaneously with compatible ones in other processes of the system (as in LOTOS):

  $$q \xrightarrow[\text{(urg)}]{g \;\mapsto\; \texttt{sync}} q'$$

---

[2] one can also define timers (as in SDL) which can be set to any positive value, decrease with progress of time and expire if they reach the value *zero*; to simplify the presentation we do not include them in this document

Where in all cases:

- g is a boolean *guard* of the transition which may depend on visible variables in the process (including clocks) and predefined tests on buffers content (e.g., emptiness).
- urg∈{**eager, delayable, lazy**} defines the *urgency type* of the transition. **eager** transitions have absolute priority over progress of time, **delayable** transitions may let time progress, but only as long as they remain enabled, whereas **lazy** transitions cannot prevent progress of time. These urgency types have been introduced in [BST98], which shows that the use of urgency predicates on transitions (instead of time progress conditions) facilitates the compositional specification of timed systems.
- input is an input of the form   "**input sig**(*reference_list*) **from buf if cond**" where
  - **sig** is a signal,
  - *reference_list* the list of variables[3] (excluding clocks) in which the received parameters are stored,
  - **buf** is the name of the buffer from which the signal should be read
  - **cond** is a time independent "post guard" defining the condition under which the received signal is accepted and it usually depends on received parameters.

  Intuitively, an input transition is enabled if its guard is true, the first signal to be consumed (according to the attributes *save*(q) and *discard*(q)) is of the form $sig(v_1, ...v_k)$ and the post guard holds (after assigning the values $v_1, ...v_k$ to the variables of the *reference_list*)
- sync is a synchronization of the form   "**sync gate** *comm_list* **if cond**"   where
  - **gate** is a synchronization gate defined at system level,
  - *comm_list* is a list of *communication offers*:
    * either an output communication offer of the form !**exp**, where the expression **exp** represents the sent value
    * or a input communication offer of the form ?**ref**, where **ref** is a local variable[3] in which the received value is stored.
  - **cond** is again a time independent post guard used to restrict the values that the process is willing to accept.

  The concept of synchronization is taken from LOTOS: the simultaneous execution of synchronization transitions concerning the same gate allows an instantaneous exchange of values between several processes. Notice that clock expressions cannot appear as communication offers.
- body is a sequence of atomic actions of the following types:
  - asynchronous *outputs* of the form   "**output sig**(*par_list*) **to buf**"   append a *signal* of the form "**sig**(*par_list*)" to the buffer **buf**.
  - usual *assignments* between discrete variables.
  - *settings* of clocks, which have the effect to assign to a clock a specific value.

---

[3] or "assignable" expressions such as elements of records or arrays

2.2 Semantics

The semantics of IF is based on concepts taken respectively from LOTOS, SDL and timed automata. We define it by translating IF systems into timed automata with urgency [BST98]. First, we show how to associate a timed automaton with each process, and then, how two timed automata can be composed into a single one[4]. Such a timed automaton can then be interpreted either using discrete or dense time depending on the verification tools and properties considered. Notice that the discrete/dense interpretation of time does not influence the translation from IF to a timed automata.

Association of a Timed Automaton with a Process: Let P= (*var-def*, Q, cTRANS) be a process definition in the system Sys and furthermore:

- Let BUF be a set of buffer environments $\mathcal{B}$, representing possible contents of the buffers of the system, on which — depending on the declared buffer type — all necessary primitives are defined: e.g. "get the first signal of a given buffer, taking into account the *save* and the *discard* attributes of the control state", "append a signal at the end of a buffer", etc.
- Let ENV be a set of environments $\mathcal{E}$ defining the set of valuations of all discrete variables defined in the system Sys (the local and the global ones)

The semantics of the process P is the timed automaton $[P] = (Q \times \text{ENV} \times \text{BUF},$ TRANS) where

- $Q \times \text{ENV} \times \text{BUF}$ is the set of states, for which we extend the attributes of control states in a natural manner, e.g. $tpc(q,(\mathcal{E},\mathcal{B}))$ is the partial evaluation of $tpc(q)$ in $(\mathcal{E},\mathcal{B})$. Notice that the set of data environments ENV can be split into $\text{ENV}_{loc} \times \text{ENV}_{glob}$ where ENV_{loc} concerns only local variables of the process and ENV_{glob} concerns the global variables of the system.
- TRANS is the set of transitions of the timed automaton obtained from control transitions by the following two rules:
  1. For any input or internal transition
  $$q \xrightarrow[\text{(urg)}]{g \;\mapsto\; (\text{sig}(x_1...x_n), \text{buf}, \text{cond})\; ;\; \text{body}} q' \in \text{cTRANS}$$
  and for any $(\mathcal{E},\mathcal{B}) \in \text{VAL}$, the transition
  $$(q,(\mathcal{E},\mathcal{B})) \xrightarrow[\text{(urg)}]{\ell\,:\, g' \;\mapsto\; \text{body}'} (q',(\mathcal{E}',\mathcal{B}')) \in \text{TRANS} \qquad \text{if}$$
     - g' is the the partial evaluation of g in $(\mathcal{E},\mathcal{B})$, which is an expression depending only on clocks.
     - let $\mathcal{B}''$ be the buffer environment obtained after consuming $\text{sig}(v_1...v_n)$ in buffer buf (and after elimination of appropriate signals of the *discard*(q) attribute and saving of the signals of the *save*(q) attribute)

---

[4] Notice that the semantics is compositional in the sense that, in order to associate a timed automaton with a system one can also first compose the system into a unique process and then associate a timed automaton with this process

- let $\mathcal{E}''=\mathcal{E}[v_1...v_n/x_1...x_n]$ is obtained by assigning v_i to x_i,
- the post guard cond evaluates to true in the environment $(\mathcal{E}'',\mathcal{B}'')$
- $(\mathcal{E}',\mathcal{B}')$ is obtained from $(\mathcal{E}'',\mathcal{B}'')$ by executing all the assignments of the body, and by appending all signals required by outputs in the body.
- body' is the sequence of settings of clocks which remain as such in the timed automaton,
- ℓ is an appropriate label used for tracing.

2. For any synchronization transition of the form

$$q \xrightarrow[\text{(urg)}]{g \;\mapsto\; c \;:\; !exp_1 \;?y_2 \;...\; :\; cond} q' \in \text{cTRANS}$$

and for any $(\mathcal{E},\mathcal{B})\in\text{VAL}$, the transition

$$(q,(\mathcal{E},\mathcal{B})) \xrightarrow[\text{(urg)}]{\ell \;:\; g' \;\mapsto\; skip} (q',(\mathcal{E}',\mathcal{B}')) \in \text{TRANS} \qquad \text{if}$$

- g' is the the partial evaluation of g in $(\mathcal{E},\mathcal{B})$,
- the expression exp_i evaluates to the value v_i in $(\mathcal{E},\mathcal{B})$,
- $\mathcal{E}'=\mathcal{E}[v_2...v_j.../y_2...y_j...]$ for some v_j belonging to the domain of y_j,
- the post guard cond evaluates to true in the environment $\mathcal{E}'$,
- the label ℓ is equal to c $!v_1$ $!v_2$ ...

Composition of Models: The timed automaton associated with a system of the form $Sys = (glob\text{-}def,\text{PROCS},S)$ is obtained by composing the timed automata of processes according to the composition expression S. The composition rules presented correspond to the *and*-parallel composition described in [BST98].

Let $[P_i] = (Q_i\times\text{VAL},\text{TRANS}_i)_{i=1,2}$ be the timed automata associated with processes or subsystems of Sys — where VAL concerns only all global variables and is of the form $\text{ENV}_{glob} \times \text{BUF}$ and the valuations of local variables are integrated into the set of control states Q_i — and C a set of gates. Then, $[P_1[C]P_2] = [P_1] [C] [P_2] = (Q\times\text{VAL},\text{TRANS})$ where

- $Q= Q_1\times Q_2$ where $\begin{aligned} init((q_1,q_2)) &= init(q_1) \wedge init(q_2) \\ stable((q_1,q_2)) &= stable(q_1) \wedge stable(q_2) \\ tpc((q_1,q_2)) &= tpc(q_1) \wedge tpc(q_2) \end{aligned}$

- TRANS is the smallest set of transitions obtained by the following two rules: the first one applies to all transitions of TRANS_1 which are not synchronizations on gates in C and there is also a symmetric rule for transitions of TRANS_2.

$$\frac{(q_1,\mathcal{V}) \xrightarrow[\text{(urg)}]{\ell \;:\; g \;\mapsto\; body} (q_1',\mathcal{V}') \in \text{TRANS}_1 \quad \text{and} \quad \neg stable(q_1) \vee stable(q_2)}{((q_1,q_2),\mathcal{V}) \xrightarrow[\text{(urg)}]{\ell \;:\; g \;\mapsto\; body} ((q_1',q_2),\mathcal{V}') \in \text{TRANS}}$$

The requirement on stableness implies that there is no interleaving in non stable states; they are transient states, such that a finite sequence of transitions between to stable states can be considered as *one* atomic transition. The second rule concerns the synchronizations on gates c $\in$C

$$\frac{(q_1, \mathcal{V}) \xrightarrow[\text{(u1)}]{\ell:\ g_1\ \mapsto\ \text{skip}} (q_1', \mathcal{V}') \in \text{TRANS}_1 \quad \text{and}}{(q_2, \mathcal{V}) \xrightarrow[\text{(u2)}]{\ell:\ g_2\ \mapsto\ \text{skip}} (q_2', \mathcal{V}') \in \text{TRANS}_2}$$

$$\frac{}{((q_1, q_2), \mathcal{V}) \xrightarrow[\text{(urg)}]{\ell:\ g_1 \wedge g_2\ \mapsto\ \text{skip}} ((q_1', q_2'), \mathcal{V}') \in \text{TRANS}}$$

In this rule, the synchronization of two transitions with the same urgency attribute result in a transition with this attribute, the composition of an **eager** transition with any other transition results in an **eager** one, an in order to compose a **lazy** with a **delayable** transition, one needs to decompose the delayable one into two transitions, an **eager** and a **lazy** one, which under a reasonable restriction is always possible [BST98].

The Semantics of Timed Automata The model of time of IF is that of communicating timed automata with urgency introduced in [BST98]. Each process has a number of clocks which increase with progress of time (either in a discrete or continuous manner). Clocks can be "tested" in the guards and "set" in the bodies of the transitions. In this model, time is considered global, that is, it progresses synchronously in all processes of the system. The main problem is "when can time progress?". In timed automata [ACD93], time progress is defined by means of "invariants" associated with each state, such that time is allowed to progress as long the invariant expression evaluates to true. The main problem with this model is that it allows not to express urgency of transitions. A model avoiding this problem is obtained by associating with every transition a *deadline* (a predicate stronger than the guard), meaning that, whenever the deadline predicate evaluates to true, the transition has priority over time progress. In [BST98], it has been shown that a much simpler model using just three possible *urgency* attributes, instead of deadlines, is sufficient: *eager* transitions have always priority over time, *delayable* transitions may let time progress, but only as long as they remain enabled, and *lazy* transitions cannot prevent time from progressing. This is the time model we have chosen in IF[5].

The semantics of timed automata with urgency is defined in [BST98]. Let $A = (Q, \text{TRANS})$ be a timed automaton. Let TIME be a set of environments for clocks, where $\mathcal{T} \in \text{TIME}$ defines for every clock a value in a time domain T (positive integers or reals). Setting a clock affects $\mathcal{T}$ by changing the value of the set clock to the specified value. Progress of time by an amount δ transforms the valuation $\mathcal{T}$ into the valuation $\mathcal{T} \boxplus \delta$ in which the values of all clocks are increased by δ.

The semantics of A is defined by the labeled transition system $(Q \times \text{TIME}, \rightarrow)$ where the transition relation $\rightarrow$ consists of two types of transitions, discrete ones and time progress transitions:

---

[5] in order to include the model of timed automata, we allow associate an explicit *tpc* attribute with control states, but we don't present this feature here

- For any transition $q_1 \xrightarrow[\text{(urg)}]{\ell \,:\, \mathbf{g} \,\mapsto\, \mathbf{body}} q_2 \in \text{TRANS}$ and $\mathcal{T} \in \text{TIME}$, there exists a discrete transition of the form $(q_1, \mathcal{T}) \xrightarrow{\ell} (q_2, \mathcal{T}')$ if
  - the guard $\mathbf{g}$ evaluates to $\mathtt{true}$ in $\mathcal{T}$,
  - and $\mathcal{T}$' is obtained from $\mathcal{T}$ by executing all clock settings of the $\mathbf{body}$.
- in any state $(q, \mathcal{T})$, time can progress by the amount δ, that is

$$(q, \mathcal{T}) \xrightarrow{\text{time: } \delta} (q, \mathcal{T} \boxplus \delta)$$

if time can progress in all states $(q, \mathcal{T} \boxplus \delta')$ for $0 \leq \delta' < \delta$, where time can progress in a state $(q, \mathcal{T})$ if and only if the following conditions hold:
  - *stable*(q), that means time progresses only in stable, never in transient states
  - *no* **eager** transition is enabled in $(q, \mathcal{T})$
  - for each **delayable** transition $\mathtt{tr}$ enabled in $(q, \mathcal{T})$, there exists a positive amount of time ϵ, such that $\mathtt{tr}$ remains enabled when time progresses by ϵ. That means enabled delayable transitions allow time to progress, but only as long as they remain enabled.

3   IF and Other Formalisms

IF is a formalism for the description of asynchronous systems at a programming language level. It has not been designed with the aim to replace specification languages such as LOTOS, SDL, but as a general intermediate representation for them, in particular for SDL. The expressiveness of IF and its adaptedness as an intermediate representation for some specification formalisms are discussed below.

3.1   SDL

The definition of SDL (Specification and Description Language) started in 1974 and it has been standardized by CCITT in 1988 [IT94]. SDL is based on extended finite state machines communicating asynchronously via queues. There exists a formal semantics of the language defined in [IT94], various authors have criticized it and proposed alternative ones, such as [Bro91, BMU98, God91] to name only a few of them. Currently, SDL is widely accepted by the industrial community. This is due mainly to the fact that SDL development is supported by methodologies [OFMP+94] and commercial tools [Ver96, AB93] in all phases from requirement analysis, design and validation to implementation. However, the validation capabilities of the commercial tools are rather limited with respect to the ones existing in the academic community.

There is no standard semantics of time defined for SDL and each tool uses its own. For example, *Object*GEODE uses a very "synchronous" time concept where time can only progress when the system is blocked (in terms of IF that means all transitions are eager), whereas in other tools time can always progress (all transitions are lazy). This shows that the currently implemented notions of time

file formats, or libraries of internal data structures. For this purpose several well-defined interfaces (APIs) must be provided.

In the remainder of the section we present the overall architecture of the already existing environment and some of its related components. In the future new connections with existing tools and new analysis modules may be added. Figure 4 describes the existing (plain arrows) and planned (dashed arrows) connections of this environment. However this figure does not represent which tools are part of the IF distribution and which are interconnections with other existing tools.

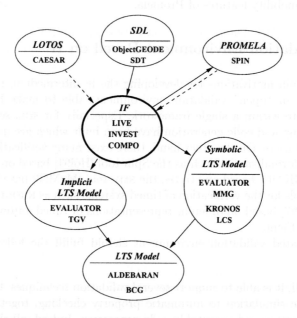

Fig. 1. An open validation environment for IF

4.1   Overall Architecture

Our IF validation environment is built upon two levels of program representations, each of them being accessed through a well-defined API.

The syntactic level allows to consult and modify the abstract tree on an IF program. Since all the variables, timers, buffers and the communication structure are still explicit, high-level transformations based on static analysis (such as *live variable* computation) or program abstraction can be applied. Moreover, this API is also well suited to implement translators between IF and other specification formalisms.

The execution model level gives access to the LTS representing the semantics of the IF program. The following three APIs are those offered in CADP for different types of representations. In the IF environment, also mixed representations are used.

- The **implicit enumerative representation** is based on the OPEN-CAESAR [Gar98] philosophy. It consists in a set of C functions and data structures allowing to compute on demand the successors of a given state. This piece of C code is generated by the IF compiler, and it can be linked with a "generic" exploration program performing on the fly analysis (deadlock detection, model-checking, test-case generation, ...).
- In the **symbolic representation** (called SMI [Boz97]) sets of states and transitions of the LTS are expressed by their characteristic functions over a set of finite variables. These functions are implemented in terms of decision diagrams (BDDs [Bry86] and MDDs). Existing applications based on this API are symbolic model-checking and minimal model generation.
- Finally, the **explicit enumerative representation** simply consists in an LTS file format with an associated access library. Although such an explicit representation is not suitable for handling large systems globally, it is still useful in practice to minimize some of its abstractions with respect to bisimulation based relations (like in *compositional generation*, see below).

Below, we discuss the tools being part of the IF verification environment and some external tools for which exists a strong connection.

CADP   [FGK+96, BFKM97] is a tool set for the verification of LOTOS specifications. It has been developed and by VERIMAG and the VASY team of INRIA Rhône-Alpes. We briefly present here two of its verifiers which are also part of the IF environment:

- ALDEBARAN compares and minimizes finite LTSs with respect to various *simulation* or *bisimulation* relations. This allows the comparison of the observable behavior of a specification with its expected one, described at a more abstract level.
- EVALUATOR is a "on-the-fly" model-checker for formulas of the alternating-free μ-calculus [Koz83].

MMG   [FKM93], developed at VERIMAG is a minimization tool based on a partition refinement algorithm combined with a reachable state space computation [BFH90]. This tools works on the symbolic SMI interface.

ObjectGEODE   [Ver96] is a commercial tool set developed by VERILOG supporting SDL, MSC and OMT. It includes graphical editors and compilers for each of these formalisms. It also provides a C code generator and a simulator to help the user to interactively debug an SDL specification.

*Object*GEODE also provides an API offering a set of functions and data structures to access the abstract tree generated from an SDL specification. Our translation tool (SDL2IF) uses this abstract tree to generate an operationally equivalent IF specification.

KRONOS [Yov97], developed at VERIMAG is a model-checker for symbolic verification of TCTL formulae on communicating timed automata. The current connection with the IF/CADP environment is as follows: control states and discrete variables are expressed using the IF/CADP implicit enumerative representation whereas clocks are expressed using an appropriate symbolic representation (particular polyhedra). Currently we are working on a more efficient translation of SDL timers into clocks.

TGV [FJJV97] is a test sequence generator built upon CADP jointly by VERIMAG and the PAMPA project of IRISA. TGV aims to automatically generate test cases for conformance testing of distributed systems. Test cases are computed during the exploration of the model and they are selected by means of *test purposes*. Test purposes characterize some abstract properties that the system should have and one wants to test, given trees of labels, decorated with verdicts "ok" and "fail".

INVEST [BLO98] is a symbolic verification tool based on the interaction with the theorem prover PVS [OSR93] computing abstractions and invariants on a set of guarded command processes communicating through shared variables. It has been developed jointly by VERIMAG, the university of Kiel and SRI. We have implemented translations between this formalism and IF, allows us to compute abstract systems.

LIVE [BFG99a] is a tool developed at VERIMAG. It transforms an IF specifications into an equivalent IF specification with a smaller state graph by means of static analysis. Presently, only simple algorithms, such as constant variable elimination and dead variable resetting (a variable which at some control point is never used before assigned again, is set to some default value) are implemented. Even this very simple analysis is very efficient, as a reduction of the state space by a factor 100 is common. In the future, we intend also to implement algorithms building weaker abstractions, for example elimination of irrelevant variables.

COMPO is a tool being developed at VERIMAG for compositional generation of minimal models associated with IF programs. This compositional generation method has already been applied for specification formalisms based on *rendez-vous* communication, and has been shown efficient in practice [GLS96, Val96, KM97]. It has not been investigated for systems based on communication via buffers, may be, because buffers raise several difficulties or due to the lack of suitable representations and tools. The potential benefit of this approach is illustrated on an example in the next section.

5   An Illustrating Example

We present a simple example to illustrate the IF formalism and related verification tools. We consider a *token ring*, that is a system of n stations (processes) S_1,

... S_n, connected in a circular network, in which a station is allowed to access some shared resource R only when it "owns" a particular message, the *token*. If the network is unreliable it is necessary to recover from token loss. This can be done using a *leader election algorithm* [Lan77, CR79] to determine a station responsible for generating a new token.

signal
    close(pid);
    open(pid);
    claim(pid, bool);
    token;
buffer
    Q1 : **queue** :lossy **of** claim, token;
    Q2 : **queue** :lossy **of** claim, token;
    Q3 : **queue** :lossy **of** claim, token;
    Q4 : **queue** :lossy **of** claim, token;

sync
    S1 ||| S2 ||| S3 ||| S4
end;
process S1;
var
    worried : timer;
    round, rnd: bool;
    adr: pid;
    . ...

Table 1. IF global definitions

Table 1 shows the global definitions of the IF specification corresponding to the particular protocol considered in [GM97]. The signals **open** and **close** denote the access and the release of the shared resource (here a part of the environment). The signals **token** and **claim** are the messages circulating on the ring.

All stations S_i are identical up to their identity and described by an IF process as the one of Figure 2. The timer **worried** is set when the station waits for the token and reset when it receives it. On expiration of the timer **worried** token loss is assumed and an election phase is started. The "alternating bit" **round** is used to distinguish between valid claims (emitted during the current election phase) and old ones (cancelled by a token reception). In the **idle** state, a station may either receive the token from its neighbor (then it reaches the **critical** state and can access the resource) or receive the timer expiration signal (then it emits a claim stamped with its **address** and the current value of **round**) or receive a claim from its neighbor. A received claim is "filtered" if its associated **address** is smaller than its own address and transmitted unchanged if it is greater. If its own valid claim is received, this station becomes elected and generates a new token.

Model Generation: We summarize in Table 2 the size of the models obtained from the token-ring protocol using three generation methods: directly from the initial IF program (global generation), using the live variable reduction (global + live) and using a compositional generation strategy (compositional + live).

The most spectacular reduction is obtained by the live reduction: the reduced model is about 100 times smaller than the one obtained by simultaneous generation, while preserving *all* properties (models 1 and 2 are strongly bisimilar). This is explained by the fact that only a few variables are live in each state: in

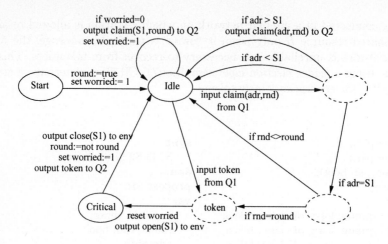

Fig. 2. The behavior of station S_1

the idle state the live variables are round and worried, in the critical state only round is live, while variables adr and rnd are never live.

model	generation method	states	transitions
1.	global	537891	2298348
2.	global + live	4943	19664
3.	compositional + live	1184	4788

Table 2. Models obtained for the token ring example

More reduction is achieved by the following compositional generation strategy yielding an LTS branching bisimilar to the original one:

1. We split the IF description into two parts, the first one contains processes S_1 and S_2 and the second one processes S_3 and S_4. For each one of these descriptions, the internal buffer between the two processes is *a priori* bounded to two places. Note that, when a bounded buffer overflows during simulation, a special *overflow* transition occurs in the corresponding execution sequence.
2. The LTS associated with each description is generated considering the "most general" environment providing any potential input. As claim and token can be transmitted at any time, *overflow* transitions appear in the generated LTSS.
3. In each LTS the input and output transitions relative to the internal buffers (Q_2 and Q_4) are hidden (i.e., renamed to the special τ action); then the

two LTSs are reduced w.r.t an equivalence relation preserving the properties under verification. For the sake of efficiency we have chosen the branching bisimulation [vGW89] preserving all the safety properties (e.g. mutual exclusion).

4. The reduced LTSs are then translated back into an IF process (without variables), and the resulting processes are combined into a single global IF description with only two buffers (Q_1 and Q_3). It turns out that the LTS generated from this new description contains no *overflow* transitions (they have been cut off during the second composition, which confirms the hypothesis on the maximal size of the internal buffers).

Verification: We are interested in checking that the shared resource is accessed in mutual exclusion. For this, we consider as visible only the **open** and **close** actions.

Mutual exclusion property can be rephrased as follows: *after every* **open**(S_i) *(station i enters the critical section) the only possible visible action is* **close**(S_i) *(station i leaves the critical section) possibly after a number of internal moves τ.* This property can be expressed in the μ-calculus (see below) and verified with EVALUATOR, on any of the generated models.

$$\bigwedge_{i=S_1}^{S_4} \nu X. \left([\mathbf{open}(S_i)] \ \neg \mu Y. \left(\langle \overline{\{\mathbf{close}(S_i), \tau\}} \rangle T \ \vee \ \langle \tau \rangle Y \right) \ \wedge \ [*]X \right)$$

Another approach to verify mutual exclusion is to compare the model of the specification with an abstract one expressing the desired behavior. For instance, after hiding of all actions different from **close**(S_i) and **open**(S_i), the minimal model for branching bisimulation of our example specification is the one shown in Figure 3. The reductions and comparisons have been carried out using ALDEBARAN.

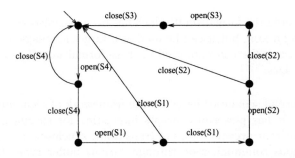

Fig. 3. The reduced behavior of the token ring.

Test Generation: We illustrate the use of TGV to extract test cases for the token ring protocol. We want to test the property stating that a station filters a received claim with a smaller address than its own and transmits it unchanged if it is greater. We chose a test purpose expressing that after S_4 has sent its claim, it will be transmitted unchanged by station S_1, then by S_2 and finally by S_3. The generated test case is shown in figure 4.

```
+----------------------------------------------------------------------+
|                      Test Case Dynamic Behaviour                     |
+----------------------------------------------------------------------+
| Test Case Name   : castest                                           |
| Group            :                                                   |
| Purpose          :                                                   |
| Default          :                                                   |
| Comments         :                                                   |
+----+-------+-----------------------------+----------+----------+-----+
| Nr | Label | Behaviour Description       | Cts Ref  | Verdict  | C   |
+----+-------+-----------------------------+----------+----------+-----+
|  1 |       | s3? claim                   | claim3   | INCONC   |     |
|  2 |       | s2? claim                   | claim2   | INCONC   |     |
|  3 |       | s1? claim                   | claim1   | INCONC   |     |
|  4 |       | s4? claim                   | claim0   |          |     |
|  5 |       |   s1! claim, St tclaim      | claim0   |          |     |
|  6 |       |     s3? claim, Cl tclaim    | claim3   | INCONC   |     |
|  7 |       |     s2? claim, Cl tclaim    | claim2   | INCONC   |     |
|  8 |       |     s1? claim, Cl tclaim    | claim1   | INCONC   |     |
|  9 |       |     s1? claim, Cl tclaim    | claim4   |          |     |
| 10 |       |       s2! claim, St tclaim  | claim4   |          |     |
| 11 |       |         s3? claim, Cl tclaim| claim3   | INCONC   |     |
| 12 |       |         s2? claim, Cl tclaim| claim2   | INCONC   |     |
| 13 |       |         s1? claim, Cl tclaim| claim1   | INCONC   |     |
| 14 |       |         s2? claim, Cl tclaim| claim5   |          |     |
| 15 |       |           s3! claim, St tclaim| claim5 |          |     |
| 16 |       |             s3? claim, Cl tclaim| claim3| INCONC  |     |
| 17 |       |             s2? claim, Cl tclaim| claim2| INCONC  |     |
| 18 |       |             s1? claim, Cl tclaim| claim1| INCONC  |     |
| 19 |       |             s3? claim, Cl tclaim| claim6| (PASS)  |     |
| 20 |       |             ? tclaim        |          | FAIL     |     |
| 21 |       |           ? tclaim          |          | FAIL     |     |
| 22 |       |         ? tclaim            |          | FAIL     |     |
+----+-------+-----------------------------+----------+----------+-----+
```

Fig. 4. TTCN test case

6   Conclusion and Perspectives

We have presented the formalism IF which has been designed as an intermediate representation for SDL, but it can be used as a target language for other FDT as it contains most of the concepts used in these formalisms. The use of IF offers several advantages:

- IF has a formal semantics based on the framework of communicating timed automata. It has powerful concepts interesting for specification purposes, such as different urgency types of transitions, synchronous communication, asynchronous communication through various buffer types (bounded, unbounded, lossy, ...), and communications through shared variables.
- IF programs can be accessed at different levels through a set of well defined APIs. These include not only several low-level model representations (symbolic, enumerative, ...) but also higher level program representation, where data and communication structures are still explicit. Using these APIs several tools have been already interconnected within an open environment able to cover a wide spectrum of validation methods.

Our translator from SDL to IF has already been used successfully to analyze real-life SDL specifications with CADP and SPIN, and is actually being used to experiment different semantics of time for SDL using the connection with the KRONOS tool.

A concept which is not provided in IF is dynamic creation of new process instances of processes and parameterization of processes; this is due to the fact that in the framework of algorithmic verification, we consider only static configurations. However, it is foreseen in the future to handle some kind of parameterized specifications and to translate also systems with bounded process creation.

The results obtained using the currently implemented static analysis and abstractions methods are very encouraging. For each type of analysis, we built a module taking an IF specification as input and which generates a *reduced* one. This architecture allows to chain several modules to benefit in a modular way from multiple reductions applied to the same initial specification. We envisage to experiment more sophisticated analysis, such as constraints propagation, and more general abstraction techniques. This will be achieved either by developing dedicated components or through the connections with INVEST.

The IF package is available at `http://www-verimag.imag.fr/DIST_SYS/IF`.

References

[AB93]   Telelogic AB. *SDT Reference Manual.*
           http://www.telelogic.se/solution/tools/sdt.asp, 1993.

[ACD93]   R. Alur, C. Courcoubetis, and D.L. Dill. Model Checking in Dense Real
           Time. *Information and Computation*, 104(1), 1993.

[BB88]   T. Bolognesi and E. Brinksma. Introduction to the ISO Specification
           Language LOTOS. *ISDN*, 14(1), jan 1988.

[BD98]   D. Bošnački and D. Dams. Integrating Real Time into Spin: A Prototype
           Implementation. In *Proceedings of the FORTE/PSTV XVIII Conference*,
           1998.

[BDHS99]   D. Bošnački, D. Dams, L. Holenderski, and N. Sidorova. Verifying the
           MASCARA Protocol in SPIN. submitted to the SPIN'99 Workshop, mai
           1999.

[BFG+98]   M. Bozga, J-C. Fernandez, L. Ghirvu, S. Graf, L. Mounier, J.P. Krimm,
           and J. Sifakis. The Intermediate Representation IF. Technical report,
           Verimag, 1998.

[BFG99a]   M. Bozga, J.-C. Fernandez, and L. Ghirvu. State Space Reduction based
           on Live Variables Analysis. In *Proceedings of SAS'99, Venezia, Italy*,
           LNCS, September 1999. to appear.

[BFG+99b] M. Bozga, J.-C. Fernandez, L. Ghirvu, S. Graf, J.P. Krimm, L. Mounier,
           and J. Sifakis. IF: An Intermediate Representation for SDL and its
           Applications. In *Proceedings of SDL-FORUM'99, Montreal, Canada*,
           June 1999.

[BFH90]   A. Bouajjani, J.-C. Fernandez, and N. Halbwachs. Minimal Model Gen-
           eration. In *Proceedings of CAV'90, Rutgers, New Jersey*, volume 3 of
           DIMACS, pages 85–92, June 1990.

[BFKM97]   M. Bozga, J.-C. Fernandez, A. Kerbrat, and L. Mounier. Protocol Veri-
           fication with the Aldebaran Toolset. *STTT*, 1(1+2):166–183, December
           1997.
[BLO98]   S. Bensalem, Y. Lakhnech, and S. Owre. Computing Abstractions of In-
           finite State Systems Compositionally and Automatically. In *Proceedings
           of CAV'98, Vancouver, Canada*, volume 1427 of *LNCS*, June 1998.
[BMU98]   J.A. Bergstra, C.A. Middelburg, and Y.S. Usenko. Discrete Time Process
           Algebra and the Semantics of SDL. Technical Report SEN-R9809, CWI,
           June 1998.
[Boz97]   M. Bozga. SMI: An Open Toolbox for Symbolic Protocol Verification.
           Technical Report 97-10, Verimag, Sep 1997.
[Bro91]   M. Broy. Towards a Formal Foundation of the Specification and Descrip-
           tion Language SDL. *Formal Aspects on Computing*, 1991.
[Bry86]   R.E. Bryant. Graph Based Algorithms for Boolean Function Manipula-
           tion. *IEEE Transactions on Computation*, 35(8), 1986.
[BST98]   S. Bornot, J. Sifakis, and S. Tripakis. Modeling Urgency in Timed Sys-
           tems. In *International Symposium: Compositionality - The Significant
           Difference, Holstein, Germany*, volume 1536 of *LNCS*, 1998.
[CR79]   E. Chang and R. Roberts. An Improved Algorithm for Decentralized
           Extrema-Finding in Circular Configurations of Processes. *Communica-
           tions of ACM*, 22(5), 1979.
[CT96]   C. Courcoubetis and S. Tripakis. Extending Promela and Spin for Real
           Time. In *Proceedings of TACAS'96*, volume 1055 of *LNCS*, 1996.
[FGK⁺96]   J.-C. Fernandez, H. Garavel, A. Kerbrat, R. Mateescu, L. Mounier, and
           M. Sighireanu. CADP: A Protocol Validation and Verification Toolbox.
           In *Proceedings of CAV'96, New Brunswick, USA*, volume 1102 of *LNCS*,
           July 1996.
[FJJV97]   J.-C. Fernandez, C. Jard, T. Jéron, and C. Viho. An Experiment in Au-
           tomatic Generation of Test Suites for Protocols with Verification Tech-
           nology. *SCP*, 29, 1997.
[FKM93]   J.-C. Fernandez, A. Kerbrat, and L. Mounier. Symbolic Equivalence
           Checking. In *Proceedings of CAV'93, Heraklion, Greece*, volume 697 of
           LNCS, 1993.
[Gar98]   H. Garavel. OPEN/CÆSAR: An Open Software Architecture for Veri-
           fication, Simulation, and Testing. In *Proceedings of TACAS'98, Lisbon,
           Portugal*, volume 1384 of *LNCS*, 1998.
[GLS96]   S. Graf, G. Lüttgen, and B. Steffen. Compositional Minimisation of
           Finite State Systems using Interface Specifications. *Formal Aspects of
           Computation*, 3, 1996.
[GM97]   H. Garavel and L. Mounier. Specification and Verification of Distributed
           Leader Election Algorithms for Unidirectional Ring Networks. *SCP*, 29,
           1997.
[God91]   J.C. Godskesen. An Operational Semantic Model for Basic SDL. Tech-
           nical Report TFL RR 1991-2, Tele Danmark Research, 1991.
[GS90]   H. Garavel and J. Sifakis. Compilation and Verification of LOTOS Spec-
           ifications. In *Proceedings of the 10th PSTV, Ottawa, Canada*, June 1990.
[HNSY94]   T.A. Henzinger, X. Nicollin, J. Sifakis, and S. Yovine. Symbolic Model
           Checking for Real-Time Systems. *Information and Computation*, 111(2),
           1994.
[Hoa84]   C.A.R. Hoare. *Communicating Sequential Processes*. Prentice Hall In-
           ternational, 1984.

[Hol91]   Gerard J. Holzmann. *Design and Validation of Computer Protocols.*
             Prentice Hall Software Series, 1991.

[ISO88]   ISO/IEC. LOTOS — A Formal Description Technique Based on the
             Temporal Ordering of Observational Behaviour. Technical Report 8807,
             International Organization for Standardization — Information Process-
             ing Systems — Open Systems Interconnection, 1988.

[IT94]   ITU-T. *Recommendation Z-100. Specification and Description Language
             (SDL) and Annexes F.2: Static Semantics and F.3: Dynamic Semantics.*
             1994.

[KM97]   J.P. Krimm and L. Mounier. Compositional State Space Generation
             from LOTOS Programs. In *Proceedings of TACAS'97, Enschede, The
             Netherlands*, volume 1217 of *LNCS*, 1997.

[Koz83]   D. Kozen. Results on the Propositional μ-Calculus. In *Theoretical Com-
             puter Science.* North-Holland, 1983.

[Lan77]   G. Le Lann. Distributed Systems – Towards a Formal Approach. In
             Information Processing 77. IFIP, North Holland, 1977.

[LL97]   L. Leonard and G. Leduc. An Introduction to ET-LOTOS for the De-
             scription of Time-Sensitive Systems. *Computer Networks and ISDN Sys-
             tems*, (29), 1997.

[LPY97]   K.G. Larsen, P. Petterson, and W. Yi. UPPAAL: Status & Develop-
             ments. In *Proceedings of CAV'97, Haifa, Israel*, volume 1254 of *LNCS*,
             1997.

[McM93]   K.L. McMillan. *Symbolic Model Checking: an Approach to the State
             Explosion Problem.* Kluwer Academic Publisher, 1993.

[Mil80]   R. Milner. A Calculus of Communication Systems. In *LNCS*, number 92.
             1980.

[OFMP⁺94]   A. Olsen, O. Færgemand, B. Møller-Pederson, R. Reed, and J.R.W.
             Smith. *Systems Engineering Using SDL-92.* North-Holland, 1994. ISBN
             0444 898727.

[OSR93]   S. Owre, N. Shankar, and J.M. Rushby. A Tutorial on Specification and
             Verification Using PVS. Technical report, Computer Science Laboratory,
             SRI International, February 1993.

[Que98]   J. Quemada. Final Comitee Draft on Enhancements to LOTOS. Tech-
             nical report, ISO/IEC JTC1/SC33/WG9, April 1998.

[Sig99]   M. Sighireanu. *Contribution at the Definition and Implementation of
             E-LOTOS.* PhD thesis, Université Joseph Fourier, Grenoble, 1999.

[Val96]   A. Valmari. Compositionality in State Space Verification. In *Application
             and Theory of Petri Nets*, volume 1091 of *LNCS*, 1996.

[Ver96]   Verilog. Object*GEODE SDL Simulator - Reference Manual.*
             http://www.verilogusa.com/solution/pages/ogeode.htm, 1996.

[vGW89]   R.J. van Glabbeek and W.P. Weijland. Branching-Time and Abstraction
             in Bisimulation Semantics. CS R8911, CWI, 1989.

[Yov97]   S. Yovine. KRONOS: A Verification Tool for Real-Time Systems. *STTT*,
             1(1-2), Dec 1997.

In section 3, we shall prove that the verification problem of such algorithms is undecidable, i.e. no computers with finite memory can answer such a queustion. Since the verification problem is extremely difficult, we instead develop an automatic approximation method which can answer the safety of a large class of such algorithms regardless of the number of processes. The idea is to construct a finite *collective image set (CIS)* whose elements are reachable state images describing the behaviors of all implementations with any number of processes. Engineers' intelligence and experiences in design and verification is encoded in the mapping from states to images in CIS's and seems to result in small CIS's even for complicate data-structures. For safety analysis, if we can construct a finite CIS which contains no images of states violating the safety specification, then it is good enough to conclude that the algorithm is safe for any number of processes. However if there is a state image violating the safety specification in the CIS, then no conclusion can be made because the image may be included due to insufficient approximation precision.

With the known high complexities of most verification problem models[1, 2, 14, 22, 23], it is clear that current technology cannot identify a large class of concurrent algorithms subject to efficient verification. On the other hand, we argue that our technology can serve to identify such a large class of "well-designed" concurrent algorithms which can be efficiently verified. In section 5, we shall establish the mighty lemma 3 which allows us to eliminate much combinatorial complexity in CIS without sacrifising approximation precision. In section 6, we shall analyze our method on the modified MCS algorithm (in example 1) in which local pointers are set to null whenever the current values of the pointers will not be used in the future. The modification is consistent with good programming practice of elimination of "stray" pointers. The interesting thing here is that our method can generate a small CIS of size 1619 for the modified MCS algorithm while fails to do so for the original one. This shows that our verification method is indeed more efficient for "good" designs.

We shall adopt the following notations. Given a set or sequence K, $|K|$ is the number of elements in K. For each element e in K, we also write $e \in K$. We let $\mathcal{N}$ be the set of nonnegative integers.

2 Related Work

Apt and Kozen already showed that in general verification of systems with unknown number of concurrent processes is undecidable[3]. This means that such verification problems are extremely hard and we can only rely on semi-decision procedures or, as in this work, approximation algorithms to answer them. Otherwise, we can also investigate to find out decidable subclasses of the problem. In the following, we briefly describe some of the related work.

Browne, Clarke, and Grumberg [5] use bisimulation equivalence relation between global state graphs of systems of different sizes. The equivalence relation must be strong enough for the method to work. Thus the construction of the equivalence relation is difficult to mechanize.

Clarke, Grumberg, and Jha[11] propose to use regular languages to specify properties in a linear network with unknown number of processes. Then state-equivalence relation is defined based on the regular languages and a mechanical method is defined to synthesize a network invariant $\mathcal{I}$ in the hope that $\mathcal{I}$ can be contained by the specification. But there is no guarrantee that $\mathcal{I}$ is a model of the specification even if the system indeed satisfies the specification. Moreover, it is not known whether using the specification regular languages to derive equivalence class properly perserves the reasonings behind the system design. Lesens, Halbwachs, and Raymond[17] furthered the approach by designing a language for the specification in systems with complex structures and by using fixed-point resolution with different heuristics to calculate many network invariants. Compared to our approach, we argue that the technique of CIS better captures the design reasoning that the relations between processes in different states are far more important than the actual numbers of processes in different states. We believe in verifying complex systems, without utilizing the reasoning behind the system designs, state-explosion problem cannot be properly dealt with.

Kurshan and McMillan[16] proposes to use network structural induction which is not guarranteed to terminate. Also inductive hypothesis is difficult to construct, although once it is ready, the whole approach is usually very efficient. Compared to our approach, we are using an approximation algorithm which captures the engineers' view of linear list. Users only have to guess the value of bound B, used in CIS construction, which for many real-world concurrent algorithms, small value like 1 will do.

Emerson and Naamjoshi[12] specialized on static token ring networks. They prove that for certain properties, verification on small size networks can be used to guarrantee the verification of large size networks. In contrast, our method is applicable to all different configurations of *"dynamic"* networks of processes.

Boigelot and Godefroid[7] choose to use state-space exploration to handle the verification problems of systems with unbounded FIFO queues. Their state-space representation is constructed by collapsing FIFO queues. Their approach does not guarrantee termination.

Recently, the author also has researched on the technique of collective quotient structures on dynamic linear networks [20]. The idea is similar to that of CIS in that they both collapse state-spaces of all implementations into single structures. However my work here is more general for pointer data-structures which allows the development of lemma 3, in section 5, and can lead to significant reduction in time and space complexity.

3   Concurrent Algorithms and Safety Bound Problem

We are dealing with concurrent algorithms with a local data structure for each process. The address of a data structure can be viewd as the identity of the corresponding process. We shall have the convention that if a process is named p, then p is also the address of process p's data-structure.

Two types of variables can be declared. The first is the type of *enumerate variables* with predefined finite integer value ranges. For convenience, we can also give symbolic names to those integer values. Traditionally, *false* is interpreted as 0 while *true* as 1. The second is the type of *pointers (address variables)* to processes (data-stuctures). As in example 1, L is a pointer to the tail of a queue. Variables can be declared as *global* variables which all processes can access, or *local* variables of a process which only the declaring process can directly access. The same name can be used to represent the respective local variables of different processes. For example, in example 1, different processes access different variables which are all locally called `locked`.

Test can be made to determine if an enumerate type variable's content equals to a constant, if a pointer is `null`, or if two pointers point to the same process. We can also assign a constant to an enumerate type variable or to assign a process address to a pointer. In the following, we shall first formally define the syntax and semantics of our systems, and then define the safety bound problem.

3.1   Syntax of Algorithm Descriptions

Conceptually, a concurrent algorithm S is a tuple $(\text{Enu}_g, \text{Ptr}_g, \text{Enu}_l, \text{Ptr}_l, A(P))$ where Enu_g and Enu_l are respectively the sets of *global* and *local enumerate variables* (as in Pascal programming language), Ptr_g and Ptr_l are respectively the sets of *global* and *local pointers*, and $A(P)$ is the *process program template*, with *process identifier* symbol P.

Given algorithm $S = (\text{Enu}_g, \text{Ptr}_g, \text{Enu}_l, \text{Ptr}_l, A(P))$, a *process predicate* pred of S can be used to describe the triggering condition of state transitions and has the following syntax.

$$
\begin{aligned}
pred &::= exp_1 = exp_2 \mid ref_1 = ref_2 \mid \neg pred \mid pred_1 \vee pred_2 \\
exp &::= c \mid x \mid z \mid y \to x \mid w \to x \\
ref &::= \text{null} \mid P \mid w \mid y \mid w \to y \mid y_1 \to y_2
\end{aligned}
$$

where $c \in \mathcal{N}$, $x \in \text{Enu}_l$, $z \in \text{Enu}_g$, $w \in \text{Ptr}_g$, and $y \in \text{Ptr}_l$. Traditional shorthands are $exp_1 \neq exp_2 \equiv \neg(exp_1 = exp_2)$, $ref_1 \neq ref_2 \equiv \neg(ref_1 = ref_2)$, $pred_1 \wedge pred_2 \equiv \neg((\neg pred_1) \vee (\neg pred_2))$, and $pred_1 \Rightarrow pred_2 \equiv (\neg pred_1) \vee pred_2$, Thus a process may operate on conditions of the global and local variables, and also on the local variables of the processes pointed to by global pointers. We let Predicate_S be the set of all process predicates of S.

Once the triggering condition is satisfied by a running process, the process may execute a finite sequence, say *actseq*, of actions to update the state information. The finite sequence *actseq* of actions has the following syntax.

$$
\begin{aligned}
actseq &::= \mid act\ actseq \\
act &::= lhsexp := exp; \mid lhsref := ref; \\
lhsexp &::= x \mid z \mid w \to x \mid y \to x \\
lhsref &::= y \mid w \mid w \to y \mid y_1 \to y_2
\end{aligned}
$$

Here *exp* and *ref* are defined as in the syntax of process predicates. *act* defines what an *action* looks like. The set of all finite sequences of actions of S is named Aseqset_S.

Given a concurrent algorithm $S = (\text{Enu}_g, \text{Ptr}_g, \text{Enu}_l, \text{Ptr}_l, A(P))$, $A(P)$ is the program template for each process with identifier symbol P. Program template $A(P)$ has the syntax similar to that of finite-state automata. $A(P)$ is conceptually a tuple (Q, q_0, E, τ, π) with the following restrictions.

- Q is a finite set of operation modes.
- $q_0 \in Q$ is the initial operation mode.
- $E \subseteq Q \times Q$ is the set of transitions among operation modes.
- $\tau : E \mapsto \text{Predicate}_S$ is a mapping which defines the triggering condition of each transition.
- $\pi : E \mapsto \text{Aseqset}_S$ is a mapping which defines the action sequence performed at the happening of each transition. *Atomicity of the transition is assumed.*

We do require that there is a variable mode $\in \text{Enu}_l$ which records the current operation mode of the corresponding process. However, while drawing $A(P)$ as an automaton, we omit the description of mode values in the triggering conditions and action sequences for simplicity and clarity.

3.2 Computation of Systems

Let Π be the set of all processes (conceptually represented by either their identifiers, or their data-structure addresses) in an implementation. For each enumerate-type variable x, we let D_x be $\{0\}$ unioned with the set of all constants assigned to x in process program $A(P)$ labeled in all transition's assignment sequence. Especially, $D_{\text{mode}} = Q$ and mode $= 0$ means the process is in its initial operation mode.

A *process state* π is a mapping from $\text{Enu}_l \cup \text{Ptr}_l$ to $\mathcal{N} \cup \Pi \cup \{\text{null}\}$ such that $\pi(x) \in D_x$ if $x \in \text{Enu}_l$; and $\pi(x) \in \Pi \cup \{\text{null}\}$ if $x \in \text{Ptr}_l$.

A *global state* of $S\Pi$ is a pair (ψ, ϕ) with the following restrictions.

- ψ is a mapping from $\text{Enu}_g \cup \text{Ptr}_g$ to $\mathcal{N} \cup \Pi \cup \{\text{null}\}$ such that $\psi(x) \in D_x$ if $x \in \text{Enu}_g$; and $\psi(x) \in \Pi \cup \{\text{null}\}$ if $x \in \text{Ptr}_g$.
- ϕ is a mapping from Π to the set of all process states running algorithm A.

Given a global state $\nu = (\psi, \phi)$, a process $p \in \Pi$, and a process predicate *pred* $\in$ Predicate_S, we define the relation of p *satisfies pred* at ν, written $p, \nu \models pred$, in the following inductive way. Assume that $x \in \text{Enu}_l$, $z \in \text{Enu}_g$, $y, y_1, y_2 \in \text{Ptr}_l$, and $w \in \text{Ptr}_g$.

- $p, \nu \models \text{exp}_1 = \text{exp}_2$ iff $\text{value}(p, \nu, \text{exp}_1) = \text{value}(p, \nu, \text{exp}_2)$
- $\text{value}(p, \nu, c) = c$
- $\text{value}(p, \nu, x) = \phi(p)(x)$
- $\text{value}(p, \nu, z) = \psi(z)$
- $\text{value}(p, \nu, y \to x) = \phi(\phi(p)(y))(x)$
- $\text{value}(p, \nu, w \to x) = \phi(\psi(w))(x)$
- $p, \nu \models \text{ref}_1 = \text{ref}_2$ iff $\text{value}(p, \nu, \text{ref}_1) = \text{value}(p, \nu, \text{ref}_2)$
- $\text{value}(p, \nu, \text{null}) = \text{null}$
- $\text{value}(p, \nu, P) = p$

- $\text{value}(p, \nu, w) = \psi(w)$
- $\text{value}(p, \nu, y) = \phi(p)(y)$
- $\text{value}(p, \nu, w \to y) = \phi(\psi(w))(y)$
- $\text{value}(p, \nu, y_1 \to y_2) = \phi(\phi(p)(y_1))(y_2)$
- $p, \nu \models \neg pred$ iff it is not the case that $p, \nu \models pred$
- $p, \nu \models pred_1 \vee pred_2$ iff $p, \nu \models pred_1$ or $p, \nu \models pred_2$

Given an action act of S, the new global state obtained by applying act to p at ν, written next_state(p, ν, act), is defined in the following way.

- $(\psi', \phi') = \text{next\_state}(p, \nu, x := exp;)$ is identical to ν
  except that $\phi'(p)(x) = \text{value}(p, \nu, exp)$.
- $(\psi', \phi') = \text{next\_state}(p, \nu, z := exp;)$ is identical to ν
  except that $\psi'(z) = \text{value}(p, \nu, exp)$.
- $(\psi', \phi') = \text{next\_state}(p, \nu, w \to x := exp;)$ is identical to ν
  except that $\phi'(\psi(w))(x) = \text{value}(p, \nu, exp)$.
- $(\psi', \phi') = \text{next\_state}(p, \nu, y \to x := exp;)$ is identical to ν
  except that $\phi'(\phi(p)(y))(x) = \text{value}(p, \nu, exp)$.
- $(\psi', \phi') = \text{next\_state}(p, \nu, y := ref;)$ is identical to ν
  except that $\phi'(p)(y) = \text{value}(p, \nu, ref)$.
- $(\psi', \phi') = \text{next\_state}(p, \nu, w := ref;)$ is identical to ν
  except that $\psi'(w) = \text{value}(p, \nu, ref)$.
- $(\psi', \phi') = \text{next\_state}(p, \nu, w \to y := ref;)$ is identical to ν
  except that $\phi'(\psi(w))(y) = \text{value}(p, \nu, ref)$.
- $(\psi', \phi') = \text{next\_state}(p, \nu, y_1 \to y_2 := ref;)$ is identical to ν
  except that $\phi'(\phi(p)(y_1))(y_2) = \text{value}(p, \nu, ref)$.

Given an action sequence $act_1 \dots act_n \in \text{Aseqset}_S$, we let next_state$(p, \nu, act_1 act_2 \dots act_n) = \text{next\_state}(p, \text{next\_state}(p, \nu, act_1), act_2 \dots act_n)$.

The *initial state* (ψ_0, ϕ_0) of an implementation $S\Pi$ must satisfies the following restrictions: (1) $\psi_0(z) = 0$ for all $z \in \text{Enu}_g$, (2) $\psi_0(w) = \text{null}$ for all $w \in \text{Ptr}_g$, (3) $\phi_0(p)(x) = 0$ for all $p \in \Pi$ and $x \in \text{Enu}_l$, and (4) $\phi_0(p)(y) = \text{null}$ for all $p \in \Pi$ and $y \in \text{Ptr}_l$. We assume that processes interact with *interleaving semantics* in the granularity of transitions, that is at any moment, at most one process can execute a transition. Interleaving semantics is well-accepted in verification theory for its simplicity. From the viewpoint of languages, such an atomicity may be difficult to implement. Since our focus is on verification and modelling, instead of implementation, we believe such an atomicity is important in modelling embedded systems in which natural world atomic transitions can only be emulated by several algorithm actions.

A *computation* of an implementation $S\Pi$ is a (finte or infinite) sequence $\rho = \nu_0 \nu_1 \dots \nu_k \dots \dots$ of global states with $\nu_k = (\psi_k, \phi_k)$ for all $k \geq 0$ such that

- ν_0 is the initial state of $S\Pi$; and
- for each ν_k with $k > 0$, there is a $p \in \Pi$ and transition from q to q' such that $p, \nu_{k-1} \models \tau(q, q')$ and next_state$(p, \nu_{k-1}, \pi(q, q')) = \nu_k$.

3.3 Safety Bound Problem and Its Undecidability

The computation definition of our algorithm implementations is independent of the real names used for each process in Π. Never the names of processes are used to affect the behaviors of our implementations. Instead, only the relation among processes in various process states is important. Thus it is better if we can present our safety analysis problem regardless of the actual names used for processes. Given a global state $\nu = (\psi, \phi)$ of an implementation $S\Pi$ and a process predicate $pred$, $\mathbf{count}_{pred}(\nu)$ is the number of processes satisfying $pred$ at ν, i.e. $|\{p \mid p \in \Pi; p, \nu \models pred\}|$. A computation $\rho = \nu_0 \nu_1 \ldots \nu_k \ldots \ldots$ of $S\Pi$ violates safety property $pred$ with bound $c \in \mathcal{N}$ iff there is a $k \geq 0$ such that $\mathbf{count}_{pred}(\nu_k) > c$.

The *safety bound problem* instance SBP($S, pred, c$) is to determine if for all finite sets Π of processes and all computation ρ of $S\Pi$, ρ does not violate safety property $pred$ with bound c. Such a problem framework can be used to verify process state reachability problem[14] which is a special case of SBP($S, pred, c$) with $c = 1$. Also mutual exclusion problem can be formulated with $c = 1$. Reader-Writer problem can be formulated with c set to the number of readers.

Example 2. : Consider the modified MCS algorithm in example 1. The critical section is in mode 4. A process can enter the critical section only if its local variable locked is true. Thus the safety bound problem for the mutual exclusion to critical section can be formulated as SBP(S, locked $= true, 1$) which answers "true" iff along any computation ρ of all implementations, no more than one process can have locked $= true$ simultaneously.   ‖

However, such a problem is extremely difficult to answer. In fact, we can show SBP($S, pred, 1$) for a given S and $pred$ is undecidable, i.e. there is no computer with finite amount of memories capable of answering SBP($S, pred, 1$). Lemma 1 proves this by reducing two-counter machine halting problem[15] to SBP($S, pred, 1$). A two-counter machine M has a finite-state control and two counters which can hold any natural numbers. The finite-state control can increment a counter, decrement a counter, or transit between finitely many operation modes by testing whether a particular counter contains zero. It is known that two-counter machine can emulate Turing machine whose halting problem cannot be answered by any computers with finite amount of memories.

Lemma 1. : *Two-counter machine halting problem is reducible to SBP(S, pred, 1).*

Proof : Due to page-limit, we shall only give a sketch of the proof. Suppose we are given a two-counter machine M. We want to show that we can construct a concurrent algorithm S such that M reaches its final state iff there is an implementation $S\Pi$ such that there is a process in Π which also reaches its corresponding local final state. We shall implement two stacks to emulate the two counters respectively with pointers linking together adjacent elements in the stacks. The first (second) stack's height of $S\Pi$ emulates the content of the first (second) counter of M. Suppose in the computation of M to reach its final state, counter 1 and 2 have maximum contents v_1 and v_2 respectively. Then there exists a Π, of $3 + v_1 + v_2$ processes, which makes the construction works.

The halting state of M is encoded in *pred*. The first transiting process in the computation will be used to emulate the finite-state control. The second and third transiting processes in the computation will respectively be used to emulate the stack bottoms for the two counters. Then each increment operation of a counter will need one process to be pushed onto the corresponding stacks. If there is not enough number of processes for the increment operations in the implementation, then the computation simply halts in a state without satisfying *pred*. Each decrement operation of a counter will need the top process in the corresponding stack to be popped. Testing for zero value of a counter can be implemented by asking if the stack top process is equal to the stack bottom process for the corresponding counter. In this way, we can construct S and *pred* such that SBP(S, *pred*, 1) answers true iff M reaches its halting state.   ∥

4   Collective Image Set

With lemma 1 and many similar complexity results[1, 2, 14, 22, 23], it is clear that classic verification technology is not able to handle the complexity incurred by verification problems for concurrent algorithms with sophisticate data-structures. However, we have observed that classic verification theory does not distinguish "well-behaved" systems from "bad" systems. In many algorithms for concurrent systems, the number of processes is usually not a crucial factor in the correctness of systems.

Our CIS is a set whose elements are global state images which are finite recordings of multisets of process information patterns. A multiset is conceptually a set which allows an element to repeat many times. Mathematically, it is a mapping from a domain to $\mathcal{N}$. We say that process p *points to* process p' (and p' is called a *reference* of p) in state (ψ, ϕ) if there is either a $y \in \text{Ptr}_l$ such that $\phi(p)(y) = p'$ or a $w \in \text{Ptr}_g$ such that $\psi(w) = p'$. State of each process p is collapsed down to a *PDSI (process data-structure image)* which only records information that process p can read from the local variables of itself and its global or local references.

A global state image, called *GDSI (global data-structure image)*, is treated as a finite recording of a multiset of PDSI's of the participating processes. It is finite because when more than B, a constant chosen by users, processes have the same PDSI in a global state, they are only recorded by a flag (∞ here) which denotes that the number of processes in that PDSI exceeds B. By viewing the GDSI's as a multiset, we treat all processes in a symmetric way without the price for the management of process identifier permutation [13]. With the constant B, we are able to map states of infinitely many implememtations down to finitely many global state images. To choose a value for B, users should have the intuition that when more than B processes are of a PDSI, the actual number of such processes is not important. For example, for many mutual exclusion algorithms, if there are either 3 or 4 processes in the waiting queue, the processes in each PDSI's exhibit the same behavior pattern. For example, to pass over the right to the critical section, the process in the critical section (of one PDSI) passes the right to the head process in the waiting queue (of another PDSI). The behavior pattern only depends on whether there is a process in the waiting queue. According to our observation, many algorithms work with such reasoning. For a lot of mutual exclusion protocols, small value of B like 1 will work and the CIS's exhibit simple regularity.

In the following subsections, we shall define rigorously the image mapping of global states of implementations. Then we shall define the *transitions*, among GDSI's, which corresponds to transition rules described in $A(P)$.

We need the following conventions regarding number systems respecting a bound B. Let $\mathcal{N}^\infty = \mathcal{N} \cup \{\infty\}$ where ∞ means any number greater than B. For any $c \in \mathcal{N}$, $c < \infty$. For any $c, d \in \mathcal{N}^\infty$, $c \le \infty$ and $c + \infty = \infty + d = \infty$.

Given any two numbers c and B in $\mathcal{N}^\infty$, we let $c^{(B)} = c$ if $c \le B$; $c^{(B)} = \infty$ if $c > B$. Finally, $[0, B]^{(\infty)} = \{0, 1, \dots, B\} \cup \{\infty\}$.

4.1   Pointer Data-Structure Images

The global-state images in our method is characterized by finite sets of propositional atoms. We shall first define *PSI (process state images)* as building blocks to construct PDSI. PSI represents the observation a process can make without going through pointers. The PSI of process p at state $\nu = (\psi, \phi)$, in symbols $\mathrm{PSI}(p, \nu)$, is a finite set of atoms constructed in the following way.

$$
\begin{aligned}
& \{x = c \mid x \in \mathrm{Enu}_l; c \in D_x; c = \phi(p)(x)\} \\
& \cup \{z = c \mid z \in \mathrm{Enu}_g; c \in D_x; c = \psi(z)\} \\
& \cup \{P = y \mid y \in \mathrm{Ptr}_l; p = \phi(p)(y)\} \\
& \cup \{P = w \mid w \in \mathrm{Ptr}_g; p = \psi(w)\} \\
\mathrm{PSI}(p, \nu) = & \cup \{y = \mathrm{null} \mid y \in \mathrm{Ptr}_l; \phi(p)(y) = \mathrm{null}\} \\
& \cup \{w = \mathrm{null} \mid w \in \mathrm{Ptr}_g; \psi(w) = \mathrm{null}\} \\
& \cup \{y = w \mid y \in \mathrm{Ptr}_l; w \in \mathrm{Ptr}_g; \phi(p)(y) = \psi(w)\} \\
& \cup \{y_1 = y_2 \mid y_1, y_2 \in \mathrm{Ptr}_l; \phi(p)(y_1) = \phi(p)(y_2)\} \\
& \cup \{w_1 = w_2 \mid w_1, w_2 \in \mathrm{Ptr}_g; \phi(p)(w_1) = \phi(p)(w_2)\}
\end{aligned}
$$

Here we use P to symbolically represent the address p of the corresponding process. Note that we conveniently define PSI's to also record information on global variables. Thus in our GDSI defined later, PSI's of all processes must all agree on the informations of those global variables. Conveniently, we shall let PSIset be the set of all PSI's.

Our process image, the PDSI (*process data-structure image (PDSI)*) of a process p in a state $\nu = (\psi, \phi)$ with bound B, in symbols $\mathbf{PDSI}^{(B)}(p, \nu)$, is graphically shown in figure 2 and only records

- the PSI's of p and p's global and local references;
- the equality among p and p's references' references (i.e. if the references point back); and
- the multiset of incoming local pointers from peer processes to p with bound B (ILM$^{(B)}$ for *incoming link multiset* with bound B, will be defined later).

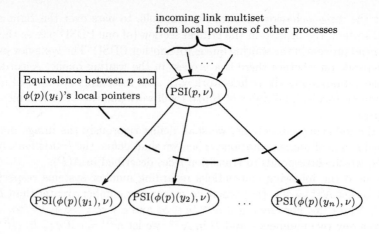

Fig. 2. Information of PDSI

Intuitively, PDSI of a process p records the information that p can infer by at most one dereferencing through its local and global pointers. In the following, we shall make the definition of PDSI more precise.

The *incoming link multiset (ILM)* of process p at state $\nu = (\psi, \phi)$, in symbols $\text{ILM}(p, \nu)$, records those peer processes which have p as their global or local references. When a transiting process p changes the PSI of itself and its references, the PDSI's of processes with p as their references will also be changed. To propagate such waves of PDSI changes, we need information in $\text{ILM}(p, \nu)$ to enumerate the possibilities. Formally speaking, for all $\lambda \in \text{PSIset}$ and $y \in \text{Ptr}_l$ in an algorithm implementation $S\Pi$,

$$\text{ILM}(p, \nu)(\lambda, y) = |\{(p', y) \mid p' \in \Pi; \text{PSI}(p', \nu) = \lambda; \phi(p')(y) = p\}|$$

To respect bound B, we let $(\text{ILM}(p, \nu))^{(B)}$ be a mapping from the domain to $[0, B]^{(\infty)}$ such that for all $\lambda \in \text{PSIset}$ and $y \in \text{Ptr}_l$, $(\text{ILM}(p, \nu))^{(B)}(\lambda, y) = (\text{ILM}(p, \nu)(\lambda, y))^{(B)}$.

Given an algorithm, it is clear that the number of different possible PDSI's at states of all implementations is finite. We let $\text{PDSIset}^{(B)}$ be the set of all possible PDSI's with bound B.

The *global data-structure image (GDSI)* χ of a state $\nu = (\psi, \phi)$ with bound B, in symbols $\mathbf{GDSI}^{(B)}(\nu)$, is a mapping from $\text{PDSIset}^{(B)}$ to $[0, B]^{(\infty)}$ such that for all $\mu \in \text{PDSIset}^{(B)}$, if $\mathbf{GDSI}^{(B)}(\nu)(\mu) \neq \infty$, it means that there are exactly $\mathbf{GDSI}^{(B)}(\nu)(\mu)$ processes in ν whose PDSI's are μ; otherwise, it means that there are more than B processes in ν whose PDSI's are μ. Since GDSI's are constructed with finite set of atomic propositions and constant B, it is clear that the number of GDSI's is finite.

Notationally, we let $\text{GDSIset}^{(B)}$ be the set of all distinct GDSI's with B.

4.2   Transitions among GDSI's

We let $\mathbf{xtion}_e(\chi, \chi')$ be the relation, between χ and χ', which is true iff from GDSI χ, we can transit to GDSI χ' through transition rule e. $\mathbf{xtion}_e(\chi, \chi')$ can be computed by the following nondeterministic procedure.

A. Nondeterministically choose PDSI's in χ corresponding to the transiting process and its references.
B. If they are inconsistent, then answer *false* and stop.
C. Change the PSI's and PDSI's of those chosen PDSI's according to the meaning of transition rule e.
D. Nondeterministically propagate the changes to other unchosen PDSI's according to the ILM recordings of those chosen PDSI's.
E. After all propagations are done, if χ is changed to χ', answer *true*; else answer *false*.

The steps are written in nondeterministic style for simplicity. If and only if one of the executions end up with return value *true*, then χ can go to χ' with transition rule e. In practice, they have to be implemented with recursive procedure-calls. In each level of the recursion, a choice is made and recorded in the recursion stack.

We shall demonstrate the working of the above-mentioned procedure for the transition rule from mode 0 in the modified MCS algorithm (figure 1). The rule in guarded command language is

$$\mathtt{mode} = 0 \rightarrow (\mathtt{mode} := 1; \mathtt{prev} := L; L := P;)$$

In step A, in case we choose $\mu \in \mathrm{PDSIset}^{(B)}$, with $\chi(\mu) \neq 0$, for either the transiting process or one of its references, what we actually do is to create a new PDSI μ' in χ with $\chi(\mu') = 1$ to represent the chosen process. Then we have to decrement the value of $\chi(\mu)$ respecting bound B. That is, if $\chi(\mu) \neq \infty$, then the decremented value can either be ∞ or B nondeterministically; otherwise, the decremented value is $\chi(\mu) - 1$.

Suppose that we pick μ_P as the transiting process with $\chi(\mu_P) = \infty$. According to our modification to MCS algorithm, the two local pointers: prev and next of μ_P both point to null. For convenience, we shall adopt notations like $\mu_P \rightarrow \mathtt{prev}$ for the PDSI which represents the reference prev of PDSI μ_P in a GDSI. $\mu_P \rightarrow \mathtt{mode}$ also has the same intuition. The only other reference which μ_P can make is through global pointer L. Suppose that we pick μ_L with $\mu_L \rightarrow \mathtt{mode} = 2$ as the global reference L. It can be shown from our CIS construction that $\chi(\mu_L) = 1$. This is natural because a global pointer can only point to one process. Thus after step A, we have the following pictorial description of those chosen PDSI's.

Note since our modification to MCS algorithm eliminates strayed pointers (see appendix), $\mu_L \rightarrow \mathtt{prev}$, if not null, will be unique in χ, i.e., $\chi(\mu_L \rightarrow \mathtt{prev}) = 1$. Suppose after a nondeterministic choice of μ_P and μ_L, χ is changed to χ_A.

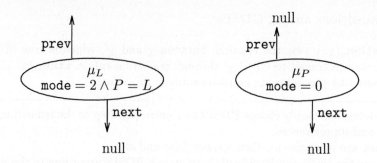

In step B, consistency among the chosen PDSI's has to be checked. For example, if μ_L requires that the local pointer next of PDSI $\mu_L \to$ prev does not point back to PDSI μ_L, then we have to check whether this requirement is compatible with the recordings in $\mu_L \to$ prev.

After step C, the transition is executed, and the configuration among the chosen PDSI's changes to the following for the above-mentioned Modified MCS algorithm scenario.

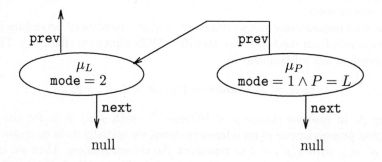

Till this step, there is no need to update χ_A.

In step D, the propagation may go in three directions. First, we have to non-deterministically modify the reference information of those unchosen processes with references as one of the chosen processes. In this scenario, since global reference L is reassigned to μ_P, the global side-effect of this step is to update the global references of all PDSI's in χ_A so that every PDSI knows that μ_P has become the new L. Especially, we have to check if there is any PDSI $\bar{\mu}$ with $\bar{\mu} \to$ next points to the unique previously globally referenced μ_L and changes the recording of $\bar{\mu} \to$ next.

Second, we have to modify the ILM recordings of the references' of those chosen PDSI's if those chosen PDSI's are PSI-modified. In our scenario, we have to nondeterminstically pick a PDSI corresponding to $\mu_L \to$ prev and changes its ILM recordings. With the side-effect nondeterministically propagated, we assume that χ_A is changed to χ_D to reflect the propagation.

Third, the new PDSI's of the chosens have to be collapsed with the PDSI's in χ_D respecting bound B. In this scenario, there will be two such PDSI's, one modified from μ_P (say μ'_P) and the other from μ_L (say μ'_L), to be added into χ_D again. In case that $\chi_D(\mu'_L) = B$ or ∞, then $\chi_D(\mu'_L)$ should be changed to ∞; otherwise, $\chi_D(\mu'_L)$ is incremented by one.

In Step E, if and only if we found that χ_D is changed to be equal to χ', we shall answer *true*. The performance of the procedure can be enhanced with symbolic manipulation techniques[6, 8]. We are still investigating the details.

5 Safety Bound Verfication with CIS

The following lemma shows that CIS is indeed a conservative approximation of all reachable states from the initial states of all implementation.

Lemma 2. *Given a concurrent algorithm S with X as the set of GDSI's of initial states of all implementations, the minimal set Reachable satisfying the following conditions:*

- *$X \subseteq$ Reachable; and*
- *for all $\chi \in$ Reachable and $\chi' \in$ GDSIset such that $\mathbf{xtion}_e(\chi, \chi') = true$ for some transition rule e, $\chi' \in$ Reachable.*

is a super set of GDSI's of all reachable states of all implementaions of S.

Proof : Our GDSI overapproximates a global state by filtering out information over bound B. While nondeterministically computing $\mathbf{xtion}_e(\chi, \chi')$ for some GDSI's χ, χ' and transition rule e, overapproximation is also done by considering all possibilities with regard to the precision bound setup by B. Thus in the construction of *Reachable*, only overapproximation has been done and underapproximation is never done. Considering all these, we infer that *Reachable* is indeed a superset of GDSI's of reachable states of all implementaions of S.   ‖

By just naive enumerating all the GDSI's reachable from the initial state in an algorithm implementation, we will easily bump into combinatorial explosion of complexity because each PDSI can be mapped to any number in $[0, B]^{(\infty)}$. However, we can take advantage of our interleaving semantics to eliminate much of such complexity. The idea is based on lemma 3. A GDSI χ' contains another GDSI χ, in symbols $\chi \subseteq \chi'$, if for every PDSI $\mu \in \text{PDSIset}^{(B)}$, $\chi(\mu) \leq \chi'(\mu)$.

Lemma 3. *Suppose we have two GDSI's $\chi \subseteq \chi'$. Then for every GDSI sequence $\chi_0 \chi_1 \cdots \cdots$ with $\chi_0 = \chi$, we can construct another GDSI sequence $\chi'_0 \chi'_1 \cdots \cdots$ with $\chi'_0 = \chi'$ such that for all $k \geq 0$, $\chi_k \subseteq \chi'_k$ and χ_k and χ'_k may go to χ_{k+1} and χ'_{k+1} respectively with the same transition rule.*

Proof : A pictorial explanation of this fact is in figure 3. The relation can happen because in a concurrent system without invariance conditions specified for the operation modes, we can withhold those PDSI's in χ' but not in χ from firing transitions.   ‖

Now we shall present our approximation algorithm for safety bound problem with finite GDSI set as our CIS. We shall take advantage of lemma 3 such that two GDSI's χ, χ' will not be in the CIS simultaneously if $\chi \subseteq \chi'$.

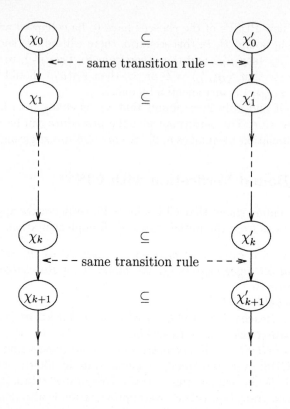

Fig. 3. Containing relation between GDSI sequences

Given a $\chi \in \text{GDSIset}^{(B)}$, $\mathbf{count}_{pred}(\chi)$ is also the number, respecting bound B, of PDSI's satisfying *pred* in χ. Formally speaking,

$$\mathbf{count}_{pred}(\chi) = \left(\Sigma_{(\theta,\beta) \in U_A^{(B)}; (\bigwedge_{a \in \theta} a) \Rightarrow pred} \chi((\theta,\beta)) \right)^{(B)}$$

Now we have the procedure **Safety_Bound**() in table 1 to embody our safety bound verification method in details. Note in statements (2.2.2) and (2.2.3), we delete those GDSI's contained by other GDSI's in V according to lemma 3.

The complexity of the method is polynomial to the number of GDSI's of states which then depends on $A(P)$ and B. A rough complexity analysis follows. The equivalence relation among pointers in a PDSI basically partitions global pointers, local pointers of P, the local pointers of references of P, the local pointers of references of those process pointed to by global pointers. The total number of pointers involved is $H = 1 + (|\text{Ptr}_g| + |\text{Ptr}_l|)(1 + |\text{Ptr}_l|)$ which is square to the size of S. The number of different partitions on these many pointers is roughly in the complexity of factorial to H. This will be the dominating factor in the complexity. Considering the values of $\text{ILM}^{(B)}$, we can deduce that the number of different PDSI's is roughly $O((B+1)^{|\text{PSIset}|2^H}) = O(2^{|S|^2 \log B})$. Since GDSI

```
/* S is an algorithm with transition rule set E.
/* pred is a process predicate describing the dangerous property.
/* C is the number of processes allowed in critical section.
/* B is the bound used in GDSI's. It is assumed C ≤ B. */
Safety_Bound(S, pred, C, B) {
(1)  Generate the initial GDSI χ₀; let V := {χ₀}; W := V;
(2)  Repeat until W = ∅. {
     (1) If there is a χ ∈ V such that count_pred(χ) > C, report "don't know" and
         stop.
     (2) Let W := {χ₂ | χ₁ ∈ W; χ₂ ∈ GDSIset⁽ᴮ⁾; ∃e ∈ E(xtion_e(χ₁, χ₂))} − V;
     (3) Let V := V ∪ W;
     }
(3)  Report "SAFE!"
}
```

Table 1. Safety analysis with CIS

are mappings from PDSI's to $[0, B]^{(\infty)}$, the total number of different GDSI's is then $(B+2)^{O(2^{|S|^2 \log B})} = 2^{2^{O(|S|^2 \log B + \log \log B)}} = 2^{2^{O(|S|^2 \log B)}}$. Thus our approach in each iteration of B value is of complexity doubly exponential to $|S|^2 \log B$.

For a lot of mutual exclusion protocols, small value of B like 1 will work and the CIS's exhibit simple regularity. The complexity analyses for MCS mutual-exclusion algorithm in section 6 shall justify our claim.

6   On Mellor-Crummy & Scott's Algorithm

We shall prove that our method indeed can verify Mellor-Crummy & Scott's (MCS) locking algorithm[18] for mutual exclusion in concurrent systems. MCS locking algorithm is a provenly correct algorithm requiring little shared memory. We believe that our method can verify many such algorithms with small B values regardless of the number of processes. The following lemma shows that our method can verify the modified version. A similar one can be used to prove for the original version.

Lemma 4. : *In the CIS constructed for MCS locking algorithm as shown in figure 1 with $B = 1$ and lemma 3, there is no image χ with $\text{count}_{mode=4}(\chi) > 1$.*
Proof : A transition rule e is executed by a process in exactly the same way as step C of xtion_e is operated on the corresponding PDSI's. Steps A, B, D, E are nondeterministically performed to properly maintain the counts in the multisets and in the ILM's to consider all possibilities respecting the bound B. Only the transiting PDSI with the local $\text{locked} = true$ can make its-successor-in-the-queue's locked true. With $B = 1$, we know in a GDSI whether there is only one PDSI with the local $\text{locked} = true$.

Intially, all PDSI's are in mode 0 with their local locked = *false*. From that point on, we want to make sure that given two GDSI's χ, χ' and a transition rule e with $\textbf{xtion}_e(\chi, \chi') = \textit{true}$, if $\textbf{count}_{\texttt{locked}=\textit{true}}(\chi) \leq 1$, then $\textbf{count}_{\texttt{locked}=\textit{true}}(\chi') \leq 1$. The first PDSI detecting prev = null while leaving mode 1, will enter mode 4 with locked set to true. This is the only situation when we can go from $\textbf{count}_{\texttt{locked}=\textit{true}}(\chi) = 0$ to $\textbf{count}_{\texttt{locked}=\textit{true}}(\chi') = 1$.

According to the algorithm, only the PDSI with locked = *true* can set the locked of other PDSI's to *true*. Immediately before setting the other PDSI's to *true* with transition rule

$$\text{mode} = 7 \rightarrow \begin{pmatrix} \texttt{mode} := 0; \\ \texttt{locked} := \textit{false}; \\ \texttt{next} \rightarrow \texttt{locked} := \textit{true}; \\ \texttt{next} := \texttt{null}; \end{pmatrix}$$

the PDSI must first reset its own locked. With $B = 1$, we know that $\textbf{count}_{\texttt{locked}=\textit{true}}(\chi)$ and $\textbf{count}_{\texttt{locked}=\textit{true}}(\chi')$ will both be one. Considering both the two cases when a new PDSI has its local locked set to *true*, we find that $\textbf{count}_{\texttt{locked}=\textit{true}}(\chi') = 1$. We thus concluded that our CIS does not have a GDSI in which more than one PDSI's have their locked = *true*.   ‖

We want to point out that our proof for lemma 4 is very much like a human proof for MCS algorithm. This shows that our method indeed reasons at an abstractness level similar to that of humans. Now we proceed to analyze the size of the CIS with $B = 1$ for the modified MCS locking algorithm, in figure 1, which has the good property that once a process is in mode=0, its local pointers will all be set to null and no other processes will have local pointers pointing to it again. This make the data-structure pretty much "clean" without "stray" pointers. Thus the number of different GDSI's solely depends on the different possibilities of PDSI's near the queue head, noted by H, and tail as shown in figure 4. We thus have the following case analysis.

- *In case there is only one PDSI in the queue.* Then $H \rightarrow$ mode $\in \{1, 4, 5\}$ and there are 3 possibilities.
- *In case there are two PDSI's in the queue.* The values of $H \rightarrow$ next and $L \rightarrow$ prev depend on $H \rightarrow$ mode and $L \rightarrow$ mode. When $H \rightarrow$ mode $\in [1, 6]$, $L \rightarrow$ mode $\in [1, 3]$. When $H \rightarrow$ mode $= 7$, $L \rightarrow$ mode $= 3$. This accounts for $6 \times 3 + 1 = 19$ possibilities.
- *In case there are three PDSI's in the queue.* Similar to the reasoning in last item, we have $(6 \times 3 + 1) \times 3 = 57$ possibilities.
- *In case there are more than three PDSI's in the queue.* Assume the second PDSI in the queue is H' while the last second is L'. The values of $H' \rightarrow$ next and $L' \rightarrow$ prev depends on the modes of the third and the last third PDSI's in the queue. Also the ILM's of H' and L' also depend on the third and the last third PDSI's in the queue. Moreover, all other PDSI's will be mapped to ∞ according to lemma 3. Again, we have $(6 \times 3 + 1) \times 3 \times 3 \times 3 \times 3 = 1539$ possibilities.

Summing up all the possibilities in addition to the initial GDSI, we have $3 + 19 + 57 + 1539 + 1 = 1619$ different GDSI's in our final CIS where the "1" represents the initial GDSI which maps the initial PDSI to ∞ and everything else to zero.

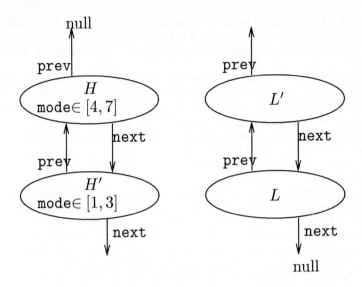

Fig. 4. PDSI pattern for modified MCS algorithm

7   Conclusion

With the known worst-case complexities of most verification problems in theory, it is apparent that the current technology of model-checking is incapable of verifying nontrivial software systems. We believe such a dilemma results from the fact that current verification theory does not distinguish "good" design from "bad" design. We argue our CIS technology is a successful example to verify well-designed concurrent systems in which relations among different PDSI groups are more important than both the actuagl numbers of processes in each PDSI group and the actual values of all pointers. We feel hopeful our technology can be extended to verify well-designed concurrent systems with other types of infinite behaviors.

Acknowledgment

I sincerely thank the reviewers of FM'99 whose comments and suggestions have greatly improved the quality of the manuscript.

References

[1] R. Alur, C. Courcoubetis, D.L. Dill. Model Checking in Dense Real-Time, Information and Computation **104**, pp.2-34 (1993).
[2] R. Alur, T.A. Henzinger. Real-Time Logics: Complexity and Expressiveness. Information and Computation **104**, pp.35-77 (1993).

[3] K.R. Apt, D.C. Kozen. Limits for Automatic Verification on finite-state concurrent systems. Information Processing Letters, 22:307-309, 1986.

[4] F. Balarin. Approximate Reachability Analysis of Timed Automata. IEEE RTSS, 1996.

[5] M.C. Browne, E.M. Clarke, O. Grumberg. Reasoning about Networks with Many Identical Finite State Processes. Information and Computation **81**, 13-31, 1989.

[6] J.R. Burch, E.M. Clarke, K.L. McMillan, D.L.Dill, L.J. Hwang. Symbolic Model Checking: 10^{20} States and Beyond, IEEE LICS, 1990.

[7] B. Boigelot, P. Godefroid. Symbolic Verification of Communication Protocols with Infinite State Spaces using QDDs. CAV 1996, LNCS, Springer-Verlag.

[8] R.E. Bryant. Graph-based Algorithms for Boolean Function Manipulation, IEEE Trans. Comput., C-35(8), 1986.

[9] E. Clarke and E.A. Emerson. Design and Synthesis of Synchronization Skeletons using Branching-Time Temporal Logic, Proceedings of Workshop on Logic of Programs, Lecture Notes in Computer Science 131, Springer-Verlag, 1981.

[10] E. Clarke, E.A. Emerson, and A.P. Sistla. Automatic Verification of Finite-State Concurrent Systems Using Temporal Logic Specifications, ACM Transactions on Programming Languages and Systems 8(2), 1986, pp. 244-263.

[11] E.M. Clarke, O. Grumberg, S. Jha. Verifying Parameterized Networks using Abstraction and Regular Languages. CONCUR'95, LNCS 962, Springer-Verlag.

[12] E.A. Emerson, K.S. Namjoshi. Reasoning about Rings. ACM POPL, 1995.

[13] E.A. Emerson, A.P. Sistla. Utilizing Symmetry when Model-Checking under Fairness Assumptions: An Automata-Theoretic Approach. ACM TOPLAS, Vol. **19**, Nr. 4, July 1997, pp. 617-638.

[14] S.M. German, A.P. Sistla. Reasoning about Systems with Many Processes. Journal of ACM, Vol. 39, No. 3, July 1992, pp.675-735.

[15] J.E. Hopcroft, J.D. Ullman. Introduction to Automata Theory, Languages, and Computation, Addison-Wesley, 1979.

[16] R.P. Kurshan, K.L. McMillan. A Structural Induction Theorem for Processes. Information and Computation **117**, 1-11(1995).

[17] D. Lesens, N. Halbwachs, P. Raymond. Automatic Verification of Parameterized Linear Networks of Processes. ACM POPL, 1997.

[18] J.M. Mellor-Crummey, M.L. Scott. "Algorithms for Scalable Synchronization on Shared-Memory Multiprocessors." ACM Transactions on Computer Systems, Vol. 9, No.1, Feb. 1991, pp.21-65.

[19] X. Nicolin, J. Sifakis, S. Yovine. Compiling real-time specifications into extended automata. IEEE TSE Special Issue on Real-Time Systems, Sept. 1992.

[20] F. Wang. Automatic Verification of Dynamic Linear Lists for All Number of Processes. Technical Report TR-IIS-98-019, Institute of Information Science, Academia Sinica, 1998.

[21] F. Wang, C.T. Lo. Procedure-Level Verification of Real-Time Concurrent Systems. Real-Time Systems Journal, Vol. 16, Nr. 1, Jan. 1999, Kluwer Academic Publishers. Preliminary version in Proceedings of the 1996 FME, Oxford, Britain, LNCS 1051, Springer-Verlag.

[22] F. Wang, A. Mok. RTL and Refutation by Positive Cycles, in Proceedings of the Formal Methods Europe Symposium, Barcelona, Spain, Octobor 1994, LNCS 873.

[23] F. Wang, A.K. Mok, E.A. Emerson. Real-Time Distributed System Specification and Verification in APTL. ACM TOSEM, Vol. 2, No. 4, Octobor 1993, pp. 346-378.

[24] H. Wong-Toi. Symbolic Approximations for Verifying Real-Time Systems. Ph.D. thesis, Stanford University, 1995.

A   Original MCS Locking Algorithm

The modification follows good programming practice and can significantly reduce verification complexity. Two modifications in the modified MCS algorithm are

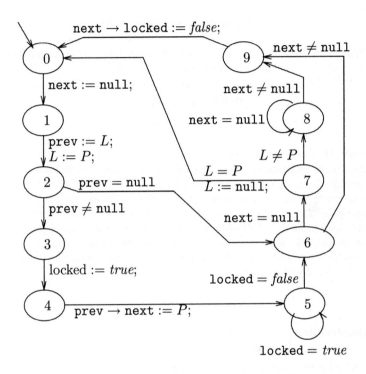

Fig. 5. original MCS locking algorithm

made. First, *true* and *false* for variable locked is interchanged in the modified version to be consistent with our initial state restrictions.

Second, local pointers are set to null as soon as the contents of the local pointers will not be used again. This is consistent with good programming practice. For example, in our modified algorithm, when a process releases the lock, it then also set its next to null because it is not meant in the queue already. However, in the original algorithm, this local next can still outdately point to some random process. Without cautious management, such "stray" local pointers can be mistakenly used.

The Use of the B Formal Method for the Design and the Validation of the Transaction Mechanism for Smart Card Applications

Denis Sabatier[1] and Pierre Lartigue[2]

[1] Steria Méditerranée - Equipe AtelierB 530, rue F.Joliot 13791 Aix-en-Provence
denis.sabatier@steria.fr
[2] Gemplus Research Lab - Av Pic de Bertagne 13881 Gemenos
pierre.lartigue@gemplus.com

Abstract. This document describes an industrial application of the B method in smart card applications. In smart card memory, data modification may be interrupted due to a card withdrawal or a power loss, the EEPROM memory may result in an unstable state and the values subsequently read, may be erroneous. The transaction mechanism provides a secure means for modifying data located in the EEPROM. As the security in smart card application is paramount, the use of the B formal method brings high confidence and provides mathematical proofs that the design of the transaction mechanism fulfills the security requirements

1. Introduction

The EEPROM memory is used for permanently storing data in smart cards. In normal operation mode, when the card is pulled out of the terminal and the power is turned off, the information stored in the EEPROM is preserved.

Due to its electronic characterization and to its physical constraints, a modification of data is not performed in a single and atomic operation. Instead, this process may take up to a few milliseconds. This lapse of time is required for electronically charging the memory cells and reaching a steady state that enables permanent retention of the information. If the power is turned off, or the card is unexpectedly pulled out while a memory cell is being written, the electronic charge may not be sufficient for retaining the information in a durable way. Values obtained from subsequent accesses to the memory may be non-deterministic.

The transaction is a software mechanism that prevents errors from these misuses; it enables modification of data in a secure way: the data are all correctly modified or their values are left unchanged.

This insures the coherence among data simultaneously modified within a transaction.

J. Wing, J. Woodcock, J. Davies (Eds.): FM'99, Vol. I, LNCS 1708, pp. 348-368, 1999.
© Springer-Verlag Berlin Heidelberg 1999

A transaction can be initiated, terminated or canceled at any time by the application. Nevertheless, in case of a card pull-out, a transaction must always be terminated in a way which provides data integrity.

Overview of the Transaction Mechanism

The transaction mechanism provides a means to update several data in an "atomic" way. This feature is of great importance to keep the coherence among data which are simultaneously modified.

Within a transaction, it is required that every data value is either correctly modified or left unchanged: if a card withdrawal occurs while a transaction is activated, the system shall preserve each data initial value.

In the example depicted bellow, the modification of data shall change the state of the memory from "State0" to "State1" in the absence of errors.

In case of an uncompleted modification process, the memory may be changed to an unwanted state "State2". Then, the transaction shall restore the initial state "State0".

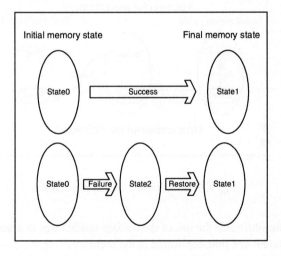

Fig. 1. Overall transaction mechanism

The Backup Level

Prior to any modification or update, the data must be copied (duplicated) in a special location of the EEPROM called the "backup zone". The process of copying the data in the backup zone is performed by the backup mechanism and may itself be interrupted if the card is withdrawn or if the power is turned off.

Once the copy is performed, data values can be modified freely, without risking a card pull-out.

If several data are modified within a transaction, their copies are piled-up in the backup zone. In case of a card pull-out, their values shall be restored by the system by the "rollback" process at the next card insertion.

Once a transaction is terminated, and if no error has occurred, the data stored in the backup zone are discarded. This is performed by the "commit" process.

Then, for security reasons, the backup zone shall be cleared.

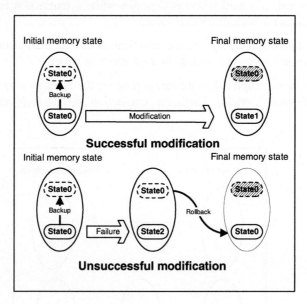

Fig. 2. Transaction and backup mechanisms

The above figure illustrates the use of the backup mechanism in a transaction:
- The data "State0" are first duplicated in the memory,
- The successful data modifications change the subset of memory "State0" to "State1"; the duplicated data then become useless, and they shall be discarded.
- Conversely, in case of a modification failure ("State2" is obtained instead of "State1"), the duplicated data are restored to retrieve the original state of the memory ("State0").

2. The Functional Requirements and the Security Properties

The use of formal methods in industrial applications requires first to identify, state and clarify the functional and security requirements together with the environment assumptions. This task may involve re-expressing the requirements in an informal text (French, English, etc..). This task is preliminary to the formalisation step. Many omissions and inconsistencies may already be found at this early stage of the process.

For the sake of conciseness, only the most important requirements of the transaction mechanism are listed below. Each requirement is labeled to facilitate the traceability of the formal representation.

Functional Requirements

FUN1	The transaction mechanism shall insure that a modification of data in the EEPROM is always performed in a safe way: the data is either correctly modified or its value is left unchanged.
FUN2	At any time of the transaction process, the card may be withdrawn and the power may be turned off.
FUN3	At any time, the application may abort a transaction. The state of the memory shall be brought back to its original state.
FUN4	Nested transactions are not supported: a transaction must be terminated before a new one is started.

Security Requirements

SEC1	To avoid risks of data disclosure, the transaction mechanism shall not permanently retain information, and the backup zone shall be cleared after use.
SEC2	The transaction mechanism shall be resistant to card pull-out.

Environment Assumptions

ENV1	The backup mechanism must not rely on any specific hardware device nor on chip features. It must be generic enough to be implemented on any type of component.
ENV2	Any unpredictable memory behavior due to defective aging cells and over-stressed modifications is out of the scope of the backup mechanism.

3. The Formal Modeling

The formal modeling technique that we use for our application does not consist in directly constructing the software algorithm. Instead, we shall obtain it in a rigorous way, from the main requirements using the refinement mechanism. We consider that the system dynamics are expressed through asynchronous events.
Each event is characterized by two components:

- a trigger that we call "guard", specifying some (but not all) necessary conditions for the event to occur,
- the action which modifies the global data of the system when the guard is valid.

The development is made in several refinements: each step must refine its preceding level. The transition to the next level is characterized by a transformation of the state abstract data to more concrete data, and of course, by the refinement of the events.

The events in refinements can be obtained in several ways:
1. A concrete event directly refines its abstract counterpart (possible strengthening of the guard and translation of the action section to take into account the new data space),
2. An abstract event is split into several concrete refining events. Combined together, the new concrete events shall refine the abstract one.
3. Addition of new concrete events which do not have abstract counterparts. However, the new concrete events must refine the abstract virtual event "skip".

Usually, the model development begins with an abstract model featuring very few events. At the beginning of the model development, we attempt to add events using modalities (2) and (3).

These events provide an implementation of the algorithm.

As a card pull-out may occur at any time during the transaction process, it appears very suitable and effective to represent the system by events.

4. The Abstract Model

Scope

The abstract model provides a high level representation of the functional requirements and the security properties. It aims at stating in a non-ambiguous way the main requirements which must be fulfilled throughout the whole software development life cycle.

The scope of the formal model is to provide a comprehensive representation of *one transaction*. We assume that the backup zone is cleared before a transaction begins. It ends with the data either correctly updated or left unchanged. In both cases, the backup zone must be cleared before exiting from the transaction process.

Should this model be used in a more complex application, the whole transaction process can be re-started several times, but its validity and robustness is demonstrated once.

Variables / Invariants

The following section introduces the main entities which are used in the model of the abstract machine:

The function "Memory0" represents the EEPROM memory of the smart card. It is a total function from the set of addresses to the set of values (at this stage of the formal representation, we do not take into consideration whether a memory element is a byte, a short integer, etc...).

$$Memory0 \in DATAZONE \longrightarrow DATUM$$

The partial function "NewState0" identifies the subset of elements to be overridden in the memory during the transaction. The variable "NewState0" denotes the final status of the transaction system. It is an abstract representation of the anticipated EEPROM memory state when the transaction is terminated. The "NewState0" variable is only used for formally identifying the expected final memory status, and for formally demonstrating that it will be reached by the system. The variable "NewState0" is an abstract variable called a "prophecy variable":

$$NewState0 \in DATAZONE \nrightarrow DATUM$$

Events

The event "Transaction" describes, from an abstract point of view, the functional properties of the system. It behaves in two different ways as described by the "CHOICE" statement (see below):

- the total function "Memory0" is correctly updated by the partial function "NewState0", **or**
- the function "Memory0" is left unchanged ("skip" statement).

```
Transaction ≙
    CHOICE
            Memory0 := Memory0 ⊲ NewState0
    OR
            skip
    END;
```

Remark 1. *In the above expression, "Memory0" is overridden by the function "NewState0": Memory0 := Memory0 ⊲ NewState0.*

5. The First Refinement

Scope

In this refinement, the transaction mechanism is performed in several successive steps, each of them shall be modeled by an event. We introduce the backup zone for storing copies of the data which are modified in the transaction.

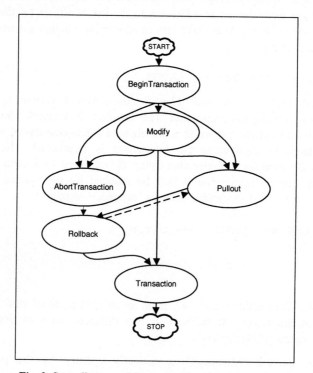

Fig. 3. State diagram of the transaction abstract model.

It is assumed that the backup zone is empty before starting the transaction and it must be demonstrated that it is also empty when the transaction is finished (aborted or normally terminated).

The modeling technique enables refinement of the abstract model by "zooming" in the event "Transaction". This process is also elicited as "time stretching"; it allows the introduction of the events "BeginTransaction", "Modify", "Rollback", "Pullout" and

"AbortTransaction". The transaction mechanism can be represented as a state machine (see above).

Variables and Invariants

In this section, we introduce the major variables and entities of the refinement model: The variables „NewState1" and „Memory1" are identical to the abstract level. The variable „CardState1" represents the state of the transaction mechanism:

```
CardState1 ∈ {START, BACKUP, MODIFIED, WITHDRAWN,
INIROLLBACK,ROLLBACK,  STOP}
```

The variable "BackMemory1" is a partial function which indicates the data which are duplicated in the backup zone:

```
BackMemory1 ∈ DATAZONE ⇸ DATUM
```

Before starting a transaction, it is assumed that the backup zone is cleared and when a transaction is terminated, the backup zone must also be cleared:

```
CardState1 ∈ {START, STOP} ⇒ BackMemory1=∅   (1)
```

The variable "MemoryInit1" is an abstract variable, which indicates the state of the memory, before the transaction is started. It can be considered as a snapshot of the memory just before the transaction is started:

```
MemoryInit1 ∈ DATAZONE ⟶ DATUM
```

At any time, except at the end of a transaction, the initial state of the memory "MemoryInit1" can be restored using the backup data "BackMemory1". One should notice that, when the transaction is terminated, the backup zone is cleared *(BackMemory1=∅)*; it is then impossible to retrieve "MemoryInit1" from "Memory1":

```
CardState1 ≠ STOP ⇒ MemoryInit1=Memory1◁BackMemory1 (2)
```

From the above expressions (1) and (2), it can be deduced that "MemoryInit1" equals "Memory1" when the transaction is started:

```
CardState1 = START ⇒ Memory1 = MemoryInit1
```

The process of modifying the data is considered complete when the EEPROM memory at the beginning of the transaction "MemoryInit", has been overridden by the data "NewState1":

```
CardState1 = MODIFIED ⇒
          (Memory1 = MemoryInit1 ◁ NewState1)
```

Events

A transaction is initiated by the event "BeginTransaction" and it can only be triggered when the system state is "START". This operation is an abstract operation; its only purpose is to switch the system state from "START" to "BACKUP".

The event "Modify" is an abstract event which indicates that the modifications have been performed and the memory is completely updated. The way the modifications have been realized is not described at this level of the formalisation:

```
Modify ≙
    SELECT CardState1 = BACKUP
    THEN
            Memory1 := Memory1 ◁ NewState1
            || BackMemory1 := (dom(NewState1) Memory1)
            || CardState1 := MODIFIED
    END;
```

The event "AbortTransaction" may be triggered by the application at any time before or after the modification of data is performed (*CardState1 ∈{BACKUP,MODIFIED}*). This corresponds to a willful action of the programmer, and the memory must be changed back to its original state (i.e before the transaction was started). Then the system must start the restore/rollback process:

```
AbortTransaction ≙
    SELECT CardState1 ∈ {BACKUP,MODIFIED}
    THEN
            CardState1 := INIROLLBACK
    END;
```

The event "Rollback" restores the initial state of the memory by overriding "Memory1" with the backed up data "BackMemory1":

```
Rollback ≙
    SELECT CardState1 ∈ {INIROLLBACK, WITHDRAWN}
    THEN
            Memory1 := Memory1 ◁ BackMemory1 ||
            CardState1 := ROLLBACK
    END;
```

The "Pullout" event is an abstract description of a physical and mechanical phenomenon. Its only goal is to make sure that the card pull-out event does not break the invariant statements of the backup mechanism. It will not be implemented, and it is not part of the backup algorithm.

The security requirements of the transaction mechanism are thus fulfilled by demonstrating that the "Pullout" event does not hamper the backup process. The backup mechanism is then formally proved to be resistant to card withdrawals that may occur at any time.

At this level of the refinement process, the "Pullout" event only indicates that the transaction system must proceed with rolling back the data located in the backup zone. This is indicated by switching the state variable CardState1 to "WITHDRAWN: the only possible event to be elected now becomes "ROLLBACK":

```
Pullout ≜
    SELECT CardState1 ≠ STOP
    THEN
            CardState1 := WITHDRAWN
    END;
```

The "Transaction" event has been refined by several new events as described above. It only consists now in erasing the backup data "BackMemory1" and switching the state variable " CardState1" to STOP:

```
Transaction =

    SELECT CardState1 ∈ {ROLLBACK,MODIFIED}
    THEN
            BackMemory1 := ∅ ‖
            CardState1 := STOP
    END;
```

6. The Second Refinement

Scope

In the first refinement, the modification of the data was performed in a single event called "Modify".

In reality, a transaction may be performed by several partial data modifications. The goal of this refinement is to introduce two new events "BuffModify" and "BuffBackup" which represent iterative buffer modifications.

The transaction is complete when all partial buffer modifications have been performed correctly as described in the abstract model.

The action performed by the abstract specification of the "Modify" event, is now replaced by an undefined number of iterations of the events "BuffBackup" and "BuffModify".

One should notice that the card is likely to be withdrawn at any time, and in particular before or after the events "BuffBackup" and "BuffModify". This implies that the "Pullout" event may be triggered at any time during the transaction.

The following picture depicts the different states of the transaction system:

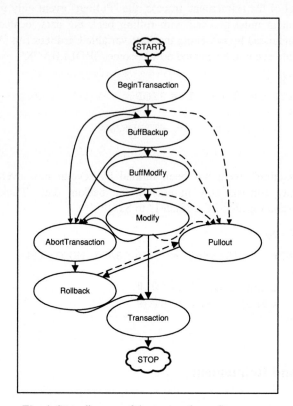

Fig. 4. State diagram of the transaction refinement

Variables and Invariants

The variables "NewState2", "Memory2", "MemoryInit2", "BackMemory2" are identical to their counterparts in the previous level.

Besides, the value "BUFFBACKUP" is added to the possible states of "CardState2":

```
CardState2 ∈ {START, BACKUP, MODIFIED, WITHDRAWN,
INIROLLBACK, ROLLBACK, STOP, BUFFBACKUP}
```

The Variable "NewMemory2" is a function representing a buffer which is updated at each iteration of the sequence defined by the event "BuffBackup" followed by "BuffModify":

```
NewMemory2 ∈ DATAZONE ⤖ DATUM
```

Events

The event "BuffBackup" updates the buffer "NewMemory2". At this level of the abstract model, no particular constraint is imposed on the buffer: it can be of any size and may take any value represented by the partial function "l_new_memory".

The expression of "BackMemory2" shown below indicates that the subset of memory to be overridden by "NewMemory2" is entirely backed up in the backup zone.

One should also notice that if an element is backed up several times, it is only required that the backup zone stores its oldest values. This requirement is of great importance to be able to retrieve the original state of the memory. It is expressed by the expression: BackMemory2:=(dom(l_new_memory) Memory2)◁ BackMemory2

```
BuffBackup ≙
     SELECT CardState2 = BACKUP
     THEN
            ANY l_new_memory
            WHERE
                l_new_memory : DATAZONE ⇸ DATUM
            THEN
            BackMemory2:=(dom(l_new_memory)  Memory2)◁
                                              BackMemory2
            ‖ CardState2 := BUFFBACKUP
            ‖ NewMemory2 := l_new_memory
            END
     END;
```

The sequencing of the events "BuffBackup" and "BuffModify", is imposed by their guards; it insures that the memory buffer is backed up before being modified by "NewMemory2".

The expression of "BuffModify" is straightforward as the modification of the memory is performed by overriding "Memory2" by the buffer "NewMemory2":

```
BuffModify ≙
     SELECT (CardState2 = BUFFBACKUP)
     THEN
            Memory2 := Memory2 ◁ NewMemory2
            ‖ CardState2 := BACKUP
     END;
```

Remark 2. In the above expression,"CardState2" is changed to "BACKUP". This implies that, in absence of card withdrawal, the only eligible future events will be "BuffBackup" or "Modify" (see above and after).

The event "Modify" is now refined by an abstract event. Its guard provides the conditions of termination of the memory modification $Memory2 = MemoryInit2 \lhd NewState2$:

```
Modify ≜
    SELECT CardState2 = BACKUP  ∧
           (Memory2 = MemoryInit2 ⊲ NewState2)
    THEN
           CardState2 := MODIFIED
    END;
```

We must notice that the model does not provide any evidence that the sequence of events "BuffBackup" and "BuffModify" will terminate and that the final state described by "NewState2" is reached.

Instead, the model only indicates that for a transaction to terminate, the complete set of modifications defined by "NewState2" shall be performed by several buffer modifications.

It is the application's responsibility to demonstrate that the transaction events are correctly used, and that the memory modifications predicted by the abstract variable "NewState" are indeed realised.

7. The 3rd Refinement

Scope

The 3rd refinement describes the High Level design of the transaction system: the backup zone is now described as a stack.

For the sake of simplicity, if a data value is required to be backed up several times within a transaction, it is duplicated in the backup zone and piled up in the stack: the system does not perform any checks to reduce the amount of duplicated data.

Similarly, the rollback mechanism consists in restoring the backed up buffers in the reverse order to insure that their oldest values are restored in the memory.

Variables and Invariants

The backup zone is described as a stack and the buffers are piled-up and numbered using increasing numbers. The variable "Top3" represents the number of backed up buffers:

```
Top3 ∈ NATURAL
```

The variable "SavedBuff3" is a total function which associates each buffer to its corresponding number. A buffer is described as a subset of the memory (a partial function from "DATAZONE" to "DATUM") :

```
SavedBuff3 ∈ 1..Top3 ⟶ (DATAZONE ⇸ DATUM)
```

The variable "Add3" identifies the set of all backed up elements. It is an abstract variable. It is used as an intermediate variable to facilitate and simplify the predicate expressions of the invariants:

```
Add3 ⊆ DATAZONE ∧
Add3=dom(union(SavedBuff3[1..top3])
```

The variable "Mark3" indicates for each backed up element belonging to "Add3" , the corresponding buffer number of its first occurrence in the backup zone:

```
Mark3 ∈ Add3 ⟶ 1..Top3 ∧
(∀ad | (ad ∈ Add3 ⇒
Mark3(ad)=min({tt| tt ∈ 1..Top3 ∧ ad∈ dom(SavedBuff3(tt))}))
```

"Mark3" is an abstract variable which is used for gluing the variable "BackMemory2" as defined in the previous level to the variable "SavedBuff3". The following statement indicates that the backed up data identified by "BackMemory2" are also marked in the backup zone by the "Mark3" variable. In case of a rollback, these values shall be restored in the memory:

```
Add3 = dom(BackMemory2)∧
∀ad|(ad ∈ Add3 ⇒
           BackMemory2(ad) = (SavedBuff3(Mark3(ad)))(ad))
```

The following figure provides a graphic representation of the entities listed above. In this example, the element "el1" is backed up twice (in the buffers n°2 and n°3 respectively). The function "Mark3" indicates that the first occurrence of the element "el1" in the backup zone is in the buffer n°2. The variable "Top3" is equal to 3:

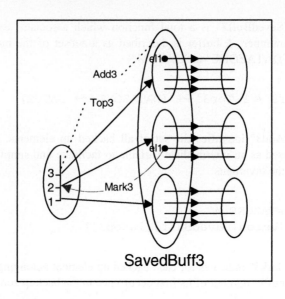

Fig. 5. Abstract representation of the backup zone

Event

The events defined in this refinement have similar meanings to those of the previous level but their expressions are modified to take into account the new variables defined above. The BuffBackup event illustrates these changes:

- the function "NewMemory3" is updated by some partial function "l_new_memory" and the variable "CardState3" is switched to "BUFFBACKUP",
- the buffer of data *(dom(l_new_memory) Memory3)* which will be modified by "NewMemory3" is appended to the backup zone stack "SavedBuff3". Its index is set to "Top3+1". The global expression is: *SavedBuff3 := SavedBuff3 ∪ {Top3+1↦(dom(l_new_memory) Memory3)}.*
- the variable "Top3" representing the index of the last buffer is incremented, *Top3:=Top3+1,*
- the elements of memory which are not already backed up in the backup zone *((dom(l_new_memory)-Add3)* are tagged with the value "Top3+1" and added to "Mark3" *(Mark3:=Mark3∪ (dom(l_new_memory)-Add3)*{Top3+1}.*

The expression of the event "BuffBackup" is shown below:

```
BuffBackup ≙
     SELECT CardState3 = BACKUP
     THEN
             ANY l_new_memory
```

WHERE
    l_new_memory $\in$ DATAZONE $\rightarrowtail$ DATUM
THEN
    CardState3 := BUFFBACKUP
  ‖ NewMemory3 := l_new_memory
  ‖ SavedBuff3 := SavedBuff3 $\cup$
    {Top3+1$\mapsto$(dom(l_new_memory) Memory3)}
  ‖ Top3 := Top3+1
  ‖ Mark3 := Mark3 $\cup$
    (dom(l_new_memory)-Add3)*{Top3+1}
  ‖ Add3 := Add3 $\cup$ dom(l_new_memory)
END
    END
END

8. The 4th Refinement

Scope

The 4th refinement is used for technical and simplification purposes. In the 3rd refinement, several abstract variables were introduced for gluing the variables with those of the 2nd level. These variables are not required anymore in the 4th refinement ("Mark3" and "Add3") and they are simply removed.

The formal expression of the invariant clause and of the events is identical to the previous model, purged of the predicates and the useless variables.

Variables and Invariants

The variables at the 4th refinement are all identical to the variables of the 3rd refinements, except for "Mark3" and "Add3" which are simply removed. They are labeled "CardState4", "NewMemory4" and the gluing is straightforward:

(CardState4 = CardState3) $\wedge$
(NewMemory4 = NewMemory3) etc..

Proof

As the refinement only consists in a simplification of the previous model, the resulting proof obligations are either obvious or automatically demonstrated by the Prover.

9. The 5th Refinement

Scope

The 5th refinement consists in modeling the modification and the constraints on the global variables resulting from a card pull-out.

As a card pull-out may occur at any time during the backup process, we might think it necessary for each event to model its counterpart when the card is withdrawn.

It can be easily stated that the only case where a card withdrawal may alter the transaction mechanism is when the backup memory or the data memory are modified. An erroneous modification in the backup zone might prevent the system from being able to restore the initial state of the memory. Similarly, an erroneous modification of the memory may cause the system not to reach its final expected condition.

As a consequence, two new events are introduced to provide a formal expression of the card withdrawal during the processes of backing up and buffer modification: "BuffBackupPullout" and "BuffModifyPullout".

The demonstration of the proof obligation generated by these new events provide evidence that the global invariants of the transaction system are not broken by the "Pullout" events.

They are introduced in the model in place of the "Pullout" event when the system state is either "BACKUP" or "BUFFBACKUP". The guard of "Pullout" is then simply restricted (or strengthened).

When the card is plugged back in the terminal after a pull-out, it is assumed that:
- *only the last buffer of the backup zone may be erroneous (the only case where the last buffer may be erroneous is when the card has been pulled-out while the backup was in progress),*
- *all buffers but the last one are necessarily correct.*

As a consequence, *all valid buffers* in the backup zone require to be rolled back after a card pull-out.

At this level of abstraction, it is assumed that:
- the last buffer is considered invalid if the card is withdrawn while the backup is in progress (the other buffers are all valid),
- all buffers in the backup zone are valid if the card is withdrawn at any other time.

Variables and Invariants

The variable "LstBufVal5" is a simple Boolean value which indicates the last buffer validity:

```
LstBufVal5 ∈ BOOL
```

All variables except "Top5" and "SavedBuff5", are identical to the 4th refinement and are labeled "CardState5", "NewMemory5" etc...

In normal operating mode (no card pull-out), the variables "Top5" and "SavedBuff5" are identical to their counterparts in the previous refinement, and the last buffer is assumed to be correct. This is stated as follows:

```
(LstBufVal5 = TRUE
 ⇒ (Top5 = Top4 ∧ SavedBuff5 = SavedBuff4))
```

In case of a card pull-out occurring while the backup is in progress, the last buffer is declared erroneous *(LstBufVal5 = FALSE)*. It comes out that all buffers of the backup zone except the last one, match with the previous refinement *(1..Top4) SavedBuff5=SavedBuff4*. The last erroneous buffer is simply added on top of the backup stack *(Top5=Top4+1)*. This is expressed as follows:

```
LstBufVal5 = FALSE
 ⇒ ((Top5=Top4+1)∧(1..Top4) SavedBuff5=SavedBuff4)
```


Events

The event "BuffBackupPullout" is similar to its counterpart "BuffBackup" except that the stack "SavedBuffer5" is updated by a buffer "1_back" which is not related to "NewMemory5": *SavedBuff5:=SavedBuff5∪{Top5+1↦1_back}*.

The Boolean "LstBufVal5" is set FALSE:

```
BuffBackupPullout ≙
    SELECT CardState5 = BACKUP
    THEN
            ANY 1_back
            WHERE
                1_back ∈ DATAZONE ⇸ DATUM
            THEN
                CardState5 := BUFFBACKUP
             ‖ SavedBuff5:=SavedBuff5∪{Top5+1↦1_back}
             ‖ Top5 := Top5+1
             ‖ LstBufVal5 := FALSE
            END
    END
```

Similarly, the event "BuffModifyPullout" is identical to the event "BuffModify" except that the buffer which is appended to the memory is not equal to "NewMemory5" (it can be of any kind).

Proofs

The demonstration of the proof obligations provides evidence that the events "BuffBackupPullout" and "BuffModifyPullout" fulfill the invariant predicates. They must preserve the following statements:

- all buffers of the backup zone except the last one are identical to the previous refinement,
- the last buffer is erroneous if the card is pulled-out while the backup is in progress; it shall not be restored by the rollback process.

10. The 6th Refinement

The 6th refinement is used for technical and simplification purposes.

11. The 7th Refinement

The 7th refinement provides an implementation of the backup zone. Each buffer of the backup zone consists of a header and a set of values. The header provides the necessary information for restoring number of data values in the memory: the start address of the buffer zone and the length (number of data) of the buffer.

A supplementary checksum is added to the Header. It is assumed that the checksum is able to determine in a non-ambiguous way the validity of the buffer.

The details of the computation of the checksum are out of the scope of this article. The formal representation only states that the validity of the last buffer determined by the variable "LstBuffVal5" (see 5th refinement) can be substituted by the computation of a checksum value. Nevertheless, we must notice that the checksum calculation must prevent misinterpretation caused by simultaneous errors occurring together in the buffer data and in the checksum itself.

12. The 8th,9th, and 10th Refinements

The last three refinements of the development provide the complete algorithm of the transaction system. Several pointers are introduced for managing the backup and the rollback processes.

For the sake of efficiency, these pointers are located in the RAM memory. This implies that their values are lost when the card is pulled out. This is modelled by erasing their values in the pull-out events (setting their values to zero for example). The formal model provides evidence that the algorithm is resistant to card pull-out, and the pointer values can be retrieved by a well designed scanning of the backup zone, and by analysing the header structures: checksum, size of the buffer data etc..

13. The Last Refinement / The Implementation Level

The last refinement is called the implementation. It provides the complete backup algorithm and is translated into the C language.

The process of code generation needs to transform an event based architecture into a sequential program which can be run by a smart card processor.

This can be obtained by first transforming the SELECT statements of the events into a PRE statement; the events must now be considered as pre-conditioned operations.

The sequencing of these operations is performed by a "scheduler" which is responsible for calling the operations in a way that complies with the pre-conditions. The scheduler is defined in a separate B machine, and its correctness is verified by the demonstration of the Proof Obligations.

The actual version of the "B0 checker" and "C" translator AtelierB tools, do not support the SELECT clauses in the implementation. The transformation of the SELECT clauses into PRE statements must be done in a specific B abstract machine. This must be performed manually or by a script command; the traceability between the original model and the transformed one can be easily demonstrated. Although we must keep in mind that no proof obligation can be generated during this process.

14. Code Generation

The design of the transaction mechanism using the B formal method has been carried out in parallel with a traditional design using the C language.

The generation of the source code from the B model has been performed manually and its effectiveness in terms of code size, memory and stack is strictly comparable to the traditional design:

- The same number of variables and pointers on the backup stack has been used in both designs,

- In order match the code size of the original design, some optimizations have been required for translating the event based model: all operations of the transaction model have been in-lined in the "scheduler" calls to reduce the processor stack and improve the execution speed.

15. Conclusion

The use of the B method for the design of the transaction mechanism has been greatly beneficial for the following reasons:

- formal description of the functional and security requirements, together with the environment assumptions,
- formal validation of the detailed design and the pseudo-code algorithm,
- reduction of the validation task load,
- 100% of the Proof Obligations of the project (over 1500 in total) have been demonstrated in interactive mode with no added lemmas.

The transcription of C source code from the implementation level has been performed manually as no automatic translator is available for smart Card applications.

The results in terms of code size, memory and stack is strickly comparable to the original design.

The design of an automatic translator is one of our concerns:

- It shall be able to generate a source code which is compact enough to be used in the smart card applications,

- It must be flexible enough to meet the peculiarities of compilers and chips which are used in the industry,

- It should also take into account the programming recommandation to improve the security of the design.

Acknowledgements

Many Thanks to J.R Abrial for his contribution to the design of the B model, and to Savy Kong for his commitment and his enthusiasm in the project during the summer of '98.

References

1. Abrial J-R, *The B-Book: Assigning programs to meanings*. Edited by Cambridge University Press (1996)
2. Abrial J-R and Mussat L, *Introducing Dynamic Constraints in B*. D.Bert (Editor): Proceedings of the Second International B Conference B'98: Recent Advances in the Development and Use of the B Method, April 1998, Springer.
3. Abrial J-R. and Mussat L, *Specification and Design of a Transmission Protocol by Successive Refinements Using B*. in Mathematical Methods in Program Development, Edited by M. Broy and B. Schieder, Springer Verlag (1997)

Météor:
A Successful Application of B in a Large Project

Patrick Behm, Paul Benoit, Alain Faivre, and Jean-Marc Meynadier

Matra Transport International
48-56 rue Barbès 92120 Montrouge
tel : +33 (0) 1 49 65 70 00 fax : +33 (0) 1 49 65 70 93
{behm,benoit,faivre,meynadier}@matra-transport.fr

Abstract. The automatic train operating system for METEOR, the first driverless metro in the city of Paris, is designed to manage the traffic of the vehicles controlled automatically or manually. This system, developed by Matra Transport International for the RATP, requires a very high level of dependability and safety for the users and the operator. To achieve this, the safety critical software located in the different control units (ground, line and on-board) was developed using the B formal method together with the Vital Coded Processor. This architecture thus ensures an optimum level of safety agreed with the customer. This experience with the METEOR project has convinced Matra Transport International of the advantages of using this B formal method for large-scale industrial developments.

1 Introduction

Matra Transport International has developed railway-automated systems with very strong dependability and safety needs (Sacem, Val, Maggaly, Météor). The complexity of the new systems leads to realise most of the functions by software even for safety functions. The validation of the software design is therefore of the utmost importance to guarantee the absence of catastrophic situations. To prevent software design errors and to reach *zero-fault*, Matra Transport International has chosen the B method to develop and validate safety critical software. The formal process has been fully applied for the first time to develop the automatic train operation system, which equips Météor, the new metro line 14 in Paris (France).

1.1 Historic

The use of formal method in the french railway industry was introduced for the SACEM system, an automatic train control system asked by RATP, the transit authority in Paris, in the beginning of 1980. The consortium of manufacturers in charge of this project decided to develop single software using a new technology to secure it, the VCP[1] technique, instead of diversified software using the

---

[1] Vital Coded Processor

J. Wing, J. Woodcock, J. Davies (Eds.): FM'99, Vol. I, LNCS 1708, pp. 369–387, 1999.
© Springer-Verlag Berlin Heidelberg 1999

redundancy concept. The VCP technique consists in protecting each software information by a redundant code, checked at run-time. Because the software was not doubled, a *zero default* design was required. Moreover, validation by testing was not considered as sufficient by RATP; so, they asked manufacturers to use a new approach based on formal method.

The process was the following one:

1. the functional software requirements were re-written in a formal language;
2. the software source code, written in Modula 2 language, was completed with *pre-assertions* and *post-assertions* and checked with a partially automated program proof activity;
3. a check between formal specification and code assertions was manually performed.

Despite the heaviness of this process and its weak automation, the confidence achieved by this first application had convinced RATP. For the following tender, the Météor line, they demanded the use of formal method for safety critical software development. Matra Transport International was chosen in 1992 to develop the automatic train operation system for the Météor line, using the B method [Abr96] for the safety critical software.

1.2   Météor

The new metro line, number 14, in Paris (France), is in operation since October 15th 1998 between *Tolbiac-Nationale* at south-east of Paris and *Madeleine* at north-west. It is connected with two main junctions of the metro network, *Gare de Lyon* and *Chatelet*. This line was designed to reach traffic of 40.000 passengers per hour and per direction with an interval between train down to 85 s. on "peak hours". This new line is managed by the automatic train operation system developed by Matra Transport International. This automatic guideway transportation system allows to manage automatic driverless trains together with non-equipped manually driven trains. It was designed to meet strong requirements such as a high quality of service (user's point of view), an easy operation management and a strong safety level.

The automatic train system is made up of four main subsystems:

1. *PA-SIG*[2], the automatic pilot and signalling system,
2. the operation control centre,
3. the platform doors,
4. the audio-video system.

The *PA-SIG* is the only subsystem that includes safety critical software. This subsystem controls the running and stopping of every trains, and controls opening and closing of doors located in trains and platforms. It ensures that the speed

---

[2] Pilote Automatique et SIGnalisation

of trains is safely guaranteed and controls electrical traction power, routes, doors and sends back alarms from passengers to the operation control centre. The automatic train operation system has a distributed architecture with:

1. line equipment located in the operation control centre,
2. wayside equipment dispatched along the track,
3. on-board equipment.

All of them are linked together through a high-speed transmission network to exchange information. At any point of the track, wayside equipment and on-board equipment are also able to mutually exchange numerical information.

The operation control centre allows the operators to monitor the pre-established operating train programs for each day and to supervise all the events received by the network. To ensure their work, operators have:

1. an optical track diagram which displays on run time a detailed picture of the track with the position of every trains,
2. video screens which display what is happening inside trains or on platforms,
3. communication means to speak with passengers in train or in station,
4. terminals which allow them to act on the system by sending orders.

Platform doors prevent people from falling on to the track. Exchange of passengers between trains and platforms is authorised when trains are correctly stopped in stations. In this case, platform doors and train doors are just facing together. In case of failure, emergency doors allow evacuation of the passengers when the trains are not correctly stopped.

Audio and video communication allow the security of passengers with the help of supervision or direct communication between passengers and operators in the operation control centre.The system has to meet a high level of availability.

1.3   Safety Critical Software

The automatic pilots (on-board, wayside and line equipment) run on a safety computer using the VCP technique. The VCP environment delivers basic services such as inputs/ouputs, hardware/software interfaces and safe computing. According to safety analysis performed at system and equipment levels, the software of the automatic pilots is split into two products (Figure 1):

1. safety critical software which corresponds to vital functionalities,
2. non safety critical software.

Each of them is running on a specific microprocessor board. The safety critical software is sequential and cyclic (with a basic cycle of 360 ms), single task and non-interruptible. This feature enables the use of a formal method such as B.

In the other hand, considering a validated *Software Requirements* document, software failures can be classified into two categories:

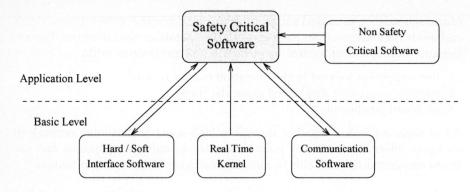

Fig. 1. Safety Critical Software of Météor

1. *design or coding errors.*
   In that case, the source code does not fulfil the *Software Requirements* document.
2. *errors in the code production chain (compiling, linking,...) or resulting from hardware failures.*
   In that case, program execution is not correct with respect to the meaning of the source code.

The VCP technique detects the second category of errors. The goal of using the B formal method is to protect against the first one by developing a single software program aiming to be bug-free.

2   Industrialisation of the B Method

Evidently, at the beginning of the Météor project, the B technology was far from being mature enough for a large industrial application. As it stood, B provided a set of mathematical modelling tools, formal validation obligations and a prototype toolkit to control and to prove rather small models. The first trials pointed out how great was the risk of elaborating, from the first level of abstraction, models very difficult to prove and even more difficult to refine into code, and revealed that the toolkit could not deal with large software components. In particular, the feasibility of a 100% proven development was not guaranteed.

Moreover, there was no answer to the question of introducing such a method into an existing lifecycle in the context of an industry. Usually, the realisation of safety critical software involves two teams:

1. the development team, which elaborates the specification of the software, designs it, and validates it, from a functional point of view;
2. the validation team, which carries out specific safety analysis, such as *Functional Safety Analysis* or *Software Errors Effect Analysis* to demonstrate that the execution of the software will not lead to a dangerous situation.

How the use of a formal method impacts this organisation and their two processes? Moreover, we were concerned about the level of education required for the use of B. Could our engineers be efficient with it, or is it reserved for experts?

An important work program was required and it was decided to go for the following objectives:

1. to define the new processes for the development and the validation teams, benefiting from the use of B;
2. to elaborate a methodological reference book enabling an efficient application of B, both for the design and the validation processes;
3. to bring the toolkit performances to the required level to handle large volumes of modelling, and particularly to improve proof techniques;
4. to link the method with the protection technique of code compilation and execution used at Matra Transport International.

In the next paragraphs we present the results of a 4-year program of industrialisation of B, associating RATP, Matra Transport International and Stéria Méditérranée.

2.1   The Development Process

The formal development cycle is shown in Figure 2 against the conventional development cycle.

This development cycle consists of the following two main steps:

1. the modelisation phase in which an abstract model of the informal software requirements is elaborated;
2. the design phase which, in successive steps, transforms the abstract model into a concrete one, ready to be translated into code.

The Modelisation Phase. The input document of this phase is the *Software Requirements* document which specifies the requirements to be met by the software product, in compliance with the design choices decided at the system, subsystem and equipment levels. It includes the functional requirements, i.e. what the software has to do, as well as operational and implementation constraints (e.g. the use of the VCP technique for the software product and the maximum time allowed for it).

This document is written in natural language. The aim of the modelisation phase is to formalise the functional requirements: an abstract model is elaborated using the B notation. This model must include all the functional features included in the *Software Requirements* document, regardless, as far as possible, of how it will be implemented afterwards.

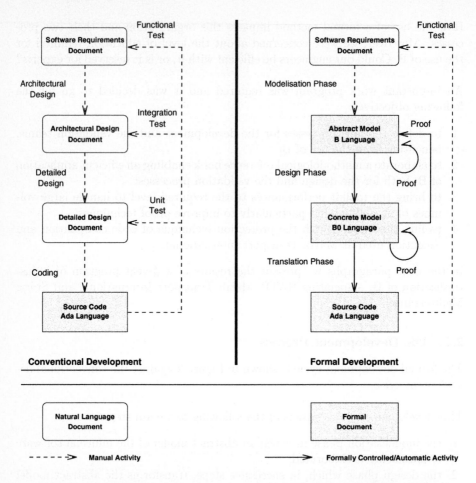

Fig. 2. Formal development cycle vs. conventional development cycle

Although the two lifecycles may look similar, there is an important difference with a conventional development. In a formal development, the abstract model is complete, i.e. no other functional information is required to implement the software product, and it gives only the highest level of the software architecture. On the contrary, the architectural design document of a conventional development gives most of the architecture, but is not concerned with the precise semantics of each box of the architecture.

Moreover, the abstract model includes properties, enabling a consistency proof of the model. The safety properties which are explicitly expressed in the *Software Requirements* document are formalised in the model. They may appear in the invariant clause of the abstract model if they must be satisfied by all the states of the system; if they deal with the dynamics of a particular function, they are included as post-conditions in the specification of the operation which formalises the function.

The consistency of the abstract model is carried out by means of the following tools:

1. the proof obligation generator; this tool produced all the mathematical theorems (called *lemmas*) to be proven;
2. the automatic and the interactive proof tools; the automatic proof tool attempts to prove each lemma. The automatic proof of the most difficult lemmas may fail; then, the interactive proof tool is used for these lemmas, the developer guides the proof by defining special proof tactics or by adding mathematical rules. These rules are validated within the framework of the formal validation activities.

As said before, the elaboration of an abstract model, completed with respect to the *Software Requirements* document, totally proven and good enough to be the firm basis for the design, is a very complex activity; it would not be effective without an efficient methodological reference environment.

A *B Method Book* [BMB99] was elaborated and enriched for several years to address this problem. It included guidelines for each step of the development. As far as the modelisation phase is concerned, the book includes:

1. rules to build the abstract model. In particular it provides :
   - restrictions to the B language (e.g. *Machines* without parameters),
   - architecture rules (e.g. the *INCLUDES* and *USES* clauses are not used),
   - specific rules for the modelisation of data and functions,
   - modelling examples relating to the notions often used in the *Software Requirements* document (e.g. several automaton model schemas are developed),
   - modelisation rules to ease the proofs (i.e. to reduce the number of lemmas produced and to get more simple lemmas).
2. rules to interface the formally specified software with software products which are not formally developed and/or reused;
3. guidelines for the interactive proofs.

The *B Method Book* enables better control of the modelisation phase. Beyond this step, it can be considered that an extremely hard to prove model stems from a defect of the model itself. This is why the rate of automatic proof is used as an indicator of the quality of the models: an abstract model must reach the 90% level of automatic proof before it is allowed to be implemented.

A very interesting demonstration of the efficiency of this book is that, in our experience, very few feedback coming from the design phase demand modifications of the abstract model, in spite of the difference of these two levels.

The Design Phase. The objective of this phase is to transform the abstract model into a concrete model, written in a subset of the B language, the B0 language, which enables automatic translation into code. During this phase, major design decisions have to be taken, fitting the operational requirements of the software product.

From a technical point of view, the refinement work from abstraction to pseudo-code includes several aspects:

1. data reification: the set of abstract data must be transformed into a set of data of basic type (integer, boolean, array). Links between these two sets are precisely given to enable the proof;
2. architecture refinement: the architecture of the abstract model has to be completed to get the implementation architecture;
3. structure refinement: the dynamics of the operations must be expressed using basic control structures (sequence, alternative, loop);
4. the validation of the concrete model with respect to the abstract one.

Again, our *B Method Book* provides a vital help to achieve the design phase. Starting from the idea that many design choices may be systematically decided, it describes the process the user has to follow:

1. the book recommends to complete first the architecture refinement in a very systematic way;
2. the structure refinement is then guided with predefined schemas for each substitution (*if*, *case*, non deterministic substitution, etc.); a special chapter explains how to build loops and how to implement abstract iterators;
3. the data reification is postponed as far as possible; for this step, a data reification dictionary is provided; it gives schemas of refinement for each type of abstract data which usually occurs in the abstract models, together with formal link between the abstraction and the suggested concrete data.

Validation of the concrete model with respect to its abstraction is again carried out using the proof obligation generator, the automatic and interactive provers. Proof activities are widely facilitated by the use of the standard schemas for architecture refinement and data reification of the *B Method Book*: specific tactics have been introduced for them. Again, the rate of automatic proof is used as a quality indicator: concrete models are reworked until 80% of the produced lemmas are automatically proven[3].

Translation into Ada Code. The translation of the concrete model, written in the B0 language, into Ada code is automatic and made by a double chain

---

[3] These rates express our current practice of the method in a given release of the toolkit. We hope they will continue to increase progressively as the power of the proof techniques and the efficiency of our methodological referential will improve.

of translators. The tool takes into account most of the *Vital Coded Processor* constraints, which were previously handled by the developer[4].

Evidently, the Ada code produced can be read, but not modified: otherwise the proof effort would be ruined. Beyond this restriction, the Ada code is considered as an intermediate language used to interface the compilation line: for the user's point of view, B0 is the implementation language.

2.2   The Validation Process

The validation process takes into account all the activities necessary to obtain the conviction that the critical functions are safely implemented. These activities follow and complete the safety analyses achieved beforehand on system, subsystem and equipment specifications.

This validation process springs from the following observations:

1. The proof activity, carried out during the formal development phase, guarantees the internal consistency of the first abstract B model and the consistency between the various phases of the formal development.
2. The proof activity, realised by automatic and interactive tools, is considered as a double chain, that is, a validation chain which is independent from the design activity of the B models carried out by the development teams.

In that context, the validation tasks to be performed are as follows:

1. verification of the abstract B model, resulting from the modelisation phase with respect to the informal *Software Requirements* document,
2. verification of interfaces between B models and operating features developed conventionally,
3. validation of all the mathematical rules, added during proof activities of the development phases,
4. verification of the translation of concrete B0 models into Ada source code,
5. functional test based validation.

This highlights the test based validation phase compared with that of a conventional development. In particular, the validation by proofs during modelisation and design phases makes unnecessary:

1. the unit tests, which validate the code of the procedures against their detailed design;
2. the integration tests, which validate, step by step, that the modules fit to one another, according to the design.

---

[4] Some constraints cannot be automatically carried out; they must be handled in the concrete model.

Furthermore, it is interesting to notice that one major advantage of the B method is to enable the validation during the development phases, and not after the elaboration of the code.

As for development activities, a *B Validation Book* [BVB99] was elaborated and enriched during the project. It details the validation activies and provides guidelines for each step of the validation.

Verification of Models Coming from the Formal Development Phase. This task guarantees the consistency and the completeness of the abstract B model coming from the formal development phase in comparison with the informal *Software Requirements* document. These requirements, and particularly the safety properties, can be converted into invariant properties or substitutions in the operations of the B models.

This is the most important step in validation activities since the following software products generated during design phase until software execution on a target machine, will be under the control of the B Method and then of the VCP technique.

This is also the most complicated step because of the informal aspect of the initial *Software Requirements* document which prevents any automation of that verification.

A detailed and complete analysis is carried out on B models compared with functional specifications. The proof activities guarantee that concrete B models stemming from the design phase strictly refined the validated abstract B models. Therefore, no additional activity is necessary to validate these concrete models.

Verification of B/Non-B Interfaces. Ada components produced by the formal B process can be interfaced with software components conventionally developed in Ada. Among these components are, for example, the operating features which are not classified as safety critical or data files which describe topology of railroad and which are calculated by others tools independently from the B development.

For each of these components, not expressed in B, and interfaced with B models, there is a corresponding formal specification, called basic machine. These basic machines contain all the information necessary for the proof of the B components which refer to them, that is, the assumptions necessary for the correct execution of the automatically generated code. Not observing these assumptions may generate a risk of inconsistency between the code corresponding to the basic machines, which has been manually generated, and the code of the components, which has been automatically generated through the toolkit.

Basic machines represent two main types of operating features:

1. Non safety critical operating features: from a safety point of view, nothing can be guaranteed concerning their results. In this case, the associated basic machines stipulate that the B components which call upon these operating features must be capable of accepting any execution result.
2. Safety critical operating features, not developed in B: in this case, the associated basic machines specify the properties expected by the proof from these operating features.

Example 1 ((Safety properties about stations and platforms)). A platform belongs to a single station and a station is associated with a maximum of two platforms.

Example 2 ((Safety properties about shunting.)). If the position of a shunting is not uncontroled, its value must be right or left.

A detailed and complete conformity analysis is equally carried out on corresponding Ada code compared with basic machines and *Software Requirements* document.

Validation of the Added Proof Rules. The rules added by the developers during the interactive proof step must be correct, that is, they must preclude wrongfully proving lemmas.

The validation of these rules includes various preliminary steps which make it possible to ensure that they are correctly written and really useful. Next, the actual mathematical proof is carried out.

In an initial step, a tool attempts to automatically prove the largest number of added rules. The rules which are not proven in this phase are then listed and undergo a manual mathematical demonstration which is as complete and as rigorous as possible: each step in the proof must be accompanied by an explicit reference to the *B-Book* (definition, theorem, property) or to general mathematical knowledge which corroborates it.

Any rule that cannot be proven either because it is false, or because it is too complex, can result from an incorrect formulation of the informal functional requirements.

Verification of Translated Ada Source Code. The safety of translation between B0 and VCP-Ada is guaranteed by the use of a double chain: two translators B0/VCP-Ada were independently developed. The correctness comparison between results issued on both sides of the double chain is assured by the VCP technique itself.

Functional Test Based Validation. The objective of the functional tests is to validate the code with respect to the *Software Requirements* document. Although this activity is redundant with all previous validation activities, we have kept it within the framework of Météor in order to assess the setting up formal methodology. This validation activity is divided between the development team for nominal tests and the validation team which completes test coverage with borderline cases. Notice that, if it were technically possible, tests on the abstract model, rather than on the code, could suffice.

2.3   Industrialisation of the Toolkit

The initial release of the toolkit we had at the end of 1994 was far from satisfying the needs of Météor. An ambitious program of evolution has enabled to take its performances to the level required. Among qualitative improvements, several evolutions of the B language were implanted (e.g. abstract constants, use of variables in B0). Especially, quantitative improvements have been realised from tests bench defined in terms of volume of formal models, time of processing and automatic proof cover. Among qualitative improvements, several evolutions of the B language were implanted (e.g. abstract constants, use of variables in B0). This last point is fundamental since the totality of the safety critical applications of Météor was expected to represent about 30,000 lemmas. A 10% increase of the automatic proof coverage saves 3,000 lemmas!

Table 1. Adequacy of releases for Météor

Release	Date	Type checking of B models	Automatic and interactive proofs	Translation into Ada code	Safe translation into Ada code
1.6	12/94	Inadequate	Inadequate	No translator	NO
2.4	3/96	Uncomplete	Inadequate	No translator	NO
2.9	9/96	OK	Difficult	OK	NO
3.3	10/97	OK	OK	OK	OK

On the basis of an internal benchmark of lemmas, here are the coverage of the automatic prover for the different releases of the toolkit.

Table 2. Number of lemmas to be proven interactively

Release	Automatic proof coverage	Expected number of lemmas to be proven interactively
1.6	35%	19,500
2.9	60%	12,000
3.3	80%	6,000

3 Météor

3.1 Organisation

The development and validation activities of the safety critical software are carried out by three teams: the development teams, the support team, the validation team.

Development Teams. Each safety critical software product (for wayside, on-board, control-centre equipment) is developped by one development team. A development team is in charge of the whole development of their software from the *Software Requirements* document to the software/hardware integration. A team includes about two third of engineers trained in B.

Concerning the formal model, the teams carry out the following activities:

1. *production of the abstract and concrete models.*
   Two main documents are used for this:
   (a) the *Software Requirements* document, to produce the abstract model,
   (b) the *B Method Book*, in order to use B efficiently.
   The models are elaborated in a rigorous compliance to these documents.
2. *cross-reading of the abstract model.*
   Every component of the abstract model written by a developer is cross-read by another developper of the same team in order to verify its conformity with regards to the software requirements.
3. *automatic and interactive proof of these models.*
   A developper makes the complete proofs of his models. The interactive proof begins only when the model is mature enough in order to avoid to make proof several times. During the interactive proof, the developper may add new mathematical rules.
4. *documentation of the models.*
   Two documents are produced. The *Abstract Model* document gives the traceability of the abstract model with the *Software Requirements* document and justifies the modelisation choices. The *Concrete Model* document mainly justifies the design decisions taken in the refinement steps.

Validation Team. Validation activities on safety critical software are realised by a software validation team in a RAMS department, strictly independent from development teams, the general mission of which is to guarantee the dependability (reliability, availability, maintainability and safety) of the automated transportation systems and automatic train control systems developed by Matra Transport International.

This team carries out the following activities:

1. *verificatin of consistency and completness of the abstract models with regards to the* Software Requirements *document.*

2. *verification of the interfaces between B and non-B.*
   The Ada code of each basic machine is verified to be conform with the corresponding B machine and with the *Software Requirements* document.
3. *validation of the added proof rules.*
   Each rule that is not proven by the *automatic rules prover* is proven by hand.
4. *verification of the proof.*
   All the proof generation process is validated. The proof activity is automatically run again in order to verify that all the lemmas are proven.

Support Team. This team is made of engineers expert on the B method. It carries out the following activities:

1. *support of the development and validation teams.*
   If one encounters any problem when using the method or the tools he can ask to the support team.
2. *reviews of the formal models.*
   Each component produced by the developpers is reviewed by the support team in order to verify its conformity to the rules of the *B Method Book*. It will guarantee in particular that the proof will keep feasible and as easy as possible.
3. *reviews of the added mathematical rules.*
   Each rule added by a developper is reviewed in order to verify that it is mathematically correct. At this step the verification is not complete: the reviewer just read the rule and convinces himself that the rule seems right. If the rule is considered as wrong, the developper will have to remove or change the rule and make another proof.
4. *cross-reading the abstract model.*
   Each component of the model written by a developper is cross-read by the support team in order to verify that it is provable and easy to read.
5. *reviews of the verification analysis.*
   Each analysis produced by the validation team during verification activities is reviewed by the support team in order to control its conformity to the rules of the *B Validation Book*.

Links Between the Teams. During the development of the software the support team works together with the development team. The development is considered as finished when:

1. the system and software requirements specification are considered as fully mature,
2. all the reviews have been passed,
3. all the proof have been done,
4. all the nominal functional tests have been passed successfully.

Then the products (formal models, added rules, ada sources) are given to the validation team.

The link between the support and the development or validation team is strong. On the other hand, development and validation teams work independently.

Training. Three courses are provided by the support team.

1. *Basic common course.*
   The objective is to make people familiar with B models, in order for them to be able to read and understand B models, on the basis of the *B-Book*. People from development and validation teams are attending this one-week course.
2. *Development course.*
   The objective of this one-week course is to teach how to elaborate large abstract models in B, to prove them and to derive proven concrete models, on the basis of the *B method Book*.
3. *Validation course.*
   The objective of this one-week course is to teach how to validate a development with B, on the basis of the *B Validation Book*.

4 Results

In the following paragraphs, we give figures and considerations about the three safety critical software products of the Météor project.

Ada. Table 3 gives the size of each software in lines of Ada (blank lines and commentary lines are excluded), instructions of Ada and Ada packages.

Table 3. Metrics about Ada

Software Product	Lines of Ada	Instructions of Ada	Ada Packages
Wayside	37,000	22,000	305
On-Board	30,000	20,000	160
Line	19,000	15,000	165
Total	86,000	57,000	630

B Model. Table 4 gives the size in lines of B (blank lines and commentary lines are excluded), number of lemmas generated and number of rules added. Moreover 556 common rules (not specific to a software product) have also been added.

It is interesting to note that we have about 1 lemma for 4 lines of B.

For each equipment, the number of lines of B is greater than the number of lines of Ada because it includes the number of lines of B in the concrete *and* the abstract model. The ratio between the number of lines of Ada and that of B0 is about 1.1.

Table 4. Metrics about B

Software Product	Lines of B	Lemmas	Rules
Wayside	50,000	13,600	477
On-Board	40,000	7,600	322
Line	25,000	6,600	1
Total	115,000	27,800	800

Proof. Table 5 gives the number of lemmas automatically proven by the tool customized by the 556 commun rules and the dedicated proof tactics and the number of lemmas proven interactively.

Table 5. Proof metrics

Software Product	Lemmas	% Automatically Proven Lemmas	% Automatically Proven Lemmas Tool customized	Interactively Proven Lemmas
Wayside	13,600	79 %	89 %	1,463
On-Board	7,600	84 %	90 %	775
Line	6,600	80 %	99 %	16
Total	27,800	81 %	92 %	2,254

Moreover, nearly 60% of the added rules are automatically proven by tools.

Proof of Abstract and Concrete Model. Table 6 gives the repartition of the number of lemmas between the abstract model and the concrete model.

Table 6. Proof metrics for the Abstract Model and the Concrete Model

Software Product	Abstract Model Lemmas	Concrete Model Lemmas	% Abstract Model Lemmas	% Concrete Model Lemmas
Wayside	2,400	11,300	18 %	82 %
On-Board	2,300	5,300	30 %	70 %
Line	1,500	5,000	23 %	77 %
Total	6,200	21,600	22 %	78 %

We can notice that the concrete model generates about 3/4 of the lemmas.

Errors Found by Proof. Many errors have been found during proof activities. Nevertheless, as development and proof are closely linked, no figure is available.

Several errors have been found by the validation team on the mathematical rules added. It is interesting to notice that they did not correspond to bugs in the models but only bugs in the proof: they were fixed without any change in the model and, consequently, in the Ada code.

Errors Found by Testing. We have obtained the following results:

1. functional validation on host computer: no bug found;
2. integration validation on target computer: no bug found;
3. on-site tests: no bug found;
4. since the line operates: no bug found.

This is clearly a very unusual situation: in comparaison with a previous unformal development of less complex safety critical software products, the different phases of validation have revealed several tens of errors. Several releases were necessary before the acceptance tests.

5   Conclusion

5.1   B: An Efficient Method for Industrial Applications

The Météor project has demonstrated how a formal development method such as B could be successfully applied in the context of a large industrial application. This success is established by several points.

B Is Not a Method Reserved for Experts. Even if a team of B experts has supported the development and validation works, most of the engineers of the development and the validation teams were newcomers in formal method (with only two weeks for training). Moreover, most of our engineers get quickly efficient and enjoy the method.

B Can Be Integrated in an Industrial Process of Development. In particular, the usual preliminary/detailed design phases can be substituted by the modelisation/design phases and the validation activies can be adapted. Moreover, very few feedback from the concrete models asked rework on the abstract models.

The Complete Proof of a Complex Software Is Feasible. 100% of proof obligations and added rules were proven, in spite of the large amount of lemmas and the complexity of many of them.

Using B, You May Expect that No Bug Will Be Found after the Development. Since no bug was found out by the validation work on host computer and target computer, nor during tests on the real line, the *zero-fault* objective can be claimed to be reached.

Formal Development Is Cost Effective. The formal development and validation were kept within the initial budget and delay. We have established that a formal development is not more expensive than a conventional development with a far better level of quality, regardless the gain obtained in the maintenance phase. This result is all the more significant as Météor is our first industrial application.

The main key points that led to the previous statements are the following:

1. a very careful preparation was needed to define how a formal method could be integrated into an existing organisation, taking into account the previous practices of software development and validation;
2. efficient methodological guidelines were developed and improved for development and validation activities: the *B Method Book* and the *B Validation Book*;
3. the toolkit was continuously improved to reach the operational level requested by Météor, thanks to a work program between Matra Transport International, RATP and Stéria Méditérranée.

Above all, the best evidence of success is that the use of B is generalised for the development of safety critical software in Matra Transport International.

5.2   What's Next

Producing the Concrete Models Automatically. An analysis of the Météor models pointed out that many refinements from abstract to concrete models were similar. Moreover, since all the semantics of the program are defined in the abstract model, it seemed possible to automatically produce in many cases the concrete models according to the abstract model. Promising results have already been obtained [BM99], allowing important cost saving.

Using B on Non Safety Critical Software. The development of the safety critical software of Météor using the B method does not make costs rise. Since reductions of cost are still possible (e.g. using the automatic production of the concrete models), it may be worth to use the B method even for non safety critical software. Experiments are in progress to demonstrate this point.

B at the System Level. The B method is currently used at the software level. Nevertheless, it seems very interesting to bring the formalisation effort up to the highest project level, in order to better prepare the system architecture and to rigorously check its validity. Others experiments, using extensions of the B language, are at the moment in progress on system level.

References

[Abr96]   Abrial J.R., *The B-Book* (1996).

[BMB99]   Burdy L., Dollé D., *B Method Book*; Internal document ref. DRL/XT/39.2617.98/DD/AA (1999).

[BVB99]   Faivre A., Milonnet C., *B Validation Book*; Internal document ref. DSF/XT/32.1374.96/CM/CM (1999).

[BM99]   Burdy L., Meynadier J.-M., Automatic Refinement; BUGM at FM'99 (1999)

initialisation $C, a_1, \ldots, a_n := I_C, I_1 \ldots I_n$, application constraint $P(C, a_1, \ldots, a_n)$,and operations $op_1 C, \ldots, op_k C$. Note that in ASSO the notation $a : t$ means an attribute a has a type t in a similar sense to an object member variable. It should not be confused with the ASCII B notation's use of the colon for set membership $\in$. For a class C, the following basic operations are available:

ADD C $(x, v_1, \ldots, v_n)$	Insert object x with attribute values $v_1, \ldots, v_n$ into C.
REM C (x)	Remove object x from C.
SKIP C	Does nothing in C.
CHANGE C a_i (x, v_i)	Update value of attribute a_i of object x in C to v_i.

The weakest precondition semantics for a base operation op in C are given via the equivalence on any arbitrary predicate R:

$$[op\, C\ (par\_list)\,]R \Leftrightarrow \exists v' \cdot (R' \wedge \mathrm{PRE}_C(op\, C\ (par\_list)) \wedge prd_C\ (op\, C\ (par\_list)))$$

where v' is a list of primed variables of the class, $C', a'_1, \ldots a'_n$ and R' is the result of priming all variables in R, representing the variables of C after the operation. We define the relationship between the pre and post variables using the before-after predicate prd_C a predicate which holds for pairs of states similar to that used to specify operations in VDM and Z. In B, the predicate is subscripted with a variable x; in ASSO we subscript the predicate with a class C. We then define the predicate $prd_C(S)$ for an operation S following ([2], §6.3.3) as:

$$prd_C(S) \Leftrightarrow \neg[S](C' \neq C) \vee (a'_1 \neq a_1) \vee \ldots \vee (a'_n \neq a_n)$$

Thus we have for the base operations of ASSO;

$prd_C(\mathrm{ADD}\ C\ (x, v_1, \ldots, v_n)) =$
$\quad (C' = C \cup \{x\}) \wedge (a'_1 = a_1 \lessdot \{(x, v_1)\}) \wedge \ldots \wedge (a'_n = a_n \lessdot \{(x, v_n)\})$
$prd_C(\mathrm{REM}\ C\ (x)) = (C' = C - \{x\}) \wedge (a'_1 = \{x\} \vartriangleleft a_1) \wedge \ldots \wedge (a'_n = \{x\} \vartriangleleft a_n)$
$prd_C(\mathrm{SKIP}\ C) = (C' = C) \wedge (a'_1 = a_1) \wedge \ldots \wedge (a'_n = a_n)$
$prd_C(\mathrm{CHANGE}\ C\ a_i\ (x, v_i)) =$
$\quad (C' = C) \wedge (a'_1 = a_1) \wedge \ldots \wedge (a'_i = a_i \lessdot \{(x, v_i)\}) \wedge \ldots \wedge (a'_n = a_n)$

We differ from [3] by explicitly including the *precondition* of the base operations:

$PRE_C(\mathrm{ADD}\ C\ (x, v_1, \ldots, v_n)) = x \in S \wedge x \notin C \wedge v_1 \in t_1 \wedge \ldots \wedge v_n \in t_n$
$PRE_C(\mathrm{REM}\ C\ (x)) = x \in C$
$PRE_C(\mathrm{SKIP}\ C) = true$
$PRE_C(\mathrm{CHANGE}\ C\ a_i\ (x, v_i)) = x \in C \wedge v_i \in t_i$

The following constructors can be applied recursively to the basic operations:

PRE P THEN $op\ C$ (par_list) END	Pre-conditioning.
$P \rightarrow op\ C$ (par_list)	Guarding.
CHOICE $op_1\ C$ (par_list) OR $op_2\ C$ (par_list) END	Choice.
ANY y WHERE P THEN $op\ C$ (par_list) END	Unbounded-choice.

Here, P is a predicate on the variables of class C, op C (par_list) op_1 C (par_list) and op_2 C (par_list) are operations on C and y is a variable distinct from the variables of C. Pre-conditioning specifies a the *preconditioned transformation*: op C (par_list) for the states satisfying P and is undetermined otherwise. Guarding specifies a *partial transformation*: op C (par_list) for the states satisfying P and abort otherwise. Choice specifies a *non-deterministic transformation* between op_1 C (par_list) and op_2 C (par_list). Unbounded-choice specifies an *unbounded non deterministic transformation* defined by replacing any value of y satisfying P in op C (par_list).

The weakest precondition semantics for a constructed operation op in C are:

$$[\,op\ C\ (par\_list)\,]R \Leftrightarrow \exists v'\cdot(R' \wedge prd_C\ (op\ C\ (par\_list)))$$

The before-after predicate for the operation constructors is as follows:

prd_C (**PRE** P **THEN** op C (par_list) **END**) $= P \Rightarrow prd_C$ $(op$ C $(par\_list))$
prd_C $(P \rightarrow op$ C $(par\_list)) = P \wedge prd_C$ $(op$ C $(par\_list))$
prd_C (**CHOICE** op_1 C (par_list) **OR** op_2 C (par_list) **END**) $=$
    prd_C $(op_1$ C $(par\_list)) \wedge prd_C$ $(op_2$ C $(par\_list))$
prd_C (**ANY** y **WHERE** P **THEN** op C (par_list) **END**) $=$
    $\exists y\cdot(P \wedge prd_C$ $(op$ C $(par\_list))$ if y is not in C'.

A class has a set of *class constraints*:

$$class\text{-}constraints_C = C \subseteq U \wedge a_1 \in C \rightarrow t_1 \wedge \ldots \wedge a_n \in C \rightarrow t_n$$

That is that all objects in C must be of the given set and every attribute on C can be regarded as a *total function* on the class. The class constraints are preserved by the valid operations on the class.

Additional (explicit) application constraints may be associated with the class in the form of a predicate I_C which have to be preserved by all class's operations. Given operation op with precondition P the consistency obligation is given by:

$$I_C \wedge P \Rightarrow [S]I_C$$

Note that this is the same as the proof obligation on invariants in B. However, the class constraints do not need to be proved.

Further, in class C there is a distinguished operation $Init_C$ which initialises the class and can assign *any* value to the class variables. Consequently, the class constraints cannot be guaranteed to hold for $Init_C$ and thus there is an initialisation obligation to show that they are established.

1. **INCLUDE** *the class machines* $T_{class}(C)$, *and* $T_{class}(C')$.
2. *Add to the* **INVARIANT** *the implicit is-a* constraint.*
3. *For each operation* $op_C(x, u_1, \ldots, u_j)$ *in* $T_{class}(C)$ *and* $op_{C'}(x, v_1, \ldots, v_k)$ *in* $T_{class}(C')$, *where x is a common instance identifier variable, form the combined operation:*

$$op(x, u_1, \ldots, u_j, v_1, \ldots, v_k) = op_C(x, u_1, \ldots, u_j) \parallel op_{C'}(x, v_1, \ldots, v_k)$$

Theorem 3. *The translation T_{top} is sound.*

Proof. (Sketch). If C is a root class, then $T_{top}(C) = T_{class}(C)$, which is sound by the above theorem. If C *is-a* C'*, then we need only show part 3 of the definition of soundness. We can assume that the machines $T_{class}(C)$, and $T_{class}(C')$ are sound. Thus we have for each operation its C and its correspondent in C':

$$[op(par\_list)] \; R \Leftrightarrow [T_{class}(op)(T_{class}(par\_list))] \; R$$
$$[op'(par\_list)] \; R \Leftrightarrow [T_{class}(op')(T_{class}(par\_list))] \; R$$

Thus we have (omitting *par_list* for clarity)

$$[op] \; R \wedge [op'] \; R \Leftrightarrow [T_{class}(op)] \; R \wedge [T_{class}(op')] \; R$$

As C and C' have independent state variables, from [2], §7.1.3, we have that:

$$[op] \; R \wedge [op'] \; R \Leftrightarrow [op \parallel op'] \; R$$
$$[T_{class}(op)] \; R \wedge [T_{class}(op')] \; R \Leftrightarrow [T_{class}(op) \parallel T_{class}(op')] \; R$$

And we are done.

As the operations have been proven to be correct, then these operations do not need to be reproven to be consistent by virtue of the structure of ASSO, and it is unnecessary to generate a top-level machine to establish consistency against the inherent constraints of the *is-a** relation.

4   Refinement in ASSO

ASSO has two complementary forms of refinement:

- *Behavioural Refinement.* Operations are refined towards implementation by reducing non-determinism, weakening preconditions, and reducing partiality of operations. Such a refinement between classes C_1, C_2 is denoted: $C_1 \Leftarrow C_2$.

— *Data Refinement.* ASSO data refinement consists of a stepwise decomposition of classes organised into a specialisation hierarchy, representing a conceptual schema. A set of smaller specialisation hierarchies is generated step by step until a set of disjoint classes is obtained, which defines the ASSO logical schema having separate classes for each intersection class. The ASSO data refinement uses the Partitioning Method, a recursive algorithm working on graphs. Such a refinement between classes C_1, C_2 is denoted: $C_1 \equiv C_2$.

To verify an ASSO refinement, the relationship which links the corresponding consistency proof obligations of any two *behaviourally* refined schemas must be logical implication. The relationship which links corresponding consistency proof obligations before and after partition is logical equivalence. The partitioning algorithm ensures that this holds without proof.

5   Behavioural Refinement

Behavioural refinement modifies operations, whilst preserving the consistency of the operations. Thus we can define a behavioural refinement as follows.

Definition 5. *Given ASSO operations* op_1 *and* op_2 *where* op_1 *terminates and satisfies the constraints* P *(that is* $P \Rightarrow [\, op_1 \,]P$*) and if* op_2 *terminates and satisfies* P' *such that:* $trm(op_1) \subseteq trm(op_2) \land P \Rightarrow P'$*, then we can say that* op_2 *is a refinement of* op_1 *with respect to* P*, written* $op_1 \Leftarrow op_2$*.*

We can then use this definition to define refinement of classes.

Definition 6. *Given classes* C_1 *and* C_2 *which have the same instances, attributes, application constraints and operation names, then*

$$C_1 \Leftarrow C_2 \text{ if and only if } \forall\, op_{C_1} \in C_1 \cdot op_{C_1} \Leftarrow op_{C_2}$$

with respect to the implicit and explicit constraints of C_1*.*

Thus we can prove the refinement of a classes by considering the refinement of each of its operations in turn (including the implicitly specialised ones). Note that the similar proposition for B does not hold.

The forms of behavioural refinement above satisfy this definition of refinement.

Theorem 4. *Weakening the precondition, reducing partiality, and reducing nondeterminism are all refinements.*

Proof. We assume that we have classes C_1, C_2 with implicit and explicit constraints on C_1, P. Then a given op_{C_1} is transformed into op_{C_2} and we show that $op_{C_1} \Leftarrow op_{C_2}$.

Weakening the precondition. If $PRE(op_{C_1}) \Rightarrow PRE(op_{C_2})$, then $pre(op_{C_1}) \subseteq pre(op_{C_2})$. So by definition, $trm(op_{C_1}) \subseteq trm(op_{C_2})$. As the substitution of the operation has not changed, $rel(op_{C_1}) = \{trm(op_{C_1})\} \lhd rel(op_{C_2})$ (where $\lhd$ is domain restriction), P is preserved by op_{C_2} and hence $trm(op_{C_1}) \subseteq trm(op_{C_2} \land P \Rightarrow P'$ and thus it is a refinement.

Reducing partiality. If $trm(op_{C_1}) \subseteq trm(op_{C_2})$, again the operation's substitution has not changed, so $rel(op_{C_1}) = \{trm(op_{C_1})\} \lhd rel(op_{C_2})$ and P is preserved by op_{C_2}, hence: $trm(op_{C_1}) \subseteq trm(op_{C_2}) \land P \Rightarrow P'$ and it is a refinement.

Reducing non-determinism. In this case there two properties: $pre(op_{C_1}) = pre(op_{C_2})$, hence: $trm(op_{C_1}) = trm(op_{C_2})$, and $rel(op_{C_2}) \subseteq rel(op_{C_1})$ that is the before-after relation becomes more restricted. Thus for any $(s, s') \in rel(op_{C_2})$, $(s, s') \in rel(op_{C_1})$, so P holds and we have a refinement.

> class   *student* **is-a*** *person* **with**   (*matriculation*:N
>   *init.student*() $\widehat{=}$ *student, matriculation* := {},{}
>   *new.student*(*pers*) $\widehat{=}$
>   **PRE**   *pers* $\in$ *PERSON* $-$ *student*
>   **THEN**   *ADD student*(*pers*, $\max(\text{ran}(matriculation))+ 1$)
>   **END**   )

Figure 4: A Behavioural Refinement of *new. student*

ASSO refinement is *compositional*. That is, in a Structured Database Schema, if a class is refined, then the whole schema is refined. This is captured in the following theorem.

Theorem 5. *If C_1 and C_1 are classes, and the Structured Database Schema C_1 is-a* C_2 is constructed, where there are no explicit application constraints between the classes, then the following two properties hold:*

i). *If $C_1 \Leftarrow C_1'$ then C_1 is-a* $C_2 \Leftarrow C_1'$ is-a* C_2.*
ii). *If $C_2 \Leftarrow C_2'$ then C_1 is-a* $C_2 \Leftarrow C_1$ is-a* C_2'.*

Thus we can say that is-a* is monotonic with respect to refinement.

Proof. (Sketch): i). If $C_1 \Leftarrow C_1'$ then for any operation $op = op_{C_1} \parallel op_{C_2}$. Therefore if $op_{C_1} \Leftarrow op_{C_1'}$, then as S and R have independent variables, we have $op_{C_1} \parallel op_{C_2} \Leftarrow op_{C_1'} \parallel op_{C_2}$. A similar argument holds for ii).

Thus we can perform *modular refinement* on ASSO schemas. This too is in contrast to B where the compositional structures are not in general monotonic through refinement.

---

structured database schema
   database1
class   *person−employee* **of** *PERSON* **with**   (*income:N*
     constraints $\forall$ *p* ($p{\in}$***person−employee*** $\Rightarrow$ ***income*(*p*)$\geq$ 1000**)
     init.person−employee() = *person, income* := {},{}
     new.person(*pers, i*) $\widehat{=}$
        PRE   *pers* $\in$ *PERSON* − (*person−employee*) $\wedge$ *i* $\geq$ 1000
        THEN
           ADD person−employee(*pers, i*)
        END ;
     del.person−employee(*person*) $\widehat{=}$
        PRE   *pers* $\in$ *person−employee*
        THEN   *REM person−employee*(*pers*)
        END   )
class   *student* **is-a*** *person−employee* **with**   (*matriculation:N*
     constraints $\forall$ ***s1, s2*** (*s1*${\in}$***student*** $\wedge$ *s2*${\in}$***student*** $\wedge$ *s1* $\neq$ *s2* $\Rightarrow$
        matriculation(*s1*)$\neq$*matriculation*(*s2*))
     init.student() $\widehat{=}$ *student, matriculation* := {},{}
     new.student(*pers*) $\widehat{=}$
        PRE   *pers* $\in$ *PERSON* − *student*
        THEN
           ANY   *m* **WHERE**   *m* $\in$ *N* $\wedge$ *m* $\notin$ ran(*matriculation*)
           THEN   *ADD student*(*pers, m*)
           END
        END   )

Figure 5: The first SDBS generated by a partitioning step.

The SDBS in Figure 1 defines the non-deterministic operation *new.student*; it selects any new value for the matriculation number which has not been used before. A more determined version of *new.student* is given in Figure 4 (constraint omitted). In this case, the value of the new *matriculation* is one greater than the maximum of all the existing matriculation numbers. This new class *student1* is a refinement of *student*, and thus by Theorem 5, the structured database schema formed by replacing *student* with *student1* in *database* is also a refinement.

5.1   An Example of Data Refinement

The Partitioning algorithm is complex, and its details are omitted here. To demonstrate its effect, we apply the first step of the partition method to the example in Figure 1.

---

structured database schema
   database2
class   *person•employee* of   *PERSON* **with**   (*income:N*
   constraints $\forall$ *p* (*p∈person•employee* $\Rightarrow$ *income(p)*$\geq$ **1000**)
   init.person•employee() = person, income := {},{}
   new.person(pers, i) $\widehat{=}$
      PRE   *pers* $\in$ *PERSON* $-$ (*person•employee*) $\wedge$ *i* $\geq$ 1000
      THEN   *ADD person•employee(pers, i)*
      END ;
   del.person•employee(person) $\widehat{=}$
      PRE   *pers* $\in$ *person•employee*
      THEN   *REM person•employee(pers)*
      END)
class   *student* **is-a*** *person•employee* **with**   (*matriculation:N*
   constraints $\forall$ *s1, s2* (*s1∈student* $\wedge$ *s2∈student* $\wedge$ *s1* $\neq$ *s2* $\Rightarrow$
   matriculation(s1)$\neq$*matriculation(s2)*))
   init.student() $\widehat{=}$ *student, matriculation* := {},{}
   new.student(pers) $\widehat{=}$
      PRE   *pers* $\in$ *PERSON* $-$ *student*
      THEN
         ANY   *m* **WHERE**   *m* $\in$ *N* $\wedge$ *m* $\notin$ ran(*matriculation*)
         THEN   *ADD student(pers, m)*
         END
      END)

Figure 6: The second SDBS generated by a partitioning step.

The initial top-level class *person* has been decomposed into two: the class disjoint from the class *employee*, producing the SDBS given in Figure 5, and the intersection class with the class *employee* generating the structured database schema given in Figure 6. In this latter, the new class intialisation and constraints of *employee*, and the operations on this class are parallel compositions of the corresponding operations on the classes *person* and *employee*. Each SDBS also takes a copy of the subclass *student* implicitly splitting this class between the two partitions of *person*. This partitioning can be continued to generate a logical schema of disjoint classes.

5.2   The Relationship between the Types of ASSO Refinement

Behavioural refinement and partitioning are not independen t in ASSO; partitioning also modifies operations. Consider a class A with an operation op on one class instance which we represent as a function on its state $op : A \rightarrow A'$. Then if A is partitioned with respect to a class B, it is divided into two sections: $A \bullet B$ and $A - B$. The operation is also partitioned: $op_{A \bullet B} : A \bullet B \rightarrow (A \bullet B)'$, and $op_{A-B} : A - B \rightarrow (A - B)'$. These two new operations can be combined into a new one which refines the original:

$$op \Leftarrow op_{A \bullet B} \parallel op_{A-B}$$

This holds as these operations on the class A do not depend on the values of B, which may or may not be present in the new classes. Thus partitioning is well behaved with respect to behavioural refinement for operations that only access one class instance. However, if more than one class instance is referenced, problems can occur. Consider the following example. Within the class A we define the following ASSO operation:

$remove\_either(p, q) =$
    PRE $p \in A \land q \in A$
    THEN CHOOSE REM A p
        OR   REM A q
        END
    END

If A is partitioned with respect to class B, the following two operations result:

$remove\_either_{A \bullet B}(p, q) =$
    PRE $p \in A \bullet B \land q \in A \bullet B$
    THEN CHOOSE REM $A \bullet B$ p
        OR   REM $A \bullet B$ q
        END
    END

$remove\_either_{A-B}(p, q) =$
    PRE $p \in A-B \land q \in A-B$
    THEN CHOOSE REM $A-B$ p
        OR   REM $A-B$ q
        END
    END

Clearly this does not partition the operation as not all the of the domain has been covered. The parameters could also satisfy the preconditions: $p \in A \bullet B \land q \in A-B$ or $p \in A - B \land q \in A \bullet B$. Thus there are two other operations which should be generated to produce a valid partition of the operation.

refinement of the original operation. Since the partitioning algorithm preserves the equivalence of the models, refinement proofs in this case are unnecessary.

Thus in both cases ASSO refinement is B refinement, and Theorem 7 follows.

Theorem 7. *If SDBS S, represented by B Abstract Machine M, is refined into a set of Structured Database Schema R, and R is represented by B Abstract Machine N, then N is a B-refinement of M.*

As behavioural refinement of operations is a B refinement, it can be validated using B tools, through the translation of ASSO schema. Translating an ASSO refinement into B exploits some properties of the two languages. As in a B refinement the abstract invariant has to be respected by the refining machine, it does not need to be repeated. Also we only define the refinement relation between the top-level machine of each class. For example, the systematic translation of the behavioural refinement in Figure 4 into B notation and proof using the B-Toolkit [4] confirms that both *student1* is a refinement of *student*, and also that the structured database schema *database1*, formed by replacing *student* by *student1* in *database* is indeed a refinement.

6   Conclusions

ASSO is a formal methodology which has advantages for the design of databases compared to the other formal methods currently used in industrial applications. The *is-a** relationship between structured database schema and the Partitioning Method are original aspects of both formal methods and the database areas, providing a higher-level of conceptual design to the database developer, exploiting the results in conceptual schemas dating back from the late 70s.

The results in this paper give three things:

i.   a firm foundation for the development of databases within ASSO in terms of the semantics of B;

ii. an established proof theory for demonstrating the consistency and correctness of ASSO models;

iii. tools developed to support B which can be used to support ASSO.

The restricted subset of B's features used by ASSO allow a relationship to be established in a straighforward manner.

ASSO should also be compared with approaches to Object-Oriented design within B, for example [9, 10, 12, 13, 22]. ASSO offers a different approach which in specialisation offers different properties in inheritance of operations. Also, by considering object-oriented databases with structuring and inheritance, we go further than the relational approach of specifiying databases in B in [21].

To progress further with ASSO, including using it on practical problems, it is proposed to design tools which aid the user to construct an ASSO design, control its structure, to prove properties, and to move towards an implementation. The ASSO tools can be based on a part of the B Toolkit, together with new tools, such as those supporting partitioning. An initial design for these tools, which integrate with the B-Toolkit, is discussed in [18].

Acknowledgements

This work has been supported by the CNR short-term mobility programme, 1998. The authors would like to thank the chairman of the B track of FM99 and the anonymous referees for their useful comments and suggestions.

References

[1] S Abiteboul, R Hull and V Vianu: *Foundations of Databases*, Addison-Wesley, 1995.

[2] J-R Abrial: *The B-Book: Assigning Programs to Meaning*, Cambridge University Press, 1996.

[3] R Andolina and E. Locuratolo: *ASSO: behavioral specialisation modelling.* In: Jaakkola H (ed) Information Modelling and Knowledge Bases VIII, IOS Press, 1997.

[4] B-Core (UK) Ltd. *The B-Toolkit Welcome page* URL <http://www.b-core.com>

[5] N. Bhalla: *Object-oriented data models: a perspective and comparative review,* Journal of Information Science, 1991.

[6] D. Castelli, and E. Locuratolo: *A Formal Notation for Database Conceptual Schema Specifications.* Information Modelling and Knowledge Bases VI, Jaakkola, H. (ed), IOS Press, 1994.

[7] D. Castelli and E. Locuratolo: *ASSO - A formal database design methodology* In Jaakkola H (ed) Information Modelling and Knowledge Bases VI, IOS Press, 1995.

[8] E W Dijkstra., and S Scholten: *Predicate Calculus and Program Semantics,* Springer-Verlag, 1990.

[9] P Facon, R Laleau and H P Nguyen: *Mapping object diagrams into B specifications.* In Bryant A, Semmens L T (eds) proceedings of the Methods Integration Workshop, Leeds, UK, Springer-Verlag, 1996

[10] P Facon, R Laleau and H P Nguyen: *Dèrivation de spècification formelles B à partir de spècifications semi-formelles de systèmes d'information.* Habrias H (ed) proceedings of the 1st Conference on the B Method, Nantes, France, 1996.

[11] R. Hull and R. King: *Semantic database modeling: survey, application, and research issues.* ACM Computing Surveys, 19(**3**) 1987

[12] K Lano and H Haughton: *Improving the process of system specification and refinement in B.* In: Till D (ed) proceedings of the 6th Refinement Workshop, Workshops in Computing, Springer-Verlag, 1994.

[13] K Lano: *The B Language and Method. A Guide to Practical Formal Development.* Springer-Verlag, 1996.

[14] E. Locuratolo: *Evolution as a formal database design methodology.* In Proceedings of symposium on Software Technology (SoST'97), Buenos Aires, 1997.

[15] E. Locuratolo and R. Rabitti F: *Conceptual classes and system classes in object databases.* Acta Informatica, 35(**3**):181-210, 1998.

[16] E.Locuratolo:*Database reengineering as modelling* IEI report B4-43, 1998.

[17] E. Locuratolo, and B.M. Matthews: *On the relationship between ASSO and B* In proceedings of the 8th European-Japanese conference on Information Modelling and Knowledge Bases, Vammala, Finland, May 1998.

[18] E. Locuratolo, and B.M. Matthews: *ASSO: A formal methodology of Conceptual Database Design* ERCIM Workshop on Formal Methods for Industrial Critical Systems, 1999.

[19] B.M. Matthews, B Ritchie, and J.C. Bicarregui: *Synthesising structure from flat specifications.* Proceedings of the B Conference, Montpelier, France, April 1998.

[20] B.M. Matthews and E. Locuratolo: *Translating Structured Database Schemas into Abstract Machines.* In proceedings of the 2nd Irish Workshop on Formal Methods, Cork, Ireland, 1998.

[21] K-D Schewe, J W Schmidt and I Wetzel: *Specification and refinement in an integrated database application environment.* Prehn S, Toetenel W J (eds) proceedings of VDM'91, 4th Int. Symp. of VDM Europe, Springer-Verlag, 1991

[22] R Shore: *An object-oriented approach to B.* Habrias H (ed) proceedings of the 1st Conference on the B Method, Nantes, France, 1996.

Interpreting the B-Method
in the Refinement Calculus

Yann Rouzaud

LSR-IMAG, Grenoble, France
Laboratoire Logiciels Systèmes Réseaux - Institut IMAG (CNRS - INPG - UJF)
BP 72, F-38402 Saint-Martin d'Hères Cedex
Tel +33 4 76827219 - Fax +33 4 76827287
Yann.Rouzaud@imag.fr
"Stream: Foundations and Methodology"
"Mini-Track: B-Method"

Abstract. In this paper, we study the B-Method in the light of the theory of refinement calculus. It allows us to explain the proof obligations for a refinement component in terms of standard data refinement. A second result is an improvement of the architectural condition of [PR98], ensuring global correctness of a B software system using the SEES primitive.

1 Introduction

The B-Method ([Abr96]) is a methodology for formal software development. It has industrial tools (B-toolkit, Atelier B) and has been successfully applied to the MTOR system, equipping the new line of subway in Paris ([Met]).

It is well known that the refinement theory of the B-Method is based on weakest precondition semantics ([Dij76]). However, curiously, no attempt has be made to establish a formal link between the theory of B, as exposed in the B-Book, and the now standard theory of refinement calculus. The primary goal of this paper is a study of this relationship.

Refinement calculus was first investigated by Back ([Ba78]), and further independently rediscovered by Morgan ([Mo88]) and Morris ([Mor87]). A good starting point to the subject is [BW98]. Its aim is to formalize the development of programs by stepwise refinement ([Wi71]). By removing the healthiness conditions of [Dij76] (which are necessary for an executable program), a continuum is obtained between specifications and programs. Indeed, specifications are programs (and programs are specifications). The theory is now mature; potential applications in the B-Method are discussed in the conclusion of this paper.

Our paper is organized as follows. Section 2 introduces the refinement calculus, defining the notions of predicate transformers and refinement, and the standard notion of data refinement. Section 3 presents another notion of data refinement. It is called data refinement through an invariant. It is this notion which is used in the B-Method, for the proof obligations of a refinement component. The relationship between the two notions of data refinement is established.

J. Wing, J. Woodcock, J. Davies (Eds.): FM'99, Vol. I, LNCS 1708, pp. 411–430, 1999.
© Springer-Verlag Berlin Heidelberg 1999

Section 4 describes the primitive language of substitutions of the B-Method. Substitutions are interpreted in terms of predicate transformers. Section 5 describes the notion of refinement in the B-Method, and relates it to standard data refinement. This section ends up with an example of valid data refinement, which is not expressible within the B-Method. Section 6 begins with an example showing that the SEES primitive of the B-Method can break the global correctness of a B-software. Using our analysis of the B-Method in terms of the refinement calculus, we exhibit an architectural condition ensuring global correctness. This analysis corrects and extends the work done in [PR98]. Finally, Section 7 concludes this work, by giving some directions of future work.

2   Predicate Transformers

Refinement calculus can be modelized using set transformers, or, equivalently, using predicate transformers. We choose the second model, because it explicitly deals with variables, which will be useful when dealing with common variables. This section is taken from [Wri94] and [BW90]. It reminds the main results and fixes the notation for the sequel.

2.1   States, Predicates, Commands, and Refinement

In programs, each variable x is associated with a set of values D_x. For any set of variables v, a state is a function mapping every x in v to some value in D_x, and the state space Σ_v is the set of states on v.

A predicate on v is a function from Σ_v to $Bool$, where $Bool = \{ff, tt\}$ is the ordered (with the order $ff < tt$) set of boolean values. $Pred_v$, the predicate space on v, is the complete boolean lattice of predicates on v, with the implication order $\leq$: $P \leq Q$ holds iff $P \Rightarrow Q$ holds universally (*false* is the bottom element and *true* is the top element).

A predicate on v can be extended to a predicate on v, w by adding new variables w. In this paper, we do not use explicit notation for this change of view. Substitutions $[d/v]$ in Σ_v are extended to $Pred_v$ in the usual way. If $Q \in Pred_{u,v}$, the renaming of v by w in Q, $Q[w/v]$, denotes the equivalent predicate in $Pred_{u,w}$.

$$\bigwedge_{i \in I} Q_i = \bigwedge \{Q_i \cdot i \in I\} \quad \text{and} \quad \bigvee_{i \in I} Q_i = \bigvee \{Q_i \cdot i \in I\}$$

are respectively the meet and the join of the family $(Q_i)_{i \in I}$. Quantified predicates are defined as follows:

$$\forall v \cdot P = \bigwedge_{d \in D_v} P[d/v] \quad \text{and} \quad \exists v \cdot P = \bigvee_{d \in D_v} P[d/v].$$

A predicate transformer is a monotonic function from predicates to predicates. $Mtran_{u \to v}$ is the complete lattice of predicate transformers from $Pred_v$ to $Pred_u$ ([Wri94] denotes it $Mtran_{u \leftarrow v}$). A predicate transformer $S \in Mtran_{u \to v}$ is identified with a command which executes from an initial state in Σ_u and, if it terminates, which gives a state in Σ_v (this is the weakest precondition approach, due to [Dij76]). In this paper, we shall indifferently use the terms command and predicate transformer.

For commands $S \in Mtran_{u \to v}$ and $T \in Mtran_{v \to w}$, sequential composition $S; T \in Mtran_{u \to w}$ is such that $(S; T)(Q) = S(T(Q))$.

For each lattice $Mtran_{u \to v}$, commands $magic$ and $abort$ are top and bottom elements: $magic(Q) = true$ and $abort(Q) = false$. For $Mtran_{u \to u}$, $skip$ is the identity command: $skip(Q) = Q$.

For two commands $S, T \in Mtran_{u \to v}$, the refinement order $S \leq T$ holds iff $S(Q) \leq T(Q)$ holds for all $Q \in Pred_v$.

2.2 Properties of Commands

Let $S \in Mtran_{u \to v}$ be a command, P, Q be predicates on v, and $(Q_i)_{i \in I}$ be a non-empty family of predicates on v. We have:

1. monotonicity: $P \leq Q \Rightarrow S(P) \leq S(Q)$
2. and-distributivity: $S(\bigwedge_{i \in I} Q_i) \leq \bigwedge_{i \in I} S(Q_i)$
3. or-distributivity: $\bigvee_{i \in I} S(Q_i) \leq S(\bigvee_{i \in I} Q_i)$

The following definitions are standard:

1. S is non-miraculous if $S(false) = false$
2. S is always terminating if $S(true) = true$
3. S is conjunctive if $S(\bigwedge_{i \in I} Q_i) = \bigwedge_{i \in I} S(Q_i)$
4. S is disjunctive if $S(\bigvee_{i \in I} Q_i) = \bigvee_{i \in I} S(Q_i)$

For instance, substitutions in the B-Method are conjunctive commands. See [BW92] for a study of sublanguages and their relationship.

2.3 Adjoint Commands

Let $S \in Mtran_{u \to v}$ be an always terminating disjunctive command. Then there exists a unique always terminating conjunctive command $S^\tau \in Mtran_{v \to u}$ such that $S; S^\tau \leq skip$ and $skip \leq S^\tau; S$. S^τ is the right adjoint of S. Dually, for each always terminating conjunctive command $S \in Mtran_{u \to v}$, there exists a unique always terminating disjunctive command $S^1 \in Mtran_{v \to u}$ such that $S^1; S \leq skip$ and $skip \leq S; S^1$. We have:

$$S^\tau(P) = \bigvee \{Q \cdot S(Q) \leq P\} \quad \text{and} \quad S^1(P) = \bigwedge \{Q \cdot P \leq S(Q)\}$$

Let R be a relation $R(u, v)$ and let α, β be commands such that $\forall Q$ on v, $\alpha(Q) = \exists v \cdot (R \wedge Q)$ and $\forall Q'$ on u, $\beta(Q') = \forall u \cdot (R \Rightarrow Q')$. Then we have: $\alpha^\tau = \beta$ and $\beta^1 = \alpha$.

Proof.

1. We write $P = \bigvee_{i \in D_w}(P_i \wedge w = i)$.

$$\begin{aligned}
S(\forall w \cdot P) &= S(\bigwedge_{d \in D_w} P[d/w]) && \text{definition of quantifiers} \\
&\leq \bigwedge_{d \in D_w} S(P[d/w]) && \text{and-distributivity} \\
&= \bigwedge_{d \in D_w} S((\bigvee_{i \in D_w}(P_i \wedge w = i))[d/w]) && \text{definition of } P \\
&= \bigwedge_{d \in D_w} S(P_d) && \text{calculus} \\
&= \bigwedge_{d \in D_w} (\bigvee_{i \in D_w}(S(P_i) \wedge w = i))[d/w] \\
&= \bigwedge_{d \in D_w} S_w(P)[d/w] && \text{definition of } S_w \\
&= \forall w \cdot S_w(P) && \text{definition of quantifiers}
\end{aligned}$$

2. Since S is conjunctive, the inequality in the demonstration above becomes an equality.

3. Q can be written as $Q = (\bigvee_{j \in J} w = w_j) = \bigvee_{j \in J}(true \wedge w = w_j)$.

$$\begin{aligned}
S_w(Q) &= \bigvee_{j \in J}(S(true) \wedge w = w_j) && \text{definition of } Q \\
&= S(true) \wedge \bigvee_{j \in J} w = w_j && \text{factorisation} \\
&= S(true) \wedge Q && \text{definition of } Q
\end{aligned}$$

4. $P = \bigvee_{i \in I}(P_i \wedge w = w_i)$ and $Q = (\bigvee_{j \in J} w = w_j) = \bigvee_{j \in J}(true \wedge w = w_j)$.
   So $P \vee Q = \bigvee_{k \in K}(R_k \wedge w = w_k)$, where:
   (a) $K = I + J = \{(0, i) \cdot i \in I\} \cup \{(1, j) \cdot j \in J\}$
       i.e. K is the disjoint union of I and J;
   (b) if $k = (0, i)$ then $w_k = w_i$ and $R_k = P_i$;
   (c) if $k = (1, j)$ then $w_k = w_j$ and $R_k = true$.

$$\begin{aligned}
S_w(P \vee Q) &= \bigvee_{k \in K}(S(R_k) \wedge w = w_k) \\
&= \bigvee_{i \in I}(S(P_i) \wedge w = w_i) \vee \bigvee_{j \in J}(S(true) \wedge w = w_j) \\
&= S_w(P) \vee (S(true) \wedge Q)
\end{aligned}$$

3.2   Data Refinement through an Invariant

Definition 2. Let a, c be disjoint sets of variables, $S \in Mtran_{a \to a}$ and $T \in Mtran_{c \to c}$ be commands and I be a predicate $I(a, c)$. We denote by $S \leq_I T$ the fact that S is data refined by T through I. Then

$$S \leq_I T \quad \text{iff} \quad I \wedge S(true) \Rightarrow T_a(\neg S_c(\neg I)).$$

This definition must be adapted when common variables occur:

Definition 3. Let a, c, g be disjoint sets of variables, $S \in Mtran_{a,g \to a,g}$ and $T \in Mtran_{c,g \to c,g}$ be commands, and I be a predicate $I(a, c, g)$.

$$S \leq_I T \quad \text{iff} \quad I \wedge g = g' \wedge S(true) \Rightarrow T'_{a,g}(\neg S_{c,g'}(\neg(I \wedge g = g')))$$

where g' are fresh variables (i.e. new and different from a, c, g) and $T' \in Mtran_{c,g' \to c,g'}$ is such that $T'(Q) = T(Q[g/g'])[g'/g]$.

For instance, let $D_g = D_{g'} = \mathbb{N}$, $S(Q) = Q[g + 1/g]$, $T(Q) = Q[g + 1/g]$, and $I = true$. For simplicity, we assume that sets a and c are empty.

1. $S_{c,g'}(\neg(I \wedge g = g')) = S_{c,g'}(\bigvee_{d \in D_{g'}}(g \neq d \wedge g' = d))$
$$= \bigvee_{d \in D_{g'}}(S(g \neq d) \wedge g' = d)$$
$$= \bigvee_{d \in D_{g'}}(g + 1 \neq d \wedge g' = d) \ = \ (g + 1 \neq g').$$

2. So $\neg S_{c,g'}(\neg(I \wedge g = g')) = (g + 1 = g') = \bigvee_{d \in D_g}(d + 1 = g' \wedge g = d).$

3. $T'_{a,g}(\neg S_{c,g'}(\neg(I \wedge g = g'))) = \bigvee_{d \in D_g}(T'(d+1=g') \wedge g=d)$
$$= \bigvee_{d \in D_g}(T(d+1=g)[g'/g] \wedge g=d)$$
$$= \bigvee_{d \in D_g}((d+1=g+1)[g'/g] \wedge g=d)$$
$$= \bigvee_{d \in D_g}(d+1=g'+1 \wedge g=d) = (g+1=g'+1)$$

3.3 Equivalence of Data Refinement Definitions

Property 2. Let u, v be disjoint sets of variables, $S \in Mtran_{u \to u}$ be a command, Q_1 be a predicate on u, v and Q_2 be a predicate on v. Then:

$$\forall u \cdot S(\forall v \cdot (Q_1 \Rightarrow Q_2)) \leq \forall u, v \cdot (\neg S_v(\neg Q_1) \Rightarrow Q_2)$$

Proof.

$$\forall u \cdot S(\forall v \cdot (Q_1 \Rightarrow Q_2)) \leq \forall u, v \cdot S_v(Q_1 \Rightarrow Q_2) \qquad \text{property 1.1}$$
$$= \forall u, v \cdot S_v(\neg Q_1 \vee Q_2)$$
$$= \forall u, v \cdot (S_v(\neg Q_1) \vee (S(true) \wedge Q_2)) \qquad \text{property 1.4}$$
$$= \forall u, v \cdot (\neg S_v(\neg Q_1) \Rightarrow S(true) \wedge Q_2)$$
$$\leq \forall u, v \cdot (\neg S_v(\neg Q_1) \Rightarrow Q_2)$$

Property 3. Let a, c be disjoint sets of variables, $S \in Mtran_{a \to a}$ and $T \in Mtran_{c \to c}$ be commands, I be a predicate on a, c, and $\alpha \in Mtran_{c \to a}$ be $\alpha(Q) = \exists a \cdot (I \wedge Q)$. Then $S \leq_I T \Rightarrow S \leq_\alpha T$.

Proof. Let Q be a predicate on c.

1. $\forall a, c \cdot (I \wedge S(\forall c \cdot (I \Rightarrow Q))) \leq \forall a, c \cdot S(\forall c \cdot (I \Rightarrow Q)) \qquad \text{predicate calculus}$
$$\leq \forall a, c \cdot (\neg S_c(\neg I) \Rightarrow Q) \qquad \text{property 2}$$
$$\leq \forall a, c \cdot (T_a(\neg S_c(\neg I)) \Rightarrow T_a(Q)) \quad \text{monotonicity}$$
2. Assume $S \leq_I T$, that is $\forall a, c \cdot (I \wedge S(true) \Rightarrow T_a(\neg S_c(\neg I)))$. So we have to prove $S \leq_\alpha T$. Because α has the right form, we may use the second of the four equivalent formulations of forward data refinement: $\alpha; S; \alpha^r \leq T$, that is: $\forall a, c \cdot (I \wedge S(\forall c \cdot (I \Rightarrow Q)) \Rightarrow T(Q)).$
3. Given a, c, assume $I \wedge S(\forall c \cdot (I \Rightarrow Q))$.
4. $\forall c \cdot (I \Rightarrow Q) \Rightarrow true$, so $S(true)$ holds by monotonicity, so does $T_a(\neg S_c(\neg I))$.
5. Using step 1, $T_a(Q)$ holds.
6. $T_a(Q) = T(Q)$, because Q is a predicate on c.

Property 4. Let a, c be disjoint sets of variables, $S \in Mtran_{a \to a}$ and $T \in Mtran_{c \to c}$ be commands, I be a predicate on a, c, and $\alpha \in Mtran_{c \to a}$ be $\alpha(Q) = \exists a \cdot (I \wedge Q)$. If S is conjunctive then $S \leq_\alpha T \Rightarrow S \leq_I T$.

Proof (the idea of P_1 and P_2 comes from [CU89]). Assume $S \leq_\alpha T$: for any a, c such that $I \wedge S(true)$, we have to prove $T_a(\neg S_c(\neg I))$. Let $a_0 \in D_a$, $P_1 = \neg S_c(\neg I)[a_0/a]$ and $P_2 = \forall c \cdot (I \Rightarrow P_1)$.

1. $S(P_2) = \forall c \cdot S_c(I \Rightarrow P_1)$ property 1.2

      $= \forall c \cdot S_c(\neg I \vee P_1)$ predicate calculus

      $= \forall c \cdot (S_c(\neg I) \vee (S(true) \wedge P_1))$ property 1.4

2. Using predicate calculus:

$$S(P_2)[a_0/a] = (\forall c \cdot (S_c(\neg I) \vee (S(true) \wedge P_1)))[a_0/a]$$
$$= \forall c \cdot (S_c(\neg I)[a_0/a] \vee (S(true)[a_0/a] \wedge P_1[a_0/a]))$$
$$= \forall c \cdot (S_c(\neg I)[a_0/a] \vee (S(true)[a_0/a] \wedge \neg S_c(\neg I)[a_0/a]))$$
$$= \forall c \cdot (S_c(\neg I)[a_0/a] \vee S(true)[a_0/a])$$
$$= (\forall c \cdot (S_c(\neg I) \vee S(true)))[a_0/a]$$

So $S(P_2) = \forall c \cdot (S_c(\neg I) \vee S(true))$.

3. We have $S(true) \Rightarrow S(P_2)$, so $I \wedge S(true) \Rightarrow I \wedge S(P_2)$. Hence $T(\exists a \cdot (I \wedge P_2))$ because $S \leq_\alpha T$.

4. Given any c, let a be such that $I \wedge P_2$ holds; we have $I \wedge P_2 = I \wedge \forall c \cdot (I \Rightarrow P_1)$, so $I \Rightarrow P_1$, so P_1 holds. Hence $\forall c \cdot (\exists a \cdot (I \wedge P_2) \Rightarrow \neg S_c(\neg I)[a_0/a])$.

5. By monotonicity, $\forall c \cdot (T(\exists a \cdot (I \wedge P_2)) \Rightarrow T(\neg S_c(\neg I)[a_0/a]))$.

6. We have: $T(\exists a \cdot (I \wedge P_2)) = T(\exists a \cdot (I \wedge P_2))[a_0/a]$

and $T(\neg S_c(\neg I)[a_0/a]) = T_a(\neg S_c(\neg I))[a_0/a]$.

So $T(\exists a \cdot (I \wedge P_2))[a_0/a] \Rightarrow T_a(\neg S_c(\neg I))[a_0/a]$,

hence: $T(\exists a \cdot (I \wedge P_2)) \Rightarrow T_a(\neg S_c(\neg I))$.

7. Finally, $T_a(\neg S_c(\neg I))$ holds.

Property 4 does not hold for non-conjunctive commands. For example, let $D_a = D_c = \mathbb{N}$, $S(Q) = Q[1/a] \vee Q[2/a]$, $T(Q) = Q[1/c] \vee Q[2/c]$, and $I = (a = c)$. Then $\alpha(Q) = \exists a \cdot (a = c \wedge Q) = Q[c/a]$ and $S \leq_\alpha T$ holds. But $T_a(\neg S_c(\neg I)) = T_a(\neg((1 \neq c) \vee (2 \neq c))) = T_a(false) = false$.

Theorem 1. Let a, c, g be disjoint sets of variables, $S \in Mtran_{a,g \to a,g}$ and $T \in Mtran_{c,g \to c,g}$ be commands, I be a predicate on a, c, g, and $\alpha \in Mtran_{c,g \to a,g}$ be $\alpha(Q) = \exists a \cdot (I \wedge Q)$. Then:

(1)	$S \leq_I T \Rightarrow S \leq_\alpha T$
(2)	$S \leq_I T \Leftrightarrow S \leq_\alpha T$ if S is conjunctive

Proof. Let g' be fresh variables, $T' \in Mtran_{c,g' \to c,g'}$ be a command such that $T'(Q) = T(Q[g/g'])[g'/g]$, and $\beta \in Mtran_{c,g' \to c,g}$ be $\beta(Q) = \exists g \cdot (g = g' \wedge Q) = Q[g'/g]$. So $\beta; \alpha \in Mtran_{c,g' \to a,g}$.

1. We have : $T'; \beta(Q) = T'(Q[g'/g]) = T(Q[g'/g][g/g'])[g'/g] = T(Q)[g'/g] = \beta; T(Q)$. So $\beta; T = T'; \beta$ and $T \leq_\beta T'$.

2. By transitivity: $S \leq_{\beta;\alpha} T' \Leftrightarrow S \leq_\alpha T$

3. But $\beta; \alpha(Q) = \exists g \cdot (g = g' \wedge \exists a \cdot (I \wedge Q)) = \exists a, g \cdot (I \wedge g = g' \wedge Q)$.

4. Now the results hold by applying properties 3 and 4 with S, T', $I \wedge g = g'$ and $\beta; \alpha$ (the variable spaces are disjoint).

4   The Language of Substitutions

In this section, we present the substitutions of the B-Method, and we interpret them as commands.

The primitive language of substitutions is given in Fig. 3, where x is a list of variables, E is a list of expressions, P is a formula, S and T are substitutions. Substitutions have a formula transformer semantics. Let Q be a formula and S be a substitution: $[S]Q$ is the weakest precondition establishing Q. For the unbounded choice substitution, we assume that Q has no free occurrence of x (otherwise, a renaming can be done). The B-Book, page 287, establishes that substitutions are monotonic (through implication) and conjunctive.

S	$[S]Q$	name of substitution	$U(S)$	$M(S)$
skip	Q	do nothing	$\emptyset$	$\emptyset$
$x := E$	$Q[E/x]$	simple	$Var(E)$	$\{x\}$
$P \mid S$	$P \wedge [S]Q$	precondition	$Var(P) \cup U(S)$	$M(S)$
$S \parallel T$	$[S]Q \wedge [T]Q$	bounded choice	$U(S) \cup U(T)$	$M(S) \cup M(T)$
$P \Longrightarrow S$	$P \Rightarrow [S]Q$	guard	$Var(P) \cup U(S)$	$M(S)$
$@x \cdot S$	$\forall x \cdot [S]Q$	unbounded choice	$U(S) - \{x\}$	$M(S) - \{x\}$

Fig. 3. Definition of substitutions; used and modified variables.

Let $Var(E)$ and $Var(P)$ be the sets of free variables of an expression E and of a formula P. In Fig. 3, $U(S)$ is the set of used variables in the substitution S and $M(S)$ is the set of modified variables.

Now, let $Var(S) = U(S) \cup M(S)$. First, we note that the notation $[S]Q$ can be reused for a predicate $Q \in Pred_{Var(S)}$, because the involved operators in formulae have homolog ones in predicates. So a substitution S is obviously interpreted as a predicate transformer $[\![S]\!]$ in $Mtran_{Var(S) \to Var(S)}$: $[\![S]\!](Q) = [S]Q$ for all $Q \in Pred_{Var(S)}$.

In practice, there are many other substitutions involved in B-components (machine, refinement, implementation) with another (verbose) syntax. However, all these substitutions are reducible to the primitive language of substitutions. For instance, the substitution PRE P THEN S END is equivalent to $P \mid S$. Moreover, these substitutions are used under the context of the variables v of the B-component. For such substitutions S, we must consider their extension $[\![S]\!]_w$, where $w = v - Var(S)$.

Some substitution constructors (for instance, the parallel operator "$\parallel$" and the sequence operator ";") are indirectly defined, using the normalized form theorem[1]: any substitution S can be written as:

---

[1] Its demonstration in the B-Book is flawed, but it can be easily repaired, by explicitly dealing with the set of involved variables.

$$S = \text{trm}(S) \mid @v' \cdot (\text{prd}_v(S) \Longrightarrow v := v')$$

where $v = Var(S)$, v' are fresh variables, $\text{trm}(S) = [S](v = v)$ (it is $[\![S]\!](true)$), and $\text{prd}_v(S) = \neg[S](v' \neq v)$. So, it suffices to define a substitution by giving its trm and prd, with the requirement: $\neg\, \text{trm}(S) \Rightarrow \text{prd}_v(S)$, where S is the newly defined substitution and $v = Var(S)$ (see [Du97, Du99]; see also property 6.4.1, page 297 of the B-Book). For instance, for the parallel operator[2], we have: $\text{trm}(S\|T) = \text{trm}(S) \wedge \text{trm}(T)$, and $\text{prd}_{v,w}(S\|T) = (\text{trm}(S) \wedge \text{trm}(T) \Rightarrow \text{prd}_v(S) \wedge \text{prd}_w(T))$, where $v = Var(S)$ and $w = Var(T)$ are disjoint sets of variables.

5   Refinement in the B-Method

In this section, we describe the notion of refinement, as defined in the B-Book, and we relate it to the results of Section 3.

5.1   Refinement Component and Proof Obligations.

A refinement component is defined as a differential to be added to a component. A refinement component can have proper variables which are linked to variables of the refined component by a *gluing invariant*. Moreover, refined operations must be stated on the new variables.

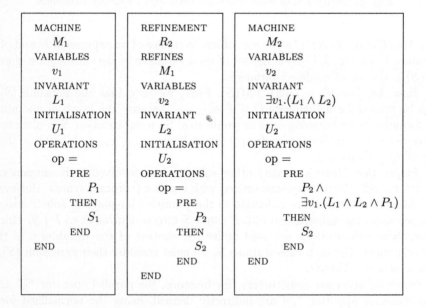

Fig. 4. Refinement R_2 of M_1, seen as an independent machine M_2.

---

[2] We use the definition of [Du97].

The proof obligations for machine M_1 of Fig. 4 are:

1. Initialisation: $[U_1]L_1$
2. Operation op: $L_1 \wedge P_1 \Rightarrow [S_1]L_1$

The proof obligations for refinement R_2 of Fig. 4 are, provided that there are no common variables (B-Book, p. 530):

1. Initialisation: $[U_2]\neg[U_1]\neg L_2$
2. Operation op: $L_1 \wedge L_2 \wedge P_1 \Rightarrow P_2 \wedge [S_2]\neg[S_1]\neg L_2$

In the most general case, there is a chain of refinements $M_1, R_2, \ldots, R_n$ to be considered. The proof obligation for an operation of R_n is, provided that M_1 and its refinements have no common variables:

$$L_1 \wedge L_2 \wedge \ldots \wedge L_n \wedge P_1 \wedge \ldots \wedge P_{n-1} \Rightarrow P_n \wedge [S_n]\neg[S_{n-1}]\neg L_n \ .$$

5.2   Refinement in B and Data Refinement

In the B-Book, the theory of refinement is presented in a set-transformer fashion. Then sufficient conditions of previous subsections are established. To do that, Abrial introduces a "substitution" W (the quotation marks come from the B-Book, pages 513 and 517): let a and c be the sets of abstract and concrete variables, supposed distinct, with corresponding sets of values D_a, D_c, and let R be a total relation from D_c to D_a (i.e $\forall c \exists a \cdot R(c, a)$); then $str(W)(q) = \overline{R[\bar{q}]}$, for all $q \subseteq D_c$ (in fact, Abrial defines W in a context of "external" variables, then drops them, page 519 ; we decided to directly present W without those variables).

W is not a true substitution, because initial and final state spaces are distinct. But it corresponds to a command $[\![W]\!] \in Mtran_{a \to c}$: $[\![W]\!](Q) = \forall c \cdot (R \Rightarrow Q)$ for all $Q \in Pred_c$. So, $[\![W]\!]$ is the right adjoint of the command $\alpha \in Mtran_{c \to a}$: $\alpha(Q) = \exists a \cdot (R \wedge Q)$, for all $Q \in Pred_a$. Hence, refinement in B is forward data refinement, and its presentation in the B-Book follows the third of the four equivalent formulations: $S \leq_\alpha T \Leftrightarrow S; \alpha^r \leq \alpha^r; T$.

Page 528, Property 11.2.5 shows that data refinement through an invariant implies forward data refinement. So, the proof obligations of the B-Method correspond to data refinement through an invariant. They are simpler, because it is assumed that the refined component is already proved (see Property 11.2.3, page 526 of the B-Book).

5.3   A Data Refinement Inexpressible in the B-Method

The example of Fig. 5 is taken from [GM93].

In machine M_1, variable I_2 determines how many times the operation $incr$ is active (in [GM93], I_2 is called a prophecy variable). Machine M_1 is data refined by machine M_2, through the command α:

$$\alpha(Q) = \forall I_2 \cdot ((B_2 = \mathsf{true} \Rightarrow I_2 = 0) \wedge I_1 + I_2 \leq 10 \Rightarrow Q)$$

```
MACHINE
    M₁
VARIABLES
    I₁, I₂
INVARIANT
    I₁ ∈ 0..10 ∧ I₂ ∈ 0..10
INITIALISATION
    I₁ := 0 ‖ I₂ :∈ 0..10
OPERATIONS
    incr =
        IF
            I₂ ≠ 0
        THEN
            I₁, I₂ := I₁ + 1, I₂ − 1
        END
END
```

```
MACHINE
    M₂
VARIABLES
    I₁, B₂
INVARIANT
    I₁ ∈ 0..10 ∧ B₂ ∈ BOOL
INITIALISATION
    I₁ := 0 ‖ B₂ :∈ BOOL
OPERATIONS
    incr =
        CHOICE
            IF
                B₂ = false ∧ I₁ < 10
            THEN
                I₁ := I₁ + 1
            END
        OR
            B₂ := true
        END
END
```

Fig. 5. A backward data refinement.

This is a backward data refinement ([Wri94]): the non-deterministic choice in the initialisation of I_2 in M_1 is made later in M_2 (it is done in the operation *incr*).

This data refinement cannot be established in the B-Method, where only forward data refinement is allowed.

6   The SEES Primitive

In this section, we exhibit an example of an incorrect B software system, where all components are locally correct. The problem relies upon a misuse of the composition primitives IMPORTS and SEES. We show that those primitives can cause aliasings between variables. Unsoundness of the construction can be determined at the command interpretation level. Then, we exhibit an architectural condition, ensuring global correctness.

First, the semantics of IMPORTS and SEES primitives of the B-Method are reminded :

– The IMPORTS primitive links implementations to abstract machines, and is used to build the state of a machine on to the state of imported machines. This primitive does not introduce sharing, so it allows to build a layered software.

– The SEES primitive allows the sharing of an abstract machine. This primitive can be used in a machine, a refinement or an implementation. Variables of a seen machine can only be consulted, and must not be modified by the seeing components. Notice that a SEES primitive must be preserved in a development: if a machine is seen at a given level, it must be seen in subsequent refinements.

In [PR98], we exhibited an architectural condition, ensuring global correctness of a B software system, when SEES occurrences are only in implementations. We extend this work, dealing with SEES occurrences at all levels.

6.1   An Example

The example given in Fig. 7 exhibits an architecture (Fig. 6) which is incorrect, in the sense that local proofs of correctness do not guarantee global correctness (this example was accepted by Atelier B [AtB], up to version 3.2: proof obligations discharged and architecture not rejected). Note that the conclusion is identical if machines A_2 and A_3 are seen by the implementation of A_1 instead of being imported.

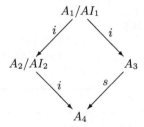

Fig. 6. Architecture of the example.

All machines and implementations are locally correct. But, the effective code of the operation Op_1 (Fig. 8) can be built by replacement, as defined for the meaning of the operation call (B-Book page 314-316 and 556), and extended for passing through a chain of refinements in [PR98]. In this case, the substitution reduces to rr := FALSE, what is obviously incorrect.

6.2   An Aliasing Problem

In this subsection, we go back to monotonicity through $\leq_\alpha$, as explained in Section 2. We show that the lack of global correctness of a B software system using SEES primitive occurs because monotonicity cannot be applied.

Let $C\langle X\rangle$ be a command, built by using X and some monotonic (through $\leq_\alpha$) command constructors, where X is a variable denoting an unknown command.

```
MACHINE
    A₁
OPERATIONS
    rr ← Op₁ = rr := TRUE
END
```

```
IMPLEMENTATION
    AI₁
REFINES
    A₁
IMPORTS
    A₂, A₃
OPERATIONS
    rr ← Op₁ =
        VAR V₁, V₂ IN
            V₁ ← Val₃ ; Op₂ ;
            V₂ ← Val₃ ;
            rr := bool(V₁=V₂)
        END
END
```

```
MACHINE
    A₂
OPERATIONS
    Op₂ = skip
END
```

```
MACHINE
    A₃
SEES
    A₄
OPERATIONS
    rr ← Val₃ = rr ← Val₄
END
```

```
IMPLEMENTATION
    AI₂
REFINES
    A₂
IMPORTS
    A₄
OPERATIONS
    Op₂ = Mod₄
END
```

```
MACHINE
    A₄
VARIABLES
    X₄
INVARIANT
    X₄ ∈ 0..1
INITIALISATION
    X₄ := 0
OPERATIONS
    rr ← Val₄ = rr := X₄ ;
    Mod₄ = X₄ := 1 - X₄
END
```

Fig. 7. A complete example

```
rr ← Op₁ =
    VAR V₁, V₂ IN
        V₁ := X₄ ; X₄ := 1-X₄ ; V₂ := X₄ ;
        rr := bool(V₁=V₂)
    END
```

Fig. 8. Code of the Op_1 operation

We assume that $X \in Mtran_{a \to a}$ and that C ranges over variables g, distinct from a, so $C\langle X \rangle \in Mtran_{a,g \to a,g}$. Hence X must be extended to X_g to be used in C. For instance, $C\langle X \rangle = [1/g]; X_g$, so that $C\langle X \rangle(Q) = X_g(Q)[1/g]$.

Let $S \in Mtran_{a \to a}$, $T \in Mtran_{c \to c}$ and $\alpha \in Mtran_{c \to a}$ be commands, such that a, c, g are distinct and $S \leq_\alpha T$ holds. Obviously, $S_g \leq_{\alpha_g} T_g$, so, by monotonicity: $C\langle S \rangle \leq_{\alpha_g} C\langle T \rangle$.

Now, let $S \in Mtran_{a \to a}$, $T \in Mtran_{c,g \to c,g}$ and $\alpha \in Mtran_{c,g \to a}$ be commands, such that $S \leq_\alpha T$. For instance, $S = skip$, $T = [2/g]$, and $\alpha = [c/a]$. In this case, there is no refinement relation between the extended predicate transformers: $S_g \not\leq_{\alpha_g} T_g$, and monotonicity cannot be applied[3]. As counterexample, we have: $C\langle S \rangle = [1/g]; skip = [1/g]$, and $C\langle T \rangle = [1/g]; [2/g] = [2/g]$.

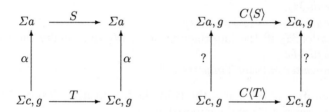

Fig. 9. An aliasing problem: concrete variable g occurs in the context $C\langle X \rangle$.

So the problem clearly comes from an aliasing between the variables of the using context of a command and the concrete variables of its refinement (see Fig.9).

We can now explain the example in the light of this analysis: in implementation AI_1, the operation Op_2 of machine A_2 is used in the context X_4, because AI_1 imports A_3, which sees A_4 (where X_4 is defined). In the implementation AI_2, the concrete variable is X_4, because AI_2 imports A_4; hence, an alias occurs.

Prohibiting this aliasing phenomenon by rejecting every aliasing architecture would be a too drastic solution. Such an architecture is globally correct if we can ensure that, when an aliasing phenomenon appears, the refined operation does not modify the global variables. In terms of commands: let $S \in Mtran_{a \to a}$,

---

[3] In [PR98], monotonicity was mistakenly applied.

$T \in Mtran_{c,g \to c,g}$ and $\alpha \in Mtran_{c,g \to a}$ be commands, such that $S \leq_\alpha T$. Let $C\langle X \rangle \in Mtran_{a,g \to a,g}$ be a command constructor.

> If for all $Q \in Pred_g$ and for all $d \in D_g$, $T(Q[d/g]) = T(Q)[d/g]$,
> then $S_g \leq_{\alpha_g} T_g$, so $C\langle S \rangle \leq_{\alpha_g} C\langle T \rangle$.

Applying this condition to the B-Method can be done either by a fine analysis of operations, or by simply ensuring, by architectural restrictions, that the refined operations *cannot* modify global variables. In the following, we investigate the latter approach.

6.3   Dependency Relations

Definition 4.

1. C_1 *s* M_2 iff the component C_1 (a machine, a refinement or an implementation) sees the machine M_2.
2. M_1 *sees* M_2 iff the implementation of M_1 sees the machine M_2.
3. M_1 *imports* M_2 iff the implementation of M_1 imports the machine M_2.
4. M_1 *uses* M_2 iff the implementation of M_1 sees or imports M_2:
   $$uses = sees \cup imports.$$
5. M_1 *depends_on* M_2 iff the implementation of M_1 is built by using M_2:
   $$depends\_on = uses^+.$$
6. M_1 *can_consult* M_2 iff the implementation of M_1 can consult the variables of the code of M_2:
   $$can\_consult = (uses^*; sees).$$
7. M_1 *can_alter* M_2 iff the implementation of M_1 can modify the variables of the code of M_2:
   $$can\_alter = (uses^*; imports).$$

Relational notation is the one of the B-Method: transitive closure $(^+)$, reflexive and transitive closure $(^*)$ and composition $(;)$.

6.4   Framework Hypotheses

Our analysis is based on the following assumptions, stated in the B-Book:

1. The dependency graph has no cycle: $depends\_on \cap id = \emptyset$, where id is the identity relation.
2. If a machine M sees a machine N, refinements of M must see N: $s \subseteq sees$.
3. A machine is imported only once: $imports^{-1}$ is a (partial) function.
4. An implementation cannot see and import the same machine:
   $$sees \cap imports = \emptyset.$$
5. Variables of two distinct components (at clause VARIABLES) are distinct. So common variables in components can only occur when a SEES primitive is used. Moreover, in a refinement chain, a variable cannot disappear, then reappear at a lower level.
6. If a component C sees a machine N, variables of N cannot be referenced in the invariant of C, and only consulting operations of N can be called in C.

6.5   Ensuring Monotonicity

Let M_1 be an abstract machine, and let I_1 be its implementation.

1. Assume I_1 imports a machine M_2. Since a machine can be imported only once, variables of M_2 cannot be modified elsewhere: this case is safe.
2. Assume I_1 sees M_2 (this case covers the case when M_1 sees M_2). To ensure that variables of M_2 are not modified elsewhere, it suffices to have:
$$can\_alter \cap sees = \emptyset.$$
3. A similar analysis can be done when M_2 is indirectly seen by I_1. For example, I_1 sees or imports a machine M_3, which sees M_2 (a longer chain of SEES between M_3 and M_2 may be allowed). In this case, I_1 may call an operation of M_3 which consults a variable of M_2. To ensure that the variable cannot be modified elsewhere:
$$can\_alter \cap (uses; sees^+) = \emptyset.$$
4. These two cases are treated by the condition:
$$can\_alter \cap ((imports; sees^+) \cup (sees^+)) = \emptyset.$$
5. This condition is too restrictive in the special case where global correctness is a consequence of local correctness: when the modification of the variable is explicit in the operation. For example, I_1 imports M_3 which sees M_1 (the chain of sees may be longer), and I_1 also imports M_1. In this case, local proof obligations cannot be satisfied. So it suffices to consider:
$$(uses; can\_alter) \cap ((imports; sees^+) \cup (sees^+)) = \emptyset.$$
6. We now analyse the fact that variables of a seen machine cannot appear in the invariant of the seeing component. For example, in the architecture of Fig. 10, machine B_4 is only seen in the implementation BI_3 of B_3. Variables of B_3 are necessarily independent of variables of B_4, so they cannot be modified by an operation of B_2. So the condition becomes:
$$(uses; can\_alter) \cap ((imports; s^+) \cup (sees; s^*)) = \emptyset.$$

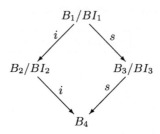

Fig. 10. A correct architecture (SEES are only in implementations).

So the sufficient architectural condition ensuring global correctness is:

$$\boxed{(uses; can\_alter) \cap ((imports; s^+) \cup (sees; s^*)) = \emptyset}$$

6.6   Simplifying Architectural Condition

Architectural condition can be reduced, if we use the following hypothesis, which is not stated in the B-Book:

> *If a machine M is indirectly seen through a chain of* SEES *primitives from a component C, possibly via an* IMPORTS *primitive, then M must be directly in the scope of a* SEES *or* IMPORTS *primitive in C.*

Using dependency relations, this hypothesis becomes:

1. For a machine or a refinement: $s^+ \subseteq s$,
2. For an implementation: $s^+ \subseteq s \cup imports$,
3. $imports; s^+ \subseteq sees \cup imports$.

This hypothesis is consistent with the non-transitivity of the SEES primitive. It imposes that each variable which can appear in a proof obligation of a component C is in the direct scope of its definition. With this hypothesis, architectural condition can be simplified, because chains of SEES primitives no more need to be considered. We have:

1. $imports; s^+ \subseteq sees \cup imports$.
2. $sees; s^* = sees \cup sees; s^+ \subseteq sees; s \cup sees; imports \subseteq sees \cup imports \cup sees; imports$.
3. So architectural condition is ensured by:
   $(uses; can\_alter) \cap (sees \cup imports \cup sees; imports) = \emptyset$.
4. Because a machine is imported only once, $(uses; can\_alter) \cap (imports \cup sees; imports) = \emptyset$, so condition becomes: $(uses; can\_alter) \cap sees = \emptyset$.
5. Because $can\_alter = imports \cup (uses; can\_alter)$ and $imports \cap sees = \emptyset$ (an implementation cannot see and import the same machine), we have: $(uses; can\_alter) \cap sees = can\_alter \cap sees$.

In consequence, architectural condition becomes:

$$\boxed{can\_alter \cap sees = \emptyset}$$

7   Conclusion

We have studied the B-Method in the light of the refinement calculus. The main results are:

1. an explanation of the proof obligations of a B-refinement in terms of standard refinement (this is Theorem 1);
2. an explanation of the SEES problem ([PR98]) in terms of abusive use of monotonicity, in presence of aliasing;
3. a sufficient architectural condition ensuring global correctness of a B-software.

An immediate perspective would be the definition of a sharing primitive, allowing several machines to see and modify the same machine. To be useful, variables of shared machines should be allowed in invariants of sharing components, so we should enforce the architectural condition. It is probable that this architectural condition would be too restrictive, so a fine analysis of operations would be necessary, to precisely know where the variables are modified.

We think that our kind of investigation is useful for studying evolution of the B-Method, because known results of refinement calculus can be directly applied, and current research can be a food for thought. The following list is not exhaustive:

1. New substitution constructors could be defined, using the results of [BB98] (the authors note that the B parallel operator ∥ is equivalent to their derived product, for conjunctive commands). In [BPR96], we introduced a ⊗ operator, extending ∥ when variables are shared; it looks like the fusion operator of [BB98].
2. Object-oriented extension could be studied, in the light of [MS97].
3. A current research in B is its application to distributed systems ([AM98]). A comparative study with action systems ([BK83], referenced in [AM98]) would be useful. This work has already begun ([BuW96], [WS96]).

Acknowledgment

We thank Pierre Berlioux for his careful reading of Section 3 and for useful suggestions.

References

[Abr96]   J-R. Abrial, *The B-Book*, Cambridge University Press, 1996.
[AM98]   J-R. Abrial, L. Mussat, *Introducing Dynamic Constraints in B*, In Second B International Conference, D. Bert editor, LNCS 1393, 83–128, Springer, 1998.
[AtB]   Steria Méditerranée, *Le Langage B. Manuel de référence version 1.5*, S.A.V. Steria, BP 16000, 13791 Aix-en-Provence cedex 3, France.
[Ba78]   R. J. R. Back, *On the Correctness of Refinement Steps in Program Development*, Report A-1978-4, Dept. of Computer Science, University of Helsinki, 1978.
[BB98]   R. J. R. Back, M. Butler, *Fusion and Simultaneous Execution in the Refinement Calculus*, Acta Informatica 35, 921–949, 1998.
[BK83]   R. J. R. Back, R. Kurki-Suonio, *Decentralisation of Process Nets with Centralized Control*, In 2nd ACM SIGACT-SIGOPS Symp. on Principles of Distributed Computing, 131–142, 1983.
[BW90]   R. J. R. Back, J. von Wright, *Refinement calculus I: Sequential Nondeterministic Programs*, In Stepwise Refinement of Distributed Systems, J. W. de-Bakker, W. P. deRoever, G. Rozenberg, editors, LNCS 430, 42–66, Springer, 1990.

[BW92]   R. J. R. Back, J. von Wright, *Combining Angels, Demons and Miracles in Program Specifications*, Theoretical Computer Science 100, 365–383, 1992.

[BW98]   R. J. R. Back, J. von Wright, *Refinement Calculus - A Systematic Introduction*, Springer, 1998.

[BPR96]   D. Bert, M-L. Potet, Y. Rouzaud, *A Study on Components and Assembly Primitives in B*, In First Conference on the B Method, 47–62, H. Habrias editor, 1996.

[BuW96]   M. Butler, M. Walden, *Distributed System Development in B*, In First Conference on the B Method, 155–168, H. Habrias editor, 1996.

[CU89]   W. Chen, J. T. Udding, *Towards a Calculus of Data Refinement*, In Mathematics of Program Construction, J. L. A. van de Snepsheut editor, LNCS 375, 197–218, Springer, 1989.

[Dij76]   E. W. Dijkstra, *A Discipline of Programming*, Prentice-Hall, 1976.

[Du97]   S. Dunne, *Parallel Composition*, In B-Talk and BUG mailing-lists, http://estas1.inrets.fr:8001/ESTAS/BUG/WWW/MailArchives/, 97-12/msg00003.html and 98-01/msg00003.html.

[Du99]   S. Dunne, *The Safe Machine: a new specification construct for B*, In Proceedings of FM'99, World Congress on Formal Methods, Toulouse, 1999.

[GM93]   P. H. B. Gardiner, C. Morgan, *A Single Complete Rule for Data Refinement*, Formal Aspects of Computing, 5, 367–392, 1993. Reprinted in [Mo92].

[GP85]   D. Gries, J. Prins, *A New Notion of Encapsulation*, in Proc. of Symp. on Languages Issues in Programming Environments, SIGPLAN, 131–139, 1985.

[Met]   Line 14: Meteor operation, http://www.ratp.fr (available in english).

[MS97]   A. Mikhajlova, E. Sekerinski, *Class Refinement and Interface Refinement in Object-Oriented Programs*, In FME'97, J. Fitzgerald, C. Jones, P. Lucas editors, LNCS 1313, 82–101, Springer, 1997.

[Mo88]   C. Morgan, *The Specification Statement*, ACM TOPLAS 10(3), July 1988. Reprinted in [Mo92].

[Mo92]   C. Morgan, *On the Refinement Calculus*, Springer-Verlag, 1992.

[Mor87]   J. Morris, *A Theoretical Basis for Stepwise Refinement and the Programming Calculus*, Science of Computer Programming 9, 287–306, 1987.

[PR98]   M-L. Potet, Y. Rouzaud, *Composition and Refinement in the B-Method*, In Second B International Conference, D. Bert editor, LNCS 1393, 46–65, Springer, 1998.

[WS96]   M. Walden, K. Sere, *Refining Action Systems within B-Tool*, In FME'96, M-C. Gaudel, J. Woodcock editors, LNCS 1051, 84–103, Springer, 1996.

[Wi71]   N. Wirth, *Program Development by Stepwise Refinement*, CACM 14(4), 221–227, 1971.

[Wri94]   J. von Wright, *The Lattice of Data Refinement*, Acta Informatica 31, 105–135, 1994.

Compositional Symmetric Sharing in B

Martin Büchi and Ralph Back

Åbo Akademi University
Turku Centre for Computer Science
Lemminkäisenkatu 14A, 20520 Turku, Finland
{Martin.Buechi, Ralph.Back}@abo.fi,
http://www.abo.fi/~{mbuechi, backrj}

Abstract. Sharing between B constructs is limited, both on the specification and the implementation level. The limitations stem from the single writer/multiple readers paradigm, restricted visibility of shared variables, and structural constraints to prevent interference. As a consequence, applications with inherent sharing requirements have to either be described as large monolithic constructs or be underspecified, leading to a loss of modularity respectively certain desirable properties being unprovable.

We propose a new compositional symmetric shared access mechanism based on roles describing rely/guarantee conditions. The mechanism provides for multiple writers on shared constructs, visibility of shared variables in the accessors' invariants, and controlled aliasing. Use is uniform in machines, refinements, and implementations. Sharing is compositional: all proof obligations are local and do not require knowledge of the other accessors' specifications, let alone their or the shared construct's implementation.

Soundness of the mechanism is established by flattening.

1 Introduction

The B method provides support for modularization and, herewith, for information hiding, compositionality of module operations, reusability of modules, and decomposition of proofs [4, 5]. Modules can be combined using a number of different mechanisms. Refinement being 'almost' monotonic with respect to the composition mechanisms, most proof obligations arise on a per module base. The few additional restriction on the global structure can be checked automatically. In this compositional approach, we can focus on a part of a large system, establish desired properties for this part, and be guaranteed that these properties hold in the complete system.

To achieve compositionality [8] and independent refinement, sharing is restricted in B. Sharing is based on the single writer/multiple readers paradigm. If several constructs access a shared construct, only one accessor (writer) can modify the state of the shared construct. The other accessors (readers) are limited to read-only access, respectively to calling inquiry operations. To ensure that invariants cannot be invalidated, only the single writer is allowed to reference variables of the shared construct in its invariant. Because of these limitations, applications with inherent sharing requirements cannot be handled satisfactorily, as described in Sect. 2.2.

J. Wing, J. Woodcock, J. Davies (Eds.): FM'99, Vol. I, LNCS 1708, pp. 431–451, 1999.

We introduce a new sharing mechanism that overcomes the single writer and the variable visibility restrictions. Multiple constructs can have write access to a shared construct and reference shared variables in their invariants. The mechanism is compositional: all proof obligations arise on a per module base and only a few automatically checkable restrictions on the sharing graph are required for global correctness. The key element are freely specifiable accessor roles, which determine how the different accessors can use the shared construct. Adherence to these role specifications guarantees that the accessors do not invalidate each others invariants.

Role specifications can be considered as guarantee conditions in the sense of Cliff Jones [15] with the rely conditions being given by the other roles. Rely/guarantee conditions (also known as assumption/commitment specifications) have been developed as a compositional proof method for shared variable and message-passing concurrency with interleaving semantics. This paper shows that the same theory is also applicable to modular sequential systems with sharing.

Section 2 reviews the existing sharing mechanisms and illustrates a shortcoming on a concrete example. Throughout the paper we use numbered variations of the same example. In Sect. 3 we take the problem to its roots, analyzing the reasons for the existing restrictions. Section 4 introduces the new mechanism. We provide further details of the sharing mechanism in Sect. 5. In Sect. 6 we list the complete syntax, the proof obligations, the visibility rules, and the well-formedness criteria for the composition graph. Using flattening of constructs, we prove the soundness of the proposed mechanism in Sect. 7. Sect. 8 lists related work and draws the conclusions.

2   The Problem

2.1   Review of Existing Composition Mechanisms

B has three different constructs: machines, refinements, and implementations, distinguished by different syntactic restrictions. Machines express original specifications. Refinements are intermediate constructs. An implementation denotes the end of a refinement chain and contains executable code. In addition to behavioral specifications, refinements and implementations contain data refinement relations in form of gluing invariants. Machines can be parameterized. Parameters are instantiated by the single writer.

The B method has four mechanisms to compose constructs. The different mechanisms can be used in different constructs. The target of a composition is always a machine.

INCLUDES   The *INCLUDES* clause can appear in machines and refinements. It can be understood as textual inclusion with the restriction that variables of the included machine can only be modified indirectly through operations of the included machine so that the invariant of the included machine is preserved. The including construct instantiates the parameters of the included machine and can reference variables of the included machine in the invariant. The including construct becomes the focus of refinement, the included construct doesn't have to be implemented unless it is also imported.

USES The *USES* clause can only appear in machines. It provides for limited sharing on the specification level. Any number of machines can use a shared machine. All using and the used machine must be included into a common machine, which becomes the focus of refinement. The using machines cannot be refined. They have read-only access to the shared machine and can reference shared variables in their invariants. To guarantee that the including machine, which is the only writer, does not invalidate the invariants of the using machines, the using machines' invariants have to be proved upon inclusion.

SEES The *SEES* clause can appear in any construct. It provides for read only access to a shared machine. Variables of the seen machine cannot be referenced in the invariant of the seeing construct. Without this restriction, the invariant of the seeing machine could be invalidated by the construct with write access to the seen machine.

IMPORTS The *IMPORTS* clause can only appear in implementations. The importing machine instantiates the parameters of the imported machine, can call both inquiry and modification operations and can reference variables of the imported machine in its invariant. Imported machines can be seen by any number of other constructs.

Summary The *INCLUDES* and *USES* clauses can be considered as weak or syntactic relations [5]. Their aim is to combine text of machine specifications; this structure is not reflected in subsequent refinements or in the final implementation. *SEES* and *IMPORTS* on the other hand are strong relations as the shared code will remain visible as a module in the final implementation.

2.2 A Problem with the Existing Mechanisms

In this subsection, we illustrate a shortcoming of the existing sharing mechanisms with a concrete example. The example's main characteristic are its inherent sharing requirements.

We consider a control system for a manufacturing plant consisting of various devices, such as robot arms and conveyor belts. Each device is controlled by its own software module, the central *Run* operation of which is periodically called by a scheduler. Whenever a device controller notices an error, the device is stopped and an alarm is registered in a central database. The plant operator can list the active alarms on the screen and deactivate alarms after fixing their cause. The devices check whether all their alarms have been deactivated and if so resume work.

The database is shared between all the device controllers and the monitoring console. They all need both read and write access: the device controllers need to check for active alarms and enter new alarms, the monitoring console needs to list active alarms and change the activity status of alarms.

How do we specify, refine, and implement such an architecture using B's existing composition mechanisms? Let us first look at the specification. Since the devices are to a certain degree independent and since multiple instances of the same device type can

When the console sets an alarm it invalidates the invariant of *ConveyorBelt2* if *running* is *TRUE*. A construct with write access to a shared machine may invalidate any other accessor's invariant, if the latter references variables of the shared machine.

Such undesirable interferences cannot be ruled out with local proofs for any of the three machines *Database2*, *ConveyorBelt2*, or *Console2*. They require either a global approach or a modular approach with noninterference proofs like [20]. In both cases we would loose the benefits of independent refinement provided by a compositional theory [25].

Hence we have to choose between having multiple writers without the possibility to reference variables of the shared machine in any of the accessors' invariants or the current single writer paradigm. Not being able at to reference variables of the shared machine in any of the accessors' invariants is too restrictive, precluding the proving of many properties. For example, we cannot prove that the conveyor belt is only running if there are no active alarms because the variable *activeAlarms* of *Database2* is not visible in the invariant of *ConveyorBelt2*.

The same problems of destroying each other's invariants exist on the refinement and implementation levels. In addition to the local invariant, also the gluing invariant, expressing the data refinement relation, could be invalidated if we were to allow multiple writers [23].

On the positive side, we can note that multiple writers never invalidate the invariant of the shared machine as all modifications are done through operation calls.

4   Role-Based Access

To guarantee interference freedom among multiple accessors of a common machine, only the possible modifications to the shared variables are relevant. We define these effects in form of access *roles* as part of the shared machine. Accessing constructs declare which role(s) they play. The accessors guarantee to perform only modifications allowed by the declared role(s). In return, they can rely on the other accessors adhering to their roles. Let construct A accesses a shared machine in role R_1. If the other roles $R_2, ..., R_n$ maintain the invariant of A, then any accessor in role R_i $(i \in 2..n$ maintains the invariant of A. Thus, we can both specify and refine accessor A without knowing the other accessors' specifications or implementations.

Because a library machine might foresee multiple sharing scenarios and because a custom machine might be used in multiple instances with different sharing, we allow the definition of multiple *contracts* with different roles.

4.1   Role Specifications

We illustrate the concept on our plant control system. This time, the conveyor belt creates the alarms reacting to sensors and an emergency stop button. The monitoring console is used to deactivate alarms. *Database3* defines a contract *SingleDevice* with two roles *Creator* and *Controller*, intended to capture the accesses by *ConveyorBelt3* and *Console3* respectively. An instance of *Database3* with contract *SingleDevice* can have at most two accessors, one for each role.

MACHINE Database3
CONTRACTS
   SingleDevice $\hat{=}$
      Creator = **ANY** type **WHERE** type∈NAT **THEN** NewAlarm(type) **END**,
      Controller = **ANY** aa **WHERE** aa∈activeAlarms**THEN** ResetAlarm(aa) **END**
VARIABLES alarms, activeAlarms, alarmType
INVARIANT alarms⊆NAT ∧ activeAlarms⊆alarms ∧ alarmType∈alarms→NAT
INITIALISATION alarms, activeAlarms, alarmType:=∅, ∅, ∅
OPERATIONS
   aa ← NewAlarm(type) $\hat{=}$
     PRE type∈NAT **THEN**
      ANY nn **WHERE** nn∈NAT-alarms **THEN**
      aa, alarms:=nn, alarms∪{nn} ‖
      activeAlarms, alarmType(nn):=activeAlarms∪{nn}, type
     END
    END;
   ResetAlarm(aa) $\hat{=}$ **PRE** aa∈activeAlarms
    THEN activeAlarms:=activeAlarms-{aa} **END**;
   nof ← NofActiveAlarms $\hat{=}$ nof:=**card**(activeAlarms);
   . . .
END

We specify the set of alarms as a subset of *NAT* and the active alarms as a subset of all alarms. The attribute *alarmType* is a functions from *alarms* to *NAT*. More on this approach of mapping records/classes to B, including proper treatments of finiteness, can be found in [18, 6].

4.2   Accesses

The machine *ConveyorBelt3* declares that it accesses the *Database3* as *Creator* in a *SingleDevice* contract. We use a '*!*' as separator of the qualified identifier because the dot is reserved for possible renaming.

MACHINE ConveyorBelt3
ACCESSES Database3!SingleDevice **AS** Creator
VARIABLES running
INVARIANT running∈BOOL ∧ (running=TRUE ⇒ activeAlarms=∅)
INITIALISATION running:=TRUE
OPERATIONS
   rr ← Run $\hat{=}$
    CHOICE
     ANY type **WHERE** type∈0. .8
      THEN NewAlarm(type) ‖ running, rr:=FALSE, FALSE **END**
    OR running, rr:=**bool**(activeAlarms=∅), **bool**(activeAlarms=∅)
    END;
   EmergencyStop $\hat{=}$ **BEGIN** NewAlarm(9) ‖ running:=FALSE **END**
END

The operations *Run* and *EmergencyStop* have to act as refinements of *Creator* ‖ *skip* on the state space of the *Database*, which is clearly the case. This also implies, that inquiry operations can be freely called by any accessor.

Furthermore, we need to show that another construct, accessing *Database3* in the second role *Controller* cannot invalidate the invariant of *ConveyorBelt3*. To this aim, we show that the role specification *Controller* executed like an operation on the combined state space of *Database3* and *ConveyorBelt3* maintains the latter's invariant. This is the case, because *Controller* can only deactivate alarms. Deactivation is unproblematic because the second conjunct of the invariant of *ConveyorBelt3* is an implication and not an equality.

4.3   Refining and Implementing Accesses

Refinements and the implementation of *ConveyorBelt3* have to make the same changes to the variables of the shared machine *Database3*.

We assume *Motor3* to be a machine controlling the power of the motor and *Sensor3* a sensor that is activated if a load on the conveyor belt is about to fall off the edge.

```
IMPLEMENTATION ConveyorBelt3′ REFINES ConveyorBelt3
ACCESSES Database3!SingleDevice AS Creator
IMPORTS M.Motor3, S.Sensor3
INVARIANT running=M.on
OPERATIONS
    rr ← Run ≙
      VAR ss, nof IN
        ss ← S.ReadSensor;
        IF ss=TRUE THEN M.ShutOff; NewAlarm(0)
        ELSE nof ← NofActiveAlarms; IF nof=0 THEN M.TurnOn END
        END
      END;
    EmergencyStop ≙ BEGIN M.ShutOff; NewAlarm(9) END
END
```

Instead of accessing the database itself, the implementation *ConveyorBelt3′* could also import another machine that accesses the database and performs the changes.

4.4   Instantiation

In the existing composition mechanisms, the single writer also instantiates the machine parameters of the utilized machine. In our new mechanism, instantiation is separate from access using the *INSTANTIATES* clause, which specifies the machine, the contract, and the values of the parameters, if any. For example, we might have an implementation *Main3′*, which imports the accessors and instantiates the shared database:

```
IMPLEMENTATION Main3′ REFINES Main3
INSTANTIATES Database3!SingleDevice
IMPORTS ConveyorBelt3, Console3
```

Every accessed copy of a shared machine must be instantiated exactly once in an implementation, naming the same contract as all accessors. Renaming can be performed in the *ACCESSES* and *INSTANTIATES* clauses, thus allowing multiple instances with possibly different contracts. The renaming of the construct containing the *INSTANTI-ATES* clause determines the number of instances.

5   Further Aspects of Role-Based Access

5.1   Replicated Roles

In the previous section we have used role-based access for a plant control with a single device. In reality, we have many devices, which all have almost identical role specifications. Rather than requiring textual duplication, we introduce a replication mechanism over a constant set. Thus, we can define the role *Creator* of *Database4* as follows:

MACHINE Database4
CONTRACTS
   MultipleDevices $\hat{=}$
     Creator(no$\in$0..19) $=$
      ANY type **WHERE** type$\in$10$\times$no..10$\times$no+9 **THEN** NewAlarm(type) **END**,

This example definition allows 20 accessors in the role of creators, one for each value between 0 and 19. The replicator *no* may be used inside the scope of the role definition like a constant. A construct that accesses a shared machine in a replicated role has to indicate its replication value. The conveyor belt could be defined as:

MACHINE ConveyorBelt4
ACCESSES Database4!MultipleDevices **AS** Creator(0)

For the non-interference proofs the other replicated roles have to be considered like different role specifications. In the example, we would have to prove that *Creator(nn)* for $nn\in1..19$ maintains the invariant of *ConveyorBelt4*. This is the case if we adapt the invariant of *ConveyorBelt3* as below and adjusting the *Run* operation correspondingly.

INVARIANT
   running$\in$BOOL $\wedge$ (running=TRUE $\Rightarrow$ activeAlarms$\cap$(alarmType^{-1}[0..9])=$\emptyset$)

5.2   Form of Role Specifications

As shown in the examples, role specifications take the format of normal B operations. Traditionally, rely/guarantee conditions are expressed as predicates over the current and the next state of variables. However, we feel that operation-like specifications are more in line with B.

As a guiding principle, we allow the same statements as in operations of a refinement that includes the accessed machine. Thus, multiple substitutions, sequencing, and nondeterministic choice are all allowed, but loops are not. Variables can be read directly, but modified through operation calls only. To gain sufficient expressiveness, either loops or direct modifications should be made legal.

We do not have to prove that operation calls in role specifications satisfy the preconditions of the called operations, because we perform these proofs for the actual accessors. As an engineering aid, the tools should nevertheless support conformance proofs for role specifications. Precondition violating role specifications do not give the accessor more freedom, but make the non-interference proofs for other accessors more difficult.

The role specifications, like any module interfaces, should be very simple compared to the code of the actual accessors. Hence, roles are described like operations, rather than full machines with variables that maintain their values between calls. Such specifications would require full-blown construct refinement with gluing invariants between role and local variables in accessors and also more complex non-interference proofs. The simple format suffices in most cases and is, combined with some coding tricks modifying the operation specifications, as general as full machines.

The relative simplicity of the role specifications compared to the code of the actual accessors reduces the complexity of the non-interference proofs. The simplification of the non-interference proofs for all other accessors on all refinement levels by far outweighs the additional burden of the single role adherence proof.

An overly weak role specification makes it easy to prove role adherence, but impossible to guarantee non-interference for other accessors. An overly strong specification causes the opposite problem. Writing the role specifications is a design step, like any other definition of module interaction.

5.3   Adherence to Role Specifications

An operation of an accessor adheres to a role specification if it either acts as a refinement of the specification or as *skip* on the state space of the accessed machine. We add *skip* as an implicit choice to every role specification. This corresponds to the guarantee condition being reflexive [15], respectively the stuttering transition being built into the semantics [3, 17].

Whether an operation O that refines a role specification R is called multiple times or whether O acts as a refinement of $R\hat{}$ $(=skip\|R\|(R;R)\| \dots)$ has the same effect for the other accessors. This corresponds to the guarantee condition being transitive [15], respectively mumbling being built into the semantics. Explicitly allowing mumbling makes the proofs more difficult and can –provided we allow direct write access or loops in role specifications– always be replaced with a weaker role specification. For simplicity, we do not consider mumbling in this paper.

In the initialization of the accessors we only allow inquiry operations of the accessed machine to be called. Otherwise we would have to define an order in which the accessors are initialized and could not assume the shared machine to be in its initial state when the accessors are initialized. The initializations acting as *skip* on the accessed machine, they automatically adhere to the role specifications.

5.4   Sharing Structure

Sharing is used to get multiple access paths to the same data. In the presence of independent refinement, we need some structural restrictions to control aliasing. In this section, we give two examples of what could go wrong without such structural restrictions. A full account of the restriction is given in Sect. 6.4.

We adopt the following notation in figures: The primed constructs are the implementations refining the unprimed machines. Multiple instances of an accessed machine –if present– are graphically indicated by duplication to make collaborations clear. We

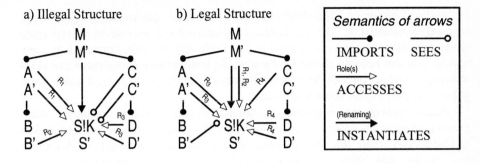

Fig. 2. Illustration of Legal and Illegal Composition Graphs

append the name of the actual contract to the name of the accessed machine. The access arrows are adorned by the role(s) and possibly the replication values, the instantiation arrow by the possible renaming. In a slight abuse of notation, it would also be possible to visualize roles as UML style interfaces (circles) attached to the shared machine. However, our notion of roles and that of UML interfaces is not identical because our roles contain guarantee conditions rather than the signatures of callable operations.

Consider a machine A that accesses a shared machine S (left branch of Fig. 2 a). The implementation A' also accesses S and furthermore imports B. Machine B does not access S, but the implementation B' does. Even if we locally prove that the operations of A' act as a refinements of the operations of A, this property might not hold in the complete system. A' may call operations of B and, thereby, unknowingly modify S. This might lead to S being modified differently than specified in A, B' observing S in a state where the gluing invariant of B' does not hold, and A' violating preconditions of operations of S. This problem is due to A' accessing S both traceably and untraceably. The problem is not bound to B only accessing S in the implementation. An invisible access could also be created if B' would not access S directly, but import a machine E that accesses S.

Without constraints on the composition graph, also the interaction between the old and the new composition mechanism can lead to problems. A seeing construct C' (right branch of Fig. 2 a) assume that the state of the seen machine S does not change during the execution of an operation of C'. To enforce this, the seeing construct C' can only call inquiry operations. In proofs of C', no substitutions are made on the state of the seen machine S. If C' could indirectly modify S, global correctness would be invalidated. This could, for example, happen if the seeing machine imports a third machine D, the implementation of which accesses S. Thus, we need restrictions on the structure of the development to ban such architectures.

5.5 Emulating the Existing Composition Mechanisms

The existing composition primitives *IMPORTS* and *SEES* can be emulated using *ACCESSES* and *INSTANTIATES* as follows: A contract permitting a single writer with full access rights and an infinite number of readers with a *skip* role specification is added to the shared construct. Then, *IMPORTS* can be replaced with an access in the writer role and an instantiation. The *SEES* clauses are replaced with accesses in the replicated reader role. Because the existing mechanisms *IMPORTS* and *SEES* capture a frequent special case and because abolishing them would require more complicated global restrictions based not only on the structure but also the semantics of roles, it makes sense to have all mechanisms at our disposition.

Promotion of operations (turning operations of a utilized machine into proper operations of the utilizing construct) would only be possible in combination with *ACCESSES* in trivial cases where the other accessors do not make any observable modifications (e.g., for the single writer in the above emulation contract). Furthermore, promotion of operations is much less important with *ACCESSES*, because the latter provides for multiple writers. Therefore, we do not consider the promotion of operations from accessed machines, but rather count promotion as a further reason to also keep the existing import mechanism.

The *USES* mechanism cannot be emulated because it dictates that the used machine be included into another machine whereas an accessed machine cannot be included. *INCLUDES*, being a copying rather than a sharing mechanism, cannot be emulated with *ACCESSES*.

6   Formal Definitions

6.1   Syntax

We give the following extended syntax definitions [2, p 715ff] for machines, refinements, and implementations:

MACHINE	REFINEMENT	IMPLEMENTATION
Machine_Header	Machine_Header	Machine_Header
CONSTRAINTS	REFINES	. . .
Predicate	Id_List	VALUES
CONTRACTS	ACCESSES	Predicate
Contract_List	Access_List	ACCESSES
ACCESSES	INSTANTIATES	Access_List
Access_List	Inst_List	INSTANTIATES
INSTANTIATES	SETS	Inst_List
Inst_List	. . .	IMPORTS
USES		. . .
. . .		

Contract_List, *Access_List*, and *Inst_List* are defined as follows:

Syntactic Category	Definition
Contract_List	Contract; Contract_List
	Contract
Contract	Contract_Name $\,\widehat{=}\,$ Role_List

Syntactic Category	Definition
Role_List	Role, Role_List
	Role
Role	Role_Name = Statement
	Role_Name(Replicator $\in$ Set) = Statement
Access_List	Access; Access_List
	Access
Access	Machine_Name!Contract_Name **AS** Acc_Role_List
	Renamed_Name.Machine_Name!Contract_Name
	AS Acc_Role_List
Acc_Role_List	Acc_Role, Acc_Role_List
	Acc_Role
Acc_Role	Role_Name
	Role_Name(Simple_Term)
Inst_List	Inst, Inst_List
	Inst
Inst	Machine_Name!Contract_Name
	Machine_Name!Contract_Name(Expression_List)
	Renamed_Name.Machine_Name!Contract_Name
	Renamed_Name.Machine_Name!Contract_Name(Expression_List)

Contract_Name, Role_Name, Replicator, Machine_Name, and *Renamed_Name* all stand for *Identifier*. The form of the role specification is discussed in detail in Sect. 5.2.

6.2   Proof Obligations

We give the proof obligations for machines and implementations containing an *ACCESSES* clause. The rules for refinements are analogous. As noted in Sect. 5.2, the *CONTRACTS* clause does not give rise to any proof obligations. We leave out sets, constants and assertions as the respective proof obligations are unchanged. Figure 3 gives an overview of the proof obligations.

MACHINE $M_s(P_s)$
CONSTRAINTS C_s
CONTRACTS
  $K \mathrel{\widehat{=}}$
    $R_1 = F_1,$
    $R_2 = F_2$
VARIABLES X_s
INVARIANT I_s
INITIALISATION U_s
OPERATIONS
  $u_s \leftarrow O_s(w_s) \mathrel{\widehat{=}}$
    PRE Q_s **THEN** V_s **END**
END

MACHINE $M_1(P_1)$
CONSTRAINTS C_1
ACCESSES
  $M_s!K$ **AS** R_1
VARIABLES X_1
INVARIANT I_1
INITIALISATION U_1
OPERATIONS
  $u_1 \leftarrow O_1(w_1) \mathrel{\widehat{=}}$
    PRE Q_1 **THEN** V_1 **END**
END

IMPLEMENTATION
  $M_1'(P_1)$
REFINES M_1
ACCESSES
  $M_s!K$ **AS** R_1
CONCRETE_VARS
  X_1'
INVARIANT I_1'
INITIALISATION U_1'
OPERATIONS
  $u_1 \leftarrow O_1(w_1) \mathrel{\widehat{=}}$
    BEGIN V_1' **END**
END

We use the abbreviations A_1 for $P_1 \in \mathcal{P}_1(\text{INT})$ and A_s for $P_s \in \mathcal{P}_1(\text{INT})$. Occurrences of O_s in U_1, V_1, U_1', V_1', F_1, and F_2 should be replaced by V_s with the parameters substituted accordingly [2, p 314ff]. As in [2] we do not make this substitution explicit in the proof obligations.

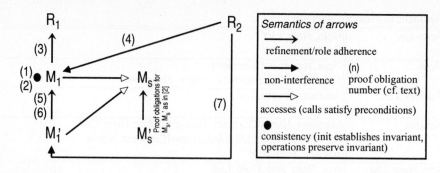

Fig. 3. Proof Obligations for an Accessing Machine and Implementation

Machine M_1 The first proof obligation of M_1 states that the initialization must establish the invariant. The role of the accessed machine is similar to the one of an included machine, except that its parameters are not actualized [2, p 331ff].

$$A_1 \wedge C_1 \wedge A_s \wedge C_s \Rightarrow [U_s][U_1]l_1 \tag{1}$$

The next obligation concerns the preservation of the invariant of the accessing machine by its operations:

$$A_1 \wedge C_1 \wedge l_1 \wedge Q_1 \wedge A_s \wedge C_s \wedge l_s \Rightarrow [V_1]l_1 \tag{2}$$

The third obligation states that the operations of the accessor must conform to the declared role. Note that there is no corresponding obligation for the initialization because the latter may not call modification operations of the accessed machine. Because both the role specification F_s and the operation O_1 operate on X_s, renaming must be performed. Let $\hat{X}_s$ be a fresh set of variables, then we get

$$A_1 \wedge C_1 \wedge l_1 \wedge Q_1 \wedge A_s \wedge C_s \wedge l_s \wedge \hat{X}_s = X_s \Rightarrow [[X_s := \hat{X}_s]V_1] \neg [F_1 \| \mathbf{skip}] \neg (\hat{X}_s = X_s) \tag{3}$$

If a construct accesses a machine in multiple roles, its operations have to conform to the nondeterministic choice of the two roles. Thus, if M_1 were to access M_s as R_1 and R_2, then F_1 would have to be replaced by $F_1 \| F_2$.

The fourth obligation concerns the interference freedom by all other roles, which in our case is only R_2.

$$A_1 \wedge C_1 \wedge l_1 \wedge A_s \wedge C_s \wedge l_s \Rightarrow [F_2]l_1 \tag{4}$$

For replicated roles, we have to prove non-interference for all replication values except for the one of the accessor in question. Let us assume the following replications $R_1(g_1 \in G_1)$ and $R_2(g_2 \in G_2)$ and let M_1 access M_s as $R_1(h_1)$. Then we get the following three obligations:

$$h_1 \in G_1 \tag{4'}$$
$$A_1 \wedge C_1 \wedge l_1 \wedge A_s \wedge C_s \wedge l_s \wedge g_1 \in G_1 - \{h_1\} \Rightarrow [F_1]l_1$$
$$A_1 \wedge C_1 \wedge l_1 \wedge A_s \wedge C_s \wedge l_s \wedge g_2 \in G_2 \Rightarrow [F_2]l_1$$

Replication not only avoids duplication of role specifications, it also leads to a reduction of the overal proof burden by combining many similar non-interference obligations.

The proof obligations for operation calls (satisfy precondition) are unchanged.

Implementation M_1' For the implementation M_1' we have 3 proof obligations. The first two proof obligations concerning initialization and operation refinement are similar to those of an implementation that imports another machine [2, p 597ff].

$$A_1 \wedge C_1 \wedge A_s \wedge C_s \Rightarrow [U_s][U_1'] \neg [U_1] \neg I_1' \tag{5}$$

The second proof obligation is for the operation refinement. The 1-to-1 data refinement of the shared variables is explicit in this obligation $(\hat{X}_s = X_s)$.

$$A_1 \wedge C_1 \wedge I_1 \wedge I_1' \wedge Q_1 \wedge A_s \wedge C_s \wedge I_s \wedge \hat{X}_s = X_s \Rightarrow \tag{6}$$
$$[[u_1 := \hat{u}_1][X_s := \hat{X}_s]V_1'] \neg [V_1] \neg ([X_s := \hat{X}_s]I_1' \wedge \hat{u}_1 = u_1 \wedge \hat{X}_s = X_s)$$

For sharing in the implementation only, we have to prove adherence rather than 1-to-1 data refinement in the implementation. The third and last obligation concerns the interference freedom. As noted above for machines, it should be replicated if some of the roles are.

$$A_1 \wedge C_1 \wedge I_1 \wedge I_1' \wedge A_s \wedge C_s \wedge I_s \Rightarrow [F_2]I_1' \tag{7}$$

If M or M_1' also instantiates M_s, say P_s with N_s, then A_s can be replaced by the stronger predicate $P_s = N_s$ in the above proof obligations. In this case we have the additional proof obligation that the actual parameters satisfy the constraints, as for *INCLUDES* and *IMPORTS*.

6.3   Visibility Rules

For brevity, we only summarizes some key aspects of the visibility rules here. In the *CONTRACTS* clause we allow only read access to variables. A construct's own sets and constants as well as those of seen machines are allowed as parameters of instantiations. To prevent cyclic dependencies, sets and constants of included, used, imported, and accessed machines are, on the other hand, not visible in the *INSTANTIATES* clause.

Only a construct's own sets and constants and those of seen machines, but not those of imported machines may be used as parameters of instantiations. In their initializations, accessors can call only inquiry operations of an accessed construct.

If a construct A only instantiates, but does not access B, then none of the objects of B are visible in A. Like *SEES*, but unlike *INCLUDES*, *ACCESSES* is not transitive. If machine A includes, uses, sees, imports, or accesses B and B accesses C, then the objects of C are not visible in A. It is, however, possible that A also accesses C (Fig. 2 b).

6.4   Well-Formedness of the Composition Graph

The well formedness criteria for the composition graph concerning *ACCESSES* to guarantee global correctness are presented below. They are simple enough to be checked automatically.

Similar checks are already performed for the existing composition mechanisms [2, 21]. For simplicity, we talk about 'accessed machines' instead of renamed instances thereof.

The following conditions can be verified by the type checker on a per-construct base:

1. If a machine, a refinement, or an included machine thereof accesses a machine M_s as R of contract K then this construct's implementation must either access M_s as R of contract K or import exactly one machine that contains such an access.
2. If a machine, a refinement, or an included machine thereof accesses a machine M_s as $R_1, \ldots, R_i$ of contract K then this construct's implementation may not access M_s in any other roles nor import a machine accessing M_s in any other roles. (The proof obligation for operation refinement would not allow modifications not covered by $R_1, \ldots, R_i$ anyhow.)
3. A construct and one of its included machines cannot access the same machine in the same role.
4. If a machine, a refinement, or an included machine thereof contains an instantiation, then all further refinements and the implementation must either contain the same instantiation with the same parameters or include/import without renaming a machine containing such an instantiation.

The following conditions must be checked globally for complete projects:

1. Every accessed machine is instantiated exactly once in an implementation.
2. Every shared machine is accessed at most once in each role, respectively for each replication value, by an implementation
3. All accesses and the instantiation of a machine are for the same contract.
4. An accessed machine cannot be included or imported. This also implies that neither a used nor a using machine can be accessed.
5. A seen machine must either be instantiated or imported.

To present the remaining architectural condition, we extend the notation of [21]. The relational notation is as in B: '$+$' denotes the transitive non-reflexive closure, '$*$' the transitive and reflexive closure, and ';' composition.

1. M_1 *sees* M_2 iff the implementation of M_1 sees the machine M_2.
2. M_1 *m_sees* M_2 iff machine M_1 sees machine M_2.
3. M_1 *imports* M_2 iff the implementation of M_1 imports the machine M_2.
4. M_1 *accesses* M_2 iff the implementation of M_1 accesses the machine M_2.
5. M_1 *depends_on* M_2 iff the implementation of M_1 is built utilizing M_2:
   $depends\_on \mathrel{\widehat{=}} (sees \cup imports \cup accesses)^+$.
6. M_1 *can_alter* M_2 iff the implementation of M_1 can alter the variables of M_2:
   $can\_alter \mathrel{\widehat{=}} depends\_on^*; (imports \cup accesses)$.

7. M_1 *any_accesses* M_2 iff M_1, one of its refinements, or its implementation accesses the machine M_2.
8. M_1 *(imp_acc M_s)* M_2 iff the implementation of M_1 imports the machine M_2 and M_2 accesses M_s.
9. M_1 *traceably_accesses* M_2 iff M_1 accesses M_2 through a chain of imports, in which all machines access M_2:
    M_1 *traceably_accesses* M_2 $\hat{=}$ M_1 *(imp_acc M_2)*; accesses M_2.*
10. M_1 *untraceably_accesses* M_2 iff M_1 indirectly accesses M_2 in a way other than an imports chain, in which all machines access M_2:
    untraceably_accesses $\hat{=}$ *(depends_on; accesses)-traceably_accesses.*
11. M_1 *instantiates* M_2 iff the implementation of M_1 instantiates the machine M_2.
12. M_1 *references* M_2 iff the implementation of M_1 references the machine M_2: *references $\hat{=}$ (sees$\cup$imports$\cup$accesses$\cup$instantiates)$^+$.*
13. *id* is the identity relation.

The composition graph must then satisfy the following condition:

$$((\text{sees} \cup \text{imports} \cup \text{accesses}); \text{can\_alter}) \cap \tag{i}$$
$$(((\text{imports} \cup \text{accesses}); \text{m\_sees}^+) \cup (\text{sees}; \text{m\_sees}^*)) = \emptyset \land$$
$$\text{any\_accesses} \cap \text{untraceably\_accesses} = \emptyset \land \tag{ii}$$
$$\text{references} \cap \text{id} = \emptyset \tag{iii}$$

The first conjunct states that a seen machine must not be modified. The second conjunct asserts that no construct accesses the same machine directly and untraceably. The third conjunct excludes cyclic dependencies.

The right branch of Fig. 2 a) violates the first conjunct of the above condition, the left branch violates the second conjunct. M' not accessing S has nothing to do with the violations; the corresponding access in the left figure is just shown as an additional option.

7   Soundness

In this section we give a partial proof of the soundness of our new shared access mechanism. We syntactically merge a shared machine and all its accessing machines into a new machine and the implementation of the shared machine along with the implementations of the accessors into a new implementation. Then we show that all the proof obligations of these two constructs, which do not contain the new mechanism, are implied by the obligations of the individual constructs. Namely, the invariant of the merged machine holds and the implementation is a correct refinement.

Because we have substitutions of both V_s and V'_s for O_s, we have to indicate which body is used. We write $[O_s \backslash V_s]$ for this extended substitution which includes the parameters, e.g., $[O_s \backslash V_s] (a \leftarrow O_s(b))$ equals $[u_s, w_s := a, b]V_s$ if u_s is the output and w_s the input parameter of O_s. We assume here that operations are not recursive.

Let M_s, M_1, and M'_1 be as in Sect. 6.2. Furthermore, let M_2 and M'_2 be like M_1 and M'_1 respectively, but with index '2'. With M'_S as in Fig. 4, we get the two merged constructs M and M' (Fig. 4). Note that V'_s gets substituted for O_s in the implementation M'.

```
IMPLEMENTATION          MACHINE M(P₁, P₂, Pₛ)       IMPLEMENTATION
  M's(Pₛ)                 CONSTRAINTS                   M'(P₁, P₂, Pₛ)
REFINES Mₛ                  C₁ ∧ C₂ ∧ Cₛ             REFINES M
CONCRETE_VARS             VARIABLES X₁, X₂, Xₛ        CONCRETE_VARS
  X'ₛ                      INVARIANT I₁ ∧ I₂ ∧ Iₛ       X'₁, X'₂, X'ₛ
INVARIANT I'ₛ             INITIALISATION              INVARIANT I'₁ ∧ I'₂ ∧ I'ₛ
INITIALISATION U'ₛ          Uₛ; [Oₛ\Vₛ](U₁ ‖ U₂)     INITIALISATION
OPERATIONS               OPERATIONS                    U'ₛ; [Oₛ\V'ₛ](U'₁; U'₂)
  uₛ ← Oₛ(wₛ) ≙            u₁ ← O₁(w₁) ≙            OPERATIONS
    BEGIN V'ₛ END            PRE Q₁ THEN                u₁ ← O₁(w₁) ≙
END                           [Oₛ\Vₛ]V₁                   BEGIN [Oₛ\V'ₛ]V'₁ END;
                           END;                          u₂ ← O₂(w₂) ≙
                         u₂ ← O₂(w₂) ≙                    BEGIN [Oₛ\V'ₛ]V'₂ END
                           PRE Q₂ THEN              END
                             [Oₛ\Vₛ]V₂
                           END
                       END
```

Fig. 4. Flattened Constructs

Theorem 1. *If all proof obligations of* M_s*,* M'_s*,* M_1*,* M'_1*,* M_2*, and* M'_2 *are true ([2, p 763ff], Sect. 6.2), then all proof obligations of* M *and* M' *hold.*

Several soundness proofs of the rely/guarantee method for shared variable systems have been given in the literature for different formalisms [24, 27, 1, 12]. The proof of this theorem is very similar.

8   Summary

8.1   Related Work

The use of assumptions and commitments to achieve compositionality in program verification was first proposed by Francez and Pnueli [11]. Jones introduced rely/guarantee conditions as a method for top-down program development [15]. Ketil Stølen has added wait-conditions to handle synchronization and auxiliary variables to increase expressiveness [24]. Jones himself applied the idea to object-oriented systems [16]. Rely/guarantee specifications have also been incorporated into temporal logic-based formalisms, thereby also capturing certain liveness properties: Collete added them to UNITY [7] and Abadi and Lamport to TLA [1]. Misra and Chandy have first used assumption/commitment specifications for message passing systems [19]. A unifying overview of shared variable and message passing assumption/commitment specifications is given by [26].

Neither VDM nor Z have an equally powerful modularization mechanism as B, although some constructions have been suggested [9, 13]. RAISE, Cogito, and other related formalisms provide different forms of modularization. However, we are not aware of any compositional symmetric shared access mechanism comparable to ours.

Both Jones [15] and Stølen [24] combined rely/guarantee specifications with a VDM like logic and syntax. However, their aim was to reason about concurrent programs only and they have not investigated rely/guarantee specifications in VDM for modular sharing. Whereas existing work has mostly focused on the use of assumption/commitment specifications for concurrent system, this paper has applied them to achieve compositionality in sequential systems with shared components.

Role-based contracts for different forms of collaborations have been proposed, e.g., by Helm et al for object-oriented systems [14] and by Francez and Forman for interacting processes [10]. Role-based specifications expressing rely/guarantee conditions as part of the shared construct are believed to be new. Traditionally, a rely/guarantee pair is part of each component to be composed. Centralization of all rely/guarantee specifications is possible in our case because only a single component is shared, whereas most other approaches handle mutual sharing. Our benefit is that all proofs for an accessor can be performed without knowing the other accessors.

Pioneering work in explaining the existing B composition mechanisms and their interplay with refinement has been done by Bert, Potet, and Rouzaud [5, 21].

8.2   Conclusions

We have extended the B method with a compositional symmetric shared access mechanism that overcomes the limitations of the single-writer restriction and the limited visibility of shared variables of the existing mechanisms. Based on rely/guarantee conditions expressed as accessor roles of the shared construct, the new mechanism is compositional, providing for independent refinement without the need to know the other accessors. The abstraction of possible modifications into compact role specifications simplifies the non-interference proofs. The new mechanism provides for flexible sharing on all levels; applications with sharing requirements can be specified, refined, and implemented without loss of modularity or underspecification as has been the case with the existing mechanisms. Uniform applicability in all constructs, replicated roles, multiple contracts, and good integration with existing composition mechanism add to the flexibility of the new mechanism.

For the new mechanism, we have given formal definitions of the syntax, the proof obligations, the visibility rules, and the restrictions on the composition graph. A partial soundness proof completes the paper.

Acknowledgments. Marina Waldén and Emil Sekerinski provided detailed comments on earlier drafts. We would also like to thank Wolfgang Weck for a number of fruitful discussions on the topic. The referees' comments are gratefully acknowledged.

References

[1] Martín Abadi and Leslie Lamport. Conjoining specifications. *ACM Transactions on Programming Languages and Systems*, 17(3):507–534, 1995.

[2] J. R. Abrial. *The B Book: Assigning Programs to Meanings*. Cambridge University Press, 1996.

[3] R. Back and J. von Wright. Trace refinement of action systems. In *CONCUR 94*, pages 367–384. LNCS 836, Springer Verlag, 1994.

[4] J. A. Bergstra, J. Heering, and P. Klint. Module algebra. *Journal of the ACM*, 37(2):335–372, 1990.

[5] Didier Bert, Marie-Laure Potet, and Yann Rouzaud. A study on components and assembly primitives in B. In *Proceedings of the first B conference*, pages 47–62, 3 rue du Maréchal Joffre, BP 34103, 44041 Nantes Cedex 1, 1996. IRIN Institut de recherche en informatique de Nantes.

[6] Martin Büchi. The B Bank. In Emil Sekerinski and Kaisa Sere, editors, *Program Development by Refinement: Case Studies Using the B Method*, chapter 4, pages 115–180. Springer Verlag, 1998. http://www.abo.fi/~mbuechi/publications/BBook.html.

[7] Pierre Collette. Application of the composition principle to UNITY-like specifications. In *Proceedings of TAPSOFT 93*, pages 230–242. LNCS 668, Springer Verlag, 1993.

[8] Willem-Paul de Roever. The quest for compositionality—a survey of assertion-based proof systems for concurrent programs, part I: Concurrency based on shared variables. In F.J. Neuhold and G. Chroust, editors, *Proceedings of the IFIP Working Conference "The role of abstract models in computer science"*, pages 181–205. North-Holland, 1985.

[9] J.S. Fitzgerald and C. B. Jones. Modularizing the formal description of a database system. In *VDM'90: VDM and Z – Formal Methods in Software Development*, pages 189–210. LNCS 428, Springer Verlag, 1990.

[10] N. Francez and I. Forman. *Interacting Processes: A Multiparty Approach to Coordinated Distributed Programming*. ACM Press, 1996.

[11] Nissim Francez and Amir Pnueli. A proof method for cyclic programs. *Acta Informatica*, 9:133–157, 1978.

[12] Peter Grønning, Thomas Qvist Nielsen, and Hans Henrik Løvengreen. Refinement and composition of transition-based rely-guarantee specifications with auxiliary variables. In *Proceedings of the 10th Conference on Foundations of Software Technology and Theoretical Computer Science*, pages 332–348. LNCS 472, Springer Verlag, 1990.

[13] I. J. Hayes and L. P. Wildman. Towards libraries for Z. In J. P. Bowen and J. E. Nicholls, editors, *Z User Workshop: Proceedings of the Seventh Annual Z User Meeting*, Workshops in Computing. Springer Verlag, 1993.

[14] Richard Helm, Ian M. Holland, and Dipayan Gangopadhyay. Contracts: Specifying behavioral compositions in object-oriented systems. In *Proceedings of OOPSLA/ECOOP '90*, pages 169–180, 1990.

[15] Cliff B. Jones. Specification and design of (parallel) programs. In *Proceedings of IFIP'83*, pages 321–332. North Holland, 1983.

[16] Cliff B. Jones. Accomodating interference in the formal design of concurrent object-based programs. *Formal Methods in System Design*, 8(2):105–122, March 1996.

[17] Leslie Lamport. The temporal logic of actions. *ACM Transactions of Programming Languages and Systems*, 16(3):872–923, 1994.

[18] Kevin Lano. Integrating formal and structured methods in object-oriented system development. In S.J. Goldsack and S.J.H. Kent, editors, *Formal Methods and Object Technology*. Springer Verlag, 1996.

[19] J. Misra and M. Chandy. Proofs of networks of processes. *IEEE Software Engineering*, 7(4):417–426, 1981.

[20] S. Owicki and D. Gries. An axiomatic proof technique for parallel programs. *Acta Informatica*, 6:319–340, 1976.

[21] Marie-Laure Potet and Yann Rouzaud. Composition and refinement in the B-method. In *Proceedings of the second B conference*, pages 46–65. LNCS 1393, Springer Verlag, 1998.

[22] Emil Sekerinski and Kaisa Sere, editors. *Program Develoment by Refinement: Case Studies Using the B Method*. FACIT. Springer Verlag, 1998.

[23] Kaisa Sere and Marina Waldén. Data refinement of remote procedures. In *Proceedings of TACS 97*, pages 267–294. LNCS 1281, Springer Verlag, 1997.

[24] Ketil Stølen. *Development of Parallel Programs on Shared Data-Structures*. PhD thesis, University of Manchester, 1990. Available as technical report UMCS-91-1-1.

[25] Qiwen Xu. On compositionality in refining concurrent systems. In J. He, J. Cooke, and P. Wallis, editors, *Proceedings of the BCS FACS 7th Refinement Workshop*. Electronic Workshops in Computing, Springer Verlag, 1996.

[26] Qiwen Xu, Antonio Cau, and Pierre Collette. On unifying assumption-commitment style proof rules for concurrency. In *Proceedings of CONCUR 94*, pages 267–282. LNCS 836, Springer Verlag, 1994.

[27] Qiwen Xu, Willem-Paul de Roever, and Jifeng He. The rely-guarantee method for verifying shared variable concurrent programs. *Formal Aspects of Computing*, 9(2):149–174, 1997.

Structural Embeddings: Mechanization with Method

César Muñoz[1] and John Rushby[2]*

[1] Institute for Computer Applications in Science and Engineering (ICASE)
Mail Stop 132C, 3 West Reid Street
NASA Langley Research Center
Hampton VA 23681-2199
munoz@icase.edu
[2] Computer Science Laboratory
SRI International
333 Ravenswood Avenue
Menlo Park, CA 94025, USA
rushby@csl.sri.com

Abstract. The most powerful tools for analysis of formal specifications are general-purpose theorem provers and model checkers, but these tools provide scant methodological support. Conversely, those approaches that do provide a well-developed method generally have less powerful automation. It is natural, therefore, to try to combine the better-developed methods with the more powerful general-purpose tools. An obstacle is that the methods and the tools often employ very different logics.

We argue that methods are separable from their logics and are largely concerned with the structure and organization of specifications. We propose a technique called *structural embedding* that allows the structural elements of a method to be supported by a general-purpose tool, while substituting the logic of the tool for that of the method. We have found this technique quite effective and we provide some examples of its application. We also suggest how general-purpose systems could be restructured to support this activity better.

1 Introduction

In recent years, the capabilities of theorem provers oriented towards support of formal methods (we call them *verification systems*) have increased enormously. Systems such as ACL2 [23], Coq [5], Eves [42], HOL [27], Isabelle [36], and PVS [30] each come with a very rich specification language and a battery of decision procedures and proof strategies highly tuned to their logic. Some also provide convenient access to model checkers or to specialized decision procedures through built-in embeddings and interpretations, and some are able to generate

---

* This work was supported by National Science Foundation grant CCR-9509931 while the first author was an International Fellow at SRI International.

J. Wing, J. Woodcock, J. Davies (Eds.): FM'99, Vol. I, LNCS 1708, pp. 452–471, 1999.

efficiently executable code. This integration of rich specification languages with powerful automation allows general-purpose verification systems to attack very complex problems in a broad spectrum of domains [40].

A commonly-cited drawback to the use of these systems, is their lack of methodological support for the global process of specification and software development: with their emphasis on deductive support, the overall structure of a development is relegated to an external (informal or formal) methodology with little automated support. For this reason, some people complain that there is little method in formal methods.

On the other hand, formal notations such as B [1], VDM [22], Z [44], and the requirements methodologies that employ tabular specifications [25,43,19] emphasize the methodological aspects of software specification and development. That is to say, they suggest how specifications should be structured and organized, how different specifications should be related to each other and to executable programs, and what theorems (i.e., "proof obligations") should be posed and proved in order to gain confidence in a specification or in the correctness of a refinement. These methods provide a formal notation and sometimes provide automated support for their methodological aspects, but usually their logic is supported only by relatively limited and specialized theorem provers, so that it can be tedious to discharge proof obligations, and difficult to establish properties of the overall specification.

It is natural to ask whether the complementary strengths of general-purpose verification systems and of the more methodical formal notations can be combined in some way. One way to do this is by a *semantic embedding* of the formal notation within the logic of the verification system. Two variants have been identified: *deep* and *shallow* embeddings [10].

In a deep embedding, the language and semantics of the method are fully formalized as an object in the logic of the specification language. In this case, it is possible to prove meta-theoretical properties of the embedded method, but the statement and proof of properties for a particular application require painful encoding into the formalized semantics. In the shallow approach, there is a syntactic translation of the objects of the method into semantically equivalent objects in the language of the verification system. In this case, meta-theoretical properties cannot be stated, but the encoding and analysis of particular applications is simpler.

Both of these approaches consider the formal notation as a unity and do not separate method from logic. This is consistent with the way most formal methods are presented—the methodological aspects of B, for example, are described in terms of a certain set theory [1], and a certain logic of partial terms is introduced to support the method of tabular specifications [34].

We question whether such unity—the tight coupling of method and logic— really is necessary. To our thinking, the method-specific aspects tend to be at the outermost, or "structural" levels of the specification language, and are not very sensitive to the actual logic employed for expressions inside the structure.

For example, the tabular method employs tables to specify aspects of a system's requirements or behavior, but is largely indifferent to the logic in which table entries are specified, provided that it possesses certain attributes (e.g., an adequate treatment of partial functions).

Given this perspective, we propose a new kind of embedding, in which the structural part of a method is embedded in the logic of the verification system (by means of either a shallow or a deep embedding, but most commonly the former), while the logic part of the method (its notation for expressions) is simply *replaced* by that of the verification system. By fitting the structural language elements of a method around a well-supported logic, we get the best of both worlds, and quite cheaply. Of course, this will not satisfy those who require the authentic language of a particular formal method, but it provides an attractive way to support the "style" of such a method, or to add methodological discipline to the raw logic of a verification system.

In this paper we study this variation on embedding, which we call *structural embedding*. The paper is organized as follows. We give an overview of the notions involved in this kind of embedding in Section 2 and we describe examples in Sections 3, and 4. The final section compares this approach with others, and discusses how general-purpose verification systems could be restructured to better support this type of activity.

2   Structural Embedding

A formal method provides a specification language, which is built on a particular logic. Since formal methods are intended to organize formal specifications, the specification language is invariably structured in several syntactic levels. Usually, the outermost level concerns some notion of "module" and relationships among these, while the innermost level provides the expression language.

Different names are used for the top-level module constructs in different specification languages: for example, machines in B, schemas in Z, theories in PVS. Specification languages usually provide several mechanisms to combine their modules in order to build large-scale systems. Most of the method in a formal method is expressed at this level. For example, invariants may be specified at the module level, giving rise to proof obligations on the operations specified within each module, or refinement relationships may be specified across modules, giving rise to further proof obligations.

An *embedding* is a semantic encoding of one specification language into another, intended to allow tools for the one to be extended to the other. In our context, we are interested in embedding the specification language of a formal method into that of a verification system. Using embeddings, the complementary strengths of several formal methods and verification systems can be combined to support different aspects of verified software development.

The semantics of the language of a formal method can be encoded in a verification system either by using an extra-logical translation (i.e., a kind of compiler), in which case we speak of a *shallow* embedding; or it can be defined directly in the specification language of the verification system, and in this case we talk of a *deep* embedding [10]. In a *structural* embedding, which is orthogonal to both of these, only the outermost level of the specification language is embedded in the logic of the verification system. The innermost level of the specification language is directly *replaced*, not embedded, by the expression language of the verification system. The logical framework of the embedded notation relies completely on the specification language of the verification system.

We can describe the way this works as follows. Let $\mathcal{L}_{\mathrm{FM}}$ and $\mathcal{L}_{\mathrm{VS}}$ be the specification languages of a formal method and a verification system, respectively. By language abuse, we use the same symbols for their logics. We use the judgment $S \models_{\mathcal{L}} P$ to mean that P is a property satisfied by the specification S in the logic $\mathcal{L}$. In these terms, a semantic embedding is a translation $\_^* : \mathcal{L}_{\mathrm{FM}} \mapsto \mathcal{L}_{\mathrm{VS}}$ satisfying

$$S \models_{\mathcal{L}_{\mathrm{FM}}} P \;\Rightarrow\; \mathcal{L}_{\mathrm{FM}}\_in\_\mathcal{L}_{\mathrm{VS}} \wedge S^* \models_{\mathcal{L}_{\mathrm{VS}}} P^*$$

where $\mathcal{L}_{\mathrm{FM}}\_in\_\mathcal{L}_{\mathrm{VS}}$ is the set of axioms and definitions in $\mathcal{L}_{\mathrm{VS}}$ encoding the semantics of $\mathcal{L}_{\mathrm{FM}}$. The shallow or deep degree of the embedding depends on the information contained in $\mathcal{L}_{\mathrm{FM}}\_in\_\mathcal{L}_{\mathrm{VS}}$.

For a structural embedding, we consider that $\mathcal{L}_{\mathrm{FM}}$ consist of two sub-languages $\mathcal{L}_{\mathrm{FM}} = \mathcal{L}^o_{\mathrm{FM}} \cup \mathcal{L}^i_{\mathrm{FM}}$, where $\mathcal{L}^o_{\mathrm{FM}}$ represents the outermost level of language, and $\mathcal{L}^i_{\mathrm{FM}}$ represents the innermost one. First, we construct $\mathcal{L}'_{\mathrm{FM}} = \mathcal{L}^{o\prime}_{\mathrm{FM}} \cup \mathcal{L}_{\mathrm{VS}}$, which replaces the inner language by that of the verification system and adjusts $\mathcal{L}^o_{\mathrm{FM}}$ (as $\mathcal{L}^{o\prime}_{\mathrm{FM}}$) to accommodate its new context while preserving its "intent." There is no formal relationship or mechanical translation between $\mathcal{L}_{\mathrm{FM}}$ and $\mathcal{L}'_{\mathrm{FM}}$—the goal is simply to preserve the ideas and intent of the method to the extent possible.

A structural embedding is then a translation $\_^* : \mathcal{L}^{o\prime}_{\mathrm{FM}} \mapsto \mathcal{L}_{\mathrm{VS}}$, which is extended to $\_^* : \mathcal{L}'_{\mathrm{FM}} \mapsto \mathcal{L}_{\mathrm{VS}}$ in the obvious way (as the identity on $\mathcal{L}_{\mathrm{VS}}$) satisfying

$$S \models_{\mathcal{L}'_{\mathrm{FM}}} P \;\Rightarrow\; \mathcal{L}^{o\prime}_{\mathrm{FM}}\_in\_\mathcal{L}_{\mathrm{VS}} \wedge S^* \models_{\mathcal{L}_{\mathrm{VS}}} P^*$$

where $\mathcal{L}^{o\prime}_{\mathrm{FM}}\_in\_\mathcal{L}_{\mathrm{VS}}$ is the set of axioms and definitions in $\mathcal{L}_{\mathrm{VS}}$ encoding the semantics of $\mathcal{L}^{o\prime}_{\mathrm{FM}}$. Notice that the semantics of $\mathcal{L}^i_{\mathrm{FM}}$ are not embedded, and that both of shallow and deep embedding are still possible for $\mathcal{L}^{o\prime}_{\mathrm{FM}}$.

To preserve intent in a structural embedding requires that well-formedness of specifications is preserved in both logics. That is,

$$\models_{\mathcal{L}_{\mathrm{FM}}} Sound_{\mathcal{L}_{\mathrm{FM}}}(S) \;\Leftrightarrow\; \mathcal{L}'_{\mathrm{FM}}\_in\_\mathcal{L}_{\mathrm{VS}} \models_{\mathcal{L}_{\mathrm{VS}}} Sound_{\mathcal{L}_{\mathrm{VS}}}(S^*).$$

By $Sound_{\mathcal{L}}(S)$, we mean the set of formulas (proof obligations) that guarantees some method-specific well-formedness property of specification S in logic $\mathcal{L}$ (e.g., the checks for overlapping or missing conditions in a tabular specification). Formal methods are often concerned with metalogical relationships between specifications (e.g., that one should be a refinement of another, or that one should be an invariant for the other), and *Sound* is then extended to the proof obligations that ensure satisfaction of the desired relationship. Notice that *Sound* is parameterized by the logic. In practice, we expect that *Sound* relies only on very general properties of a logic, so that proof obligations retain their intuitive content under the structural embedding.

In the following two sections we present concrete examples of structural embeddings.

3   The B-Method in PVS

In this first example, we describe a structural embedding of the B-method in the higher-order logic of PVS.

The B-method [1] is a state-oriented formal method mainly intended for development of sequential systems. The underlying logic of the method is a set theory with a first-order predicate calculus. PVS [30] is a verification system whose specification language is a higher-order logic with a type system. PVS does not come with a particular built-in methodology.

3.1   An Overview of the B-Method

In B, specifications are structured in modules called *machines*. Machines can be of three kinds: *abstract machines*, *refinements*, and *implementations*. Each kind of machine corresponds to a different stage of software development. The initial specification of a problem is given by a set of abstract machines. Refinements allows data reification of specifications. Final refinements, those that are not intended to be refined anymore, are called implementations.

A machine is an abstract description of the statics and dynamics of a system. Statics are given by a state declaration: constants, properties of the constants, variables, and an invariant (a property satisfied by the state of the machine). Dynamics are given by operations or services provided by the machine. In contrast to other stated oriented methods, operations in B are not specified by *before-after* predicates, but by an equivalent mechanism of predicate transformers called *generalized substitutions*.

Large software development is supported using several composition mechanisms. These mechanisms give different access privileges to the operations or to the local variables of an external machine. In this way, it is possible to build complex machines incrementally by using previously defined ones. Thus, by using the unified notation of machines, B supports the complete life cycle of software development.

Several cases studies of developments in B are reported in [7]. That work pointed out some drawbacks of the B-method:

- Although typing conditions can be handled using the set theory provided by B, mathematical objects such as variables or functions are not explicitly typed. In some cases this "free-typing" style obscures the specifications.

- The generalized substitutions mechanism encourages the writing of algorithmic specifications. Some kind of operations could be more naturally expressed by before-after predicates. The same conclusion was drawn by Bicarregui and Ritchie in [8].
- Support for data types is limited. In particular, record types are absent in the B notation.
- Proof obligations usually deal with type conditions that could be easily solved by a type checker.
- B imposes a very rigid discipline. For instance, parameters of a machine are restricted to be scalars or uninterpreted sets. In some cases such restrictions seem to be very strong.

Most of these criticisms concern the limitation of the formal notation rather than the methodological aspects of B. We argue that it is possible to separate the abstract machine mechanism from its specification language, and to use the expression language of PVS instead of that of B. In this way, we combine the best features of each technique: the methodology of B, and the expressiveness and richness (and automation) of the specification language of PVS.

3.2   An Example: A Drinks Dispenser Machine

To concretize our ideas, we present in Figure 1 an example of a drinks dispenser specification written in B by Leno and Haughton [24]. The specification is, for most of the parts, self-explanatory.

At first glance, the expressions of the machine `Dispenser` could be easily translated to PVS. For instance, the invariant

$$\texttt{dstate} \in \texttt{DSTATE} \land \texttt{given} \in \texttt{NAT} \land \texttt{given} \leq \texttt{lifetime}$$

literally corresponds to the PVS expression

```
member(dstate,DSTATE) AND member(given,NAT) AND given <= lifetime.
```

However, the PVS specification language is fully-typed while the B notation is not. For instance, although it is possible to define a set in PVS containing all the natural numbers, the normal way to handle a property like `given` $\in$ `NAT` in PVS is by using a type declaration `given:NAT`—the natural numbers are a basic type in PVS, whereas they are a predefined set in B.[1] Thus, in PVS, the invariant is reduced to

$$\texttt{given} \texttt{ <= } \texttt{lifetime}.$$

and its other two clauses become typing judgments.

---

[1] In fact, in B, `NAT` is the predefined set of naturals numbers between 1 and `maxint`, where `maxinit` is not known a priori. PVS can also represent this as a type: `subrange(1,maxint)`.

```
Dispenser_in_PVS [ lifetime:nat ] : MACHINE
BEGIN
  TYPES
    DSTATE = {stocked, unstocked}

  CONSTANTS
    ok : nat = 0
    notok : nat = 1

  VARIABLES
    dstate : DSTATE
    given : nat

  INVARIANT
    given <= lifetime

  INITIALIZATION
    dstate := unstocked ||
    given := 0

  OPERATIONS
    restock =
      dstate := stocked

    give_drink =
      PRE dstate = stocked AND given < lifetime THEN
        dstate :: DSTATE ||
        given := given + 1
      END

    is_stocked : nat =
      IF dstate = stocked THEN
        ok
      ELSE
        notok
      ENDIF

    count : nat =
      given

END Dispenser_in_PVS
```

Fig. 2. The Drinks Dispenser Machine Structurally Embedded in PVS

The general type defined for `Dispenser_in_PVS` is

```
Dispenser_in_PVS_Type : TYPE = [#
  dstate:DSTATE,
  given:nat
#]
```

(Record types in PVS are declared by using the brackets `[#,#]`. Instances of a record type are given between `(#,#)` parentheses. Record and function overriding are indicated in PVS by the `WITH` construct.)

The invariant of the machine is handled by the following type:

```
Dispenser_in_PVS : TYPE =
  { self: Dispenser_in_PVS_Type | given(self) <= lifetime }
```

An operation op of a machine M with inputs $i_1:I_1, \ldots, i_n:I_n$ and outputs $o_1:O_1, \ldots, o_m:O_m$, is translated into PVS as a function `op(`$i_1:I_1, \ldots, i_n:I_n$`)(self:M) : [`$o_1:O_1, \ldots, o_m:O_m$`,self_out:M]`. If op has no inputs and outputs, its signature is simply `op(self:M):M`. For instance:

```
restock(self:Dispenser_in_PVS) : Dispenser_in_PVS =
  LET self =
    self WITH [
      dstate := stocked
    ] IN
  self
```

Generalized substitutions are interpreted as PVS expressions dealing with record field overriding, function updating, set operations, and typing conditions. Certain kinds of compositions are supported by using the importing mechanism of PVS. The complete embedding is described in [28].

Soundness of a B machine corresponds to type correctness of the PVS theory embedding it. Therefore, the proof obligations to be checked are just the type correctness conditions (TCCs) generated by the PVS type system, and so it is possible to use the automation provided by the PVS type-checker and theorem prover. The type correctness conditions generated for the PVS embedding of a B machine guarantee that the initial state satisfies the invariant and that the invariant is preserved by the operations.

PVS generates four TCCs for the machine `Dispenser_in_PVS`. All of them are automatically discharged by the theorem prover. For instance, the TCC corresponding to the initialization clause is

```
init_TCC1 :

  |-------
{1} (∀ (self):
          self = (# dstate := unstocked, given := 0 #) ⇒
          0 ≤ lifetime)
```

The embedding that we have described corresponds to a shallow structural embedding. That is, meta-theoretical properties about the abstract machine notation cannot be proved. It has been completely implemented by a front-end tool called PBS [28]. An alternative deeper embedding has been proposed in [9]. That work formalizes the generalized substitution mechanism of the B-method in the higher-order logic of Coq and PVS. In this case, it is possible to verify meta-theoretical properties about generalized substitutions.

3.4   The PBS System

PBS works like a compiler. It takes as input a file *m.bps* containing an abstract machine and generates its corresponding embedding as a PVS theory in the file *m.pvs*. We have rewritten several examples of abstract machines from [24, 1, 29] in PBS. The results obtained are satisfactory according to our expectations: trivial type conditions are discharged automatically by the type checker of PVS, and most of the other proof obligations can be solved by the automated decision procedures and strategies provided by its theorem prover.

Table 1 summarizes one of these developments. Client, Product, and Invoice are part of an invoice system developed in [1]. The example provides the basic functionality of a data processing system. During the development, the type checker of PVS allowed us to find some minor errors in the specification given in [1].

Machine	PBS (in lines)	PVS theory (in lines)	TCCs	Auto proved
Client	56	83	12	100%
Product	66	92	18	83%
Invoice	125	166	48	87%

Table 1. Metrics of Some Examples

Büchi [11, 12] describes a prototypical banking application implemented in two commercial tools supporting the B-method: Atelier B from Steria and the B-Toolkit from B-Core. Bank is the largest machine of that system, and we have rewritten it in PBS. In Table 2, we compare our metrics for this example with those given by Büchi. [3]

The difference between the size of the files is due to the fact that many properties are attached to the types of the variables and parameters in the PBS specification and therefore need not be repeated in the invariant and the pre-conditions to the operations, making the specification shorter. The proof obligations of the PBS and B machines do not correspond one-to-one either: recall that proof obligations in PBS machines are generated by the type checker

---

[3] For these developments we are using PVS Version 2.3.

Machine	File length (in lines)	Proof obligations	Auto proved
Bank in PBS	232	47	94%
Bank in B	362	49	95%

Table 2. Comparison Between B and PBS Machines

of PVS, which is able to solve some type conditions internally, and to subsume some type conditions in others.

A feature introduced in PVS Version 2.3 allows PVS "ground terms" (i.e., executable definitions applied to concrete data) to be evaluated via compilation into Lisp. The compiler (due to N. Shankar) uses sophisticated static analysis to eliminate some of the inefficiencies of applicative programs, so that compiled PVS executes extremely rapidly. Combined with the refinement mechanism of the B-Method, this provides good support for rapid prototyping, testing, and code generation. For example, by refining the PVS choice function that interprets the ANY construct of B into a linear search, we obtain a rapid prototype for the B-Bank that can perform many thousand Bank operations (create an account, make a deposit, perform a balance enquiry, etc.) per second.

PBS and some of the examples that we have developed are available electronically at: http://www.csl.sri.com/~munoz/src/PBS.

4 Tabular Representations

Several methods for documentation and analysis of requirements make some use of tabular specifications. These include methods such as SCR and CoRE that are derived from the "four variable model" of Parnas [35], the RSML notation of Leveson [25], and the decision tables of Sherry [43]. All these methods can be considered as having two levels of "structure" above their base logic: the top level provides the attributes that are unique to each method, but the lower level is broadly similar across all of them: it is the use of tables to define functions by cases. A simple example is the following definition of the function $sign(x)$, which returns $-1, 0$, or 1 according to whether its integer argument is negative, zero, or positive.

$$sign(x) = \begin{array}{|c|c|c|} \hline x < 0 & x = 0 & x > 0 \\ \hline -1 & 0 & +1 \\ \hline \end{array}$$

This is an example of a piecewise continuous function that requires definition by cases, and the tabular presentation provides two benefits.

- It provides a visually attractive presentation of the definition that eases comprehension.
- It makes the cases explicit, thereby allowing checks that none of them overlap and that none have been forgotten.
  The checks for forgotten and overlapping cases generate proof obligations that have been shown to be a potent tool for error detection [19].

The structural properties of tables interact with well-definedness concerns for the underlying logic, as seen in the following table from [33, Figure 1] where the applications of the (real-valued) square root function in the second and third rows can only be shown to be well-defined (that is, to have nonnegative arguments) when the corresponding row constraints are taken into account.

	$y = 27$	$y > 27$	$y < 27$
$x = 3$	$27 + \sqrt{27}$	$54 + \sqrt{27}$	$y^2 + 3$
$x < 3$	$27 + \sqrt{-(x-3)}$	$y + \sqrt{-(x-3)}$	$y^2 + (x-3)^2$
$x > 3$	$27 + \sqrt{x-3}$	$2 \times y + \sqrt{x-3}$	$y^2 + (3-x)^2$

Another interaction is seen when tables allow "don't care" and blank entries (which must be shown to be unreachable).

An example of the latter is the quotient lookup table for an SRT divider shown at right. The notorious Pentium FDIV bug was due to bad entries in similar table. The triangular-shaped blank regions at top and bottom of these tables are never referenced by the division algorithm; the Pentium error was that certain entries believed to be in this inaccessible region, and containing arbitrary data, were, in fact, sometimes referenced during execution [37]. Proof obligations to show that such regions truly are unreachable can help avoid such errors [39, 26].

Notice that the logic required to provide an interpretation for tables with blank entries must be one that provides either partial functions, or dependent typing.

	000	001	010	011	100	101	110	111
01010								2
01001						2	2	2
01000					2	2	2	2
00111			2	2	2	2	2	2
00110		2	2	2	2	2	2	2
00101	2	2	2	2	2	2	2	1
00100	2	2	2	2	c	1	1	1
00011	2	c	1	1	1	1	1	1
00010	1	1	1	1	1	1	1	1
00001	1	1	1	1	e	0	0	0
00000	0	0	0	0	0	0	0	0
11111	0	0	0	0	0	0	0	0
11110	-1	-1	d	d	0	0	0	0
11101	-1	-1	-1	-1	-1	-1	-1	-1
11100	a	b	-1	-1	-1	-1	-1	-1
11011	-2	-2	-2	b	-1	-1	-1	-1
11010	-2	-2	-2	-2	-2	-2	b	-1
11001	-2	-2	-2	-2	-2	-2	-2	-2
11000			-2	-2	-2	-2	-2	-2
10111				-2	-2	-2	-2	-2
10110						-2	-2	-2
10101							-2	-2

Parnas [34] proposes a partial term logic similar to that of Beeson [6, Section 5] for dealing with these complexities. Parnas' approach is perfectly satisfactory, but we contend that tables are a structural element that can be hosted, with suitable adjustments and restrictions, on almost any logic.

In particular, the predicate and dependent typing of PVS [41], although quite different to Parnas' logic, provides an adequate foundation for a very rich set of tabular constructions. The structural embedding of tables into PVS is a shallow one that differs from the PBS embedding of B by being integrated directly into PVS using an intermediate COND construct [31]. It would have been perfectly feasible to use an external translation similar to that of PBS, but tables seemed of sufficiently general utility that we preferred a more tightly integrated implementation. The specific tabular constructions of SCR, RSML, and Sherry can then be encoded into the generic PVS tables using techniques described in [31].

The structural embedding of tables in PVS can be compared with an alternative approach where theorem provers have been used as back-ends to method-specific table analyzers. One example is RSML, where proof obligations generated by a dedicated tool have been submitted to a BDD-based tautology checker [18], PVS [17], and the Stanford Validity Checker (SVC) [32]. In all these cases, the back-end tools are used only to examine proof obligations that ensure no overlapping or forgotten cases: they do not have access to other specification properties (e.g., they would not be able to state or prove that $sign(x)$ is idempotent). With the structural embedding in PVS, however, the full specification is available for analysis; [31] describe examples where PVS is used to analyze (by theorem proving and model checking) properties of tabular specifications that extend beyond simple consistency of the tables themselves.

5   Comparison, Recommendation, and Conclusion

A formal *method* provides guidance and discipline in the application of formal mathematics to the processes of specification, design, and implementation of software and hardware systems. Verification systems, theorem provers, and model checkers can provide mechanized support for the analysis of such formal descriptions. If we want both method and mechanization, there seem to be four basic choices.

- Develop mechanized support for the chosen method from the ground up. The B tools exemplify this approach.
- Develop front-end tools for the chosen method and use existing verification systems and model checkers for back-end reasoning support. For example, the front end tools may generate proof obligations that are submitted to a theorem prover. Some of the tools developed for RSML and SCR exemplify this approach.
- Provide an embedding of the chosen method into the logic supported by a verification system. Embeddings of VDM in PVS and Isabelle exemplify this approach.
- Add method to an existing verification system or model checker. Structural embeddings are one way to do this: we take the structural or "method" level of the language from an existing method and wrap it around the logic of a verification system (or, dually, we take an existing method and replace the "logic" level of its language by that of a verification system). The structural embedding of B in PVS by the PBS tool exemplifies this approach.

The "ground up" approach potentially can deliver the most seamless integration, but incurs the very high cost of developing a customized theorem prover for the chosen method. It is not just that theorem provers are large and complex tools, and therefore expensive to develop and maintain. The largest cost is the hidden one of gaining the experience necessary to build an effective theorem prover: these systems require delicate judgments concerning how to integrate interaction and automation, how to combine rewriting and decision procedures, how to decide combinations of theories, how to integrate decision procedures with heuristics, and how to combine an expressive notation with effective deductive support. It is no accident that the most effective verification systems come from groups that have been building them for a decade or more, and that have learned from many failures.

The "back-end" approach can be an effective way to discharge proof obligations, but does not allow the verification system to provide any other kind of deductive support. For example, as noted, the RSML table analyzer generates proof obligations that have been submitted to several different theorem proving components, but these tools see only the proof obligations and do not have access to the full specification. When a different kind of analysis is desired—for example, checking of invariants—then a different translator and a different back end tool (e.g., a model checker) may be required [13]. By contrast, the structural embedding of tables in PVS allows all the capabilities of PVS to be applied to the full specification, including use of its model checker to examine invariants [31].

Checking of proof obligations with a back-end tool is not without difficulties. First is the question of compatibility between the logic of the method and that of the back-end tool. The choices are between embedding the logic of the method in that of the tool, and simply replacing the former by the latter when generating proof obligations. Pratten [38] describes a tool that adopts the former approach: it generates a PVS representation of proof obligations for the B method that conform to the standard semantics of B given in [1]. The RSML table analyzer adopts the latter approach (which can also be considered a shallow embedding, since RSML specifications use a simple fragment of first order logic). Second is the issue of providing an adequate formalization of all the supporting theories required for a given specification. For example, formal analysis of a program that uses a data structure to represent a graph will require access to a formalization of some fragment of graph theory. If supporting theories are written in the notation of the formal method, then analysis will be complicated by their embedding into the language of the verification system; also, supporting theories should generally be written in a way that supports effective deduction (e.g., by presenting definitions and lemmas in a form that is convenient for rewriting), and this may be contrary to the style of the method. If the supporting theories are written directly in the language of the verification system, then the intended method is not followed to the full extent, and the specifier must master two different specification languages and styles.

Traditional shallow and deep embeddings also suffer from the drawbacks just outlined. Furthermore, the difficulties of embedding a formal specification language in a different logic are greater when the full notation is to be supported, rather than just its proof obligations. Agerholm [2] describes a shallow embedding of VDM-SL into PVS that transforms VDM-SL constructs to similar PVS constructs, and Agerholm, Bicarregui and Maharaj [3] describe an extension of this approach to support refinements. Although the constructs are often similar, they are not identical, so the semantics of the VDM-SL specifications are not fully preserved by this embedding. Agerholm and Frost [4] describe an alternative embedding of VDM-SL into Isabelle; here, the semantics are preserved but the embedding is correspondingly more difficult.

Whenever the notation of one method is supported by the logic and mechanization of another (whether as a back-end or by embedding), there is tension between supporting the semantics of the former vs. fully exploiting the mechanization of the latter. And if one notation is supported by more than one tool, there is the additional concern that each will provide slightly different semantics.

Structural embeddings sidestep these concerns because they do not claim to preserve the full semantics of the original method. A structural embedding of VDM, for example, would be similar to the first of the two VDM embeddings mentioned above, except that the logic of VDM would be *replaced* by that of the verification system concerned, and a traditional embedding would be provided only for the outermost, or structural level of the VDM language (e.g., its notions of state and of refinement). Of course, the resulting system would not support true VDM any more than PBS supports true B, and this would be a fatal defect for some users. However, we believe that others will value the methodological contributions of VDM, or B, more than the idiosyncrasies of their logics and would be happy to trade those logics for others in return for better automated support of their preferred method.

There are some potential difficulties, however, to this approach. In the first place, even quite good verification systems are not uniformly effective, and the encodings produced by structural embeddings may take them into areas where they perform poorly. For example, one of the proof obligations generated by the RSML checker caused PVS to go into an apparently endless computation [17] (this was a back-end application rather than a structural embedding but the problem would be the same in either case). In fact, PVS had discovered that the formula was not a propositional tautology within a couple of seconds (which is all the user wanted to know), and then spent the next several days trying to calculate a minimal set of subgoals to return to the user (there were well over 1,000). Design choices made in the expectation that the user is conducting an interactive proof of a human-generated conjecture may be inappropriate when dealing with formulas generated by mechanical translation.

A related problem is that most interactive verification systems assume that a human is guiding the process, and they therefore provide only rudimentary interfaces for other programs. A deeper manifestation of the same design philosophy is the monolithic, closed nature of most verification systems: it is almost impossible for outside programs to interact with their components or to query their internal data structures, and correspondingly difficult to create customized capabilities.

Our recommendation (which is hardly original) is that verification systems should be restructured into open collections of components with well-defined application programming interfaces (APIs) that allow other programs to invoke their capabilities. A cluster of components interacting through a shared intermediate language might be a suitable overall architecture.[4] A front-end providing structural embedding for some formal method could then communicate with the verification system through its intermediate language and its APIs.

Some embedding tools have already adopted a similar architecture, but with only monolithic verification systems connected to their intermediate languages. Gravell and Pratten [15] describe a tool that automates conventional embedding of a formal notation within the logic of a verification system. The tool, called JavaLIL, has been used for the embedding of Z specifications into the higher-order logics of PVS and HOL [14]. Gravell and Pratten justly bemoan difficulties caused by the monolithic, closed character of the verification systems used. In a similar vein, Jacobs et al. [21, 20] describe a tool called LOOP to support embeddings of object oriented languages in general-purpose verification systems.

Structural embedding does not serve the same ends as these tools: its purpose is not to support the full language of an existing formal method, but to capture just its *methodological* attributes and to support those in conjunction with the language of an existing verification system. We believe that those for whom methodology and mechanized support are more important than the authentic language of a specific formal method may find that a structural embedding provides a cost-effective way to achieve their goals.

Of course, structural embedding does not solve all the problems of providing effective automated support for formal methods. There is more to a method than just its deductive aspects (although deductive support is the *sine qua non* of truly *formal* methods): a fully supported method also supplies automated assistance in documentation and traceability, prototyping and code development, testing and validation, and the project management that ties all these together. We would hope that these capabilities could be created by customizing (or, if necessary, developing) generic tools that support these functions, and that such generic tools could be incorporated in the open architecture described previously.

Acknowledgments The authors would like to thank N. Shankar and the anonymous referees for constructive criticism and helpful comments.

---

[4] This is the approach adopted by the SAL (Symbolic Analysis Laboratory) project at SRI, Berkeley and Stanford. However, SAL is intended to promote cooperative use of complete tools such as model checkers and theorem provers, not the components of such tools; its focus is the use of abstraction in analysis of concurrent systems represented as transition systems.

References

[1] J.-R. Abrial. *The B-Book—Assigning Programs to Meanings.* Cambridge University Press, 1996.

[2] Sten Agerholm. Translating specifications in VDM-SL to PVS. In Joakim von Wright, Jim Grundy, and John Harrison, editors, *Theorem Proving in Higher Order Logics: 9th International Conference, TPHOLs '96,* volume 1125 of *Lecture Notes in Computer Science,* pages 1–16, Turku, Finland, August 1996. Springer-Verlag.

[3] Sten Agerholm, Juan Bicarregui, and Savi Maharaj. On the verification of VDM specification and refinement with PVS. In Juan Bicarregui, editor, *Proof in VDM: Case Studies,* FACIT (Formal Approaches to Computing and Information Technology), chapter 6, pages 157–190. Springer-Verlag, London, UK, 1997.

[4] Sten Agerholm and Jacob Frost. An Isabelle-based theorem prover for VDM-SL. In Elsa Gunter and Amy Felty, editors, *Theorem Proving in Higher Order Logics: 10th International Conference, TPHOLs '97,* volume 1275 of *Lecture Notes in Computer Science,* pages 1–16, Murray Hill, NJ, August 1997. Springer-Verlag.

[5] B. Barras, S. Boutin, C. Cornes, J. Courant, J.C. Filliatre, E. Giménez, H. Herbelin, G. Huet, C. Muñoz, C. Murthy, C. Parent, C. Paulin, A. Saïbi, and B. Werner. The Coq Proof Assistant Reference Manual – Version V6.1. Technical Report 0203, INRIA, August 1997.

[6] Michael J. Beeson. Towards a computation system based on set theory. *Theoretical Computer Science,* 60:297–340, 1988.

[7] J.C. Bicarregui, D.L. Clutterbuck, G. Finnie, H. Haughton, K. Lano, H. Lesan, D.W.R.M. Marsh, B.M. Matthews, M.R. Moulding, A.R. Newton, B. Ritchie, T.G. A. Rushton, and P.N. Scharbach. Formal methods into practice: Case studies in the application of the B method. *IEE Proc. Software Engineering,* 144(2):119–133, 1997.

[8] J.C. Bicarregui and B. Ritchie. Invariants, frames and postconditions: A comparison of the VDM and B notations. *IEEE Transactions on Software Engineering,* 21(2):79–89, February 1995.

[9] J.-P. Bodeveix, M. Filali, and C. Muñoz. A formalization of the B-method in Coq and PVS. Manuscript, 1999.

[10] R. Boulton, A. Gordon, M.J.C. Gordon, J. Herbert, and J. van Tassel. Experience with embedding hardware description languages in HOL. In *Proc. International Conference on Theorem Provers in Circuit Design: Theory, Practice and Experience,* pages 129–156, Nijmegen, June 1992. IFIP TC10/WG 10.2, North-Holland.

[11] M. Büchi. The B bank: A complete case study. In *Proc. ICFEM98,* pages 190–199. IEEE Press, December 1998.

[12] Martin Büchi. The B bank. In Emil Sekerinski and Kaisa Sere, editors, *Program Development by Refinement: Case Studies Using the B Method,* FACIT (Formal Approaches to Computing and Information Technology), chapter 4, pages 115–180. Springer-Verlag, London, UK, 1999.

[13] William Chan, Richard J. Anderson, Paul Beame, Steve Burns, Francesmary Modugno, David Notkin, and Jon D. Rees. Model checking large software specifications. *IEEE Transactions on Software Engineering,* 24(7):498–520, July 1998.

[14] Andrew M. Gravell and Chris H. Pratten. Embedding a formal notation: Experiences of automating the embedding of Z in the higher order logics of PVS and HOL. In Grundy and Newey [16], pages 73–84. Available at http://www.staff.ecs.soton.ac.uk/~amg/javalil/efn.ps.gz.

[15] Andrew M. Gravell and Chris H. Pratten. A prototype generic tool supporting the embedding of formal notations. In Grundy and Newey [16], pages 63–72. Available at http://www.staff.ecs.soton.ac.uk/~amg/javalil/agt.ps.gz.

[16] Jim Grundy and Malcolm Newey, editors. *Theorem Proving in Higher Order Logics: Emerging Trends 11th International Conference, TPHOLs '98, Supplementary Proceedings*, Canberra, Australia, September 1998. Technical Report 98-08, Department of Computer Science, Australian National University.

[17] Mats P. E. Heimdahl and Barbara J. Czerny. Using PVS to analyze hierarchical state-based requirements for completeness and consistency. In *IEEE High-Assurance Systems Engineering Workshop (HASE '96)*, pages 252–262, Niagara on the Lake, Canada, October 1996.

[18] Mats P. E. Heimdahl and Nancy G. Leveson. Completeness and consistency in hierarchical state-based requirements. *IEEE Transactions on Software Engineering*, 22(6):363–377, June 1996.

[19] Constance L. Heitmeyer, Ralph D. Jeffords, and Bruce G. Labaw. Automated consistency checking of requirements specifications. *ACM Transactions on Software Engineering and Methodology*, 5(3):231–261, July 1996.

[20] Ulrich Hensel, Marieke Huisman, Bart Jacobs, and Hendrik Tews. Reasoning about classes in object-oriented languages: Logical models and tools. In Chris Hankin, editor, *Programming Languages and Systems: 7th European Symposium On Programming (ESOP)*, volume 1381 of *Lecture Notes in Computer Science*, pages 105–121, Lisbon, Portugal, March 1998. Springer-Verlag.

[21] Bart Jacobs, Joachim van den Berg, Marieke Huisman, Martijn van Berkum, Ulrich Hensel, and Hendrick Tews. Reasoning about Java classes. In *Proceedings, Object-Oriented Programming Systems, Languages and Applications (OOPSLA '98)*, pages 329–340, Vancouver, Canada, October 1998. Association for Computing Machinery. Proceedings issued as ACM SIGPLAN Notices Vol. 33, No. 10, October 1998.

[22] C.B. Jones. *Systematic Software Development Using VDM*. Prentice-Hall International, Englewood Cliffs, New Jersey, second edition, 1990. ISBN 0-13-880733-7.

[23] Matt Kaufmann and J Strother Moore. An industrial strength theorem prover for a logic based on Common Lisp. *IEEE Transactions on Software Engineering*, 23(4):203–213, April 1997.

[24] K. Lano and H. Haughton. *Specification in B*. Imperial College Press, 1996.

[25] Nancy G. Leveson, Mats Per Erik Heimdahl, Holly Hildreth, and Jon Damon Reese. Requirements specification for process-control systems. *IEEE Transactions on Software Engineering*, 20(9):684–707, September 1994.

[26] Paul S. Miner and James F. Leathrum, Jr. Verification of IEEE compliant subtractive division algorithms. In Mandayam Srivas and Albert Camilleri, editors, *Formal Methods in Computer-Aided Design (FMCAD '96)*, volume 1166 of *Lecture Notes in Computer Science*, pages 64–78, Palo Alto, CA, November 1996. Springer-Verlag.

[27] M.J.C. Gordon and T.F. Melham. *Introduction to HOL: A Theorem Proving Environment for Higher Order Logic*. Cambridge University Press, 1993.

[28] C. Muñoz. PBS: Support for the B-method in PVS. Technical Report SRI-CSL-99-01, SRI International, February 1999.

[29] University of Teesside. B-resource. Available at http://www-scm.tees.ac.uk/bresource/welcome.html.

[30] S. Owre, J. M. Rushby, and N. Shankar. PVS: A prototype verification system. In Deepak Kapur, editor, *11th International Conference on Automated Deduction*

(CADE), volume 607 of *Lecture Notes in Artificial Intelligence*, pages 748–752, Saratoga, NY, June 1992. Springer-Verlag.

[31] Sam Owre, John Rushby, and N. Shankar. Integration in PVS: Tables, types, and model checking. In Ed Brinksma, editor, *Tools and Algorithms for the Construction and Analysis of Systems (TACAS '97)*, volume 1217 of *Lecture Notes in Computer Science*, pages 366–383, Enschede, The Netherlands, April 1997. Springer-Verlag.

[32] David Y. W. Park, Jens U. Skakkebæk, Mats P. E. Heimdahl, Barbara J. Czerny, and David L. Dill. Checking properties of safety critical specifications using efficient decision procedures. In Mark Ardis, editor, *Second Workshop on Formal Methods in Software Practice (FMSP '98)*, pages 34–43, Clearwater Beach, FL, March 1998. Association for Computing Machinery.

[33] David Lorge Parnas. Tabular representation of relations. Technical Report CRL Report 260, Telecommunications Research Institute of Ontario (TRIO), Faculty of Engineering, McMaster University, Hamilton, Ontario, Canada, October 1992.

[34] David Lorge Parnas. Predicate logic for software engineering. *IEEE Transactions on Software Engineering*, 19(9):856–862, September 1993.

[35] David Lorge Parnas and Jan Madey. Functional documents for computer systems. *Science of Computer Programming*, 25(1):41–61, October 1995.

[36] L. C. Paulson. *Isabelle: A Generic Theorem Prover*, volume 828 of *Lecture Notes in Computer Science*. Springer-Verlag, 1994.

[37] Vaughan Pratt. Anatomy of the Pentium bug. In *TAPSOFT '95: Theory and Practice of Software Development*, volume 915 of *Lecture Notes in Computer Science*, pages 97–107, Aarhus, Denmark, May 1995. Springer-Verlag.

[38] C.H. Pratten. An introduction to proving AMN specifications with PVS and the AMN-PROOF tool. In Henri Habrias, editor, *Proc. Z Twenty Years On—What Is Its Future*, pages 149–165. IRIN-IUT de Nantes, October 1995.

[39] H. Rueß, N. Shankar, and M. K. Srivas. Modular verification of SRT division. In Rajeev Alur and Thomas A. Henzinger, editors, *Computer-Aided Verification, CAV '96*, volume 1102 of *Lecture Notes in Computer Science*, pages 123–134, New Brunswick, NJ, July/August 1996. Springer-Verlag.

[40] John Rushby. PVS bibliography. Technical report, Computer Science Laboratory, SRI International, Menlo Park, CA. Constantly updated; available at http://www.csl.sri.com/pvs-bib.html.

[41] John Rushby, Sam Owre, and N. Shankar. Subtypes for specifications: Predicate subtyping in PVS. *IEEE Transactions on Software Engineering*, 24(9):709–720, September 1998.

[42] Mark Saaltink, Sentot Kromodimoeljo, Bill Pase, Dan Craigen, and Irwin Meisels. An EVES data abstraction example. In J. C. P. Woodcock and P. G. Larsen, editors, *FME '93: Industrial-Strength Formal Methods*, volume 670 of *Lecture Notes in Computer Science*, pages 578–596, Odense, Denmark, April 1993. Springer-Verlag.

[43] Lance Sherry. Apparatus and method for controlling the vertical profile of an aircraft. United States Patent 5,337,982, August 16, 1994.

[44] J.M. Spivey. *Introducing Z: A Specification Language and its Formal Semantics*. Cambridge University Press, 1988.

The Safe Machine: A New Specification Construct for B

Steve Dunne

School of Computing and Mathematics, University of Teesside
Middlesbrough, TS1 3BA, UK
s.e.dunne@tees.ac.uk

Abstract. We compare the role of state invariants in Z and other state-based formalisms with that of abstract machine invariants in B. We argue a case for bringing B into line with the other formalisms in its use of invariants, and show how this can be achieved by one small extension to B's underlying semantics concerning the multiple composition operator, which has in any case already been proposed by others from different motivations. We illustrate the utility of our proposal with a small specification example, our Electronic Thesaurus.

1 Introduction

The role of the state invariant in a Z specification of a sequential system is surely familiar to all; it has been amply described by many authors; the source most frequently cited is perhaps [8]. The Z specifier conventionally incorporates $\Delta State$ in his description of each of his system's operations, and $State$ (or $State'$) in his description of his system's initialisation. We can regard the state invariant as embodying all common required safe aspects of behaviour factored out from the individual operations, allowing those operations to be expressed all the more succinctly. Whatever else he asserts in their descriptions, as long as he adheres to this convention our Z specifier's operations and initialisation will necessarily respect the state invariant: his specifications are inherently "safe". In asserting some further specific effect of an operation the Z specifier may of course unwittingly contradict the state invariant, but the result of doing so is not thereby to compromise the operation's safety: rather, it is implicitly to precondition the operation so as to render it inapplicable wherever the contradiction obtains. We will call this use of the state invariant in specification a *constructive* one. It means the state invariant is an integral part of the specification. Other formalisms which employ state invariants in the same constructive manner within specification include VDM [6] and the Refinement Calculus [7].

The role of the machine invariant in B is somewhat different from the constructive one described above: it plays no direct part in the specifier's expression of his abstract machine's initialisation or operations, but rather serves as a safety template against which those operations and initialisation must be checked *a posteriori*. Weakening an abstract machine's invariant, even to the ultimate extent where it serves merely to type the machine's variables, does not change the

J. Wing, J. Woodcock, J. Davies (Eds.): FM'99, Vol. I, LNCS 1708, pp. 472–489, 1999.
© Springer-Verlag Berlin Heidelberg 1999

meaning of the machine *per se*, though confidence in its validity as an expression of its user's requirements would be diminished if the consistency of its operations and initialisation has been checked only against this weakened invariant. The B specifier's only incentive to ensure his machine's invariant is as tight as possible is such a concern for validity. Indeed, one might even imagine –perish the thought– an unscrupulous specifier deliberately underspecifying his state invariant so as to avoid some tedious consistency proof obligations.

In this paper we set out to explore how the invariant of a B abstract machine might be conscripted to play a more constructive part in the specification of that machine's operations and initialisation. Having first identified an appropriate state invariant for his machine we would like the B specifier to be able to utilise it in specifying its initialisation and operations. This is in contrast to the current situation where, by obliging him to formulate his initialisation and operations without reference to his machine invariant but in a way which ensures they are consistent with that invariant, B might be said to be coercing the specifier into engaging in what is really a proto-implementation activity rather than one of pure specification. In any realm of engineering-description a consistency-checking need is usually symptomatic of some underlying duplication of description: the best way to avoid inconsistency is to describe everything just once. The proper place for consistency checking is *between* successive steps of design on the path to implementation, but not *within* any one design stage where it just betokens descriptive redundancy. We will look to Z for inspiration as to how such consistency checking might be eliminated in B: that is, we seek a means by which our B user can specify B abstract machines which are inherently safe. We will show that the key to this lies in a natural extention of the notion of multiple composition of generalised substitutions which already exists in B.

2   Some B Preliminaries

In the B literature generalised substitutions are usually understood in the context of an abstract machine with known state variables and a known invariant. A substitution therefore tends to be identified with the operation it characterises within that machine. We take a somewhat different standpoint here: our generalised substitutions will have an existence independent of any particular machine context; or, rather, we will regard a generalised substitution as inducing its own primitive context we call its *frame*. After explaining frames, we use them to describe a useful general notion of *refinement* between arbitrary pairs of substitutions. We also introduce the ideas of "totalising" a partly feasible substitution by formulating its *weakest feasible completion*, and of "normalising" a non-deterministic choice substitution, both of which will be needed later.

2.1   Substitutions and Frames

We call a collection of variables a *frame*. If a frame comprises only one variable, then the frame and its single constituent variable are synonymous. If u and v are frames, then

$$u, v$$

denotes the new frame obtained by merging u and v, and

$$u \setminus v$$

denotes the residual frame obtained by removing from u any variables it shares with v. In particular, note that

$$u, v \ = \ v, u \qquad \text{and} \qquad u, (v \setminus u) \ = \ u, v$$

We call the collection of variables on which a generalised substitution acts its *active frame*. If S is a generalised substitution we denote its active frame by *frame*(S). A substitution may make passive reference to variables outside its active frame. For example, the active frame of $x := y$ is just x although it makes passive reference to y too. The active frame may be empty as in *skip*, or as in $x < 7 \mid skip$ which makes only passive reference to x. We distinguish between *skip* and $x := x$ since they have different active frames. We also have that

$$frame(S \parallel T) \ = \ frame(S), frame(T)$$

When one abstract machine is included in another the operations of the former can be invoked as substitutions in the latter. The active frame of an invoked operation comprises *all* the variables of that operation's native machine, not just the active frame of its operation body therein. If *opbody* denotes that body and r denotes the residual native machine variables outside *opbody*'s active frame, the invoked operation is therefore equivalent to

$$opbody \parallel r := r$$

By incorporating the residual $r := r$ above we depart from the orthodox interpretation of operation invocation, which simply syntactically replaces the operation name by *opbody*. We contend our interpretation is preferable since it provides referential transparency over the way an operation is defined. For example, in a given machine we would recognise the two operations defined respectively with bodies *skip* and $x := x$ as having the same meaning, and therefore we would desire that their invocations in any including machine have the same meaning too.

2.2   Refinement of Substitutions

A generalised substitution S with active frame s is said to be *refined* by another generalised substitution T with active frame t, written

$$S \ \sqsubseteq \ T$$

if for any predicate Q without free variables in $t \setminus s$

$$[S]Q \ \Rightarrow \ [T]Q$$

Essentially T must be able to establish anything that S can establish. T's active frame will usually encompass that of S. One obvious exception is the rather pathological case of *magic* (i.e. *false* $\implies$ *skip*) which though having an empty active frame refines anything. If T has a wider active frame than S we can interpret this as T employing its own "local" variables outside the scope of S. The free-variables constraint we imposed on Q above reflects the local nature within T of these variables of $t \setminus s$.

2.3   Weakest Feasible Completion of a Substitution

In the Z literature a Z operation schema is always interpreted as a totally feasible operation, even when it has a restricted domain of before-states on which it can be applied. Indeed, the actual restriction predicate extracted from the schema property by hiding primed and !-decorated variables is called the *precondition* of the operation. The operational interpretation is that the operation is always invocable, although unsafe to invoke outside its precondition because there the effect will be unpredictable, perhaps even abortive. There is thus no concept of restricted feasibility for a Z operation, but only one of restricted safe applicability.

In hindsight we can see Z would probably have been better served by an interpretion of its schema preconditions as feasibility guards. Certainly, Z's current interpretation of schema preconditions makes a reasonable intuitive operational interpretation of other Z constructs unfortunately problematic: the schema disjunction of two operation schemas cannot in general be operationally interpreted as a non-deterministic choice between those two operations; nor can the schema sequential composition of two operation schemas always be operationally interpreted as a sequential composition of those operations. Interpreting schema preconditions as feasibility guards would resolve such anomalies at a stroke.

Happily, the syntax of generalised substitutions, in common with VDM and the Refinement Calculus, does distinguish between preconditions and guards. We can still impose a Z-like "total" interpretation of any substitution by explicitly preconditioning it by its own feasibility guard. We call this derivation the *weakest feasible completion* of the substitution. We define the weakest feasible completion of S as

$$fis(S) \mid S$$

where $fis(S)$ is the feasibility guard of S, defined as $\neg \ [S]false$. Interpreting our substitutions as weakest precondition predicate transformers, the above expresses a substitution which concurs with S where the latter is feasible but cannot be guaranteed to establish anything when applied where S is infeasible –unlike S itself which by definition can establish anything at all in those circumstances. If S is already total $fis(S)$ reduces to *true* and therefore, as one would expect, S is its own weakest feasible completion. The weakest feasible completion of *magic* is *abort*. Extracting the feasibility guard of a generalised substitution is a purely syntactic manipulation, so deriving the weakest feasible completion of a substitution is straightforward.

2.4   Normalising a Non-deterministic Choice

Consider the non-deterministic choice substitution $x := 3 \; [] \; y := 4$. Its two component substitutions have different frames x and y. We can rewrite such a choice as

$$x, y := 3, y \; [] \; x, y := x, 4$$

without changing its meaning, so that the two components now have identical active frames. This is what we term *normalising* a non-deterministic choice. More generally if S and T are two generalised substitutions, let u denote $frame(S) \setminus frame(T)$ and let v denote $frame(T) \setminus frame(S)$; then we can express $S[]T$ in normalised form as

$$(S \; || \; v := v) \; [] \; (T \; || \; u := u)$$

2.5   Classical Multiple Composition in B

In [1] Abrial defines the multiple composition $S \; || \; T$ of generalised substitutions S and T only when S and T have disjoint active frames. He also forbids the multiple composition $op1 \; || \; op2$ of two operations $op1$ and $op2$ from the same native machine, though the pathological example he exhibits on page 317 of [1] provides only a pragmatic illustration of the need for the prohibition, not a deep explanation for it. Our new interpretation of operation invocation allows us to infer the same prohibition as a particular consequence of his general edict on the disjointness of frames. This is because we now recognise that $op1$ and $op2$, by being from the same native machine, have the same active frame.

On page 308 of [1] Abrial gives these definitions of $trm(S \; || \; T)$ and $prd(S \; || \; T)$, where S and T act respectively on disjoint frames x and y:

$trm(S \; || \; T)$	$trm(S) \wedge trm(T)$
$prd_{x,y}(S \; || \; T)$	$prd_x(S) \wedge prd_y(T)$

The above *prd* definition is flawed. To see this we note that for any generalised substitution U, $prd(U) \vee trm(U)$ is a tautology.

Proof: Let U's active frame be u. We assert the following true disjunction:

$u = u' \vee true$

whence $\{a \vee b = \neg a \Rightarrow b\}$

$u \neq u' \Rightarrow true$

whence $\{$monotonicity of $[U]\}$

$[U]u \neq u' \Rightarrow [U]true$

whence $\{$definition of $trm(U)\}$

$[U]u \neq u' \Rightarrow trm(U)$

whence $\{a \Rightarrow b = \neg\, a \lor b\}$

$\neg\, [U]u \neq u' \lor trm(U)$

whence $\{$definition of $prd(U)\}$

$prd(U) \lor trm(U)$ QED

Abrial's above definitions of $trm(S \parallel T)$ and $prd(S \parallel T)$ do not uphold the tautology. For example, they give us

$$trm(abort \parallel magic) = false$$

$$prd(abort \parallel magic) = false$$

which cannot be the case for any generalised substitution. We can correct the flaw by amending the definition of $prd(S \parallel T)$ to

$prd_{x,y}(S \parallel T)$	$(trm(T) \Rightarrow prd_x(S)) \land (trm(S) \Rightarrow prd_y(T))$

We hasten to reassure B users this flaw in Abrial's definition of $prd(S \parallel T)$ is benign, since it in no way invalidates the rest of the treatment of multiple composition in [1]. Our correction therefore, though technically justified, is of little practical significance.

3 Generalising Multiple Composition

It is a fact that the characterisation of $S \parallel T$ in terms of trm and prd described in the previous section remains perfectly sound even if we dispense with Abrial's requirement that the active frames of S and T be disjoint. We are by no means the first to make this observation: Bert *et al* [4] characterise exactly such an operator, which they call their "new composition of substitutions" and denote by $S \otimes T$; in [5] Chartier describes how in his formalisation of the Generalised Substitution Language in Isabelle/HOL it seems more natural to define $\parallel$ without any explicit disjoint frames requirement. Both authors observe that their more general operators coincide exactly with Abrial's $\parallel$ whenever the frames of the two participating substitutions do happen to be disjoint. We propose to follow Chartier by retaining the symbol $\parallel$ to represent such a generalisation of Abrial's multiple composition, justifying this by representing that we haven't changed $\parallel$'s meaning, but merely extended its domain of application. We will indulge ourselves, however, with a change in terminology: we will refer to our generalised $\parallel$ as a *parallel composition* of substitutions.

3.1   Re-write Rules for ||

In section 7.1.2 of [1] Abrial gives a comprehensive set of re-write rules by which the multiple composition operator || can always be systematically eliminated from any generalised substitution expression. The existence of such a set of rules reveals that || is not, after all, a fundamental operator of the Generalised Substitution Language. In essence, it is really no more than a convenient syntactic shorthand for expressing substitutions which could always be alternatively expressed without it. Our extension of Abrial's multiple composition into our parallel composition doesn't change ||'s status as an operator which can always be eliminated by application of re-write rules. We do, though, have to consider carefully the impact of our extension on those re-write rules: it turns out we have to augment Abrial's existing battery of re-write rules for || with one more; we also have to qualify one of his existing rules, as we will show below.

A New Re-write Rule for ||.   This new rule[1] captures the meaning of applying two simple substitutions in parallel on the same variable:

Syntax	Definition
$x := E \mathbin{\|} x := F$	$E = F \implies x := E$

It expresses that a parallel composition of two simple substitutions on the same variable is only feasible if those substitutions are assigning identical values.

Distributing || through Non-deterministic Choice.   One of Abrial's existing re-write rules, expressed as

$$(S [] T) \ \| \ U \ = \ (S \ \| \ U) \ [] \ (T \ \| \ U)$$

allows us to distribute multiple composition through non-deterministic choice unconditionally. With our more general parallel composition we have to be a little more circumspect about such a distribution: it is in fact only valid once the non-deterministic choice concerned has been normalised. To see why this is so, consider the following parallel composition:

$$(x := 3 \ [] \ skip) \ \| \ x := 7$$

If we just unconditionally distribute the || through the [] we obtain

$$(x := 3 \ \| \ x := 7) \ [] \ (skip \ \| \ x := 7)$$

which reduces to *magic* [] $x := 7$ and thence $x := 7$. But if we directly calculate the *prd* of our parallel composition we have

---

[1]   It was originally suggested by Andy Galloway.

$prd((x := 3 \;[]\; skip) \;||\; x := 7)$

$= \{\text{defn of } prd(S \;||\; T)\}$

$prd(x := 3 \;[]\; skip) \;\wedge\; prd(x := 7)$

$= \{\text{defn of } prd\}$

$\neg\, [x := 3 \;[]\; skip]x \neq x' \;\wedge\; \neg\, [x := 7]x \neq x'$

$= \{\text{apply substitutions and simplify}\}$

$(x' = 3 \vee x = x') \;\wedge\; x' = 7$

$= \{\text{boolean algebra}\}$

$(x' = 3 \wedge x' = 7) \;\vee\; (x = x' \wedge x' = 7)$

$=$

$false \;\vee\; x = x' = 7$

$=$

$x = x' = 7$

which is not $prd(x := 7)$ but rather $prd(x = 7 \Longrightarrow x := 7)$.

We try again, but this time we will normalise the non-deterministic choice first before we distribute the $||$. Since $skip$ has an empty frame, the normalised form of $x := 3 \;[]\; skip$ is just $x := 3 \;[]\; (skip \;||\; x := x)$ which reduces to $x := 3 \;[]\; x := x$. So we have

$(x := 3 \;[]\; skip) \;||\; x := 7$

$= \{\text{normalise the non-deterministic choice}\}$

$(x := 3 \;[]\; x := x) \;||\; x := 7$

$= \{\text{now distribute } || \text{ through } []\}$

$(x := 3 \;||\; x := 7) \;[]\; (x := x \;||\; x := 7)$

$= \{3 = 7 \text{ is false, so the lefthand choice collapses to magic}\}$

$magic \;[]\; (x := x \;||\; x := 7)$

$= \{\text{magic disappears in non-deterministic choice}\}$

$x := x \;||\; x := 7$

$= \{\text{applying our new re-write rule}\}$

$x = 7 \Longrightarrow x := 7$

which accords completely with our prd calculation above.

3.2   Fusion

When both operands share the same active frame, or when one operand's active frame is completely contained within that of the other, our generalised $\parallel$ corresponds to what Back and Butler [2, 3] call, within the more general context of all monotonic predicate transformers [2], their *fusion* operator.

If we think of S and T as embodying two separate operational requirements on the same state-space, then their "fusion" is simply the logical conjunction of those requirements. Fusion therefore reduces demonic non-determinism. For example

$$x : (5 < x) \parallel x : (x < 10)$$

is equivalent to

$$x : (5 < x < 10)$$

If S and T represent contradictory requirements then their fusion becomes infeasible. For example, as we saw earlier,

$$x := 3 \parallel x := 7$$

collapses to *magic*. Our $\parallel$ is more general than either fusion or Abrial's multiple composition because, unlike either of them, its operands can have arbitrarily overlapping frames. For example

$$x, y := 1, 2 \parallel y, z := z, y$$

is meaningful. It reduces, in fact, to

$$z = 2 \implies x, y, z := 1, 2, y$$

3.3   Abrial's Pathological Example Revisited

We now consider the pathological example of a multiple composition given on page 317 of [1] to which we alluded earlier. It consists of a machine with frame x, y and invariant

$$x \in NAT \wedge y \in NAT \wedge x \leq y$$

with the following pair of operations

$$incx \mathrel{\widehat{=}} x < y \mid x := x + 1$$
$$decy \mathrel{\widehat{=}} x < y \mid y := y - 1$$

The parallel composition $inx \parallel decy$ is now expressible, noting our introduction of a residual $r := r$ in each operation body, as

---

[2] Generalised substitutions model only the positively conjunctive subclass of such transformers.

$$(x < y \mid x := x + 1 \parallel y := y) \parallel (x < y \mid y := y - 1 \parallel x := x)$$

thence

$$(x < y \mid x, y := x + 1, y) \parallel (x < y \mid x, y := x, y - 1)$$

thence

$$x < y \mid x = x + 1 \wedge y = y - 1 \implies x, y := x, y$$

thence

$$x < y \mid false \implies x, y := x, y$$

thence

$$x < y \mid magic$$

Although entirely infeasible inside its precondition $x < y$, we conclude that $incx \parallel decy$ is certainly safe: that is to say, wherever it is applicable it (miraculously) preserves the machine's invariant. So the parallel composition of two invoked operations from the same machine can now safely be permitted. It is interpreted as the fusion of the two operations concerned. Often, as in this case, it will simply yield an infeasible substitution.

3.4   A Categorical Definition of Parallel Composition

Since the ultimate destiny of most generalised substitutions in B is refinement into implementation code, the following alternative characterisation of $\parallel$ directly in terms of refinement is apt:

> For generalised substitutions S and T with respective active frames x and y, $S \parallel T$ is the unique generalised substitution with active frame x, y satisfying the following universal property for any generalised substitution U:

$$S \parallel T \quad \sqsubseteq \quad U$$

$$\Leftrightarrow$$

$$trm(T) \mid S \quad \sqsubseteq \quad U \quad \wedge \quad trm(S) \mid T \quad \sqsubseteq \quad U$$

That is to say, in the lattice of generalised substitutions ordered by refinement, $S \parallel T$ is the refinement supremum of the pair of substitutions

$$trm(T) \mid S \qquad \text{and} \qquad trm(S) \mid T$$

In other words, it is the "least-refined" co-refinement of these two substitutions. This alternative characterisation is important for builders of tools to support the B method since it indicates how we can directly "refine away" a parallel composition instead of having to eliminate it from a specification using the rewrite rules.

4   Intrinsically Safe Abstract Machines

Having developed our parallel composition operator for substitutions we can now employ it to formulate our desired new notion of a safe abstract machine. In order to do this we need first to coin some more B terminology –the "characteristic" operation and "characteristic" initialisation of an abstract machine– as explained in the next subsection.

4.1   Characteristic Operation and Initialisation

In conventional Z, $\Delta State$ represents the least-deterministic operation on $State$ which maintains the invariant of $State$. Conventionally any other operation specified on $State$ will incorporate $\Delta State$, and so can be deconstructed as a conjunction of operation $\Delta State$ with a second, usually unsafe operation. Now consider a B abstract machine with variable x and invariant Inv. We will use the names *Establish* for the generalised substitution

$x : Inv$

and *Preserve* for the generalised substitution

$Inv \mid x : Inv$

Establish expresses the least-deterministic safe initialisation of our machine. We call it our machine's *characteristic* initialisation. *Preserve* characterises an operation preconditioned by Inv and guaranteeing, providing the before-state is within Inv, to deliver an after-state also satisfying Inv. It is, in short, the least-deterministic safe operation for our machine –the exact B counterpart of Z's $\Delta State$ operation. We call it our machine's *characteristic* operation.

4.2   Making an Abstract Machine Safe

An arbitrary initialisation of our machine will be made safe by parallel composition with its characteristic initialisation *Establish*. Such a composite initialisation will inherit from *Establish* the certainty of establishing Inv. Similarly, an arbitrary operation body of our machine will be made safe by parallel composition with its characteristic operation *Preserve*.

We give a small example. Consider the following machine:

MACHINE
$$M$$

VARIABLES
$$x, y$$

INVARIANT
$$x \in \mathbb{N} \land$$
$$y \in \mathbb{N} \land$$
$$x + y = 100$$

INITIALISATION
$$x := 0$$
OPERATIONS
$$incx \mathrel{\widehat{=}} x := x + 1 \quad ;$$
$$incy \mathrel{\widehat{=}} y := y + 1$$
END

Of course, M is manifestly unsafe since its initialisation and its operations all flout its invariant. *Establish* for M is the substitution

$$x, y : (x \in \mathbb{N} \wedge y \in \mathbb{N} \wedge x + y = 100)$$

and *Preserve* is the substitution

$$x \in \mathbb{N} \wedge y \in \mathbb{N} \wedge x + y = 100 \mid x, y : (x \in \mathbb{N} \wedge y \in \mathbb{N} \wedge x + y = 100)$$

or equivalently in Abstract Machine Notation

PRE
$$x \in \mathbb{N} \wedge y \in \mathbb{N} \wedge x + y = 100$$
THEN
$$x, y : (x \in \mathbb{N} \wedge y \in \mathbb{N} \wedge x + y = 100)$$
END

Now we will "repair" M by parallel-composing its initialisation with *Establish* and its operations with *Preserve*. We obtain the following machine:

MACHINE
$$SafeM$$
VARIABLES
$$x, y$$
INVARIANT
$$x \in \mathbb{N} \wedge$$
$$y \in \mathbb{N} \wedge$$
$$x + y = 100$$
INITIALISATION
$$x := 0 \quad \|$$
$$x, y : (x \in \mathbb{N} \wedge y \in \mathbb{N} \wedge x + y = 100)$$
OPERATIONS
$$safe\_incx \mathrel{\widehat{=}}$$
$$x := x + 1 \quad \|$$
PRE
$$x \in \mathbb{N} \wedge y \in \mathbb{N} \wedge x + y = 100$$
THEN
$$x, y : (x \in \mathbb{N} \wedge y \in \mathbb{N} \wedge x + y = 100)$$
END $\quad ;$

$$safe\_incy \; \widehat{=}$$
$$y := y + 1 \quad \|$$
$$\textbf{PRE}$$
$$x \in \mathbb{N} \wedge y \in \mathbb{N} \wedge x + y = 100$$
$$\textbf{THEN}$$
$$x, y : (x \in \mathbb{N} \wedge y \in \mathbb{N} \wedge x + y = 100)$$
$$\textbf{END}$$

END

Our "repaired" initialisation reduces to

$$x, y := 0, 100$$

The "repaired" operations *safe_incx* and *safe_incy* are infeasible, since they both contain non-trivial guards. For example, *safe_incx* reduces to

$$\textbf{PRE}$$
$$x \in \mathbb{N} \wedge y \in \mathbb{N} \wedge x + y = 100$$
$$\textbf{THEN}$$
$$\textbf{SELECT}$$
$$x < 100$$
$$\textbf{THEN}$$
$$x, y := x + 1, y - 1$$
$$\textbf{END}$$
$$\textbf{END}$$

Our goal is to reflect faithfully in B all the recognised Z conventions in operation specification, so it remains for us to "totalise" our repaired operations *safe_incx* and *safe_incy* by taking their weakest feasible completions. In practice this means changing guards into preconditions. Thus we finally arrive at the following definitions of our total operations *tot_incx* and *tot_incy*:

$$tot\_incx \; \widehat{=}$$
$$\textbf{PRE}$$
$$x \in \mathbb{N} \wedge y \in \mathbb{N} \wedge x + y = 100 \; \wedge$$
$$x < 100$$
$$\textbf{THEN}$$
$$x, y := x + 1, y - 1$$
$$\textbf{END}$$

and

$$tot\_incy \; \widehat{=}$$
$$\textbf{PRE}$$
$$x \in \mathbb{N} \wedge y \in \mathbb{N} \wedge x + y = 100 \; \wedge$$
$$y < 100$$
$$\textbf{THEN}$$
$$x, y := x - 1, y + 1$$
$$\textbf{END}$$

4.3   A New Specification Construct for B

We have just seen how an arbitrary abstract machine can be made feasible and safe after the manner of conventional Z, by

1. parallel-composing its actual and characteristic initialisations;
2. parallel-composing each of its actual operations with its characteristic operation;
3. "totalising" the resulting composite operations by taking their weakest completions.

This leads us to propose a new syntactic category for B which we will call a *SAFE_MACHINE*. Each safe machine can be syntactically expanded to an equivalent safe ordinary abstract machine by the systematic process we have just described. For example, suppose we have

SAFE_MACHINE
$$SM$$
VARIABLES
$$x$$
INVARIANT
$$Inv$$
INITIALISATION
$$U$$
OPERATIONS
$$op1 \cong S \;\; ;$$
$$op2 \cong T$$
END

We can syntactically expand SM into the abstract machine

MACHINE
$$SM$$
VARIABLES
$$x$$
INVARIANT
$$Inv$$
INITIALISATION
$$U \;||\; (x : Inv)$$
OPERATIONS
$$op1 \cong (Inv \land fis(S \;||\; x : Inv)) \mid (S \;||\; x : Inv) \;\; ;$$
$$op2 \cong (Inv \land fis(T \;||\; x : Inv)) \mid (T \;||\; x : Inv)$$
END

At this point the machine SM can be further reduced by applying our elimination rules for $||$, and so be expressed as a classical B machine. Alternatively we can by utilising our characteristic refinement rules for $||$ choose to refine SM directly into a conventional B refinement or implementation.

4.4   How Safe Is a Safe Machine?

It could be argued that –paradoxically– a Safe Machine would be far from safe for another developer to introduce into his own development, since its operations' real preconditions are not explicit in its text. This would be quite true if indeed its author simply published the unqualified source text of his Safe Machine into his organisation's software component catalogue. Clearly we must insist that the translation tool which translates his Safe Machine into its corresponding conventional B abstract machine must also extract the real precondition of each operation in an explicit form. This should then be used to annotate the text of the Safe Machine which will ultimately appear in the component catalogue.

5   The Electronic Thesaurus

We now discuss a more significant application which illustrates the expressive power of our new safe machine construct. A thesaurus is essentially a grouping of the words of a language such that all the words in any given group are associated in meaning. Some words will appear in more than one group because they have several different meanings. Suppose we wish to specify an electronic thesaurus. We will assume the given sets $GROUP$ and $WORD$. We could model the thesaurus simply as the relation

$$contains : GROUP \leftrightarrow WORD$$

or alternatively as the function

$$comprises : GROUP \rightarrow \mathbb{F}_1 \, WORD$$

Some of the maintenance operations we wish to specify will be easier to express in terms of the relation *contains* while others will be easier to express in terms of the function *comprises*. For example, establishing a new group with its inaugural set of words is best expressed using *comprises*. Removing an individual thesaurus entry, on the other hand, is best expressed using *contains*, since when we remove the last or only word from a group we must also dis-establish the group itself. If we were specifying our thesaurus as a classical B abstract machine we would have to commit ourselves to either one representation or the other. Inevitably the choice we are forced to make will result in some of our operations being difficult to express. Using a definition to represent the omitted component would be to no avail, because defined identifiers cannot be actively updated in machine operations.

In contrast, by specifying our thesaurus as a safe machine we gain the best of both worlds. We declare the state of the thesaurus to consist of both the relation and the function. We link these together via the machine invariant thus:

SAFE_MACHINE

Thesaurus

SETS

> $GROUP$;
> $WORD$

VARIABLES

> $contains, comprises$

INVARIANT

> $contains \in GROUP \leftrightarrow WORD \wedge$
> $comprises \in GROUP \twoheadrightarrow \mathbb{F}_1\ WORD \wedge$
> $comprises = \lambda\, gg\ .\ (gg \in \mathrm{dom}\ contains \mid contains[\{gg\}])$

INITIALISATION

> $contains := \{\}$

OPERATIONS

> $new\_group(words) \mathrel{\widehat{=}}$
>
> > **PRE**
> > $words \in \mathbb{F}_1\ WORD \wedge$
> > $\mathrm{dom}\ comprises \neq GROUP$
> > **THEN**
> > > **ANY**
> > > > gg
> > > **WHERE**
> > > > $gg \in GROUP - \mathrm{dom}\ comprises$
> > > **THEN**
> > > > $comprises(gg) := words$
> > > **END**
> > **END** ;
>
> $remove\_entry(gg, ww) \mathrel{\widehat{=}}$
>
> > **PRE**
> > $gg \in GROUP \wedge ww \in WORD \wedge$
> > $gg \mapsto ww \in contains$
> > **THEN**
> > > $contains := contains - \{gg \mapsto ww\}$
> > **END**

END

The extra complexity of the *Thesaurus* safe machine's invariant is amply compensated by the ease with which its operations are subsequently expressed. A full *Thesaurus* would of course involve many more operations than the two we have presented above, so the benefit would be correspondingly magnified.

6   On Framing

There are no completely free lunches, and so there is a price to pay by the B developer for being relieved of the obligation to take explicit steps to ensure his operations preserve his machine's invariant. When he is writing an operation of a Safe Machine he can no longer be certain that any machine state variable which he hasn't explicitly changed will in fact remain unchanged. Some will doubtless argue that this robs us of so convenient a facet of our B operations as to render the whole concept of a Safe Machine impractical.

We would counter that the concern can adequately be addressed by appropriate framing –that is, encapsulating of variables inside subsidiary machines. If two variables can be changed independently we should question why they are framed in the same machine, rather than being encapsulated in separate subsidiary machines included by the original one.

7   Conclusion

We contrasted B's current use of machine invariants in a purely passive verification role during specification, against Z's more constructive use of state invariants in specification. We argued that, in the context of specification, the Z usage is to be preferred, since it gives more expressive leverage to the specifier and frees him from the obligation to demonstrate his specifications are consistent, because they will automatically be so. We have shown how a single straightforward and very natural extension to just one of the constructors of B's Generalised Substitution Language is the only change needed in B's underlying semantics to provide us with a means of writing B specifications which constructively use their machine invariants. We have seen how the $\Delta State$ construction so familiar to Z users has a direct analogy in B as the characteristic operation of an abstract machine which we have called $Preserve$. We have shown how fusing $Preserve$ with the particular body of an abstract machine operation is guaranteed to produce a safe operation which respects the machine invariant.

Along the way we have made various proposals to complete the theory of the multiple composition operator in B. We have also introduced a number of other subsidiary new constructions, which we hope may themselves prove to be of value in helping to promote a deeper appreciation of some of B's underlying concepts.

Acknowledgements

I am indebted to my Teesside colleagues Bill Stoddart and Richard Shore, and to Andy Galloway of York, for countless fruitful discussions on many of the ideas in this paper. I also wish to thank my anonymous referees for their encouraging comments.

References

[1] J.-R. Abrial. *The B-Book: Assigning Programs to Meanings.* Cambridge University Press, 1996.

[2] R.J.R. Back and M.J. Butler. Exploring summation and product operators in the refinement calculus. In B. Moller, editor, *Mathematics of Program Construction*, number 947 in Lecture Notes in Computer Science, pages 128–158. Springer Verlag, 1995.

[3] R.J.R. Back and M.J. Butler. Fusion and simultaneous execution in the refinement calculus. *Acta Informatica*, 35(11):921–940, 1998.

[4] D. Bert, M.-L. Potet, and Y. Rouzaud. A study on components and assembly primitives in B. In H. Habrias, editor, *Proceedings of the First B Conference*, pages 47–62. IRIN, Nantes, 1996.

[5] P Chartier. Formalisation of B in Isabelle/HOL. In D. Bert, editor, *B'98: Recent Advances in the Development and Use of the B Method; Proceedings of the Second International B Conference, Montpellier, France*, number 1393 in Lecture Notes in Computer Science, pages 66–82. Springer Verlag, 1998.

[6] C.B. Jones. *Systematic Software Development Using VDM (2nd edn).* Prentice-Hall, 1990.

[7] C. Morgan. *Programming from Specifications (2nd edn).* Prentice Hall International, 1994.

[8] J.M. Spivey. *The Z Notation: a Reference Manual (2nd edn).* Prentice Hall International, 1992.

csp2B: A Practical Approach to Combining CSP and B

Michael Butler

Dept of Electronics & Computer Science
University of Southampton
Highfield
Southampton SO17 1BJ
United Kingdom
M.J.Butler@ecs.soton.ac.uk
www.ecs.soton.ac.uk/~mjb

Abstract. This paper describes the tool csp2B which provides a means of combining CSP-like descriptions with standard B specifications. The notation of CSP provides a convenient way of describing the order in which the operations of a B machine may occur. The function of the tool is to convert CSP-like specifications into standard machine-readable B specifications which means that they may be animated and appropriate proof obligations may be generated. Use of csp2B means that abstract specifications and refinements may be specified purely using CSP or using a combination of CSP and B. The translation is justified in terms of an operational semantics.

1 Introduction

In the B method [1], a system is specified as an abstract machine consisting of some state and some operations acting on that state. Originally B was intended for the development of sequential systems. Influenced by Action Systems [3], recent work has shown how B may be used in the development of distributed systems [2, 5, 7]. In these approaches, the state of a machine may be used to model the global state of a distributed system and its operations may represent events that change the state of the system. Refinement in this approach involves partitioning the global state amongst the nodes of the system to localise events. Events are guarded by conditions on the state and may only be executed when their guard is enabled.

However, while B is suitable for modelling distributed activity in terms of events, it is weaker at modelling sequential activity. Typically one has to introduce an abstract 'program counter' to order the execution of actions. This can be a lot less transparent than the way in which one orders action execution in process algebras such as CSP [9] and CCS [10].

The csp2B tool converts CSP-like descriptions of system behaviour into standard machine-readable B specifications. The resulting B specifications can be input to a tool such as *Atelier B* from Steria and *The B-Toolkit* from B-Core

J. Wing, J. Woodcock, J. Davies (Eds.): FM'99, Vol. I, LNCS 1708, pp. 490–508, 1999.
© Springer-Verlag Berlin Heidelberg 1999

which means that they may be animated and appropriate proof obligations may be generated.

The tool supports a CSP-like process notation containing prefixing ($\rightarrow$), choice ($[]$) and the deadlocked process *STOP*. It does not support an internal nondeterminism operator. Internal nondeterminism may be modelled using nondeterministic operations in B. Parallel composition is supported but only at the outermost level, that is, a system can be described using a parallel composition of purely sequential processes. Interleaving of multiple instances of similar processes is also supported.

Given a CSP description of a system, the tool generates a B machine containing variables corresponding to the implicit states of the CSP processes, i.e., abstract program counters. For each event in the alphabet of the CSP description, a B operation is generated which is guarded appropriately and which updates the abstract program counters appropriately. It is possible to declare that a CSP description constrains the behaviour of a standard existing B machine, in which case, a guarded call to the corresponding operation in that existing machine is embedded in each generated operation.

We take an operational approach to the semantics of the CSP and B combination and show that the composition of a CSP process with a B machine is compositional with respect to refinement.

Section 2 gives an overview of the tool and how it may be used, while Section 3 discusses the semantics of the CSP notation used and how it relates to B.

The csp2B tool itself may be downloaded from `http://www.ecs.soton.ac.uk/~mjb/csp2B`.

2   Tool Overview

The csp2B tool converts CSP-like descriptions of system behaviour into B machines. CSP provides a very convenient way of specifying the order in which operations may be invoked. Consider the following CSP specification of a vending machine (written in the source notation of csp2B[1]):

MACHINE   *VendingMachine*

    ALPHABET   *Coin   Tea   Coffee*

    PROCESS   *VM* = *AwaitCoin*   WHERE
          AwaitCoin = *Coin* $\rightarrow$ *DeliverDrink*
        DeliverDrink = *Tea* $\rightarrow$ *AwaitCoin*
                $[]$ *Coffee* $\rightarrow$ *AwaitCoin*
    END
  END .

---

[1] The tool supports an ascii version of CSP and the full syntax may be found in [6].

This describes a machine that has three operations, *Coin*, *Tea* and *Coffee* (called the *alphabet* of the machine) whose behaviour is dictated by a CSP process *VM* that may be in one of two states *AwaitCoin* and *DeliverDrink*. *VM* specifies that, in the state *AwaitCoin*, *Coin* is the only operation that may be invoked while, in the *DeliverDrink* state, both the *Tea* and *Coffee* operations may be invoked. *VM* will initially be in the *AwaitCoin* state. *VM* is described by a mutually recursive set of equations and each recursive call on a right-hand side must be preceded by at least one event (in the terminology of CSP, each recursive call must be guarded). From the above CSP description, csp2B will generate the following B machine:

MACHINE   *VendingMachine*
SETS   *VMState* = { *AwaitCoin*, *DeliverDrink* }
VARIABLES   *VM*
INVARIANT   *VM* ∈ *VMState*
INITIALISATION   *VM* := *AwaitCoin*

OPERATIONS

   Coin ≙ SELECT   *VM* = *AwaitCoin*   THEN   *VM* := *DeliverDrink*   END;

   Tea ≙ SELECT   *VM* = *DeliverDrink*   THEN   *VM* := *AwaitCoin*   END;

   Coffee ≙ SELECT   *VM* = *DeliverDrink*   THEN   *VM* := *AwaitCoin*   END

END .

The operations of the generated machine are described using SELECT statements. These provide a means of specifying reactive systems in which operations are only enabled in certain states. A statement of the form

   SELECT   *G*   THEN   *S*   END

is enabled only in those states for which the guard *G* is true. The generated B machine contains a 'control' variable named *VM*, the same as the name of the main process in the CSP description, of type *VMState*. The operations are guarded by and make assignments to this variable appropriately.

   The semantics of B operations is given in terms of weakest preconditions. For statement *S* and postcondition *Q*, $[S]Q$ represents the weakest precondition under which *S* is guaranteed to terminate in a state satisfying *Q*. The guard of a B operation *S* is defined using $[S]$ as follows[2] [2, 11]:

$$grd(S) \; \hat{=} \; \neg \, [S] \; false \; .$$

---

[2] $[S]$ *false* represents those initial states in which *A* could establish any postcondition, i.e., behave miraculously. An action is said to be enabled when it cannot behave miraculously, i.e., when ¬ $[S]$ *false* holds.

From this it is easy to show that

$$grd(\text{ SELECT } G \text{ THEN } S \text{ END }) \ = \ G \wedge grd(S)$$
$$grd(\ x := E \ ) \ = \ true \ .$$

2.1 Nested Prefixing

Nested prefixing in a CSP description is supported by the tool. For example, the vending machine could have been specified using a single equation:

$$AwaitCoin \ = \ Coin \rightarrow (Tea \rightarrow AwaitCoin \ [] \ Coffee \rightarrow AwaitCoin) \ .$$

In this case, the process enters an implicit unnamed state immediately after the *Coin* event. The tool will generate a fresh name for each such implicit state in the CSP description. For the above example, csp2B will generate a fresh name for this state based on the name on the left hand side of the equation as follows:

SETS *VMState* = { *AwaitCoin*, *AwaitCoin_1* }

Coin $\hat{=}$ SELECT *VM* = *AwaitCoin* THEN *VM* := *AwaitCoin_1* END .

2.2 Parallel Processes

It is possible to have more than one process description in a single CSP specification. For example, if for some reason we wanted the vending machine to always alternate between delivering tea and coffee, we could add a process, in this case called *Alternate*, as follows:

MACHINE *VendingMachine*

    ALPHABET *Coin* *Tea* *Coffee*

    PROCESS *VM* = *AwaitCoin* WHERE ... END

    PROCESS *Alternate* = *Alt*
    CONSTRAINS *Tea* *Coffee* WHERE
       Alt = *Coffee* $\rightarrow$ *Tea* $\rightarrow$ *Alt*
    END
END .

The (optional) *CONSTRAINS* clause in the *Alternate* process signifies that this process description only constrains the *Tea* and *Coffee* operations and places no constraint on when the *Coin* operation may occur.

In the generated machine, the operations constrained by more than one process will be composed of several parallel SELECT statements. For example, the *Coffee* action will be as follows:

Coffee $\hat{=}$
    SELECT *VM* = *DeliverDrink* THEN *VM* := *AwaitCoin* END
    ||
    SELECT *Alternate* = *Alt* THEN *Alternate* := *Alt_1* END .

The guard of a parallel statement satisfies the following [1]:

$$grd(S \parallel T) \quad = \quad trm(S) \wedge trm(T) \; \Rightarrow \; grd(S) \wedge grd(T) \; .$$

Here, $trm(S)$ is the termination condition of S. The tool always generates statements from CSP descriptions whose termination condition is always true (such as the SELECT statements for *Coffee* above). In that case, $grd(S \parallel T) = grd(S) \wedge grd(T)$. This means that events common to several processes will only be enabled when each of those processes is willing to engage in that event. This corresponds to the CSP notion of parallel composition (see Section 3.4).

2.3   Parameterised Events and Indexing

In the manner of channels in CSP, events may be parameterised by input parameters $(Ev?x)$ or output parameters $(Ev!y)$. When translated into B, these parameters will correspond to the input and output parameters of an operation. Also, processes may be indexed by parameters and these index parameters become state variables in the generated B machine. As an example of each of these, consider the following two process equations:

$$Idle \quad = \quad In?f \rightarrow Remember(f)$$
$$Remember(f) \quad = \quad Out!f \rightarrow Idle \; .$$

In the terminology of CSP, *In* and *Out* are input and output channels respectively. Process *Idle* inputs a value f on channel *In* and then behaves as *Remember* indexed by f. *Remember(f)* outputs the index value on channel *Out* and then behaves as *Idle*.

The input parameter acts as a bound variable and its scope is the syntactic process term which the event prefixes. The output value may be defined by any B expression. The input and output parameters must be declared in the alphabet of a CSP specification in the form:

$$(y1, y2, ...) \longleftarrow OpName(x1 : T1, x2 : T2, ...) \; .$$

The types of the input parameters are needed for the generated B machine, but the output types are not needed as they are inferred by a B tool. Types are any B expression. The event in the CSP description is written in the form

$$OpName?x1?x2?...!y1!y2!...$$

A file transfer service that inputs files and then outputs them may be specified as follows:

```
MACHINE  FileTransfer
SETS  Byte
DEFINITIONS  File == seq Byte
ALPHABET  Send(f : File)   f ⟵ Receive
    PROCESS  Copy = Idle  WHERE
        Idle  =  Send?f → Remember(f)
        Remember(g : File)  =  Receive!g → Idle
    END
END .
```

The indexing variable g in this specification becomes a state variable of type *File* in the generated B machine. It is called g to distinguish it from the input and output parameter f of the *Send* and *Receive* operations. The *Send* operation assigns the value of its input parameter f to the variable g while the *Receive* operation reads from g. Within a PROCESS description the same indexing variable may be used in several equations and each occurrence will refer to the same variable in the generated machine.

Notice that the above specification contains a standard B SETS clause and a standard B DEFINITIONS clause. These will be carried over into the generated machine.

Idle could also be declared using nested prefixing as follows:

$$Idle \;=\; Send?f \rightarrow Receive!f \rightarrow Idle \; .$$

In this case, as well as introducing a name for the implicit state immediately after the *Send* event, csp2B also introduces a variable to store the input value f. This is because f remains in scope until the recursive call to *Idle* and, as is the case here, may be referred to. Whenever an event with an input parameter is not immediately followed by a recursive call, then a new state variable will be introduced to the generated B machine to store that input parameter.

The actual value for a process index in a recursive call may be any B expression. Furthermore, IF – THEN – ELSE statements may be used in process descriptions and the guard may be any B predicate. This is illustrated by the following example:

```
MACHINE  BUFFER(T)
ALPHABET  In(x : T)    x ⟵ Out
    PROCESS  InitBuffer  =  Buffer([ ])  WHERE
        Buffer(s : seq T)  =
            IF   s = [ ]
            THEN  In?x → Buffer([x])
            ELSE    In?x → Buffer(s ⌢ [x])
                 [] Out!first(s) → Buffer(tail(s))
        END
END .
```

Input parameters may also be 'dot' parameters, which means that a process is only willing to accept a particular value as input rather than being willing to accept any value. This is illustrated by the following CSP example:

$$Free \;=\; Lock?u \rightarrow Locked(u)$$

$$Locked(v : USER) \;=\; \begin{aligned} & Access.v \rightarrow Locked(v) \\ & [] \; Unlock.v \rightarrow Free \; . \end{aligned}$$

Here, any user u may lock some shared resource. Once it has been locked by u only that user may access or unlock the resource. A dot argument for an event may be any B expression and corresponds to an input parameter of an operation. A clause is added to the guard of the generated operation to constrain the input parameter so that it equals the dot value. For example, the *Access* operation generated from the above CSP would be:

$$Access(u) \ \hat{=} \ \text{SELECT} \ P = Locked \wedge u = v \ \text{THEN} \ \textit{skip} \ \text{END}.$$

In the case that a CSP specification consists of more than one process, each output parameter of an operation may be determined by at most one of the processes, though different processes may determine different output parameters for the same operation.

2.4   Interleaving

A process may be defined as an interleaved composition of a set of indexed instances of a process. This is illustrated in the following example:

```
MACHINE  MultiFileTransfer
ALPHABET  Send(u : User,  v : User,  f : File)
             f ⟵ Receive(u : User,  v : User)
    PROCESS  MultiCopy  =    ||| u, v.Copy[u, v]  WHERE
         Copy[u, v]  =  Send.u.v?f → Receive.u.v!f → Copy[u, v]
    END
  END .
```

Here, *MultiCopy* is defined as the interleaved composition of an indexed set of instances of *Copy*, where *Copy* is indexed by a pair of variables u, v, both of type *User*. The indexing variables for the interleaving are placed in square brackets rather than round brackets because they are treated differently to standard process parameters. In the translation to B, the state of the process is represented by a function from the indexing set to the appropriate control type and an operation refers to the point in this function determined by its indexing input parameters. With the above example, two functions, representing the control states and the input parameter f, are generated. Both these functions take pairs of users as arguments corresponding to the indexing parameters of *Copy*. Each operation is indexed by a pair of users and accesses the functions at a point determined by the indexing pair of users. The generated machine is illustrated in Figure 1. Note that the operations of this machine have preconditions which constrain the input parameters as well as guards. The preconditions are required in B to determine the types of the input parameters.

2.5   Conjunction

A CSP machine may be used to constrain the execution order of a standard B machine. Consider the B machine shown in Figure 2 which contains a variable representing a counter and operations for incrementing, decrementing and reading the counter.

MACHINE *MultiFileTransfer*
SETS *MultiCopyState* = { *Copy, Copy_1* }
VARIABLES *MultiCopy, f_1*
INVARIANT
    $MultiCopy \in (User \times User) \rightarrow MultiCopyState$ ∧
    $f\_1 \in (User \times User) \rightarrow File$
INITIALISATION $MultiCopy := \lambda u, v.(u \in User \land v \in User \mid Copy)$

OPERATIONS

    $Send(u, v, f) \;\hat{=}$
        PRE $u \in User \land v \in User \land f \in File$ THEN
            SELECT $MultiCopy(u, v) = Copy$
            THEN $MultiCopy(u, v) := Copy\_1$ || $f\_1(u, v) := f$
        END
    END;

    $f \longleftarrow Receive(u, v) \;\hat{=}$
        PRE $u \in User \land v \in User$ THEN
            SELECT $MultiCopy(u, v) = Copy\_1$
            THEN $MultiCopy(u, v) := Copy$ || $f := f\_1(u, v)$
        END
    END
END

Fig. 1. Generated machine for *MultiFileTransfer*.

The ordering of these operations may be further constrained by the CSP specification shown in Figure 3. This process description forces a user v to lock the counter before it can be manipulated by v and prevents other users from manipulating it while it is locked by v. Notice that the process description places no constraint on the x parameter of the *Inc* and *Dec* operations nor does it constrain the *Read* operation.

The CONJOINS clause in Figure 3 signifies that the CSP specification is constraining the B machine *CounterActs*. For each event name *OpName* in the alphabet of the CSP specification, the conjoined machine should have a corresponding operation called *OpName_Act* as shown in the *CounterActs* machine of Figure 2.

The B machine generated by csp2B from the *Counter* specification of Figure 3 will include the *CounterActs* machine using the machine inclusion mechanism of B. Each operation, *OpName*, in the generated machine will include a guarded call to the corresponding *OpName_Act* operation of the included machine. That is, if S represents the parallel composition of the statements generated from the

MACHINE *BUFFER_Acts(T)*
VARIABLES *s*
INVARIANT $s \in \text{seq } T$
INITIALISATION $s := [\ ]$

OPERATIONS
    $In\_Act(x) \;\hat{=}\; \text{PRE } x \in T \text{ THEN } s := s \frown [x] \text{ END};$

    $Out\_Act(u, x) \;\hat{=}\; \text{PRE } x \in T \wedge s \neq [\ ] \text{ THEN } s := tail(s) \text{ END}$
END

Fig. 4. B part of buffer.

MACHINE *BUFFER(T)*
CONJOINS *BUFFER_Acts(T)*
ALPHABET $In(x \in T)$ $x \longleftarrow Out$

    PROCESS *InitBuffer* = *Buffer*
    CONSTRAINS *In* $y \longleftarrow Out$ WHERE
        Buffer =
            IF $s = [\ ]$
                THEN *In* → *Buffer*
                ELSE *In* → *Buffer*   [ ]   *Out!first(s)* → *Buffer*
    ENDEND

Fig. 5. CSP part of buffer.

incoming file is stored in the variable *afile* while an outgoing file comes from the variable *bfile*. The contents of *afile* are gradually transferred to *bfile* using a byte-wise transmission protocol. The CSP part describes the ordering of events whereby both sides in a transmission agree to start a transmission (*OpenReq* followed by *OpenResp*), then transfer each bit using a succession of *Trans* events and then finish the transmission. Operations such as *OpenReq* that do not appear in the abstract specification *FileTransfer* nor in the conjoined machine *FileTransferRefinement* are all *skip* actions and have been omitted here.

The refinement invariant used to prove the refinement is included in the CSP specification of Figure 6. This invariant refers to the abstract and concrete control variables (*Copy* and *ByteWise* respectively) and, when deriving the invariant, it was useful to be able to perform the translation of the CSP description in order to see an explicit representation of its state and state transitions. The invariant is then added to the CSP specification and the translation performed again. The invariant is copied over into the generated B machine and is used by the proof obligation generator of a B tool.

MACHINE   *File TransferRefinement*
REFINES   *File Transfer*
CONJOINS   *File TransferRefinementActs(Byte)*

INVARIANT
$(ByteWise \in \{BW_1, BW_2\} \Rightarrow f\_1 = afile) \wedge$
$(ByteWise = Transfer \Rightarrow f\_1 = bfile \frown afile) \wedge$
$(ByteWise = Transfer\_1 \Rightarrow f\_1 = bfile)$
$\wedge$
$(Copy = Idle \Leftrightarrow ByteWise \in \{BW, Transfer\_2\}) \wedge$
$(Copy = Idle\_1 \Leftrightarrow ByteWise \in \{BW\_1, BW\_2, Transfer, Transfer\_1\})$

ALPHABET   *Send(f : File)* $f \longleftarrow Receive$
                 OpenReq   OpenResp   TransBlock   EndTrans   Ack

PROCESS   *ByteWise* = *BW* WHERE
    $BW = Send \rightarrow OpenReq \rightarrow OpenResp \rightarrow Transfer$
    Transfer =
        IF   *afile* = [ ]
            THEN $EndTrans \rightarrow Receive \rightarrow Ack \rightarrow BW$
            ELSE $TransBlock \rightarrow Transfer$
END
END

Fig. 6. CSP part of *File Transfer* refinement.

3   Semantic Issues

In [9], Hoare takes a denotational approach to the semantics of CSP by defining the Failure-Divergences model for processes. It is also possible to take an operational approach by considering processes as Labelled Transition Systems (LTS) in the manner of Milner's CCS [10]. The B machine generated from a CSP specification may be viewed as an LTS and, for this reason we, take an operational approach to justifying the semantics of the csp2B translation. Roscoe [12] shows how the denotational and operational models of CSP are linked.

In the absence of CSP processes being allowed to access the state variables of conjoined B machines, the semantics is entirely compositional. That is, the semantics of the combination of several CSP processes conjoined with a B machine (viewed as an LTS) is precisely CSP parallel composition. This entails monotonicity of refinement allowing the B machine to be refined independently. However, as we shall see, this compositionality fails when sharing of state variables occurs. First we consider the case where no sharing of variables occurs and look at normal forms for CSP processes and how they define an LTS.

MACHINE *FileTransferRefinementActs(Byte)*
VARIABLES *afile, bfile*
INVARIANT *afile ∈ File ∧ bfile ∈ File*

OPERATIONS

> *Send_Act(f)* ≙ PRE *f ∈ File* THEN *afile := f* END;
>
> *f ⟵ Receive_Act* ≙ *f := bfile*;
>
> *TransBlock_Act* ≙ *bfile := bfile ⌢ (first afile)* || *afile := tail(afile)*

END

Fig. 7. B part of *FileTransfer* refinement.

3.1   Normal Form

In the notation supported by csp2B, a process is described by a set of equations
of the form

$$I_i(v) \;=\; P_i \;,$$

where I_i is a process identifier and P_i is a process term which may contain
several process identifiers. A process term P is said to be in *normal form* either
if $P = STOP$ or if P is a choice in which each branch is a boolean-guarded event
prefixing a recursive call to another process identifier, that is,

$$P \;=\; Q_1 \;[\!] \;\cdots\; [\!]\; Q_n \;,$$

where each Q_i is of the form

$$\text{IF} \quad G \quad \text{THEN} \quad a \to I(e) \;.$$

Here I must be the identifier on the left of a process equation and not a more
complicated process term. The event a may contain input, output and dot parameters. We assume that choice is associative and commutative.

There is an important syntactic restriction in csp2B which requires that all
recursive calls are prefixed by an event and this includes recursive calls in the
branches of an IF-statement. This ensures that any set of syntactically-correct
process equations may be transformed to normal form.

IF-statements are distributed through a term using the following transformations:

$$\text{IF} \quad G \quad \text{THEN} \quad P \quad \text{ELSE} \quad Q = (\text{IF} \quad G \quad \text{THEN} \quad P)\,[\!]\,(\text{IF} \; \neg \, G \quad \text{THEN} \quad Q)$$
$$\text{IF} \quad G \quad \text{THEN} \quad (P \;[\!]\; Q) = (\text{IF} \quad G \quad \text{THEN} \quad P)\,[\!]\,(\text{IF} \quad G \quad \text{THEN} \quad Q)$$
$$\text{IF} \quad G \quad \text{THEN} \quad (\text{IF} \quad H \quad \text{THEN} \quad P) = (\text{IF} \quad G \wedge H \quad \text{THEN} \quad P) \;.$$

Nested prefixing is normalised by introducing new equations. An equation of the form

$$I(v) \; = \; (\text{IF } G \text{ THEN } a \to P) \; \| \; Q \; ,$$

where P is not a process identifier, is replaced by the pair of equations

$$I(v) \; = \; (\text{IF } G \text{ THEN } a \to J(v, w)) \; \| \; Q$$
$$J(v, w) \; = \; P$$

Here, J is some fresh process identifier and w is the list of input parameters in the event a (with renaming to fresh variables where necessary to avoid name clashes). The introduction of w is necessary because P may refer to any input parameters of a.

Terms involving $STOP$ are simplified as follows:

$$\text{IF } G \text{ THEN } STOP \; = \; STOP$$
$$STOP \; \| \; P \; = \; P.$$

In the case that a set of process equations has different parameter lists, then the parameter lists are extended to the merge of all the parameters. For example, a pair of process equations

$$I(v) \; = \; a \to J(e)$$
$$J(w) \; = \; b \to I(f) \; ,$$

becomes

$$I(v, w) \; = \; a \to J(v, e)$$
$$J(v, w) \; = \; b \to I(f, w) \; .$$

3.2   Labelled Transition Systems

A process specification consisting of a set of normal-form equations defines an LTS. The state space is the cartesian product of the set of process identifiers with the type of the indexing parameters. We continue to write elements of this state space as $I(v)$. The labels of the LTS are the parameterised event names. A label may consist of several components $c.i.j.$ and an event of the form $c.i?y!k$ stands for the set of labels $\{ \; c.i.j.k \; | \; j \in Y \; \}$, where Y is the type of input parameter y. The LTS may make a transition labelled $a.i.j.k$ from state $I(v)$ to $I'(v')$, written

$$I(v) \; \xrightarrow{a.i.j.k} \; I'(v') \; , \tag{1}$$

if the set of normalised equation contains an equation of the form

$$I(v) \; = \; \cdots \; \| \; \text{IF } G(v) \text{ THEN } a.i?y!k \to I'(V(y)) \; \| \; \cdots \; , \tag{2}$$

and $G(v)$ holds and $v' = V(j)$.

In converting a CSP specification to B, csp2B normalises the set of equations as described previously and then constructs a B machine corresponding to the LTS. The state space is represented by the state variables of the machine, the labels are represented by the operation names (along with input and output parameters) and the transitions are represented by the operations. The B machine contains state variables (v) corresponding to the list of indexing parameters as well as a special control variable (p) typed over the set of process identifiers from the left hand sides of the equations. For each event name a in the alphabet of the CSP process, the B machine contains an operation of the form

$$z \longleftarrow a(x, y) \,\hat{=}\, S_a \ ,$$

where S_a is constructed in the following manner: For each occurrence of event a in a normalised CSP process equation of the form (2), the B operation has a SELECT branch of the form:

$$\text{SELECT} \ \ G(v) \wedge p = I \wedge x = i \ \ \text{THEN} \ \ p, v, z := I', V(y), k \ \ \text{END} \ . \quad (3)$$

The clause $x = i$ ensures that the input value x matches the dot value i. All the branches of S_a are composed using the B choice operator $S \,[\!]\, T$.

We briefly outline why the LTS defined by the set of normalised equations is the same as the LTS defined by the constructed B machine. In order to define when a transition is allowed by a B operation, we use the notion of conjugate weakest precondition defined as follows [11]:

$$\langle S \rangle Q \,\hat{=}\, \neg \, [S] \neg \, Q \ .$$

$\langle S \rangle Q$ represents the weakest precondition under which it is possible for S to establish Q (as opposed to the guarantee provided by $[S]Q$). If the machine contains an operation of the form

$$z \longleftarrow a(x, y) \,\hat{=}\, S_a$$

then the transition

$$I(w) \overset{a.i.j.k}{\longrightarrow} I'(w') \quad (4)$$

is possible in state $I(w)$ provided

$$\langle \ p, v, x, y := I, w, i, j \ ; \ \ S_a \ \rangle \ (p, v, z = I', w', k) \quad (5)$$

holds. That is, provided it is possible for S_a to establish an outcome in which p and v equal $I'(w')$ and z equals k when p, v, x, y are initialised appropriately.

Now, a process equation of the form (2) enables a transition of the form (4) in state $I(w)$ when $G(w)$ holds. Using (5), it is easy to show that this is precisely the same condition under which the choice branch (3) allows this transition. Furthermore transition (4) is allowed if there is some occurrence of event a in some normalised CSP process equation. Likewise, the constructed B operation allows the transition if there is some choice branch that allows it which follows from:

$$\langle S \ [\!] \ T \rangle Q \ = \ \langle S \rangle Q \ \lor \ \langle T \rangle Q \ . \tag{6}$$

Thus the transition relation $\xrightarrow{a.i.j.k}$ defined by the set of normalised CSP process equations is the same as the transition relation defined by the constructed B machine.

3.3   Interleaving

The csp2B tool supports interleaving of processes at the outermost level only. This interleaving has the form $|||\ i.P[i]$ where all of the instances $P[i]$ behave in a similar way except for the indexing of event labels by i. Such an interleaving represents multiple instance of $P[i]$ running in parallel where the parallel instances do not interact with each other in any way. This interleaving is modelled as a single large LTS whose state is modelled by replicated instances of the state that a single $P[i]$ would normally have. Thus, if the LTS for a single $P[i]$ would normally have a state space Σ and i ranges over an indexing set I, then the state space of the large LTS is $I \to \Sigma$. This is the basis for the translation to B of interleaving described in Section 2.4.

3.4   Compositionality

The parallel composition of two LTS's P and Q is an LTS $P \parallel Q$ formed by taking the cartesian product of their state spaces and merging common actions. If a is common to P and Q, then their composition has a transition labelled a as defined by the following rule:

$$\frac{I \xrightarrow{a} I' \in P \quad \land \quad J \xrightarrow{a} J' \in Q}{(I, J) \xrightarrow{a} (I', J') \in P \parallel Q \ .} \tag{7}$$

This models synchronised parallelism since both P and Q must be in states that enable a for a to be enabled in $P \parallel Q$. Events that are present in only one of the processes result in transitions that have no effect on the other process. Thus, if a is an event of P but not of Q, then the composition has a transition defined by the following rule:

$$\frac{I \xrightarrow{a} I' \in P}{(I, J) \xrightarrow{a} (I', J) \in P \parallel Q \ .}$$

Similarly for the case where a is an event of Q only.

When generating a B machine from parallel processes and a conjoined machine, csp2B composes the appropriate statements using the B parallel operator. Thus, given two parallel processes P and Q, csp2B constructs an operation of the form $S \parallel T$ for the generated B machine, where S is constructed from P and T is constructed from Q in the usual way. The following result about the B parallel operator is important in showing that this corresponds to the LTS definition of parallel composition: Let S be a statement that assigns to x only and let T be a statement that assigns to y only. Let M be a predicate that depends on x only and let N be a statement that depends on y only. If $trm(S) = trm(T) = true$, then

$$\langle S \parallel T \rangle (M \wedge N) \;=\; \langle S \rangle M \;\wedge\; \langle T \rangle N \; . \tag{8}$$

Using this result, it is easy to show that the relationship between transitions allowed by S and T and those allowed by $S \parallel T$ is precisely that of (7). Thus, in the absence of variable sharing, the parallel composition used by csp2B corresponds to the CSP definition of parallelism.

An important consequence of this result is that, since CSP parallel composition is monotonic with respect to refinement, a conjoined machine may be refined separately while maintaining the refinement of the overall system. Refinement of CSP processes is defined in terms of the Failures-Divergences model. Based on [11, 13], [5] defines the Failures-Divergences semantics of B machines and shows that refinement of B machines corresponds to refinement at the Failures-Divergences level[4].

3.5   Divergence and Nontermination

In the above presentation, we have assumed that systems never diverge. This will always be the case for CSP processes written in the notation supported by csp2B since it does not contain a hiding operator. However, Morgan [11] shows that it is appropriate to equate nontermination of operations with divergent behaviour and the operations of a conjoined B machine may be nonterminating in some states, e.g., operations of the form PRE M THEN S END. This situation may be dealt with by introducing a special bottom state modelling divergence to the LTS model along with several extra transition rules. Alternatively, one may directly define the failures and divergences of a B machine using conjugate weakest-precondition formulae in the manner of [11]. (We have found this latter approach to be the most convenient.) Either way one can show that the correspondence between CSP parallelism, and the composition used in the construction of B machines by csp2B, holds. Such a proof is presented in detail in [4]. We presented an LTS-style justification in this paper since it is simpler (though less comprehensive) and portrays the essence of the translation.

The potential presence of nontermination in a conjoined operation makes it essential to guard calls to the conjoined machine, i.e., if S is the operation constructed from a CSP process and T is a call to the conjoined machine, then the operation in the generated B machine has the form:

---

[4] Strictly speaking, for this correspondence to hold, an extra condition on refinement of B machines is introduced which requires that the guard of an abstract operation implies the guard of a concrete operation.

$$S \parallel \text{SELECT } grd(S) \text{ THEN } T \text{ END} . \tag{9}$$

If T was not guarded by $grd(S)$, then the composition of S and T would be enabled in any state in which T is nonterminating, even if S is not enabled in that state. This arises from the definition of $S \parallel T$, and we have, for example, that

$$\text{SELECT } false \text{ THEN } skip \text{ END} \parallel abort \quad = \quad abort .$$

Guarding T avoids the possibility of the composition being enabled in states where S is not enabled. It is not necessary to guard S since it is constructed from a nondivergent CSP process and will therefore be fully terminating.

3.6   Variable Sharing

In the case where a CSP process refers to the state variables of a conjoined machine, the compositionality result no longer holds. This is because the CSP processes cannot be given an independent CSP semantics if they refer to variables outside their control. Interaction between processes in CSP is based purely on interaction via synchronised events and allowing them to access the state of another machine would allow for stronger interaction that just synchronisation over shared events.

In the case where sharing of variables occurs, the semantics of the whole system is given by normalising the CSP processes in the usual way and collapsing the results, along with the conjoined machine, into a single large LTS. This single large then needs to be refined as a whole. Of course the modularity provided by B for structuring developments can still be availed of, and the whole system does not have to be represented as a single B machine, rather its semantics are those of a single LTS.

4   Conclusions

We have presented an outline of the functionality of the csp2B tool and provided an operational-semantic justification for the way in which it translates CSP to B. The supported CSP notation provides a powerful way of describing ordering constraints for reactive system development and enhances the standard B notation. The tool provides a useful extension to the B Method and can easily be used in conjunction with existing B tools.

An interesting feature of the tool is that it accepts expressions, types and predicates written in standard B notation, copying them directly to the generated B machine. This means that it supports quite a rich CSP notation.

There are features of CSP that are not supported by the tool, namely non-determinism, event hiding and arbitrary (i.e., not just at the outermost level) parallel composition and interleaving. Supporting these features would result in a lot of complexity in the generated B machines. For example, extra flag variables would have to be introduced to model the CSP nondeterministic choice operator.

Some of these features can be achieved directly in the B part of a specification. Nondeterminism can be modelled in the B part using nondeterministic constructs of B. Event hiding may be modelled using the notion of internal operations in B machines as introduced in [5]. The tool has been applied to a larger example (a form of distributed database) [8] than those presented here and the restrictions in the supported CSP notation did not prove a hindrance.

References

[1] J.-R. Abrial. *The B-Book*. Cambridge University Press, 1996.

[2] J.-R. Abrial and L. Mussat. Introducing dynamic constraints in B. In D. Bert, editor, *Second International B Conference*, April 1998.

[3] R.J.R. Back and R. Kurki-Suonio. Decentralisation of process nets with centralised control. In *2nd ACM SIGACT-SIGOPS Symp. on Principles of Distributed Computing*, pages 131–142, 1983.

[4] M.J. Butler. *A CSP Approach To Action Systems*. D.Phil. Thesis, Programming Research Group, Oxford University, 1992.

[5] M.J. Butler. An approach to the design of distributed systems with B AMN. In J.P. Bowen, M.G. Hinchey, and D. Till, editors, *10th International Conference of Z Users (ZUM'97)*, volume LNCS 1212, pages 223 – 241. Springer–Verlag, April 1997.

[6] M.J. Butler. csp2B User Manual. Available from http://www.ecs.soton.ac.uk/~mjb/csp2B, 1999.

[7] M.J. Butler and M. Waldén. Distributed system development in B. In H. Habrias, editor, *First B Conference*, November 1996.

[8] P. Hartel, M. Butler, A. Currie, P. Henderson, M. Leuschel, A. Martin, A. Smith, U. Ultes-Nitsche, and B. Walters. Questions and answers about ten formal methods. In *Proc. 4th Int. Workshop on Formal Methods for Industrial Critical Systems*, Trento, Italy, Jul 1999. http://www.dsse.ecs.soton.ac.uk/techreports/99-1.html.

[9] C.A.R. Hoare. *Communicating Sequential Processes*. Prentice–Hall, 1985.

[10] R. Milner. *Communication and Concurrency*. Prentice–Hall, 1989.

[11] C.C. Morgan. Of wp and CSP. In W.H.J. Feijen, A.J.M. van Gasteren, D. Gries, and J. Misra, editors, *Beauty is our business: a birthday salute to Edsger W. Dijkstra*. Springer–Verlag, 1990.

[12] A.W. Roscoe. *The Theory and Practice of Concurrency*. Prentice–Hall, 1998.

[13] J.C.P. Woodcock and C.C. Morgan. Refinement of state-based concurrent systems. In D. Bjørner, C.A.R. Hoare, and H. Langmaack, editors, *VDM '90*, volume LNCS 428, pages 340–351. Springer–Verlag, 1990.

Test Criteria Definition for B Models

Salimeh Behnia [1], Hélène Waeselynck [2]

[1] LAAS-CNRS and INRETS
[2] LAAS-CNRS
7, avenue du Colonel Roche, 31077 Toulouse Cedex 4, France
{behnia, waeselyn}@laas.fr

Abstract. Test criteria are defined in order to guide the selection of subsets of the input domain to be covered during testing. A unification of two categories of test criteria, program based and specification based, is presented. Such a unification is possible for B models because the specification, refinement concepts and implementation are captured in one notation. The notion of control flow graph is extended to handle the abstract constructs of the generalized substitution language, and a link between the coverage of the graph and the coverage of the before-after predicate is established. A set of criteria for the coverage of the control flow graph is proposed. These criteria are partially ordered according to their stringency, so that the coverage strategy may be tuned according to the complexity of the operation under test.

1   Introduction

Testing is a partial verification technique that consists in exercising a target piece of software by supplying it with a sample of input values. Since exhaustive testing is generally not tractable, the tester is faced with the problem of selecting a proper subset of the input domain. The selection is guided by *test criteria* that specify a set of elements to be covered during testing. This paper focuses on the definition of test criteria for B models. It extends previous work establishing a validation framework for the B development process [13]. The aim is to track down specification faults originating from a misunderstanding of the functional requirements, or from the failure to adequately express an understood requirement.

The B formal development process can be seen as a series of stages where more and more concrete models of the application are built, the final code being just a compiled version of the most concrete one. In order to validate these models, we have defined a uniform testing framework, irrespective of the development stage and of whether the test inputs are supplied to the final code or to the formal models [13]. Within the uniform framework, we wish to be equipped with coverage criteria that can be applied not only to the most abstract model (i.e. before refinement), but also to any intermediate model obtained during development. This must be so because, in typical B projects, the smallest meaningful model with respect to the functional requirements is likely to involve a few steps of refinement (see e.g. the modeling approach adopted by the French railway industry [2]). As a result, the target model to

J. Wing, J. Woodcock, J. Davies (Eds.): FM'99, Vol. I, LNCS 1708, pp. 509-529, 1999.
© Springer-Verlag Berlin Heidelberg 1999

be covered   may involve abstract constructs of the B notation, or implementation ones, or a mix of both.

Covering a program and covering an abstract specification correspond to different approaches in the literature on testing. Structural analysis of programs (see e.g. [9]) is usually based on a compact view of their control structure, the control flow graph, that may be supplemented with data flow information. Examples of related criteria are All-Statements, All-Branches or All-Paths, demanding the coverage of the nodes (resp. edges, paths) of the graph: such approaches may be easily transferred to the most concrete B models whose allowed syntactic constructs are similar to program statements. As regards specification based testing, existing approaches vary depending on the used formalism. In case of model-based specifications like Z and VDM, test criteria exploit the structure of the before-after predicates [8, 10]: they demand the coverage of a set of disjunctive cases extracted from the original predicates. As exemplified by [11], such approaches can be transferred to B models, by producing the before-after predicates corresponding to generalized substitutions.

A unification of both categories of criteria, program based and specification based, is presented in this paper. This is done by extending the notion of control flow graph to handle the abstract constructs of the generalized substitution language, and by showing that the coverage of this graph is related to the coverage of the before-after predicate. Such a unification is possible for B models because the specification, refinement concepts and implementation are captured in one notation.

After a very brief overview of the B method (Section 2), we introduce our uniform testing framework for B models, and explain its relation with the problem addressed in this paper (Section 3). In Section 4, we present some specification based and program based structural criteria that have been proposed in the literature. The unification of these structural approaches to cover B models is proposed in Section 5. In Section 6, we define a new set of criteria that are partially ordered according to their stringency. These criteria are illustrated by a simple example.

2   Overview of the B Method

The B method due to J-R. Abrial [1] is a model-based approach for the incremental development of specifications and their refinements down to an implementation. Proof obligations accompany the construction of the software.

The *abstract machine* is the basic element of a B development. It characterizes a machine which has an invisible memory and a number of keys. The values stored in the memory form the *state* of the machine, whereas the various keys are the *operations* that a user is able to activate in order to modify the state. A unique Abstract Machine Notation (AMN) is used for the description of machines at various levels of abstraction, in MACHINE, REFINEMENT and IMPLEMENTATION components.

The *declarative part* of a component describes its encapsulated state according to set-theoretic model and first order logic. The invariant states the static laws that the data must obey, whatever the operation applied.

Various *composition clauses* are defined in the B method, in order to be able to develop large software systems. Refinement is introduced by means of the REFINES clause. As soon as the refined version of an abstract machine becomes too complicated, it is decomposed into smaller components, through the IMPORTS clause. The IMPORTS clause proceeds according to the layered paradigm: the importing machine uses the service offered by the ones imported from lower layers. Those lower layer machines are then independently refined and decomposed into smaller components. Other clauses introduced in [1] are INCLUDES, USES, SEES and EXTENDS that enrich the formal text of a component according to specific composition rules.

The *execution part* of a component, which specifies the dynamics, contains the initialization and some operations which are described under the form of a precondition and an action. The corresponding syntactic structures are interpreted in the *generalized substitution language*. The generalized substitutions (see Table 1) are predicate transformers: $[S]R$ denotes the weakest precondition for substitution S to establish postcondition R. For example, for the simple substitution $X := X + 1$ and the postcondition $X = 5$ to be established, we have: $[X := X + 1] X = 5 \Leftrightarrow X + 1 = 5 \Leftrightarrow X = 4$. To facilitate the development of abstract machines, syntactic sugar is introduced. For example, $P \mid S$ is rewritten as PRE P THEN S END.

Table 1. A Subset of Generalized Substitution: x denotes a variable, E is an expression, R and P are predicates, S and T are generalized substitutions

Syntactic Category	Syntax	Semantics
Simple substitution	$x := E$	$[x := E] R \Leftrightarrow$ replacing all free occurrences of x in R by E
no-op	skip	$[skip] R \Leftrightarrow R$
Preconditioning	$P \mid S$	$[P \mid S] R \Leftrightarrow P \wedge [S] R$
Bounded choice	$S \, \acute{e} \, T$	$[S \, \acute{e} \, T] R \Leftrightarrow [S] R \wedge [T] R$
Guarded substitution	$P \Rightarrow S$	$[P \Rightarrow S] R \Leftrightarrow P => [S] R$
Unbounded choice	$@x . S$	$[@x . S] R \Leftrightarrow \forall x.[S] R$ where x is not free in R

Preconditioned substitutions are related to the notion of *termination*. Given a substitution S, trm (S) denotes the predicate that holds if and only if S terminates:

$$trm(S) \Leftrightarrow [S](x = x)$$

The concept of guarded substitutions is related to the one of feasibility. It would be possible to specify *infeasible* substitutions able to establish any postcondition: this clearly happens when the guard cannot hold. Given a substitution S working with variable x, mir (S) (miracle) and its negation fis (S) (feasible) are defined as:

$$mir \, (S) \Leftrightarrow [S](x \neq x) \qquad\qquad fis \, (S) \Leftrightarrow \neg \, [S](x \neq x)$$

The before-after predicate corresponding to substitution S working with variable x is defined by $prd_x (S)$, where the after-value is denoted by priming the variable:

$$prd_x \Leftrightarrow \neg \, [S](x' \bullet x)$$

The following properties are demonstrated in the B-Book:

(a) fis $(S) \Leftrightarrow \mathrm{E}x' \cdot prd_x (S)$ (b) $S = trm \, (S) \mid @x' \cdot (prd_x (S) \Rightarrow x := x')$

Property (a) indicates that a substitution is feasible (at x) if some after value x' is reachable from the before-value x, and property (b) states that a substitution is completely characterized by trm and prd.

Checking the mathematical consistency of a MACHINE component involves proving that its initialization establishes the invariant and that each operation, called within its precondition, terminates and preserves the invariant. Checking the correctness of a REFINEMENT or an IMPLEMENTATION involves checking that the initialization and the operations preserve the semantics of their corresponding more abstract versions. The composition clauses allow the proof to be modular, abstract machines being constructed in an incremental fashion from smaller, already proved components.

3   Purpose of a Uniform Testing Framework

Criteria based on formal models are typically used when testing a program against its specification. However, in our case, the search for such criteria arises in the context of on-going research on the validation of the formal models themselves [4, 12, 13].

The B development process can be seen as a series of stages where more and more concrete models of the application are built. Refinement is typically used both to replace abstract constructs of the notation by programmable ones, *and* to gradually introduce functional requirements into the models. It may be the case that some user requirements are captured only at the end of the process. Then validation may be done by testing the final code, which is a compiled version of the most concrete model. But it is better methodology to capture requirements in earlier stages. This also permits earlier validation, provided that there is a means to test B models. Several B animators already exist or are under development: hence the idea of a uniform framework, irrespective of whether the test cases are supplied to the final code or the models.

Our previous work covers two aspects: (i) identification of the development stages where intermediate testable models are obtained and (ii) formalization of the notions of test sequence and test oracle for the corresponding models, the test oracle being the mechanism for determining acceptance or rejection of the output results.

The first aspect identifies the models that may be the target of validation. The B method calls for the incremental development of abstract machines: the formal text corresponding to an abstract machine is split in smaller components linked by composition clauses. In order to be able to reason about the observable behavior specified in this way, we have defined a flattening algorithm that gives the abstract machine resulting from a set of B components [12]. For example, in Figure 1, *Model 1* is the abstract machine obtained by flattening Main.mch, A.mch and B.mch. The set of B components that can be flattened must satisfy architectural conditions that have been identified. The refinement relation can be applied to flattened abstract machines: in Figure 1, *Model 1* is refined by *Model 2*. Using this partial relation we may construct a hierarchy of flattened machines in decreasing order of abstraction: the top of the hierarchy is the model containing no REFINES or IMPORTS clauses; the bottom of the hierarchy is the final model to be automatically translated into a programming language; intermediate flattened models form the various development stages.

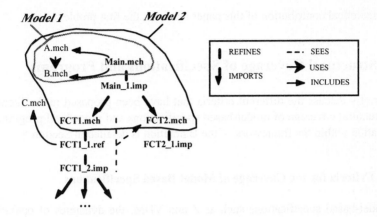

Fig. 1. Identification of development stages

The second aspect specifies what is to be controlled and what is to be observed when testing such models. A test sequence contains a finite sequence of calls to the operations of the machine, beginning with its initialization. It contains no reference to the state variables encapsulated in the machine: due to the hiding principle, the state of an abstract machine must be indirectly controlled and observed through calls to its operations. The oracle checks are defined in relation to the B notion of correctness, namely refinement. This allows us to take advantage of the formality of the B method: given a test sequence, acceptance of the results supplied by a model implies acceptance of the results supplied by proved refinements of this model. We also explored the practical consequences of these definitions in terms of required animation facilities.

The problem of test data selection was not addressed by our previous work. The criteria used for this purpose may refer to elements drawn from the structural analysis of the target B model, or the functional analysis of user requirements, or both. A typical approach could be to select functional test sequences and to supplement them by additional cases to achieve a target coverage of the B model. But the notion of model coverage requires further theoretical investigation: within the uniform framework, we wish to be equipped with criteria that can be applied to abstract models as well as concrete ones. Note that the same problem would arise if our aim was to test the final program against its B specification: the most abstract model is likely to be loose with respect to some required functional features, so that we would also have to consider a refined version of it.

Let us mention that the coverage of models actually involves two problems:

1. identification of test cases for individual operations. Such cases may depend on both the operation's input parameter and the current state of the abstract machine.

2. sequencing of operation calls. As test cases generated in the previous step depend on the internal state, their coverage necessitate to bring the abstract machine to the corresponding before state.

The theoretical contribution of this paper concerns the first problem.

4   Structural Coverage of Specifications and Programs

We briefly discuss the different criteria that have been proposed in the literature for the structural coverage of model-based specifications and procedural programs. Their unification within the framework of the B notation is detailed in Section 5.

4.1   Criteria for the Coverage of Model-Based Specifications

In model-based specifications such as Z and VDM, the dynamics of operations are expressed by means of a predicate relating the inputs (input parameters and before state) to the outputs (output parameters and after state). Such a before-after predicate may be used to derive a set of test cases for each operation. Existing approaches first flatten the specification of the operation, recursive definitions being unfolded a bounded number of times. Then they exploit the propositional structure of the resulting predicate to obtain a partition of the input domain: the corresponding test strategy will be to force (at least) one input to come from each subdomain. Since the analyzed predicate is based on the first order logic and set theory, these approaches cannot be fully automated.

The approach proposed by [8] is to reduce the predicate into a Disjunctive Normal Form (DNF) whose disjuncts yield the subdomains of the partition. As the transformation proceeds, the following rules are applied:

- $A \lor B$ is split into three disjoint cases $A \land B$, $\neg A \land B$ and $A \land \neg B$.
- $A => B$ is split into two disjoint cases $\neg A$ and $A \land B$.

An operation op is thus decomposed into disjoint cases op_i characterizing relations between input and output subdomains. Constraints involving only input parameters, or state variables, etc. may be extracted by existentially quantifying the other variables. For example, let us assume that operation op is working with formal parameters v_in, v_out and state variable s. We also adopt the convention that the after value of s is denoted by priming the identifier. Then, $\exists v\_out, s' \cdot op_i$ and $\exists v\_in, s \cdot op_i$ yield the input and output subdomains for each op_i.

Another approach [10] rewrites the operation predicate as $\bigvee_i (X_i \land Y_i)$ where:

- predicates X_i refer only to the inputs;
- predicates Y_i refer to the outputs.

The rewritten operation predicate is not necessarily in DNF, because X_i and Y_i may contain disjunctions. The idea is not to separate constraints that apply to the same category of variables. For example $(v\_in = 0 \lor v\_in = 1) \land (v\_out = v\_in + 1)$ has the desired form $X_i \wedge Y_i$. As argued by the author, predicate X_i needs not to be further split: it characterizes an input subdomain with uniform behavior. However, at that stage, a partition of the input domain is not yet obtained because the predicates may overlap. Disjoint subdomains are produced by forming their disjunction and applying the same rule as [8] to split it. For example, if the rewritten predicate was:

$$(X_1 \wedge Y_1) \vee (X_2 \wedge Y_2)$$

Then the resulting partition of the input domain would be:

$$X_1 \wedge X_2 \qquad\qquad \neg X_1 \wedge X_2 \qquad\qquad X_1 \wedge \neg X_2.$$

This partition is coarser than the one of [8] since the individual X_i have not been expanded. However, even [10] faces a scalability problem. As pointed out by the author, a specification in the form $\bigwedge_i (X_i \vee Y_i)$ with $1 \le i \le n$ would be rewritten as the disjunction of 2^n predicates.

Both approaches can be further refined by considering boundary cases and expansion of set-theoretic operators. For example, $x \le a$ may be split into two cases $x = a$, $x < a$; $e \in S_1 \cup S_2$ may be split into three cases $e \in S_1 \cap S_2$, $e \in S_1 - S_2$, $e \in S_2 - S_1$.

The partition analysis of each operation is used by the authors to produce a finite state automaton (FSA) from the model-based specification. The aim is to address the problem of the sequencing of test cases. The corresponding techniques are not presented in this paper.

4.2   Structural Coverage of Programs

Structural criteria have been defined for procedural programs (see e.g. [9]). Structural analysis of procedures is usually based on the analysis of their control flow graph that may be supplemented by data flow information. The source code is divided into basic blocks, i.e. single entry, single exit sequences of statements. Then, the control flow graph is constructed by making each basic block a node and drawing an arc for each possible transfer of control from one basic block to another. The control flow graph may be annotated by data flow information to mark the locations where a variable is assigned a value and the ones where it is used.

The execution of the procedure in response to one input can be seen as the exercising of one path in the graph: hence structural criteria for procedures are path selection criteria. For example, All-Statements (resp. All-Branches, All-Paths) requires the selection of a set of paths such as each node of the graph (resp. edge, path) is traversed at least once. There may be a large – if not infinite – number of paths due to the presence of loops: some specific criteria demand the coverage of a bounded number of iterations. Other data-flow criteria involve the coverage of subpaths between the definitions and uses of the variables. Finally, control and data flow criteria may be refined by considering boundary cases, or by expanding branch Boolean expressions (see e.g. [7]). All these criteria can be partially ordered according to their stringency.

Note that there may be infeasible paths in the graph, i.e. paths for which no test data can be found: such paths are excluded from the above criteria so that All-Paths actually demands the coverage of feasible paths, etc. Since the identification of infeasible paths is undecidable in the general case, none of the above approaches can be fully automated.

Note also that most of the above criteria do not define a partition of the input domain: All-Paths does, because the input subdomains associated to two distinct paths are disjoint; but the input subdomains induced by weaker criteria, like All-Branches, may (and generally will) overlap.

5   Unification of Structural Approaches for B Models

As explained in Section 3, the uniform testing framework has to cope with flattened B models obtained at any development stage. Structural approaches for the coverage of before-after predicates can theoretically be applied whatever the level of abstraction (Section 5.1) but, as already mentioned, these approaches face a scalability problem. Structural approaches defined for procedural programs can be applied to the most concrete models that contain only programmable constructs (Section 5.2). We propose an extension of the notion of control flow graph that can be applied to abstract constructs as well (Section 5.2), so that it can serve as a basis for structural analysis at any development stage. We also show that coverage criteria for this graph can be related to coverage criteria defined from the corresponding before-after predicate.

5.1   Partition Analysis of B Operations from Before-After Predicates

The work introduced in [8] is within the framework of VDM specifications, while [10] is working with Z specifications. However, both approaches may be transferred to other model-based specifications, including B specifications. B operations are specified by generalized substitutions, but it is possible to use the translation into before-after predicate (see Section 2), and perform the partition analysis as described in Section 4.1. Nevertheless, as will be explained below, the partition analysis has to be adapted to the target B notation, in order to account for the notion of well-defined B.

Like [8] in the VDM approach, we assume that the operation is called within its precondition, and that the before state satisfies the invariant. Moreover, for the before-after predicate to have a meaning, we have to take into account contextual information about the sets and constants given for the abstract machine. The predicate corresponding to contextual information is precisely defined in the B-Book (see e.g. the expression of the proof obligation that an operation preserves the invariant).

Now, let us assume that the operation to be analyzed is in the form:

$$\text{PRE } P \text{ THEN } S \text{ END}$$

From Section 2, property (a) of generalized substitutions, we may notice that the existential quantification of the before-after predicate of S, used by [8] to hide the after state and output values, gives us fis (S). Then, the input domain of the operation to be partitioned into subdomains may be expressed as:

$$\text{context} \wedge \text{invariant} \wedge P \wedge \text{fis } (S) \tag{1}$$

Applying the transformation into disjoint cases, one must be careful not to generate ill-defined cases. To illustrate the problem, let us assume that the partition analysis generates the following intermediate formula, where f is a partial function:

$$\neg(x \in \text{dom } (f) \wedge f(x) = y)$$

Applying the approaches described in Section 4.1, the formula would be further split into three disjoint cases:

$$x \notin \text{dom } (f) \wedge f(x) \bullet y \qquad x \notin \text{dom } (f) \wedge f(x) = y \qquad x \in \text{dom } (f) \wedge f(x) \bullet y$$

The first two cases are ill-defined: $f(x)$ is meaningless since x does not belong to the domain of function f.

The problem of well-defined B has been investigated in [3]: the concern was to tackle ill-defined proof obligations. The adopted solution was to 1) generate additional proof obligations of the well-definedness of models; 2) propose a deduction system such that the proof of a well-defined lemma does not introduce ill-defined formulæ. Our work is based on their definition of well-definedness. Assuming that the original predicate is well-defined, the concern is not to introduce ill-definedness during the separation into cases. The well-definedness of predicates is given in [3] by means of Δ_p operator and the well-definedness of substitutions by means of Δ_s operator. In Figure 2, we give a subset of rules defining Δ_p and Δ_s operators to which we will refer afterwards. We also give a theorem defined in [3] which states that predicate transformation of a well-defined substitution is also well-defined.

$$\Delta_p \neg P \equiv \Delta_p P \qquad\qquad \Delta_s (S \parallel T) \equiv \Delta_s S \wedge \Delta_s T$$
$$\Delta_p (P \wedge Q) \equiv \Delta_p P \wedge (P => \Delta_p Q) \qquad \Delta_s (P \Rightarrow S) \equiv \Delta_p P \wedge (P => \Delta_s S)$$
$$\Delta_p (P \vee Q) \equiv \Delta_p P \wedge (\neg P => \Delta_p \qquad \Delta_s (S \, \tilde{N} \, T) \equiv \Delta_s S \wedge \Delta_s T$$
$$Q)$$
$$\Delta_p (P => Q) \equiv \Delta_p P \wedge (P => \Delta_p Q) \qquad \Delta_s ((@x \cdot S) \equiv \forall x \cdot \Delta_s S$$

$$\textbf{Theorem:} \qquad \Delta_p I \wedge \Delta_s S => \Delta_p ([S]I)$$

Fig. 2. Inductive rules from the definition of Δ_p and Δ_s operators in [3]

Note that the rules for Δ_p correspond to an interpretation of the logical *and* (resp. *or*) operator as the *and then* (resp. *or else*) operator provided by some programming languages. Accordingly, a safe separation of the previous formula would give us only two well-defined disjoint cases:

$$x \notin \text{dom } (f) \qquad\qquad x \in \text{dom } (f) \wedge f(x) \bullet y$$

Restricting the formulæ manipulations to safe ones, the partition analysis could be theoretically applied to any intermediate model obtained during a B development: the translation from substitution to before-after predicate can be performed whatever the level of abstraction. Similarly, the application of the approach to refinements was also suggested by [8], in the framework of wide spectrum notations such as VDM-SL. But the problem of scalability is all the more acute as the model is detailed.

5.2   Control Flow Graph of B0 Substitutions

The subset of the B language that can be used in an IMPLEMENTATION component is called B0. In Table 2, we show the substitutions of B0 together with their control flow subgraphs. As these substitutions are similar to the statements of the classical procedural languages, their adopted control flow representations are similar to the ones proposed in the literature for programming language statements.

Table 2. Control flow representation of B0 substitutions: X and W are (lists of) variables; E is an (a list of) expression(s); F is an expression; S, $S1$, $S2$, Sn are substitutions; P, I and V are predicates; $L1$ is a (list of) constant(s); and $\mathbf{O}$ is the subgraph corresponding to a substitution

Substitution	CF graph	Substitution	CF graph
Assignment substitution: $X := E$		Operation call: $X \leftarrow \mathrm{op}(E)$	
IF substitution: IF P THEN $S1$ ELSE $S2$ END		CASE substitution: CASE F OF EITHER $L1$ THEN $S1$ OR ... ELSE Sn END	
Local variable: VAR W IN S END		WHILE substitution: WHILE P DO S INVARIANT I VARIANT V END	

These substitutions can be sequenced using the ";" operator. This operator is equivalent to the well-known ";" operator in programming languages and means that the related substitutions follow each other. This operator, in terms of construction of a control flow graph, means that the subgraphs of corresponding substitutions must be put one after the other. This is done systematically using the subgraphs of Table 2: the exiting edge of a substitution is merged with the incoming edge of its subsequent substitution. In order to complete the control flow graph, a start node before the first substitution and an end node after the last substitution of an operation are also added.

The control flow graph obtained in this way can possibly be simplified into a more compact form. For example, in control flow graphs it is typical to represent by nodes maximum length blocks of uninterrupted sequences of assignments (see e.g. [5] on the control flow graph representation of programs).

The substitutions of B0 are essentially syntactic constructions that are proposed in order to ease the use of the language. They can be rewritten using the basic generalized substitutions. For example, the rewriting of the IF substitution is the following:

$$(P \Rightarrow S1) \text{ À } (\neg P \Rightarrow S2)$$

As can be seen in subgraphs of Table 2, the existence of several subpaths leaving a node is because of existence of a decision in the substitution (IF, CASE, WHILE substitutions or other forms of these substitutions). In terms of basic generalized substitutions, this corresponds to the bounded choice between guarded substitutions. If we rewrite the original substitution S as $\text{ñ}_i \, S_i$, each substitution S_i gives us a path on the control flow graph. Note that the control flow graph of the substitution $\text{ñ}_i \, S_i$ is not the same as the control flow graph of the original substitution S, but the paths on both graphs are the same. As usual when testing loops, the WHILE substitution will be unfolded to be traversed a bounded number of times.

The rewriting is possible because of the following equivalence rules that have been proved in the B-Book [1]:

$(S1 \text{ ñ } S2) \, ; \, S3 = (S1 \, ; \, S3) \text{ ñ } (S2 \, ; \, S3)$ $S1 \, ; \, (S2 \text{ ñ } S3) = (S1 \, ; \, S2) \text{ ñ } (S1 \, ; \, S3)$

$P \Rightarrow (S1 \text{ ñ } S2) = (P \Rightarrow S1) \text{ ñ } (P \Rightarrow S2)$ $@x \cdot (S1 \text{ ñ } S2) = (@x \cdot S1) \text{ ñ } (@x \cdot S2)$

According to the Δ_s operator defined in [3] (see Figure 2) for the well-definedness of a substitution, the rewriting does not introduce ill-defined substitutions. We have demonstrated this for all rewriting rules. In Figure 3, we show that the rewriting rule for the guarded substitution is well-defined.

$$
\begin{aligned}
\Delta_s (P \Rightarrow (S1 \; \bullet \; S2)) &\Leftrightarrow \Delta_p \, P \wedge (P => \Delta_s (S1 \; \bullet \; S2)) \\
&\Leftrightarrow \Delta_p \, P \wedge (P => (\Delta_s S1 \; \wedge \Delta_s S2)) \\
&\Leftrightarrow \Delta_p \, P \wedge (P => \Delta_s S1 \; \wedge P => \Delta_s S2) \\
&\Leftrightarrow \Delta_s (P \Rightarrow S1) \wedge \Delta_s (P \Rightarrow S2) \\
&\Leftrightarrow \Delta_s ((P \Rightarrow S1) \text{ ñ } (P \Rightarrow S2))
\end{aligned}
$$

Fig. 3. Well-definedness of the rewriting rule for guarded substitution

Just as in the control flow graph of programs, all of the paths on the graph may not be feasible. The predicate fis of the rewritten substitution gives the feasible paths of the control flow graph: fis $(\bullet_i \, S_i) \Leftrightarrow \vee_i$ fis (S_i). This shows that path selection techniques can be expressed in terms of predicate coverage.

5.3   Structural Coverage of Generalized Substitutions

In the previous section, only B0 substitutions have been discussed. We will now propose an extension to the notion of control flow graph in order to be able to also consider abstract substitutions of the B language.

The bounded choice substitution can be used at different levels of development in MACHINE, REFINEMENT and IMPLEMENTATION components. In an IMPLEMENTATION component the specification must be deterministic. Therefore, the bounded choice substitution is used only in the context of a decision, i.e. the component substitutions are guarded with mutually exclusive predicates whose disjunction is true (e.g. P and $\neg P$). In a MACHINE or REFINEMENT component the bounded choice substitution may be used in a non-deterministic manner: the substitution $S = S1 \bullet S2$ means that the substitution S can be implemented by further implementing either $S1$ or $S2$. In order to represent this substitution in a control flow graph, we propose the subgraph of Table 3. As can be noticed, this subgraph is similar to the subgraph of B0's IF substitution but there are no predicates associated to the incoming arcs of subgraphs of $S1$ and $S2$; $S1$ and $S2$ may or may not be guarded substitutions, or the guards may not be exclusive. Therefore, the coverage of this subgraph must be given an operational interpretation. We adopt the operational interpretation that is based on the notion of correct executable interpretation of model-based specifications investigated for Z notation in [6], also discussed in the context of testing B models via animation [13]. It is argued that a correct interpretation of a non-deterministic specification should offer many alternative outputs. In the same manner, if for some input data both component substitutions of the bounded choice are feasible, both branches of the subgraph will be covered.

Table 3. Control flow representation of bounded choice, parallel and guarded substitutions: S, $S1$, $S2$ are substitutions; P is a predicate; O is the subgraph corresponding to a substitution

Substitution	CF graph	Substitution	CF graph
Bounded Choice Substitution: CHOICE $S1$ OR $S2$ $\equiv S1 \sqcap S2$ END		Parallel Substitution: $S1 \parallel S2$	
Guarded Substitution: SELECT P THEN S $\equiv P \Rightarrow S$ END			

As the substitutions of an IMPLEMENTATION component are deterministic, an execution of these substitutions will correspond to only one complete path on the corresponding control flow graph. This will no more be the case for more abstract substitutions of MACHINE or REFINEMENT components that may contain non-deterministic substitutions. An "execution" (by animation) of such substitutions may not correspond to only one path on the control flow graph but to a set of paths. We call a *path-combination* the set of paths that are covered at the same time by test data.

Besides non-determinism, another issue that must be considered is the notion of infeasible specifications. There is no proof of feasibility in the B method. While it would be possible for a MACHINE or REFINEMENT component to contain infeasible substitutions, if the development ends up with a set of proved IMPLEMENTATIONs, then it is sure that the specification is feasible. If in a machine or refinement component a miracle has been specified, there may be no feasible paths for some input data. This will be the case when all guards evaluate to false. Because of infeasible substitutions, a path-combination may also be the empty set.

In Table 3, we also propose a control flow subgraph for guarded and parallel substitutions. The guarded substitution $P \Rightarrow S$ means that the substitution S is only feasible when the guard is true. In the same manner, the subgraph of the substitution S is covered only if the guard is true. The parallel substitution $S = S1 \parallel S2$ indicates the simultaneous execution of substitutions $S1$ and $S2$. The parallelism in this case means that both substitutions, working with distinct variables, can be performed independently. A parallel substitution is feasible if and only if both component substitutions are feasible. So if for some input cases one of the substitutions is not feasible, the subgraph of the parallel substitution is not covered.

Like the other substitutions, an original substitution S containing parallel substitutions can be rewritten in the form $\bullet_i S_i$ so that each S_i will be a path on the control flow graph. The following equivalence rules have been proved in the B-Book:

$$(S1 \bullet S2) \parallel S3 = (S1 \parallel S3) \bullet (S2 \parallel S3) \qquad S1 \parallel (S2 \bullet S3) = (S1 \parallel S2) \bullet (S1 \parallel S3)$$

Note that for parallel substitutions a subpath on a control flow graph is not the same as the classical subpaths on a program control flow graph. For example considering the control flow graph of Figure 4, we only have two paths and not three. These are the paths that we get after rewriting the original substitution.

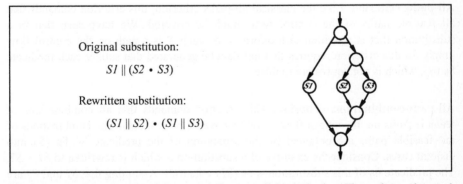

Original substitution:

$S1 \parallel (S2 \bullet S3)$

Rewritten substitution:

$(S1 \parallel S2) \bullet (S1 \parallel S3)$

Fig. 4. An example of a control flow graph for a parallel substitution. The paths on the graph are $S1 \parallel S2$ and $S1 \parallel S3$

The last basic generalized substitution that must be considered is preconditioned substitution. Actually, the construction of control flow graph assumes that the precondition, the invariant and the context holds. This assumption, which is the same as Equation 1, in Section 5.1, when analyzing before-after predicates, is necessary in order to be able to reason about the feasibility of substitutions. For example, consider the feasibility of preconditioned substitution $P \mid S$: fis $(P \mid S) \Leftrightarrow P \Rightarrow$ fis (S). According to [3], S and fis (S) may be ill-defined if the precondition does not hold.

To conclude, consider an operation PRE P THEN S END, in which S may contain abstract and concrete substitutions. We have seen in Section 5.1 that in order to have a partition of the input domain, predicate transformations, like the ones proposed by [8], may be performed on fis (S). We have also seen that a control flow graph can be constructed from S, and that after rewriting the substitution S so that the choices are pushed out, the feasible paths on the graph are fis $(\bullet_i S_i) \Leftrightarrow \vee_i$ fis (S_i). This means that path coverage criteria defined for this control flow graph are equivalent to partitioning fis (S) into (possibly overlapping) cases.

6   Coverage Criteria for Generalized Substitutions

The extended control flow graph permits us to define a hierarchy of criteria that are applicable to models in different levels of abstraction. The hierarchy of criteria allows to tune the test stringency according to the abstraction level of the analyzed B model.

6.1   Definition of Criteria

The first three criteria that we will define in this section, concern the coverage of the control flow graph. Each criterion can be further refined by considering the coverage of predicates of guards.

All-paths criterion. Like the classical all-paths criterion, this criterion demands that all feasible paths of the control flow graph be covered. We have seen that in a substitution that is rewritten in the form $\bullet_i S_i$, each S_i is a path on the control flow graph. So this criterion requires that test data be generated that satisfy each predicate fis (S_i), which is not equivalent to false.

All-path-combinations criterion. This criterion demands that all combinations of feasible paths on the control flow graph be covered by test data. The combinations of the feasible paths are obtained by the separation of the predicate $\vee_i$ fis (S_i) into disjoint cases. Consider the example of a substitution S which is rewritten to $S1 \bullet S2$. The predicate fis of this substitution is fis $(S1) \vee$ fis $(S2)$. Assuming that $S1$ and $S2$ are well-defined, the predicates fis $(S1)$ and fis $(S2)$ are also well-defined (see theorem in Figure 2, defined in [3]). So the predicate fis $(S1) \vee$ fis $(S2)$ can be separated into the following three disjoint cases, without generating ill-defined terms:

fis $(S1) \wedge$ fis $(S2)$ or $\neg$fis $(S1) \wedge$ fis $(S2)$ or   fis $(S1) \wedge \neg$fis $(S2)$

The separation of the predicate $\vee_i$ fis (S_i) will generate at most $2^i - 1$ cases. This is an upper bound because some of the cases may be simplified to false. For example, there may be some paths on the control flow graph that are exclusive, that is if one is feasible the other one will always be infeasible. For the substitutions of IMPLEMENTATION components, i.e. deterministic and feasible operations, this criterion is equivalent to all-paths criterion.

All-expanded-path-combinations criterion. In the previous criterion, it has been required to consider combinations in which some of paths on the control flow graph are infeasible. There may also be several cases in which a path is infeasible: the substitution $P \Rightarrow S$ may be infeasible either if the guard P is false or if the substitution S is infeasible; the substitution $S \| T$ may be infeasible if either substitutions S or T, or both of them are infeasible. The all-expanded-path-combinations demands that each of these cases be considered separately. In order to do this, we will separate the negation of the predicate fis of guarded and parallel substitutions into disjoint cases.

According to the definition of Δ_s operator for guarded substitutions defined in [3] (see Figure 2), the component substitution of a guarded substitution may be ill-defined if the predicate of guard is false. To avoid generating ill-defined terms, we will use a safe separation into disjoint cases for the negation of the predicate fis of guarded substitutions:

$$\neg\text{fis}\ (P \Rightarrow S) \Leftrightarrow \neg(P \wedge \text{fis}\ (S)) \qquad \text{is separated into} \qquad \neg P \quad \text{or} \quad P \wedge \neg\text{fis}\ (S)$$

For the parallel substitutions, the negation of the predicate fis can be separated into three disjoint cases. This is because the Δ_s of the parallel substitution (see Figure 2) states that both component substitutions are well-defined if the parallel substitution is well-defined.

$$\neg\text{fis}\ (S \| T) \Leftrightarrow \neg(\ \text{fis}\ (S) \wedge \text{fis}\ (T)) \qquad \text{is separated into} \qquad \begin{array}{ll} \neg\text{fis}\ (S) \wedge \neg\text{fis}\ (T) & \text{or} \\ \neg\text{fis}\ (S) \wedge \text{fis}\ (T) & \text{or} \\ \text{fis}\ (S) \wedge \neg\text{fis}\ (T) & \end{array}$$

Coverage of predicates of guards. In the previous criteria, we have considered the structure of the operators of the Generalized Substitution Language and we have proposed different ways in which they can be covered. We may also consider the structure of predicates of guards. If a predicate of guard can be broken into simpler predicates, we may define different ways in covering these predicates. In order to cover a predicate of guard, we propose the following separation into disjoint cases for disjunction and implication operators and for negation of a conjunction operator:

$$\begin{array}{llll} A \vee B & \text{is separated into} & A \quad \text{or} & \neg A \wedge B \\ A \Rightarrow B & \text{is separated into} & \neg A \quad \text{or} & A \wedge B \\ \neg(A \wedge B) & \text{is separated into} & \neg A \quad \text{or} & A \wedge \neg B \end{array}$$

All of the above criteria can be further refined by requiring that each predicate of guard be separated at least once during testing. For example, all-paths plus predicate coverage criterion requires that all feasible paths on the control flow graph be covered and that every predicate of guard be separated into disjoint cases at least once. The above separations are safe separations that will not generate ill-defined terms. They are based on the definition of the well-definedness operator Δ_p for predicates [3] (see Figure 2).

There are other predicate coverage criteria that have been proposed in the literature for the structural coverage of decisions in a program (e.g. [7] in avionics domain). Such criteria could be used as well.

6.2   Hierarchy of the Criteria

The hierarchy of the criteria that we have defined in the previous section is shown in Figure 5. The relation between criteria is the *inclusion* relation [9]. Criterion A includes criterion B, if and only if each test set that covers A also covers B. The inclusion relation between our criteria is easily found according to their definition. The all-path-combination criterion demands that all combinations of feasible paths be covered and in this way includes all-paths criterion which demands only that all feasible paths be covered. The all-expanded-path-combination criterion demands that all combinations of feasible paths be covered, distinguishing between the different cases in which a path may not be feasible, and so it includes all-path-combination criterion. Each of these criteria is included by the same criteria plus the coverage of predicates of guards, in the way that it demands that each predicate be separated at least once during testing.

These criteria are defined in order to cover specifications in different levels of abstraction, which may contain non-deterministic and infeasible constructs. After the all-paths criterion we may retrieve the classical structural coverage criteria that have been defined for programs.

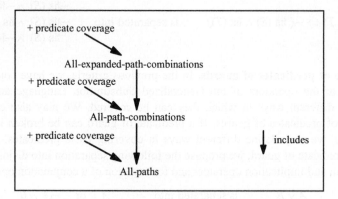

Fig. 5. The hierarchy of the coverage criteria.

It is also interesting to compare these criteria with the approach proposed in [8] for the generation of test cases from VDM specifications. In this approach, test cases are generated for each operation by partition analysis of the corresponding before-after predicate: logical disjunction and implication operators are decomposed into disjoint cases (see Section 4.1). This approach is more stringent than our criteria. First, let us mention that the cases that we have identified from the structure of the substitution operators correspond to disjunctions in the before-after predicate. For example, prd_x $(S1 \cdot S2) \Leftrightarrow \text{prd}_x$ $(S1) \vee \text{prd}_x$ $(S2)$. The same applies to the cases identified from the guard predicates. Then, the criterion of [8] is at least as stringent as all-expanded-path-combinations plus the coverage of all of the predicates of guards. But in addition, in [8], test cases may be generated that partition the output space. Consider the following simple example:

$$\text{IF } x > 0 \text{ THEN } y := x \text{ ELSE } y := 1 \text{ END}$$

The approach of [8] will generate three test cases:

$$(1) \ x = 1 \qquad\qquad (2) \ x > 1 \qquad\qquad (3) \ x \leq 0$$

For the first branch of IF, i.e. when $x > 0$, two cases are generated: in case (1) the output result is the same as the one that would be obtained through the other branch of IF, i.e. $y = 1$; in case (2) the output result is different. The distinction of these cases arises from a partition of output space. It is also worth noting that if the approach of [8] is applied to B models, generated test cases may contain ill-defined terms.

Let us recall that the approach proposed in [8] causes serious problems of scalability. Even for a small and simple specification a large number of test cases may be generated. As we work directly with the substitutions and not with the before-after predicates, we are able to distinguish between cases that are generated from the structure of substitution operators and cases that correspond to the structure of guard predicates. This has permitted us to define criteria with different degrees of stringency, so that the coverage strategy may be tuned according to the complexity of the operation.

6.3   Example

In this section, we will illustrate by means of an example, the criteria that we have defined in the previous section. The application of these criteria will permit to identify (possibly overlapping) subsets of the input domain in order to generate test data.

Consider the example of Figure 6. The specification can be written using the basic substitutions:

$$S = (@ww \cdot ww \in 0..4 \Rightarrow n1 := ww) \cdot$$
$$(special\_n = \text{TRUE} \Rightarrow (((n1 = 0 \vee n1 = 1) \Rightarrow n1 := n1 + 1) \parallel$$
$$(n2 > n1 \Rightarrow n2 := n1)))$$

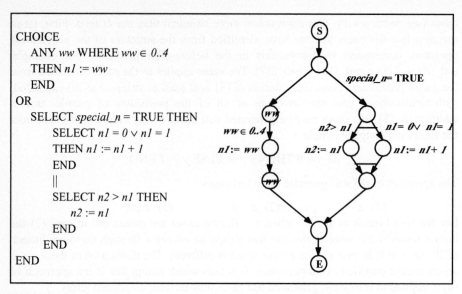

CHOICE
   ANY *ww* WHERE *ww* ∈ *0..4*
   THEN *n1* := *ww*
   END
OR
   SELECT *special_n* = TRUE THEN
      SELECT *n1 = 0* ∨ *n1 = 1*
      THEN *n1* := *n1 + 1*
      END
      ||
      SELECT *n2 > n1* THEN
         n2 := *n1*
      END
   END
END

Fig. 6. The control flow graph of a substitution. The substitution is considered in the following context : $n1 \in NAT \wedge n2 \in NAT \wedge$ special_n $\in BOOL$

This substitution needs not be rewritten. Let *S1* and *S2* designate each component of the bounded choice substitution. The predicate fis (*S*) is:

$$\text{fis } (S) \Leftrightarrow \text{fis } (@ww \cdot ww \in 0..4 \Rightarrow n1 := ww) \vee$$
$$\text{fis } (special\_n = TRUE \Rightarrow (((n1 = 0 \vee n1 = 1) \Rightarrow n1 := n1 + 1) \|$$
$$(n2 > n1 \Rightarrow n2 := n1)))$$
$$\Leftrightarrow \text{fis } (S1) \vee \text{fis } (S2)$$

The all-paths criterion requires the coverage of each feasible path on the control flow graph, so we have to produce test data that satisfy the following two predicates:

$$\text{fis } (S1) \quad \exists ww \cdot ww \in 0..4$$
$$\Leftrightarrow$$
$$\text{fis } (S2) \quad special\_n = TRUE \wedge (n1 = 0 \vee n1 = 1) \wedge n2 > n1$$
$$\Leftrightarrow$$

The first path is always feasible (fis (*S1*) always holds). In order to cover the second path a single test data, for example *special_n* = TRUE $\wedge$ *n1* = *0* $\wedge$ *n2* = *1*, is sufficient. If we want also to cover the predicates of guards, the predicate (*n1* = *0* $\vee$ *n1* = *1*) will be separated. In order to cover this predicate, the previous test can be completed by test data *special_n* = TRUE $\wedge$ *n1* = *1* $\wedge$ *n2* = *2*.

The all-path-combination criteria is more demanding than all-paths criterion. It requires that all combinations of feasible paths be covered by test data. The predicate fis (*S*) will be separated into disjoint cases:

$$\text{fis } (S1) \wedge \text{fis } (S2) \Leftrightarrow special\_n = TRUE \wedge (n1 = 0 \vee n1 = 1) \wedge n2 > n1$$
$$\neg\text{fis } (S1) \wedge \text{fis } (S2) \Leftrightarrow FALSE$$
$$\text{fis } (S1) \wedge \neg\text{fis } (S2) \Leftrightarrow \neg(special\_n = TRUE \wedge (n1 = 0 \vee n1 = 1) \wedge n2 > n1)$$

Two test data will be sufficient in order to satisfy the above predicates. For example, we may complete test data *special_n* = TRUE $\wedge$ *n1* = *0* $\wedge$ *n2* = *1* by test data *special_n* = FALSE.

Finally, the all-expanded-path-combination criterion requires to distinguish between different cases in which a path may be infeasible. Consider the last predicate generated in the all-path-combinations criterion, in which the substitution *S2* is not feasible. Each component of *S2*, that can make the substitution infeasible, will be considered separately. So we have to complete the previous test data in order to satisfy the following predicates:

$$\text{special\_n} \quad = \quad \text{FALSE}$$

$$\text{special\_n} = \text{TRUE} \quad \wedge \; \neg(n1 = 0 \vee n1 = 1) \wedge \neg(n2 > n1)$$

$$\text{special\_n} = \text{TRUE} \quad \wedge \quad (n1 = 0 \vee n1 = 1) \wedge \neg(n2 > n1)$$

$$\text{special\_n} = \text{TRUE} \quad \wedge \; \neg(n1 = 0 \vee n1 = 1) \wedge (n2 > n1)$$

These cases are the result of the safe separation of the guarded substitution and the separation of the parallel substitution into disjoint cases.

7   Conclusion

A unified approach to the structural coverage of B models has been proposed. This approach was initially considered in a testing framework in which intermediate B models obtained in different stages of development are object to validation. As the smallest meaningful model with respect to user requirements may involve several steps of refinement and decomposition into logical layers, the B models that will be validated may contain abstract and concrete constructs at the same time. But the proposed approach reaches a more global aim: it can also be used wherever a structural analysis of B models is needed.

We have seen how a control flow graph can be constructed from the substitutions of a B operation, and how the coverage of (sets of) paths in this graph can be linked with the coverage of before-after predicates proposed for model-based specifications in the literature. The fact that we work directly with substitutions, and not with their translation into before-after predicate, has allowed us to distinguish between cases that may be extracted from the structure of substitution operators (like the bounded choice) and cases that may be extracted from the structure of guard predicates. Moreover, the approach takes into account the notion of well-definedness for both predicates and substitutions, so that ill-defined cases are never generated. We end up with a set of criteria whose stringency can be partially ordered according to the inclusion relation. The aim is to be able to tune the test strategy to the complexity of the model to be analyzed. While the fine partition analysis of [8] may be applicable to simple abstract models, it is expected to become untractable as complexity is gradually entered into the models; for the most concrete models obtained at late development stages, only weak path selection criteria (e.g. statement coverage) may be adopted. Our criteria fill the gap between these specification based and program based strategies.

The presented criteria apply to the coverage of individual B operation. As mentioned earlier, separate analysis of each operation is not sufficient: their joint dependency on the encapsulated state must also be considered to design test sequences. The approaches proposed in [8, 10] yield a finite state automaton representing all valid sequences of operation calls: both the states and transitions of the automaton are derived from the partition analysis of the operations. We will investigate whether such approaches are applicable to realistic B models, at least at the earliest stages of the development process.

As regards tool support, it would be worth studying whether our criteria may be implemented using existing environment like B-CASTING [11]. CASTING is a generic approach meant for the generation of test data from formal specification: a first prototype instantiating this approach in the case of the B notation has been developed. The extraction of test cases works with an attributed grammar of the notation, while the generation of data is performed using a constraint solver. We are currently investigating the possibility of expressing the parsing of B substitutions induced by our criteria in terms of rules similar to the ones given in [11].

However, it is not expected that the generation of test data from the models can be fully automated. An alternative approach could be to generate test sequences using some other means, and to obtain an a posteriori assessment of the supplied coverage. The assessment could be performed by instrumenting the target B models, so that we obtain a trace of the parts of the operation substitutions that are traversed during animation. We have started preliminary work to address this problem. Our first conclusion is that it should be possible to mark the nodes that are traversed by insertion of simple substitutions, but the coverage analysis from the resulting trace has still to be formalized.

Acknowledgments. We sincerely thank our colleague, Pascale Thévenod-Fosse, for her detailed reading and helpful suggestions in the preparation of this paper.

References

1. Abrial, J.R.: The B-Book – Assigning Programs to Meanings, Cambridge University Press (1996)
2. Behm, P., Desforges, P., Mejia, F.: Application de la méthode B dans l'industrie ferroviaire, In: Application des techniques formelles au logiciel, ARAGO 20, OFTA, ISBN 2-906028-06-1 (1997) 59-87
3. Behm, P., Burdy, L., Meynadier, J.M.: Well Defined B, In: Proceedings of 2nd International B Conference, LNCS No. 1393, April (1998) 29-45
4. Behnia, S., Waeselynck, H.: External Verification of a B Development Process, In: Proceedings of 9th European Workshop on Dependable Computing, May (1998) 93-96
5. Bieman, J.M., Baker, A.L., Clites, P.N., Gustafson, D.A., Melton, A.C.: A Standard Representation of Imperative Language Programs for Data Collection and Software Measures Specification, The Journal of Systems and Software 8 (1998) 13-37

6. Breuer, P.T., Bowen, J.P.: Towards Correct Executable Semantics for Z, In: Proceedings of the Z User Workshop, (1994) 185-209
7. Chilenski, J.J., Miller, S.P.: Applicability of Modified Condition/Decision Coverage to Software Testing, Software Engineering Journal, September (1994) 193-200
8. Dick, J., Faivre, A.: Automating the generation and sequencing of test cases from model-based specifications, In: Proceedings of the International Formal Methods Europe Symposium, (1993) 268-284
9. Frankl, P.G., Weyuker, E.J.: An Applicable Family of Data Flow Testing Criteria, IEEE Transaction on Software Engineering, Vol. 4, No. 10, October (1988) 1483-1498
10. Hierons, R.M.: Testing from a Z Specification, Software Testing, Verification and Reliability, Vol. 7 (1997) 19-33
11. Van Aertryck, L., Benveniste, M., Le Métayer, D.: CASTING: a Formally Based Software Testing Generation Method, In: Proceedings of 1st International Conference on Formal Engineering Methods, IEEE Computer Society, November (1997)
12. Waeselynck, H., Behnia, S.: Towards a Framework for Testing B Models, LAAS Report No. 97225, June (1997)
13. Waeselynck, H., Behnia, S.: B Model Animation for External Verification, In: Proceedings of 2nd International Conference on Formal Engineering Methods, IEEE Computer Society, December (1998) 36-45

though we might choose not to write § in the latter example. Bunches can also be used as a type system, as in the declaration **var** x : *nat* (perhaps with restrictions for easy implementation). Any bunch, including the empty bunch *null*, can be used as a type. For example, the declaration **var** x : 1 says that x can take on one value, 1.

Bunches can also be used in arithmetic expressions, where the arithmetic operators distribute over bunch union (comma):

$$nat = 0, nat + 1$$

We write functions in a standard way, as in the example $\lambda n : nat \cdot n + 1$. Function application is by juxtaposing the function name and its arguments, e.g., $f\ x$. The domain of a function is obtained by the Δ operator. If the function body does not use its variable, we may write just the domain and body with an arrow between. For example, $2 \rightarrow 3$ is a function that maps 2 to 3, which we could have written $\lambda n : 2 \cdot 3$ with n unused.

When the domain of a function is an initial segment of the natural numbers, we sometimes use a list notation, as in [3; 5; 2; 5]. The empty list is [*nil*] (*nil* without square parentheses is the empty string). We also use the asymmetric notation [$m; ..n$] for a list of integers starting with m and ending before n. List length is #, and catenation is $^{+}$ (raised plus). A list of characters, such as "*abc*" can be written within quotes.

All functions we use in this paper apply to elements, and thus application of a function f distributes over bunch union, i.e.,

$$f\ null = null \qquad f\ (A, B) = f\ A, f\ B$$

A union of functions applied to an argument gives the union of the results, i.e., $(f, g)\ x = fx, gx$. A function f is included in a function g according to the *function inclusion law*.

$$(f : g) = ((\Delta g : \Delta f) \wedge (\forall x : \Delta g \cdot fx : gx))$$

Thus we can prove $(f : A \rightarrow B) = ((A : \Delta f) \wedge (\forall a : A \cdot fa : B))$. Using inclusion both ways round, we find function equality is as usual.

$$(f = g) = ((\Delta f = \Delta g) \wedge (\forall x : \Delta f \cdot fx = gx))$$

list T consists of all lists with items of type T. By defining *list* as $list = \lambda T : \Delta list \cdot 0, ..\#(list\ T) \rightarrow T$, *list T* can be used as a type.

The selective union $f \mid g$ of functions f and g is a function that behaves like f when applied to an argument in the domain of f, and otherwise behaves like g. It is similar to Z's function extension.

$$\Delta(f \mid g) = \Delta f, \Delta g$$
$$(f \mid g)x = \textbf{if } x : \Delta f \textbf{ then } f\ x \textbf{ else } g\ x$$

One of the uses of selective union is to write a selective list update. For example, if $L = [2; 5; 3; 4]$ then $2 \rightarrow 6 \mid L = [2; 5; 6; 4]$. Another use is to create a record structure. Define *PERSON* as follows.

$$PERSON = \text{"}name\text{"} \rightarrow list\ char \mid \text{"}age\text{"} \rightarrow nat$$

Declare variable p of type *PERSON* and assign p as follows.

$$p := \text{``name''} \rightarrow \text{``Smith''} \mid \text{``age''} \rightarrow 33$$

We can access the name field of p by dereferencing: $p\,\text{``name''}$.

2.2 Functional Refinement

A *refinement* relation can also be applied to functions. A function P is refined by a function S if and only if all results that are satisfactory according to S are also satisfactory according to P. Formally, this is just bunch inclusion, $S : P$. When writing refinements, we prefer to write the problem, P, on the left, and the solution, S, on the right. Thus, we write $P \mathrel{:\cdot} S$ (informally read as "P is refined by S"), which means $S : P$.

2.3 Real-Time and Concurrency

Predicative programming is well-suited to specifying and reasoning about real-time, concurrent, and communicating systems. To talk about time, a time variable t is used; the theory need not be changed at all. The interpretation of t as time is justified by how it is used. t is used as the initial time (where execution starts), and t' for final time (where execution ends). To allow for nontermination, the domain of time is a number system extended with an infinite number ∞. The number system can be naturals, reals, et cetera. The following example says that the final value of variable h should be the index of the first occurrence of x in list L, and that any program satisfying the specification must provide an execution time that is linear in the length of L.

$$(\neg\, x : L(0, ..h') \land (Lh' = x \lor h' = \#L)) \land t' \le t + \#L$$

Predicative programming includes notations for concurrent specification and for communication. We will not use the communication notations explicitly herein, but we will use concurrency; we direct the reader to [6] for details on communication.

The independent composition operator $\parallel$ applied to specifications P and Q is defined so that $P \parallel Q$ (pronounced "P parallel Q") is satisfied by a machine that behaves according to P and at the same time, in parallel, according to Q. The formal meaning of $\parallel$ is as follows. Let the variables used by P and Q be denoted by σ (σ may be any number of variables, but it does not include t).

$$P \parallel Q = \exists\, \sigma_P, \sigma_Q, t_P, t_Q \cdot$$
$$P[\sigma_P/\sigma', t_P/t'] \land Q[\sigma_Q, t_Q/\sigma', t'] \land$$
$$(\sigma_P = \sigma \Rightarrow \sigma' = \sigma_Q) \land (\sigma_Q = \sigma \Rightarrow \sigma' = \sigma_P) \land t' = \max t_P\, t_Q$$

($P[a/b]$ means "substitute a for b in P".) Informally, if P leaves a variable unchanged, then Q determines the final value, while if Q leaves a value unchanged, P determines its final value. If both processes change the value, then the final value is undetermined (unless the processes agree on the final value).

We define $\parallel_{i:0,..k} P(i)$ to be $P(0) \parallel \ldots \parallel P(k-1)$ for any specification P on i.

3   Using Bunches for Object-Oriented Concepts

We now outline how bunches and predicative notation can be used to specify a core collection of OO concepts, including classes, objects, features, inheritance, and redefinition of feature semantics. Our intent is not to present a new OO theory; rather, it is a step towards being able to use OO, real-time, and concurrency together.

3.1   Specifying Classes and Objects

Several different definitions of the notion of a class have been presented in the literature. The definition of a class that we use is adapted from [9].

Definition 2. *A* **class** *is an abstract data type equipped with a possibly partial behavioural specification.*

A class consists of a number of features, which are *attributes* (representing state) or *routines* (representing computations). Routines may be further subdivided into *functions* (which return a value) and *procedures* (which can change state). No routine is both function and procedure. A class specification has three parts:

- a *class interface*, which declares all the attributes and functions of the class and gives their signatures (our convention is that class interface names end in *Int*).
- a *class definition*, which defines all the functions (our convention is that class definitions will always be in upper case).
- zero or more procedure definitions.

A separation of a class into interface and definition is useful, because it lets us define inheritance in terms of each (the concepts coincide when the interface possesses no functions). Note that our notion of interface is more general than that in Java, since we allow attributes in an interface, and the definition of some, but not necessarily all, functions. In this last respect, our notion of interface is closer to the Eiffel concept of *deferred class* [9].

We illustrate these mechanisms with a simple example: a stack of integers. The stack has one attribute, *contents*, which is a list of integers. It also has three routines, *push*, *pop*, and *top*. The interface specification of the stack, *StackInt*, declares the attributes and functions, and gives their signatures.

$$StackInt = \text{``contents''} \rightarrow list\ int \mid \text{``top''} \rightarrow int$$

A specific behavior is required for the parameterless function *top*. The definition of *top* is given in terms of *contents*, and is specified in the class definition *STACK*. (In the definition, recall that $s\,\text{``top''}$ is the record dereference syntax.)

$$STACK = \S s : StackInt \cdot s\,\text{``top''} = s\,\text{``contents''}\,(\#s\,\text{``contents''} - 1) \tag{1}$$

STACK is the bunch of all elements of *StackInt* that satisfy the definition of *top*: *top* is the last element of the list *contents*. (We could, in fact, write a generic *STACK* class, by replacing the *int* type for elements by a generic parameter *T*.)

For procedures we use a different approach, which is described in Section 3.2. In the interim, we turn to objects, which are instances of classes.

Definition 3. *An* **object** *is a variable with a class definition for its type.*

To declare an object of class *STACK*, we can write **var** *s* : *STACK*, and can access the *contents* field of object *s* by dereferencing *s*, written *s* "*contents*". A dereferenced field may be any function or attribute. To assign a value to field *contents*, we just carry out a record field assignment, written either as *s* "*contents*" := *value*, or (as a selective union), as *s* := "*contents*" → *value* | *s*. This approach does not support any notion of information hiding; visibility of features is enforced only by specifier discipline.

3.2   Specifying Procedures

The formalization of classes is sufficient for specifying attributes and functions of classes, but is insufficient for capturing procedures, i.e., routines that change the state of an invoking object.

Each procedure of a class is a predicative function that takes an instance of the class as argument, and returns a changed, new instance of the class. Suppose *f* is to be a procedure of class *C*. We define a (possibly nondeterministic) function *f* : *C* → *C*. To use *f* applied to an object *c* of class *C*, we write *c.f* which is sugar for the assignment *c* := *f*(*c*). The syntax *c.f* allows specifiers to use procedures in a syntax similar to what is found in languages like C++ or Java. This function does not have side effects; it maintains the command/query separation suggested in [9].

Returning to the stack example, the procedure *pop* would be specified as

$$pop = \lambda s : STACK \cdot \text{``}contents\text{''} \rightarrow s\text{``}contents\text{''}[0; ..\#s\text{``}contents\text{''} - 1] \mid s$$

The method to push integer *x* to a *STACK* *s* is

$$push = \lambda s : STACK \cdot \lambda x : int \cdot \text{``}contents\text{''} \rightarrow s\text{``}contents\text{''}^{+}[x] \mid s$$

push can be used by writing *s.push*(*x*), which is sugar for *s* := *push* *s* *x*. After a *push* or a *pop* has been applied to a stack *s*, the value of function *s* "*top*" will have changed. The definition of *s* "*top*" will not change, only its value.

3.3   Implementation

The preceding formalization of classes and objects is straightforward to structurally transform into an object-oriented programming language, e.g., Eiffel. A class definition *T* can be transformed into an Eiffel class T. Attributes are transformed into objects that are features of the class; for example, array *contents* of class *STACK* could be mapped to an instance of class ARRAY in Eiffel. Function definitions are transformed into bodies of functions in Eiffel; for example, the function definition of *top*, given in equation (1), can be easily transliterated into the following Eiffel function of class STACK.

```
top : INTEGER is do
   result := current.contents.item(contents.upper-1)
end
```

References to the bound variable s in (1) are replaced with references to the current object, current, in the Eiffel program. In general, a simple transliteration of predicative specification to Eiffel program will not be possible, thus refinement may have to take place beforehand.

Functions on objects in predicative notation can be transliterated into procedures of a class; explicit reference in the function to the object that is passed as an argument can be replaced by explicit reference to the current object. For example, *push* could be transliterated into the following Eiffel procedure (append is a feature of class ARRAY).

```
push( x:INTEGER ) is do
    current.contents.append(x)
end
```

3.4   Single and Multiple Inheritance

We now give a brief overview of inheritance in predicative programming. There are many different definitions and types of inheritance, e.g., see [1, 9]. The definition we use in this paper is one of *subtyping:* if a (child) class B inherits from a (parent) class C, then B can be used everywhere C can be used. We take this approach predominantly because we want to ensure behavioral compatibility between classes related by inheritance.

It is straightforward to determine if a class definition B is derived from class definition C. Since each class is just a type, we can apply bunch inclusion notation directly.

Rule 1   [Inheritance Relation] *Class B inherits from class C if $B : C$.*

This rule is valid if there are functions in the class definitions; we just apply function inclusion. When applying function inclusion, we must take care with function domains and ranges: functions are anti-monotonic in their domains, and monotonic in their ranges (see Section 2.1: function inclusion).

We also need to show how to build one class from another using inheritance. Single class inheritance is expressed in predicative notation by merging the definition or interface of the parent class with any new features that the child class will provide; this produces a definition or interface for the child class.

Definition 4. *Let C be a class definition or interface. If class B singly inherits C, then*

$$B = \text{``}b_1\text{''} \rightarrow T_1 \mid \ldots \mid \text{``}b_i\text{''} \rightarrow T_i \mid \ldots \mid \text{``}b_k\text{''} \rightarrow T_k \mid C$$

where the b_j are attribute names and T_1 through T_k are bunches.

By definition, $B : C$, because every value satisfactory to B is also satisfactory to C. In other words, class C includes all its extensions. This last fact is an artifact of the axiomatic definition of bunches in [6].

The names of attributes and functions of C and $b_1, .., b_k$ can coincide. If b_i is also the name of an attribute of C, then the attribute in C will be replaced by new attribute b_i in B. In order to maintain the subbunch relation of Rule 1, constraints must be placed on the types of the replacements. If a b_i overrides an attribute in C, then the type of the new attribute must be a subbunch of the original. This is the *contravariant* rule [9]. A discussion of the limitations and advantages of contravariance is in [9].

An implication of using selective union to specify inheritance is that in class hierarchies, the order in which features appear in class definitions or interfaces *matters*. Consider B, above: if C had appeared before all the new features b_i, then the features in C could override the new features – which is probably not what the specifier intended. To get around this complication, we follow the convention that, when using single inheritance, the parent class will always appear last in the child class interface or definition. Most OO programming languages enforce this by syntactic means. (We discuss the effect ordering of parent classes will have on multiple inheritance shortly).

Procedures of a parent class are inherited by a child class in the following sense. If there is a procedure $f : C \rightarrow C$, and class B inherits from C, then f can be applied to objects of class B, and type correctness is guaranteed on the use of f, because $B : C$. Therefore, f can be specialized for the methods of class B. New procedures can also be added to child classes. However, arbitrary procedure addition is not possible, because new procedures may falsify constraints specified in a parent class. Thus a new non-vacuous procedure h (i.e., a procedure that does not map everything to the empty bunch) of child class C that inherits from parent B must guarantee, for all $c : C$, that $h(c) : B$.

3.4.1 Overriding and Redefinition

We have defined inheritance in terms of selective union, which allows us to override features of a parent class in a child class. In particular, it lets us give different definitions to functions in child classes than are present in parent classes; this allows us to specify a kind of *redefinition*. In a class definition, functions can always be redefined (as is the case with Java and Eiffel, but not C++).

Let C be a class definition with function $f : T$, and possibly some more attributes. Let $BInt$ inherit from C. By construction, $BInt : C$. Redefine function f in the class definition B as follows.

$$B = \S b : BInt \cdot (b\text{``}f\text{''} = body)$$

where *body* is a subbunch of T. Function f in B can therefore have a definition *body* different from that given to f in the definition of C. There are constraints on the redefinition *body*: a definition for f is inherited from C, say P. In the class definition for B, function f is being further constrained. Thus, the new constraint that $b\text{``}f\text{''} = body$ is effectively being conjoined with the original constraint P from class C. Thus, whatever new definition of f is provided must not contradict the original definition. That is, the specification

$$b\text{``}f\text{''} = P \wedge b\text{``}f\text{''} = body$$

must be satisfiable; this can be ensured by making *body* a refinement of the original definition P. This is akin to the correctness constraints on redefinition in Eiffel [9].

Procedure redefinition can be simulated by overloading procedure names; each instance of the procedure is defined on a different class in a hierarchy. The types of arguments to the procedure dictate the instance of the procedure that is to be used. New procedures must satisfy the constraints of the parent class.

Redefinition allows us to support a form of dynamic binding of functions, where the instance of a function that is used in a call is dependent on the dynamic type of an object, rather than its static type. Suppose we have a class A with feature f, and class B inherits from A and redefines f. Declare a list of instances of A, and an instance of B, and set element 3 of a to reference b.

$$\textbf{var } a : \textit{list } A \cdot \textbf{var } b : B \cdot \text{``3''} \rightarrow b \mid a$$

The static type of $a(3)$ is A; its dynamic type is B. A call to $a(3)$ "f" will use the B version of f.

3.4.2 Multiple Inheritance

Multiple inheritance allows a child class to have more than one parent. It has been suggested as being useful in describing the complex class relationships that occur in domain modeling, as well as for building reusable object-oriented libraries. In predicative programming, we can easily adopt the simple yet powerful Eiffel approach to multiple inheritance. We summarize some details here.

Multiple inheritance, in predicative programming, takes two or more parent class definitions or interfaces, and produces a child class definition or interface (to simplify the discussion, we will refer only to 'parent' and 'child' classes, which we allow to mean class definitions or class interfaces). We first provide a preliminary definition of multiple inheritance, and then touch on its limitations.

Definition 5. *Let* $C_1, .., C_k$ *be classes. If B multiply inherits from* $C_1, .., C_k$ *then*

$$B = C_1 \mid C_2 \mid \ldots \mid C_k$$

B can also add new features and these new features can override attributes or functions in any of $C_1, .., C_k$. *The restriction on overriding is that the types of the overriding features must be subtypes of the original features.*

3.4.3 Name Clashes

Suppose that the name of a feature is declared in two or more parents, and the parents are multiply inherited. Should there be one or two occurrences of the shared name in the derived class? Following [9], we can treat this problem syntactically, and use one of two mechanisms to resolve name clashes.

1. Order the base classes in the definition of the derived class, so as to override those features that we do not want in the derived class. In this way, we can select the reoccurring feature that we want to inherit in the derived class.
   Unlike multiple inheritance in some languages, in predicative programming the order in which base classes are multiply inherited *does* matter, and we can use this to our advantage to resolve name clashes.
2. Apply a renaming to all the commonly named features of the base classes in order to eliminate name clashes. This approach can be used in Eiffel [9]. An example is shown in Fig. 1: attribute a is common to both $C1$ and $C2$. If we need two occurrences of the attribute in the derived class D, we rename the occurrences of a in the definition of D.

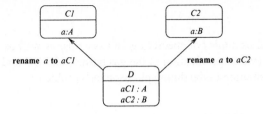

Fig.1. Renaming to avoid name clashes

Renaming in predicative notation is just substitution. The definition of class D, from Fig. 1 would be $D = C1[aC1/a] \mid C2[aC2/a]$, where $aC1$ and $aC2$ are fresh names of features. D can add new attributes and functions as necessary. We place one restriction on the names of new features like $aC1$: they cannot take on any of the names that are being changed.

If we rename features to avoid clashes in a child, the child is no longer (provably) a subtype of its parents. The proof rule for inheritance involving multiple parents and renaming is therefore slightly more complex.

Rule 2 [Multiple Inheritance Relation] *Let D inherit from both classes $C1$ and $C2$, and suppose name a is shared between $C1$ and $C2$. D is derived from $C1$ if there exists a substitution $[a/aC1]$ such that $D[a/aC1] : C1$ (and similarly for $C2$).*

Feature renaming must also be applied to the procedures of $C1$ and $C2$ that are inherited by D. If a method $f : C1 \rightarrow C1$ uses the attribute $a : A$ and $a : B$ is an attribute of class $C2$, then class D must have a new procedure, say $Df : D \rightarrow D$, with definition

$$Df = f[aC1/a]$$

Multiple inheritance can be expressed and used in predicative notation, but it is not always convenient to use the renaming facility to avoid its problems: the specifier must keep track of all the renamings. For large OO specifications, this will be impractical. Automated support for keeping track of renamings, e.g., as provided by a compiler, is essential for this solution to be feasible.

3.4.4   Repeated Inheritance If a class is a descendent of another through two or more paths, then repeated inheritance has occurred. Under repeated inheritance in bunch notation, a function or attribute from a common ancestor will yield a single method or attribute if it is inherited under a single name (this matches the notion of *virtual base class* in C++). If a renaming is applied to one or more features, a derived class can have two or more instances of a feature; [9] gives examples of when this is useful. The solution that we applied for resolving name clashes can also be used in resolving repeated inheritance (as is the case with Eiffel).

4   Examples

We present several examples of specifying OO systems, as well as combining use of OO and real-time (via a specification of the gas burner) and OO and concurrency (in a specification of a solution to the dining philosopher's problem).

4.1   Sequences and Queues

Our first example simply aims at illustrating the main concepts of the previous sections. We define a *SEQUENCE* class, and derive a *QUEUE* class from it. A sequence consists of the following features: a list *contents* of data elements; an *add* procedure, which puts an element x at position i of the sequence; a *delete* procedure, which removes the element at position i of the sequence; a *get* function, which returns the element at position i, or $-\infty$ if there is no element at i; and, an *empty* function. We first provide a class interface, *SeqInt*, where the sequence is to contain integers. *SeqInt* declares the attributes plus the signatures of *index* and *empty*.

$$SeqInt = \quad \text{``contents''} \rightarrow list\ int$$
$$\mid \text{``get''} \rightarrow (nat \rightarrow int) \mid \text{``empty''} \rightarrow bool$$

This interface has two functions, *get* and *empty*, which we now define.

$$SEQUENCE = \S s : SeqInt \cdot$$
$$s\text{``empty''} = (\#s\text{``contents''} = 0) \wedge$$
$$s\text{``get''} = (\lambda i : nat \cdot \textbf{if}\ i < \#s\text{``contents''}\ \textbf{then}\ s\text{``contents''}(i)\ \textbf{else}\ -\infty)$$

We next specify the method *add*. If an addition at index i occurs where an entry exists, the entry at index i is overwritten with x; otherwise, catenation occurs.

$$add = \lambda s : SEQUENCE \cdot \lambda i : nat \cdot \lambda x : int \cdot$$
$$\textbf{if}\ 0 \leq i < \#s\text{``contents''}\ \textbf{then}\ \text{``contents''} \rightarrow (i \rightarrow x \mid s\text{``contents''}) \mid s$$
$$\textbf{else}\ \text{``contents''} \rightarrow (s\text{``contents''}{}^{+}[x]) \mid s$$

The *delete* method is defined as follows: to remove an entry that exists, all following entries are shifted left by one; otherwise, the sequence is returned unchanged.

$$delete = \lambda s : SEQUENCE \cdot \lambda i : nat \cdot$$
$$\textbf{if}\ (0 \leq i < \#s\text{``contents''})\ \textbf{then}$$
$$\text{``contents''} \rightarrow (s\text{``contents''}[0;\ ..i]{}^{+}s\text{``contents''}[i+1;\ ..\#s\text{``contents''}]) \mid s$$
$$\textbf{else}\ s$$

The **then** branch of the *delete* method can be refined using standard predicative techniques. The ability to use standard refinement in developing programs is one benefit of using predicative programming in specifying object-oriented systems. To refine the **then** branch, we introduce a new recursive function, *shift*, which takes three arguments:

a sequence s, a pivot element i (everything to the right of i is shifted left one index), and a counter j. It is recursively defined as follows.

$$shift = \lambda s : SEQUENCE \cdot \lambda i,j : nat \cdot$$
$$\textbf{if } j \geq \#s\,\text{``contents''} - 1 \textbf{ then } [nil]$$
$$\textbf{else if } j = i \textbf{ then } [s\,\text{``contents''}(i+1)]^+ shift\ s\ i\ (j+2)$$
$$\textbf{else } [s\,\text{``contents''}(j)]^+ shift\ s\ i\ (j+1)$$

Using the functional refinement laws from [6], it is straightforward to prove that

$$delete :\cdot \lambda s : SEQUENCE \cdot \lambda i : nat \cdot \textbf{if } 0 \leq i < \#s\,\text{``contents''} \textbf{ then } shift\ s\ i\ 0 \textbf{ else } s$$

The refined specification is implementable in any language that supports lists and recursion.

SEQUENCE can now be used in constructing a QUEUE class. QUEUE is like a SEQUENCE, except it is used in FIFO order. We derive a QUEUE class from SEQUENCE, adding a new state attribute called *cursor*, which is an index to the front of the QUEUE, and a new function called *head*, which gives the element at the head of the queue. First we specify the interface of the new class.

$$QueueInt = \text{``cursor''} \rightarrow 0 \mid \text{``head''} \rightarrow int \mid SEQUENCE$$

To define the function *head*, we give a class definition for QUEUE.

$$QUEUE = \S q : QueueInt \cdot q\,\text{``head''} = q\,\text{``get''}\ q\,\text{``cursor''}$$

head is the value stored in the *contents* attribute, in entry *cursor*. It follows immediately that QUEUE : SEQUENCE (since SEQUENCE includes all its extensions), and so QUEUE is derived from SEQUENCE.

We now specify the procedures of QUEUE; in doing so, we specialize procedures of SEQUENCE. There are two: *enqueue*, which adds an element to the rear of the QUEUE, and *dequeue*, which removes the front-most element of the QUEUE. To *enqueue* an element, we carry out an *add* in the last position in the sequence. *enqueue* changes only those parts of the queue q that are affected by *add*.

$$enqueue = \lambda q : QUEUE \cdot \lambda x : int \cdot add\ q\ (\#q\,\text{``contents''})\ x \mid q$$

add returns a SEQUENCE, which is part of a QUEUE. The selective union in the body of *enqueue* therefore overrides the SEQUENCE fields of q, while not changing the parts of q that are only defined in QUEUE.

To *dequeue* an element, we *delete* the element at position *cursor*.

$$dequeue = \lambda q : QUEUE \cdot delete\ q\ (q\,\text{``cursor''}) \mid q$$

4.2   Quadrilaterals

The quadrilaterals example is described in [15]; it is used to compare several different object-oriented methods based on Z. The example requires specifying different sorts of quadrilaterals which may be used in a drawing system.

The shapes of interest in the system are: a *quadrilateral*, the general four-sided figure; a *parallelogram*, a *quadrilateral* that has parallel opposite sides; a *rhombus*, a *parallelogram* with identical-length sides; a *rectangle*, which is a *parallelogram* with perpendicular sides; and, a *square*, which is both a *rectangle* and a *rhombus*.

We assume the existence of a class *VECTOR*. The usual vector operations, such as addition, are available. *VECTOR* also has a zero. The edges of a four-sided figure are defined first as a list, $EdgesInt = (0, ..4) \rightarrow VECTOR$. Then, a class definition is provided, ensuring that the edges form a closed figure.

$$EDGES = \S e : EdgesInt \cdot (e0 + e1 + e2 + e3 = 0)$$

A quadrilateral class consists of edges and a position vector, the latter intended to be used in drawing the quadrilateral on the screen. The class definition of *QUAD* is

$$QUAD = \text{``edges''} \rightarrow EDGES \mid \text{``pos''} \rightarrow VECTOR$$

The class hierarchy in the quadrilateral system is depicted in Fig. 2, using BON notation. Each ellipse represents a class in the system, while directed edges indicate inheritance relationships. Inheritance will be defined predominantly on interfaces (though there are many other ways to use inheritance to specify this system).

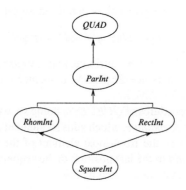

Fig.2. The class hierarchy

We construct the classes in the system by inheritance. In the process, we add a function *angle* to each class, where *angle* is the angle between edge 0 and 1. The hierarchy is described by first specifying class interfaces. Then, class definitions are provided, which give further details on constraints specific to each class.

$ParInt = \text{``angle''} \rightarrow real \mid QUAD$ $RectInt = ParInt$

$RhomInt = ParInt$ $SquareInt = RhomInt \mid RectInt$

Renaming of attributes from *ParInt* in *SquareInt* and *RhomInt* does not have to be done, since we need only one occurrence of each of *ParInt*'s attributes. In *SquareInt*, it is expressed that a square is both a rectangle and a rhombus. However, since both *RectInt* and *RhomInt* have the same class interface, their merge simplifies to *ParInt*.

The derivation hierarchy states that a parallelogram is a quadrilateral, a rhombus is a parallelogram, et cetera. But there are extra constraints associated with these special-case quadrilaterals—e.g., that a rectangle is a parallelogram with perpendicular sides. These constraints can be placed in the class definitions.

$$SQUARE = \S s : SquareInt \cdot IsSquare(s\,\text{``edges''}) \wedge s\,\text{``angle''} = \pi/2$$

$$RECTANGLE = \S r : RectInt \cdot IsRect(r\,\text{``edges''}) \wedge r\,\text{``angle''} = \pi/2$$

$$RHOMBUS = \S r : RhomInt \cdot IsRhom(r\,\text{``edges''}) \wedge r\,\text{``angle''} = cos^{-1}(\ldots)$$

$$PARALLELOGRAM = \S p : ParInt \cdot IsPar(p\,\text{``edges''}) \wedge p\,\text{``angle''} = cos^{-1}(\ldots)$$

We omit the full definitions of the *angle* methods of *RHOMBUS* and *PARALLELOGRAM* (they are in [15]). *IsRect* is *true* if and only if the list of edges forms a rectangle ($\cdot$ in the body of *IsRect* is dot product.)

$$IsRect = \lambda e : EDGES \cdot (e0 \cdot e1 = 0 \wedge e0 + e2 = 0)$$

The predicates *IsSquare*, *IsPar*, and *IsRhom* are similar. We next define a procedure to translate a quadrilateral's position by a vector.

$$TranslateQuad = \lambda q : QUAD \cdot \lambda v : VECTOR \cdot \text{``pos''} \rightarrow q\,\text{``pos''} + v \mid q$$

To build a translation procedure on rhombi, for example, we specialize *TranslateQuad*.

$$TranslateRhom = \lambda r : RHOMBUS \cdot \lambda v : VECTOR \cdot TranslateQuad\ r\ v \mid r$$

The generic quadrilateral initialization method is as follows. It can be reused in the initializers of the other classes.

$$InitQuad = \lambda q : QUAD \cdot \lambda e : EDGES \cdot \lambda v : VECTOR \cdot \text{``edges''} \rightarrow e \mid \text{``pos''} \rightarrow v \mid q$$

4.3   A real-Time Example: Gas Burner

The gas burner problem has been treated by many researchers [14]. The problem is to specify the control of a gas burner. The inputs of the burner come from a sensor, a thermometer, and a thermostat. The inputs are:

- a real *temp*, indicating the actual temperature,
- a real *desired*, indicating the desired temperature,
- a boolean *flame*, indicating whether there is a flame.

The outputs of the burner are

- *gas*, which is set to *on* if the gas is on, or to *off* if the gas is off,
- *spark*, which maintains the gas and causes a spark for the purposes of ignition.

Heat is wanted when the actual temperature falls ϵ below the desired temperature, and is not wanted when the actual temperature rises ϵ above the desired temperature. ϵ is small enough to be unnoticeable, but large enough to prevent rapid oscillation.

To obtain heat, the spark should be applied to the gas for at least 1 second (to give it a chance to ignite and to allow the flame to become stable). A safety regulation states that the gas must not remain on and unlit for more than 3 seconds. Another regulation states that when the gas is shut off, it must not be turned on again for at least 20 seconds to allow any accumulated gas to clear. And finally, the gas burner must respond to its inputs within 1 second.

We formulate an object-oriented, real-time specification. Thus, we will need to talk about time. As discussed in Section 2.3, to talk about time, global time variables are introduced and are manipulated. In a pure OO specification, there are no global variables. In order to talk about real-time, we therefore formulate a simple class definition, $TIME$, which will be used to represent the passage of time over the lifetime of an object. $TIME$ has one attribute, t, of type $real$.

$$TIME = \text{``}t\text{''} \rightarrow real$$

($TIME$ can be used to introduce a local clock. To introduce a system clock, $TIME$ can be inherited by the $root$ class in our system, from which computation will begin.) We also specify, implicitly, a function $addtime$, which will be used to describe a nondeterministic increase in time. $addtime$ takes three real numbers r_1, r_2, r_3, as parameters, and satisfies the following property.

$$r_1 + r_2 \leq addtime\ r_1\ r_2\ r_3 \leq r_1 + r_3$$

The similar specification $takeone$, which takes one real number r_1 as a parameter, will be used to specify a nondeterministic increase in time of $at\ most$ one second.

$$r_1 < takeone\ r_1 < r_1 + 1$$

The gas burner will be specified as a class. We begin by specifying its interface, giving the names of the attributes and functions local to the class.

$$BurnerInt = \text{``}temp\text{''} \rightarrow real \mid \text{``}desired\text{''} \rightarrow real \mid$$
$$\text{``}flame\text{''} \rightarrow bool \mid \text{``}spark\text{''} \rightarrow bool \mid \text{``}gas\text{''} \rightarrow status \mid$$
$$\text{``}cold\text{''} \rightarrow bool \mid \text{``}hot\text{''} \rightarrow bool \mid TIME$$

In its interface, the burner inherits from $TIME$. The bunch $status$ is $status = on, off$. Now, we can define the functions of the class.

$$BURNER = \S b : BurnerInt \cdot$$
$$b\text{``}cold\text{''} = (b\text{``}temp\text{''} < b\text{``}desired\text{''} - \epsilon) \wedge$$
$$b\text{``}hot\text{''} = (b\text{``}temp\text{''} \geq b\text{``}desired\text{''} + \epsilon \wedge b\text{``}flame\text{''})$$

This completes the specification of the burner's attributes and functions. Now we specify its procedures.

$$gas\_on = \lambda b : BURNER \cdot \text{``}gas\text{''} \rightarrow on \mid b$$
$$gas\_off = \lambda b : BURNER \cdot \text{``}gas\text{''} \rightarrow off \mid b$$

gas_on and *gas_off* are used to turn the gas on or off, on request. The next two procedures, *ignite* and *cutoff*, are responsible for igniting the spark of the burner (leaving it on for between 1 and 3 seconds) and for turning the spark off.

$$ignite = \lambda b : BURNER \cdot \text{``spark''} \rightarrow \top \mid \text{``}t\text{''} \rightarrow (addtime\ b\text{``}t\text{''}\ 1\ 3) \mid b$$
$$cutoff = \lambda b : BURNER \cdot \text{``spark''} \rightarrow \bot \mid b$$

Finally, the procedure *wait* causes the burner to wait for 20 to 21 seconds.

$$wait = \lambda b : BURNER \cdot \text{``}t\text{''} \rightarrow (addtime\ b\text{``}t\text{''}\ 20\ 21) \mid b$$

The behaviour of the burner system can now be specified as two procedures, *too_hot* and *too_cold*. *too_cold* tests if the temperature is too cold; if it is, the gas is turned on, and the spark is ignited for at most three seconds, then it is cut off, and the test is repeated; if it is not too cold, one unit of time is taken, and then the test is repeated.

$$too\_cold = \lambda b : BURNER \cdot$$

if $b\text{``}cold\text{''}$ **then**

$$too\_hot\ cutoff\ ignite\ gas\_on\ b$$

else $too\_cold\ (\text{``}t\text{''} \rightarrow takeone\ b\text{``}t\text{''} \mid b)$

too_hot is as follows. If the temperature is too hot, then the gas is shut off and the burner waits for 20 to 21 seconds; then the temperature is tested. If it is not too hot, then one unit of time is taken, and then the test is repeated.

$$too\_hot = \lambda b : BURNER \cdot$$

if $b\text{``}hot\text{''}$ **then**

$$too\_cold\ wait\ gas\_off\ b$$

else $too\_hot\ (\text{``}t\text{''} \rightarrow takeone\ b\text{``}t\text{''} \mid b)$

The OO specification of the gas burner is then

$$\textbf{var}\ b : BURNER \cdot b.too\_hot\ \lor\ b.too\_cold$$

4.4   A Concurrent Example: Dining Philosophers

As a final example, we formulate a simple concurrent and object-oriented specification of the dining philosophers synchronization problem. We assume that we have five philosophers who are either thinking, eating, or hungry. The philosophers are sitting at a circular table which is laid with only five chopsticks, placed between neighbouring philosophers. From time to time, philosophers get hungry and try to pick up the two nearest chopsticks. A philosopher can pick up one chopstick at a time, and cannot pick up a chopstick in the hand of a neighbour. When a hungry philosopher has both his chopsticks at the same time, he eats without releasing the chopsticks. When he is finished eating, he puts down both chopsticks and starts to think again.

We commence by assuming that we have a class called *SEMAPHORE*, used to represent the standard synchronization tool. This class has two procedures, *semwait* and *semsignal*. We also assume that we have used *SEMAPHORE* to specify a class called *CONDITION*, which specifies *condition constructs* for critical regions. This class has a queue, for waiting processes, associated with it as well as two procedures: *csignal*, which resumes exactly one suspended process, and *cwait*, which makes the invoking process wait until another invokes *csignal*. Formulations of both semaphores and condition constructs can be found in [12]. We will use these classes to specify the mutual exclusion required in the dining philosophers problem, via a *monitor.*

A monitor allows safe, effective sharing of objects among several concurrent processes. Monitors assure mutual exclusion; only one process at a time can be active within the monitor. A monitor is a class, consisting of two semaphores, *mutex* (used to orchestrate entrance to and exit from the monitor) and *next* (on which signaling processes may suspend themselves), and a counter *next_count*, which keeps track of the number of waiting processes. It also has two procedures, *enter* and *leave*, used by a process to enter and leave the monitor. Here is the class definition.

$$MONITOR = \text{``mutex''} \rightarrow SEMAPHORE \mid \text{``next''} \rightarrow SEMAPHORE \mid \text{``next\_count''} \rightarrow int$$

The *enter* procedure calls *semwait* on the *mutex* semaphore.

$$enter = \lambda m : MONITOR \cdot \text{``mutex''} \rightarrow (semwait\ m\text{``mutex''}) \mid m$$

Similarly, procedure *leave* exits the invoking process from the monitor. If the number of waiting processes is 0, *semsignal* is called on *mutex*, and the invoking process leaves the monitor; otherwise, *semsignal* is called on *next*.

$$leave = \lambda m : MONITOR \cdot$$
$$\quad \textbf{if } m\text{``next\_count''} > 0 \textbf{ then } \text{``next''} \rightarrow (semsignal\ m\text{``next''}) \mid m$$
$$\quad \textbf{else } \text{``mutex''} \rightarrow (semsignal\ m\text{``mutex''}) \mid m$$

We next specify a philosopher as a class definition, *PHIL*. This class has two attributes, *state* (recording whether the philosopher is thinking, hungry, or eating), and *self*, which is a condition construct used for synchronization (it is used to delay a philosopher when he is hungry but unable to obtain the needed chopsticks).

$$PHIL = \text{``state''} \rightarrow Status \mid \text{``self''} \rightarrow CONDITION$$

(The bunch *Status* is *thinking, hungry, eating*.) The procedures for *PHIL* are used to change the state of an invoking object to one of *hungry* or *thinking*.

$$sethungry = \lambda p : PHIL \cdot \text{``state''} \rightarrow hungry \mid p$$
$$setthinking = \lambda p : PHIL \cdot \text{``state''} \rightarrow thinking \mid p$$

A philosopher uses the *eat* procedure to move to the eating state. A move to the eating state requires a call to the *csignal* procedure of class *CONDITION*, which resumes a suspended process. Thus, a call *p.eat* (where *p* is a philosopher) changes the philosopher's state to *eating*, and calls the *csignal* procedure of the philosopher's *self* attribute.

$$eat = \lambda p : PHIL \cdot \text{``self''} \rightarrow (csignal\ p\text{``self''}) \mid \text{``state''} \rightarrow eating \mid p$$

The dining philosophers system is specified as a class, *DINING*, which is a *MONITOR* extended with a list of five philosophers (we use the short-hand [5 * *PHIL*] for a list of five philosophers).

$$DINING = \text{``phils''} \rightarrow [5 * PHIL] \mid MONITOR$$

The *DINING* system has several procedures. The first procedure we specify, *test*, takes a number k in the range $0 \le k \le 4$, moves philosopher k to *eating* status if possible, and signals that change in philosopher status to the system. A philosopher can move to *eating* only if he can obtain both the chopsticks to his sides and he is hungry. We view this procedure as *private*; it will only be used by other procedures in the dining philosopher system, and is not an entry procedure of the monitor.

$test = \lambda d : DINING \cdot \lambda k : 0, ..5 \cdot$

> **if** $(d\text{``phils''}(k-1 \bmod 5)\text{``state''} \ne eating \wedge d\text{``phils''}(k)\text{``state''} = hungry \wedge$
>
> $d\text{``phils''}(k+1 \bmod 5)\text{``state''} \ne eating)$
>
> **then**
>
> $\text{``phils''} \rightarrow k \rightarrow (eat\, d\text{``phils''}(k)) \mid d$
>
> **else** d

(Informally, this specification reads "if I am hungry, and my neighbours aren't eating, then I will eat, otherwise, I won't change.")

The procedure *putdown* is used when the philosopher is finished eating. The procedure puts philosopher i into a *thinking* state (i.e., the chopsticks are dropped). Then, the *test* procedure is applied to both of the neighbours of philosopher i, to see if they can start to eat.

$putdown = \lambda d : DINING \cdot \lambda i : 0, ..5 \cdot$

> $test$
>
> $(test\ (\text{``phils''} \rightarrow i \rightarrow setthinking\, d\text{``phils''}(i) \mid d)\ (i-1 \bmod 5))$
>
> $(i+1 \bmod 5)$

The first argument of the inner-most *test* call sets philosopher i to thinking; *test* is then applied to the neighbours: philosopher $i - 1 \bmod 5$, then philosopher $i + 1 \bmod 5$. However, this specification of *putdown* ignores synchronization issues. In order for a call to *putdown* to synchronize with the actions of all other philosophers, *putdown* must be embedded in synchronization primitives; that is, the process must enter the monitor, then it may execute, and then it leaves the monitor. This is expressed in the procedure *entry_putdown*.

$entry\_putdown = \lambda d : DINING \cdot \lambda i : 0, ..5 \cdot leave\ (putdown\ (enter\, d \mid d)\ i) \mid d$

The procedure *pickup* sets a philosopher to *hungry*, then attempts to pickup the chopsticks. If the attempt succeeds, he eats, but if he cannot pickup the chopsticks, he suspends himself by a call to the *wait* procedure of class *DINING*.

$pickup = \lambda d : DINING \cdot \lambda i : 0, ..5 \cdot$

> $wait\ (test\ (\text{``phils''} \rightarrow i \rightarrow sethungry\, d\text{``phils''}(i) \mid d)\ i)\ i$

The first argument to *test* sets philosopher i to *hungry*, then tests him. Either this call succeeds and the philosopher eats, or it returns and he waits. *wait* is as follows. If philosopher i is eating, it does nothing. Otherwise (if the philosopher is thinking or hungry) it calls *cwait* on the philosopher, delaying him.

$$wait = \lambda d : DINING \cdot \lambda i : 0, ..5 \cdot$$
$$\textbf{if } (d\text{``phils''}(i)\text{``state''} = eating) \textbf{ then } d$$
$$\textbf{else ``phils''} \to i \to \text{``self''} \to (cwait\ d\text{``phils''}(i)\text{``self''}) \mid d$$

As was the case with *putdown*, the specification of *pickup* ignores synchronization. Thus, we must extend *pickup* with synchronization details, i.e., make it an entry procedure of the monitor. This is expressed in procedure *entry_pickup*.

$$entry\_pickup = \lambda d : DINING \cdot \lambda i : 0, ..5 \cdot leave\ (pickup\ (enter\ d \mid d)\ i) \mid d$$

The initialization of the *DINING* class will be to set all philosophers to the *thinking* state, and to initialize the monitor (which amounts to initializing the semaphores).

$$init = \lambda d : DINING \cdot \text{``phils''} \to 0 \to setthinking\ d\text{``phils''}(0) \mid$$
$$\text{``phils''} \to 1 \to setthinking\ d\text{``phils''}(1) \mid$$
$$\text{``phils''} \to 2 \to setthinking\ d\text{``phils''}(2) \mid$$
$$\text{``phils''} \to 3 \to setthinking\ d\text{``phils''}(3) \mid$$
$$\text{``phils''} \to 4 \to setthinking\ d\text{``phils''}(4) \mid$$
$$\text{``mutex''} \to 1 \mid \text{``next''} \to 0 \mid d$$

The dining philosophers system can then be specified as follows. We first declare an object, d, of type *DINING*. The object must be initialized, and then it will enter an indefinite concurrent iteration.

$$\textbf{var } d : DINING \cdot d.init.\ iterate$$

where

$$iterate = (\|_{i:0,..5}\ d.entry\_pickup(i).\ Eat.\ d.entry\_putdown(i)).\ iterate$$

The procedure *Eat* performs the activity of eating the food; we leave it unspecified. This specification will not allow deadlock, nor will it allow two neighbours to eat simultaneously. However, it is possible for a philosopher to starve to death. We leave the amendment of this as an exercise for the reader.

5 Discussion and Conclusions

That the predicative programming notation can be used to directly specify many key object-oriented concepts is not surprising, since the notation is sufficient to model any form of computation. Without having to change the notation, we can express key object concepts and still make use of the standard predicative method and all its features, such as timing, concurrency, and refinement.

Part of the reason for the simplicity of specifying object-oriented concepts is due to the bunch notation for types. In the predicative notation, all types are based upon a bunch representation, including lists and records. Because of this, classes and functions can be developed from bunch notation, and therefore object instantiation can be given its usual interpretation as variable declaration. This differs from the approach in [4], where objects are specified in terms of their effect on a global system state. Furthermore, inheritance can be given an interpretation akin to that which is available in many programming languages. The interpretation, as selective union, is easy to implement in any programming language that has lists, arrays, or records (overriding of a field can be implemented as assignment to the field of a record instance).

The formalization of OO concepts is not without limitations. Visibility and export of features is left entirely up to the discipline of the specifier; there is no equivalent to C++'s `public` or `private` notation, nor Eiffel's **export** clause. Further, it might be useful to be able to include procedures within a class definition (though see Utting [16], who argues that non-encapsulation of procedures is useful), but it is not possible within the existing type system of predicative programming. Encapsulation of procedures is left informal, based on the signatures of the features. However, procedures can be specified, and are associated with objects and classes by type rules: procedures associated with a class are only (consistently) applicable to objects of that class or of a child class. Misusing procedures results in unsatisfiable specifications.

A key benefit of using predicative programming to specify and reason about object-oriented systems, is that all existing predicative theory applies immediately to such specifications. This implies that we can specify and reason about key object-oriented concepts, as well as the real-time, interactive, concurrent, and timing characteristics of systems, using one notation and method, as the examples in Section 4 showed. A heterogeneous notation, in the sense of [10, 13], does not have to be created in order to integrate the concepts of OO, real-time, and concurrency.

In the future, we intend to work on improving and extending the object-oriented theory, and will formulate examples that combine use of OO and predicative programming's communication features.

Acknowledgements. We thank the reviewers for their very detailed comments. We thank NSERC for support.

References

[1] M. Abadi and L. Cardelli. *A Theory of Objects*, Springer-Verlag, 1996.

[2] A. Bunkenburg and J. Morris. Formal Bunch Theory. Draft.

[3] R. Duke, G. Rose, and G. Smith. Object-Z: A Specification Language advocated for the description of standards. *Computer Standards and Interfaces* **17**(5), 1995.

[4] A. Hall. Specifying and Interpreting Class Hierarchies in Z. In *Proc. Eighth Z User Meeting,* Workshops in Computing Series, Springer-Verlag, 1994.

[5] E.C.R. Hehner. Bunch Theory: A Simple Set Theory for Computer Science. *Information Processing Letters* **12**(1), 1981.

[6] E.C.R. Hehner. *A Practical Theory of Programming,* Springer-Verlag, 1993.

[7] K. Lano. *Formal Object-Oriented Development*, Springer-Verlag, 1995.

[8] B. Mahony and J.S. Dong. Blending Object-Z and Timed CSP: an introduction to TCOZ. In *Proc. ICSE '98*, IEEE Press, 1998.

[9] B. Meyer. *Object-Oriented Software Construction,* Second Edition, Prentice-Hall, 1997.

[10] R.F. Paige. Heterogeneous Notations for Pure Formal Method Integration. *Formal Aspects of Computing* **10**(3):233-242, June 1999.

[11] R.F. Paige. Integrating a Program Design Calculus and UML. To appear in *The Computer Journal*, 1999.

[12] A. Silberschatz and P. Galvin. *Operating System Concepts* 5e, Addison-Wesley, 1997.

[13] G. Smith. A Semantic Integration of Object-Z and CSP. In *Proc. FME'97*, LNCS 1313, Springer-Verlag, 1997.

[14] E.V. Sorenson, A.P. Ravn, and H. Rischel. Control Program for a gas burner, Technical Report ID/DTH EVS2, Computer Science Department, Technical University of Denmark, Lyngby, Denmark, 1989.

[15] S. Stepney, R. Barden, and D. Cooper. *Object-Orientation in Z*, Springer-Verlag, 1992.

[16] M. Utting. *An Object-Oriented Refinement Calculus with Modular Reasoning.* PhD Dissertation, University of New South Wales, October 1992.

Applications of Structural Synthesis of Programs

Enn Tyugu[1], Mihhail Matskin[2], and Jaan Penjam[3]

[1] Department of Teleinformatics, Royal Institute of Technology, Kista, Sweden
tyugu@it.kth.se
[2] Department of Computer and Information Science, Norwegian University of Science
and Technology, Trondheim, Norway
Mihhail.Matskin@idi.ntnu.no
[3] Institute of Cybernetics, Tallinn, Estonia
Jaan.Penjam@cs.ioc.ee

Abstract. This is an experience report on the automatic and hidden
usage of program synthesis in several application domains. The structural synthesis of programs has been implemented in an object-oriented
programming environment NUT and used for development of simulation
software, engineering calculations software, implementing a benchmark
for safety critical systems and development of highly interactive visual
modeling of radar coverage of landscape.

1 Introduction

This paper presents experience of using a formal method of software development that is applied completely automatically, and hidden from the user. The
advantage is that we do not introduce errors during the process of usage of a
formal method in this case. The obvious disadvantages are high requirements to
the reliability and performance of complex automatic operations that are hidden
from the user.

Actually, there are few synthesis methods sufficiently mature for automatic
usage. Here we refer to the following two practically applied systems where automatic program synthesis plays a central role: Specware [20] and Amphion [12].
Specware is a tool for creating applications from a set of specifications of its
parts. The specifications are given in an algebraic style in the language called
Slang. They are joined into larger specifications in a formal way specified in
terms of categories. Specware includes a visual tool for drawing diagrams of
categories for composing the specifications. Although Specware is intended for
the interactive usage, the composition of specifications and development of an
implementation is highly automated. Another automated system with deductive
program synthesis is Amphion – a program for constructing programs from preprogrammed subroutines in a library. This system is domain-oriented and it is
used for solving problems in planetary astronomy. Using the experience in program synthesis gained with Amphion, its authors have developed Meta-Amphion
– a tool for implementing domain-oriented synthesizers [13].

We are dealing with deductive program synthesis, and are concerned not only
of the synthesis process, but also of getting correct specifications as the reliable

J. Wing, J. Woodcock, J. Davies (Eds.): FM'99, Vol. I, LNCS 1708, pp. 551–569, 1999.
© Springer-Verlag Berlin Heidelberg 1999

material for synthesis. The complete verification/validation of specifications is in principle an unsolvable task, therefore we try to give to software developers specification tools which are intuitive and easy to use. As a consequence, we have had also another and completely different motivation of our research – development of a sufficiently general method of semantic processing of specifications which is applicable in compilers of a wide class of problem-oriented languages.

The main part of this paper is a presentation of applications of program synthesis in several problem domains: design of mechanical drives, implementation of a safety-critical system, analysis of dynamics of a hydraulic system for controlling ailerons of an aircraft, calculating radar coverage of a landscape and simulation of a network of mobile telephone communication. These applications are all implemented in the NUT programming environment where the program synthesis is used hiddenly and automatically. We start with brief descriptions of the synthesis method and the programming environment.

2   Structural Synthesis of Programs

Structural synthesis of programs (SSP) is a deductive program synthesis method based on the idea that one can construct programs taking into account only their structural properties. We use this idea for constructing programs from small as well as large modules whose behavior we do not describe in detail. Each preprogrammed module is supplied with a specification used as an axiom stating under which conditions the module can be applied and which postconditions will be satisfied after its execution. However, the specification does not specify explicitly the relation between the input and output of the module.

The SSP uses an implicative fragment of the intuitionistic propositional calculus with restricted nestedness of implications. Intuitionistic logic guarantees simplicity of program extraction from proofs: programs are realizations of formulae and can be represented in typed lambda calculus. The general form of formulae is

$$(\underline{A} \to B)\& \ldots \&(\underline{C} \to D) \to (\underline{E} \to F) \tag{1}$$

where, for any symbol W, $\underline{W}$ denotes $W_1\&W_2\&\ldots\&W_n$ or $W_1, W_2, ..., W_n$ or empty (depending on context). If we assume that propositional letters $\underline{X}, Y, \ldots$ denote computability of objects $\underline{x}, y, \ldots$, then an implication $\underline{X} \to Y$ has the following meaning "y is computable from $\underline{x}$". An implication of this form can be either a specification of a preprogrammed module (i.e. an axiom), or a goal specifying the program to be synthesized. In the case of an axiom we can show the module under the arrow as follows: $\underline{X} \underset{f}{\to} Y$.

The nested implications $\underline{A} \to B, ..., \underline{C} \to D$ in an axiom of the form (1) are called subtasks. They state subgoals, which must be achieved in order to apply the module with this axiom. They provide generality to the logical language, indeed, they play a role similar to atoms in the body of a Prolog clause.

Program development based on SSP is sometimes called propositional logic programming, because, first, it is a kind of logic programming, and, second, it uses a propositional logic [15].

The fragment of the intuitionistic propositional calculus used in SSP is still expressive enough for deductively equivalent encoding of arbitrary intuitionistic propositional formulae [15]. The derivability problem in the intuitionistic propositional calculus is known to be PSPACE complete, consequently, the proof search in SSP is PSPACE complete. Still, efficient algorithms exist for practical cases of synthesis where restrictions on structural complexity of specifications are known [18].

A natural way to extend the SSP could be to use a more general theory of constructive types, e.g. proposed by P. Martin Löf [5]. However, we have been afraid of loosing the efficiency by introducing this extension.

3   NUT Programming Environment

The NUT programming environment is an Unix/Linux-based tool that combines object-oriented and visual programming paradigms with automatic program synthesis. The object-oriented concept of a class is extended in such a way that a class can serve as a complete specification for program synthesis [16]. The NUT language includes two parts: a specification language and a procedural language. We outline the specification language here and present a small example.

3.1   Specification Language

There are built-in classes for primitive data types: <u>num</u>, <u>bool</u>, <u>text</u>, <u>prog</u>, <u>any</u>. The last is a universal class, which should be narrowed to any well-defined class before a more detailed specification will be needed. A class is specified as a collection of declarations of the following form (C is a class name):

Superclass declaration
<u>super</u> C;   - C is a superclass

Component declaration
<u>var</u> A : C;   - A is a new component
                                          which has a class C

Method declaration
<u>rel</u> R : <axiom> <program>; - R is a new method
                                          (the name R may be omitted.)

Equality declaration
<u>rel</u> A = B;   - A and B are components with
                                          the same value

Equation declaration

> <u>rel</u> e1 = e2;   - e1, e2 are arithmetic expressions
> which define a constraint on the
> variables occurring in them

A complete description of the NUT language can be found in [17].

3.2   An Example

A simple example of logical circuits description illustrates the usage of basic constructs of the language and program synthesis [14]. We describe `inverter`, and-port and `nand`-port as classes of basic elements, and a logical circuit is described as a set of the interconnected basic elements.

INVERTER

> <u>var</u> InINV, OutINV: <u>bool</u>;
> <u>rel</u> inv: InINV -> OutINV
> {OutINV := <u>not</u> InINV}

INVERTER has two boolean primitive type specifiers `InINV` and `OutINV`. The method `inv` specifies computations of `OutINV` from `InINV` which are performed by sequence of statements (body of the method) in the curly brackets. This method will be translated into the following axiom: $InINV \xrightarrow{inv} OutINV$ where inv refers to the body of the method, i. e. to {OutINV := <u>not</u> InINV}.

AND

> <u>var</u> InAND1, InAND2, OutAND: <u>bool</u>;
> <u>rel</u> and: InAND1,InAND2->OutAND
> {OutAND:=InAND1 & InAND2}

NAND

> <u>super</u> INVERTER;
> <u>super</u> AND;
> <u>var</u> InNAND1, InNAND2, OutNAND: <u>bool</u>;
> <u>rel</u> InAND1 = InNAND1; InAND2 = InNAND2;
>   OutNAND = OutINV; InINV = OutAND;
> nand: InNAND1, InNAND2 -> OutNAND{<u>specification</u>}

Let us follow the (automatic) translation of the class **NAND** into the set of axioms. Each equality is translated into two axioms, e.g. $InAND1 \xrightarrow{asg} InNAND1$ and $InNAND1 \xrightarrow{asg} InAND1$, where asg is the name of the standard function performing assignment. The keyword `specification` in the last method indicates that a function for the `nand` method should be synthesized automatically.

Other equalities and methods give the following set of axioms in the sequential form where and, inv and asg indicate methods which implement the corresponding formulae:

$\vdash InINV \xrightarrow[inv]{} OutINV;$ $\qquad$ $\vdash InAND1\&InAND2 \xrightarrow[and]{} OutAND;$

$\vdash InAND1 \xrightarrow[asg]{} InNAND1;$ $\qquad$ $\vdash InNAND1 \xrightarrow[asg]{} InAND1;$

$\vdash InAND2 \xrightarrow[asg]{} InNAND2;$ $\qquad$ $\vdash InNAND2 \xrightarrow[asg]{} InAND2;$

$\vdash OutNAND \xrightarrow[asg]{} OutINV;$ $\qquad$ $\vdash OutINV \xrightarrow[asg]{} OutNAND;$

$\vdash InINV \xrightarrow[asg]{} OutAND;$ $\qquad$ $\vdash OutAND \xrightarrow[asg]{} InINV;$

(Also axioms describing a class as a data structure which can be composed and decomposed are always introduced. We don't use them in the present example, and don't show them here.)

The theorem to be proven is $\vdash InNAND1, InNAND2 \to OutNAND$. Using the set of formulae and the inference rules of SSP $((\to -)$ - implication elimination and $(\to +)$ - implication introduction), the following proof can be made:

$$InNAND1(in1) \vdash InNAND1(in1); \quad \vdash InNAND1 \xrightarrow[asg]{} InAND1;$$

$$InNAND2(in2) \vdash InNAND1(in2); \quad \vdash InNAND2 \xrightarrow[asg]{} InAND2;$$

$$\overline{InNAND1(in1) \vdash InAND1(asg(in1)); \quad InNAND2(in2) \vdash InAND2(asg(in2));}(\to -)$$

$$\vdash InAND1\&InAND2 \xrightarrow[and]{} OutAND$$

$$\overline{InNAND1(in1), InNAND2(in2) \vdash OutAND(and(asg(in1), asg(in2)));}(\to -)$$

$$\vdash OutAND \xrightarrow[asg]{} InINV;$$

$$\overline{InNAND1(in1), InNAND2(in2) \vdash InINV(asg(and(asg(in1), asg(in2))));}(\to -)$$

$$\vdash InINV \xrightarrow[inv]{} OutINV;$$

$$\overline{InNAND1(in1), InNAND2(in2) \vdash OutINV(inv(asg(and(asg(in1), asg(in2)))));}(\to -)$$

$$\vdash OutINV \xrightarrow[asg]{} OutNAND$$

$$\overline{InNAND1(in1), InNAND2(in2) \vdash OutNAND(asg(inv(asg(and(asg(in1), asg(in2))))))}(\to -)$$

$$\overline{\vdash InNAND1\&InNAND2 \xrightarrow[\lambda in1 \ in2.asg(inv(asg(and(asg(in1),asg(in2)))))]{} OutAND}(\to +)$$

Q.E.D.

The extracted program is as follows

$$\lambda in1 \ in2.asg(inv(asg(and(asg(in1), asg(in2)))))$$

or after optimization which removes assignments (asg) for equalities from the formulae

$$\lambda in1 \ in2.inv(and(in1, in2))$$

The classes above can be used for description of different logical circuits. For example, the circuit from Fig. 1 1 can be specified by the following class in NUT.

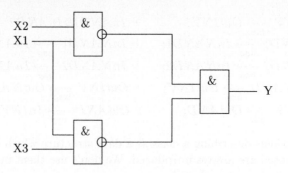

Fig. 1. A logical circuit

SCHEMA
```
    var X1, X2, X3, Y:bool;
        A1:NAND InNAND1=X1, InNAND2=X2;
        A2:NAND InNAND1=X1, InNAND2=X3;
        A3:AND InAND1=A1.OutNAND, InAND2=A2.OutNAND,
                OutAND=Y;
```

Some possible goals are as follows.

```
G1:X1, X2, X3 → Y {specification };
G2:X1, X2, X3 → A1.OutNAND, A2.OutNAND {specification };
G3:X1, X2 → A1.OutNAND {specification };
G4:X1, X3 → A2.OutNAND {specification };
```

Programs for solving these goals are synthesized in a manner similar to the synthesis of the nand method.

This small example should give an idea how classes are used in specification. The approach is, however, scalable and the next sections demonstrate its application for specifications containing thousands of axioms and objects.

4   Solving Numerical Problems in Mechanical Engineering

This is a problem domain where the structural synthesis of programs has been in use for a long time, and applications are in the form of numerous packages. Fig. 2 (taken with permission from [8]) shows a set of packages and their interrelations in mechanical design which have been developed or are under the development with the SSP tools. The largest is a package for calculating tear and wear of gears in gearboxes, used during several years in the Tallinn Excavators Factory.

Mathematical models of typical machine parts: shafts, springs, housings etc. are traditionally presented as sets of algebraic equations and tabulated functions. Such a model is used in two different ways: either for checking the suitability

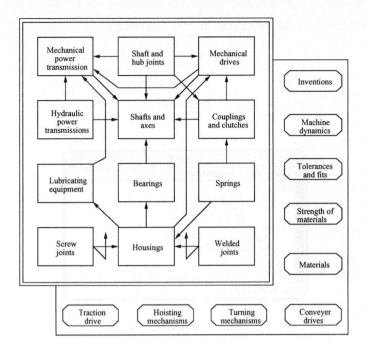

Fig. 2. CAD packages in mechanical engineering

of a given design by calculating the stresses and comparing them with their admissible values, or for calculating the dimensions of a device (machine part) from given design data. Traditionally, there are different programs for these two tasks. Applying the SSP, one can use one and the same mathematical model for both tasks, stating only different goals. Still, developing one universal model for a problem domain could be a difficult task. Object-orientedness and visual tools of the NUT system enable one to develop a set of concepts representing the ontology of a problem domain in such a detail that it becomes easy to specify each particular case of design in this ontology. We present here a simple example: development of a visual language for calculating loads and kinematics of gearboxes, introducing in this way also visual tools of the NUT system.

We start from the ontology for the problem domain. In the present case, the ontology consists of one concept: a gear (toothed wheel) and its features: diameter D, rotations per second n, linear speed v, torque T, tangential force F, module of teeth m and number of teeth z. The concept of gear is specified as a class, and its features, which are numeric parameters in this case, become instance variables of the class. Fig. 3 shows a specification of the gear in a NUT class window. We can see the usage of equations in the class specification. An equation is always interpreted in NUT as a set of methods, one for every variable which can be computed from the equation. For instance, the equation

$$D = m * z;$$

gives three methods whose axioms are the following:

$$m, z \rightarrow D$$

$$D, m \rightarrow z$$

$$D, z \rightarrow m$$

```
                          gear
File Edit Graphics
 rel
     v = 3.14*n*D/1000;
     D = m*z;
     F = 1000*T/(0.5*D);
 alias
     tangential=(v,m,F);
     axial=(n,T);


 Not modified
```

Fig. 3. Class of gear

There are two data structures **tangential** and **axial** specified in this class. These structures will be used for connecting gears tangentially and axially.

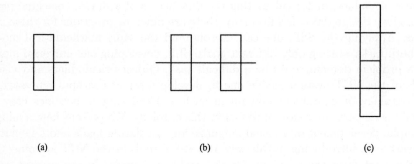

(a)   (b)   (c)

Fig. 4. Visual ontology of gears: (a) am image; (b) connected axially; (c) connected tangentially

Having specified the class **gear**, we associate an image with this class. This is done in a graphics image editor window opened from the Graphics menu of the class window visible in Fig. 3. The image of a gear, familiar to mechanical engineers, is simply a rectangle with an axis through it, Fig. 4,a. The ends of the axis should be defined as ports (graphical elements) by associating them with the name **axial** used in the class **gear**. These ports are for connecting gears axially as shown in Fig. 4,b. Connecting two images via ports means equality of of objects associated with ports. Looking at the class definition, we see that the axial connection of gears means equality of their torques and rotations per second. Also horizontal sides of the gear are defined as ports, for tangential connection in this case, Fig. 4,c. According to the specification, the tangential connection means equality of forces F, moduli m, and velocities v of the connected gears. This gives us a visual language for specifying kinematics of gearboxes which is sufficient for solving computational problems about kinematics and loads in gearboxes.

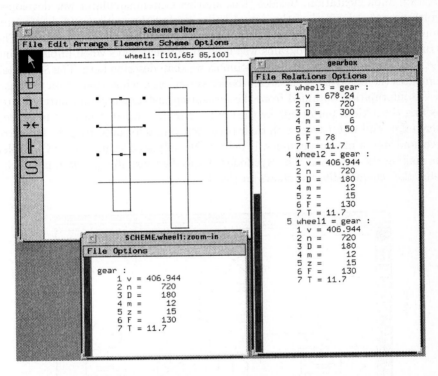

Fig. 5. Specification of a gearbox and results of computation

Fig. 5 shows a visual specification of a gearbox and results of some computations visualized for the gearbox and a gear in the NUTs built-in object windows. The example demonstrates how simple the development of a visual language can be for a restricted engineering domain, if a tradition of graphical representation of objects (gearboxes in this case) exists. This technique was used in building the packages for mechanical engineering.

5   Implementing Steam Boiler Control System

In [1] an informal, but quite precise requirements specification of a boiler control system was presented as a benchmark for application of formal methods. The task was to develop a provably correct implementation of the control system. We solved the task by using the NUT language for encoding the refined requirements and synthesizing programs from these specifications [2]. The automatic synthesis guarantees correctness of the programs with respect to the requirements.

The control program consists of two parts: SysModel - simulator for the prediction of the behavior of the physical system, and Controler - control algorithm implementation. Besides that, another system simulator was developed which operated instead of the actual boiler during the testing and demonstration phases. Considerable part of the latter was identical to the SysModel. The structural synthesis of programs was used in different ways when implementing the simulator and the control algorithm as we shall describe here. The SysModel simulates the behavior of the steam-boiler system as a whole, partly on the basis of the information obtained from the measuring instruments, and partly by reflecting the actions performed by the Controler. It compares also the measured steam flow and water level with their predicted values for detecting the failure of level and steam measuring units. It delivers the adjusted values to the Controler for making the decisions. The SysModel is specified visually on the top level by using the scheme editor as shown in Fig. 6.

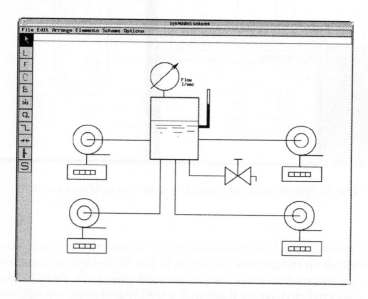

Fig. 6. Visual specification of SysModel of boiler system

Components of the SysModel represent physical units and are specified as subclasses of the class Device:

```
class Device
        var
                OK: bool;         % true if operating correctly
                name: text;       % name of a device
                mode: text;       % operation mode
                time: num;        % current time
                Dt: num;          % time step
        init
                Dt := 5;
                OK := true;
```

In particular, class `Boiler` is a subclass of `Device` and `BoilerParameters`, and represents the configuration of the boiler environment, including a valve and pumps:

```
class Boiler
        super Device, BoilerParameters;
        var
                valve: Valve;
                P1, P2, P3, P4: any;
                p, q, v: num;     % throughput of all pumps,
                                  %water level, steam flow,
        alias
                Pumps = (P1, P2, P3, P4);
```

Class `BoilerModel` is a subclass of `Boiler`, it represents the actual mathematical model of the boiler, and includes numerous equations in the same form as written in the requirements specification [1]. It is a complete specification of boiler as a physical device suitable for synthesis of programs for finding different sets of values of parameters (raw, calculated, adjusted).

Another part of the control system - the `Controler` was implemented in a different way. It was designed as a production system. Rules given in the initial requirements specification were represented as methods of the class `ControlerRules`. Axioms served as guards of the rules. A goal for synthesis fired the rules which satisfied the firing conditions. Fairness of the set of rules had to be verified manually after writing all the rules.

6   Analysis of Hydraulic Systems

This is a problem domain where structural synthesis has been used for solving a number of large problems. We describe here two of them. Several years ago G. Grossschmidt introduced a multi-pole method of description of models of elements and subsystems of hydraulic systems [7]. This enabled him to develop a rich set of models of components of hydraulics which appeared well suited for implementation in the visual environment provided by NUT, and has been used in simulation of hydraulic systems of aircrafts, cars and machine tools. The paper [6] describes analysis of statics and dynamics of an airplane aileron position control – a work done under a contract with the Antonov Airplane Plant in Kiev, Ukraine. The position control mechanism of ailerons is an electro-hydraulic servo drive. Because of the extremely high requirements for the static, steady-state and dynamic characteristics of the control system, a detailed simulation is required. The model includes a multitude of nonlinear and changing relations with many loops. Analysis of static and steady-state characteristics is done in principle in the way as we described for gears. The difference lies in the complexity of models which does not cause practical difficulties. The NUT synthesizer can handle tens of thousands of variables and thousands of axioms which is sufficient for solving the present problem.

Analysis of dynamics is performed by means of simulation of the mechanism described as a network of interconnected components in the NUT scheme editor window. The main simulation procedure is implemented as a method of a process class used as a superclass of the whole control system model. As the process class is used in many applications, we describe its simplified version here.

```
class process
        var
                timestep : num;
                time : num;
                state, nextstate, initstate : any;
                result : table;
        rel
                (state -> nextstate) -> (initstate -> result)
                                {<simulation program>};
        alias
                state = (all.state);
                nextstate = (all.nextstatte);
                initstate = (all.initstate);
```

The alias statements in NUT define state, nextstate and initstate as structures (vectors) of variables with same names taken from components of the model. The axiom

$$(state \rightarrow nextstate) \rightarrow (initstate \rightarrow result)$$
$$\{<simulation\ program>\};$$

states that the result is computable from the given initstate as soon as an algorithm can be synthesized for computing nextstate from the given state. The simulation program is a loop over given time with the given timestep, computing nextstate and substituting nextstep for the step at each repetition.

Another problem concerns a load-sensitive hydraulic drive shown in Fig. 7. The functional elements of the drive are actuator AC, hydraulic cylinder HC, check valve CHV, electro-hydraulic proportion valve EHPV, elasticity EL, flow

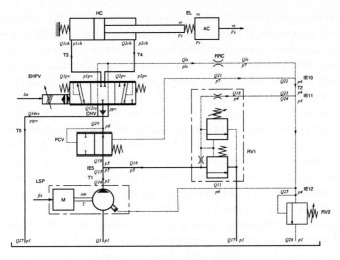

Fig. 7. Load-sensing pump

control valve FCV, interface elements (tee couplings) IE1,..., IE12, load-sensing pump LSP, driving motor M, hydraulic resistance RRC, relief valves RV1 and RV2, tubes T1,..., T5. This problem concerns a stiff dynamic system, i.e. a system where both high and low frequencies are essential for obtaining a correct solution. This complicates the simulation task – one has to perform a large number of simulation steps in order to obtain required precision for the high frequencies, and to cover sufficiently long time for the slower part of the system. The total number of objects involved only in simulation of the hydraulic cylinder with tubes is already more than 50 000.

7   Design and Analysis of Radar Coverage

Modeling of a surveillance radar coverage (see an example of output of this package in Fig. 8), performed under the contracts with Estonian Ministry of Defense and Estonian National Maritime Board is an example where the user interface with volatile graphical objects has been useful. It means that graphical elements drawn from the program can be kept connected to instance variables of the object referred to in the drawing command. As a consequence, manual manipulation, (moving, reshaping etc.) of the image causes corresponding changes of the connected object. For instance, when calculations show that the radar cannot reach a certain point from a hill because of the shadow of a large object, one can find a new position for the radar by moving the image of radar (the dot in the center of the coverage picture) to another point and introduce new coordinates before the next iteration of the modeling.

The package of radar coverage analysis interoperates with the digital map including information about types of earth ground, buildings and their reflection properties. A specification of the radar coverage model uses classes of radars, i.e.

sets of equations and parameters that describe characteristics of certain radar device and its properties of propagation of electromagnetic radiation (see details in [3]). There are also classes that describe attenuation of electromagnetic energy in atmosphere and models for different meteorological conditions such as rain, fog and clouds that can affect to the propagation of radar waves. In particular, we were interested in radar waves propagation when coastal area should be watched. Very different models of clutter must be used and switched on/off when the radar turns its beam from a water surface to land and back. This is an example of a real application of the system where hundreds and thousands of objects and geographical constraints must be taken into account. The program synthesis used provides correct computations of new surveillance state after changes in the specification of the model caused by moving radar positions or declaring changes in weather conditions, for instance.

To achieve the appropriate efficiency, the package has been implemented on the basis of the distributed NUT system [22] built upon PVM software. General control structure of the modeling task is represented as a method with subtasks (see section 2) where a subtask specifies a computation of the coverage by one radar. The distributed NUT assigns automatically these subtasks to available computers and spawns corresponding processes. The planning and computation of the coverage of different radars is performed in parallel and the results are returned to main process that visualizes integrated coverage as shown by example in Fig. 8.

Some administrative and domain-specific control structures useful for development of parallel NUT programs were described in [22]. In our case, there is quite little attention to be paid to synchronization as radars do not communicate while working. For efficiency reasons, we have to deal carefully with resources management here. The program synthesis turned to be useful also for balancing the work load of workstations for parallel computing.

8   Simulation of Mobile Communication

The problem to be considered is analysis of accessibility for sites of wireless communication networks [11]. This example demonstrates all specification facilities of the NUT system. The main blocks are station and client which are basic nodes of a network to be modeled. Here we consider a GSM type network where objects of class Station refer to base stations i.e. non-movable radio transmission centers that have channels where clients can take a connection. Another class – Client (e.g. mobile phone) is a moving transmitter that may try to find free channel from a nearby base station. A client can use only one channel at a time, but while moving, the client has to change the base station or channel every time when transmission quality is not good enough to keep existing connection.

We assume using the dynamic channel assignment algorithm [4] when defining classes of mobile communication environment. Besides the classes Station and Client mentioned above, we need also a class Channel specifying

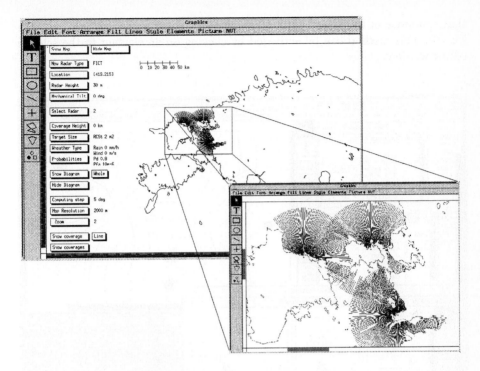

Fig. 8. Modeling of radar coverage

quality characteristics of the channel. There can be remarkable power losses
in the channel caused by environmental conditions or long distance between
sites connected. The noise in the channel created by other radio transmitters or
coming from space is another reason why a client should lift transmission power
or cancel connection. There are methods in the class Channel to compute these
characteristics by request of clients or stations.

A client has the functionality to establish and keep connection to a base
station nearby by choosing current channel in use and to achieve the best quality
of connection using as little energy as possible. Clients check the beacon signals
from base stations to decide from which station the received signal is highest
and negotiate with the base stations assigned to them about characteristics and
availability of channels. This functionality is implemented by the class Client.

The class Station specifies computations that a base stations has to perform
for replying requests from clients as well as establishing of paths between clients
that want to communicate.

To simulate a mobile network with respect to its real-time behavior, interactive graphics becomes useful. Here we specify base stations and clients in a
scheme editor window. Images of clients and stations have a point whose coordinates are passed to the object and can be used for further computations.
Stations and clients have the method Locate for visualizing their actual posi-

tion and state in the specific graphical output window (upper right window in Fig. 9). This method can be activated by clicking on an element in the scheme editor window.

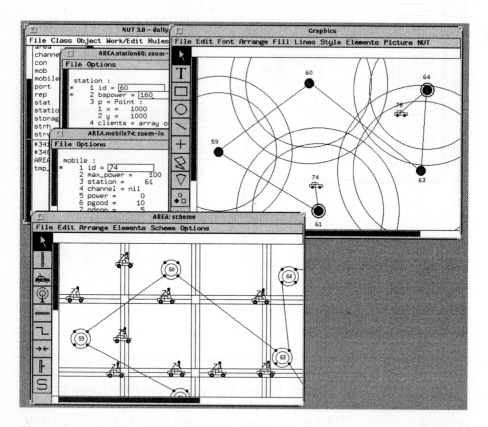

Fig. 9. Simulation of wireless communication (antennas and cars present base stations and clients/mobiles respectively)

The system allows to specify processes in the scheme editor window (moving a car ahead by a specified distance and/or changing radiation conditions, for example) that may influence the reliability of channels in use. Program synthesis is used for construction of algorithms that provide visualization of new situation in the environment and to compute the corresponding new communication paths between sites. Traditional routing algorithms can be used for modeling of path establishing processes. A specialization of the planning mechanism of NUT system to get a program for path search in mobiles network has been discussed but not implemented yet.

9   Concluding Remarks

Applications of the structural synthesis of programs presented here are selected from various problem domains bearing in mind their practical usefulness and credibility. They all have been presented already as technical reports or even journal papers. However, with exception of the boiler control problem, they are written from the point of view of a particular application domain. For instance, the papers on the analysis of hydraulic systems [7, 6] give detailed description of models of hydraulic components and results of the analysis, but mention the software aspect only briefly. The boiler control example has been included into the present paper as a solution of a well-known benchmark. Our aim in selecting just these application examples has been to demonstrate the practical applicability of completely automatic program synthesis in problem domains, varying from simple engineering calculations to simulation of complex dynamic systems and parallel computing on a set of workstations. The fact that we use structural synthesis of programs has no principal importance. The main message of our presentation is that the deductive synthesis of program is sufficiently mature for automatic usage in software practice. One important lesson learned from our applications is that the automatic synthesis of programs should be supported by conventional software development tools: visual editor, object oriented programming language for implementing preprogrammed parts of the software etc. This seems to be true for any automatic application of formal methods. One can say it in another way: the synthesis is only one of the features of software development environments. It should be available for applications where it can be useful, and the amount of synthesis used may vary largely from one application to another. In our case, the synthesis appeared useful for developing visual specification languages, simulation software, and highly interactive computing even in the case of considerable amount of number-crunching.

10   Acknowledgements

This work was partially financed by Andersen Consulting Research Foundation and Estonian Science Foundation (grant #2238). We would like to thank M. Addibpour, A. Kalja, T. Tiidemann, J. Pahapill, G. Grossschmidt and V. Kotkas for their kind support with information.

References

[1] Abrial, J.-R., Börger, E., Langemaack, H.: The Stem-Boiler Control Specification Problem. A Problem Suggestion for the Dagstuhl Meeting on Methods for Semantics and Specification, Lecture Notes Computer Science Vol. 1165, Springer-Verlag, Berlin Heidelberg New York (1997)

[2] Addibpour, M., Tyugu, E.: Structural Synthesis of Programs from Refined User Requirements (Programming Boiler Control in NUT). Lecture Notes Computer Science Vol. 1165, Springer-Verlag, Berlin Heidelberg New York (1997)

[3] Blake, L.V.: A Guide to Basic Pulse-Radar Maximum-Range Calculation. Part 1. Equations, Definitions, and Aids to Calculation. Naval Research Laboratory Report 6930, AS 701 321 (1969)

[4] Chuang, J.: Performance Issues and Algorithms for Dynamic Channel Assignment. IEEE Journal on Selected Areas in Communications, **11**, 6 (1993) 955-963

[5] Coquand, T., Nordström, B., Smith, J.M.: Type Theory and Programming, Bulletin of the EATCS, Vol. 52 (1994) 203-228

[6] Grossschmidt, G., Pahapill, J.: Computing the Statics and Dynamics of Airplane Aileron Position Control Using the NUT Language. Proc. Estonian Acad. Sci. Engineering, **1**, 1 (1995) 32-50

[7] Grossschmidt, G., Vanaveski, J.: Composing Multi-Pole-Model Block Schemes for a Load-Sensing Hydraulic Drive. Proc. Estonian Acad. Sci. Engineering, **3**, 4 (1998) 209-224

[8] Kalja, A., Tiidemann, T.: A Conceptual Framework for Software Developing in Mechanical CAD. In Leinonen, T. (ed.): Proc. of OST-97 Symposium on Machine Design, Acta Univ. Oulu, C 109 (1997) 120 - 128

[9] Kalja, A., Tiidemann, T.: Supporting Mechanical Design with Visual Programming in the NUT Environment. In Leinonen, T. (ed.): Proc. of OST-98 Symposium on Machine Design, Acta Univ. Oulu, C 130 (1998) 163 -172

[10] Kotkas, V.: Intelligent Software Tools for Data Communication Modeling. In: László Varga (ed.): Proc. of the Fourth Symposium on Programming Languages and Software Tools, Department of General Computer Science, Eötvös Loránd University, Budapest (1995) 279 - 287

[11] Kotkas, V., Harf, M., Lõugas, R., Kann, E.: Positions of Coastal Radars Around Tallinn Bay. Final Report on the Contract, Institute of Cybernetics, Tallinn, (1998) - in Estonian

[12] Lowry, M., Philpot, A., Pressburger, T., Underwood, I.: Amphion: Automatic Programming for Scientific Subroutine Libraries. In Proc. 8th Int. Symp. on Methodologies for Intelligent Systems, Lecture Notes Computer Science Vol. 869, Springer-Verlag, Berlin Heidelberg New York (1994) 326-335

[13] Lowry, M., van Baalen, J.: Meta-Amphion: Synthesis of Efficient Domain-Specific Program Synthesis Systems. Automated Software Engineering, **4** (1997) 199-241

[14] Matskin, M., Komorowski, J.: Partial Structural Synthesis of Programs. Fundamenta Informaticae **31** (1997) 125-144

[15] Mints, G.: Propositional Logic Programming. In: J. Hayes et al. (eds.): Machine Intelligence, Vol. 12, Clarendon Press, Oxford (1991) 17 - 37

[16] Tyugu, E.: Using Classes as Specifications for Automatic Construction of Programs in the NUT System. Automated Software Engineering, **1**, (1994) 315 - 334

[17] Uustalu, T., Kopra, U., Kotkas, V., Matskin, M., Tyugu, E.: The NUT Language Report. The Royal Institute of Technology (KTH), TRITA-IT R 94:14 (1994)

[18] Uustalu, T., Tyugu, E.: Higher-Order Functional Constraint Networks. In: Mayoh, B. et al.(eds.): Constraint Programming. NATO ASI Series F, Vol. 131, Springer-Verlag, Berlin Heidelberg New York (1994) 116 - 139

[19] Uuustalu, T.: Aspects of Structural Synthesis of Programs. The Royal Institute of Technology (KTH), TRITA-IT 95:09 (1995)

[20] Srinivas, Y.V., Jüllig, R.: Specware: Formal Support for Composing Software. In Proc. of the Conf. on Mathematics of Program Construction, Lecture Notes Computer Science Vol. 947, Springer-Verlag, Berlin Heidelberg New York (1995)

[21] Stickel, M., Waldinger, R., Lowry, M., Pressburger, T., Underwood, I.: Deductive Composition of Astronomical Software from Subroutine Libraries. In: Bundy A., (ed.): Automated Deduction, Lecture Notes Computer Science Vol. 814, Springer-Verlag, Berlin Heidelberg New York (1994)

[22] Vlassov, V., Addibpour, M., Tyugu, E.: NUTS: a Distributed Object-Oriented Platform with High Level Communication Functions. Computers and Artificial Intelligence, **17**, 4 (1998) 305-335

Towards a Compositional Approach to the Design and Verification of Distributed Systems*

Michel Charpentier and K. Mani Chandy

California Institute of Technology
Computer Science Department
{charpov,mani}@cs.caltech.edu

Abstract. We are investigating a component-based approach for formal design of distributed systems. In this paper, we introduce the framework we use for specification, composition and communication and we apply it to an example that highlights the different aspects of a compositional design, including top-down and bottom-up phases, proofs of composition, refinement proofs, proofs of program texts, and component reuse.

Key-words: component-based design, distributed systems, formal specification, formal verification, temporal logic, UNITY.

1   A Compositional Approach

1.1   Introduction

Component technology is becoming increasingly popular. Microsoft's COM, Java-Soft's beans, CORBA, and new trade magazines devoted to component technology attest to the growing importance of this area. Component-based software development is having an impact in the development of user interfaces. Such systems often have multiple threads (loci of control) executing in different components that are synchronized with each other. These systems are examples of reactive systems in which components interact with their environments. Component technology has advantages for reactive systems, but it also poses important challenges including the following:

- How do we specify components? Specifications must deal with both progress and safety, and they must capture the relationship between each component and its environment. What technologies will support large repositories of software components, possibly even world-wide webs of components, such that component implementations can be discovered given component specifications?
- Electronic circuit design is an often-cited metaphor for building software systems using component technologies. Phrases such as *plug and play*, and *wiring components together*, are used in software design. These approaches

---

* This work is supported by a grant from the Air Force Office of Scientific Research.

J. Wing, J. Woodcock, J. Davies (Eds.): FM'99, Vol. I, LNCS 1708, pp. 570–589, 1999.

to software design work only if there are systematic methods of proving specifications of composed systems from specifications of components.

Further, we would like to propose methods in which the proof obligations for the designer who puts components together is made easier at the expense of the component designer. The idea is that component designers add component specifications, implementations, and proofs into a repository. An implementation of a component may, in turn, be a composition of other components. We want the composer's work to become easier by exploiting the effort in specification, implementation and proof that is invested in building the component repository.

– Mechanical proof checkers and theorem provers can play an important role in building high-confidence repositories of software components, though the widespread use of these technologies may be decades away. The challenge is to develop theories of composition that can be supported by mechanical provers.

1.2 Proposition

The basis for our framework is the UNITY formalism which provides a way to describe fair transition systems and which uses a small set of temporal logic operators. The formalism is extended with a theory of composition which relies on two forms of composition: *existential* (a system property holds if it holds in at least one component) and *universal* (a system property holds if it holds in all components). We also extend standard UNITY with a new temporal operator (*follows*) which allows us to represent asynchronous point-to-point communication at a logical level.

We obtain a simpler framework by restricting its expressive power: we do not deal with *all* temporal specifications, *all* forms of composition and *all* types of communication. However, we need to know if such a framework can be applied to a wide class of problems and if it can be used to develop simple proofs. These two points can be explored by using the framework to design several distributed systems.

Through the example described in this paper, we show that this framework can be used to specify generic and specific components, to describe communication between them, to handle refinement proofs (classical UNITY proofs) related to top-down steps, program text correctness proofs ("almost" classical UNITY proofs) and compositional proofs related to bottom-up steps. This paper describes a first step towards developing a simple compositional methodology for reactive systems.

The remainder of the paper is organized as follows. In the next section, we define the different aspects of the framework we are using. The following section presents the architecture of a resource allocation example and introduces the required formal steps we have to complete in order to achieve the design. The next sections are each devoted to a part of this design. One proof of each kind (refinement, composition and program text correctness) is given in the paper. All other proofs can be found in the technical report [11].

2 Framework

The framework we use is based on a UNITY-like logic and programming notation [5, 28, 27]. The traditional UNITY form of program composition (*union*) is used. However, at the logical level, we use the notions of *existential* and *universal* properties. A *guarantees* operator, that provides existential specifications, is introduced [6, 7]. We further extend UNITY with an abstraction of communication, based on temporal operators described in [12, 9, 13, 37].

2.1 Basis

A program (describing a component behavior) consists of a set of typed variables, an *initially* predicate, which is a predicate on program states, a finite set of atomic commands C, and a subset D of C of commands subjected to a weak fairness constraint: every command in D must be executed infinitely often. The set C contains at least the command *skip* which leaves the state unchanged.

Program composition is defined to be the union of the sets of variables and the sets C and D of the components, and the conjunction of the *initially* predicates. Such a composition is not always possible. Especially, composition must respect variable locality and must provide at least one initial state (the conjunction of initial predicates must be logically consistent). We use $F * G$ to denote the boolean: *Programs F and G can be composed*. The system resulting from that composition is denoted by $F \| G$.

To specify programs and to reason about their correctness, we use UNITY logical operators as defined in [28, 27]. However, when dealing with composition, one must be careful whether to use the *strong* or the *weak* form of these operators. The strong (sometimes called *inductive*) form is the one obtained when *wp* calculus is applied to statements *without* using the substitution axiom [5, 28, 27]. The weak form is either the one obtained when the substitution axiom is used or the one defined from the *strongest invariant* (which are equivalent) [34, 28, 27]. Strong operators are subscripted with s and weak operators are subscripted with w. No subscript means that either form can be used. The strong form of an operator is logically stronger than the weak form. We give the definitions of temporal operators in terms of the program text:

$$
\begin{array}{ll}
\text{init } p \;\triangleq\; [\textit{initially} \Rightarrow p] & p \text{ next}_w\, q \;\triangleq\; (SI \wedge p) \text{ next}_s\, q \\
\text{transient } p \;\triangleq\; \langle \exists c : c \in D : [p \Rightarrow wp.c.\neg p] \rangle & \text{stable}_w\, p \;\triangleq\; p \text{ next}_w\, p \\
p \text{ next}_s\, q \;\triangleq\; \langle \forall c : c \in D : [p \Rightarrow wp.c.q] \rangle & \text{always } p \;\triangleq\; [SI \Rightarrow p] \\
\text{stable}_s\, p \;\triangleq\; p \text{ next}_s\, p & \\
\text{invariant } p \;\triangleq\; (\text{init } p) \wedge (\text{stable}_s\, p) & \\
\end{array}
$$

where SI denotes the strongest invariant of the program (i.e. the conjunction of all invariants).

The *leads-to* operator, denoted by $\mapsto$, is the strongest solution of:

$\begin{array}{lll}
\textit{Transient} & : & [\,\texttt{transient}\ q\ \Rightarrow\ \textit{true}\ \mapsto\ \neg q\,] \\
\textit{Implication} & : & [p \Rightarrow q]\ \Rightarrow\ [p\ \mapsto\ q] \\
\textit{Disjunction} & : & \textit{For any set of predicates }S: \\
& & [\,\langle\forall p : p \in \mathcal{S} : p\ \mapsto\ q\rangle\ \Rightarrow\ \langle\exists p : p \in \mathcal{S} : p\rangle\ \mapsto\ q\,] \\
\textit{Transitivity} & : & [\,p\ \mapsto\ q \wedge q\ \mapsto\ r \Rightarrow p\ \mapsto\ r\,] \\
\textit{PSP} & : & [\,p\ \mapsto\ q \wedge s\ \texttt{next}_w\ t\ \Rightarrow\ (p \wedge s)\ \mapsto\ (q \wedge s) \vee (\neg s \wedge t)\,]
\end{array}$

Note that *transient* has no weak form and *leads-to* has no strong form, and that *always* is the weak form of *invariant* (which is strong).

$X \cdot F$ means that property X holds in program F. Traditionally, monotonicity is expressed with a set of *stable* properties. In order to avoid the repetition of this set of *stable* properties, we define the shortcut:

$$x \nearrow_{\leqslant} \cdot F\ \triangleq\ (\forall k :: \texttt{stable}_w\ k \leqslant x \cdot F)$$

which means that x never decreases in F in isolation (the weak form of *stable* is used and nothing is said about x when F is composed with other components). When there is no ambiguity, we omit the order relation and simply write $x \nearrow$.

Since we are dealing with distributed systems, we assume no variable can be written by more than one component. We consider three kinds of component variables: input ports, output ports and local variables. Input ports can only be read by the component; output ports and local variables can be written by the component and by no other component.

The fact that an output port or a local variable cannot be written by another component is referred to as the *locality* principle. Formally, if variable v is writable only by component F and *env* is a possible environment of F ($F * env$), then:

$$\forall k :: \texttt{stable}_s\ (v = k) \cdot env$$

i.e., v is left unchanged by the statements of F's environment.

2.2   Composition

We use a compositional approach introduced in [6, 7], based on *existential* and *universal* characteristics. A property is existential when it holds in any system in which at least *one* component has the property. A property is universal when it holds in any system in which *all* components have the property. Of course, any existential property is also universal. We use the formal definition of [10] which is slightly different from the original definition in [7]:

$\begin{array}{ll}
X \textit{ is existential} & \triangleq\ \langle\forall F, G : F * G : X \cdot F \vee X \cdot G \Rightarrow X \cdot F\|G\rangle \\
X \textit{ is universal} & \triangleq\ \langle\forall F, G : F * G : X \cdot F \wedge X \cdot G \Rightarrow X \cdot F\|G\rangle
\end{array}$

Another element of the theory is the *guarantees* operator, from pairs of properties to properties. Given program properties X and Y, the property X **guarantees** Y is defined by:

$$X\ \textbf{guarantees}\ Y \cdot F\ \triangleq\ \langle\forall G : F * G : (X \cdot F\|G) \Rightarrow (Y \cdot F\|G)\rangle$$

Properties of type *init*, *transient* and *guarantees* are existential and properties of type *next$_s$*, *stable$_s$* and *invariant* are universal. All other types are neither existential nor universal, but can appear on any side of *guarantees* to provide an existential property.

2.3   Communication

All the communication involved in a system is described with input and output ports. Formally, an input (resp. output) port is the *history* of all messages received (resp. sent) through this port. Note that ports are monotonic with respect to the prefix relation. We need to introduce a temporal operator to describe communication delays between these ports, as well as some notations to handle easily finite sequences of messages.

Follows. To represent the unbounded nondeterministic delay introduced by some components (including the underlying network), we use a *follows* temporal operator inspired form [12, 9, 13, 37].

Definition 1 ($\boxtimes$). *For any pair of* state expressions *(in particular variables)* x and $`x$, and an order relation $\leqslant$, we define $`x \boxtimes x$ *(" $`x$ follows x ") with respect to $\leqslant$:*

$$`x \boxtimes x \triangleq (x \nearrow_\leqslant) \wedge (`x \nearrow_\leqslant) \wedge (\text{always } `x \leqslant x) \wedge (\forall k :: k \leqslant x \mapsto k \leqslant `x)$$

Intuitively, $`x \boxtimes x$ means that $x$ and $`x$ are nondecreasing and $`x$ is always trailing $x$ (wrt the order $\leqslant$), but $`x$ eventually increases (at least) to the current value of x.

Follows can be used in conjunction with functions on histories to describe different kinds of transformational components. Deterministic components are described with specifications of the form "*Out* $\boxtimes f.In$", while nondeterministic components use the "$f.Out \boxtimes In$" form. In particular, network components (unbounded channels) are specified by "*Out* $\boxtimes In$."

The following properties are referred to as "follows theorems":

$$`x \boxtimes x \wedge f \text{ increasing function} \Rightarrow f.`x \boxtimes f.x$$
$$"x \boxtimes `x \wedge `x \boxtimes x \qquad\qquad\;\; \Rightarrow "x \boxtimes x$$
$$`x \boxtimes x \wedge `y \boxtimes y \qquad\qquad\;\; \Rightarrow `x \cup `y \boxtimes x \cup y \text{ (for sets or bags)}$$

Notations on Histories

Definition 2 (/). *Given a (finite) sequence Seq and a set S of integers, Seq/S represents the subsequence of Seq for indexes in S:*

$$|Seq/S| \triangleq \text{card}([1..|Seq|] \cap S) \text{ and}$$
$$\langle \forall k : 1 \leqslant k \leqslant |Seq/S| : (Seq/S)[k] \triangleq Seq[\langle \min n : \text{card}(S \cap [1..n]) \geqslant k : n \rangle] \rangle$$

$|Seq|$ denotes the length of sequence Seq. Note that we do not force values in S to be valid indexes of Seq. Actually, the condition under which k is a valid index of Seq/S is $(1 \leqslant k \leqslant |Seq| \wedge k \in S)$.

Definition 3 ($\sqsubseteq_{\mathcal{R}}$). *Given a binary relation $\mathcal{R}$, we define the corresponding weak prefix relationship between sequences, denoted by $\sqsubseteq_{\mathcal{R}}$:*

$$Q \sqsubseteq_{\mathcal{R}} Q' \triangleq |Q| \leqslant |Q'| \wedge \langle \forall k : 1 \leqslant k \leqslant |Q| : Q[k] \ \mathcal{R} \ Q'[k] \rangle$$

Note that $\sqsubseteq_{=}$ is the traditional prefix relationship. In the paper, we are only using $\sqsubseteq_{\leqslant}$ and $\sqsubseteq_{\geqslant}$ on sequences of integers.

3 The Resource Allocation Example

3.1 The Different Steps of the Design

We shall design a resource allocation system. We require that all clients handle shared resources correctly.

In a first step, we specify what the clients are doing with respect to these resources (spec. $\langle 3 \rangle$) and what the correctness constraints of the system are (spec. $\langle 2 \rangle$). We deduce, in a systematic way, how a resource allocator should behave to provide that correctness (spec. $\langle 4 \rangle$). We then use a generic network specification (spec. $\langle 5 \rangle$) and develop a compositional proof to show that if all components satisfy their specifications, then the global system also satisfies its specification (proof C1 sect. 4.2).

Next, we design a resource allocator satisfying the previous specification. We build the general allocator by composing a simpler single-client allocator and some generic components (possibly found in a component library). So, we specify how the single-client allocator should behave (spec. $\langle 10 \rangle$), pick a generic merge component (spec. $\langle 6 \rangle$), a generic distributor component (spec. $\langle 7 \rangle$) and connect all these components with a network (spec. $\langle 8 \rangle$). We obtain an allocator that enjoys additional properties, compared to the allocator we need for our system. Since such properties may be reused later in another design, we specify formally this resulting allocator (spec. $\langle 9 \rangle$) and prove that it is actually obtained from the chosen components (proof C2 in [11]). We also prove that this allocator implements the allocator we needed (proof R1 sect. 5.2).

To complete the development, we have to design a client program and a single-client allocator program. Starting from the specifications we obtained ($\langle 3 \rangle$ and $\langle 10 \rangle$), we write two programs we hope to satisfy the given specifications. We observe that the resulting programs (prog. sect. 6.1 and prog. sect. 7.1) have more properties than requested. Again, since such properties can be reused, we express formally these behaviors (spec. $\langle 11 \rangle$ and spec. $\langle 12 \rangle$), prove that the texts satisfy these specifications (proofs T1 sect. 6.3 and T2 in [11]) and, of course, that these specifications are stronger than requested (proofs R2 and R3 in [11]).

The different steps of this design are summarized in fig. 1. Each specification $\langle n \rangle$ is described in the corresponfing figure fig. n.

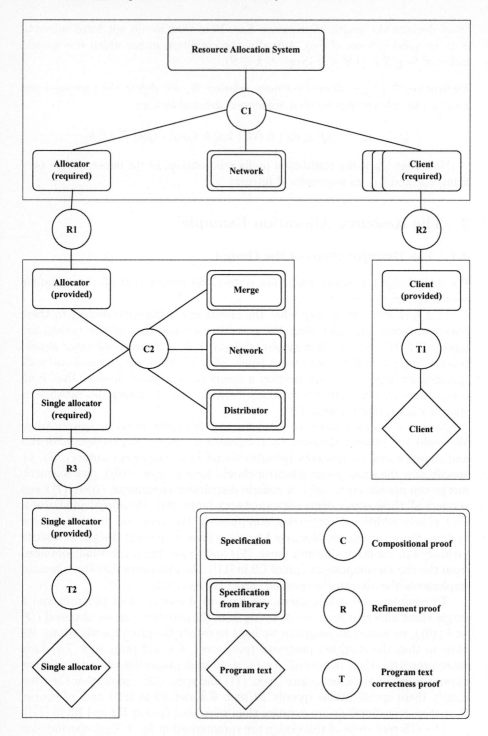

Fig. 1. General design.

3.2   Notations

Resources are modeled as tokens. All tokens are indivisible and identical. Tokens are not created or destroyed. All the messages exchanged between the resource allocator and its clients have the same type: integer (the number of tokens requested, given or released). $Tokens.h$ is the total number of tokens in history h (i.e. $Tokens.h = \sum_{k=1}^{|h|} h[k]$).

All clients have the same generic behavior. They send requests for resources through a port ask, receive these resources through a port giv, and release the resources through a port rel. Clients variables are prefixed with $Client_i$. The allocator has three arrays of ports, ask, giv and rel, prefixed by $Alloc$. A network is responsible for transporting messages from $Client_i.ask$ to $Alloc.ask_i$, from $Alloc.giv_i$ to $Client_i.giv$, and from $Client_i.rel$ to $Alloc.rel_i$. A valid initial state is a state where all ports histories are empty and where the resource allocator has a stock of NbT tokens.

4   From a Resource Allocation System towards an Allocator and Clients

4.1   Components Specifications

The global correctness we expect from the resource allocation system is expressed in the traditional way. A safety property states that clients never share more tokens than there exists in the system. A liveness property guarantees that all client requests are eventually satisfied (Fig. 2).

$$\textbf{always}\quad \sum_i (Tokens.Client_i.giv - Tokens.Client_i.rel) \leqslant NbT \qquad (1)$$
$$\forall i, h :: h \sqsubseteq Client_i.ask \;\mapsto\; h \sqsubseteq_{\leqslant} Client_i.giv \qquad (2)$$

Fig. 2. Resource allocation system specification.

The client's specification is also intuitive. The safety part is that clients never ask for more tokens than there exist. The liveness part guarantees that clients return all the tokens they get, when these tokens are satisfying a request (unrequested tokens or tokens in insufficient number may not be returned) (Fig. 3).

$$true\ \textbf{guarantees}\ ask \nearrow \wedge\ rel \nearrow \qquad (3)$$
$$true\ \textbf{guarantees always}\ \langle \forall k :: ask[k] \leqslant NbT \rangle \qquad (4)$$
$$giv \nearrow\ \textbf{guarantees}\ \forall h :: h \sqsubseteq giv \wedge h \sqsubseteq_{\geqslant} ask \;\mapsto\; Tokens.rel \geqslant Tokens.h \qquad (5)$$

Fig. 3. Client specification (required).

The allocator specification is almost derived from the client specification. In particular, there is a strong correspondence between the right-hand sides of clients *guarantees* and the left-hand side of the allocator *guarantees*. The global safety, which is the responsibility (mostly) of the allocator also appears in the specification (Fig. 4).

$$\textit{true } \textbf{guarantees } \forall i :: giv_i \nearrow \tag{6}$$

$$(\forall i :: rel_i \nearrow) \textbf{ guarantees always } \sum_i (Tokens.giv_i - Tokens.rel_i) \leqslant NbT \tag{7}$$

$$\begin{array}{c} \forall i :: ask_i \nearrow \wedge rel_i \nearrow \\ \wedge \qquad \textbf{always } \langle \forall i, k :: ask_i[k] \leqslant NbT \rangle \\ \wedge \; \forall i, h :: h_i \sqsubseteq giv_i \wedge h_i \sqsubseteq_\geqslant ask_i \; \mapsto \; Tokens.rel_i \geqslant Tokens.h_i \\ \textbf{guarantees} \\ \forall i, h :: h \sqsubseteq ask_i \; \mapsto \; h \sqsubseteq_\leqslant giv_i \end{array} \tag{8}$$

Fig. 4. Allocator specification (required).

The network specification relies on the *follows* operator. Output ports are connected to corresponding input ports with $\boxtimes$ which provides both safety and liveness (Fig. 5).

$$\begin{array}{c} \forall i :: \\ Client_i.ask \nearrow \textbf{ guarantees } Alloc.ask_i \; \boxtimes \; Client_i.ask \\ Alloc.giv_i \nearrow \textbf{ guarantees } Client_i.giv \; \boxtimes \; Alloc.giv_i \\ Client_i.rel \nearrow \textbf{ guarantees } Alloc.rel_i \; \boxtimes \; Client_i.rel \end{array} \tag{9}$$

Fig. 5. Network specification.

4.2   Composition Proof

The following two proofs are built as chains. Because they are existential, *guarantees* properties hold in the global system. Then, applying *follows* theorems to the right-hand side of a *guarantees*, we deduce a property that can be injected into the left-hand side of another *guarantees* property, which allows us to use the right-hand side of this new *guarantees* property, and so on until we reach the desired global correctness property.

Property (1).

Proof. In the resource allocation system:

$$\{\text{Specification (3)}\}$$
$$\forall i :: Client_i.rel \nearrow$$
$$\Rightarrow \{\text{Specification (9), follows definition}\}$$
$$\forall i :: Alloc.rel_i \nearrow$$
$$\Rightarrow \{\text{Specification (7)}\}$$
$$\textbf{always } \sum_i (Tokens.Alloc.giv_i - Tokens.Alloc.rel_i) \leqslant NbT$$
$$\Rightarrow \{\text{Specifications (6), (3) and (9), follows theorems}\}$$
$$\textbf{always } \sum_i (Tokens.Client_i.giv - Tokens.Client_i.rel) \leqslant NbT$$

$\square$

Property (2).

Proof. In the resource allocation system:

{Specification (3)}
$\forall i :: Client_i.ask \nearrow \land Client_i.rel \nearrow$
$\Rightarrow$ {Specification (9), follows definition}
$\forall i :: Alloc.ask_i \nearrow \land Alloc.rel_i \nearrow$
$\Rightarrow$ {Specification (4)}
$\quad \forall i :: Alloc.ask_i \nearrow \land Alloc.rel_i \nearrow$
$\land \forall i :: \mathsf{always} \langle \forall k :: Client_i.ask[k] \leqslant NbT \rangle$
$\Rightarrow$ {Specification (9), follows definition, calculus}
$\quad \forall i :: Alloc.ask_i \nearrow \land Alloc.rel_i \nearrow$
$\land \mathsf{always} \langle \forall i, k :: Alloc.ask_i[k] \leqslant NbT \rangle$
$\Rightarrow$ {Specification (6)}
$\quad \forall i :: Alloc.ask_i \nearrow \land Alloc.rel_i \nearrow$
$\land \mathsf{always} \langle \forall i, k :: Alloc.ask_i[k] \leqslant NbT \rangle$
$\land \forall i :: Alloc.giv_i \nearrow$
$\Rightarrow$ {Specification (9), follows definition}
$\quad \forall i :: Alloc.ask_i \nearrow \land Alloc.rel_i \nearrow$
$\land \mathsf{always} \langle \forall i, k :: Alloc.ask_i[k] \leqslant NbT \rangle$
$\land \forall i :: Client_i.giv \nearrow$
$\Rightarrow$ {Specification (5)}
$\quad \forall i :: Alloc.ask_i \nearrow \land Alloc.rel_i \nearrow$
$\land \mathsf{always} \langle \forall i, k :: Alloc.ask_i[k] \leqslant NbT \rangle$
$\land \forall i, h_i :: h_i \sqsubseteq Client_i.giv \land h_i \sqsubseteq_{\geqslant} Client_i.ask \mapsto Tokens.Client_i.rel \geqslant$
$Tokens.h_i$
$\Rightarrow$ {Specification (9), follows definition, transitivity of $\mapsto$ }
$\quad \forall i :: Alloc.ask_i \nearrow \land Alloc.rel_i \nearrow$
$\land \mathsf{always} \langle \forall i, k :: Alloc.ask_i[k] \leqslant NbT \rangle$
$\land \forall i, h :: h_i \sqsubseteq Alloc.giv_i \land h_i \sqsubseteq_{\geqslant} Alloc.ask_i \mapsto Tokens.Alloc.rel_i \geqslant$
$Tokens.h_i$
$\Rightarrow$ {Specification (8)}
$\quad \forall i, h :: h \sqsubseteq Alloc.ask_i \mapsto h \sqsubseteq_{\leqslant} Alloc.giv_i$
$\Rightarrow$ {Specification (9), follows definition}
$\quad \forall i, h :: h \sqsubseteq Client_i.ask \mapsto h \sqsubseteq_{\leqslant} Client_i.giv$

$\qquad\qquad\qquad\qquad\qquad\qquad\qquad\qquad\qquad\qquad\qquad\qquad$ □

5 From a Single-Client Allocator to a General Allocator

5.1 Components Specifications

The first component we use is a fair merge. It merges N input channels (In) into one output channel (Out). Furthermore, it provides, for each output message, the number of the channel where it comes from ($iOut$) (Fig. 6). This merge component is fair: No input channel can be ignored indefinitely. A merge component is nondeterministic.

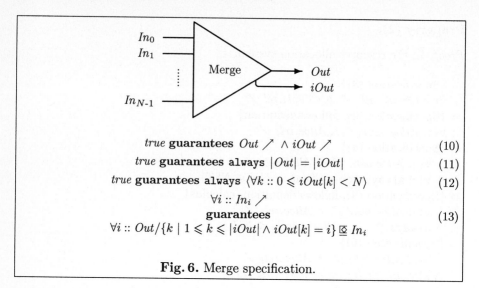

$$true \text{ guarantees } Out \nearrow \wedge iOut \nearrow \tag{10}$$

$$true \text{ guarantees always } |Out| = |iOut| \tag{11}$$

$$true \text{ guarantees always } \langle \forall k :: 0 \leqslant iOut[k] < N \rangle \tag{12}$$

$$\begin{array}{c} \forall i :: In_i \nearrow \\ \textbf{guarantees} \\ \forall i :: Out/\{k \mid 1 \leqslant k \leqslant |iOut| \wedge iOut[k] = i\} \; \boxtimes \; In_i \end{array} \tag{13}$$

Fig. 6. Merge specification.

The main merge specification is (13). This specification only constrains values when indexes are present (and indexes when values are present): it requires that there is no value without the corresponding index, and no index without the corresponding value (11). Moreover, specification (13) does not constrain values corresponding to nonvalid indexes. So, we require that there are no nonvalid indexes (12). Finally, these specifications force the output to be monotonic *in length* only (some value may still be replaced by another, changing the corresponding index at the same time). Therefore, we add the constraint (10). We obtain the specification in fig. 6.

The distributor component is the dual of the merge: If the k-th value in iIn is j, then the distributor outputs the k-th value of In to Out_j, provided that j is a correct index, i.e. $0 \leqslant j < N$. A distributor component is fair: If indexes are present, the input channel cannot be ignored indefinitely. A distributor component is deterministic.

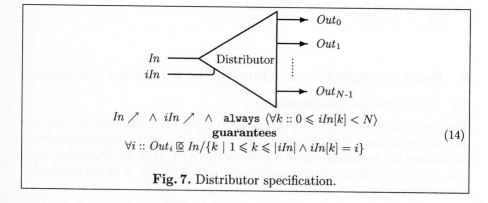

$$\begin{array}{c} In \nearrow \wedge iIn \nearrow \wedge \textbf{ always } \langle \forall k :: 0 \leqslant iIn[k] < N \rangle \\ \textbf{guarantees} \\ \forall i :: Out_i \; \boxtimes \; In/\{k \mid 1 \leqslant k \leqslant |iIn| \wedge iIn[k] = i\} \end{array} \tag{14}$$

Fig. 7. Distributor specification.

The distributor main specification is similar to the corresponding merge specification (Fig. 7). One important difference is the left-hand side of the *guarantees*: We have to assume that the indexes provided in *iIn* are correct. The difficulties we had with the merge, leading us to add several specifications, do not appear here. In particular, the monotonicity of outputs is a theorem.

We now combine these merge and distributor components with a simple allocator that only deals with a unique client. The requests are merged towards this simple allocator. Their origins are transfered directly to a distributor which is responsible for sending the tokens given by the allocator to the right addresses. Releases are also merged towards the simple allocator. Their origins are not used. All four components are connected via a network described with follows relations (Fig. 8).

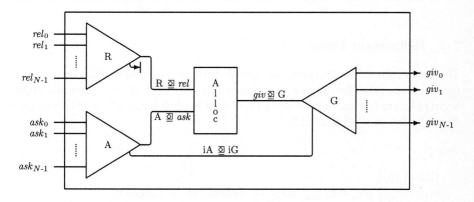

Fig. 8. General allocator architecture and network specification.

The allocator we build from this composition provides a specification stronger than the required specification $\langle 4 \rangle$. The difference is that the origin of releases is completely ignored. Therefore, the resulting allocator only cares about the *total* number of tokens coming back. This allows clients to exchange tokens and a client can return tokens received by another client. This leads to a weaker assumption in the left-hand side of the liveness property (Fig. 9).

$$true \text{ \textbf{guarantees} } \forall i :: giv_i \nearrow \tag{15}$$

$$(\forall i :: rel_i \nearrow) \text{ \textbf{guarantees always} } \sum_i (Tokens.giv_i - Tokens.rel_i) \leqslant NbT \tag{16}$$

$$\begin{aligned} &\qquad\qquad \forall i :: ask_i \nearrow \wedge rel_i \nearrow \\ \wedge &\qquad\qquad \textbf{always } \langle \forall i,k :: ask_i[k] \leqslant NbT \rangle \\ \wedge\ &\forall h :: \langle \forall i :: h_i \sqsubseteq giv_i \wedge h_i \sqsubseteq_{\geqslant} ask_i \rangle \mapsto \sum_i Tokens.rel_i \geqslant \sum_i Tokens.h_i \\ &\qquad\qquad\qquad \textbf{guarantees} \\ &\qquad\qquad \forall i,h :: h \sqsubseteq ask_i \mapsto h \sqsubseteq_{\leqslant} giv_i \end{aligned} \tag{17}$$

Fig. 9. Allocator specification (provided).

The previous construction relies on a single-client allocator. Its specification is derived from specification $\langle 9 \rangle$ for $N = 1$ (Fig. 10).

$$true \text{ \bf guarantees } giv \nearrow \tag{18}$$

$$rel \nearrow \text{ \bf guarantees always } Tokens.giv - Tokens.rel \leqslant NbT \tag{19}$$

$$\begin{array}{c} ask \nearrow \; \wedge \; rel \nearrow \\ \wedge \qquad \text{\bf always } \langle \forall k :: ask[k] \leqslant NbT \rangle \\ \wedge \; \forall h :: h \sqsubseteq giv \wedge h \sqsupseteq_{\geqslant} ask \; \mapsto \; Tokens.rel \geqslant Tokens.h \\ \text{\bf guarantees} \\ \forall h :: h \sqsubseteq ask \; \mapsto \; h \sqsubseteq_{\leqslant} giv \end{array} \tag{20}$$

Fig. 10. Single-client allocator specification (required).

5.2 Refinement Proof

We need to show that the provided specification $\langle 9 \rangle$ is stronger than the required specification $\langle 4 \rangle$. The only proof obligation is that $(17) \Rightarrow (8)$. Since the right-hand sides are the same, we have to prove that the left-hand side of (8) is stronger than the left-hand-side of (17).

Proof.

$\quad \{$lhs of $(8)\}$
$\quad \forall i, h :: h_i \sqsubseteq giv_i \wedge h_i \sqsupseteq_{\geqslant} ask_i \; \mapsto \; Tokens.rel_i \geqslant Tokens.h_i$
$\Rightarrow \{rel_i \nearrow, \; Tokens.rel_i \nearrow, \; \text{PSP}\}$
$\quad \forall h :: \langle \forall i :: h_i \sqsubseteq giv_i \wedge h_i \sqsupseteq_{\geqslant} ask_i \rangle \; \mapsto \; \langle \forall i :: Tokens.rel_i \geqslant Tokens.h_i \rangle$
$\Rightarrow \{\text{calculus}\}$
$\quad \forall h :: \langle \forall i :: h_i \sqsubseteq giv_i \wedge h_i \sqsupseteq_{\geqslant} ask_i \rangle \; \mapsto \; \sum_i Tokens.rel_i \geqslant \sum_i Tokens.h_i$
$\quad \{$lhs of $(17)\}$

$\hfill \square$

The composition proof, i.e. the proof that the components connected as described in fig. 8 provide the general allocator specification $\langle 9 \rangle$ is given in [11].

6 Clients

6.1 Model

A client has a variable T which represents the size of the next request. We do not specify how T is chosen. However, its value must always be in the range $1..NbT$. In the following program, we use the nondeterminism of UNITY programs to generate a random value for T. Requests for tokens are built by appending the value of T to the history of requests. There is exactly one *rel* message produced for each *giv* message received that satisfies the condition (enough tokens to serve the request). Such a client can send several requests before one request is answered, and can receive several answers before it releases one.

Program *Client*
Declare
    giv : *input history*;
    ask, *rel* : *output history*;
    T : *bag of colors*;
Initially
    $1 \leqslant T \leqslant NbT$;
Assign (*weak fairness*)
    $rel := rel \bullet giv[|rel| + 1]$ **if** $|rel| < |giv| \wedge giv[|rel| + 1] \geqslant ask[|rel| + 1]$
Assign (*no fairness*)
    $\|\ T := (T \bmod NbT) + 1$
    $\|\ ask := ask \bullet T$
End

6.2   Provided Specification

The client model provides a different (and stronger) liveness than requested. It is only requested that clients return the right *total* number of tokens. However, this client always return *all* the tokens corresponding to a request in a single message (Fig. 11). The refinement proof ($\langle 11 \rangle \Rightarrow \langle 3 \rangle$) is given in [11].

$$
\begin{array}{lr}
\textit{true } \textbf{guarantees } ask \nearrow \wedge rel \nearrow & (21) \\
\textit{true } \textbf{guarantees always } \langle \forall k :: ask[k] \leqslant NbT \rangle & (22) \\
giv \nearrow \textbf{ guarantees } \forall h :: h \sqsubseteq giv \wedge h \sqsubseteq_{\geqslant} ask \ \mapsto \ h \sqsubseteq rel & (23)
\end{array}
$$

Fig. 11. Client specification (provided).

6.3   Correctness Proof

Property (21). Properties in the right-hand side of the *guarantees* are strongly satisfied by the client text (i.e. the corresponding strong property holds). Because they only refer to local variables, they also hold strongly in other components. Then, since strong *stable* properties are universal, they hold in the global system.

Property (22). The same argument is applied, using the following inductive invariant:

$$\textbf{invariant } \langle \forall k :: ask[k] \leqslant NbT \rangle \wedge (T \leqslant NbT)$$

which is local and stronger than the required *always* property.

Property (23).

Lemma 24.

$$\forall h, k :: \texttt{transient}\ rel = k \wedge k \sqsubseteq h \wedge h \sqsubseteq giv \wedge h \sqsubseteq_\geqslant ask \cdot Client \qquad (24)$$

Proof. We use the fact that $(\texttt{transient}\ q) \wedge [p \Rightarrow q] \Rightarrow (\texttt{transient}\ p)$:

$rel = k \wedge k \sqsubseteq h \wedge h \sqsubseteq giv \wedge h \sqsubseteq_\geqslant ask$
$\Rightarrow$ {Definition of $\sqsubseteq_\geqslant$, calculus}
$rel = k \wedge |rel| < |h| \leqslant |giv| \wedge \langle \forall n : 1 \leqslant n \leqslant |h| : giv[n] \geqslant ask[n] \rangle$
$\Rightarrow$ {Calculus}
$rel = k \wedge |rel| \leqslant |giv| \wedge \langle \forall n : 1 \leqslant n \leqslant |rel| + 1 : giv[n] \geqslant ask[n] \rangle$
$\Rightarrow$ {Choose $n = |rel| + 1$}
$rel = k \wedge |rel| \leqslant |giv| \wedge giv[|rel| + 1] \geqslant ask[|rel| + 1]$
{From the first program statement}
is *transient* for any k

$\square$

Proof (specification (23)). In any composed system:

{From lemma (24), existentiality of *transient*}
$\qquad (rel = k \wedge k \sqsubseteq h \wedge h \sqsubseteq giv \wedge h \sqsubseteq_\geqslant ask)$
$\qquad \longmapsto \ \neg(rel = k \wedge k \sqsubseteq h \wedge h \sqsubseteq giv \wedge h \sqsubseteq_\geqslant ask)$
$\Rightarrow$ {$giv \nearrow$ from lhs, $ask \nearrow$, PSP}
$rel = k \wedge k \sqsubseteq h \wedge h \sqsubseteq giv \wedge h \sqsubseteq_\geqslant ask \ \longmapsto \ rel \neq k$
$\Rightarrow$ {$rel \nearrow$, PSP}
$rel = k \wedge k \sqsubseteq h \wedge h \sqsubseteq giv \wedge h \sqsubseteq_\geqslant ask \ \longmapsto \ k \sqsubseteq rel$
$\Rightarrow$ {Induction on $|h| - |k|$}
$rel = k \wedge k \sqsubseteq h \wedge h \sqsubseteq giv \wedge h \sqsubseteq_\geqslant ask \ \longmapsto \ rel = h$
$\Rightarrow$ {Weakening}
$rel = k \wedge k \sqsubseteq h \wedge h \sqsubseteq giv \wedge h \sqsubseteq_\geqslant ask \ \longmapsto \ h \sqsubseteq rel$
$\Rightarrow$ {Disjunction over k}
$rel \sqsubseteq h \wedge h \sqsubseteq giv \wedge h \sqsubseteq_\geqslant ask \ \longmapsto \ h \sqsubseteq rel$
$\Rightarrow$ {Disjunction $[(p \wedge r \ \longmapsto \ q) \Rightarrow ((p \vee q) \wedge r \ \longmapsto \ q)]$}
$(rel \sqsubseteq h \vee h \sqsubseteq rel) \wedge h \sqsubseteq giv \wedge h \sqsubseteq_\geqslant ask \ \longmapsto \ h \sqsubseteq rel$
$\Rightarrow$ {$\texttt{always}\ rel \sqsubseteq giv$ holds in system, hence $h \sqsubseteq giv \Rightarrow (rel \sqsubseteq h \vee h \sqsubseteq rel)$}
$h \sqsubseteq giv \wedge h \sqsubseteq_\geqslant ask \ \longmapsto \ h \sqsubseteq rel$

$\square$

7   The Single-Client Allocator

7.1   Model

The allocator uses a variable T to store the number of available tokens. It simply answers an unsatisfied request if there are enough tokens in T. The allocator also looks into its release port and "consumes" messages to increase T. It keeps track of the number of consumed messages in NbR.

Program *Alloc*
Declare
    ask, rel : *input history*;
    giv : *output history*;
    T : *bag of colors*;
    NbR : *int*;
Initially
    $T = NbT \wedge NbR = 0$
Assign (*weak fairness*)
    $giv, T := giv \bullet ask[|giv| + 1], T - ask[|giv| + 1]$
        if $|ask| > |giv| \wedge T \geqslant ask[|giv| + 1]$
  ⫿ $T, NbR := T + rel[NbR + 1], NbR + 1$ **if** $|rel| > NbR$
End

7.2   Provided Specification

The previous model provides a specification for the single client allocator stronger than the required specification $\langle 10 \rangle$.

The main difference is that this allocator waits for a request before it sends tokens (27). This is not explicitly required in specification $\langle 10 \rangle$. Especially, we can imagine an allocator able to *guess* some clients requests, using, for instance, some knowledge that several clients have exactly the same behavior (client i asked for n tokens, therefore client j will also ask for n tokens.). The only constraint is that tokens given to a client correspond (possibly in the future) to a request from that client. Then, since this allocator does not send tokens without requests, it can expect the return of *all* the tokens it sent, which changes the left-hand side of the liveness property (28). Intuitively, this leads to a stronger specification: Never sending tokens without request and expecting the return of all tokens is stronger than only expecting the return of tokens sent in response to a request.

The second (minor) difference is that this allocator always gives *exactly* the right number of tokens. The resulting specification is summarized in fig. 12.

$$true \ \textbf{guarantees} \ giv \ \nearrow \tag{25}$$

$$rel \ \nearrow \ \textbf{guarantees always} \ Tokens.giv - Tokens.rel \leqslant NbT \tag{26}$$

$$ask \ \nearrow \ \textbf{guarantees always} \ giv \sqsubseteq ask \tag{27}$$

$$\begin{array}{c} ask \ \nearrow \ \wedge \ rel \ \nearrow \\ \wedge \quad \textbf{always} \ \langle \forall k :: ask[k] \leqslant NbT \rangle \\ \wedge \ \forall k :: Tokens.giv \geqslant k \ \mapsto \ Tokens.rel \geqslant k \\ \textbf{guarantees} \\ \forall h :: h \sqsubseteq ask \ \mapsto \ h \sqsubseteq giv \end{array} \tag{28}$$

Fig. 12. Single-client allocator specification (provided).

The refinement proof ($\langle 12 \rangle \Rightarrow \langle 10 \rangle$) and the program text correctness proof are given in [11].

8   Conclusions

The allocator example illustrates the need, when adopting a component-based design, to switch between top-down and bottom-up approaches.

Designers are given the specification of the global system that they are designing. They propose components which can be composed to obtain the desired system. Some of the components may have been implemented earlier and may be available in a component library. Other components must be designed. These components can be implemented as compositions of other components or directly as programs. This approach is the traditional top-down approach. While building these components (by programming, or by composition), designers adopt the point of view of providers: they look at what they get and express it logically. This corresponds to a bottom-up phase.

Provided specifications and required specifications need not be the same and, in general, they are different. This is because when specifying a required behavior, one does not want to demand too much; and on the other hand, when programming a model, one does not try to obtain the weakest possible solution. If the user and the provider are forced to share some average common specification, they remain unsatisfied: "Why should I ask for things I don't need?", "Why should I hide some properties my program has?". Because we hope for reusability, a component should be finally published with its provided specification, as well as with different weaker specifications. One advantage in publishing these weak specifications is that they may allow a reuse of the component while avoiding either another refinement proof or a complex compositional proof (using directly the provided specification). These weaker specifications can be obtained from previous uses of that component. Another possibility is that the component implementor invests effort in proving several specifications of his component, and hence reduces the work of the composer who can use the most convenient specification.

As we see on the example, this approach requires three kinds of proofs: *compositional proofs*, to deduce the correctness of a system (or sub-system) from components correctness; *refinement proofs* to check that bottom-up phases provides components stronger than requested during top-down phases; *program text correctness proofs* to relate, at the bottom, program texts to logical specifications. The framework we are using, based on UNITY, extended with composition operators (*guarantees*) and a communication abstraction (*follows*), is able to handle those three types of proofs, while remaining in the minimalist spirit of UNITY.

Our goal is to develop methods for building distributed systems from components. It is important to be able to specify components in terms of input and output, and to be able to connect them formally through simple proofs. Combining a temporal operator like *follows* with some basic sequence properties seems an interesting approach. We are currently investigating how far this approach can go. We would like to express both traditional functional behaviors and useful nondeterministic behaviors (like *merge*) with a common notation that would be able to handle their interaction nicely.

Another area of interest is *universal* properties. Throughout the allocator example, all composition aspects are handled with *existential* properties. Although it it easier to use existential properties than universal properties, it seems that they can become insufficient when dealing with global complex safety properties. We are currently investigating examples involving such global complex safety properties to learn more about universally-based composition [10].

The motivation for this research is the development of large repositories of software components. Designers can discover implementations of components and use relatively simple compositional structures to create useful software systems. Widespread deployment of such repositories may be years away. Nevertheless, we believe that research to support such repositories is interesting both because it offers intellectually stimulating problems and because it is useful.

We have been working on composition in which shared variables are modified only by one component and read by others. Further, proofs are simplified if these shared variables have a monotonic structure. Existential and universal property types make proof obligations very clear, and these property types yield nice proof rules that appear, at least at this early stage in our investigation, to be well suited for mechanical theorem provers. We have started a collaboration with Larry Paulson who has successfully used *Isabelle* [33] to prove the correctness of such systems.

Much work remains to be done to achieve our goal of large repositories of software components with their proofs of correctness. This is a step in that direction.

9   Related Work

Many people have studied methods for designing systems by composition of components [1, 2] and by systematic refinement [3, 4, 16, 35]. A significant amount of work has been done on compositional methods within the UNITY framework [14, 15, 28, 27]. Composition using rely/guarantee properties and systematic specifications of interfaces have been proposed by Jones [19, 21, 22, 23, 36]. This paper differs from most of the earlier work in developing the theory of universal and existential properties and the *guarantees* operator proposed in [7].

Likewise, compositional software architectures have been covered in great detail with the software engineering community. Excellent overviews of the software process [24], technology [39] and the academic state of the art [31] are available. Existing solutions primarily focus on software engineering processes (e.g. semi-formal interface specifications [25, 18]) and language- and architecture-based approaches ([26, 30] and [8, 32, 38], respectively). Only recently has work begun to incorporate theoretically grounded compositional concepts into practice [29, 17, 37, 20].

References

[1] M. Abadi and L. Lamport. Composing specifications. *ACM Transactions on Programming Languages and Systems*, 15(1):73–132, Jan. 1993.

[2] M. Abadi and L. Lamport. Conjoining specifications. *ACM Transactions on Programming Languages and Systems*, 17(3):507–534, May 1995.

[3] R. Back. Refinement calculus, Part I: Sequential nondeterministic programs. In *REX Workshop on Stepwise Refinement of Distributed Systems*, volume 430 of *Lecture Notes in Computer Science*, pages 42–66. Springer-Verlag, 1989.

[4] R. Back. Refinement calculus, Part II: Parallel and reactive programs. In *REX Workshop on Stepwise Refinement of Distributed Systems*, volume 430 of *Lecture Notes in Computer Science*, pages 67–93. Springer-Verlag, 1989.

[5] K. M. Chandy and J. Misra. *Parallel Program Design: A Foundation*. Addison-Wesley, 1988.

[6] K. M. Chandy and B. A. Sanders. Predicate transformers for reasoning about concurrent computation. *Science of Computer Programming*, 24:129–148, 1995.

[7] K. M. Chandy and B. A. Sanders. Reasoning about program composition. Technical Report 96-035, University of Florida, Department of Computer and Information Science and Engineering, 1996.

[8] D. Chappell. *Understanding ActiveX and OLE*. Microsoft Press, 1996.

[9] M. Charpentier. *Assistance à la Répartition de Systèmes Réactifs*. PhD thesis, Institut National Polytechnique de Toulouse, France, Nov. 1997.

[10] M. Charpentier and K. M. Chandy. Examples of program composition illustrating the use of universal properties. In J. Rolim, editor, *International workshop on Formal Methods for Parallel Programming: Theory and Applications (FMPPTA'99)*, volume 1586 of *Lecture Notes in Computer Science*, pages 1215–1227. Springer-Verlag, Apr. 1999.

[11] M. Charpentier and K. M. Chandy. Towards a compositional approach to the design and verification of distributed systems. Technical Report CS-TR-99-02, California Institute of Technology, Jan. 1999. 29 pages.

[12] M. Charpentier, M. Filali, P. Mauran, G. Padiou, and P. Quéinnec. Abstracting communication to reason about distributed algorithms. In Ö. Babaoğlu and K. Marzullo, editors, *Tenth International Workshop on Distributed Algorithms (WDAG'96)*, volume 1151 of *Lecture Notes in Computer Science*, pages 89–104. Springer-Verlag, October 1996.

[13] M. Charpentier, M. Filali, P. Mauran, G. Padiou, and P. Quéinnec. Tailoring UNITY to distributed program design. In J. Rolim, editor, *International workshop on Formal Methods for Parallel Programming: Theory and Applications (FMPPTA'98)*, volume 1388 of *Lecture Notes in Computer Science*, pages 820–832. Springer-Verlag, April 1998.

[14] P. Collette. Composition of assumption-commitment specifications in a UNITY style. *Science of Computer Programming*, 23:107–125, 1994.

[15] P. Collette. *Design of Compositional Proof Systems Based on Assumption-Commitment Specifications. Application to UNITY*. Doctoral thesis, Faculté des Sciences Appliquées, Université Catholique de Louvain, June 1994.

[16] P. Gardiner and C. Morgan. Data refinement of predicate transformers. *Theoretical Computer Science*, 87:143–162, 1991.

[17] D. Garlan. Higher-order connectors. In *Proceedings of Workshop on Compositional Software Architectures*, Monterey, California, Jan. 1998.

[18] R. Helm, I. M. Holland, and D. Gangopadhyay. Contracts: Specifying behavioral compositions in object-oriented systems. In *European Conference on Object-Oriented Programming/ACM Conference on Object-Oriented Programming Systems, Languages, and Applications*, volume 25/10, pages 169–180, 1990.

[19] C. Jones. Tentative steps toward a development method for interfering programs. *ACM Transactions on Programming Languages and Systems*, 5(4):596–619, 1983.

[20] J. R. Kiniry. CDL: A component description language. In *Proceedings of the COOTS '99 Advanced Topics Workshop on Validating the Composition/Execution of Component-Based Systems*, 1999.

[21] S. Lam and A. Shankar. Specifying modules to satisfy interfaces–a state transition approach. *Distributed Computing*, 6(1):39–63, July 1992.

[22] S. Lam and A. Shankar. A theory of interfaces and modules 1: Composition theorem. *IEEE Transactions on Software Engineering*, 20(1):55–71, Jan. 1994.

[23] R. Manohar and P. Sivilotti. Composing processes using modified rely-guarantee specifications. Technical Report CS-TR-96-22, California Institute of Technology, 1996.

[24] B. Meyer. *Object-Oriented Software Construction*. Prentice-Hall, Inc., 2nd edition, 1988.

[25] B. Meyer. Applying design by contract. *IEEE Computer*, Oct. 1992.

[26] R. Milner, M. Tofte, R. Harper, and D. MacQueen. *The Definition of Standard ML (Revised)*. The MIT Press, 1997.

[27] J. Misra. A logic for concurrent programming: Progress. *Journal of Computer and Software Engineering*, 3(2):273–300, 1995.

[28] J. Misra. A logic for concurrent programming: Safety. *Journal of Computer and Software Engineering*, 3(2):239–272, 1995.

[29] O. Nierstrasz, S. Gibbs, and D. Tsichritzis. Component-oriented software development. *Communications of the ACM*, 35(9):160–165, Sept. 1992.

[30] O. Nierstrasz and T. Meijler. Requirements for a composition language. In *ECOOP'94 Workshop on Models and Languages for Coordination of Parallelism and Distribution*, pages 147–161. Springer–Verlag, 1995.

[31] O. Nierstrasz and D. Tsichritzis, editors. *Object-Oriented Software Composition*. Prentice-Hall, Inc., 1995.

[32] Object Management Group (OMG). *The Common Object Request Broker: Architecture and Specification (CORBA), revision 2.0.* Object Management Group (OMG), 2.0 edition.

[33] L. C. Paulson. *Isabelle: A Generic Theorem Prover*, volume 828 of *Lecture Notes in Computer Science*. Springer-Verlag, 1994.

[34] B. A. Sanders. Eliminating the substitution axiom from UNITY logic. *Formal Aspects of Computing*, 3(2):189–205, April–June 1991.

[35] B. A. Sanders. Data refinement of mixed specification: A generalization of UNITY. *Acta Informatica*, 35(2):91–129, 1998.

[36] N. Shankar. Lazy compositional verification. In *Compositionality: The Significant Difference. International Symposium, COMPOS'97*, volume 1536 of *Lecture Notes in Computer Science*. Springer-Verlag, 1998.

[37] P. A. G. Sivilotti. *A Method for the Specification, Composition, and Testing of Distributed Object Systems*. PhD thesis, California Institute of Technology, 256-80 Caltech, Pasadena, California 91125, Dec. 1997.

[38] Sun Microsystems, Inc. JavaBeans API specification, version 1.01. Technical report, Sun Microsystems, Inc., July 1997.

[39] C. Szyperski. *Component Software: Beyond Object-Oriented Programming*. Addison-Wesley Publishing Company, 1997.

Formal Modeling in a Commercial Setting: A Case Study

Andre Wong and Marsha Chechik

Department of Computer Science, University of Toronto,
Toronto, ON M5S 3G4, Canada,
{andre,chechik}@cs.toronto.edu,
http://www.cs.toronto.edu/~chechik

Abstract. This paper describes a case study conducted in collaboration with Nortel to demonstrate the feasibility of applying formal modeling techniques to telecommunication systems. A formal description language, SDL, was chosen by our qualitative CASE tool evaluation to model a multimedia-messaging system described by an 80-page natural language specification. Our model was used to identify errors in the software requirements document and to derive test suites, shadowing the existing development process and keeping track of a variety of productivity data.

1 Introduction

For a long time, researchers and practitioners have been seeking ways to improve productivity in the software development process. Precise documentation of software specifications has been advocated as one of the viable approaches [25]. If high quality specifications are crucial to the success of system developments, it seems logical to apply rigorous specification techniques to the requirements for ensuring their completeness and consistency.

The majority of successful applications of formal modeling have been confined to safety-critical projects [5, 13, 19] where software correctness is the pivotal goal. In contrast, the commercial software industry seeks practical techniques that can be seamlessly integrated into the existing development processes and improve productivity; absolute quality is often a desirable but not crucial objective. Although the feasibility of formal specifications has been demonstrated in commercial settings [12, 15, 23], the overall adoption of the idea has been slow. Most companies, such as the Canadian-based telecommunications company Nortel[1], opt to rely on manual inspections of natural-language specifications as the only technique to detect errors in them, even though the results have been suboptimal. If the advantages of better quality specifications, such as a better understanding of the system and less error-prone designs, do not provide an adequate justification, more benefits can be obtained by leveraging the investment

---

[1] Nortel, for the purpose of this paper, refers to the Toronto Multimedia Applications Center of Nortel Networks.

J. Wing, J. Woodcock, J. Davies (Eds.): FM'99, Vol. I, LNCS 1708, pp. 590–607, 1999.
© Springer-Verlag Berlin Heidelberg 1999

in the formalization process to other stages of the software lifecycle, i.e. generating code or test cases from the formal specifications. Not only does this amortize the cost of creating the specifications, but the productivity improvement can also be more immediate and easily measurable.

Driven by the need to shorten and improve the software development process, Nortel and the Formal Methods Laboratory at the University of Toronto have jointly proposed a pilot research project to investigate the feasibility of formal modeling techniques in a commercial setting. The goal of the project is to find means of using formal modeling to improve productivity in various stages of the software lifecycle in an economical manner. Specifically, the emphasis is placed on deriving test cases from the formal model as the Nortel engineers have expressed concerns about the feasibility of code generation for their proprietary platform.

Our exploratory project was organized as a hybrid quantitative and qualitative case study [21]. As it was extremely important to choose the right system/language combination for the formalization process, we began the study by selecting a typical system to specify and conducting a qualitative evaluation of formal modeling languages. A chosen language was applied to model the system, and the resulting model was used to identify errors in the software requirements document and to derive test suites, shadowing the existing development process. Throughout the study, we kept a variety of productivity data for comparison with similar information from the actual development process. We also noted the qualitative impact of the formalization process.

The rest of the paper is organized as follows: Section 2 provides a brief description of the software system selected for the study. Section 3 discusses the criteria used in choosing a suitable modeling language. In Section 4, we discuss the formalization process. Section 5 presents findings from the study. The experience gained during the project is summarized in Section 6. Section 7 briefly describes a usability workshop that we conducted at Nortel, and Section 8 concludes the paper.

2   System Selection

To make the project meaningful, we did not want to be directly involved in choosing a system, hoping to work on something representative of typical projects of the TorMAC division of Nortel. We also felt that it was important to do the formalization in parallel with the development cycle. Thus, a group of Nortel engineers, consisting of developers from the design team and testers from the verification team decided that we should work on a subsystem of the Operation, Administration and Maintenance (OAM) software of a multimedia-messaging system connected to a private branch exchange. The subsystem, called Service-Creator in our paper, is a voice service creation environment that lets administrators build custom telephony applications in a graphical workspace by connecting predefined voice-service components together. Figure 1 illustrates the graphical view of one such telephony application consisting of four components: *start, end, password-check,* and *fax.* When the application is activated, a call session begins at the *start* component, and a caller is required to enter a numerical password in order to retrieve a fax document from the *fax* component. The caller is directed to the *end* component if an incorrect password is entered. In both scenarios, the call session ends when the *end* component is reached.

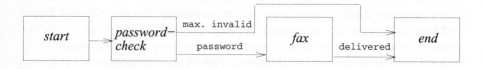

Fig. 1. A simplified telephony application example.

The lines connecting various components represent potential control flow of the call session, and the actions performed by the caller in an active component determine the output path taken. In the *password-check* component, for instance, the caller exits via the path *password* if a correct password is entered, or the path *max. invalid* if there are too many invalid password attempts.

In our study, we analyzed the run-time behavior of 15 such components, described by an 80-page natural language specification. We illustrate the approach using the password-check component, described by a 5-page natural language specification. Figure 2 shows a graphical view of this component.

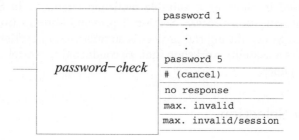

Fig. 2. The graphical view of the password-check component.

The purpose of this component is to validate digits entered by a caller against any of the passwords (up to five) defined by the administrator. For instance, the path *password 1* is taken if the entered digits match the first defined password. The caller is forced to leave the component using the *max. invalid* output if the maximum number of invalid password attempts is reached. Such attempts are also monitored on a per-call session basis, and the caller leaves via the *max. invalid/session* output if the per-call session limit is reached. The caller can also enter the *** key to retrieve the help prompt, which has a side effect of clearing the password entry, or the *#* key to exit prematurely via the *# (cancel)* path if no password has been entered. If the caller stays idle for a certain time period and has not previously keyed in any digits prior to entering the password-check component, she is assumed to be using a rotary phone and is transferred to a different voice-service component. Otherwise, one of the two delay prompts may be played depending on whether she has begun keying in the password. After two more timeouts, the caller exits via the *no response* path.

In order to generalize from the results of the study, we need a good characterization of the type of applications that ServiceCreator represents. First of all, it is clearly a reactive system in the telecommunications domain. Additionally, it has relatively stable requirements and is fairly self-contained, having a loose coupling with the underlying system. Finally, it is not very complex although non-trivial.

3   Evaluation of Modeling Methods

A successful formalization of the system in a commercial setting depends crucially on a modeling language, supported by an appropriate tool. Thus, in this section we use the term *method* to indicate both the modeling language and its tool support. The goal of the evaluation was to select a suitable modeling method to be used in the feasibility study.

Easily readable and reviewable artifacts as well as a simple notation were the two basic requirements for a modeling method to be usable in a commercial setting. Moreover, since one of the overall objectives was to amortize the cost of creating a formal specification, we began the evaluation by conducting a broad survey [31] of available tools that provided support for both modeling and testing. These constraints turned out to be extremely limiting as most of the surveyed methods either had just the modeling or just the testing support, or did not have a formal notation. Some were simply too difficult to be used in industry. We eventually narrowed down our search to the following candidates:

- *Telelogic SDT* [27]—an integrated software modeling and testing tool suite that utilizes Specification and Description Language (SDL) [16], which is based on extended finite state machines (EFSMs), for behavioral modeling and Message Sequence Charts (MSCs) [17] for component-interaction specification. MSCs, which can be used as test cases, can be derived semi-automatically from an SDL model. Alternatively, SDT can verify the correctness of the model with respect to independently created MSCs.
- *Aonix Validator/Req (V/Q)* [2]—a test generation tool that allows black-box requirements of a system to be specified in the form of parameterized UML [4] use cases. Validator/Req generates test cases for data-flow testing from the model automatically and produces documents that conform with the IEEE standard for software requirements specifications [1].
- *Teradyne TestMaster (TM)* [28]—a test generation tool that automatically generates test cases for both control-flow and limited data-flow testing from models based on EFSMs. The number of test cases can be flexibly tuned to suit different testing needs.

To perform a detailed assessment, we structured our evaluation as a feature analysis exercise [21] and refined our focus to choosing among the remaining methods using additional evaluation criteria gathered from the Nortel engineers. These criteria comprised of factors, such as usability and smooth integration, that were crucial to the use of formal modeling in their environment. After the methods were used to model the password-check component, they were ranked against the criteria based on our impressions of the tool and the models produced.

Criteria	Weighting	SDT	V/Q	TM
has modeling support	5	4	2	3
has testing support	5	3	4	5
has a gentle learning curve	4	3	5	3
produces easy-to-understand artifacts	3	4	5	4
enhances understanding of the system	4	5	3	4
works smoothly with the existing development process and tools	4	5	4	3
is scalable	3	4	2	3
has strong tool support	3	5	4	5
performs completeness or consistency checks	2	4	3	3
provides features such as multi-user support, requirements traceability and document generation	1	3	4	2
Score	N/A	137	121	124

Table 1. Comparison of modeling methods.

Table 1 shows results of this evaluation. It lists the evaluation criteria in column one, their relative importance using a scale from 1 (least important) to 5 (most important) in column two[2], and the degree the methods satisfy the criteria using a scale from 1 (unsatisfactory) to 5 (completely satisfactory) in columns three to five. In the first row, for instance, SDL scores the highest as it allows the behavioral modeling and the hierarchical partitioning of a system into concurrent processes. TestMaster has similar modeling support but a system can only be modeled as a single hierarchical EFSM from a tester's perspective. Validator/Req ranks the lowest as its scenario-based notation provides very limited modeling support. The conclusion of the evaluation was reached by comparing the final scores for the methods obtained by adding weighted scores from each criterion, making SDT the most suitable tool.

A confounding factor in feature analysis is the potentially biased opinions of the evaluator. Although we tried to ensure the objectivity of the evaluation, assignments of the scores inevitably contained our subjective judgment, and we did not feel that we could accurately evaluate such factors as usability. To

---

[2] These were assigned after consultations with Nortel engineers.

mitigate this potential problem and to gain more confidence in our assessment, we demonstrated the tools and the models to the engineers. They agreed that SDT satisfied their criteria more closely than the other tools.

4   Modeling and Testing the System

The next step was to formalize the ServiceCreator application. This formalization was undertaken by us in parallel with the actual development process. ServiceCreator was modeled as a 70-page SDL system in which the environment contained the underlying OAM software and messaging-system hardware. Out of the 15 voice-service components, 10 were modeled as separate SDL processes (see Appendix A for an example) that communicated with the environment through a "driver" SDL process. This process models the control-flow information of the telephone application. Figure 3 shows a simplified view of the "driver" process created for the application of Figure 1. This process is responsible for activating voice-service components and responding to their termination. The functionality of the five remaining components (e.g., *start* and *end*) was incorporated into the "driver" processes. A total of 23 signals were used in the SDL system; eight of them were external (used for communicating with the environment) and the rest internal. Persistent data such as the predefined passwords for the password-check component, were represented as parameters to the SDL processes.

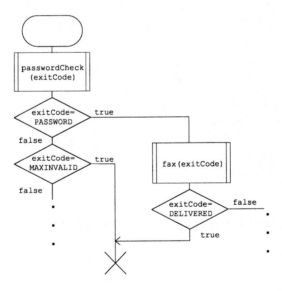

Fig. 3. A driver process for a simplified telephony application example of Fig. 1.

4.1   The Level of Abstraction

The modeling process was relatively straightforward as we encountered no major problems in modeling ServiceCreator; we also felt that a background in formal methods was not required. However, the biggest concern was to determine the appropriate level of abstraction which was dictated by two opposing needs: the model should be constructed from a black-box view to reduce its complexity, while the exact behavior of the system needs to be modeled for deriving detailed test cases. In addition, a more detailed model would help in identifying problems in the natural-language specification.

Our approach was to start from a high level of abstraction, filling in details about some parts of the behavior if the natural-language specification required it. Mostly, such details were necessary in dealing with external input. For example, in modeling the password-check component, we represented the various timeouts by an SDL timer *timeout* (see Figure 4), as the actual length of the timeouts was relatively unimportant. Processing of user input, on the other hand, required reasoning on the level of single digits. In our model, a received digit, *digit*, was actually stored in a variable *numberRecv*. While this treatment could potentially lead to large and cluttered models, we sometimes had to resort to it to be able to derive sufficiently detailed test cases.

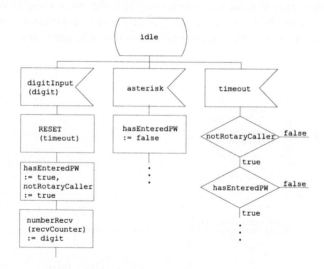

Fig. 4. A simplified fragment from the SDL model of the password-check component.

4.2   Test Case Derivation

To obtain immediate benefits from the formalization process, 120 MSCs were derived from the SDL model for testing the implementation. The derivation was not automatic: SDT recorded the interactions between the SDL system and its environment as MSCs when we animated the SDL model manually. We felt that the automation was not necessarily desirable since this exercise gave us confidence in the content and the coverage of the test cases.

During the test case derivation, we took advantage of the modular nature of the voice-service components and generated test cases for each of them separately, achieving full transition coverage in the corresponding SDL processes. However, some functionality of the system could be covered only by testing multiple components together, i.e. by integration testing. More than 20 integration test cases have been identified. For instance, to derive test cases for testing the initial timeout behavior for touch-tone callers where no passwords were keyed in, we created a telephony application model in which a caller was required to key in some digits in a component, such as a menu, prior to entering the password-check component (see Appendix B for the corresponding MSC). The procedure for deriving such test cases was as follows:

- During the modeling phase, note the cases where the input comes not only from the environment but also from other components. If some input to component A comes from component B, we say that there is a relationship between A and B.
- After the modeling phase, use the resulting model to create test cases that specifically ensure that the relationship between the components is correctly implemented.

Derivation of test cases for integration testing was the most labor-intensive part of this phase; it also required a fair bit of skill.

4.3   Specification and Implementation Problems

The SDL model and the experience gained from the formalization process allowed us to identify specification errors that escaped a series of manual inspections by Nortel engineers. As the components modeled were not particularly complicated, most of the errors we found were caused by vagueness and missing information. In fact, the most time-consuming part of the formalization process was to understand the natural-language specifications and to consult the engineers for clarifications. We estimated that these activities took as much time as the formalization process. Some of the problems found in the specification of the password-check component are presented below:

1) it was never mentioned whether the various voice prompts were interruptible, and no conventions for such behavior were defined;
2) lengths of various timeouts were not mentioned;
3) it was unclear which exit path should be taken when the administrator set two or more passwords to be the same;
4) the maximum and minimum lengths of passwords were not defined.

Some of these problems were very low criticality and could be easily fixed in the implementation. However, the testers were required to interact with the developers to clarify the correct behavior of the system, spending an unnecessarily long time in the test case execution phase (see Section 5.1). In addition, problem 4) propagated itself into the implementation. That is, a malicious caller could crash the system by entering an abnormally long password within the password-check component. Thus, this requirement omission became a critical implementation error. Moreover, since the MSCs derived from the SDL model were used to identify errors in the implementation *after* the Nortel engineers had officially completed testing of the voice-service components, we were able to observe that this implementation error had not been discovered. The reason was that the test cases were derived from the same incomplete specification and missed a critical error.

5   Findings

We began our analysis by seeking quantitative evidence to measure the effects of the formalization process on productivity. However, as the study progressed, we felt that it was also crucial to identify the qualitative factors (e.g., perceived usability of SDL and commitments from the development team) and the limitations of the study in order to reach accurate and unbiased conclusions.

Unfortunately, Nortel engineers did not keep track of many essential metrics and, due to the exploratory nature of our study, did not allow us to create a controlled environment where such metrics could be obtained. In particular, we do not know the exact amount of time it takes to fix a bug, if it is found during the inspection vs. design vs. testing phase. The lack of metrics significantly impairs our ability to draw quantitative conclusions.

5.1   Quantitative Results

The entire modeling process, which consisted of activities such as understanding and formalizing the specification as well as deriving and executing test cases, took about two person-months to complete. During this period, we kept track of a variety of productivity data in the study (column two of Table 2) for comparison with similar information from the existing development process (column three). Effort measurements in this table are approximated to the nearest person-day. Since the sizes of test cases varied greatly, we did not use a "test case" as the unit of comparison for testing-related data. Instead, we counted test units, the smallest externally visible functionality of the system, in each test case to ensure a fair comparison. Highlights from the table are summarized below:

- The *time to model* value included only the time used for modeling the SDL processes. While the modeling task did not have an equivalent in the actual development process, manual inspection was a similar activity that was also performed at the completion of the specification phase. Certainly, the formalization process was not meant to be a complete replacement. However,

Productivity Data	Study	Existing Process
Time to model (person-days)	11	N/A
Time to inspect (person-days)	N/A	50
Number of specification errors reported	56	N/A
Number of test units	269	96
Time to create test units (person-days)	7	7
Time to execute test units (person-days)	5	14
Number of implementation errors identified	50	23

Table 2. Productivity Comparisons.

if a large number of specification errors were identified in a relatively short amount of time, the modeling task could be considered a way to decrease the time for inspection. (We discuss this point later in this Section.)

- The number of specification errors reported could not be used for comparison as the Nortel engineers did not keep track of such statistics.
- More test units could be derived from the SDL model (which translated to better test coverage) in roughly the same amount of time, possibly because the model eased the creation task by providing a more in-depth understanding of the system as well as a better sense of completeness. One other reason for the difference in the quantity was that the test units from Nortel were sometimes vaguely specified (see Figure 5 for an example); the missing details contributed to a decrease in the number of test units reported.

Call the application and simulate a number of hacker attempts (such as common passwords and misspelled passwords). Verify that the application terminates the call session after the maximum number of password attempts is reached.

Fig. 5. A Nortel test case for testing the password-check component.

- The time needed for test unit execution in our study was much smaller for two major reasons: the derived test units were more detailed and thus easier to execute, and it was observed that Nortel engineers spent a lot of time revising the existing test cases because of the changes in requirements and creating more detailed test scenarios based on the vaguely specified test units. However, due to tight schedules, most testers did not document these extra units until the end of the entire testing phase, which spanned over more than four months. They admitted that some of these test units would inevitably be lost, contributing to a decrease in their total number.
- The number of implementation errors identified in the study was two times larger than that of the existing development process. Many of them were missed because testers created test cases from an incorrect and incomplete

specification, as indicated in the third row of Table 2. Problems such as incompleteness propagate to the test cases and affect the test coverage. In fact, 18 of the 50 problems could be linked to problems in the specification. Their criticality ranged from the minor ones, dealing with the availability and the interruptability of voice prompts, to the critical ones, affecting the core functionality of the voice-service components or causing the system to crush. Most of these errors resulted from undocumented assumptions or incorrect/missing error handling.

To obtain an accurate cost/benefit figure, we needed to collect additional statistics such as an average cost to fix a requirements error discovered during the inspection and the implementation phases. As we mentioned above, the Nortel development team did not keep track of such metric; however, a conservative cost/benefit estimation is still possible. Without taking the improvement in software quality into account, we can estimate the cost of formalization by subtracting the time of the modeling task from the direct savings in

- the test unit creation (0 person-days),
- the test unit execution (9 person-days), and
- the manual inspection.

The formalization process did not include a manual inspection phase, whereas the actual development took 50 person-days for it. The modeling task would come at no cost if it were to reduce the manual inspection by 2 person-days, or 4%. Of course, the actual cost/benefit figure is significantly more promising if the long-term benefits, coming from a better quality of the product, ease of maintenance and regression testing, and an ability to reuse a good specification, are taken into account.

5.2 Qualitative Observations

While all the quantitative data was in favor of the use of the formal modeling, it was clear that these results alone constituted only a part of our findings. Some observations from the formalization process that were not evident from Table 2 are discussed below.

- The most frequent complaint from the test engineers is that the missing information in the specifications often complicates the task of the test case creation. The SDL models encourage and assist developers in stating system requirements more precisely and completely, which should allow testers to create better quality (e.g., more detailed and with expected results more clearly defined) test cases and reduce the time needed for test case creation and execution. Developers should also benefit from the more complete specifications during the design and the implementation phases. This is an area where SDL can potentially significantly improve the development process. In fact, SDL has been successfully applied in the telecommunications field: from the traditional use of protocol specifications [3, 26, 8] to high level specification [22], prototyping [29], design [24], code generation [10], and testing [11] of telecommunications applications. Although the results reported in these studies were similar to ours, the goal of the studies was different: they were aimed to investigate technical advantages or a feasibility of SDL in a given environment, or were emphasizing only one of the development activities.

- As with any other formal specification technique, a successful integration of SDL into the development process requires a firm commitment from the entire development team. For instance, the developers must ensure that the SDL model is always kept consistent with the system requirements and the code, e.g. last-minute changes in the design and implementation are propagated back to the model. Testers also need to ensure that their test cases always reflect the model accurately. While this is possibly one of the biggest obstacles in applying a formal modeling technique, the advantages provided by SDL justify the extra effort.

- Compared to other formal modeling techniques, the strengths of SDL lie in its ease of use and the ability to express nontrivial behavior in a reviewable notation. Unlike many other formal modeling languages, SDL does not require an explicit use of formal logic. The graphical user-friendly notation allows developers without a strong mathematical background to effectively create EFSMs. Compared to natural language specifications, such EFSMs give a much better sense of completeness, allowing to easily detect missing scenarios, e.g., problem 1) in Section 4.3. In addition, the formal syntax helps clarify ambiguities or inconsistencies, e.g., problem 3) in the same section. However, SDL tends to blur the line between requirements and designs. If proper abstractions are not applied, the model may become too detailed and unnecessarily large, possibly duplicating the design effort.

5.3 Limitations

Based on the opinions expressed by the Nortel developers and testers, Service-Creator was representative of the types of systems they have to work with, so we are fairly confident that the results of the study would apply to similar projects in this environment. We were also fortunate to find a method which is well suited for modeling telecommunication systems. However, it would be difficult [33] to generalize our findings outside the Nortel domain, since they would depend on the current development methodology, types of applications and the choice of a modeling language/tool.

Other limitations came from the fact that we had prior experience with SDL and were not constrained by development pressures. That is, we took the time necessary to produce high quality models and detailed test cases and felt that the process was straightforward. If time pressures prevent Nortel developers from applying the modeling techniques carefully, they may not achieve equally good results. In addition, novice users of SDL would take more time and possibly create less effective models of their systems. However, we believe that appropriate training and availability of an SDL expert can ensure that Nortel engineers use the SDL system successfully.

6   Lessons Learned

We were able to show that formal modeling techniques can shorten the development cycle while improving the quality of software. This can be done by amortizing the cost of creating the model over time-intensive phases of the software development lifecycle, such as testing or code generation. However, the total decrease in the development cycle is only achievable if the formalization can be done fairly inexpensively, by utilizing an easy-to-use and review notation, formalizing only selected components, and staying at a fairly high level of abstraction. It is also essential to achieve immediate results by using the approach incrementally, that is, being able to stop at any time and get partial benefits from partial modeling. A light-weight approach to formalization has been advocated by many researchers [6, 18, 20] and applied successfully in several projects, e.g. [7, 9].

What about verification? We feel that in the current commercial environment the majority of systems do not require any verification. There is typically a lesser need for absolute assurance, but a greater need for rapid development of reasonably correct systems. In fact, our use of SDL showed that, if verification is not involved, it is not essential to use a modeling language with a fully-defined formal semantics to achieve immediate and measurable benefits.

7   Measuring Usability of SDL

There is no doubt that usability of formal modeling techniques plays an important role in their acceptance in industry [14]. An easy-to-use technique encourages experimentation and reduces the cost of integration. More importantly, the reality is that practitioners do not try to adapt to an inconvenient technique— they simply abandon it [30]. Thus, it is essential that SDL is perceived to be usable by Nortel engineers. Only then will they be willing to apply it to their projects.

To collect some information about the usability of SDL, we conducted a one-day workshop in which six Nortel engineers participated. In the first part of the workshop we provided the participants with natural language descriptions of two small software systems [32]. After inspecting the descriptions manually and noting problems in them, the participants were asked to model the described systems in SDL. By formalizing the behavior, they were able to discover many additional specification errors; some of them found even more errors than we originally seeded, i.e. the descriptions contained errors that we did not notice. A few minor usability problems were noted, but the consensus reached among the participants was that the use of a formal, yet user-friendly, notation could help uncover problems hidden in the seemingly simple exercises much more effectively than manual inspections. In the second part of the workshop we asked the participants to fill in a questionnaire. The goal of the questionnaire was to obtain opinions about the usability of SDL and its perceived role in the development environment. Some of the results are summarized in Table 3, and the rest are available in [32]. The column on the right contains an average score on the scale from 1 (strongly disagree) to 5 (strongly agree).

Statement	Score
SDL is easy to use	3.7
SDL can be used to address many of the development problems we are facing.	3.7
The use of SDL increases our understanding of the requirements and their quality.	4.2
The use of SDL lengthens the requirements analysis phase.	4.0
The use of SDL shortens the design, implementation, and testing phases.	4.1
Integrating SDL into my work routine is worthwhile and should be tried.	3.7

Table 3. Some results from the questionnaire.

Results from the questionnaire strengthened our findings that SDL is a user-friendly formal modeling technique which can be used effectively by Nortel engineers to improve their development process. Encouraged by the prospects of SDL, Nortel and University of Toronto are in the process of setting up another joint project where the engineers will carry out the formalization process themselves, and we will only observe the progress and provide consulting, if necessary. Without many limitations of our study, this new project will provide a more accurate insight into the technical and economical feasibility of SDL in a commercial setting.

8   Conclusions

In this case study we formalized the behavior of a multimedia-messaging system in a commercial setting. The success of the study was in finding a representative system, carefully selecting a suitable modeling method, and taking a lightweight formalization approach. Although we did not have access to some development metrics to fully quantify our findings, the results of the study clearly show that software requirements can be formalized effectively and economically, yielding significant improvements over the existing development process.

Acknowledgments

The authors would like to thank Albert Loe, Steve Okun, Avinash Persaud, and Shawn Turner of Nortel for their technical assistance and continual support throughout the study. We are also grateful to the anonymous referees for suggesting ways to improve the paper. The study was supported in part by Nortel Networks, NSERC, and Ontario Graduate Scholarship (OGS).

References

[1] ANSI/IEEE. "IEEE 830: IEEE Recommended Practice for Software Requirements Specifications ". *IEEE*, 1993.

[2] Aonix. "Aonix Home Page". http://www.aonix.com, September 1998.

[3] F. Belina, D. Hogrefe, and A. Sarma. *SDL with Applications from Protocol Specification*. Prentice Hall, 1991.

[4] UML Partners Consortium. "UML Proposal Document Set". *OMG documents ad/97-08-{02,03,04,05,06,07,08,09}*, September 1997.

[5] J. Crow and B.L. Di Vito. "Formalizing Space Shuttle Software Requirements". In *Workshop on Formal Methods in Software Practice*, San Diego, California, January 1996.

[6] R.E. Davis and R.L. Danielson. "Practically Formal Methods". In *Proceedings of International Conference on Software Engineering: Education and Practices*, pages 168–175. IEEE Computer Society Press, January 1996.

[7] Steve Easterbrook, Robyn Lutz, Richard Covington, John Kelly, Yoko Ampo, and David Hamilton. "Experience Using Lightweight Formal Methods for Requirements Modeling". *IEEE Transactions on Software Engineering*, 24(1):4–14, January 1998.

[8] Christian Facchi, Markus Haubner, and Ursula Hinkel. The SDL Specification of the Sliding Window Protocol Revisited. Technical Report TUM-I9614, Technische Univerität München, 1996.

[9] M.S. Feather. "Rapid Application of Lightweight Formal Methods for Consistency Analysis". *IEEE Transactions on Software Engineering*, November 1998.

[10] M.W. Froberg. "Automatic Code Generation from SDL to a Declarative Programming Language". In *Proceedings of the Sixth SDL Forum*, Darmstadt, Germany, October 1993.

[11] M. Grasmanis and I. Medvedis. "Approach to Behaviour Specification and Automated Test Generation for Telephone Exchange Systems". In *Proceedings of the Fifth SDL Forum*, Glasgow, Scotland, September 1991.

[12] Anthony Hall. "Using Formal Methods to Develop an ATC Information System". *IEEE Software*, 13(2), March 1996.

[13] Mats P.E. Heimdahl. "Lessons from the Analysis of TCAS II". In *Proceedings of the International Symposium on Software Testing and Analysis (ISSTA '96)*, San Diego, CA, January 1996.

[14] Constance Heitmeyer. "One the Need for Practical Formal Methods". In *Proceedings of 5th Int. Symp. on Real-time and Real-time Fault Tolerant Systems (FTRTFT'98)*, pages 18–26, 1998. LICS 1486.

[15] Jonathan P. Hoare. "Application of the B-Method to CICS". In M. G. Hinchey and J. P. Bowen, editors, *Applications of Formal Methods*, pages 97–124. Prentice Hall International Series in Computer Science, 1995.

[16] ITU-T. "ITU-T Recommendation Z.100: Specification and Description Language (SDL)". *ITU-T*, 1993.

[17] ITU-T. "ITU-T Recommendation Z.120: Message Sequence Chart (MSC)". *ITU-T*, 1993.

[18] Daniel Jackson and Jeannette Wing. "Lighweight Formal Methods". *IEEE Computer*, April 1996.

[19] Paul K. Joannou. "Experiences from Application of Digital Systems in Nuclear Power Plants". In *Proceedings of the Digital Systems Reliability and Nuclear Safety Workshop*, Rockville, Maryland, 1993.

[20] Cliff B. Jones. "An Invitation to Formal Methods: A Rigorous Approach to Formal Methods". *IEEE Computer*, 20(4):19, April 1996.

[21] Barbara Ann Kitchenham. "Evaluating Software Engineering Methods and Tools. Part 1". *ACM SIGSOFT Software Engineering Notes*, 21(1):11–15, January 1996.

[22] L. Mansson. "High Level Specification of a Telecom Application with SDL'92". In *Proceedings of the Sixth SDL Forum*, Darmstadt, Germany, October 1993.

[23] Peter Mataga and Pamela Zave. "Multiparadigm Specification of an AT&T Switching System". In M. G. Hinchey and J. P. Bowen, editors, *Applications of Formal Methods*, pages 375–398. Prentice Hall International Series in Computer Science, 1995.

[24] M.Kooij and L. Provoost. "Industrial Report on the Use of Abstraction in SDL/MSC". In *First Workshop of the SDL Forum Society on SDL and MSC*, Berlin, Germany, June 1998. alcatel.

[25] D.L. Parnas. "Some Theorems We Should Prove". In *Proceedings of 1993 International Conference on HOL Theorem Proving and Its Applications*, Vancouver, BC, August 1993.

[26] A. Sarma. "Modelling Broadband ISDN Protocols with SDL". In *Proceedings of the Fifth SDL Forum*, Glasgow, Scotland, September 1989.

[27] Telelogic. "Telelogic SDT Home Page". http://www.telelogic.com/solution/tools/sdt.asp, September 1998.

[28] Teradyne. "TestMaster Home Page". http://www.teradyne.com/prods/sst/ssthome.html, September 1998.

[29] H.J. Vgel, W. Kellerer, S. Karg, M. Kober, A. Beckert, and G. Einfalt. "SDL based prototyping of ISDN-DECT-PBX switching software". In *First Workshop of the SDL Forum Society on SDL and MSC*, Berlin, Germany, June 1998.

[30] Debora Weber-Wulff. "Selling Formal Methods to Industry". In J.C.P. Woodcock and P.G. Larsen, editors, *Proceedings of FME'93: Industrial Benefit of Formal Methods, First International Symposium of Formal Methods Europe*, pages 671–678, Odense, Denmark, April 1993. Springer-Verlag.

[31] Andre Wong. "The Diary of the Formal-Method Survey". http://www.cs.toronto.edu/~andre/progress.html, September 1998.

[32] Andre Wong. *"Formalizing Requirements in a Commercial Setting: A Case Study"*. M.Sc. thesis, University of Toronto, Department of Computer Science, Toronto, ON, Canada, 1999. (In preparation).

[33] Marvin V. Zelkowitz and Dolores R. Wallace. "Experimental Models for Validating Technology". *IEEE Computer*, 31(5), May 1998.

A   An SDL Block Diagram

The diagram below illustrates the SDL block diagram of the telephony application shown in Figure 1. The "driver" block (which contains a "driver" process) acts as the signal router between the environment and the SDL blocks of the voice-service components by routing the signal lists *inputSigLst* and *output-SigLst*. It is also responsible for activating the appropriate component according to the control-flow of the application and actions from the caller by using the signal *activate*. Please refer to Section 4 for more details.

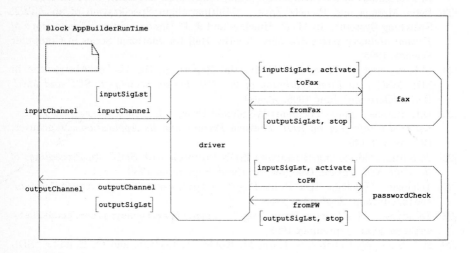

B   A Message Sequence Chart

The MSC below shows the interactions between a caller and a telephony application in ServiceCreator. The application requires a caller to press button *1* in the menu component prior to entering the password-check component. Refer to Section 4.2 for more details.

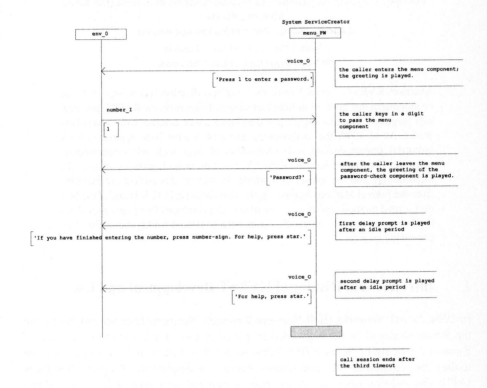

KVEST: Automated Generation of Test Suites from Formal Specifications

Igor Burdonov[1], Alexander Kossatchev[1], Alexander Petrenko[1], and Dmitri Galter[2]

[1]Institute for System Programming of Russian Academy of Science (ISP RAS),
Moscow, Russia
{Igor, Kos, Petrenko}@ispras.ru
[2]Nortel Networks, Ottawa, Canada
Galter@nortelnetworks.com

Abstract. KVEST - Kernel VErification and Specification Technology - is based on automated test generation from formal specifications in the RAISE specification language. The technology was developed under contract with Nortel Networks. As of 1999, the methodology and toolset have been applied in three industrial project dealing with verification of large-scale telecommunication software. The first project, the Kernel Verification project, gives its name to the methodology and the toolset as a whole. Results of this project are available from the Formal Methods Europe Application database [13]. It is one of the biggest formal method application presented in the database. This paper provides a brief description of the approach, comparison to related works, and statistics on completed projects.

1   Introduction. History of KVEST Development and Use

In 1994, Nortel Networks (Bell-Northern Research, Northern Telecom and Nortel are the former names of Nortel Networks) proposed Institute for System Programming of Russian Academy of Science (ISP RAS) to develop a methodology and supporting toolset for automation of conformance testing of Application Program Interfaces (API). The real-time operating system (OS) kernel was selected as a first practical target for the methodology. ISP was to rigorously describe software contract definition of the kernel and produce test suites for the kernel conformance testing.

The success of this work would allow Nortel to automate conformance testing for the next OS kernel porting and for the new release of the OS. In addition, Nortel would be able to improve its product software structure as a whole, since during software contract definition, ISP promised to establish minimal and orthogonal set of interfaces for the OS kernel.

ISP organized a joint group of researchers and developers. The team members had rich experience in operating system design, real-time systems, compiler development, and formal specification use in a systematic approach for design and testing [2, 9,10].

During the first half year, ISP developed the first version of the Kernel Interface Layer (KIL) contents and conducted a comparison analysis of the available specification methodologies. The KIL contents were approved with slight modifications. RSL (RAISE Specification Language) [11,12] was selected as the most suitable specification language.

J. Wing, J. Woodcock, J. Davies (Eds.): FM'99, Vol. I, LNCS 1708, pp. 608-621, 1999.

During next half year, ISP developed a first draft of the specification and test generation methodology and developed a prototype version of the specifications and test oracle generator. The prototype demonstrated the possibility to use formal specifications in industrial software development. Implicit specification was selected as the main kind of specification. The base principles of test coverage analysis were established. KVEST methodology uses a modification of FDNF (Full Disjunctive Normal Form) criteria for the partition of input space, test coverage and test strategy.

During the second year, product version of the specifications and tools for test generation and execution were completed. From mid-1996 to the beginning of 1997, the majority of the test suites were produced and the OS kernel was successfully tested. The number of detected latent errors exceeded expectations.

2   Terms and Basic Notions

Let there be some software system containing the functionally closed set of procedures. We need to determine the elements and functional specifications of its external interfaces, constituting the software contract, and to develop a set of test suites suitable for conformance testing of the software contract implementation. Since the elements of the software contract are procedures, we can say that this is in fact API (Application Programming Interface) testing. Here and below we will say that the API consists of a set of procedures. There are other kinds of API entities like operations, functions, methods (in C++), subroutines in Fortran, etc. We consider all the terms synonyms and will use the term *procedure* in this paper.

Let us note that we are not talking about testing some specific implementation of the software contract. It was important to build a methodology allowing to verify correctness of the software behaviour without introducing any extra limitations on the internal structure of the implementation. To stress this very important requirement, we call our specifications implementation independent.

Let us introduce some terminology. The whole software system used in the process of test execution and communicating with the system under test (SUT), is called the *test harness*. Sometimes, instead of SUT, we will use the term *target system*. The main part of the test harness is the *test drivers*. To enable the functionality of the test drivers, we need a run-time support system, which is often called a *test bed*. The test drivers are usually developed with the SUT specifics in mind while the test bed is independent of the SUT functionality.

We consider two levels of test drivers. A *basic driver* is a test driver for some target procedure that performs the following actions:

- checks that pre-conditions for the target procedure hold for a given tuple of input parameters;
- calls the target procedure with a given tuple of input parameter and records corresponding output parameters;
- assigns a verdict on the correctness of the target procedure execution results;
- collects information necessary to estimate the test coverage or investigate reasons for a fault.

A *script driver* is a test driver for some target procedure, or a set of target procedures, that performs the following actions:

- reads test options;

- generates sets of input parameters based on test options;

- calls a basic driver with some set of input parameters;

- does extra checking, if necessary, of the correctness of the target procedure execution results and assigns a verdict;

- checks if desired test coverage is complete and if not, continues to generate sets of input parameters and call the basic driver with this tuple.

A *test plan* is a program that defines the order of script driver calls with the given test options and checks the script driver call conditions and termination correctness.

Besides the set of basic and script drivers and test plan interpreter, the test harness also contains a repository and tools for test plan execution and querying the results kept in repository. The repository contains information about all test executions, code coverage metrics for different procedures with different test coverage criteria, and all situations when test drivers assigned a negative verdict.

3 KVEST Overview

KVEST methodology consists of the following steps:

- Software contract content definition;

- Specification development;

- Test suite production;

- Test execution and test result analysis.

3.1   Software Contract Content Definition

Goals:

- to provide the minimal and orthogonal interface;

- to hide internal data structures and implementation details.

Following these goals we can minimize the restrictions on the possible implementation solutions and the knowledge needed to use the software, and make it possible to develop long-term living test suites for conformance testing.

3.2   Specification Development

Goals:

- to rigorously describe functionality;

- to provide an input for test generation.

Based on the specification, KVEST can fully automatically generate the basic drivers.

3.3   Test Suite Production

Goals:

- to develop the so-called "manually developed" components (MDC) of test suites;
- to generate test suites.

Most of the MDCs are convertors between model and implementation data representation, test data structure initiators, and iterators. Based on the MDCs and the specifications, KVEST generates test suites as a whole. No customization is required once the generation is complete.

3.4   Test Execution and Test Result Analysis

Requirements of the tool for test execution and analysis are as follows:

- to automate test execution;
- to collect trace data and to calculate obtained test coverage;
- to provide browsing and navigation facilities;
- to recover the "incremental testing" target system after a fault or a crash, and to continue test execution from the point of interruption.

3.5   Specification Approach

Let us consider the specification approach in more detail. KVEST uses model-oriented specification in implicit (pre- and post- condition) form as the main form of specification. More exotic RAISE features like axiom, algebraic specifications and channels are not used in the formal specification but are used in semi-formal considerations and explanations.

Concrete examples of implicit specifications are shown below.

3.6   Testing Approach

To develop a test driver we have to solve three problems:

- how to generate an oracle, i.e. a program that assigns a verdict on the correctness of outcome for the target procedure;
- how to estimate completeness of the test coverage;
- how to enumerate combinations of the test input data.

Test oracles are very similar to post-conditions. Both functions are Boolean. They have the same parameters, and return True if the target procedure produces correct result and False otherwise. So, the generation of test oracles is quite feasible once we have the post-conditions.

Test coverage criterion is a metric defined in terms of implementation or specification. The most well known test coverage criteria in terms of implementation are:

- C1 - all statements are passed;
- C2 - all branches are passed.

In case of specification use for test coverage criteria definition, the so called domain testing approach is used. The whole input space is partitioned into areas. Each area corresponds to a class of equivalence. The partition could be derived from the specification that describes requirements on input and properties of outcome for target procedures. Both the requirements and the properties are clearly represented in pre- and post-conditions of formal specifications in implicit form. So, based on the implicit specification, we can successfully solve the problem of test coverage estimation.

There are sceptics who think that full coverage of domains, even including interesting points like a boundary layer, does not guarantee good coverage of the implementation code. Our experience shows that the average percentage of KVEST test coverage is 70% to 100% of statements in the implementation.

We distinguish two levels of the test coverage criteria. The first one is the coverage of all branches in post-conditions. The second one is the coverage of all disjuncts (elementary conjunctions) in the Full Disjunctive Normal Form (FDNF) representation of the post-condition while taking into account the pre-condition terms. KVEST allows partitioning in terms of specification branches and FDNF to be made fully automatically. One of the most difficult problems is the calculation of accessible FDNF disjuncts and removing the inaccessible FDNF disjuncts. This problem is solved in KVEST by a special technique in pre-condition design.

Monitoring of obtained test coverage is conducted on the fly by script drivers. Based on this data, the script driver may tune testing parameters and/or testing duration.

4   Test Generation Techniques

4.1   API Classification

First we should consider a classification of API. The classification determines the choice of one of the test generation techniques applicable to a procedure interface or interface of a procedure group.

We consider five main classes of API and some extensions of classes including interfaces tested in parallel and expected exceptions.

The classes are organized hierarchically. The first class establishes the strongest requirements. Each following class weakens the requirements. The requirements for the five classes are as follows:

Kind 1. The input is data that could be represented in literal (textual) form and can be produced without accounting for any interdependencies between the values of different parameters. Such procedures can be tested separately because no other target procedure is needed to generate input parameters and analyze the outcome.

Examples of interdependencies will be shown below.

Kind 2. No interdependencies exist between the input items (values of input parameters). Input does not have to be in literal form. Such procedures can be tested separately.

Example: Procedures with the pointer type input parameters.

Kind 3. Some interdependencies exist, however separate testing is possible.

Example: A procedure with two parameters, the first one is array, the second one is a value in the array.

Kind 4. The procedures cannot be tested separately, because some input can be produced only by calling another procedure from the group and/or some outcome can be analyzed only by calling other procedures.

Example: A procedure that provide stack operations and that receives the stack as a parameter.

Kind 5. The procedures cannot be tested separately. Part of the input and output data is hidden and user does not have direct access to data.

Example: Instances of OO classes with internal states; a group of procedures that share a variable not visible to the procedure user.

Exception raising extension of API classes. The specific kind of procedures that raise exceptions as a correct reaction to certain inputs.

Example: A procedure that is supposed to raise an exception after dividing by zero. If zero received as an input parameter, then this procedure must not return any return code.

4.2   Script Driver Scheme. Example of Kind 5

The above taxonomy is a good basis for the classification of test generation techniques. Kind 1 allows full automation of test generation. All other kinds need some additional effort for MDC writing. The effort gradually grows from kind 2 to kind 5. The extensions require more effort than the corresponding kinds themselves.

Complexity and effort of the MDC development is caused by the complexity of script driver writing and debugging. Below we consider only one scheme of script drivers used for kind 5 API testing. All script drivers have similar structure. The main distinction is the distribution between automatically generated components and MDCs. The kind 1 script driver is generated fully automatically, kind 2 script driver - almost automatically and so on.

The script driver is a program that is composed and compiled by KVEST. The general scheme of the script driver is defined by a formal description called a *skeleton*. The skeletons are specific to each kind of API. Each script driver consists of declarations and a body. The declarations are generated automatically based on the list of procedures under test and their specifications. The declarations include import of the procedure under test and its data structure definitions and/or import of all data and types used in the specifications.

The body of a script driver begins with the script driver option parsing. The options - parameters of the script driver as a whole - determine the depth of testing (i.e. the level of test coverage criteria, and some specific data like interval of values, duration of testing, etc.).

Before testing starts some initialization is required. For example, before testing write/read procedures we have to open a file. Such initializations are written manually. After initialization is finished, the main part of the script driver begins.

The kind 5 script driver realizes a general algorithm for traversing an abstract Finite State Machine (FSM). The goal of the algorithm is to pass all states and all possible transitions between the states. Each transition corresponds to an execution of a procedure under test.

The aforementioned data are the data used in the formal specification, the so-called *model data*. The algorithm of a script driver is related to the specification and does not depend on the implementation details outside the specification.

The most interesting aspect of the script driver algorithm is the absence of direct descriptions of the abstract FSM. Direct specification of the FSM requires extra effort, so KVEST avoids this. There are some attempts to extract FSM specification from the implicit specification [1,7]. However, no one yet can provide a fully automated way for such extraction.

Instead of a direct specification of FSM, KVEST uses its indirect, virtual representation. Such representation consists of a function-observer and a function-iterator. The function-observer calculates on the fly the current state in the abstract FSM. The function-iterator selects the next procedure from the group and generates a tuple of the input parameter values for this procedure.

Let us consider the kind 5 script driver algorithm in more detail. For example, suppose we are testing a procedure group. Say, we have passed several FSM states, which means we have called some target procedures. Now we are going to make the next transition. This elementary cycle of testing consists of the following steps:

- Calling a function-iterator that selects the next procedure from the group and prepares a tuple of input parameter values for this target procedure.

- If the iterators have managed to generate a new and correct tuple without violation of pre-conditions, then the script driver calls a corresponding basic driver with the tuple as actual parameters.

- When the basic driver returns, the control script driver checks the verdict assigned by the basic driver.

- If the verdict is False (an error has been detected), the script driver produces corresponding trace data and finishes.

- If the verdict is True (the elementary test case passed), the script driver calls the function-observer that calculates a current state, logs the state and transition and continues to traverse FSM.

Thus, we obtain all possible states and test the procedures with all needed sets of input parameters. FSM is used here as a guideline to pass through all states the needed number of times.

4.3   Test Suite Composition

Let us come back to the issue of the composition of MDCs and automatically generated components. Script drivers are composed following the requirements of the corresponding skeletons. Overall, we need five skeletons for serial testing of API kinds 1 through 5; one skeleton for parallel testing, and five skeletons for exception raising testing. Based on a corresponding skeleton and the list of target procedures and specifications, KVEST generates the script driver template. For kind 1, this template is a ready-to-use program. For the other kinds, the template includes several nests with default initiators and iterators. If a test designer does not need to add or improve anything in the nests, the template can be compiled and executed. This situation is typical for a kind 2 API. For other kinds, the test designer usually has to add some specific initiators and iterators. In any case, he or she should define FSM state observer for the script drivers of kinds 4 and 5.

The basic drivers invoked by the script drivers are generated fully automatically. The only MDCs called from basic drivers are data converters. As mentioned above, the converters transform the model data representation into the implementation representation and vice versa. A model representation is distinguished from the implementation one by the level of abstraction. For example, models may use "infinite" representation of integers, maps, relations, and other data structures suitable for specification. Sometimes model representation is very similar to the implementation one. In this case, such transformation is done by standard translation algorithm of the specification language into the implementation language.

KVEST uses implementation language independent test generators. All generators use only RSL texts as input and output. The only component written in the implementation language is the data converters. This component is out of the scope of the test generators. So, the test generation process first produces a full test suite in RSL, and then the RSL source is compiled into the implementation language. To port a KVEST test suite from one implementation language platform to another, a user should rewrite the data converters and provide RSL to the implementation language compiler, as well as a run-time support system with test bed functions.

5   Project Result Discussion and Conclusions

5.1   KVEST Applications and Statistics

As of early 1999, three projects have been completed using the KVEST technology. The first two were pursuing only code verification [3], while the third one included the re-design of old code and development of the new implementation. In all three projects, formal specifications for software contracts and test suites for conformance testing were developed.

The research on KVEST technology was conducted starting in the middle of 1994. The first year was spent on selecting the specification language, development of specification methodology principles allowing to use it in industrial-strength projects, test methodology principles and specification based test generation. At the end of the first year of research, prototype specifications of one fifth of the real OS kernel and prototype of one of the main technology tools (generator of basic drivers with test oracles) were developed.

In September 1995, works on the production version of the toolset started. Also, development of industrial specifications and the complete automated testing system was begun.

Below we provide a brief description of the three completed projects and some statistics.

A. Kernel Verification Project (Product Phase).
Target software: OS kernel of the large-scale telecommunication system.
Time period: September 1995 - February 1997.

Goals:

- to define the orthogonal and minimal interface layer of the OS kernel;
- to conduct reverse-engineering and develop formal specifications of the interface layer in RSL;
- to develop a toolset for the automated test generation and test execution;
- to generate test suites for the conformance testing of the OS kernel.

B. Feature Processing Environment (FPE) Verification Project.
Target software: Base level of call processing system;
Time period: August 1997 - December 1997.

Goals:

- to conduct reverse-engineering and develop formal specifications;
- to generate test suites.

C. Queue Utilities Re-design and Verification Project.
Target software: Management of tree-like store for queues with different disciplines.
Time period: August 1998 - December 1998.

Goals:

- to conduct reverse-engineering and develop formal specifications;
- to re-design the legacy implementation;
- to generate test suites.

Table 1: KVEST methodology statistics

Project	Size of target system in KLOC	Specifi-cation in KLOC	Generated test suites in KLOC	Effort in man months	Personal performance in KLOC per man month
Kernel Verification	200	50	900	108	1.8[a]
FPE verification	35	15	150	16	2.2
Queue utility redesign and verification[b]	9	2	90	9	1.0

a. includes tool development
b. includes re-design and re-implementation of the software in addition to analysis
    and verification. This explains the additional effort.

5.2 Related Works

In this section, we will discuss the related systems that, on one hand, build the verification process on the formal specifications, and, on the other hand, propose a rather generic technological scheme. We will not discuss the systems that propose the solutions to the specific problems that have certain theoretical value but fail attempts to introduce them in the process of verification of the industrial-strength software.

ITEX - Interactive TTCN Editor and eXecutor [14].
ITEX is a test environment for communicating systems. It includes a TTCN and ASN.1 analysis and design tool, a test simulator and support for generation of complete Executable Test Suites (ETS). Here is a brief ITEX functionality summary:

*   A Test Suite is made up of Test Cases in form of tables;

*   ITEX provides a set of highly integrated tools for development and maintenance of Abstract Test Suites (ATS) written in TTCN;

*   ITEX supports the following phases of Test Suite development: Test Case Generation, Editing, Verification, Validation and Execution.

This toolset is well integrated with SDT, an environment for design of SDL specifications. Test suites described with TTCN can be transformed to the form that allows testing both implementation in some programming language and specification in SDL.

The main shortcoming of this approach in context of our research is that it is unsuitable for API testing. TTCN does not permit declaration of pointers and other software entities that do not have textual (literal) representation.

A very serious limitation of SDL-like specifications is their explicit form. This means that it is quite easy to build models and prototypes based on them but it is very difficult to develop a system of constraints that define the union of all possible implementations. Implicit specifications overcome this problem.

ADL/ADL2 [15].

This approach is the most similar to the our group's works. From formal specifications, ADL generates test oracles and skeletons for building test drivers and documentation. A not very fundamental, but still interesting difference between ADL and KVEST is that it uses not one of the popular specification languages but extensions of C and C++ languages. In the Kernel Verification project, SPP, a similar extension of the target language, was developed during the prototyping phase. A similar kind of extension was also proposed by Liskov and Guttag[6]. There are ideas on extensions of Java and other object-oriented languages aimed at developing software in "Design-by-Contract" fashion [5]. However, despite the obvious advantages of better acceptance of such languages in the software engineering community, the concept, not to mention the common notation, is still far in the future.

The difference of the KVEST results compared to the ADL results can be explained by the difference in the range of API classes for which these methodologies can provide means for specification and automatic test generation. ADL provides adequate tools for test generation automation only for procedures whose parameters allow independent enumeration and allows testing procedures one by one. In KVEST classification, these are APIs of the first and second kind. This means that procedures with dependent parameters, procedures that require testing in a group, e.g., "open - close", or those that require testing in parallel mode, e.g., "lock - unlock", or "send - receive", are omitted. Besides, ADL does not recognize the first kind of API that permits automatic generation of the complete test suite including test case parameters and test oracles.

An interesting part of ADL is its capability to generate the natural language documentation. It is important to note that the same mechanism is used for both documentation of the target system and documentation of the test suites. It seems that the ADL authors made a conscious choice of not using any of the technologies from the Natural Language Generation field. It is easy to explain in pragmatic sense, however, it does not mean that modern natural language generation methods cannot help in the generation of the software documentation. KVEST capabilities in documentation generation are implemented in the prototype version. Still, as opposed to ADL, KVEST uses computer grammar and English dictionary for analysis and generation of natural language fragments that allows it to reduce the number of natural language errors and make the text more readable without any manual work.

ADL2 went further than KVEST in its capability of specification and testing of OO classes. This KVEST shortcoming can be explained by a corresponding RSL weakness. Extending KVEST to OO software verification is a task for 1999.

Using Test Oracles Generated from Program Documentation [8]

This work is research and as such it can not be considered a technology ready to use in industry. The main interest in this research is the analysis of difficulties and limitations that, in the authors' opinion, prevent the wide use of formal specifications during automatic testing of industrial software. D. Peters and D. Parnas and us arrived to the common understanding that those are the key problems in the task of testing automation based on formal specifications. KVEST continued research in this direction and proposed a technological scheme for partial automation of test suite development for all kinds of API.

Formal Derivation of Finite State Machines for Class Testing [7].

This work is also at the research stage. At the same time, this work is interesting in the sense that it proposes a scheme for organization of procedure group testing similar to the scheme used in KVEST. Object-Z is used as a specification language and C++ as a programming language. The task is stated as follows: to built test suites to verify conformance of the implementation to the specification using formal specifications of the methods for a class. As a test coverage criterion, the union of two criteria is used: to cover all equivalence classes that represent the areas obtained as a result of partition analysis, and then, to check results on or near the boundaries.

The authors of this work do not try to solve the problem of complete automation of test generation. Nor do they attempt to support any elements of the preparation phase with tools. Still, all the steps are described in a very systematic way and can be boiled down to various specification transformations.

Partition and boundary analysis is done manually according to the methodology proposed by the authors. In a similar way, they build the specification of oracles. Oracles, once compiled into C++, call target procedures and verify the conformance of the results to the specifications.

The most interesting part is the testing scheme which is a framework that dynamically generates test sequences of procedure calls. The framework is controlled by the FSM description which represents an abstraction of the state transition graph of the test class. The authors describe the methodology of building specifications for the classes of states and transitions between them while considering the problem of exclusion of inaccessible states.

The theoretical weakness of this approach is that it does not try to come up with a formal methodology to build transformation specifications. It is obvious that serious problems will be encountered when attempting to apply this method recommendations to the specifications of real-life complexity. In practical sense, it is clear that the process of test derivation from the specifications is mostly manual activity which limits its applicability to industrial software.

The main difference between KVEST and this work is that during testing KVEST does not need the full description of the Finite State Machine that models the states of the system under test. Instead, KVEST proposes a universal algorithm that can dynamically provide all accessible states and all possible transitions between state pairs.

5.3   Kernel Verification Prospects

The most effort-consuming work in the KVEST verification process is the reverse-engineering and specification development. This work is currently being automated. The basic idea of the approach is gradual *upwarding* of data representation in defined implementations. Upwarding is increasing of the level of abstraction [4].

During 1998, ISP conducted initial work in natural language documentation generation. The result of the experiment was a prototype demo that had been presented at the ZUM'98 conference (Berlin, September 1998).

The prototype synthesizes UNIX-like "man"-page documentation based on formal and informal components of specification. The prototype demonstrated the possibility of generating actual documentation. The consistency of the documentation is checked by means of a test execution generated from the same source, the RSL specification. This work is currently being continued to extend the variety of documentation forms and to produce more fluent natural language.

5.4   Conclusions and Future Works

KVEST experience shows that formal methods can be used in industrial software production. Level of complexity and size of KVEST applications support this thesis.

An interesting fact was derived from KVEST experience. Errors detected in KVEST projects are distributed into three categories of almost equal size. One third of errors is detected during reverse-engineering and formal specification development. Another third is detected during test execution. The analysis of the test execution results allows the detection of the typical situation that cause the wrong behaviour. Based on the analysis during repeat code inspections, we detected the last third of errors.

Note 1. Code inspection in composition with formal specification, so called "formal code inspection", can detect up to one third of the errors. Note that these errors are the most dangerous.

Note 2. Code inspection can not replace testing. Up to two thirds of errors are detected during and after testing.

Note 3. Testing is necessary to develop correct specifications. During script driver debugging, up to a half of all detected errors were the errors in the specifications. Thus, formal methods must be supported by technologies that compare formal method results with actual software by executing the target software.

The next consideration is related to the distribution of error causes. Up to one third of the errors were caused by the lack of knowledge on pre-conditions and some details of the called procedures' behavior. Because pre-conditions and variants of possible procedure behavior were not described sufficiently, users could call procedures in the wrong situations and not expect strange procedure reactions. Establishing software contracts and systematic description of the API allows the number of errors to be decreased by up to 30%.

Acknowledgments

We are pleased to acknowledge Spencer Cheng, who initiated this work and formulated the task definition; Helene Wong, who was the first team leader from Nortel side and suggested the title "Kernel Verification"; Lynn Marshall, who supervises and helps us; Marc Granic, Henri Balter, Brian Brummund and Victor Ivannikov, who provide senior management support; Richard Krol and John Shannon, who sponsored initial phases of KVEST development; and KVEST developers and users, who made a lot of contributions in clarification of KVEST approach and helped achieving goals that seemed absolutely non-realistic five years ago.

References

1. B. Algayres, Y. Lejeune, G. Hugonnet, and F. Hantz. The AVALON project: A VALidation Environment For SDL/MSC Descriptions. In *6th SDL Forum*, Darmstadt, 1993.
2. I. Burdonov, V. Ivannikov, A. Kossatchev, G. Kopytov, S. Kuznetsov. The CLOS Project: Towards an Object-Oriented Envirinment for Application Development. In *Next Generation Information System Technology, Lecture Notes in Computer Science*, Vol. 504, Springer Verlag, 1991, pp. 422-427.
3. I. Burdonov, A. Kossatchev, A. Petrenko, S. Cheng, H. Wong. Formal Specification and Verification of SOS Kernel, *BNR/Nortel Design Forum*, June 1996.
4. J. Derrick and E. Boiten. Testing Refining Test. *Lecture Notes in Computer Science*, 1493, pp. 265-283.
5. R.Kramer. iContract - The Java Design by Contract Tool. *Fourth conference on OO technology and systems (COOTS)*, 1998.
6. B. Liskov, J. Guttag. *Abstraction and Specification in Program Development*. The MIT Press, McGraw-Hill Book Company, 1986.
7. L. Murray, D. Carrington, I. MacColl, J. McDonald, P. Strooper. Formal Derivation of Finite State Machines for Class Testing. In *Lecture Notes in Computer Science*, 1493, pp. 42-59.
8. D. Peters, D. Parnas. Using Test Oracles Generated from Program Documentation. *IEEE Transactions on Software Engineering*, Vol. 24, No. 3, pp. 161-173.
9. A. K. Petrenko. Test specification based on trace description. *Software and Programming, (translated from "Programmirovanie")*, No. 1, Jan.-Feb. 1992, pp. 26-31.
10. A. K. Petrenko. Methods of debugging and monitoring of parallel programs. *Software and Programming*, No. 3, 1994.
11. The RAISE Language Group. *The RAISE Specification Language*. Prentice Hall, 1992.
12. The RAISE Language Group. *The RAISE Development Method*. Prentice Hall, 1995.

Internet resources.
13. http://www.fme-nl.org/fmadb088.html
14. http://www.kvatro.no/products/itex/itex.htm
15. http://www.sun.com/960201/cover/language.html

Feature Interaction Detection Using Testing and Model-Checking Experience Report

Lydie du Bousquet

Laboratoire LSR-IMAG, BP 72,
38402 Saint Martin d'Hères cedex, France
tel: +33 4 76 82 72 32, fax: +33 4 76 82 72 87
ldubousq@imag.fr
http://www-imag.lsr.fr/

Abstract. We present an experiment in feature interaction detection. We studied the 12 features defined for the first feature interaction contest held in association with the 5th international Feature Interaction Workshop. We used a synchronous approach for modeling features, and both, a model-checker and a test generator for revealing interactions. The first part of the paper describes the feature modeling. The second part deals with the feature interaction detection carried out with a testing tool, and the last part addresses the use of a model-checker for the detection.

1 Introduction

Telecommunication software is a variety of safety-critical software. Its requirements in terms of dependability are high since a malfunction may result in environment harm. The disastrous financial consequences of failures impose on this kind of software strong correctness and quality of service constraints.

This is why modeling, analysis and risk assessment activities take a large part of its development process. For critical components, the requirements engineering phase usually ends in a formal specification which is provided in some logics; therefore, validation can be performed in a very rigorous and formal way using proof tools and/or specification-based testing techniques. Examples of such critical pieces are protocols and telephone services.

The expansion of new telephone supplementary services (called features) has reinforced the need for formal, mathematically sound and well equiped specification and validation techniques. Indeed, a new supplementary service can change the behavior of pre-existing ones, alter them, or even crash the system. The phenomena are known as the "feature interaction problem" in the telecommunication industry [9].

Besides, one can note that a telecommunication system has most of the characteristics of reactive programs [18]. Such programs continuously react with their environment at their own speed. They must satisfy some strong timing dependencies between external events and their role is to bring about or maintain desired relationships in the environment.

J. Wing, J. Woodcock, J. Davies (Eds.): FM'99, Vol. I, LNCS 1708, pp. 622–641, 1999.

We applied a reactive synchronous approach to the feature validation problem, using Lustre [6]. Lustre is an executable specification language which can be used for programming and formally verifying (using model-checking) [11] as well as for testing [7] synchronous critical software.

In 1998, Nancy Griffeth et al. organized the first feature interaction detection tool contest [10]. This contest was held for the 5th International Workshop on Feature Interactions. We participated in this contest and our tool won the "Best Tool Award". Our approach consisted in two major points: a synchronous technology to express a model of a telecommunication system and using test techniques to detect feature interactions.

We decided to favor a testing approach for a couple of reasons.

(1) Feature interaction detection can be viewed as finding some errors in a program, and testing is the process of executing a program with the intent of finding errors [15]. Moreover, testing allows to establish the fitness or the worth of a software product for its operational mission, and interaction occurrences are strongly connected to the telecom system operations [3].

(2) It is our experience that model-checking often fails for lack of time or memory. Besides, model-checking is not appropriate to evaluate the adequacy of a property. When searching for interaction and no interaction is found, the relevance of the property must be questioned. Deciding on this relevance can be easily performed using a testing tool.

We have applied a model-checker to confirm the results which have been obtained with our testing tool, contrary to most situations where testing and proving (by deduction or model-checking) are jointly used.

In this paper, we first sum up the contest instructions (section 2). Then, we describe the synchronous approach (section 3). In sections 4 and 5, we detail three major points of our model: our definition of interaction, our approach principles and our feature composition operation. Section 6 describes the first part of our validation experiment using a test generator, and section 7 describes the second part of the validation experiment using a model-checker on the same model.

2 Feature Interaction Detection Tool Contest

The goal of this contest was to compare different feature interaction detection tools according to a single benchmark collection of twelve features. The contest had two phases. The first one required the contestants to analyze the ten first features in a five month period. The second phase required the analysis of the two last features, in sixteen days.

The contest instructions were made of the description of a network model, given as a collection of black boxes communicating with each other via defined interfaces, the description of a feature description formalism, the specification of the basic call service feature, and an informal description and the specification of the twelve features to be examined.

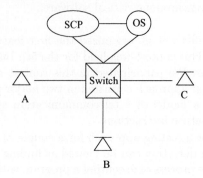

Fig. 1. The network specification

The network consists of 4 types of elements (fig. 1): some end-user equipments (telephones), a Switch, a Service Control Point (SCP) processing IN features, and an Operations System (OS) that does the billing.

A user can perform 4 actions: go off the hook, go on the hook, dial a number, a flash-hook. The telephones are assumed to have a flash button.

A service formal specification is represented as a Chisel sequence diagram [1]. Such a diagram is a directed graph whose vertices are labeled by events or messages exchanged at the various interfaces. A diagram defines the set of event sequences of a single call, one for each path through the graph. Event sequences involving multiple calls can be interleaved to define the global system activity. Figure 2 represents the Plain Old Telephone Service (POTS) diagram which stands for two phones and a single call, originated by party A.

3   Synchronous Approach and Lustre Language

To enter the contest, we have used a synchronous framework. In this section, we describe the synchronous approach.

3.1   The Synchronous Software Technology

Synchronous programs [2] are a sub-class of reactive software programs: every reaction of a program to its inputs is theoretically instantaneous. Synchronous programs have cyclic behaviors: at each tick of a global clock (also called instant of time), all inputs are read and all outputs are emitted.

Synchronous languages rely on the ideal synchrony hypothesis, which says that synchronous machines have zero-time response delay and synchronous systems are systems of dynamical equations. Practically, the synchrony hypothesis

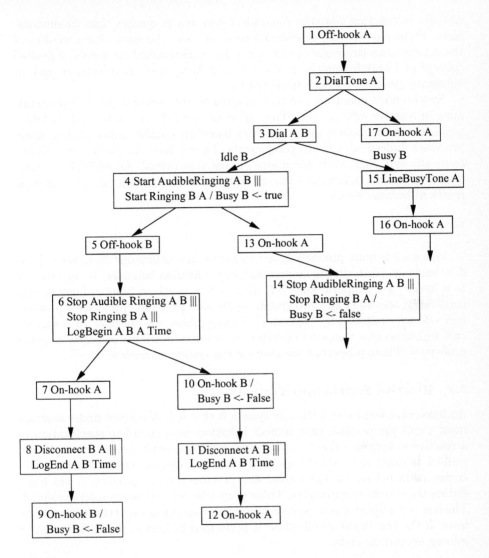

Variables:
Busy A: true between an Off-hook A event and the next On-hook A event; between a Start Ringing A B event and the next Stop Ringing A B event, if no Off-hook A intervenes; or between a Start Ringing A B event and the next On-hook A.

Ringing A B: true between a Start Ringing A B event immediately following a Dial B A event and the next Stop Ringing A B event.

AudibleRinging A B: true between a Start AudibleRinging A B event immediately following a Dial A B event and the next Stop AudibleRinging A B event. All of the POTS event sequences start and end with Busy A = False (Idle A = True).

Fig. 2. POTS formal description (Chisel diagram)

consists in checking that the program always reacts quicker than its environment. From the software developer's point of view, the main characteristics of the synchronous languages are [2]: a precise mathematical semantics, a flexible concept of hierarchy, precise notions of modularity and encapsulation, and an automatic generation of executable code.

Synchronous languages are well-adapted to the specification and programming of reactive software [11]. They allow to avoid the combinatorial explosion problem, which impairs the approaches based on parallel and communicating processes. Indeed, all parallel components of a synchronous system react simultaneously and, thus, their executions are not intertwined. An additional consequence of this characteristic is that all state transitions (which take place at each reaction) become visible.

Lustre

Our work is more precisely based on Lustre, a synchronous declarative dataflow language [4]. Lustre is an executable specification language. It corresponds to a linear past temporal logic [17] which offers usual arithmetic, boolean and conditional operators and two specific operators: **pre**, the "previous" operator, and −> the "followed-by" operator[1]. Lustre allows the specifier to define its own logical and/or temporal operators to express invariants or safety-oriented properties. Those properties are used for the system validation.

3.2   Reactive System Specification

An important feature of a reactive system is that it is developed under assumptions about the possible environment behavior. So a complete specification of a reactive system is a three step process. First, the environment has to be described, in order to be able to specify system reactions only in response to valid environment behaviors. The second step provides a set of properties, which describes the system requirements. Those properties are commonly safety-oriented. The last step objective is to provide a functional specification of the reactive software. If the functional specification is performed in Lustre, it can be compiled into an executable code.

3.3   Reactive System Validation

We focus here on the high level validation phase of reactive systems, which consists in showing that the functional specification, providing the specification of the environment, satisfies the properties.

Thus, the reactive system validation is done with respect to environment constraints. Clearly, when one is not concerned with the system robustness,

---

[1] Let E and F be two expressions of the same type denoting the sequences $(e_0, e_1, ..., e_n ...)$ and $(f_0, f_1, ..., f_n, ...)$; $\mathbf{pre}(E)$ denotes the sequence $(nil, e_0, e_1, ..., e_{n-1} ...)$ where nil is an undefined value. $E \rightarrow F$ denotes the sequence $(e_0, f_1, ..., f_n ...)$.

it makes no sense to take into account unrealistic environment behaviors. For example, in a telecommunication system, it is physically impossible to go on the hook twice without going off the hook in between. Consider a program which simulates the network reactions when some users go on the hook, go off the hook or dial a number. This program should observe for each user a sequence of actions among which "go off" et "go on" actions alternate.

The validation tool has to produce a verdict which indicates whether the program to be validated satisfies the properties under the environment assumptions (fig. 3).

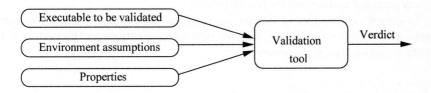

Fig. 3. Reactive system validation method

Lustre has been equipped with various dedicated validation tools: for example, a model-checker (Lesar) [11, 12] and a testing environment (Lutess) [7, 16]. Lutess is presented in section 6, and Lesar is presented in section 7.

4   Feature, Feature Composition, and Feature Interaction

Our definition of a feature relies on the feature interaction detection contest instructions. A single feature is a modification of the Plain Old Telephone Service (POTS). Thus, the POTS is successively redefined by the application of features. A feature (or a service) waits for an input and then reacts to it by producing outputs.

A general framework has been defined in [5], which inspired our approach. In this framework, let $F_1, F_2...F_n$ be a set of feature specifications, and N the network specification. Let $\oplus$ denote the composition of the network, and one or possibly several features ($N \oplus F_1 \oplus ... \oplus F_n$). Let $P_1, P_2...$ be a set of formulae expressing the respective feature requirements. Let $S \models P$ denote that the specification S satisfies (is a model of) the formula P. By definition, we say that there is an interaction when

$$\begin{cases} N \oplus F_i \models P_i, 1 \leq i \leq n \\ N \oplus F_1 \oplus ... \oplus F_n \nvDash P_1 \wedge ... \wedge P_n \end{cases} \quad \text{(T)}$$

The basic principle of our approach consists of building an executable description of the system to be studied. The network in the sense of (T) is only made of POTS, and the composition operation consists of modifying the POTS.

The POTS and each feature is represented as an automaton. This automaton results from the translation of the corresponding Chisel diagram. The automata are coded in Lustre.

Then, the composition of the POTS and the features is done in a "software unit" (fig. 4b). This unit is called a *logical telephone* (LT). There is one logical telephone for each user.

Logical telephones are gathered into a single program, which is called a *simulation program*. For the contest experiment, all the simulation programs have dealt with 4 users. These programs have been limited to up to two features (each logical telephone contains at most 2 different features). The simulation program is then used for feature interaction detection.

To detect occurrences of feature interactions, we expressed feature requirements as properties (in Lustre) and we defined interactions as the system's inability to satisfy these properties.

5   Modeling Choices

Each simulation program has been built applying the reactive system specification method (3.2). We had to identify the system environment, the functional specification of the system and some properties.

5.1   The Simulation Program Environment

The simulation program deals with the Switch and the Service Control Point. The Operations System is a passive element, which only receives some messages. Thus, it has been considered as part of the simulation environment. The end-user equipments (telephones) compose the other part of the environment (fig. 4a).

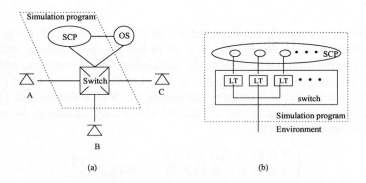

Fig. 4. Network executable specification

5.2   The Network Specification

The network executable specification (in the sense of (T)) relies only on the POTS specification. This specification is the result of a translation of a Chisel diagram into automata. The translation is performed in two steps. First, the different users involved in the feature execution and their respective actions are identified. Each user represents a "role" in the communication. For instance, POTS involves two roles: the caller and the callee.

For each role, the Chisel diagram is duplicated and then simplified to keep only the events with which it is concerned. For the POTS, we thus obtain two automata (fig. 5). Each automaton is then coded in a Lustre node. The node inputs are the user-to-switch messages. The outputs are the switch-to-user messages and the events produced for the billing systems.

Message encoding

There are 4 types of messages (ringing, display, billing messages and user action). All the messages are represented by boolean vectors. Moreover, for each message or event type, a specific message is coded. Indeed, at each cycle, a reactive synchronous program should read all its inputs and produce all its outputs. The absence of message or event is also a piece of information, and therefore, it must be "coded". For this purpose, a specific value (usually named "no_message") exists for each type of message.

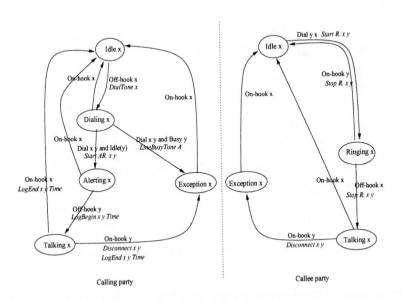

Fig. 5. The two automata for POTS

5.3   Feature Specification F_i

The feature executable specifications F_i were obtained systematically by generalizing the method used for POTS. For instance, Call Forwarding (CF) feature involves three users, the caller, the callee (the user to whom the CF is provided) and the forwarded-to user (the user to whom the call is redirected as a result of forwarding). Three automata were built.

As for POTS, the inputs of a feature executable specification are the user-to-switch messages. The outputs are also the switch-to-user messages and the events produced for the billing system. One supplementary output has been introduced: it is a boolean variable af (*active_feature*) which states whether the feature is active.

An inactive feature always emits the message "no_message". An active one can emit a message from the interface defined, or choose to answer "no_message". For instance, in the 4th vertex of POTS Chisel diagram (fig. 2), there are no display message and no billing event. So, a "no_message" can be emitted in two cases, and the boolean variable af allows us to make difference between them.

5.4   Feature Composition $\oplus$

The composition of the features is done at the switch level, in the logical telephones. We tried two different feature composition operations $\oplus_1$ and $\oplus_2$. Both rely on a multiplexing operation and on the af variables.

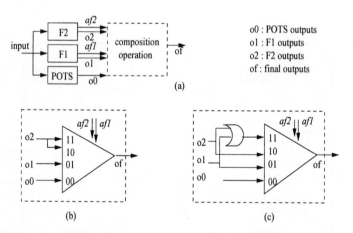

Fig. 6. Composition operations of POTS and two features

Let us consider two features $F1$ and $F2$. When the features are inactive (fig. 6a), the POTS outputs are chosen. When there is only one active feature, its outputs are chosen. When both features are active, we implemented two ways of selecting the outputs.

The first composition operation $\oplus_1$ (fig. 6b) gives priority to one feature over the other. The underlying hypothesis is: if there is an interaction between $F1$ and $F2$, it should be detected by $F1$ property violation.

The second composition operation $\oplus_2$ (fig. 6c) gives no priority to any of the features. When both features are active, the final output messages are built with a simple boolean *or* operator on each type of message. When both features produce no message, the final message is "no_message" (fig. 7a). When only one feature produces a message m, the final message is m (fig. 7b). When both features produce a message, the final message is the "composition" of both feature messages. If the messages are equal, the resulting message is unchanged; and if the messages are different, the resulting message is undefined (fig. 7c). Message codes were defined so that any composition of two different messages produces an undefined message. The second composition operation underlying hypothesis is: if there is an interaction between $F1$ and $F2$, it should be detected by $F1$ or $F2$ property violation or when an undefined message appears.

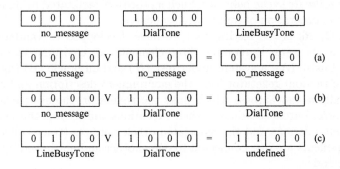

Fig. 7. Message composition for $\oplus_2$

5.5   Feature Properties

Two sets of properties are to be stated. The first one is intended to ensure the consistency of the services (POTS and feature) implementation in Lustre. For instance, the messages between the Switch and the telephones should be well-formed. The second one collects the POTS and the feature expected behavior properties. As the former set is implementation-dependent, we focus only on the latter. Those properties correspond to the feature informal requirements expressed in English.

For example, let us considered the Calling Number Delivery feature. The informal requirements are:

[CND1] CND feature enables the subscriber's telephone to receive and display the number of the originating party on an incoming call.

[CND2] For the purpose of the contest, we assume the capability of delivering the number of the calling party whenever an idle called party receives the Ringing event.

and the corresponding properties, written in Lustre, are:

$$
\left\{
\begin{array}{l}
\{\ \mathrm{CNDsubs}(x) \Leftrightarrow x \text{ is a subscriber of CND feature. } \} \\[6pt]
(1)\ \triangleright\ \mathrm{CNDsub}(x) \text{ and ConnectRequest}(z,x) \text{ and pre Idle}(x) \Rightarrow \mathrm{Display}(x,z) \\
(2)\ \triangleright\ \mathrm{CNDsub}(x) \Rightarrow \mathrm{Display}(x,z) \Leftrightarrow \mathrm{StartRinging}(x,z)
\end{array}
\right.
$$

6   Detection of Interactions Using Lutess

6.1   Lutess Testing Tool

Testing reactive systems can not easily be based on manually generated data. The software input data depend on the software outputs produced at the previous step of the software cyclic behavior. Such a process is facilitated by an automatic and dynamic generation of input data sequences.

Lutess [7, 16] is the testing tool we have developped to validate reactive synchronous software. It requires three elements: an environment description written in Lustre (A), a system under test (Π) and an oracle (B) (fig. 8). Lutess builds a random generator from the environment description and constructs automatically a test harness which links the generator, the system under test and the oracle. Lutess coordinates their executions and records the sequences of input-output relations and the associated oracle verdicts (trace collector module). Components are just connected to one another and not linked into a single executable code.

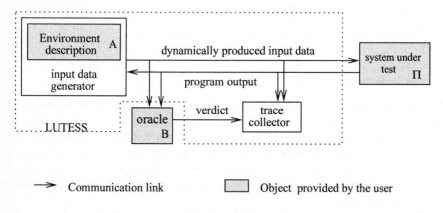

Fig. 8. Lutess

The system under test and the oracle are both synchronous and reactive executable programs, with boolean inputs and outputs. Optionally, they can be supplied as Lustre programs.

The test is operated on a single action-reaction cycle, driven by the generator. The generator simulates the environment behavior. At each cycle, the generator randomly selects an input vector which is valid with respect to the environment description (A). The chosen input vector is then sent to the system under test. This latter then reacts with an output vector and feeds back the generator with it. The generator proceeds by producing a new input vector and the cycle is repeated. The oracle observes the program inputs and outputs, and determines whether the software specification is violated. The testing process is stopped when the user-defined length of the test sequence is reached.

Basically, the Lutess generator selection algorithm chooses a valid input vector in an equally probable way. In each environment state, each valid input vector has the same probability to be selected as the others. This selection method is easy to use and requires no supplementary work for the tester. However, this selection method is not always efficient. For instance, in a 4-user simulation program, each user can dial his own number 1 time out of 4.

Lutess allows the tester to guide the generator [7]. Three methods are proposed:

- the user can define some safety properties; the selection algorithm will select inputs which potentially drive the system under test toward those properties violation;
- the user can define some scenarios (behavioral patterns); the selection algorithm will select inputs which follow the scenario;
- the user can also define input statistical (partial) distribution; the selection algorithm will produce the inputs following the given distribution.

6.2 Use of Lutess for Feature Validation

The environment constraints were mainly constraints on sequences of operations that the user can perform (e.g. a user cannot go off the hook twice in a row without going on the hook in between). These constraints may be enriched with probability distributions or specific behavioral patterns corresponding to typical sequences of users' operations.

The detection procedure consists in running Lutess over a user-defined number of exchanges between the feature executable specifications and the environment simulator. During these exchanges, the interactions are detected by the oracle which signals them by setting the verdict to false. The exchange trace and the verdict trace are compiled by Lutess in a readable format which can be subsequently analyzed to find out the reason of the interaction.

6.3 Experiment Description

78 configurations were to be tested, each including one or two features [8]. In each case, 5 to 10 feature properties were available. The test process for each

configuration involved 10 to 20 sequences of 1000 to 10000 steps each. On the whole, each configuration has been evaluated on around 1 million test cases.

Building the generator corresponding to a given environment is the most expensive part of the testing process. In our experimentations, environments included from 32 to 45 constraints, plus up to 20 testing guides.

It was always possible to perform this computation and to run the test on a Sparc Ultra-1 station with 128 MB of memory. Maximum virtual memory required amounts to 100 MB. As the number of constraints describing the environment increases, the environment generation lasts longer. For the less-constrained environments that we produced, 6 seconds on CPU were necessary, while the most-constrained environments required 2000 seconds to be generated. As a comparison, a 1000 test run lasts 120 seconds once the generator has been built[2]. One can notice that here a trade-off has to be found: the more the environment is constrained, the more relevant is the test (since the whole test case is more realistic), but the longer is the generation.

6.4 Experiment Lessons

Test Automation

From the tester's perspective, the tool allows a significant relief by automating the test. Building the oracle appeared to be the most difficult part of the testing process. One has first to master the temporal logic paradigm, then to find out the better terms to express a given property. This requires an adequate training and experience.

From the specifier's point of view, Lutess has shown to be very helpful to debug specifications. First, Lutess has been used to validate the oracles: the oracle specifications are put in place of the unit under test and a human observation is substituted for the Lutess oracle. Second, prior to the search for interactions, the service specifications to be tested have been validated using oracle properties. For instance, in the specifications, some possible transitions were missing in a diagram, or an expected output message was never sent in a given situation. These problems were automatically exhibited as oracle violations.

Composition operation and feature interaction detection

We tried the two composition operations presented in section 5.2 (fig. 6b and 6c). It appears that the second one is more efficient in terms of "quantity of feature interaction detected". Let us consider the Calling Number Delivery (CND) and Call Forward (CF) features. CND properties are given in 5.5.

As it can be noticed in figure 9, CND feature displays the number of the subscriber calling party as soon as his number is dialed. Let A be a user who is both a CND and CF subscriber, let B the forwarded-to number of A. B is also a CND subscriber. Whenever A's number is dialed when B is idle, CF

---

[2] This second phase of the testing process is proportional to the sequence length.

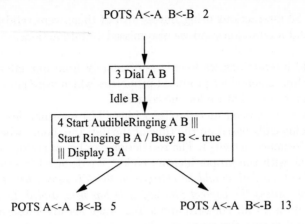

Fig. 9. CND formal description (Chisel diagram)

feature diverts the call. Moreover CND feature displays the caller's number on A's phone, but not on B's phone (because of the dialing action). Thus there are two interactions between CF and CND:

- After a call forwarding due to CF feature, the number of the calling party is not displayed even if the forwarded-to user is a CND subscriber.
- After a call forwarding due to CF feature, the number of the calling party is displayed on the callee's phone even if the forwarded-to user is idle.

When the first composition operation is used and CF feature is given the higest priority, (i.e. $POTS \oplus_1 CND \oplus_1 CF$) the second interaction does not occur. Indeed, when A's Call Forward feature is invoked, CND outputs are hidden by the CF's ones: CF is active and produce a "no_message" for the callee's display.

With the second composition operation, a feature can not completely mask another feature reaction. In this case, the second interaction appears and is detected by Lutess.

Feature subscription list configuration

An interaction may depends on the feature subscription configuration. If the subscription configuration is not adequate, some ineractions could be missed.

To use Lutess, the configurations of the feature subscription list were defined manually. Several possible configurations were chosen for each pair of features in order to decrease the probability to miss an interaction.

Importance of the properties

The Contest Committee defined a set of *valid* interactions. Those are the feature interactions that the Committee believes exist between the features as defined for the contest.

We found 83 interactions using Lutess. 3/4 of them were valid features. We found 14 invalid interactions and we also missed 19 interactions.

The invalid interactions we found result mainly from our interpretation of the informal requirements: we produced properties which were not considered to be "requirements" of a feature for the contest.

For instance, let us consider the Teen Line (TL) informal description: "TL restricts outgoing calls based on the time of the day, (i.e. hours when homework should be the primary activity). The restriction can be overridden on a per-call basis by anyone with the proper identity code." We deduced from this informal specification that *no call should be charged to the TL subscriber during the restriction hours, unless the correct identity code has been dialed.* Let us consider a user who is both a Call Forward and a Teen Line feature subscriber. When a call is forwarded during the restriction hours, the extra charges are "charged" and the TL property is thus violated. This is one of the invalid interaction we found.

Concurrently, the valid interactions we didn't find are also due to our properties, which were inadequate to reveal them. For instance, for most of the features, an on-hook action ends a phone call. This is not the case of Call Waiting (CW) feature. Thus there are some interactions between CW and some other features when a on-hook action is both interpreted as a step of the communication by CF and as the end of communication by the other features. The notion of "communication ending" was never taken into account since it was always implicit in the informal feature description.

When to stop testing ?

One of the major problem we had during this experiment phase was to decide when the test should be stopped. Since testing does not provide a definite verdict on the absence of the interaction, if no problem is found, one may wonder whether the test was significant enough to detect all interactions. Thus, to evaluate how significant were various test sequences, and increase confidence in testing, we have worked along two directions:

– since very often, a feature interaction appears during features invocation, we have produced some specific observers (i.e. properties which are included in the oracle) to measure how often a feature is invoked; thus we have checked whether interesting situations were explored during the test and so, if relevant data were produced;

– we have applied a model-checker, since we expected to evaluate the ability of such methods to detect feature interactions.

7   Detection of Interaction Using a Model-Checker (Lesar)

7.1   Lesar

Lesar [11, 12] has been designed to prove the correctness of a Lustre program with respect to some critical safety properties. A safety property usually states that a given situation will never occur or that a given statement should always hold.

- Safety properties can be checked on program abstractions. Let P a program and S a safety property to be proven. Let P' an abstraction of P. Intuitively, P' has more "behaviors" than P. Therefore, if S holds for P', it holds for P.
- Safety properties can be checked on program states rather than on execution paths.

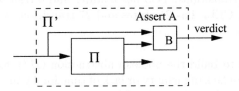

Fig. 10. Verification program structure

Lesar operates on a *verification program*. A *verification program* is a specific Lustre program Π' built out of three elements (fig. 10) [11]:

- a program Π to be verified,
- a property P expressed by a boolean expression B which should be invariably *true*,
- some assumptions on the environment (environment constraints); those assumptions are boolean expressions (A) which can be assumed to be always true.

These three elements are also those required by Lutess (fig. 8)

The verification is performed on a finite boolean state abstraction Π'' of the program Π'. Any numerical abstraction is ignored. Boolean expressions depending on numerical variables (such as comparisons) are considered nondeterministic. The verification principle is the following: proving that Π'' holds is equivalent to enumerating its finite set of states, checking that in each state (belonging to a path starting from initial state and on which the assertions are always true) and for each input vector, Π'' output evaluates to true.

9   Acknowledgments

I would like to thank Nicolas Zuanon, Remi Cave and Jérome Vassy who worked hard during the first part of the experiment, and Nicolas Halbwachs and Pascal Raymond who welcomed me at Verimag and helped me use Lesar during the second part of the experiment.

References

[1] A. Aho, S. Gallagher, N. Griffeth, C. Schell, and D. Swayne. Scf3^{TM} sculptor with chisel: Requirements engineering for communications services. In *Feature Interactions in Telecommunications Systems V*, pages 45–63. IOS Press, 1998.

[2] A. Benveniste and al. Synchronous technology for real-time systems. In *The 1994 Real-Time Conferences*, pages 104–122, Teknea, 1994.

[3] B.W. Boehm. *Software Engineering Economics*. Prentice-Hall, 1981.

[4] P. Caspi, N. Halbwachs, D. Pilaud, and J. Plaice. LUSTRE, a declarative language for programming synchronous systems. In *14th Symposium on Principles of Programming Languages (POPL 87), Munich*, pages 178–188. ACM, 1987.

[5] P. Combes and S. Pickin. Formalization of a user view of network and services for feature interaction detection. In *Feature Interactions in Telecommunications Systems*, pages 120–135. IOS Press, 1994.

[6] L. du Bousquet, F. Ouabdesselam, J.-L. Richier, and N. Zuanon. Incremental feature validation : a synchronous point of view. In *Feature Interactions in Telecommunications Systems V*, pages 262–275. IOS Press, 1998.

[7] L. du Bousquet, F. Ouabdesselam, J.-L. Richier, and N. Zuanon. Lutess: a specification-driven testing environment for synchronous software. In *21st International Conference on Software Engineering*, Los Angeles, USA, May 1999. ACM.

[8] L. du Bousquet and N. Zuanon. Feature interaction detection contest: Lutess testing tool. technical report PFL, IMAG - LSR, Grenoble, France, 1998.

[9] N. D. Griffeth and Y.-J. Lin. Extending telecommunication systems: The feature-interaction problem. In *IEEE Computer*, pages 14–18, August 1993.

[10] N.D. Griffeth, R. Blumenthal, J.-C. Gregoire, and T. Otha. Feature interaction detection contest. In K. Kimbler and L.G. Bouma, editors, *Feature Interactions in Telecommunications Systems V*, pages 327–359. IOS Press, 1998.

[11] N. Halbwachs, F. Lagnier, and C. Ratel. Programming and Verifying Real-Time Systems by Means of the Synchronous Data-Flow Programming Language LUSTRE. *IEEE Transactions on Software Engineering*, pages 785–793, september 1992.

[12] N. Halbwachs, D. Pilaud, F. Ouabdesselam, and A-C. Glory. Specifying, Programming and Verifying Real-Time Systems, using a synchronous declarative language. In *Workshop on automatic verification methods for finite state systems, LNCS 407*, Grenoble, France, 1989. Springer Verlag.

[13] L.J. Jagadeesan, C. Puchol, and J.E. Von Olnhausen. Safety Property Verification of Esterel Programs and Applications to Telecommunications Software. In *7th Conference on Computer-Aided Verification*, 1995.

[14] G. Murakami and R. Sethi. Terminal call processing in Esterel. In *Proc. IFIP 92 World Computer Congress*, Madrid, Spain, 1992.

[15] G. Myers. *The Art Of Software Testing*. Wiley-Interscience, 1979.

[16] F. Ouabdesselam and I. Parissis. Testing Synchronous Critical Software. In *5th International Symposium on Software Reliability Engineering*, Monterey, USA, 1994.

[17] D. Pilaud and N. Halbwachs. From a synchronous declarative language to a temporal logic dealing with multiform time. In *Symposium on Formal Techniques in Real Time and Fault Tolerant Systems*, Warwick, 1988. Springer Verlag.

[18] A. Pnueli. Application of temporal logic to the specification and verification of reactive systems : a survey of current trends. *Current Trends in Concurrency, LNCS, Springer-Verlag*, 224:510–584, 1986.

Emma: Developing an Industrial Reachability Analyser for SDL

Nisse Husberg[1] and Tapio Manner[2]

[1] Helsinki University of Technology, Theoretical Computer Science Laboratory,
FIN-02015 HUT, FINLAND,
Nisse.Husberg@hut.fi,
http://www.tcs.hut.fi
[2] Nokia Telecommunications, P.O.Box 300, FIN-00045 Nokia Group, FINLAND,
Tapio.Manner@ntc.nokia.com

Abstract Testing products is very expensive in the telecommunication business and remaining errors can also be very difficult to correct in a working system. In this project formal methods are used for the verification of software written in TNSDL (a dialect of SDL-88), which is used as a programming language in telecommunication products. A front-end for the PROD reachability analyser translates the TNSDL code into a high level Petri net model which can be analysed by PROD. The results are translated back to TNSDL. The *complete* TNSDL can be analysed, except some very difficult constructs like pointers. Dynamic processes, all data types, signals with parameters and even timers can be handled. The granularity of the model is very fine, SDL statements are considered atomary but can be folded if they are independent.

1 Introduction

The application of formal methods to industrial problems is not easy. Usually it is a very time consuming task to create the formal model of the system. It has to be done manually and the creator should know the real system very well and he must also be an expert of the formal system. Such persons are, however, still very unusual. Thus the creation of a formal model by hand takes a lot of time and the link between the real system and the model might be distorted.

There are, however, some areas where rather good specification languages are used, for example telecommunications where SDL [9] is quite widespread. The *Emma* project started with the goal to design a system which automatically translates SDL programs into Petri net models which could be analysed with the PROD [13] reachability analyser and the results presented in SDL terms. Both *Emma* and *PROD* are developed at the Theoretical Computer Science Laboratory (former Digital Systems Laboratory).

At Nokia Telecommunications as much as 70 % of the time must be used for testing the systems. The remaining errors must be corrected in running systems which is difficult, slow and expensive. Thus any tool which can be used to make

J. Wing, J. Woodcock, J. Davies (Eds.): FM'99, Vol. I, LNCS 1708, pp. 642–661, 1999.
© Springer-Verlag Berlin Heidelberg 1999

the verification of the systems easier would be most welcome. The TNSDL (TeleNokia SDL - a variant of SDL-88) is used in the implementation of the systems and there are approximately 2 million lines of code written in TNSDL already. Thus the *Emma* project had a good possibility to succeed in creating a useful industrial verification tool in this setting.

The model generator of *Emma* was not trivial to construct. There are data types in TNSDL like arrays and structures - things which often are left out of any academic work about formal modelling. Another problem was that there is dynamic creation of processes and dynamic targets of output statements in TNSDL. Not to speak of timers considering that the Petri net model used in PROD has no time concept. But fortunately all these problems were solved and the model generator can handle the *complete* TNSDL (with exception of rather impossible features like pointers and calls to procedures written in assembler or other programming languages).

The resulting TNSDL analyser was, however, just the first prototype. It was evaluated in a Master's thesis [6] by an engineer working at Nokia Telecommunications and the result prompted the start of a new project, *Maria*, where all the problems of the first prototype should be addressed. There is a working prototype of the *Maria* analyser but it has not yet been tested in an industrial environment. This paper describes the *Emma* analyser and the experiences gained in the *Emma* project and in the evaluation of the prototype. It was very valuable feedback for our laboratory although we have been building reachability analysers for more than 20 years.

Although *Emma* could handle the examples of TNSDL used in testing, the introduction of real TNSDL programs from the production showed that there still are quite a few problems. The problems were only partly related to TNSDL itself. Usually the most serious obstacles in applying *Emma* was the use of non-TNSDL features like calling routines written in other languages and the use of machine dependent features. But when we are taking the step from academic to industrial analysis we have to cope with this kind of problems for the foreseeable future. Although specification languages like SDL are introduced, these problems will persist on the implementation side as in TNSDL.

In this paper this problem is discussed and some solutions are proposed. In the evaluation of *Emma* about 40 out of the nearly 500 program blocks written in TNSDL for the DX 200 telecommunication system were used. This paper contains a section about the design of *Emma*, one section about the experience of using *Emma* and finally one section about the new analyser *Maria*, which will be a combination of *PROD* and *Emma*, but with many new features.

2   General Design of *Emma*

The creation of the formal model is a serious obstacle in industrial formal verification. The creator should be an expert both in the application area and in formal models. Academic personal may know a lot about formalisms and industrial engineers a lot about the system to be verified, but this knowledge is seldom easy to bring together.

In the *Emma* project the main idea was to make the modelling easy for the industrial engineer, preferably automatic. Therefore *Emma* consists of a TNSDL parser, a net model generator, a reachability analyser and a result interpreter (Figure 1). In fact, the net model generator and the result interpreter are integrated into one C++ program, **emma**.

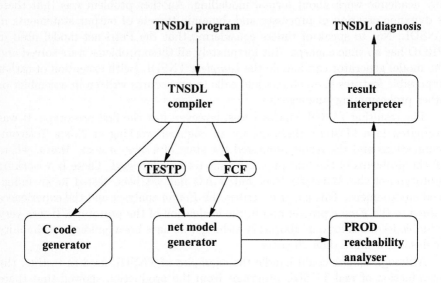

Fig.1. The *Emma* analyser.

The TNSDL parser used in *Emma* is part of the TNSDL compiler developed at Nokia Telecommunications. This compiler is used in the production and generates C code from the TNSDL source. It was only extended with a module writing the *flow control data* (FCF) to a (text) file. It can also write a text file containing the *symbol table* (TESTP) of the compiled program.

The model generator uses the *same information* as in the C code generator. Thus the model is very close to the implementation of the system thereby reducing possible modelling errors. The formal model which is verified must be a correct abstraction of the real system. As will be seen in this paper, this abstract model is difficult to create because the complexity must be kept quite low and the implementation (not only "clean" TNSDL code) causes problems.

The *PROD* reachability analyser [13] is a Petri net tool implemented in C by a student group in the early 90's, but substantially improved by Kimmo Varpaaniemi [12]. It uses an input language which is close to Predicate/transition nets (Pr/T nets) and can do on-the-fly verification of LTL properties and use reduction methods like stubborn sets and sleep sets . One problem with the model generation from TNSDL was that the data structures had to be coded into tuples of integers, which is the only data type that *PROD* knows.

The implementation of *Emma* is still on the prototype stage. Now the analyser consists of three different parts: the TNSDL compiler (internal tool at Nokia Telecommunications) which is written in C++ and runs only under Sun OS (and MS Windows NT), the **emma** program, written in C++ and using libraries from the TNSDL compiler running under Linux and the *PROD* reachability analyser written in C code and running under Linux (and MS Windows).

The experience with *Emma* showed that the idea was good, but also that the analyser should be rewritten completely and this is now done in the *Maria* project [10] which will produce a complete SDL and Petri net reachability analyser written in C++ under the Gnu public license, i.e. it will be *freely available*. The development of *Emma* is restricted to smaller bug fixes.

3   Automatic Generation of the Net Model

In principle it is not very difficult to translate SDL into Petri nets because both "languages" are designed for the description of concurrent systems. There are, however, certain problems with the data types and timers in SDL and the most important thing is to create a model which can be analysed. Reachability analysis easily generates huge graphs and even relatively simple systems can be impossible to analyse if a combinatorial explosion is allowed to take place.

When using Petri nets it is very important to decide how the *dynamic* features are modelled. The structure of the net is *static* and can not be changed by the behaviour. Fortunately, this is not necessary in high level nets, because it is easy to code the complete dynamics using the *marking* (tokens). It is even possible to use a high level net which consists of only one place and one transition, but then we are only trading the structural complexity with annotational complexity.

At first sight it seems appropriate to use one net transition to model one SDL statement. This is also possible for TNSDL except in the WHILE statement and in the call of a procedure. It is, however, not very efficient in reachability analysis because there will be too many intermediate states. If the system consists of several processes, as usually is the case, then there will be a lot of interleavings.

In *Emma* this approach is used, but in order to reduce the number of interleavings, a special *lock place* is added to the net. It is not the most optimal solution for analysis efficiency, but it allows the user to closely follow the behaviour of the system in terms of executed TNSDL statements.

The net transitions are connected using *control places*, e.g. **C1** and **C2** in Figure 3. Note that an *SDL transition* consists of a sequence of SDL statements, among others OUTPUT statements and statements referring to global variables. Thus these SDL transitions can not be treated as atomary behavioural unit as is done e.g. in ObjectGEODE [7]. *Emma* can treat sequences of SDL statements as behavioural units, but can break up SDL transitions if necessary.

3.1   Modelling Data

It is usually impossible to model the data in a real system completely. Thus it has to be limited heavily. In the analysis it makes little difference because there are a lot of symmetries which can be ignored in the verification.

The data in the SDL program is modelled in the marking of the net model. A *variable* is a *place* in the net and its value is a *token*. Because Petri nets are *resource-conscious*, the tokens which are read by a net transition are removed from the place and must be explicitly restored. A token written to a place does *not* destroy the old value, which must be removed before adding a new value.

Therefore it is necessary to use the marking of this place as a *frame*, i.e. the number and type of tokens are always the same, only the contents (the value) of the tokens is changed (Figure 2). Typically the same net transition which reads the token also returns it, possibly with a new value. This is so common that double arrowheads are used in the pictures (Figure 3).

This feature in Petri nets is quite useful when there are several instances of a variable. It is only necessary to tag the values in order to make them distinguishable. In this way *dynamic creation of processes* is quite easy to model.

One special "variable" is the *queue* used in SDL processes. It is implemented using frames although these frames are rather complex. One token at a queue place defines a slot in one queue. In *Emma* such a token is a quintuple `<.pid,spid,n,sig,par.>` consisting of the *process identifier* `pid`, the *sender process identifier* `spid`, the *queue entry number* `n`, the *signal number* `sig`, and the signal *parameter information* `par`. Because the process identifier is unique, it means that dynamic creation of processes can be handled with this model.

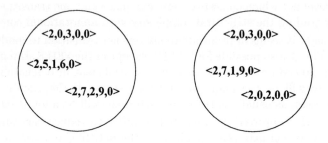

Fig.2. The queue modelled as a frame.

In the example in (Figure 2) the queue of process 2 has three entries, with the first one containing signal 6 sent from process 5, the second one has signal 9 sent from process 7, and the third one is empty. There are no parameters in the queue. When the first signal in the queue is read, the new queue (at the right) contents will be reduced to signal 9 sent from process 7 in the first entry. Note that there is no order among the tokens at a place in a Petri net. Therefore the entries must be numbered explicitly. The use of frames makes it much easier to handle the net because there are problems with testing if there is a token in a place especially if the number of tokens is not bounded.

It is possible to use one single place for all queues in the net because the process identifiers are unique. This would be useful in handling the OUTPUT statements in SDL which have *dynamically defined targets*. It was reflected upon in *Emma*, but even if it does make the model simpler, it does not have any influence on the size of the reachability graph, which is more important.

The queue needs two auxiliary places *Cursor* and *Free*, which keep track of the first free slot and the signal to be input, respectively. Note that the signal is *not* removed from the queue by the net transition corresponding to the INPUT statement in SDL - only the *Cursor* is incremented. There are several reason for this, e.g. the existence of a SAVELATEST statement in TNSDL, which may force the signal to remain in the queue. Only the net transitions which move control to another SDL state (like NEXTSTATE) will clean the stack and set the *Cursor* to zero.

The SAVE statement in SDL should move a signal from the input queue to a save queue and put the save queue back to the input queue when the SDL state is changing. In *Emma* the **Save** net transition only increments the *Cursor*. This makes the change in the state of the net very small and with smart state space storage algorithms (storing only the *change* in the state) this should keep the memory needed for the state change very small. The queue model used in the SDL modelling of the PEP tool generates a lot of intermediate states [3] resulting in a big state graph.

In *Emma* the length of the queue is fixed because *frames* are used. This is in conflict with the definition of SDL, but it has no practical significance at all. In the analysis of the systems the length of the queue must be limited very heavily or the size of the reachability graph will really explode. In our tests with rather small examples, the maximal queue lengths which could be analysed were usually shorter than five. On the other hand, in the verification of systems the errors typically can be found already using very short queues. The increase of the queue length generates a lot of similar subgraphs, but very little new behaviour.

In the new analyser *Maria* a *queue data type* is introduced in order to increase efficiency and reduce the number of intermediate states in the reachability graph.

It was easy to implement variables with simple types, but the inclusion of more complex data types turned out to be rather troublesome and an excessive amount of work was needed to implement the translation of all possible expressions found in TNSDL. Everything had to be coded using tuples of integers.

A basic problem was that the structure of the net must be determined at translation time because it cannot be changed dynamically. Thus the SDL program must be analysed very carefully before the net structure is generated. However, the net class used in PROD was powerful enough to handle the creation of processes and *recursive procedure calls* can also be modelled. The solution is to tag all the tokens in a recursive process with the depth of the recursion.

Because industrial systems often have huge or infinite state spaces it is impossible to generate the complete reachability graph first and then perform the analysis using this graph. Therefore the *on-the-fly method* must be used. It means that the graph is checked for the interesting property, e.g. a deadlock, at the same time as the graph is generated. If a deadlock is found, the process is stopped.

This makes it possible to work even with infinite state spaces, but the search strategy is extremely important. Simple search strategies like depth-first and breadth-first are not very useful in this case. Here *smart strategies*, the possibility to give the analyser some *hints* or even the use of *manual control* of the generation of the reachability graph are needed.

3.2   Dynamic Structures

The *static* structure of the net makes it impossible to change the output arcs of an **Output** net transition dynamically. When the SDL source has the target of the OUTPUT statement defined as a variable which can have several different values at run time it is necessary to generate *several* **Output** net transitions to all possible input queues. Only one of these can, however, be enabled for each instance and the size of the reachability graph is not affected.

The problems with transferring the parameters of a signal is related to the dynamical determination of the target of an OUTPUT statement in SDL.

A third problem is the dynamic determination of timer instance names. In principle a timer in SDL can have an infinite number of active instances distinguished by the parameters of the timer. Because the parameters are determined when the timer is activated, the name is determined dynamically. This causes problems as the SET statement in SDL will reset an active timer with the same parameters and set it again. The net transition must check the actual parameters with the parameters of all active timers, but it is impossible to have a variable unbounded number of active arcs in the net transition.

Thus it was necessary to have a fixed number of active timer instances for each timer in a process instance. The tuples for these timer instances are *frames* which are created at startup and remain constant in number and form during the whole analysis, except that their contents might vary.

3.3   Modelling Timers without a Time Concept

It seems impossible or at least useless to model timers in a formalism which has no concept of time at all, but in *Emma* it is done using a "window" technique. It does not even pretend to model the complete behaviour of timers, but at least a good approximation is achieved. The basic reason for this is that the communication in SDL is completely *asynchronous* and thus it is impossible to make any assumption of "when" a certain timer will expire in another process (in the same process it is possible).

In fact, the timer would be modelled in exactly the same way in a formalism having a time concept, i.e. the timer can in principle expire *at any time* seen from other processes. This will cause the reachability graph to be very big and some restriction which removes all the uninteresting paths must be used.

The solution to this problem was to implement a kind of "window", where the timer was allowed to expire. In practice, a special *lock place* (Figure 3) was introduced and the timer can only expire if this lock place has the right token. When the timer is set, the lock is closed because the **Set** net transition puts a CLOSED token into the lock place and it can be opened by any net transition which puts an OPEN token into this place. Any net transition can close the lock again. In this way a "window" is opened and the timer can expire only within the window, i.e. it will only be interleaved with the net transitions in the window - not with all net transitions in the model.

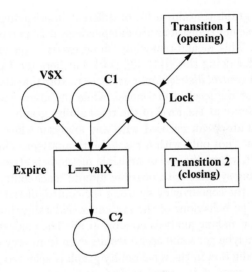

Fig.3. The timer model.

The transition **Expire** in Figure 3 is disabled until **Transition 1** puts a token $< pid, L >$ into it. After that the transition can fire if L == valX, but when **Transition 2** is fired it takes away the token in the lock place and the transition **Expire** is locked again. Note that there must always be a token (a frame) in **Lock** so that it does not interfere with the behaviour of **Transition 2**. In some paths the **Transition 2** might be fired before **Transition 1**.

The lock is closed by putting the token $< pid, L0 >$ into **Lock** (where **L0** is a value which cannot be a value of the variable **X**). In the example both transitions **Expire** and **Transition 2** will close the lock. Of course there can be much more complex situations.

The user can manually define where the lock should be opened and closed or he can let *Emma* use some algorithm for defining the window automatically. He can try different windows in critical segments of the code and see if erroneous behaviour occurs. This is probably a much faster way to analyse the system than generating a very big reachability graph (if it is possible at all).

When a timer expires, a signal is put into the queue, but this signal cannot be read until the next **Input** net transition. Therefore it is possible to keep the timer locked during the whole SDL transition, i.e. all SDL statements except INPUT and OUTPUT (affecting the same queue as the timer or having dynamical target). It is necessary to open the lock also before an **Output** net transition so that the order in the queue will not be altered - if the target of the **Output** is dynamical, it is not possible to know which queue it affects.

3.4 Limiting Concurrency

The reachability graph contains a lot of different interleavings of the same net transitions. If these net transitions are independent, it is unnecessary to consider but one of them. This means removing "unnecessary" concurrency. There are several methods for doing this ([11], [2], [14]), but here the *lock* mechanism can also be used as an *control distributor* or *sequencer*. Note that this method reduces the concurrency *at the level of the model*, while the above mentioned methods reduce the complexity at the level of the reachability graph.

Control distributors can be used with any analyser which can take the net model as an input - not only with a reachability analyser. This is important in the *Emma* project, where the use of multiple methods is stressed.

Especially in big systems with possibly infinite reachability graphs it can be necessary to limit the concurrency by using the control distributor very heavily. This can change the behaviour of the system considerably, but it might be the price to be paid for making analysis possible at all. The analyst can try different possibilities and maybe get some useful results even from very complex systems.

The biggest reduction in the reachability graph is achieved if control is given to a process only when it is necessary and given away again by the following net transition. Because the SDL processes can interfere with each other *only* by asynchronous communication, the only interesting windows are around **Output** and **Input** net transitions.

A more general form of a control distributor place is a *counter place*. It can be used to control the number of processes created etc. Each time a certain net transition fires, it decrements the counter and when it is zero, the net transition cannot fire any more. By making the system to put fresh tokens in the counter place in certain cases, the dynamics of the system can be controlled in a very sophisticated way.

It must be stressed that these *approximative* methods are fundamentally different from those used in [11], [2], [14], where the reduction is proved to retain the interesting properties. In an *industrial* analyser the use of *partial* analysis is often more interesting because the main objective is to *find errors quickly*. Note, however, that this approach is based on a formal model and that *exhaustive* analysis can be used as well.

Typically the work with *Emma* would consist of doing a lot of partial analysis checking for errors and at the end an exhaustive analysis would be done (perhaps taking several weeks). In an industrial environment an exhaustive analysis is, however, seldom possible to do at all because of the huge (often infinite) reachability graph.

4   Experiences from Industrial Verification

When the first prototype of *Emma* was ready, a project was started to evaluate its usefulness in a real industrial environment. It was not possible to do an evaluation in the university because the conditions are quite different. A good academic tool is not necessarily very useful in an industrial setting.

Emma was tested at Nokia Telecommunications by Tapio Manner, who had some experience of *Emma* but did not take part in the development directly. We got very valuable feedback needed in the next stage of the development of the analyser.

The evaluation was not only a test of *Emma* using more complex TNSDL programs but a test of its usefulness as a tool in the software development of the entire DX 200 system. The importance is in the analysis of the concurrent behaviour of the entire system instead of separate program blocks.

There are some details in the DX 200 source code which are not analysable with the *Emma* analyser. Some of them were already documented in [5] and [4]. During the evaluation some new problems were found. These are divided into five categories: *other programming languages, pointers, linking, DX 200 specific features* and *bugs*. The bugs are only a temporary quality problem in the prototype, but the other four categories represent DX 200 implementation details which were not addressed in the design of the *Emma* analyser.

4.1   Other Programming Languages

The telecommunication systems developed at Nokia Telecommunications are implemented using several programming languages. A good deal of the asynchronous communicating processes belong to program blocks written in PL/M, C or assembler. The operating system interface and many other basic services appear as *synchronous services* in libraries, not necessarily written in TNSDL.

The *Emma* analyser can read only TNSDL descriptions, the programs and synchronous services written in other languages are outside the scope of the analyser. To *Emma* these parts of the system are unknown – possible effects on the system state can not be detected.

However, *Emma* is not completely powerless in this case. It can model the effect of an external synchronous service by a random value. This gives a partial model of the synchronous service. If a better model is needed, it must be modelled manually as a TNSDL process or directly as a Petri net. This only takes us back to square one, i.e. to the situation before *Emma* was created.

Some C source code may also be included within the TNSDL source code file. The MACRO feature in TNSDL supports the use of in-line C language macros implementing either synchronous services or data type operators. The macros are mainly used for reasons of efficiency. The macros cause the same kind of problems as the external synchronous services implemented as procedures.

Analysing the concurrent behaviour of the complete system with only partial access to the system description is impossible. This is why the inaccessibility to the parts written in other languages is probably one of the greatest shortcomings in *Emma* from the industrial point of view. Some ideas how to get the behaviour of these black boxes more visible to *Emma* is presented in Section 5.

4.2   Pointers

Pointers can be used to optimise the use of stacks with respect to size and time by avoiding the copying of large structures to the stack in procedure calls. Pointers can also be used to make changes in structures transparent to interfaces: adding a new field to a structure does not require rewriting related procedure prototypes. A pointer is a very convenient in implementing dynamical data structures. These are important in reserving a minimal amount of memory while retaining flexibility to meet peak size needs.

Parameter passing, especially to external synchronous services, is where pointers probably are used most frequently. Many synchronous services can be rewritten not to use pointers in their interface, but it is questionable whether this is reasonable in general. Section 5 discusses some widely used cases which are transformable to program code without pointers.

4.3   Linking

In an industrial system it is not only the program code that defines the behaviour. For example, the linking of modules in TNSDL is a rather complex operation where the *visibility* of procedures can be restricted.

The linkable modules of processes in TNSDL are composed into a linkable module of the entire program block. The object files of TNSDL modules can be linked into any of these linkable modules. Every link of the TNSDL module places one copy of the object code into the target module. In addition to possibly many physical copies of TNSDL module with binding, the visibility of procedures of the TNSDL module can be restricted. As this is defined outside the TNSDL source code, *Emma* expects the TNSDL modules to be linked into a single shared copy of module in the program block. If this is not the case the model represents something else than was defined in TNSDL source code.

4.4   DX 200 Specific Features

To increase the fault tolerance there are spare units in DX 200 storing backup values. This system is not fully transparent to the programs. There are a few statements having attributes tuning the fault tolerance features. For example the OUTPUT statement can contain implementation-dependent attribute specifications, which are needed in certain situations causing the operating system to deliver the message to the destination process in a specific way such as "delete the message if the receiver is in a spare unit" or "put the message into the receiver's message queue even if this would cause queue-length quota to be exceeded".

What happens to the system when the working unit and the spare unit for some logical computer unit change their roles on the fly is something that the analysis with *Emma* can not handle.

4.5 Bugs

During the tests several bugs were found and many of them were successfully corrected. However, there are still some problems which will be corrected only in the new version, i.e. in the *Maria* analyser. One of these is the handling of *union types*. This is a problem in TNSDL because the programmers often use a union type as a formal parameter in a procedure to save space. The actual parameter type is known only when the procedure is called. The new analyser *Maria* has a complete type system and the union types will be handled by it.

4.6 Testing with Real Programs

The purpose of the tests was to show how *Emma* copes with real TNSDL programs, and learn what kind of modifications must be made in order to get them analysed with *Emma*.

The extensive test suite that was developed can later be used in testing future versions of *Emma*. This work produced a lot of workarounds, i.e. methods of adapting the source code to analysis with *Emma*. For industrial application there is a need to design a new front-end which processes the TNSDL source code used in the production. Now editing one of the smallest program blocks according to the suggested workarounds takes days, which is intolerable.

In Section 5 it is described which constructs in the TNSDL source code must be handled to make the analysis possible. The following list shows how common each problem is by giving the proportion of program blocks involved. All of these problems can be solved by the methods in Section 5. Note that some of problems can not be solved without changing the behaviour of the TNSDL system to some extent.

5 Preparing TNSDL Source Code for the Analysis

Many tools are presented using some examples which work very nicely, but here we use "dirty" production programs which we try to verify using *Emma*. It was difficult to find a program which could be analysed directly. Usually some TNSDL source code modification was necessary, in some cases a rewriting of the code was necessary. This is, however, still very far from creating a formal model manually. Table 5 shows the frequency of the most important problems encountered during the evaluation.

Table1. Problem Frequency

The Problem Source	Ratio in %
pointer	98
external synchronous services	100
union	71
memset	55
memcpy	33
block without implementation	100
output attributes	14

Pointers are probably causing most of the problems because *Emma* does not handle pointers. Clearly the necessity for manual modifications impedes common use of the *Emma* system because pointers are used in every TNSDL program studied in this work. It is, however, possible to do some modifications automatically, but manual modification will always be at least a partial solution to deal with pointers. Most of the guidelines given in this section are actually procedures precise enough for automatic implementation.

The second group of changes is related to *synchronous services*. Most of the changes are due to the use of pointers in parameters, but it is convenient to handle this separate from detailed pointer discussion.

The internal behaviour of a synchronous service is unknown to *Emma*, only the interface is known. In most cases, the only option available is to simulate the interface and ignore the behaviour. In some cases, we can build a TNSDL implementation for an external synchronous service. There are also external synchronous services that can be ignored without problems.

5.1   Modelling Synchronous Services

Some of the synchronous services have no effect on the analysis at all like those offered by the program block CLUGEN which typically are procedures that display data at terminal monitors. All use of these external synchronous services can be left out of the analysis. To speed up the removal of irrelevant synchronous services a tool program **emmastrip** was made when preparing the program blocks for the tests. The tool is described in more detail in Section 5.5.

When the behaviour of a synchronous service is absolutely essential to the analysis one can write partial substitutions called *stubs* in TNSDL, or even completely replace some synchronous services with TNSDL programs. In TNSDL, the functions from the ANSI C library defined in `string.h` can be used. There exist synchronous service definitions for them in the TNSDL library. Fortunately one can replace the C statements with equivalent TNSDL statements.

memset conversion example The following example demonstrates the results of performing such a translation. Consider the given data type definitions:

```
TYPE struct1_t
    REPRESENTATION STRUCT
        big     word;
        pos     bool;
    ENDSTRUCT;
ENDTYPE struct1_t;

TYPE struct2_t
    REPRESENTATION STRUCT
        digit   byte;
        ptr     bytepointer;
        string  array(2) of character;
        stru    struct1_t;
    ENDSTRUCT;
ENDTYPE struct2_t;
...
DCL
    x struct2_t;
...
```

If a piece of source code has as its original form

```
TASK memset(x, 0, SIZEOF(struct2_t));
```

then applying the translation rules results in

```
TASK x.digit := 0;
TASK x.ptr := NIL;
TASK x.string(0) := character(0);
TASK x.string(1) := character(0);
TASK x.stru.big = 0;
TASK x.stru.pos = F;
```

memcpy(target, source, size); is normally used to copy data between variables of the same data type. Copying between differing data types is normally an error, and is not considered further here. With this simplification `memcpy` turns into an assignment of the value of one variable to another variable. With simple data types a simple assignment statement will do, but with structures the assignment must be performed field by field as in initialisations in the `memset` case. TNSDL allows direct assignment of arrays, which makes their treatment easy [1].

The predefined variable `UNINTERPRETED_SIGNAL_DATA` is a special case where the array must be copied entry by entry up to `UNINTERPRETED_SIGNAL_LENGTH`. A simple array assignment will not do because the size of `UNINTERPRETED_SIG-NAL_DATA` is not known at compilation time.

The untagged union type is a problem in *Emma*, but it will be solved in the *Maria* analyser, which has a union type.

---

[1] Surprisingly TNSDL assignment with arrays is more efficient in machine code than `memcpy`

Some software designers always build a structure for a union. The structure has two fields: the union field and a tag field indicating the type used in the union field at any specified moment. In this case, the analysis engineer has the possibility to write a DECISION statement which handles all possible alternatives correctly. The tag field does not allow automatic transformation because it is not specified exactly how to refer to each of the union members.

The principle is the same for handling many other functions like memmove which copies a number of bytes from one memory address to another, strcpy which is a special case of memcpy, strncpy which is a variant of strcpy and strncmp which compares two strings byte by byte.

Efficiency Considerations As always in reachability analysis it is very important to take the effect on the size of the reachability graph into consideration also when some functions are replaced by TNSDL code. When TNSDL arrays are initialised as in the memset case it is possible to choose between writing a TASK statement for each array index, or using a loop.

1) Straight code:

```
TASK ai(0) := 0;
TASK ai(1) := 0;
TASK ai(2) := 0;
TASK ai(3) := 0;
TASK ai(4) := 0;
etc. up to 7
```

2) Loop:

```
DCL i byte;
...
WHILE (i < SIZEOF(ai));
    TASK ai(i) := 0;
ENDWHILE;
```

These alternatives were added to a system consisting of one program block and one master process. The master process contained originally only the START SDL transition which ended in a STOP statement and the net model consisted of 27 places and 3 net transitions giving a reachability graph with 2 nodes.

Adding the straight code increased the net model with 9 places and 8 transitions giving a reachability graph with 8 more nodes. Adding a loop increased the net model with 5 places and 5 transitions, but resulting in a reachability graph with 34 additional nodes. The result suggests that loops should be avoided.

Concatenating assignments of local variables within a TNSDL transition into a single net transition would reduce the size of the reachability graph. A simple rule is that all local variable assignments where the left hand side (that is the target of assignment) is not used in the right hand size of an assignment or as by-reference argument of a procedure call or in any other expression can be concatenated without distorting analysis.

This is really a question for the model generator in *Emma*. It is possible to join multiple assignments in a TNSDL transition into a single net transition as long as the set of input places is distinct from the set of output places as suggested by Markus Malmqvist [5].

5.2   Data Type Related Changes

Because of the problems with union data types all data types of this kind must be changed. There are basically three alternatives:

- Change a UNION type into a structure. If the size of the data type is not essential the changed source code behaves identically except for the growth in memory consumption.
- Replace a UNION type with a structure where only one of the union's alternatives exist. Then remove all source code related to the alternatives.
- Remove the UNION type completely and all source code related to it.

In the next generation analyser, Maria, the problems related to the union data type are solved elegantly by connecting the data type to a value for every piece of data in a union.

5.3   Handling Pointers

Due to extensive use of pointers a large portion of the TNSDL source code would require modifications to make the source code understandable to *Emma*. In many situations, the only possible way to modify programs to pointer-less is to completely remove statements containing pointer interpretation. In addition to the fact that such removals are time consuming to perform, they might change the concurrent behaviour. This is the main reason why the analysis engineer must consider very carefully whether to remove or replace a problematic statement.

In this section, a few possible ways to handle TNSDL pointers are defined. They are designed to allow *Emma* analysis with very limited preparations. Easy access to the analysis is essential if one wants to include it into a set of normal software development activities, much in the same way as *lint* variants are used in professional C source code development.

Neglecting pointers can cause trouble in cases where pointers are used in expressions of DECISION statements for example resulting in loss of some executions paths. These paths may contain OUTPUT or NEXTSTATE statements. To have the source code make sense syntactically we must consider the entire expression, not just pointers. We could simply use some default, e.g. FALSE.

To avoid infinite loops it is suggested that the (sub)expressions containing pointer handling in a WHILE loop condition are interpreted as FALSE by default. The only exception to this is the NOT expression: with NOT operators the outermost NOT must evaluate to FALSE. The outermost here does not mean code such as NOT(T OR NOT(expr)) but code such as NOT(NOT(expr)).

The complete removal of pointers is a very harsh treatment of the original TNSDL source code and should be avoided.

If all accesses to an object to which a pointer refers ($ and ->) were interpreted somehow, complete removal would be necessary only for references accessing an address of an object (@). It is suggested that the default values for $ and -> dereferences evaluates to the initialisation value of the corresponding data type as in the memset case. The default interpretation does not give much more precision to analysis compared to complete removal. What it gives is a closer relationship between the original source code and a more complete path in the interpreted reachability graph because fewer statements are removed.

A better way is to let the user specify a value for a pointer expression or give a replacement for a statement containing a pointer. These could be specified in the option file of *Emma*.

5.4   DX 200 Specific Features

This section describes how the DX 200 specific features mainly related to fault tolerance issues can be eliminated from the source code.

Usually addressing a message is done by using the process identifier available in predefined TNSDL variables SELF, PARENT, OFFSPRING and SENDER. The most common exception is the start-up messages using the signal route definition in the routing file. In some rare backup related situations, neither of these methods will do but we must determine the process identifier dynamically, for example if it is necessary to change the computer information of the sender from the spare unit to the working unit. Such treatment of backup strategies is quite out of the scope of *Emma* and such modifications may be commented out without problems in the analysis.

There are also cases where a process identifier is not only changed, but built from scratch. Should this happen there is no way *Emma* could construct the address of a receiver.

The OUTPUT statement can contain implementation-dependent attribute specifications. The following is an example of this use of attributes and how it should be commented out:

```
OUTPUT print_char_s TO special_pid /*, SET GROUP=funny_c,
                                PRIORITY=max_priority-1*/;
```

5.5   Tool Set

Most of the changes to the TNSDL source code files must be done manually before feeding them into the *Emma* analyser. To make preparation easier some tools were made to find possible sources of problems and to automate some of the changes as defined in this section. All of them alter either the TNSDL source code or the FCF and TESTP files generated by the TNSDL compiler.

emmastrip removes the calls of synchronous services not relevant to the analysis of concurrency. This is a very useful tool because it succeeded in removing a great number of problematic statements in every program block in the sample programs.

chkptr investigates TNSDL source code modules and reports any use of pointers. This is useful in pinpointing statements requiring special attention. The chkptr is a simple Bourne shell script using basic Unix tools to do the search efficiently. It simply searches for occurrences of @, $, and ->.

6   The New Modular Analyser *Maria*

Emma was intended to be a modular analyser but it was impossible to achieve this goal using *PROD*, which is implemented in a very "non-modular" way and difficult to develop further. Together with the problems concerning complex data types this caused us to start designing a completely new analyser, *Maria* (Modular Reachability Analyser, Figure 4). This project [10], financed by TEKES, started in 1998 and will result in a free analyser (under Gnu Public License) with front-ends for both standard SDL (possibly SDL-2000) and TNSDL, in addition to typed (sorted) Pr/T nets.

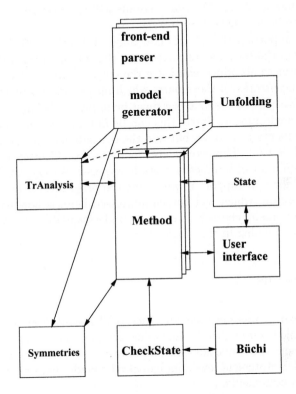

Fig.4. The *Maria* analyser.

The new analyser should be easy to connect to other tools like Design/CPN [1] and [8] which have very good graphical front-ends. It is also important that new analysis methods can easily be added to the analyser because there is no method which would be the best for all kinds of systems. Thus we need a number of different specialised analysis methods.

The experience from applying *Emma* to industrial programs showed that substantial changes and simplifications have to be made to make any analysis at all possible. As mentioned it is a real problem to handle huge and infinite reachability graphs. Therefore the new analyser will have methods for on-the-fly, but also *partial* reachability analysis. In *Emma* there are some options which can give a partial analysis, but these possibilities must be expanded considerably.

These approximative methods use the *same* model which is used for complete (and usually very time consuming) reachability analysis. They are used mainly for fast debugging or when complete analysis is impossible. It is considered important also that the user can guide the analysis to those portions of the code which he considers most sensitive to errors.

Storing the reachability graph is not very efficient in *Emma*. A graph with only 35 000 nodes may need as much as 150 Mbytes. This must be made much better in the new analyser. The *State* module will be implemented using efficient techniques like incremental state storage.

The most important thing is *not* how many states the analyser can generate, because most of those states are correct and thus of no interest. What we really need are new methods which can leave the correct states out of the generated graph and concentrates on those parts which may contain problems.

The *user interface* of the analyser must be improved before it can be used in an industrial environment. Partly this can be obtained by making interfaces to other tools as mentioned above, but also the reachability analysis must be easier to follow and control. This would also increase the efficiency of the analysis, especially when a lot of interactive work is required. As suggested above, there is also a need for tool support in *preparing* the programs for analysis. Another important question, which will not be addressed here, is how to make a good interface to the model checker. It must be understandable also for an engineer without special training in time logic.

7   Conclusions

The *Emma* project was unexpectedly successful because the *complete* TNSDL could be handled *automatically*, including complex data types, dynamic processes and timers. The analysis can be performed with a very fine granularity down to the SDL statement level, but can also be made coarser e.g. for sequences of independent statements.

Although successful on the pure TNSDL level, the evaluation at Nokia Telecommunications showed that there still is a lot to do before the analysis can be performed automatically in a real industrial environment. This is mainly a question of preparing the TNSDL programs for the analysis. It should be noted, however, that this preparatory work, even as it stands now, is just a fraction of the work which has to be done in manual design of a formal model.

A future project for implementing a *new more powerful analyser*, *Maria* is already under way at the Theoretical Computer Science Laboratory. It will implement many of the ideas behind *Emma* which could not be realised in the settings available earlier. This is a very research intensive project but the driving force will be the needs of the practical software engineering involved in the design and maintenance of distributed concurrent systems.

The construction of *Emma* and the industrial evaluation of it has shown that it is possible to build an industrial analyser for a *complete* and *real* programming language using high level Petri nets. The first prototype has brought good experience and the industrial feedback shows the direction of further development.

The aim with the *Maria* project is to make this new analyser useful both for academic prototyping and industrial analysis.

8 Acknowledgements

Special thanks to Esa Kettunen who initiated the *Emma* project while working at Nokia Telecommunications, which completely financed the project. This work has partly been supported also by the ETX program of TEKES - the Technology Development Centre in Finland.

References

[1] Design/CPN Home Page. http://www.daimi.aau.dk/CPnets/.

[2] P. Godefroid. Partial-Order Methods for the Verification of Concurrent Systems - An Approach to the State-Explosion Problem. Phd thesis, University of Liege, November 1994.

[3] Berndt Grahlmann. *Parallel Programs as Nets.* Phd thesis, Universität Hildesheim, September 1998.

[4] Tero Jyrinki. Dynamical Analysis of SDL Programs with Predicate/Transition Nets. Technical report, Helsinki University of Technology, Digital Systems Laboratory, April 1997.

[5] Markus Malmqvist. Methodology of Dynamical Analysis of SDL Programs Using Predicate/Transition Nets. Technical report, Helsinki University of Technology, Digital Systems Laboratory, April 1997.

[6] Tapio Manner. Extending Verification of Industrial TNSDL Programs with Formal Methods Using Emma. Master's thesis, Helsinki University of Technology, Theoretical Computer Science Laboratory, November 1998.

[7] ObjectGEODE Home Page. http://www.verilogusa.com/solution/geode.htm.

[8] SDT Home Page. http://www.telelogic.se/.

[9] CCITT Specification and Description Language (SDL). Technical Report Z.100 (1993), ITU-T, June 1994.

[10] Theoretical Computer Science Laboratory, Helsinki University of Technology. *Maria - a Modular Reachability Analyzer*, October 1 1998. Unpublished research plan 4.0.

[11] Antti Valmari. State Space Generation: Efficiency and Practicality. PhD thesis 55, Tampere University of Technology, Tampere, Finland, 1988.

[12] Kimmo Varpaaniemi. On th Stubborn Set Method in Reduced State Space Generation. Research Report 51, Digital Systems Laboratory, Helsinki University of Technology, FIN-02015 HUT, Finland, May 1998.

[13] Kimmo Varpaaniemi, Jaakko Halme, Kari Hiekkanen, and Tino Pyssysalo. PROD Reference Manual. Technical Report 13, Digital Systems Laboratory, Helsinki University of Technology, FIN-02150 ESBO, Finland, August 1995.

[14] François Vernadat, Pierre Azéma, and François Michel. Covering Step Graph. In J. Billington and W. Reisig, editors, *Application and Theory of Petri Nets 1996*, volume 1091 of *LNCS*, pages 516–535. Springer-Verlag, 1996.

Correctness Proof of the Standardized Algorithm for ABR Conformance

Jean-François Monin and Francis Klay

France Télécom CNET DTL/MSV, Technopôle Anticipa
2 av. Pierre Marzin, 22307 Lannion, France
JeanFrancois.Monin@cnet.francetelecom.fr

Abstract. Conformance control for ATM cells is based on a real-time reactive algorithm which delivers a value depending on inputs from the network. This value must always agree with a well defined theoretical value. We present here the correctness proof of the algorithm standardized for the ATM transfer capability called ABR. The proof turned out a key argument during the standardization process of ABR.

1 Introduction

We want to present in this paper an unusual (at least to our knowledge) application of formal methods in telecommunications, though it is closely related to a protocol. There is now quite a long tradition in using formal languages in this area, even standardized ones. They are based on communicating (extended) finite state machines (e.g. Estelle, SDL, Promela) or process algebra (e.g. Lotos). Verification based on model checking [16, 8] or simulation [14] has also been successfully employed. Typically, you model the protocol at hand, using one of the above formalisms, and then you try to verify that bad things like unexpected messages, deadlocks and so on never happen. To this effect you may use temporal logic formulas or observers and automated verification tools. This approach turns out very useful because the global behavior of a system made of several concurrent components is difficult to grasp.

In the problem we deal with here, complexity does not lie in parallelism or message interleaving, but in a single sequential, short, real-time and reactive algorithm. This algorithms runs on a key device for an ATM Transfer Capability called ABR (see below). It handles a small scheduler and delivers a value which depends on inputs from the network. We essentially have to prove that the value delivered by the device always agrees with (more precisely: is not smaller than) a theoretical value whose computation is not feasible under realistic assumptions. The correctness proof presented here has been a key argument in the standardization process of ABR.

The technique used is basically the calculus of weakest preconditions. However real time comes into the picture: not only the mathematical expression of the problem involves functions of the time, but invariants themselves involve such functions: a scheduler predicts values in the future. In order to make the result as convincing as possible (a must in the context of standardization) we do not hesitate to make proof steps explicit and before anything we start from a very simple and declarative specification $\mathcal{S}_d$. At a later stage, we describe the state space of the device under study, as well as associated invariants. Unfortunately specification $\mathcal{S}_d$ is technically not well suited to the correctness proof. A bit of theory has to be developed, in order to get an equivalent but more tractable computational specification $\mathcal{S}_c$. The invariant to be proved is then stated in terms of $\mathcal{S}_c$ and the proof can be carried out thanks to preliminary lemmas related to $\mathcal{S}_c$. This paper aims at giving the details of this work. Note that the specification and the whole proof have been completely formalized with CoQ [5], an automated proof assistant based on type theory [15].

The rest of this paper is organized as follows. Section 2 describes the problem as well as the stakes for telecommunications. Section 3 states the specifications called $\mathcal{S}_d$ and $\mathcal{S}_c$ above and explains how to get the latter from the former. Section 4 describes the state space with its invariant and sketches the main steps of the proof (the standardized algorithm and technical details of its correctness proof are respectively given in appendix A and B). We end with concluding remarks and related work in section 5.

2   Context and Motivation

2.1   Conformance Control in ATM

In an ATM (Asynchronous Transfer Mode) network, data packets (cells) sent by a user must not exceed a rate which is defined by a contract negotiated between the user and the network. Several modes for using an ATM network, called "ATM Transfer Capabilities" (ATCs) have been defined. Each ATC may be seen as a generic contract between the user and the network, saying that the network must guarantee the negotiated *quality of service* (QoS), defined by a number of characteristics like maximum cell loss or transfer delay, provided the cells sent by the user conform to the negotiated traffic parameters (for instance, their rate must be bounded by some value). The conformance of cells sent by the user is checked using an algorithm called GCRA (generic control of cell rate algorithm). In this way, the network is protected against users misbehaviors and keeps enough resources for delivering the required QoS to well behaved users.

In fact, a new ATC cannot be accepted (as an international standard) without an efficient conformance control algorithm, and some evidence that this algorithm has the intended behavior.

For the ATC called ABR (Available Bit Rate), considered here, a simple but inefficient algorithm had been proposed in a first stage. Reasonably efficient algorithms proposed later turned out to be fairly complicated. This situation has been settled when one of them, due to Christophe Rabadan, has been proved correct in relation to the simple one: this algorithm is now part of the I.371.1 standard [13]. The first version of the proof was hand written. The main invariants discovered during this process are included in I.371.1. Later on, the proof has been completely formalized and mechanically verified with CoQ [5].

2.2   The Case of ABR

In some of the most recently defined ATCs, like ABR, the allowed cell rate (ACR) may vary during the same session, depending on the current congestion state of the network. Such ATCs are designed for irregular sources, that need high cell rates from time to time, but that may reduce their cell rate when the network is busy. A servo-mechanism is then proposed in order to let the user know whether he can send data or not. This mechanism has to be well defined, in order to have a clear traffic contract between user and network. The key is an adaptation of the public algorithm for checking conformance of cells.

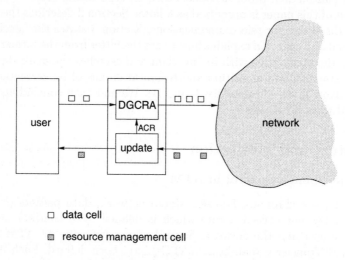

□ data cell

▩ resource management cell

Fig. 1. conformance control

An abstract view of the protocol ABR is given in fig. 1 (actually, resource management (RM) cells are sent by the user, but only their transmission from the network to the user is relevant here; details are available in [17]). The conformance control algorithm for ABR has two parts. The first one is called DGCRA (dynamic GCRA). It just checks that the rate of data cells emitted by the user is not higher than a value which is approximately Acr, the allowed cell rate. Excess cells may be discarded by DGCRA. Note that, in the case of ABR, Acr depends on time: its value has to be known each time a new data cell comes from the user. This part is quite simple and is not addressed here. The complexity lies in the computation of $Acr(t)$ ("update" in fig. 1), which depends on the sequence of values (ER_n) carried by resource management cells coming from the network. By a slight abuse of notation, the cell carrying ER_n will be called itself ER_n.

Of course, $Acr(t)$ depends only on cells ER_n whose arrival time t_n is such that $t_n < t$ (we order resource management cells so that $t_n < t_{n+1}$ for any n). In ABR, a resource management cell carries a value of Acr, that should be reached as soon as possible. At first sight, $\text{Acr}(t)$ should then be simply the last ER_i received at time t, i.e. ER_i with $i = \text{last}(t)$, where $\text{last}(x)$ is the only integer such that $t_i \leq x < t_{i+1}$. Unfortunately, because of electric propagation time and various transmission mechanisms, the user is aware of this expected value only after a delay. Taking the user's reaction time τ observed by the control device into consideration, that is, the overall round trip time between the control device and the user, $\text{Acr}(t)$ should then be ER_i with $i = \text{last}(t - \tau)$. But τ may vary in turn. ITU-T considers that a lower bound τ_3 and an upper bound τ_2 for τ are established during the negotiation phase of each ABR connection. Hence, a cell arriving from the user at time t on DGCRA may legitimately have been emitted using any rate ER_i such that i is between $\text{last}(t - \tau_2)$ and $\text{last}(t - \tau_3)$. Any rate less than or equal to any of these values, or, equivalently less than or equal to the maximum of them, should then be allowed. Therefore, $\text{Acr}(t)$ is taken as the maximum of these ER_i.

Actually the standards committee did not give these explanations, but directly specified the set of ER_i under the equivalent form (2) below.

2.3   Effective Computation of $\text{Acr}(t)$

ITU-T committee considered that a direct computation of $\text{Acr}(t)$ is not feasible at reasonable cost with current technologies: it would amount to compute the maximum of several hundreds integers each time a cell is received from the user. However, it is not difficult to see that $\text{Acr}(t)$ is constant on any interval that contains no value among $\{t_n + \tau \mid \tau = \tau_2 \vee \tau = \tau_3\}$. In other words, $\text{Acr}(t)$ is determined by a sequence of values. It then becomes possible to use a scheduler handling future changes of $\text{Acr}(t)$. This scheduler is updated when a new cell ER_n is received. Roughly, if s is the current time, ER_n will be taken into account at time $s + \tau_3$, while ER_{n-1} will not be taken into account after $s + \tau_2$.

The control conformance algorithm considered here exploits this idea, with the further constraint that only a small amount of memory is allocated to the scheduler. This means that some information is lost. *Filtering is performed in such a way that the actual value of* $\text{Acr}(t)$ *is greater or equal to its theoretical value, as defined above.*

3   Ideal ACR

3.1   Declarative Specification

The declarative specification ($\mathcal{S}_d$ in the introduction) of the ideal value or Acr is given by (1) and (2) under assumption (3). We are given a sequence of RM cells (ER_i) whose arrival date are respectively (t_i); the desired allowed cell rate at time t is defined by :

$$\text{Acr}(t) = \max\{\text{ER}_i \mid i \in I(t)\}, \tag{1}$$

where I is the interval defined by :

$$i \in I(t) \quad \text{iff} \quad (t - \tau_2 < t_i \leq t - \tau_3) \vee (t_i \leq t - \tau_2 < t_{i+1}) . \tag{2}$$

The t_i are taken in increasing order :

$$t_1 < t_2 < \ldots t_n < \ldots \tag{3}$$

The following equivalent characterization of $I(t)$ is easier to handle:

$$i \in I(t) \quad \text{iff} \quad t_i + \tau_3 \leq t < t_{i+1} + \tau_2 \tag{4}$$

The initial (inefficient) ABR conformance control algorithm was a direct computation of Acr according to (1).

3.2   Specification Using only Finite Knowledge

In practice, only finite prefixes of the sequence (t_i) are available. Then we have to take into account that, given a list l of length $\sharp l$ of RM cells (ER_i) whose arrival date are respectively (t_i), t_{i+1} makes sense only for $i < \sharp l$. However, if we consider that $t_{\sharp l+1} = \infty$, (4) boils down to $\sharp l \in I(t)$ iff $t_{\sharp l} \leq t - \tau_3$. With this intuition in mind we introduce

$$\text{Approx}(l, t) = \max\{ER_i \mid i \in I_a(l, t)\}, \tag{5}$$

where $I_a(l, t)$ is similar to $I(t)$:

$$i \in I_a(l, t) \quad \text{iff} \quad \left\{ \begin{array}{ll} i \in I(t) & \wedge \quad i < \sharp l \\ \vee & \\ t_i \leq t - \tau_3 & \wedge \quad i = \sharp l . \end{array} \right. \tag{6}$$

The list l we consider depends on time : $l(s)$ contains all indices i such that $t_i \leq s$, where s represents the current time. The following lemma, whose meaning is that it is enough to compute $\text{Approx}(l(s), t)$, is easy to prove :

Lemma 1.
(i) The value of Approx *at t becomes stable after $t - \tau_3$:*

$$\forall s \geq t - \tau_3, \quad \text{Approx}(l(s), t) = \text{Approx}(l(t - \tau_3), t) .$$

(ii) $\text{Approx}(l(s), t)$ *is an exact approximation of* $\text{Acr}(t)$ *for $s \geq t - \tau_3$:*

$$\forall t, \quad \text{Acr}(t) = \text{Approx}(l(t - \tau_3), t) .$$

Unless otherwise stated s will remain implicit in the following : we will note just l instead of $l(s)$. In the same way, variables like Efi (see below) actually handled by the algorithm denote a value that also depends on s, but will be noted just Efi. We also assume without loss of generality that ER_0 is equal to the initial value of Acr; if the algorithm starts at s_0, this amounts to stating $t_0 = s_0 - \tau_3$ and for $i > 0$, $t_i > s_0$:

$$t_0 = s_0 - \tau_3 < s_0 < t_1 < t_2 < \ldots t_{\#l} \,. \tag{7}$$

Note that hereafter, $\#l$ is the number of the last element of l.

The will use the following explicit characterization of $I_a(l,t)$:

$$i \in I_a(l,t) \text{ iff } \begin{cases} t_i + \tau_3 \leq t < t_{i+1} + \tau_2 & \wedge \quad i < \#l \\ \vee \\ t_i + \tau_3 \leq t & \wedge \quad i = \#l \,. \end{cases} \tag{8}$$

In particular, for $t' \geq t \geq t_{\#l} + \tau_3$, we have $i \in I_a(l,t')$ implies $i \in I_a(l,t)$, hence the following lemma :

Lemma 2. Approx(l,t) is decreasing after $t_{\#l} + \tau_3$:

$$\forall t, t', t_{\#l} + \tau_3 \leq t \leq t' \Rightarrow \text{Approx}(l,t') \leq \text{Approx}(l,t) \,.$$

It is also easy to see that for any t greater than $t_{\#l} + \tau_2$, the only i of $I_a(l,t)$ is $\#l$, hence the following lemma :

Lemma 3.

$$\forall t, \quad t_{\#l} + \tau_2 \leq t \quad \Rightarrow \quad i \in I_a(l,t) \text{ iff } i = \#l, \tag{9}$$

$$\forall t, \quad t_{\#l} + \tau_2 \leq t \quad \Rightarrow \quad \text{Approx}(l,t) = \text{ER}_{\#l}. \tag{10}$$

3.3   Computing Approx in an Incremental Way

Initially (at time $s_0 = t_0 + \tau_3$), we have $l = \langle t_0 \rangle$. The characterization (8) of I_a yields then

$$i \in I_a(\langle t_0 \rangle, t) \quad \text{iff} \quad s_0 \leq t \wedge i = 0 \,.$$

Then we get (as desired):

$$\forall t, \quad s_0 \leq t \Rightarrow \text{Approx}(\langle t_0 \rangle, t) = \text{ER}_0 \,. \tag{11}$$

We now consider the adjunction of a new t_n at the end of l. The new list is denoted by $l^\frown t_n$, and we have $n = \#l + 1 = \#(l^\frown t_n)$. Three cases have to be considered : $i < n-1$, $i = n-1$ and $i = n$. We can further assume that $t < t_n + \tau_2$, because lemma 3 gives us directly the result if $t_n + \tau_2 \leq t$. The assumption $t < t_n + \tau_2$ is especially useful for $i = n-1$. Using (8) we see that

- for $i < n-1$, $i \in I_a(l,t)$ iff $t_i + \tau_3 \leq t < t_{i+1} + \tau_2$ iff $i \in I_a(l^\frown t_n, t)$,
- for $t < t_n + \tau_2$, $n-1 \in I_a(l,t)$ iff $t_{n-1} + \tau_3 \leq t$ iff $n-1 \in I_a(l^\frown t_n, t)$,
- $n \in I_a(l^\frown t_n, t)$ iff $t_n + \tau_3 \leq t$.

Hence we can verify that :

- for $t < t_n + \tau_3$, $i \in I_a(l^\frown t_n, t)$ iff $i \in I_a(l, t)$,
- for $t_n + \tau_3 \leq t < t_n + \tau_2$, $i \in I_a(l^\frown t_n, t)$ iff $i \in I_a(l, t) \vee i = n$,
- for $t_n + \tau_2 \leq t$, $i \in I_a(l^\frown t_n, t)$ iff $i = n$ (by (9)).

Thus we get the following way of computing the value of $\mathrm{Approx}(l^\frown t_n, t)$ from the value of $\mathrm{Approx}(l, t)$ (this what we called $\mathcal{S}_c$ in the introduction):

Lemma 4. *The value of* $\mathrm{Approx}(l^\frown t_n, t)$ *is given by :*

	$t < t_n + \tau_3$	$t_n + \tau_3 \leq t < t_n + \tau_2$	$t_n + \tau_2 \leq t$
$\mathrm{Approx}(l^\frown t_n, t)$	$\mathrm{Approx}(l, t)$	$\max(\mathrm{Approx}(l, t), \mathrm{ER}_n)$	ER_n

.

A simple but useful consequence of lemma 4 is :

Lemma 5.

$$\forall\, l, t, t_n, \mathrm{ER}_n, M,$$
$$\mathrm{Approx}(l, t) \leq M \,\wedge\, \mathrm{ER}_n \leq M \quad \Rightarrow \quad \mathrm{Approx}(l^\frown t_n, t) \leq M. \quad (12)$$

4   Proof of Algorithm B'

The enhanced algorithm B proposed by CNET (hereafter called B') computes an upper bound of Approx. More precisely, at the current instant s, the state $e(s)$ handled by B' defines a function $\mathrm{Ub}(e(s), t)$ greater than $\mathrm{Approx}(l(s), t)$ for any $t \geq s$ and not defined for $t < s$.

Running the algorithm consists of changing the state e into a e'. Such a step is called a *transition*. Here we have essentially two kinds of transitions: the first is fired when receiving a new RM cell, the second is fired when the current time reaches the date for a scheduled event.

We basically use standard calculus of weakest preconditions [9] with notations taken from B [1]. Our treatment of time is inspired by timed automata of [3] and the synchrony hypothesis of synchronous languages [11]. We assume that our system reacts more quickly than its environment : state transitions induced by the arrival of a RM cell or due to the scheduler are finished before the arrival of a new RM cell. This assumption depends on the technology used in the real device and can be checked on it. It is then safe to consider that a transition takes no time. Timed automata consider two kinds of transitions: "continuous" ones concerning time evolution (modeled by clocks) and "discrete" ones concerning the state.

Here we just need to assume the existence of an external clock, with an internal value s that can be read but not written by programming means. We model the progress of time by an implicit assignment

$$s := \text{current date},$$

for instance $s := t_k$ when the kth RM cell is received. The new value of s cannot be smaller than its old value, and we also constrain the new value in a way such that no event arose in the meantime (we assume that the scheduler is reliable). Formally, we consider transitions of the form

$$\langle s, e \rangle \longrightarrow \langle s', e' \rangle$$

with $s \leq s'$ and such that nothing happened between s and s', and where e' is the new state obtained from s after running a transition of algorithm B'. This is made explicit in assumptions (G_e) and (G_i) below. It may happen that an internal event is scheduled at a time t_k. In that case, the internal event has to be handled first.

Transitions are modeled by program assignments or "generalized substitutions" in the terminology of B.

4.1 Components of the State

The state e is made of 5 variables :

- ACR, the current ACR;
- Efi, the next ACR if nothing new happens;
- tfi, the date at which Efi will be active if nothing new happens;
- Ela, containing the value of the last known order ($ER_{\sharp l}$);
- tla, the date at which Ela will be active if nothing new happens.

As an optimization trick, there is a sixth variable Emx whose value is just the maximum of Efi and Ela.

4.2 Transitions

The algorithm reacts either when receiving a new ER_n, i.e. when the current time reaches t_n (this is called an external event in the sequel), or when the current time reaches tfi (this is called an internal event in the sequel). Each transition changes the current state; an internal event is scheduled if and only if tfi is greater than the current time.

4.3 Invariant

Here we want to ensure that B' provides an ACR which cannot be less than the ideal value $\text{Acr}(s)$. To this effect we prove that the following property is invariant. The current time is noted s.

$$\text{Approx}(l, s) \leq \text{ACR} \tag{I_{main}}$$

I_{main} is itself a consequence of the following conjunction.

$$\text{Emx} = \max(\text{Efi}, \text{Ela}) \tag{I_{max}}$$
$$\text{Ela} = \text{ER}_{\#l} \tag{I_{Ela}}$$
$$\text{tfi} \leq \text{tla} \leq t_{\#l} + \tau_2 \tag{I_{fil}}$$
$$\text{tfi} \leq s \Rightarrow \forall t, \ s \leq t \Rightarrow \text{Approx}(l, t) \leq \text{ACR} \tag{I_{tfs}}$$
$$\text{ACR} < \text{Efi} \Rightarrow \text{tfi} \leq t_{\#l} + \tau_3 \tag{I_{Et1}}$$
$$\text{Efi} < \text{Ela} \Rightarrow \text{tla} \leq t_{\#l} + \tau_3 \tag{I_{Et2}}$$
$$\text{tfi} = \text{tla} \Rightarrow \text{Efi} = \text{Ela} \tag{I_{ttE}}$$
$$\forall t \quad s \leq t < \text{tfi} \Rightarrow \text{Approx}(l, t) \leq \text{ACR} \tag{I_{Ub1}}$$
$$\forall t \quad \text{tfi} \leq t < \text{tla} \Rightarrow \text{Approx}(l, t) \leq \text{Efi} \tag{I_{Ub2}}$$
$$\forall t \quad \text{tla} \leq t \Rightarrow \text{Approx}(l, t) \leq \text{Ela} . \tag{I_{Ub3}}$$

We define

$$\text{Inv} = I_{max} \wedge I_{Ela} \wedge I_{fil} \wedge I_{tfs} \wedge I_{Et1} \wedge I_{Et2} \wedge I_{ttE} \wedge I_{Ub1} \wedge I_{Ub2} \wedge I_{Ub3}.$$

Invariants I_{Ub1}, I_{Ub2} and I_{Ub3} mean that $\text{Approx}(l, t) \leq \text{Ub}(e, t)$ for $t \geq s$, where the function $\text{Ub}(e, t)$ is defined by: $\text{Ub}(e, t) = \text{ACR}$ for $s \leq t < \text{tfi}$, $\text{Ub}(e, t) = \text{Efi}$ for $\text{tfi} \leq t < \text{tla}$, $\text{Ub}(e, t) = \text{Ela}$ for $\text{tla} \leq t$. In the sequel we use the following consequence of I_{max}, I_{Ub2} and I_{Ub3}:

$$\forall t \quad \text{tfi} \leq t \Rightarrow \text{Approx}(l, t) \leq \text{Emx} . \tag{I_{Apx}}$$

Lemma 6. Inv *implies* I_{main}.

Proof. We have either $\text{tfi} \leq s$ or $s < \text{tfi}$. Apply respectively I_{tfs} and I_{Ub1} with $t = s$.

4.4   Initial State

Initially we have $l = \langle t_0 \rangle$, $\#l = 0$ and we want to show that Inv is true in the initial state defined by:

$$\text{tfi} = \text{tla} = s_0, \text{ACR} = \text{Emx} = \text{Efi} = \text{Ela} = \text{ER}_0 \quad \text{(initial value of Acr)}.$$

Formally, we consider the substitution S_0:

$$S_0 \overset{\text{df}}{=} l, \text{ACR}, \text{Emx}, \text{Efi}, \text{Ela}, \text{tfi}, \text{tla} := \langle t_0 \rangle, \text{ER}_0, \text{ER}_0, \text{ER}_0, \text{ER}_0, s_0, s_0$$

and we show $[S_0]\text{Inv}$. The proof is very easy.

4.5   External Event

Let s be the current time. Let k be an abbreviation for $\sharp l + 1$. We consider a transition from s to $s' = t_k$ (and consistently of $e(s)$ to $e(t_k)$) only if $s \le t_k$ and there is no internal event between s and t_k. Formally, the following guard is taken for granted:

$$s \le t_k \;\wedge\; (\texttt{tfi} \le s \vee t_k < \texttt{tfi}). \tag{G_e}$$

At time t_k, the list l becomes then $l^\frown t_k$. Formally, the following substitution is always taken into account:

$$\mathsf{T_e} \;\stackrel{\mathrm{df}}{=}\; s, l := t_k, l^\frown t_k.$$

The complete pseudo-code and the proof are given is appendixes A and B.

4.6   Internal Event

Let s be the current time. We consider a transition from s to $s' = \texttt{tfi}$ (and consistently of $e(s)$ to $e(\texttt{tfi})$) only if $s < \texttt{tfi}$ and there is no external event between s and $\texttt{tfi}$. Formally, the following guard is taken for granted:

$$t_{\sharp l} \le s \le \texttt{tfi} \le t_{\sharp l+1}. \tag{G_i}$$

The substitution $\mathsf{T_i} \;\stackrel{\mathrm{df}}{=}\; s := \texttt{tfi}.$ is also taken into account. Let $\mathsf{S_i}$ be the substitution

$$\mathsf{S_i} \;\stackrel{\mathrm{df}}{=}\; \mathsf{T_i} \;\|\; \texttt{ACR}, \texttt{tfi}, \texttt{Efi}, \texttt{Emx} := \texttt{Efi}, \texttt{tla}, \texttt{Ela}, \texttt{Ela}.$$

In appendix B we show: $\mathrm{Inv} \wedge (G_i) \Rightarrow [\mathsf{S_i}]\mathrm{Inv}$.

4.7   Observing Intermediate States

Let s be the current time. We consider a transition from $\langle s, e \rangle$ to $\langle s', e \rangle$ only if $s \le s'$ and there is no event between s and s'. Actually s' may be equal to t_k but must remain less than $\texttt{tfi}$ (when real time reaches $\texttt{tfi}$, $\mathsf{S_i}$ must run). Formally, the following guard is taken for granted:

$$s \le s' \;\wedge\; (\texttt{tfi} \le s \vee s' < \texttt{tfi}) \;\wedge\; \\ (\forall i,\; t_i \le s \vee s' \le t_i) \;\wedge\; s = t_{\sharp l+1} \Rightarrow s' = t_{\sharp l+1}. \tag{G_o}$$

The transition is modeled by the substitution: $\mathsf{T_o} \;\stackrel{\mathrm{df}}{=}\; s := s'.$ In appendix B we show $\mathrm{Inv} \wedge (G_o) \Rightarrow [\mathsf{T_o}]\mathrm{Inv}$.

4.8   Main Theorem

Our main result is an easy consequence of previous lemmas.

Theorem 1. *At any time s we have* $\mathrm{Acr}(s) \le \mathsf{ACR}$.

Proof. Using lemma 1 we know that $\mathrm{Acr}(s) = \mathrm{Approx}(l, s)$. As Inv is actually an invariant, lemma 6 yields $\mathrm{Approx}(l, s) \le \mathsf{ACR}$, hence the result.

5   Discussion and Related Work

For engineers working in the context of standardization, theorem 1 is much more convincing than the similar theorem involving Approx instead of Acr. However it is clear for us that the computational characterization of Approx (lemma 4) is much more suited for reasoning about B'. In a first attempt, we tried to prove directly the invariant Inv using (1) and (2). This resulted in shallow areas and even holes in the manual proof.

We also submitted the problem of the correctness of B' to other research teams, in order to assess other approaches. It is too early (and beyond the scope of this paper) to compare the results of these works, we just give some hints. Model checking using classical and temporal automata is experimented in the framework of FORMA (http://www-verimag.imag.fr/FORMA), a project founded by the French government which aims at experimenting various formal methods on industrial case studies. In the two first attempts, the property to be checked corresponded to theorem 1, but modeling Acr contributed to an explosion of the number of states. Moreover the tools used—UPPAAL [6] and MEC [4]—allowed only fixed numeric values for τ_2, τ_3 and ER_i. Checking the algorithm could be carried through for small values. Later on, good results within two different frameworks have been obtained by L. Fribourg [10] and B. Bérard [7], with specifications based on Approx instead of Acr. In one framework, they used the parameterized temporized automata of Hytech [12], and in the other an automated proof search procedure due to Revesz [18] was extended to timed automata. In both cases τ_2, τ_3, etc. were symbolic parameters and the desired property could be checked without the help of Inv. In our case, Inv has been incrementally constructed while attempting to prove I_{tfs} and I_{Ub1}, following the steps given in appendix B. Note that such calculations are boring and error prone: this is why we felt that the proof should be checked with a proof assistant. Indeed, our experiment with CoQ [15] showed that one of the proofs of appendix B was wrong (but could be repaired, fortunately !). A detailed comparison between the approaches mentioned above will be done in a forthcoming paper.

Finally, let us say a word on two attempts using B. At CNET we (with G. Blorec) tried to use this method on this case study two years ago. At first sight B should be well suited, because of our systematic use of substitution calculus. But we failed to handle time and the very notion of scheduler in a nice way; our specification was heavy and many proof obligations could not be discharged. Recently, Abrial worked on this problem using an event oriented variant of B and he succeeded to reconstruct an algorithm different from the one standardized in I.371, but where the design decisions are much clearer [2].

Our current feeling is that specialized procedures or methods can discharge boring and painful parts in the verification process, but are really successful only on "predigested" specifications like $\mathcal{S}_c$, in contrast with $\mathcal{S}_d$. On the other side, general purpose frameworks and tools like type theory and CoQ are helpful on the whole process but still require much more interaction from the user on the parts automatically handled by specialized methods. Work is in progress for integrating both kind of techniques in the same tool.

Acknowledgement

The problem has been submitted by Christophe Rabadan, who is the main author of the algorithm studied in this document. This work has benefited of very fruitful discussions with him and Annie Gravey. Many improvements are also due to the comments of anonymous referees.

References

[1] J.-R. Abrial. *The B-Book: Assigning Programs to Meanings.* Cambridge University Press, 1996.

[2] J.-R. Abrial. Développement de l'algorithme ABR. Personal communication, 1999.

[3] R. Alur and D. L. Dill. A theory of timed automata. *Theoretical Computer Science*, 126(2):183–235, April 1994.

[4] A. Arnold. MEC: A system for constructing and analysing transition systems. In J. Sifakis, editor, *Proceedings of the International Workshop on Automatic Verification Methods for Finite State Systems*, volume 407 of *LNCS*, pages 117–132, Berlin, June 1990. Springer.

[5] Bruno Barras and all. The coq proof assistant reference manual : Version 6.1. Technical Report RT-0203, INRIA, 1997.

[6] J. Bengtsson, K. G. Larsen, F. Larsson, P. Pettersson, and Wang Yi. UPPAAL: a tool suite for the automatic verification of real-time systems. In R. Alur, T. A. Henzinger, and E. D. Sontag, editors, *Hybrid Systems III*, volume 1066 of *Lecture Notes in Computer Science*, pages 232–243. Springer-Verlag, 1996.

[7] B. Bérard and L. Fribourg. Automated verification of a parametric real-time program: the ABR conformance protocol. In *CAV'99*, Lecture Notes in Computer Science. Springer-Verlag, 1999. To appear.

[8] D. Clark, E. M. Emerson, and A. P. Sistla. Automatic verification of finite state concurrent systems using temporal logic specifications: a practical approach. In *Proc. 10th ACM Symp. on Principles of Programming Languages*, 1983.

[9] E. W. Dijkstra. *A Discipline of Programming.* Prentice-Hall, Englewood Cliffs, NJ, 1976.

[10] L. Fribourg. A closed-form evaluation for extended timed automata. Research Report LSV-98-2, Lab. Specification and Verification, ENS de Cachan, Cachan, France, March 1998. 17 pages.

[11] N. Halbwachs. *Synchronous Programming of Reactive Systems.* Kluwer Academic Publishers, 1993.

[12] T. A. Henzinger, P.-H. Ho, and H. Wong-Toi. HYTECH: A model checker for hybrid systems. *Lecture Notes in Computer Science*, 1254:460–463, 1997.

[13] ITU-T. *Traffic control and congestion control in B-ISDN.* Recommendation I.371.1.

[14] C. Jard, J.-F. Monin, and R. Groz. Development of Veda, a Prototyping Tool for Distributed Algorithms. *IEEE Transactions on Software Engineering*, 14(3):339–352, march 1988.

[15] Jean-François Monin. Proving a real time algorithm for ATM in Coq. In E. Gimenez and C. Paulin-Mohring, editors, *Types for Proofs and Programs*, volume 1512 of *LNCS*, pages 277–293. Springer Verlag, 1998.

[16] J. P. Queille and J. Sifakis. Specification and verification of concurrent systems in CESAR. In *Proc. 5th Int'l Symp. on Programming*, Lecture Notes in Computer Science, Vol. 137, pages 337–371. SV, Berlin/New York, 1982.

[17] Christophe Rabadan. L'ABR et sa conformité. NT DAC/ARP/034, CNET, 1997.

[18] P. Z. Revesz. A closed-form evaluation for Datalog queries with integer (gap)-order constraints. *Theoretical Computer Science*, 116(1):117–149, August 1993.

A   Pseudo-code for Algorithm B'

When real time reaches t_k :

if $t_k <$ tfi **then**
  if Emx $\leq$ ER$_k$ **then**
    if tfi $< t_k + \tau_3$ **then**
      if $t_k + \tau_3 <$ tla $\vee$ tfi $=$ tla **then**
        Emx $:=$ ER$_k$ $\|$ Ela $:=$ ER$_k$ $\|$ tla $:= t_k + \tau_3$
      else
        Emx $:=$ ER$_k$ $\|$ Ela $:=$ ER$_k$
    else
      if ACR $\leq$ ER$_k$ **then**
        Emx $:=$ ER$_k$ $\|$ Efi $:=$ ER$_k$ $\|$ Ela $:=$ ER$_k$ $\|$ tfi $:= t_k + \tau_3$ $\|$ tla $:= t_k + \tau_3$
      else
        Emx $:=$ ER$_k$ $\|$ Efi $:=$ ER$_k$ $\|$ Ela $:=$ ER$_k$ $\|$ tla $:=$ tfi
  else
    if ER$_k <$ Ela **then**
      Efi $:=$ Emx $\|$ Ela $:=$ ER$_k$ $\|$ tla $:= t_k + \tau_2$
    else
      Efi $:=$ Emx $\|$ Ela $:=$ ER$_k$
else
  if ACR $\leq$ ER$_k$ **then**
    Efi $:=$ ER$_k$ $\|$ Ela $:=$ ER$_k$ $\|$ Emx $:=$ ER$_k$ $\|$ tfi $:= t_k + \tau_3$ $\|$ tla $:= t_k + \tau_3$
  else
    Efi $:=$ ER$_k$ $\|$ Ela $:=$ ER$_k$ $\|$ Emx $:=$ ER$_k$ $\|$ tfi $:= t_k + \tau_2$ $\|$ tla $:= t_k + \tau_2$

When real time reaches tfi:

ACR $:=$ Efi $\|$ tfi $:=$ tla $\|$ Efi $:=$ Ela $\|$ Emx $:=$ Ela

If tfi $= t_k$, we run the algorithm for tfi, then the algorithm for t_k.

B   Proof of Algorithm B'

Remark 1. Proof obligations concerning the preservation of I_{tfs} and of I_{Ub1} have the form $[S_n] \dots s \leq t \Rightarrow \dots$, where S_n includes T_e: we then have to prove $\dots t_k \leq t \Rightarrow \dots$ Under the assumption (G_e), $t_k \leq t$ yields in fact $s \leq t$, we may apply hypotheses of the form $\dots s \leq t \Rightarrow \dots$ if Inv holds at time s.

Remark 2. We consider proof obligations of the form $[S]\mathrm{Inv}$, where $[S]$ is a substitution. It is decomposed into $[S]I_{max}$, $[S]I_{Ela}$, $[S]I_{fil}$, $[S]I_{tfs}$, $[S]I_{Et1}$, $[S]I_{Et2}$, $[S]I_{ttE}$, $[S]I_{Ub1}$, $[S]I_{Ub2}$ and $[S]I_{Ub3}$. Some of them are immediate, for instance $\mathrm{Efi} < \mathrm{ER}_k \Rightarrow t_k + \tau_3 \leq t_k + \tau_3$ or $\mathrm{Ela} < \mathrm{Ela} \Rightarrow \mathrm{tla} \leq t_{\#l} + \tau_3$. They are skipped in order to save space.

Case 1

if $t_k < \mathrm{tfi}$ **then if** $\mathrm{Emx} \leq \mathrm{ER}_k$ **then if** $\mathrm{tfi} < t_k + \tau_3$
  then if $t_k + \tau_3 < \mathrm{tla} \lor \mathrm{tfi} = \mathrm{tla}$
  then $\mathrm{Emx} := \mathrm{ER}_k \parallel \mathrm{Ela} := \mathrm{ER}_k \parallel \mathrm{tla} := t_k + \tau_3$

Let S_1 be the substitution $S_1 \overset{\mathrm{df}}{=} T_e \parallel \mathrm{Emx}, \mathrm{Ela}, \mathrm{tla} := \mathrm{ER}_k, \mathrm{ER}_k, t_k + \tau_3$. This transition is correct if :

$$\mathrm{Inv} \quad \land \quad (G_e) \quad \land$$
$$t_k < \mathrm{tfi} \quad \land \qquad\qquad\qquad\qquad (G_{11})$$
$$\mathrm{Emx} \leq \mathrm{ER}_k \quad \land \qquad\qquad\qquad (G_{12})$$
$$\mathrm{tfi} < t_k + \tau_3 \quad \land \qquad\qquad\quad (G_{13})$$
$$(t_k + \tau_3 < \mathrm{tla} \lor \mathrm{tfi} = \mathrm{tla}) \qquad \Rightarrow \qquad (G_{14})$$
$$[S_1]\mathrm{Inv}.$$

Proof. We assume Inv, (G_e), (G_{11}), (G_{12}), (G_{13}), (G_{14}), and we prove $[S_1]\mathrm{Inv}$.

- $[S_1]I_{max}$, that is $\mathrm{ER}_k = \max(\mathrm{Efi}, \mathrm{ER}_k)$: by I_{max} and (G_{12}).
- $[S_1]I_{fil}$, that is $\mathrm{tfi} \leq t_k + \tau_3 \leq t_k + \tau_2$: trivial from (G_{13}).
- $[S_1]I_{tfs}$, that is $\mathrm{tfi} \leq t_k \Rightarrow \forall t, t_k \leq t \Rightarrow \mathrm{Approx}(l^\frown t_k, t) \leq \mathrm{ACR}$: absurd hypothesis, given (G_{11}).
- $[S_1]I_{Et1}$, that is $\mathrm{ACR} < \mathrm{Efi} \Rightarrow \mathrm{tfi} \leq t_k + \tau_3$: the conclusion comes from (G_{13}).
- $[S_1]I_{ttE}$, that is $\mathrm{tfi} = t_k + \tau_3 \Rightarrow \mathrm{Efi} = \mathrm{ER}_k$: absurd hypothesis, given (G_{13}).
- $[S_1]I_{Ub1}$, that is $\forall t, t_k \leq t < \mathrm{tfi} \Rightarrow \mathrm{Approx}(l^\frown t_k, t) \leq \mathrm{ACR}$:
  for t such that $t_k \leq t < \mathrm{tfi}$, we get $t < t_k + \tau_3$ by (G_{13}), then lemma 4 yields $\mathrm{Approx}(l^\frown t_k, t) = \mathrm{Approx}(l, t)$; we also have $s < t_k < \mathrm{tfi}$ by (G_e), then we can apply I_{Ub1} (see remark 1), and finally we get
  $\mathrm{Approx}(l^\frown t_k, t) = \mathrm{Approx}(l, t) \leq \mathrm{ACR}$.
- $[S_1]I_{Ub2}$, that is $\forall t, \mathrm{tfi} \leq t < t_k + \tau_3 \Rightarrow \mathrm{Approx}(l^\frown t_k, t) \leq \mathrm{Efi}$:
  first remark that $\mathrm{Approx}(l^\frown t_k, t) = \mathrm{Approx}(l, t)$ by lemma 4; (G_{14}) gives either $t_k + \tau_3 < \mathrm{tla}$, or $\mathrm{tfi} = \mathrm{tla}$;

- in the former case, $\text{Approx}(l, t) \leq \text{Efi}$ by I_{Ub2}, hence the result;
- in the latter case, I_{ttE} yields $\text{Efi} = \text{Ela}$, and $\text{tla} = \text{tfi} \leq t$ yields $\text{Approx}(l, t) \leq \text{Ela}$ by I_{Ub3}, hence the result.

— $[\text{S}_1]\text{I}_{\text{Ub3}}$, that is $\forall t,\ t_k + \tau_3 \leq t \Rightarrow \text{Approx}(l^\frown t_k, t) \leq \text{ER}_k$:
we show $\forall t,\ t_k + \tau_3 \leq t \Rightarrow \text{Approx}(l^\frown t_k, t) = \text{ER}_k$:
for t such that $t_k + \tau_3 \leq t$, we have $\text{tfi} \leq t$ by (G_{13}), then $\text{Approx}(l, t) \leq$
$\text{Emx} \leq \text{ER}_k$ by I_{Apx} and (G_{12}); lemma 4 yields either
$\text{Approx}(l^\frown t_k, t) = \max(\text{Approx}(l, t), \text{ER}_k)$ or $\text{Approx}(l^\frown t_k, t) = \text{ER}_k$; in
both cases, we see that $\text{Approx}(l^\frown t_k, t) = \text{ER}_k$.

Case 2

if $t_k < \text{tfi}$ **then if** $\text{Emx} \leq \text{ER}_k$ **then if** $\text{tfi} < t_k + \tau_3$ **then**
 if $t_k + \tau_3 < \text{tla} \lor \text{tfi} = \text{tla}$ **then**
 else $\text{Emx} := \text{ER}_k \ \|\ \text{Ela} := \text{ER}_k$

Let S_2 be the substitution $\text{S}_2 \stackrel{\text{df}}{=} \text{T}_e \ \|\ \text{Emx}, \text{Ela} := \text{ER}_k, \text{ER}_k$. This transition is correct if :

$$
\begin{aligned}
\text{Inv} \ \wedge \ \ (G_e) \ \ \wedge & \\
t_k < \text{tfi} \ \ \wedge & \qquad (G_{11}) \\
\text{Emx} \leq \text{ER}_k \ \ \wedge & \qquad (G_{12}) \\
\text{tfi} < t_k + \tau_3 \ \ \wedge & \qquad (G_{13}) \\
\text{tla} \leq t_k + \tau_3 \ \ \wedge & \qquad (G_{24}) \\
\text{tfi} \neq \text{tla} \ \ \Rightarrow & \qquad (G_{25}) \\
[\text{S}_2]\text{Inv}. &
\end{aligned}
$$

Proof. $[\text{S}_2]\text{I}_{\max}$, $[\text{S}_2]\text{I}_{\text{tfs}}$ and $[\text{S}_2]\text{I}_{\text{Et1}}$, are proved as in case 1.

— $[\text{S}_2]\text{I}_{\text{fil}}$, that is $\text{tfi} \leq \text{tla} \leq t_k + \tau_2$: trivial from I_{fil} (G_{24}).
— $[\text{S}_2]\text{I}_{\text{Et2}}$, that is $\text{Efi} < \text{ER}_k \Rightarrow \text{tla} \leq t_k + \tau_3$: the conclusion is (G_{24}).
— $[\text{S}_2]\text{I}_{\text{ttE}}$, that is $\text{tfi} = \text{tla} \Rightarrow \text{Efi} = \text{ER}_k$: absurd hypothesis, given (G_{25}).
— $[\text{S}_2]\text{I}_{\text{Ub1}}$, that is $\forall t,\ t_k \leq t < \text{tfi} \Rightarrow \text{Approx}(l^\frown t_k, t) \leq \text{ACR}$:
using (G_{13}), lemma 4 and I_{Ub1} (see remark 1), we have
$\text{Approx}(l^\frown t_k, t) = \text{Approx}(l, t) \leq \text{ACR}$.
— $[\text{S}_2]\text{I}_{\text{Ub2}}$, that is $\forall t,\ \text{tfi} \leq t < \text{tla} \Rightarrow \text{Approx}(l^\frown t_k, t) \leq \text{Efi}$:
$\text{Approx}(l^\frown t_k, t) = \text{Approx}(l, t)$ by lemma 4 and (G_{24}); $\text{Approx}(l, t) \leq \text{Efi}$
by I_{Ub2}, hence the result.
— $[\text{S}_2]\text{I}_{\text{Ub3}}$, that is $\forall t,\ \text{tla} \leq t \Rightarrow \text{Approx}(l^\frown t_k, t) \leq \text{ER}_k$:
we have $\text{tfi} \leq t$ by I_{fil}, then $\text{Approx}(l, t) \leq \text{Emx} \leq \text{ER}_k$ by I_{Apx} and (G_{12});
taking $M = \text{ER}_k$ in lemma 5 gives $\text{Approx}(l^\frown t_k, t) \leq \text{ER}_k$.

Case 3

if $t_k < \mathtt{tfi}$ then if $\mathtt{Emx} \leq \mathrm{ER}_k$ then if $\mathtt{tfi} < t_k + \tau_3$ then
 else if $\mathrm{ACR} \leq \mathrm{ER}_k$ then
 $\mathtt{Emx} := \mathrm{ER}_k \parallel \mathtt{Efi} := \mathrm{ER}_k \parallel \mathtt{Ela} := \mathrm{ER}_k \parallel \mathtt{tfi} := t_k + \tau_3 \parallel \mathtt{tla} := t_k + \tau_3$

Let S_3 be the substitution

$$\mathsf{S}_3 \overset{\mathrm{df}}{=} \mathsf{T}_e \parallel \mathtt{Efi}, \mathtt{Ela}, \mathtt{Emx}, \mathtt{tfi}, \mathtt{tla} := \mathrm{ER}_k, \mathrm{ER}_k, \mathrm{ER}_k, t_k + \tau_3, t_k + \tau_3.$$

This transition is correct if :

$$
\begin{aligned}
\mathrm{Inv} \quad &\wedge \quad (G_e) \quad \wedge \\
&t_k < \mathtt{tfi} \quad \wedge &&(G_{11}) \\
&\mathtt{Emx} \leq \mathrm{ER}_k \quad \wedge &&(G_{12}) \\
&t_k + \tau_3 \leq \mathtt{tfi} \quad \wedge &&(G_{33}) \\
&\mathrm{ACR} \leq \mathrm{ER}_k \quad \Rightarrow &&(G_{34}) \\
&[\mathsf{S}_3]\mathrm{Inv}.
\end{aligned}
$$

Proof.

- $[\mathsf{S}_3]\mathrm{I}_{\mathrm{Ub1}}$, that is $\forall t,\ t_k \leq t < t_k + \tau_3 \Rightarrow \mathrm{Approx}(l^\frown t_k, t) \leq \mathrm{ACR}$: using lemma 4 and $\mathrm{I}_{\mathrm{Ub1}}$ (see remark 1), we have $\mathrm{Approx}(l^\frown t_k, t) = \mathrm{Approx}(l, t) \leq \mathrm{ACR}$.
- $[\mathsf{S}_3]\mathrm{I}_{\mathrm{Ub3}}$, that is $\forall t,\ t_k + \tau_3 \leq t \Rightarrow \mathrm{Approx}(l^\frown t_k, t) \leq \mathrm{ER}_k$: we show $\forall t,\ t_k + \tau_3 \leq t \Rightarrow \mathrm{Approx}(l^\frown t_k, t) = \mathrm{ER}_k$; we have either $t < \mathtt{tfi}$ or $\mathtt{tfi} \leq t$;
  - in the first case, $\mathrm{Approx}(l, t) \leq \mathrm{ACR} \leq \mathrm{ER}_k$ by $\mathrm{I}_{\mathrm{Ub1}}$ (see remark 1; here $t_k \leq t$ comes from $t_k \leq t_k + \tau_3 \leq t$) and (G_{34});
  - in the second case, $\mathrm{Approx}(l, t) \leq \mathtt{Emx} \leq \mathrm{ER}_k$ by $\mathrm{I}_{\mathrm{Apx}}$ and (G_{12});
  hence $\mathrm{Approx}(l, t) \leq \mathrm{ER}_k$ is always true; using lemma 4 we get $\mathrm{Approx}(l^\frown t_k, t) = \mathrm{ER}_k$ for t such that $t_k + \tau_3 \leq t$.

Case 4

if $t_k < \mathtt{tfi}$ then if $\mathtt{Emx} \leq \mathrm{ER}_k$
 then if $\mathtt{tfi} < t_k + \tau_3$ then
 else $\mathtt{Emx} := \mathrm{ER}_k \parallel \mathtt{Efi} := \mathrm{ER}_k \parallel \mathtt{Ela} := \mathrm{ER}_k \parallel \mathtt{tla} := \mathtt{tfi}$

Let S_4 be the substitution

$$\mathsf{S}_4 \overset{\mathrm{df}}{=} \mathsf{T}_e \parallel \mathtt{Efi}, \mathtt{Ela}, \mathtt{Emx}, \mathtt{tla} := \mathrm{ER}_k, \mathrm{ER}_k, \mathrm{ER}_k, \mathtt{tfi}.$$

This transition is correct if :

$$
\begin{aligned}
\mathrm{Inv} \quad &\wedge \quad (G_e) \quad \wedge \\
&t_k < \mathtt{tfi} \quad \wedge &&(G_{11}) \\
&\mathtt{Emx} \leq \mathrm{ER}_k \quad \wedge &&(G_{12}) \\
&t_k + \tau_3 \leq \mathtt{tfi} \quad \wedge &&(G_{33}) \\
&\mathrm{ER}_k < \mathrm{ACR} \quad \Rightarrow &&(G_{44}) \\
&[\mathsf{S}_4]\mathrm{Inv}.
\end{aligned}
$$

Proof.

- $[S_4]I_{fil}$, that is $\mathtt{tfi} \leq \mathtt{tfi} \leq t_k + \tau_2$:
  we have $\mathtt{tfi} \leq t_{\#l} + \tau_2 = t_{k-1} + \tau_2 \leq t_k + \tau_2$ by I_{fil}, definition of $\#l$ and (7).
- $[S_4]I_{tfs}$, that is $\mathtt{tfi} \leq t_k \Rightarrow \forall t,\, t_k \leq t \Rightarrow \mathrm{Approx}(l^\frown t_k, t) \leq \mathsf{ACR}$: hypothesis absurd, given (G_{11}).
- $[S_4]I_{Et1}$, that is $\mathsf{ACR} < \mathsf{ER}_k \Rightarrow \mathtt{tfi} \leq t_k + \tau_3$: absurd hypothesis, given (G_{44}).
- $[S_4]I_{Ub1}$, that is $\forall t,\, t_k \leq t < \mathtt{tfi} \Rightarrow \mathrm{Approx}(l^\frown t_k, t) \leq \mathsf{ACR}$:
  by I_{Ub1} (see remark 1) and $t < \mathtt{tfi}$, we have $\mathrm{Approx}(l, t) \leq \mathsf{ACR}$; taking $M = \mathsf{ACR}$ in lemma 5 and using (G_{44}) yields $\mathrm{Approx}(l^\frown t_k, t) \leq \mathsf{ACR}$.
- $[S_4]I_{Ub3}$, that is $\forall t,\, \mathtt{tfi} \leq t \Rightarrow \mathrm{Approx}(l^\frown t_k, t) \leq \mathsf{ER}_k$: we show
  $\forall t,\, \mathtt{tfi} \leq t \Rightarrow \mathrm{Approx}(l^\frown t_k, t) = \mathsf{ER}_k$; for t such that $\mathtt{tfi} \leq t$, we have
  $\mathrm{Approx}(l, t) \leq \mathsf{Emx} \leq \mathsf{ER}_k$ by I_{Apx} and (G_{12}); we have $t_k + \tau_3 \leq \mathtt{tfi} \leq t$ by
  (G_{33}), then lemma 4 yields either $\mathrm{Approx}(l^\frown t_k, t) = \max(\mathrm{Approx}(l, t), \mathsf{ER}_k)$
  or $\mathrm{Approx}(l^\frown t_k, t) = \mathsf{ER}_k$; in both cases, we see that $\mathrm{Approx}(l^\frown t_k, t) = \mathsf{ER}_k$.

Case 5

if $t_k < \mathtt{tfi}$ **then if** $\mathsf{Emx} \leq \mathsf{ER}_k$ **then else if** $\mathsf{ER}_k < \mathsf{Ela}$
  then $\mathtt{Efi} := \mathsf{Emx}$ $\|$ $\mathsf{Ela} := \mathsf{ER}_k$ $\|$ $\mathtt{tla} := t_k + \tau_2$

Let S_5 be the substitution

$$S_5 \overset{\mathrm{df}}{=} T_e \ \| \ \mathtt{Efi}, \mathsf{Ela}, \mathtt{tla} := \mathsf{Emx}, \mathsf{ER}_k, t_k + \tau_2.$$

This transition is correct if :

$$
\begin{aligned}
&\mathrm{Inv} \ \wedge \ (G_e) \ \wedge \\
&\quad t_k < \mathtt{tfi} \ \wedge && (G_{11}) \\
&\quad \mathsf{ER}_k < \mathsf{Emx} \ \wedge && (G_{52}) \\
&\quad \mathsf{ER}_k < \mathsf{Ela} \quad \Rightarrow && (G_{53}) \\
&\quad [S_5]\mathrm{Inv}.
\end{aligned}
$$

Proof. $[S_5]I_{fil}$ and $[S_5]I_{tfs}$ are similar to $[S_4]I_{fil}$ and $[S_4]I_{tfs}$

- $[S_5]I_{max}$, that is $\mathsf{Emx} = \max(\mathsf{Emx}, \mathsf{ER}_k)$: by (G_{52}).
- $[S_5]I_{Et1}$, that is $\mathsf{ACR} < \mathsf{Emx} \Rightarrow \mathtt{tfi} \leq t_k + \tau_3$: we have $\mathtt{Efi} < \mathsf{Ela}$ or $\mathsf{Ela} \leq \mathtt{Efi}$;
    - in the first case, $\mathtt{tfi} \leq \mathtt{tla} \leq t_{\#l} + \tau_3$ by I_{fil} and I_{Et2};
    - in the second case, $\mathsf{Emx} = \mathtt{Efi}$, then $\mathtt{tfi} \leq t_{\#l} + \tau_3$ by I_{Et1} and I_{max};
  in both cases, $\mathtt{tfi} \leq t_{k-1} + \tau_3 \leq t_k + \tau_3$ by definition of $\#l$ and (7).
- $[S_5]I_{Et2}$, that is $\mathsf{Emx} < \mathsf{ER}_k \Rightarrow t_k + \tau_2 \leq t_k + \tau_3$:
  the hypothesis $\mathsf{Emx} < \mathsf{ER}_k$ is absurd given (G_{52}).
- $[S_5]I_{ttE}$, that is $\mathtt{tfi} = t_k + \tau_2 \Rightarrow \mathsf{Emx} = \mathsf{ER}_k$:
  we have $\mathtt{tfi} \leq t_{\#l} + \tau_2 = t_{k-1} + \tau_2 < t_k + \tau_2$ by I_{fil}, definition of $\#l$ and (7);
  then the hypothesis $\mathtt{tfi} = t_k + \tau_2$ is absurd.
- $[S_5]I_{Ub1}$, that is $\forall t,\, t_k \leq t < \mathtt{tfi} \Rightarrow \mathrm{Approx}(l^\frown t_k, t) \leq \mathsf{ACR}$:
  by I_{Ub1} (see remark 1) and $t < \mathtt{tfi}$, we have $\mathrm{Approx}(l, t) \leq \mathsf{ACR}$; we also
  have $\mathtt{tfi} \leq t_k + \tau_3$ or $t_k + \tau_3 < \mathtt{tfi}$;

- in the first case, $\text{Approx}(l^\frown t_k, t) = \text{Approx}(l, t) \leq \text{ACR}$ by lemma 4;
- in the second case, $\text{ER}_k < \text{Emx} \leq \text{ACR}$ by (G_{52}) and contraposition of $[S_5]I_{\text{Et1}}$ shown above; taking $M = \text{ACR}$ in lemma 5 yields $\text{Approx}(l^\frown t_k, t) \leq \text{ACR}$.
- $[S_5]I_{\text{Ub2}}$, that is $\forall t,\ \text{tfi} \leq t < t_k + \tau_2 \Rightarrow \text{Approx}(l^\frown t_k, t) \leq \text{Emx}$:
  for t such that $\text{tfi} \leq t$, we have $\text{Approx}(l, t) \leq \text{Emx}$, by I_{Apx}; taking $M = \text{Emx}$ in lemma 5 and using (G_{52}) yields $\text{Approx}(l^\frown t_k, t) \leq \text{Emx}$.
- $[S_5]I_{\text{Ub3}}$, that is $\forall t,\ t_k + \tau_2 \leq t \Rightarrow \text{Approx}(l^\frown t_k, t) \leq \text{ER}_k$:
  by lemma 4, we have $\forall t,\ t_k + \tau_2 \leq t \Rightarrow \text{Approx}(l^\frown t_k, t) = \text{ER}_k$.

Case 6

if $t_k < \text{tfi}$ **then if** $\text{Emx} \leq \text{ER}_k$ **then else if** $\text{ER}_k < \text{Ela}$ **then**
   else $\text{Efi} := \text{Emx}\ \|\ \text{Ela} := \text{ER}_k$

Let S_6 be the substitution

$$S_6 \overset{\text{df}}{=} T_e\ \|\ \text{Efi}, \text{Ela} := \text{Emx}, \text{ER}_k.$$

This transition is correct if :

$$
\begin{aligned}
\text{Inv}\ &\wedge\ (G_e)\ \wedge \\
&t_k < \text{tfi}\ \wedge && (G_{11}) \\
&\text{ER}_k < \text{Emx}\ \wedge && (G_{52}) \\
&\text{Ela} \leq \text{ER}_k && (G_{63}) \\
&\quad\Rightarrow \\
&[S_6]\text{Inv}.
\end{aligned}
$$

Proof. $[S_6]I_{\text{Et1}}$ and $[S_6]I_{\text{Et2}}$ are similar to $[S_5]I_{\text{Et1}}$ and $[S_5]I_{\text{Et2}}$.

- $[S_6]I_{\max}$, that is $\text{Emx} = \max(\text{Emx}, \text{ER}_k)$: by (G_{52}).
- $[S_6]I_{\text{fil}}$, that is $\text{tfi} \leq \text{tla} \leq t_k + \tau_2$: we have
  $\text{tfi} \leq \text{tla} \leq t_{\sharp l} + \tau_2 = t_{k-1} + \tau_2 \leq t_k + \tau_2$ by I_{fil}, definition of $\sharp l$ and (7).
- $[S_6]I_{\text{tfs}}$, that is $\text{tfi} \leq t_k \Rightarrow \forall t,\ t_k \leq t \Rightarrow \text{Approx}(l^\frown t_k, t) \leq \text{ACR}$:
  the hypothesis is absurd given (G_{11}).
- $[S_6]I_{\text{ttE}}$, that is $\text{tfi} = \text{tla} \Rightarrow \text{Emx} = \text{ER}_k$:
  we use a weakened form of (G_{52}):

$$\text{ER}_k \leq \text{Emx}; \qquad\qquad (G_{52'})$$

  assuming $\text{tfi} = \text{tla}$, we have $\text{Efi} = \text{Ela} = \text{Emx}$ by $I_{\max}$, then $\text{Emx} = \text{Ela} \leq \text{ER}_k$ by (G_{63}); $\text{Emx} \leq \text{ER}_k$ and $(G_{52'})$ yields $\text{Emx} = \text{ER}_k$.
- $[S_6]I_{\text{Ub1}}$, that is $\forall t,\ t_k \leq t < \text{tfi} \Rightarrow \text{Approx}(l^\frown t_k, t) \leq \text{ACR}$:
  by I_{Ub1} (see remark 1) and $t < \text{tfi}$, we have $\text{Approx}(l, t) \leq \text{ACR}$; we also have $\text{tfi} \leq t_k + \tau_3$ or $t_k + \tau_3 < \text{tfi}$;
  - in the first case, $\text{Approx}(l^\frown t_k, t) = \text{Approx}(l, t) \leq \text{ACR}$ by lemma 4;
  - in the second case, $\text{ER}_k < \text{Emx} \leq \text{ACR}$ by (G_{52}) and contraposition of $[S_6]I_{\text{Et1}}$ shown above; taking $M = \text{ACR}$ in lemma 5 yields $\text{Approx}(l^\frown t_k, t) \leq \text{ACR}$.

- $[S_6]I_{Ub2}$, that is $\forall t$, $\mathtt{tfi} \leq t < \mathtt{tla} \Rightarrow \mathrm{Approx}(l^\frown t_k, t) \leq \mathtt{Emx}$:
  for t such that $\mathtt{tfi} \leq t$, we have $\mathrm{Approx}(l, t) \leq \mathtt{Emx}$, by I_{Apx}; taking $M = \mathtt{Emx}$
  in lemma 5 and using (G_{52}) yields $\mathrm{Approx}(l^\frown t_k, t) \leq \mathtt{Emx}$.
- $[S_6]I_{Ub3}$, that is $\forall t$, $\mathtt{tla} \leq t \Rightarrow \mathrm{Approx}(l^\frown t_k, t) \leq \mathrm{ER}_k$:
  for t such that $\mathtt{tla} \leq t$, we have $\mathrm{Approx}(l, t) \leq \mathtt{Ela} \leq \mathrm{ER}_k$ by I_{Ub3} and
  (G_{63}); taking $M = \mathrm{ER}_k$ in lemma 5 yields $\mathrm{Approx}(l^\frown t_k, t) \leq \mathrm{ER}_k$.
  Note that if we can ensure $t_k + \tau_3 \leq \mathtt{tla} \leq t$, we can show
  $\forall t$, $\mathtt{tla} \leq t \Rightarrow \mathrm{Approx}(l^\frown t_k, t) = \mathrm{ER}_k$.

Case 7

if $t_k < \mathtt{tfi}$ **then else if** $\mathrm{ACR} \leq \mathrm{ER}_k$ **then**
   $\mathtt{Efi} := \mathrm{ER}_k \parallel \mathtt{Ela} := \mathrm{ER}_k \parallel \mathtt{Emx} := \mathrm{ER}_k \parallel \mathtt{tfi} := t_k + \tau_3 \parallel \mathtt{tla} := t_k + \tau_3$

Let S_7 be the substitution

$$S_7 \overset{\mathrm{df}}{=} T_e \parallel \mathtt{Efi}, \mathtt{Ela}, \mathtt{Emx}, \mathtt{tfi}, \mathtt{tla} := \mathrm{ER}_k, \mathrm{ER}_k, \mathrm{ER}_k, t_k + \tau_3, t_k + \tau_3.$$

This transition is correct if :

$$
\begin{aligned}
\mathrm{Inv} \quad \wedge \quad &(G_e) \quad \wedge \\
&\mathtt{tfi} \leq t_k \quad \wedge && (G_{71}) \\
&\mathrm{ACR} \leq \mathrm{ER}_k \quad \Rightarrow && (G_{72}) \\
&[S_7]\mathrm{Inv}.
\end{aligned}
$$

Proof.

- $[S_3]I_{Ub1}$, that is $\forall t$, $t_k \leq t < t_k + \tau_3 \Rightarrow \mathrm{Approx}(l^\frown t_k, t) \leq \mathrm{ACR}$:
  we remark that $\mathtt{tfi} \leq s$ by (G_e) and (G_{71}), then $\mathrm{Approx}(l, t) \leq \mathrm{ACR}$ by
  I_{tfs} (see remark 1); using lemma 4 we have $\mathrm{Approx}(l^\frown t_k, t) = \mathrm{Approx}(l, t)$,
  hence $\mathrm{Approx}(l^\frown t_k, t) \leq \mathrm{ACR}$.
- $[S_3]I_{Ub3}$, that is $\forall t$, $t_k + \tau_3 \leq t \Rightarrow \mathrm{Approx}(l^\frown t_k, t) \leq \mathrm{ER}_k$:
  we show $\forall t$, $t_k + \tau_3 \leq t \Rightarrow \mathrm{Approx}(l^\frown t_k, t) = \mathrm{ER}_k$; we remark that $\mathtt{tfi} \leq s$
  by (G_e) and (G_{71}), then $\mathrm{Approx}(l, t) \leq \mathrm{ACR} \leq \mathrm{ER}_k$ by I_{tfs} (see remark 1;
  here $t_k < t$ comes from $t_k < t_k + \tau_3 \leq t$) and (G_{72}); using the assumption
  $t_k + \tau_3 \leq t$ and lemma 4, we know that $\mathrm{Approx}(l^\frown t_k, t)$ is either equal to
  $\max(\mathrm{Approx}(l, t), \mathrm{ER}_k)$ or to ER_k, that is, in both cases, to ER_k.

Case 8

if $t_k < \mathtt{tfi}$ **then else if** $\mathrm{ACR} \leq \mathrm{ER}_k$ **then else**
   $\mathtt{Efi} := \mathrm{ER}_k \parallel \mathtt{Ela} := \mathrm{ER}_k \parallel \mathtt{Emx} := \mathrm{ER}_k \parallel \mathtt{tfi} := t_k + \tau_2 \parallel \mathtt{tla} := t_k + \tau_2$

Let S_8 be the substitution

$$S_8 \overset{\mathrm{df}}{=} T_e \parallel \mathtt{Efi}, \mathtt{Ela}, \mathtt{Emx}, \mathtt{tfi}, \mathtt{tla} := \mathrm{ER}_k, \mathrm{ER}_k, \mathrm{ER}_k, t_k + \tau_2, t_k + \tau_2.$$

This transition is correct if :

$$\begin{aligned}
\text{Inv} \quad &\wedge \quad (G_e) \quad \wedge \\
&\texttt{tfi} \le t_k \quad \wedge \\
&\text{ER}_k < \text{ACR} \qquad \Rightarrow \\
&[\text{S}_8]\text{Inv}.
\end{aligned}$$

(G_{71})

(G_{82})

Proof.

- $[\text{S}_8]\text{I}_{\text{tfs}}$ and $[\text{S}_8]\text{I}_{\text{Ub2}}$ are similar to $[\text{S}_7]\text{I}_{\text{tfs}}$ and $[\text{S}_7]\text{I}_{\text{Ub2}}$, replacing τ_3 with τ_2.
- $[\text{S}_8]\text{I}_{\text{Et1}}$, that is $\text{ACR} < \text{ER}_k \Rightarrow t_k + \tau_2 \le t_k + \tau_3$: the hypothesis $\text{ACR} < \text{ER}_k$ is absurd given (G_{82}).
- $[\text{S}_8]\text{I}_{\text{Ub1}}$, that is $\forall t,\ t_k \le t < t_k + \tau_2 \Rightarrow \text{Approx}(l^\frown t_k, t) \le \text{ACR}$: for t such that $t_k \le t$, we have $\texttt{tfi} \le s$ by (G_e) and (G_{71}), then $\text{Approx}(l, t) \le \text{ACR}$ by I_{tfs} (see remark 1); taking $M = \text{ACR}$ in lemma 5 and using (G_{82}) yields $\text{Approx}(l^\frown t_k, t) \le \text{ACR}$.
- $[\text{S}_8]\text{I}_{\text{Ub3}}$, that is $\forall t,\ t_k + \tau_2 \le t \Rightarrow \text{Approx}(l^\frown t_k, t) \le \text{ER}_k$: by lemma 4, we have $\forall t,\ t_k + \tau_2 \le t \Rightarrow \text{Approx}(l^\frown t_k, t) = \text{ER}_k$.

Internal Event. We prove: $\text{Inv} \wedge (G_i) \Rightarrow [\text{S}_i]\text{Inv}$.

Proof.

- $[\text{S}_i]\text{I}_{\text{Ela}}$, that is $\texttt{Ela} = \text{ER}_{\#l}$: from I_{Ela}.
- $[\text{S}_i]\text{I}_{\text{fil}}$, that is $\texttt{tla} \le \texttt{tla} \le t_{\#l} + \tau_2$: we have $\texttt{tla} \le t_{\#l} + \tau_2$ by I_{fil}.
- $[\text{S}_i]\text{I}_{\text{tfs}}$, that is $\texttt{tla} \le \texttt{tfi} \Rightarrow \forall t,\ \texttt{tfi} \le t \Rightarrow \text{Approx}(l, t) \le \texttt{Efi}$: $\texttt{tla} \le \texttt{tfi}$ and I_{fil} yields $\texttt{tfi} = \texttt{tla}$, then $\texttt{Efi} = \texttt{Ela}$ by I_{ttE}; we then have to show that for t such that $\texttt{tla} \le t$, we have $\text{Approx}(l, t) \le \texttt{Ela}$: we just apply I_{Ub3}.
- $[\text{S}_i]\text{I}_{\text{Et1}}$, that is $\texttt{Efi} < \texttt{Ela} \Rightarrow \texttt{tla} \le t_{\#l} + \tau_3$: it is just I_{Et2}.
- $[\text{S}_i]\text{I}_{\text{Ub1}}$, that is $\forall t\ \texttt{tfi} \le t < \texttt{tla} \Rightarrow \text{Approx}(l, t) \le \texttt{Efi}$: it is just I_{Ub2}.
- $[\text{S}_i]\text{I}_{\text{Ub3}}$, that is $\forall t\ \texttt{tla} \le t \Rightarrow \text{Approx}(l, t) \le \texttt{Ela}$: for t such that $\texttt{tla} \le t$, we have $s \le \texttt{tla} \le t$ by (G_i); we can then apply I_{Ub3}, which yields $\text{Approx}(l, t) \le \texttt{Ela}$.

Observation Event. We prove: $\text{Inv} \wedge (G_o) \Rightarrow [\text{T}_o]\text{Inv}$.

Proof.

- $[\text{T}_o]\text{I}_{\text{tfs}}$, that is $\texttt{tfi} \le s' \Rightarrow \forall t,\ s' \le t \Rightarrow \text{Approx}(l, t) \le \text{ACR}$: from $\texttt{tfi} \le s'$ and (G_o) we get $\texttt{tfi} \le s$; for t such that $s' \le t$, we have $s \le t$ by (G_o) then $\text{Approx}(l, t) \le \text{ACR}$ by I_{tfs}.
- $[\text{T}_o]\text{I}_{\text{Ub1}}$, that is $\forall t\ s' \le t < \texttt{tfi} \Rightarrow \text{Approx}(l, t) \le \text{ACR}$: for t such that $s' \le t < \texttt{tfi}$ we have $s < s' \le t < \texttt{tfi}$ by (G_o), then $\text{Approx}(l, t) \le \text{ACR}$ by I_{Ub1}.

Verifying a Distributed Database Lookup Manager Written in Erlang

Thomas Arts[1] and Mads Dam[2]

[1] Computer Science Laboratory, Ericsson Utvecklings AB,
Box 1505, 125 25 Älvsjö, Sweden,
thomas@cslab.ericsson.se,
http://www.ericsson.se/cslab/~thomas/
[2] Swedish Institute of Computer Science, Box 1263, S-164 28 Kista, Sweden,
mfd@sics.se, http://www.sics.se/~mfd/home.html

Abstract. We describe a case-study in which formal methods were used to verify an important responsiveness property of a distributed database system which is used heavily at Ericsson in a number of recent products. One of the aims of the project was to verify the actual running code which is written in the distributed functional language Erlang. In a joint project between SICS and Ericsson we have over the past few years been developing a tableau-based verification tool for Erlang of considerable scope. In particular, we are capable of addressing — on the level of running program code — systems with unbounded behaviour along the many dimensions in which this happens in "real" programs, involving datatypes, recursive control structures, error handling and recovery, initialisation, and dynamic process creation. The database lookup manager considered here contains most of these features, giving rise to infinite state behaviour which is not very adequately handled using model checking or other approaches based purely on state space traversal. In the paper we introduce the case study, our approach to formalisation and verification, and discuss our experiences using the Erlang verification tool.

Industrial Applications, experience report
Keywords: Telecommunication; Proof Checker; Distributed Algorithms; Distributed Databases; Formal Verification

1 Introduction

Erlang [AVWW96, OSE98] is a functional programming language developed by Ericsson, which is used extensively for writing robust distributed telecommunication applications. Central in many of these applications is a distributed database, Mnesia [Mnesia], also written in Erlang. The Mnesia system is crucial to the robustness of almost all Erlang based product developed at Ericsson. It is, for instance, responsible for error recovery, the prompt and safe handling of which is essential in telecommunication applications. These features make the Mnesia system a rewarding object of study when trying out new verification techniques.

J. Wing, J. Woodcock, J. Davies (Eds.): FM'99, Vol. I, LNCS 1708, pp. 682–700, 1999.

The case study at hand concerns only a small part of the Mnesia system, a protocol for the evaluation of a query which is distributed over several computers in a network. The starting point for this case study was the Erlang code implementing the distributed database. The author of this code knew that the query lookup protocol was implemented in a tricky way and got interested in supporting his implementation with a clear and verified description.

We extracted, from the real implementation, the code for the distributed query evaluation protocol and added some code to provide a very simple simulated interface to parts of the system that were irrelevant for the problem at hand. The result was an Erlang program that could be seen as a very precise, and in some sense formal, description of the underlying algorithm. Isolation of the code responsible for the lookup mechanism and analysing the intended behaviour of the code resulted, as a side effect, in a clear and patentable picture of the underlying protocol [Nil99].

In Sect. 2 we present the distributed query evaluation in more detail. As input the protocol receives a database query divided into subqueries. These subqueries are distributed over the network in the form of processes on those computers where the specific data for a subquery is stored. By sending messages to the subquery processes, data is extracted from the database tables and sent along the network. One process is responsible for initialising the lookup process ring, and for collecting the resulting data. To avoid excessive delays and storage consumption, query answers are collected in segments, managed by the lookup manager. The task we set ourselves was to prove that the implementation provided a responsiveness property: that input queries are eventually being replied to.

The query lookup manager implements initialisation and query lookup phases in manners which are tightly interwoven. Both these phases are important for correct behaviour. Moreover, the code is evidently designed to cater for tables of arbitrary numbers and sizes, and for queries of arbitrary natures. Reflecting this, our aim was to prove correctness *uniformly* in these parameters, i.e. without fixing numbers and sizes of tables and queries in advance. This sort of problem is outside the scope of model checkers, symbolic or otherwise, or other techniques based purely on global state space traversal.

There are several reasons why we find this sort of verification exercise useful and interesting.

- First of all it is clearly relevant to verify the actual code rather than some abstraction of it, as this gives us more accurate and reliable information about the way the system is going to behave when it is eventually executed[1].
- Secondly, by analysing the code, and in particular, by doing so in a compositional manner, we produce verication information which is reusable as the system grows. By contrast, most approximate analyses, such as ones based on abstract interpretation (c.f. [Cri95]), tend to be global ones, not readily reusable.

---

[1] Absolute accuracy, of course, is unattainable

– Thirdly, and most significantly, the Erlang code itself is in fact already quite abstract, in the sense of providing designers and implementors with a concise set of primitives and language constructs which are efficiently implementable yet not at all far from a process calculus-like level of abstraction.
– Fourthly we have the potential to maintain strong links between running and verified code. For instance, it will very often be possible to update proofs in a fully automatic way after minor code revisions, by reapplying proof tactics.
– As a longer term perspective, we are interested in developing object and component encapsulation techniques for which a code verification capability is essential.

To realize the verification we used a tool [ADFG98], based on an approach to compositional verification which we have developed in some recent papers (c.f. [Dam98, DFG98]). The approach uses a tightly integrated mix of state-space exploration and proof-editing techniques. System properties and specifications are given in a first-order temporal logic, a variant of Park's μ-calculus [Par76] tailored, in this case, specifically to Erlang. Proof goals are stated as general Gentzen-type sequents, proved in a goal-driven fashion by refinement and loop detection. The result is a very powerful proof system which supports model checking, compositional reasoning, and general coinductive or inductive reasoning, for instance about datatypes, in a uniform framework.

In Sect. 3 we briefly describe our approach to specification. In Sect. 4 the actual verification is described and an outline of the informal proof is presented. Then, in Sect. 5, we describe in more detail our approach to formalisation of the proof, and its realisation in the verification tool. Large parts of the proof are easily automatable by tactics that perform model-checking like state exploration, or prove type adherence or termination of sequential functions. Since these tactics are often used within interactively developed proofs, our verification approach gives rise to proofs that easily become large enough (several thousand nodes) for tool support to be essential. We conclude, in Sect. 6, with some final remarks, reflecting on the approach followed and lessons learned from performing this case study.

2 A Process Verification Problem

In this section we explain the mechanism for query lookup and the property we have proved.

The database tables in which the requested information is stored are distributed over several computers. Whenever a query is formulated for the database the Erlang function `query_setup` is called to analyse the query and divide it into subqueries each addressing only one table. The subqueries are distributed over a network (by the Erlang funtion `mk_ring`) as processes located at the computer where the information is available. A request is sent to the first of the spawned processes, which reads data from a table. This results in several partially instantiated queries, which are sent to the next process. For every such partly instantiated query, the next process reads additional data from a table, resulting in further instantiations. The last process gathers all data and sends it to the requesting process. To avoid unnecessary delays in transmission, processing, and database lookup, and to avoid excessive storage consumption, query processing is split into segments.

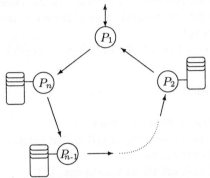

Fig. 1. Ring of processes attached to tables, with P_1 the initial process

We identify an initial process taking care of a query by partioning it into subqueries, represented by Erlang functions, whereafter for every such subquery a process is created on a computer where the subquery can find its information. All spawned processes execute the same function (viz. process_in_ring), which have one of the Erlang functions that represents the subquery as an argument. The processes are spawned in a ring configuration (by mk_ring) and the initial process may be seen as a distinguished member of this ring.

```
query_setup(Query,DBStructure) ->
   SubQueries = split_handle(Query,DBStructure),
   mk_ring(self(),SubQueries).

mk_ring(NextPid,SubQueries) ->
   case SubQueries of
     []->
       wait_for_request(NextPid);
     [Q|Qs] ->
       mk_ring(spawn(process_in_ring,[NextPid,Q,[]]),Qs)
   end.
```

In our approach we abstract from the actual computation of the subqueries and assume that this computation results in a list of functions (represented by SubQueries) with at least one element. For every such function a process is created on the appropriate machine (by spawn(process_in_ring, [NextPid,Q,[]]) where Q represents the subquery and is one of the three arguments of the spawned function process_in_ring), where the name of the machine is computed together with the subquery itself. For readability, we have chosen not to present the machine name and perform the spawning on only one machine. Spawning on several machines is done similarly, where the Erlang spawn primitive needs the machine name as an additional argument.

The function process_in_ring is spawned with three arguments, the process identifier (pid) of the next process in the ring, the function representing the subquery, and the empty list representing a local store for the process (see below for more details on this store).

After spawning the ring (Fig. 1), the initial process (P_1) executes the function[2]

```
wait_for_request(NextPid) ->
  receive
    {user_request,UserPid,NrSolutions} ->
      PacketSize = some_value_smaller(NrSolutions),
      NextPid!{[[]],PacketSize},
      counting(NextPid,UserPid,NrSolutions,[])
  end.
```

with as argument the next process in the ring (P_n). Now P_1 is ready to receive a message of the form {user_request, UserPid, NrSolutions} where the triple represents an atom user_request to identify the message type, the pid of the requesting process and the maximum number of solutions that the latter process wants to receive. Observe that, because of the asynchronous communication discipline of Erlang, a user request may arrive at the mailbox of the initial process long before it is actually processed.

Whenever this message arrives, a message is sent to the consecutive process in the ring (P_n), which is the first process able to perform a subquery lookup. The process P_1 subsequently calls the function counting, which collects all answers that the subqueries of the ring produce. The idea is that for all solutions that a process in the ring receives, it computes all new solutions using its subquery lookup function. This might result in an increase or decrease of the number of solutions. These new solutions are passed to the next process and so on, until P_1 receives the answers and can present them to the user.

However, in order not to overload the network, the processes in the ring are not sending all the answers they find, but just a fixed number given by *PacketSize*, which is dynamically determined by P_1 (via the dummy function some_value_smaller, where we abstract from the real computation) and depends on the number of requested solutions and the network load. Thus, the number *PacketSize* is sent along in the message from P_1 to the next process P_n in the ring. The latter process computes all answers it can find according to its subquery and sends at most *PacketSize* of these answers to the next process, whereas the remaining answers are kept in the store. All consecutive processes in the ring perform the same actions and eventually P_1 receives at most *PacketSize*

---

[2] In the real code this receive statement is incorporated in the function mk_ring, this has been modified for clarity of presentation.

answers. The process P_1 may now add these answers to its store and as long as the store is less than the demanded number of answers (NrSolutions) a message will be sent to the process P_n requesting to produce new answers.

```
counting(NextPid,UserPid,NrSolutions,Store) ->
  receive
    {Solutions,PacketSize} ->
      NewStore = Solutions ++ Store,
      SolutionsToGet = NrSolutions - length(NewStore),
      case {Solutions,SolutionsToGet =< 0} of
        {_,true} ->                  % enough solutions found
          UserPid!{user_response,NewStore}
        {[],_} ->                    % no more solutions in DB
          UserPid!{user_response,NewStore}
        Otherwise ->
          NextPid!{[],PacketSize},
          counting(NextPid,UserPid,NrSolutions,NewStore)
      end
  end.
```

Except for the initial processes, all other processes in the ring, i.e. $P_2, \ldots, P_n$, are evaluating the function process_in_ring.

```
process_in_ring(NextPid,Filter,Store) ->
  receive
    {Solutions,PacketSize} ->
      case PacketSize =< length(Store) of
        true ->
          {ToSend,ToStore} = split(PacketSize,Store),
          NextPid!{ToSend,PacketSize},
          NewStore = ToStore ++ flatmap(Filter,Solutions),
          process_in_ring(NextPid,Filter,NewStore);
        false ->
          NewStore = Store ++ flatmap(Filter,Solutions),
          {ToSend,ToStore} = split(PacketSize,NewStore),
          NextPid!{ToSend,PacketSize},
          process_in_ring(NextPid,Filter,ToStore)
      end
  end.
```

These processes wait for a message containing at most *PacketSize* answers of the previous process and the value *PacketSize* itself. The number of stored answers is compared to the number *PacketSize* of demanded answers and if enough answers are already in the store, these are sent along to the next process and new answers are computed. In case not enough answers are stored, first all new answers are computed, whereafter at most *PacketSize* answers are sent to the next process and all other answers are stored for the next round. Answers are computed using the function `flatmap` which applies the function `Filter` to any partially instantiated query in the list `Solutions`. The function `Filter` has been generated from the original query and the database and was given as an argument of the spawned function. We abstract from this function and only assume that `Filter` is a terminating function that results in a (probably empty) list of arguments. The function `flatmap` results in the concatenation of all lists that result from applying `Filter` to all arguments of `Solutions`, which might either be a longer or a shorter list than the `Solutions` itself. In this way, the store of the process may increase and decrease dynamically.

The function `split` divides a list in two sublists of which the length of the first list contains the first *PacketSize* elements of the list, provided that *PacketSize* is given as an argument to the function. Functions like `=<` and `++` have their usual meaning. In the verification process these functions are not considered as build-in functions, like they are in Erlang, but are specified separately.

The property that we want to verify is informally described as 'Is the retrieval of the information terminating?' In other words, given an arbitrary query and an arbitrary positive integer, whenever we build a ring corresponding to this query and send a message of the form {user_request,MyPid,Number} to the first process in the spawned ring, do we always eventually receive a message back with at most this `Number` of solutions in it?

3   The Specification Logic and Its Proof System

It is not completely trivial to come up with a correct formal rendition of the property outlined at the end of Sect. 2. A first step is to understand correctly the abstract execution mechanism of Erlang. We gave a core fragment of Erlang, involving, roughly, the features used in the present example, an SOS-style operational semantics. Among the more tricky features to model adequately is communication. In Erlang interprocess communication is asynchronous. Each process is equipped with one mailbox. Sending is non-blocking: The transmitted message is placed at the end of the mailbox belonging to the receiving process. Messages are subsequently read by retrieving the first message in the mailbox matching a given pattern. Since we need to analyse behaviour both at the level of processes and process communication and at the level of sequential function elaboration we are forcing a separation between the time at which a message packet crosses a process boundary (or: enters the schedulers domain, i.e. the process mailbox), and the time at which the packet is read from the mailbox by the receiving process.

A second step is to adequately account for the execution behaviour of processes in a formal property specification language. Our work has been based on a first-order fixed point calculus inspired by Park's μ-calculus [Par76, Koz83], extended with Erlang-specific features. In summary this logic is based on the first-order language of equality, extended with modalities reflecting state transition capabilities, least and greatest fixed points, along with a few additional primitives. Using μ-calculus correctly is by itself well known to be tricky. On the other hand we have found the μ-calculus recursive style of specification extremely natural and useful. We have used an equational style of specification, using the notation

$$prop(args) \Rightarrow body$$

for greatest fixed points (the body can be inferred from the head), and

$$prop(args) \Leftarrow body$$

for least fixed points (the head must be inferred from the body). Whereas this notation is fraught with danger (how are dependencies resolved?) a clear benefit of such a notation is that it encourages a programming language style of specification defining "larger", more complicated properties in terms of "smaller" ones.

The benefits of the equational style of specification becomes apparent, in particular, once properties are decomposed. To do this one typically needs to express state, liveness, or safety properties embedded inside another invariant which needs to adequately capture all possible ways in which the processes can interact, and the consequences of these interactions. An example of the shape of a property one obtains is (1) below.

A complication which is more semantical than due to the recursive style of specification is Erlang's asynchronous communication. Since receivers are powerless to influence the delivery of packets into receivers mailbox, for the purpose of packet delivery events, and in the absence of a suitable fairness assumption (which we have not so far implemented), it is possible for packet delivery to continuously preempt progress by the local process. In this example we have been able to bypass this problem, as the ring structure enforces a synchrony property that ensures to a sufficient extent that mailboxes do not grow in unbounded manners.

3.1   The Logic

Typical Erlang-related primitives are $the\_term = e$ to pick up the Erlang expression associated with the process under evaluation and compare this with the term e; *unevaluated* which is true if the Erlang expression under evaluation is not yet in normal form; and similar primitives for queues and process identifiers with are local or foreign to the system under consideration.

The modal operators $<\cdot>$ and $[\cdot]$ (not to be confused with the Erlang list constructors $[]$ (the nil list) and $[hd|tl]$) are used to express transition capabilities. The formula $<>\phi$ holds if an internal transistion is enabled to a state satisfying ϕ. Similarly, we have a diamond operator for the non-internal transitions for sending and receiving, viz. $<P!V>\phi$ and $<P?V>\phi$. Observe that the receive modality is "appending to recipients mailbox". The box operator is the dual of the diamond operator, expressing that a formula should hold in all states reachable in one transition from the current state.

Using least and greatest fixed point temporal properties, like liveness and safety, can easily be expressed. Furthermore simple data types, like lists and natural numbers, can be expressed using least fixed points:

$$list(L) \Leftarrow (L = []) \vee \exists H.\exists T.(list(T) \wedge (L = [H|T]))$$

Combinations of both greatest and least fixed points are used to express the complicated eventuality properties we deal with in this case-study. A representative example of the latter is the formula that expresses that the property *wait_for_input* holds for an arbitrary number of internal computation steps, until a certain shape of message is received and the property *continue* holds. The properties *wait_for_input* and *continue* will typically be mutually recursive, so let us assume that *wait_for_input* is defined in the context of a definition

$$continue \Rightarrow \cdots wait\_for\_input(\ldots) \cdots.$$

Now *wait_for_input* is defined in the following way:

$$wait\_for\_input(RightForm) \Rightarrow wait\_for\_input'(RightForm) \tag{1}$$
$$wait\_for\_input'(RightForm) \Leftarrow [] wait\_for\_input'(RightForm) \wedge$$
$$\forall P.\forall V.([P!V]false) \wedge$$
$$\forall P.\forall V.([P?V](RightForm(P, V) \wedge$$
$$continue))$$

The least fixed point ensures that the predicated process does not diverge (i.e. performs an infinite sequence of internal computation steps without ever writing an incoming message to its mailbox. The greatest fixed point on the other hand permits states satisfying *wait_for_input* infinitely often, as long as they are infinitely often separated by *continue* states.

4   Outline of the Proof

According to the informal property as stated in Sect. 2, we are dealing with two actions initiating the query lookup: first the ring is built and thereafter a request message is sent to the first process in this ring. For verification we are focusing on the outcome of the valuation of the Erlang expression:

```
Ring = spawn(query_setup, [Query, DBStructure]),
Ring!{user_request, self(), NrSolutions},
receive
     {user_response, Solutions}
end.
```

where we quantify over all possible values of *Query*, *DBStructure*, *NrSolutions* and *Solutions*. We abstract from the first two variables by assuming the function split_handle to result in a list of functions, where the real interesting issue is the length of this list, which can be any positive integer determining the number of processes in the ring. The property we address in this paper is that evaluation of this Erlang expression is terminating. Similar properties of interest are:

- The number of received answers is equal to the number of demanded answers if that many answers exist in the database.
- The set of obtained answers is independent of the packet size, provided the latter is a positive number.

Given the experience of, e.g., the *wait_for_input* formula (1) formulating the responsiveness property is not too difficult. The specification will have the following shape:

$$spec \Rightarrow spec'$$
$$spec' \Leftarrow \Box spec' \wedge \forall P.\forall V.[P!V] false \wedge$$
$$\forall P.\forall V.[P?V]((P = userpid) \wedge$$
$$\exists From.\exists N.(V = \{\texttt{user\_request}, From, N\}) \wedge \phi)$$

where ϕ expresses responsiveness in a similar style, that eventually a user response is sent to the pid *From*, before returning to a state satisfying *spec*. Several details are omitted in this description: Information about process identifiers and the store have to be carried over to the property ϕ, and assumptions concerning the return address *From*, and the types of other arguments have to be made.

The basic style of specification is one of distinguishing abstract states in which (aggregate sets of) processes may find themselves. The abstract states will often correspond to infinitely many actual states of the process. For every process we define a few abstract states and formulate which properties should hold in these states and how one property depends on the other. The processes we consider are the initial process evaluating the given Erlang expression, a ring process (which is not the initial one), and, as part of an inductive argument, a ring segment which includes the initial process.

4.1 The Ring Invariant

The basic difficulties in proving the specification to hold are the unbounded number of ring processes which can be created, and the unbounded number of query replies which can be requested. To address these difficulties we resort to induction. We identify two invariants:

1. An invariant to hold of each of the ring processes $P_2, \ldots, P_n$ (c.f. Fig. 2).
2. A sort of structural and temporal invariant for a ring segment of the shape $P_1, P_n, \ldots, P_i$ with $2 \leq i \leq n$.

Let us call the first invariant *proc_wait_for_input* and the second invariant for *rootspec*. We first need to show that *rootspec* is strong enough to derive the end specification we wish to establish, i.e. a sequent of the shape

$$x : rootspec(\cdots) \vdash x : spec(\cdots). \tag{2}$$

The task is thus to prove that *rootspec* holds of the process initially evaluating `query_setup`:

$$\text{some assumptions} \vdash proc(\texttt{query\_setup}(\cdots), \cdots) : rootspec(\cdots) \tag{3}$$

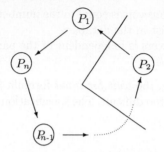

Fig. 2. Induction on number of processes in ring

Here *proc* denotes the Erlang process for which *rootspec* has to be proved. Such a process consists of the Erlang term to be evaluated, the process-identifier and the message queue associated with the process. Using straightforward, and fully automatable, state exploration techniques which we return to in the following section we can reduce (3) first to a subgoal of the shape

$$\text{some assumptions} \vdash proc(\texttt{mk\_ring}(\cdots),\cdots) : rootspec(\cdots) \qquad (4)$$

and then, by continuing state exploration, to a subgoal of the shape

$$\text{some assumptions} \vdash proc(\texttt{mk\_ring}(\cdots),\cdots) \parallel \qquad (5)$$
$$proc(\texttt{process\_in\_ring}(\cdots),\cdots) : rootspec(\cdots)$$

The idea is to prove two lemmas, one stating the correctness of `process_in_ring`,

$$\text{some assumptions} \vdash proc(\texttt{process\_in\_ring}(\cdots)) : proc\_wait\_for\_input(\cdots) \quad (6)$$

and one concerning the composability of *rootspec* with *proc_wait_for_input*,

$$C1 : rootspec(\cdots), C2 : proc\_wait\_for\_input(\cdots) \vdash C1 \parallel C2 : rootspec(\cdots) \quad (7)$$

Subgoal (7) states a compositional property of root and ring processes: putting together a (possibly aggregate) process (P_1) acting as a root with a (possibly aggregate) process acting as a ring element results in an aggregate process which again acts as a root. Obviously the correctness of this statement is crucially dependent on input and outputs being properly connected, which are matters we will not be concerned with here.

By themselves, (6) and (7) are not sufficient to conclude (5). However, using (6) and (7) it is possible to reduce to a goal which is actually an instance of the goal (4), and the remarkable fact is that, in principle, an inductive argument can be set up such that at this point the proof can be completed (c.f. [DFG98]). In realizing this proof, however, a number of complications must be attended to which we return to in Sect. 5.

4.2 Properties of the Separate Processes

We are thus left with two main subgoals, one of the shape (6), and one of the shape (7). We do not comment further on (7) other than observe that the ring process property *proc_wait_for_input* we are looking for must be strong enough to permit (7) to be proved. Instead we turn to *proc_wait_for_input*.

We start by observing the role of a special token that is initially sent by the first process (P_1) in the ring and implies termination as soon as it is also received by this process, i.e. when the token has gone through the entire ring. This special token ({[],PacketSize}), which we call the *end_token* for convenience, is repeatedly send by P_1 to P_n after initially sending {[[]],PacketSize} once. In case the number of demanded solutions is larger than the number of solutions present in the database, the process P_1 can only respond to the user when this *end_token* is received from the process P_2.

The first process in the ring P_1 plays a special role and the abstract states we distinguish for this process are

1. the process is waiting for a user_request,
2. a non-end_token is sent to the next process (P_n) and the process is waiting for a message,
3. an end_token is sent to the next process and the process is waiting for a message,
4. a non-end_token is received and not enough answers are collected,
5. the end_token is received or another token is received and enough answers are collected.

Our choice to follow the real code and not to abstract from the actual counting of the number of answers, causes the state space of this first process in the ring to be unbounded. For this reason, modelchecking is infeasible for this part of the proof as well, but with our verification tool such a proof can be handled.

States that we distinguish for the processes in the ring are characterized by whether or not they receive an end_token and whether or not they send an end_token. Crucial is the observation that after receiving an end_token once, only end_tokens can be received successively. The latter is a property of the ring and not of the process itself, but when proved for the ring, we use it in our formalization to disallow the state transition from receiving an end_token to receiving a non-end_token.

For a process in the ring ($P_2, \ldots, P_n$) we define four abstract states, depending again on the end_token:

1. the process awaits the reception of an arbitrary message,
2. the process receives an *end*-message and sends a message to the next process,
3. the process receives a non-*end*-message and sends a message to the next process,
4. the process waits for receiving a successive *end*-message.

Every state is captured in a property, but also the relation to the other abstract states is reflected in this same property using the fixed point operators.

To support discharge and, in particular, subproof sharing it seems essential to maintain a "current" proof tree, and to have rules of proof elaborate this proof tree through side effects. Observe that this makes the proof construction process very different from that of other proof editing tools (such as PVS [ROS92, Sha96], Coq [DFH+], Lego [Lego], Isabelle [Pau94],...) which maintain only the leaves, but not the internal structure of proof trees. Thus, in these tools one shares subproofs by having the user formulate lemma's which are used for several leaves. We overcome this user intervention and in case a subproof need not be performed, this is detected automatically.

5.3   Tactics

The construction of proof trees by side effects has drastic impact on the programming of tactics, for instance. The benefit, besides the support of discharge and (in particular) copy-discharge, is that the entire proof tree becomes available for inspection and navigation. In fact, to help keep the information manageable we implemented a facility for suppressing the creation on new nodes. The cost of maintaining the complete proof tree, on the other hand, is that tactics programming becomes much more difficult, and that the attractive, and very tight, connections between term and proof structure evident from e.g. type theory, get lost. So far we have implemented a rather "dirty" solution, giving users access to the basic proof rules themselves, to a set of basic rules for accessing and traversing proof trees, to a small set of tactic constructors, like sequential composition, conditional, etc, and to a higher-order tactic definition facility.

Another example is outlined on Fig. 3 which is shown less for its details than to give a general impression of the shape of tactics we used for the example. In our case study tactics were indispensable. They permitted us to produce very large parts of the proofs entirely automatically. We implemented tactics for a wide range of purposes, and of very different generality. For instance it is quite easy to implement simple proof strategies for boolean formulas as tactics.

Example 2. A coarse approximation of the Erlang function `process_in_ring` as presented in Sect. 2, just receiving an integer, incrementing it by one and passing it on:

```
process_in_ring(NextProcess) ->
   receive
     N -> NextProcess!(N+1),
          process_in_ring(NextProcess)
   end.
```

The following "wait_for_input" property expresses the behaviour of such ring processes in state transition terms:

$$wait\_for\_input(pid_1, pid_2) \Rightarrow wait\_for\_input'(pid_1, pid_2)$$
$$wait\_for\_input'(pid_1, pid_2) \Leftarrow []\, wait\_for\_input'(pid_1, pid_2)$$
$$\land \ \forall P.\forall V.[P!V]\mathit{false}$$

```
/* resolvable: Proof branch can be closed */
rule resolvable =
    eq_r() /* Node is provable equality */
    orelse id() /* Node is instance of id rule */
    orelse ...
    orelse copy_discharge() ;

/* rightexpandable: Goal can be reduced but not closed */
rule rightexpandable =
    or_r() orelse and_r() orelse ... orelse all_r
    orelse box_sem() ; /* Chase transition */

rule rightreduce =
    block
        if isleaf() /* Node is not yet reduced */
        then if resolvable ()
            then skip
            else if rightexpandable()
                then block next_above() ; rightreduce end
                else fail("rightreduce")
        else fail("rightreduce")
    end ;
```

Fig. 3. Tactic for simple "model checking"

$$\wedge \ \forall P.\forall N.[P?N]((P = pid_1) \wedge$$
$$nat(N) \rightarrow respond(pid_1, pid_2))$$

$$respond(pid_1, pid_2) \Rightarrow respond'(pid_1, pid_2)$$
$$respond'(pid_1, pid_2) \Leftarrow []respond'(pid_1, pid_2)$$
$$\wedge \ \forall P.\forall V.[P!V]((P = pid_2) \wedge$$
$$nat(V) \wedge wait\_for\_input(pid_1, pid_2))$$

Using a tactic based on `right_reduce` above the proof goal (6) was proved automatically, with subproof sharing, using 212 nodes, 1 application of discharge, and 7 applications of copy-discharge. Turning subproof sharing off the same tactic required 530 nodes and 12 applications of discharge. The size increase is due to one subproof being duplicated thrice.

For larger sequential functions than the one considered in Ex. 2 the issue of subproof sharing becomes very urgent, and it is not hard to realize that an exponential growth in proof size will be the rule rather than the exception.

Also for sequential function evaluation we found tactics very helpful. The `counting` function, for instance, appeals to a number of small auxillary functions like `length`, `split`, `flatmap`, or comparison operators like $\geq$ which are implemented as functions as well. Frequently small lemmas are needed to show

[Dam98]   M. Dam, Proving Properties of Dynamic Process Networks. *Information and Computation*, **140**, p. 95–114, 1998.

[DFG98]   M. Dam, L.-Å. Fredlund and D. Gurov, Toward Parametric Verification of Open Distributed Systems. H. Langmaack, A. Pnueli, W.-P. De Roever (eds.), *Compositionality: The Significant Difference*, Springer Verlag, 1998.

[DFH⁺]   G. Dowek, A. Felty, H. Herbelin, G. Huet, C. Murthy, C. Parent, C. Paulin-Mohring, and B. Werner. *The Coq proof assistant user guide*, Technical report, INRIA-Rocquencourt, May 1993.

[FW94]   M. Fröhlich and M. Werner. The graph visualization system daVinci – a user interface for applications. Technical Report 5/94, Department of Computer Science, Bremen University, 1994.

[Koz83]   D. Kozen, Results on the propositional μ-calculus. *Theoretical Computer Science*, 27:333–354, 1983.

[Lego]   The Lego Proof Assistant, http://www.dcs.ed.ac.uk/home/lego/.

[Mnesia]   C. Wikström, Hans Nilsson and Håkan Mattson, Mnesia Database Management System, In *Open Telecom Platform users manual*, Open Systems, Ericsson Utvecklings AB, Stockholm, Sweden, 1997.

[Nil99]   H. Nilsson, Patent application, 1999.

[OSE98]   Open Source Erlang, http://www.erlang.org, 1998.

[Par76]   D. Park, Finiteness is mu-ineffable. *Theoretical Computer Science*, 3:173–181, 1976.

[Pau94]   L. C. Paulson. *Isabelle: A Generic Theorem Prover*, LNCS 828, 1994

[ROS92]   J. Rushby, S. Owre and N. Shankar. PVS: A prototype verification system. In *Proceedings 11th Conference on Automated Deduction*, LNAI 607, pp. 748–752, 1992.

[Sha96]   N. Shankar. PVS: Combining specification, proof checking, and model checking. In *Proceedings of Formal Methods in Computer-Aided Design*, LNCS 1166, pp. 257–264, November 1996.

Secure Interoperation
of Secure Distributed Databases
An Architecture Verification Case Study

Fred Gilham, R.A. Riemenschneider, and Victoria Stavridou

Computer Science Laboratory
SRI International
{gilham,rar,victoria}@csl.sri.com

Abstract. This paper describes the process of implementing an architecture for secure distributed transaction processing, the process of verifying that it has the desired security properties, and the implementation that resulted. The implementation and verification processes provided us with valuable experience relevant to answering several questions posed by our research on transformational development of architectures. *To what extent can implementation-level architectural descriptions be derived from abstract description via application of transformations that preserve a broad class of properties, which includes satisfaction of various access control policies? To what extent can a formal derivation of a non-secure implementation-level distributed transaction processing architecture be reused in derivation of a secure architecture? Are the transformation verification techniques that we have developed sufficient for verifying a collection of transformations adequate for implementing complex secure architecture? Do our architecture hierarchies effectively fill the gap between abstract, intellectually manageable models of a complex architecture and the actual implementation?* Exploring the answers to these questions resulted in a reference implementation of an architecture for secure distributed transaction processing, and an independently interesting demonstration instance of the reference implementation.

1   Introduction

The primary focus of our research efforts is on the problem of producing *dependable system architectures*. We have recently developed the basic technology required to effectively solve this problem in the case of distributed transaction processing systems. Our solution involves extending the ACID properties that drove the development of the X/Open standard for distributed transaction processing by adding security constraints. Specifically, we added the constraint that the system must satisfy a multilevel secure access control policy. Our basic approach to defining a family of architectures that satisfy the extended requirements was described in an earlier paper [8]. This paper is devoted to describing our experiences following that approach to its logical conclusion: an implemented architecture for secure distributed transaction processing that has been proven secure.

J. Wing, J. Woodcock, J. Davies (Eds.): FM'99, Vol. I, LNCS 1708, pp. 701–717, 1999.
© Springer-Verlag Berlin Heidelberg 1999

2 Architecture Hierarchies

It is common practice to informally describe a single architecture at many levels of abstraction, and from a variety of different perspectives. For example, at a concrete level, the architecture might be described in terms of how a system is assembled from code components using connection mechanisms provided by a programming language or operating system. At a very abstract level, the same architecture might be described in terms of the data and control flow paths that link the functions the system is required to perform. At an intermediate level, the system architecture might be described in terms of clients and servers interacting through message queues.

One reason that multiple descriptions are provided is that each of these architectural descriptions is useful for some purposes, but less useful for others. Often the argument that the system has some desirable architectural property can be greatly simplified by employing an abstract description of the architecture. On the other hand, some properties require detailed analysis of low-level architectural descriptions. Another reason is that there is often a major conceptual gap between abstract architectural descriptions and the actual implementation. Descriptions at intermediate levels of abstraction break this gap down into intellectually tractable pieces, and thus can significantly increase confidence that the abstract description correctly characterizes the as-implemented architecture.

While much of the recent work on more formal architectural description languages (ADLs) has focussed on the problem of describing architectures in a way that provides a suitable basis for various formal analyses, our own work has focussed primarily on the problem of formally linking these several descriptions in an *architecture hierarchy*. The basic idea is to regard each description as a logical theory, the theory of the class of architectural structures that the description describes, and to formalize the links between the descriptions as interpretation mappings. Figure 1 shows the structure of a typical architecture hierarchy. Correctness of the hierarchy can be explicated in terms of constraints on the interpretation mappings. For example, one might require that the interpretations preserve some property of special interest (say, some security property). Or one might require that they preserve every property expressible in some language.

Our tools for constructing architecture hierarchies are based upon an incremental transformation paradigm. The result of applying a transformation to a hierarchy is a hierarchy containing additional or altered descriptions. An additional description is typically either an abstraction of another description in the hierarchy, a refinement of another description in the hierarchy, or a description at the same level of abstraction but from a different perspective (e.g., a data-oriented description that complements an existing function-oriented description). If a hierarchy has been constructed entirely by applications of transformations that are known to be generally correctness-preserving, or whose correctness in the particular instance are checked as they are applied, the hierarchy is known to be correct. Correct hierarchies formally link very abstract formal architectural descriptions, which can easily be demonstrated to satisfy system requirements,

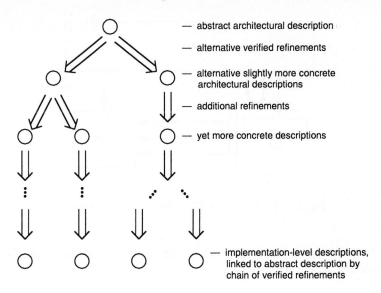

— abstract architectural description

— alternative verified refinements

— alternative slightly more concrete architectural descriptions

— additional refinements

— yet more concrete descriptions

— implementation-level descriptions, linked to abstract description by chain of verified refinements

Fig. 1. An Architecture Hierarchy

to implementation-level architectural descriptions in a way that guarantees the implementation satisfies the requirements.

3   Distributed Transaction Processing

In response to a growing demand for increased interoperability of software compoenents, a number of vendor-neutral, open software architectures have been proposed as standards. The X/Open Distributed Transaction Processing (DTP) reference architecture [17] is one of these standards. X/Open DTP is specifically intended to standardize interactions among the components of a three-tiered client/server model: resource (e.g., database) managers (RMs), an application (AP) that accesses those resources, and a transaction manager (TM). A very abstract, informal representation of this architecture — which can be found in the X/Open documents — is shown in Fig. 2.

The role of the TM is to ensure that consistency is maintained when the state of the RMs is changed by the AP. Transactions are collections of operations on the RMs. Multiple transactions can be performed concurrently. In the context of a transaction, all other transaction appear to be executed atomically. In other words, it always appears that all or none of the operations that make up a transaction have taken effect.

The X/Open documentation is informal, consisting of a mix of C header files[1] and English text describing the semantics of the functions declared in

---

[1] Since a description of how components written in languages other than C, including languages such as COBOL that do not support return values, can be accomodated is

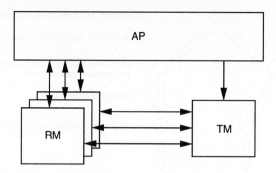

Fig. 2. The X/Open DTP Reference Architecture

the headers. The protocols for using these functions are also only semi-formally characterized.

4   Adding Security to DTP

Security requirements are ubiquitous in transaction processing, both within the defense sector and within the commercial sector. Tremendous leverage can be gained by addressing security concerns at the architectural level, because ensuring security is typically both technically challenging and expensive. Several of the open software architectures have introduced extensions to deal with security issues. For example, recent updates of OMG's CORBA specification have included security services that address fundamental security concerns in a distributed object system, based on a trusted ORB model. These services include credential-based authentication of principals and their clients, several simple privilege delegation schemes, authorization based on access control lists, audit trails, and non-repudiation services based on the ISO non-repudiation model.

One of the key security issues in DTP is enforcement of an *access control policy*, which ensures that classified resoures can only be accessed by clients with appropriate clearances. In terms of the Bell-LaPadula model [4], our proposed multilevel secure (MLS) access control policy for secure DTP can be defined by saying that the distributed transaction processing systems must have the following two properties:

- *The Simple Security Property* — A client is allowed read access to a resource only if the client's clearance level is greater than or equal to the resource's classification level.
- *The ⋆-Property* — A client is allowed write access to a resource only if the client's clearance level is less than or equal to the resource's classification level.

---

included, it is clear that the C code cannot be considered to be a formal specification of the syntax of the interface functions.

The simple security property guarantees that there is no *read-up* of data, while the ⋆-property guarantees that there is no *write-down*.

To say that a component in a DTP system is MLS means that the component satisfies the MLS access policy internally, and that all inputs to and outputs from the component are properly classified. So, for example, to say that a multilevel database management system (DBMS) is an MLS resource manager means that

- any data entered into the database is tagged with a classification level,
- any data retrieved from the database comes tagged with the same classification level that it had when it was entered, and
- no operation performed by the DBMS can result in either read-up or write-down among the subcomponents of the DBMS.

(Note that a single-level database is trivially an MLS resource manager, provided single-levelness is maintained.) Similarly, to say that the entire DTP system is MLS means that no read-up or write-down occurs between components and that inputs and outputs are properly classified.

The challenge in adding an MLS access control policy to X/Open DTP is to define an architecture which guarantees that, if the components used to build the system are MLS, then the DTP system as a whole is MLS. That this is not a trivial problem can be seen by considering a DTP system composed of an application that accesses several single-level databases, each of which has a different classification level, a very common situation. A secure DTP (SDTP) architecture must ensure that the client application does not read data classified above the application's clearance level, that it does not write data that it obtained from a highly classified database to a database classified at a lower level, and so on.

One complicating factor is that no single architectural structure is well suited to every SDTP system. It is easy to see that a single-level client AP, a single-level TM, and a collection of single-level RMs all at the same level can be linked by secure connectors to build a system that is automatically MLS secure. Extending the X/Open DTP architecture to handle such systems can be accomplished simply by adding appropriate encryption to the communication protocols. But varying single-level systems will require that the connectors linking the AP to the RMs somehow enforce the access control policy (at least in the absence of a certification that the AP satisfies security constraints beyond being MLS). One way of doing so is to introduce a Security Manager component that mediates communication between the RMs and the MLS AP, as shown in Fig. 3.

5   Defining the SDTP Hierarchy

As part of an earlier effort to develop an architectural description language suitable for defining architectural hierarchies, we defined a formal hierarchy for the X/Open DTP standard consisting of 17 SADL [9][2] specifications, linked by

---

[2] SADL, pronounced *saddle*, is an acronym for 'Structural Architecture Description Language'. The name was suggested by the fact that SADL emphasizes description of structure rather than description of the behavior of connectors, a topic quite adequately addressed by other ADLs.

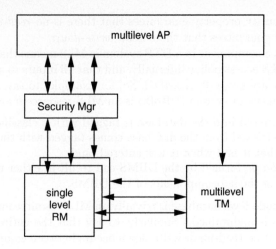

Fig. 3. SDTP Architecture for Varying Single-level Resource Managers

SADL-specified interpretation mappings. The most abstract description, shown in Fig. 4, approximately corresponds to the informal diagram shown in Fig. 2. Six levels below the most abstract description is a description at roughly the same level of abstraction as the code in the X/Open documentation. (Excerpts from this code are shown in Fig. 5.) Below this level, the hierarchy branches in several directions, reflecting, e.g., the various choices that can be made in allocating low-level interprocessor communication functions to processors.

```
x_open_abstract: ARCHITECTURE [ -> ]
   IMPORTING ALL FROM Dataflow_Relations_style
BEGIN

CONFIGURATION
   ap: TYPE <= Function
   rms: TYPE <= Function
   tm: TYPE <= Function

   the_ap: ap
   the_rms: rms
   the_tm: tm

   ar: CONSTRAINT = Dataflow(the_ap, the_rms)
   tx: CONSTRAINT = Dataflow(the_ap, the_tm)
   xa: CONSTRAINT = Dataflow(the_tm, the_rms)

END x_open_abstract
```

Fig. 4. Dataflow-Level SADL Description of X/Open Architecture

```
x_open_std_level: ARCHITECTURE [ -> ]
%% X_Open_style defines relevant
%%  properties of procedure calls;
%%  this description covers how things
%%  are hooked together
  IMPORTING ALL FROM X_Open_style , ...
BEGIN
  ...
COMPONENTS
  tm: TYPE <= ARCHITECTURE [ -> ]
     EXPORTING ALL
     BEGIN
        register: AX_Register_Procedure
          [id: X_Id, rmid: INT, flags: INT
                  -> ret: INT]
          begin: TX_Begin_Proc [ -> ret: INT]
          ...
     END tm
  ...
  the_tm:  tm
  ...


CONFIGURATION
  tx: CONSTRAINT =
        Called_From(the_tm.begin, the_ap)
           AND ...
  xa: CONSTRAINT =
        (FORALL y: rm)
         [Called_From(the_tm.register, y)
            AND ...
  ...
END x_open_std_level
```

Fig. 5. X/Open Standard-Level SADL Description of X/Open Architecture (Heavily Elided)

Our basic approach to developing a similar hierarchy for SDTP architectures was to treat SDTP as a *rearchitecting* problem: given an architecture that satisfies a set of requirements, how can that architecture be modified to satisfy an additional requirement, viz., that the MLS access policy is satisfied. The idea is to attempt to "replay" the derivation of the implementation-level architecture descriptions from the most abstract architectural description. An architecture hierarchy includes a record of the transformations used to generate the interpretations that link the descriptions. If a transformation used in the original X/Open DTP hierarchy can be shown to preserve satisfaction of the additional requirement — i.e., in this case, if the transformation can be shown to preserve the simple security property (no read-up) and the ⋆-property (no write-down)

— then the same transformation can be employed in deriving an SDTP implementation.[3]

A priori, it was not known what percentage of the design history encoded in the X/Open DTP hierarchy could be reused in the SDTP hierarchy. We therefore developed implementation-level descriptions of the three abstract architectures for SDTP that we have described in an earlier publication [8]. It turned out that over 90% of the design decisions made during the implementation of each of the three SDTP architectures could be based on decisions recorded in DTP hierarchy; conversely, every design decision in the DTP hierarchy was reused in the development of every one of the three SDTP hierarchies. In the most extreme case, the hierarchy for the "single-level, same level RMs" case is nearly identical to the DTP hierarchy, the only real difference being additional low-level decision to use an RPC mechanism that performs encryption. Thus, one important result of this case study was evidence that confirms our hypothesis that derivation replay is often an effective rearchitecting technique.

6 Verifying Security

We believe that our implementation-level SDTP architectural descriptions define architectures that have the simple security property and the $\star$-property, because we have formally proved that these properties follow from a dataflow-level description of the SDTP architectures in terms of components linked by channels that enforce security and we are in the process of formally confirming our belief that the design decisions in the SDTP hierarchies preserve security. The proofs that the design decisions preserve the desired security properties use two different verification techniques we have developed.

Many of the transformations employed in development can be shown to preserve a broad class of structural properties by showing that the implementation links they introduce into the hierarchy are *faithful interpretations* of the theory of the more abstract description in the theory of the more concrete description. To say an interpretation μ of the language of theory T_1 in theory T_2 is a faithful (theory) interpretation means that, for every sentence (i.e., closed formula) **A** in the language of T_1,

$$T_1 \vdash \mathbf{A} \quad \text{if and only if} \quad T_2 \vdash \mu(\mathbf{A})$$

In general, access control policies prohibit certain dataflow paths in the system. Simply by omitting the undesired dataflow channels from the abstract architectural description, we guarantee that no formula saying *there is a dataflow from C_1 to C_2*, where a flow from component C_1 to component C_2 would violate the access control policy, can be proved from the theory of the abstract description. Faithful interpretations cannot introduce new dataflow channels, but can

---

[3] The bindings of the variables in the transformation can, and usual do, change. But the bindings in the replay can be automatically determined from the bindings in the original derivation by tracking the correspondence between objects in the two hierarchies as the new hierarchy is constructed from the old.

only further elaborate existing channels. Therefore, transformations that can be shown to always introduce faithful interpretations can freely be used in the process of implementing a design that has been verified to be secure, without fear that security will be violated. The details of our model-theoretic method for proving that transformations always introduce faithful interpretation links has been described in a series of earlier papers [7, 13, 15]. Currently, we manually prove that transformations introduce faithful theory interpretations, though we are actively investigating the possibility of using the SRI's PVS verification system to provide automated support for the process.

On the other hand, not every interpretation link in the SDTP hierarchies has been shown to be a faithful theory interpretation. In fact, some of the transformations employed in building the hierarchies do not have the property that they always introduce faithful interpretations. For these interpretations, we apply a *checking* technique to show that the interpretation preserves the desired security properties. The basic idea is to use the interpretations that refine the architectural description to refine the proof that the descriptions have the desired security properties as well. If the result of applying the interpretation to the security proof at the more abstract level can be used to automatically obtain a security proof at the more concrete level, the implementation step has been shown to preserve security. (This technique has been described in greater detail in an earlier paper [14].) Currently, we apply the transformations to proofs manually, then use PVS to check the results. A tool that automates proof transformation is under development.

7   Implementing an SDTP Reference Architecture

In this SDTP reference implementation the RMs consist of a Security Manager (SM) that enforces the desired multilevel security policies — each of which implements a piece of the Security Manager component shown in Figure 3 — and a set of single-level RMs, which are arbitrary single-level databases. A multilevel-secure RM consists of the combination of the SM and the single-level RMs. Note that the single-level RMs are not required to provide the X/Open DTP standard services themselves; they must, however, support transaction processing.

The X/Open DTP standard specifies various services that the components of the architecture must provide and make use of. An SDTP application will make use of two services: the **TX** (Transaction Demarcation) service, and the **AR** service (the service that allows the application access to shared resources). The **TX** service is provided by the TM while the **AR** service is provided by the (multilevel) RMs the application makes use of.

The TM and RMs also make use of X/Open DTP-specified services. The service the RMs provide to the TM is called the **xa** subservice of the **XA** service. This subservice implements the interface the TM uses to perform the two-phase commit protocol. The **ax** subservice of the **XA** service is provided by the TM and allows RMs to dynamically register themselves as being under the TM's management, and unregister themselves when that management is no longer desired.

The X/Open DTP standard gives a detailed specification of the **TX** and **XA** services. The **AR** service is considered implementation-dependent because RMs may provide services other than database management, and thus the **AR** interface must allow its clients to make use of those services.

Our reference implementation of SDTP was written in Common Lisp. The advantage of using a language quite different from X/Open's choice of C is that it helped us identify and eliminate some of the "C-centric" implementation decisions that crept into the X/Open design. Common Lisp was also attractive because it enabled rapid implementation and debugging of the system. The Common Lisp package system was used to globally identify the various services and prevent name conflicts (e.g., since `open` is a standard Common Lisp function for file I/O as well as appearing in both the **TX** and **XA-xa** service, a name conflict would occur unless some method of distinguishing between these functions was employed).

A remote procedure call (RPC) facility native to the Common Lisp version we used was employed for component-to-component communication. Communication between the RMs and the single-level databases was done by means of a foreign function interface (FFI) to the native database programmatic interface library.

7.1   The TX Service

The **TX** service allows the application to open and close resource managers, start, finish or roll back transactions, obtain information about the state of a transaction, and set certain transaction characteristics.

A typical chain of events involving the application making use of the **TX** service is:

1. Tell the TM to open the RMs with the `tx:open` call.
2. Connect to the RMs and use the **AR** services of the RM for preliminary functions (such as authentication and key exchange).
3. Tell the TM to start a transaction with the `tx:begin` call.
4. Use the **AR** service of the RMs to exchange data
5. Finish the transaction by using the TM's `tx:commit` call; alternatively, abort and roll back the transaction using the `tx:rollback` call.
6. Once the desired set of transactions is completed, tell the TM to close the RMs using the `tx:close` call.

7.2   The XA Service

The **XA** service is used by the TM to communicate with the RMs and by the RMs to communicate with the TM. It is divided into two subservices as described above.

The **xa** subservice is used by the TM to communicate with the RMs to negotiate the two-phase commit protocol. A typical chain of events is:

1. The application informs the TM that it wishes to begin processing transactions (via the **ax** subservice, described below).
2. The TM uses the `xa:open` call to tell the RMs to begin listening for connections from the application.
3. The application tells the TM that it is beginning a transaction.
4. The TM issues `xa:start` calls to the RMs, telling them that a new transaction is being started.
5. After issuing one or more commands to the RMs, the application informs the TM that it wants to commit its current transaction.
6. The TM makes an `xa:prepare` call to each of the RMs. Each RM returns a value indicating that it is ready to commit.
7. The TM makes an `xa:commit` call to each of the RMs, indicating that it should commit its work.

The **ax** subservice is used by the RMs to dynamically register with the TM. Once an RM registers with the TM, it is then managed along with all the other RMs that the TM currently knows about. This feature is intended to permit RMs that are infrequently used to only be managed when they are doing actual work, thus avoiding the necessity for them to engage in the transaction protocol when they aren't processing transactions.

7.3   The AR Service

The **AR** service is the service an RM provides to allow applications to access its shared resources. The X/Open DTP standard does not specify the form this interface must take. It allows the RMs to provide standard interfaces, such as SQL, and/or custom or proprietary interfaces. The SDTP RM reference implementation currently provides a custom interface built on top of SQL.

A typical call to an **AR** service looks like the following:

```
(wire:remote-value
  rm-wire
  (ar:update *tid*
    (encrypt-string "inv_id" common-key)
    (encrypt-string new-inv-id common-key)
    (encrypt-string " " common-key)
    (encrypt-string " " common-key)))
```

where `rm-wire` is the wire or connection the application has to the resource manager, `ar:update` is the actual RPC to the **AR** service, `*tid*` is the application's thread ID and the rest of the arguments are mapped into an **update** SQL statement.

The SDTP reference implementation of the **AR** service uses encryption to secure the contents of its network communications (as do the other services). The current encryption package uses a Diffie-Hellman key exchange protocol and RC4 as its encryption mechanism.

8   Cooperating Law Enforcement Databases

As a test application for the SDTP reference implementation, we built an MLS law enforcement tracking system. This system was inspired by an FBI system called "FOIMS" (Field Office Information Management System), though of course it bears no relationship to the actual working of that system.

Our intent in building this application was to demonstrate multilevel security in a database system that was both distributed and replicated. For this reason we decided to distribute the information for State investigations and replicate the Federal information. The motivation for this was that each State would tend to query and update its own information the vast majority of the time and so it would be more efficient to keep that information on local resource managers and allow remote queries; on the other hand, Federal information would likely be queried by many States and so it would be more efficient to replicate that information across the resource managers belonging to the States.

An example of a table that contains information classified at varying security levels was the Agent Table. This table contained a unique ID number for each agent as well as the agent's name. The ID number was needed at all security levels, both to keep track of agent workloads and to ensure that each investigation had a valid agent assigned to it. However, the agent's name was considered Top Secret and so it was only available when the user making the query was authenticated at the Top Secret security level.

Another example of multilevel tables is the Investigation Tables. Each investigation was classified at a particular security level — even the fact that an investigation was being conducted on a particular individual might itself be sensitive information. For this reason, investigations that might have, say, important political implications were classified at Top Secret, while investigations that had resulted in court cases would ordinarily be public knowledge and therefore Unclassified.

Our demonstration implementation contained resource managers for two States, each of which also contained a replica of the Federal portion of the database. The application was capable of querying, updating and adding information to the relevant tables.

The SDTP reference architecture enforces the simple security property (*no read-up*) and the *-property (*no write-down*) by using a distributed Security Manager layer. These Security Managers each used a set of single-level databases for storage; the combination of the Security Manager layer and the single-level databases produced a virtual multilevel resource manager.

The Security Managers communicated with the single-level databases using the native interface provided by the database. The Security Manager would create a set of communications links to the databases and manage them so as to maintain the security constraints. When an operation was requested by a component, the Security Manager would select the set of links that were appropriate for that operation. For example, when a component requested a read operation, the Security Manager would select the links to databases serving the current security level or lower. A write operation would result in only the current security level's link being selected.

The screen dump in Fig. 6 shows the demonstration instance in operation.

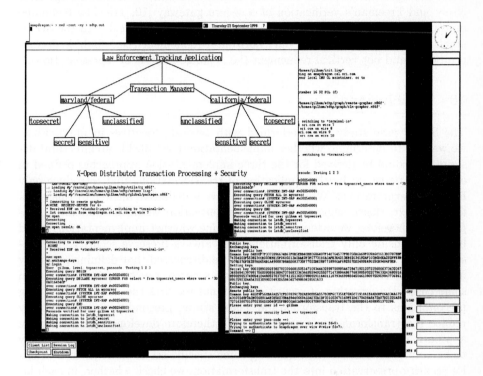

Fig. 6. SDTP Demonstration Instance in Operation

9   Related Work

A great deal of work has been devoted to transformational development of software artifacts and to (informal) architecture refinement, but very little has been done that combines both. Other than our own papers on the subject, some of the best examples are Brinksma, Jonsson, and Orava's work on connector refinement [2], work on component refinement [3], and Philipps and Rumpe's work on refinement of information flow architectures [12]. However, work on relating models of connector behavior at different levels of abstraction by Abowd, Allen, and Garlan [1], Luckham, et al. [5], and Moriconi and Qian [6] is closely related.

Similarly, a great deal of work has been devoted to developing verification of transformations, but we are unaware of any work specifically devoted developing techniques for showing that transformations always introduce faithful interpretations other than our own, with the exception of the sort of very general techniques for proving the existence of faithful interpretations found in references such as Turski and Maibaum's book [16].

Generally speaking, the security community has not been successful in formally linking security proofs to actual implementations. A notable exception is Neely and Freeman's verification of a secure gateway [10, 11]. The technique used in Neely and Freemen's case study is not adequate to deal with the SDTP architecture, because it treats only horizontal refinement (i.e., "bubble decomposition") and not vertical refinement (i.e., change in style of representation).

10   Conclusions

The SDTP case study was performed with several objectives in mind. First, we wanted to determine whether implementation-level SDTP architectural descriptions could be derived for the three implementation approaches defined in our earlier paper [8] by the application of transformations that introduce only faithful interpretations. While we do not have a definitive answer to this question, our experience suggests that such a derivation would be difficult or impossible. Therefore, we attempted to determine whether implementations could be derived using only transformations that always preserve security. The answer to this question is certainly *yes*. But we discovered that defining generally useful transformations that always preserve security can be quite difficult, in some cases. Preservation of security sometimes requires the addition of strong preconditions to the transformation. These strong preconditions can seriously reduce the transformation's generality. We therefore developed an alternative approach which allows transformations that only *sometimes* preserve security to be employed. Rather than building some specific set of sufficient conditions for security-preservation into the transformation, we check whether, in each individual application of the transformation, security has been preserved. Our approach to checking is based on a notion we call *proof-carrying architectures* [14]: the same transformation used to implement the architectural description is used to "implement" the security proof, which is carried along with the architectural description. Using a combination of showing that some transformations always introduce faithful interpretations and checking that the others preserve security in the particular case, we succeeded in manually verifying the security of all 12 implementation-level architectural descriptions (four per implementation approach).

A second objective in performing the case study was to begin to determine whether our "rearchitecting via replay" model works as well for global architectural changes (such as introducing security requirements) as it has worked in the 23 small-scale local rearchitecting case studies we have performed based on the X/Open DTP architecture.[4] As we pointed out above, the X/Open DTP derivation was very effectively reused in the defining the SDTP hierarchies. In

---

[4] The 23 studies are based on making a variety of small changes in system requirements (e.g., adding an RM) and/or implementation infrastructure (e.g., reducing the cost of interprocessor communication).

addition, our techniques for quickly estimating the cost of changes, and conservatively bounding the scope of changes, required to restore consistency in a hierarchy after a change has been introduced continued to work effectively. Therefore, we have begun the process of designing a rearchitecting tool based on this model that we believe will provide very substantial automated support for the process.

Our third objective in performing the case study was to assess the effectiveness of our transformation verification techniques on a larger stock of transformations. Although we wound up abandoning the idea of using only generally valid transformations in the development of the SDTP hierarchies, all the transformations that we believe to be generally valid were successfully verified. So, as mentioned above, we have begun to explore the process of automating these manual verifications using SRI's PVS verification system.

The final principal objective was to determine whether the lowest level architectural descriptions in the SDTP hierarchy were, in fact, implementation-level. In other words, we wanted to confirm our belief that no significant design decisions would have to be made when turning these low-level descriptions into executable code. This is crucial, because the hierarchy only effectively links the abstract architecture to the actual implementation if the gap between the lowest level description and the code is very small. If the gap is too large, confidence that the "implementation-level" descriptions of SDTP are secure provides only weak evidence that the actual implementation is secure. Our experience was that writing the code from these low-level descriptions is completely straightforward, thanks to formalizing information about implementation language facilities as SADL styles. Although this approach makes the low level implementation decisions in the SDTP hierarchies implementation language-dependent, it should hardly be surprising that choice of a programming language for the implementation affects low-level architectural design. Designs appropriate for other choices of programming language can be included by introducing additional branches in the hierarchies (although we have not done so in the case of the SDTP hierarchies we have developed). It should be noted that all these branchings would be at a level of abstraction lower than the X/Open standard, and hence they do not reduce the general utility of an SDTP standard at that same abstraction level. Based on this experience, we are planning to extend our architecture transformation toolset by including a facility for automatic generation of code for the architecture from an implementation-level description in SADL.

So it can be seen that development of the three SDTP hierarchies and the one reference implementation and demonstration instance served as a useful case study in

- transformational development of architectures,
- rearchitecting after adding a new "global" system requirement,
- transformation verification, and
- linking architectural descriptions to code.

References

[1] G. Abowd, R. Allen, and D. Garlan. Formalizing style to understand descriptions of software architecture. Technical Report CMU-CS-95-111, School of Computer Science, Carnegie Mellon University, January 1995.

[2] E. Brinksma, B. Jonsson, and F. Orava. Refining interfaces of communicating systems. In S. Abramsky and T. S. E. Maibaum, editors, *Proceedings of TAPSOFT '91*, pages 71–80. Springer-Verlag, 1991.

[3] M. Broy. Compositional refinement of interactive systems. Technical Report No. 89, Digital Systems Research Center, Palo Alto, July 1992.

[4] L. J. LaPadula and D. E. Bell. MITRE technical report 2547, Volume II. *Journal of Computer Security*, 4(2,3):239–263, 1996.

[5] D. C. Luckham, L. M. Augustin, J. J. Kenney, J. Vera, D. Bryan, and W. Mann. Specification and analysis of system architecture using Rapide. *IEEE Transactions on Software Engineering*, 21(4):314–335, April 1995.

[6] M. Moriconi and X. Qian. Correctness and composition of software architectures. In *Proceedings 2nd ACM Symposium on Foundations of Software Engineering (SIGSOFT '94)*, pages 164–174. ACM Press, 1994.

[7] M. Moriconi, X. Qian, and R. A. Riemenschneider. Correct architecture refinement. *IEEE Transactions on Software Engineering*, 21(4):356–372, April 1995. Available at http://www.csl.sri.com/sadl/tse95.ps.gz.

[8] M. Moriconi, X. Qian, R. A. Riemenschneider, and L. Gong. Secure software architectures. In *Proceedings of the 1997 IEEE Symposium on Security and Privacy*, pages 84–93, May 1997. Available at http://www.csl.sri.com/sadl/sp97.ps.gz.

[9] M. Moriconi and R. A. Riemenschneider. Introduction to SADL 1.0: A language for specifying software architecture hierarchies. Technical Report SRI-CSL-97-01, Computer Science Laboratory, SRI International, March 1997. Available at http://www.csl.sri.com/sadl/sadl-intro.ps.gz.

[10] R. B. Neely and J. W. Freeman. Structuring systems for formal verification. In *Proccedings of the IEEE Symposium on Security and Privacy*, pages 2–13, April 1985.

[11] R. B. Neely, J. W. Freeman, and M. D. Krenzin. Achieving understandable results in a formal design verification. In *Proceedings of the Computer Security Workshop II*, pages 115–124, June 1989.

[12] J. Philipps and B. Rumpe. Refinement of information flow architectures. In *Proceedings of the First IEEE International Conference on Formal Engineering Methods (ICFEM '97)*, pages 203–212, November 1997. Available at http://www4.informatik.tu-muenchen.de/papers/icfem_rumpe_1997_Publication.html.

[13] R. A. Riemenschneider. A simplified method for establishing the correctness of architectural refinements. SRI CSL Dependable System Archiecture Group, Working Paper DSA-97-02. Available at http://www.csl.sri.com/sadl/simplified.ps.gz., November 1997.

[14] R. A. Riemenschneider. Checking the correctness of architectural transformation steps via proof-carrying architectures. In *Proccedings of the First Working IFIP Conference on Software Architecture*, Kluwer Academic Press, 1999. Available at http://www.csl.sri.com/sadl/checking.ps.gz.

[15] R. A. Riemenschneider. Correct transformation rules for incremental development of architecture hierarchies. SRI CSL Dependable System Architecture

Group, Working Paper DSA-98-01. Available at `http://www.csl.sri.com/sadl/incremental.ps.gz`. February 1998.

[16] W. M. Turski and T. S. E. Maibaum. *The Specification of Computer Programs.* Addison-Wesley, 1987.

[17] X/Open Company, Apex Plaza, Forbury Road, Reading, Berkshire RG1 1AX, U.K. *Distributed Transaction Processing: Reference Model*, November 1993.

A Formal Security Model for Microprocessor Hardware

Volkmar Lotz[1], Volker Kessler[1], and Georg Walter[2]

[1] Siemens AG, Corporate Technology, D-81730 Munich,
{Volkmar.Lotz,Volker.Kessler}@mchp.siemens.de
[2] Siemens AG, D-81541 Munich

Abstract. The paper introduces a formal security model for a micro-processor hardware system. The model has been developed as part of the evaluation process of the processor product according to ITSEC assurance level E4. Novel aspects of the model are the need for defining integrity and confidentiality objectives on the hardware level without the operating system or application specification and security policy being given, and the utilisation of an abstract function and data space. The security model consists of a system model given as a state transition automaton on infinite structures, and the formalisation of security objectives by means of properties of automaton behaviours. Validity of the security properties is proved. The paper compares the model with published ones and summarises the lessons learned throughout the modelling process.

Key words: security, hardware, formal security models.

1   Introduction

When evaluating a system according to ITSEC's [8] quality assurance level E4 and beyond, the provision of a formal model of the underlying security policy is an integral part of the assessment procedure. The formal model is an "abstract statement of the important principles of security that the TOE [target of evaluation] will enforce" [8, p.33]. In general, it includes a formal specification of the security objectives and a formal system model that emphasises the security enforcing functions either by explicitly modelling them or by implicitly describing them in terms of the effects that they are expected to achieve. The goal of formalising these points is to review and get a deeper understanding of the security principles, to be able to analyse formally the validity and consistency of the security objectives, and to provide confidence that the system satisfies its security requirements by showing that the system model is adequate with respect to the security enforcing functions of the system.

In this paper we present a formal security model for microprocessor hardware that has been developed in the context of an E4 evaluation of the processor chip, and that shows some novel aspects compared to existing formal security models [10]. The most unusual feature of the work lies in the fact that the formal model has been defined for a hardware system where neither the operating system nor

J. Wing, J. Woodcock, J. Davies (Eds.): FM'99, Vol. I, LNCS 1708, pp. 718–737, 1999.
© Springer-Verlag Berlin Heidelberg 1999

the intended applications are known exactly at the time the hardware is designed, except for the fact that they will run in security sensitive environments. In particular, the security policy of the operating system as well as the applications is not yet defined, thus forcing the model to express security objectives by referring to an abstract application or operating system function space that is expected to satisfy its own security policy.

Since there is a wide range of possible applications, the hardware does not enforce a particular security policy, but rather provides basic security services on a physical and logical layer, like encryption, that can be utilised by operating systems and applications in order to maintain their security requirements. As a consequence, the security objectives of the hardware are stated in abstract terms, e.g. "legitimate access" or "undesired modifications". The above mentioned reference to higher order concepts, e.g. definition of function space and application of operating system functions, allows for an appropriate formalisation of these abstract terms.

In the following, we give a short introduction to the application domain and the hardware system to be modelled. Then, our security model is introduced in detail: we describe the system model which is based on a variant of state transition automata over infinite structures, show the formalisation of the security objectives, and give a summary of the proofs showing that the abstract system provably meets the security objectives. Though we could not refer to or adapt an already existing formal security model, our model shows some similarities concerning modelling and proof principles to published models, which will be discussed in detail.

Finally, the paper presents some of the lessons learned with respect to the pragmatic aspects of formal security modelling within an evaluation process according to E4. We are convinced that, even when not striving for certification, formal security modelling is useful. However, there are some key factors that have to be considered if the modelling work is to be successful in terms of applicability, expressiveness and, last but not least, efficiency. We will investigate these topics at the end of the paper. Furthermore, we examine whether our particular model can be used as a basis for a whole class of models for processor applications.

For reasons of exposition, the paper shows a simplified version of the original model that was submitted to the evaluation and certification process. However, the original model differs only in technical details, thus the results that have been derived can be equally applied.

2   Security Target

The target of evaluation is a security processing system with a CPU (including an encryption unit), RAM memory, ROM memory and EEPROM memory, which holds the stored data even if the power is turned off (see Fig. ??). The most important security objective is to preserve the security of information stored in the memory components. In detail, this means

- The data stored in any of the memory components shall be protected against unauthorised access or modification.
- The security relevant functions stored in any of the memory components shall be protected against unauthorised access or modification.
- As a consequence, it must not be possible to execute any hardware test routine without authorisation.

These objectives are achieved by implementing a set of security enforcing functions which mainly perform the following two tasks:

- The system passes several phases during its lifetime. The entry to the phases is controlled by a phase management, which checks different flags and gives a specified level of authorisation.
- Additionally, encryption of the memory components is implemented in hardware. Encryption utilises several keys and key sources with a chip specific random number among them.

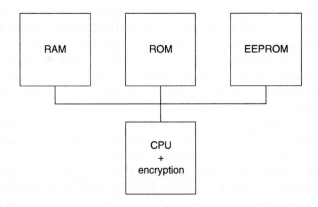

Fig. 1. Processor architecture

Though the ITSEC allow defining a security model in terms of references to existing and published models, for our application we could not make use of this option. On one hand this is due to the fact that the well-known models like Bell-LaPadula etc. refer to operating system or higher levels, where operations like reading, writing, or granting access rights form a suitable level of abstraction. For the processor hardware we do not know which kind of functionality the operating system will offer. Thus it cannot be anticipated that the system models of the given security models are adequate. We only know that there will be some functionality offered by an operating system or an application. We have to assume that executing this functionality is legitimate in any case, since operating system and application are considered to be responsible for enforcing their respective security policy.

On the other hand, among the most important modelling principles that were to be followed in our work we had the requirement of keeping the model as simple and abstract as possible without losing meaningfulness. This was motivated by the need for discussing the model with non-experts in formal methods, in particular the processor development staff, and to accelerate the evaluation process. As a consequence, we intended to define the model without using modelling aids, i.e. formal concepts that occur in the model in order to explicate its properties, but that do not have an immediate correspondence within the real system. Thus, for example, formal models relying on access control concepts including the definition of rights and the utilisation of some access control data structure could not be appropriately applied. For further comparison to existing models see Sect. 5.1.

The formal security policy model of the processor hardware consists of two parts: a system model describing the processor's behaviour on an abstract level by means of a state transition automaton with input and output, and a set of security objective specifications given as properties on automata behaviours. Thus we are able to prove the validity of the security properties with respect to the system model. Interpreting the system model in terms of the real processor then allows one to conclude with some evidence that the processor indeed meets its security objectives as required by ITSEC E4 assessment criteria.

3   System Model

In this chapter, we present the system model part of the security model in detail. We formally define the processor as a state transition system and explain why it is an appropriate abstraction of the original processor hardware. Though the explanation is informal, it is an important part of the process, since it defines the modelling relationship and is the basis for interpreting the results of formal security analysis.

3.1   General System Model

We assume the reader to be familiar with tuples, functions and (finite or infinite) sequences. We will use common notation including $\Pi_i(s)$ for tuple projection, $dom(f)$ and $rng(f)$ for function domain and range, A^* and A^∞ for finite and infinite sequences over a set A, $A^\omega = A^* \cup A^\infty$ for arbitrary sequences, and $\cdot_i$, $\circ$, $\sharp$, and $\sqsubseteq$ for selection, concatenation, length and the prefix relation on sequences, respectively.

The system model itself is defined as a variant of state transition automata over infinite structures [16].

Definition 1. *An automaton M is a tuple of five components:*

$$M = (State, In, Out, S_0, \delta)$$

not being accessible in the given state, which leads to f not being executable in this state. Deletion of a function can be defined by redefining val. If $val(f) = g$ where $g \neq \perp$, a call of f leads to the execution of the operation g. The modelling principle corresponds to viewing the data state as a memory component, which is appropriate with respect to the processor hardware (see Fig. **??**) and its security objectives.

Definition 5. *A state s is given by a triple:*

$$s \in Ph \times (F \to Val) \times (D \to Val) \ .$$

We thus have the set of states State given by :

$$State = Ph \times (F \to Val) \times (D \to Val) \ .$$

For a given state $s \in State$ we have:

- *$ph(s) = \Pi_1(s) \in Ph$ the component denoting the current phase,*
- *$data(s) = (\Pi_2(s), \Pi_3(s))$ the data state component[1],*
- *$val_s^F = \Pi_2(s)$ function state component[2] and $fct(s) = dom(\Pi_2(s))$ the set of available function identifiers,*
- *$val_s^D = \Pi_3(s)$ the data object state component and $dt(s) = dom(\Pi_3(s))$ the set of available data object identifiers.*
- *the function $val_s : O \to Val$ defined by:*
  $$val_s(o) := val_s^F(o) \ \ if \ o \in F \ ,$$
  $$val_s^D(o) \ \ if \ o \in D \ .$$

Since F and D are disjoint, val_s is well defined. We do not require the evaluation function to remain invariant throughout a particular behaviour of the automaton. Thus the model is able to capture attacks resulting from modification of functions, in particular testing software. We abbreviate an error state, which is given if the processor is in phase ∞ by e.

Among the security critical functions, the test functions possibly enabling a phase transition, play a particular role emphasised in Sect. 2. For each of them we define a predicate denoting test results.

Definition 6. *For each $f \in F_{Test}$ we define a predicate $Test_f(val_s)$. If a test predicate evaluates to true, the test is considered to be successfully passed.*

3.3   Environment Interface

The processor interacts with its environment by means of input and output. We interpret inputs as requests for the execution of operations which can be accepted or denied by the processor. Requests are assigned to a subject, with the processor manufacturer Pmf being particularly distinguished. Including subject identifiers is an abstraction from the real processor system, where the subject identity is derived from the results of an authentication mechanism.

---

[1] Note that the notion data state also refers to functions.
[2] Note that in this case $val_s^F(f)$ itself is a function.

Definition 7. *Let Sb be a set of* subject identifiers *including $Pmf \in Sb$. A* subject $sb \in Sb$ *is able to request three types of operations, two of them modelling ordinary processor operation and one modelling attack situations:*

- *$exec(sb, f)$ where $f \in F$ models the function call of f;*
- *$load(sb, o, v)$ where $o \in F \cup D$ and $v \in Val$ describes the request for modifying or adding an object o with value v;*
- *$spy(o)$ where $o \in O$ models an eavesdropping action, which is given if a subject tries to force the processor to reveal information without executing a function in F. A spy action is typically given by physical attacks on the processor hardware. Note that the definition of spy is independent of subjects, since it models an attack that should be prohibited.*
- *We also define an input selector function subject by $subject(exec(sb, f)) = sb$ and $subject(load(sb, o, v)) = sb$ where $sb \in Sb, f \in F, o \in F \cup D$ and $v \in Val$.*

Our model of the influence of operation execution, i.e. state transitions of the automaton, on the environment is abstract as well: an output value does not only model the data being output by the processor, but is assumed to include all the information that can be derived from the data. We implicitly assume a partial order on the set of output values modelling information containment, thus we can consider outputs to be elements of $Val \cup \{ok, no\}$. The special values ok and no describe outputs stating acceptance or denial of requests, or the occurrence of errors.

Definition 8. *Let $f \in F$ be a function identifier, $s \in State$ a state, and $out : Val \rightarrow Val$, $change : Val \rightarrow (F \rightarrow Val) \times (D \rightarrow Val)$ suitable selection functions, then*

- *$out(val_s^F(f)(data(s))) \in Val$ denotes the output resulting from execution of f, and*
- *$change(val_s^F(f)(data(s))) \in (F \rightarrow Val) \times (D \rightarrow Val)$ denotes the state change resulting from execution of f.*

Note that in the above definition, the term $val_s^F(f)(data(s))$ denotes the application of the current evaluation $val_s^F(f)$ of f to the current data state $data(s)$, thus specifying the results of the execution of f.

Our model of executable functions and their effects does not include function parameters. This simplifies the model significantly without restricting its expressiveness. Simply assume that, like in an assembler language, parameters are loaded to data objects and functions immediately address data objects.

From the security modelling and analysis viewpoint, our decision to explicitly model data space and function execution might be considered to provide irrelevant detail compared to a Bell-LaPadula-like approach referring to object access only. However, since our model has been part of an industrial-level IT-SEC evaluation, we were forced to keep the balance between the different system development tasks related to the formal security model: performing security analysis, serving as the top-level security specification for the evaluation target, and proving the correspondence of the model and the system implementation.Adding some more detail to the security model significantly reduced the complexity of correspondence arguments.

3.4   State Transition Function and Model Definition

Definition 9. *The formal system model is given by an automaton*

$$M = (State, In, Out, S_0, \delta) \ .$$

- $State = Ph \times (F \to Val) \times (D \to Val)$,
- $In = \{exec(sb, f) | sb \in Sb, f \in F\} \cup \{load(sb, o, v) | sb \in Sb, o \in F \cup D, v \in Val\} \cup \{spy(o) | o \in O\}$,
- $Out = Val \cup \{ok, no\}$,
- $S_0 \subset State$ *where for all* $s_0 \in S_0$ *we have* $ph(s_0) = 0$ *and* $F_{Test} \subseteq fct(s_0)$.
- $\delta \in State \times In \to \mathcal{P}(State \times Out)$ *is defined by the state transition rules below.*

It remains to define the state transition rules. For reasons of exposition, the following rule definitions in general only give those state components explicitly that are changed if a state transition occurs. In any case, all the components that are not explicitly mentioned remain invariant. Following definition 1, the state transition function is total. However, organisational and technical security measures ensure that only reasonable inputs will occur in processor applications. For example, operating system functionality is checked, and abuse of application functionality does not disclose security relevant information because of encryption. We therefore simply assume that only reasonable inputs occur. To keep things clean, we do not encode this assumption immediately in the system model, but rather state it as a property of the input sequences that may occur. In Sect. 4.1 the model is thus extended by a set of assumptions explicitly defining the notion "reasonable input". The processor's security mechanisms ensure validity of these assumptions.

We start with the definition of the state transition rules for *exec* inputs that apply to the automaton in phase 0, the construction phase. Let $s \in \{0\} \times (F \to Val) \times (D \to Val)$ be a state in this phase of the processor's life cycle

(R0.0) $\delta(s, exec(sb, f)) = (s', \text{"ok"})$ if $sb = Pmf$,
where $ph(s') = 1$, $fct(s') = fct(s) \setminus F_{Test0}$, $f \in fct(s) \cap F_{Test0}$
$val_{s'}^F = val_s^F |_{fct(s) \setminus F_{Test0}}$ and $Test_f(val_s)$

(R0.1) $\delta(s, exec(sb, f)) = (s', \text{``ok''})$ if $sb = Pmf$,
     where $ph(s') = 2$, $fct(s') = fct(s) \setminus F_{Test}$, $f \in fct(s) \cap F_{Test1}$
     $val^F_{s'} = val^F_s |_{fct(s) \setminus F_{Test}}$ and $Test_f(val_s)$

(R0.2) $\delta(s, exec(sb, f)) = (e, \text{``no''})$ if $sb = Pmf$,
     with arbitrary $data(e)$ $f \in fct(s) \cap F_{Test}$
                         and $\neg Test_f(val_s)$.

(R0.3) $\delta(s, exec(sb, f)) = (s', out(val^F_s(f)(data(s))))$ if $sb = Pmf$,
     where $ph(s') = 0$, $f \in fct(s) \setminus F_{Test}$
     $data(s') = change(val^F_s(f)(data(s)))$

(R0.4) $\delta(s, exec(sb, f)) = (s, \text{``no''})$ if $sb \neq Pmf$
                               or $f \notin fct(s)$

(R0.0) models the fact that only the hardware manufacturer is allowed to execute tests. The required test function must a member of the set of active, i.e. executable, functions. If the test succeeds, phase 1 will be entered. Note that when entering phase 1 the test functionality according to phase 0 will be deleted, i.e. removed from the set of active functions. The model does not exclude that the test is separated in different tasks that are to be executed in sequence. The essential thing is that after finishing the last part the next phase is entered. The execution of previous parts of the test is modelled by (R0.3).

(R0.1) describes the case in which a test function intended for phase 1 is inadvertently executed in phase 0. Then, the processor moves immediately to phase 2, without being able to load application functionality (cf. the rules for *load* below). Though leading to an unusable system, this state transition does not contribute to a security violation. If a test fails, the system will enter an error state as described by rule (R0.2).

In phase 0, active functions may be executed only by the processor manufacturer. This does not change the phase. Additional requirements on functions executable in phase 0, e.g. that they should not modify any of the currently available functionality, are expressed as predicates over elements of $rng(val^F_{s_0})$ and required in Sect. 4.1.

Altogether, in phase 0 only the processor manufacturer's requests for function execution are accepted by the system, all other requests will be denied as being described by (R0.4). Obviously, requests for the execution of functions that are currently not executable are denied as well, independent of the requestor.

The transition rules for *exec* inputs in phase 1, the upload phase, are defined completely analogous to those referring to phase 0. Let $s \in \{1\} \times (F \to Val) \times (D \to Val)$ be a state in the second phase of the processor's life cycle.

(R1.1) $\delta(s, exec(sb, f)) = (s', \text{"}ok\text{"})$ if $sb = Pmf$,

     where $ph(s') = 2$, $fct(s') = fct(s) \setminus F_{Test1}$, $f \in fct(s) \cap F_{Test1}$

     $val^F_{s'} = val^F_s|_{fct(s) \setminus F_{Test1}}$ and $Test_f(val_s)$

(R1.2) $\delta(s, exec(sb, f)) = (e, \text{"}no\text{"})$ if $sb = Pmf$,

     with arbitrary $data(e)$ $f \in fct(s) \cap F_{Test1}$

     and $\neg Test_f(val_s)$

(R1.3) $\delta(s, exec(sb, f)) = (s', out(val^F_s(f)(data(s))))$ if $sb = Pmf$,

     where $ph(s') = 1$, $f \in fct(s) \setminus F_{Test1}$

     $data(s') = change(val^F_s(f)(data(s)))$

(R1.4) $\delta(s, exec(sb, f)) = (s, \text{"}no\text{"})$ if $sb \neq Pmf$

     or $f \notin fct(s)$

To define the state transition rules for *exec* in phase 2, the operational phase, let $s \in \{2\} \times (F \to Val) \times (D \to Val)$. We have

(R2.1) $\delta(s, exec(sb, f)) = (s', out(val^F_s(f)(data(s))))$ if $f \in fct(s)$

     where $ph(s') = 2$,

     $data(s') = change(val^F_s(f)(data(s)))$

(R2.2) $\delta(s, exec(sb, f)) = (s, \text{"}no\text{"})$ if $f \notin fct(s)$

From the rules above it follows that in phase 2 everyone may execute the functionality that is available on the processor, regardless of the subject's role. However, the rules defined for phase 0 and 1 guarantee that there are no phase 0 and 1 test functions available in phase 2. The rules for phase 2 do not restrict the operating system or application designer in enforcing their own security policy. The means that implementing such a security policy must be part of the application functionality itself and may impose additional requirements on the data object or function state components. The detailed investigation of an application's security policy is, however, beyond the scope of a processor security model.

To complete the transition rules for *exec* we have to consider the error state. Let $e \in \{\infty\} \times (F \to Val) \times (D \to Val)$ be an error state.

(R3.1) $\delta(e, exec(sb, f_{SN})) = (e, SN)$ if $f_{SN} \in fct(e)$

(R3.2) $\delta(e, exec(sb, f)) = (e, \text{"}no\text{"})$ if $f \neq f_{SN}$

     or $f_{SN} \notin fct(e)$

In the error state the only executable function is the one revealing the processor's serial number. Any other function calls result in an error message and do not change the state.

Next, we define state transition rules for *load*. For all $s \in Ph \times (F \to Val) \times (D \to Val)$, $sb \in Sb$, $o \in O$, $v \in Val$ we have

(R4.1) $\delta(s, load(sb, o, v)) = (s', \text{"ok"})$ if $ph(s) = 1$,
      where $ph(s') = 1$, $sb = Pmf$,
      $fct(s') = fct(s) \cup \{o\}$, $o \in F_{nSec}$
      $val_{s'}^F = val_s^F|_{F \setminus \{o\}} \cup \{o \mapsto v\}$

(R4.2) $\delta(s, load(sb, o, v)) = (s, \text{"no"})$ otherwise

An upload of new functionality is only allowed in phase 1 which is considered to be the phase where the operating system and the application is brought onto the processor hardware. By definition uploadable functions are not security relevant. This emphasises that functions that are security critical on the application or operating system level are not treated as being security relevant within the processor's security model, since they do not refer to the security objectives of the processor itself. Apart from this, rule (R4.1) does not impose further restrictions on the values of o and v. If there exist additional restrictions that, for instance, address the semantics of uploaded functions to avoid undesired side effects, they are formalised by model assumptions as presented in Sect. 4.1. Besides those defined by (R4.1) no other upload attempts are allowed throughout the processor's life cycle, which is formalised by (R4.2).

Finally, the transition rules for *spy* inputs remain to be defined. Recall that our model of the *spy* operation mainly addresses attacks on the physical level whereas (even illegitimate) utilisation of available functions in order to achieve knowledge about objects is covered by the *exec* rules. Typically misuse of executable functions is subject of an operating system or application security policy and does not apply to the processor model. See Sect. 4 for our formalisation of the notion "legitimate access". Let $s \in Ph \times (F \to Val) \times (D \to Val)$ and $o \in O$.

(R5.1) $\delta(s, spy(o)) = (s, val_s(o))$ if $o \in F_{nSec} \cup D_{nSec}$
                                    and $s \neq e$

(R5.2) $\delta(s, spy(o)) \in \{(e, val_s(o)), (e, \bot), (s, \bot)\}$ if $o \in F_{Sec} \cup D_{Sec}$
                                    and $s \neq e$

(R5.3) $\delta(e, spy(o)) = (e, \bot)$

(R5.1) states that objects not being security relevant may be disclosed anyway without changing the system's state. (R5.2) describes the processor's reaction to *spy* attacks on security critical objects by three cases that may occur non-deterministically. $(e, val_{P_1}(o))$ as successor state models the case of "destructive reading": since we have to consider even attacks on physical level, e.g. inspecting the silicon with a microscope, we cannot rule out that attacks may reveal information even about security critical objects. Thus, we at least require that if an attack is successful the processor hardware will be "destroyed", i.e. cannot regularly be used further on. This is modelled by moving to the error state, with rules (R3.1) and (R3.2) formalising what is meant by "cannot regularly be used".

Depending on the kind of attack, we also may enter the case that after attacking a security critical object the processor is not being destroyed. If that occurs, no information is allowed to be disclosed, modelled by $(s, \bot)$ being the successor state. The even stronger case with $(e, \bot)$ as the successor state is included for completeness.

(R5.3) formalises the effect of *spy* attacks if the processor is already in the error state. Since the error state describes destruction of the processor as result of security enforcing functions operating on the physical, or hardware, level, we may reasonably assume that any further attack will require highly extensive resources, and thus is improbable to successfully occur. The security model gives an idealised description by defining that *spy* operations in the error state do not reveal any information regardless of the object being addressed.

The *spy* rules explicitly describe the effects of possible attacks in terms of state change and output. A more abstract modelling alternative would have been to add model assumptions as logical axioms, just like the environment assumptions stated in Sect. 4.1. We chose the above model with respect to subsequent processor design and the informal correspondence arguments, the latter being required by ITSEC E4. In particular, attacks on the physical level are among the most important attacks to be considered during processor design, and a number of security measures have been implemented to counter such attacks.

4   Formalising Security Requirements

4.1   Model Assumptions

In order to exclude pathological cases with respect to environment behaviour, we have to add some assumptions on function objects that are initially available or uploaded during a behaviour of the system. For instance, we have to exclude the case where a hostile operating system or application offers functionality executable by everyone that modifies security relevant functions, or where an application is inadvertently used to store the processor's design description.

We state three axioms that describe expectations about environment behaviours that agree with the security objectives. Since axioms address the environment, they are separated from the system model definition. However, this does not imply that the processor's security functions do not contribute to avoiding undesired consequences in case of the assumptions being violated. For example, initially available security critical functionality f can be stored in the processor's read-only memory component, thus even an $exec(sb, f')$ call of a "hostile" function f' violating axioms 1 and 2 below cannot modify f.

Axiom 1 (Integrity with respect to initially available functions)
Initially available functions only change the data object state, but not $fct(P)$ itself, i.e. for all $f \in fct(s_0)$ and for all $s \in S$ we have

$$\Pi_1(change(val_s^F(f)(data(s)))) = val_s^F \ .$$

Axiom 2 (Integrity with respect to non-security-relevant functions)
Functions $f \in F_{nSec}$ that are not security relevant only change objects that are not security relevant, i.e. elements of $D_{nInt} \cup F_{nSec}$. For all $f \in F_{nSec}$ and for all $s \in S$ we have

$$\Pi_1(change(val_s^F(f)(data(s))))|_{F_{Sec}} = val_s^F|_{F_{Sec}} \ ,$$
$$\Pi_2(change(val_s^F(f)(data(s))))|_{D_{Int}} = val_s^D|_{D_{Int}} \ .$$

Axiom 3 (Confidentiality) *Let $b = (s, in, out) \in \|M\|$ be a behaviour of M and $Val_{s_i}^{F_{Sec}} := \{val_{s_j}^F(f) \, | \, j < i, f \in F_{Sec}\}$, for $i < \sharp s$, the set of security critical functions that have been available in at least one state up to the $i-th$ state transition of b. For all $i \in \mathcal{N}$ where $ph(s_i) = 2$ and $f \in fct(s_i)$ we have*

$$out(val_{s_i}^F(f)(data(s_i))) \notin Val_{s_i}^{F_{Sec}} \ .$$

Note that Axiom 3 is stated purely for reasons of being able to conduct the security proofs. The processor's security enforcing functions guarantee that non-security-relevant functions cannot access the security critical functionality. However, to prove validity of the security properties, we also have to consider the case where an application function guesses or accidentally reveals security relevant information. This case is unlikely to occur in practice, but it has to be explicitly excluded in the security model, which is done by adding Axiom 3.

4.2   Security Properties

To complete the formal security model we have to formalise the processor security objectives that have been stated in chapter 2. The formalisation refers to the behaviours of the automaton that describes the system model and is given in definition 9.

Requirement SO1. "The hardware must be protected against unauthorised disclosure of security enforcing functionality."

In our model disclosure of information is defined by an appropriate value occurring in the output sequence of a behaviour. Only the processor manufacturer is allowed to know about the security enforcing functions. If any other subject gets to know about security enforcing functions, e.g. by means of an attack, the processor must be destroyed which in our model means that the error state is entered.

FSO 1 Let $b = (s, in, out) \in \|M\|$ and $Val_{s_i}^{F_{Sec}}$ as defined in Axiom 3. For all $j < \sharp b$ it must hold that

$$out_j \in Val_{s_j}^{F_{Sec}} \quad \Rightarrow \quad (subject(in_j) = Pmf \ \vee \ s_{j+1} = e) \ .$$

Requirement SO2. "The hardware must be protected against unauthorised modification of security enforcing functions."

Modification includes the deletion of functions. In terms of the system model the requirement states that in any behaviour the evaluation of the corresponding function object identifier always returns the same value, if the evaluation is defined for the identifier. Due to our model design, this value must correspond to the initial value of the function object. Deletion of security relevant functions which means removing the corresponding identifier from the evaluation domain is allowed in case of phase transitions. We add an additional requirement that deletion of security functions in states other than the error state is only permitted during phase transitions.

FSO 2.1 Let $b = (s, in, out) \in \|M\|$. For all $i \in \mathcal{N}$ where $s_i \neq e$ it must hold that
$$f \in F_{Sec} \cap fct(s_i) \Rightarrow val^F_{s_i}(f) = val^F_{s_0}(f) \ .$$

FSO 2.2 Let $b = (s, in, out) \in \|M\|$. For all $i \in \mathcal{N}$ where $s_{i+1} \neq e$ it must hold that
$$ph(s_i) = ph(s_{i+1}) \Rightarrow fct(s_i)|_{F_{Sec}} \subseteq fct(s_{i+1})|_{F_{Sec}} \ .$$

Requirement SO3. "The information stored in the processor's memory components must be protected against unauthorised access."

We restrict the formal definition of this requirement to the *spy* operations, since the output of available operating system or application functionality obeys the corresponding security policy which is unknown for the time being. Thus we may not exclude that an application does not consider the output of security relevant data to be harmful. Additionally, it does not suffice to solely consider output sequences, since we have to take into account destructive reading. In order to avoid compromising confidentiality, destructive reading may only occur once in a behaviour, after that the error state must be entered.

FSO 3 Let $b = (s, in, out) \in \|M\|$. For all $i \in \mathcal{N}$; $o \in F_{Sec} \cup D_{Sec}$ it must hold that

$$out_i = val_{s_i}(o) \wedge in_i = spy(o) \Rightarrow$$
$$\{s_j | j > i\} = \{e\} \wedge \{out_j | j < i, in_j = spy(o') \text{ with } o' \in F_{Sec} \cup D_{Sec}\} = \{\bot\}.$$

Requirement SO4. "The information stored in the processor's memory components must be protected against unauthorised modification."

Without knowing about the operating system and application security policy, the requirement can only be interpreted in the sense that any modification resulting from the execution of available functions is considered to be authorised. Here, available means initially existing or being uploaded by performing a *load* operation. It is the task of the operating system or application designer to only upload functions that do not violate their security policy. Besides function execution, operations or state transitions leading to data state changes are only allowed to behave in the desired way.

FSO 4 Let $b = (s, in, out) \in \|M\|$. For all $i \in \mathcal{N}$ it must hold that

$$data(s_{i+1}) = data(s_i)$$
$$\vee \; \exists sb \in Sb, \, f \in fct(s_i) : in_i = exec(sb, f)$$
$$\wedge \; data(s_{i+1}) = change(val_{s_i}^F(f)(data(s_{i+1})))$$
$$\vee \; ph(s_{i+1}) \neq ph(s_i) \wedge val_{s_{i+1}}^D = val_{s_i}^D \wedge val_{s_{i+1}}^F|_{F \backslash F_{Test}} = val_{s_i}^F|_{F \backslash F_{Test}}$$
$$\vee \; \exists sb \in Sb, \, f \in F, \, v \in Val : in_i = load(sb, f, v)$$
$$\wedge \; val_{s_{i+1}}^F|_{F \backslash \{f\}} = val_{s_i}^F|_{F \backslash \{f\}} \wedge val_{s_{i+1}}^D = val_{s_i}^D \, .$$

Requirement SO5. "It may not occur that test functions are executed in an unauthorised way."

Test functions may only executed by the processor manufacturer. Otherwise, a request for execution will be denied.

FSO 5 Let $b = (s, in, out) \in \|M\|$. For all $i \in \mathcal{N}$, $j = 0, 1$, $sb \in Sb$ it must hold that:

$$in_i = exec(sb, f) \wedge f \in F_{Testj} \quad \Rightarrow$$
$$sb = Pmf \vee (s_{i+1} \in \{s_i, e\} \wedge out_i = \text{"no"}) \, .$$

4.3 Security Proofs

Firstly, it has to be shown that the rules for the state transitions are well-defined, thus providing evidence for model consistency and adequacy. It is easy to check, because the case distinctions in the transition rule definitions are given in a constructive way. Secondly, we prove that the model defined in Definition 9 satisfies the security requirements, i.e. the following theorem holds.

Theorem 1. *Given Axioms 1 to 3, $M = (State, In, Out, S_0, \delta)$ satisfies FSO 1, 2.1, 2.2, 3, 4, 5.*

The proof is carried out either by induction on the length of behaviours (which is admissible since the properties FSO 1, 2.1, 2.2, 3, 4, 5 are safety properties) or by immediately considering the case distinctions of the definitions of the state transition functions. Proof details are left out for reason of space ([11] contains the complete proof). The proof makes also use of auxiliary lemmas like

Lemma 1. *Let $b = (s, in, out) \in \|M\|$. Then it holds for all $i, j \in \mathcal{N}$ with $j \geq i$:*

$$ph(s_j) \geq ph(s_i) \, .$$

i.e. the TOE cannot get into a previous phase, especially there is no exit from the error-state.

5   Discussion

5.1   Classification and Comparison

The "well-known" security models [10] often consider either confidentiality, e.g.
Bell-LaPadula [1], Denning [6], Goguen-Meseguer [7], Chinese Wall [9], or integrity, e.g. Biba [3], Clark-Wilson [5]. There are only a few examples like Terry-Wiseman [15] which consider both confidentiality and integrity. The security objectives of our model refer to confidentiality like FSO1 and FSO 3, and to integrity like FSO 2 and FSO 4.

In the area of security modelling there has been a long controversial debate whether the definition of *secure* should refer to states or to state transformations. Bell-LaPadula [1] called a system secure iff each (possible) state is secure. McLean pointed out that "any explication of security based on the notion of a *secure state* must fail ... The concept of a secure system must be explicated as one whose initial state is secure and whose system transform is secure" [12, p. 128]. In our model the security requirements refer to the behaviours $b = (s, in, out)$ $\in State^\omega \times In^\omega \times Out^\omega$ which includes both states and state transformations, e.g., requirement FSO 1 refers to state transformation and FSO 2 refers to states.

The BLP-model introduces an access control matrix as a mechanism to enforce the security requirements. In our model we do not introduce any security mechanisms for two reasons discussed in Sect. 2: level of operation and simplicity by avoiding modelling aids. From the modelling point of view our model description is on a higher level of abstraction and it is thus more flexible.

Note that although our model was designed for a hardware system it could be used for software or hybrid systems as well.

5.2   Practical Aspects and Lessons Learned

The work reported in this paper provides strong evidence that drawing up a formal security model is feasible as well as beneficial with respect to systems operating in a security sensitive environment, even if it is not followed by a formal development process up to some design or implementation level. The complete formal modelling work took about two months, including understanding and discussing the system design and security target, investigating modelling alternatives, discussing the model with the development staff, and supporting the evaluation process. The formal parts made up about ten percent of the whole evaluation and certification effort which was even based on existing development documents. These numbers may serve as an indicator for estimating formal modelling efforts in future evaluation processes.

However, a number of critical factors turned out to influence success and efficiency of formal security modelling. Among them there is the appropriateness of the chosen abstraction level, in particular the decision on implicit or explicit modelling of security enforcing functions. Unfortunately, there is no general methodology that helps to determine which function to explicitly model, and ITSEC leave the decision completely to the model designers. In practice, one should therefore base the decision on its estimated contribution to understandability, simplicity, and meaningfulness of the model. Take our implicit model of encryption as an example: If we had modelled encryption explicitly, we would have been forced to include additional data types (e.g., keys, random numbers, cryptograms), state components (e.g., key space, encrypted memory) and operations (key generation, key distribution, encryption, decryption) to the system model and an adversary description (including a model of the adversary's "knowledge" like [13] or [14]) to the environment model, thus being able to reduce the proof obligations concerning the *spy* operation to a set of assumptions on sound cryptosystems. We do not consider this model extension as being beneficial compared to our approach of simply stating that *spy* does not reveal useful information to the environment, since increased complexity of the model and proofs only leads to yet another set of assumptions that have to be informally interpreted in terms of the real system. As another example, explicitly modelling the phase concept of processor construction and rollout turned out to be reasonable since security objectives like FSO2.2 immediately refer to the phase model.

In order to decide upon the appropriate abstraction level and to discuss whether the system is faithfully represented (see [2] for the importance of faithful representation) it turned out to be useful to provide a first version of the formal security model as early as possible within the process and to discuss it with the system development staff. This serves two purposes: on one hand it supports the evolutionary development of the model while maintaining the representation relation and its informal interpretation, on the other hand it supports the review and understanding of the security objectives and the system's security architecture even in the early phases of the development.

Difficulties in modelling occur on a detailed level rather than with respect to general modelling concepts. Typical examples are given by incomplete case distinctions, missing parameters, or wrong handling of exceptional cases. It is therefore of crucial importance to conduct proofs showing that the model is consistent and that the abstract security properties hold with respect to the system model. With merely writing down a model errors will certainly occur. Thus proofs are necessary to provide model consistency, avoid errors in modelling details and to check model adequacy. As a prerequisite for meaningful proofs, a separation between the system model and the definition of the security objectives in the tradition of the Bell-LaPadula model is required.

Altogether, we recommend the construction of a formal security model for reasons going beyond achieving ITSEC's E4 correctness level. In particular it is the deeper and better understanding of the system and its security objectives that makes their formalisation valuable. Actually, the formal model turned out to be the key tool for understanding and assessing the security objectives, particularly by giving a precise meaning to fuzzy notions like "legitimate", "allowed", etc. that still occur in the security target. Additionally, the formalisation explicates the limitations of the security model and even the security target specification. Our particular modelling approach is considered to be beneficial mainly because of its high abstraction level that makes the model easy to understand without losing relevance and its constructive approach to the definition of the state transition function which implies completeness with respect to the abstraction level of the model. The cost-benefit ratio turned out to be adequate.

6   Conclusion

In this paper we have introduced a formal security model for a processor. The model differs from those known in the literature in that it must assume an arbitrary set of functions implemented by an operating system or an application and that it cannot refer to a particular security policy definition. Rather, abstract notions like "legitimate access" are formalised in terms of execution of functions of the actual function space and a particular operation *spy* modelling attacks to the hardware that are performed on a physical level. Besides these novel aspects, the formal approach continues a tradition of well-established modelling principles: separation of formal definitions of system model and security objectives, modelling the system as state transition automaton with input and output, and proving the validity of security objectives by inductive proofs.

The model has been defined as part of an ITSEC evaluation process according to quality assurance level E4. However, formal security modelling has turned out to be valuable even if evaluation is not desired. Formal modelling results in a deeper understanding of the system and its security aspects and is a useful tool in system development. Moreover, our experience is that the additional work required by security modelling can be done with reasonable amount of time and money spent. However, some key factors have to be taken into account, with the selection of an appropriate abstraction level and the inclusion of development staff into the modelling process among them.

The impact of formal security modelling can be increased if one can benefit from a particular modelling effort in other applications as well. We expect that our model can be adequately used as a basic model for processor applications of arbitrary kind including, for instance, software virtual machines: it shows a sufficiently high level of abstraction that, for example, does not restrict it to hardware developments, and it does not assume particular properties of an operating system that is to be loaded onto the processor system. The model assumptions included are satisfied by typical operating systems and thus do not restrict the scope. However, future work has to concentrate on adapting and parameterising the model in order to provide a generic model, or a class of models, respectively, for processor applications.

References

[1] Bell, D.E., Len LaPadula. *Secure Computer Systems: Unified Exposition and Multics Interpretation.* NTIS AD-A023588, MTR 2997, ESD-TR-75-306, MITRE Corporation, Bedford, MA, 1976.
[2] Bell, D.E. *Concerning "Modelling" of Computer Security.* Proc. of the IEEE Symp. on Security and Privacy 1988, 8-13.

[3] Biba, K.J. *Integrity Considerations for Secure Computer Systems.* NTIS AD-A039 324, MTR 3153,ESD-TR-76-372, MITRE Corporation, Bedford, MA, 1977.

[4] Broy,M. *Towards a Logical Basis for Systems Engineering.* Working Material of the 1998 Marktoberdorf Summer School on Calculational System Design 1998. Also to appear in: Broy, M.(ed.) *Calculational System Design.* Springer Verlag, NATO ASI Series F.

[5] Clark, D.C., D.R. Wilson. *Evolution of a Model for Computer Integrity.* Report of the Invitational Workshop on Data Integrity, NIST Publ. 500-168, 1989, Sect. A2, 1-3.

[6] Denning, D.E. *A Lattice Model of Secure Information Flow.* Comm. ACM Vol. 19, No. 5 (1976), 236-243.

[7] Goguen, J.A., J. Meseguer. *Security Policies and Security Models.* Proc. of the IEEE Symp. on Security and Privacy 1982, 11-20.

[8] Commission of the European Communities. *Information Technology Security Evaluation Criteria (ITSEC).* June 1991

[9] Kessler, Volker. *On the Chinese Wall Model.* Proc. of the 2nd European Symposium on Research in Computer Security (ESORICS 92) Toulouse, Springer LNCS 648, 41-54.

[10] Kessler, Volker, und Sibylle Mund. *Sicherheitsmodelle - Baupläne für die Entwicklung sicherer Systeme.* Siemens AG, Zentralabteilung Forschung und Entwicklung, München 1993.

[11] Lotz, Volkmar, Volker Kessler, Georg Walter. *Ein formales Sicherheitsmodell.* Part of the evaluation documentation (internal paper), 1999.

[12] McLean, John. *Reasoning about Security Models.* Proc. of the IEEE Symp. on Security and Privacy 1987, 123-131.

[13] Paulson, L.C. *The inductive approach to verifying cryptographic protocols.* J. Computer Security 6, 1998, 85-128.

[14] Schneider, S. *Security Properties and CSP.* Proc. of the IEEE Symp. on Security and Privacy 1996.

[15] Terry, P., S. Wiseman. *A "New" Security Policy Model.* Proc. of the IEEE Symp. on Security and Privacy 1989, 215-228.

[16] Thomas, Wolfgang. *Automata on Infinite Objects.* in: van Leeuwen, Jan (ed.). Handbook of Theoretical Computer Science, Volume B: Formal Models and Semantics. Elsevier, Amsterdam, 1990.

This means that if only events in L can be observed, then P and Q should be considered equivalent if any test which has access only to the events in L (a particular view of the process), and does not block the events in LN_p, cannot tell the difference between P and Q.

The following relationship between this form of may_p testing and the standard de Nicola/Hennessy form of may testing [dNH84] makes it clear that this is a generalisation, in that may testing is simply may_{p_0} testing for a particular partition p_0.

If p_0 is the partition that considers all events as low-level refusable events, then all events will be visible to the testing process, which has no constraints on being required to accept any of them. In this case $LR_{p_0} = \Sigma$, and H_{p_0} and LN_{p_0} are all $\varnothing$. It then turns out that may_{p_0} testing is equivalent to the standard notion of may testing. In this case, the testing process has access to all the events that the processes under test can perform; and is able to block any of them, which is exactly the situation in may testing. This is the most powerful kind of test within this framework: the one which allows the most distinctions to be made.

In fact, given any set of non-refusable events LN_p, any arbitrary CSP test T can be converted to a LN_p test T' such that P may $_p$ $T \Leftrightarrow P$ may $_p$ T' for any process P. This is achieved by introducing the extra possibility $\ldots \square RUN_{LN_p}$ to every state. No new successful executions are introduced, since whenever any of these choices are taken then there is no possibility of reaching ω; so any successful execution of $P \,\|[\,L\,]\|\, T'$ must correspond to a successful execution of $P \,\|\, T$.

This means that if two processes are equivalent under may testing for a particular set L, then the precise nature of LN_p and LR_p are not relevant—they will remain equivalent whatever the sets LN_p and LR_p happen to be, subject to their union remaining L.

Hence may testing need only be parametrised by the set L, since the finer distinctions made by LN_p and LR_p make no difference at the level of may testing.

A straightforward consequence of the definitions is as follows:

Lemma 1. *If $P \equiv_{\mathsf{may}_p} Q$ and $L_{p'} \subseteq L_p$ then $P \equiv_{\mathsf{may}_{p'}} Q$*

This lemma states that if some low-level events are promoted to become high-level events, then any processes that were previously equivalent will remain so: testing processes have access to even less information. If two processes cannot be distinguished by any tests which have access to L_p, then they will never be distinguished by any tests which have access to a smaller set of events $L_{p'} \subseteq L_p$; in fact this smaller set of tests is subsumed within the previous set of tests.

3.2 Must Testing

Must testing can be considered as the dual of may testing. In may testing, a process may pass a test if there is some successful execution. In must testing, a process must pass a test if *every* execution is successful. Since partial executions might not reach a success state because the execution has not run for long enough, attention is focused onto *complete* executions[3].

An execution e of a process P will be considered to be complete if P could be unable to extend it. This will certainly be the case if e is infinite, but it will also arise if e finishes in a stable state where only refusable events are possible—since the process might be prevented from continuing its execution. However, if there are any non-refusable events available, then the execution is not complete since it is entirely within the process' control to continue the execution.

Definition 5. *An execution e is* complete *with respect to (a set of non-refusable events) N if*

1. *e is infinite; or*
2. *e is finite, and the last state Q of e can perform neither internal transitions nor transitions from N.*

The point is to consider the execution as complete even if refusable events are possible. Such executions could be complete executions if the process is placed in a high-level environment (which the test cannot know about) in which such events are blocked.

Must testing can now be defined:

Definition 6. *If P is a process, and T is an LN_p test, then P must$_p$ T if and only if every complete execution (with respect to $LN_p \cup HN_p$) of $(P \,|[\, L_p \,]|\, T) \setminus L_p$ is successful.*

Example 1. Let P_1 be the process:

$$P_1 = h_r \to h_n \to l_r \to l_n \to P_1$$
$$\square\ l_r \to l_n \to P_1$$

Define the test $T_1 = l_n \to RUN_{l_n} \square l_r \to l_n \to \omega \to Stop$. This will succeed as long as the process under test firstly cannot perform l_n before l_r, and secondly is guaranteed to be able to accept l_r and then provide l_n.

Then P_1 must T_1. If its choice is in favour of l_r, then the complete execution is successful. If its choice is in favour of the high-level event, then the complete execution must include the second high-level event since this is not refusable, and so progress to the low-level events and hence to the success state.

On the other hand, for the test $T_2 = l_n \to \omega \to Stop$, we have that $\neg(P_1$ must $T_2)$. The test does not provide l_r, and so no low-level interaction between the process and the test is possible; the success state will not be reached.

Two processes will be must$_p$ testing equivalent if they must pass exactly the same tests:

---

[3] In the standard approach to testing, these executions are the *maximal* ones since they cannot be extended at all. In our setting they are not necessarily maximal, since finite complete executions might be extendable with refusable events

Definition 7. $P \equiv_{\mathsf{must}_p} Q$ *if and only if* $\forall T : TEST_{LN_p} \bullet (P \; \mathsf{must}_p \; T \Leftrightarrow Q \; \mathsf{must}_p \; T)$

Example 2. If

$$P_2 = h_{r2} \rightarrow h_{n2} \rightarrow l_r \rightarrow l_n \rightarrow P_2$$
$$\Box \; l_r \rightarrow l_n \rightarrow P_2$$

and

$$P_3 = h_{r2} \rightarrow h_{n2} \rightarrow l_r \rightarrow l_n \rightarrow P_3$$
$$\sqcap \; h_n \rightarrow l_r \rightarrow l_n \rightarrow P_3$$
$$\Box \; l_r \rightarrow l_n \rightarrow P_3$$

then P_1, P_2, and P_3 are all must_p equivalent. A process which interacts with them only on l_r and l_n will be unable to distinguish between them.

This means that two processes P and Q should be considered equivalent (from the point of view of the interface information) if any test which has access only to the events in L (a particular view of the process), and does not block the events in LN_p, cannot tell the difference between P and Q.

If p_0 is such that $LR_{p_0} = \Sigma$, and H_{p_0} and LN_{p_0} are all $\varnothing$, then must_{p_0} testing is equivalent to the standard notion of must testing. In this case, the testing process has access to all the events that the processes under test can perform; and is able to block any of them. This is the most powerful kind of test within this framework: it allows the most distinctions to be made.

From the point of view of must testing, it makes a difference whether the high-level events are refusable or not, since we are concerned with liveness and progress. For example, $h \rightarrow l \rightarrow Stop$ is must_p equivalent to $l \rightarrow Stop$ if h is not refusable, but the two processes are distinguishable if h is refusable. In that case the first process might be blocked from performing the event h, and never reach the stage where it offers the event l. This cannot happen for the second process. One test which distinguishes these two processes is $T = l \rightarrow \omega \rightarrow RUN_l$.

3.3   Changing Views

The notion of abstraction is bound up in the available views of a process as given by the sets L and H, and also by the distinction between refusable and non-refusable events within those sets. Varying the views on processes gives different degrees of abstraction and varies the capability of an observer to tell processes apart.

Views on a process might be varied by shifting the boundary between refusable and non-refusable events, at high and low-levels; and by shifting the boundary between levels for refusable and for non-refusable events.

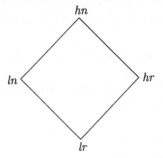

Fig. 3. The partial order $\leqslant$ on the interface partition

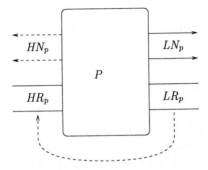

Fig. 4. Moving events from LR to HR

As the boundaries are shifted and the partition function p changes, the equivalence relation $\equiv_{\mathsf{must}_p}$ changes accordingly. The four possible locations of an event of P's interface may be ordered as in Figure 3, where higher positions for events result in *weaker* equivalence relations: those more abstract relations which identify more processes. Thus as previously observed, if all events are in LR_p then the equivalence is strongest, and in fact is equivalent to standard **must** testing; and if all events are in HN_p (or in fact a combination of HN_p and HR_p) then the equivalence is weakest, able only to identify the possibility of divergence in a process.

Each order relation in Figure 3 is associated with a lemma which supports the claim that transferring events from the lower to the higher set preserves $\equiv_{\mathsf{must}_p}$. Each edge in general corresponds to a strict weakening of $\equiv_{\mathsf{must}_p}$: new equivalences are introduced in each case. The resulting Lemma 2 collects these results together: if p is pointwise weaker than p', then must_p equivalence implies $\mathsf{must}_{p'}$ equivalence.

For example, increasing HR at the expense of LR preserves **must** testing equivalence. This scenario is illustrated in Figure 4.

Lemma 2. *If* $(\forall\, a : \Sigma.p(a) \leqslant p'(a))$ *then for any* P *and* Q, *if* $P \equiv_{\mathrm{must}_p} Q$ *then* $P \equiv_{\mathrm{must}_{p'}} Q$.

If partition p is pointwise less than partition p', then $\equiv_{\mathrm{must}_p}$ is stronger than $\equiv_{\mathrm{must}_{p'}}$.

The relation $p \leqslant p'$ (defined pointwise) can also be characterised in terms of the corresponding sets. In this case,

$$p \leqslant p' \Leftrightarrow LR_p \subseteq LR_{p'}$$
$$LR_p \cup LN_p \subseteq LR_{p'} \cup LN_{p'}$$
$$LR_p \cup HR_p \subseteq LR_{p'} \cup HR_{p'}$$

High-level non-refusable events are hidden from any interacting process, and they are urgent, so they behave as hidden events. This is made explicit in the following lemma:

Lemma 3. *For any process* P, $P \equiv_{\mathrm{must}_p} (P \setminus HN_p)$

3.4   Examples

Example 3.

$$h_n \rightarrow l_r \rightarrow Stop \equiv_{\mathrm{must}_p} l_r \rightarrow Stop$$

The non-refusability of the high-level event means that at the low level the l_r event is guaranteed to be offered.

In contrast, a refusable high-level event yields the following:

$$h_r \rightarrow l_r \rightarrow Stop \equiv_{\mathrm{must}_p} (l_r \rightarrow Stop) \sqcap Stop$$

At the low level, the event l_r might never be offered, since the high-level event could be refused in a complete execution. In this case, the low-level behaviour is described by $Stop$. However, the high-level event could also be performed, and so the possibility of the low-level event is also present.

Example 4.

$$
\begin{array}{ccc}
\begin{array}{l} h_{n1} \rightarrow l_{r1} \rightarrow Stop \\ \square \\ h_{n2} \rightarrow l_{r2} \rightarrow Stop \end{array}
& \equiv_{\mathrm{must}_p} &
\begin{array}{l} l_{r1} \rightarrow Stop \\ \sqcap \\ l_{r2} \rightarrow Stop \end{array}
\end{array}
$$

$$
\equiv_{\mathrm{must}_p}
\begin{array}{l} h_{n2} \rightarrow l_{r1} \rightarrow Stop \\ \square \\ h_{n1} \rightarrow l_{r2} \rightarrow Stop \end{array}
$$

In this example, the high-level events are non-refusable, and so one of them is guaranteed to occur in a complete execution. However, the testing process has no control over which will occur, and so the process is equivalent to one which offers a nondeterministic choice between the two low-level events. An observer who can engage only in low-level events cannot distinguish these three processes.

Observe that there is information flow from high to low in the two processes that have high-level events: the identity of the low-level event that occurs allows the identity of the preceding high-level event to be deduced.

4   Denotational Characterisations

It is useful to have a characterisation in terms of the denotational semantics for when two processes are must_p equivalent, and when they are may_p equivalent. This allows model-checkers such as FDR to be deployed in analysing processes for such equivalences.

4.1   May Equivalence

With regard to may testing, two processes will be considered equivalent with regard to a particular low-level view if their trace sets are identical when projected onto that view.

Theorem 1.

$$P \equiv_{\mathsf{may_p}} Q \Leftrightarrow traces(P \setminus H_p) = traces(Q \setminus H_p)$$

4.2   Must Equivalence

Encapsulating must testing equivalence in the most general case is not straightforward. There are two independent issues to be resolved: one concerning the appropriate way to handle the high-level events; and the other concerning how best to treat the low-level non-refusable events.

Lemma 3 indicates that non-refusable high-level events can simply be hidden. high-level refusable events should also be removed from view, but in a way which does not make them urgent (since they are not required to occur). This can be achieved by running the process in parallel with a process which might block such high-level events at any stage; and then hiding all the high-level events. This is the approach taken in [GH97], by means of a 'regulator' process.

Case 1: $LN = \varnothing$ We will begin by considering the set of low-level non-refusable events to be empty. As before, high-level urgent events can simply be hidden

Theorem 2. *If $LN = \varnothing$ then*

$$P \equiv_{\mathsf{must_p}} Q \Leftrightarrow FDI((P \,||[\, HR_p \,]||\, Chaos_{HR_p}) \setminus H_p)$$
$$= FDI((Q \,||[\, HR_p \,]||\, Chaos_{HR_p}) \setminus H_p)$$

The construction $(P \,||[\, HR_p \,]||\, Chaos_{HR_p}) \setminus H_p$ will be abbreviated $abs_p(P)$: an abstracted view of P.

This gives us a low-level view of a process: the low-level view of P is simply $(abs_p(P))$. This only has low-level events. Any two processes which exhibit this low-level behaviour are indistinguishable through that view of the process.

Case 2: $LN \neq \varnothing$ If the set of low-level non-refusable events is not empty, then there are some constraints on the low-level behaviour of the tests.

To begin with, we will consider the situation where there are no high-level events at all: every event is low-level, some are refusable and some are not.

Any *finite* complete execution must end up in a state in which all LN events are impossible for the process. This must correspond to a failure (tr, X) of the process for which $LN \subseteq X$. The events in LN which were performed should appear in the trace, since they were accessible to the tests. This corresponds to treating the events as urgent but visible, which is not an aspect of standard CSP, but which has been analysed in the context of timed CSP [DJS92]. The failures of such a process will be given as the urgent failures (with respect to LN), defined as

$$ufailures_{LN}(P) = \{(tr, X) \in failures(P) \mid LN \subseteq X\}$$

Such a set does not meet the standard axioms for CSP, as Example 5 illustrates. In fact, it turns out that it need not meet *any* of the axioms pertaining to failures: it is not necessarily prefix-closed on traces, subset closed on refusals, or even non-empty, and events need not extend either a trace or a refusal set.

Example 5. If $H = \varnothing$, $LN = \{ln\}$, and $LR = \{lr\}$, then

$$ufailures_{LN}(lr \to ln \to Stop) = \{(\langle\rangle, \{ln\}), (\langle lr, ln\rangle, \{ln\}), (\langle lr, ln\rangle, \{ln, lr\})\}$$

This set is neither prefix-closed on traces, subset closed on refusals, and on the behaviour with the empty trace the event lr can extend neither the trace (by itself) or the refusal.

A recursive process that is always willing to perform events from LN, such as $P = ln \to P$, has an empty urgent failure set. However, it is guaranteed to have infinite traces corresponding to the sequences of events from LN that it must be able to perform.

Along with the divergences and infinite traces, the urgent failures set does characterise must testing equivalence with regard to non-refusable low-level events:

Theorem 3. *If* $H = \varnothing$ *then*

$$P \equiv_{\mathsf{must}_p} Q \Leftrightarrow ufailures_{LN}(P) = ufailures_{LN}(Q)$$
$$\wedge \; divergences(P) = divergences(Q)$$
$$\wedge \; infinites(P) = infinites(Q)$$

We will refer to this triple of semantic sets of P (with respect to the partition p) as $UDI_p(P)$.

A new CSP operator $\mathsf{sticky}_{LN}(P)$ can be defined which provides a context for characterising urgent failures: $FDI(\mathsf{sticky}_{LN}(P)) = FDI(\mathsf{sticky}_{LN}(Q))$ if and only P and Q have the same urgent failures, divergences, and traces.

The sticky operator masks non-urgent failures on a set LN by introducing as many refusals as possible whenever an event from LN is possible. In particular, whenever an event l from LN is possible, then it introduces the possibility that all other events should be refused, and that l is the only possible event. This has a similar effect to making the events in LN urgent, since it is the process P itself (and not its environment) that chooses the event to be performed. In order to be consistent with the axioms of the FDI model, such events cannot be forced to occur (since the process might be in an uncooperative environment), but once P has selected an event, it will then refuse all other events.

It is defined denotationally as follows:

$$divergences(\ \text{sticky}_{LN}\ (P)) = divergences(P)$$
$$infinites(\ \text{sticky}_{LN}\ (P)) = infinites(P)$$
$$failures(\ \text{sticky}_{LN}\ (P)) = failures(P)$$
$$\cup \{(tr, X) \mid (tr \frown l, \varnothing) \in failures(P)$$
$$\wedge\ l \in LN \wedge l \notin X\}$$

Observe that $\text{sticky}_{LN}\ (P)$ has the same traces as P. It is only additional refusals that are introduced into the failure set.

In the most general case, we arrive at the following characterisation of must equivalence:

Theorem 4.

$$P \equiv_{\text{must}_p} Q \Leftrightarrow \text{sticky}_{LN}\ (abs_p(P)) = \text{sticky}_{LN}\ (abs_p(Q))$$

Note that this theorem also covers the case where $LN = \varnothing$, since in that case sticky_{LN} simply has no effect.

Observe that $\text{sticky}_{LN}\ (abs_p(P)) = abs_p(\ \text{sticky}_{LN}\ (P))$. The order in which the abstractions are performed is irrelevant.

Observe also that Theorem 3 given above can be characterised in this form:

Theorem 5. *If* $H = \varnothing$ *then*

$$P \equiv_{\text{must}_p} Q \Leftrightarrow \text{sticky}_{LN}\ (P) = \text{sticky}_{LN}\ (Q)$$

More about sticky   Different processes might map to the same result under sticky_{LN}. For example, $P_1 = ln_1 \to Stop \ \Box\ ln_2 \to Stop$ and $P_2 = ln_1 \to Stop \ \sqcap\ ln_2 \to Stop$ have different refusals, yet $\text{sticky}_{LN}\ (P_1)$ and $\text{sticky}_{LN}\ (P_2)$ have the same refusals. Hence from Theorem 3 they are equivalent under must testing.

This new operator can also be given an operational semantics, which may provide an alternative understanding of its behaviour. The process $\text{sticky}_{LN}\ (P)$ will have all the transitions that P has together with a few extra ones introduced to allow events from LN to be 'selected'. Two rules define its operational semantics:

$$\frac{P \xrightarrow{\mu} P'}{\text{sticky}_{LN}\ (P) \xrightarrow{\mu} \text{sticky}_{LN}\ (P')}$$

$$\frac{P \xrightarrow{a} P'}{\text{sticky}_{LN}(P) \xrightarrow{\tau} (a \to \text{sticky}_{LN}(P'))} \quad [\, a \in LN \,]$$

The transitions that are introduced by means of the second rule correspond to the additional failures that are introduced to $\text{sticky}_{LN}(P)$.

If the events in LN are hidden, it makes no difference whether they are abstracted by means of the sticky operator first:

$$P \setminus LN = (\,\text{sticky}_{LN}(P)) \setminus LN$$

The operational semantics for sticky point the way to a definition in terms of the standard CSP operators. This can be achieved as follows: firstly, let f_{old} and g be event renaming functions such that $f_{old}(a) = (old, a)$ for all $a \in \Sigma$, and $g(old, a) = g(new, a) = a$ for all $a \in \Sigma$, with g leaving events not of the form (a, new) or (a, old) unchanged. Define the process R_{LN} as follows:

$$R_{LN} = (old, a) : f(LN) \to (new, a) \to R_{LN}$$
$$\Box\ (old, a) : (f(\Sigma) \setminus f(LN)) \to R_{LN}$$

This process allows all events of the form (old, a), but whenever the event a is in LN, then it must perform the event (new, a) before any further events. sticky can then be defined as follows:

$$\text{sticky}_{LN}(P) = g((f(P)\,|[\,f(\Sigma)\,]|\,R_{LN}) \setminus f(LN))$$

Any sticky event $a \in LN$ of P is performed internally in this process (as (old, a)), but P is prevented from any further progress by R_{LN} until (new, a) occurs (which appears in the overall process as the original sticky event a because of the renaming g). Non-sticky events are performed as expected.

4.3   Congruence

The equivalences considered in this paper are not congruences in general, which is perhaps why they are not generally considered in the literature on testing. This fact is unsurprising, since operators can influence the behaviour of a process through its abstracted interface, and if processes differ there then they may be affected differently.

Example 6.

$$h_{r1} \to l \to Stop \equiv_{\text{must}_p} h_{r2} \to l \to Stop$$

but

$$Stop\,|[\,h_{r1}\,]|\,h_{r1} \to l \to Stop \not\equiv_{\text{must}_p} Stop\,|[\,h_{r1}\,]|\,h_{r2} \to l \to Stop$$

since the processes behave differently on the abstracted event h_{r1}, they can behave differently when placed in parallel with a process that interacts with them on that event.

Another unsurprising example concerns the event renaming where $f(h_{r1}) = l_1$, $f(h_{r2}) = h_{r2}$, and $f(l) = l$. In this case

$$f(h_{r1} \to l \to Stop) \not\equiv_{\mathsf{must}_p} f(h_{r2} \to l \to Stop)$$

Finally, an event renaming that renames a high-level refusable event to a high-level non-refusable event, but does not map high to low or low to high: $f(h_{r1}) = h_{n1}$, $f(h_{r2}) = h_{r2}$, and $f(l) = l$. In this case

$$f(h_{r1} \to l \to Stop) \not\equiv_{\mathsf{must}_p} f(h_{r2} \to l \to Stop)$$

The left hand process cannot refuse l at the low level, whereas the right hand process can.

The first two examples also illustrate may equivalences that are not preserved; the last example does preserve may equivalence.

However, many of the operators do preserve both equivalences. Prefixing, sequential composition (provided $\checkmark$ is low-level), all forms of choice, and hiding certainly do so. Parallel composition does so, provided all synchronisations are at the low level: thus interleaving preserves equivalence, as does the operator $\|[A]\|$ provided $A \subseteq L$. Event renaming $f(P)$ preserves $\equiv_{\mathsf{must}_p}$ provided the partitions are respected: so $p(f(a)) = p(a)$ for all events a is required for $\equiv_{\mathsf{must}_p}$. With $\equiv_{\mathsf{may}_p}$, we require simply that high-level events do not become low-level, so $a \in H \Rightarrow f(a) \in H$ is sufficient to guarantee preservation of equality.

5   Non-interference

Non-interference properties are generally considered in the context of a given system. The requirement is that even if an agent knows exactly how the system works, there is no information flow across particular boundaries concerned with particular activity on that system. In other words, the options available to the low-level user should not divulge any information about the high-level users' activity. High-level users' activity is concerned with events in HR; the set HN consists of those high-level events entirely within the control of the system. Knowing that the system will perform an event of HN does not leak information about high-level activity, since the high-level user is unable to prevent it.

Information flow from high to low will be prevented if P's low-level possibilities at any stage are dependent entirely on P's previous low-level behaviour, and not in terms of any high-level behaviour. This would seem to indicate that if two sequences of events have been performed, which appear the same on the low level, then the resulting processes should be equivalent.

This characterisation can be made in various ways. It has traditionally been made denotationally, and this has led to some difficulties to its relationship with refinement. If e is an execution of a process P, then $Ltrace_p(e)$ is the sequence of low-level (in the sense of the partition p) events in e.

Operationally, lack of information flow in P from high to low level might be characterised as follows:

Definition 8. *A process* P *is* interference-free *with respect to* p *if*

$$P \stackrel{e'}{\Longrightarrow} P' \wedge P \stackrel{e''}{\Longrightarrow} P'' \wedge Ltrace_p(e') = Ltrace_p(e'') \Rightarrow P' \equiv_{\mathsf{must}_p} P''$$

where $Ltrace_p(e)$ is the sequence of low-level (in the sense of the partition p) events in e. If the low-level views of two executions are the same, then the resulting processes must be indistinguishable.

In this case, we can say that P is *interference-free on* p. This is a very strong definition: it excludes nondeterministic processes, even those that can perform no high-level events, such as $P = l_{r1} \rightarrow Stop \sqcap l_{r2} \rightarrow Stop$: the distinguishable processes $l_{r1} \rightarrow Stop$ and $l_{r2} \rightarrow Stop$ are both reachable via the empty trace.

This operational definition is attractive in one sense, since it considers individually all possible processes resulting from the execution, rather than considering them all together (where the acceptable behaviour of some can mask the unacceptable behaviour of others), as is the case with the denotational 'after' operator.

This definition has the difficulty that it is dependent on the precise nature of the operational semantics for a process, and two processes that are equivalent (under must testing for example) might be treated differently by the definition. This means that it cannot be characterised denotationally, and that in general its truth or falsity is not determined from the denotational semantics.

Divergence To take an extreme example, the process which has one state and is only able to perform internal actions to that one state may be defined recursively as follows: $\perp = \perp$. It is must equivalent to $\perp \sqcap LEAK$, where $LEAK$ is a process which takes in messages on a high-level channel, and immediately communicates them on a low-level channel: $LEAK = in_H?x \rightarrow out_L!x \rightarrow LEAK$. Yet $\perp$ meets the definition, whereas $\perp \sqcap LEAK$ does not.

The desire to have no information flow preserved by refinement has led to some difficulties with regard to this example. If $\perp$ is seen as a process which does not provide information flow, but it can be refined by $LEAK$, then it is patently clear that any definition of security with respect to information flow is either going to fail on $\perp$ or else will not be preserved by refinement.

Divergence-Free Processes If the process is divergence-free, then the situation is rather better. In this case, the definition will hold of precisely those processes whose low-level behaviour is deterministic: that is, those processes P for which $abs_p(P)$ is deterministic. This coincides with Roscoe's characterisation of non-interference.

Theorem 6. *If* P *is divergence-free, then* P *is interference-free on* p *if and only if* $abs_p(P)$ *is deterministic.*

Observe that this theorem holds even if $LN \neq \varnothing$, despite the fact that tests cannot directly detect refusals of events in LN. This means that two processes might be indistinguishable under testing, yet the definition of non-interference applies differently to them. For example, consider the two processes:

$$P_1 = h_1 \rightarrow l_{n1} \rightarrow P_1 \; \square \; h_2 \rightarrow l_{n2} \rightarrow P_1$$
$$P_2 = h : \{h_1, h_2\} \rightarrow l : \{l_{n1}, l_{n2}\} \rightarrow P_2$$

If $LN = \{l_{n1}, l_{n2}\}$, then these two processes are indistinguishable at the low level. Any low-level test must always be ready to accept all events in LN, and so is able to make distinctions only on the basis of traces—and P_1 and P_2 have the same low-level traces.

On the other hand, it is clear that P_1 allows interference whereas P_2 does not, and in fact P_1 fails the definition given above whereas P_2 meets it: $abs_p(P_1)$ is non-deterministic whereas $abs_p(P_2)$ is deterministic.

This example also illustrates the point that interference-freedom is concerned with particular processes that are given. The aim in interference-freedom is not to distinguish P_1 from P_2, but rather to make deductions about high-level activity from the visible low-level activity in a given process.

6   Atomicity and Fault-Tolerance

Atomicity is a feature of particular kinds of specification, where the desired behaviour is characterised in terms of the occurrence or availability of a single event.

Typically in analysing fault tolerance, faults are modelled by the occurrence of special fault events. These might appear at certain points of a process' description, indicating that the fault can occur at that stage during the process' execution. They will then be modelled as refusable events—the environment might perform them when the process makes them 'available', but is not obliged to do so. (Generally in fact the system would be modelled so they are always available.)

The low-level activity need not be deterministic, so this is different from consideration of information flow properties.

For example, a one-place buffer that can lose its contents on the occurrence of a particular fault might be described as follows:

$$FBUFF = in?x \rightarrow out!x \rightarrow FBUFF$$
$$\square \; power\_blip \rightarrow FBUFF$$
$$\square \; power\_blip \rightarrow FBUFF$$

On the other hand, fault recovery will generally be modelled as non-refusable events: the fault recovery mechanism is under the control of the process itself, and should not be blocked by the environment.

As a primitive example, a system might undergo a fault between input and output, from which it must recover before performing output. This could be modelled, extremely crudely, as

$$FT = in?x \rightarrow out!x \rightarrow Stop$$
$$\square \; fault \rightarrow recover \rightarrow out!x \rightarrow Stop$$

The requirement on the system might be that, when the fault recovery mechanisms are out of the view of the user, then this system should look like a simple buffer taking an input to an output.

In other words, the *requirement* on the system is that it is a refinement under must_p testing of

$$SPEC = in?x \rightarrow out!x \rightarrow Stop$$

Here we have $p(fault) = hr$ and $p(recover) = hn$.

Then $SPEC \sqsubseteq_{\mathsf{must}_p} FT^4$.

If $p(fault) = hn$, then any complete execution would not be able to finish if a fault was possible—this is tantamount to *relying* on the fault to occur. In this case, $SPEC \equiv_{\mathsf{must}} FT$ again holds, but so too does the equivalence

$$in?x \rightarrow fault \rightarrow recover \rightarrow out!x \rightarrow Stop \equiv_{\mathsf{must}_p} FT$$

which relies on *fault* to occur in order to guarantee output.

Conversely, if $p(recover) = hr$ then recovery can be blocked. In this case correct behaviour cannot be guaranteed, and in fact

$$FT \equiv_{\mathsf{must}_p} in?x \rightarrow (Stop \sqcap out!x \rightarrow Stop)$$

The approach to fault-tolerant modelling suggested by this example is to treat fault events as high-level refusable events HR, to treat system recovery mechanisms as high-level non-refusable events HN, and to treat the normal part of the system, which the user interacts with, in terms of low-level events (either refusable or non-refusable as appropriate).

7   Summary

This paper has been concerned with providing a more explicit approach to the kind of abstraction that is achieved when processes are viewed through particular interfaces, and where their events can be considered as refusable or not refusable by the environment of the process. The results have reinforced the denotational approach, provided a more explicit explanation and justification, and indeed have extended that approach by considering a more general categorisation of events.

This form of abstraction has been analysed for both may and must testing with respect to a division p of the interface of the process, and the variation in the relations as p varies has also been analysed: as less control over events is provided to the testing environment (either through removal from the interface, or through non-refusability), the equivalence relations become weaker.

The may testing equivalence and refinement relations turn out to be relatively straightforward to characterise in denotational terms, and are indeed equivalent to the denotational approaches which have been traditionally taken.

---

[4] in other words, $\forall T : TEST_{LN_p} \bullet SPEC \ \mathsf{must}_p \ T \Rightarrow FT \ \mathsf{must}_p \ T$

Must testing equivalence and refinement have also resulted in the expected equivalences as far as high-level, and refusable low-level events are concerned; but the relations when low-level non-refusable events are permitted have not been previously considered. Theorem 4 provides a complete characterisation of this equivalence.

This approach to abstraction has been used in what appears to be an extremely strong operational characterisation of non-interference (or interference-freedom) which turns out to be equivalent to a previous denotational characterisation on non-divergent processes[RWW94]. We have also considered its place in the specification of fault-tolerant systems, and in the characterisation of specifications that make use of atomicity.

Acknowledgements I am grateful to Peter Ryan, Irfan Zakkiudin for discussion and comments on earlier forms of this work, to the anonymous referees for their detailed comments, and to Bill Roscoe for pointing out the CSP characterisation of sticky .

Support for this work was provided by DERA.

References

[DJS92]   J Davies, D Jackson, and S Schneider. Making things happen in Timed CSP. In *Formal Techniques for Real-Time and Fault-Tolerant Systems*, volume 573 of *Lecture Notes in Computer Science*. Springer Verlag, 1992.

[dNH84]   R de Nicola and M Hennessy. Testing equivalences for processes. *Theoretical Computer Science*, 34(1), 1984.

[GH97]   M Goldsmith and J Hulance. Application of CSP and FDR to safety-critical systems: Investigation of refinement properties of fault tolerance and prototype implementation of analysis techniques. DERA project report, 1997.

[Hen88]   M Hennessy. *Algebraic Theory of Processes*. MIT Press, 1988.

[Ros97]   A W Roscoe. *The Theory and Practice of Concurrency*. Prentice-Hall, 1997.

[RWW94]   A W Roscoe, J C P Woodcock, and L Wulf. Non-interference through determinism. In *European Symposium on Research in Computer Security*, volume 875 of *Lecture Notes in Computer Science*. Springer Verlag, 1994.

[Sch99a]   S A Schneider. Abstraction and testing. Technical Report TR-99-02, Royal Holloway, 1999.

[Sch99b]   S A Schneider. *Concurrent and real-time systems: the CSP approach*. John Wiley, 1999. to appear.

Formal Analysis of a Secure Communication Channel: Secure Core-Email Protocol

Dan Zhou and Shiu-Kai Chin

Department of Electrical Engineering and Computer Science
Syracuse University, Syracuse, New York, 13244
{danzhou, chin}@cat.syr.edu

Abstract. To construct a highly-assured implementation of secure communication channels we must have clear definitions of the security services, the channels, and under what assumptions these channels provide the desired services. We formally define secure channel services and develop a detailed example. The example is a core protocol common to a family of secure email systems. We identify the necessary properties of cryptographic algorithms to ensure that the email protocol is secure, and we verify that the email protocol provides secure services under these assumptions. We carry out the definitions and verifications in higher-order logic using the HOL theorem-prover. All our definitions and theorems are conservative extensions to the logic of HOL.

1 Introduction

Numerous security protocols are used for secure transactions in networked systems. To construct high-confidence implementations of these protocols, we need to have protocols that provide security services and to implement them correctly. One way of establish the correctness of protocols is to model, specify and verify them in higher-order logic. We demonstrate how this can be done in this paper.

Protocols such as Kerberos [14] and Needham-Schroeder [13] authentication protocols are based on message exchanges between two or more parties. In general, these protocols and the logics (such as [3]) and tools (e.g., [10]) analyzing them have assumed that a single message passing between two parties is secure if the message is appropriately encrypted and signed and if the keys for decryption and signing are kept secret. In this work, we explore the validity of this assumption by studying secure communication channels. We identify what it means for a channel to be secure and the required properties of cryptographic functions to ensure channel security.

We have two goals. First, we want precise definitions of the services desired of secure channels. Some applications require a channel with integrity where messages cannot be modified without detection. Other applications require a channel that is confidential, where only the intended recipient can read the message. We formalize these secure protections in higher-order logic as properties that secure channels should satisfy.

Second, we want clear definitions of the required properties of cryptographic algorithms used in secure channels. As we use cryptographic algorithms in protocols to

J. Wing, J. Woodcock, J. Davies (Eds.): FM'99, Vol. I, LNCS 1708, pp. 758–775, 1999.
© Springer-Verlag Berlin Heidelberg 1999

provide secure communication, the properties of these algorithms are vital in reasoning about the security properties of the secure channels. The required properties vary, depending on the particular services the channels provide and the components of the channels themselves. As an example, we formally specify a secure core-email protocol that provides confidentiality, integrity, source authentication, and non-repudiation. The protocol uses a combination of secret-key encryption, public-key encryption and digital signatures. It is common to a family of secure email systems such as Privacy Enhanced Mail (PEM) [9] and Pretty Good Privacy (PGP) [16].

We identify and specify the properties required of cryptographic algorithms for the channel to be secure. The secure core-email protocol is then verified formally to provide secure services under these assumptions. The list of required properties can serve as a reference when specific algorithms are used in actual protocol implementations.

The purpose of our work is not to invent new protocols. Rather we want to add enough formality to the protocol analysis so that we can account for security properties in concrete implementations. As a practical demonstration, we have carried out the formal development process down to the generation of C++ code of the secure core-email protocol and Privacy Enhanced Email and have reported the result in [15] . This paper concentrates on a formal analysis of the secure channel.

Our work attempts to fill the gap between previous abstract formal treatments such as Lampson and others [8], and detailed implementation descriptions such as PEM,[9]. The focus of abstract analysis in [8] is how to make secure decisions based on user statements. The correct functionality of secure channels is assumed. The focus of detailed implementation descriptions is on message structure and protocols. Definitions of security properties are missing and no attempt is made to show the protocols and operations on messages satisfy the intended security properties. This paper attempts to relate concrete implementations to abstract security properties.

There are two types of methods of analyzing protocols. There are those based on theorem proving and those based on model checking. In the category of theorem proving, specialized logics are developed to describe both protocols and their desired properties, inference rules are defined to reason about the correctness of protocols. For example, BAN logic [3] and authentication logic by Lampson and others [8] are used for describe and reason about authentication protocols. Brackin has embedded an extension of GNY logic (called BGNY logic) in higher-order logic theorem prover HOL and has developed specialized tactic in HOL to prove theorems about protocols [2]. By embedding BGNY logic in HOL as a conservative (definitional) extension, his analyzer has advantage of the mechanized theorem proving environment and guarantees the correctness of the theorems. In comparison, our work uses general higher-order logic and relies on the higher-order logic itself for specification and reasoning. Higher-order logic has been used in constructing assured implementation of computer systems [4]. Those specialized logics are more abstract than higher-order logic which our work employed. It is not clear how we can arrive at a correct implementation from protocols described in these logic without translating the protocols descriptions to a language that is closer to implementation.

In the category of model checking, protocols are described as state machines, properties are expressed either as invariants or as another state machine. NRL protocol analyzer uses first-order logic to express invariants and searches the state space (potentially exhaustively) to find if the invariants hold for the protocol [11]. Spi-calculus models both protocols and desired properties as traces and uses equivalence of processes to reason about the correctness of protocols [1]. NRL protocol analyzer provides the automation of analysis, spi-calculus is suitable for modeling concurrent systems. However they are all further away from constructing an assured implementation than ours.

For this study we use the higher-order logic theorem prover HOL [5] for formal specification and verification. We use standard predicate calculus notation. The symbols $\wedge, \vee, \neg$, and $\supset$, respectively, denote the logic operations *and, or, negation*, and *implication*, while $\forall$ and $\exists$ denote *universal* and *existential quantifications*. Function composition is denoted by the symbol $\circ$, and $f\ a$ denotes the application of function f to a. The symbol I denotes the identity function. Expression $\Gamma \vdash t$ denotes a theorem: whenever the list of logical terms in Γ are all *true*, the conclusion t is guaranteed to be *true*. Definitional extensions to the HOL system are denoted by $\vdash_{def}$.

For the rest of the paper we start by describing rigorously the cryptographic algorithms and their properties in Section 2. This is followed by the formal definitions of services of secure communication channels in Section 3. In Section 4 we present an example channel that is a secure core-email protocol common to a family of similar secure-email systems. In Section 5 we show the development of a formal theory in higher-order logic that describes the correctness of the email protocol: the theory states that the email protocol provides secure services to messages passing through it. We conclude in Section 6.

2   Overview of Cryptography

Network protocols rely on cryptographic algorithms to provide security services. Formal verification of these protocols requires formal definitions of not only the protocols themselves, but also the properties of the cryptographic algorithms they implore. Menezes and others have defined rigorously the terms related to cryptography functions such as the encryption scheme and the digital-signature scheme in [12]. Here we formalize cryptographic functions and their properties in HOL.

Before we get into any formula, we briefly describe how we have handled types.

2.1   Types and Type Conversion

There are many sets of entities exist in a cryptographic system, such as plaintexts, ciphertexts, keys and signatures. We view them as different types. A system can reject a value if it is not of a particular type. For example, if a system expects a key to be 128 bits long, then it will discard a value that is of 129 bits. We have modeled all the types in our work. When an entity is used for different purpose as different types, we use type converters which are constant functions to change types. For instance, a key is of type *key* when it is used to encrypted a message and it is of type *plaintext* when it is encrypted for transmission. We define a constant function *keyToPlaintext* to convert variables from type *key* to *plaintext*. If a variable k is of type *key*, then the type of *keyToPlaintext k* is *plaintext*.

For the simplicity of presentation we have ignored all types in this paper.

2.2 Encryption Scheme

Encryptions are used to protect the confidentiality of information. An encryption scheme consists of a set of encryption functions and a corresponding set of decryption functions. For each encryption function E, there is a unique decryption function D such that any message encrypted by E can be retrieved by D. We define *cipherPair* as a pair of uniquely associated encryption and decryption functions.

DEFINITION 1 (CIPHERPAIR) A pair of functions, E and D, is called a *cipherPair* if D is the unique left inverse of E.

$$\vdash_{def} \forall E\ D.\ cipherPair\ E\ D = (D \circ E = I)\ \wedge$$
$$(\forall D\_arb.\ (D\_arb \circ E = I) \supset (D\_arb = D))$$

One way of designing an encryption scheme is to design one algorithm for the set of encryption functions and a corresponding algorithm for the set of decryption functions. Keys are used to pick out the particular encryption and decryption functions.

2.3 Digital-Signature Scheme

Signatures are used to identify principals. A digital-signature scheme consists of a set of signing functions and a corresponding set of signature verification functions. For any entity A, signing function S_A takes a message to a signature, while verification function V_A takes a message and a signature and returns a boolean value. Function S_A is kept secret by entity A, while V_A is made known to the public and is used by others to verify A's signatures.

For a pair of functions, S_A and V_A, to be consider secure, $V_A\ (m,s)$ should return *true* if and only if s is a valid signature of A on message m and if there is no practical way for any other entity to find a pair (m,s) such that $V_A\ (m,s)$ is *true*.

We define *DSPair* as a pair of uniquely associated signing and signature verification functions.

DEFINITION 2 (DSPAIR) A *DSpair* is a pair of functions—a signing function *Sign* and a verification function V—such that, for every message m, $V\ (m,s)$ is *true* if and only if s is a valid signature on m. The signing function *Sign* is a one-to-one function.

$$\vdash_{def} \forall Sign\ V.$$
$$DSPair\ Sign\ V =$$
$$(\forall m\ s.\ V\ (m,s) = (s = Sign\ m))\ \wedge$$
$$(\forall m1\ m2.\ (Sign\ m1 = Sign\ m2) \supset (m1 = m2))$$

A digital signature is uniquely associated with a signer and the information being signed, while a signature on paper is uniquely associated with a signer. When we move from paper signatures to digital signatures, we gain the ability to associate the information with a signature and, we lose the ability to uniquely identify a signer from the signature. With a digital signature, we can conclude that only entity A could have generated the signature on message m. However, it is not practical for anyone to fake a particular signature by a particular signer on chosen information.

Digital-signature schemes can be designed analogously for encryption schemes. One algorithm is designed for the set of signing functions, and a corresponding algorithm is designed for the set of verification functions. Keys are also used to pick out the particular signing and verification functions.

2.4   Secret-Key Cryptography

Secret-key cryptography uses the same key to specify its encryption and decryption transformations. We define *secKeyPair* to name the encryption function, decryption function, and the secret key used in *cipherPair*.

DEFINITION 3 (SECKEYPAIR) Functions (*encryptS k*) and (*decryptS k*) constitute a *cipherPair*.

$\vdash_{def}$ $\forall encryptS\ decryptS\ k.$
    secKeyPair encryptS decryptS k = cipherPair (*encryptS k*) (*decryptS k*)

2.5   Public-Key Cryptography

Public-key cryptography uses two keys to specify its transformations: a private key, d_k, known only to the owner and a corresponding public key, e_k, accessible by the world. When used for an encryption scheme, the public key is used for encryption and the private key is used for decryption. When used for a signature scheme, the private key is used for signing and the public key is used for verification. These two keys form a unique key pair.

We define *pubKeyPair* to name the encryption function, the decryption function, and the pair of public and private keys used in *cipherPair*.

DEFINITION 4 (PUBKEYPAIR) Functions (*encryptS ek*) and (*decryptP dk*) constitute a *cipherPair*.

$\vdash_{def}$ $\forall encryptP\ decryptP\ ek\ dk.$
    pubKeyPair encryptP decryptP (*ek, dk*) =
    cipherPair (*encryptP ek*) (*decryptP dk*)

We define *DSKeyPair* to name the signing function, the signature verification function, and the pair of public and private keys used in *DSPair*.

DEFINITION 5 (DSKEYPAIR) Functions (*sign sk*) and (*verify vk*) constitute a *DSPair*.

$\vdash_{def}$ $\forall sign\ verify\ vk\ sk.$
    DSKeyPair sign verify (*vk,sk*) = *DSPair* (*sign sk*) (*verify vk*)

3   Formal Definition of Security Services of Channels

A channel is a means of communication, a mechanism for entities to make statements [8]. A secure channel provides security services to messages such as confidentiality and source authentication, which are essential to network-system services such as establishing identities of entities and granting access to system resources.

To be able to formally analyze secure channels, we define the confidential channel and the source-authentic channel in this section.

A channel between a sender A and a receiver B consists of a sender process, a receiver process, and a network that transmits information from the sender process to the receiver process. Sender A makes a `statement` through a `package` generated by the sender process. Receiver B receives the `statement` recovered from the `package` by the receiver process (Fig. 1). A package has the necessary header information for the particular services the channel provides.

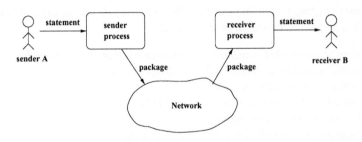

Fig. 1. A communication channel between entities A and B

3.1   Confidential Channel

A typical informal definition of confidentiality is as follows. Confidentiality implies that you know who the receiver is. A channel is confidential if the intended recipient can derive the statement from a received package while nobody else can. For example, sender A makes a statement *msgA* to receiver B through a communication channel consisting of the sender process *sendTo*, the receiver process *receiveByB*, and the network. Sender A's process *sendTo* generates a package *envelopeA* and transmits it to B's receiver process through the network. Entity B's receiver process receives a package *envelopeB* and recovers a statement *msgB* using *receiveByB*. If the package *envelopeA* arrives intact at B's process, then B recovers the statement *msgA*. Another entity C, which is also on the network, can observe the package. However, even if the package *envelopeA* arrives intact at C's process, C will not be able to recover the statement *msgA* (Fig. 2).

Formal definition based on the above description is as follows.

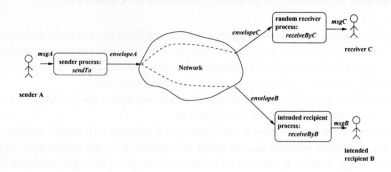

Fig. 2. A confidential channel

DEFINITION 6 (CONFCHANNEL) A confidential channel allows user A to send a statement through a package, knowing that regardless of who gets the package, only intended recipient B can read the statement in the package.

$\vdash_{def}$ $\forall sendTo\ receiveByB\ envelopeA\ msgA\ envelopeB\ msgB\ recipientB.$
      $confChannel\ sendTo\ receiveByB\ envelopeA\ msgA$
        $envelopeB\ msgB\ recipientB =$
        $(envelopeA = sendTo\ recipientB\ msgA) \supset$
        $(((envelopeB = envelopeA) \supset$
        $(msgB = receiveByB\ recipientB\ envelopeB) \supset$
        $(msgB = msgA)) \wedge$
        $(\forall receiveByC\ envelopeC\ msgC\ receiverC.$
        $(envelopeC = envelopeA) \supset$
        $(msgC = receiveByC\ receiverC\ envelopeC) \supset$
        $(msgC = msgA) \supset$
        $(receiverC = recipientB)))$

3.2   Source Authentication Channel

Source authentication implies that you know who the real sender is. A channel adds source authentication to statements if the receiver process can derive the source of a received statement when the received package passes an authenticity check. For example, sender A makes a statement $msgA$ to receiver B through a communication channel consisting of the sender process $sendFromA$, the network, the receiver process $receive$, and authenticity check $authChk$. Sender A sends a package $envelopeA$ through $sendFromA$ to B. Receiver B receives a package $envelopeB$ and recovers a statement $msgB$. If the package $envelopeA$ arrives intact at B's process, it will pass the authenticity check ($authChk\ senderA$) and B will recover the statement $msgA$. Suppose another entity D, which is also on the network and has full control of its process $sendFromD$, sends a package $envelopeD$ to B and claims that it is from A. If the package $envelopeD$ arrives intact at B's process, it will not pass the authenticity check (*authChk senderA*). This is illustrated in Fig. 3. The formal definition of authentic channel is as follows.

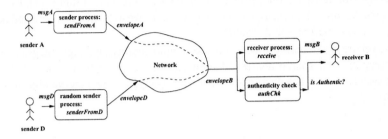

Fig. 3. A channel with source-authentication protection

DEFINITION 7 (AUTHCHANNEL) A channel provides source authentication service to a statement sent between A and B if it provides a way to certify the originator of the statement to the recipient.

$\vdash_{def}$ $\forall authChk\ sendFromA\ receive\ envelopeA\ msgA\ envelopeB\ msgB\ senderA.$
  authChannel authChk sendFromA receive envelopeA msgA
    envelopeB msgB senderA =
  $(msgB = receive\ envelopeB) \supset$
  $(((envelopeA = sendFromA\ senderA\ msgA) \supset$
  $(envelopeB = envelopeA) \supset$
  $(authChk\ senderA\ envelopeB \wedge (msgB = msgA))) \wedge$
  $(\forall sendFromD\ envelopeD\ msgD\ originatorD.$
  $(envelopeD = sendFromD\ originatorD\ msgD) \supset$
  $(envelopeB = envelopeD) \supset$
  authChk senderA envelopeB $\supset$
  $((originatorD = senderA) \wedge (msgB = msgD))))$

A channel providing source-authentication service to statements also provides integrity service to the statements. If a statement in a package is corrupt, the source of the statement is the source of the corruption, hence the package will not pass the source authentication check.

4   Secure Core-Email Protocol

In the last section we studied the services of secure channels. In this and the next sections, we show one example channel—secure core-email protocol—that provides these services. In this section we define the protocol rigorously. In the next section we verify that the protocol is secure.

Our example of secure channels is a secure core-email protocol. We have studied secure email systems PEM, PGP, and X.400. These systems differ from one another in message structures and the certificate hierarchies, among other things [7]. However, their cores that provide security services are the same. We extracted this core and named it "secure core-email protocol" (ScEP).

The secure core-email protocol provides confidentiality, message integrity, source authentication, and source non-repudiation services. It protects messages through a combination of secret-key encryption, public-key encryption, and digital-signature generation.

4.1   Sender Process

The sender process of ScEP is as follows. We refer to the content of an email as message. First, the process randomly generates a per-message data encryption key (DEK) and uses it as a secret key to encrypt the message. Second, it computes the message digest of the message using a hash function and computes the digital signature of the message by signing the message digest with the sender's private key. It then encrypts the digital signature with DEK. Last, the process encrypts DEK with the intended recipient's public key. The output of the sender process is a 4-tuple: (sender's public key, encrypted DEK, encrypted digital signature, encrypted message). Fig. 4 illustrates the sender process.

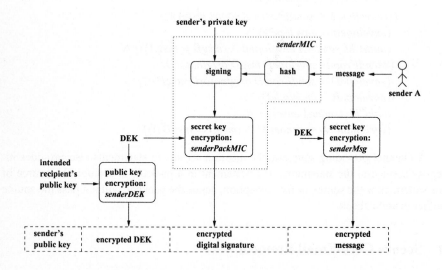

Fig. 4. Sender process of the secure core-email protocol: *enMailSender*

Table 1. Functions in the sender process *enMailSender*

Name	Definition and Description
senderDEK	packs DEK by encrypt it with receiver's public key: *senderDEK encryptP ekeyB DEK = encryptP ekeyB DEK*
senderMsg	packs a message by encrypt it with DEK: *senderMsg encryptS DEK message = encryptS DEK message*
senderGenMIC	generates a digital signature of a message by signing the message digest: *senderGenMIC sign hash skeyA message =* *sign skeyA (hash message)*
senderPackMIC	packs the digital signature of a message: *senderPackMIC encryptS DEK MIC = encryptS DEK MIC*
senderMIC	generates and packs the digital signature of a message: *senderMIC encryptS sign hash skeyA DEK message =* *((senderPackMIC encryptS DEK) o* *(senderGenMIC sign hash skeyA))* *message*

We define the sender process *enMailSender* in HOL as follows. The functions that appear in Fig. 4 and in the definition of *enMailSender* are also defined in HOL and are listed in Table 1. The variables appeared in the definitions are described in Table 2.

DEFINITION 8 (ENMAILSENDER) Process *enMailSender* generates an email by encrypting and signing a message.

$\vdash_{def}$ *∀encryptP encryptS sign hash vkeyA ekeyB DEK skeyA message.*
    enMailSender encryptP encryptS sign hash vkeyA ekeyB DEK skeyA
      message =
    (vkeyA,
    senderDEK encryptP ekeyB DEK,
    senderMIC encryptS sign hash skeyA DEK message,
    senderMsg encryptS DEK message)

4.2 Receiver Process

The receiver process of ScEP reverses the sender process to recover the message. The receiver process expects a 4-tuple as input, the same 4-tuple that is the output of the sender process. To process a received email, the receiver process first accesses the fields of the email to get the sender's public key, encrypted DEK, encrypted digital signature, and the encrypted message. The receiver process then recovers the per-message encryption key DEK by decrypting the encrypted DEK using the receiver's private key. It then uses DEK to retrieve message and digital signature by decrypting the encrypted message and the encrypted digital signature respectively. Finally, it checks the trustworthiness of the received message by checking the recovered digital signature against

Table 2. Variables in the sender and receiver processes

Name	Description
DEK	data encryption key
decryptP	public key decryption function
decryptS	secret key decryption function
ekeyB	receiver's public key (for encryption)
enDEK	encrypted DEK
enMIC	encrypted digital signature
enMsg	encrypted message
encryptP	public key encryption function
encryptS	secret key encryption function
envelope	email, 4-tuple with sender's public key
flag	indication of the trustworthiness of a received email
hash	hash function
message	content of an email
privateKey	constant function, naming the corresponding private key given a public key
rxEnvelope	received email
rxMessage	received message in rxEnvelope
skeyA	sender's private key (for message signing)
sign	signing function
txEnvelope	transmitted email
txMessage	transmitted message in txEnvelope
verify	signature verification function
vkeyA	sender's public key (for signature verification)

the recovered message: it computes the message digest of the message using the hash function and verifies the digital signature against the message digest using the sender's public key. The receiver process is illustrated in Fig. 5.

We define the receiver process *enMailReceiver* in HOL as follows. The functions that appear in Fig. 5 and in the definition of *enMailReceiver* are also defined in HOL and are listed in Table 3. The variables appeared in the definitions are described in Table 2.

DEFINITION 9 (ENMAILRECEIVER) Process *enMailReceiver* retrieves *message* from an encrypted-signed mail.

$\vdash_{def}$ $\forall decryptP$ *decryptS verify hash dkeyB envelope.*
      enMailReceiver decryptP decryptS verify hash dkeyB envelope =
        (*enMailVerMIC decryptP decryptS verify hash dkeyB envelope,*
        enMailRetMsg decryptP decryptS dkeyB envelope)

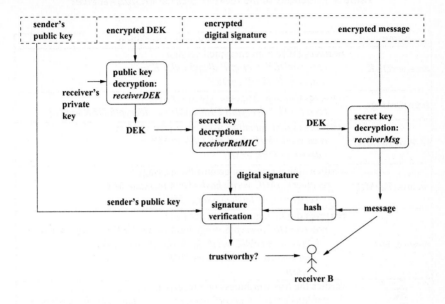

Fig. 5. Receiver process of secure core-email protocol: *enMailReceiver*

4.3 Secure Email System

A system that follows ScEP consists of a sender process and a receiver process. The cryptographic functions used by the sender and receiver processes must have proper properties. The required properties of these functions are:

- (*encryptS DEK*), (*decryptS DEK*) comprises a *cipherPair*. *DEK* is a secret key.
- (*encryptP ekeyB*), (*decryptP dkeyB*) comprises a *cipherPair*. The pair (*ekeyB, dkeyB*) is a public-key pair.
- (*sign skeyA*), (*verify vkeyA*) comprises a *DSpair*. The pair (*vkeyA, skeyA*) is a public-key pair.
- The received email contains a valid public key for signature verification, and the public key has a corresponding private key for signing messages.

We define secure email system in HOL as follows. The function *privateKey* names the corresponding private key given a public key. It is defined as a constant in HOL. The variables appeared in the definitions are described in Table 2.

DEFINITION 10 (ENMAILSYSTEM) Encrypted-signed-message   mail   system *enMailSystem* consists of the sender process *enMailSender* and the receiver process *enMailReceiver*, whose keys make up digital signature key pairs and cipher key pairs.

$\vdash_{def}$ $\forall encryptP\ encryptS\ decryptP\ decryptS\ sign\ verify\ hash\ vkeyA\ skeyA$
$ekeyB\ dkeyB\ DEK\ txEnvelope\ txMessage\ rxEnvelope\ rxMessage\ flag.$

Table 3. Functions in the receiver process *enMailReceiver*

Name	Definition and Description
receiverDEK	retrieves DEK from encrypted version: *receiverDEK decryptP dkeyB enDEK =* *decryptP dkeyB enDEK*
receiverMsg	retrieves message from encrypted version: *receiverMsg decryptS DEK enMsg = decryptS DEK enMsg*
receiverRetMIC	retrieves digital signature from encrypted version: *receiverRetMIC decryptS DEK enMIC =* *decryptS DEK enMIC*
receiverVerMIC	verifies digital signature against the message: *receiverVerMIC verify hash vkeyA message MIC =* *verify vkeyA (hash message, MIC)*
receiverMIC	retrieves digital signature and verifies it: *receiverMIC decryptS verify hash vkeyA DEK message enMIC =* *((receiverVerMIC verify hash vkeyA message) o* *(receiverRetMIC decryptS DEK))* *enMIC*
enMailVerMIC	verifies the trustworthiness of a received mail: *enMailVerMIC decryptP decryptS verify hash dkeyB envelope =* *(let (vkeyA, enDEK, enMIC, enMsg) = envelope in* *let DEK = receiverDEK decryptP dkeyB enDEK in* *let message = receiverMsg decryptS DEK enMsg in* *receiverMIC decryptS verify hash vkeyA DEK message enMIC)*
enMailRetMsg	retrieves the message from a received mail: *enMailRetMsg decryptP decryptS dkeyB envelope =* *(let (vkeyA, enDEK, enMIC, enMsg) = envelope in* *let DEK = receiverDEK decryptP dkeyB enDEK in* *receiverMsg decryptS DEK enMsg)*
enMailRetSender	retrieves the sender's public key from a received mail: *enMailRetSender envelope =* *(let (vkeyA, enDEK, enMIC, enMsg) = envelope in vkeyA)*

enMailSystem encryptP encryptS decryptP decryptS sign verify
  hash vkeyA skeyA ekeyB dkeyB DEK txEnvelope txMessage
  rxEnvelope rxMessage flag =
(txEnvelope =
enMailSender encryptP encryptS sign hash vkeyA ekeyB DEK
  skeyA txMessage) ∧
((flag,rxMessage) =
enMailReceiver decryptP decryptS verify hash dkeyB rxEnvelope) ∧
secKeyPair encryptS decryptS DEK ∧
pubKeyPair encryptP decryptP (ekeyB, dkeyB) ∧
DSKeyPair sign verify (vkeyA, skeyA) ∧
DSKeyPair sign verify

(enMailRetSender rxEnvelope,
*   privateKey (enMailRetSender rxEnvelope))*

To simplify the protocol we have ignored the selection of cryptographic functions used by the sender and receiver processes. However, in the HOL definitions of these two processes the cryptographic functions are taken as parameters.

We have also ignored the necessary verification of certificates. A certificate is a document issued by a certificate authority certifying an entity's public key, much like the entries in telephone directory. A certificate contains an entity's name and public key and is signed by the certification authority. Anyone with certificate authority's public key can verify a certificate, hence can establish a channel where a public key speaks for the entity. In ScEP we identify as the source of an email the public key of an entity, not the entities itself.

In ScEP, the sender's public-key pair is used for signing and signature verification; the receiver's public-key pair is used for encryption and decryption. It is possible that entities in the network use different public-key pairs for different purposes: one pair for signing and signature verification, and one pair for encryption and decryption.

5   Formal Verification of Secure Communication Channels

In the last section we formally defined the ScEP system. A ScEP system can be regarded as a channel between a sender and a receiver that provides confidentiality and source authentications to the statements. In ScEP, a sender identifies an intended recipient of a statement with the recipient's public key and, a receiver identifies the source of a statement with the sender's public key contained in the received package. The channel between a sender A and a receiver B is broken down into three sub-channels: a channel C_A between A and a key k_A that A holds, a channel C_B between B and a key k_B that B holds, and a channel $C_{k_A k_B}$ between k_A and k_B. The composition of these three channels is channel C_{AB} between entity A and B. (Fig. 6.)

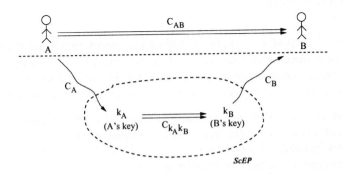

Fig. 6. Communication channels between entities A and B

In this work we concentrate on the analysis of ScEP, which is a channel between two entities' keys. In Section 3 we defined confidential and source authentic channels based on entities. To verify that this channel provides secure services, we redefine the confidential and source authentic channels to be based on keys.

5.1   Confidential Channel

Because both public-key and secret-key encryption are used in ScEP and they use keys differently, we redefine confidential channels for each case. With a public-key encryption a channel is confidential if, when A sends B a statement encrypted with B's public key, only the entity with B's private key can recover the statement in the package. With a secret-key encryption a channel is confidential if, when A sends B a statement encrypted with a secret key k, only the entity knows the secret k can recover the statement in the package. The definitions of these two confidential channels in HOL are as follows.

DEFINITION 11 (CONFCHANNELPUB)   A channel is confidential if only the entity with knowledge of the intended recipient's private key can read the statement in the package. Parameters $ekeyB$ and $dkeyB$ respectively denote the public and private keys of the intended recipient. Parameter $keyC$ denotes a quantity that an arbitrary entity C uses to retrieves the statement.

$\vdash_{def}$ $\forall sendTo\ receiveByB\ envelopeA\ msgA\ envelopeB\ msgB\ (ekeyB, dkeyB).$
$\qquad confChannelPUB\ sendTo\ receiveByB\ envelopeA\ msgA$
$\qquad\quad envelopeB\ msgB\ (ekeyB, dkeyB) =$
$\qquad\quad (envelopeA = sendTo\ ekeyB\ msgA) \supset$
$\qquad\quad (((envelopeB = envelopeA) \supset$
$\qquad\quad (msgB = receiveByB\ dkeyB\ envelopeB) \supset$
$\qquad\quad (msgB = msgA)) \land$
$\qquad\quad (\forall receiveByC\ envelopeC\ msgC\ keyC.$
$\qquad\quad (envelopeC = envelopeA) \supset$
$\qquad\quad (msgC = receiveByC\ keyC\ envelopeC) \supset$
$\qquad\quad (msgC = msgA) \supset$
$\qquad\quad (keyC = dkeyB)))$

DEFINITION 12 (CONFCHANNELSEC)   A channel is confidential if only the entity with knowledge of a shared secret key can read the statement in the package. Parameter $secretAB$ is the shared secret between the sender and the intended recipient. Parameter $keyC$ denotes a quantity that an arbitrary entity C uses to retrieve the statement.

$\vdash_{def}$ $\forall sendTo\ receiveByB\ envelopeA\ msgA\ envelopeB\ msgB\ secretAB.$
$\qquad confChannelSec\ sendTo\ receiveByB\ envelopeA\ msgA$
$\qquad\quad envelopeB\ msgB\ secretAB =$
$\qquad\quad (envelopeA = sendTo\ secretAB\ msgA) \supset$
$\qquad\quad (((envelopeB = envelopeA) \supset$
$\qquad\quad (msgB = receiveByB\ secretAB\ envelopeB) \supset$
$\qquad\quad (msgB = msgA)) \land$

$(\forall receiveByC\ envelopeC\ msgC\ keyC.$
$(envelopeC = envelopeA) \supset$
$(msgC = receiveByC\ keyC\ envelopeC) \supset$
$(msgC = msgA) \supset$
$(keyC = secretAB)))$

However, with Definitions 11 and 12 of confidential channel, we are unable to prove the ScEP provides the confidentiality services. There are two reasons:

1. There are several ways to identify entities [6]. The previous definitions used "what an entity knows" (e.g. *dkeyB*) to identify the entity. This is not suitable for our model. A better alternative is to use "what an entity can do" (e.g. *receiveByB dkeyB*) to identify the entity. The definition of *confChannelPub* is rewritten as an example:

DEFINITION 13 (CONFCHANNELPUB') Definition of confidential channel where an entity is identified by "what he can do".

$\vdash_{def} \forall sendTo\ receiveByB\ envelopeA\ msgA\ envelopeB\ msgB\ (ekeyB,\ dkeyB).$
    $confChannelPub'\ sendTo\ receiveByB\ envelopeA\ msgA$
    $envelopeB\ msgB\ (ekeyB, dkeyB) =$
$\forall receiveByC\ envelopeC\ msgC\ keyC.$
    $(envelopeA = sendTo\ ekeyB\ msgA) \supset$
    $(envelopeC = envelopeA) \supset$
    $(msgC = receiveByC\ keyC\ envelopeC) \supset$
    $((msgC = msgA) = (receiveByC\ keyC = receiveByB\ dkeyB))$

2. To prove the ScEP is a confidential channel, we need to assume that the encryption and decryption functions used satisfy the following property:

DEFINITION 14 (CIPHERPROP) If E and D constitute a *cipherPair*, then D is the only function that can decipher a message encrypted by E.

$\vdash_{def} \forall E\ D.$
    $cipherProp\ E\ D =$
    $cipherPair\ E\ D \supset$
    $(\forall m\ D\_arb.\ (D\_arb\ (E\ m) = m) \supset (D\_arb = D))$

However, any constant function D_arb is going to satisfy $(D\_arb\ (E\ m) = m)$ for some value m. Therefore, there is no pair of functions E and D that has the property *cipherProp*.

5.2 Source Authentication Channel

We redefine a source-authentic channel based on public-key cryptography because only the public-key digital signature is used in ScEP. A channel provides source-authentic service to a statement if, only when A sends B a statement sealed with A's signature will the channel certifies the statement as coming from A. In Definition 7 we derive the source of a statement according to how a package is generated from the statement. One way of generating a package, usually adopted by a person of authority, is to check the validity of a statement and signs it to indicate the source of the statement. We refine the source-authentic channel based on this approach in HOL:

DEFINITION 15 (AUTHCHANNELDS) A channel provides source authentication services to statements if it certifies the origins of the received statements. Parameter *sealA* denotes sender A's action of validating a statement and signing it. Parameter *sealD* denotes a function that an arbitrary entity D uses to sign a statement. The function *retSeal* retrieves the seal of the mail and the function *retSender* retrieves the public key of the sender. Function *authChk* is the authentication check of the mail.

$$\vdash_{def} \forall authChk\ sealA\ retSeal\ retSender\ envelopeA\ msgA\ envelopeB\ msgB$$
$$vkeyA\ skeyA.$$
$$authChannelDS\ authChk\ sealD\ retSeal\ retSender\ envelopeA\ msgA$$
$$envelopeB\ msgB\ (vkeyA,skeyA) =$$
$$(\forall sealD\ envelopeD\ msgD\ keyD.$$
$$(envelopeB = envelopeD) \supset$$
$$(retSeal\ envelopeD = sealD\ keyD\ msgD) \supset$$
$$(vkeyA = retSender\ envelopeB) \supset$$
$$(authChk\ envelopeB =$$
$$(sealD\ keyD\ msgD = sealA\ skeyA\ msgB)))$$

In this definition, we equate two entities by their ability to generate a particular signature s such that $(verify\ vkeyA\ (msgB, s))$ is *true*. A stronger equivalence between two entities would be by equating their signing ability such as $(signA\ skeyA)$ and $(signD\ keyD)$. This is necessary for the following theorem because, as discussed in Section 2.3, a digital signature is uniquely associated with a signer and the information being signed, rather than with a signer alone.

The following theorem shows that a ScEP system provides a source-authentic channel to statements.

THEOREM 16 (ENAUTHENTIC) A ScEP system provides a source authentication channel to statements.

$$\vdash enMailSystem\ encryptP\ encryptS\ decryptP\ decryptS\ sign\ verify\ hash$$
$$vkeyA\ skeyA\ ekeyB\ dkeyB\ txDEK\ envelopeA\ msgA$$
$$envelopeB\ msgB\ flag \supset$$
$$authChannelDS\ (enMailVerMIC\ decryptP\ decryptS\ verify\ hash\ dkeyB)$$
$$(senderGenMIC\ sign\ hash)$$
$$(enMailRetMIC\ decryptP\ decryptS\ dkeyB)$$
$$enMailRetSender\ envelopeA\ msgA\ envelopeB\ msgB\ (vkeyA,skeyA) \wedge$$
$$(flag =$$
$$enMailVerMIC\ decryptP\ decryptS\ verify\ hash\ dkeyB\ envelopeB)$$

6   Conclusion

Our objectives were to specify security properties and their implementation mechanisms, so we could prove the implementation mechanisms satisfied the desired properties. These mechanisms form the core of several secure email protocols such as PGP and PEM. The services we looked at were confidentiality and source authenticity. At this time we have proved the implementations satisfy the source-authenticity service. We are currently working on verifying confidentiality service. This will likely require a reformulation of confidentiality as it relates to implementation.

References

[1] M. Abadi and A. Gordon. A calculus for cryptographic protocols: the spi calculus. *Information and Computation*, 148(1):1–70, January 1999. Also appeared as SRC Research Report 149.

[2] Stephen H. Brackin. A HOL Extension of GNY for Automatically Analyzing Cryptographic Protocols. In *Proceedings of 9th IEEE Computer Security Foundation Workshop*, pages 62–76, June 1996.

[3] M. Burrows, M. Abadi, and R. Needham. A Logic of Authentication. *ACM Transactions on Computer Systems*, 8(1):18–36, February 1990. Also appeared as SRC Research Report 39.

[4] M.J.C. Gordon. Why Higher-Order Logic is a Good Formalism for Specifying and Verifying Hardware. In G. Milne and P.A. Subrahmanyam, editors, *VLSI specification, verification and synthesis*. North Holland, 1986.

[5] M.J.C. Gordon. A Proof Generating System for Higher-Order Logic. In G. Birtwistle and P. A. Subramanyam, editors, *VLSI specification, verification and synthesis*. Kluwer, 1987.

[6] Roberto Gorrieri and Paul Syverson. Varieties of Authentication. In *Proceedings of 11th IEEE Computer Security Foundations Workshop*, pages 79–82, 1998.

[7] Charlie Kaufman, Radia Perlman, and Mike Speciner. *Network Security Private Communication in a Public World*. Prentice Hall, New Jersey, 1995.

[8] Butler Lampson, Martin Abadi, Michael Burrows, and Edward P. Wobber. Authentication in Distributed Systems: Theory and Practice. *ACM Transactions on Computer Systems*, 10(4):265–310, November 1992. Also appeared as SRC Research Report 83.

[9] J. Linn. Privacy Enhancement for Internet Electronic Mail: Part I: Message Encryption and Authentication Procedures. RFC 1421, DEC, February 1993. ftp: ds.internic.net.

[10] G. Lowe. Casper: A Compiler for the Analysis of Security Protocols. In *Proceedings of 10th IEEE Computer Security Foundations Workshop*, pages 18–30, 1997.

[11] Catherine A. Meadows. The NRL Protocol Analyzer: An Overview. In *The Proceedings of Second International Conference on the Practical Applications of Prolog*, April 1994.

[12] Alfred J. Menezes, Paul C. van Oorschot, and Scott A. Vanstone. *Handbook of Applied Cryptography*. CRC Press, New York, 1996.

[13] R.M. Needham and M.D. Schroeder. Using Encryption for Authentication in Large Networks of Computers. *Communications of the ACM*, 21:993–999, 1978.

[14] Jennifer G. Steiner, Clifford Neuman, and Jeffrey I. Schiller. Kerberos: An Authentication Service for Open Network Systems. In *Proceedings of the USENIX Winter Conference*, pages 191–202, February 1988.

[15] Dan Zhou, Joncheng C. Kuo, Susan Older, and Shiu-Kai Chin. Formal Development of Secure Email. In *Proceedings of the 32nd Hawaii International Conference on System Sciences*, January 1999.

[16] P.R. Zimmermann. *The Official PGP User's Guide*. MIT Press, Cambridge, Massachusetts, 1995.

Probabilistic Polynomial-Time Equivalence and Security Analysis

P. Lincoln[*, 1], J. Mitchell[**, 2], M. Mitchell[* * *, 2], and A. Scedrov[†, 3]

[1] Computer Science Laboratory, SRI International
[2] Department of Computer Science, Stanford University
[3] Department of Mathematics, University of Pennsylvania

Abstract. We use properties of observational equivalence for a probabilistic process calculus to prove an authentication property of a cryptographic protocol. The process calculus is a form of π-calculus, with
probabilistic scheduling instead of nondeterminism, over a term language
that captures probabilistic polynomial time. The operational semantics
of this calculus gives priority to communication over private channels, so
that the presence of private communication does not affect the observable
probability of visible actions. Our definition of observational equivalence
involves asymptotic comparison of uniform process families, only requiring equivalence to within vanishing error probabilities. This definition
differs from previous notions of probabilistic process equivalence that require equal probabilities for corresponding actions; asymptotics fit our
intended application and make equivalence transitive, thereby justifying
the use of the term "equivalence." Our security proof uses a series of lemmas about probabilistic observational equivalence that may well prove
useful for establishing correctness of other cryptographic protocols.

1 Introduction

Protocols based on cryptographic primitives are commonly used to protect access
to computer systems and to protect transactions over the internet. Two well-
known examples are the Kerberos authentication scheme [KNT94, KN93], used
to manage encrypted passwords, and the Secure Sockets Layer [FKK96], used
by internet browsers and servers to carry out secure internet transactions. Over
the past decade or two, a variety of methods have been developed for analyzing
and reasoning about such protocols. These approaches include specialized logics
such as BAN logic [BAN89], special-purpose tools designed for cryptographic
protocol analysis [KMM94], as well as theorem proving [Pau97a, Pau97b] and
model-checking methods using general purpose tools [Low96, Mea96, MMS97,
Ros95, Sch96].

* Partially supported by DoD MURI "Semantic Consistency in Information Ex-
change," ONR Grant N00014-97-1-0505.
** Additional support from NSF CCR-9629754.
* * * Additional support from Stanford University Fellowship.
† Additional support from NSF Grant CCR-9800785.

J. Wing, J. Woodcock, J. Davies (Eds.): FM'99, Vol. I, LNCS 1708, pp. 776–793, 1999.
© Springer-Verlag Berlin Heidelberg 1999

In two previous papers [LMMS98, MMS98], we outlined a framework for protocol analysis employing assumptions different from those used in virtually all other formal approaches. Specifically, most formal approaches use a basic model of adversary capabilities which appears to have developed from positions taken by Needham and Schroeder [NS78] and a model presented by Dolev and Yao [DY83]. This set of modeling assumptions treats cryptographic operations as "black-box" primitives, with plaintext and ciphertext treated as atomic data that cannot be decomposed into sequences of bits. Furthermore, as explained in [MMS97, Pau97a, Sch96], there are limited ways for an adversary to learn new information. For example, if a decryption key is sent over the network "in the clear," it can be learned by the adversary. However, it is not possible for the adversary to learn the plaintext of an encrypted message unless the entire decryption key has already been learned. Generally, the adversary is treated as a nondeterministic process that may attempt any possible attack, and a protocol is considered secure if no possible interleaving of actions results in a security breach. The two basic assumptions of this model, perfect cryptography coupled with nondeterministic computation on the part of the adversary, provide an idealized setting in which protocol analysis becomes relatively tractable. However, this model reduces the power of the adversary relative to real-world conditions. As a result, it is possible to prove a protocol correct in this standard model, even when the protocol is vulnerable to simple deterministic attacks.

Our goal is to establish a framework that can be used to analyze protocols (and, potentially, other computer security components) under the standard assumptions of complexity-based cryptography. In [LMMS98], we outlined a refinement of spi-calculus [AG97] that requires a calculus of communicating probabilistic polynomial-time processes and an asymptotic form of observational equivalence. We proposed basic definitions of the key concepts and discussed the potential of this framework by examining some extremely simple protocols. The sequential fragment of our calculus is developed in more detail in [MMS98], where a precise correspondence is proved between a modal-typed lambda calculus and probabilistic polynomial-time computation. In the present paper, we test our basic definitions by considering further applications and develop a more refined probabilistic semantics. Using our improved semantics, we sketch a proof of correctness for a less trivial protocol. Specifically, we prove correctness of a mutual authentication protocol proposed by Bellare and Rogaway [BR94]. This security proof involves some reasoning about a specific form of asymptotic probabilistic observational equivalence for our process calculus. Since, to the best of our knowledge, there has been no previous work on process equivalence up to some error tolerance, this argument and the difficulties we have encountered motivate further investigation into resource-bounded probabilistic semantics and information hiding.

In addition to relying on the basic relation between observational equivalence and security properties developed in the spi-calculus [AG97], we have drawn inspiration from the cryptography-based protocol studies of Bellare and Rogaway [BR94, BR95]. In these studies, a protocol is represented as a set of oracles, each corresponding to one input-output step by one principal. These oracles are each available to the adversary, which is represented by a probabilistic polynomial-time oracle Turing machine. There are some similarities to our setting, since an adversary has access to each input-output step by a principal by sending and receiving data on the appropriate ports. However, there are some significant technical and methodological differences. In our setting, the protocol and the adversary are both expressed in a formal language. The use of a formal language allows for proof techniques that are based on either the syntactic structure of the protocol or on the semantic properties of all expressible adversaries. We have found the specification method we have adopted from spi-calculus to be relatively natural and more systematic than the specifications used by Bellare and Rogaway. In particular, it appears that our specification of authentication is stronger than the one used in [BR94], requiring us to prove more about the observable properties of a protocol execution. Finally, by structuring our proof around observational equivalence, we are led to develop general methods for reasoning about probabilistic observational equivalence that should prove useful in analyzing other protocols.

2   Process Calculus for Protocol Analysis

A protocol consists of a set of programs that communicate over some medium in order to achieve a certain task. Typically, these programs are parameterized by a *security parameter* k, with the idea that increasing the value of k makes the protocol more secure. Often, k is just the length of the keys used in the protocol since it is expected that longer encryption keys make decryption more difficult.

For simplicity, we will consider only those protocols that require some fixed number of communications, independent of the security parameter. In other words, the number of messages sent back and forth before the protocol completes does not increase, even as the security parameter is "cranked up," although the length of the keys used throughout the protocol will increase. This simplification is appropriate for most handshake protocols, key-exchange protocols and authentication protocols. (Many widely-used protocols, including he authentication phase of SSL, serve as examples of "real-world" protocols where the number of messages remains fixed, even as the security parameter is increased.) We are in the process of extending our process calculus to allow looping, which will allow us to deal with more complex protocols, such as those used to prove zero-knowledge. In the present paper, however, we present methods for reasoning about asymptotic observational equivalence that rely on having a fixed bound on the depth of the concurrent process execution tree, and are therefore inappropriate for protocols where the number of messages depends on the security parameter.

Following the work of Abadi and Gordon [AG97], we express security properties of a protocol P by writing an idealized protocol Q which is "patently secure." (Typically, Q requires magic machinery not available in real computational environments, such as perfect random number generators or perfectly secure communication channels.) Then, we endeavor to show that, for any adversary, the interactions between the adversary and P have the same observable behavior as the interactions between the adversary and Q. If this condition holds, we can replace the ideal protocol Q with the realizable protocol P, without compromising security.

The adversary may then be thought of as a *process context*, at which point the task of reasoning about security is reduced to the task of reasoning about observational equivalence (also called observational congruence). Our framework is a refinement of the spi-calculus approach in that we replace nondeterministic computation with probabilistic polynomial-time computation while simultaneously shifting from a standard observational equivalence to an asymptotic form of observational equivalence.

2.1   Syntax

The syntax of our probabilistic polynomial-time calculus consists of *terms* and *processes*. The process portion of the language is a bounded subset of asynchronous π-calculus. However, readers familiar with the traditional π-calculus will note the absence of scope extrusion, or the ability to pass channel names. These omissions are purposeful, and necessary, in order that the expressive power of the calculus correspond to what is commonly believed reasonable in the cryptographic community. It is best to think of the calculus presented here as a notationally familiar means of expressing parallelism and communication, rather than to compare it directly to more traditional forms of π-calculus.

The term portion of the language is used to express all data dependent computation. All terms have natural number type, so the only values communicated from process to process are natural numbers. We do not present a formal grammar or semantics for the term calculus (although we did so in [MMS98]). For the purposes of this paper, the important consideration is that the term language be able to express precisely the probabilistic polynomial time functions from integers to integers. (Therefore, an alternative formalism to that employed in [MMS98] would be probabilistic Turing machine descriptions, together with explicit polynomial time limits, and the understanding that a Turing machine computation that exceeds its time limit outputs zero.) Because the syntax of the term language is not critical for the level of analysis presented in this paper, we use pseudo-code to express terms throughout the paper.

In the grammar below, P varies over processes, T over terms, x over term variables, and c over a countably infinite set C of channel names. The set of well-formed processes is given by the following grammar:

$$
\begin{array}{lll}
P ::= & 0 & \text{(termination)} \\
& (\nu c).P & \text{(private channel)} \\
& c(x).P & \text{(input)} \\
& \bar{c}\langle T \rangle & \text{(output)} \\
& [T = T].P & \text{(match)} \\
& P \mid P & \text{(parallel composition)}
\end{array}
$$

To simplify the presentation of our probabilistic scheduling conventions, we partition the set C of channel names into two disjoint subsets: the *private channel names* and the *public channel names*. Any name c bound with (νc) must be a "private" channel name.

Communication between separate principals of a protocol will normally take place across public channels. Private channels are used to communicate between processes that are considered part of a single principal. Typically, these processes would be running on a single machine, and their communication would therefore be invisible to other machines on the network. Private channels are also used to express offline initialization steps in a protocol, such as the exchange of keys prior to the beginning of some communication.

Private channels are also used in writing specifications; there, they are used to transfer information between processes in a way that is secure by fiat. Often this information is transmitted in encrypted form in the actual implementation; the statement of observational equivalence expresses the fact that encrypted communication should behave similarly to totally private communication.

We often sweeten our process descriptions with a little syntactic sugar. We write $!_n P$ to mean the n-fold parallel composition of P with itself. We write LET $x = y$ IN P as shorthand for $(\nu c).(\bar{c}\langle y\rangle \mid c(x).P)$ where c is some private channel not occurring in P. As usual, we say P is closed if all variables in P are bound.

2.2   Probabilistic Scheduling

Traditional process calculi assume nondeterministic scheduling of computations. In particular, when there are several steps which could be chosen next, the one actually chosen is selected nondeterministically. One motivation for this point of view is derived from failure analysis. If one wishes to prove a mission-critical system to be one hundred percent reliable, it is important to consider all possible interleavings of computation in order to see whether any of them yield an unacceptable outcome.

However, from the point of view of realistic security analysis, nondeterminism gives too much power to the adversary. For example, an adversary allowed to choose a number nondeterministically may just select the key required to decrypt the message. Security analysis, however, is founded on the notion that such an event can happen only with negligible probability, and is therefore of limited concern.

For the sake of concreteness, and to provide an introduction to our notation and methodology, we consider a simple protocol in which one party, A, wishes to send a message securely to another party, B, using public-key encryption. A will attempt to accomplish this feat by encrypting the message with B's k-bit public key (K_b). In the notation commonly found in the literature, this protocol would be expressed as:

$$A \to B : \{\mathsf{msg}\}_{K_b}$$

The notation $A \to B$ indicates a message from A to B, while $\{x\}_y$ is commonly used to indicate a message (plaintext) x encrypted under key y. In our system, we would describe the protocol as

$$\overline{AB}\langle encrypt(K_b, \mathsf{msg})\rangle$$

The channel name AB is used to indicate that the message is being sent from A to B. Of course, an adversary might intercept or modify the message, so the channel name serves only as a mnemonic.

We assume that an evil adversary wishes to discover the message msg. If we allow the adversary to consist of the parallel composition of 3 processes E_0, E_1 and E, scheduled nondeterministically, then the message can be discovered. Specifically, we let

$$
\begin{aligned}
E_0 &= !_k \overline{E}\langle 0\rangle \\
E_1 &= !_k \overline{E}\langle 1\rangle \\
E &= E(b_0).\ \dots\ E(b_{k-1}).\ AB(x).\\
&\quad \overline{Public}\langle decrypt(conc(b_0, \dots, b_{k-1}), \mathsf{msg})\rangle
\end{aligned}
$$

Processes E_0 and E_1 each send k bits on the same channel. The intruder E reads the message from A to B, nondeterministically reads the bits from E_0 and E_1 in such an order so as to obtain B's private key, and decrypts the message. Although at first one might think that eliminating nondeterminism from the term calculus would be sufficient, this example demonstrates that nondeterminism cannot be allowed even at the level of the process calculus.

Our probabilistic operational semantics is in the same spirit as Milner's reaction relation approach [Mil92], which was inspired by the Chemical Abstract Machine of Berry and Boudol [BB90]. Simply put, the reduction step is the "reaction" between a process ready to output on a channel and a process ready to receive input on that same channel. Our operational semantics provides a means of calculating, at any point, which processes are eligible to interact, and then of choosing probabilistically from among this set.

There are actually two sources of randomness in the execution of a process. The first, just discussed, is in the choice of which processes will execute next. The second comes in the computation of terms, which themselves perform probabilistic computations. Specifically, for any closed term T there is a finite set of possible values $T_1, \dots, T_k$ such that the probability of T evaluating to T_i is p_i and $\sum_{i=1,k} p_i = 1$.

Our goal is to devise an intuitively plausible probabilistic semantics that refines the standard nondeterministic semantics of π-calculus and allows us to model faithfully the security phenomena of interest. Subject to these two primary goals, we would also like to have as many natural equivalences as possible. For example, all other things being equal, we would like parallel composition to be associative. The first goal, refining the standard nondeterministic semantics, means that our operational semantics will induce some probability distribution on the set of execution sequences allowed by the nondeterministic semantics. We assign probabilities in a "local" manner, independent of the history of prior steps leading to any process state.

That communications on private channels be unobservable is of the utmost importance in our framework. For example, it is vital that

$$P \quad \cong \quad (\nu c).(\,\bar{c}\langle 0 \rangle \mid c(x).P\,)$$

when x does not occur free in P. In words, we want any process P to be equivalent to the process that transmits some value on a private channel, discards the result of that communication, and then proceeds as P. After all, given that private channels are considered private, out-of-band communication mechanisms, there is no way that an adversary should be able to observe the private communication.

In order to guarantee unobservability, we must ensure not only that the contents of the transmission are unavailable to the adversary, but also that the existence of the transmission cannot become known. In particular, the communication must not skew the probability of other actions in the process as the adversary might otherwise be able to distinguish the processes by sampling the behavior of the (supposedly equivalent) processes.

Consider the following concrete example:

$$\overline{A}\langle 0 \rangle \mid \overline{A}\langle 1 \rangle.$$

We would like this process to be equivalent to:

$$((\nu c).(\bar{c}\langle 0 \rangle \mid c(x).\overline{A}\langle 0 \rangle)) \mid \overline{A}\langle 1 \rangle.$$

However, if our operational semantics were to select from all possible next steps with equal probability, then the first process would output a 0 followed by a 1 one half of the time, and the sequence $1, 0$ the other half of the time. The introduction of the private channel in the second process would bias the computation so that the $0, 1$ sequence would occur with only twenty-five percent probability while the $1, 0$ sequence would occur with seventy-five percent probability. In other words, the most obvious probabilistic scheduling rules yield a situation in which the introduction of a silent action changes the behavior of the process as a whole. The solution we have chosen is to give priority to silent actions, allowing them to occur before any reductions involving public channels. We thereby keep the probability of scheduling silent actions from interfering with the scheduling of observable actions.

2.3   Operational Semantics

The probabilistic operational semantics of processes is given in three parts. The first part is essentially a structural equivalence, in the same sprit as Milner's structural-equivalence-based semantics for π-calculus [Mil92], presented using multisets of subprocesses instead of a syntactic transformation of process expressions. The second part determines the set of eligible process combinations, each consisting of either a matching output and input, or a single process that requires evaluation of a conditional test. The third part of the operational semantics is the definition of the execution graph of a process, which consists of edges between sets of schedulable processes, each edge labeled with a probability and any visible communication that may appear as a result of the computation step.

The basic computation steps of our process calculus are either a communication, consisting of an output and matching input, or a guarded process whose guard is to be evaluated. Therefore, a *schedulable process* is a process of one of the following three forms: $c(x).Q$, called an *output process*, $\bar{c}\langle T \rangle$, called an *input process*, or $[T_1 = T_2].Q$, called a *guarded process*.

If P is any process, then the multiset $S(P)$ of *schedulable subprocesses of* P is defined inductively as follows:

$$S(P) = \begin{cases} \emptyset & \text{if } P = 0 \\ S(Q) & \text{if } P = (\nu c).Q \\ \{P\} & \text{if } P \text{ is } schdulable \\ S(P_1) \cup S(P_2) & \text{if } P = P_1|P_2 \end{cases}$$

Since the semantics of a process P is determined by $S(P)$, we can think of P and Q as structurally equivalent if $S(P)$ and $S(Q)$ are identical multisets.

The execution of a process consists of selecting one computation step from the set of schedulable subprocesses. To simplify a later definition, we say a singleton $[T_1 = T_2].Q$ is an *eligible computation*, and a pair $(\bar{c}\langle T \rangle, c(x).Q)$ is an *eligible computation*. Due to priority of internal actions over external ones, communication will only occur if there are no eligible guarded processes, and communication on public channels will occur only if there are no eligible computations on a private channel.

The *execution graph* $G(P)$ of process P has nodes that are multisets of schedulable processes and arcs labeled with probabilities. In addition to the probability that a transition will occur, an arc may also be labeled with a channel name and value, if the transition involves communication on a public channel. The probabilities will depend on both the probabilistic scheduling of subprocesses, and the probabilistic evaluation of terms (explained in [MMS98]). Intuitively, if $S(P) = \{P_1, \ldots, P_n\}$, we select uniformly at random from among the eligible computations of the highest priority. More specifically, the root of $G(P)$ is the multiset $S(P)$ of schedulable processes of P. The arcs of $G(P)$ are determined as follows:

- There is an arc from multiset $R = R' \cup \{[T_1 = T_2].Q\}$ to $R \cup S(Q)$ with probability p if there are k eligible guarded processes in R, the probability that T_1 and T_2 evaluate to the same value is r, and $p = r/k$.
- There is an arc from multiset $R = R' \cup \{\bar{c}\langle T \rangle, c(x).Q\}$ to $R \cup S([v/x]Q)$ with probability p if there are no guarded processes in R, there are k eligible communications along private channels in R, the probability that T evaluates to v is r, and $p = r/k$.
- There is an arc from multiset $R = R' \cup \{\bar{c}\langle T \rangle, c(x).Q\}$ to $R \cup S([v/x]Q)$, labeled with probability p and pair $\langle c, v \rangle$ if there are no guarded processes in R, there are no eligible communications along private channels, there are

k eligible communications along public channels in R, the probability that T evaluates to v is r, and $p = r/k$.

The nodes of $G(P)$ are all sets of schedulable processes that lie along a path from the root of $G(P)$.

Intuitively, we assume that public communications are externally observable, while the evaluation of guards and private communication are not. Formally, an *observation* is a sequence of pairs $\langle c, v \rangle$, each consisting of a public channel name and a value. We say an observation o *occurs* in the execution of P if o is a subsequence of the labels along a path in $G(P)$. For example, the observation $\langle c, 1 \rangle, \langle d, 2 \rangle$ occurs in the execution of $\bar{c}\langle 1 \rangle | \bar{c}\langle 2 \rangle | \bar{d}\langle 2 \rangle$. The probability of a path in $G(P)$ is the product of all the probabilities along the path, and the *probability of observation* o in the execution of P is the sum of the probabilities of all paths in $G(P)$ on which o occurs.

3 Process Equivalence

Two processes P and Q are observationally equivalent, written $P \simeq Q$, if any program $\mathcal{C}[P]$ containing P has the same observable behavior as the program $\mathcal{C}[Q]$ with Q replacing P. To make this more precise for a specific programming language $\mathcal{L}$, we assume the language definition gives rise to some set of *program contexts,* each context $\mathcal{C}[\ ]$ consisting of a program with a "hole" (indicated by empty square brackets $[\ ]$) in which to insert a phrase of the language, and some set *Obs* of concrete *observable actions,* such as integer or string outputs. We also assume that there is some semantic evaluation relation $\overset{eval}{\rightsquigarrow}$, with $M \overset{eval}{\rightsquigarrow} v$ meaning that evaluation or execution of the program M produces the observable action v.

We perform an *experiment* on a process P by placing it in a context $\mathcal{C}[\ ]$, running the resulting process, and seeing whether or not a particular observable v occurs. The main idea underlying the concept of observational equivalence is that the properties of a program that matter are precisely the properties that can be observed by experiment. Although we presented the basic form of observational equivalence below in [LMMS98], we repeat the basic motivation here for completeness. We now commit ourselves to uniform families of processes and contexts (in which all members of a family represented by the same expression, but parameterized by some natural number), mirroring the usual assumptions regarding protocols and security parameters mentioned earlier.

3.1 Definition of Equivalence

For the process language considered in this paper, we are interested in contexts that distinguish between processes. (We will not need to consider observational equivalence of terms.) Therefore, the contexts of interest are process expressions with a "hole", given by the following grammar

$$\mathcal{C}[\ ] ::= [\ ] \quad | \quad n(x).\mathcal{C}[\ ] \quad | \quad P|\mathcal{C}[\ ] \quad | \quad \mathcal{C}[\ ]|Q \quad |$$
$$(\nu c).\mathcal{C}[\ ] \quad | \quad \bar{c}\langle T \rangle \quad | \quad [M = N]\mathcal{C}[\ ]$$

A process observation will be a communication event on a public channel. More specifically, we let *Obs* be the set of all possible observations, *i.e.*, the set of pairs $\langle n, m \rangle$, where n is a public channel name and m is an integer. We write $P \overset{eval}{\leadsto} o$ if evaluation of process expression P results in the observation $o \in Obs$.

Intuitively, given program phrases P and Q, context $\mathcal{C}[\,]$ and observation o, it seems reasonable to compare the probability that $\mathcal{C}[P] \overset{eval}{\leadsto} o$ to the probability that $\mathcal{C}[Q] \overset{eval}{\leadsto} o$. However, since a probability distribution is an infinite entity, it is not clear how to "observe" a distribution. We might run $\mathcal{C}[P]$ some number of times, count how many times o occurs, and then repeat the series of experiments for $\mathcal{C}[Q]$. If the probabilities are very different, then we might be able to observe this difference (with high confidence) by a few runs of each program. However, if the probabilities are very close, then it might take many more runs of both programs to distinguish them.

As a first step toward developing a workable notion of observable equivalence, we define computational indistinguishability within factor ϵ by saying that $P \simeq_\epsilon Q$ if

$$\forall \mathcal{C}[\,]. \ \forall v \in Obs. \ |\mathrm{Prob}[\mathcal{C}[P] \overset{eval}{\leadsto} v] - \mathrm{Prob}[\mathcal{C}[Q] \overset{eval}{\leadsto} v]| \leq \epsilon$$

An immediate difficulty with $\simeq_\epsilon$ is that it is not a transitive relation. Moreover, it is not clear how to differentiate large ϵ from small ϵ. Specifically, we would like to draw a distinction between sets of processes that are "close" in behavior from those that are "far apart." Intuitively, the distinction should have something to do with running time, since it takes more trials to distinguish random variables that differ by a small amount than to distinguish random variables that differ by a large amount.

We can bring concepts from asymptotic complexity theory to bear on the situation if the processes P and Q under consideration are actually families of processes indexed by natural numbers. This point of view fits our intended application, since, as mentioned earlier, cryptographic primitives and security protocols are generally defined with some security parameter that may be increased if greater resistance to tampering is required.

A *process family* P is a process of the form $\mathsf{n}(n).P'$. If P is a process family, we write P_n for $(\nu \mathsf{n}).(\bar{\mathsf{n}}\langle n \rangle \mid P)$. A context family is the analogous construction, but with a single hole permitted in the body of P. Let us assume that $P = \{P_n\}_{n \geq 0}$ and $Q = \{Q_n\}_{n \geq 0}$ are process families and $\mathcal{C}[\,] = \{\mathcal{C}_n[\,]\}_{n \geq 0}$ a family of contexts. We assume that the running times of P_n, Q_n and $\mathcal{C}_n[\,]$ are bounded by polynomials in n. Then for function f, we define *asymptotic equivalence within* f for two process families P and Q by writing $P \simeq_f Q$ if

$$\forall \mathcal{C}[\,]. \forall o \in Obs. \exists n_0. \forall n \geq n_0.$$
$$|\mathrm{Prob}[\mathcal{C}_n[P_n] \overset{eval}{\leadsto} o] - \mathrm{Prob}[\mathcal{C}_n[Q_n] \overset{eval}{\leadsto} o]| \leq f(n)$$

In words, P and Q are asymptotically equivalent within f if, for every computational experiment given by a context family and an observable value, the

$$E \in GNDC_{\lhd}^{\alpha} \qquad \textit{iff} \qquad E \parallel_C Top \lhd \alpha(E) \qquad\qquad \blacksquare$$

In particular, if the hypotheses of the proposition above hold then it is sufficient to check that $\alpha(E)$ is satisfied when E is composed to the most general (i.e., most powerful) environment Top. This is useful, since permits to make only one single check, in order to prove that a property holds whatever attacker we choose. We also have the following corollary for the congruence induced by $\lhd$:

Corollary 1. *Let $\lhd$ be a pre-congruence w.r.t. $\parallel_C$ and let $\equiv = \lhd \cap \lhd^{-1}$. If there exist two processes $Nil, Top \in \mathcal{E}_C^{\phi_X}$ such that for every process $X \in \mathcal{E}_C^{\phi_X}$ we have $Nil \lhd X \lhd Top$ then*

$$E \in GNDC_{\equiv}^{\alpha} \qquad \textit{iff} \qquad E \parallel_C Nil \equiv E \parallel_C Top \equiv \alpha(E) \qquad\qquad \blacksquare$$

3.2   Trace Equivalence

Most of the security properties that have been proposed for the analysis of security protocols are based on the simple notion of *traces*: two processes are equivalent if they exactly show the same execution sequences (called *traces*). In order to formally define traces, we need a transition relation which does not consider internal τ moves. This can be defined as follows:

Definition 3. *The expression $E \overset{\alpha}{\Longrightarrow} E'$ is a shorthand for $E(\overset{\tau}{\longrightarrow})^* E_1 \overset{\alpha}{\longrightarrow} E_2(\overset{\tau}{\longrightarrow})^* E'$, where $(\overset{\tau}{\longrightarrow})^*$ denotes a (possibly empty) sequence of τ labelled transitions. Let $\gamma = \alpha_1 \ldots \alpha_n \in (Act \setminus \{\tau\})^*$ be a sequence of actions; then $E \overset{\gamma}{\Longrightarrow} E'$ if and only if there exist $E_1, E_2, \ldots, E_{n-1} \in \mathcal{E}$ such that $E \overset{\alpha_1}{\Longrightarrow} E_1 \overset{\alpha_2}{\Longrightarrow} \cdots \overset{\alpha_{n-1}}{\Longrightarrow} E_{n-1} \overset{\alpha_n}{\Longrightarrow} E'$.* $\blacksquare$

We define *trace preorder* ($\leq_{trace}$) and *trace equivalence* ($\approx_{trace}$) as follows:

Definition 4. *For any $E \in \mathcal{E}$ the set $T(E)$ of traces associated with E is $T(E) = \{\gamma \in (Act \setminus \{\tau\})^* \mid \exists E' : E \overset{\gamma}{\Longrightarrow} E'\}$. F can execute all the traces of E (notation $E \leq_{trace} F$) iff $T(E) \subseteq T(F)$. E and F are trace equivalent (notation $E \approx_{trace} F$) iff $E \leq_{trace} F$ and $F \leq_{trace} E$, i.e., iff $T(E) = T(F)$.* $\blacksquare$

It is possible to prove that trace preorder $\leq_{trace}$ is a pre-congruence with respect to value-passing CCS operators.

Now we can provide the description of the most powerful intruder in the trace setting. It can be defined by using a family of processes $(Top_{trace}^C)_\phi$ each representing the instance of the enemy with knowledge ϕ.

$$(Top_{trace}^C)_\phi = \sum_{c \in C} c(x).(Top_{trace}^C)_{\phi \cup \{x\}} + \sum_{\substack{c \in C \\ m \in \mathcal{D}(\phi) \cap Msg(c)}} \bar{c}m.(Top_{trace}^C)_\phi$$

The following holds:

Proposition 2. *If $X \in \mathcal{E}_C^{\phi_X}$ then $X \leq_{trace} (Top_{trace}^C)_{\phi_X}$.* $\blacksquare$

So, we have proved that there exists a top of the set $\mathcal{E}_C^{\phi_X}$ with respect to $\leq_{trace}$ and it is indeed $(Top_{trace}^C)_{\phi_X}$. These result, together with the fact that $\leq_{trace}$ is a pre-congruence with respect to $\|_C$ allow us to apply Proposition 1 obtaining the following result for the family of $\leq_{trace}$-based $GNDC_{\leq_{trace}}^{\alpha}$ properties:

Corollary 2. *For every function* $\alpha : \mathcal{E} \to \mathcal{E}$

$$E \in GNDC_{\leq_{trace}}^{\alpha} \qquad \text{iff} \qquad E \underset{C}{\|} (Top_{trace}^C)_{\phi_X} \leq_{trace} \alpha(E) \qquad \blacksquare$$

Note that this corollary holds for every possible α. So, every property which is based on trace pre-congruence can be checked statically. We show how we can directly apply this result on our simple running example.

Example 3. Consider again protocol P of Example 1. We would like to check that no intruder is able to fake message m_A if it does not know the shared key k_{AB}. We do this by checking that $P \in GNDC_{\leq_{trace}}^{\overline{out}\,m_A}$. Indeed, if this holds then even in the presence of any enemy X, the process B only receives message m_A and no fake is possible. We assume that $c \in C$, $\phi_X = \emptyset$ and, as before, $Msg(c) = \{\{m\}_k \mid m \in M, k \in K\}$. By corollary 2 we have that $P \in GNDC_{\leq_{trace}}^{\overline{out}\,m_A}$ if and only if $P' \overset{\text{def}}{=} P \|_C (Top_{trace}^C)_\emptyset \leq_{trace} \overline{out}\,m_A$. Since every action a, executed by the enemy and such that $chan(a) \neq c$ will never synchronize with P, then it is easy to see that $P' \approx_{trace} P \|_C (Top_{trace}^{\{c\}})_\emptyset$. Now, if A and B communicate together we have $P' \overset{\overline{out}\,m_A}{\Longrightarrow} (\underline{0} \| \underline{0} \| (Top_{trace}^{\{c\}})_\emptyset) \setminus \{c\}$ which can do nothing else. Otherwise, A and B could communicate with the enemy. Note that $(Top_{trace}^{\{c\}})_\emptyset$ can only read from channel c since it has no knowledge. So, the only possible move is the one where it intercepts the message from A:

$$P' \overset{\tau}{\longrightarrow} (\underline{0} \| B(k_{AB}) \| (Top_{trace}^{\{c\}})_{\{m_A\}_{k_{AB}}}) \setminus \{c\}$$

It is easy to see that $(Top_{trace}^{\{c\}})_{(\{m_A\}_{k_{AB}})}$ can only either read again from c or send $\{m_A\}_{k_{AB}}$ on c. Indeed, it cannot decrypt the message since it does not know the key and it cannot send other "kind" of messages on c such as pairs composed by two instances of $\{m_A\}_{k_{AB}}$ because of how is defined $Msg(c)$. Since none is sending messages on c we have only one possible execution:

$$(\underline{0} \| B(k_{AB}) \| (Top_{trace}^{\{c\}})_{\{m_A\}_{k_{AB}}}) \setminus \{c\} \overset{\overline{out}\,m_A}{\Longrightarrow} (\underline{0} \| \underline{0} \| (Top_{trace}^{\{c\}})_{\{m_A\}_{k_{AB}}}) \setminus \{c\}$$

We conclude that the only trace executable by P' is $\overline{out}\,m_A$, thus $P' \leq_{trace} \overline{out}\,m_A$ and $P \in GNDC_{\leq_{trace}}^{\overline{out}\,m_A}$. It is analogously possible to prove that $P \in GNDC_{\leq_{trace}}^{\overline{out}\,m_A}$ even when ϕ_X is not empty (the enemy could know some private messages or keys) and we simply require that $k_{AB} \notin \mathcal{D}(\phi_X)$. $\qquad \blacksquare$

4   Some Examples of Security Properties

In this section we want to show the generality of $GNDC_\lhd^\alpha$ properties. In particular we show that a number of existing formal definitions of security properties can be redefined as $GNDC_\lhd^\alpha$ ones, with particular instantiations of α and $\lhd$.

4.1 Non Deducibility on Compositions

Non Deducibility on Compositions (NDC, for short) [9, 10] has been proposed as a generalization of the classical idea of *Non-Interference* [11] to non-deterministic systems. Non-Interference tries to capture whether a certain group of processes G is able to "interfere" in some way with another group G', i.e., if what is done by processes in G has some effect on the execution of processes in G'. Sometimes Non-Interference properties are also called *Information Flow* properties, since an interference of G with G' can be seen as a information flow from the first group to the second one. A classical application of these properties is *multilevel security* [3] where H represent a set of "classified" (high level) processes that should be forbidden to send any data to L (low level), i.e., to interfere with L. In [8] NDC has also been applied to the verification of security protocols.

Since $GNDC_\triangleleft^\alpha$ is a generalization of NDC it can be instantiated in order to obtain NDC and also the *bisimulation* based NDC, called BNDC. We first redefine in our extended language the original definitions: we consider C as the set of channels that classified processes H use when trying to interfere with the processes L. Thus, H corresponds to $\mathcal{E}_C^{\phi_X}$ and NDC can be defined as follows:

Definition 5. *E is NDC if and only if* $\forall \Pi \in \mathcal{E}_C^{\phi_X}$, $E \setminus C \approx_{trace} E \|_C \Pi$.   ∎

where the only difference with respect to the definition given in the original model is that the knowledge of processes $\Pi \in H$ is bounded by ϕ_X. In the extended model, this is required to guarantee reliable encryption. NDC requires that high level processes $\mathcal{E}_C^{\phi_X}$ are not able to change the low level behaviour of the system represented by $E \setminus C$. As a matter of fact $E \setminus C$ is the system where no high level activity is allowed. If it is equivalent to $E \|_C \Pi$ this clearly means that Π is not able to modify in any way the execution of E.

We can obtain a bisimulation based NDC by simply substituting $\approx_{trace}$ with $\approx_{bisim}$. We do not define bisimulation here, since we will not use it directly, but we only mention that it is a strong observational equivalence which requires that two bisimilar processes are able to simulate each other step by step (see, e.g., [20] for more details).

Definition 6. *E is BNDC if and only if* $\forall \Pi \in \mathcal{E}_C^{\phi_X}$, $E \setminus C \approx_{bisim} E \|_C \Pi$.   ∎

Note that NDC and BNDC correspond to $GNDC_{\approx_{trace}}^{E \setminus C}$ and $GNDC_{\approx_{bisim}}^{E \setminus C}$, respectively. For NDC it is also possible to apply Corollary 1 obtaining an interesting static characterization.

Proposition 3. *E is NDC   iff $E \|_C (Top_{trace}^C)_{\phi_X} \approx_{trace} E \setminus C$.*   ∎

This result is the analogous of the one in [9]. Note that here we have found it as a particular case of the more general result of Corollary 1.

For BNDC we cannot give an analogous static characterization. Indeed, to the best of our knowledge, the only preorder whose kernel is the weak bisimulation, is the weak bisimulation itself. Thus, in this case, we cannot find suitable processes *Nil* and *Top*. As a matter of fact, such processes would result to be bisimilar.

It is worthwhile noticing that there are several similarities with a related problem in temporal logic, namely *module checking*. Given a finite system, which is able to interact with its environment, the *module checking* problem is the task of verifying that for every environment the induced behaviour of the system satisfies a certain temporal logic formula. Interestingly, if the formula expresses only safety properties (i.e. trace based properties) then the problem is reduced to check the system in composition with the environment which enables every system transition (the most general one!). But if the formula expresses also liveness properties then problem becomes very difficult and it is no more sufficient to consider the most general environment (see [19] for a deeper discussion).

4.2   The Agreement Property

In this section we show that also the approach proposed in [15] for the analysis of authentication properties, inside the framework of CSP [12] process algebra, can be rephrased in terms of our specification schema. The basic idea of the *Agreement* property is the following:

"A protocol guarantees to an initiator A *Agreement* with a responder B on a set of data items ds if, whenever A (acting as initiator) completes a run of the protocol, apparently with responder B, then B has previously been running the protocol, apparently with A, and B was acting as responder in his run, and the two agents agreed on the data values corresponding to all the variables in ds, and each such run of A corresponds to a unique run of B".

What is technically done in the *Agreement* property is to have for each party an action representing the running of the protocol and another one representing the completion of it. For example, consider an action $commit\_res(B, A, d)$ representing a correct termination of B as a responder that is convinced to communicate with A and agrees on data in d. Moreover we have an action $running\_ini(A, B, d)$ that represents the fact that A is running the protocol as initiator, apparently with B and with data d. If we have these two actions specified in the protocol, the *Agreement* property requires that when B executes $commit\_res(B, A, d)$ then A has previously executed $running\_ini(A, B, d)$. This means that every time B completes the protocol with A convinced that the relevant data are the ones represented by d, then A must have been running the protocol with B using exactly the data in d.

As done in [15], we assume that the actions representing the running and the commit are correctly specified in the protocol. We can see them as output actions over two particular channels $running\_ini$ and $commit\_res$. For simplicity, we only analyze the case where A is the initiator and B is the responder, and the set ds of variables is composed only by d which can assume values in a set D. However, the specification can be easily extended in order to cover all the cases studied in [15]. Function $\alpha(E)$ can be defined as follows:

$$E' = Top_{trace}^{Sort(E) \setminus \{running\_ini, commit\_res\}}$$
$$E''(x,y) = \sum_{d \in D} running\_ini(x,y,d) \ . \ \overline{commit\_res}(y,x,d)$$
$$\alpha_{Agree}(E) = E' \parallel E''(A,B)$$

Given E, $\alpha(E)$ represents the most general system which satisfies the agreement property and has the same sort as E. As a matter of fact in $\alpha(E)$ the action $\overline{running\_ini}(A,B,d)$ always precedes $\overline{commit\_res}(B,A,d)$ for every datum d, and every combination of the other actions of E can be executed. In order to analyze more than one session, it is sufficient to consider an extended α which has several processes $E''(A,B)$ in parallel. For example, for n sessions we can consider the following:

$$\alpha_{Agree}(E) = E' \parallel \underbrace{E''(A,B) \parallel \ldots \parallel E''(A,B)}_{n}$$

We want that even in the presence of an hostile process, E does not execute traces that are not in $\alpha(E)$,i.e., we require that $E \parallel_C X \leq_{trace} \alpha(E)$. So we can give the following definition:

Definition 7. *E satisfies Agreement iff E is* $GNDC_{\leq_{trace}}^{\alpha_{Agree}(E)}$. ∎

Note that in [15] it is only required that *Agreement* holds when the system is composed with a particular intruder, which turns out to be equivalent to the most general one. In the following we exploit Proposition 1 in order to formally prove that such a (static) requirement is indeed sufficient (and necessary) to guarantee our *GNDC*-based version of *Agreement*. As a matter of fact, by Corollary 2 we immediately have the following result:

Proposition 4. *E satisfies Agreement iff* $E \parallel_C (Top_{trace}^C)_{\phi_X} \leq_{trace} \alpha_{Agree}(E)$. ∎

In [15], other versions of *Agreement* are defined. We can rephrase all of them in our model by simply changing the α function. [5]

4.3   Message-Oriented Authentication

Now, we consider the message-based approach to authentication defined in [24, 26] using the CSP language. The idea is to observe when a set of messages T authenticates another set of messages R. Informally, T authenticates R if the occurrence of some element of T implies the occurrence of some element of R (it is required that T and R are disjoint). When a system P satisfies this property we say that P satisfies T **authenticates** R.

In [24] the net is represented by a process *Medium* which acts like a router by receiving and forwarding to the correct process the messages. In CSP, it is

---

[5] Indeed, *recentness* cannot be immediately rephrased in our CCS-based model, because of the difference in handling communication with respect to CSP. This could be overcome by extending our language with time as done in [19]. This is only related to the differences in the model, and is not caused by a weakness of our schema.

possible to observe the communication between the processes and the medium since they are not "internalized" as in CCS. However, we can simulate this by assuming that the $Medium$ echoes every routing of messages through particular output actions on two reserved channels $trans$ and rec. For example $\overline{trans}\,(A, B, m)$ corresponds to the sending of message m from A to B and, symmetrically, $\overline{rec}\,(B, A, m)$ represents the reception of it. In this way we can observe communication as done in CSP. Sets T and R range over these reserved actions. We can now define the $\alpha_{auth_R^T}(E)$ function as follows:

$$\alpha_{auth_R^T}(E) = E'$$
$$E' = \left(\sum_{\substack{a\,\in\,Act \\ a\,\notin\,R\,\cup\,T}} a.E'\right) + \sum_{\substack{a\,\in\,Act \\ a\,\in\,R}} a.E''$$
$$E'' = Top_{trace}^{Sort(E)}$$

Process $\alpha_{auth_R^T}(E)$ can execute actions in T only after it has executed some actions in R. Indeed we note that it moves to E'', where it can execute also actions in T, only after it performs at least one action in R. This is exactly what we require by our system E and $\alpha(E)$ is indeed the most general system (with the same sort as E) satisfying T **authenticates** R. So we can give the following definition:

Definition 8. E satisfies T **authenticates** R iff E is $GNDC_{\leq trace}^{\alpha_{auth_R^T}(E)}$. ∎

As in the section above, we can prove that the approach followed in [24], where it is considered only the most powerful intruder, guarantees that the property holds in the presence of whatever hostile process. By Corollary 2 we obtain that:

Proposition 5. E satisfies T **authenticates** R iff $E \parallel_C (Top_{trace}^C)_{\phi_X} \leq_{trace} \alpha_{auth_R^T}(E)$. ∎

4.4   Non-repudiation

In this section, we show that also non-repudiation properties can be formulated within the $GNDC$ schema. Non repudiation protocols have the aim of producing evidence about the execution of services, among parties that do not trust each other (see [27, 28]).

In [25] Schneider shows how to apply verification methods based on CSP process algebra to the analysis of a (fair) non repudiation protocol proposed in [27]. Among the non repudiation properties studied in [25, 28], we briefly recall:

- *Non Repudiation of Origin (NRO)* is intended to protect the receiver from the false denial of another party to have sent a message.
- *Non Repudiation of Receipt (NRR)* is intended to protect the sender form the false denial of another party to have received a message.

Roughly speaking, the analysis performed by Schneider is similar to his message based authentication (see section above). As an example, consider NRO verification: if the receiver is able to produce an evidence of the sending of a certain message m, then, actually, m should have been sent. In other words, such an evidence should "authenticate" m (in the sense of message-based authentication).

Non-repudiation protocols are not concerned with communication among two or more parties in an hostile environment. So, at a first glance, the $GNDC$ schema seems to be not applicable. However, the parties do not trust each other, and in particular, one of them could try to act maliciously in order to obtain some advantage. We will show that this malicious party may be considered as the hostile environment in a $GNDC$ schema.

In the verification of NRO (NRR) we assume that a Judge should be able to establish that a certain message has been sent (received) if he obtains some evidence of it from the receiver (sender). This verification should be carried out by simply assuming that both the sender and the receiver have not sent on the net some information which could invalidate the evidence. In particular, the Judge cannot assume that they have followed the protocol. For this reason, Schneider models both the sender and the receiver similarly to the most general intruder. In order to apply the $GNDC$ schema, we consider a weaker (but still reasonable) notion of NRO; in particular, we require that if the receiver B, after following the protocol, is able to give evidence of origin, then the sender A has actually sent that message. We call this NRO with honest receiver NRO_{hr}. It can be simply encoded as $GNDC$ schema by considering a process E_B where we only have the receiver B plus the possible communication medium (but we do not specify A):

$$\forall X_A \in \mathcal{E}_C^{\phi_A} \quad X_A \parallel_C E_B \leq_{trace} \alpha^{wnro}(E_B) \tag{2}$$

Now, if R is the set of all the actions where m is sent as message and ev_of_or is the action which signals that B has evidence of origin of m, then $\alpha^{wnro}(E_B)$ can be defined as $\alpha_{auth_R^{\{ev\_of\_or\}}}(E_B)$. [6] Analogously, we define non-repudiation of origin with honest sender, i.e., NRO_{hs}. This property can be encoded in the $GNDC$ schema (2) by simply considering process E_A instead of E_B and by quantifying over processes which have the initial knowledge ϕ_B. Symmetrically to E_B, in E_A only A and the possible medium are given, while B is left unspecified.

We can now define *weak-NRO* as the intersection of NRO_{hr} and NRO_{hs}, i.e., $E_A, E_B \in GNDC_{\leq_{trace}}^{\alpha^{wnro}}$. An analogous definition may be given for *weak-NRR*, even though the situation is slightly more complicated since, in this case, also liveness properties should be considered. We do not address this issue in details, since we prefer to focus our attention to another property which is also based on liveness. The property is *fairness* [28]:

---

[6] Indeed, there is a slight limitation due to the necessity of preventing the communication of information that could invalidate the proof of evidence. This can be treated in our model as done in [25].

– *Fairness*: At no point in the protocol run does either of participants have an advantage. In other words no one of the party can get his own evidence and avoid the other to get his corresponding evidence.

As observed in [25], this property cannot be defined as a safety property (i.e. nothing bad happens). Indeed we have to prove that whenever one of the two participants obtains his own evidence, then the other must be in the position to get his own evidence too. This can be seen as a liveness property (i.e. something good happens). For this reason, in the analysis of this property it is used the *failure* model instead of the trace one. As a matter of fact, failure equivalence is actually able to observe potential deadlocks in the executions, and so it permits to see if something can be executed or not (i.e., if an evidence can be obtained or not). The verification technique for the fairness property proposed in [25] directly fits in the $GNDC$ schema. Indeed, it is reasonable to assume that an agent can require fairness from the other only in the case he behaves correctly, i.e., if it follows the protocol. For example, the *fairness* for the sender A of receiving evidence of message receipt can be defined as in (2) with a suitable relation $\leq_{failure}$ which takes into account failures, and a function α^{fair} which models the fact that after the receiver gets evidence of the origin (ev_of_or) then the sender have the possibility to obtain his own evidence of receipt (ev_of_re). This is modeled in α^{fair} by making the action ev_of_re always executable after that ev_of_or has been engaged.

4.5   Authentication in the Spi-Calculus

In [2, 1] an interesting notion of authentication is proposed. The basic idea is the following: consider a protocol $P(M)$, which tries to transmit message M from one party (say A) to another one (say B). The authentication of the message M is checked by verifying if $P(M)$ is equivalent to a specification $P_{spec}(M)$ where M is always delivered correctly. In $P_{spec}(M)$ the receiver B always knows M and whatever happens on the communication channel, B will continue its execution exactly as it had received the correct message M. In other words, $P_{spec}(M)$ represents the situation where M is always received and no enemy is able to substitute it with a different message. If $P(M)$ is equivalent to $P_{spec}(M)$ then also $P(M)$ is clearly able to avoid any possible attack. The language used in [2, 1] is the spi-calculus. Moreover the may-testing equivalence (see [5]) is used in order to check that $P(M)$ is equivalent to $P_{spec}(M)$ with respect to any possible interaction with the (hostile) environment. The definition of authentication in the spi-caluclus is given as follows:

Definition 9. *P(M) guarantees authentication if and only if for all M we have that P(M) is may-testing equivalent to $P_{spec}(M)$*   ∎

It seems reasonable to rephrase this property in our model as follows:

Definition 10. *Let P(M) be a protocol where the parties communicates over the set C of channels. P(M) guarantees authentication iff for all M we have that $P(M) \in NDC$.*   ∎

NDC is the one defined in Section 4.1. In particular, $P(M) \in NDC$ requires that $P(M)$ composed with whatever enemy X is (trace) equivalent to $P(M) \backslash C$. Since C represents the set of channels over which the parties communicate, then $P(M) \backslash C$ corresponds to our secure specification $P_{spec}(M)$ where no enemy is able to modify the execution of the protocol. In the spi-calculus the system is checked against all the possible interactions with the (hostile) environment through the use of the may-testing equivalence. Here we do it explicitly through the quantification over X which is the base of the $GNDC$ schema.

Indeed, Definitions 9 and 10 are based on two quite different models. As a matter of fact, in the spi-calculus it is possible to send a channel as a message, thus giving the possibility of creating dynamically a new secure channel. However, we are quite confident that NDC, as defined in our model, is strong enough to detect the attacks shown in [2]. Note also that NDC can be statically characterized, thus permitting a simplification of the verification task. We are presently working on a formal comparison of these two definitions in the spi-calculus setting. It is worthwhile noticing that the knowledge of the enemy is handled differently in our model and in the spi-calculus. In CryptoSPA, we assume that the initial knowledge of the enemy is represented by ϕ_X. In the spi-calculus we find a complementary modeling of this since there is no specification of the initial knowledge on the enemy, and the restriction operator is exploited in order to guarantee that some information is kept secret from anyone other than the parties of the protocol. Indeed, the restriction operator of the spi-calculus can be seen as a generator of fresh names that cannot be guessed by any (whatever powerful!) enemy. Note that, given a protocol P in the spi-calculus, we can obtain ϕ_X by simply requiring that the restricted names in P are not in ϕ_X (in this sense we have a complementary modeling of knowledge).

4.6   Comparison

In this section we show one of the advantages in having a uniform treatment of security properties, namely the possibility of studying the relationships among them in a fairly simple way. First, we show that NDC may be seen as a sufficient condition for every property which is based on trace-preorder. This result is interesting since it relates NDC (first proposed for modeling information flow security) to properties which has been proposed for completely different purposes, e.g., authentication. The result holds for what we will call *good candidates* for a function α, i.e., processes E such that $E \backslash C \leq_{trace} \alpha(E)$. This condition is quite reasonable since we certainly want that at least the protocol under no attacks (i.e., $E \backslash C$) "satisfies" $\alpha(E)$.

Proposition 6. *Let $\alpha(E)$ be a function between processes and let E be a good candidate for α, i.e., $E \backslash C \leq_{trace} \alpha(E)$. Then, E is $GNDC^{E \backslash C}_{\approx_{trace}}$ implies that E is $GNDC^{\alpha(E)}_{\leq_{trace}}$.* ∎

Note that if a function α does not have good candidates then it represents an empty property (no process satisfies it). Note also that every process E is a good candidate for $GNDC^{E \backslash C}_{\approx_{trace}}$.

The result above shows that $GNDC^{E\backslash C}_{\approx_{trace}}$ is stronger that $GNDC^{\alpha_{Agree}(E)}_{\leq_{trace}}$ and $GNDC^{\alpha_{auth}(E)}_{\leq_{trace}}$ for their respective good candidates. This is quite intuitive since $GNDC^{E\backslash C}_{\approx_{trace}}$ basically requires that the protocol behaviour is completely preserved even under attacks. So if E satisfies a certain property under no attacks (i.e., it is a food candidate), then $GNDC^{E\backslash C}_{\approx_{trace}}$ will preserve such a property also under every possible attack.

In general, we observe that if $\lhd \subseteq \lhd'$ then $GNDC^{\alpha}_{\lhd} \subseteq GNDC^{\alpha}_{\lhd'}$, furthermore if for all $E \in \mathcal{E}$ we have $\alpha(E) \lhd \alpha'(E)$ then $GNDC^{\alpha}_{\lhd} \subseteq GNDC^{\alpha'}_{\lhd}$.

Indeed, both *Agreement* and *message-authentication* are based on traces and so the relations between them can be easily derived by comparing their relative α. Here, we give an example of comparison of such properties in the simple case of a single run between a sender A and a receiver B. Moreover we also assume that we have no variables to agree on. We consider $T = \{commit(B,A)\}$ and $R = \{running(A,B)\}$. It is easy to prove that, for all $E \in \mathcal{E}$:

$$\alpha_{agree}(E) \leq_{trace} \alpha_{auth\genfrac{}{}{0pt}{}{\{commit(B,A)\}}{\{running(A,B)\}}}(E).$$

We also give a simple example of how it is possible to exploit property comparisons in the verification of protocols. We consider a slight variant of example 1 where messages $running(A,B)$ and $commit(B,A)$ are suitably inserted.

$$A(m,k) \overset{\text{def}}{=} [\langle m,k\rangle \vdash_{enc} x]running(A,B).\bar{c}\,x$$
$$B(k) \overset{\text{def}}{=} c(y).[\langle y,k\rangle \vdash_{dec} z]commit(B,A)$$
$$P \overset{\text{def}}{=} A(m_A,k_{AB}) \parallel B(k_{AB})$$

It is easy to see that the composed system P is a good candidate for α_{agree}, and so also for α_{auth}, when we consider $C = \{c\}$. Moreover by using arguments similar to the ones of Example 3, we can prove that $P \in GNDC^{E\backslash C}_{\approx_{trace}}$. Thus by proposition 6 we get that $P \in GNDC^{\alpha_{agree}}_{\leq_{trace}}$ and $P \in GNDC^{\alpha_{auth}}_{\leq_{trace}}$, where $\alpha_{auth} = \alpha_{auth\genfrac{}{}{0pt}{}{\{commit(B,A)\}}{\{running(A,B)\}}}(E)$.

5 Conclusions

In this paper we have proposed a uniform method for defining computer security properties. In doing so, we have tried to exploit some underlying ideas of existing proposals rather than giving a completely new approach. Actually, we did not try to obtain a universal definition for all possible security properties; our aim was indeed to find a quite flexible and useful schema that could help in reasoning about different properties. Indeed, we have shown the flexibility of our proposal by rephrasing on it a number of existing definitions, some of which have completely different aims (e.g., Non-Interference, authentication and non-repudiation).

We think that a uniform schema for the definition of security properties could have several advantages. First, it allows to study the relationships among different security properties. For example, we have shown that NDC may be seen as the strongest property definable for a certain protocol since it requires that the action of any intruder does not modify in any way the observable behaviour of the protocol. Other formal relationships between security properties can be easily established by simply reasoning on α and $\vartriangleleft$. As a future work we will try to give a general taxonomy of security properties, which could extend and possibly integrate the one for information flow given in [9] and the one for authentication protocol properties studied in [15]. We are presently studying if also other security properties can be conveniently defined in our general framework.

By using a unique model and a unique schema it is possible to develop more general theories which could then be applied to a number of definitions by simply instantiating them. For example, we have shown that the static characterization result, which permits to check a property only against the most general intruder, can be easily applied to all the trace-semantics based properties. It would be interesting to extend some proof techniques for the analysis of authentication protocols (e.g., the ones developed in [14, 26, 7]), in order to deal with the GNDC schema. In this way they could also be applied for the analysis of other GNDC security properties.

Another interesting point is that the $GNDC$ schema itself suggests new analysis techniques. Indeed, the analysis of $GNDC$-like properties may be seen as example of *module checking*, i.e. model checking of systems which have to interact with arbitrary environments. Thus compositional analysis concepts exploited in [19] for the analysis of such problems may be recasted also for the analysis of security problems. This approach has been successfully followed in [17, 18] where an automated methodology for the analysis of GNDC like properties over protocols with a finite behaviour has been developed. This methodology does not require the specification of a particular intruder and may be thus adopted also when the hypothesis of proposition 1 does not hold.

Acknowledgements: We would like to thank Prof. Roberto Gorrieri for the interesting hints and discussions on the topic of this paper. Furthermore, we wish to thank the anonymous referees for their helpful comments and suggestions.

References

[1] M. Abadi and A. D. Gordon. Reasoning about cryptographic protocols in the spi calculus. In *Proceedings of CONCUR'97*, pages 59–73. LNCS 1243, 1997.

[2] M. Abadi and A. D. Gordon. A calculus for cryptographic protocols: The spi calculus. *Information and Computation*, 148(1):1–70, 1999.

[3] D. E. Bell and L. J. La Padula. Secure computer systems: Unified exposition and multics interpretation. *ESD-TR-75-306, MITRE MTR-2997*, March 1976.

[4] C. Bodei, P. Degano, R. Focardi, and C. Priami. Authentication via localized names. In *Proceedings of CSFW'99*, pages 98–110. IEEE press, 1999.

[5] R. De Nicola and M. Hennessy. Testing equivalences for processes. *Theoretical Computer Science*, 34:83–133, 1984.

[6] D. Dolev and A. Yao. On the security of public key protocols. *IEEE Transactions on Information Theory*, 29(2), 1983.

[7] A. Durante, R. Focardi, and R. Gorrieri. CVS: A compiler for the analysis of cryptographic protocols. In *Proceedings of CSFW'99*, pages 203–212. IEEE press, 1999.

[8] R. Focardi, A. Ghelli, and R. Gorrieri. Using non interference for the analysis of security protocols. In *Proceedings of DIMACS Workshop on Design and Formal Verification of Security Protocols*, 1997.

[9] R. Focardi and R. Gorrieri. A classification of security properties for process algebras. *Journal of Computer Security*, 3(1):5–33, 1994/1995.

[10] R. Focardi and R. Gorrieri. The compositional security checker: A tool for the verification of information flow security properties. *IEEE Transactions on Software Engineering*, 23(9):550–571, 1997.

[11] J. A. Goguen and J. Meseguer. Security policy and security models. In *Proc. of the 1982 Symposium on Security and Privacy*, pages 11–20. IEEE Press, 1982.

[12] C. A. R. Hoare. *Communicating Sequential Processes*. Prentice-Hall, 1985.

[13] R. Kemmerer, C. Meadows, and J. Millen. Three systems for cryptographic protocol analysis. *Journal of Cryptology*, 7(2):79–130, 1994.

[14] G. Lowe. Breaking and fixing the Needham-Schroeder public-key protocol using FDR. In *Proceedings of TACAS'96*, pages 146–166. LNCS 1055, 1996.

[15] G. Lowe. A hierarchy of authentication specification. In *Proceedings of the 10th Computer Security Foundation Workshop*, pages 31–43. IEEE press, 1997.

[16] W. Marrero, E. Clarke, and S. Jha. A model checker for authentication protocols. In *Proc. of DIMACS Workshop on Design and Formal Verification of Security Protocols*. Rutgers University, Sep. 1997.

[17] F. Martinelli. Languages for description and analysis of authentication protocols. In *Proceedings of ICTCS'98*, pages 304–315. World Scientific, 1998.

[18] F. Martinelli. Partial model checking and theorem proving for ensuring security properties. In *Proceedings of CSFW'98*, pages 44–52. IEEE press, 1998.

[19] F. Martinelli. *Formal Methods for the Analysis of Open Systems with Applications to Security Properties*. PhD thesis, University of Siena, Feb. 1999.

[20] R. Milner. *Communication and Concurrency*. Prentice-Hall, 1989.

[21] J. C. Mitchell, V. Shmatikov, and U. Stern. Finite-State Analysis of SSL 3.0. In *7th USENIX Security Symposium*, 1998.

[22] P. Y. A. Ryan and S. Schneider. Process algebra and non-interference. In *Proceedings of CSFW'99*, pages 214–227. IEEE press, 1999.

[23] A. W. Roscoe. *The Theory and Practice of Concurrency*. Prentice-Hall, 1997.

[24] S. Schneider. Security Properties and CSP. In *Proceedings of the 1996 Symposium on Security and Privacy*, pages 174–187. IEEE Press, 1996.

[25] S. Schneider. Formal analysis of a non-repudiation protocol. In *Proceedings of CSFW'98*, pages 54–65. IEEE Press, 1998.

[26] S. Schneider. Verifying authentication protocols in CSP. *IEEE Transactions on Software Engineering*, 24(9), September 1998.

[27] J. Zhou and D. Gollmann. A fair non-repudiation protocol. In *Proc. of Symposium in Research in Security and Privacy*, pages 55–61. IEEE Press, 1996.

[28] J. Zhou and D. Gollmann. Towards verification of non-repudiation protocols. In *International Refinement Workshop and Formal Methods Pacific*, 1998.

Group Principals and the Formalization of Anonymity

Paul F. Syverson[1]* and Stuart G. Stubblebine[2]**

[1] Center for High Assurance Computer Systems,
Naval Research Laboratory, Washington, DC 20375, USA,
syverson@itd.nrl.navy.mil
[2] CertCo, 55 Broad St. - Suite 22, New York, NY 10004, USA,
stubblebine@{cs.columbia.edu, CertCo.com}
http://www.cs.columbia.edu/~stu

Abstract. We introduce the concept of a group principal and present a number of different classes of group principals, including threshold-group-principals. These appear to naturally useful concepts for looking at security. We provide an associated epistemic language and logic and use it to reason about anonymity protocols and anonymity services, where protection properties are formulated from the intruder's knowledge of group principals. Using our language, we give an epistemic characterization of anonymity properties. We also present a specification of a simple anonymizing system using our theory.

1 Introduction

Though principals are typically viewed as atomic, there is no reason we cannot consider the knowledge and actions taken by a group. Hence, the basic notion of a group principal. This notion appears to be a useful concept for reasoning about various properties of electronic commerce and security protocols. One such principal is a threshold-group-principal. Such a principal allows us to express properties of threshold cryptosystems [13]. Although we do not pursue this in the present paper, we believe we can give a straightforward characterization not only of threshold cryptography including signatures and confidentiality, but also (once time is introduced into our language) such things as proactive security [5] and mobile adversaries [19]. Another group principal is the or-group principal. It is useful for characterising security properties relating to anonymity.

We demonstrate the applicability of our theory by examining the issue of anonymity and privacy. Studies have shown that privacy is a great concern for users of electronic commerce. Numerous protocols have emerged for protecting the anonymity of individuals. These protocols have been in the areas of protecting general Internet communications [23], commercial transactions [25], web based communications [21, 1], email [9, 18], and electronic cash [28]. However,

---

* Work by this author supported by ONR.
** Work by this author was also performed at AT&T Research.

J. Wing, J. Woodcock, J. Davies (Eds.): FM'99, Vol. I, LNCS 1708, pp. 814–833, 1999.
© Springer-Verlag Berlin Heidelberg 1999

little work has been done on formally representing or analyzing privacy in such protocols.

In this paper, we provide an epistemic language and logic and use it to reason about anonymity protocols and anonymity services. We also describe an associated model of computation. Using our language, we give an epistemic characterization of various anonymity properties. As far as we know, these basic properties have not been set out previously.

We develop the idea of looking at the environment as not a single entity for which all messages must pass, but one with individual components with different characteristics. In our model, the environment principal is no different from system principals. When you send a message you send it to an environment principal, likewise for receiving messages. All uncertainty in communication is represented in the environment principals; so, any sent message is immediately received, and all received messages have been sent by some principal. In this way, we are able specify environments particular to the threat model at hand.

We demonstrate our approach with a simple example. Typically, we have a single intruder which is a distributed group principal, composed of environment and/or (compromised) system principals. Each principal is specified by a knowledge program. Compromised principals run distinct programs from their reliable counterparts. It is also possible to have multiple intruders, each with their own separate goals, though we do not present any examples of this in this paper.

This paper does not address temporal features directly, other than to differentiate past and present (much as in [2]). Thus any timing attack on an anonymity system is beyond its scope. Temporal reasoning is expected to be added in future work, and there is no reason to expect difficulty in doing so. Indeed, the knowledge programs set out in this paper are derived from the knowledge-based programs of [11, 12], and those include temporal operators by default.

The seminal work setting out properties, goals, and mechanisms for anonymity in communication is that of Chaum (cf., e.g., [6, 7]). Our work is the first we are aware to give an epistemic characterization of anonymity properties. However, anonymity properties have been formally defined in CSP [22]. And, in [20] a formal notation was given for specifying anonymity protocols; however, that notation was not designed to specify anonymity properties or to be used in formal analysis. Also, others have defined interesting rigorous but informal notions of security properties [21].

The remainder of this paper is as follows. In Section 2 we present our model including the definitions of various types of group principals. In Section 3 we present the formal language. In Section 4 we present the logic. In Section 5 we present anonymity properties. In Section 6 we present our knowledge programs. In Section 7 we present a specification of the anonymizer protocol. In Section 8 we present our conclusions.

2   Model

Our system model is essentially built from and extends model elements described in [11] and elsewhere. We give a sketch of our model here.

2.1   Atomic Principals

There is a set of *atomic principals* $\{P_1, \ldots, P_n\}$. These are similar to the 'ordinary' principals that one associates with distributed computing. However, unlike others, we do not distinguish the environment in the model. Also, unlike others, the environment may be several (possibly disconnected) principals. Environment principals are made up of these atomic principals, just as system principals are.

2.2   Actions

Each principal can perform any one of a set of *actions* at each time. The actions that can be performed are $send(M, P_i, P_j)$, $receive(M, P_j, P_i)$, representing the sending of a message $M \in \mathcal{M}$ (the set of messages) from P_i to P_j and its receipt by P_j from P_i respectively. Principals may also perform internal operations, $int\_action(\{M_1, \ldots, M_n\}, P_i)$. This represents principal P_i performing some internal operation on the messages in the set $\{M_1, \ldots, M_n\}$, for example encryption, concatenation, decryption, etc. Principals may also do nothing at a given time. This is indicated by the performance of the null action Λ. Two particular internal actions, *record* and *purge*, will be discussed presently. We follow the example of [10] and subsequent work, that all messages are sent to the environment or received from the environment. We can thus make the simplifying assumption that all sent messages are received immediately. Any message loss, delay, modification, etc. can be represented by the actions of the environment. So, exactly one of P_i and P_j in any $send(M, P_i, P_j)$ or $receive(M, P_j, P_i)$ is always an environmental principal.

2.3   States

Each principal has a *local state*. Local states are assumed to be unique; although principals may not always be able to distinguish all of even their own local states. A state s_i local to principal P_i at time t is given by

$$s_i \triangleq \langle state\_id, history, log, facts, recent \rangle$$

The *history*, is the sequence of actions that have been performed locally. The *log*, is the sequence of local actions that have been logged. Similar to the local history, the local log is complete in having an entry for each time. But, since the log reflects the local time, entries are recorded as $\langle a, t \rangle$ where $t = localtime(t')$ is the time on the local clock when t' is the actual time, and t' is the actual time that a occurred. We assume that the real clock is fine enough to reflect the occurrence of all events in the system. Thus, an advance of the real clock need not imply an advance on all local clocks, but an advance on any local clock implies an advance on the real clock. Since principals may or may not keep track of local actions, and may even 'forget' them, the log may contain a null-log-entry $\perp$ for any time t. This is not the same as a null-action Λ, which may occur in both the local history and the local log and indicates that no action was performed at that time. We also keep track of any facts that may be known by a principal, such as the public key of a local server. These are collected in a set *facts*. In a principal's initial state all of the fields except *state_id* and *facts* should be empty sequences.

We keep track of actions and of facts by means of a *record* action. *record* is defined on *recent* $\cup$ *knowledge*. (The constitution of both *recent* and *knowledge* will be set out below.): For an action $a \in$ *recent*, *record*(a) has the effect of placing $\langle a, localtime(t_a) \rangle \rangle$ in the local log. For a known formula φ, *record*(φ) has the effect of placing φ in the set of facts *facts*. We also allow sets of recent actions and sets of known formulae in the domain of *record*. The way that *record* works for these sets should be obvious from the case for individual actions and known formulae. *purge* is similarly defined on entries in *log* and facts in *facts*. $purge(\{\langle a_{i_1}, t_{i_1} \rangle, \ldots, \langle a_{i_m}, t_{i_m} \rangle\})$ has the effect of removing those log entries from the log and replacing them with $\perp$. $purge(\{\varphi_1, \ldots, \varphi_m\})$ has the effect of removing those formulae from the set of recorded facts. The recent actions *recent*, are actions that were effectively performed recently and are remembered even though they have not been logged. *recent* is always a tail segment of *history* and never includes *record* or *purge* actions.

We will introduce composite (group) principals presently. Nonetheless, each *global state* is completely determined by a tuple of the local states of all atomic principals. A *run* is a sequence of global states indexed by (actual) times, where the any local state occurring in the global state at time t is such that the relevant principal is in that local state at (actual time) t.

2.4   Knowledge

In a given local state, knowledge is entirely determined by the log, the set of facts, and the recent actions. We include in the set of formulae, *knowledge*, the closure of what is known from those three sources. More precisely we have: (1) If an action is known to a principal because it is in the log or is recent, then the principal knows that he performed that action. So, for example, if $receive(M, P_i, P_j) \in$ *recent* or if $receive(M, P_i, P_j) \in log$ then M **received from** P_j $P_i \in$ *knowledge*. (2) If $\varphi \in$ *facts*, then $\varphi \in$ *knowledge*. (3) If φ can be derived from other members of *knowledge* by the axioms, then $\varphi \in$ *knowledge*. That P knows φ is represented in our language by $\Box_P \varphi$. The dual of $\Box_P$ is $\Diamond_P$. (There are certain generic axioms for adding to the knowledge of principals, e.g., $(\Box_P \varphi \land \Box_P (\varphi \supset \psi)) \supset \Box_P \psi$. So, if $\varphi, (\varphi \supset \psi) \in$ *knowledge*, then $\psi \in$ *knowledge*. Axioms for knowledge will be briefly discussed below in section 4.)

2.5   Group Principals

Ordinarily, we think of principals atomically. In particular, when evaluating protocols in the Dolev-Yao framework, we view all communication as going through a single environmental principal, typically identified as the intruder. For example, anything sent between principals A and B is assumed to be known to the intruder as is anything sent between principals C and D. However, the intruder between A and B may not be able to directly communicate with the intruder between C and D. They may only be able to communicate via 'honest' principals, e.g., one intruder can signal the other by causing an honest principal between them to send certain messages to the other. (Cf. [26] for more discussion of this model of computation in a hostile environment.) This naturally engenders a view of the environment as a distributed group principal. Similarly, sets of honest principals trying to solve some threshold computation (e.g., decryption or signature) may be thought of in this way. We will find it useful to have various types of *group principals* to model these and other circumstances.

There are four kinds of group principal, *collective-group* ($\star G$), *and-group* ($\&G$), *or-group* ($\oplus G$), and *threshold-group*($n - G$). Each type of group principal is distinguished by how the knowledge and actions of the principal is determined by the knowledge and actions of the members of that principal. The set of group principals $\mathcal{G}$ is defined as follows: for any nonempty set of atomic principals G, $\star G$, $\&G$, and $\oplus G$ are all groups (of the indicated type). And, $n - G$ is a (threshold) group provided that $n \leq |G|$.

collective group principal: Given any set of atomic principals G, $\star G$ is a distributed group viewed collectively. What the group knows is what is known by combining the knowledge of all the group members. (This is the concept of distributed knowledge in [11].) The group actions are those taken by the group collectively. For example, if something is sent or received by any member of the group then it is sent (received) by the group. However, it may also be the case that the group performs some action, e.g., elect a leader and possible successors, that is not performed by any one of the members. In this example, each member might vote for one leader, but the succession is determined by the total number of votes received, in diminishing order.

and-group principal: written $\&G$ for an and-group of members of G, is a distributed group viewed conjunctively. We also write $(P_1 \wedge \ldots \wedge P_n)$ for the and-group of principals P_1 through P_n. What the and-group knows is what every member of the group knows. (This is the concept of everyone knowledge in [11].) The group actions are those taken by each member of the group. Thus, $\&G$ said (received) messsage M if each member of G said (received) M.

or-group principal: written $\oplus G$ for an or-group of members of G, is a distributed group viewed disjunctively. We also write $(P_1 \vee \ldots \vee P_n)$ for the or-group of principals P_1 through P_n. What the or-group knows is what at least one member of the group knows. (This does not have a correlate in [11].) The group actions are those taken by at least one member of the group. Thus, $\oplus G$ said (received) messsage M if at least one member of G said (received) M.

threshold group principal: written $n - G$ for a given threshold n and group G. What the n-threshold group $n - G$ knows is anything known by any collective subgroup contained in G of cardinality at least n. (This does not have a correlate in [11].) Suppose two subgroups $G', G'' \subseteq G$ s.t. $|G'| \geq n$ and $|G''| \geq n$. Ordinarily, if $\Box_{G'} \varphi$ and $\Box_{G''} (\varphi \supset \psi)$, we cannot conclude anything more specific than that $\Box_{\star(G' \cup G'')} \psi$. But, if G is an n-threshold group, then it follows that $\Box_{n-G} \psi$. Thus, it follows that $\Box_{G'} \psi$ (and $\Box_{G'} (\varphi \supset \psi)$) and $\Box_{G''} \psi$ (and $\Box_{G''} \varphi$). Another way to characterize an n-threshold group is as an or-group of collective groups, each with cardinality of at least n. Thus if $G' = \{G_1, \ldots, G_m\}$ is the set of all collective subgroups of G s.t. $|G_i| \geq n$, then

$$n - G \triangleq \oplus G' \text{ (which is } (G_1 \vee \ldots \vee G_m))$$

What the n-threshold group $n - G$ does is what is done by any subgroup contained in G of cardinality at least n. Thus, $n - G$ said (received) anything said (received) by any subgroup of cardinality at least n.

3   Formal Language

Let A and B be principals, M be a message, and φ be a formula. We assume without explanation the usual logical connectives and formula building using them. Any formula is also a message, though not vice versa.

Actions. There are send and receive actions. We can record and purge both send and receive actions.

```
send(M, A, B)
receive(M, B, A)
```

Also, if s-r-action is a send or receive action, then we also have the purging and recording of send and receive actions.

```
purge(s-r-action)
record(s-r-action)
```

We will find it useful to have the following macro (eliminable definition):

$$\text{action}(X, A, B, \text{remember});$$

is a macro for

$$\text{action}(X, A, B); \text{record}(\text{action}(X, A, B)) ;$$

Said and Received Formula. These are formulae expressing the sending and receiving of messages, as well as of any formulae implicit in the sending or receiving of such messages.

> A **said** M
> A **received** M
> A **said to** B M
> B **received from** A M

That a formula represents the whole message sent or received is denoted by the use of quotation marks. These refer not to the bit string, but to the parsing of that string without any encryption, decryption, deconcatenation, etc[1]. So, for example, were A to send the message $\{M\}_K$ (where A knew K), then A **said** "$\{M\}_K$" and A **said** M would be true, but A **said** "M" would not.

Message Extensions. Message fields may have an origin and destination. We express this using either "to" or "from" or using both extensions.

> (X **from** A **to** B)

We can further qualify certain features of a message that are common to anonymity protocols. These features include an indication of the ultimate destination of a message using "for".

> (X **for** B)

Another feature common to anonymity protocols is referencing a prior message. This is common for query-response (request-response) protocols.

> R **in response to** Q

Encryptions and Key Possession. Messages may also be encrypted. The encryption of M with K and A's possession of K^{-1} are expressed as follows.

> $\{M\}_K$
> A **has** K^{-1}

Runs Formula. A principal running a knowledge program is expressed.

> A **runs** `program_name`

Knowledge. If φ is a formula in the language, and A a principal, we can express that A knows φ and that A knows possibly φ, by the following formulae respectively.

> $\Box_A\,\varphi$
> $\Diamond_A\,\varphi$

---

[1] In particular, this is not meant to be an opaque context. Thus, values may be substituted for variable names.

Did Formula. The following allow us to express any action done by a principal, as a formula. For example, suppose A, performed some action `action`. This is expressed by the following. (It might be possible to replace the following two types of formulae with one type and an appropriate temporal operator. However, we choose to keep the number of modal operator types that we use to a minimum for the present.)

A **did** (`action`)

If the action is being done now (i.e, *recently* according to our model), we can express this as:

A **does** (`action`)

4   Logic

We set out here our axioms and rules. Those for knowledge and propositional reasoning are standard. For background consult [11, 8, 16].

Propositional and Epistemic Logic. Knowledge is characterized by the **S5** axioms. Our only rules are modus ponens and necessitation (knowledge generalization):

Modus Ponens: From φ and $\varphi \supset \psi$ infer ψ.

Knowledge Generalization: From $\vdash \varphi$ infer $\vdash \Box_P \varphi$.

It is important to recall that knowledge generalization does not allow us to infer that P knows φ for arbitrary formulae φ. Rather, if φ is a theorem (i.e., derivable from axioms alone with no assumptions) then $\Box_P \varphi$ is also a theorem. In other words, all principals are expected to know all logical truths. Now for the axioms.

Ax1. All tautologies of propositional logic are axioms.

As mentioned before, $\Box_P$ and $\Diamond_P$ are duals. This means that these are interchangeable according to the definition: $\Box_P \varphi \leftrightarrow \neg \Diamond_P \neg \varphi$ (for any formula φ). Given formulae φ and ψ the knowledge axioms are as follows. (N.B. These axioms, together with the above rules and axiom, constitute **S5**, the most standard and well understood knowledge logic for distributed computing. The axioms may not all be ultimately necessary for intended applications. However, we begin with **S5** and leave the possible elimination of unnecessary axioms for future work.)

Ax2. Distribution Axiom, **K**: $\Box_P (\varphi \supset \psi) \supset (\Box_P \varphi \supset \Box_P \psi)$
Ax3. Truth Axiom, **T**: $\Box_P \varphi \supset \varphi$
Ax4. Positive Introspection Axiom, **4**: $\Box_P \varphi \supset \Box_P \Box_P \varphi$
Ax5. Negative Introspection Axiom **5**: $\neg \Box_P \varphi \supset \Box_P \neg \Box_P$

Simplifying Said and Received Formulae. These formulae may be simplified in the obvious ways. We do not list all of these, but simply give representative examples:

Ax6. *A* **said to** *B* *M* $\supset$ *A* **said** *M*
Ax7. *B* **received from** *A* *M* $\supset$ *B* **received** *M*
Ax8. *A* **said to** *B* $(M_1, \ldots, M_n)$ $\supset$ *A* **said to** *B* M_i (where $i \in \{1, \ldots, n\}$)

Assume K is an encryption key and K^{-1} the corresponding decryption key (in the symmetric case $K = K^{-1}$).

Ax9. $(A$ **said** $\{M\}_K \wedge A$ **has** $K^{-1}) \supset A$ **said** M
Ax10. $(B$ **received** $\{M\}_K \wedge B$ **has** $K^{-1}) \supset B$ **received** M

Note that we do *not* have any axioms reflecting authentication principles, as in [2] or its successors.

Message extensions may be removed in said and received formulae. Let *extensions*(φ) be the set of all messages that are extensions of φ. Then, for any $\psi \in$ *extensions*(φ) we have the following axioms:

Ax11. *A* **said** $\psi \supset A$ **said** φ
Ax12. *B* **received** $\psi \supset B$ **received** φ

Thus, for example, the following is a theorem of our logic:

A **said** "$(X$ **for** $C)$ **from** A **to** B" $\supset$
$(A$ **said** X **from** $A \wedge A$ **said** $(X$ **for** $C)$ **to** $B \wedge A$ **said** $X)$

Sending and Receiving. Message delivery is guaranteed. Sending corresponds to saying exactly, and likewise for receiving.

Ax13. *A* **did** (send(M, A, B)) $\leftrightarrow$ *B* **did** (receive(M, B, A))
Ax14. *A* **did** (send(M, A, B)) $\leftrightarrow$ *A* **said to** *B* "M "
Ax15. *B* **did** (receive(M, B, A)) $\leftrightarrow$ *B* **received from** *A* "M"

Record Implies Did. This axiom expresses that an entity recording and action implies that it performed the action.

Ax16. *A* **did** (record(s-r-action)) $\supset$ *A* **did** (s-r-action)

Doing and Knowing What Was Done. These axioms express the conditions under which a principal knows what it has done as well as the relation between **does** and **did**.

Ax17. *A* **did** (s-r-action, remember) $\wedge \neg A$ **did** (purge(s-r-action)) $\supset$
    $\Box_A$ *A* **did** (s-r-action)
Ax18. *A* **does** (s-r-action) $\supset \Box_A$ *A* **does** (s-r-action)
Ax19. *A* **does** (s-r-action) $\supset$ *A* **did** (s-r-action)

Group Axioms. These axioms relate to formulae involving group principals. We mention here only the basic ones that will be useful in the rest of the paper. Let $G = \{P_1, \ldots, P_n\}$. And, let $\varphi(G)$ be a formula with one or more (free) occurrences of G and $\varphi(P/G)$ be the formula that results from replacing every (free) occcurrence of G in φ with P.

Ax20. $\varphi(\&G) \leftrightarrow (\varphi(P_1/G) \wedge \ldots \wedge \varphi(P_n/G))$
Ax21. $\varphi(\oplus G) \leftrightarrow (\varphi(P_1/G) \vee \ldots \vee \varphi(P_n/G))$

5 Anonymity Properties

The goal of any system or protocol we will be examining is to provide some type of anonymity, that is to hide some fact about a principal or set of principals from some adversary. This can be broken into two parts. The piece of information to be protected and the nature of that protection. In this section, we will set out a characterization of both pieces.

5.1 Condenda (i.e., Things to Be Hidden)

We might want to hide that a principal is the originator of a message or that some pair of principals are the originator and intended recipient, respectively, of a message, etc. For profile security, we may wish to hide that two messages originating from the same principal in fact originated at that principal or more strongly that they originated at any one principal.

5.2 Condens (i.e., Types of Hiding)

The various facts just described that are to be hidden from view may be hidden to varying degrees. We will now set out the various types of anonymity that can be achieved with respect to each of these. The principal from whom they are to be hidden is always the intruder, I. The exact nature of the intruder will vary from context to context; it may include insiders and/or outsiders to the system running active or merely passive attacks. No matter how the intruder is implemented, we are always able represent the types of anonymity with respect to an abstract intruder, I. This allows for a succinct statement of properties; however, since the following are not stated with respect to a particular principal, technically they are formula schemata rather than formulae. In practice we always specify a particular principal for the condens. In the future, we might allow actual principal variables, but we do not attempt such here. Similarly, we might consider existential quantification over principals, e.g., to reflect the hiding of arbitrary profiles, whether or not they are associated with any given principal (more generally, n-tuple of principals).

We first set out some assumptions. Our main assumption is that all condenda are of the form $\varphi(P)$. In other words, they are single formulae in which a single principal name occurs (freely). Our restriction to single principals is just for simplicity and uniformity of presentation. The generalization from hiding P **said** X to hiding P **said to** Q X is straightforward. Our restriction to single formulae is minimal. For example, if we wish to hide profiling information about P, e.g., that several facts about P are associated, this is generally expressible in a single formula, such as $\varphi(P) \supset \psi(P)$. We do not attempt to represent the hiding of arbitrary formulae of the language that do not involve principal names at all. It is unclear what role these would play in anonymity protection. However, we may explore this possibility in the future should need arise. Our next major assumption is that condenda are true of only one principal. Thus, for any formula $\varphi(P)$ for which we are considering the anonymity provided by a system or protocol, we assume

$$\Box_I \, (\varphi(P) \wedge \varphi(Q) \supset P = Q)$$

We also assume that any condendum is actually true. That is, we are not worried about trying to prevent the conclusion or even suspicion that P **said** X in the case when P did not say X.

Unknown

   $\neg(\Diamond_I \, \varphi(P))$

   In our current logic and language, this is basically impossible. It is logically equivalent to $\Box_I \, \neg\varphi(P)$. Thus, by axiom Ax3, this cannot be true if $\varphi(P)$ is true (which we assume). Therefore, everyone is always a suspect. The only possibility for a principal to be unknown would be if we partitioned the set of principal names so that some were meaningless to the intruder. We do not consider such an extension in this paper.

$(\geq n)$-anonymizable

   $\Diamond_I \, \varphi(P) \supset (\Diamond_I \, \varphi(P_1) \wedge \ldots \wedge \Diamond_I \, \varphi(P_{n-1}))$

   We assume here and in the following definitions that distinct names denote distinct principals. This says that if P is a suspect wrt φ then there are $n-1$ other principals (and possibly more) who are also suspects. If there are precisely $n-1$ other principals such that $\Diamond_I \, \varphi(P_i)$ when $\Diamond_I \, \varphi(P)$, we have the more exact property of being n-anonymizable. Similarly for the properties below.

Possible Anonymity

   $\Diamond_I \, \varphi(P) \wedge \Diamond_I \, \neg\varphi(P)$

   The intruder cannot rule out $\varphi(P)$ but cannot rule out $\neg\varphi(P)$. Basically, he has no knowledge about this condendum.

$(\leq n)$-suspected

   $\Box_I \, (\varphi(P) \vee \varphi(P_1) \vee \ldots \vee \varphi(P_{n-1}))$

   The intruder has narrowed things down to no more than n suspects, one of which is P.

$(\geq n)$-anonymous

   $\Diamond_I \, \varphi(P) \wedge \Diamond_I \, \varphi(P_1) \wedge \ldots \wedge \Diamond_I \, \varphi(P_{n-1})$

   The intruder has narrowed things down to no fewer than n suspects, one of which is P.

($\leq m$)-suspected implies ($\geq n$)-anonymous

$\Box_I \, (\varphi(P) \vee \varphi(P_1) \vee \ldots \vee \varphi(P_{m-1})) \supset (\Diamond_I \, \varphi(P) \wedge \Diamond_I \, \varphi(P_1) \wedge \ldots \wedge \Diamond_I \, \varphi(P_{n-1}))$

Here $n \leq m$. The idea is that even if the intruder has narrowed things down to m or fewer suspects, he cannot narrow down who is φ to fewer than n. In the case where $n = m$, proving this property is like saying "OK, let's assume for the sake of argument that the intruder has narrowed it down to m suspects. By this property, he cannot do any better than that." This is stronger than a simple bound on intruder knowledge: it is a bound even when we assume a given degree of knowledge for the intruder.

Exposed

$\Box_I \, \varphi(P)$

We say a formula is exposed if the intruder knows the truth of the formula, i.e., he knows exactly who it is that φ.

5.3   Other Characterizations of Anonymity

Ours is by no means the first attempt to characterize anonymity. Reiter and Rubin present a range of "degrees of anonymity" in [21] from "absolute privacy" to "provably exposed". There are two important differences between their approach and ours. First, their definitions are not given in a formal language and are not designed to have a formal specification or analysis. Second, their approach is probabilistic while ours is possibilistic. We will return to this point presently.

A formal characterization of anonymity has been given in terms of CSP in [22]. The basic idea there is to describe a system by means of a process P and a renaming function f and to consider a system anonymous if mapping the process to the image of f and back yields the same process. Space precludes a clear setting out of their characterization. Put no doubt too succinctly, with respect to our characterization above, the parameters allow one to vary the principal P and the formula φ and perhaps the intruder doing the observation. Thus, one can capture many different condenda and different intruders. However, it appears that there is only one condens that they consider. On the other hand, they have the advantage of expressing things entirely in terms of CSP, which is a well understood formalism. The logic in this paper is meant as an alternative, not a replacement for the CSP approach. As different people have different tastes regarding the approach with which they are comfortable, it is good to have alternatives. One approach seems to have a more succinct and intuitive expression of properties while the other has an existing framework and analysis tool. In any case, they are not necessarily mutually exclusive. It is conceivable that one could have a process algebra semantics for a logic such as in this paper. We might thereby take a step towards combining the advantages of theorem provers and model checker, such as in the NRL Protocol Analyzer.

Like Schneider and Sidiropoulos, our characterizations of anonymity are possibilistic rather than probabilistic. And, like them we would hope to bring in probabilistic language at some point. However, there is reason to think that most of the contributions will occur on the possibilistic front.

First, it is often difficult to assign probabilities. In our case this is both because we are concerned with the nonprobabilistic behaviour of users at the system interface and because any assignment of probabilities based on expected behavior may be altered by an active intruder. Assigning probabilities can also be misleading if not done correctly. For example, if 99 out of 100 remailers only forward messages from one client to a second remailer, we might be tempted to think that messages coming through the second remailer have a 99 percent chance of being from that client. But, a moments reflection will show this to be incorrect. Second, even when probabilities can be assigned, adding probabilistic expressiveness to a formal language usually greatly adds to the complexity of specification and analysis.

Both of these points are well illustrated in the information flow security literature. The basic concept of noninterference as introduced in [15] is possibilistic, and most of the analysis, system design, and development of related properties that has gone on since then has been of a possibilistic nature. In fact, the only substantial systems built to date that have been been designed to be noninterfering in any sense have taken a possibilistic approach. Nonetheless, it is possible to give a probabilistic characterization of noninterference [4, 17]. And,a system satisfying these probabilistic properties is clearly more secure. Nonetheless, virtually no significant design or analysis has been done in this area, no doubt due to the complexity. (Some recent encouraging advances have been made by Volpano and Smith [27].) This state of affairs has been mirrored on the formal level as well. There have been possibilistic characterizations of many possibilistic noninterference properties in a variety of formalisms, including notably epistemic logic [3, 14]. And, there have even been some epistemic characterizations of probabilistic noninterference [24]. But, again, most of the development as well as discussion of more complex systems has been in terms of possibilistic properties. Our expectation is that the situation is likely to be analogous when formally analyzing anonymity. Probabilistic characterizations may still be applied to substantial systems, for example *Crowds*, but it is unclear if these will prove both general and amenable to formal specification or analysis.

6   Knowledge Programs

Systems and environments that we discuss will be specified via *knowledge programs* following the approach of Fagin et al. [11, 12]. All our knowledge programs have the following form:

case of
    if [*knowledge test #1*]
      do [*action #1*]
    if [*knowledge test #2*]
      do [*action #2*]
    ⋮
end case

Knowledge tests are conjunctions of formulae where each conjunct is preceded by $\Box_P$ or $\neg\Box_P$ for some principal P. Actions are performed by the principal running the program. Each action given in the consequent of a clause may be a series of actions to be performed by the principal. The knowledge test and action given in any one clause are considered atomic. At any one time, at most one clause of the program will fire. Also, in a properly specified knowledge program, knowledge tests should be mutually exclusive. Thus, at any one time, only one clause of a properly specified program can fire. In the execution of a knowledge program, recent actions, defined in the model in section 2, are ones taken during the execution of the current clause.[2]

As noted above in section 2, the system environment can be viewed as a group principal made up of many smaller environments. We will now examine this point in more detail. Our reasons are at least twofold: (1) The environment programs we will set out presently are very simple. Thus, they serve as an accessible introduction to knowledge programs. (2) The environment programs we will set out are generic and will be used to describe the environment for subsequently presented examples.

6.1   Generic Environment Programs

The following programs describe environments between the various principals. Recall that we assume message delivery is guaranteed; all uncertainty, delay, etc. is reflected in the behavior of the environment. Note also that the clauses for environment principals are often simpler than for system principals. This is because the environments we set out here are not doing anything based on message content other than the **to** or **from** fields; they simply forward any message they receive or block it, possibly recording the events. More sophisticated environments, e.g., doing selective forwarding based on message content or timing, are possible. We will not describe them here.

We typically assume a single environment between any two system principals. This we call a *pairwise*[3] environment. In some sense, the communication graph for the system is fully connected, but with an environment principal between any two system principals (much as in [26], although our environments need not be hostile). However, in practice many of these environment principals will

---

[2] Unlike the "knowledge-based programs" of [11, 12], our knowledge programs do not have "standard tests" (those not involving epistemic operators) because we have yet to see a need for these tests in any of the examples we have looked at; although, there is no reason they could not be added in if needed. There are also more important differences. We have placed all uncertainty in the principals (including explicitly represented environment principals). Thus, e.g., all sent messages are received, and all received messages were sent by someone, albeit possibly an environment principal.

[3] It is might seem natural to call these 'atomic environments'. However, a complex environment that, e.g., forwards messages between two principals based on the traffic it sees between two others could not be reduced to such atomic principals. Hence, this would be a misnomer. Detailed discussion of such environments is beyond the scope of this paper.

simply block any transmission they receive. And, we will not bother to specify these in cases where there is obviously no direct communication between the two principals or we do not care if there is (and so can assume that there is not). Also, we are often more interested in an environment principal that is a distributed group of the pairwise environment principals just mentioned, for example, when we consider several distinct clients sending queries through the Anonymizer. We now give some examples of basic environments, from which more complex environments can be built.

A reliable environment between principals is one that simply passes any messages sent between them without any alteration, delay, recording, etc.

Reliable_Environment_Program :
   if $[\Box_E\ E$ **received from** P_i "M **to** P_j" $\land\ \neg\Box_E\ E$ **said to** P_j "M **to** P_j "]
     do [send(M to P_j, E, P_j)]

A remembering environment between principals is just like the reliable environment except that it keeps track of all messages it passes.

Remembering_Environment_Program :
   if $[\Box_E\ E$ **received from** P_i "M **to** P_j" $\land\ \neg\Box_E\ E$ **said to** P_j "M **to** P_j "]
     do [record(receive(M to P_j, E, P_i)) ;
          send(M **to** P_j, E, P_j, remember)]

A simple blocking environment is one that simply blocks (drops) all messages that pass through it. It thus does no action, i.e., Λ. But, to explicitly contrast it with the next environment, we give it the following redundant description.

Simple_Blocking_Environment_Program :
   if $[\Box_E\ E$ **received from** P_i "M **to** P_j" $\land\ \neg\Box_E\ E$ **said to** P_j "M **to** P_j "]
     do $[\Lambda]$

A remembering blocking environment is one that blocks (drops) all messages that pass through it, but records the message receptions.

Remembering_Blocking_Environment_Program :
   if $[\Box_E\ E$ **received from** P_i "M **to** P_j" $\land\ \neg\Box_E\ E$ **said to** P_j "M **to** P_j "]
     do [record(receive(M to P_j, E, P_i))]

An environment may forward only messages sent from or to a selected principal (possibly a group principal). By selecting which traffic it forwards, the environment may reveal traffic information to other parts of the intruder elsewhere, e.g., in a system employing chained remailers or other forwarding mechanisms. A pairwise environment that selects based on sender or receiver would be trivial. It would simply block (or forward) all messages in one direction and block or forward all messages in the other direction. This is thus the first presented example of an environment that will typically only be used to describe an environment that is a group principal. We set out an example of an environment that selectively forwards only messages from a particular principal, P_0. The program itself is virtually identical to that of the remembering environment, except that it only forwards if the sending principal is the particular principal specified.

Sender_Selecting_Environment_Program(P_0) :
 if $[\Box_E$ (E **received from** P_i "M **to** P_j" $\wedge$ $P_i = P_0$) $\wedge$
  $\neg\Box_E$ E **said to** P_j "M **to** P_j "]
 do $[\text{record}(\text{receive}(M \text{ to } P_j, E, P_i))$;
  $\text{send}(M \text{ to } P_j, E, P_j, \text{remember})$]

Despite the fact that some environments are not reducible to pairwise environments, pairwise environments will serve as basic building blocks in many cases. We therefore find it useful to refer to them succinctly. Let '$E_{P_i P_j}$' denote the environment between system principals P_i and P_j. Thus, $E_{P_i P_j}$ **runs** *Program* means that messages between P_i and P_j are delivered according to Program. Note also that this is meant to cover messages in both directions. Thus, we assume $E_{P_j P_i} = E_{P_i P_j}$.

6.2 Theorems for Environment Programs

In the course of our analysis, we will have to assess what various principals have or have not done and what they know or don't know. This information comes primarily from the program specifications, the assumptions about who is running what program, and what initial messages are sent and facts known. A main way we are able to formally derive things based on the knowledge programs is by means of program theorems. These have the general form:

$$(P \text{ runs } Program \wedge precondition) \supset postcondition$$

However, for the purposes of the analysis we do in this paper, we can more specifically assume that the only way for the postcondition to obtain is for the principal to run the program and the precondition to hold. This allows us to strengthen the form to:

$$(P \text{ runs } Program \wedge precondition) \leftrightarrow postcondition$$

We present examples of these program theorems below. They can be generated automatically from the corresponding knowledge programs. This will ultimately be useful for automated analysis. For now we must be content to set them out by hand.

A1. (E **runs** Reliable_Environment_Program $\wedge$
 E **did** ($\text{receive}(M \text{ to } P_j, E, P_i)$)) $\leftrightarrow$ E **did** ($\text{send}(M \text{ to } P_j, E, P_j)$)
A2. (E **runs** Remembering_Environment_Program $\wedge$
 E **did** ($\text{receive}(M \text{ to } P_j, E, P_i)$)) $\leftrightarrow$
 $\text{record}(\text{receive}(M \text{ to } P_j, E, P_i)$) ; $\text{send}(M \text{ to } P_j, E, P_j, \text{remember})$
A3. (E **runs** Simple_Blocking_Environment_Program $\wedge$
 E **did** ($\text{receive}(M \text{ to } P_j, E, P_i)$)) $\leftrightarrow$ E **did** (Λ)

A4. (E **runs** Remembering_Blocking_Environment_Program $\wedge$
    E **did** (receive(M **to** P_j, E, P_i))) $\leftrightarrow$
    E **did** (record(receive(M **to** P_j, E, P_i)))
A5. (E **runs** Sender_Selecting_Environment_Program $\wedge$
    receive(M **to** P_j, E, P_i) **did** ($\wedge$)$P_i = P_0$) $\leftrightarrow$
    E **did** (record(receive(M **to** P_j, E, P_i))) ;
    send(M **to** P_j, E, P_j, remember))

7   Anonymizer Example

Space precludes presenting more than the knowledge programs for our example.
We here describe the standard analysis procedure to be followed if space permitted. We would begin by setting out the knowledge programs that characterize
the system principals when operating properly (uncompromised). We would then
proceed to the analysis. This consists of (1) setting out the condenda, (2) giving the contexts, i.e., setting out the specific system and environment principals
and the programs they are running, and specifying the intruder (here is where
we would specify compromised principals if necessary), (3) giving the program
theorems (relating pre- and postconditions to the programs being run), and (4)
assessing the anonymity protections afforded by the given programs under the
given conditions.

7.1   Anonymizer Knowledge Programs

The Anonymizer [1] is a Web proxy service that receives queries submitted by
a client, strips off any identifying information, and forwards the query to the
relevant server. When replies are received from the server, it forwards these back
to the client. We will now give knowledge programs that specify an anonymizer,
a client, and a server. For our purposes, we assume multiple clients and possibly
multiple anonymizers; however, it is only necessary to assume one server.

Variables for principal names should be fairly intuitive. We assume that there
is one environment $E_{\oplus CA_j}$ between an anonymizer A_j and the set of clients C,
that use it and one environment $E_{A_j S}$ between an anonymizer A_j and a server
S. The variable Q represents a query and R represents a response to a query.
We also assume that communication between a client C_i and the corresponding
user U_i occurs without any intervening environment. For contexts where this is
not true, it should be clear how to add in the relevant environment principal.
Client_Program$_{C_i}$:
case of
    if [$\square_{C_i}$ C_i **received** "(Q **for** S) **from** U_i" $\wedge$
        $\neg\square_{C_i}$ C_i **said to** $E_{\oplus CA_j}$ "(Q **for** S) **from** C_i **to** A_j "]
    do [send((Q **for** S) **from** C_i **to** A_j, C_i, $E_{\oplus CA_j}$, remember)]
    if [$\square_{C_i}$ (C_i **received from** $E_{\oplus CA_j}$ "R **in response to** Q **from** A_j" $\wedge$
        C_i **said to** $E_{\oplus CA_j}$ "(Q **for** S) **from** C_i **to** A_j ") $\wedge$
        $\neg\square_{C_i}$ C_i **said to** U_i "R **in response to** Q **from** S "]

do [send(R in response to Q from S, C_i, U_i) ;
    purge(send((Q for S) from C_i to A_j, C_i, $E_{\oplus CA_j}$))]
end case

Anonymizer_Program$_{A_j}$:
case of
  if [$\Box_{A_j}$ A_j received from $E_{\oplus CA_j}$ "(Q for S) from C_i to A_j" $\wedge$
     $\neg\Box_{A_j}$ A_j said to $E_{A_j S}$ "Q from A_j to S "]
  do [send(Q from A_j to S, A_j, $E_{A_j S}$, remember) ;
    purge(receive((Q for S) from C_i to A_j, A_j, $E_{\oplus CA_j}$)) ;
      record(receive((Q for S) from C_i to A_j, A_j, $E_{\oplus CA_j}$))]
  if [$\Box_{A_j}$ (A_j received from $E_{A_j S}$ "R in response to Q from S" $\wedge$
    A_j received from $E_{\oplus CA_j}$ "(Q for S) from C_i to A_j") $\wedge$
  $\neg\Box_{A_j}$ A_j said to $E_{\oplus CA_j}$ "(R in response to Q from S) from A_j to C_i "]
  do [send((R in response to Q from S) from A_j to C_i, A_j, $E_{A_j C_i}$) ;
      purge(receive((Q for S) from C_i to A_j, A_j, $E_{A_j C_i}$)) ;
purge(send(Q from A_j to S, A_j, $E_{A_j S}$))]
end case

Server_Program$_S$:
case of
  if [$\Box_S$ S received from $E_{A_j S}$ "Q from A_j to S" $\wedge$
    $\neg\Box_S$ S said to $E_{A_j S}$ "R in response to Q from S to A_j "]
  do [send(R in response to Q from S to A_j, S, $E_{A_j S}$) ;
    record(receive(Q from A_j to S, S, $E_{A_j S}$))]
end case
The above assumes the server logs queries (but not responses).

7.2 Anonymizer Condenda

As noted above, we have no space to set out our analysis. Nonetheless, we at least state the condenda that the Anonymizer is expected to hide. The following are examples of formulae that should be hidden from the intruder. The operating environment and the nature of the intruder will be set out below, in addition to demonstrations of the level of condendum hiding afforded against specified intruders in specified environments.

G1 C_i said (Q for S)
G2 C_i received R in response to Q from S
G3 C_i received R in response to Q
G4 S said R in response to Q $\supset$ C_i said Q

8   Conclusion

We have introduced the basic notion of a group principal and an associated model, language, and logic. We have demonstrated the utility of these by defining anonymity properties and specifying an anonymity protocol. Space limitations preclude presenting the analysis of that protocol with respect to anonymity.

Even if we had space to set it out, the assessment by hand of anonymity in the example we have specified is tedious and complex. In fact it would be infeasible to provide the quantitative by-hand assessments of anonymity we envision for complex systems involving many principals. However, with the theory established in this paper, we have a starting point for investigating suitable automated analysis techniques such as incorporating the use of model checkers.

Another direction for future work is the analysis of other types of security properties using our characterization of group principals. In particular, we believe we can ultimately give a characterization of such things as threshold cryptography and proactive security.

Acknowledgements: We thank Cathy Meadows and the anonymous referees for helpful comments and suggestions.

References

[1] The Anonymizer. http://www.anonymizer.com

[2] Michael Burrows, Martín Abadi, and Roger Needham. *A Logic of Authentication*, Research Report 39, Digital Systems Research Center, February 1989.

[3] P. Bieber and F. Cuppens. A logical view of secure dependencies. *Journal of Computer Security*, 1(1):99–129, 1992.

[4] Randy Browne. *Stochastic Non-Interference: Temporal Stochastic Processes Without Covert Channels*. Odyssey Research Associates, Ithaca, NY, November 1989. unpublished manuscript.

[5] R. Canetti, R. Gennaro, A. Herzberg, and D. Naor. "Proactive Security: Long-term Protection Against Break-ins", *CryptoBytes*, vol. 3, no. 1, Spring 1997, pp. 1–ff. (Available at http://www.rsa.com/rsalabs/pubs/cryptobytes/)

[6] D. Chaum. "Untraceable Electronic Mail, Return Addresses, and Digital Pseudonyms", *Communications of the ACM*, v. 24, n. 2, Feb. 1981, pp. 84-88.

[7] D. Chaum, "Security without Identification: Transaction Systems to Make Big Brother Obsolete", *CACM* (28,10), October 1985, pp. 1030–1044.

[8] Brian F. Chellas. *Modal Logic: An Introduction,* Cambridge University Press, Cambridge, 1980.

[9] L. Cottrell. *Mixmaster and Remailer Attacks,*
http://obscura.obscura.com/~loki/remailer/remailer-essay.html

[10] D. Dolev and A. Yao, "On the Security of Public Key Protocols", *IEEE Transactions on Information Theory*, 29(2): 198–208, March 1983.

[11] R. Fagin, J. Halpern, Y. Moses, and M. Vardi, *Reasoning About Knowledge*, The MIT Press, 1995.

[12] Ronald Fagin, Joseph Y. Halpern, Yoram Moses, and Moshe Y. Vardi, "Knowledge-Based Programs", *Distributed Computing* 10(4): 199–225, 1997.

[13] P. Gemmell. "An Introduction to Threshold Cryptography", *CryptoBytes*, vol. 2, no. 3, Winter 1997, pp. 7–12. (Available at
http://www.rsa.com/rsalabs/pubs/cryptobytes/)

[14] Janice Glasgow, Glenn MacEwen, and Prakash Panangaden. A logic for reasoning about security. *ACM Transactions on Computer Systems*, 10(3):226–264, August 1992.

[15] J. A. Goguen and J. Meseguer. Security policies and security models. In *Proceedings of the 1982 IEEE Computer Society Symposium on Security and Privacy*, Oakland, CA, 1982.

[16] Robert Goldblatt. *Logics of Time and Computation, 2nd edition*, volume 7 of *CSLI Lecture Notes*, CSLI Publications, Stanford, 1992.

[17] James W. Gray, III. Toward a mathematical foundation for information flow security. *Journal of Computer Security*, 1(3):255–294, 1992. A preliminary version appears in Proc. 1991 IEEE Symposium on Research in Security and Privacy, Oakland, CA, May, 1991.

[18] C. Gülcü and G. Tsudik. "Mixing Email with *Babel*", *1996 Symposium on Network and Distributed System Security*, San Diego, February 1996.

[19] R. Ostrovsky and M. Yung. "How to Withstand Mobile Virus Attacks", *Proc. 10th ACM Symposium on Principles of Distributed Computation (PODC91)*, ACM Press, 1991, pp. 51–59.

[20] M. Reed, P. Syverson, and D. Goldschlag. "Protocols using Anonymous Connections: Mobile Applications", *Security Protocols: 5th International Workshop, Paris, France, April 1997, Proceedings*, B. Christianson, B. Crispo, M. Lomas, and M. Roe, eds., LNCS vol. 1361, Springer-Verlag, 1998, pp. 13–23.

[21] M. Reiter and A. Rubin. *Crowds: Anonymity for Web Transactions*, DIMACS Technical Reports 97-15, April 1997 (revised August 1997).

[22] S. Schneider and A. Sidiropoulos. "CSP and Anonymity", *ESORICS 96*, E. Bertino, H. Kurth, G. Martella, and E. Montolivio, eds., LNCS vol. 1146, Springer-Verlag, 1996, pp. 198–218.

[23] P. Syverson, D. Goldschlag, and M. Reed. "Anonymous Connections and Onion Routing", *Proceedings of the 1997 IEEE Symposium on Security and Privacy*, Oakland, CA, IEEE CS Press, May 1997, pp. 44–54.

[24] Paul F. Syverson and James W. Gray, III. The epistemic representation of information flow security in probabilistic systems. In *Proc. 8th IEEE Computer Security Foundations Workshop*, pages 152–166, County Kerry, Ireland, June 1995.

[25] Stuart G. Stubblebine, Paul F. Syverson, and David M. Goldschlag, "Unlinkable Serial Transactions: Protocols and Applications", to appear in *ACM Transactions on Information Systems and Security*.

[26] Paul F. Syverson, "A Different Look at Secure Distributed Computation", in 10th *IEEE Computer Security Foundations Workshop (CSFW10)*, IEEE CS Press, pp. 109–115, June 1997.

[27] Dennis Volpano and Geoffrey Smith, "Probabilistic Noninterference in a Concurrent Language", in 11th *IEEE Computer Security Foundations Workshop (CSFW11)*, IEEE CS Press, pp. 34–43, June 1998.

[28] Peter Wayner. *Digital Cash: Commerce on the Net*, AP Professional, Chestnut Hill, Mass., 1996.

Developing BON as an Industrial-Strength Formal Method

Richard F. Paige and Jonathan S. Ostroff

Department of Computer Science, York University,
Toronto, Ontario M3J 1P3, Canada.
{paige,jonathan}@cs.yorku.ca

Abstract. The emerging Unified Modelling Language has been touted as merging the best features of existing modelling languages, and has been adopted by leading companies and vendors as a universal software modelling language. Some researchers are also looking to UML as a basis for formal methods development. A less known approach is BON (the Business Object Notation), which is based on the principles of seamlessness, reversibility and design by contract, making it an ideal basis for industrial-strength formal methods development of object-oriented software. In this paper, we argue that BON is much more suited for the application of formal methods than UML. We describe the properties that an industrial-strength formal method must have, show how algorithm refinement can be done in BON (as an example of using BON for formal development), and contrast BON with other approaches, including UML, Z, B and VDM.

1 Introduction

"UML is in the middle of of a standardization process with the Object Management Group, and I expect it will be the standard modeling language in the future." Martin Fowler, **UML Distilled** [5].

The emerging Unified Modelling Language has been touted as merging the best features of existing software design notations, and has been adopted by leading companies and vendors as a universal software modelling language. Some researchers are also looking to UML as a basis for the application of formal methods in software development [4]. A less known approach is the Business Object Notation (BON) [21]. BON addresses roughly the same problem space as UML. We argue in this paper that BON is much more suited for the application of formal methods than UML and other alternatives.

In the previous decade, many companies made a move from C to C++ in the hope of developing more reliable software. This move may not have resulted in the the the expected gains — or worse, may actually have impeded software development and maintenance [8]. We have to ask ourselves whether the move to UML may also be premature.

The UML notation summary of approximately sixty pages makes its syntax as difficult to master as any of the most opaque formal methods, even without any formal semantics. A notation that supports every conceivable feature is not necessarily the best notation for development. Rather, what is needed is an integrated set of features

J. Wing, J. Woodcock, J. Davies (Eds.): FM'99, Vol. I, LNCS 1708, pp. 834–853, 1999.

that capture the essence of software abstractions, and which are directly mappable to implementation (and the reverse, from implementation to abstractions) so that the development can proceed seamlessly. Finally, a notion of software contracting in which clients and suppliers have obligations and benefits is needed as a basis for formal specification and analysis of software products. BON is just such a method, and its focus on seamlessness, reversibility and design by contract make it an ideal basis for industrial-strength formal methods development of object-oriented software.

In this paper, we outline the BON method of Walden and Nerson [21]. We explain how BON satisfies a number of criteria that have been suggested as being essential for a mathematical method to be industrially applicable. Our thesis is that BON provides a superior method for building large-scale, reliable, reusable software systems, and allows emphasis of mathematical or informal development, as the software engineer sees fit. Further, we attempt to suggest why the BON specification language has significant advantages over widely used informal and formal approaches like UML (with its constraint language, OCL), Z, and B.

The paper is organized as follows. We commence by suggesting a number of criteria for an industrial-strength formal method. BON is then presented, and an example is used to illustrate how BON supports the design of large systems, and how it can be used as a purely mathematical method. In presenting the use of BON as a formal method, we demonstrate an example of *method reuse*, and show that Z algorithm refinement rules can be reused and applied with only minor syntactic changes to BON specifications. We discuss which industrial-strength criteria BON does not currently support, and how we plan to amend these limitations. Finally, we contrast BON with other approaches, and consider future work.

2   Criteria for an Industrial-Strength Formal Method

An industrial-strength formal method is a mathematically based technique that is applicable to large-scale, complex software development problems. We suggest several properties that such a method might possess, synthesized from the experience of others, particularly [7, 22], and our own findings.

An industrial-strength formal method should satisfy at least the following.

1. *Restrictability of formality*, the ability to restrict the use of formal techniques – e.g., specification and verification – to those aspects of the development that require them [22].
2. *Gradual introduction capabilities*, the ability to introduce formality gradually, over time, into a development setting [17, 22].
3. *Tool support,* for both standard software engineering tasks like compilation, debugging, version control, and diagramming, as well as for formal manipulations.
4. *Modularity,* the ability of the formal method to produce modular designs [14].
5. *Seamlessness.* The method should apply to the full software life cycle, in a way that minimizes the gaps between successive activities.
6. *Education.* The method must be founded on an appropriate educational programme.

We now consider each aspect in more detail, and suggest why it is important for any industrial-strength formal method to satisfy all.

2.1   Restrictability of Formality

Formality in software development is often expensive to use, and it is typically infeasible to apply in full. Software systems are usually too large and too complex to fully develop via formal methods. Further, formal method use often depends on having clear, precise requirements; for a system with vague requirements, formal methods may be of only minimal help.

It should therefore be possible for engineers to use formality only when their experience and education suggests that it is appropriate. Specifications that are deemed to be complex by engineers should be subject to formal techniques, and those requirements that are either too vague, or are straightforward to specify and implement via informal techniques, can be handled differently.

Some critical system components may need to be developed formally, in which case restrictability is not an issue. However, we can view the development of such systems as being at one end of the spectrum of use of formality: that part where only formal methods are used. Thus, all industrial-strength formal methods need to be restrictable.

Because we require restrictability of formality, we should be able to use other informal techniques for developing the remaining components of our system. It should be possible to directly code some components, produce others by reuse, formally specify and informally develop others, and even abstract specifications from programs. An implication of restrictability is that it will be useful for specification languages to be *wide-spectrum* [9], encompassing both abstract, mathematical specifications, as well as an executable programming language subset.

Restrictability is also useful for coping with complex specifications and their refinements. When refining significant specifications, invariably the engineer loses track of the initial specification after only a small number of refinement steps: it is hard to maintain a view of the context in which the refinement is taking place. Restrictability, in cooperation with modularity (see Section 2.4, below) can help in ensuring that the engineer does not lose track of the refinement context.

2.2   Gradual Introduction of Formality

Many software development projects do not currently use formal methods, and so if it is desired to move towards the use of mathematical methods, they need to be introduced into the existing engineering macro- and micro-processes. Ideally, the introduction needs to be done so that the engineers and managers can adapt to the use of the new methods, evaluate the use of formal techniques (primarily with respect to their own processes), and decide the extent to which formality is usable in their context; this may have to be done on a project-by-project basis.

Thus, it should be possible to produce a migration path for a formal method, so that its use can be brought into practice gradually over time. With gradual introduction, it is possible to assess the effectiveness of the formal method in the development setting, and to determine the appropriate extent in which formality should be used. Gradual introduction is important in helping to fit formal methods to the development context— and in particular, to the macro-process in which formality is being used.

Gradual introduction goes hand-in-hand with restrictability: if one has a restrictable formal method, then one can gradually introduce it over time. An ideal form of restrictability is one in which the developers can change the extent of use of formality even while development is ongoing. In particular, if it is discovered that the current extent of use of formality is inappropriate, developers should be able to change the extent of use without altering the rest of the specification, design, and development.

2.3   Tool Support

Industrial-sized software engineering projects usually require industrial-strength tools to support development. In projects that do not apply formality, tool support is typically for diagramming, design, and animation (e.g., via CASE tools), configuration management and version control, compilation and debugging. For industrial-strength formal methods, tools should also exist to support the production, syntax, and type-checking of specifications, as well as automatic or semi-automatic discharge of the proof obligations that arise in refinements. Tools may also be provided to help manage any refinement or verification process. Analysis tools should be as transparent to the engineer as possible, and, ideally, should be integrated or integrable with other standard development tools, like the aforementioned CASE systems, compilers, and debuggers. In integrating analysis tools with other development tools, an *integrated development environment*, or *application framework* may have to be produced in order to simplify communication between tools, and to hide the tool integration details from the software engineers.

2.4   Modularity

A modular software design is often a quality software design, in part, because it can lead to maintainable software [14]. If a software system is designed and implemented as a set of precisely specified interacting modules, then software maintenance can be easier to carry out. A common form of a module in software design is a *class* [14].

Modularity is an essential quality in an industrial-strength formal method. Modularity lets developers focus their attentions on small parts of a system at a time. Small parts of a system can be easier to understand and develop; therefore, usually, small parts of a system are easier to formally analyze. Further, if developers are able to restrict their attentions at one time to small parts of the system, they will be less likely to lose track of the context in which the formal analysis is being carried out. A formal method that can be applied to a class or a package, for example, will be applied strictly to the functions and procedures of the class or package. A modular software development method thus allows developers to focus their attentions on separate components of the system.

Simply having a modular software development method does not guarantee the production of quality systems, nor does it guarantee maintainability. Design principles, e.g., for obtaining cohesive, low-coupled modules, must still be followed.

2.5   Seamlessness

A seamless method is one that can be applied to the entire software life cycle (analysis through to implementation and maintenance). The method is devised in such a way so as to minimize the gaps that exist between successive development activities. Seamlessness attempts to recognize the unity that exists in software development activities. Whether we are analyzing a problem, designing a solution, or implementing code, the same intellectual challenges arise and the same structuring mechanisms are needed.

A seamless method, such as BON, provides many benefits. For one, semantic gaps (impedence mismatches) can be avoided when making transitions between development steps. Mismatches between analysis and design, design and implementation, etc., have caused significant trouble in software development. Further, by using one form of model from the start of development, a close correspondence between the problem description and the solution description can be maintained. Finally, seamlessness facilitates reversibility, the inevitable backward adjustments that must occur during development.

Reversing a process is inevitable in software development. Invariably, when implementing a program, a developer learns that the software could accomplish its tasks better. The method should support the developer in making backward adjustments when they are discovered. Seamlessness is essential in facilitating this task.

2.6   Education

For a method or tool to be used and accepted within industry, it must be taught in an educational programme. This is certainly the case with formal methods, which require a solid mathematical and Computer Science background to understand and apply. Teaching a formal method or using a software tool in a university programme can have a significant effect on practice. The paper [16] raises the example of Spice in the domain of electrical engineering. Electrical engineering programmes taught differential equations and used the Spice tool; now, Spice is part of the toolset of electrical engineers, and is widely applied outside of the university environment. Methods and tools of similar strength, soundness, and ease of use are needed for the practice of software engineering. And educational programmes founded on such methods and tools are essential for software engineering to become a professional discipline.

3   BON: Towards an Industrial-Strength Formal Method

An ideal industrial-strength formal method satisfies the properties listed and outlined in the previous section. We now suggest a method that satisfies some, but not all, of these properties. In the next section, we explain changes or extensions to the method that need to be made to support all of the properties given in Section 2.

The Business Object Notation (BON) [21] is a method possessing a recommended process as well as a graphical and a separate textual notation for specifying and describing object-oriented systems. The notation provides mechanisms for specifying inheritance and usage relationships between classes, and has a small collection of techniques for expressing dynamic relationships (e.g., message passing). The notation also includes an *assertion language* for specifying preconditions and postconditions of class features as well as class properties. It is supported by the EiffelCase tool [14].

BON was designed to support three main techniques: seamlessness (discussed in Section 2.5), reversibility (the ability to extract BON graphical specifications from programs automatically), and software contracting (discussed in Section 3.1). As a result, BON provides only a small collection of powerful modeling features that guarantee seamlessness and full reversibility on the static modeling notations.

The fundamental specification construct in BON is the class. A BON class has a name, an optional *class invariant*, and a collection of *features*. A feature may be a query—which returns a value and does not change the system state—or a command, which does change system state. BON does not include a separate notion of attribute. Conceptually, an attribute should be viewed as a query returning the value of some hidden state information. Thus, identical syntax is used for accessing and writing attributes as for queries; this is the so-called *uniform access* principle [14].

Fig. 1 contains a short example of a BON graphical specification of a class *CITIZEN*. Class features are in the middle section of the diagram, while the class invariant is at the bottom. The invariant is a predicate (conjoined terms are separated by semicolons) that must be *true* whenever an instance of the class is used by another object (in the invariant @ refers to the current object). Class *CITIZEN* has seven queries, and one command. In particular the class has a query *single* (which results in a *BOOLEAN*) and a command *divorce*, which changes the state of an object. Class *SET* is a generic class with the usual operators (e.g., $\in$, *add*).

Feature behaviour is written using *contracts*, in a pre- and postcondition form. Preconditions of features are annotated with question marks in boxes, while postconditions are annotated with exclamation marks in boxes. Visibility of features is expressed by sectioning and use of the feature clause. By default, features are accessible to client classes; this can be changed by writing a new section of the class interface and prefixing the section with a list of client classes that may access the features.

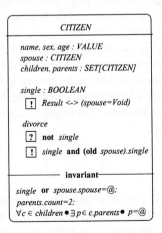

Fig.1. Class Interface for *CITIZEN*

3.1   Design by Contract

The pre- and postconditions of BON feature specifications are called contracts. The notion of design by contract [14] is central to BON. Each feature of a class has a contract, and interactions between the class and *client* classes must be via this contract. The contract is part of the official documentation of the class; the class specification and the contract are not separated. The feature contract places obligations on the client of the feature (who must establish the precondition) and supplies benefits to the client of the feature (who can rely that the feature will establish the postcondition).

Design by contract is tightly integrated into BON. The recommended BON process suggests providing contracts for all features, written using the BON assertion language. BON obeys all rules with respect to contracts that Eiffel does. In particular, BON obeys the Eiffel rules with respect to redefinition of features that have contracts: a feature that has its semantics redefined in a subclass can only weaken the precondition and strengthen the postcondition of the feature in the parent class.

3.2   The BON Assertion Language

Contracts in BON are written in an assertion language, a dialect of predicate logic. Assertions are statements about object properties. These statements can be expressed directly, using predicate logic, or indirectly by combining boolean queries from individual objects. The basic assertion language contains the usual elements, such as propositional and arithmetic operators and constants. Expressions constructed from these elements are easy to translate into executable code; effectively, this subset of the BON assertion language is the Eiffel assertion language.

The BON predicate logic can be used when more expressive power is needed. The predicate logic introduces set operations (e.g., membership, union), and universal and existential quantifiers. The quantifier notation in BON is akin to that used in the Logic E of Gries and Schneider [6] (with a few minor syntactic differences).

The BON assertion language can also be used to refer to the prestate in the postcondition of a feature. The **old** keyword, applied to an expression *expr*, refers to the value of *expr* before the feature was called. **old** can be used to specify how values returned by queries may change as a result of executing a command. Most frequently, **old** is used to express changes in abstract attributes. For example, *count* = **old** *count* + 1 specifies that *count* is increased by one.

3.3   Seamlessness

BON was originally designed to work seamlessly with Eiffel; in particular, the syntax of textual BON closely resembles Eiffel's syntax for pre- and postconditions. Making a transition from a BON specification to an Eiffel program is often easier than transitioning to alternative languages (e.g., Java or C++), because Eiffel supports pre- and postconditions (including the **old** keyword) as well as class invariants. The EiffelCase tool supports the automatic generation of Eiffel code from BON specifications, as well as the full reverse engineering of specifications from code.

In this paper, we view an Eiffel specification as a special case of a BON specification: one that just happens to be immediately executable. We therefore view BON as a wide-spectrum language, which supports easy refinement of (abstract) BON specifications into (concrete) Eiffel programs.

3.4   Architectural Diagrams

A great deal of the value of BON comes from its assertion language, but also from its ability to clearly and precisely specify architectural elements of an object-oriented design. BON provides a small selection of *relationships* that can be used to specify how classes, in a design, interact. There are two ways in which classes can interact in BON.

- *Inheritance:* one class can inherit behavior from one or more parent classes.
- *Client-supplier:* one class uses a second class in some way. This is used to specify the 'has-a' or 'part-of' relationships between classes.

Fig. 2 contains a non-trivial architectural diagram using BON, demonstrating examples of both inheritance and client-supplier. Classes are drawn as ellipses. Thin vertical arrows (e.g., between *EXP* and *SD*) represent inheritance. Double-line arrows with thick heads (e.g., between *FTS* and *TRANSITION*) represent client-supplier. Dashed boxes are *clusters*, which encapsulate subsystems; clusters are a purely syntactic notion. Inheritance and client-supplier relationships are recursively extended to be applicable to clusters, as the figure shows.

The EiffelCase drawing tool supports production and browsing of such diagrams, as well as automatic code generation from the diagrams, and the reverse engineering of such diagrams from Eiffel programs. The CASE tool works cooperatively with the EiffelBench compiler and debugger, the latter of which can be used to syntax and type check specifications (that do not use quantifiers).

3.5   Algorithm Refinement in BON

With BON, the use of mathematics is restrictable; an engineer need not formally specify the behavior of features or classes. But BON can also be used in a completely mathematical manner. That is, BON specifications can be treated as mathematical expressions, and formal analysis and reasoning can be applied to these expressions.

Let us consider an example, for implementation correctness, i.e., for showing that an implementation of a class in Eiffel satisfies a specification of a class in BON. This is a feature-by-feature process, carried out by showing that each Eiffel feature implementation satisfies its corresponding BON feature specification. Implementation correctness can be a verification process or a refinement process; in the latter, implementation and proof are developed hand-in-hand. We consider the refinement process here.

Suppose that we have a feature S in a class that also possesses attributes a. The feature also introduces local variables v. A *specification* associated with feature S is a predicate with free variables a or v, where a free variable may optionally be prefixed with the keyword **old**.

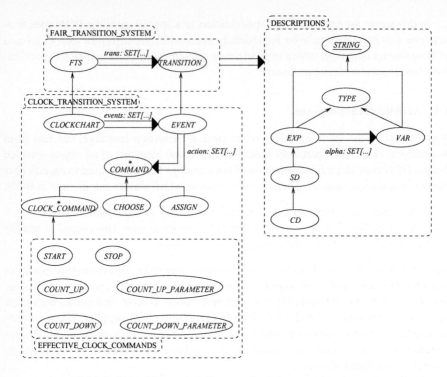

Fig.2. BON architectural diagram for fair transition systems

There is one particular specification associated with a feature that is of most interest to us in refinement; this specification arises when a feature has a contract. This specification, **spec** S, formally describes the meaning of the feature based on the contract. Suppose we have feature S with **require** clause P and **ensure** clause Q (P and Q each include the invariant). The **require** clause of S is a predicate on the prestate of the object, while the **ensure** clause is a predicate on the pre- and poststate. The meaning of this specification is given by **spec** S, defined below.

$$\textbf{spec } S \quad \hat{=} \quad (\textbf{old } P) \rightarrow Q$$

If the precondition **old** P is *false*, then any behavior will satisfy the specification.

An algorithm refinement relationship can be defined for BON feature specifications, allowing the stepwise refinement of a specification down to the level of an Eiffel program. This is possible for two reasons: because BON is part of a seamless development method that can result in Eiffel programs; and, because we will allow a specification to appear wherever Eiffel allows a statement.

In BON, refinement is just implication. Suppose we have a feature T that we think refines S. S is refined by T (written $S \sqsubseteq T$) if

$$\forall \textbf{old } \sigma, \sigma \bullet (\textbf{spec } S \leftarrow \textbf{spec } T)$$

where σ is the attributes of the class in which feature S occurs. In a refinement, we need only concern ourselves with the attributes of the class; this can reduce the complexity of the proof obligations that we must discharge in refinement.

Refinement of a BON specification (or verification of a program against a BON specification) can be applied to large software systems, because the refinement relationship $\sqsubseteq$ is monotonic over class relationships. Suppose we have a class A, with a number of feature specifications, which we want to refine to code. The process is as follows. First, determine **ind** A, the set of all classes that A directly depends on (via inheritance or client-supplier). Then, determine **spec** A, the set of contracts for all features in A (including inherited features). To refine A to an Eiffel program, we must refine each contract of A, i.e.,

$$\forall s \in \textbf{spec } A \bullet s \sqsubseteq \textbf{body } s$$

where **body** s is an implementation of s in Eiffel. To carry out this process, we *only* need **spec** A and the contracts of **ind** A. We do not need any implementations of **ind** A, nor do we (in most cases) need to consider the entire system. Thus, refinement can be done compositionally, feature by feature.

The ultimate goal of algorithm refinement is to formally derive a program from a specification. Because BON works seamlessly with Eiffel it is simplest to refine BON specifications into Eiffel. This requires us to provide rules for refining BON specifications into Eiffel.

An interesting result associated with BON refinement rules is that we can *reuse* all existing Z refinement rules — such as those from [23] — assuming that a consistent notation for distinguishing pre- and poststate is used (we will use BON's **old** notation to distinguish prestate from poststate). In other words, a valid refinement rule for Z is a valid refinement rule for BON features. This follows from Theorem 1.

Theorem 1. *Let S and T be BON specifications as described above, and let $\sqsubseteq_Z$ be the Z definition of refinement (see [20], or the proof below). Then, under syntax,*

$$S \sqsubseteq_Z T \to S \sqsubseteq T$$

Proof. Expand the definitions of $\sqsubseteq_Z$ and $\sqsubseteq$. The PVS theorem prover discharges the proof automatically, after applying the definitions, using one instance of (grind). The PVS specification of the conjecture used to discharge the proof is as follows (in the theory, p and q are the pre- and postcondition of S, while u and v are the pre- and postcondition of T). Equational proof details can be found in [18].

```
refmaps : THEORY
BEGIN
 STATETYPE : TYPE
 old_s, s  : VAR STATETYPE
 p(old_s:STATETYPE)    : bool
 q(old_s,s:STATETYPE)  : bool
 u(old_s:STATETYPE)    : bool
 v(old_s,s:STATETYPE)  : bool

 refmapping : CONJECTURE
   (FORALL old_s, s :
      (p(old_s) IMPLIES (u(old_s) AND
      (v(old_s,s) IMPLIES q(old_s,s))))
      IMPLIES
      ((u(old_s) IMPLIES v(old_s,s)) IMPLIES
      (p(old_s) IMPLIES q(old_s,s))))
 END refmaps
```

An implication of this theorem is that we do not have to formulate new refinement rules for BON, and can make use of the extensive collection of Z refinement rules that already exist, providing that we transform the Z syntax into BON's syntax.

We can use the refinement rules in Wordsworth [23] with BON. Wordsworth treats Z schemas as summarizing the operation of programs written in a simple guarded command language. Values of program variables before and after the execution of the corresponding program make up the declaration part of the schema, and the predicate part expresses the relation between those values induced by the execution of the schema. We can do the same, treating BON feature contracts as summarizing the operation of Eiffel programs. Here are some examples, translated into BON syntax. In the following, let S, A, and B be BON feature specifications. We extract the precondition of a feature with the **pre** operator, and the postcondition with the **post** operator. Assume that refinement is being done within a single class, with attributes x and y (we use σ to stand for both x and y). We use $\sqsubseteq$ to denote the refinement relation.

First, we consider how to introduce an assignment statement in a refinement.

Rule 2 *Introducing assignment. Let e be an expression whose type is compatible (based on the BON/Eiffel notion of compatibility [14]) with x. Then $S \sqsubseteq x := e$ if*

$$\forall\, \textbf{old}\ \sigma, \sigma \bullet (\textbf{pre}\ S \wedge (x = \textbf{old}\ e) \wedge (y = \textbf{old}\ y)) \rightarrow \textbf{post}\ S$$

The effect of the assignment $x := e$ is formally described by the BON specification

> **require** *true*
>
> **ensure** $x = \textbf{old}\ e \wedge y = \textbf{old}\ y$

The next rule is for introducing a selection. A selection has the following form.

> **if** c_1 **then** P_1 **elseif** c_2 **then** P_2 ... **else** P_k **end**

where the c_i are conditions and the P_i specifications. In the refinement rule, we consider the two-branch case, which generalizes in the obvious way to the multi-branch setting.

Rule 3 *Introducing if. Let b be a BOOLEAN expression. Then*

$$S \;\sqsubseteq\; \textbf{if } b \textbf{ then } A \textbf{ else } B \textbf{ end}$$

providing that

$$\forall\, \sigma, \textbf{old } \sigma \bullet (\textbf{spec } S \wedge b) \leftarrow \textbf{spec } A$$
$$\forall\, \sigma, \textbf{old } \sigma \bullet (\textbf{spec } S \wedge \neg\, b) \leftarrow \textbf{spec } B$$

This rule is a formalization of the notion of refinement by *cases* [9].

The refinement rules become more complicated when we consider sequencing and repetition, because of the need to introduce intermediate states. Before we consider the rule for sequencing, we introduce some new notation, allowing us to talk about intermediate states. We annotate specifications with primes (e.g., A') to indicate systematic addition of primes to *variable names* used within the specification. This notation is borrowed from [23]. However, we must make one slight adaptation in BON, because of its use of **old** to distinguish pre- and poststate: a prime applied to an **old** expression removes the **old** keyword. Here is an example.

$$(x = \textbf{old } y \wedge y = \textbf{old } (x + y))'$$
$$= x' = y \wedge y' = (x + y)$$

Now we can provide a rule for introducing sequencing.

Rule 4 *Introducing sequencing. $S \sqsubseteq A$; B providing that*

$$\textbf{pre } S \rightarrow \textbf{pre } A$$
$$(\textbf{pre } S \wedge \textbf{spec } A) \rightarrow (\textbf{pre } B)'$$
$$(\textbf{pre } S \wedge \textbf{spec } A \wedge \textbf{spec } B') \rightarrow (\textbf{spec } S)[\_'/\_]$$

*where, in the last line, the notation $X[\_'/\_]$ reads "substitute primed versions of variables for unprimed versions of variables in X" (and don't change the **old** variables).*

Finally, we can give a rule for introducing a loop. We use Wordsworth's initialized loop rule. Loops in Eiffel have the following syntax.

$$Loop \;\widehat{=}\; \textbf{from } Init \textbf{ until } b \textbf{ loop } P \textbf{ end}$$

Init and *P* are specifications with **require** and **ensure** clauses, while b is a boolean expression.

> **Rule 5** *Introducing an initialized loop. Let b be a boolean expression, I a loop invariant, and Loop a loop as above. Then S ⊑ Loop if*
>
> $$\textbf{pre } S \rightarrow \textbf{pre } Init$$
> $$\textbf{pre } S \wedge \textbf{spec } Init \rightarrow I$$
> $$\textbf{pre } S \wedge I \wedge b \rightarrow \textbf{spec } S$$
> $$\textbf{pre } S \wedge I \wedge \neg b' \rightarrow (\textbf{pre } P)'$$
> $$\textbf{pre } S \wedge I \wedge \neg b' \wedge (\textbf{spec } P)' \rightarrow I[\_'/\_]$$

We have shown that Z refinement rules can be applied to BON. We intend to develop a collection of refinement rules, written directly in BON, and expect the rules to be simpler to write and use than the reused ones.

Refinement (and verification) in BON is industrial-strength; it is restrictable and can be applied on a class-by-class and feature-by-feature manner. Further, with BON there is no system-level validity check that has to be discharged to show system correctness. To show that a system is correct, we must verify all classes (including the root class). When the root class is finally verified, the system has been shown to be correct.

3.6   Example of Refinement

This section illustrates a simple example of refinement in BON, demonstrating the use of Z refinement rules with BON. The refinement will transform a BON specification into an Eiffel program.

The problem we will solve is a simple one, taken from [23], to find the maximum of a non-empty array (or sequence) of integers. We suppose that we have a class, *FOO*, that includes a feature that will be used to determine the maximum of the array. This class has the following BON specification.

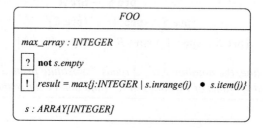

Fig.3. Class *FOO* for refinement example

The array for the computation is a feature *s* of the class. The function *max_array* calculates the maximum of the array. The function introduces a local variable, *i*, as a loop index. A local variable *result*, automatically declared for the function, will hold the result of the computation. The introduction of these variables is formally defined by existential quantification over the specification. The notation $s.item(j)$ is the Eiffel syntax for the array index operation. $s.capacity$ is the maximum size of the array, while $s.lower$ and $s.upper$ are its lower and upper bounds. $s.inrange(i)$ is *true* iff i is in range of the subscripts of s.

We can now refine the specification to code. Clearly, the implementation will require a loop. The first step of the refinement will introduction such a loop, with invariant

$$I \,\widehat{=}\, result = max\{j : INTEGER \mid s.lower \leq j \leq i \bullet s.item(j)\} \land i \leq s.upper \land s = \textbf{old}\ s$$

and guard $b \,\widehat{=}\, (i = s.upper)$. The first refinement step is

$$\textbf{spec}\ max\_array$$
$$\sqsubseteq \textbf{from spec}\ P$$
$$\textbf{until}\ i = s.upper$$
$$\textbf{loop spec}\ Q\ \textbf{end}$$

where

$$\textbf{spec}\ P \;=\; i = s.lower \land result = s.item(s.lower)$$
$$\textbf{spec}\ Q \;=\; i = \textbf{old}\ i + 1 \land result = max\{\textbf{old}\ result, s.item(i)\}$$

and where *max* is extended to sets as in [20]. The proof obligations that must be discharged are as follows.

$$\textbf{not}\ s.empty \rightarrow true$$

i.e., that the precondition of *max_array* establishes the precondition of the initialization.

$$\textbf{not}\ s.empty \land i = s.lower \land result = s.item(s.lower) \rightarrow I$$

i.e., that the initialization together with the precondition of *max_array* establish the invariant; this is *true*, by one application of the one-point rule.

$$\textbf{not}\ s.empty \land I \land b \rightarrow (\textbf{not old}\ s.empty \rightarrow$$
$$result = max\{j : INTEGER \mid s.inrange(j) \bullet s.item(j)\})$$

which is also *true*, by simplification.

$$\textbf{not}\ s.empty \land I \land \neg b' \rightarrow true$$

i.e., that the invariant and negated guarded together establish the precondition of the loop body (which is clearly *true*).

$$\textbf{not}\ s.empty \land I \land \neg b' \land i' = i + 1 \land result' = max\{result, s.item(i')\} \rightarrow I[\_'/\_]$$

i.e., that the body of the loop maintains the invariant. (We should also demonstrate termination, but this is straightforward and omitted.)

The body of the loop, **spec** Q, can be refined as follows

$$\textbf{spec}\ Q \sqsubseteq i := i + 1;\ result := result.max(s.item(i))$$

(*max* is a feature of the class *INTEGER*.) The initialization can be implemented as

$$i := s.lower;\ result := s.item(i)$$

This refinement follows similar steps to a refinement of the same problem in Z.

3.7   BON and the Criteria

In Section 2, we suggested six criteria for an industrial-strength formal method. We now very briefly discuss the criteria, and how BON supports – or fails to support them. In Section 4, we discuss extensions to BON which can help eliminate these limitations.

1. *Restrictability.* The use of mathematics in BON specifications is under the control of the software engineer, for both specification and for formal manipulations like refinement. Each feature of each class may be given a contract written in predicate logic, or in an executable subset. The contract may be written as comments. Or the contract may be omitted entirely. Further, refinement need only be applied to those features that the engineer wants. The engineer can therefore restrict use of formality to those parts of the system they believe, in their judgment, require mathematics for specification or refinement.

2. *Gradual introduction.* Because BON has restrictable use of formality, gradual introduction can be obtained by a software engineer carefully managing the extent of use of formality over time, in some process.

3. *Tool support.* BON has CASE tool support [14], and this tool is integrated with an Eiffel compiler and debugger. It does not possess version control tool support (tools like RCS or CVS can be used on the side), nor analysis tools, e.g., theorem provers, simulators, and model checkers.

4. *Modularity.* BON is a pure object-oriented notation, and is therefore modular. It also provides a clustering notation to support modularity at the system level.

5. *Seamlessness.* BON is part of a seamless method that produces Eiffel programs. This method is reversible: BON specifications can be produced from Eiffel.

6. *Education.* BON is not as widely taught as other object-oriented approaches, e.g., UML. It is being taught in some universities throughout the world, and by consultants. Our experience in teaching BON at all levels of an undergraduate programme is that it is appropriate and superior to other methods for introducing and teaching object-oriented concepts. We discuss this more in Section 6 and elsewhere [16].

   Meyer [14] suggests that object-oriented software construction, with design by contract – which BON supports – is a gentle progressive exposure to formal techniques that doesn't overwhelm the students and allows them to produce real software. Our experience agrees with this, but we add that the teaching must be founded on an appropriate course in logic and calculation, e.g., supplied by the text [6].

4   Making BON Industrial-Strength

BON does not satisfy all of the criteria listed in Section 3. In particular, it has no tool support for refinement or formal analysis regarding classes and contracts, and it is not yet appropriate for reactive and real-time systems. In this section we outline our plans for extending BON so that it satisfies the properties listed in Section 3.

We see three clear areas for extension and development of BON.

1. *Education:* teaching the notation and method. We discuss this more in the conclusions and elsewhere [16].

2. *Analytic tools:* providing support for proof, discussed in Section 4.1.

3. *Extension to real-time and reactive systems,* discussed in Section 4.2.

4.1   Analytic Tools

The current toolset for BON consists of the EiffelCase tool, which is integrated with a collection of base libraries, a compiler/debugger, a GUI builder, and a number of smaller supporting tools. The CASE tool is capable of generating BON diagrams (akin to those in Figs. 1 and 2), of generating Eiffel code automatically from diagrams, and can reverse-engineer diagrams from Eiffel programs. Such tools are constantly under further development. No tools currently exist for formal analysis of BON specifications, e.g., for simulation or proof.

Our current research is focusing on providing analytic tools for BON. We are proceeding by providing links between BON and PVS. BON and PVS will be linked by a general- purpose translator, based on the EiffelLex and EiffelParse libraries and automated tools, which will generate PVS theories from BON specifications. The PVS theories can then be subjected to rigorous analytic manipulation, e.g., involving proof of properties, consistency, and implementability.

The basic mapping from simple BON specifications to PVS is straightforward: a single class is mapped into a PVS theory. Class features can be mapped into PVS variables, boolean functions, or functions on local state variables. An example is given below, for a single class *PASSWORD_MANAGEMENT* and a PVS theory `password`.

class *PASSWORD_MANAGEMENT* **feature**

$alarm, operate : BOOLEAN$

$p1 : PASSWORD$

$i : INTEGER$

$--$ initially $\neg\ alarm \wedge \neg\ operate \wedge (i = 0) \wedge (p1 = \ldots)$

$verify\_user(p : PASSWORD)$

require $\neg\ alarm \wedge \neg\ operate$

ensure $(g_1 \rightarrow e_1) \wedge (g_2 \rightarrow e_2) \wedge (g_3 \rightarrow e_3)$

invariant $i \geq 0$

end

where

$g_1 = \textbf{old}\ i < 6 \wedge \textbf{old}\ p1 = p$

$g_2 = \textbf{old}\ i < 6 \wedge \textbf{old}\ p1 \neq p$

$g_3 = \textbf{old}\ i \geq 6 \wedge \textbf{old}\ p1 \neq p$

$e_1 = (i = 0) \wedge operate \wedge \neg\ alarm \wedge (p1 = \textbf{old}\ p1)$

$e_2 = (i = \textbf{old}\ i + 1) \wedge \neg\ operate \wedge \neg\ alarm \wedge (p1 = \textbf{old}\ p1)$

$e_3 = (i = 0) \wedge \neg\ operate \wedge alarm \wedge (p1 = \textbf{old}\ p1)$

Our proposed tool will map this automatically into the following PVS theory, with the conjecture `implementability` added by the user.

```
password : THEORY begin
passwordtype: TYPE
alarm, old_alarm, operate, old_operate: VAR bool
i, old_i: VAR nat
p1,p2,old_p1: VAR passwordtype

verify_user(i,old_i,operate,alarm,p1,old_p1,p2):bool =
    (NOT old_alarm AND NOT old_operate)
    IMPLIES
    ((old_i<6 AND old_p1=p2 IMPLIES
       (i=0) AND operate AND NOT alarm AND p1=old_p1)
     AND
     (old_i<6 AND old_p1 /= p2 IMPLIES
       (i=old_i+1) AND NOT operate AND NOT alarm AND p1=old_p1)
     AND
     (old_i >= 6 AND old_p1 /= p2 IMPLIES
       alarm AND NOT operate AND i=0 AND p1=old_p1))

implementability: CONJECTURE
    (EXISTS i, operate, alarm, p1:
    NOT old_alarm AND NOT old_operate
    IMPLIES
    verify_user(i,old_i,operate,alarm,p1,old_p1,p2))
  end password
```

The PVS specification includes a boolean function, `verify_user`, as well as a user-added conjecture. The conjecture `implementability` is to ensure that the *verify_user* specification is implementable.

In general, a BON specification will involve many classes interacting in client-supplier and inheritance relationships. A simple class-to-theory mapping will not suffice. Here, we intend to map BON classes to PVS types, and to treat objects as PVS variables. Features of BON classes will be transformed into functions on objects. This is akin to the work reported in [10] which maps Java to PVS. There may be advantages to mapping select BON classes to PVS datatypes, but it is not yet clear if this can be automated, nor if the datatype mechanism is sufficiently expressive. An advantage with mapping BON to PVS is that we do not need to transform BON specifications (and hence Eiffel programs) into an intermediate representation (as is done in [10]), because BON and Eiffel specifications include contracts.

Work is underway, starting January 1999, on a translator from BON to PVS.

4.2   Real-Time

Currently, BON does not provide support for reasoning about temporal properties of systems. This makes it difficult to develop real-time, object-oriented programs with BON. Eiffel currently provides support for concurrency [14], so it would be a useful extension to be able to talk about concurrency and real-time properties at the level of BON. We are proposing to extend the BON assertion language to real-time temporal logic [15], and to extend the BON toolset to support writing such specifications.

We also are proposing to support the temporal logic dialect of BON with a combined theorem prover and model checker, namely STeP, so as to provide automated analytic tools for reasoning about such specifications. The integration of the extended BON toolset with STeP will follow the work reported in [12], which considered integrating a visual toolset with STeP for a different (non-object-oriented) notation.

5   Related Work

The development of so-called 'industrial-strength' software engineering methods that have a sound yet practical mathematical basis is of current interest. Powerful general-purpose methods, such as B [1], VDM [11], and those based upon Z have seen success, as have more specialized methods. We now briefly contrast some of these alternatives — particularly Z, UML combined with the Object Constraint Language, VDM and B — with BON. A detailed comparison of BON and UML can be found in [19].

5.1   BON Compared with Z and UML

Two widely used approaches are Z and UML; a great deal of past and current research has focused on these notations.

The Z notation is mathematical and, as we have discussed, can be used for refinement. However, Z is not modular (except at the level of an operation) – hence the development of object-oriented and modular dialects of the notation – and therefore provides only minimal support for producing modular – and hence reusable, and maintainable systems. It is left to the discipline of the software engineer to use Z so that maintainable, reusable designs are produced.

UML is the current focus of much activity; it is quickly becoming a 'standard' notation for object-oriented modeling. It has recently been combined with the Object Constraint Language (OCL), to provide better support for formal modeling and design by contract. The Precise UML group has studied formalizing parts of the notation [4]. In terms of the criteria discussed in Section 2, UML (including the OCL) satisfies most of the criteria: restrictability, gradual introduction, tool support, and modularity are clearly satisfied, although tools for supporting the UML and OCL are needed. In terms of education, suitable textbooks for the UML are beginning to appear, but more are needed. Where UML falls short is with seamlessness: it is difficult to have seamless development with UML and the OCL, because of the auxiliary use of finite state machines for object semantics, data modelling, and stereotypes [19]. Seamlessness for UML is usually supported only for a subset of the language. Further, even though design by contract can be used with UML and OCL, it is not well-supported, as a number of examples in [19] demonstrate.

5.2   BON Contrasted with VDM and B

The Vienna Development Method [11] has seen industrial success, primarily in Europe. The method supports specification in a pre- and postcondition style, not unlike BON, using the logic of partial functions. It is supported by tools for proof and refinement. Its fundamental specification component is the operation.

The B method [1] was developed by Abrial and has been applied successfully to substantial software engineering problems. The method uses the modular abstract machine notation for specification. Refinement relationships between machines are used to produce executable programs from specifications. The B Method has tools (the B-Tool and Atelier B) that support semi-automatic generation of code from specifications.

The SPECTRUM project [3, 13] has focused on combining VDM and B. In this method, VDM is to be used for specification and validation, while B is to be used for development of the specification, via refinement and code generation. The integration provides techniques for synthesizing B designs from flat VDM specifications. The integration provides the benefits of both VDM and B: expressive specification, tool support, and modularity. It also provides restrictability of both B and VDM, and therefore the means to gradually introduce one or the other method into practice.

With BON, no integration is necessary to provide expressive specification capabilities or modularity; the method supports these features by default. Further, BON also provides restrictability of the use of mathematics, unlike VDM integrated with B. Finally, BON is object-oriented, whereas B combined with VDM is a modular notation. For the purposes of building reusable, maintainable systems, object-oriented methods can provide significant advantages over methods that are not object-oriented [14].

An advantage that VDM+B has over BON is in tool support; the B-Tool and IFAD VDM are powerful toolsets that support proof and refinement. Similar tools are required for BON, and are currently under development.

6 Conclusions

BON provides a solid foundation for a software engineering method that is practical and has a sound theoretical basis. It provides fundamental techniques, like object-orientation, restrictability of formalism, and tool support, that can be further supplemented by a suitable educational programme and analytic tools.

BON, and other object-oriented methods, are not always appropriate for software development, e.g., systems with complicated real-time constraints, information processing systems, concurrent systems, and operating system kernels. Tool support for BON, especially with regards to formal analysis, needs to be improved. However, the basic techniques that BON supports — restrictability, object-orientation, and design-by-contract — provide a method for immediate practical use, as well as a foundation for further research and development.

Our experience is that BON is also a suitable method for introducing object-oriented methods to students. We use BON in our third year software design and OO programming courses, and introduce its basic concepts to our first-year students. The notation has proven to be teachable, and the students find that it is easy to quickly apply in nontrivial projects. More details on our experiences and plans for teaching using BON can be found in [16].

References

[1] J.-R. Abrial. *The B-Book*, Cambridge, 1996.
[2] L. Baresi and M. Pezze. Toward Formalizing Structured Analysis, *ACM Trans. Soft. Eng. Method.* 7(1), January 1998.
[3] J. Bicarregui, B. Matthews, and B. Ritchie. Investigating the integration of two formal methods. In *Proc. FMICS '98*, CWI, 1998.

[4]   A. Evans, R. France, K. Lano, and B. Rumpe. The UML as a Formal Modeling Notation. *Computer Standards and Interfaces* **19**(7), 1998.

[5]   M. Fowler. *UML Distilled*, Addison-Wesley, 1997.

[6]   D. Gries and F. Schneider. *A Logical Approach to Discrete Math*, Springer, 1993.

[7]   A. Hall. Seven Myths of Formal Methods. *IEEE Software,* September 1990.

[8]   L. Hatton. Does OO Sync with How We Think? *IEEE Software*, May/June 1998.

[9]   E.C.R. Hehner. *A Practical Theory of Programming*, Springer-Verlag, 1993.

[10] B. Jacobs et al. Reasoning about Java Classes (Preliminary Report). In *Proc. OOP-SLA'98*, ACM Press, Oct. 1998.

[11] C.B. Jones. *Systematic Software Development using VDM*, Prentice-Hall, 1990.

[12] L. Lo. *Modular Design for Reactive Systems*, MSc Thesis, Department of Computer Science, York University, 1998.

[13] B. Matthews, B. Ritchie, and J. Bicarregui. Synthesizing structure from flat specifications. In *Proc. B'98*, LNCS 1393, Springer-Verlag, 1998.

[14] B. Meyer. *Object-Oriented Software Construction*, Prentice-Hall, 1997.

[15] J.S. Ostroff. *Temporal Logic for Real-Time Systems*, Wiley, 1989.

[16] J.S. Ostroff and R.F. Paige. Formal Methods in the Classroom: The Logic of Real-Time Software Design. In *Proc. Real-Time Software Engineering Education Workshop'98*, IEEE Press, 1999.

[17] R.F. Paige. A Meta-Method for Formal Method Integration. In *Proc. FME'97*, LNCS 1313, Springer, 1997.

[18] R.F. Paige. Heterogeneous Notations for Pure Formal Method Integration. *Formal Aspects of Computing* **10**(3):233-242, June 1999.

[19] R.F. Paige and J.S. Ostroff. A Comparison of BON and UML. Technical Report CS-1999-03, York University, May 1999.

[20] J.M. Spivey. *The Z Notation: A Reference Manual*, Prentice-Hall, 1989.

[21] K. Walden and J.-M. Nerson. *Seamless Object-Oriented Software Development*, Prentice-Hall, 1995.

[22] D. Weber-Wulff. Selling Formal Methods to Industry. In *Proc. FME '93*, LNCS 670, Springer-Verlag, 1993.

[23] J. Wordsworth. *Software Development with Z*, Addison-Wesley, 1994.

On the Expressive Power of OCL[*]

Luis Mandel[1] and María Victoria Cengarle[2]

[1] Forschungsinstitut für Angewandte Software-Technologie (FAST e. V.)
Arabellastr. 17, D-81925 Munich, Germany
mandel@fast.de
[2] Ludwig-Maximilians-Universität München.
Oettingenstr. 67, D-80538 Munich, Germany
cengarle@informatik.uni-muenchen.de

Abstract. This paper examines the expressive power of OCL in terms of navigability and computability. First the expressive power of OCL is compared with the relational calculus; it is showed that OCL is not equivalent to the relational calculus. Then an algorithm computing the transitive closure of a binary relation –operation that cannot be encoded in the relational calculus– is expressed in OCL. Finally the equivalence of OCL with a Turing machine is pondered.

1 Introduction

The Object Constraint Language (OCL), developed within IBM and based on IBEL (Integrated Business Engineering Language, IBM) and on Syntropy [4], is part of the Unified Modeling Language (UML) from version 1.1 on. This extension has been designed to augment a class diagram with additional information which cannot be otherwise expressed by UML diagrams; previous versions of UML have only allowed the definition of constraints as annotations in an informal textual way. OCL allows the definition of integrity constraints at the user level, and it has also been used for the formalization of the metamodel of UML. The introduction of a constraint language is an important step towards the formalization of system specification. Constraints represent necessary conditions for a domain to constitute a model of the static aspects of the specified system. OCL is based on standard set theory and it was designed to specify invariants of classes and types in the class model, to specify type invariant of stereotypes, to describe pre- and postconditions on operations and methods, to describe guards; it is also suited to specify queries in the database sense. That is, OCL can be used to write expressions that evaluate to "true" or "false" and also to write expressions that once evaluated return the values respectively satisfying the constraint specified by those query expressions.

In [6] some weak points of OCL have been shown, for example the difference between data values and object instances is not clear. Normally data values are immutable whereas objects (or class instances) are mutable. The term

---

[*] This work was partially supported by the Bayerische Forschungsstiftung.

J. Wing, J. Woodcock, J. Davies (Eds.): FM'99, Vol. I, LNCS 1708, pp. 854–874, 1999.
© Springer-Verlag Berlin Heidelberg 1999

value/object as well as the term subtype/subclass is not consistently used in the specification document of OCL [9]. In fact, the specification document is very informal and not even the examples given there are consistent with their English explanation. Moreover there it is said that an OCL expression can be part of a guard but neither examples nor explanation of how guards work are given. Some steps have been done in order to formalize it, for example in [10] a formal semantics of OCL has been proposed.

This paper aims at examining the completeness of OCL. We show that OCL is not powerful enough to denote any query expression of the relational calculus. However, by means of OCL it is possible to calculate the transitive closure of a relation. We also show that any primitive recursive function can be calculated by an OCL expression, and hint that OCL is not Turing complete.

The paper is organized as follows. Section 2 briefly introduces "OCL by examples." Section 3 studies the expressive power of OCL: Section 3.1 demonstrates that the expressiveness of OCL is *not* as powerful as the relational calculus, in Section 3.2 it is shown how the transitive closure of a relation can be computed in OCL, and in Section 3.3 the Turing incompleteness of OCL is shown. Finally in Section 4 some conclusions are drawn.

2 OCL Examples

This section briefly introduces the OCL language using the example of a class hierarchy of a diagram editor; see Fig. 1. The editor supports the notion of group of graphic elements. A document consists of pages, and a page consists of graphic elements. Graphic elements are either geometric figures or groups of at least two graphic elements; a graphic element can be member of at most one group. Graphic elements can be moved, rotated, etc. Geometric figures are either one dimensional (points and curves) or two dimensional (circles, ellipses, etc.). Two dimensional figures can be filled with a color.

The diagram of Fig. 1 can be enhanced with OCL constraints that further restrict the possible system states. OCL expressions are either of an OCL predefined type or of a class of the class model to which the expressions are attached. OCL expressions compute values without changing the system state. OCL uses dot notation for accessing the attributes of objects. The attribute `radius` of the class `Circle` is accessed by the expression `Circle.radius`. If all the instances of that class are restricted to have a positive radius, a constraint `Circle.radius > 0` can be written. The result type of this expression is `Boolean`, establishing an invariant for the class `Circle`. Alternatively, one can write

```
Circle
    self.radius > 0   -- two dashes precede a comment
```

where the name of the class underlined is the *context* of the constraint, and an occurrence of `self` in it refers to any instance of that class.

A basic data structure of OCL is `Set`. The expression `self.vertices` in the context `Polygon` computes the set of all the vertices of a polygon object and returns a value of type `Set(Point)`. A further data structure `Bag` which stands

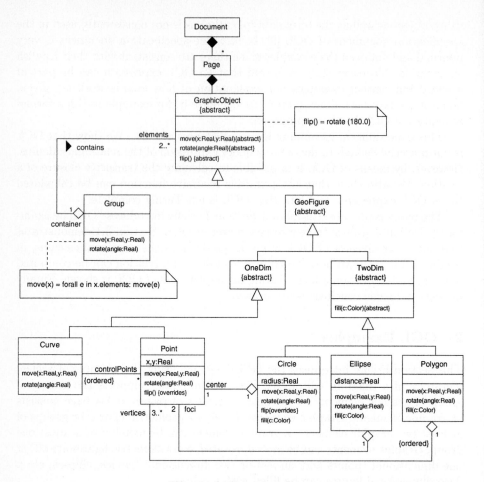

Fig. 1. A diagram editor

for a multiset, i.e. a set with possibly repeated elements. Besides sets and bags another data structure is `Sequence` as usual denoting ordered bags. All these data structures are parametric, one writes `Set(T)`, `Bag(T)`, and `Sequence(T)` for T a type, and sets, bags, and sequences are subtypes of the abstract parametric class `Collection`. In the context of <u>Group</u> the query `self.elements` returns a set whose cardinality is calculated by applying the *feature* `size` associated with collections:

<u>Group</u>
    self.elements->size

The result of this expression is of type `Integer` and is restricted to values greater than or equal to 2 by the multiplicity at the `elements` end of the aggregation `contains` between `Group` and `GraphicObject`.

OCL provides universal and existential quantification. A constraint of the Polygon class is that any two vertex points of a polygon must be in different positions. This is expressed using the feature forAll as follows:

```
Polygon
    self.vertices->forAll(p1, p2 : Point |
    (p1.x = p2.x and p1.y = p2.y) implies p1 = p2)
```

This expression has type Boolean.

OCL also allows the navigation through the information using queries. For instance, the bag containing the surface of each circle with center p can be computed using the feature collect as in the following expression (where the classname with small initial is used if the association end has no rolename):

```
    p.circle->collect(3.14*radius)
```

whose result type is Bag(Real).

allInstances is a feature associated with any type that returns the set of all instances of the given type. For example the set of polygons which are triangles is calculated as follows:

```
    Polygon.allInstances->select(p : Polygon | p.vertices->size = 3)
```

A powerful feature of collections is iterate, by means of it many other ones can be implemented. iterate traverses a collection, performs a calculation with each of its elements, and stores the results in an accumulator, whose last value is the result of the iterate expression. For instance the sum of the surfaces of all the circles present in the model is calculated by the following expression:

```
    Circle.allInstances->iterate(c : Circle ;        -- iteration variable
    sum : Real = 0                          -- accumulator with initial value 0
    |   sum + 3.14 * c.radius * c.radius)           -- new value of sum
    --   ^^^ this occurrence of sum refers to its rvalue
```

A more involved example is the calculation of the set of all the polygons with at least one vertex in common with a given polygon p0:

```
    Polygon.allInstances->iterate(p1 : Polygon ;
    cv : Set(Polygon) = Set{}    -- accumulator, initially the empty set
    |   if p1 <> p0 and
            (p1.vertices->intersection(p0.vertices))->notEmpty
        then cv->including(p1) else cv endif)
```

It is worth mentioning that OCL does not have the concept of tuple. Moreover collections (i.e. sets, sequences and bags), which could be used to simulate tuple functions, are flat, that is, in OCL there is no possibility to create a set of sets, for example (if a query returns a set of sets, then this result is flattened).

3   Completeness

This section examines the expressive power of OCL from three different viewpoints. First we ponder if the operations of the relational calculus can be formulated in OCL, second we try to compute the transitive closure of a relation (which is an operation that cannot be expressed by means of the relational calculus), and third we consider the Turing completeness of OCL.

3.1 Equivalence of OCL and Relational Calculus

In this section we show that OCL is not complete in the sense defined by Ullman (see [13]) i.e. it is not possible to express in OCL the five basic operations of the relational algebra. We also show that some of the derived expressions of the relational algebra are primitive of OCL or can be expressed using OCL. Given that OCL does not have the concept of tuple, some operations like for instance the projection trivially cannot be expressed in OCL.

There are three abstract query languages, namely the relational algebra, the tuple relational calculus, and the domain relational calculus. They are all equivalent in expressive power to the each other and were proposed by Codd [3] to represent the *minimun capability of any reasonable query language using the relational model*. Moreover, as stated in [13]:

A language that can (at least) simulate tuple calculus, or equivalently, relational algebra or domain calculus, is said to be *complete*.

Query languages for the relational model break down into two broad classes:

algebraic languages: queries are expressed by applying operators to relations;
predicate calculus languages: a desired set of tuples is described by specifying a predicate the tuples must satisfy.

As shown in the previous section, on the one hand OCL expressions define the set of elements satisfying a constraint expression, and on the other some operators can be applied to sets of instances. Therefore OCL follows a mixed model. We now consider how to express the operations of the relational algebra in OCL.

Union is a primitive operation for collections in OCL and is expressed as:

```
set->union(set2 : Set(T)) : Set(T)
bag->union(bag2 : Bag(T)) : Bag(T)
sequence->union(sequence2 : Sequence(T)) : Sequence(T)
```

Both collections must be of the same type; only the union of sets and bags is allowed.

Difference is also a primitive operation for sets and is expressed as follows:

```
set - (set2 : Set(T)) : Set(T)
```

Difference is not defined for other subtypes of collection.

Cartesian product is not directly expressible in OCL.[1] Moreover, if an OCL expression computes a value of type T, then T either is a class present in the

---

[1] The only mention of Cartesian product in [9] is when introducing the extended variant of the forAll operation, namely the one with more than one iterator: `collection->forAll(e1,e2 | <Boolean-expression-on-e1-and-e2>)`, which in fact is a forAll on the Cartesian product of the collection with itself. The result of an expression of this form is Boolean.

Fig. 2. Cartesian product

class diagram being navigated or is a primitive type of OCL; in other words, any operation that computes values of another type cannot be expressed in OCL. However, if it is indispensable to add to a class diagram constraints only expressible using the Cartesian product of classes R and S, then a further class RS should be included, associated with R and S as shown in Fig. 2, and the following OCL expression should be attached that guarantees that the set of instances of RS in fact always is the Cartesian product of R and S:

```
R.allInstances->union(S.allInstances)->forAll(r, s : oclAny
|   if r.oclType.name=s.oclType.name
    then true
    else RS.allInstances->exists( t : RS | t.r=r and t.s=s) endif)
```

We take the union of the set of instances of class R and the set of instances of class S, and test if every two elements of this set either are of the same type (given that we cannot compare types, we compare their names) or there is an instance of class RS such that it is associated to both of them. Note that R.allInstances is of type Set(R) and S.allInstances is of type Set(S), and then the union of these two sets is of type Set(oclAny) where oclAny is the supertype of all types in the model. An alternative is to build a set of pairs (r,s) with r an instance of R and s an instance of S, where pairs are simulated by sequences of two elements. Unfortunately this is impossible since in OCL all collections of collections are automatically flattened. Still we can build a sequence {r1,s1,r1,s2,...,r1,sN,r2,s1,...,rM,sN} such that any subsequence {rI,sJ} (i.e. a subsequence of two elements beginning at an odd position) represents an element of the Cartesian product of R and S, such that conversely if r is an instance of R and s is an instance of S then there is a subsequence {r,s} of rs beginning at an odd position. This is achieved as follows:

```
R.allInstances->iterate(r : R ;
rs : Sequence(oclAny) = Sequence{}
|   S.allInstances->iterate(s : S ;
    rs1 : Sequence(oclAny) = rs
    |   rs1->append(r)->append(s)
)   )
```

rs is the sequence encoding the Cartesian product of R and S, which is of type Sequence(oclAny) since we do not know of another supertype of both R and S. The accumulator rs1 is needed because the return value of the inner iteration is the last value of its accumulator, and then rs can be properly updated.

Projection is possible for just one attribute using the `collect` on collections:

```
collection->collect(attrName)
```

The result of such an expression is `Bag(T)` if T is the type of values for `attrName`; in order to eliminate duplicates, one can use the operation `asSet` of bags:

```
collection->collect(attrName)->asSet
```

and in this way a result of type `Set(T)` is obtained. Given that the Cartesian product is not expressible in OCL, the projection on more than one attribute cannot be expressed in OCL either.[2] If we need the projection of the set of instances of a class on more than one attribute, say a1, ..., aN, then –similarly to the alternative proposed for the Cartesian product– we can build the sequence of $n \times m$ values (where $n = N$ and m is the number of instances currently present in the class, say R, to be projected) as follows:

```
R.allInstances->iterate(r : R ;
proj : Sequence(oclAny) = Sequence{}
|    proj->append(r.a1)->...->append(r.aN))
```

Selection can be expressed by using the `select` operation on collections:

```
collection->select(Boolean-expr)
```

Some derived operations have also a representation in OCL.

Intersection is a primitive in OCL for sets and bags, and is written as follows:

```
set->intersection(set2 : Set(T)) : Set(T)
set->intersection(bag : Bag(T)) : Set(T)
bag->intersection(bag2 : Bag(T)) : Bag(T)
bag->intersection(set : Set(T)) : Set(T)
```

Join of two relations is the selection of those tuples of a Cartesian product whose i-th component is in the relation θ with the corresponding $(r+j)$-th component. Given that we cannot compute Cartesian products, we assume that there is a class RS whose set of instances invariantly is the Cartesian product of the sets of instances of classes R and S (cf. paragraph on Cartesian product above) and we compute the join of R and S w.r.t. attributes a and b in the relation `theta` (assuming that θ is expressible in OCL) as follows:

```
RS.allInstances->select( t : RS | t.r.a theta t.s.b )
```

If alternatively we have built the sequence rs = {r1,s1,...} (see above paragraph on Cartesian product), then the join can likewise be stored in a sequence as follows:

```
Sequence{1..(rs->size)/2}->iterate(i : Integer ;
join : Sequence(oclAny) = Sequence{}
|    if (rs->at(2*i-1)).a theta (rs->at(2*i)).b
     then join->append(rs->at(2*i-1))->append(rs->at(2*i))
     else join endif)
```

---

[2] Notice that in general it cannot be ensured that the projection of a set of instances of a class (i.e. a set of n-tuples) is of a type present in the model, thus an operation returning such a set is not expressible in OCL; cf. discussion above on Cartesian products in OCL.

Here `rs` is the sequence containing the Cartesian product of R and S, and `Sequence{1..(rs->size)/2}` is the sequence of integer numbers between 1 and the size of `rs` (which we know of even length) divided by two, whose elements are used to index the sequence `rs`. Each element in `rs` at an odd position is an element of R and each element in `rs` at an even position is an element of S; each element in `rs` at an odd position is paired with its following in `rs`. If their a resp. b attribute are in the relation `theta`, then both of them are stored in the result accumulator `join`. (Note that, given that we cannot store values in variables, in the above algorithm we should replace every one the four occurrences of `rs` by the algorithm computing it, besides the first which could also be replaced by `R.allInstances->size * S.allInstances->size`. This fact would represent a problem if two different computations of `rs` yield sequences in different order.)

Natural join is similarly calculated: if `a1, ..., aN` are all the attributes in both R and S with the same name, then

```
RS.allInstances->select( t : RS | t.r.a1 = t.s.a1 and
                        ... t.r.aN = t.s.aN )
```

or alternatively

```
Sequence{1..(rs->size)/2}->iterate(i : Integer ;
join : Sequence(oclAny) = Sequence{} |
    if (rs->at(2*i-1)).a1 = (rs->at(2*i)).a1 and
    ... (rs->at(2*i-1)).aN = (rs->at(2*i)).aN
    then join->append(rs->at(2*i-1))->append(rs->at(2*i))
    else join endif)
```

The obvious conclusion is that OCL is incomplete. Completeness can be achieved by just including a concept of tuple functions (or creation of virtual classes) and a mechanism for creating instances of any type or class. These instances are of course not meant to be included to the current model of the class diagram but to allow navigation on a higher level of abstraction. The question is if in an object-oriented environment this is needed: one can argue that projection is not necessary since one can handle the whole object and use only the attrbutes of interest, and that if the Cartesian product is needed then the classes involved will be anyway connected in some form or another (e.g. by an association).

3.2   Transitive Closure of a Relation

Data manipulation languages normally have capabilities beyond those of relational calculus, like *arithmetic* operations, *assignment* commands, and *aggregate* functions. Often algebraic expressions must involve some arithmetic operations like $a < b + c$; notice that e.g. $+$ does not appear in the relational algebra. The assignment of a computed relation to be the value of a relation name is undoubtedly useful, see discussion about Cartesian product or projection in the previous section. Furthermore some operations like sum, average, max, min are also desirable as aggregate functions, that can be applied to columns of a relation to obtain a single quantity. For these reasons a (complete) query language with such capabilities is said to be *more than complete* [13, p. 175]. OCL includes the following arithmetic and aggregate functions:

type of operands	operations
Real	$=, +, -, *, /$, abs, floor, max, min, $<, >, <=, >=$
Integer	$=, +, -, *, /$, abs, div, mod, max, min
Boolean	$=$, or, xor, and, not, implies, if-then-else[3]
String	$=$, size, concat, toUpper, toLower, substring
Enumeration	$=, <>$

Notice that `Integer` is a subclass of `Real`, that is, for each formal parameter of type `Real` an actual parameter of type `Integer` can be used. OCL does not include assignment commands.

Some languages are *more than complete* even after eliminating the above mentioned functions. For example QBE (Query-by-Example, see [13]) allows the computation of the transitive closure of a relation. The transitive closure R^+ of a relation $R \subseteq A \times A$ is the least transitive relation containing R:

1. $xRy \Rightarrow xR^+y$;
2. $(x\ R^+\ y \wedge y\ R^+\ z) \Rightarrow xR^+z$;
3. if S satisfies (1) and (2), then $R^+ \subseteq S$.

The transitive closure of a relation cannot be expressed in relational algebra or relational calculus; see [2, 1]. The transitive closure of a relation is needed in our example of Fig. 1 if we want to ensure that no instance of `Group` is (recursively) an element of itself, since what we require is the non-reflexivity of the transitive closure of the relation `contains`. In the remainder of this section we study how to express this constraint in OCL.

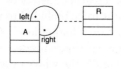

Fig. 3. An association class R from class A to class A

First of all what we need is a relation that, as R above, is a subset of the Cartesian product of a set A with itself. In the framework of UML class diagrams, the easiest is to have an association class (and not just an association name) as depicted in Fig. 3. We therefore lift the association name `contains` to an

---

[3] In the specification document [9] of OCL, the `if-then-else` operation is listed among the `Boolean` ones, of course just the first argument of an `if-then-else` operation has to be of type `Boolean` and its result value is of the (least) supertype of the types of the `then`-branch and of the `else`-branch.

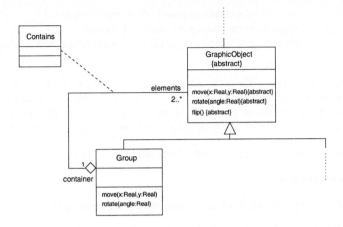

Fig. 4. The Contains association class

association class as pictured in Fig. 4. Notice that the relation Contains might include pairs of objects of different classes, like an instance of Group containing an instance of (a subclass of the abstract class) GeoFigure. The subset (which we call r) of instances of Contains that includes only the desired pairs, namely r = Contains ∩ (Group × Group), can be computed as follows:

```
-- algorithm computing r included in Group x Group:
Contains.allInstances->iterate(pair : Contains;
r : Set(Contains) = Set{}
|    if pair.elements.oclIsTypeOf(Group)
     then r->including(pair) else r endif)
```

Let us remark that, in the above query, every pair is just one pair of an instance of Group and a single instance of GraphicObject, which can be referred to by container resp. elements. The class GraphicObject is abstract, that means, any of its instances must be an instance of any of its concrete subclasses. In the iteration, therefore, we only include those pairs whose GraphicObject-component is of type Group. Now the Warshall's algorithm (see e.g. [5]) can be applied to r and in this way a new set s of instances of Contains is computed that is the transitive closure of r:

```
-- algorithm computing s, the transitive closure of r:
Group.allInstances->iterate(g3 : Group ;
s : Set(Contains) = r
|    Group.allInstances->iterate(g2 : Group ;
   s2 : Set(Contains) = s
   |    Group.allInstances->iterate(g1 : Group ;
      s1 : Set(Contains) = s2
      |    if s1->exists(c1,c2 : Contains |
              (c1.container=g1 and c1.elements=g2) or
              (c1.container=g1 and c1.elements=g3 and
```

```
            c2.container=g3 and c2.elements=g2)   )
        then s1->including(c) else s1 endif
      -- where: c : Contains with c.container=g1 and c.elements=g2
)   )   )
```

In the above algorithm the sets s1 and s2 had to be declared in order for s to be properly updated. The variant of exists with two iterators used in this algorithm is inexistent in OCL. However, given the equivalences $(\exists x)\varphi \equiv \neg(\forall x)\neg\varphi$ and $(\exists x)(\exists y)\varphi \equiv \neg(\forall x)\neg(\exists y)\varphi \equiv \neg(\forall x)\neg\neg(\forall y)\neg\varphi \equiv \neg(\forall x)(\forall y)\neg\varphi$,

```
collection->exists(e1,e2 | <Boolean-expr-on-e1-and-e2>)
```

is the abbreviation we use for

```
not collection->forAll(e1,e2 | not <Boolean-expr-on-e1-and-e2>).
```

The OCL constraint we are looking for is the non-reflexivity of the set s:

```
not s->exists(d : Contains | d.container=d.elements)
```

The desired OCL constraint is therefore the following:

```
not
Group.allInstances->iterate(g3 : Group ;
s : Set(Contains) = Contains.allInstances->iterate(pair : Contains;
                r : Set(Contains) = Set{}
                |   if pair.elements.oclIsTypeOf(Group)
                    then r->including(pair) else r endif
                )
|   Group.allInstances->iterate(g2 : Group ;
    s2 : Set(Contains) = s
    |   Group.allInstances->iterate(g1 : Group ;
        s1 : Set(Contains) = s2
        |   if s1->exists(c1,c2 : Contains |
              (c1.container=g1 and c1.elements=g2) or
              (c1.container=g1 and c1.elements=g3 and
               c2.container=g3 and c2.elements=g2)   )
            then s1->including(c) else s1 endif
          -- where: c : Contains with c.container=g1 and c.elements=g2
)   )   )->exists(d : Contains | d.container=d.elements)
```

Here we discover a problem: the instance c of Contains with c.container=g1 and c.elements=g2, necessary when computing s for recording partial paths, cannot be created. This instance is not meant to be added to the actual state of the model, the same as many sets and such that can be calculated using OCL are not meant to be added to the actual state of the model. Furthermore, and differently to what was remarked in Section 3.1 about Cartesian product and projection, we are not trying to generate an instance of an unknown type but of a type present in the class diagram. An alternative would be to manipulate, instead of a set s of instances of Contains, a set s' of pairs of instances of Group (represented by a sequence of length two) such that, if the sequence {g1,g2} belongs to s', then there is a path in r from g1 to g2. Unfortunately this is impossible since within OCL all collections of collections are automaticaly flattened (it is not specified what type has the result of flattening a set of sequences).

The third idea that comes to mind, in order to overcome nested collections, is to manipulate a sequence t with an even number of elements such that if g1 and g2 belong to t, g1 is at an odd position i of t, and g2 is at position i+1, then there is a path in r from g1 to g2. This seems to be a satisfactory solution, the problematic sentence s1->including(c) could then be replaced by t1->append(g1)->append(g2) (also in this case we need auxiliary variables t1 and t2). Now, the initial value of t is not r but

```
t : Sequence(Group)
= r->iterate(pair : Contains ;
    res : Sequence(Group) = Sequence{}
  |   res->append(pair.container)->append(pair.elements))
```

Also the algorithm computing the transitive closure of r has to be accordingly adapted wherever s, s1 or s2 are used. There is just one more place where one of these variables is used, namely when the existence is asked of two pairs c1 and c2 in s1 that satisfy certain property. Now we have to look for the existence of two subsequences of length two both beginning at an odd position and satisfying the same property. We access the subsequences using an index that points to their position in t. We replace the test

```
s1->exists(c1,c2 : Contains |
(c1.container=g1 and c1.elements=g2) or
(c1.container=g1 and c1.elements=g3 and
 c2.container=g3 and c2.elements=g2)  )
```

by the following

```
Sequence{1..(t1->size)/2}->exists(i,j : Integer |
(t1->at(2*i-1) = g1 and t1->at(2*i) = g2) or
(t1->at(2*i-1) = g1 and t1->at(2*i) = g3 and
 t1->at(2*j-1) = g3 and t1->at(2*j) = g2)          )
```

where Sequence{1..(t1->size)/2} is the sequence of integer numbers between 1 and the size of t1 (which we know of even length) divided by two, and the elements of this sequence are used to index the sequence t1.

Finally in a similar way we can test the non-reflexivity of t:

```
not Sequence{1..(t->size)/2}->exists(i : Integer
 |   t->at(2*i-1) = t->at(2*i)               )
```

There is still a last hurdle to surmount. t is just a mnemonic we have used, that has to be replaced by the algorithm that computes it, since we cannot use a variable. t occurs three times in the above test of non-reflexivity, and we would like to calculate it only once. Moreover, if we replace each one of the three occurrences of t in the test above, then we cannot be sure that each instance of the sequence is equal to another one, and in particular when testing if t->at(2*i) = t->at(2*i+1) it is absolutely necessary that both t's at each side of the equation are equal. The only constructs using new names are the operations iterating on collections, and of them only `iterate` allows for a variable of an arbitrary type (namely the accumulator) and the assignment of an arbitrary value to this variable. But the last value of the accumulator is the return value of an `iterate`, and we need a `Boolean`. We can therefore just *assume* that the different occurrences of the algorithm computing t return always the same sequence. The resulting algorithm is as follows:

```
not Sequence{1..(
    -- t
    Group.allInstances->iterate(g3 : Group ;
    t : Sequence(Group) = -- r
        Contains.allInstances->iterate(pair : Contains;
        r : Set(Contains) = Set{}
        |   if pair.elements.oclIsTypeOf(Group)
            then r->including(pair) else r endif
        )->iterate(pair : Contains ;
        res : Sequence(Group) = Sequence{}
        |   res->append(pair.container)->append(pair.elements)
        )
    |   Group.allInstances->iterate(g2 : Group ;
        t2 : Sequence(Group) = t
        |   Group.allInstances->iterate(g1 : Group ;
            t1 : Sequence(Group) = t2
            |   if Sequence{1..(t1->size)/2}->exists(i,j : Integer |
                    (t1->at(2*i-1) = g1 and t1->at(2*i) = g2) or
                    (t1->at(2*i-1) = g1 and t1->at(2*i) = g3 and
                    t1->at(2*j-1) = g3 and t1->at(2*j) = g2)         )
                then t1->append(g1)->append(g2) else t1 endif
    )   )   )
    ->size)/2}->exists(i : Integer
|   -- t
    Group.allInstances->iterate(g3 : Group ;
    t : Sequence(Group) = -- r
        Contains.allInstances->iterate(pair : Contains;
        r : Set(Contains) = Set{}
        |   if pair.elements.oclIsTypeOf(Group)
            then r->including(pair) else r endif
        )->iterate(pair : Contains ;
        res : Sequence(Group) = Sequence{}
        |   res->append(pair.container)->append(pair.elements)
        )
    |   Group.allInstances->iterate(g2 : Group ;
        t2 : Sequence(Group) = t
        |   Group.allInstances->iterate(g1 : Group ;
            t1 : Sequence(Group) = t2
            |   if Sequence{1..(t1->size)/2}->exists(i,j : Integer |
                    (t1->at(2*i-1) = g1 and t1->at(2*i) = g2) or
                    (t1->at(2*i-1) = g1 and t1->at(2*i) = g3 and
                    t1->at(2*j-1) = g3 and t1->at(2*j) = g2)         )
```

```
                    then t1->append(g1)->append(g2) else t1 endif
    )    )    )
    ->at(2*i-1) =
    -- t
    Group.allInstances->iterate(g3 : Group ;
    t : Sequence(Group) = -- r
        Contains.allInstances->iterate(pair : Contains;
        r : Set(Contains) = Set{}
        |    if pair.elements.oclIsTypeOf(Group)
             then r->including(pair) else r endif
        )->iterate(pair : Contains ;
        res : Sequence(Group) = Sequence{}
        |    res->append(pair.container)->append(pair.elements)
        )
    |    Group.allInstances->iterate(g2 : Group ;
        t2 : Sequence(Group) = t
        |    Group.allInstances->iterate(g1 : Group ;
            t1 : Sequence(Group) = t2
            |    if Sequence{1..(t1->size)/2}->exists(i,j : Integer |
                    (t1->at(2*i-1) = g1 and t1->at(2*i) = g2) or
                    (t1->at(2*i-1) = g1 and t1->at(2*i) = g3 and
                     t1->at(2*j-1) = g3 and t1->at(2*j) = g2)          )
                then t1->append(g1)->append(g2) else t1 endif
    )    )    )
    ->at(2*i)
)
```

Although the computation capabilities for computing the transitive closure of a binary relation are present in OCL, here again a concept of tuple functions would have made the above algorithm considerably simpler. At this point we want to remark the notion of *relational completeness* as formulated in [8, p. 94]:

> In language implementations, the following two operations are needed to assure relational completeness:
> (a) The ability to represent assignments, that is, the ability to create new relations to store the results of relational algebra operations that are also relations. [...]
> (b) The ability to compute transitive closures which enables recursion and/or nesting of relational algebra operations to express expressions of arbitrary complexity. [...]

Also Codd (see [3]) asserted the need for more than complete languages, providing tuple and aggregate functions.

3.3   Turing Completeness

This section addresses the Turing completeness of OCL. We show that primitive recursive functions are expressible in OCL and hint why general recursive functions cannot be expressed in OCL. In order to do so, we show that LOOP-programs can and WHILE-programs cannot be written in OCL (see [11]).

The syntax of LOOP-programs is as follows:

$$P ::= X \text{ <- } X + C \mid X \text{ <- } X - C \mid \text{LOOP } X \text{ DO } P \text{ END} \mid P \text{ ; } P$$
$$X ::= x_0 \mid x_1 \mid x_2 \mid \ldots \qquad \qquad (variables)$$
$$C ::= 0 \mid 1 \mid 2 \mid \ldots \qquad \qquad (constants)$$

The semantics of LOOP-programs is straightforward. The value assignment x_i <- $x_j + c$ is interpreted as usual, that is, the new value of the variable x_i is the value of x_j plus c. The value assignment x_i <- $x_j - c$ is the non-negative subtraction, that is, if $c > x_j$ then the new value of x_i is 0 otherwise the value of x_j minus c. A LOOP-program of the form P_1 ; P_2 is interpreted as the execution of P_1 and afterwards the execution of P_2. Finally a LOOP-program of the form LOOP x_i DO P END is interpreted as follows: the program P is executed n times, where n is the value of the variable x_i *at the beginning* (i.e. the change of the value of x_i within P does not affect the number of repetitions). Given a LOOP-program that computes a k-ary function f, it is assumed that the input values $n_1, \ldots, n_k$ are initially stored in the variables $x_1, \ldots, x_k$, that any other variable has initial value 0, and that the result $f(n_1, \ldots, n_k)$ is stored in the variable x_0 after execution of the program.

LOOP-programs are WHILE-programs, and additionally if P is a WHILE-program then WHILE $x_i \neq 0$ DO P END is a WHILE-program. The semantics of the new construct is the following: the program P is repeatedly executed as long as the value of x_i is different from 0. (The LOOP construct becomes superfluous, LOOP x DO P END can be simulated by WHILE $y \neq 0$ DO P ; $y := y - 1$ END.)

Every LOOP-program can be computed by an OCL expression. Indeed, given a LOOP-program P computing a k-ary function and using auxiliary variables $x_{k+1}, \ldots, x_r$, we write an OCL expression that manipulates an array vals$_1$ of $r + 1$ values (representing the values of the variables $x_0, \ldots, x_r$) and returns the first value of this array after executing the translation of P:

```
Sequence{1..1}->iterate(it : Integer ; -- iterator, will be ignored
vals₁ : Sequence(Integer) = {0,n₁,...,nₖ, 0,....,0 }
```
$$\underbrace{}_{(r-k) \text{ times}}$$
```
|     trans(P,1)
)->first
```

The return value of the above expression is the first value of the sequence vals$_1$ after (iterating one time) the execution of $trans(P, 1)$. Initially vals$_1$ stores the value n_i for the variable x_i ($i = 1, \ldots, k$) and 0 otherwise. In general, the return value of $trans(P, n)$ with $n \in \mathbb{N}$ is stored in vals$_n$. The OCL expression $trans(P, n)$ is defined by induction on P as follows:

- The translation $trans(P, n)$ of a program P of the form x_i <- $x_j + c$ depends on i and j and is defined by:
  - $trans(x_i$ <- $x_i + c, n) =$
    ```
    valsₙ->iterate(val : Integer ;
    newvals : Sequence(Integer) = Sequence{}
    ```

```
|   if newvals->size = i
    then newvals->append(val+c)
    else newvals->append(val) endif)
```
- if $i > j$, then
$trans(x_i$ <- $x_j + c, n) =$
```
valsₙ->iterate(val : Integer ;
newvals : Sequence(Integer) = Sequence{}
|   if newvals->size = i
    then newvals->append(newvals->at(j+1)+c)
    else newvals->append(val) endif)
```
- if $i < j$, then
$trans(x_i$ <- $x_j + c, n) =$
```
valsₙ->iterate(val : Integer ;
newvals : Sequence(Integer) = Sequence{}
|   if newvals->size = j
    then (newvals->subSequence(1,i))              -- (1)
        ->append(val+c)
        ->union(newvals->subSequence(i+2,j)) -- (2)
        ->append(val)
    else newvals->append(val) endif)⁴
```

- The translation $trans(P, n)$ of a program P of the form x_i <- $x_j - c$ depends not only on i and j but also on the values of x_j and c, and is defined by:
  - $trans(x_i$ <- $x_i - c, n) =$
  ```
  valsₙ->iterate(val : Integer ;
  newvals : Sequence(Integer) = Sequence{}
  |   if newvals->size = i
      then newvals->append(if val<c then 0 else val-c endif)
      else newvals->append(val) endif)
  ```
  - if $i > j$, then
  $trans(x_i$ <- $x_j - c, n) =$
  ```
  valsₙ->iterate(val : Integer ;
  newvals : Sequence(Integer) = Sequence{}
  |   if newvals->size = i
      then newvals->append(if newvals->at(j+1)<c then 0
                          else newvals->at(j+1)-c endif)
      else newvals->append(val) endif)
  ```
  - if $i < j$, then
  $trans(x_i$ <- $x_j - c, n) =$
  ```
  valsₙ->iterate(val : Integer ;
  newvals : Sequence(Integer) = Sequence{}
  |   if newvals->size = j
      then (newvals->subSequence(1,i))              -- (1)
          ->append(if val<c then 0 else val-c endif)
  ```

---

⁴ Notice that $i < j$ implies $i + 1 \leq j$, therefore it might be incorrect to speak of the subsequence of newvals starting at $i + 2$ and ending at j, see statement above commented with (2). The same w.r.t. the sentence commented with (1) if $i = 0$. [9] does specify the result of extracting a subsequence whose upper position number is less than its lower position number, we therefore assume that in such a case the subsequence is empty.

```
                ->union(newvals->subSequence(i+2,j)) -- (2)
                ->append(val)
          else newvals->append(val) endif)
```
[5]

- $trans($LOOP x_i DO P END$, n) =$
```
Sequence{1..valsn->at(i+1)}->iterate(it : Integer ; -- will be ignored
valsn+1 : Sequence(Integer) = valsn
|  trans(P,n + 1))
```
- $trans(P_1$; $P_2, n) =$
```
Sequence{1..2}->iterate(step : Integer ;
valsn+1 : Sequence(Integer) = valsn
|  if step = 1 then trans(P1,n + 1) else trans(P2,n + 1) endif)
```

The number n accompanying the definition of $trans$ allows for the definition of new variables that do not shadow previously (in the outer block) defined ones.

So for instance the function $f(n, m) = n + m$ is computed by the program X0 <- X1 + X2 and can be encoded as the following LOOP-program P

```
X0 <- X1 + 0 ;     -- P1
LOOP X2 DO         -- P2
    X0 <- X0 + 1   -- P21
END
```

which is translated to OCL by successively calculating $trans$ as follows:

```
1. Sequence{1..1}->iterate(it : Integer ;
   vals1 : Sequence(Integer) = {0,n,m} | trans(P,1))->first
2. Sequence{1..1}->iterate(it : Integer ;
   vals1 : Sequence(Integer) = {0,n,m}
   |  Sequence{1..2}->iterate(step : Integer ;
      vals2 : Sequence(Integer) = vals1
      |  if step = 1 then trans(P1,2) else trans(P2,2) endif) )->first
3. Sequence{1..1}->iterate(it : Integer ;
   vals1 : Sequence(Integer) = {0,n,m}
   |  Sequence{1..2}->iterate(step : Integer ;
      vals2 : Sequence(Integer) = vals1
      |  if step = 1
         then vals2->iterate(val : Integer ;
              newvals : Sequence(Integer) = Sequence{}
              |  if newvals->size = 1
                 then (newvals->subSequence(1,0))->append(val+0)
                     ->union(newvals->subSequence(0+2,1))->append(val)
                 else newvals->append(val)
                 endif)
         else Sequence{1..vals2->at(2+1)}->iterate(it : Integer ;
              vals3 : Sequence(Integer) = vals2
              |  trans(P21,3))
         endif)
   )->first
```

---

[5] Here again we assume that the subsequence (1) of newvals starting at 1 and ending at i is empty if $i = 0$, and that the subsequence (2) of newvals starting at $i+2$ and ending at j is empty if $i + 1 = j$.

```
4. Sequence{1..1}->iterate(it : Integer ;
   vals1 : Sequence(Integer) = {0,n,m}
   |  Sequence{1..2}->iterate(step : Integer ;
      vals2 : Sequence(Integer) = vals1
      |  if step = 1
         then vals2->iterate(val : Integer ;
                 newvals : Sequence(Integer) = Sequence{}
                 |  if newvals->size = 1
                    then (newvals->subSequence(1,0))->append(val+0)
                         ->union(newvals->subSequence(0+2,1))->append(val)
                    else newvals->append(val)
                    endif)
         else Sequence{1..vals2->at(2+1)}->iterate(it : Integer ;
                 vals3 : Sequence(Integer) = vals2
                 |  vals3->iterate(val : Integer ;
                    newvals : Sequence(Integer) = Sequence{}
                    |  if newvals->size = 0
                       then newvals->append(val+1)
                       else newvals->append(val) endif)
              )
         endif)
   )->first
```

We now prove that the OCL expression defined in terms of a LOOP-program computes the same function.

Proposition 1. *Let P be a LOOP-program used in a context where only variables among $x_0, \ldots, x_r$ are used. For any $m_0, \ldots, m_r, m'_0, \ldots, m'_r \in \mathbb{N}$, for any $n \in \mathbb{N}$, if the variable x_i changes its value from m_i to m'_i $(i = 0, \ldots, r)$ after the execution of P, then $vals_n$ changes its value from $\{m_0, \ldots, m_r\}$ to $\{m'_0, \ldots, m'_r\}$ after the execution of $trans(P, n)$.*

Proof. The thesis is proved by induction on the structure of P.

- (P is x_i <- $x_j \pm c$)
  Trivial.
- (P is LOOP x_j DO P' END)
  $trans(P, k) = $ Sequence{1..$vals_k$->at(j+1)}->iterate(i : Integer ;
           $vals_{k+1}$: Sequence(Integer) = $vals_k$
           | $trans(P', k+1)$)
  By IH, for any $m_1, \ldots, m_r, m'_1, \ldots, m'_r \in \mathbb{N}$, for any $n \in \mathbb{N}$, if the variable x_i changes its value from m_i to m'_i $(i = 1, \ldots, r)$ after the execution of P', then $vals_n$ changes its value from $\{m_0, \ldots, m_r\}$ to $\{m'_0, \ldots, m'_r\}$ after the execution of $trans(P', n)$, in particular for $n = k + 1$.
  Therefore, if $vals_k = \{l_0, \ldots, l_r\}$, then $vals_k$->at(j+1) $= l_j$, $vals_{k+1}$ is initialized by $trans(P, k)$ with the value of $vals_k$, and if after l_j successive executions of P' the variable x_i changes its value from l_i to l'_i, then after

l_j successive executions of $trans(P', k + 1)$ $\texttt{vals}_{k+1}$ changes its value from $\{l_0, \ldots, l_r\}$ to $\{l'_0, \ldots, l'_r\}$.

Given that the last value of $\texttt{vals}_{k+1}$ is the return value of $trans(P, k)$, the thesis holds.

$-$ (P is P_1 ; P_2)

$trans(P, k) =$ Sequence{1..2}->iterate(step : Integer ;

                $\texttt{vals}_{k+1}$: Sequence(Integer) = $\texttt{vals}_k$

            | if step = 1

                then $trans(P_1, k + 1)$ else $trans(P_2, k + 1)$ endif)

This case is also trivial by IH.

$\square$

Hence, every LOOP function is also computable using an OCL expression.

Consider now the WHILE construct of WHILE-programs. The iterating construct $\texttt{iterate}$ runs through a collection (randomly ordered if not a sequence) from its beginning to its end. Thus, an $\texttt{iterate}$ terminates if, and only if, the collection is finite. Notice that, on the one hand and according to [9, p. 13], there are three ways of getting a collection:

1. by a literal, e.g. Set{1,2,5,3}, or
2. by a navigation, e.g. Polygon self.vertices, or
3. by operations on collections, e.g. set->union(set2).

The first two possibilities return a finite collection, and finite collections are closed under the operations mentioned as third possibility.[6] But, on the other hand, the feature $\texttt{allInstances}$ associated with the type $\texttt{oclType}$ of types returns a set; see [9, p. 20]. That is, by writing $\texttt{Integer.allInstances}$ (or even $\texttt{Real.allInstances}$) we could also obtain an infinite collection.

In any way, an $\texttt{iterate}$ either performs a previously determined number of iterations or does not terminate, since there is no possibility of interrupting an $\texttt{iterate}$ (like e.g. the $\texttt{break}$ command of C). In other words, the WHILE construct cannot be encoded in OCL, and thus semidecidable problems in general cannot be solved using OCL.

Therefore, given that the class of primitive recursive functions coincides with the class of LOOP-computable functions and that the class of μ-recursive functions coincides with the class of WHILE-computable functions (see [11]), OCL allows only for the definition of primitive recursive functions (or totally undefined functions if $\texttt{Integer.allInstances}$ is a valid OCL expression).

4 Conclusions

OCL brought to UML 1.1 two advantages: At metalevel it has been used for the definition of the UML metamodel and at user level it can be used to describe additional constraints about the objects in the model, constraints that cannot be described in a graphic way. OCL can also be used as a navigation language. We

---

[6] This is also true for the negation given the (implicit) closed world assumption.

have shown that OCL is not as expressive as the relational calculus and therefore it is incomplete as query language in the database sense. On the other hand we have shown that in OCL the transitive closure of a relation, operation that cannot be expressed in relational calculus, can be computed by an OCL expression (assuming some kind of determinism when constructing twice a sequence); the resulting code is somehow tricky and neither intuitive nor easy to read. Both relational completeness and an easier to read OCL expression computing the transitive closure of a binary relation can be achieved by just adding a concept of tupling. Finally we demonstrated that OCL can compute any primitive recursive function and hinted that not any recursive function can be computed by an OCL expression; in other words, OCL is not equivalent to a Turing machine.

Since we first wrote this article, a book [14] on OCL was published that completes the original OCL specification with many and detailed examples; unfortunately, some questions like e.g. the result type of flattening collections in general is still missing. Due to the ambiguities, some inconsistencies and the lack of formality of the OCL specification some authors have suggested to replace it by other well-founded language such as EER (see [6]) or CASL (see [12] and also [7]). It is expected that new revisions of UML will also bring to the community a new revised version of OCL or, may be better, a new approach to facilitate navigation and specification of model properties in a formal way.

References

[1] A. V. Aho and J. D. Ullman. Universality of data retrieval languages. In *Sixth ACM Symposium on Principles of Programming Languages (POPL 79, proceedings)*, pages 110–117, 1979.

[2] P. Atzeni and V. D. Antonellis. *Relational database theory*. The Benjamin/-Cummings Publishing Company, Inc., 1993.

[3] E. F. Codd. Relational Completeness of Data Base Sublanguages. In R. Rustin, editor, *Data Base Systems*, pages 65–98. Prentice Hall, Englewood Cliffs, New Jersey, 1972.

[4] S. Cook and J. Daniels. *Designing Object Systems—Object Oriented Modeling with Syntropy*. Prentice Hall, 1994.

[5] J. L. Gersting. *Mathematical Structures for Computer Science*. Computer Science Press, 3rd edition, 1993.

[6] M. Gogolla and M. Richters. On Constraints and Queries in UML. In M. Schader and A. Korthaus, editors, *Proc. UML'97 Workshop 'The Unified Modeling Language - Technical Aspects and Applications'*, pages 109–121. Physica-Verlag, Heidelberg, 1997.

[7] P. D. Mosses. CoFI: The common framework initiative for algebraic specification and development. In M. Bidoit and M. Dauchet, editors, *TAPSOFT '97: Proceedings of the Seventh Joint Conference on Theory and Practice of Software Development, 7th International Joint Conference CAAP/FASE*, number 1214 in LNCS, Lille, France, Apr. 1997. Springer.

[8] E. Ozkarahan. *Database Machines and Database Management*. Prentice Hall, 1986.

[9] RATIONAL Software Corporation. *Object Constraint Language Specification*, Sept. 1997. Version 1.1. Available at www.rational.com/uml/.

[10] M. Richters and M. Gogolla. On Formalizing the UML Object Constraint Language OCL. In T.-W. Ling, editor, *Proc. 17th Int. Conf. Conceptual Modeling (ER'98)*. Springer, Berlin, LNCS, 1998.

[11] U. Schöning. *Theoretische Informatik – kurzgefaßt*. Spektrum Akademischer Verlag, 2nd edition, 1995.

[12] The CoFI Task Group on Language Design. CASL: The common algebraic specification language: Summary. Available at `www.brics.dk/Projects/CoFI/Documents/CASL/Summary/`, 1998.

[13] J. D. Ullman. *Principles of Database Systems*. Computer Software Engineering Series. Computer Science Press, 1982.

[14] J. B. Warmer and A. B. Kleppe. *The Object Constraint Language: Precise Modeling with UML*. Addison-Wesley, 1999.

A Systematic Approach to Transform OMT Diagrams to a B Specification

Eric Meyer and Jeanine Souquières

LORIA - Université Nancy 2 - UMR 7503 ,
Campus scientifique, BP 239,
54506 Vandœuvre-les-Nancy Cedex - France,
Tel: +33 3.83.59.20.42   Fax: +33 3.83.41.30.79
{meyer,souquier}@loria.fr

Abstract. This paper presents a systematic transformation of semi-formal specifications expressed with OMT notations into formal specifications. The object model is first transformed into a specification composed of a set of B machines. Then each component of the dynamic model is transformed and integrated into the previous specification leading to a single specification. Transformations are presented as generic templates. When using these templates, the generated specification is automatically proved within the B prover relatively to the invariant preservation.

1   Introduction

Early phases of software development are crucial for the quality of software. The usefulness of formal specifications is now well accepted. But formal specifications are difficult to develop and to understand. More effort has been spent to develop new languages than to provide methodological guidance for using existing ones. But it does not suffice to hand a language description to specifiers and to expect them to be able to produce formal specifications. Moreover, formal specifications techniques are not well integrated with the analysis phase of software engineering.

Today, software engineers in industry mostly use semi-formal techniques like data-flow diagrams, entity-relationship diagrams, finite state machines or decision tables. Object oriented approaches and notations like OMT [15], Fusion [4] or UML [16] are now quite popular. These techniques have the advantage that they support the intuitive understanding of specification by graphical representations. They are useful for understanding problems and for the documentation allowing a better communication with customers. Sophisticated tool support is widely available. However, semi-formal techniques do not perform the transition from informal to formal texts. Therefore, the resulting specifications can be subject to misinterpretations. This makes them an insecure basis for the development contract.

Our approach aims at a better support of the early phases of the software development, thus contributing to a better quality of the specification. It votes

J. Wing, J. Woodcock, J. Davies (Eds.): FM'99, Vol. I, LNCS 1708, pp. 875–895, 1999.
© Springer-Verlag Berlin Heidelberg 1999

to combine semi-formal diagrammatical descriptions with formal specifications, providing a bridge from the informal object oriented modelling concepts to the formal notation. It starts from the object and the dynamic models of the OMT method. Then these models are translated into a B specification [2] using predefined generic templates. We focus on producing formalisations that can directly support verification and validation activities, and for which mechanical support exists.

In this paper, we focus on the definition of the B generic templates issued from the object and dynamic OMT diagrams. Section 2 presents the OMT approach developing the object and the dynamic models. Section 3 is about the translation of these diagrams into a single B specification. Details are given on the definition of each component and on their integration into a single specification. Translations are defined as B generic predefined templates. In section 4, we discuss about the proof of these templates using the B tool. Section 5 presents the state of the art and a summary of our contributions concludes the paper.

2   An Overview of Part of the OMT Notations

The goal of OMT is to model systems using object-oriented concepts. The underlying method [15] integrates analysis, conception and coding activities, using three kind of models: the object, the dynamic and the functional ones.

The object model is the core of these model, it defines the static structure of the information manipulated by the application in terms of classes and the relationships among them. The dynamic model describes the evolution of the objects. It is defined by state diagrams. Automatons with a finite number of states are associated to all or a part of the classes. They present the different states of an object, transitions between these states and events that can be sent or received. The functional model defines the transformation of data in the system. Classically, it is issued from the data flow diagrams in the Yourdon and Ward [21] approach.

In this section, we summarise the different components of the object and dynamic models.

2.1   Object Model

Object model (see Fig. 1) provides a graphical notation for modelling objects, classes and their relationships to one another. They are easy to understand. The object model comes in two varieties of static diagrams: class diagrams showing generic descriptions of possible systems and object diagrams describing particular instantiations of systems. In most case, a system is built with several class diagrams plus occasional object diagrams illustrating complicated data structures.

Classes. A generic class diagram is presented in Fig. 1. Classes are drawn as boxes. A class ($Class_i$) describes a graph of objects with similar properties given

by a list of typed attributes ($AttrList_i$) and common behaviour expressed by
a list of operations ($OperList_i$). A parameterized class is specified by including
a list of formal typed parameters: $Class_i < Param_i : Type_{par} >$. Type and
initial values for attribute can be specified as $Attr_i : Type_{att} = Val_{att}$. Input
and output parameters of an operation can optionally be defined: $Op_i(arg :
Type_{arg}) : Type_{op}$. The attribute and operation sections of the class box can be
omitted to reduce detail in the overview. A class can have a multiplicity indicator
($mult_j$ for $class_j$), drawn as a small expression in the upper right corner; it
indicates how many instances of the class can exist at a time.

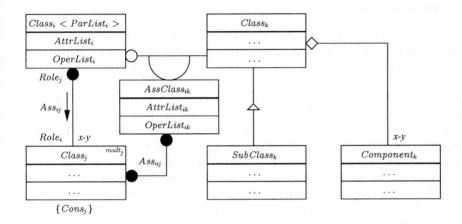

Fig. 1. A generic object model

Relations. Classes can be related to each other establishing structural relationships between objects of different classes. An association (Ass_{ij} in Fig. 1) relates
two classes, either more by a line. It can have a name with an arrow showing
which way the name is read. Each end of an association is a role ($Role_i, Role_j$).
Each role can be named, describing how its class is considered by the other class.
Each role indicates the cardinality of its class that restricts the number of class
instances that can be associated to one instance of the other. Cardinality can
be 1 (no marker), 0-1 (drawn by $\circ$), 0 or more (drawn by $\bullet$), or some other
integer range value (indicated by an expression as $x - y$). An association can
be considered as a class itself ($AssClass_{ik}$) with its own attributes, operations
and associations. In addition to associations, inheritance relationship between a
superclass ($Class_k$) and its subclass ($SubClass_k$) can be represented as a triangle
with a line from the apex to the superclass and one line from the baseline to
each subclass.

Aggregation. Aggregation is the "part-whole" or "a-part-of" relationship in
which objects representing the components of something are associated to an
object representing the entire assembly. Aggregation is a tightly coupled form of

association with some extra semantics. Aggregations are drawn like associations, except a small diamond indicating the assembly end of the relationship. Aggregation is shown in Fig. 1 : $Class_k$ is defined by the aggregation $Component_k$.

Constraints. It is useful in some cases to restrict the values that objects or links can assume. A constraint is a restriction on values expressed as a predicate attached to a class or an association. It is enclosed in braces and placed near the elements it constrains (see $Cons_j$ for the $Class_j$ in Fig. 1).

2.2   Dynamic Model

The dynamic model (see Fig. 2) based on state diagrams is a complement to the object model. It shows the local behaviour of the objects of a class. It presents abstractions of sets of possible states for objects, and which events change the state. A state is a function of the attributes values and the links of the object. An object can realize within a state some operations which do not modify its state, these operations are called activities or internal actions. An activity is an ongoing operation that takes time to complete whereas internal actions are instantaneously operations triggered by events. A change of state is called a transition and is triggered by an event which is something happening at a moment. An action can be connected to a transition, specifying what would be done in association with the state transition. As actions, events can be sent by objects to other objects. State diagrams are not drawn for all classes, only for those that have a number of well-defined states and where the behaviour is affected and changed by different events. They can be drawn for the system as a whole.

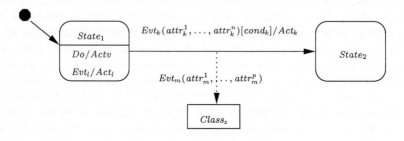

Fig. 2. A generic dynamic model

A state diagram is a directed graph whose nodes are states ($State_1$, $State_2$ in Fig. 2) and whose directed arcs are transitions. A transition is annotated by an event (Evt_k) and can optionally be followed by one or several attributes ($attr_x^y$) into brackets. A condition ($cond_k$) considered as a guard for the transition can be specified between hooks, actions (Act_k) are noted on the transition after the event and the guard. Activities or internal actions are represented within the states. An activity ($Actv$) is noted after the keyword (Do) and internal actions (Act_l) follow the name of the associated event (Evt_l). When an object sends an event to another object, it is represented by an arrow in dotted lines that goes from the associated transition to a box denoting the name of the destination object class ($Classe_z$), the arrow is annotated by the event sent ($Evt_m(attr_m^1, ..., attr_m^p)$). Finally, the entry point in a state diagram is denoted by a full circle and an arrow toward the initial state.

3   From OMT Diagrams to a B Specification

This section presents the B method and a systematic transformation of the two previous OMT models into a B specification.

Created by Jean-Raymond Abrial, the B method [2] is a formal software development method that covers the software process from the specification to the implementation. B notations are based on the mathematical concepts of set theory, the language of generalised substitutions and the first order logic. Specifications are composed of abstract machines similar to modules or classes; they consist of a set of variables, properties on these variables called the invariant and operations. The state of the system, i.e. the set of variables values, is only modifiable by methods (operations). Various possibilities of machine links are given allowing large systems to be specified, and modular and reusable text to be produced. The B model is then refined, i.e. specialized, until a complete implementation of the software system is obtained. Refinement can be seen as an implementation technique but also as a gradually specification technique enabling progressive inclusion of details. In every stage of the specification, proof obligations are generated verifying that the operations preserve the invariant of the system. Refinement are proven correct by generation and proof of refinement proofs.

Note that, in this discussion, we don't take into account the evolution of B proposed by Abrial and Mussa in [1, 3].

3.1   From an Object Model to a B Specification

For each concept introduced in the section 2.1, we discuss its formalisation and define a B generic template. Then we build a B specification for the whole object model showing how the different components are distributed in various abstract machines.

Classes. Classes are expressed by abstract machines. If they are parameterized, names of formal parameters are expressed in brackets after the name of the machine and typed by a predicate inside the CONSTRAINTS clause. An abstract machine Class$_i$ describes a deferred set CLASS$_i$ of the possible instances of a class $Class_i$. The set of existing instances is modelled by a variable class$_i$ constrained to be a subset of CLASS$_i$. For each attribute $Attr_i$, a variable attr$_i$

SETS	$state_i, \dots$
$\quad STATE_i = \{state_1, state_2\}$	INVARIANT
VARIABLES	$\quad state_i \in class_i \rightarrow STATE_i \wedge$

Fig. 10. Template for the state

An alternative state representation is proposed by Lano [10] in which each state of the diagram is represented by a subset of an existing instances set. Modification of a state is processed by moving the objects from one state set to the other. This approach has the advantage to generate proof obligations which are more simple and easier to resolve, but it becomes infeasable once the number of states is important.

Transitions. Each event is formalized by an operation. This operation is parameterized by the target objects and the eventual parameters of the event. Parameters are typed by a predicate in the precondition of the operation. The operation is defined by a SELECT substitution which has as many cases as transitions where the event appears. The operation modifies the state of the object and calls the operations associated to actions and events specified in the transition. As presented below, an action is formalized by a B operation, this operation results from the object model and will be completed by the functional model translation. Actitivities are extra actions which take care that the object is in the appropriate state.

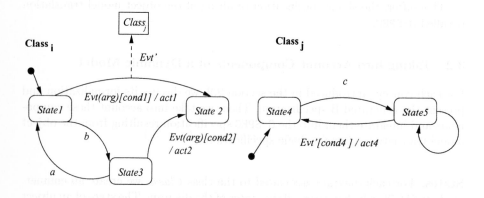

Fig. 11. State diagrams for $Class_i$ and $Class_j$

The translation of an event Evt used in the $Class_i$ state diagram (see fig. 11) is presented in Fig. 12.

$$\begin{array}{l|l}
\texttt{Evt}(c_i, \texttt{arg}) = & \texttt{SELECT}\ \ \texttt{state}_i(c_i) = \texttt{state1} \land \texttt{cond1} \\
\texttt{PRE} & \quad\texttt{THEN}\ \ \texttt{state}_i(c_i) := \texttt{state2} \parallel \texttt{act1} \parallel \texttt{Evt}' \\
\quad c_i \in \texttt{class}_i \land & \texttt{WHEN}\ \ \texttt{state}_i(c_i) = \texttt{state3} \land \texttt{cond2} \\
\quad \texttt{arg} \in \texttt{Type}_{\texttt{arg}} & \quad\texttt{THEN}\ \ \texttt{state}_i(c_i) := \texttt{state2} \parallel \texttt{act2} \\
\texttt{THEN} & \texttt{ELSE skip END} \\
& \texttt{END}
\end{array}$$

Fig. 12. Template for an event

Integrating the Dynamic Model into the O-SPEC Specification. We have presented the formalization of each concept of the dynamic model. This section is devoted to the integration of these concepts into a whole specification, taking into account that an object model has been first defined, formalised with the O-SPEC specification.

The B formalization of states of a class *Class_i* must be defined in the abstract machine associated to this class. We consider that a state is a data of a class and therefore must be formalized in the abstract machine defining this class.

When translating transitions, several concepts have been identified. We present now separately each of them, and express the needed conditions.

- Target objects: they are instances of different classes. These instances are reached via the set of existing instances (variable $\texttt{class}_i$ for the class $Class_i$). Thus, the machines where these various variables are defined must be accessible in the machine where we formalize target objects.
- Firing conditions: they are predicates on attributes and associations of a class. We saw previously that attributes and associations of a class can be specified in different machines (not fixed association). The firing condition has to be introduced in a machine which reaches data of both others.
- Action calls: they are operations which modify the data of a class or an association and are formalized by translation of object and functional models. We distinguish between the actions which modify attributes of a class and those which modify associations. The first ones are specified in the machine representing the class and the second ones are defined in the machine modelling the association. Here, we are constrained by several obligations: the necessity to include machines where actions are defined and if we are in the machine which defines the action, the necessity to rewrite its definition in the body of the operation which calls it.
- Access and modification of states: states are formalized by variables defined as a total function from a set of existing instances to an enumerated set of all the possible states. The access to a variable is possible outside the machine where it is defined whether it belongs to the set of included or used machines. The modification of a variable is authorized outside the machine **A** where it is defined only by the use of its modification operations. The machine **A** must then be included.
- Communication with other events: sending an event by another one is expressed by an operation call. The constraints inherent in the event call are

We start by specifying two generic models (see Fig. 14): an object and a dynamic one. These models gather the principal components of the OMT notation and are expressed here as general as possible.

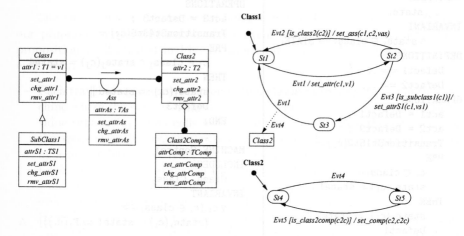

Fig. 14. Generic OMT models

The object model presents *Class1* and *Class2* classes linked by an *Ass* association. The *Class2* class is aggregated by the *Class2Comp* optional component. A *SubClass1* subclass inherits from *Class1*. Attributes and operations are defined for each class and association. The dynamic model is expressed by two state diagrams associated to *Class1* and *Class2* classes. Objects of *Class1* have three possible states (*St1, St2, St3)*, the change of the state is triggered by *Evt1, Evt2* and *Evt3* events. When the *Evt1* event occurs in the *St3* state, it sends to *Class2* an *Evt4* event. *Evt3* and *Evt4* are internal events. Actions are associated to transitions, they modify the data of the *Class1* class, the *Ass* association or the *SubClass1* subclass. The state diagram associated to *Class2* is composed of two states (*St4, St5)*, two events *Evt4, Evt5* and an action which updates the aggregation.

We apply our transformation templates on OMT models, obtaining a B specification (SPEC-B), the structure of which is represented graphically in Fig. 15.

The correction of a B specification is done by generating and proving proof obligations. These proof obligations verify that operations preserve the invariant of the system. We thus generate the proof obligations for SPEC-B using the B tool [19]; 236 proof obligations were generated, they were all automatically proven by the B prover as shown in table 3.

The generated SPEC-B specification is automatically proved within the B Tool. It is proved relatively to the invariant generated by the transformation of the generic specification.

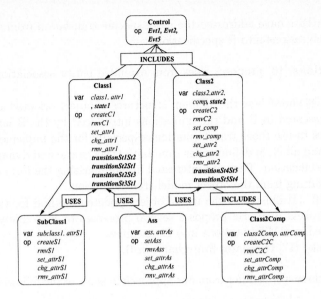

Fig. 15. Structure of the SPEC–B specification

Table 3. Proof results

COMPONENT	Obv	nPO	nUn	%Pr
Ass	5	6	0	100
Class1	28	23	0	100
Class2	71	34	0	100
Class2Comp	10	8	0	100
Control	37	3	0	100
SubClass1	5	6	0	100
TOTAL	156	80	0	100

The specification is modular since the used templates facilitate its decomposition into a set of B machines. The proof is then decomposed. When specifying a real problem, we have to instantiate these templates. The part corresponding to the predefined templates is automatically proved. The creative work of the specification will add new proof obligations linked to constraints between components corresponding to the problem and its domain knowledge. The proof of this creative part remains to be done.

5 Related Work

Many studies have proposed to combine semi-formal and formal methods. Several projects have studied the problem of integrating SSADM and Z [14], OMT and LOTOS [20] - VDM [7] or Z [5, 6].

Next authors have addressed the more specific translation from OMT semi-formal specifications into B specifications:

- Nagui-Raiss [13] proposes rules from extended entity association diagrams to B.
- Shore [18] shows how the different structures of object-oriented analysis can be represented in B and the limitations introduced by the B language. He proposes to use those transformations especially for the implementation.
- Facon and all [9, 8] defines rules from both OMT static and dynamic models to B specification. They are interested in modularizing the formal specification resulting from the object model transformation.
- Lano [10, 11] illustrates the use of object-oriented method for the development process in B. He proposes several processes to map analysis models expressed in OMT notations into B machines.
- Sekerinsky [17] translates Statecharts in B.

But all these works differ from our approach in some of the following aspects:

- They do not deal with the aggregation and contraints in the object model.
- Most studies do not differentiate between the various cases of attributes or associations. We give here a systematic transformation of attributes depending on their features and of associations depending on their cardinalities.
- Consistency between the models is not treated. Our proposition integrates the dynamic model into the B specification resulting from the object model translation, leading to a single specification.
- Most studies have not investigated all the advantages of this approach: we show here how this approach improves the proof process.
- This paper presents the transformation using generic templates, taking particular care to remain the most generic and general as possible.

6   Conclusion

In this paper, we have presented an intuitive semantic for the set of concepts used in the OMT object and dynamic models. A B generic template has been defined for each component as well as their integration into a single specification. Rules have been explicited to merge informations coming from both object and dynamic OMT models, providing an integrated view of dynamic and static requirements. Advantages for using these templates are:

- the translation from OMT object and dynamic diagrams into a B specification is done in a systematic way,
- in the formal specification, the two object and dynamic OMT models are combined giving a single specification,
- a proof of the invariant preservation for the resulting B specification is automatically done by the B-tool.

Currently, in our approach we consider B and OMT as two idependant formalisms, regarding those as two views of the specification construction and taking the advantages of each one.

A number of features of the OMT notations have been left out. These remain the subject of further research. We currently study refinement, with the idea of applying it either on the OMT models or on the B specification. An idea is to use the concepts of sub-systems, composite-objects and composite states introduced in the OMT notations and see if they can be related to the B refinement.

Tools are expected in order to automatically transform the OMT diagrams into a B specification. We aim to integrate the templates defined below as operators in the PROPLANE model [12]. The PROPLANE approach is related to process modelling, methodological aspects are expressed outside the language by way of development operators. Operators are applied to development steps which are composed of both a workplan describing the followed reasoning and the specification.

References

[1] J.R. Abrial. Extending B without Changing it (for Developing Distributed Systems). In H. Habrias, editor, *Putting Into Practice Methods and Tools for Information System Design - 1st Conference on the B Method*, Nantes (F), November 1996.

[2] J.R. Abrial. *The B Book - Assigning Programs to Meanings.* Cambridge University Press, 1996. ISBN 0-521-49619-5.

[3] J.R. Abrial and L. Mussat. Introducing Dynamic Constraints in B. In D. Bert, editor, *B'98: Recent Advances in the Development and Use of the B Method - 2nd International B Conference*, number 1393 in Lecture Notes in Computer Science, Montpellier (F), April 1998. Springer-Verlag.

[4] D. Coleman, P. Arnold, St. Bodoff, Ch. Dollin, H. Gilchrist, F. Hayes, and P. Jeremaes. *Object-Oriented Development: The Fusion Method.* Prentice Hall, 1994.

[5] S. Dupuy, Y. Ledru, and M. Chabre-Peccoud. Integrating OMT and Object-Z. In *BCS FACS/EROS ROOM Workshop*, London (UK), June 1997.

[6] S. Dupuy, Y. Ledru, and M. Chabre-Peccoud. Translating the OMT Dynamic Model into Object-Z*. In *ZUM'98: The Z Formal Specification Notation - 11th International Conference of Z Users*, number 1493 in Lecture Notes in Computer Science, Berlin (D), September 1998.

[7] P. Facon and R. Laleau. Des modèles d'objets aux spécifications formelles ensemblistes. *Revue Ingénierie des Systèmes d'Information*, 4(2), 1996.

[8] P. Facon, R. Laleau, and H.P. Nguyen. Dérivation de spécifications formelles B à partir de spécifications semi-formelles de systèmes d'information. In H. Habrias, editor, *Putting Into Practice Methods and Tools for Information System Design - 1st Conference on the B Method*, Nantes (F), November 1996.

[9] P. Facon, R. Laleau, and H.P. Nguyen. Mapping Object Diagrams into B Specifications. In A. Bryant and L. Semmens, editors, *Methods Integration Workshop*, Electronic Workshops in Computing (eWiC), Leeds (UK), March 1996. Springer-Verlag.

[10] K. Lano. *The B Language and Method: A Guide to Practical Formal Development.* FACIT. Springer-Verlag, 1996. ISBN 3-540-76033-4.

[11] K. Lano, H. Haughton, and P. Wheeler. *Formal Methods and Object Technology*, chapter Integrating Formal and Structured Methods in Object-Oriented System Development, pages 113–157. FACIT. Springer-Verlag, 1996. S.J. Goldsack and S.J.H. Kent eds.

[12] N. Lévy and J. Souquières. Modelling Specification Construction by Successive Approximations. In M. Johnson, editor, *6th International AMAST Conference*, pages 351–364, Sydney (A), 1997. Springer Verlag 1349.

[13] N. Nagui-Raiss. A formal Software Specification Tool Using The Entity-Relationship Model. In *13th International Conference on the Entity-Relationship Approach*, number 881 in Lecture Notes in Computer Science, Manchester (UK), December 1994. Springer-Verlag.

[14] F. Polack, M. Whiston, and K. Pronk. The SAZ Project: Integration SSADM and Z. In *International Symposium Formal Methods Europe*, number 670 in Lecture Notes in Computer Science, Odense (DK), April 1993. Springer-Verlag.

[15] J. Rumbaugh, M. Blaha, W. Premerlani, F. Eddy, and W. Lorensen. *Object-Oriented Modeling and Design*. Prentice Hall Inc. Englewood Cliffs, 1991.

[16] J. Rumbaugh, I. Jacobson, and G. Booch. *The Unified Modeling Language Reference Guide*. Addison-Wesley, 1998. ISBN 020130998X.

[17] E. Sekerinski. Graphical Design of Reactive Systems. In D. Bert, editor, *B'98: Recent Advances in the Development and Use of the B Method - 2nd International B Conference*, number 1393 in Lecture Notes in Computer Science, Montpellier (F), April 1998. Springer-Verlag.

[18] R. Shore. An Object-Oriented Approach to B. In H. Habrias, editor, *Putting Into Practice Methods and Tools for Information System Design - 1st Conference on the B Method*, Nantes (F), November 1996.

[19] STERIA - Technologies de l'Information, Aix-en-Provence (F). *Atelier B, Manuel Utilisateur*, 1998. Version 3.5.

[20] E. Wand, H. Richter, and B. Cheng. Formalizing and integrating the dynamic model within OMT. In *19th International Conference on Software Engineering*, Boston (USA), July 1997.

[21] P.T. Ward. How to Integrate Object Orientation with Structured Analysis and Design. In *IEEE Software*. March 1989.

Appendix

Table 4. Association (Ass_{ij}) translations according to the most frequently used cardinalities (C_i, C_j)

		c_j		
	0-1	**1**	**0 or more**	**1 or more**
0-1	$ass_{ij} \in class_i \mathbin{>\!\!+\!\!>} class_j$	$ass_{ij} \in class_i \mathbin{>\!\!\rightarrow} class_j$	$ass_{ij}^{-1} \in class_j \mathbin{+\!\!\rightarrow} class_i$	$ass_{ij}^{-1} \in class_j \mathbin{+\!\!\twoheadrightarrow} class_i$
1	$ass_{ij} \in class_i \mathbin{>\!\!+\!\!>} class_j$	$ass_{ij} \in class_i \mathbin{>\!\!\rightarrow\!\!\!\rightarrow} class_j$	$ass_{ij}^{-1} \in class_j \longrightarrow class_i$	$ass_{ij}^{-1} \in class_j \twoheadrightarrow class_i$
c_i 0 or more	$ass_{ij} \in class_i \mathbin{+\!\!\rightarrow} class_j$	$ass_{ij} \in class_i \longrightarrow class_j$	$ass_{ij} \in class_i \leftrightarrow class_j$	$ass_{ij} \in class_i \leftrightarrow class_j$ $\wedge\, ran(ass_{ij}) = class_j$
1 or more	$ass_{ij} \in class_i \mathbin{+\!\!\twoheadrightarrow} class_j$	$ass_{ij} \in class_i \twoheadrightarrow class_j$	$ass_{ij} \in class_i \leftrightarrow class_j$ $\wedge\, dom(ass_{ij}) = class_i$	$ass_{ij} \in class_i \leftrightarrow class_j$ $\wedge\, dom(ass_{ij}) = class_i$ $\wedge\, ran(ass_{ij}) = class_j$

Verifying Consistency and Validity of Formal Specifications by Testing*

Shaoying Liu

Faculty of Information Sciences
Hiroshima City University, Japan
shaoying@cs.hiroshima-cu.ac.jp
http://www.sel.cs.hiroshima-cu.ac.jp/~liu/

Abstract. Detecting faults in specifications can help reduce the cost and risk of software development because incorrect implementation can be prevented early. This goal can be achieved by verifying the consistency and validity of specifications. In this paper we put forward *specification testing* as a practical technique for verification and validation of formal specifications. Our approach is to derive *proof obligations* from a specification and then test them, in order to detect faults leading to the violation of consistency or validity of the specification. We describe proof obligations for various consistency properties of a specification, and suggest the use of five strategies for testing them. We provide a method for testing implicit specifications by evaluation rather than by prototyping, and criteria for interpreting the meaning of test results.

1 Introduction

It is desirable and important to detect faults in a specification (for requirements or design) before it is implemented, in order to reduce the cost and risk of software development [1, 2]. Faults may arise if the consistency of the specification is violated or the user requirements are misrepresented by the specification. A specification is consistent if there exists a computational model for its implementation. A specification is valid if it expresses the user requirements satisfactorily.

To support verification and validation of formal specifications, we suggest *specification testing* as a practical technique. Our target is to deal with implicit or nonprocedural specifications, possibly involving pre and postconditions like those in VDM [3] or Z [4]. Such a specification is often not executable, but can often be evaluated for a given input and output. In addition, we also expect to deal with the complex constructs composed of implicit formal specifications for components. Our approach is to combine the ideas of formal proof and program

* This work is supported in part by the Ministry of Education of Japan under Grant-in-Aid for Scientific Research on Priority Areas (A) (No. 09245105), Grant-in-Aid for Scientific Research (B) (No. 11694173), and Grant-in-Aid for Scientific Research (C) (No. 11680368)

J. Wing, J. Woodcock, J. Davies (Eds.): FM'99, Vol. I, LNCS 1708, pp. 896–914, 1999.
© Springer-Verlag Berlin Heidelberg 1999

testing. The principle of this combination is that formal proof obligations indicate what to verify for what purpose, whereas testing offers the idea of using test cases to check proof obligations.

1.1   Specification Testing

By specification testing, we mean presentation of inputs and outputs to a specification, and evaluation to obtain a result—usually a truth value. As the postcondition of an implicit operation usually describes the relation between its inputs and outputs, an evaluation of the postcondition needs both inputs and outputs. This is slightly different from program testing, as discussed in detail later in this section. Our concrete approach to testing is to derive a proof obligation expressing the consistency property of the *testing target* (e.g., invariant, operation, composition of operations), and then test the proof obligation with test cases—selected inputs and outputs. The proof obligation is a necessary prerequisite for the testing target to be consistent in terms of the semantics of the formal specification language in which the target is written. For this reason, the proof obligation is usually derived based on the semantics of the testing target.

Similar to conventional program testing [5], testing a specification also consists of three steps: (1) test case generation; (2) evaluation of proof obligations that are logical expressions derived from the specification; and (3) analysis of test results, as illustrated in Figure 1. Two methods for generating test cases can be used. One is to produce test cases based on the proof obligations derived from the specification. This is similar to *structural testing* for programs where test cases are based on examination of program structure. In this method, there is no need to provide expected test results, because the meaning of the testing is interpreted based on the established criteria (which is mainly for checking consistency). Another method is based on informal user requirements. This is similar to *functional testing* for programs, where test cases are based on a functional description of the program. In this method, expected test results are required, in order to check whether or not the specification expresses satisfactorily the user requirements. An evaluation of a logical expression is a process of computing the expression with a test case to yield **true** or **false**. Analysis of test results determines the nature of the test, and possibly indicates the existence of faults in the specification.

To test an entire specification, *unit testing* and *integration testing* can be conducted for different objectives. Unit testing aims to detect faults in each component which can be an invariant, operation or object; whereas integration testing tries to uncover faults occurring in the integration of operations (e.g., functional compositions by control constructs or message communications), and to check whether the required services are specified satisfactorily.

When testing an operation (which can be a method for object-oriented specification language like Object-Z [6]), it is necessary to treat the state variables before and after the operation, for example, $\overleftarrow{x}$ and x in VDM [3]; x and x' in Z [4], as

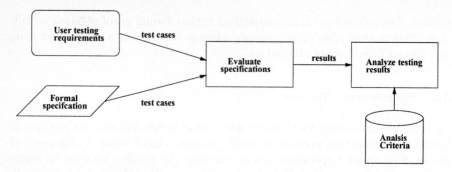

Fig. 1. The process of specification testing

inputs and outputs of the operation, respectively. This will allow an evaluation of the postcondition of the operation and a verification of whether the change of the state by this operation is satisfactory in both its consistency and validity.

Specification testing has two major differences from program testing. To test the specification of an operation, for example, we need test cases for both input and output variables, whereas we need only for input variables to run the program in program testing (although we need to supply the expected results for test results analysis). Another difference is that testing a specification involves evaluation of logical expressions but does not involve running any program, which allows the system to be tested before its implementation, whereas testing a program entails running the program.

1.2   Related Work

Specification testing is much less researched than program testing, and only a few reports are in the literature. Testing implicit formal specifications is especially not well studied. In contrast to this situation, *specification-based testing* for programs has attracted much more attention from the research community.

An early and important work on testing formal specifications was done by Kemmerer [2]. He argued that testing specifications early in the software life cycle to discover whether a formal specification has a *satisfiable* implementation and whether the specification satisfies its critical and desired functional requirements can help ensure the reliability of systems and reduce cost. Kemmerer proposed two approaches to testing nonprocedural formal specifications, and applied them to specifications written in the *Ina Jo* language. One is *by prototyping*, that is, transforming a nonprocedural specification into a procedural form and then using the latter as a rapid prototype for testing. The other approach is *by symbolic execution*, that is, performing a symbolic execution of the sequence of operations and checking the resultant symbolic values to see if they define the desired set of resultant states.

Recent work on testing object-oriented formal specifications was undertaken by Chen and Liu [7]. We suggested using specification testing as an alternative to *theorem proving* in order to verify whether the required properties are satisfied by the specification for finite test cases. However, the proposed technique was applied only to specification components (e.g., invariants, methods), not to their integration. No well-defined criteria for test case generation were given either.

Specification-based testing is another area of research related to specification testing [8, 9, 10]. Although related to each other, specification testing and specification-based testing are different in a number of ways. First, their targets are different. The former aims to test the specification itself, whereas the latter aims to test the program that implements the specification. Second, the former tries to detect faults in requirements and design, whereas the latter attempts to find faults in the program which may lead to violation of the specification. Third, test cases are not necessarily generated based on the structure of the specification for the former, whereas for the latter test cases are generated based on the structure of the specification. Finally, testing specifications involves evaluation of logical expressions, whereas specification-based testing entails running the program.

1.3   Contributions

We make three major contributions in this paper. Firstly, we suggest a new approach to testing implicit formal specification by evaluation of proof obligations derived from the specification. Secondly, we suggest the use of five strategies for testing logical expressions, which can be applied to test proof obligations for consistency and specifications themselves for validity. Finally, we provide criteria for interpreting the meaning of a test result to determine whether or not a fault is found by the test.

We apply the proposed approach to SOFL (Structured Object-based Formal Language), and describe proof obligations for verifying consistency properties of the SOFL constructs: invariants, condition processes (similar to VDM operations), condition data flow diagrams which integrate condition processes, and decompositions of condition processes.

We choose SOFL to apply the proposed technique, because SOFL integrates the advantages of classical data flow diagrams, Petri nets, and VDM-SL, and has begun to be applied to real projects [11, 12, 13]. Due to this feature, the technique applied to SOFL specifications in this paper can also be applied to commonly used data flow diagrams, Petri nets and model-oriented formal specifications, such as VDM, Z, and B-method [14]. For the sake of space, no introduction to SOFL is given in this paper. The reader who is interested in the details of SOFL can refer to the author's previous publications [11, 15, 12].

The remainder of this paper is organized as follows. Section 2 describes strategies for testing logical expressions in general which can be applied to test proof obligations. Section 3 discusses *unit testing*, including testing of specification invariants and condition processes. Section 4 focuses on *integration testing* to show how to test condition data flow diagrams. Section 5 addresses the issue of verifying decomposition of condition processes. Finally, in section 6 we give conclusions and outline future research.

2   Testing Logical Expressions

As described previously, the fundamental step in testing a specification is to test the logical expressions that represent the proof obligations derived from the specification. In this section we discuss strategies for testing logical expressions.

Definition 2.1 Let $P(x_1, x_2, \ldots, x_n)$ be a logical expression containing free variables $x_1, x_2, \ldots, x_n$. A *test case* for P is *a group of values* $v_1, v_2, \ldots, v_n$ bound to $x_1, x_2, \ldots, x_n$, respectively, and a *test set* for P is *a non-empty set of test cases*.

Note that a test set for P can be a single test case as well.

Definition 2.2 Let P be a logical expression. A *test suite* for P is a set of pairs $\{(T_c^1, E_r^1), (T_c^2, E_r^2), \ldots, (T_c^m, E_r^m)\}$ where T_c^i ($i = 1\ldots m$) are test cases and E_r^i are expected results corresponding to test cases T_c^i.

As testing a logical expression involves evaluation of the expression to either **true** or **false**, each E_r^i in fact is a truth value.

Definition 2.3 Let P be a logical expression and T_d a test set for P. A *test* of P is a set of evaluations of P with all the test cases in the test set T_d.

Definition 2.4 Let P be a logical expression and T_s a test suite for P. A *test report* of P can be one of the two forms. One is a set of triplets $\{(T_c^1, E_r^1, A_r^1), (T_c^2, E_r^2, A_r^2), \ldots, (T_c^m, E_r^m, A_r^m)\}$ where T_c^i ($i = 1\ldots m$) are test cases; E_r^i and A_r^i are expected and actual results corresponding to test cases T_c^i, respectively. Another form is a set of pairs $\{(T_c^1, A_r^1), (T_c^2, A_r^2), \ldots, (T_c^m, A_r^m)\}$.

For example, suppose $P \equiv x > 0 \land x < 10/y$, where $\equiv$ means "is defined syntactically as"; x and y denote a real number and an integer, respectively, then

(1) $(x = 2.0, y = 5)$ is a test case for P.

(2) $\{(x = -1.0, y = 4), (x = 1.0, y = 0), (x = 1.5, y = 2)\}$ is a test set for P.

(3)

x	y	E_r
-1.0	4	false
1.0	0	true
1.5	2	true

shows a test suite for P.

(4)

x	y	E_r	P
-1.0	4	false	false
1.0	0	true	*
1.5	2	true	true

shows a test report of P, where * is a logical value, representing "undefined".

For convenience, it is assumed that logical expressions under discussion are in disjunctive normal form (DNF). The primary intent is that each clause in each logical expression is tested independently.

We suggest five strategies for testing logical expressions with different objectives, each imposing a different constraint on selection of test cases.

Let $P \equiv P_1 \vee P_2 \vee \cdots \vee P_n$ be a disjunctive normal form and $P_i \equiv Q_i^1 \wedge Q_i^2 \wedge \cdots \wedge Q_i^m$ be a conjunction of relational expressions Q_i^j which are atomic components, where $i = 1...n$ and $j = 1...m$. We treat a quantified expression as an atomic logical expression (the same level as a relational expression) in P_i. When generating a test case for a universal quantifier, for example $\forall_{x \in \mathbf{nat}} \cdot x + 1 > x$, we generate a finite subset of the infinite natural number type **nat**, say $\{0, 1, ..., 1000\}$, to replace **nat** in this quantified expression. Let T_d be a test set for P.

Strategy 1 Evaluate P with T_d to **true** and **false**, respectively.

This strategy is illustrated by table 1.

Table 1. Strategy 1

P
true
false

Strategy 2 Evaluate P_i with T_d for every $i = 1...n$ to **true** and **false**, respectively.

Table 2 explains this strategy.

Table 2. Strategy 2

P_1	P_2	P_3	...	P_n
true	$\star$	$\star$	...	$\star$
false	$\star$	$\star$	...	$\star$
$\star$	true	$\star$	...	$\star$
$\star$	false	$\star$	...	$\star$
.	.	.	...	.
.	.	.	...	.
.	.	.	...	.
$\star$	$\star$	$\star$	...	true
$\star$	$\star$	$\star$	...	false

where $\star$ denotes either **true** or **false**.

Although it is possible to test the cases of each disjunct P_i being **true** and **false** respectively by using this strategy, we cannot guarantee that each disjunct be evaluated to **true** while every other disjunct to **false**. To overcome this weakness, a strengthened strategy is given as follows.

Strategy 3 Evaluate P_i with T_d to **true** while all $P_1, \ldots, P_{i-1}, P_{i+1}, \ldots, P_n$ to **false**, and to **false** while all $P_1, \ldots, P_{i-1}, P_{i+1}, \ldots, P_n$ to **true**, respectively.

This strategy is illustrated by table 3.

However, for some logical expressions, for example, $x > 0 \lor x > 3$, it is impossible to directly apply this strategy because when $x > 3$ evaluates to **true**, there is no way to evaluate $x > 0$ to **false**. In this case, either the logical expression (or the corresponding specification) needs to be modified or **Strategy 2** needs to be applied.

Table 3. Strategy 3

P_1	P_2	P_3	...	P_n
true	false	false	...	false
false	true	false	...	false
false	false	true	...	false
.	.	.	...	.
.	.	.	...	.
.	.	.	...	.
false	false	false	...	true

Strategy 4 When evaluating P_i to **true** with T_d, evaluate every Q_i^j to **true**. When evaluating P_i to **false**, evaluate Q_i^j to **false** for every $j = 1...m$, respectively.

This strategy is for testing a disjunct of P which is a conjunction of sub-expressions. Table 4 illustrates this strategy.

Table 4. Strategy 4

Q_1	Q_2	Q_3	...	Q_m
true	true	true	...	true
false	$\star$	$\star$	...	$\star$
$\star$	false	$\star$	...	$\star$
.	.	.	...	.
.	.	.	...	.
.	.	.	...	.
$\star$	$\star$	$\star$	...	false

Strategy 5 When evaluating P_i to **true** with T_d, evaluate every Q_i^j to **true**. When evaluating P_i to **false**, evaluate Q_i^j to **false** while all $Q_i^1, \ldots, Q_i^{j-1}, Q_i^{j+1}$, ..., Q_i^n to **true**.

This strategy imposes a stronger restriction on evaluation of conjuncts than previous one. It is illustrated by table 5.

By convention in program testing, a *successful test* means that a fault is detected by the test, whereas a *failed test* means that no fault is detected by the test. We also follow this convention in this paper.

Table 5. Strategy 5

Q_1	Q_2	Q_3	...	Q_n
true	true	true	...	true
false	true	true	...	true
true	false	true	...	true
true	true	false	...	true
.	.	.	...	.
.	.	.	...	.
.	.	.	...	.
true	true	true	...	false

3   Unit Testing

Unit testing includes testing of invariants and condition processes.

3.1   Testing Invariants

For brevity, our discussion focuses on invariants which involve only a single bound variable. The same testing method can be easily extended to invariants containing multiple bound variables.

Let an invariant Inv be

forall$[x$ **inset** $D \mid P(x)]$

where D can be a basic type (e.g., integers, natural numbers) or a constructed type. For the meaning of SOFL operators occurring in this paper, see Appendix A.

The invariant describes a property of all the elements of the type D which is expected to be sustained throughout the entire system. To enable the invariant to serve this purpose, it is necessary to ensure that the invariant is defined

Definition 4.1 Let $T_d = \{T_1, T_2, \ldots, T_n\}$ be a test set for the proof obligation 2. If every single evaluation of this expression with each T_i ($i = 1 \ldots n$) satisfies the condition that when $(pre_{A_1} \wedge post_{A_1}(x_1)) \wedge (pre_{A_2} \wedge post_{A_2}(x_2)) \wedge \cdots \wedge (pre_{A_n} \wedge post_{A_n}(x_n))$ evaluates to **true**, pre_B also evaluates to **true**, then the test with T_d is a failed test. Otherwise, if there exists any T_i such that pre_B evaluates to **false** whereas $(pre_{A_1} \wedge post_{A_1}(x_1)) \wedge (pre_{A_2} \wedge post_{A_2}(x_2)) \wedge \cdots \wedge (pre_{A_n} \wedge post_{A_n}(x_n))$ evaluates to **true**, the test with T_d is a successful test.

This definition provides a precise rule for determining whether or not a fault is detected by a test. For the sake of space, we do not give further illustration of this kind of testing by examples.

4.2   Testing Conditional Constructs

There are three kinds of conditional constructs in SOFL: IF-THEN, IF-THEN-ELSE and CASE, as given in Figure 2(b) and (c). As testing of these constructs share the same nature as for sequential constructs, we try to keep the discussion as brief as necessary.

IF-THEN The construct of this kind is illustrated by the graphical representation on the left hand side in Figure 2(b). Its proof obligation is:

$$pre \wedge post(x) \wedge C(x) \Rightarrow pre_B \tag{3}$$

where pre is the precondition of the preceding condition process; $post(x)$ is the sub-logical expression of its postcondition which contains variable x; and pre_B is the precondition of the condition process B.

The rule for determining a successful test or failed test for sequential constructs given in **Definition 4.1** can be applied to testing expression 3 if substituting $pre \wedge post(x) \wedge C(x)$ for $(pre_{A_1} \wedge post_{A_1}(x_1)) \wedge (pre_{A_2} \wedge post_{A_2}(x_2)) \wedge \cdots \wedge (pre_{A_n} \wedge post_{A_n}(x_n))$.

IF-THEN-ELSE This construct is illustrated by the graphical representation on the right hand side in Figure 2(b). Its proof obligation is

$$pre \wedge post(x) \wedge C(x) \Rightarrow pre_{B1} \tag{4}$$

$$pre \wedge post(x) \wedge \neg C(x) \Rightarrow pre_{B2} \tag{5}$$

Testing this proof obligation can be performed by testing expressions 4 and 5 respectively with the same method used for **IF-THEN** constructs.

CASE A CASE construct represents a multiple selection which is depicted by Figure 2(c). Its proof obligation is

$$pre \wedge post(x) \wedge C_i(x) \Rightarrow pre_{B_i} \tag{6}$$

$$pre \wedge post(x) \wedge \neg(C_1(x) \vee \cdots \vee C_n(x)) \Rightarrow pre_{B_{n+1}} \tag{7}$$

where $i = 1...n$.

If x satisfies condition $C_i(x)$, the precondition of the associated condition process B_i needs to be assured by the conjunction $pre \wedge post(x) \wedge C_i(x)$ so that the condition process B_i can be fired correctly. If x does not satisfy any of $C_1(x), \ldots, C_n(x)$, the precondition of condition process B_{n+1} must be assured for firing B_{n+1} correctly.

Again, testing this proof obligation can be performed by testing expressions 6 and 7 respectively with the same method used for **IF-THEN** constructs.

5   Testing Decompositions

A complete SOFL specification is a structured hierarchy of CDFDs, in which a condition process at one level may be decomposed into a CDFD at a lower level. The decomposition of a condition process defines how its inputs are transformed to its outputs in detail. While it needs to implement the specified functions of the high level condition process, the decomposition may also provide some additional functions under the constraint of the high level condition process specification in a strict *refinement* manner. That is, the decomposition must be a refinement of the high level condition process.

The rules for operational refinement have been well studied by researchers in the field [16, 3]. Those rules can also be applied to the decomposition of condition processes in SOFL.

Suppose a condition process OP is decomposed into a CDFD G. Let pre_{OP} and $post_{OP}$ denote the pre and postconditions of OP, respectively. Let pre_G and $post_G$ represent the pre and postconditions of G, respectively. The proof obligation for the decomposition

$$pre_{OP} \Rightarrow pre_G \tag{8}$$

$$pre_{OP} \wedge post_G \Rightarrow post_{OP} \tag{9}$$

must be satisfied by OP and G.

then 5 additional transitions have been fired, and 3 additional states have been reached, which brings the transition coverage to 53% and the state coverage to 87%.

Improving the Coverage Evaluation with Backtracking. With the method presented in the previous section, states and transitions are only marked during the fault detection phase. However, if some transitions have been fired in the passive homing sequence, and are not fired again in the fault detection phase, they will not be considered as fired in this evaluation. Thus, the coverage evaluation will be less than the actual coverage. In order to improve this coverage evaluation, we also need to mark the states and transitions that were fired during the first phase. This is done by backtracking the actual states and transitions that have been fired in the passive homing sequence. The algorithms introduced below (algorithm 1 and algorithm 2) are extensions of the algorithm given in [2]. Since we mentioned that we can use the same approach for observable nondeterministic finite state machine as for deterministic finite state machines, we give their formal definition.

Definition 1. *An observable nondeterministic finite state machine is a five-tuple $M = (S, s_0, I, O, \delta)$, where*
    S is a finite nonempty set of states,
    s_0 is the initial state,
    I is a finite set of input symbols,
    O is a finite set of output symbols, and
    $\delta : S \times I \times O \to S$ is a transition function.
    $s' = \delta(s, a, o)$ means that there is a transition from s to s' labelled with a/o.

Algorithm 1 (Test coverage). This procedure can be inserted either between the passive homing and the fault detection procedures, or after the fault detection procedure, just before computing the coverage (the latter is better in a real-time environment). We denote $Pred(s', a, o)$ the set of predecessors of state s' for transitions labelled with a/o: $Pred(s', a, o) = \{s \in S \land \delta(s, a, o) = s'\}$.
Input: a specification FSM *Spec*, the current state *scur*, a trace $s = a_1/o_1, ...,$ a_k/o_k reflecting a behaviour of an implementation *Imp* up to *scur*.
Output: the set of transitions that were fired in the course of the trace up to *scur*.

```
begin
    L := {s_cur}; /* Current state */
    L' := ∅;
    for (j = k-1) downto 1 do /* backtrack */
        for each s ∈ L do
            for each s' ∈ Pred(s, a_j, o_j) do
                add s' in L' ;
            end
```

```
            end
            L := L';
            L' := ∅;
        end
        /* go down the trace again */
        j:=1;
        while [(| L |> 1) ∧ (j ⩽ k − 1)] do
            for each s ∈ L do
                add δ(s, a_k, o_k) in L';
            end
            L := L' ;
            L' := ∅ ;
            j := j +1;
        end
        while (j ⩽ k − 1) do
            mark transition (s, a_k/o_k, δ(s, a_k, o_k)) in Spec ;
            replace s by δ(a, a_k, o_k) in L;
        end
    end
```

This method will work best if the singleton was obtained because only one candidate accepted the last transition; results will not be as good if the singleton happened because two (or more) paths of the automaton converge towards a single state. This phenomenon is independent of the actual algorithm: if two paths converge during the passive homing sequence, determining which one was actually followed is an undecidable problem. Let us consider two examples to illustrate this:

- Consider again the trace that was used in the example. If we backtrack step by step and then walk down the path again, we can find the transitions that were fired during the passive homing sequence, namely transitions t_8, t_{12}, t_{15}, t_7, t_3 and t_1. If we take them into account to evaluate the coverage, 14 different transitions have been fired, which makes for a 82% transition coverage and a 100% state coverage. In this case, the backtracking procedure has allowed us to improve the coverage significantly.
- On the other hand, let us now assume that the trace had begun with

$$b/2 \quad c/3 \quad b/2 \quad a/1$$

for the same FSM. Then, the passive homing sequence shows that the current state is state 5 after 4 transitions. With backtracking, we can find out that the last two transitions were transitions t_9 followed by transition t_8, but we cannot determine whether the initial state was state 6, with transitions t_{14} and t_{13}, or state 1 with transitions t_3 and t_2, as both paths converge towards state 5. In this example, despite the convergence, backtracking has allowed us to mark two transitions and two states.

      else if $[((|\mathcal{L}| = \infty)$ **and** "there are no undefined variables in $\boldsymbol{x}$")]

          end_homing:=true;

      k:=k+1;

  end

/* Fault detection */

r:=1;

while $([(\exists\delta(s, a_{k+r}, o_{k+r}, P_t)) \wedge (P_t(\boldsymbol{x}))]$ **and** [end_of_file=false]) **do**

  mark transition $(s, "a_{k+r}/o_{k+r}", \delta(s, a_{k+r}, o_{k+r}, P_t));$

  s:=$\delta(s, a_{k+r}, o_{k+r}, P_t);$

  $\boldsymbol{x} := A_t(\boldsymbol{x});$

  r:=r+1;

end

if (end_of_file=false)

  return fault;

end

/* Predicate evaluation function*/

eval$(P_t, \boldsymbol{x})$

  result := FALSE;

  if $(P_t(\boldsymbol{x})$ cannot be evaluated)

    result :=TRUE;

  else if $(P_t(\boldsymbol{x}) = $ TRUE)

    result := TRUE;

  return result;

end

Algorithm 4 (procedure: Adding $A(x)$ to newX list).

  begin

    $\boldsymbol{y}:=\boldsymbol{x};$

    For each component y_i of $\boldsymbol{y}$ **do**

      if $[(x_i=$UNDEFINED) **and** (a clause of the predicate is $(x_i=$val$))]$

        $y_i := $ val;

    end

    $\boldsymbol{y} := A(\boldsymbol{y});$

    Add $\boldsymbol{y}$ to the list newX;

  end

Algorithm 5 (procedure: Synthesis of possible values).

  begin

    for each variable x_i

      read the list of variables x_i

```
            if (at least one of the values is UNDEFINED)
                x_i := UNDEFINED;
            if (there are at least two different values)
                x_i := UNDEFINED;
            else /*every value is defined and equal to val_i*/
                x_i := val_i;
        end
    end
```

5 An Experiment with the GSM-MAP Protocol

In this section we present an application of the passive testing tool that implements the algorithms described in the previous section. The application is the testing in isolation for the MAP-DSM process (MAP-Dialogue State Machine). MAP-DSM is a component process of the GSM-MAP protocol (Global System for Mobile communication-Mobile Application Part) [3]. In order to understand this application we provide a short description of the GSM-MAP protocol and the new approach for the SDL modelling of the MAP-DSM process. Finally, we describe the results obtained using the passive testing tool for the random simulations of this process.

5.1 GSM-MAP Protocol

The GSM-MAP protocol describes the signalling functions required in the SS7 signalling system in order to offer the services needed in a mobile network. The machine associated with the GSM-MAP protocol provides the set of services SSM (Service State Machine), for which we distinguish the requesting and the performing services. All these services need the establishment of a dialogue between the requesting and performing entities, dialogue which is coordinated by the MAP-DSM process. This process is responsible for the establishment of the dialogue, transmission and reception of messages, data verification and verification that the context does not change during the dialogue.

5.2 A New Approach for the SDL Modelling of the MAP-DSM Process

It must be mentioned here that we have already performed some researches for the testing of the MAP-DSM process [1], but because of its complexity these tests were done only for a partial behaviour of this process. Our original approach for the SDL modelling of the MAP-DSM process intends to reduce the complexity of this component in order to be able to test its global behaviour.

The modelisation of the MAP-DSM process has been performed in the SDL language. The SDL language [7] is a formal description technique, standardized by ITU (International Telecommunication Union). SDL is largely used in the telecommunication industry to make the formal specification of communication

	main	proc1	proc2	composed automaton
main states (SDL)	8	2	2	
transition branches (SDL)	46	25	25	
internal variables (SDL)	21	21	21	
states (reachability graph)	3362	3446	2738	
transitions (reachability graph)	17475	100421	97205	
states (minimized machine)	24	6	6	60
transitions (minimized machine)	176	352	316	2136

Table 1. Information on the size of automata

5.3 MSC Traces

The global MAP-DSM specification in SDL was used to obtain traces: more specifically, random simulations of the specification were generated using Verilog's ObjectGEODE Simulator [13] and saved as Message Sequence Charts (MSCs) [8] in order to obtain traces conformant to the specification (Fig. 8). These MSCs were then translated into our trace format before being processed by the passive testing tool (Fig. 9).

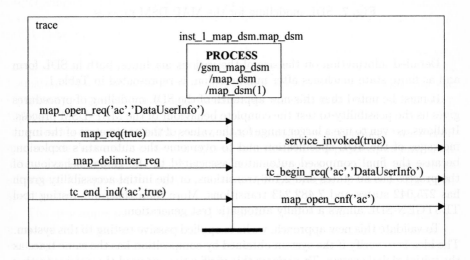

Fig. 8. A sample MSC example

Our passive testing tool uses traces in the following format: each line represents an input/output pair as a quoted string "i/o", where i is a (possibly parametrised) signal and o is a sequence of 1 or more (possibly parametrised) signals. A *NULL* signal as output means that no output was observed. Parameters are included within square brackets. "*map_req[true]/service_invoked[true]*"

```
"map_open_req['ac','DataUserInfo']/NULL"
"map_req[true]/service_invoked[true]"
"map_delimiter_req/tc_begin_req['DataUserInfo']"
"tc_end_ind['ac',true]/map_open_cnf['ac']"
```

Fig. 9. MSC translated into trace format

means that the system received the signal *map_req* with the parameter value *true* as and responded with the signal *service_invoked* with the parameter value *true*.

5.4 Results Obtained

The first results were the detection of discrepancies between the global SDL specification and the behaviour of the FSM obtained through the decomposition/composition process. These discrepancies were detected within 10 input/output pairs after the end of the passive homing sequence and were reported as faults by the passive testing software. They turned out to be mostly due to some variable values that were inconsistent between the various processes. This allowed us to correct these inconsistencies in the specification. After correction, tests were rerun with the same traces, and no faults were detected, which was the expected outcome. In order to assess our tool, faults were also added manually in some of the traces. Those faults were detected within a few input/output pairs after they occurred.

Traces varied from 1,000 to about 12,500 input/output pairs. Computation time varied between 0.04 to 0.14 seconds on a Sun Ultra1. Transition coverage varied between 5% and 25% of the transitions, and state coverage varied between 56% and 71% of the states. The global coverage, obtained by taking into account all the states reached in the various experiments, and all the transitions, was 86% of the states and 46% of the transitions.

6 Conclusion and Future Work

In this paper, we have applied passive testing techniques to a real protocol, the GSM-MAP. The experiments we performed showed that passive testing is a promising technique. It can be applied to test systems where active testing is hard to perform or where no control is possible over the system to be tested. It can also be very useful to improve the specification used as a reference. In fact, some of the discrepancies we found during the experiments were produced by ambiguities in the specification used as a reference rather than by errors of the observed system.

In order to assess the passive testing algorithm and its coverage evaluation, random simulations of the SDL specification of the protocol were saved as MSCs, representing execution traces. A number of faults were detected during our experiments. These faults reflected real differences between the global

SDL execution traces and the behaviour of the EFSM obtained through the decomposition/composition process.

The EFSM we considered for our experiments was in the form of a reachability graph obtained by the exhaustive simulation of the SDL specification of the system. Our future work will be on the application of our methods directly on an EFSM specification.

7 Acknowledgements

We are indebted to David Lee, who helped us with very useful discussions on this subject.

References

[1] R. Anido, A. Cavalli, T. Macavei, L. Paula Lima Jr, M. Clatin, and M. Phalippou. Testing a real protocol with the aid of verification techniques. In *XXII SEMISH*, Brazil, August 1996.

[2] David Lee et al. Passive testing and applications to network management. In *ICNP'97 International Conference on Network Protocols*, Atlanta, Georgia, October 1997.

[3] ETSI. *Digital cellular telecommunication system (Phase 2+); Mobile Application Part (MAP) specification (GSM 09.02)*. ETSI, August 1996.

[4] A. Ghedamsi, R. Dssouli, and G.v. Bochmann. Diagnostic tests for single transition faults in non-deterministic finite state machines. In *IWPTS'92 International Workshop on Protocol Test Systems*, September 1992.

[5] Melania Ionescu and Ana Cavalli. Test imbriqu du protocole GSM-MAP. In *CFIP'99, Colloque Francophone sur l'Ingnierie des protocoles*, Nancy, France, April 1999.

[6] ISO and ITU-T. *Open distributed Processing - Reference Model - Part 2: Foundations*. International Standard 10746-2/ITU-T Recommendation X.902. ITU-T, 1995.

[7] ITU. *Recommendation Z.100: Specification and Description Language (SDL)*. International Standard Z.100. ITU, Geneva, 1993.

[8] ITU-T. *Recommendation Z.120: Message Sequence Chart*. International Standard Z.120. ITU-T, 1994.

[9] L. Paula Lima and A. Cavalli. A pragmatic approach to generating test sequences for embedded systems. In *Proceedings of the IFIP IWTCS'97*, Cheju Island, Korea, September 1997.

[10] S. Naito and M. Tsunoyama. Fault detection for sequential machines by transition tour. In *Proc. IEEE Computer Conference*, 1981.

[11] B. Sarikaya and G. v. Bochmann. Obtaining normal form specifications for protocols. In *Computer Network Usage: Recent Experiences*. Elsevier Science Publishers, 1986.

[12] Charles L. Seitz. An approach to designing checking experiments based on a dynamic model. In Z. Kohavi and A. Paz, editors, *Theory of Machines and Computations*. Academic Press, 1972.

[13] Verilog. *ObjectGEODE SDL Simulator - Reference manual*, 1997.

Author Index

Lecture Notes in Computer Science

For information about Vols. 1–1619
please contact your bookseller or Springer-Verlag

Vol. 1663: F. Dehne, A. Gupta. J.-R. Sack, R. Tamassia (Eds.), Algorithms and Data Structures. Proceedings, 1999. IX, 366 pages. 1999.

Vol. 1664: J.C.M. Baeten, S. Mauw (Eds.), CONCUR'99. Concurrency Theory. Proceedings, 1999. XI, 573 pages. 1999.

Vol. 1666: M. Wiener (Ed.), Advances in Cryptology – CRYPTO '99. Proceedings, 1999. XII, 639 pages. 1999.

Vol. 1667: J. Hlavička, E. Maehle, A. Pataricza (Eds.), Dependable Computing – EDCC-3. Proceedings, 1999. XVIII, 455 pages. 1999.

Vol. 1668: J.S. Vitter, C.D. Zaroliagis (Eds.), Algorithm Engineering. Proceedings, 1999. VIII, 361 pages. 1999.

Vol. 1671: D. Hochbaum, K. Jansen, J.D.P. Rolim, A. Sinclair (Eds.), Randomization, Approximation, and Combinatorial Optimization. Proceedings, 1999. IX, 289 pages. 1999.

Vol. 1672: M. Kutylowski, L. Pacholski, T. Wierzbicki (Eds.), Mathematical Foundations of Computer Science 1999. Proceedings, 1999. XII, 455 pages. 1999.

Vol. 1673: P. Lysaght, J. Irvine, R. Hartenstein (Eds.), Field Programmable Logic and Applications. Proceedings, 1999. XI, 541 pages. 1999.

Vol. 1674: D. Floreano, J.-D. Nicoud, F. Mondada (Eds.), Advances in Artificial Life. Proceedings, 1999. XVI, 737 pages. 1999. (Subseries LNAI).

Vol. 1675: J. Estublier (Ed.), System Configuration Management. Proceedings, 1999. VIII, 255 pages. 1999.

Vol. 1976: M. Mohania, A M. Tjoa (Eds.), Data Warehousing and Knowledge Discovery. Proceedings, 1999. XII, 400 pages. 1999.

Vol. 1677: T. Bench-Capon, G. Soda, A M. Tjoa (Eds.), Database and Expert Systems Applications. Proceedings, 1999. XVIII, 1105 pages. 1999.

Vol. 1678: M.H. Böhlen, C.S. Jensen, M.O. Scholl (Eds.), Spatio-Temporal Database Management. Proceedings, 1999. X, 243 pages. 1999.

Vol. 1679: C. Taylor, A. Colchester (Eds.), Medical Image Computing and Computer-Assisted Intervention – MICCAI'99. Proceedings, 1999. XXI, 1240 pages. 1999.

Vol. 1680: D. Dams, R. Gerth, S. Leue, M. Massink (Eds.), Theoretical and Practical Aspects of SPIN Model Checking. Proceedings, 1999. X, 277 pages. 1999.

Vol. 1682: M. Nielsen, P. Johansen, O.F. Olsen, J. Weickert (Eds.), Scale-Space Theories in Computer Vision. Proceedings, 1999. XII, 532 pages. 1999.

Vol. 1683: J. Flum, M. Rodríguez-Artalejo (Eds.), Computer Science Logic. Proceedings, 1999. XI, 580 pages. 1999.

Vol. 1684: G. Ciobanu, G. Păun (Eds.), Fundamentals of Computation Theory. Proceedings, 1999. XI, 570 pages. 1999.

Vol. 1685: P. Amestoy, P. Berger, M. Daydé, I. Duff, V. Frayssé, L. Giraud, D. Ruiz (Eds.), Euro-Par'99 Parallel Processing. Proceedings, 1999. XXXII, 1503 pages. 1999.

Vol. 1687: O. Nierstrasz, M. Lemoine (Eds.), Software Engineering – ESEC/FSE '99. Proceedings, 1999. XII, 529 pages. 1999.

Vol. 1688: P. Bouquet, L. Serafini, P. Brézillon, M. Benerecetti, F. Castellani (Eds.), Modeling and Using Context. Proceedings, 1999. XII, 528 pages. 1999. (Subseries LNAI).

Vol. 1689: F. Solina, A. Leonardis (Eds.), Computer Analysis of Images and Patterns. Proceedings, 1999. XIV, 650 pages. 1999.

Vol. 1690: Y. Bertot, G. Dowek, A. Hirschowitz, C. Paulin, L. Théry (Eds.), Theorem Proving in Higher Order Logics. Proceedings, 1999. VIII, 359 pages. 1999.

Vol. 1691: J. Eder, I. Rozman, T. Welzer (Eds.), Advances in Databases and Information Systems. Proceedings, 1999. XIII, 383 pages. 1999.

Vol. 1692: V. Matoušek, P. Mautner, J. Ocelíková, P. Sojka (Eds.), Text, Speech and Dialogue. Proceedings, 1999. XI, 396 pages. 1999. (Subseries LNAI).

Vol. 1693: P. Jayanti (Ed.), Distributed Computing. Proceedings, 1999. X, 357 pages. 1999.

Vol. 1694: A. Cortesi, G. Filé (Eds.), Static Analysis. Proceedings, 1999. VIII, 357 pages. 1999.

Vol. 1695: P. Barahona, J.J. Alferes (Eds.), Progress in Artificial Intelligence. Proceedings, 1999. XI, 385 pages. 1999. (Subseries LNAI).

Vol. 1696: S. Abiteboul, A.-M. Vercoustre (Eds.), Research and Advanced Technology for Digital Libraries. Proceedings, 1999. XII, 497 pages. 1999.

Vol. 1697: J. Dongarra, E. Luque, T. Margalef (Eds.), Recent Advances in Parallel Virtual Machine and Message Passing Interface. Proceedings, 1999. XVII, 551 pages. 1999.

Vol. 1698: M. Felici, K. Kanoun, A. Pasquini (Eds.), Computer Safety, Reliability and Security. Proceedings, 1999. XVIII, 482 pages. 1999.

Vol. 1699: S. Albayrak (Ed.), Intelligent Agents for Telecommunication Applications. Proceedings, 1999. IX, 191 pages. 1999. (Subseries LNAI).

Vol. 1701: W. Burgard, T. Christaller, A.B. Cremers (Eds.), KI-99: Advances in Artificial Intelligence. Proceedings, 1999. XI, 311 pages. 1999. (Subseries LNAI).

Vol. 1702: G. Nadathur (Ed.), Principles and Practice of Declarative Programming. Proceedings, 1999. X, 434 pages. 1999.

Vol. 1703: P. Laurence, T. Kropf (Eds.), Correct Hardware Design and Verification Methods. Proceedings, 1999. XI, 366 pages. 1999.

Vol. 1704: Jan M. Żytkow, J. Rauch (Eds.), Principles of Data Mining and Knowledge Discovery. Proceedings, 1999. XIV, 593 pages. 1999. (Subseries LNAI).

Vol. 1705: H. Ganzinger, D. McAllester, A. Voronkov (Eds.), Logic for Programming and Automated Reasoning. Proceedings, 1999. XII, 397 pages. 1999. (Subseries LNAI).

Vol. 1707: H.-W. Gellersen (Ed.), Handheld and Ubiquitous Computing. Proceedings, 1999. XII, 390 pages. 1999.

Vol. 1708: J.M. Wing, J. Woodcock, J. Davies (Eds.), FM'99 – Formal Methods. Proceedings Vol. I, 1999. XVIII, 937 pages. 1999.

Vol. 1709: J.M. Wing, J. Woodcock, J. Davies (Eds.), FM'99 – Formal Methods. Proceedings Vol. II, 1999. XVIII, 937 pages. 1999.